APR 01 1998

D1100058

CRIME STATE RANI
1998

Crime in the 50 United States

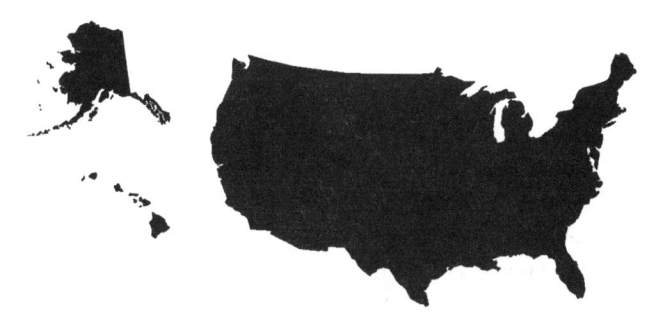

Editors:
Kathleen O'Leary Morgan, Scott Morgan and Mark Uhlig
Associate Editor: Kim Tiffany

MORGAN
QUITNO

Morgan Quitno Press
© Copyright 1998, All Rights Reserved

512 East 9th Street, P.O. Box 1656
Lawrence, KS 66044-8656
USA

800-457-0742 or 785-841-3534
http://www.morganquitno.com

Fifth Edition

ISBN:
1-56692-328-X
ISSN:
1077-4408

Crime State Rankings 1998 sells for $49.95 ($5.00 shipping) and is only available in paper binding. For those who prefer ranking information tailored to a particular state, we also offer *Crime State Perspectives*, state-specific reports for each of the 50 states. These individual guides provide information on a state's data and rank for each of the categories featured in the national *Crime State Rankings* volume. Perspectives sell for $19.00 or $9.50 if ordered with *Crime State Rankings*. If you are interested in city and metropolitan crime data, we offer *City Crime Rankings, 4th Edition* ($37.95 paper). If health statistics are your interest, please ask about our annual *Health Care State Rankings* ($49.95 paper). If you are interested in a general view of the states, please ask about our annual *State Rankings* ($49.95 paper). We also offer the data in our books on diskette. Shipping is $5.00 per order.

Fifth Edition
Printed in the United States of America
March 1998

PREFACE

This fifth edition of *Crime State Rankings* offers a wealth of crime-related information in a straightforward, easy-to-understand format. With 508 tables of state information, it offers a solid collection of crime and law enforcement data. The good news for this year is that crime in the United States continues to decline. However because crime rates are still higher than what many of us remember, our concern about the safety of our communities certainly has not diminished.

Important Notes About *Crime State Rankings 1998*

This book is the result of a year-round effort to find and filter basic information regarding crime. We have examined each table, updated most of them, remove others and added new data of interest. Designed with simplicity as its driving force, *Crime State Rankings 1998* presents a straightforward view of crime in the 50 United States.

New to the book this year is a table showing data from the National Criminal Victimization Survey. This annual study collects crime data based on interviews of crime victims. Its 1996 national findings (they are not broken down by state) are shown in the appendix. These numbers are particularly interesting when compared to the FBI's data (see our "Offense" chapter) which are collected from law enforcement agency reports.

All states in the tables of this book are ranked on a high to low basis. Any ties among states are shown alphabetically for a given ranking. Numbers reported in parentheses "( )" are negative numbers. For tables with national totals (as opposed to rates, per capita's, etc.) we include a separate column showing what percent of the national total each individual state's total represents. This column is headed by "% of USA." This percentage figure is particularly interesting when compared with a state's share of the nation's population for a particular year. The appendix contains population tables to aid in these comparisons.

Now, a word of caution. You will not find crime rankings in any publication of the FBI or US Department of Justice. Officials of these agencies fear that rankings create misleading perceptions. They correctly point out that crime levels are affected by many different factors, such as population density, economic conditions, education levels, citizen awareness and climate. Assessing the safety of a state based on rankings alone is not accurate or wise. Crime ranking information must be used carefully and we certainly do not want to be irresponsible in our presentation of the data. However, rankings do allow states to compare themselves to other states and also enable leaders to track their crime situation from one year to the next. Used within the proper context, rankings often tell a very interesting and important story.

Crime State Perspectives and Other Books

In addition to *Crime State Rankings 1998,* Morgan Quitno publishes several other time-saving and frustration-free reference books. For those interested in crime information for just one state, we once again are offering our *Crime State Perspective* series of publications. These 21-page, comb-bound reports feature data and ranking information for an individual state pulled from *Crime State Rankings 1998.* (For example, *New York Crime in Perspective* contains crime information about the state of New York only.) When purchased individually, *Crime State Perspectives* sell for $19. When purchased with a copy of *Crime State Rankings 1998,* these handy quick reference guides are just $9.50.

Other volumes of interest to researchers include *City Crime Rankings,* currently in its fourth edition. This 400-page reference compares all cities of 75,000 population or more and all metropolitan areas (some as small as 65,000 population) in 40 categories of crime each. Numbers of crimes, rates and trends over one and five years are presented for all major crime categories reported by the FBI. ($37.95; paper cover; $5.00 shipping)

General state statistics or state health care information are the focus of *State Rankings* and *Health Care State Rankings.* The first of these, *State Rankings,* provides a general view of the states. Statistics are featured in a wide variety of categories including agriculture, transportation, government finance, health, population, crime, education, social welfare, energy and environment. In its ninth edition for 1998, this book has received great acclaim for its ease of use and simple presentation of state data. Following the same format as the book you are holding, *Health Care State Rankings* focuses on state health issues instead of crime. Included in this volume are data on health care facilities, providers, insurance and finance, incidence of disease, mortality, physical fitness, natality and reproductive health. Both *State Rankings* and *Health Care State Rankings* sell for $49.95 (paper cover) plus $5.00 shipping. *State Perspectives* and *Health Care State Perspectives* are also available for each of these books, selling for $19 individually or $9.50 if purchased with their corresponding national volume. We also offer the data in our books on diskette (.dbf format for PC). If you would like a brochure or further information, please call us at 1-800-457-0742.

In closing, many thanks to those of you who call or write with suggestions or comments. Your ideas are always helpful and make our books better each year. Thanks also to the hard working librarians and government workers who help us with information, explanations and general support. If you have a suggestion for us, please don't be shy about sending it our way.

THE EDITORS

WHICH STATE IS THE MOST DANGEROUS?

Louisiana is back! After having topped our Most Dangerous State list for two consecutive years (1994 and 1995) Louisiana dropped to second in 1996 and then third in 1997. But this year it came roaring back to reclaim its title. At the safer end of the scale, the appropriately named Peace Garden State of North Dakota is once again the nation's Safest State.

To determine the rankings, we used the same methodology as our annual Safest/Most Dangerous City and Metropolitan Area awards. For those announcements, awarded in conjunction with our annual *City Crime Rankings* book, we joined forces with MONEY Magazine.

The Methodology

Six basic crime factors were used to determine our results: murder, rape, robbery, aggravated assault, burglary and motor vehicle theft. States were ranked based on how well their rates for each of these crimes compared to the national average for that crime.

In addition to these calculations, each factor also was weighted to reflect which crimes Americans fear the most. The basis of this weighting system was derived from a poll taken as part of the Safest and Most Dangerous City awards. This year's poll showed that respondents were most fearful of burglary, followed motor vehicle theft, robbery, aggravated assault, rape and finally murder. Remember, this is not to say that Americans think burglary is worse than murder. It simply means that fortunately for most of us, murder is not viewed as a very real threat as compared to having our homes broken into while we're away. Using these responses, weights were calculated for each of the six crime factors (see box on this page) and applied to the final

1998 MOST DANGEROUS STATE

RANK	STATE	SUM	'97	RANK	STATE	SUM	'97
1	Louisiana	47.08	3	26	Indiana	(15.57)	27
2	Florida	45.95	2	27	Ohio	(19.31)	28
3	Nevada	41.88	1	28	Massachusetts	(19.63)	26
4	Maryland	36.74	4	29	Colorado	(20.74)	31
5	New Mexico	35.20	7	30	Kansas	(21.71)	31
6	South Carolina	24.87	11	31	Hawaii	(22.43)	29
7	California	24.12	5	32	Connecticut	(23.50)	32
8	Tennessee	23.17	9	33	Minnesota	(26.55)	33
9	Arizona	18.79	6	34	Pennsylvania	(27.49)	34
10	Illinois	16.08	8	35	Utah	(29.50)	35
11	Michigan	11.68	12	36	Rhode Island	(33.57)	36
12	Georgia	8.20	17	37	Virginia	(34.87)	38
13	Alaska	7.40	10	38	Kentucky	(36.66)	37
14	Texas	5.77	15	39	Nebraska	(39.49)	41
15	Oklahoma	1.93	13	40	Wisconsin	(45.93)	39
16	New York	(0.46)	14	41	Idaho	(50.61)	40
17	North Carolina	(1.46)	18	42	Wyoming	(53.48)	44
18	Delaware	(1.66)	16	43	Montana	(54.46)	43
19	Mississippi	(4.34)	19	44	Iowa	(55.59)	42
20	Alabama	(4.45)	21	45	West Virginia	(57.87)	45
21	Missouri	(8.22)	20	46	South Dakota	(59.02)	46
22	Washington	(9.49)	22	47	Vermont	(61.65)	47
23	Arkansas	(11.25)	25	48	Maine	(61.85)	48
24	New Jersey	(13.95)	24	49	New Hampshire	(63.66)	49
25	Oregon	(14.51)	23	50	North Dakota	(70.20)	50

FACTORS CONSIDERED AND WEIGHT GIVEN:
(all rates per 100,000 population)

1. Murder Rate (13.9%) (Table 329)
2. Rape Rate (14.8%) (Table 348)
3. Robbery Rate (17.8%) (Table 354)
4. Aggravated Assault Rate (15.7%) (Table 369)
5. Burglary Rate (19.9%) (Table 389)
6. Motor Vehicle Theft Rate (18.0%) (Table 399)

formula. The farther a state's score (shown as "SUM" in the chart) is below the national crime average, the better it placed in the rankings; the farther above the national crime average, the worse a state ranked in the final list.

Morgan Quitno Press takes pride in presenting facts in a nonbiased, objective manner. A central theme of our books is our clear presentation of data, with the analysis and interpretation left to our readers. Yet these awards can also be a useful, if subjective, tool. Annually since 1991 we have named the "Most Livable State" based on data from our *State Rankings* series. In 1993, we began the "Healthiest State" award based on data from our *Health Care State Rankings* series.

The reaction from naming a "Most Dangerous State" is always interesting. Some state leaders accept it with resignation and inform their citizens of the steps they are taking to improve. Others take more of a "kill the messenger" approach. While it doesn't affect our rankings, it certainly keeps us on our toes. Almost two-thirds of states can boast declining violent crime rates over the past five years. Louisiana's violent crime rate has fallen more than 5 percent. Yet with crime dropping in most parts of the country, it takes more than that for Louisiana to improve when judged against its fellow states.

THE EDITORS

TABLE OF CONTENTS

I. Arrests

II. Corrections

TABLE OF CONTENTS (continued)

TABLE OF CONTENTS (continued)

III. Drugs and Alcohol

IV. Finance

TABLE OF CONTENTS (continued)

V. Juveniles

TABLE OF CONTENTS (continued)

VI. Law Enforcement

TABLE OF CONTENTS (continued)

VII. Offenses

TABLE OF CONTENTS (continued)

Urban/Rural Crime

TABLE OF CONTENTS (continued)

TABLE OF CONTENTS (continued)

1992 Crimes

VIII. Appendix

IX. Sources

X. Index

I. ARRESTS

Important Note Regarding Arrest Numbers

The state arrest numbers reported by the FBI and shown in tables 1 to 36 are only from those law enforcement agencies that submitted complete arrests reports for 12 months in 1996. Reports from law enforcement agencies in Illinois, Mississippi, Kentucky and Tennessee represented less than half of their state populations. Thus the rates for these states may be somewhat skewed.

The rates were calculated by the editors using population totals provided by the FBI for those jurisdictions reporting. Using these FBI population figures, we first determined what percentage the FBI numbers represented of each state's total resident population. Next, using 1996 US Census Bureau state estimates for the state, we multiplied the percentages derived from the FBI population figures into the Census Bureau's total population estimates. The resulting population is the base that was used to determine arrests per 100,000 population. The national rate was calculated in the same manner.

Reported Arrests in 1996

National Total = 11,088,352 Reported Arrests*

ALPHA ORDER					RANK ORDER			

RANK	STATE	ARRESTS	% of USA
19	Alabama	215,361	1.94%
42	Alaska	34,180	0.31%
12	Arizona	299,937	2.70%
21	Arkansas	198,776	1.79%
1	California	1,573,555	14.19%
17	Colorado	217,716	1.96%
27	Connecticut	154,446	1.39%
44	Delaware	26,667	0.24%
NA	Florida**	NA	NA
14	Georgia	250,064	2.26%
35	Hawaii	65,258	0.59%
33	Idaho	78,229	0.71%
11	Illinois	301,870	2.72%
23	Indiana	162,253	1.46%
31	Iowa	89,972	0.81%
NA	Kansas**	NA	NA
37	Kentucky	56,688	0.51%
22	Louisiana	177,083	1.60%
38	Maine	54,319	0.49%
15	Maryland	242,128	2.18%
26	Massachusetts	155,962	1.41%
7	Michigan	378,119	3.41%
16	Minnesota	221,193	1.99%
39	Mississippi	51,625	0.47%
13	Missouri	272,065	2.45%
NA	Montana**	NA	NA
36	Nebraska	59,007	0.53%
29	Nevada	123,823	1.12%
41	New Hampshire	34,735	0.31%
6	New Jersey	396,784	3.58%
32	New Mexico	87,259	0.79%
3	New York	824,639	7.44%
4	North Carolina	505,310	4.56%
45	North Dakota	21,205	0.19%
8	Ohio	377,034	3.40%
28	Oklahoma	153,537	1.38%
25	Oregon	159,691	1.44%
10	Pennsylvania	346,773	3.13%
40	Rhode Island	41,058	0.37%
18	South Carolina	215,578	1.94%
43	South Dakota	32,960	0.30%
24	Tennessee	160,461	1.45%
2	Texas	1,020,750	9.21%
30	Utah	120,600	1.09%
NA	Vermont**	NA	NA
9	Virginia	375,677	3.39%
20	Washington	208,713	1.88%
34	West Virginia	70,538	0.64%
5	Wisconsin	459,506	4.14%
46	Wyoming	20,107	0.18%

RANK	STATE	ARRESTS	% of USA
1	California	1,573,555	14.19%
2	Texas	1,020,750	9.21%
3	New York	824,639	7.44%
4	North Carolina	505,310	4.56%
5	Wisconsin	459,506	4.14%
6	New Jersey	396,784	3.58%
7	Michigan	378,119	3.41%
8	Ohio	377,034	3.40%
9	Virginia	375,677	3.39%
10	Pennsylvania	346,773	3.13%
11	Illinois	301,870	2.72%
12	Arizona	299,937	2.70%
13	Missouri	272,065	2.45%
14	Georgia	250,064	2.26%
15	Maryland	242,128	2.18%
16	Minnesota	221,193	1.99%
17	Colorado	217,716	1.96%
18	South Carolina	215,578	1.94%
19	Alabama	215,361	1.94%
20	Washington	208,713	1.88%
21	Arkansas	198,776	1.79%
22	Louisiana	177,083	1.60%
23	Indiana	162,253	1.46%
24	Tennessee	160,461	1.45%
25	Oregon	159,691	1.44%
26	Massachusetts	155,962	1.41%
27	Connecticut	154,446	1.39%
28	Oklahoma	153,537	1.38%
29	Nevada	123,823	1.12%
30	Utah	120,600	1.09%
31	Iowa	89,972	0.81%
32	New Mexico	87,259	0.79%
33	Idaho	78,229	0.71%
34	West Virginia	70,538	0.64%
35	Hawaii	65,258	0.59%
36	Nebraska	59,007	0.53%
37	Kentucky	56,688	0.51%
38	Maine	54,319	0.49%
39	Mississippi	51,625	0.47%
40	Rhode Island	41,058	0.37%
41	New Hampshire	34,735	0.31%
42	Alaska	34,180	0.31%
43	South Dakota	32,960	0.30%
44	Delaware	26,667	0.24%
45	North Dakota	21,205	0.19%
46	Wyoming	20,107	0.18%
NA	Florida**	NA	NA
NA	Kansas**	NA	NA
NA	Montana**	NA	NA
NA	Vermont**	NA	NA
	District of Columbia**	NA	NA

Source: Federal Bureau of Investigation
"Crime in the United States 1996" (Uniform Crime Reports, October 4, 1997)
*By law enforcement agencies submitting complete reports to the F.B.I. for 12 months in 1996. The F.B.I. estimates
15,168,100 reported and unreported arrests occurred in 1996. See important note at beginning of this chapter.
**Not available.*

Reported Arrest Rate in 1996

National Rate = 5,838.2 Reported Arrests per 100,000 Population*

RANK	STATE	RATE	RANK	STATE	RATE
33	Alabama	5,225.9	1	Illinois	10,961.1
20	Alaska	6,353.2	2	Wisconsin	8,934.6
12	Arizona	7,187.6	3	Missouri	8,799.0
5	Arkansas	8,369.5	4	New Mexico	8,682.5
35	California	5,044.3	5	Arkansas	8,369.5
9	Colorado	7,701.3	6	Mississippi	8,168.5
22	Connecticut	6,109.4	7	Nevada	7,891.8
11	Delaware	7,187.9	8	Tennessee	7,755.5
NA	Florida**	NA	9	Colorado	7,701.3
29	Georgia	5,550.8	10	Kentucky	7,410.2
30	Hawaii	5,511.7	11	Delaware	7,187.9
15	Idaho	6,680.5	12	Arizona	7,187.6
1	Illinois	10,961.1	13	Wyoming	7,155.5
37	Indiana	4,925.7	14	North Carolina	7,040.7
43	Iowa	3,905.0	15	Idaho	6,680.5
NA	Kansas**	NA	16	Louisiana	6,642.3
10	Kentucky	7,410.2	17	Utah	6,554.3
16	Louisiana	6,642.3	18	New York	6,542.7
40	Maine	4,441.5	19	South Dakota	6,526.7
24	Maryland	6,015.6	20	Alaska	6,353.2
46	Massachusetts	3,098.2	21	Texas	6,148.7
38	Michigan	4,793.6	22	Connecticut	6,109.4
32	Minnesota	5,255.2	23	Virginia	6,081.9
6	Mississippi	8,168.5	24	Maryland	6,015.6
3	Missouri	8,799.0	25	South Carolina	5,893.3
NA	Montana**	NA	26	Ohio	5,867.3
36	Nebraska	4,971.1	27	Oregon	5,828.1
7	Nevada	7,891.8	28	Washington	5,570.1
42	New Hampshire	3,924.9	29	Georgia	5,550.8
34	New Jersey	5,182.0	30	Hawaii	5,511.7
4	New Mexico	8,682.5	31	North Dakota	5,354.8
18	New York	6,542.7	32	Minnesota	5,255.2
14	North Carolina	7,040.7	33	Alabama	5,225.9
31	North Dakota	5,354.8	34	New Jersey	5,182.0
26	Ohio	5,867.3	35	California	5,044.3
39	Oklahoma	4,651.2	36	Nebraska	4,971.1
27	Oregon	5,828.1	37	Indiana	4,925.7
45	Pennsylvania	3,719.9	38	Michigan	4,793.6
41	Rhode Island	4,386.5	39	Oklahoma	4,651.2
25	South Carolina	5,893.3	40	Maine	4,441.5
19	South Dakota	6,526.7	41	Rhode Island	4,386.5
8	Tennessee	7,755.5	42	New Hampshire	3,924.9
21	Texas	6,148.7	43	Iowa	3,905.0
17	Utah	6,554.3	44	West Virginia	3,863.0
NA	Vermont**	NA	45	Pennsylvania	3,719.9
23	Virginia	6,081.9	46	Massachusetts	3,098.2
28	Washington	5,570.1	NA	Florida**	NA
44	West Virginia	3,863.0	NA	Kansas**	NA
2	Wisconsin	8,934.6	NA	Montana**	NA
13	Wyoming	7,155.5	NA	Vermont**	NA
				District of Columbia**	NA

Source: Morgan Quitno Press using data from Federal Bureau of Investigation
"Crime in the United States 1996" (Uniform Crime Reports, October 4, 1997)
*By law enforcement agencies submitting complete reports to the F.B.I. for 12 months in 1996. These rates based on population estimates for areas under the jurisdiction of those agencies reporting. Arrest rate based on the F.B.I. estimate of total arrests is 5,717.7 reported and unreported arrests per 100,000 population. See important note at beginning of this chapter. **Not available.

Reported Arrests for Crime Index Offenses in 1996

National Total = 2,054,605 Reported Arrests*

ALPHA ORDER

RANK	STATE	ARRESTS	% of USA
21	Alabama	37,032	1.80%
42	Alaska	6,835	0.33%
11	Arizona	57,689	2.81%
28	Arkansas	25,427	1.24%
1	California	370,478	18.03%
26	Colorado	30,057	1.46%
25	Connecticut	30,937	1.51%
41	Delaware	7,246	0.35%
NA	Florida**	NA	NA
16	Georgia	47,301	2.30%
35	Hawaii	12,397	0.60%
33	Idaho	12,766	0.62%
10	Illinois	59,323	2.89%
24	Indiana	31,567	1.54%
31	Iowa	16,072	0.78%
NA	Kansas**	NA	NA
34	Kentucky	12,414	0.60%
17	Louisiana	41,893	2.04%
36	Maine	10,838	0.53%
13	Maryland	52,481	2.55%
22	Massachusetts	33,587	1.63%
8	Michigan	61,867	3.01%
20	Minnesota	38,720	1.88%
39	Mississippi	8,419	0.41%
14	Missouri	48,464	2.36%
NA	Montana**	NA	NA
38	Nebraska	8,718	0.42%
30	Nevada	21,073	1.03%
44	New Hampshire	4,912	0.24%
6	New Jersey	71,757	3.49%
32	New Mexico	14,172	0.69%
3	New York	129,002	6.28%
4	North Carolina	85,957	4.18%
46	North Dakota	2,422	0.12%
9	Ohio	61,789	3.01%
27	Oklahoma	29,659	1.44%
19	Oregon	39,300	1.91%
5	Pennsylvania	71,812	3.50%
40	Rhode Island	8,046	0.39%
18	South Carolina	39,827	1.94%
43	South Dakota	5,602	0.27%
23	Tennessee	33,093	1.61%
2	Texas	165,474	8.05%
29	Utah	23,581	1.15%
NA	Vermont**	NA	NA
12	Virginia	56,303	2.74%
15	Washington	47,667	2.32%
37	West Virginia	10,069	0.49%
7	Wisconsin	67,778	3.30%
45	Wyoming	2,782	0.14%

RANK ORDER

RANK	STATE	ARRESTS	% of USA
1	California	370,478	18.03%
2	Texas	165,474	8.05%
3	New York	129,002	6.28%
4	North Carolina	85,957	4.18%
5	Pennsylvania	71,812	3.50%
6	New Jersey	71,757	3.49%
7	Wisconsin	67,778	3.30%
8	Michigan	61,867	3.01%
9	Ohio	61,789	3.01%
10	Illinois	59,323	2.89%
11	Arizona	57,689	2.81%
12	Virginia	56,303	2.74%
13	Maryland	52,481	2.55%
14	Missouri	48,464	2.36%
15	Washington	47,667	2.32%
16	Georgia	47,301	2.30%
17	Louisiana	41,893	2.04%
18	South Carolina	39,827	1.94%
19	Oregon	39,300	1.91%
20	Minnesota	38,720	1.88%
21	Alabama	37,032	1.80%
22	Massachusetts	33,587	1.63%
23	Tennessee	33,093	1.61%
24	Indiana	31,567	1.54%
25	Connecticut	30,937	1.51%
26	Colorado	30,057	1.46%
27	Oklahoma	29,659	1.44%
28	Arkansas	25,427	1.24%
29	Utah	23,581	1.15%
30	Nevada	21,073	1.03%
31	Iowa	16,072	0.78%
32	New Mexico	14,172	0.69%
33	Idaho	12,766	0.62%
34	Kentucky	12,414	0.60%
35	Hawaii	12,397	0.60%
36	Maine	10,838	0.53%
37	West Virginia	10,069	0.49%
38	Nebraska	8,718	0.42%
39	Mississippi	8,419	0.41%
40	Rhode Island	8,046	0.39%
41	Delaware	7,246	0.35%
42	Alaska	6,835	0.33%
43	South Dakota	5,602	0.27%
44	New Hampshire	4,912	0.24%
45	Wyoming	2,782	0.14%
46	North Dakota	2,422	0.12%
NA	Florida**	NA	NA
NA	Kansas**	NA	NA
NA	Montana**	NA	NA
NA	Vermont**	NA	NA
	District of Columbia**	NA	NA

Source: Federal Bureau of Investigation
    "Crime in the United States 1996" (Uniform Crime Reports, October 4, 1997)
*By law enforcement agencies submitting complete reports to the F.B.I. for 12 months in 1996. The F.B.I. estimates 2,775,000 reported and unreported arrests for crime index offenses occurred in 1996. Crime index offenses consist of murder, forcible rape, robbery, aggravated assault, burglary, larceny-theft, motor vehicle theft and arson. See important note at beginning of this chapter. **Not available.

3

Reported Arrest Rate for Crime Index Offenses in 1996

National Rate = 1,081.8 Reported Arrests per 100,000 Population*

<table>
<tr><td colspan="3">ALPHA ORDER</td><td colspan="3">RANK ORDER</td></tr>
<tr><th>RANK</th><th>STATE</th><th>RATE</th><th>RANK</th><th>STATE</th><th>RATE</th></tr>
<tr><td>35</td><td>Alabama</td><td>898.6</td><td>1</td><td>Illinois</td><td>2,154.1</td></tr>
<tr><td>16</td><td>Alaska</td><td>1,270.4</td><td>2</td><td>Delaware</td><td>1,953.1</td></tr>
<tr><td>9</td><td>Arizona</td><td>1,382.4</td><td>3</td><td>Kentucky</td><td>1,622.7</td></tr>
<tr><td>23</td><td>Arkansas</td><td>1,070.6</td><td>4</td><td>Tennessee</td><td>1,599.5</td></tr>
<tr><td>19</td><td>California</td><td>1,187.6</td><td>5</td><td>Louisiana</td><td>1,571.4</td></tr>
<tr><td>24</td><td>Colorado</td><td>1,063.2</td><td>6</td><td>Missouri</td><td>1,567.4</td></tr>
<tr><td>17</td><td>Connecticut</td><td>1,223.8</td><td>7</td><td>Oregon</td><td>1,434.3</td></tr>
<tr><td>2</td><td>Delaware</td><td>1,953.1</td><td>8</td><td>New Mexico</td><td>1,410.1</td></tr>
<tr><td>NA</td><td>Florida**</td><td>NA</td><td>9</td><td>Arizona</td><td>1,382.4</td></tr>
<tr><td>25</td><td>Georgia</td><td>1,050.0</td><td>10</td><td>Nevada</td><td>1,343.1</td></tr>
<tr><td>26</td><td>Hawaii</td><td>1,047.0</td><td>11</td><td>Mississippi</td><td>1,332.1</td></tr>
<tr><td>21</td><td>Idaho</td><td>1,090.2</td><td>12</td><td>Wisconsin</td><td>1,317.9</td></tr>
<tr><td>1</td><td>Illinois</td><td>2,154.1</td><td>13</td><td>Maryland</td><td>1,303.9</td></tr>
<tr><td>31</td><td>Indiana</td><td>958.3</td><td>14</td><td>Utah</td><td>1,281.6</td></tr>
<tr><td>42</td><td>Iowa</td><td>697.6</td><td>15</td><td>Washington</td><td>1,272.1</td></tr>
<tr><td>NA</td><td>Kansas**</td><td>NA</td><td>16</td><td>Alaska</td><td>1,270.4</td></tr>
<tr><td>3</td><td>Kentucky</td><td>1,622.7</td><td>17</td><td>Connecticut</td><td>1,223.8</td></tr>
<tr><td>5</td><td>Louisiana</td><td>1,571.4</td><td>18</td><td>North Carolina</td><td>1,197.7</td></tr>
<tr><td>37</td><td>Maine</td><td>886.2</td><td>19</td><td>California</td><td>1,187.6</td></tr>
<tr><td>13</td><td>Maryland</td><td>1,303.9</td><td>20</td><td>South Dakota</td><td>1,109.3</td></tr>
<tr><td>43</td><td>Massachusetts</td><td>667.2</td><td>21</td><td>Idaho</td><td>1,090.2</td></tr>
<tr><td>39</td><td>Michigan</td><td>784.3</td><td>22</td><td>South Carolina</td><td>1,088.8</td></tr>
<tr><td>33</td><td>Minnesota</td><td>919.9</td><td>23</td><td>Arkansas</td><td>1,070.6</td></tr>
<tr><td>11</td><td>Mississippi</td><td>1,332.1</td><td>24</td><td>Colorado</td><td>1,063.2</td></tr>
<tr><td>6</td><td>Missouri</td><td>1,567.4</td><td>25</td><td>Georgia</td><td>1,050.0</td></tr>
<tr><td>NA</td><td>Montana**</td><td>NA</td><td>26</td><td>Hawaii</td><td>1,047.0</td></tr>
<tr><td>41</td><td>Nebraska</td><td>734.5</td><td>27</td><td>New York</td><td>1,023.5</td></tr>
<tr><td>10</td><td>Nevada</td><td>1,343.1</td><td>28</td><td>Texas</td><td>996.8</td></tr>
<tr><td>45</td><td>New Hampshire</td><td>555.0</td><td>29</td><td>Wyoming</td><td>990.0</td></tr>
<tr><td>32</td><td>New Jersey</td><td>937.1</td><td>30</td><td>Ohio</td><td>961.5</td></tr>
<tr><td>8</td><td>New Mexico</td><td>1,410.1</td><td>31</td><td>Indiana</td><td>958.3</td></tr>
<tr><td>27</td><td>New York</td><td>1,023.5</td><td>32</td><td>New Jersey</td><td>937.1</td></tr>
<tr><td>18</td><td>North Carolina</td><td>1,197.7</td><td>33</td><td>Minnesota</td><td>919.9</td></tr>
<tr><td>44</td><td>North Dakota</td><td>611.6</td><td>34</td><td>Virginia</td><td>911.5</td></tr>
<tr><td>30</td><td>Ohio</td><td>961.5</td><td>35</td><td>Alabama</td><td>898.6</td></tr>
<tr><td>36</td><td>Oklahoma</td><td>898.5</td><td>36</td><td>Oklahoma</td><td>898.5</td></tr>
<tr><td>7</td><td>Oregon</td><td>1,434.3</td><td>37</td><td>Maine</td><td>886.2</td></tr>
<tr><td>40</td><td>Pennsylvania</td><td>770.3</td><td>38</td><td>Rhode Island</td><td>859.6</td></tr>
<tr><td>38</td><td>Rhode Island</td><td>859.6</td><td>39</td><td>Michigan</td><td>784.3</td></tr>
<tr><td>22</td><td>South Carolina</td><td>1,088.8</td><td>40</td><td>Pennsylvania</td><td>770.3</td></tr>
<tr><td>20</td><td>South Dakota</td><td>1,109.3</td><td>41</td><td>Nebraska</td><td>734.5</td></tr>
<tr><td>4</td><td>Tennessee</td><td>1,599.5</td><td>42</td><td>Iowa</td><td>697.6</td></tr>
<tr><td>28</td><td>Texas</td><td>996.8</td><td>43</td><td>Massachusetts</td><td>667.2</td></tr>
<tr><td>14</td><td>Utah</td><td>1,281.6</td><td>44</td><td>North Dakota</td><td>611.6</td></tr>
<tr><td>NA</td><td>Vermont**</td><td>NA</td><td>45</td><td>New Hampshire</td><td>555.0</td></tr>
<tr><td>34</td><td>Virginia</td><td>911.5</td><td>46</td><td>West Virginia</td><td>551.4</td></tr>
<tr><td>15</td><td>Washington</td><td>1,272.1</td><td>NA</td><td>Florida**</td><td>NA</td></tr>
<tr><td>46</td><td>West Virginia</td><td>551.4</td><td>NA</td><td>Kansas**</td><td>NA</td></tr>
<tr><td>12</td><td>Wisconsin</td><td>1,317.9</td><td>NA</td><td>Montana**</td><td>NA</td></tr>
<tr><td>29</td><td>Wyoming</td><td>990.0</td><td>NA</td><td>Vermont**</td><td>NA</td></tr>
<tr><td></td><td></td><td></td><td></td><td>District of Columbia**</td><td>NA</td></tr>
</table>

Source: Morgan Quitno Press using data from Federal Bureau of Investigation
    "Crime in the United States 1996" (Uniform Crime Reports, October 4, 1997)
*By law enforcement agencies submitting complete reports to the F.B.I. for 12 months in 1996. These rates based on population estimates for areas under the jurisdiction of those agencies reporting. Arrest rate based on the F.B.I. estimate of reported and unreported arrests for crime index offenses is 1,046.0 arrests per 100,000 population. See important note at beginning of this chapter. **Not available.*

4

Reported Arrests for Violent Crime in 1996

National Total = 548,146 Reported Arrests*

ALPHA ORDER

RANK	STATE	ARRESTS	% of USA
14	Alabama	10,980	2.00%
36	Alaska	1,520	0.28%
19	Arizona	9,025	1.65%
26	Arkansas	5,279	0.96%
1	California	146,092	26.65%
27	Colorado	5,211	0.95%
25	Connecticut	6,365	1.16%
35	Delaware	1,789	0.33%
NA	Florida**	NA	NA
17	Georgia	9,816	1.79%
37	Hawaii	1,488	0.27%
40	Idaho	1,372	0.25%
11	Illinois	12,685	2.31%
20	Indiana	8,283	1.51%
31	Iowa	3,120	0.57%
NA	Kansas**	NA	NA
29	Kentucky	4,192	0.76%
15	Louisiana	9,962	1.82%
41	Maine	895	0.16%
10	Maryland	12,711	2.32%
9	Massachusetts	14,224	2.59%
5	Michigan	20,573	3.75%
24	Minnesota	6,395	1.17%
38	Mississippi	1,393	0.25%
16	Missouri	9,877	1.80%
NA	Montana**	NA	NA
42	Nebraska	800	0.15%
30	Nevada	3,608	0.66%
44	New Hampshire	539	0.10%
6	New Jersey	20,032	3.65%
34	New Mexico	2,181	0.40%
2	New York	54,426	9.93%
4	North Carolina	26,880	4.90%
46	North Dakota	154	0.03%
8	Ohio	17,420	3.18%
23	Oklahoma	6,525	1.19%
28	Oregon	4,304	0.79%
7	Pennsylvania	19,744	3.60%
32	Rhode Island	2,409	0.44%
12	South Carolina	11,917	2.17%
43	South Dakota	686	0.13%
21	Tennessee	8,090	1.48%
3	Texas	33,827	6.17%
33	Utah	2,244	0.41%
NA	Vermont**	NA	NA
13	Virginia	11,417	2.08%
22	Washington	6,559	1.20%
39	West Virginia	1,391	0.25%
18	Wisconsin	9,335	1.70%
45	Wyoming	411	0.07%

RANK ORDER

RANK	STATE	ARRESTS	% of USA
1	California	146,092	26.65%
2	New York	54,426	9.93%
3	Texas	33,827	6.17%
4	North Carolina	26,880	4.90%
5	Michigan	20,573	3.75%
6	New Jersey	20,032	3.65%
7	Pennsylvania	19,744	3.60%
8	Ohio	17,420	3.18%
9	Massachusetts	14,224	2.59%
10	Maryland	12,711	2.32%
11	Illinois	12,685	2.31%
12	South Carolina	11,917	2.17%
13	Virginia	11,417	2.08%
14	Alabama	10,980	2.00%
15	Louisiana	9,962	1.82%
16	Missouri	9,877	1.80%
17	Georgia	9,816	1.79%
18	Wisconsin	9,335	1.70%
19	Arizona	9,025	1.65%
20	Indiana	8,283	1.51%
21	Tennessee	8,090	1.48%
22	Washington	6,559	1.20%
23	Oklahoma	6,525	1.19%
24	Minnesota	6,395	1.17%
25	Connecticut	6,365	1.16%
26	Arkansas	5,279	0.96%
27	Colorado	5,211	0.95%
28	Oregon	4,304	0.79%
29	Kentucky	4,192	0.76%
30	Nevada	3,608	0.66%
31	Iowa	3,120	0.57%
32	Rhode Island	2,409	0.44%
33	Utah	2,244	0.41%
34	New Mexico	2,181	0.40%
35	Delaware	1,789	0.33%
36	Alaska	1,520	0.28%
37	Hawaii	1,488	0.27%
38	Mississippi	1,393	0.25%
39	West Virginia	1,391	0.25%
40	Idaho	1,372	0.25%
41	Maine	895	0.16%
42	Nebraska	800	0.15%
43	South Dakota	686	0.13%
44	New Hampshire	539	0.10%
45	Wyoming	411	0.07%
46	North Dakota	154	0.03%
NA	Florida**	NA	NA
NA	Kansas**	NA	NA
NA	Montana**	NA	NA
NA	Vermont**	NA	NA
	District of Columbia**	NA	NA

Source: Federal Bureau of Investigation
 "Crime in the United States 1996" (Uniform Crime Reports, October 4, 1997)
*By law enforcement agencies submitting complete reports to the F.B.I. for 12 months in 1996. The F.B.I. estimates 729,900 reported and unreported arrests for violent crimes occurred in 1996. Violent crimes are offenses of murder, forcible rape, robbery and aggravated assault. See important note at beginning of this chapter.
**Not available.

Reported Arrest Rate for Violent Crime in 1996

National Rate = 288.6 Reported Arrests per 100,000 Population*

ALPHA ORDER				RANK ORDER		
RANK	STATE	RATE		RANK	STATE	RATE
15	Alabama	266.4		1	Kentucky	548.0
13	Alaska	282.5		2	Delaware	482.2
26	Arizona	216.3		3	California	468.3
22	Arkansas	222.3		4	Illinois	460.6
3	California	468.3		5	New York	431.8
31	Colorado	184.3		6	Tennessee	391.0
19	Connecticut	251.8		7	North Carolina	374.5
2	Delaware	482.2		8	Louisiana	373.7
NA	Florida**	NA		9	South Carolina	325.8
24	Georgia	217.9		10	Missouri	319.4
39	Hawaii	125.7		11	Maryland	315.8
41	Idaho	117.2		12	Massachusetts	282.6
4	Illinois	460.6		13	Alaska	282.5
20	Indiana	251.5		14	Ohio	271.1
38	Iowa	135.4		15	Alabama	266.4
NA	Kansas**	NA		16	New Jersey	261.6
1	Kentucky	548.0		17	Michigan	260.8
8	Louisiana	373.7		18	Rhode Island	257.4
43	Maine	73.2		19	Connecticut	251.8
11	Maryland	315.8		20	Indiana	251.5
12	Massachusetts	282.6		21	Nevada	230.0
17	Michigan	260.8		22	Arkansas	222.3
35	Minnesota	151.9		23	Mississippi	220.4
23	Mississippi	220.4		24	Georgia	217.9
10	Missouri	319.4		25	New Mexico	217.0
NA	Montana**	NA		26	Arizona	216.3
44	Nebraska	67.4		27	Pennsylvania	211.8
21	Nevada	230.0		28	Texas	203.8
45	New Hampshire	60.9		29	Oklahoma	197.7
16	New Jersey	261.6		30	Virginia	184.8
25	New Mexico	217.0		31	Colorado	184.3
5	New York	431.8		32	Wisconsin	181.5
7	North Carolina	374.5		33	Washington	175.0
46	North Dakota	38.9		34	Oregon	157.1
14	Ohio	271.1		35	Minnesota	151.9
29	Oklahoma	197.7		36	Wyoming	146.3
34	Oregon	157.1		37	South Dakota	135.8
27	Pennsylvania	211.8		38	Iowa	135.4
18	Rhode Island	257.4		39	Hawaii	125.7
9	South Carolina	325.8		40	Utah	122.0
37	South Dakota	135.8		41	Idaho	117.2
6	Tennessee	391.0		42	West Virginia	76.2
28	Texas	203.8		43	Maine	73.2
40	Utah	122.0		44	Nebraska	67.4
NA	Vermont**	NA		45	New Hampshire	60.9
30	Virginia	184.8		46	North Dakota	38.9
33	Washington	175.0		NA	Florida**	NA
42	West Virginia	76.2		NA	Kansas**	NA
32	Wisconsin	181.5		NA	Montana**	NA
36	Wyoming	146.3		NA	Vermont**	NA
					District of Columbia**	NA

Source: Morgan Quitno Press using data from Federal Bureau of Investigation
   "Crime in the United States 1996" (Uniform Crime Reports, October 4, 1997)
*By law enforcement agencies submitting complete reports to the F.B.I. for 12 months in 1996. These rates based
on population estimates for areas under the jurisdiction of those agencies reporting. Arrest rate based on the F.B.I.
estimate of reported and unreported arrests for violent crimes is 275.1 arrests per 100,000 population. See
important note at beginning of this chapter. **Not available.

Reported Arrests for Murder in 1996

National Total = 14,447 Reported Arrests*

ALPHA ORDER

RANK	STATE	ARRESTS	% of USA
12	Alabama	402	2.78%
37	Alaska	28	0.19%
17	Arizona	253	1.75%
19	Arkansas	227	1.57%
1	California	2,492	17.25%
28	Colorado	113	0.78%
27	Connecticut	115	0.80%
39	Delaware	19	0.13%
NA	Florida**	NA	NA
18	Georgia	246	1.70%
35	Hawaii	51	0.35%
36	Idaho	29	0.20%
5	Illinois	767	5.31%
26	Indiana	123	0.85%
38	Iowa	27	0.19%
NA	Kansas**	NA	NA
33	Kentucky	64	0.44%
10	Louisiana	418	2.89%
40	Maine	15	0.10%
7	Maryland	625	4.33%
29	Massachusetts	93	0.64%
2	Michigan	1,220	8.44%
25	Minnesota	145	1.00%
30	Mississippi	84	0.58%
14	Missouri	338	2.34%
NA	Montana**	NA	NA
40	Nebraska	15	0.10%
22	Nevada	174	1.20%
43	New Hampshire	12	0.08%
13	New Jersey	349	2.42%
31	New Mexico	72	0.50%
4	New York	1,136	7.86%
6	North Carolina	697	4.82%
46	North Dakota	6	0.04%
15	Ohio	329	2.28%
20	Oklahoma	216	1.50%
24	Oregon	147	1.02%
8	Pennsylvania	511	3.54%
42	Rhode Island	13	0.09%
16	South Carolina	324	2.24%
44	South Dakota	9	0.06%
21	Tennessee	206	1.43%
3	Texas	1,157	8.01%
32	Utah	66	0.46%
NA	Vermont**	NA	NA
11	Virginia	417	2.89%
23	Washington	157	1.09%
34	West Virginia	55	0.38%
9	Wisconsin	477	3.30%
45	Wyoming	8	0.06%

RANK ORDER

RANK	STATE	ARRESTS	% of USA
1	California	2,492	17.25%
2	Michigan	1,220	8.44%
3	Texas	1,157	8.01%
4	New York	1,136	7.86%
5	Illinois	767	5.31%
6	North Carolina	697	4.82%
7	Maryland	625	4.33%
8	Pennsylvania	511	3.54%
9	Wisconsin	477	3.30%
10	Louisiana	418	2.89%
11	Virginia	417	2.89%
12	Alabama	402	2.78%
13	New Jersey	349	2.42%
14	Missouri	338	2.34%
15	Ohio	329	2.28%
16	South Carolina	324	2.24%
17	Arizona	253	1.75%
18	Georgia	246	1.70%
19	Arkansas	227	1.57%
20	Oklahoma	216	1.50%
21	Tennessee	206	1.43%
22	Nevada	174	1.20%
23	Washington	157	1.09%
24	Oregon	147	1.02%
25	Minnesota	145	1.00%
26	Indiana	123	0.85%
27	Connecticut	115	0.80%
28	Colorado	113	0.78%
29	Massachusetts	93	0.64%
30	Mississippi	84	0.58%
31	New Mexico	72	0.50%
32	Utah	66	0.46%
33	Kentucky	64	0.44%
34	West Virginia	55	0.38%
35	Hawaii	51	0.35%
36	Idaho	29	0.20%
37	Alaska	28	0.19%
38	Iowa	27	0.19%
39	Delaware	19	0.13%
40	Maine	15	0.10%
40	Nebraska	15	0.10%
42	Rhode Island	13	0.09%
43	New Hampshire	12	0.08%
44	South Dakota	9	0.06%
45	Wyoming	8	0.06%
46	North Dakota	6	0.04%
NA	Florida**	NA	NA
NA	Kansas**	NA	NA
NA	Montana**	NA	NA
NA	Vermont**	NA	NA
	District of Columbia**	NA	NA

Source: Federal Bureau of Investigation
   "Crime in the United States 1996" (Uniform Crime Reports, October 4, 1997)
*By law enforcement agencies submitting complete reports to the F.B.I. for 12 months in 1996. The F.B.I. estimates 19,020 reported and unreported arrests for murder occurred in 1996. Murder includes nonnegligent manslaughter. See important note at beginning of this chapter.
**Not available.

Reported Arrest Rate for Murder in 1996

National Rate = 7.6 Reported Arrests per 100,000 Population*

ALPHA ORDER

RANK ORDER

RANK	STATE	RATE	RANK	STATE	RATE
9	Alabama	9.8	1	Illinois	27.9
25	Alaska	5.2	2	Louisiana	15.7
21	Arizona	6.1	3	Maryland	15.5
11	Arkansas	9.6	3	Michigan	15.5
16	California	8.0	5	Mississippi	13.3
32	Colorado	4.0	6	Nevada	11.1
29	Connecticut	4.5	7	Missouri	10.9
26	Delaware	5.1	8	Tennessee	10.0
NA	Florida**	NA	9	Alabama	9.8
22	Georgia	5.5	10	North Carolina	9.7
30	Hawaii	4.3	11	Arkansas	9.6
38	Idaho	2.5	12	Wisconsin	9.3
1	Illinois	27.9	13	New York	9.0
33	Indiana	3.7	14	South Carolina	8.9
45	Iowa	1.2	15	Kentucky	8.4
NA	Kansas**	NA	16	California	8.0
15	Kentucky	8.4	17	New Mexico	7.2
2	Louisiana	15.7	18	Texas	7.0
45	Maine	1.2	19	Virginia	6.8
3	Maryland	15.5	20	Oklahoma	6.5
39	Massachusetts	1.8	21	Arizona	6.1
3	Michigan	15.5	22	Georgia	5.5
35	Minnesota	3.4	22	Pennsylvania	5.5
5	Mississippi	13.3	24	Oregon	5.4
7	Missouri	10.9	25	Alaska	5.2
NA	Montana**	NA	26	Delaware	5.1
44	Nebraska	1.3	26	Ohio	5.1
6	Nevada	11.1	28	New Jersey	4.6
42	New Hampshire	1.4	29	Connecticut	4.5
28	New Jersey	4.6	30	Hawaii	4.3
17	New Mexico	7.2	31	Washington	4.2
13	New York	9.0	32	Colorado	4.0
10	North Carolina	9.7	33	Indiana	3.7
41	North Dakota	1.5	34	Utah	3.6
26	Ohio	5.1	35	Minnesota	3.4
20	Oklahoma	6.5	36	West Virginia	3.0
24	Oregon	5.4	37	Wyoming	2.8
22	Pennsylvania	5.5	38	Idaho	2.5
42	Rhode Island	1.4	39	Massachusetts	1.8
14	South Carolina	8.9	39	South Dakota	1.8
39	South Dakota	1.8	41	North Dakota	1.5
8	Tennessee	10.0	42	New Hampshire	1.4
18	Texas	7.0	42	Rhode Island	1.4
34	Utah	3.6	44	Nebraska	1.3
NA	Vermont**	NA	45	Iowa	1.2
19	Virginia	6.8	45	Maine	1.2
31	Washington	4.2	NA	Florida**	NA
36	West Virginia	3.0	NA	Kansas**	NA
12	Wisconsin	9.3	NA	Montana**	NA
37	Wyoming	2.8	NA	Vermont**	NA
			NA	District of Columbia**	NA

Source: Morgan Quitno Press using data from Federal Bureau of Investigation
"Crime in the United States 1996" (Uniform Crime Reports, October 4, 1997)
*By law enforcement agencies submitting complete reports to the F.B.I. for 12 months in 1996. These rates based on population estimates for areas under the jurisdiction of those agencies reporting. Arrest rate based on the F.B.I. estimate of reported and unreported arrests for murder is 7.2 arrests per 100,000 population. See important note at beginning of this chapter. **Not available.

Reported Arrests for Rape in 1996

National Total = 24,347 Reported Arrests*

<table>
<tr><td colspan="4">ALPHA ORDER</td><td colspan="4">RANK ORDER</td></tr>
<tr><td>RANK</td><td>STATE</td><td>ARRESTS</td><td>% of USA</td><td>RANK</td><td>STATE</td><td>ARRESTS</td><td>% of USA</td></tr>
<tr><td>18</td><td>Alabama</td><td>456</td><td>1.87%</td><td>1</td><td>California</td><td>3,134</td><td>12.87%</td></tr>
<tr><td>36</td><td>Alaska</td><td>113</td><td>0.46%</td><td>2</td><td>Texas</td><td>2,316</td><td>9.51%</td></tr>
<tr><td>28</td><td>Arizona</td><td>252</td><td>1.04%</td><td>3</td><td>Michigan</td><td>1,673</td><td>6.87%</td></tr>
<tr><td>22</td><td>Arkansas</td><td>444</td><td>1.82%</td><td>4</td><td>New York</td><td>1,568</td><td>6.44%</td></tr>
<tr><td>1</td><td>California</td><td>3,134</td><td>12.87%</td><td>5</td><td>Ohio</td><td>1,113</td><td>4.57%</td></tr>
<tr><td>19</td><td>Colorado</td><td>454</td><td>1.86%</td><td>6</td><td>Pennsylvania</td><td>1,095</td><td>4.50%</td></tr>
<tr><td>25</td><td>Connecticut</td><td>308</td><td>1.27%</td><td>7</td><td>New Jersey</td><td>910</td><td>3.74%</td></tr>
<tr><td>30</td><td>Delaware</td><td>155</td><td>0.64%</td><td>8</td><td>Virginia</td><td>790</td><td>3.24%</td></tr>
<tr><td>NA</td><td>Florida**</td><td>NA</td><td>NA</td><td>9</td><td>Minnesota</td><td>782</td><td>3.21%</td></tr>
<tr><td>23</td><td>Georgia</td><td>395</td><td>1.62%</td><td>10</td><td>North Carolina</td><td>771</td><td>3.17%</td></tr>
<tr><td>32</td><td>Hawaii</td><td>128</td><td>0.53%</td><td>11</td><td>Wisconsin</td><td>697</td><td>2.86%</td></tr>
<tr><td>41</td><td>Idaho</td><td>83</td><td>0.34%</td><td>12</td><td>Washington</td><td>651</td><td>2.67%</td></tr>
<tr><td>17</td><td>Illinois</td><td>457</td><td>1.88%</td><td>13</td><td>South Carolina</td><td>625</td><td>2.57%</td></tr>
<tr><td>29</td><td>Indiana</td><td>178</td><td>0.73%</td><td>14</td><td>Missouri</td><td>619</td><td>2.54%</td></tr>
<tr><td>43</td><td>Iowa</td><td>77</td><td>0.32%</td><td>15</td><td>Maryland</td><td>610</td><td>2.51%</td></tr>
<tr><td>NA</td><td>Kansas**</td><td>NA</td><td>NA</td><td>16</td><td>Massachusetts</td><td>584</td><td>2.40%</td></tr>
<tr><td>35</td><td>Kentucky</td><td>117</td><td>0.48%</td><td>17</td><td>Illinois</td><td>457</td><td>1.88%</td></tr>
<tr><td>20</td><td>Louisiana</td><td>445</td><td>1.83%</td><td>18</td><td>Alabama</td><td>456</td><td>1.87%</td></tr>
<tr><td>44</td><td>Maine</td><td>75</td><td>0.31%</td><td>19</td><td>Colorado</td><td>454</td><td>1.86%</td></tr>
<tr><td>15</td><td>Maryland</td><td>610</td><td>2.51%</td><td>20</td><td>Louisiana</td><td>445</td><td>1.83%</td></tr>
<tr><td>16</td><td>Massachusetts</td><td>584</td><td>2.40%</td><td>20</td><td>Oklahoma</td><td>445</td><td>1.83%</td></tr>
<tr><td>3</td><td>Michigan</td><td>1,673</td><td>6.87%</td><td>22</td><td>Arkansas</td><td>444</td><td>1.82%</td></tr>
<tr><td>9</td><td>Minnesota</td><td>782</td><td>3.21%</td><td>23</td><td>Georgia</td><td>395</td><td>1.62%</td></tr>
<tr><td>33</td><td>Mississippi</td><td>123</td><td>0.51%</td><td>24</td><td>Tennessee</td><td>335</td><td>1.38%</td></tr>
<tr><td>14</td><td>Missouri</td><td>619</td><td>2.54%</td><td>25</td><td>Connecticut</td><td>308</td><td>1.27%</td></tr>
<tr><td>NA</td><td>Montana**</td><td>NA</td><td>NA</td><td>26</td><td>Oregon</td><td>298</td><td>1.22%</td></tr>
<tr><td>42</td><td>Nebraska</td><td>82</td><td>0.34%</td><td>27</td><td>Nevada</td><td>290</td><td>1.19%</td></tr>
<tr><td>27</td><td>Nevada</td><td>290</td><td>1.19%</td><td>28</td><td>Arizona</td><td>252</td><td>1.04%</td></tr>
<tr><td>38</td><td>New Hampshire</td><td>104</td><td>0.43%</td><td>29</td><td>Indiana</td><td>178</td><td>0.73%</td></tr>
<tr><td>7</td><td>New Jersey</td><td>910</td><td>3.74%</td><td>30</td><td>Delaware</td><td>155</td><td>0.64%</td></tr>
<tr><td>40</td><td>New Mexico</td><td>85</td><td>0.35%</td><td>31</td><td>Utah</td><td>154</td><td>0.63%</td></tr>
<tr><td>4</td><td>New York</td><td>1,568</td><td>6.44%</td><td>32</td><td>Hawaii</td><td>128</td><td>0.53%</td></tr>
<tr><td>10</td><td>North Carolina</td><td>771</td><td>3.17%</td><td>33</td><td>Mississippi</td><td>123</td><td>0.51%</td></tr>
<tr><td>45</td><td>North Dakota</td><td>25</td><td>0.10%</td><td>34</td><td>West Virginia</td><td>118</td><td>0.48%</td></tr>
<tr><td>5</td><td>Ohio</td><td>1,113</td><td>4.57%</td><td>35</td><td>Kentucky</td><td>117</td><td>0.48%</td></tr>
<tr><td>20</td><td>Oklahoma</td><td>445</td><td>1.83%</td><td>36</td><td>Alaska</td><td>113</td><td>0.46%</td></tr>
<tr><td>26</td><td>Oregon</td><td>298</td><td>1.22%</td><td>37</td><td>Rhode Island</td><td>106</td><td>0.44%</td></tr>
<tr><td>6</td><td>Pennsylvania</td><td>1,095</td><td>4.50%</td><td>38</td><td>New Hampshire</td><td>104</td><td>0.43%</td></tr>
<tr><td>37</td><td>Rhode Island</td><td>106</td><td>0.44%</td><td>39</td><td>South Dakota</td><td>89</td><td>0.37%</td></tr>
<tr><td>13</td><td>South Carolina</td><td>625</td><td>2.57%</td><td>40</td><td>New Mexico</td><td>85</td><td>0.35%</td></tr>
<tr><td>39</td><td>South Dakota</td><td>89</td><td>0.37%</td><td>41</td><td>Idaho</td><td>83</td><td>0.34%</td></tr>
<tr><td>24</td><td>Tennessee</td><td>335</td><td>1.38%</td><td>42</td><td>Nebraska</td><td>82</td><td>0.34%</td></tr>
<tr><td>2</td><td>Texas</td><td>2,316</td><td>9.51%</td><td>43</td><td>Iowa</td><td>77</td><td>0.32%</td></tr>
<tr><td>31</td><td>Utah</td><td>154</td><td>0.63%</td><td>44</td><td>Maine</td><td>75</td><td>0.31%</td></tr>
<tr><td>NA</td><td>Vermont**</td><td>NA</td><td>NA</td><td>45</td><td>North Dakota</td><td>25</td><td>0.10%</td></tr>
<tr><td>8</td><td>Virginia</td><td>790</td><td>3.24%</td><td>46</td><td>Wyoming</td><td>18</td><td>0.07%</td></tr>
<tr><td>12</td><td>Washington</td><td>651</td><td>2.67%</td><td>NA</td><td>Florida**</td><td>NA</td><td>NA</td></tr>
<tr><td>34</td><td>West Virginia</td><td>118</td><td>0.48%</td><td>NA</td><td>Kansas**</td><td>NA</td><td>NA</td></tr>
<tr><td>11</td><td>Wisconsin</td><td>697</td><td>2.86%</td><td>NA</td><td>Montana**</td><td>NA</td><td>NA</td></tr>
<tr><td>46</td><td>Wyoming</td><td>18</td><td>0.07%</td><td>NA</td><td>Vermont**</td><td>NA</td><td>NA</td></tr>
<tr><td></td><td></td><td></td><td></td><td></td><td>District of Columbia**</td><td>NA</td><td>NA</td></tr>
</table>

Source: Federal Bureau of Investigation
   "Crime in the United States 1996" (Uniform Crime Reports, October 4, 1997)
*By law enforcement agencies submitting complete reports to the F.B.I. for 12 months in 1996. The F.B.I. estimates 33,050 reported and unreported arrests for rape occurred in 1996. Forcible rape is the carnal knowledge of a female forcibly and against her will. Assaults or attempts to commit rape by force or threat of force are included. See important note at beginning of this chapter. **Not available.

Reported Arrest Rate for Rape in 1996

National Rate = 12.8 Reported Arrests per 100,000 Population*

<table>
<tr><td colspan="3">ALPHA ORDER</td><td colspan="3">RANK ORDER</td></tr>
<tr><td>RANK</td><td>STATE</td><td>RATE</td><td>RANK</td><td>STATE</td><td>RATE</td></tr>
<tr><td>30</td><td>Alabama</td><td>11.1</td><td>1</td><td>Delaware</td><td>41.8</td></tr>
<tr><td>3</td><td>Alaska</td><td>21.0</td><td>2</td><td>Michigan</td><td>21.2</td></tr>
<tr><td>44</td><td>Arizona</td><td>6.0</td><td>3</td><td>Alaska</td><td>21.0</td></tr>
<tr><td>6</td><td>Arkansas</td><td>18.7</td><td>4</td><td>Missouri</td><td>20.0</td></tr>
<tr><td>34</td><td>California</td><td>10.0</td><td>5</td><td>Mississippi</td><td>19.5</td></tr>
<tr><td>16</td><td>Colorado</td><td>16.1</td><td>6</td><td>Arkansas</td><td>18.7</td></tr>
<tr><td>24</td><td>Connecticut</td><td>12.2</td><td>7</td><td>Minnesota</td><td>18.6</td></tr>
<tr><td>1</td><td>Delaware</td><td>41.8</td><td>8</td><td>Nevada</td><td>18.5</td></tr>
<tr><td>NA</td><td>Florida**</td><td>NA</td><td>9</td><td>South Dakota</td><td>17.6</td></tr>
<tr><td>35</td><td>Georgia</td><td>8.8</td><td>10</td><td>Washington</td><td>17.4</td></tr>
<tr><td>32</td><td>Hawaii</td><td>10.8</td><td>11</td><td>Ohio</td><td>17.3</td></tr>
<tr><td>38</td><td>Idaho</td><td>7.1</td><td>12</td><td>South Carolina</td><td>17.1</td></tr>
<tr><td>14</td><td>Illinois</td><td>16.6</td><td>13</td><td>Louisiana</td><td>16.7</td></tr>
<tr><td>45</td><td>Indiana</td><td>5.4</td><td>14</td><td>Illinois</td><td>16.6</td></tr>
<tr><td>46</td><td>Iowa</td><td>3.3</td><td>15</td><td>Tennessee</td><td>16.2</td></tr>
<tr><td>NA</td><td>Kansas**</td><td>NA</td><td>16</td><td>Colorado</td><td>16.1</td></tr>
<tr><td>17</td><td>Kentucky</td><td>15.3</td><td>17</td><td>Kentucky</td><td>15.3</td></tr>
<tr><td>13</td><td>Louisiana</td><td>16.7</td><td>18</td><td>Maryland</td><td>15.2</td></tr>
<tr><td>43</td><td>Maine</td><td>6.1</td><td>19</td><td>Texas</td><td>14.0</td></tr>
<tr><td>18</td><td>Maryland</td><td>15.2</td><td>20</td><td>Wisconsin</td><td>13.6</td></tr>
<tr><td>28</td><td>Massachusetts</td><td>11.6</td><td>21</td><td>Oklahoma</td><td>13.5</td></tr>
<tr><td>2</td><td>Michigan</td><td>21.2</td><td>22</td><td>Virginia</td><td>12.8</td></tr>
<tr><td>7</td><td>Minnesota</td><td>18.6</td><td>23</td><td>New York</td><td>12.4</td></tr>
<tr><td>5</td><td>Mississippi</td><td>19.5</td><td>24</td><td>Connecticut</td><td>12.2</td></tr>
<tr><td>4</td><td>Missouri</td><td>20.0</td><td>25</td><td>New Jersey</td><td>11.9</td></tr>
<tr><td>NA</td><td>Montana**</td><td>NA</td><td>26</td><td>New Hampshire</td><td>11.8</td></tr>
<tr><td>39</td><td>Nebraska</td><td>6.9</td><td>27</td><td>Pennsylvania</td><td>11.7</td></tr>
<tr><td>8</td><td>Nevada</td><td>18.5</td><td>28</td><td>Massachusetts</td><td>11.6</td></tr>
<tr><td>26</td><td>New Hampshire</td><td>11.8</td><td>29</td><td>Rhode Island</td><td>11.3</td></tr>
<tr><td>25</td><td>New Jersey</td><td>11.9</td><td>30</td><td>Alabama</td><td>11.1</td></tr>
<tr><td>36</td><td>New Mexico</td><td>8.5</td><td>31</td><td>Oregon</td><td>10.9</td></tr>
<tr><td>23</td><td>New York</td><td>12.4</td><td>32</td><td>Hawaii</td><td>10.8</td></tr>
<tr><td>33</td><td>North Carolina</td><td>10.7</td><td>33</td><td>North Carolina</td><td>10.7</td></tr>
<tr><td>42</td><td>North Dakota</td><td>6.3</td><td>34</td><td>California</td><td>10.0</td></tr>
<tr><td>11</td><td>Ohio</td><td>17.3</td><td>35</td><td>Georgia</td><td>8.8</td></tr>
<tr><td>21</td><td>Oklahoma</td><td>13.5</td><td>36</td><td>New Mexico</td><td>8.5</td></tr>
<tr><td>31</td><td>Oregon</td><td>10.9</td><td>37</td><td>Utah</td><td>8.4</td></tr>
<tr><td>27</td><td>Pennsylvania</td><td>11.7</td><td>38</td><td>Idaho</td><td>7.1</td></tr>
<tr><td>29</td><td>Rhode Island</td><td>11.3</td><td>39</td><td>Nebraska</td><td>6.9</td></tr>
<tr><td>12</td><td>South Carolina</td><td>17.1</td><td>40</td><td>West Virginia</td><td>6.5</td></tr>
<tr><td>9</td><td>South Dakota</td><td>17.6</td><td>41</td><td>Wyoming</td><td>6.4</td></tr>
<tr><td>15</td><td>Tennessee</td><td>16.2</td><td>42</td><td>North Dakota</td><td>6.3</td></tr>
<tr><td>19</td><td>Texas</td><td>14.0</td><td>43</td><td>Maine</td><td>6.1</td></tr>
<tr><td>37</td><td>Utah</td><td>8.4</td><td>44</td><td>Arizona</td><td>6.0</td></tr>
<tr><td>NA</td><td>Vermont**</td><td>NA</td><td>45</td><td>Indiana</td><td>5.4</td></tr>
<tr><td>22</td><td>Virginia</td><td>12.8</td><td>46</td><td>Iowa</td><td>3.3</td></tr>
<tr><td>10</td><td>Washington</td><td>17.4</td><td>NA</td><td>Florida**</td><td>NA</td></tr>
<tr><td>40</td><td>West Virginia</td><td>6.5</td><td>NA</td><td>Kansas**</td><td>NA</td></tr>
<tr><td>20</td><td>Wisconsin</td><td>13.6</td><td>NA</td><td>Montana**</td><td>NA</td></tr>
<tr><td>41</td><td>Wyoming</td><td>6.4</td><td>NA</td><td>Vermont**</td><td>NA</td></tr>
<tr><td></td><td></td><td></td><td></td><td>District of Columbia**</td><td>NA</td></tr>
</table>

Source: Morgan Quitno Press using data from Federal Bureau of Investigation
   "Crime in the United States 1996" (Uniform Crime Reports, October 4, 1997)
*By law enforcement agencies submitting complete reports to the F.B.I. for 12 months in 1996. These rates based on population estimates for areas under the jurisdiction of those agencies reporting. Arrest rate based on the F.B.I. estimate of reported and unreported arrests for rape is 12.5 arrests per 100,000 population. See important note at beginning of this chapter. **Not available.

Reported Arrests for Robbery in 1996

National Total = 121,781 Reported Arrests*

ALPHA ORDER				RANK ORDER			
RANK	STATE	ARRESTS	% of USA	RANK	STATE	ARRESTS	% of USA
14	Alabama	2,042	1.68%	1	California	25,398	20.86%
40	Alaska	164	0.13%	2	New York	24,240	19.90%
18	Arizona	1,617	1.33%	3	Texas	7,094	5.83%
27	Arkansas	923	0.76%	4	Pennsylvania	6,698	5.50%
1	California	25,398	20.86%	5	New Jersey	5,654	4.64%
31	Colorado	590	0.48%	6	Ohio	4,065	3.34%
19	Connecticut	1,609	1.32%	7	North Carolina	4,034	3.31%
33	Delaware	397	0.33%	8	Maryland	4,007	3.29%
NA	Florida**	NA	NA	9	Michigan	3,646	2.99%
15	Georgia	1,875	1.54%	10	Illinois	3,279	2.69%
30	Hawaii	678	0.56%	11	Virginia	2,635	2.16%
43	Idaho	117	0.10%	12	Missouri	2,527	2.08%
10	Illinois	3,279	2.69%	13	Wisconsin	2,055	1.69%
29	Indiana	852	0.70%	14	Alabama	2,042	1.68%
36	Iowa	282	0.23%	15	Georgia	1,875	1.54%
NA	Kansas**	NA	NA	16	Massachusetts	1,747	1.43%
28	Kentucky	885	0.73%	17	South Carolina	1,736	1.43%
22	Louisiana	1,372	1.13%	18	Arizona	1,617	1.33%
39	Maine	189	0.16%	19	Connecticut	1,609	1.32%
8	Maryland	4,007	3.29%	20	Nevada	1,387	1.14%
16	Massachusetts	1,747	1.43%	21	Minnesota	1,382	1.13%
9	Michigan	3,646	2.99%	22	Louisiana	1,372	1.13%
21	Minnesota	1,382	1.13%	23	Oregon	1,343	1.10%
35	Mississippi	316	0.26%	24	Washington	1,253	1.03%
12	Missouri	2,527	2.08%	25	Tennessee	1,159	0.95%
NA	Montana**	NA	NA	26	Oklahoma	965	0.79%
42	Nebraska	125	0.10%	27	Arkansas	923	0.76%
20	Nevada	1,387	1.14%	28	Kentucky	885	0.73%
41	New Hampshire	131	0.11%	29	Indiana	852	0.70%
5	New Jersey	5,654	4.64%	30	Hawaii	678	0.56%
34	New Mexico	339	0.28%	31	Colorado	590	0.48%
2	New York	24,240	19.90%	32	Utah	403	0.33%
7	North Carolina	4,034	3.31%	33	Delaware	397	0.33%
46	North Dakota	11	0.01%	34	New Mexico	339	0.28%
6	Ohio	4,065	3.34%	35	Mississippi	316	0.26%
26	Oklahoma	965	0.79%	36	Iowa	282	0.23%
23	Oregon	1,343	1.10%	37	West Virginia	271	0.22%
4	Pennsylvania	6,698	5.50%	38	Rhode Island	208	0.17%
38	Rhode Island	208	0.17%	39	Maine	189	0.16%
17	South Carolina	1,736	1.43%	40	Alaska	164	0.13%
44	South Dakota	63	0.05%	41	New Hampshire	131	0.11%
25	Tennessee	1,159	0.95%	42	Nebraska	125	0.10%
3	Texas	7,094	5.83%	43	Idaho	117	0.10%
32	Utah	403	0.33%	44	South Dakota	63	0.05%
NA	Vermont**	NA	NA	45	Wyoming	18	0.01%
11	Virginia	2,635	2.16%	46	North Dakota	11	0.01%
24	Washington	1,253	1.03%	NA	Florida**	NA	NA
37	West Virginia	271	0.22%	NA	Kansas**	NA	NA
13	Wisconsin	2,055	1.69%	NA	Montana**	NA	NA
45	Wyoming	18	0.01%	NA	Vermont**	NA	NA
					District of Columbia**	NA	NA

Source: Federal Bureau of Investigation
"Crime in the United States 1996" (Uniform Crime Reports, October 4, 1997)
*By law enforcement agencies submitting complete reports to the F.B.I. for 12 months in 1996. The F.B.I. estimates 156,270 reported and unreported arrests for robbery occurred in 1996. Robbery is the taking or attempting to take anything of value by force or threat of force. See important note at beginning of this chapter.
**Not available.

Reported Arrest Rate for Robbery in 1996

National Rate = 64.1 Reported Arrests per 100,000 Population*

ALPHA ORDER				RANK ORDER		
RANK	STATE	RATE		RANK	STATE	RATE
18	Alabama	49.6		1	New York	192.3
32	Alaska	30.5		2	Illinois	119.1
27	Arizona	38.7		3	Kentucky	115.7
26	Arkansas	38.9		4	Delaware	107.0
8	California	81.4		5	Maryland	99.6
37	Colorado	20.9		6	Nevada	88.4
11	Connecticut	63.6		7	Missouri	81.7
4	Delaware	107.0		8	California	81.4
NA	Florida**	NA		9	New Jersey	73.8
24	Georgia	41.6		10	Pennsylvania	71.9
13	Hawaii	57.3		11	Connecticut	63.6
44	Idaho	10.0		12	Ohio	63.3
2	Illinois	119.1		13	Hawaii	57.3
34	Indiana	25.9		14	North Carolina	56.2
42	Iowa	12.2		15	Tennessee	56.0
NA	Kansas**	NA		16	Louisiana	51.5
3	Kentucky	115.7		17	Mississippi	50.0
16	Louisiana	51.5		18	Alabama	49.6
38	Maine	15.5		19	Oregon	49.0
5	Maryland	99.6		20	South Carolina	47.5
28	Massachusetts	34.7		21	Michigan	46.2
21	Michigan	46.2		22	Texas	42.7
31	Minnesota	32.8		22	Virginia	42.7
17	Mississippi	50.0		24	Georgia	41.6
7	Missouri	81.7		25	Wisconsin	40.0
NA	Montana**	NA		26	Arkansas	38.9
43	Nebraska	10.5		27	Arizona	38.7
6	Nevada	88.4		28	Massachusetts	34.7
39	New Hampshire	14.8		29	New Mexico	33.7
9	New Jersey	73.8		30	Washington	33.4
29	New Mexico	33.7		31	Minnesota	32.8
1	New York	192.3		32	Alaska	30.5
14	North Carolina	56.2		33	Oklahoma	29.2
46	North Dakota	2.8		34	Indiana	25.9
12	Ohio	63.3		35	Rhode Island	22.2
33	Oklahoma	29.2		36	Utah	21.9
19	Oregon	49.0		37	Colorado	20.9
10	Pennsylvania	71.9		38	Maine	15.5
35	Rhode Island	22.2		39	New Hampshire	14.8
20	South Carolina	47.5		39	West Virginia	14.8
41	South Dakota	12.5		41	South Dakota	12.5
15	Tennessee	56.0		42	Iowa	12.2
22	Texas	42.7		43	Nebraska	10.5
36	Utah	21.9		44	Idaho	10.0
NA	Vermont**	NA		45	Wyoming	6.4
22	Virginia	42.7		46	North Dakota	2.8
30	Washington	33.4		NA	Florida**	NA
39	West Virginia	14.8		NA	Kansas**	NA
25	Wisconsin	40.0		NA	Montana**	NA
45	Wyoming	6.4		NA	Vermont**	NA
					District of Columbia**	NA

Source: Morgan Quitno Press using data from Federal Bureau of Investigation
   "Crime in the United States 1996" (Uniform Crime Reports, October 4, 1997)
*By law enforcement agencies submitting complete reports to the F.B.I. for 12 months in 1996. These rates based on population estimates for areas under the jurisdiction of those agencies reporting. Arrest rate based on the F.B.I. estimate of reported and unreported arrests for robbery is 58.9 arrests per 100,000 population. See important note at beginning of this chapter. **Not available.

Reported Arrests for Aggravated Assault in 1996

National Total = 387,571 Reported Arrests*

<table>
<tr><td colspan="4">ALPHA ORDER</td><td colspan="4">RANK ORDER</td></tr>
<tr><td>RANK</td><td>STATE</td><td>ARRESTS</td><td>% of USA</td><td>RANK</td><td>STATE</td><td>ARRESTS</td><td>% of USA</td></tr>
<tr><td>12</td><td>Alabama</td><td>8,080</td><td>2.08%</td><td>1</td><td>California</td><td>115,068</td><td>29.69%</td></tr>
<tr><td>36</td><td>Alaska</td><td>1,215</td><td>0.31%</td><td>2</td><td>New York</td><td>27,482</td><td>7.09%</td></tr>
<tr><td>18</td><td>Arizona</td><td>6,903</td><td>1.78%</td><td>3</td><td>Texas</td><td>23,260</td><td>6.00%</td></tr>
<tr><td>27</td><td>Arkansas</td><td>3,685</td><td>0.95%</td><td>4</td><td>North Carolina</td><td>21,378</td><td>5.52%</td></tr>
<tr><td>1</td><td>California</td><td>115,068</td><td>29.69%</td><td>5</td><td>Michigan</td><td>14,034</td><td>3.62%</td></tr>
<tr><td>26</td><td>Colorado</td><td>4,054</td><td>1.05%</td><td>6</td><td>New Jersey</td><td>13,119</td><td>3.38%</td></tr>
<tr><td>24</td><td>Connecticut</td><td>4,333</td><td>1.12%</td><td>7</td><td>Ohio</td><td>11,913</td><td>3.07%</td></tr>
<tr><td>35</td><td>Delaware</td><td>1,218</td><td>0.31%</td><td>8</td><td>Massachusetts</td><td>11,800</td><td>3.04%</td></tr>
<tr><td>NA</td><td>Florida**</td><td>NA</td><td>NA</td><td>9</td><td>Pennsylvania</td><td>11,440</td><td>2.95%</td></tr>
<tr><td>16</td><td>Georgia</td><td>7,300</td><td>1.88%</td><td>10</td><td>South Carolina</td><td>9,232</td><td>2.38%</td></tr>
<tr><td>40</td><td>Hawaii</td><td>631</td><td>0.16%</td><td>11</td><td>Illinois</td><td>8,182</td><td>2.11%</td></tr>
<tr><td>37</td><td>Idaho</td><td>1,143</td><td>0.29%</td><td>12</td><td>Alabama</td><td>8,080</td><td>2.08%</td></tr>
<tr><td>11</td><td>Illinois</td><td>8,182</td><td>2.11%</td><td>13</td><td>Louisiana</td><td>7,727</td><td>1.99%</td></tr>
<tr><td>17</td><td>Indiana</td><td>7,130</td><td>1.84%</td><td>14</td><td>Virginia</td><td>7,575</td><td>1.95%</td></tr>
<tr><td>29</td><td>Iowa</td><td>2,734</td><td>0.71%</td><td>15</td><td>Maryland</td><td>7,469</td><td>1.93%</td></tr>
<tr><td>NA</td><td>Kansas**</td><td>NA</td><td>NA</td><td>16</td><td>Georgia</td><td>7,300</td><td>1.88%</td></tr>
<tr><td>28</td><td>Kentucky</td><td>3,126</td><td>0.81%</td><td>17</td><td>Indiana</td><td>7,130</td><td>1.84%</td></tr>
<tr><td>13</td><td>Louisiana</td><td>7,727</td><td>1.99%</td><td>18</td><td>Arizona</td><td>6,903</td><td>1.78%</td></tr>
<tr><td>41</td><td>Maine</td><td>616</td><td>0.16%</td><td>19</td><td>Missouri</td><td>6,393</td><td>1.65%</td></tr>
<tr><td>15</td><td>Maryland</td><td>7,469</td><td>1.93%</td><td>20</td><td>Tennessee</td><td>6,390</td><td>1.65%</td></tr>
<tr><td>8</td><td>Massachusetts</td><td>11,800</td><td>3.04%</td><td>21</td><td>Wisconsin</td><td>6,106</td><td>1.58%</td></tr>
<tr><td>5</td><td>Michigan</td><td>14,034</td><td>3.62%</td><td>22</td><td>Oklahoma</td><td>4,899</td><td>1.26%</td></tr>
<tr><td>25</td><td>Minnesota</td><td>4,086</td><td>1.05%</td><td>23</td><td>Washington</td><td>4,498</td><td>1.16%</td></tr>
<tr><td>39</td><td>Mississippi</td><td>870</td><td>0.22%</td><td>24</td><td>Connecticut</td><td>4,333</td><td>1.12%</td></tr>
<tr><td>19</td><td>Missouri</td><td>6,393</td><td>1.65%</td><td>25</td><td>Minnesota</td><td>4,086</td><td>1.05%</td></tr>
<tr><td>NA</td><td>Montana**</td><td>NA</td><td>NA</td><td>26</td><td>Colorado</td><td>4,054</td><td>1.05%</td></tr>
<tr><td>42</td><td>Nebraska</td><td>578</td><td>0.15%</td><td>27</td><td>Arkansas</td><td>3,685</td><td>0.95%</td></tr>
<tr><td>32</td><td>Nevada</td><td>1,757</td><td>0.45%</td><td>28</td><td>Kentucky</td><td>3,126</td><td>0.81%</td></tr>
<tr><td>45</td><td>New Hampshire</td><td>292</td><td>0.08%</td><td>29</td><td>Iowa</td><td>2,734</td><td>0.71%</td></tr>
<tr><td>6</td><td>New Jersey</td><td>13,119</td><td>3.38%</td><td>30</td><td>Oregon</td><td>2,516</td><td>0.65%</td></tr>
<tr><td>33</td><td>New Mexico</td><td>1,685</td><td>0.43%</td><td>31</td><td>Rhode Island</td><td>2,082</td><td>0.54%</td></tr>
<tr><td>2</td><td>New York</td><td>27,482</td><td>7.09%</td><td>32</td><td>Nevada</td><td>1,757</td><td>0.45%</td></tr>
<tr><td>4</td><td>North Carolina</td><td>21,378</td><td>5.52%</td><td>33</td><td>New Mexico</td><td>1,685</td><td>0.43%</td></tr>
<tr><td>46</td><td>North Dakota</td><td>112</td><td>0.03%</td><td>34</td><td>Utah</td><td>1,621</td><td>0.42%</td></tr>
<tr><td>7</td><td>Ohio</td><td>11,913</td><td>3.07%</td><td>35</td><td>Delaware</td><td>1,218</td><td>0.31%</td></tr>
<tr><td>22</td><td>Oklahoma</td><td>4,899</td><td>1.26%</td><td>36</td><td>Alaska</td><td>1,215</td><td>0.31%</td></tr>
<tr><td>30</td><td>Oregon</td><td>2,516</td><td>0.65%</td><td>37</td><td>Idaho</td><td>1,143</td><td>0.29%</td></tr>
<tr><td>9</td><td>Pennsylvania</td><td>11,440</td><td>2.95%</td><td>38</td><td>West Virginia</td><td>947</td><td>0.24%</td></tr>
<tr><td>31</td><td>Rhode Island</td><td>2,082</td><td>0.54%</td><td>39</td><td>Mississippi</td><td>870</td><td>0.22%</td></tr>
<tr><td>10</td><td>South Carolina</td><td>9,232</td><td>2.38%</td><td>40</td><td>Hawaii</td><td>631</td><td>0.16%</td></tr>
<tr><td>43</td><td>South Dakota</td><td>525</td><td>0.14%</td><td>41</td><td>Maine</td><td>616</td><td>0.16%</td></tr>
<tr><td>20</td><td>Tennessee</td><td>6,390</td><td>1.65%</td><td>42</td><td>Nebraska</td><td>578</td><td>0.15%</td></tr>
<tr><td>3</td><td>Texas</td><td>23,260</td><td>6.00%</td><td>43</td><td>South Dakota</td><td>525</td><td>0.14%</td></tr>
<tr><td>34</td><td>Utah</td><td>1,621</td><td>0.42%</td><td>44</td><td>Wyoming</td><td>367</td><td>0.09%</td></tr>
<tr><td>NA</td><td>Vermont**</td><td>NA</td><td>NA</td><td>45</td><td>New Hampshire</td><td>292</td><td>0.08%</td></tr>
<tr><td>14</td><td>Virginia</td><td>7,575</td><td>1.95%</td><td>46</td><td>North Dakota</td><td>112</td><td>0.03%</td></tr>
<tr><td>23</td><td>Washington</td><td>4,498</td><td>1.16%</td><td>NA</td><td>Florida**</td><td>NA</td><td>NA</td></tr>
<tr><td>38</td><td>West Virginia</td><td>947</td><td>0.24%</td><td>NA</td><td>Kansas**</td><td>NA</td><td>NA</td></tr>
<tr><td>21</td><td>Wisconsin</td><td>6,106</td><td>1.58%</td><td>NA</td><td>Montana**</td><td>NA</td><td>NA</td></tr>
<tr><td>44</td><td>Wyoming</td><td>367</td><td>0.09%</td><td>NA</td><td>Vermont**</td><td>NA</td><td>NA</td></tr>
<tr><td></td><td></td><td></td><td></td><td></td><td>District of Columbia**</td><td>NA</td><td>NA</td></tr>
</table>

Source: Federal Bureau of Investigation
    "Crime in the United States 1996" (Uniform Crime Reports, October 4, 1997)
*By law enforcement agencies submitting complete reports to the F.B.I. for 12 months in 1996. The F.B.I. estimates 521,570 reported and unreported arrests for aggravated assault occurred in 1996. Aggravated assault is an attack for the purpose of inflicting severe bodily injury. See important note at beginning of this chapter.
**Not available.

13

Reported Arrest Rate for Aggravated Assault in 1996

National Rate = 204.1 Reported Arrests per 100,000 Population*

ALPHA ORDER

RANK ORDER

RANK	STATE	RATE		RANK	STATE	RATE
15	Alabama	196.1		1	Kentucky	408.6
10	Alaska	225.8		2	California	368.9
22	Arizona	165.4		3	Delaware	328.3
24	Arkansas	155.2		4	Tennessee	308.8
2	California	368.9		5	North Carolina	297.9
26	Colorado	143.4		6	Illinois	297.1
19	Connecticut	171.4		7	Louisiana	289.8
3	Delaware	328.3		8	South Carolina	252.4
NA	Florida**	NA		9	Massachusetts	234.4
23	Georgia	162.0		10	Alaska	225.8
41	Hawaii	53.3		11	Rhode Island	222.4
37	Idaho	97.6		12	New York	218.0
6	Illinois	297.1		13	Indiana	216.5
13	Indiana	216.5		14	Missouri	206.8
33	Iowa	118.7		15	Alabama	196.1
NA	Kansas**	NA		16	Maryland	185.6
1	Kentucky	408.6		17	Ohio	185.4
7	Louisiana	289.8		18	Michigan	177.9
43	Maine	50.4		19	Connecticut	171.4
16	Maryland	185.6		20	New Jersey	171.3
9	Massachusetts	234.4		21	New Mexico	167.7
18	Michigan	177.9		22	Arizona	165.4
38	Minnesota	97.1		23	Georgia	162.0
28	Mississippi	137.7		24	Arkansas	155.2
14	Missouri	206.8		25	Oklahoma	148.4
NA	Montana**	NA		26	Colorado	143.4
44	Nebraska	48.7		27	Texas	140.1
35	Nevada	112.0		28	Mississippi	137.7
45	New Hampshire	33.0		29	Wyoming	130.6
20	New Jersey	171.3		30	Pennsylvania	122.7
21	New Mexico	167.7		31	Virginia	122.6
12	New York	218.0		32	Washington	120.0
5	North Carolina	297.9		33	Iowa	118.7
46	North Dakota	28.3		33	Wisconsin	118.7
17	Ohio	185.4		35	Nevada	112.0
25	Oklahoma	148.4		36	South Dakota	104.0
39	Oregon	91.8		37	Idaho	97.6
30	Pennsylvania	122.7		38	Minnesota	97.1
11	Rhode Island	222.4		39	Oregon	91.8
8	South Carolina	252.4		40	Utah	88.1
36	South Dakota	104.0		41	Hawaii	53.3
4	Tennessee	308.8		42	West Virginia	51.9
27	Texas	140.1		43	Maine	50.4
40	Utah	88.1		44	Nebraska	48.7
NA	Vermont**	NA		45	New Hampshire	33.0
31	Virginia	122.6		46	North Dakota	28.3
32	Washington	120.0		NA	Florida**	NA
42	West Virginia	51.9		NA	Kansas**	NA
33	Wisconsin	118.7		NA	Montana**	NA
29	Wyoming	130.6		NA	Vermont**	NA
					District of Columbia**	NA

Source: Morgan Quitno Press using data from Federal Bureau of Investigation
    "Crime in the United States 1996" (Uniform Crime Reports, October 4, 1997)
*By law enforcement agencies submitting complete reports to the F.B.I. for 12 months in 1996. These rates based on population estimates for areas under the jurisdiction of those agencies reporting. Arrest rate based on the F.B.I. estimate of reported and unreported arrests for aggravated assault is 196.6 arrests per 100,000 population.   See important note at beginning of this chapter. **Not available.

Reported Arrests for Property Crime in 1996

National Total = 1,506,459 Reported Arrests*

ALPHA ORDER					RANK ORDER			
RANK	STATE		ARRESTS	% of USA	RANK	STATE	ARRESTS	% of USA
21	Alabama		26,052	1.73%	1	California	224,386	14.89%
42	Alaska		5,315	0.35%	2	Texas	131,647	8.74%
8	Arizona		48,664	3.23%	3	New York	74,576	4.95%
28	Arkansas		20,148	1.34%	4	North Carolina	59,077	3.92%
1	California		224,386	14.89%	5	Wisconsin	58,443	3.88%
23	Colorado		24,846	1.65%	6	Pennsylvania	52,068	3.46%
24	Connecticut		24,572	1.63%	7	New Jersey	51,725	3.43%
41	Delaware		5,457	0.36%	8	Arizona	48,664	3.23%
NA	Florida**		NA	NA	9	Illinois	46,638	3.10%
16	Georgia		37,485	2.49%	10	Virginia	44,886	2.98%
34	Hawaii		10,909	0.72%	11	Ohio	44,369	2.95%
33	Idaho		11,394	0.76%	12	Michigan	41,294	2.74%
9	Illinois		46,638	3.10%	13	Washington	41,108	2.73%
25	Indiana		23,284	1.55%	14	Maryland	39,770	2.64%
31	Iowa		12,952	0.86%	15	Missouri	38,587	2.56%
NA	Kansas**		NA	NA	16	Georgia	37,485	2.49%
37	Kentucky		8,222	0.55%	17	Oregon	34,996	2.32%
19	Louisiana		31,931	2.12%	18	Minnesota	32,325	2.15%
35	Maine		9,943	0.66%	19	Louisiana	31,931	2.12%
14	Maryland		39,770	2.64%	20	South Carolina	27,910	1.85%
29	Massachusetts		19,363	1.29%	21	Alabama	26,052	1.73%
12	Michigan		41,294	2.74%	22	Tennessee	25,003	1.66%
18	Minnesota		32,325	2.15%	23	Colorado	24,846	1.65%
39	Mississippi		7,026	0.47%	24	Connecticut	24,572	1.63%
15	Missouri		38,587	2.56%	25	Indiana	23,284	1.55%
NA	Montana**		NA	NA	26	Oklahoma	23,134	1.54%
38	Nebraska		7,918	0.53%	27	Utah	21,337	1.42%
30	Nevada		17,465	1.16%	28	Arkansas	20,148	1.34%
44	New Hampshire		4,373	0.29%	29	Massachusetts	19,363	1.29%
7	New Jersey		51,725	3.43%	30	Nevada	17,465	1.16%
32	New Mexico		11,991	0.80%	31	Iowa	12,952	0.86%
3	New York		74,576	4.95%	32	New Mexico	11,991	0.80%
4	North Carolina		59,077	3.92%	33	Idaho	11,394	0.76%
46	North Dakota		2,268	0.15%	34	Hawaii	10,909	0.72%
11	Ohio		44,369	2.95%	35	Maine	9,943	0.66%
26	Oklahoma		23,134	1.54%	36	West Virginia	8,678	0.58%
17	Oregon		34,996	2.32%	37	Kentucky	8,222	0.55%
6	Pennsylvania		52,068	3.46%	38	Nebraska	7,918	0.53%
40	Rhode Island		5,637	0.37%	39	Mississippi	7,026	0.47%
20	South Carolina		27,910	1.85%	40	Rhode Island	5,637	0.37%
43	South Dakota		4,916	0.33%	41	Delaware	5,457	0.36%
22	Tennessee		25,003	1.66%	42	Alaska	5,315	0.35%
2	Texas		131,647	8.74%	43	South Dakota	4,916	0.33%
27	Utah		21,337	1.42%	44	New Hampshire	4,373	0.29%
NA	Vermont**		NA	NA	45	Wyoming	2,371	0.16%
10	Virginia		44,886	2.98%	46	North Dakota	2,268	0.15%
13	Washington		41,108	2.73%	NA	Florida**	NA	NA
36	West Virginia		8,678	0.58%	NA	Kansas**	NA	NA
5	Wisconsin		58,443	3.88%	NA	Montana**	NA	NA
45	Wyoming		2,371	0.16%	NA	Vermont**	NA	NA
						District of Columbia**	NA	NA

Source: Federal Bureau of Investigation
    "Crime in the United States 1996" (Uniform Crime Reports, October 4, 1997)
*By law enforcement agencies submitting complete reports to the F.B.I. for 12 months in 1996. The F.B.I. estimates 2,045,600 reported and unreported arrests for property crime occurred in 1996. Property crimes are offenses of burglary, larceny-theft, motor vehicle theft and arson. See important note at beginning of this chapter.
**Not available.

Reported Arrest Rate for Property Crime in 1996

National Rate = 793.2 Reported Arrests per 100,000 Population*

ALPHA ORDER

RANK	STATE	RATE
37	Alabama	632.2
16	Alaska	987.9
8	Arizona	1,166.2
22	Arkansas	848.3
31	California	719.3
21	Colorado	878.9
19	Connecticut	972.0
2	Delaware	1,470.9
NA	Florida**	NA
24	Georgia	832.1
20	Hawaii	921.4
18	Idaho	973.0
1	Illinois	1,693.5
32	Indiana	706.9
41	Iowa	562.2
NA	Kansas**	NA
14	Kentucky	1,074.8
6	Louisiana	1,197.7
26	Maine	813.0
15	Maryland	988.1
46	Massachusetts	384.6
43	Michigan	523.5
28	Minnesota	768.0
12	Mississippi	1,111.7
4	Missouri	1,248.0
NA	Montana**	NA
36	Nebraska	667.1
11	Nevada	1,113.1
44	New Hampshire	494.1
35	New Jersey	675.5
7	New Mexico	1,193.1
39	New York	591.7
25	North Carolina	823.1
40	North Dakota	572.7
34	Ohio	690.5
33	Oklahoma	700.8
3	Oregon	1,277.2
42	Pennsylvania	558.5
38	Rhode Island	602.2
29	South Carolina	763.0
17	South Dakota	973.5
5	Tennessee	1,208.5
27	Texas	793.0
9	Utah	1,159.6
NA	Vermont**	NA
30	Virginia	726.7
13	Washington	1,097.1
45	West Virginia	475.2
10	Wisconsin	1,136.4
23	Wyoming	843.8

RANK ORDER

RANK	STATE	RATE
1	Illinois	1,693.5
2	Delaware	1,470.9
3	Oregon	1,277.2
4	Missouri	1,248.0
5	Tennessee	1,208.5
6	Louisiana	1,197.7
7	New Mexico	1,193.1
8	Arizona	1,166.2
9	Utah	1,159.6
10	Wisconsin	1,136.4
11	Nevada	1,113.1
12	Mississippi	1,111.7
13	Washington	1,097.1
14	Kentucky	1,074.8
15	Maryland	988.1
16	Alaska	987.9
17	South Dakota	973.5
18	Idaho	973.0
19	Connecticut	972.0
20	Hawaii	921.4
21	Colorado	878.9
22	Arkansas	848.3
23	Wyoming	843.8
24	Georgia	832.1
25	North Carolina	823.1
26	Maine	813.0
27	Texas	793.0
28	Minnesota	768.0
29	South Carolina	763.0
30	Virginia	726.7
31	California	719.3
32	Indiana	706.9
33	Oklahoma	700.8
34	Ohio	690.5
35	New Jersey	675.5
36	Nebraska	667.1
37	Alabama	632.2
38	Rhode Island	602.2
39	New York	591.7
40	North Dakota	572.7
41	Iowa	562.2
42	Pennsylvania	558.5
43	Michigan	523.5
44	New Hampshire	494.1
45	West Virginia	475.2
46	Massachusetts	384.6
NA	Florida**	NA
NA	Kansas**	NA
NA	Montana**	NA
NA	Vermont**	NA
	District of Columbia**	NA

*Source: Morgan Quitno Press using data from Federal Bureau of Investigation
"Crime in the United States 1996" (Uniform Crime Reports, October 4, 1997)*
*By law enforcement agencies submitting complete reports to the F.B.I. for 12 months in 1996. These rates based on population estimates for areas under the jurisdiction of those agencies reporting. Arrest rate based on the F.B.I. estimate of reported and unreported arrests for property crime is 771.1 arrests per 100,000 population. See important note at beginning of this chapter. **Not available.*

Reported Arrests for Burglary in 1996

National Total = 264,193 Reported Arrests*

ALPHA ORDER					RANK ORDER			
RANK	STATE	ARRESTS	% of USA		RANK	STATE	ARRESTS	% of USA
24	Alabama	3,845	1.46%		1	California	61,140	23.14%
41	Alaska	852	0.32%		2	Texas	20,737	7.85%
13	Arizona	5,969	2.26%		3	North Carolina	15,429	5.84%
26	Arkansas	3,243	1.23%		4	New York	13,212	5.00%
1	California	61,140	23.14%		5	New Jersey	9,166	3.47%
29	Colorado	2,469	0.93%		6	Pennsylvania	8,995	3.40%
21	Connecticut	4,197	1.59%		7	Maryland	7,780	2.94%
42	Delaware	794	0.30%		8	Michigan	7,779	2.94%
NA	Florida**	NA	NA		9	Ohio	7,418	2.81%
14	Georgia	5,930	2.24%		10	Wisconsin	6,817	2.58%
37	Hawaii	1,381	0.52%		11	Virginia	6,518	2.47%
36	Idaho	1,474	0.56%		12	Louisiana	6,127	2.32%
19	Illinois	4,350	1.65%		13	Arizona	5,969	2.26%
28	Indiana	2,609	0.99%		14	Georgia	5,930	2.24%
33	Iowa	1,802	0.68%		15	South Carolina	5,787	2.19%
NA	Kansas**	NA	NA		16	Washington	5,659	2.14%
34	Kentucky	1,699	0.64%		17	Missouri	5,011	1.90%
12	Louisiana	6,127	2.32%		18	Massachusetts	4,362	1.65%
30	Maine	2,099	0.79%		19	Illinois	4,350	1.65%
7	Maryland	7,780	2.94%		20	Oklahoma	4,253	1.61%
18	Massachusetts	4,362	1.65%		21	Connecticut	4,197	1.59%
8	Michigan	7,779	2.94%		22	Nevada	4,185	1.58%
25	Minnesota	3,697	1.40%		23	Oregon	3,885	1.47%
32	Mississippi	1,824	0.69%		24	Alabama	3,845	1.46%
17	Missouri	5,011	1.90%		25	Minnesota	3,697	1.40%
NA	Montana**	NA	NA		26	Arkansas	3,243	1.23%
40	Nebraska	962	0.36%		27	Tennessee	3,159	1.20%
22	Nevada	4,185	1.58%		28	Indiana	2,609	0.99%
44	New Hampshire	551	0.21%		29	Colorado	2,469	0.93%
5	New Jersey	9,166	3.47%		30	Maine	2,099	0.79%
38	New Mexico	1,210	0.46%		31	Utah	1,863	0.71%
4	New York	13,212	5.00%		32	Mississippi	1,824	0.69%
3	North Carolina	15,429	5.84%		33	Iowa	1,802	0.68%
46	North Dakota	252	0.10%		34	Kentucky	1,699	0.64%
9	Ohio	7,418	2.81%		35	West Virginia	1,595	0.60%
20	Oklahoma	4,253	1.61%		36	Idaho	1,474	0.56%
23	Oregon	3,885	1.47%		37	Hawaii	1,381	0.52%
6	Pennsylvania	8,995	3.40%		38	New Mexico	1,210	0.46%
39	Rhode Island	1,079	0.41%		39	Rhode Island	1,079	0.41%
15	South Carolina	5,787	2.19%		40	Nebraska	962	0.36%
43	South Dakota	747	0.28%		41	Alaska	852	0.32%
27	Tennessee	3,159	1.20%		42	Delaware	794	0.30%
2	Texas	20,737	7.85%		43	South Dakota	747	0.28%
31	Utah	1,863	0.71%		44	New Hampshire	551	0.21%
NA	Vermont**	NA	NA		45	Wyoming	281	0.11%
11	Virginia	6,518	2.47%		46	North Dakota	252	0.10%
16	Washington	5,659	2.14%		NA	Florida**	NA	NA
35	West Virginia	1,595	0.60%		NA	Kansas**	NA	NA
10	Wisconsin	6,817	2.58%		NA	Montana**	NA	NA
45	Wyoming	281	0.11%		NA	Vermont**	NA	NA
						District of Columbia**	NA	NA

Source: Federal Bureau of Investigation
    "Crime in the United States 1996" (Uniform Crime Reports, October 4, 1997)
*By law enforcement agencies submitting complete reports to the F.B.I. for 12 months in 1996. The F.B.I. estimates
364,800 reported and unreported arrests for burglary occurred in 1996. Burglary is the unlawful entry of a structure
to commit a felony or theft. Attempts are included.   See important note at beginning of this chapter.
**Not available.

Reported Arrest Rate for Burglary in 1996

National Rate = 139.1 Reported Arrests per 100,000 Population*

<table>
<tr><td colspan="3">ALPHA ORDER</td><td colspan="3">RANK ORDER</td></tr>
<tr><td>RANK</td><td>STATE</td><td>RATE</td><td>RANK</td><td>STATE</td><td>RATE</td></tr>
<tr><td>37</td><td>Alabama</td><td>93.3</td><td>1</td><td>Mississippi</td><td>288.6</td></tr>
<tr><td>12</td><td>Alaska</td><td>158.4</td><td>2</td><td>Nevada</td><td>266.7</td></tr>
<tr><td>18</td><td>Arizona</td><td>143.0</td><td>3</td><td>Louisiana</td><td>229.8</td></tr>
<tr><td>20</td><td>Arkansas</td><td>136.5</td><td>4</td><td>Kentucky</td><td>222.1</td></tr>
<tr><td>7</td><td>California</td><td>196.0</td><td>5</td><td>North Carolina</td><td>215.0</td></tr>
<tr><td>39</td><td>Colorado</td><td>87.3</td><td>6</td><td>Delaware</td><td>214.0</td></tr>
<tr><td>10</td><td>Connecticut</td><td>166.0</td><td>7</td><td>California</td><td>196.0</td></tr>
<tr><td>6</td><td>Delaware</td><td>214.0</td><td>8</td><td>Maryland</td><td>193.3</td></tr>
<tr><td>NA</td><td>Florida**</td><td>NA</td><td>9</td><td>Maine</td><td>171.6</td></tr>
<tr><td>22</td><td>Georgia</td><td>131.6</td><td>10</td><td>Connecticut</td><td>166.0</td></tr>
<tr><td>28</td><td>Hawaii</td><td>116.6</td><td>11</td><td>Missouri</td><td>162.1</td></tr>
<tr><td>24</td><td>Idaho</td><td>125.9</td><td>12</td><td>Alaska</td><td>158.4</td></tr>
<tr><td>14</td><td>Illinois</td><td>158.0</td><td>13</td><td>South Carolina</td><td>158.2</td></tr>
<tr><td>43</td><td>Indiana</td><td>79.2</td><td>14</td><td>Illinois</td><td>158.0</td></tr>
<tr><td>44</td><td>Iowa</td><td>78.2</td><td>15</td><td>Tennessee</td><td>152.7</td></tr>
<tr><td>NA</td><td>Kansas**</td><td>NA</td><td>16</td><td>Washington</td><td>151.0</td></tr>
<tr><td>4</td><td>Kentucky</td><td>222.1</td><td>17</td><td>South Dakota</td><td>147.9</td></tr>
<tr><td>3</td><td>Louisiana</td><td>229.8</td><td>18</td><td>Arizona</td><td>143.0</td></tr>
<tr><td>9</td><td>Maine</td><td>171.6</td><td>19</td><td>Oregon</td><td>141.8</td></tr>
<tr><td>8</td><td>Maryland</td><td>193.3</td><td>20</td><td>Arkansas</td><td>136.5</td></tr>
<tr><td>41</td><td>Massachusetts</td><td>86.7</td><td>21</td><td>Wisconsin</td><td>132.5</td></tr>
<tr><td>35</td><td>Michigan</td><td>98.6</td><td>22</td><td>Georgia</td><td>131.6</td></tr>
<tr><td>38</td><td>Minnesota</td><td>87.8</td><td>23</td><td>Oklahoma</td><td>128.8</td></tr>
<tr><td>1</td><td>Mississippi</td><td>288.6</td><td>24</td><td>Idaho</td><td>125.9</td></tr>
<tr><td>11</td><td>Missouri</td><td>162.1</td><td>25</td><td>Texas</td><td>124.9</td></tr>
<tr><td>NA</td><td>Montana**</td><td>NA</td><td>26</td><td>New Mexico</td><td>120.4</td></tr>
<tr><td>42</td><td>Nebraska</td><td>81.0</td><td>27</td><td>New Jersey</td><td>119.7</td></tr>
<tr><td>2</td><td>Nevada</td><td>266.7</td><td>28</td><td>Hawaii</td><td>116.6</td></tr>
<tr><td>46</td><td>New Hampshire</td><td>62.3</td><td>29</td><td>Ohio</td><td>115.4</td></tr>
<tr><td>27</td><td>New Jersey</td><td>119.7</td><td>30</td><td>Rhode Island</td><td>115.3</td></tr>
<tr><td>26</td><td>New Mexico</td><td>120.4</td><td>31</td><td>Virginia</td><td>105.5</td></tr>
<tr><td>32</td><td>New York</td><td>104.8</td><td>32</td><td>New York</td><td>104.8</td></tr>
<tr><td>5</td><td>North Carolina</td><td>215.0</td><td>33</td><td>Utah</td><td>101.3</td></tr>
<tr><td>45</td><td>North Dakota</td><td>63.6</td><td>34</td><td>Wyoming</td><td>100.0</td></tr>
<tr><td>29</td><td>Ohio</td><td>115.4</td><td>35</td><td>Michigan</td><td>98.6</td></tr>
<tr><td>23</td><td>Oklahoma</td><td>128.8</td><td>36</td><td>Pennsylvania</td><td>96.5</td></tr>
<tr><td>19</td><td>Oregon</td><td>141.8</td><td>37</td><td>Alabama</td><td>93.3</td></tr>
<tr><td>36</td><td>Pennsylvania</td><td>96.5</td><td>38</td><td>Minnesota</td><td>87.8</td></tr>
<tr><td>30</td><td>Rhode Island</td><td>115.3</td><td>39</td><td>Colorado</td><td>87.3</td></tr>
<tr><td>13</td><td>South Carolina</td><td>158.2</td><td>39</td><td>West Virginia</td><td>87.3</td></tr>
<tr><td>17</td><td>South Dakota</td><td>147.9</td><td>41</td><td>Massachusetts</td><td>86.7</td></tr>
<tr><td>15</td><td>Tennessee</td><td>152.7</td><td>42</td><td>Nebraska</td><td>81.0</td></tr>
<tr><td>25</td><td>Texas</td><td>124.9</td><td>43</td><td>Indiana</td><td>79.2</td></tr>
<tr><td>33</td><td>Utah</td><td>101.3</td><td>44</td><td>Iowa</td><td>78.2</td></tr>
<tr><td>NA</td><td>Vermont**</td><td>NA</td><td>45</td><td>North Dakota</td><td>63.6</td></tr>
<tr><td>31</td><td>Virginia</td><td>105.5</td><td>46</td><td>New Hampshire</td><td>62.3</td></tr>
<tr><td>16</td><td>Washington</td><td>151.0</td><td>NA</td><td>Florida**</td><td>NA</td></tr>
<tr><td>39</td><td>West Virginia</td><td>87.3</td><td>NA</td><td>Kansas**</td><td>NA</td></tr>
<tr><td>21</td><td>Wisconsin</td><td>132.5</td><td>NA</td><td>Montana**</td><td>NA</td></tr>
<tr><td>34</td><td>Wyoming</td><td>100.0</td><td>NA</td><td>Vermont**</td><td>NA</td></tr>
<tr><td></td><td></td><td></td><td></td><td>District of Columbia**</td><td>NA</td></tr>
</table>

Source: Morgan Quitno Press using data from Federal Bureau of Investigation
"Crime in the United States 1996" (Uniform Crime Reports, October 4, 1997)
*By law enforcement agencies submitting complete reports to the F.B.I. for 12 months in 1996. These rates based on population estimates for areas under the jurisdiction of those agencies reporting. Arrest rate based on the F.B.I. estimate of reported and unreported arrests for burglary is 137.5 arrests per 100,000 population. See important note at beginning of this chapter. **Not available.

Reported Arrests for Larceny and Theft in 1996

National Total = 1,096,488 Reported Arrests*

<u>ALPHA ORDER</u>

RANK	STATE	ARRESTS	% of USA
22	Alabama	20,472	1.87%
41	Alaska	3,983	0.36%
7	Arizona	39,197	3.57%
27	Arkansas	16,156	1.47%
1	California	130,242	11.88%
21	Colorado	20,716	1.89%
24	Connecticut	18,599	1.70%
40	Delaware	4,468	0.41%
NA	Florida**	NA	NA
15	Georgia	29,385	2.68%
34	Hawaii	8,021	0.73%
33	Idaho	9,188	0.84%
10	Illinois	33,548	3.06%
25	Indiana	18,198	1.66%
31	Iowa	10,281	0.94%
NA	Kansas**	NA	NA
38	Kentucky	5,446	0.50%
19	Louisiana	24,236	2.21%
35	Maine	7,175	0.65%
17	Maryland	26,104	2.38%
29	Massachusetts	13,321	1.21%
14	Michigan	29,842	2.72%
18	Minnesota	24,872	2.27%
39	Mississippi	4,744	0.43%
13	Missouri	29,919	2.73%
NA	Montana**	NA	NA
36	Nebraska	6,428	0.59%
30	Nevada	11,722	1.07%
44	New Hampshire	3,618	0.33%
6	New Jersey	39,845	3.63%
32	New Mexico	10,131	0.92%
3	New York	53,983	4.92%
5	North Carolina	40,752	3.72%
46	North Dakota	1,833	0.17%
12	Ohio	32,502	2.96%
28	Oklahoma	16,016	1.46%
16	Oregon	27,430	2.50%
8	Pennsylvania	35,596	3.25%
42	Rhode Island	3,944	0.36%
20	South Carolina	20,792	1.90%
43	South Dakota	3,915	0.36%
23	Tennessee	19,550	1.78%
2	Texas	100,021	9.12%
26	Utah	17,848	1.63%
NA	Vermont**	NA	NA
9	Virginia	34,643	3.16%
11	Washington	33,286	3.04%
37	West Virginia	6,419	0.59%
4	Wisconsin	46,144	4.21%
45	Wyoming	1,957	0.18%

<u>RANK ORDER</u>

RANK	STATE	ARRESTS	% of USA
1	California	130,242	11.88%
2	Texas	100,021	9.12%
3	New York	53,983	4.92%
4	Wisconsin	46,144	4.21%
5	North Carolina	40,752	3.72%
6	New Jersey	39,845	3.63%
7	Arizona	39,197	3.57%
8	Pennsylvania	35,596	3.25%
9	Virginia	34,643	3.16%
10	Illinois	33,548	3.06%
11	Washington	33,286	3.04%
12	Ohio	32,502	2.96%
13	Missouri	29,919	2.73%
14	Michigan	29,842	2.72%
15	Georgia	29,385	2.68%
16	Oregon	27,430	2.50%
17	Maryland	26,104	2.38%
18	Minnesota	24,872	2.27%
19	Louisiana	24,236	2.21%
20	South Carolina	20,792	1.90%
21	Colorado	20,716	1.89%
22	Alabama	20,472	1.87%
23	Tennessee	19,550	1.78%
24	Connecticut	18,599	1.70%
25	Indiana	18,198	1.66%
26	Utah	17,848	1.63%
27	Arkansas	16,156	1.47%
28	Oklahoma	16,016	1.46%
29	Massachusetts	13,321	1.21%
30	Nevada	11,722	1.07%
31	Iowa	10,281	0.94%
32	New Mexico	10,131	0.92%
33	Idaho	9,188	0.84%
34	Hawaii	8,021	0.73%
35	Maine	7,175	0.65%
36	Nebraska	6,428	0.59%
37	West Virginia	6,419	0.59%
38	Kentucky	5,446	0.50%
39	Mississippi	4,744	0.43%
40	Delaware	4,468	0.41%
41	Alaska	3,983	0.36%
42	Rhode Island	3,944	0.36%
43	South Dakota	3,915	0.36%
44	New Hampshire	3,618	0.33%
45	Wyoming	1,957	0.18%
46	North Dakota	1,833	0.17%
NA	Florida**	NA	NA
NA	Kansas**	NA	NA
NA	Montana**	NA	NA
NA	Vermont**	NA	NA
	District of Columbia**	NA	NA

Source: Federal Bureau of Investigation
    "Crime in the United States 1996" (Uniform Crime Reports, October 4, 1997)
*By law enforcement agencies submitting complete reports to the F.B.I. for 12 months in 1996. The F.B.I. estimates 1,486,300 reported and unreported arrests for larceny and theft occurred in 1996. Larceny and theft is the unlawful taking of property without use of force, violence or fraud. Attempts are included. Motor vehicle thefts are excluded. See important note at beginning of this chapter. **Not available.

Reported Arrest Rate for Larceny and Theft in 1996

National Rate = 577.3 Reported Arrests per 100,000 Population*

ALPHA ORDER

RANK	STATE	RATE
35	Alabama	496.8
16	Alaska	740.3
8	Arizona	939.3
21	Arkansas	680.3
41	California	417.5
18	Colorado	732.8
17	Connecticut	735.7
2	Delaware	1,204.3
NA	Florida**	NA
23	Georgia	652.3
22	Hawaii	677.4
12	Idaho	784.6
1	Illinois	1,218.2
31	Indiana	552.5
38	Iowa	446.2
NA	Kansas**	NA
19	Kentucky	711.9
9	Louisiana	909.1
27	Maine	586.7
24	Maryland	648.5
46	Massachusetts	264.6
44	Michigan	378.3
26	Minnesota	590.9
14	Mississippi	750.6
6	Missouri	967.6
NA	Montana**	NA
32	Nebraska	541.5
15	Nevada	747.1
42	New Hampshire	408.8
33	New Jersey	520.4
3	New Mexico	1,008.1
39	New York	428.3
29	North Carolina	567.8
37	North Dakota	462.9
34	Ohio	505.8
36	Oklahoma	485.2
4	Oregon	1,001.1
43	Pennsylvania	381.8
40	Rhode Island	421.4
28	South Carolina	568.4
13	South Dakota	775.2
7	Tennessee	944.9
25	Texas	602.5
5	Utah	970.0
NA	Vermont**	NA
30	Virginia	560.8
11	Washington	888.3
45	West Virginia	351.5
10	Wisconsin	897.2
20	Wyoming	696.4

RANK ORDER

RANK	STATE	RATE
1	Illinois	1,218.2
2	Delaware	1,204.3
3	New Mexico	1,008.1
4	Oregon	1,001.1
5	Utah	970.0
6	Missouri	967.6
7	Tennessee	944.9
8	Arizona	939.3
9	Louisiana	909.1
10	Wisconsin	897.2
11	Washington	888.3
12	Idaho	784.6
13	South Dakota	775.2
14	Mississippi	750.6
15	Nevada	747.1
16	Alaska	740.3
17	Connecticut	735.7
18	Colorado	732.8
19	Kentucky	711.9
20	Wyoming	696.4
21	Arkansas	680.3
22	Hawaii	677.4
23	Georgia	652.3
24	Maryland	648.5
25	Texas	602.5
26	Minnesota	590.9
27	Maine	586.7
28	South Carolina	568.4
29	North Carolina	567.8
30	Virginia	560.8
31	Indiana	552.5
32	Nebraska	541.5
33	New Jersey	520.4
34	Ohio	505.8
35	Alabama	496.8
36	Oklahoma	485.2
37	North Dakota	462.9
38	Iowa	446.2
39	New York	428.3
40	Rhode Island	421.4
41	California	417.5
42	New Hampshire	408.8
43	Pennsylvania	381.8
44	Michigan	378.3
45	West Virginia	351.5
46	Massachusetts	264.6
NA	Florida**	NA
NA	Kansas**	NA
NA	Montana**	NA
NA	Vermont**	NA
	District of Columbia**	NA

Source: Morgan Quitno Press using data from Federal Bureau of Investigation
   "Crime in the United States 1996" (Uniform Crime Reports, October 4, 1997)
*By law enforcement agencies submitting complete reports to the F.B.I. for 12 months in 1996. These rates based
on population estimates for areas under the jurisdiction of those agencies reporting. Arrest rate based on the F.B.I.
estimate of reported and unreported arrests for larceny and theft is 560.3 arrests per 100,000 population. See
important note at beginning of this chapter. **Not available.*

Reported Arrests for Motor Vehicle Theft in 1996

National Total = 132,023 Reported Arrests*

ALPHA ORDER					RANK ORDER				
RANK	STATE		ARRESTS	% of USA	RANK	STATE		ARRESTS	% of USA
23	Alabama		1,586	1.20%	1	California		30,766	23.30%
39	Alaska		452	0.34%	2	Texas		9,917	7.51%
13	Arizona		3,109	2.35%	3	Illinois		8,566	6.49%
33	Arkansas		632	0.48%	4	New York		6,930	5.25%
1	California		30,766	23.30%	5	Pennsylvania		6,753	5.12%
28	Colorado		1,379	1.04%	6	Maryland		5,527	4.19%
22	Connecticut		1,596	1.21%	7	Wisconsin		4,966	3.76%
43	Delaware		186	0.14%	8	Ohio		3,840	2.91%
NA	Florida**		NA	NA	9	Minnesota		3,470	2.63%
20	Georgia		1,920	1.45%	10	Missouri		3,306	2.50%
25	Hawaii		1,472	1.11%	11	Virginia		3,273	2.48%
35	Idaho		603	0.46%	12	Oregon		3,221	2.44%
3	Illinois		8,566	6.49%	13	Arizona		3,109	2.35%
17	Indiana		2,282	1.73%	14	Michigan		2,998	2.27%
32	Iowa		685	0.52%	15	Oklahoma		2,417	1.83%
NA	Kansas**		NA	NA	16	North Carolina		2,388	1.81%
31	Kentucky		1,038	0.79%	17	Indiana		2,282	1.73%
29	Louisiana		1,366	1.03%	18	New Jersey		2,172	1.65%
37	Maine		525	0.40%	19	Tennessee		2,115	1.60%
6	Maryland		5,527	4.19%	20	Georgia		1,920	1.45%
24	Massachusetts		1,554	1.18%	21	Washington		1,850	1.40%
14	Michigan		2,998	2.27%	22	Connecticut		1,596	1.21%
9	Minnesota		3,470	2.63%	23	Alabama		1,586	1.20%
41	Mississippi		416	0.32%	24	Massachusetts		1,554	1.18%
10	Missouri		3,306	2.50%	25	Hawaii		1,472	1.11%
NA	Montana**		NA	NA	26	Nevada		1,456	1.10%
40	Nebraska		437	0.33%	27	Utah		1,433	1.09%
26	Nevada		1,456	1.10%	28	Colorado		1,379	1.04%
45	New Hampshire		153	0.12%	29	Louisiana		1,366	1.03%
18	New Jersey		2,172	1.65%	30	South Carolina		1,115	0.84%
34	New Mexico		607	0.46%	31	Kentucky		1,038	0.79%
4	New York		6,930	5.25%	32	Iowa		685	0.52%
16	North Carolina		2,388	1.81%	33	Arkansas		632	0.48%
44	North Dakota		170	0.13%	34	New Mexico		607	0.46%
8	Ohio		3,840	2.91%	35	Idaho		603	0.46%
15	Oklahoma		2,417	1.83%	36	West Virginia		561	0.42%
12	Oregon		3,221	2.44%	37	Maine		525	0.40%
5	Pennsylvania		6,753	5.12%	38	Rhode Island		503	0.38%
38	Rhode Island		503	0.38%	39	Alaska		452	0.34%
30	South Carolina		1,115	0.84%	40	Nebraska		437	0.33%
42	South Dakota		193	0.15%	41	Mississippi		416	0.32%
19	Tennessee		2,115	1.60%	42	South Dakota		193	0.15%
2	Texas		9,917	7.51%	43	Delaware		186	0.14%
27	Utah		1,433	1.09%	44	North Dakota		170	0.13%
NA	Vermont**		NA	NA	45	New Hampshire		153	0.12%
11	Virginia		3,273	2.48%	46	Wyoming		119	0.09%
21	Washington		1,850	1.40%	NA	Florida**		NA	NA
36	West Virginia		561	0.42%	NA	Kansas**		NA	NA
7	Wisconsin		4,966	3.76%	NA	Montana**		NA	NA
46	Wyoming		119	0.09%	NA	Vermont**		NA	NA
						District of Columbia**		NA	NA

Source: Federal Bureau of Investigation
"Crime in the United States 1996" (Uniform Crime Reports, October 4, 1997)
*By law enforcement agencies submitting complete reports to the F.B.I. for 12 months in 1996. The F.B.I. estimates 175,400 reported and unreported arrests for motor vehicle theft occurred in 1996. Motor vehicle theft includes the theft or attempted theft of a self-propelled vehicle. Excludes motorboats, construction equipment, airplanes and farming equipment. See important note at beginning of this chapter. **Not available.

Reported Arrest Rate for Motor Vehicle Theft in 1996

National Rate = 69.5 Reported Arrests per 100,000 Population*

ALPHA ORDER

RANK	STATE	RATE
35	Alabama	38.5
11	Alaska	84.0
14	Arizona	74.5
45	Arkansas	26.6
8	California	98.6
30	Colorado	48.8
19	Connecticut	63.1
28	Delaware	50.1
NA	Florida**	NA
33	Georgia	42.6
4	Hawaii	124.3
26	Idaho	51.5
1	Illinois	311.0
17	Indiana	69.3
43	Iowa	29.7
NA	Kansas**	NA
3	Kentucky	135.7
27	Louisiana	51.2
31	Maine	42.9
2	Maryland	137.3
40	Massachusetts	30.9
37	Michigan	38.0
12	Minnesota	82.4
18	Mississippi	65.8
6	Missouri	106.9
NA	Montana**	NA
38	Nebraska	36.8
10	Nevada	92.8
46	New Hampshire	17.3
44	New Jersey	28.4
20	New Mexico	60.4
23	New York	55.0
39	North Carolina	33.3
31	North Dakota	42.9
21	Ohio	59.8
15	Oklahoma	73.2
5	Oregon	117.6
16	Pennsylvania	72.4
24	Rhode Island	53.7
42	South Carolina	30.5
36	South Dakota	38.2
7	Tennessee	102.2
22	Texas	59.7
13	Utah	77.9
NA	Vermont**	NA
25	Virginia	53.0
29	Washington	49.4
41	West Virginia	30.7
9	Wisconsin	96.6
34	Wyoming	42.3

RANK ORDER

RANK	STATE	RATE
1	Illinois	311.0
2	Maryland	137.3
3	Kentucky	135.7
4	Hawaii	124.3
5	Oregon	117.6
6	Missouri	106.9
7	Tennessee	102.2
8	California	98.6
9	Wisconsin	96.6
10	Nevada	92.8
11	Alaska	84.0
12	Minnesota	82.4
13	Utah	77.9
14	Arizona	74.5
15	Oklahoma	73.2
16	Pennsylvania	72.4
17	Indiana	69.3
18	Mississippi	65.8
19	Connecticut	63.1
20	New Mexico	60.4
21	Ohio	59.8
22	Texas	59.7
23	New York	55.0
24	Rhode Island	53.7
25	Virginia	53.0
26	Idaho	51.5
27	Louisiana	51.2
28	Delaware	50.1
29	Washington	49.4
30	Colorado	48.8
31	Maine	42.9
31	North Dakota	42.9
33	Georgia	42.6
34	Wyoming	42.3
35	Alabama	38.5
36	South Dakota	38.2
37	Michigan	38.0
38	Nebraska	36.8
39	North Carolina	33.3
40	Massachusetts	30.9
41	West Virginia	30.7
42	South Carolina	30.5
43	Iowa	29.7
44	New Jersey	28.4
45	Arkansas	26.6
46	New Hampshire	17.3
NA	Florida**	NA
NA	Kansas**	NA
NA	Montana**	NA
NA	Vermont**	NA
	District of Columbia**	NA

Source: Morgan Quitno Press using data from Federal Bureau of Investigation
 "Crime in the United States 1996" (Uniform Crime Reports, October 4, 1997)
*By law enforcement agencies submitting complete reports to the F.B.I. for 12 months in 1996. These rates based on population estimates for areas under the jurisdiction of those agencies reporting. Arrest rate based on the F.B.I. estimate of reported and unreported arrests for motor vehicle theft is 66.1 arrests per 100,000 population. See important note at beginning of this chapter. **Not available.

Reported Arrests for Arson in 1996

National Total = 13,755 Reported Arrests*

ALPHA ORDER					RANK ORDER			
RANK	STATE		ARRESTS	% of USA	RANK	STATE	ARRESTS	% of USA
28	Alabama		149	1.08%	1	California	2,238	16.27%
43	Alaska		28	0.20%	2	Texas	972	7.07%
13	Arizona		389	2.83%	3	Pennsylvania	724	5.26%
32	Arkansas		117	0.85%	4	Michigan	675	4.91%
1	California		2,238	16.27%	5	Ohio	609	4.43%
18	Colorado		282	2.05%	6	New Jersey	542	3.94%
25	Connecticut		180	1.31%	7	Wisconsin	516	3.75%
46	Delaware		9	0.07%	8	North Carolina	508	3.69%
NA	Florida**		NA	NA	9	Oregon	460	3.34%
19	Georgia		250	1.82%	10	Virginia	452	3.29%
42	Hawaii		35	0.25%	11	New York	451	3.28%
30	Idaho		129	0.94%	12	Oklahoma	448	3.26%
27	Illinois		174	1.26%	13	Arizona	389	2.83%
22	Indiana		195	1.42%	14	Maryland	359	2.61%
24	Iowa		184	1.34%	15	Missouri	351	2.55%
NA	Kansas**		NA	NA	16	Washington	313	2.28%
41	Kentucky		39	0.28%	17	Minnesota	286	2.08%
21	Louisiana		202	1.47%	18	Colorado	282	2.05%
29	Maine		144	1.05%	19	Georgia	250	1.82%
14	Maryland		359	2.61%	20	South Carolina	216	1.57%
31	Massachusetts		126	0.92%	21	Louisiana	202	1.47%
4	Michigan		675	4.91%	22	Indiana	195	1.42%
17	Minnesota		286	2.08%	23	Utah	193	1.40%
40	Mississippi		42	0.31%	24	Iowa	184	1.34%
15	Missouri		351	2.55%	25	Connecticut	180	1.31%
NA	Montana**		NA	NA	26	Tennessee	179	1.30%
36	Nebraska		91	0.66%	27	Illinois	174	1.26%
35	Nevada		102	0.74%	28	Alabama	149	1.08%
38	New Hampshire		51	0.37%	29	Maine	144	1.05%
6	New Jersey		542	3.94%	30	Idaho	129	0.94%
39	New Mexico		43	0.31%	31	Massachusetts	126	0.92%
11	New York		451	3.28%	32	Arkansas	117	0.85%
8	North Carolina		508	3.69%	33	Rhode Island	111	0.81%
45	North Dakota		13	0.09%	34	West Virginia	103	0.75%
5	Ohio		609	4.43%	35	Nevada	102	0.74%
12	Oklahoma		448	3.26%	36	Nebraska	91	0.66%
9	Oregon		460	3.34%	37	South Dakota	61	0.44%
3	Pennsylvania		724	5.26%	38	New Hampshire	51	0.37%
33	Rhode Island		111	0.81%	39	New Mexico	43	0.31%
20	South Carolina		216	1.57%	40	Mississippi	42	0.31%
37	South Dakota		61	0.44%	41	Kentucky	39	0.28%
26	Tennessee		179	1.30%	42	Hawaii	35	0.25%
2	Texas		972	7.07%	43	Alaska	28	0.20%
23	Utah		193	1.40%	44	Wyoming	14	0.10%
NA	Vermont**		NA	NA	45	North Dakota	13	0.09%
10	Virginia		452	3.29%	46	Delaware	9	0.07%
16	Washington		313	2.28%	NA	Florida**	NA	NA
34	West Virginia		103	0.75%	NA	Kansas**	NA	NA
7	Wisconsin		516	3.75%	NA	Montana**	NA	NA
44	Wyoming		14	0.10%	NA	Vermont**	NA	NA
						District of Columbia**	NA	NA

Source: Federal Bureau of Investigation
"Crime in the United States 1996" (Uniform Crime Reports, October 4, 1997)
*By law enforcement agencies submitting complete reports to the F.B.I. for 12 months in 1996. The F.B.I. estimates 19,000 reported and unreported arrests for arson occurred in 1996. Arson is the willful burning of or attempt to burn a building, vehicle or another's personal property. See important note at beginning of this chapter.
**Not available.

Reported Arrest Rate for Arson in 1996

National Rate = 7.2 Reported Arrests per 100,000 Population*

ALPHA ORDER

RANK	STATE	RATE
41	Alabama	3.6
36	Alaska	5.2
12	Arizona	9.3
39	Arkansas	4.9
22	California	7.2
9	Colorado	10.0
23	Connecticut	7.1
46	Delaware	2.4
NA	Florida**	NA
35	Georgia	5.5
44	Hawaii	3.0
7	Idaho	11.0
29	Illinois	6.3
30	Indiana	5.9
17	Iowa	8.0
NA	Kansas**	NA
37	Kentucky	5.1
20	Louisiana	7.6
5	Maine	11.8
13	Maryland	8.9
45	Massachusetts	2.5
15	Michigan	8.6
26	Minnesota	6.8
27	Mississippi	6.6
6	Missouri	11.4
NA	Montana**	NA
19	Nebraska	7.7
28	Nevada	6.5
33	New Hampshire	5.8
23	New Jersey	7.1
40	New Mexico	4.3
41	New York	3.6
23	North Carolina	7.1
43	North Dakota	3.3
11	Ohio	9.5
2	Oklahoma	13.6
1	Oregon	16.8
18	Pennsylvania	7.8
4	Rhode Island	11.9
30	South Carolina	5.9
3	South Dakota	12.1
14	Tennessee	8.7
30	Texas	5.9
8	Utah	10.5
NA	Vermont**	NA
21	Virginia	7.3
16	Washington	8.4
34	West Virginia	5.6
9	Wisconsin	10.0
38	Wyoming	5.0

RANK ORDER

RANK	STATE	RATE
1	Oregon	16.8
2	Oklahoma	13.6
3	South Dakota	12.1
4	Rhode Island	11.9
5	Maine	11.8
6	Missouri	11.4
7	Idaho	11.0
8	Utah	10.5
9	Colorado	10.0
9	Wisconsin	10.0
11	Ohio	9.5
12	Arizona	9.3
13	Maryland	8.9
14	Tennessee	8.7
15	Michigan	8.6
16	Washington	8.4
17	Iowa	8.0
18	Pennsylvania	7.8
19	Nebraska	7.7
20	Louisiana	7.6
21	Virginia	7.3
22	California	7.2
23	Connecticut	7.1
23	New Jersey	7.1
23	North Carolina	7.1
26	Minnesota	6.8
27	Mississippi	6.6
28	Nevada	6.5
29	Illinois	6.3
30	Indiana	5.9
30	South Carolina	5.9
30	Texas	5.9
33	New Hampshire	5.8
34	West Virginia	5.6
35	Georgia	5.5
36	Alaska	5.2
37	Kentucky	5.1
38	Wyoming	5.0
39	Arkansas	4.9
40	New Mexico	4.3
41	Alabama	3.6
41	New York	3.6
43	North Dakota	3.3
44	Hawaii	3.0
45	Massachusetts	2.5
46	Delaware	2.4
NA	Florida**	NA
NA	Kansas**	NA
NA	Montana**	NA
NA	Vermont**	NA

District of Columbia**   NA

Source: Morgan Quitno Press using data from Federal Bureau of Investigation
"Crime in the United States 1996" (Uniform Crime Reports, October 4, 1997)
*By law enforcement agencies submitting complete reports to the F.B.I. for 12 months in 1996. These rates based on population estimates for areas under the jurisdiction of those agencies reporting. Arrest rate based on the F.B.I. estimate of reported and unreported arrests for arson is 7.2 arrests per 100,000 population. See important note at beginning of this chapter. **Not available.

Reported Arrests for Weapons Violations in 1996

National Total = 161,158 Reported Arrests*

ALPHA ORDER

RANK	STATE	ARRESTS	% of USA
23	Alabama	2,381	1.48%
38	Alaska	490	0.30%
13	Arizona	3,981	2.47%
21	Arkansas	2,527	1.57%
1	California	31,281	19.41%
20	Colorado	2,535	1.57%
27	Connecticut	1,898	1.18%
41	Delaware	342	0.21%
NA	Florida**	NA	NA
17	Georgia	2,946	1.83%
40	Hawaii	432	0.27%
34	Idaho	703	0.44%
8	Illinois	6,240	3.87%
28	Indiana	1,758	1.09%
36	Iowa	600	0.37%
NA	Kansas**	NA	NA
32	Kentucky	964	0.60%
25	Louisiana	2,034	1.26%
42	Maine	310	0.19%
12	Maryland	4,023	2.50%
30	Massachusetts	1,293	0.80%
6	Michigan	6,572	4.08%
18	Minnesota	2,665	1.65%
39	Mississippi	439	0.27%
11	Missouri	4,717	2.93%
NA	Montana**	NA	NA
35	Nebraska	636	0.39%
26	Nevada	1,977	1.23%
44	New Hampshire	126	0.08%
9	New Jersey	5,699	3.54%
33	New Mexico	850	0.53%
3	New York	10,338	6.41%
4	North Carolina	7,967	4.94%
46	North Dakota	75	0.05%
10	Ohio	4,725	2.93%
19	Oklahoma	2,580	1.60%
24	Oregon	2,245	1.39%
14	Pennsylvania	3,571	2.22%
37	Rhode Island	514	0.32%
15	South Carolina	3,149	1.95%
43	South Dakota	182	0.11%
16	Tennessee	3,039	1.89%
2	Texas	13,544	8.40%
31	Utah	1,252	0.78%
NA	Vermont**	NA	NA
5	Virginia	7,287	4.52%
22	Washington	2,497	1.55%
29	West Virginia	1,335	0.83%
7	Wisconsin	6,346	3.94%
45	Wyoming	93	0.06%

RANK ORDER

RANK	STATE	ARRESTS	% of USA
1	California	31,281	19.41%
2	Texas	13,544	8.40%
3	New York	10,338	6.41%
4	North Carolina	7,967	4.94%
5	Virginia	7,287	4.52%
6	Michigan	6,572	4.08%
7	Wisconsin	6,346	3.94%
8	Illinois	6,240	3.87%
9	New Jersey	5,699	3.54%
10	Ohio	4,725	2.93%
11	Missouri	4,717	2.93%
12	Maryland	4,023	2.50%
13	Arizona	3,981	2.47%
14	Pennsylvania	3,571	2.22%
15	South Carolina	3,149	1.95%
16	Tennessee	3,039	1.89%
17	Georgia	2,946	1.83%
18	Minnesota	2,665	1.65%
19	Oklahoma	2,580	1.60%
20	Colorado	2,535	1.57%
21	Arkansas	2,527	1.57%
22	Washington	2,497	1.55%
23	Alabama	2,381	1.48%
24	Oregon	2,245	1.39%
25	Louisiana	2,034	1.26%
26	Nevada	1,977	1.23%
27	Connecticut	1,898	1.18%
28	Indiana	1,758	1.09%
29	West Virginia	1,335	0.83%
30	Massachusetts	1,293	0.80%
31	Utah	1,252	0.78%
32	Kentucky	964	0.60%
33	New Mexico	850	0.53%
34	Idaho	703	0.44%
35	Nebraska	636	0.39%
36	Iowa	600	0.37%
37	Rhode Island	514	0.32%
38	Alaska	490	0.30%
39	Mississippi	439	0.27%
40	Hawaii	432	0.27%
41	Delaware	342	0.21%
42	Maine	310	0.19%
43	South Dakota	182	0.11%
44	New Hampshire	126	0.08%
45	Wyoming	93	0.06%
46	North Dakota	75	0.05%
NA	Florida**	NA	NA
NA	Kansas**	NA	NA
NA	Montana**	NA	NA
NA	Vermont**	NA	NA
	District of Columbia**	NA	NA

Source: Federal Bureau of Investigation
  "Crime in the United States 1996" (Uniform Crime Reports, October 4, 1997)
*By law enforcement agencies submitting complete reports to the F.B.I. for 12 months in 1996. The F.B.I. estimates
216,200 reported and unreported arrests for weapons violations occurred in 1996. Weapons violations include
illegal carrying and possession. See important note at beginning of this chapter.
**Not available.

Reported Arrest Rate for Weapons Violations in 1996

National Rate = 84.9 Reported Arrests per 100,000 Population*

ALPHA ORDER

RANK	STATE	RATE
34	Alabama	57.8
14	Alaska	91.1
12	Arizona	95.4
9	Arkansas	106.4
10	California	100.3
15	Colorado	89.7
24	Connecticut	75.1
13	Delaware	92.2
NA	Florida**	NA
31	Georgia	65.4
39	Hawaii	36.5
33	Idaho	60.0
1	Illinois	226.6
37	Indiana	53.4
42	Iowa	26.0
NA	Kansas**	NA
4	Kentucky	126.0
23	Louisiana	76.3
44	Maine	25.3
11	Maryland	100.0
43	Massachusetts	25.7
18	Michigan	83.3
32	Minnesota	63.3
28	Mississippi	69.5
2	Missouri	152.6
NA	Montana**	NA
36	Nebraska	53.6
4	Nevada	126.0
46	New Hampshire	14.2
25	New Jersey	74.4
17	New Mexico	84.6
19	New York	82.0
8	North Carolina	111.0
45	North Dakota	18.9
26	Ohio	73.5
22	Oklahoma	78.2
20	Oregon	81.9
38	Pennsylvania	38.3
35	Rhode Island	54.9
16	South Carolina	86.1
40	South Dakota	36.0
3	Tennessee	146.9
21	Texas	81.6
29	Utah	68.0
NA	Vermont**	NA
7	Virginia	118.0
30	Washington	66.6
27	West Virginia	73.1
6	Wisconsin	123.4
41	Wyoming	33.1

RANK ORDER

RANK	STATE	RATE
1	Illinois	226.6
2	Missouri	152.6
3	Tennessee	146.9
4	Kentucky	126.0
4	Nevada	126.0
6	Wisconsin	123.4
7	Virginia	118.0
8	North Carolina	111.0
9	Arkansas	106.4
10	California	100.3
11	Maryland	100.0
12	Arizona	95.4
13	Delaware	92.2
14	Alaska	91.1
15	Colorado	89.7
16	South Carolina	86.1
17	New Mexico	84.6
18	Michigan	83.3
19	New York	82.0
20	Oregon	81.9
21	Texas	81.6
22	Oklahoma	78.2
23	Louisiana	76.3
24	Connecticut	75.1
25	New Jersey	74.4
26	Ohio	73.5
27	West Virginia	73.1
28	Mississippi	69.5
29	Utah	68.0
30	Washington	66.6
31	Georgia	65.4
32	Minnesota	63.3
33	Idaho	60.0
34	Alabama	57.8
35	Rhode Island	54.9
36	Nebraska	53.6
37	Indiana	53.4
38	Pennsylvania	38.3
39	Hawaii	36.5
40	South Dakota	36.0
41	Wyoming	33.1
42	Iowa	26.0
43	Massachusetts	25.7
44	Maine	25.3
45	North Dakota	18.9
46	New Hampshire	14.2
NA	Florida**	NA
NA	Kansas**	NA
NA	Montana**	NA
NA	Vermont**	NA
	District of Columbia**	NA

Source: Morgan Quitno Press using data from Federal Bureau of Investigation
   "Crime in the United States 1996" (Uniform Crime Reports, October 4, 1997)
*By law enforcement agencies submitting complete reports to the F.B.I. for 12 months in 1996. These rates based on population estimates for areas under the jurisdiction of those agencies reporting. Arrest rate based on the F.B.I. estimate of reported and unreported arrests for weapons violations is 81.5 arrests per 100,000 population. See important note at beginning of this chapter. **Not available.

Reported Arrests for Driving Under the Influence in 1996

National Total = 1,013,932 Reported Arrests*

ALPHA ORDER

RANK	STATE	ARRESTS	% of USA
17	Alabama	18,919	1.87%
40	Alaska	4,373	0.43%
8	Arizona	32,398	3.20%
18	Arkansas	18,656	1.84%
1	California	199,536	19.68%
9	Colorado	29,599	2.92%
31	Connecticut	9,489	0.94%
46	Delaware	146	0.01%
NA	Florida**	NA	NA
7	Georgia	32,538	3.21%
38	Hawaii	4,733	0.47%
28	Idaho	11,176	1.10%
42	Illinois	2,894	0.29%
20	Indiana	16,088	1.59%
27	Iowa	12,051	1.19%
NA	Kansas**	NA	NA
39	Kentucky	4,403	0.43%
29	Louisiana	10,757	1.06%
33	Maine	7,984	0.79%
19	Maryland	17,913	1.77%
23	Massachusetts	15,431	1.52%
4	Michigan	46,506	4.59%
6	Minnesota	33,348	3.29%
36	Mississippi	5,740	0.57%
21	Missouri	15,873	1.57%
NA	Montana**	NA	NA
32	Nebraska	8,617	0.85%
34	Nevada	7,473	0.74%
37	New Hampshire	5,074	0.50%
12	New Jersey	24,486	2.41%
26	New Mexico	12,595	1.24%
14	New York	24,031	2.37%
3	North Carolina	71,411	7.04%
44	North Dakota	1,992	0.20%
13	Ohio	24,049	2.37%
15	Oklahoma	21,658	2.14%
16	Oregon	20,449	2.02%
10	Pennsylvania	29,296	2.89%
45	Rhode Island	1,881	0.19%
24	South Carolina	15,326	1.51%
41	South Dakota	4,187	0.41%
25	Tennessee	14,427	1.42%
2	Texas	75,497	7.45%
35	Utah	7,410	0.73%
NA	Vermont**	NA	NA
11	Virginia	28,100	2.77%
22	Washington	15,495	1.53%
30	West Virginia	9,817	0.97%
5	Wisconsin	37,470	3.70%
43	Wyoming	2,640	0.26%

RANK ORDER

RANK	STATE	ARRESTS	% of USA
1	California	199,536	19.68%
2	Texas	75,497	7.45%
3	North Carolina	71,411	7.04%
4	Michigan	46,506	4.59%
5	Wisconsin	37,470	3.70%
6	Minnesota	33,348	3.29%
7	Georgia	32,538	3.21%
8	Arizona	32,398	3.20%
9	Colorado	29,599	2.92%
10	Pennsylvania	29,296	2.89%
11	Virginia	28,100	2.77%
12	New Jersey	24,486	2.41%
13	Ohio	24,049	2.37%
14	New York	24,031	2.37%
15	Oklahoma	21,658	2.14%
16	Oregon	20,449	2.02%
17	Alabama	18,919	1.87%
18	Arkansas	18,656	1.84%
19	Maryland	17,913	1.77%
20	Indiana	16,088	1.59%
21	Missouri	15,873	1.57%
22	Washington	15,495	1.53%
23	Massachusetts	15,431	1.52%
24	South Carolina	15,326	1.51%
25	Tennessee	14,427	1.42%
26	New Mexico	12,595	1.24%
27	Iowa	12,051	1.19%
28	Idaho	11,176	1.10%
29	Louisiana	10,757	1.06%
30	West Virginia	9,817	0.97%
31	Connecticut	9,489	0.94%
32	Nebraska	8,617	0.85%
33	Maine	7,984	0.79%
34	Nevada	7,473	0.74%
35	Utah	7,410	0.73%
36	Mississippi	5,740	0.57%
37	New Hampshire	5,074	0.50%
38	Hawaii	4,733	0.47%
39	Kentucky	4,403	0.43%
40	Alaska	4,373	0.43%
41	South Dakota	4,187	0.41%
42	Illinois	2,894	0.29%
43	Wyoming	2,640	0.26%
44	North Dakota	1,992	0.20%
45	Rhode Island	1,881	0.19%
46	Delaware	146	0.01%
NA	Florida**	NA	NA
NA	Kansas**	NA	NA
NA	Montana**	NA	NA
NA	Vermont**	NA	NA
	District of Columbia**	NA	NA

Source: Federal Bureau of Investigation
    "Crime in the United States 1996" (Uniform Crime Reports, October 4, 1997)
*By law enforcement agencies submitting complete reports to the F.B.I. for 12 months in 1996. The F.B.I. estimates
1,467,300 reported and unreported arrests for driving under the influence occurred in 1996. Includes driving any
vehicle while drunk or under the influence of liquor or narcotics. See important note at beginning of this chapter.
**Not available.

27

Reported Arrest Rate for Driving Under the Influence in 1996

National Rate = 533.9 Reported Arrests per 100,000 Population*

ALPHA ORDER

RANK ORDER

RANK	STATE	RATE	RANK	STATE	RATE
29	Alabama	459.1	1	New Mexico	1,253.2
8	Alaska	812.8	2	Colorado	1,047.0
11	Arizona	776.4	3	North Carolina	995.0
10	Arkansas	785.5	4	Idaho	954.4
19	California	639.6	5	Wyoming	939.5
2	Colorado	1,047.0	6	Mississippi	908.2
38	Connecticut	375.4	7	South Dakota	829.1
46	Delaware	39.4	8	Alaska	812.8
NA	Florida**	NA	9	Minnesota	792.3
15	Georgia	722.3	10	Arkansas	785.5
37	Hawaii	399.7	11	Arizona	776.4
4	Idaho	954.4	12	Oregon	746.3
45	Illinois	105.1	13	Wisconsin	728.6
27	Indiana	488.4	14	Nebraska	725.9
24	Iowa	523.0	15	Georgia	722.3
NA	Kansas**	NA	16	Tennessee	697.3
21	Kentucky	575.6	17	Oklahoma	656.1
35	Louisiana	403.5	18	Maine	652.8
18	Maine	652.8	19	California	639.6
32	Maryland	445.0	20	Michigan	589.6
42	Massachusetts	306.5	21	Kentucky	575.6
20	Michigan	589.6	22	New Hampshire	573.3
9	Minnesota	792.3	23	West Virginia	537.6
6	Mississippi	908.2	24	Iowa	523.0
25	Missouri	513.4	25	Missouri	513.4
NA	Montana**	NA	26	North Dakota	503.0
14	Nebraska	725.9	27	Indiana	488.4
28	Nevada	476.3	28	Nevada	476.3
22	New Hampshire	573.3	29	Alabama	459.1
40	New Jersey	319.8	30	Virginia	454.9
1	New Mexico	1,253.2	31	Texas	454.8
44	New York	190.7	32	Maryland	445.0
3	North Carolina	995.0	33	South Carolina	419.0
26	North Dakota	503.0	34	Washington	413.5
39	Ohio	374.2	35	Louisiana	403.5
17	Oklahoma	656.1	36	Utah	402.7
12	Oregon	746.3	37	Hawaii	399.7
41	Pennsylvania	314.3	38	Connecticut	375.4
43	Rhode Island	201.0	39	Ohio	374.2
33	South Carolina	419.0	40	New Jersey	319.8
7	South Dakota	829.1	41	Pennsylvania	314.3
16	Tennessee	697.3	42	Massachusetts	306.5
31	Texas	454.8	43	Rhode Island	201.0
36	Utah	402.7	44	New York	190.7
NA	Vermont**	NA	45	Illinois	105.1
30	Virginia	454.9	46	Delaware	39.4
34	Washington	413.5	NA	Florida**	NA
23	West Virginia	537.6	NA	Kansas**	NA
13	Wisconsin	728.6	NA	Montana**	NA
5	Wyoming	939.5	NA	Vermont**	NA
				District of Columbia**	NA

Source: Morgan Quitno Press using data from Federal Bureau of Investigation
"Crime in the United States 1996" (Uniform Crime Reports, October 4, 1997)
*By law enforcement agencies submitting complete reports to the F.B.I. for 12 months in 1996. These rates based
on population estimates for areas under the jurisdiction of those agencies reporting. Arrest rate based on the F.B.I.
estimate of reported and unreported arrests for driving under the influence is 553.1 arrests per 100,000 population.
See important note at beginning of this chapter. **Not available.

Reported Arrests for Drug Abuse Violations in 1996

National Total = 1,128,647 Reported Arrests*

ALPHA ORDER

RANK	STATE	ARRESTS	% of USA
22	Alabama	14,647	1.30%
44	Alaska	1,619	0.14%
13	Arizona	24,348	2.16%
27	Arkansas	11,640	1.03%
1	California	252,974	22.41%
25	Colorado	12,950	1.15%
18	Connecticut	16,479	1.46%
43	Delaware	1,764	0.16%
NA	Florida**	NA	NA
12	Georgia	24,522	2.17%
40	Hawaii	3,470	0.31%
37	Idaho	3,991	0.35%
5	Illinois	52,903	4.69%
29	Indiana	11,047	0.98%
32	Iowa	6,570	0.58%
NA	Kansas**	NA	NA
31	Kentucky	6,663	0.59%
20	Louisiana	14,993	1.33%
38	Maine	3,789	0.34%
9	Maryland	32,952	2.92%
15	Massachusetts	22,262	1.97%
7	Michigan	33,398	2.96%
24	Minnesota	14,025	1.24%
35	Mississippi	4,239	0.38%
14	Missouri	22,692	2.01%
NA	Montana**	NA	NA
36	Nebraska	4,128	0.37%
30	Nevada	8,753	0.78%
41	New Hampshire	2,756	0.24%
4	New Jersey	56,075	4.97%
33	New Mexico	6,185	0.55%
2	New York	135,316	11.99%
6	North Carolina	35,658	3.16%
46	North Dakota	640	0.06%
8	Ohio	33,030	2.93%
23	Oklahoma	14,360	1.27%
19	Oregon	15,493	1.37%
11	Pennsylvania	25,474	2.26%
39	Rhode Island	3,773	0.33%
17	South Carolina	20,841	1.85%
42	South Dakota	1,788	0.16%
26	Tennessee	12,479	1.11%
3	Texas	78,440	6.95%
28	Utah	11,114	0.98%
NA	Vermont**	NA	NA
10	Virginia	27,261	2.42%
21	Washington	14,707	1.30%
34	West Virginia	4,346	0.39%
16	Wisconsin	21,232	1.88%
45	Wyoming	861	0.08%

RANK ORDER

RANK	STATE	ARRESTS	% of USA
1	California	252,974	22.41%
2	New York	135,316	11.99%
3	Texas	78,440	6.95%
4	New Jersey	56,075	4.97%
5	Illinois	52,903	4.69%
6	North Carolina	35,658	3.16%
7	Michigan	33,398	2.96%
8	Ohio	33,030	2.93%
9	Maryland	32,952	2.92%
10	Virginia	27,261	2.42%
11	Pennsylvania	25,474	2.26%
12	Georgia	24,522	2.17%
13	Arizona	24,348	2.16%
14	Missouri	22,692	2.01%
15	Massachusetts	22,262	1.97%
16	Wisconsin	21,232	1.88%
17	South Carolina	20,841	1.85%
18	Connecticut	16,479	1.46%
19	Oregon	15,493	1.37%
20	Louisiana	14,993	1.33%
21	Washington	14,707	1.30%
22	Alabama	14,647	1.30%
23	Oklahoma	14,360	1.27%
24	Minnesota	14,025	1.24%
25	Colorado	12,950	1.15%
26	Tennessee	12,479	1.11%
27	Arkansas	11,640	1.03%
28	Utah	11,114	0.98%
29	Indiana	11,047	0.98%
30	Nevada	8,753	0.78%
31	Kentucky	6,663	0.59%
32	Iowa	6,570	0.58%
33	New Mexico	6,185	0.55%
34	West Virginia	4,346	0.39%
35	Mississippi	4,239	0.38%
36	Nebraska	4,128	0.37%
37	Idaho	3,991	0.35%
38	Maine	3,789	0.34%
39	Rhode Island	3,773	0.33%
40	Hawaii	3,470	0.31%
41	New Hampshire	2,756	0.24%
42	South Dakota	1,788	0.16%
43	Delaware	1,764	0.16%
44	Alaska	1,619	0.14%
45	Wyoming	861	0.08%
46	North Dakota	640	0.06%
NA	Florida**	NA	NA
NA	Kansas**	NA	NA
NA	Montana**	NA	NA
NA	Vermont**	NA	NA
	District of Columbia**	NA	NA

Source: Federal Bureau of Investigation
   "Crime in the United States 1996" (Uniform Crime Reports, October 4, 1997)
*By law enforcement agencies submitting complete reports to the F.B.I. for 12 months in 1996. The F.B.I. estimates 1,506,200 reported and unreported arrests for drug abuse violations occurred in 1996. Includes offenses relating to possession, sale, use, growing and manufacturing of narcotic drugs. See important note at beginning of this chapter.
**Not available.

Reported Arrest Rate for Drug Abuse Violations in 1996

National Rate = 594.3 Reported Arrests per 100,000 Population*

ALPHA ORDER				RANK ORDER		
RANK	STATE	RATE		RANK	STATE	RATE
32	Alabama	355.4		1	Illinois	1,921.0
41	Alaska	300.9		2	New York	1,073.6
13	Arizona	583.5		3	Kentucky	871.0
21	Arkansas	490.1		4	Maryland	818.7
5	California	810.9		5	California	810.9
24	Colorado	458.1		6	Missouri	733.9
9	Connecticut	651.9		7	New Jersey	732.3
22	Delaware	475.5		8	Mississippi	670.7
NA	Florida**	NA		9	Connecticut	651.9
18	Georgia	544.3		10	New Mexico	615.4
42	Hawaii	293.1		11	Utah	604.0
35	Idaho	340.8		12	Tennessee	603.1
1	Illinois	1,921.0		13	Arizona	583.5
36	Indiana	335.4		14	South Carolina	569.7
43	Iowa	285.2		15	Oregon	565.4
NA	Kansas**	NA		16	Louisiana	562.4
3	Kentucky	871.0		17	Nevada	557.9
16	Louisiana	562.4		18	Georgia	544.3
39	Maine	309.8		19	Ohio	514.0
4	Maryland	818.7		20	North Carolina	496.8
25	Massachusetts	442.2		21	Arkansas	490.1
28	Michigan	423.4		22	Delaware	475.5
37	Minnesota	333.2		23	Texas	472.5
8	Mississippi	670.7		24	Colorado	458.1
6	Missouri	733.9		25	Massachusetts	442.2
NA	Montana**	NA		26	Virginia	441.3
34	Nebraska	347.8		27	Oklahoma	435.0
17	Nevada	557.9		28	Michigan	423.4
38	New Hampshire	311.4		29	Wisconsin	412.8
7	New Jersey	732.3		30	Rhode Island	403.1
10	New Mexico	615.4		31	Washington	392.5
2	New York	1,073.6		32	Alabama	355.4
20	North Carolina	496.8		33	South Dakota	354.1
46	North Dakota	161.6		34	Nebraska	347.8
19	Ohio	514.0		35	Idaho	340.8
27	Oklahoma	435.0		36	Indiana	335.4
15	Oregon	565.4		37	Minnesota	333.2
44	Pennsylvania	273.3		38	New Hampshire	311.4
30	Rhode Island	403.1		39	Maine	309.8
14	South Carolina	569.7		40	Wyoming	306.4
33	South Dakota	354.1		41	Alaska	300.9
12	Tennessee	603.1		42	Hawaii	293.1
23	Texas	472.5		43	Iowa	285.2
11	Utah	604.0		44	Pennsylvania	273.3
NA	Vermont**	NA		45	West Virginia	238.0
26	Virginia	441.3		46	North Dakota	161.6
31	Washington	392.5		NA	Florida**	NA
45	West Virginia	238.0		NA	Kansas**	NA
29	Wisconsin	412.8		NA	Montana**	NA
40	Wyoming	306.4		NA	Vermont**	NA
					District of Columbia**	NA

Source: Morgan Quitno Press using data from Federal Bureau of Investigation
  "Crime in the United States 1996" (Uniform Crime Reports, October 4, 1997)
*By law enforcement agencies submitting complete reports to the F.B.I. for 12 months in 1996. These rates based on population estimates for areas under the jurisdiction of those agencies reporting. Arrest rate based on the F.B.I. estimate of reported and unreported arrests for drug abuse violations is 567.8 arrests per 100,000 population. See important note at beginning of this chapter. **Not available.

Reported Arrests for Sex Offenses in 1996

National Total = 70,619 Reported Arrests*

ALPHA ORDER

RANK	STATE	ARRESTS	% of USA
30	Alabama	409	0.58%
36	Alaska	313	0.44%
8	Arizona	2,238	3.17%
28	Arkansas	501	0.71%
1	California	15,724	22.27%
18	Colorado	1,218	1.72%
27	Connecticut	686	0.97%
42	Delaware	214	0.30%
NA	Florida**	NA	NA
14	Georgia	1,837	2.60%
32	Hawaii	367	0.52%
34	Idaho	326	0.46%
9	Illinois	2,137	3.03%
24	Indiana	865	1.22%
41	Iowa	234	0.33%
NA	Kansas**	NA	NA
39	Kentucky	260	0.37%
19	Louisiana	1,024	1.45%
35	Maine	319	0.45%
16	Maryland	1,407	1.99%
21	Massachusetts	981	1.39%
13	Michigan	1,899	2.69%
26	Minnesota	743	1.05%
38	Mississippi	284	0.40%
11	Missouri	1,995	2.83%
NA	Montana**	NA	NA
36	Nebraska	313	0.44%
20	Nevada	1,017	1.44%
40	New Hampshire	251	0.36%
12	New Jersey	1,977	2.80%
43	New Mexico	141	0.20%
3	New York	5,064	7.17%
5	North Carolina	2,547	3.61%
45	North Dakota	83	0.12%
10	Ohio	2,105	2.98%
21	Oklahoma	981	1.39%
17	Oregon	1,303	1.85%
7	Pennsylvania	2,311	3.27%
31	Rhode Island	371	0.53%
25	South Carolina	855	1.21%
44	South Dakota	130	0.18%
29	Tennessee	468	0.66%
2	Texas	5,361	7.59%
23	Utah	968	1.37%
NA	Vermont**	NA	NA
6	Virginia	2,326	3.29%
15	Washington	1,719	2.43%
33	West Virginia	330	0.47%
4	Wisconsin	3,942	5.58%
46	Wyoming	75	0.11%

RANK ORDER

RANK	STATE	ARRESTS	% of USA
1	California	15,724	22.27%
2	Texas	5,361	7.59%
3	New York	5,064	7.17%
4	Wisconsin	3,942	5.58%
5	North Carolina	2,547	3.61%
6	Virginia	2,326	3.29%
7	Pennsylvania	2,311	3.27%
8	Arizona	2,238	3.17%
9	Illinois	2,137	3.03%
10	Ohio	2,105	2.98%
11	Missouri	1,995	2.83%
12	New Jersey	1,977	2.80%
13	Michigan	1,899	2.69%
14	Georgia	1,837	2.60%
15	Washington	1,719	2.43%
16	Maryland	1,407	1.99%
17	Oregon	1,303	1.85%
18	Colorado	1,218	1.72%
19	Louisiana	1,024	1.45%
20	Nevada	1,017	1.44%
21	Massachusetts	981	1.39%
21	Oklahoma	981	1.39%
23	Utah	968	1.37%
24	Indiana	865	1.22%
25	South Carolina	855	1.21%
26	Minnesota	743	1.05%
27	Connecticut	686	0.97%
28	Arkansas	501	0.71%
29	Tennessee	468	0.66%
30	Alabama	409	0.58%
31	Rhode Island	371	0.53%
32	Hawaii	367	0.52%
33	West Virginia	330	0.47%
34	Idaho	326	0.46%
35	Maine	319	0.45%
36	Alaska	313	0.44%
36	Nebraska	313	0.44%
38	Mississippi	284	0.40%
39	Kentucky	260	0.37%
40	New Hampshire	251	0.36%
41	Iowa	234	0.33%
42	Delaware	214	0.30%
43	New Mexico	141	0.20%
44	South Dakota	130	0.18%
45	North Dakota	83	0.12%
46	Wyoming	75	0.11%
NA	Florida**	NA	NA
NA	Kansas**	NA	NA
NA	Montana**	NA	NA
NA	Vermont**	NA	NA
	District of Columbia**	NA	NA

Source: Federal Bureau of Investigation
   "Crime in the United States 1996" (Uniform Crime Reports, October 4, 1997)
*By law enforcement agencies submitting complete reports to the F.B.I. for 12 months in 1996. The F.B.I. estimates 95,800 reported and unreported arrests for sex offenses occurred in 1996. Excludes forcible rape, prostitution and commercialized vice. Includes statutory rape and offenses against chastity, common decency, morals and the like. See important note at beginning of this chapter. **Not available.

Reported Arrest Rate for Sex Offenses in 1996

National Rate = 37.2 Reported Arrests per 100,000 Population*

ALPHA ORDER				RANK ORDER		
RANK	STATE	RATE		RANK	STATE	RATE
46	Alabama	9.9		1	Illinois	77.6
5	Alaska	58.2		2	Wisconsin	76.6
7	Arizona	53.6		3	Nevada	64.8
39	Arkansas	21.1		4	Missouri	64.5
9	California	50.4		5	Alaska	58.2
13	Colorado	43.1		6	Delaware	57.7
28	Connecticut	27.1		7	Arizona	53.6
6	Delaware	57.7		8	Utah	52.6
NA	Florida**	NA		9	California	50.4
14	Georgia	40.8		10	Oregon	47.6
24	Hawaii	31.0		11	Washington	45.9
27	Idaho	27.8		12	Mississippi	44.9
1	Illinois	77.6		13	Colorado	43.1
31	Indiana	26.3		14	Georgia	40.8
45	Iowa	10.2		15	New York	40.2
NA	Kansas**	NA		16	Rhode Island	39.6
21	Kentucky	34.0		17	Louisiana	38.4
17	Louisiana	38.4		18	Virginia	37.7
32	Maine	26.1		19	North Carolina	35.5
20	Maryland	35.0		20	Maryland	35.0
41	Massachusetts	19.5		21	Kentucky	34.0
36	Michigan	24.1		22	Ohio	32.8
43	Minnesota	17.7		23	Texas	32.3
12	Mississippi	44.9		24	Hawaii	31.0
4	Missouri	64.5		25	Oklahoma	29.7
NA	Montana**	NA		26	New Hampshire	28.4
30	Nebraska	26.4		27	Idaho	27.8
3	Nevada	64.8		28	Connecticut	27.1
26	New Hampshire	28.4		29	Wyoming	26.7
33	New Jersey	25.8		30	Nebraska	26.4
44	New Mexico	14.0		31	Indiana	26.3
15	New York	40.2		32	Maine	26.1
19	North Carolina	35.5		33	New Jersey	25.8
40	North Dakota	21.0		34	South Dakota	25.7
22	Ohio	32.8		35	Pennsylvania	24.8
25	Oklahoma	29.7		36	Michigan	24.1
10	Oregon	47.6		37	South Carolina	23.4
35	Pennsylvania	24.8		38	Tennessee	22.6
16	Rhode Island	39.6		39	Arkansas	21.1
37	South Carolina	23.4		40	North Dakota	21.0
34	South Dakota	25.7		41	Massachusetts	19.5
38	Tennessee	22.6		42	West Virginia	18.1
23	Texas	32.3		43	Minnesota	17.7
8	Utah	52.6		44	New Mexico	14.0
NA	Vermont**	NA		45	Iowa	10.2
18	Virginia	37.7		46	Alabama	9.9
11	Washington	45.9		NA	Florida**	NA
42	West Virginia	18.1		NA	Kansas**	NA
2	Wisconsin	76.6		NA	Montana**	NA
29	Wyoming	26.7		NA	Vermont**	NA
					District of Columbia**	NA

Source: Morgan Quitno Press using data from Federal Bureau of Investigation
"Crime in the United States 1996" (Uniform Crime Reports, October 4, 1997)
*By law enforcement agencies submitting complete reports to the F.B.I. for 12 months in 1996. These rates based on population estimates for areas under the jurisdiction of those agencies reporting. Arrest rate based on the F.B.I. estimate of reported and unreported arrests for sex offenses is 36.1 arrests per 100,000 population. See important note at beginning of this chapter. **Not available.*

32

Reported Arrests for Prostitution and Commercialized Vice in 1996

National Total = 81,036 Reported Arrests*

<table>
<tr><td colspan="4">ALPHA ORDER</td><td colspan="4">RANK ORDER</td></tr>
<tr><th>RANK</th><th>STATE</th><th>ARRESTS</th><th>% of USA</th><th>RANK</th><th>STATE</th><th>ARRESTS</th><th>% of USA</th></tr>
<tr><td>32</td><td>Alabama</td><td>263</td><td>0.32%</td><td>1</td><td>California</td><td>17,393</td><td>21.46%</td></tr>
<tr><td>37</td><td>Alaska</td><td>185</td><td>0.23%</td><td>2</td><td>New York</td><td>9,148</td><td>11.29%</td></tr>
<tr><td>10</td><td>Arizona</td><td>2,460</td><td>3.04%</td><td>3</td><td>Illinois</td><td>7,780</td><td>9.60%</td></tr>
<tr><td>34</td><td>Arkansas</td><td>235</td><td>0.29%</td><td>4</td><td>Texas</td><td>6,277</td><td>7.75%</td></tr>
<tr><td>1</td><td>California</td><td>17,393</td><td>21.46%</td><td>5</td><td>Michigan</td><td>3,628</td><td>4.48%</td></tr>
<tr><td>17</td><td>Colorado</td><td>1,178</td><td>1.45%</td><td>6</td><td>Nevada</td><td>3,458</td><td>4.27%</td></tr>
<tr><td>25</td><td>Connecticut</td><td>550</td><td>0.68%</td><td>7</td><td>Pennsylvania</td><td>2,779</td><td>3.43%</td></tr>
<tr><td>38</td><td>Delaware</td><td>146</td><td>0.18%</td><td>8</td><td>Ohio</td><td>2,697</td><td>3.33%</td></tr>
<tr><td>NA</td><td>Florida**</td><td>NA</td><td>NA</td><td>9</td><td>Massachusetts</td><td>2,615</td><td>3.23%</td></tr>
<tr><td>31</td><td>Georgia</td><td>283</td><td>0.35%</td><td>10</td><td>Arizona</td><td>2,460</td><td>3.04%</td></tr>
<tr><td>27</td><td>Hawaii</td><td>385</td><td>0.48%</td><td>11</td><td>New Jersey</td><td>2,316</td><td>2.86%</td></tr>
<tr><td>44</td><td>Idaho</td><td>7</td><td>0.01%</td><td>12</td><td>Wisconsin</td><td>2,134</td><td>2.63%</td></tr>
<tr><td>3</td><td>Illinois</td><td>7,780</td><td>9.60%</td><td>13</td><td>Missouri</td><td>1,723</td><td>2.13%</td></tr>
<tr><td>15</td><td>Indiana</td><td>1,355</td><td>1.67%</td><td>14</td><td>Maryland</td><td>1,630</td><td>2.01%</td></tr>
<tr><td>33</td><td>Iowa</td><td>254</td><td>0.31%</td><td>15</td><td>Indiana</td><td>1,355</td><td>1.67%</td></tr>
<tr><td>NA</td><td>Kansas**</td><td>NA</td><td>NA</td><td>16</td><td>Virginia</td><td>1,195</td><td>1.47%</td></tr>
<tr><td>28</td><td>Kentucky</td><td>380</td><td>0.47%</td><td>17</td><td>Colorado</td><td>1,178</td><td>1.45%</td></tr>
<tr><td>30</td><td>Louisiana</td><td>359</td><td>0.44%</td><td>18</td><td>Minnesota</td><td>1,176</td><td>1.45%</td></tr>
<tr><td>40</td><td>Maine</td><td>47</td><td>0.06%</td><td>19</td><td>Tennessee</td><td>1,172</td><td>1.45%</td></tr>
<tr><td>14</td><td>Maryland</td><td>1,630</td><td>2.01%</td><td>20</td><td>South Carolina</td><td>1,026</td><td>1.27%</td></tr>
<tr><td>9</td><td>Massachusetts</td><td>2,615</td><td>3.23%</td><td>21</td><td>Oregon</td><td>930</td><td>1.15%</td></tr>
<tr><td>5</td><td>Michigan</td><td>3,628</td><td>4.48%</td><td>22</td><td>North Carolina</td><td>914</td><td>1.13%</td></tr>
<tr><td>18</td><td>Minnesota</td><td>1,176</td><td>1.45%</td><td>23</td><td>Washington</td><td>780</td><td>0.96%</td></tr>
<tr><td>41</td><td>Mississippi</td><td>19</td><td>0.02%</td><td>24</td><td>Utah</td><td>772</td><td>0.95%</td></tr>
<tr><td>13</td><td>Missouri</td><td>1,723</td><td>2.13%</td><td>25</td><td>Connecticut</td><td>550</td><td>0.68%</td></tr>
<tr><td>NA</td><td>Montana**</td><td>NA</td><td>NA</td><td>26</td><td>Rhode Island</td><td>529</td><td>0.65%</td></tr>
<tr><td>43</td><td>Nebraska</td><td>13</td><td>0.02%</td><td>27</td><td>Hawaii</td><td>385</td><td>0.48%</td></tr>
<tr><td>6</td><td>Nevada</td><td>3,458</td><td>4.27%</td><td>28</td><td>Kentucky</td><td>380</td><td>0.47%</td></tr>
<tr><td>39</td><td>New Hampshire</td><td>62</td><td>0.08%</td><td>29</td><td>New Mexico</td><td>365</td><td>0.45%</td></tr>
<tr><td>11</td><td>New Jersey</td><td>2,316</td><td>2.86%</td><td>30</td><td>Louisiana</td><td>359</td><td>0.44%</td></tr>
<tr><td>29</td><td>New Mexico</td><td>365</td><td>0.45%</td><td>31</td><td>Georgia</td><td>283</td><td>0.35%</td></tr>
<tr><td>2</td><td>New York</td><td>9,148</td><td>11.29%</td><td>32</td><td>Alabama</td><td>263</td><td>0.32%</td></tr>
<tr><td>22</td><td>North Carolina</td><td>914</td><td>1.13%</td><td>33</td><td>Iowa</td><td>254</td><td>0.31%</td></tr>
<tr><td>46</td><td>North Dakota</td><td>2</td><td>0.00%</td><td>34</td><td>Arkansas</td><td>235</td><td>0.29%</td></tr>
<tr><td>8</td><td>Ohio</td><td>2,697</td><td>3.33%</td><td>35</td><td>West Virginia</td><td>210</td><td>0.26%</td></tr>
<tr><td>36</td><td>Oklahoma</td><td>187</td><td>0.23%</td><td>36</td><td>Oklahoma</td><td>187</td><td>0.23%</td></tr>
<tr><td>21</td><td>Oregon</td><td>930</td><td>1.15%</td><td>37</td><td>Alaska</td><td>185</td><td>0.23%</td></tr>
<tr><td>7</td><td>Pennsylvania</td><td>2,779</td><td>3.43%</td><td>38</td><td>Delaware</td><td>146</td><td>0.18%</td></tr>
<tr><td>26</td><td>Rhode Island</td><td>529</td><td>0.65%</td><td>39</td><td>New Hampshire</td><td>62</td><td>0.08%</td></tr>
<tr><td>20</td><td>South Carolina</td><td>1,026</td><td>1.27%</td><td>40</td><td>Maine</td><td>47</td><td>0.06%</td></tr>
<tr><td>42</td><td>South Dakota</td><td>16</td><td>0.02%</td><td>41</td><td>Mississippi</td><td>19</td><td>0.02%</td></tr>
<tr><td>19</td><td>Tennessee</td><td>1,172</td><td>1.45%</td><td>42</td><td>South Dakota</td><td>16</td><td>0.02%</td></tr>
<tr><td>4</td><td>Texas</td><td>6,277</td><td>7.75%</td><td>43</td><td>Nebraska</td><td>13</td><td>0.02%</td></tr>
<tr><td>24</td><td>Utah</td><td>772</td><td>0.95%</td><td>44</td><td>Idaho</td><td>7</td><td>0.01%</td></tr>
<tr><td>NA</td><td>Vermont**</td><td>NA</td><td>NA</td><td>45</td><td>Wyoming</td><td>3</td><td>0.00%</td></tr>
<tr><td>16</td><td>Virginia</td><td>1,195</td><td>1.47%</td><td>46</td><td>North Dakota</td><td>2</td><td>0.00%</td></tr>
<tr><td>23</td><td>Washington</td><td>780</td><td>0.96%</td><td>NA</td><td>Florida**</td><td>NA</td><td>NA</td></tr>
<tr><td>35</td><td>West Virginia</td><td>210</td><td>0.26%</td><td>NA</td><td>Kansas**</td><td>NA</td><td>NA</td></tr>
<tr><td>12</td><td>Wisconsin</td><td>2,134</td><td>2.63%</td><td>NA</td><td>Montana**</td><td>NA</td><td>NA</td></tr>
<tr><td>45</td><td>Wyoming</td><td>3</td><td>0.00%</td><td>NA</td><td>Vermont**</td><td>NA</td><td>NA</td></tr>
<tr><td></td><td></td><td></td><td></td><td></td><td>District of Columbia**</td><td>NA</td><td>NA</td></tr>
</table>

Source: Federal Bureau of Investigation
   "Crime in the United States 1996" (Uniform Crime Reports, October 4, 1997)
*By law enforcement agencies submitting complete reports to the F.B.I. for 12 months in 1996. The F.B.I. estimates 99,000 reported and unreported arrests for prostitution and commercialized vice occurred in 1996. Includes keeping a bawdy house, procuring or transporting women for immoral purposes. Attempts are included. See important note at beginning of this chapter. **Not available.

Reported Arrest Rate for Prostitution and Commercialized Vice in 1996

National Total = 42.7 Reported Arrests per 100,000 Population*

<table>
<tr><td colspan="3"><u>ALPHA ORDER</u></td><td colspan="3"><u>RANK ORDER</u></td></tr>
<tr><td>RANK</td><td>STATE</td><td>RATE</td><td>RANK</td><td>STATE</td><td>RATE</td></tr>
<tr><td>37</td><td>Alabama</td><td>6.4</td><td>1</td><td>Illinois</td><td>282.5</td></tr>
<tr><td>21</td><td>Alaska</td><td>34.4</td><td>2</td><td>Nevada</td><td>220.4</td></tr>
<tr><td>4</td><td>Arizona</td><td>59.0</td><td>3</td><td>New York</td><td>72.6</td></tr>
<tr><td>35</td><td>Arkansas</td><td>9.9</td><td>4</td><td>Arizona</td><td>59.0</td></tr>
<tr><td>7</td><td>California</td><td>55.8</td><td>5</td><td>Tennessee</td><td>56.6</td></tr>
<tr><td>14</td><td>Colorado</td><td>41.7</td><td>6</td><td>Rhode Island</td><td>56.5</td></tr>
<tr><td>28</td><td>Connecticut</td><td>21.8</td><td>7</td><td>California</td><td>55.8</td></tr>
<tr><td>18</td><td>Delaware</td><td>39.4</td><td>8</td><td>Missouri</td><td>55.7</td></tr>
<tr><td>NA</td><td>Florida**</td><td>NA</td><td>9</td><td>Massachusetts</td><td>51.9</td></tr>
<tr><td>38</td><td>Georgia</td><td>6.3</td><td>10</td><td>Kentucky</td><td>49.7</td></tr>
<tr><td>23</td><td>Hawaii</td><td>32.5</td><td>11</td><td>Michigan</td><td>46.0</td></tr>
<tr><td>45</td><td>Idaho</td><td>0.6</td><td>12</td><td>Ohio</td><td>42.0</td></tr>
<tr><td>1</td><td>Illinois</td><td>282.5</td><td>12</td><td>Utah</td><td>42.0</td></tr>
<tr><td>16</td><td>Indiana</td><td>41.1</td><td>14</td><td>Colorado</td><td>41.7</td></tr>
<tr><td>34</td><td>Iowa</td><td>11.0</td><td>15</td><td>Wisconsin</td><td>41.5</td></tr>
<tr><td>NA</td><td>Kansas**</td><td>NA</td><td>16</td><td>Indiana</td><td>41.1</td></tr>
<tr><td>10</td><td>Kentucky</td><td>49.7</td><td>17</td><td>Maryland</td><td>40.5</td></tr>
<tr><td>31</td><td>Louisiana</td><td>13.5</td><td>18</td><td>Delaware</td><td>39.4</td></tr>
<tr><td>40</td><td>Maine</td><td>3.8</td><td>19</td><td>Texas</td><td>37.8</td></tr>
<tr><td>17</td><td>Maryland</td><td>40.5</td><td>20</td><td>New Mexico</td><td>36.3</td></tr>
<tr><td>9</td><td>Massachusetts</td><td>51.9</td><td>21</td><td>Alaska</td><td>34.4</td></tr>
<tr><td>11</td><td>Michigan</td><td>46.0</td><td>22</td><td>Oregon</td><td>33.9</td></tr>
<tr><td>27</td><td>Minnesota</td><td>27.9</td><td>23</td><td>Hawaii</td><td>32.5</td></tr>
<tr><td>42</td><td>Mississippi</td><td>3.0</td><td>24</td><td>New Jersey</td><td>30.2</td></tr>
<tr><td>8</td><td>Missouri</td><td>55.7</td><td>25</td><td>Pennsylvania</td><td>29.8</td></tr>
<tr><td>NA</td><td>Montana**</td><td>NA</td><td>26</td><td>South Carolina</td><td>28.0</td></tr>
<tr><td>43</td><td>Nebraska</td><td>1.1</td><td>27</td><td>Minnesota</td><td>27.9</td></tr>
<tr><td>2</td><td>Nevada</td><td>220.4</td><td>28</td><td>Connecticut</td><td>21.8</td></tr>
<tr><td>36</td><td>New Hampshire</td><td>7.0</td><td>29</td><td>Washington</td><td>20.8</td></tr>
<tr><td>24</td><td>New Jersey</td><td>30.2</td><td>30</td><td>Virginia</td><td>19.3</td></tr>
<tr><td>20</td><td>New Mexico</td><td>36.3</td><td>31</td><td>Louisiana</td><td>13.5</td></tr>
<tr><td>3</td><td>New York</td><td>72.6</td><td>32</td><td>North Carolina</td><td>12.7</td></tr>
<tr><td>32</td><td>North Carolina</td><td>12.7</td><td>33</td><td>West Virginia</td><td>11.5</td></tr>
<tr><td>46</td><td>North Dakota</td><td>0.5</td><td>34</td><td>Iowa</td><td>11.0</td></tr>
<tr><td>12</td><td>Ohio</td><td>42.0</td><td>35</td><td>Arkansas</td><td>9.9</td></tr>
<tr><td>39</td><td>Oklahoma</td><td>5.7</td><td>36</td><td>New Hampshire</td><td>7.0</td></tr>
<tr><td>22</td><td>Oregon</td><td>33.9</td><td>37</td><td>Alabama</td><td>6.4</td></tr>
<tr><td>25</td><td>Pennsylvania</td><td>29.8</td><td>38</td><td>Georgia</td><td>6.3</td></tr>
<tr><td>6</td><td>Rhode Island</td><td>56.5</td><td>39</td><td>Oklahoma</td><td>5.7</td></tr>
<tr><td>26</td><td>South Carolina</td><td>28.0</td><td>40</td><td>Maine</td><td>3.8</td></tr>
<tr><td>41</td><td>South Dakota</td><td>3.2</td><td>41</td><td>South Dakota</td><td>3.2</td></tr>
<tr><td>5</td><td>Tennessee</td><td>56.6</td><td>42</td><td>Mississippi</td><td>3.0</td></tr>
<tr><td>19</td><td>Texas</td><td>37.8</td><td>43</td><td>Nebraska</td><td>1.1</td></tr>
<tr><td>12</td><td>Utah</td><td>42.0</td><td>43</td><td>Wyoming</td><td>1.1</td></tr>
<tr><td>NA</td><td>Vermont**</td><td>NA</td><td>45</td><td>Idaho</td><td>0.6</td></tr>
<tr><td>30</td><td>Virginia</td><td>19.3</td><td>46</td><td>North Dakota</td><td>0.5</td></tr>
<tr><td>29</td><td>Washington</td><td>20.8</td><td>NA</td><td>Florida**</td><td>NA</td></tr>
<tr><td>33</td><td>West Virginia</td><td>11.5</td><td>NA</td><td>Kansas**</td><td>NA</td></tr>
<tr><td>15</td><td>Wisconsin</td><td>41.5</td><td>NA</td><td>Montana**</td><td>NA</td></tr>
<tr><td>43</td><td>Wyoming</td><td>1.1</td><td>NA</td><td>Vermont**</td><td>NA</td></tr>
<tr><td></td><td></td><td></td><td></td><td>District of Columbia**</td><td>NA</td></tr>
</table>

Source: Morgan Quitno Press using data from Federal Bureau of Investigation
"Crime in the United States 1996" (Uniform Crime Reports, October 4, 1997)
*By law enforcement agencies submitting complete reports to the F.B.I. for 12 months in 1996. These rates based on population estimates for areas under the jurisdiction of those agencies reporting. Arrest rate based on the F.B.I. estimate of reported and unreported arrests for prostitution and commercialized vice is 37.3 arrests per 100,000 population. See important note at beginning of this chapter. **Not available.

Reported Arrests for Offenses Against Families and Children in 1996

National Total = 103,800 Reported Arrests*

ALPHA ORDER					RANK ORDER			
RANK	STATE	ARRESTS	% of USA		RANK	STATE	ARRESTS	% of USA
22	Alabama	1,160	1 12%		1	Ohio	22,860	22.02%
42	Alaska	162	0.16%		2	New Jersey	16,911	16.29%
13	Arizona	1,920	1.85%		3	North Carolina	7,057	6.80%
19	Arkansas	1,219	1.17%		4	Texas	4,841	4.66%
33	California	679	0.65%		5	Wisconsin	4,063	3.91%
16	Colorado	1,651	1.59%		6	Georgia	3,240	3.12%
12	Connecticut	2,016	1.94%		7	Massachusetts	3,113	3.00%
45	Delaware	100	0.10%		8	Missouri	3,068	2.96%
NA	Florida**	NA	NA		9	Virginia	2,971	2.86%
6	Georgia	3,240	3.12%		10	Michigan	2,798	2.70%
14	Hawaii	1,865	1.80%		11	Maryland	2,150	2.07%
38	Idaho	434	0.42%		12	Connecticut	2,016	1.94%
35	Illinois	541	0.52%		13	Arizona	1,920	1.85%
20	Indiana	1,170	1.13%		14	Hawaii	1,865	1.80%
40	Iowa	257	0.25%		15	New Mexico	1,710	1.65%
NA	Kansas**	NA	NA		16	Colorado	1,651	1.59%
29	Kentucky	872	0.84%		17	South Carolina	1,423	1.37%
23	Louisiana	1,143	1.10%		18	Utah	1,378	1.33%
41	Maine	217	0.21%		19	Arkansas	1,219	1.17%
11	Maryland	2,150	2.07%		20	Indiana	1,170	1.13%
7	Massachusetts	3,113	3.00%		21	New York	1,162	1.12%
10	Michigan	2,798	2.70%		22	Alabama	1,160	1.12%
32	Minnesota	714	0.69%		23	Louisiana	1,143	1.10%
30	Mississippi	864	0.83%		24	Oklahoma	1,096	1.06%
8	Missouri	3,068	2.96%		25	Nevada	1,080	1.04%
NA	Montana**	NA	NA		26	Tennessee	1,009	0.97%
27	Nebraska	979	0.94%		27	Nebraska	979	0.94%
25	Nevada	1,080	1.04%		28	Pennsylvania	978	0.94%
44	New Hampshire	106	0.10%		29	Kentucky	872	0.84%
2	New Jersey	16,911	16.29%		30	Mississippi	864	0.83%
15	New Mexico	1,710	1.65%		31	West Virginia	789	0.76%
21	New York	1,162	1.12%		32	Minnesota	714	0.69%
3	North Carolina	7,057	6.80%		33	California	679	0.65%
46	North Dakota	67	0.06%		34	Oregon	630	0.61%
1	Ohio	22,860	22.02%		35	Illinois	541	0.52%
24	Oklahoma	1,096	1.06%		36	Washington	486	0.47%
34	Oregon	630	0.61%		37	Rhode Island	457	0.44%
28	Pennsylvania	978	0.94%		38	Idaho	434	0.42%
37	Rhode Island	457	0.44%		39	South Dakota	266	0.26%
17	South Carolina	1,423	1.37%		40	Iowa	257	0.25%
39	South Dakota	266	0.26%		41	Maine	217	0.21%
26	Tennessee	1,009	0.97%		42	Alaska	162	0.16%
4	Texas	4,841	4.66%		43	Wyoming	128	0.12%
18	Utah	1,378	1.33%		44	New Hampshire	106	0.10%
NA	Vermont**	NA	NA		45	Delaware	100	0.10%
9	Virginia	2,971	2.86%		46	North Dakota	67	0.06%
36	Washington	486	0.47%		NA	Florida**	NA	NA
31	West Virginia	789	0.76%		NA	Kansas**	NA	NA
5	Wisconsin	4,063	3.91%		NA	Montana**	NA	NA
43	Wyoming	128	0.12%		NA	Vermont**	NA	NA
						District of Columbia**	NA	NA

Source: Federal Bureau of Investigation
    "Crime in the United States 1996" (Uniform Crime Reports, October 4, 1997)
*By law enforcement agencies submitting complete reports to the F.B.I. for 12 months in 1996. The F.B.I. estimates 149,800 reported and unreported arrests for offenses against families and children occurred in 1996. Includes nonsupport, neglect, desertion or abuse of family and children. See important note at beginning of this chapter.
**Not available.

35

Reported Arrest Rate for Offenses Against Families and Children in 1996

National Rate = 54.7 Reported Arrests per 100,000 Population*

<table>
<tr><td colspan="3">ALPHA ORDER</td><td colspan="3">RANK ORDER</td></tr>
<tr><td>RANK</td><td>STATE</td><td>RATE</td><td>RANK</td><td>STATE</td><td>RATE</td></tr>
<tr><td>34</td><td>Alabama</td><td>28.1</td><td>1</td><td>Ohio</td><td>355.7</td></tr>
<tr><td>32</td><td>Alaska</td><td>30.1</td><td>2</td><td>New Jersey</td><td>220.9</td></tr>
<tr><td>23</td><td>Arizona</td><td>46.0</td><td>3</td><td>New Mexico</td><td>170.1</td></tr>
<tr><td>19</td><td>Arkansas</td><td>51.3</td><td>4</td><td>Hawaii</td><td>157.5</td></tr>
<tr><td>46</td><td>California</td><td>2.2</td><td>5</td><td>Mississippi</td><td>136.7</td></tr>
<tr><td>16</td><td>Colorado</td><td>58.4</td><td>6</td><td>Kentucky</td><td>114.0</td></tr>
<tr><td>10</td><td>Connecticut</td><td>79.7</td><td>7</td><td>Missouri</td><td>99.2</td></tr>
<tr><td>35</td><td>Delaware</td><td>27.0</td><td>8</td><td>North Carolina</td><td>98.3</td></tr>
<tr><td>NA</td><td>Florida**</td><td>NA</td><td>9</td><td>Nebraska</td><td>82.5</td></tr>
<tr><td>13</td><td>Georgia</td><td>71.9</td><td>10</td><td>Connecticut</td><td>79.7</td></tr>
<tr><td>4</td><td>Hawaii</td><td>157.5</td><td>11</td><td>Wisconsin</td><td>79.0</td></tr>
<tr><td>28</td><td>Idaho</td><td>37.1</td><td>12</td><td>Utah</td><td>74.9</td></tr>
<tr><td>37</td><td>Illinois</td><td>19.6</td><td>13</td><td>Georgia</td><td>71.9</td></tr>
<tr><td>29</td><td>Indiana</td><td>35.5</td><td>14</td><td>Nevada</td><td>68.8</td></tr>
<tr><td>43</td><td>Iowa</td><td>11.2</td><td>15</td><td>Massachusetts</td><td>61.8</td></tr>
<tr><td>NA</td><td>Kansas**</td><td>NA</td><td>16</td><td>Colorado</td><td>58.4</td></tr>
<tr><td>6</td><td>Kentucky</td><td>114.0</td><td>17</td><td>Maryland</td><td>53.4</td></tr>
<tr><td>26</td><td>Louisiana</td><td>42.9</td><td>18</td><td>South Dakota</td><td>52.7</td></tr>
<tr><td>38</td><td>Maine</td><td>17.7</td><td>19</td><td>Arkansas</td><td>51.3</td></tr>
<tr><td>17</td><td>Maryland</td><td>53.4</td><td>20</td><td>Rhode Island</td><td>48.8</td></tr>
<tr><td>15</td><td>Massachusetts</td><td>61.8</td><td>20</td><td>Tennessee</td><td>48.8</td></tr>
<tr><td>29</td><td>Michigan</td><td>35.5</td><td>22</td><td>Virginia</td><td>48.1</td></tr>
<tr><td>39</td><td>Minnesota</td><td>17.0</td><td>23</td><td>Arizona</td><td>46.0</td></tr>
<tr><td>5</td><td>Mississippi</td><td>136.7</td><td>24</td><td>Wyoming</td><td>45.6</td></tr>
<tr><td>7</td><td>Missouri</td><td>99.2</td><td>25</td><td>West Virginia</td><td>43.2</td></tr>
<tr><td>NA</td><td>Montana**</td><td>NA</td><td>26</td><td>Louisiana</td><td>42.9</td></tr>
<tr><td>9</td><td>Nebraska</td><td>82.5</td><td>27</td><td>South Carolina</td><td>38.9</td></tr>
<tr><td>14</td><td>Nevada</td><td>68.8</td><td>28</td><td>Idaho</td><td>37.1</td></tr>
<tr><td>42</td><td>New Hampshire</td><td>12.0</td><td>29</td><td>Indiana</td><td>35.5</td></tr>
<tr><td>2</td><td>New Jersey</td><td>220.9</td><td>29</td><td>Michigan</td><td>35.5</td></tr>
<tr><td>3</td><td>New Mexico</td><td>170.1</td><td>31</td><td>Oklahoma</td><td>33.2</td></tr>
<tr><td>45</td><td>New York</td><td>9.2</td><td>32</td><td>Alaska</td><td>30.1</td></tr>
<tr><td>8</td><td>North Carolina</td><td>98.3</td><td>33</td><td>Texas</td><td>29.2</td></tr>
<tr><td>40</td><td>North Dakota</td><td>16.9</td><td>34</td><td>Alabama</td><td>28.1</td></tr>
<tr><td>1</td><td>Ohio</td><td>355.7</td><td>35</td><td>Delaware</td><td>27.0</td></tr>
<tr><td>31</td><td>Oklahoma</td><td>33.2</td><td>36</td><td>Oregon</td><td>23.0</td></tr>
<tr><td>36</td><td>Oregon</td><td>23.0</td><td>37</td><td>Illinois</td><td>19.6</td></tr>
<tr><td>44</td><td>Pennsylvania</td><td>10.5</td><td>38</td><td>Maine</td><td>17.7</td></tr>
<tr><td>20</td><td>Rhode Island</td><td>48.8</td><td>39</td><td>Minnesota</td><td>17.0</td></tr>
<tr><td>27</td><td>South Carolina</td><td>38.9</td><td>40</td><td>North Dakota</td><td>16.9</td></tr>
<tr><td>18</td><td>South Dakota</td><td>52.7</td><td>41</td><td>Washington</td><td>13.0</td></tr>
<tr><td>20</td><td>Tennessee</td><td>48.8</td><td>42</td><td>New Hampshire</td><td>12.0</td></tr>
<tr><td>33</td><td>Texas</td><td>29.2</td><td>43</td><td>Iowa</td><td>11.2</td></tr>
<tr><td>12</td><td>Utah</td><td>74.9</td><td>44</td><td>Pennsylvania</td><td>10.5</td></tr>
<tr><td>NA</td><td>Vermont**</td><td>NA</td><td>45</td><td>New York</td><td>9.2</td></tr>
<tr><td>22</td><td>Virginia</td><td>48.1</td><td>46</td><td>California</td><td>2.2</td></tr>
<tr><td>41</td><td>Washington</td><td>13.0</td><td>NA</td><td>Florida**</td><td>NA</td></tr>
<tr><td>25</td><td>West Virginia</td><td>43.2</td><td>NA</td><td>Kansas**</td><td>NA</td></tr>
<tr><td>11</td><td>Wisconsin</td><td>79.0</td><td>NA</td><td>Montana**</td><td>NA</td></tr>
<tr><td>24</td><td>Wyoming</td><td>45.6</td><td>NA</td><td>Vermont**</td><td>NA</td></tr>
<tr><td></td><td></td><td></td><td></td><td>District of Columbia**</td><td>NA</td></tr>
</table>

Source: Morgan Quitno Press using data from Federal Bureau of Investigation "Crime in the United States 1996" (Uniform Crime Reports, October 4, 1997)
*By law enforcement agencies submitting complete reports to the F.B.I. for 12 months in 1996. These rates based on population estimates for areas under the jurisdiction of those agencies reporting. Arrest rate based on the F.B.I. estimate of reported and unreported arrests for offenses against families and children is 56.5 arrests per 100,000 population. See important note at beginning of this chapter. **Not available.*

Percent of Crimes Cleared in 1996

National Percent = 21.7% Cleared*

<table>
<tr><td colspan="3"><u>ALPHA ORDER</u></td><td colspan="3"><u>RANK ORDER</u></td></tr>
<tr><td>RANK</td><td>STATE</td><td>PERCENT</td><td>RANK</td><td>STATE</td><td>PERCENT</td></tr>
<tr><td>NA</td><td>Alabama**</td><td>NA</td><td>1</td><td>South Dakota</td><td>31.8</td></tr>
<tr><td>4</td><td>Alaska</td><td>28.4</td><td>2</td><td>Wyoming</td><td>29.2</td></tr>
<tr><td>41</td><td>Arizona</td><td>18.5</td><td>3</td><td>Delaware</td><td>28.7</td></tr>
<tr><td>7</td><td>Arkansas</td><td>27.5</td><td>4</td><td>Alaska</td><td>28.4</td></tr>
<tr><td>31</td><td>California</td><td>20.6</td><td>5</td><td>Nebraska</td><td>28.1</td></tr>
<tr><td>20</td><td>Colorado</td><td>22.8</td><td>6</td><td>Wisconsin</td><td>27.7</td></tr>
<tr><td>35</td><td>Connecticut</td><td>20.1</td><td>7</td><td>Arkansas</td><td>27.5</td></tr>
<tr><td>3</td><td>Delaware</td><td>28.7</td><td>8</td><td>Maine</td><td>27.4</td></tr>
<tr><td>NA</td><td>Florida**</td><td>NA</td><td>9</td><td>Idaho</td><td>26.2</td></tr>
<tr><td>28</td><td>Georgia</td><td>21.9</td><td>10</td><td>North Dakota</td><td>25.7</td></tr>
<tr><td>43</td><td>Hawaii</td><td>15.8</td><td>11</td><td>Kentucky</td><td>25.2</td></tr>
<tr><td>9</td><td>Idaho</td><td>26.2</td><td>11</td><td>Virginia</td><td>25.2</td></tr>
<tr><td>NA</td><td>Illinois**</td><td>NA</td><td>13</td><td>Pennsylvania</td><td>24.4</td></tr>
<tr><td>38</td><td>Indiana</td><td>19.4</td><td>14</td><td>Nevada</td><td>24.2</td></tr>
<tr><td>39</td><td>Iowa</td><td>18.9</td><td>15</td><td>Tennessee</td><td>24.0</td></tr>
<tr><td>NA</td><td>Kansas**</td><td>NA</td><td>16</td><td>Minnesota</td><td>23.7</td></tr>
<tr><td>11</td><td>Kentucky</td><td>25.2</td><td>17</td><td>New York</td><td>23.3</td></tr>
<tr><td>29</td><td>Louisiana</td><td>21.6</td><td>18</td><td>Massachusetts</td><td>23.1</td></tr>
<tr><td>8</td><td>Maine</td><td>27.4</td><td>18</td><td>Missouri</td><td>23.1</td></tr>
<tr><td>26</td><td>Maryland</td><td>22.3</td><td>20</td><td>Colorado</td><td>22.8</td></tr>
<tr><td>18</td><td>Massachusetts</td><td>23.1</td><td>21</td><td>North Carolina</td><td>22.6</td></tr>
<tr><td>44</td><td>Michigan</td><td>13.9</td><td>21</td><td>South Carolina</td><td>22.6</td></tr>
<tr><td>16</td><td>Minnesota</td><td>23.7</td><td>21</td><td>Texas</td><td>22.6</td></tr>
<tr><td>31</td><td>Mississippi</td><td>20.6</td><td>24</td><td>Oregon</td><td>22.5</td></tr>
<tr><td>18</td><td>Missouri</td><td>23.1</td><td>25</td><td>Ohio</td><td>22.4</td></tr>
<tr><td>NA</td><td>Montana**</td><td>NA</td><td>26</td><td>Maryland</td><td>22.3</td></tr>
<tr><td>5</td><td>Nebraska</td><td>28.1</td><td>27</td><td>West Virginia</td><td>22.1</td></tr>
<tr><td>14</td><td>Nevada</td><td>24.2</td><td>28</td><td>Georgia</td><td>21.9</td></tr>
<tr><td>40</td><td>New Hampshire</td><td>18.8</td><td>29</td><td>Louisiana</td><td>21.6</td></tr>
<tr><td>33</td><td>New Jersey</td><td>20.2</td><td>30</td><td>Washington</td><td>21.1</td></tr>
<tr><td>42</td><td>New Mexico</td><td>16.6</td><td>31</td><td>California</td><td>20.6</td></tr>
<tr><td>17</td><td>New York</td><td>23.3</td><td>31</td><td>Mississippi</td><td>20.6</td></tr>
<tr><td>21</td><td>North Carolina</td><td>22.6</td><td>33</td><td>New Jersey</td><td>20.2</td></tr>
<tr><td>10</td><td>North Dakota</td><td>25.7</td><td>33</td><td>Rhode Island</td><td>20.2</td></tr>
<tr><td>25</td><td>Ohio</td><td>22.4</td><td>35</td><td>Connecticut</td><td>20.1</td></tr>
<tr><td>37</td><td>Oklahoma</td><td>19.5</td><td>36</td><td>Utah</td><td>19.7</td></tr>
<tr><td>24</td><td>Oregon</td><td>22.5</td><td>37</td><td>Oklahoma</td><td>19.5</td></tr>
<tr><td>13</td><td>Pennsylvania</td><td>24.4</td><td>38</td><td>Indiana</td><td>19.4</td></tr>
<tr><td>33</td><td>Rhode Island</td><td>20.2</td><td>39</td><td>Iowa</td><td>18.9</td></tr>
<tr><td>21</td><td>South Carolina</td><td>22.6</td><td>40</td><td>New Hampshire</td><td>18.8</td></tr>
<tr><td>1</td><td>South Dakota</td><td>31.8</td><td>41</td><td>Arizona</td><td>18.5</td></tr>
<tr><td>15</td><td>Tennessee</td><td>24.0</td><td>42</td><td>New Mexico</td><td>16.6</td></tr>
<tr><td>21</td><td>Texas</td><td>22.6</td><td>43</td><td>Hawaii</td><td>15.8</td></tr>
<tr><td>36</td><td>Utah</td><td>19.7</td><td>44</td><td>Michigan</td><td>13.9</td></tr>
<tr><td>45</td><td>Vermont</td><td>10.4</td><td>45</td><td>Vermont</td><td>10.4</td></tr>
<tr><td>11</td><td>Virginia</td><td>25.2</td><td>NA</td><td>Alabama**</td><td>NA</td></tr>
<tr><td>30</td><td>Washington</td><td>21.1</td><td>NA</td><td>Florida**</td><td>NA</td></tr>
<tr><td>27</td><td>West Virginia</td><td>22.1</td><td>NA</td><td>Illinois**</td><td>NA</td></tr>
<tr><td>6</td><td>Wisconsin</td><td>27.7</td><td>NA</td><td>Kansas**</td><td>NA</td></tr>
<tr><td>2</td><td>Wyoming</td><td>29.2</td><td>NA</td><td>Montana**</td><td>NA</td></tr>
<tr><td></td><td></td><td></td><td></td><td>District of Columbia</td><td>7.9</td></tr>
</table>

Source: Federal Bureau of Investigation (unpublished data)
*Includes murder, rape, robbery, aggravated assault, burglary, larceny-theft and motor vehicle theft. A crime is considered cleared when at least one person is arrested, charged and turned over to the court for prosecution. Clearances recorded in 1996 may be for crimes which occurred in prior years. Several crimes may be cleared by the arrest of one person while the arrest of many persons may clear only one crime.
**Not available.

Percent of Violent Crimes Cleared in 1996

National Percent = 47.3% Cleared*

RANK	STATE (ALPHA ORDER)	PERCENT		RANK	STATE (RANK ORDER)	PERCENT
NA	Alabama**	NA		1	Nebraska	71.5
4	Alaska	65.1		2	South Dakota	71.2
42	Arizona	39.1		3	Wyoming	69.2
14	Arkansas	54.5		4	Alaska	65.1
27	California	47.8		5	Maine	63.4
11	Colorado	57.7		6	Idaho	61.5
30	Connecticut	46.7		7	Minnesota	61.2
8	Delaware	59.7		8	Delaware	59.7
NA	Florida**	NA		9	Virginia	58.9
32	Georgia	46.1		10	Wisconsin	58.5
41	Hawaii	40.2		11	Colorado	57.7
6	Idaho	61.5		12	Rhode Island	55.7
NA	Illinois**	NA		13	West Virginia	55.3
37	Indiana	43.0		14	Arkansas	54.5
16	Iowa	53.5		14	North Dakota	54.5
NA	Kansas**	NA		16	Iowa	53.5
24	Kentucky	49.8		17	South Carolina	53.4
38	Louisiana	41.4		18	North Carolina	52.3
5	Maine	63.4		19	Tennessee	52.2
35	Maryland	44.8		20	Oklahoma	51.2
23	Massachusetts	50.4		21	Washington	51.1
45	Michigan	33.3		22	Texas	50.9
7	Minnesota	61.2		23	Massachusetts	50.4
43	Mississippi	38.8		24	Kentucky	49.8
27	Missouri	47.8		25	Vermont	49.1
NA	Montana**	NA		26	Pennsylvania	48.6
1	Nebraska	71.5		27	California	47.8
40	Nevada	40.5		27	Missouri	47.8
33	New Hampshire	45.6		29	Ohio	47.4
34	New Jersey	45.5		30	Connecticut	46.7
44	New Mexico	34.1		31	Oregon	46.6
36	New York	43.8		32	Georgia	46.1
18	North Carolina	52.3		33	New Hampshire	45.6
14	North Dakota	54.5		34	New Jersey	45.5
29	Ohio	47.4		35	Maryland	44.8
20	Oklahoma	51.2		36	New York	43.8
31	Oregon	46.6		37	Indiana	43.0
26	Pennsylvania	48.6		38	Louisiana	41.4
12	Rhode Island	55.7		39	Utah	40.9
17	South Carolina	53.4		40	Nevada	40.5
2	South Dakota	71.2		41	Hawaii	40.2
19	Tennessee	52.2		42	Arizona	39.1
22	Texas	50.9		43	Mississippi	38.8
39	Utah	40.9		44	New Mexico	34.1
25	Vermont	49.1		45	Michigan	33.3
9	Virginia	58.9		NA	Alabama**	NA
21	Washington	51.1		NA	Florida**	NA
13	West Virginia	55.3		NA	Illinois**	NA
10	Wisconsin	58.5		NA	Kansas**	NA
3	Wyoming	69.2		NA	Montana**	NA
					District of Columbia	20.7

Source: Federal Bureau of Investigation (unpublished data)
Includes murder, rape, robbery and aggravated assault. A crime is considered cleared when at least one person is arrested, charged and turned over to the court for prosecution. Clearances recorded in 1996 may be for crimes which occurred in prior years. Several crimes may be cleared by the arrest of one person while the arrest of many persons may clear only one crime.
***Not available.*

Percent of Murders Cleared in 1996

National Percent = 66.7% Cleared*

RANK	STATE	PERCENT
NA	Alabama**	NA
15	Alaska	76.7
39	Arizona	59.0
9	Arkansas	83.0
38	California	59.9
18	Colorado	74.7
24	Connecticut	72.8
31	Delaware	65.5
NA	Florida**	NA
14	Georgia	77.2
3	Hawaii	87.5
6	Idaho	85.0
NA	Illinois**	NA
20	Indiana	74.4
34	Iowa	63.8
NA	Kansas**	NA
30	Kentucky	66.3
42	Louisiana	49.8
11	Maine	80.0
36	Maryland	60.6
35	Massachusetts	63.7
37	Michigan	60.0
18	Minnesota	74.7
27	Mississippi	70.4
17	Missouri	76.1
NA	Montana**	NA
4	Nebraska	87.2
44	Nevada	44.7
1	New Hampshire	105.6
8	New Jersey	83.1
45	New Mexico	42.5
33	New York	64.8
12	North Carolina	78.6
28	North Dakota	70.0
32	Ohio	65.0
7	Oklahoma	84.8
29	Oregon	68.4
21	Pennsylvania	74.2
40	Rhode Island	52.0
10	South Carolina	80.6
2	South Dakota	100.0
23	Tennessee	73.0
25	Texas	72.4
43	Utah	48.4
41	Vermont	50.0
16	Virginia	76.4
13	Washington	78.4
22	West Virginia	73.9
5	Wisconsin	86.8
26	Wyoming	72.2

RANK	STATE	PERCENT
1	New Hampshire	105.6
2	South Dakota	100.0
3	Hawaii	87.5
4	Nebraska	87.2
5	Wisconsin	86.8
6	Idaho	85.0
7	Oklahoma	84.8
8	New Jersey	83.1
9	Arkansas	83.0
10	South Carolina	80.6
11	Maine	80.0
12	North Carolina	78.6
13	Washington	78.4
14	Georgia	77.2
15	Alaska	76.7
16	Virginia	76.4
17	Missouri	76.1
18	Colorado	74.7
18	Minnesota	74.7
20	Indiana	74.4
21	Pennsylvania	74.2
22	West Virginia	73.9
23	Tennessee	73.0
24	Connecticut	72.8
25	Texas	72.4
26	Wyoming	72.2
27	Mississippi	70.4
28	North Dakota	70.0
29	Oregon	68.4
30	Kentucky	66.3
31	Delaware	65.5
32	Ohio	65.0
33	New York	64.8
34	Iowa	63.8
35	Massachusetts	63.7
36	Maryland	60.6
37	Michigan	60.0
38	California	59.9
39	Arizona	59.0
40	Rhode Island	52.0
41	Vermont	50.0
42	Louisiana	49.8
43	Utah	48.4
44	Nevada	44.7
45	New Mexico	42.5
NA	Alabama**	NA
NA	Florida**	NA
NA	Illinois**	NA
NA	Kansas**	NA
NA	Montana**	NA
	District of Columbia	23.9

Source: Federal Bureau of Investigation (unpublished data)
*Includes nonnegligent manslaughter. A crime is considered cleared when at least one person is arrested, charged and turned over to the court for prosecution. Clearances recorded in 1996 may be for crimes which occurred in prior years. Several crimes may be cleared by the arrest of one person while the arrest of many persons may clear only one crime.
**Not available.*

Percent of Rapes Cleared in 1996

National Percent = 51.8% Cleared*

ALPHA ORDER

RANK	STATE	PERCENT
NA	Alabama**	NA
29	Alaska	48.1
40	Arizona	32.6
6	Arkansas	62.7
23	California	50.2
21	Colorado	51.7
23	Connecticut	50.2
5	Delaware	64.5
NA	Florida**	NA
13	Georgia	56.9
3	Hawaii	66.3
30	Idaho	46.8
NA	Illinois**	NA
27	Indiana	49.0
37	Iowa	38.4
NA	Kansas**	NA
35	Kentucky	41.5
31	Louisiana	44.9
34	Maine	43.2
12	Maryland	57.3
19	Massachusetts	52.7
39	Michigan	34.7
17	Minnesota	55.4
31	Mississippi	44.9
7	Missouri	61.1
NA	Montana**	NA
4	Nebraska	65.6
45	Nevada	25.1
42	New Hampshire	31.7
20	New Jersey	52.2
44	New Mexico	26.8
15	New York	55.9
10	North Carolina	58.7
28	North Dakota	48.5
21	Ohio	51.7
9	Oklahoma	58.8
33	Oregon	44.0
11	Pennsylvania	58.1
38	Rhode Island	36.4
25	South Carolina	49.5
18	South Dakota	54.0
13	Tennessee	56.9
8	Texas	59.8
43	Utah	31.5
40	Vermont	32.6
2	Virginia	69.5
26	Washington	49.3
36	West Virginia	41.3
1	Wisconsin	74.7
16	Wyoming	55.6

RANK ORDER

RANK	STATE	PERCENT
1	Wisconsin	74.7
2	Virginia	69.5
3	Hawaii	66.3
4	Nebraska	65.6
5	Delaware	64.5
6	Arkansas	62.7
7	Missouri	61.1
8	Texas	59.8
9	Oklahoma	58.8
10	North Carolina	58.7
11	Pennsylvania	58.1
12	Maryland	57.3
13	Georgia	56.9
13	Tennessee	56.9
15	New York	55.9
16	Wyoming	55.6
17	Minnesota	55.4
18	South Dakota	54.0
19	Massachusetts	52.7
20	New Jersey	52.2
21	Colorado	51.7
21	Ohio	51.7
23	California	50.2
23	Connecticut	50.2
25	South Carolina	49.5
26	Washington	49.3
27	Indiana	49.0
28	North Dakota	48.5
29	Alaska	48.1
30	Idaho	46.8
31	Louisiana	44.9
31	Mississippi	44.9
33	Oregon	44.0
34	Maine	43.2
35	Kentucky	41.5
36	West Virginia	41.3
37	Iowa	38.4
38	Rhode Island	36.4
39	Michigan	34.7
40	Arizona	32.6
40	Vermont	32.6
42	New Hampshire	31.7
43	Utah	31.5
44	New Mexico	26.8
45	Nevada	25.1
NA	Alabama**	NA
NA	Florida**	NA
NA	Illinois**	NA
NA	Kansas**	NA
NA	Montana**	NA
	District of Columbia	23.8

Source: Federal Bureau of Investigation (unpublished data)
*Forcible rape including attempts. However, statutory rape without force and other sex offenses are excluded. A crime is considered cleared when at least one person is arrested, charged and turned over to the court for prosecution. Clearances recorded in 1996 may be for crimes which occurred in prior years. Several crimes may be cleared by the arrest of one person while the arrest of many persons may clear only one crime.
**Not available.

Percent of Robberies Cleared in 1996

National Percent = 26.8% Cleared*

ALPHA ORDER				RANK ORDER		
RANK	STATE	PERCENT		RANK	STATE	PERCENT
NA	Alabama**	NA		1	South Dakota	58.3
40	Alaska	22.4		2	Maine	44.7
41	Arizona	22.3		3	Minnesota	39.9
9	Arkansas	34.4		4	North Dakota	39.7
36	California	24.9		5	Oklahoma	38.4
14	Colorado	32.7		6	Idaho	38.1
34	Connecticut	25.1		6	Nebraska	38.1
21	Delaware	28.6		8	Virginia	37.2
NA	Florida**	NA		9	Arkansas	34.4
19	Georgia	29.0		10	Oregon	33.6
23	Hawaii	28.1		11	North Carolina	33.5
6	Idaho	38.1		12	Wisconsin	33.4
NA	Illinois**	NA		13	South Carolina	33.0
38	Indiana	24.8		14	Colorado	32.7
29	Iowa	25.5		15	New Hampshire	32.5
NA	Kansas**	NA		16	Ohio	31.8
27	Kentucky	26.5		17	Texas	30.0
43	Louisiana	17.8		18	New York	29.8
2	Maine	44.7		19	Georgia	29.0
39	Maryland	23.5		20	Pennsylvania	28.8
23	Massachusetts	28.1		21	Delaware	28.6
44	Michigan	13.3		21	Washington	28.6
3	Minnesota	39.9		23	Hawaii	28.1
42	Mississippi	21.4		23	Massachusetts	28.1
25	Missouri	27.6		25	Missouri	27.6
NA	Montana**	NA		26	Wyoming	26.6
6	Nebraska	38.1		27	Kentucky	26.5
36	Nevada	24.9		28	New Jersey	26.2
15	New Hampshire	32.5		29	Iowa	25.5
28	New Jersey	26.2		30	Rhode Island	25.2
45	New Mexico	13.0		30	Tennessee	25.2
18	New York	29.8		30	Utah	25.2
11	North Carolina	33.5		30	West Virginia	25.2
4	North Dakota	39.7		34	Connecticut	25.1
16	Ohio	31.8		35	Vermont	25.0
5	Oklahoma	38.4		36	California	24.9
10	Oregon	33.6		36	Nevada	24.9
20	Pennsylvania	28.8		38	Indiana	24.8
30	Rhode Island	25.2		39	Maryland	23.5
13	South Carolina	33.0		40	Alaska	22.4
1	South Dakota	58.3		41	Arizona	22.3
30	Tennessee	25.2		42	Mississippi	21.4
17	Texas	30.0		43	Louisiana	17.8
30	Utah	25.2		44	Michigan	13.3
35	Vermont	25.0		45	New Mexico	13.0
8	Virginia	37.2		NA	Alabama**	NA
21	Washington	28.6		NA	Florida**	NA
30	West Virginia	25.2		NA	Illinois**	NA
12	Wisconsin	33.4		NA	Kansas**	NA
26	Wyoming	26.6		NA	Montana**	NA
					District of Columbia	7.3

Source: Federal Bureau of Investigation (unpublished data)
Robbery is the taking of anything of value by force or threat of force. Attempts are included. A crime is considered cleared when at least one person is arrested, charged and turned over to the court for prosecution. Clearances recorded in 1996 may be for crimes which occurred in prior years. Several crimes may be cleared by the arrest of one person while the arrest of many persons may clear only one crime.
***Not available.*

Percent of Aggravated Assaults Cleared in 1996

National Percent = 57.9% Cleared*

ALPHA ORDER				RANK ORDER		
RANK	STATE	PERCENT		RANK	STATE	PERCENT
NA	Alabama**	NA		1	South Dakota	78.7
3	Alaska	77.3		2	Nebraska	78.0
43	Arizona	46.0		3	Alaska	77.3
26	Arkansas	59.3		4	Wyoming	75.4
22	California	60.3		5	Maine	74.0
11	Colorado	67.2		6	Delaware	73.5
16	Connecticut	62.8		7	Wisconsin	73.4
6	Delaware	73.5		8	Minnesota	72.3
NA	Florida**	NA		9	Virginia	71.1
34	Georgia	53.7		10	Rhode Island	69.1
42	Hawaii	47.0		11	Colorado	67.2
14	Idaho	65.1		12	Pennsylvania	66.0
NA	Illinois**	NA		12	Tennessee	66.0
39	Indiana	49.7		14	Idaho	65.1
20	Iowa	60.9		15	West Virginia	64.9
NA	Kansas**	NA		16	Connecticut	62.8
17	Kentucky	62.2		17	Kentucky	62.2
36	Louisiana	53.0		18	New Jersey	61.3
5	Maine	74.0		19	Washington	61.0
21	Maryland	60.7		20	Iowa	60.9
31	Massachusetts	56.2		21	Maryland	60.7
44	Michigan	41.7		22	California	60.3
8	Minnesota	72.3		23	North Dakota	60.1
41	Mississippi	47.6		24	Ohio	59.8
33	Missouri	55.9		25	New Hampshire	59.6
NA	Montana**	NA		26	Arkansas	59.3
2	Nebraska	78.0		27	North Carolina	59.2
35	Nevada	53.4		28	Texas	58.1
25	New Hampshire	59.6		29	South Carolina	58.0
18	New Jersey	61.3		30	Vermont	57.5
45	New Mexico	41.6		31	Massachusetts	56.2
32	New York	56.1		32	New York	56.1
27	North Carolina	59.2		33	Missouri	55.9
23	North Dakota	60.1		34	Georgia	53.7
24	Ohio	59.8		35	Nevada	53.4
36	Oklahoma	53.0		36	Louisiana	53.0
38	Oregon	51.7		36	Oklahoma	53.0
12	Pennsylvania	66.0		38	Oregon	51.7
10	Rhode Island	69.1		39	Indiana	49.7
29	South Carolina	58.0		40	Utah	47.8
1	South Dakota	78.7		41	Mississippi	47.6
12	Tennessee	66.0		42	Hawaii	47.0
28	Texas	58.1		43	Arizona	46.0
40	Utah	47.8		44	Michigan	41.7
30	Vermont	57.5		45	New Mexico	41.6
9	Virginia	71.1		NA	Alabama**	NA
19	Washington	61.0		NA	Florida**	NA
15	West Virginia	64.9		NA	Illinois**	NA
7	Wisconsin	73.4		NA	Kansas**	NA
4	Wyoming	75.4		NA	Montana**	NA
					District of Columbia	34.1

Source: Federal Bureau of Investigation (unpublished data)

*Aggravated assault is an attack for the purpose of inflicting severe bodily injury. A crime is considered cleared when at least one person is arrested, charged and turned over to the court for prosecution. Clearances recorded in 1996 may be for crimes which occurred in prior years. Several crimes may be cleared by the arrest of one person while the arrest of many persons may clear only one crime.

**Not available.

Percent of Property Crimes Cleared in 1996

National Percent = 18.1% Cleared*

ALPHA ORDER				RANK ORDER		
RANK	**STATE**	**PERCENT**		**RANK**	**STATE**	**PERCENT**
NA	Alabama**	NA		1	South Dakota	29.2
10	Alaska	22.7		2	Wyoming	26.6
37	Arizona	16.4		3	Maine	26.0
6	Arkansas	24.1		4	Wisconsin	25.5
41	California	15.1		5	North Dakota	24.7
17	Colorado	19.8		6	Arkansas	24.1
33	Connecticut	17.2		7	Delaware	23.7
7	Delaware	23.7		7	Idaho	23.7
NA	Florida**	NA		9	Nebraska	23.3
20	Georgia	19.2		10	Alaska	22.7
42	Hawaii	14.7		11	Virginia	22.0
7	Idaho	23.7		12	Nevada	21.6
NA	Illinois**	NA		13	Minnesota	21.5
37	Indiana	16.4		14	Pennsylvania	20.9
39	Iowa	16.2		15	Kentucky	20.8
NA	Kansas**	NA		16	Oregon	20.3
15	Kentucky	20.8		17	Colorado	19.8
28	Louisiana	18.5		17	Missouri	19.8
3	Maine	26.0		19	Ohio	19.4
30	Maryland	18.2		20	Georgia	19.2
32	Massachusetts	17.5		21	New York	19.0
44	Michigan	11.0		21	North Carolina	19.0
13	Minnesota	21.5		21	Tennessee	19.0
27	Mississippi	18.6		21	West Virginia	19.0
17	Missouri	19.8		25	Texas	18.9
NA	Montana**	NA		26	Washington	18.7
9	Nebraska	23.3		27	Mississippi	18.6
12	Nevada	21.6		28	Louisiana	18.5
31	New Hampshire	17.6		29	Utah	18.4
35	New Jersey	16.6		30	Maryland	18.2
43	New Mexico	14.1		31	New Hampshire	17.6
21	New York	19.0		32	Massachusetts	17.5
21	North Carolina	19.0		33	Connecticut	17.2
5	North Dakota	24.7		34	Rhode Island	16.8
19	Ohio	19.4		35	New Jersey	16.6
40	Oklahoma	15.7		35	South Carolina	16.6
16	Oregon	20.3		37	Arizona	16.4
14	Pennsylvania	20.9		37	Indiana	16.4
34	Rhode Island	16.8		39	Iowa	16.2
35	South Carolina	16.6		40	Oklahoma	15.7
1	South Dakota	29.2		41	California	15.1
21	Tennessee	19.0		42	Hawaii	14.7
25	Texas	18.9		43	New Mexico	14.1
29	Utah	18.4		44	Michigan	11.0
45	Vermont	9.0		45	Vermont	9.0
11	Virginia	22.0		NA	Alabama**	NA
26	Washington	18.7		NA	Florida**	NA
21	West Virginia	19.0		NA	Illinois**	NA
4	Wisconsin	25.5		NA	Kansas**	NA
2	Wyoming	26.6		NA	Montana**	NA
					District of Columbia	4.5

Source: Federal Bureau of Investigation (unpublished data)
*Property crimes are offenses of burglary, larceny-theft and motor vehicle theft. A crime is considered cleared when at least one person is arrested, charged and turned over to the court for prosecution. Clearances recorded in 1996 may be for crimes which occurred in prior years. Several crimes may be cleared by the arrest of one person while the arrest of many persons may clear only one crime.
**Not available.

43

Percent of Burglaries Cleared in 1996

National Percent = 13.7% Cleared*

ALPHA ORDER				RANK ORDER		
RANK	STATE		PERCENT	RANK	STATE	PERCENT
NA	Alabama**		NA	1	South Dakota	21.0
7	Alaska		18.3	1	Virginia	21.0
42	Arizona		8.2	3	Wyoming	20.3
6	Arkansas		19.2	4	Maine	20.2
29	California		12.9	5	Wisconsin	19.5
33	Colorado		12.2	6	Arkansas	19.2
36	Connecticut		11.4	7	Alaska	18.3
10	Delaware		16.8	8	Nevada	17.4
NA	Florida**		NA	9	Massachusetts	17.0
18	Georgia		14.2	10	Delaware	16.8
40	Hawaii		9.9	11	Kentucky	16.6
20	Idaho		14.0	12	Maryland	16.2
NA	Illinois**		NA	12	North Carolina	16.2
39	Indiana		10.7	14	Pennsylvania	16.1
41	Iowa		8.7	15	Missouri	15.7
NA	Kansas**		NA	15	New York	15.7
11	Kentucky		16.6	17	Ohio	14.9
20	Louisiana		14.0	18	Georgia	14.2
4	Maine		20.2	19	Texas	14.1
12	Maryland		16.2	20	Idaho	14.0
9	Massachusetts		17.0	20	Louisiana	14.0
43	Michigan		7.7	22	North Dakota	13.8
32	Minnesota		12.3	23	Nebraska	13.4
26	Mississippi		13.0	24	New Jersey	13.2
15	Missouri		15.7	24	South Carolina	13.2
NA	Montana**		NA	26	Mississippi	13.0
23	Nebraska		13.4	26	Tennessee	13.0
8	Nevada		17.4	26	West Virginia	13.0
33	New Hampshire		12.2	29	California	12.9
24	New Jersey		13.2	30	Oklahoma	12.5
44	New Mexico		7.3	31	Oregon	12.4
15	New York		15.7	32	Minnesota	12.3
12	North Carolina		16.2	33	Colorado	12.2
22	North Dakota		13.8	33	New Hampshire	12.2
17	Ohio		14.9	33	Rhode Island	12.2
30	Oklahoma		12.5	36	Connecticut	11.4
31	Oregon		12.4	37	Utah	11.3
14	Pennsylvania		16.1	38	Washington	11.0
33	Rhode Island		12.2	39	Indiana	10.7
24	South Carolina		13.2	40	Hawaii	9.9
1	South Dakota		21.0	41	Iowa	8.7
26	Tennessee		13.0	42	Arizona	8.2
19	Texas		14.1	43	Michigan	7.7
37	Utah		11.3	44	New Mexico	7.3
45	Vermont		6.8	45	Vermont	6.8
1	Virginia		21.0	NA	Alabama**	NA
38	Washington		11.0	NA	Florida**	NA
26	West Virginia		13.0	NA	Illinois**	NA
5	Wisconsin		19.5	NA	Kansas**	NA
3	Wyoming		20.3	NA	Montana**	NA
					District of Columbia	5.0

Source: Federal Bureau of Investigation (unpublished data)
Burglary is the unlawful entry of a structure to commit a felony or theft. Attempts are included. A crime is considered cleared when at least one person is arrested, charged and turned over to the court for prosecution. Clearances recorded in 1996 may be for crimes which occurred in prior years. Several crimes may be cleared by the arrest of one person while the arrest of many persons may clear only one crime.
**Not available.*

Percent of Larcenies and Thefts Cleared in 1996

National Percent = 20.2% Cleared*

ALPHA ORDER

RANK	STATE	PERCENT
NA	Alabama**	NA
11	Alaska	24.4
30	Arizona	20.0
10	Arkansas	25.1
41	California	17.6
18	Colorado	21.7
28	Connecticut	20.2
5	Delaware	27.2
NA	Florida**	NA
29	Georgia	20.1
43	Hawaii	16.3
6	Idaho	25.7
NA	Illinois**	NA
37	Indiana	18.1
37	Iowa	18.1
NA	Kansas**	NA
16	Kentucky	22.0
23	Louisiana	21.0
2	Maine	27.3
32	Maryland	19.7
36	Massachusetts	18.4
44	Michigan	12.7
13	Minnesota	23.1
23	Mississippi	21.0
22	Missouri	21.2
NA	Montana**	NA
8	Nebraska	25.2
8	Nevada	25.2
35	New Hampshire	18.7
27	New Jersey	20.4
40	New Mexico	17.8
16	New York	22.0
33	North Carolina	19.5
6	North Dakota	25.7
23	Ohio	21.0
42	Oklahoma	16.9
14	Oregon	22.6
12	Pennsylvania	23.3
34	Rhode Island	18.9
39	South Carolina	18.0
1	South Dakota	30.7
14	Tennessee	22.6
26	Texas	20.8
31	Utah	19.9
45	Vermont	9.5
19	Virginia	21.6
20	Washington	21.5
21	West Virginia	21.3
2	Wisconsin	27.3
2	Wyoming	27.3

RANK ORDER

RANK	STATE	PERCENT
1	South Dakota	30.7
2	Maine	27.3
2	Wisconsin	27.3
2	Wyoming	27.3
5	Delaware	27.2
6	Idaho	25.7
6	North Dakota	25.7
8	Nebraska	25.2
8	Nevada	25.2
10	Arkansas	25.1
11	Alaska	24.4
12	Pennsylvania	23.3
13	Minnesota	23.1
14	Oregon	22.6
14	Tennessee	22.6
16	Kentucky	22.0
16	New York	22.0
18	Colorado	21.7
19	Virginia	21.6
20	Washington	21.5
21	West Virginia	21.3
22	Missouri	21.2
23	Louisiana	21.0
23	Mississippi	21.0
23	Ohio	21.0
26	Texas	20.8
27	New Jersey	20.4
28	Connecticut	20.2
29	Georgia	20.1
30	Arizona	20.0
31	Utah	19.9
32	Maryland	19.7
33	North Carolina	19.5
34	Rhode Island	18.9
35	New Hampshire	18.7
36	Massachusetts	18.4
37	Indiana	18.1
37	Iowa	18.1
39	South Carolina	18.0
40	New Mexico	17.8
41	California	17.6
42	Oklahoma	16.9
43	Hawaii	16.3
44	Michigan	12.7
45	Vermont	9.5
NA	Alabama**	NA
NA	Florida**	NA
NA	Illinois**	NA
NA	Kansas**	NA
NA	Montana**	NA

District of Columbia   4.7

Source: Federal Bureau of Investigation (unpublished data)
*Larceny and theft is the unlawful taking of property without use of force, violence or fraud. Attempts are included. Motor vehicle thefts are excluded. A crime is considered cleared when at least one person is arrested, charged and turned over to the court for prosecution. Clearances recorded in 1996 may be for crimes which occurred in prior years. Several crimes may be cleared by the arrest of one person while the arrest of many persons may clear only one crime. **Not available.

Percent of Motor Vehicle Thefts Cleared in 1996

National Percent = 14.0% Cleared*

ALPHA ORDER			RANK ORDER		
RANK	**STATE**	**PERCENT**	**RANK**	**STATE**	**PERCENT**
NA	Alabama**	NA	1	Wyoming	40.7
15	Alaska	19.3	2	South Dakota	39.8
38	Arizona	11.1	3	Maine	35.1
5	Arkansas	30.6	4	North Dakota	32.0
41	California	9.5	5	Arkansas	30.6
14	Colorado	21.4	6	Idaho	29.5
37	Connecticut	12.1	7	Virginia	27.9
42	Delaware	9.2	8	Minnesota	27.7
NA	Florida**	NA	9	North Carolina	25.6
13	Georgia	22.2	10	Nebraska	24.3
39	Hawaii	10.9	11	Kentucky	23.7
6	Idaho	29.5	12	Wisconsin	22.7
NA	Illinois**	NA	13	Georgia	22.2
26	Indiana	16.0	14	Colorado	21.4
22	Iowa	17.1	15	Alaska	19.3
NA	Kansas**	NA	16	Ohio	18.5
11	Kentucky	23.7	17	Mississippi	18.3
35	Louisiana	12.8	17	Missouri	18.3
3	Maine	35.1	19	Oregon	17.8
33	Maryland	13.8	20	West Virginia	17.6
30	Massachusetts	14.9	21	Utah	17.3
43	Michigan	8.5	22	Iowa	17.1
8	Minnesota	27.7	23	New Hampshire	16.8
17	Mississippi	18.3	24	Vermont	16.7
17	Missouri	18.3	25	Texas	16.6
NA	Montana**	NA	26	Indiana	16.0
10	Nebraska	24.3	27	Oklahoma	15.9
36	Nevada	12.2	28	Pennsylvania	15.7
23	New Hampshire	16.8	29	South Carolina	15.3
45	New Jersey	5.6	30	Massachusetts	14.9
44	New Mexico	7.2	31	Rhode Island	14.3
40	New York	10.4	32	Tennessee	14.0
9	North Carolina	25.6	33	Maryland	13.8
4	North Dakota	32.0	34	Washington	13.1
16	Ohio	18.5	35	Louisiana	12.8
27	Oklahoma	15.9	36	Nevada	12.2
19	Oregon	17.8	37	Connecticut	12.1
28	Pennsylvania	15.7	38	Arizona	11.1
31	Rhode Island	14.3	39	Hawaii	10.9
29	South Carolina	15.3	40	New York	10.4
2	South Dakota	39.8	41	California	9.5
32	Tennessee	14.0	42	Delaware	9.2
25	Texas	16.6	43	Michigan	8.5
21	Utah	17.3	44	New Mexico	7.2
24	Vermont	16.7	45	New Jersey	5.6
7	Virginia	27.9	NA	Alabama**	NA
34	Washington	13.1	NA	Florida**	NA
20	West Virginia	17.6	NA	Illinois**	NA
12	Wisconsin	22.7	NA	Kansas**	NA
1	Wyoming	40.7	NA	Montana**	NA
				District of Columbia	3.3

Source: Federal Bureau of Investigation (unpublished data)
*Motor vehicle theft includes the theft or attempted theft of a self-propelled vehicle. Excludes motorboats, construction equipment, airplanes and farming equipment. A crime is considered cleared when at least one person is arrested, charged and turned over to the court for prosecution. Clearances recorded in 1996 may be for crimes which occurred in prior years. Several crimes may be cleared by the arrest of one person while the arrest of many persons may clear only one crime. **Not available.

II. CORRECTIONS

II. CORRECTIONS (continued)

Prisoners in State Correctional Institutions in 1997

National Total = 1,108,096 State Prisoners*

RANK	STATE	PRISONERS	% of USA	RANK	STATE	PRISONERS	% of USA
17	Alabama	22,076	1.99%	1	California	153,010	13.81%
40	Alaska	3,741	0.34%	2	Texas	136,599	12.33%
15	Arizona	23,176	2.09%	3	New York	69,530	6.27%
29	Arkansas	9,539	0.86%	4	Florida	64,713	5.84%
1	California	153,010	13.81%	5	Ohio	47,248	4.26%
26	Colorado	12,840	1.16%	6	Michigan	43,784	3.95%
22	Connecticut	15,608	1.41%	7	Illinois	40,425	3.65%
35	Delaware	5,313	0.48%	8	Georgia	36,329	3.28%
4	Florida	64,713	5.84%	9	Pennsylvania	34,703	3.13%
8	Georgia	36,329	3.28%	10	North Carolina	32,334	2.92%
37	Hawaii	4,491	0.41%	11	Virginia	28,673	2.59%
39	Idaho	4,105	0.37%	12	Louisiana	28,382	2.56%
7	Illinois	40,425	3.65%	13	New Jersey	27,766	2.51%
20	Indiana	17,549	1.58%	14	Missouri	23,687	2.14%
33	Iowa	6,636	0.60%	15	Arizona	23,176	2.09%
32	Kansas	7,790	0.70%	16	Maryland	22,415	2.02%
25	Kentucky	13,858	1.25%	17	Alabama	22,076	1.99%
12	Louisiana	28,382	2.56%	18	South Carolina	21,021	1.90%
47	Maine	1,559	0.14%	19	Oklahoma	19,931	1.80%
16	Maryland	22,415	2.02%	20	Indiana	17,549	1.58%
28	Massachusetts	11,907	1.07%	21	Tennessee	15,827	1.43%
6	Michigan	43,784	3.95%	22	Connecticut	15,608	1.41%
34	Minnesota	5,348	0.48%	23	Mississippi	14,639	1.32%
23	Mississippi	14,639	1.32%	24	Wisconsin	13,965	1.26%
14	Missouri	23,687	2.14%	25	Kentucky	13,858	1.25%
44	Montana	2,295	0.21%	26	Colorado	12,840	1.16%
41	Nebraska	3,431	0.31%	27	Washington	12,732	1.15%
30	Nevada	8,617	0.78%	28	Massachusetts	11,907	1.07%
46	New Hampshire	2,153	0.19%	29	Arkansas	9,539	0.86%
13	New Jersey	27,766	2.51%	30	Nevada	8,617	0.78%
36	New Mexico	4,692	0.42%	31	Oregon	7,899	0.71%
3	New York	69,530	6.27%	32	Kansas	7,790	0.70%
10	North Carolina	32,334	2.92%	33	Iowa	6,636	0.60%
50	North Dakota	739	0.07%	34	Minnesota	5,348	0.48%
5	Ohio	47,248	4.26%	35	Delaware	5,313	0.48%
19	Oklahoma	19,931	1.80%	36	New Mexico	4,692	0.42%
31	Oregon	7,899	0.71%	37	Hawaii	4,491	0.41%
9	Pennsylvania	34,703	3.13%	38	Utah	4,154	0.37%
42	Rhode Island	3,293	0.30%	39	Idaho	4,105	0.37%
18	South Carolina	21,021	1.90%	40	Alaska	3,741	0.34%
45	South Dakota	2,177	0.20%	41	Nebraska	3,431	0.31%
21	Tennessee	15,827	1.43%	42	Rhode Island	3,293	0.30%
2	Texas	136,599	12.33%	43	West Virginia	3,003	0.27%
38	Utah	4,154	0.37%	44	Montana	2,295	0.21%
49	Vermont	1,187	0.11%	45	South Dakota	2,177	0.20%
11	Virginia	28,673	2.59%	46	New Hampshire	2,153	0.19%
27	Washington	12,732	1.15%	47	Maine	1,559	0.14%
43	West Virginia	3,003	0.27%	48	Wyoming	1,468	0.13%
24	Wisconsin	13,965	1.26%	49	Vermont	1,187	0.11%
48	Wyoming	1,468	0.13%	50	North Dakota	739	0.07%
					District of Columbia	9,739	0.88%

Source: U.S. Department of Justice, Bureau of Justice Statistics
    "Prison and Jail Inmates at Midyear 1997 (January 1998, NCJ-167247)
*As of June 30, 1997. Totals include inmates sentenced to more than one year and those sentenced to a year or less or with no sentence. Does not include 110,160 prisoners under federal jurisdiction. State and federal prisoners combined total 1,218,256.

State Prisoner Incarceration Rate in 1997

National Rate = 401 State Prisoners per 100,000 Population*

ALPHA ORDER

RANK ORDER

RANK	STATE	RATE
7	Alabama	499
18	Alaska	396
8	Arizona	484
21	Arkansas	368
10	California	466
26	Colorado	330
27	Connecticut	322
13	Delaware	442
12	Florida	443
9	Georgia	476
35	Hawaii	258
25	Idaho	339
24	Illinois	340
31	Indiana	296
39	Iowa	232
29	Kansas	302
22	Kentucky	355
2	Louisiana	651
48	Maine	118
16	Maryland	417
30	Massachusetts	301
11	Michigan	454
49	Minnesota	114
5	Mississippi	505
14	Missouri	438
35	Montana	258
44	Nebraska	201
5	Nevada	505
45	New Hampshire	183
23	New Jersey	346
35	New Mexico	258
20	New York	383
19	North Carolina	385
50	North Dakota	104
15	Ohio	422
3	Oklahoma	599
40	Oregon	226
34	Pennsylvania	288
42	Rhode Island	203
4	South Carolina	542
31	South Dakota	296
33	Tennessee	294
1	Texas	677
43	Utah	202
47	Vermont	152
17	Virginia	412
40	Washington	226
46	West Virginia	163
38	Wisconsin	256
28	Wyoming	304

RANK	STATE	RATE
1	Texas	677
2	Louisiana	651
3	Oklahoma	599
4	South Carolina	542
5	Mississippi	505
5	Nevada	505
7	Alabama	499
8	Arizona	484
9	Georgia	476
10	California	466
11	Michigan	454
12	Florida	443
13	Delaware	442
14	Missouri	438
15	Ohio	422
16	Maryland	417
17	Virginia	412
18	Alaska	396
19	North Carolina	385
20	New York	383
21	Arkansas	368
22	Kentucky	355
23	New Jersey	346
24	Illinois	340
25	Idaho	339
26	Colorado	330
27	Connecticut	322
28	Wyoming	304
29	Kansas	302
30	Massachusetts	301
31	Indiana	296
31	South Dakota	296
33	Tennessee	294
34	Pennsylvania	288
35	Hawaii	258
35	Montana	258
35	New Mexico	258
38	Wisconsin	256
39	Iowa	232
40	Oregon	226
40	Washington	226
42	Rhode Island	203
43	Utah	202
44	Nebraska	201
45	New Hampshire	183
46	West Virginia	163
47	Vermont	152
48	Maine	118
49	Minnesota	114
50	North Dakota	104
	District of Columbia	1,373

Source: U.S. Department of Justice, Bureau of Justice Statistics
   "Prison and Jail Inmates at Midyear 1997 (January 1998, NCJ-167247)
*As of June 30, 1997. Includes only inmates sentenced to more than one year. Does not include federal incarceration rate of 35 prisoners per 100,000 population. State and federal combined incarceration rate is 436 prisoners per 100,000 population.

Prisoners in State Correctional Institutions in 1996

National Total = 1,059,336 State Prisoners*

ALPHA ORDER

RANK ORDER

RANK	STATE	PRISONERS	% of USA	RANK	STATE	PRISONERS	% of USA
16	Alabama	21,495	2.03%	1	California	141,535	13.36%
40	Alaska	3,583	0.34%	2	Texas	129,937	12.27%
14	Arizona	22,143	2.09%	3	New York	68,721	6.49%
29	Arkansas	9,430	0.89%	4	Florida	64,333	6.07%
1	California	141,535	13.36%	5	Ohio	45,314	4.28%
28	Colorado	11,742	1.11%	6	Michigan	41,884	3.95%
22	Connecticut	14,975	1.41%	7	Illinois	38,373	3.62%
34	Delaware	5,148	0.49%	8	Georgia	34,808	3.29%
4	Florida	64,333	6.07%	9	Pennsylvania	33,939	3.20%
8	Georgia	34,808	3.29%	10	North Carolina	30,671	2.90%
37	Hawaii	3,693	0.35%	11	Virginia	28,827	2.72%
39	Idaho	3,623	0.34%	12	New Jersey	27,753	2.62%
7	Illinois	38,373	3.62%	13	Louisiana	26,673	2.52%
20	Indiana	16,582	1.57%	14	Arizona	22,143	2.09%
33	Iowa	6,176	0.58%	15	Maryland	22,118	2.09%
32	Kansas	7,462	0.70%	16	Alabama	21,495	2.03%
24	Kentucky	12,652	1.19%	17	South Carolina	20,814	1.96%
13	Louisiana	26,673	2.52%	18	Missouri	20,541	1.94%
47	Maine	1,468	0.14%	19	Oklahoma	19,134	1.81%
15	Maryland	22,118	2.09%	20	Indiana	16,582	1.57%
27	Massachusetts	11,996	1.13%	21	Tennessee	15,634	1.48%
6	Michigan	41,884	3.95%	22	Connecticut	14,975	1.41%
35	Minnesota	5,040	0.48%	23	Mississippi	13,785	1.30%
23	Mississippi	13,785	1.30%	24	Kentucky	12,652	1.19%
18	Missouri	20,541	1.94%	25	Wisconsin	12,105	1.14%
44	Montana	2,162	0.20%	26	Washington	12,059	1.14%
41	Nebraska	3,248	0.31%	27	Massachusetts	11,996	1.13%
31	Nevada	8,064	0.76%	28	Colorado	11,742	1.11%
45	New Hampshire	2,050	0.19%	29	Arkansas	9,430	0.89%
12	New Jersey	27,753	2.62%	30	Oregon	8,564	0.81%
36	New Mexico	4,528	0.43%	31	Nevada	8,064	0.76%
3	New York	68,721	6.49%	32	Kansas	7,462	0.70%
10	North Carolina	30,671	2.90%	33	Iowa	6,176	0.58%
50	North Dakota	640	0.06%	34	Delaware	5,148	0.49%
5	Ohio	45,314	4.28%	35	Minnesota	5,040	0.48%
19	Oklahoma	19,134	1.81%	36	New Mexico	4,528	0.43%
30	Oregon	8,564	0.81%	37	Hawaii	3,693	0.35%
9	Pennsylvania	33,939	3.20%	38	Utah	3,643	0.34%
42	Rhode Island	3,226	0.30%	39	Idaho	3,623	0.34%
17	South Carolina	20,814	1.96%	40	Alaska	3,583	0.34%
46	South Dakota	2,049	0.19%	41	Nebraska	3,248	0.31%
21	Tennessee	15,634	1.48%	42	Rhode Island	3,226	0.30%
2	Texas	129,937	12.27%	43	West Virginia	2,679	0.25%
38	Utah	3,643	0.34%	44	Montana	2,162	0.20%
49	Vermont	1,096	0.10%	45	New Hampshire	2,050	0.19%
11	Virginia	28,827	2.72%	46	South Dakota	2,049	0.19%
26	Washington	12,059	1.14%	47	Maine	1,468	0.14%
43	West Virginia	2,679	0.25%	48	Wyoming	1,458	0.14%
25	Wisconsin	12,105	1.14%	49	Vermont	1,096	0.10%
48	Wyoming	1,458	0.14%	50	North Dakota	640	0.06%
					District of Columbia	9,763	0.92%

Source: U.S. Department of Justice, Bureau of Justice Statistics
"Prison and Jail Inmates at Midyear 1997 (January 1998, NCJ-167247)

*As of June 30, 1996. Totals include inmates sentenced to more than one year and those sentenced to a year or less or with no sentence. Does not include 103,722 prisoners under federal jurisdiction. State and federal prisoners combined total 1,163,058.

Percent Change in Number of State Prisoners: 1996 to 1997

National Percent Change = 4.6% Increase*

<table>
<tr><td colspan="3">ALPHA ORDER</td><td colspan="3">RANK ORDER</td></tr>
<tr><td>RANK</td><td>STATE</td><td>PERCENT CHANGE</td><td>RANK</td><td>STATE</td><td>PERCENT CHANGE</td></tr>
<tr><td>37</td><td>Alabama</td><td>2.7</td><td>1</td><td>Hawaii</td><td>21.6</td></tr>
<tr><td>29</td><td>Alaska</td><td>4.4</td><td>2</td><td>North Dakota</td><td>15.5</td></tr>
<tr><td>27</td><td>Arizona</td><td>4.7</td><td>3</td><td>Wisconsin</td><td>15.4</td></tr>
<tr><td>41</td><td>Arkansas</td><td>1.2</td><td>4</td><td>Missouri</td><td>15.3</td></tr>
<tr><td>11</td><td>California</td><td>8.1</td><td>5</td><td>Utah</td><td>14.0</td></tr>
<tr><td>9</td><td>Colorado</td><td>9.4</td><td>6</td><td>Idaho</td><td>13.3</td></tr>
<tr><td>33</td><td>Connecticut</td><td>4.2</td><td>7</td><td>West Virginia</td><td>12.1</td></tr>
<tr><td>36</td><td>Delaware</td><td>3.2</td><td>8</td><td>Kentucky</td><td>9.5</td></tr>
<tr><td>46</td><td>Florida</td><td>0.6</td><td>9</td><td>Colorado</td><td>9.4</td></tr>
<tr><td>29</td><td>Georgia</td><td>4.4</td><td>10</td><td>Vermont</td><td>8.3</td></tr>
<tr><td>1</td><td>Hawaii</td><td>21.6</td><td>11</td><td>California</td><td>8.1</td></tr>
<tr><td>6</td><td>Idaho</td><td>13.3</td><td>12</td><td>Iowa</td><td>7.4</td></tr>
<tr><td>24</td><td>Illinois</td><td>5.3</td><td>13</td><td>Nevada</td><td>6.9</td></tr>
<tr><td>20</td><td>Indiana</td><td>5.8</td><td>14</td><td>Louisiana</td><td>6.4</td></tr>
<tr><td>12</td><td>Iowa</td><td>7.4</td><td>15</td><td>Maine</td><td>6.2</td></tr>
<tr><td>29</td><td>Kansas</td><td>4.4</td><td>15</td><td>Mississippi</td><td>6.2</td></tr>
<tr><td>8</td><td>Kentucky</td><td>9.5</td><td>15</td><td>Montana</td><td>6.2</td></tr>
<tr><td>14</td><td>Louisiana</td><td>6.4</td><td>15</td><td>South Dakota</td><td>6.2</td></tr>
<tr><td>15</td><td>Maine</td><td>6.2</td><td>19</td><td>Minnesota</td><td>6.1</td></tr>
<tr><td>40</td><td>Maryland</td><td>1.3</td><td>20</td><td>Indiana</td><td>5.8</td></tr>
<tr><td>50</td><td>Massachusetts</td><td>(0.7)</td><td>21</td><td>Nebraska</td><td>5.6</td></tr>
<tr><td>28</td><td>Michigan</td><td>4.5</td><td>21</td><td>Washington</td><td>5.6</td></tr>
<tr><td>19</td><td>Minnesota</td><td>6.1</td><td>23</td><td>North Carolina</td><td>5.4</td></tr>
<tr><td>15</td><td>Mississippi</td><td>6.2</td><td>24</td><td>Illinois</td><td>5.3</td></tr>
<tr><td>4</td><td>Missouri</td><td>15.3</td><td>25</td><td>Texas</td><td>5.1</td></tr>
<tr><td>15</td><td>Montana</td><td>6.2</td><td>26</td><td>New Hampshire</td><td>5.0</td></tr>
<tr><td>21</td><td>Nebraska</td><td>5.6</td><td>27</td><td>Arizona</td><td>4.7</td></tr>
<tr><td>13</td><td>Nevada</td><td>6.9</td><td>28</td><td>Michigan</td><td>4.5</td></tr>
<tr><td>26</td><td>New Hampshire</td><td>5.0</td><td>29</td><td>Alaska</td><td>4.4</td></tr>
<tr><td>47</td><td>New Jersey</td><td>0.0</td><td>29</td><td>Georgia</td><td>4.4</td></tr>
<tr><td>35</td><td>New Mexico</td><td>3.6</td><td>29</td><td>Kansas</td><td>4.4</td></tr>
<tr><td>41</td><td>New York</td><td>1.2</td><td>32</td><td>Ohio</td><td>4.3</td></tr>
<tr><td>23</td><td>North Carolina</td><td>5.4</td><td>33</td><td>Connecticut</td><td>4.2</td></tr>
<tr><td>2</td><td>North Dakota</td><td>15.5</td><td>33</td><td>Oklahoma</td><td>4.2</td></tr>
<tr><td>32</td><td>Ohio</td><td>4.3</td><td>35</td><td>New Mexico</td><td>3.6</td></tr>
<tr><td>33</td><td>Oklahoma</td><td>4.2</td><td>36</td><td>Delaware</td><td>3.2</td></tr>
<tr><td>47</td><td>Oregon</td><td>0.0</td><td>37</td><td>Alabama</td><td>2.7</td></tr>
<tr><td>38</td><td>Pennsylvania</td><td>2.3</td><td>38</td><td>Pennsylvania</td><td>2.3</td></tr>
<tr><td>39</td><td>Rhode Island</td><td>2.1</td><td>39</td><td>Rhode Island</td><td>2.1</td></tr>
<tr><td>44</td><td>South Carolina</td><td>1.0</td><td>40</td><td>Maryland</td><td>1.3</td></tr>
<tr><td>15</td><td>South Dakota</td><td>6.2</td><td>41</td><td>Arkansas</td><td>1.2</td></tr>
<tr><td>41</td><td>Tennessee</td><td>1.2</td><td>41</td><td>New York</td><td>1.2</td></tr>
<tr><td>25</td><td>Texas</td><td>5.1</td><td>41</td><td>Tennessee</td><td>1.2</td></tr>
<tr><td>5</td><td>Utah</td><td>14.0</td><td>44</td><td>South Carolina</td><td>1.0</td></tr>
<tr><td>10</td><td>Vermont</td><td>8.3</td><td>45</td><td>Wyoming</td><td>0.7</td></tr>
<tr><td>49</td><td>Virginia</td><td>(0.5)</td><td>46</td><td>Florida</td><td>0.6</td></tr>
<tr><td>21</td><td>Washington</td><td>5.6</td><td>47</td><td>New Jersey</td><td>0.0</td></tr>
<tr><td>7</td><td>West Virginia</td><td>12.1</td><td>47</td><td>Oregon</td><td>0.0</td></tr>
<tr><td>3</td><td>Wisconsin</td><td>15.4</td><td>49</td><td>Virginia</td><td>(0.5)</td></tr>
<tr><td>45</td><td>Wyoming</td><td>0.7</td><td>50</td><td>Massachusetts</td><td>(0.7)</td></tr>
<tr><td></td><td></td><td></td><td></td><td>District of Columbia</td><td>(0.2)</td></tr>
</table>

Source: U.S. Department of Justice, Bureau of Justice Statistics
"Prison and Jail Inmates at Midyear 1997 (January 1998, NCJ-167247)
*From June 30, 1996 to June 30, 1997. Includes inmates sentenced to more than one year and those sentenced to a year or less or with no sentence. The percent change in number of prisoners under federal jurisdiction during the same period was a 6.2% increase. The combined state and federal increase was 4.7%.

Percent Change in State Prisoner Incarceration Rate: 1996 to 1997

National Percent Change = 3.4% Increase*

ALPHA ORDER

RANK ORDER

RANK	STATE	PERCENT CHANGE		RANK	STATE	PERCENT CHANGE
33	Alabama	2.5		1	Massachusetts	69.1
7	Alaska	11.5		2	Wisconsin	22.5
44	Arizona	0.6		3	North Dakota	15.6
31	Arkansas	2.8		4	Hawaii	14.7
14	California	6.4		5	Missouri	14.4
11	Colorado	7.8		6	West Virginia	13.2
43	Connecticut	0.9		7	Alaska	11.5
26	Delaware	4.0		7	Idaho	11.5
48	Florida	(1.1)		9	Utah	11.0
39	Georgia	1.7		10	Kentucky	9.2
4	Hawaii	14.7		11	Colorado	7.8
7	Idaho	11.5		12	Iowa	7.4
17	Illinois	5.6		13	Louisiana	6.5
20	Indiana	5.3		14	California	6.4
12	Iowa	7.4		15	Vermont	6.3
21	Kansas	4.5		16	South Dakota	6.1
10	Kentucky	9.2		17	Illinois	5.6
13	Louisiana	6.5		17	Minnesota	5.6
19	Maine	5.4		19	Maine	5.4
41	Maryland	1.0		20	Indiana	5.3
1	Massachusetts	69.1		21	Kansas	4.5
24	Michigan	4.1		21	Montana	4.5
17	Minnesota	5.6		23	Ohio	4.2
27	Mississippi	3.9		24	Michigan	4.1
5	Missouri	14.4		24	Nebraska	4.1
21	Montana	4.5		26	Delaware	4.0
24	Nebraska	4.1		27	Mississippi	3.9
36	Nevada	2.4		28	Washington	3.7
29	New Hampshire	3.4		29	New Hampshire	3.4
47	New Jersey	(0.3)		30	Oklahoma	3.3
38	New Mexico	2.0		31	Arkansas	2.8
40	New York	1.1		32	Texas	2.7
50	North Carolina	(3.0)		33	Alabama	2.5
3	North Dakota	15.6		33	Pennsylvania	2.5
23	Ohio	4.2		33	Rhode Island	2.5
30	Oklahoma	3.3		36	Nevada	2.4
37	Oregon	2.3		37	Oregon	2.3
33	Pennsylvania	2.5		38	New Mexico	2.0
33	Rhode Island	2.5		39	Georgia	1.7
45	South Carolina	0.4		40	New York	1.1
16	South Dakota	6.1		41	Maryland	1.0
46	Tennessee	0.3		41	Wyoming	1.0
32	Texas	2.7		43	Connecticut	0.9
9	Utah	11.0		44	Arizona	0.6
15	Vermont	6.3		45	South Carolina	0.4
49	Virginia	(2.1)		46	Tennessee	0.3
28	Washington	3.7		47	New Jersey	(0.3)
6	West Virginia	13.2		48	Florida	(1.1)
2	Wisconsin	22.5		49	Virginia	(2.1)
41	Wyoming	1.0		50	North Carolina	(3.0)
					District of Columbia	(4.9)

Source: Morgan Quitno Press using data from U.S. Department of Justice, Bureau of Justice Statistics
"Prison and Jail Inmates at Midyear 1997 (January 1998, NCJ-167247)
*From June 30, 1996 to June 30, 1997. Includes only inmates sentenced to more than one year. The percent change in rate of prisoners under federal jurisdiction during the same period was a 6.1% increase. The combined state and federal increase was 3.8%.

Percent Change in State Prisoner Incarceration Rate: 1993 to 1997

National Percent Change = 24.5% Increase*

ALPHA ORDER				RANK ORDER		
RANK	STATE	PERCENT CHANGE		RANK	STATE	PERCENT CHANGE
34	Alabama	15.8		1	Massachusetts	95.5
50	Alaska	(11.2)		2	Texas	75.8
40	Arizona	12.6		3	West Virginia	66.3
41	Arkansas	12.5		4	Wisconsin	54.2
20	California	26.6		5	North Dakota	48.6
22	Colorado	26.0		6	Idaho	44.9
48	Connecticut	0.6		7	Missouri	42.2
42	Delaware	12.2		8	Montana	41.8
37	Florida	15.4		9	Mississippi	39.9
26	Georgia	23.0		10	South Dakota	37.0
17	Hawaii	30.3		11	Oregon	36.1
6	Idaho	44.9		12	Kansas	33.6
35	Illinois	15.6		13	Iowa	33.3
28	Indiana	18.4		13	Pennsylvania	33.3
13	Iowa	33.3		15	Utah	32.9
12	Kansas	33.6		16	Nebraska	31.4
18	Kentucky	29.6		17	Hawaii	30.3
24	Louisiana	24.7		18	Kentucky	29.6
47	Maine	1.7		19	Wyoming	27.7
45	Maryland	8.9		20	California	26.6
1	Massachusetts	95.5		21	North Carolina	26.2
44	Michigan	9.7		22	Colorado	26.0
25	Minnesota	23.9		23	New Mexico	25.2
9	Mississippi	39.9		24	Louisiana	24.7
7	Missouri	42.2		25	Minnesota	23.9
8	Montana	41.8		26	Georgia	23.0
16	Nebraska	31.4		27	Virginia	19.1
33	Nevada	16.4		28	Indiana	18.4
32	New Hampshire	16.6		28	Oklahoma	18.4
39	New Jersey	15.0		30	Rhode Island	18.0
23	New Mexico	25.2		31	Tennessee	17.6
46	New York	8.2		32	New Hampshire	16.6
21	North Carolina	26.2		33	Nevada	16.4
5	North Dakota	48.6		34	Alabama	15.8
35	Ohio	15.6		35	Illinois	15.6
28	Oklahoma	18.4		35	Ohio	15.6
11	Oregon	36.1		37	Florida	15.4
13	Pennsylvania	33.3		38	Washington	15.3
30	Rhode Island	18.0		39	New Jersey	15.0
43	South Carolina	11.1		40	Arizona	12.6
10	South Dakota	37.0		41	Arkansas	12.5
31	Tennessee	17.6		42	Delaware	12.2
2	Texas	75.8		43	South Carolina	11.1
15	Utah	32.9		44	Michigan	9.7
49	Vermont	(1.3)		45	Maryland	8.9
27	Virginia	19.1		46	New York	8.2
38	Washington	15.3		47	Maine	1.7
3	West Virginia	66.3		48	Connecticut	0.6
4	Wisconsin	54.2		49	Vermont	(1.3)
19	Wyoming	27.7		50	Alaska	(11.2)
					District of Columbia	(11.4)

Source: Morgan Quitno Press using data from U.S. Department of Justice, Bureau of Justice Statistics
"Prison and Jail Inmates at Midyear 1997 (January 1998, NCJ-167247) and
"Correctional Populations in the United States, 1993" (October 1995, NCJ-156241)

*From December 31, 1993 to June 30, 1997. Includes only inmates sentenced to more than one year. The percent change in rate of prisoners under federal jurisdiction during the same period was a 25.0% increase. The combined state and federal increase was 24.6%.

52

State Prison Population as a Percent of Highest Capacity in 1996

National Percent = 116% of Highest Capacity*

ALPHA ORDER

RANK	STATE	PERCENT
35	Alabama	99
10	Alaska	135
22	Arizona	111
29	Arkansas	101
1	California	203
19	Colorado	118
NA	Connecticut**	NA
16	Delaware	121
47	Florida	89
24	Georgia	107
5	Hawaii	151
29	Idaho	101
8	Illinois	138
33	Indiana	100
5	Iowa	151
39	Kansas	98
12	Kentucky	131
33	Louisiana	100
35	Maine	99
42	Maryland	96
7	Massachusetts	150
35	Michigan	99
35	Minnesota	99
47	Mississippi	89
27	Missouri	102
17	Montana	120
13	Nebraska	130
24	Nevada	107
27	New Hampshire	102
2	New Jersey	167
45	New Mexico	94
29	New York	101
18	North Carolina	119
29	North Dakota	101
11	Ohio	134
9	Oklahoma	136
26	Oregon	105
3	Pennsylvania	156
43	Rhode Island	95
23	South Carolina	108
21	South Dakota	113
40	Tennessee	97
43	Texas	95
49	Utah	86
40	Vermont	97
4	Virginia	152
15	Washington	125
46	West Virginia	90
13	Wisconsin	130
19	Wyoming	118

RANK ORDER

RANK	STATE	PERCENT
1	California	203
2	New Jersey	167
3	Pennsylvania	156
4	Virginia	152
5	Hawaii	151
5	Iowa	151
7	Massachusetts	150
8	Illinois	138
9	Oklahoma	136
10	Alaska	135
11	Ohio	134
12	Kentucky	131
13	Nebraska	130
13	Wisconsin	130
15	Washington	125
16	Delaware	121
17	Montana	120
18	North Carolina	119
19	Colorado	118
19	Wyoming	118
21	South Dakota	113
22	Arizona	111
23	South Carolina	108
24	Georgia	107
24	Nevada	107
26	Oregon	105
27	Missouri	102
27	New Hampshire	102
29	Arkansas	101
29	Idaho	101
29	New York	101
29	North Dakota	101
33	Indiana	100
33	Louisiana	100
35	Alabama	99
35	Maine	99
35	Michigan	99
35	Minnesota	99
39	Kansas	98
40	Tennessee	97
40	Vermont	97
42	Maryland	96
43	Rhode Island	95
43	Texas	95
45	New Mexico	94
46	West Virginia	90
47	Florida	89
47	Mississippi	89
49	Utah	86
NA	Connecticut**	NA
	District of Columbia	89

Source: U.S. Department of Justice, Bureau of Justice Statistics
    "Prisoners in 1996" (June 1997, NCJ-164619)
*As of December 31, 1996. Federal prison population is at 125% of highest rated capacity.
**Not available.

Prisoners in State Correctional Institutions: Year End 1996

National Total = 1,074,976 State Prisoners*

<table>
<tr><td colspan="4"><u>ALPHA ORDER</u></td><td colspan="4"><u>RANK ORDER</u></td></tr>
<tr><td>RANK</td><td>STATE</td><td>PRISONERS</td><td>% of USA</td><td>RANK</td><td>STATE</td><td>PRISONERS</td><td>% of USA</td></tr>
<tr><td>17</td><td>Alabama</td><td>21,760</td><td>2.02%</td><td>1</td><td>California</td><td>146,049</td><td>13.59%</td></tr>
<tr><td>40</td><td>Alaska</td><td>3,716</td><td>0.35%</td><td>2</td><td>Texas</td><td>132,383</td><td>12.31%</td></tr>
<tr><td>14</td><td>Arizona</td><td>22,493</td><td>2.09%</td><td>3</td><td>New York</td><td>69,709</td><td>6.48%</td></tr>
<tr><td>29</td><td>Arkansas</td><td>9,407</td><td>0.88%</td><td>4</td><td>Florida</td><td>63,763</td><td>5.93%</td></tr>
<tr><td>1</td><td>California</td><td>146,049</td><td>13.59%</td><td>5</td><td>Ohio</td><td>46,174</td><td>4.30%</td></tr>
<tr><td>27</td><td>Colorado</td><td>12,438</td><td>1.16%</td><td>6</td><td>Michigan</td><td>42,349</td><td>3.94%</td></tr>
<tr><td>22</td><td>Connecticut</td><td>15,007</td><td>1.40%</td><td>7</td><td>Illinois</td><td>38,852</td><td>3.61%</td></tr>
<tr><td>35</td><td>Delaware</td><td>5,110</td><td>0.48%</td><td>8</td><td>Georgia</td><td>35,139</td><td>3.27%</td></tr>
<tr><td>4</td><td>Florida</td><td>63,763</td><td>5.93%</td><td>9</td><td>Pennsylvania</td><td>34,537</td><td>3.21%</td></tr>
<tr><td>8</td><td>Georgia</td><td>35,139</td><td>3.27%</td><td>10</td><td>North Carolina</td><td>30,647</td><td>2.85%</td></tr>
<tr><td>37</td><td>Hawaii</td><td>4,011</td><td>0.37%</td><td>11</td><td>Virginia</td><td>27,655</td><td>2.57%</td></tr>
<tr><td>39</td><td>Idaho</td><td>3,832</td><td>0.36%</td><td>12</td><td>New Jersey</td><td>27,490</td><td>2.56%</td></tr>
<tr><td>7</td><td>Illinois</td><td>38,852</td><td>3.61%</td><td>13</td><td>Louisiana</td><td>26,779</td><td>2.49%</td></tr>
<tr><td>20</td><td>Indiana</td><td>16,960</td><td>1.58%</td><td>14</td><td>Arizona</td><td>22,493</td><td>2.09%</td></tr>
<tr><td>33</td><td>Iowa</td><td>6,342</td><td>0.59%</td><td>15</td><td>Maryland</td><td>22,050</td><td>2.05%</td></tr>
<tr><td>32</td><td>Kansas</td><td>7,756</td><td>0.72%</td><td>16</td><td>Missouri</td><td>22,003</td><td>2.05%</td></tr>
<tr><td>25</td><td>Kentucky</td><td>12,910</td><td>1.20%</td><td>17</td><td>Alabama</td><td>21,760</td><td>2.02%</td></tr>
<tr><td>13</td><td>Louisiana</td><td>26,779</td><td>2.49%</td><td>18</td><td>South Carolina</td><td>20,446</td><td>1.90%</td></tr>
<tr><td>48</td><td>Maine</td><td>1,426</td><td>0.13%</td><td>19</td><td>Oklahoma</td><td>19,593</td><td>1.82%</td></tr>
<tr><td>15</td><td>Maryland</td><td>22,050</td><td>2.05%</td><td>20</td><td>Indiana</td><td>16,960</td><td>1.58%</td></tr>
<tr><td>28</td><td>Massachusetts</td><td>11,796</td><td>1.10%</td><td>21</td><td>Tennessee</td><td>15,626</td><td>1.45%</td></tr>
<tr><td>6</td><td>Michigan</td><td>42,349</td><td>3.94%</td><td>22</td><td>Connecticut</td><td>15,007</td><td>1.40%</td></tr>
<tr><td>34</td><td>Minnesota</td><td>5,158</td><td>0.48%</td><td>23</td><td>Mississippi</td><td>13,859</td><td>1.29%</td></tr>
<tr><td>23</td><td>Mississippi</td><td>13,859</td><td>1.29%</td><td>24</td><td>Wisconsin</td><td>12,991</td><td>1.21%</td></tr>
<tr><td>16</td><td>Missouri</td><td>22,003</td><td>2.05%</td><td>25</td><td>Kentucky</td><td>12,910</td><td>1.20%</td></tr>
<tr><td>44</td><td>Montana</td><td>2,293</td><td>0.21%</td><td>26</td><td>Washington</td><td>12,527</td><td>1.17%</td></tr>
<tr><td>41</td><td>Nebraska</td><td>3,287</td><td>0.31%</td><td>27</td><td>Colorado</td><td>12,438</td><td>1.16%</td></tr>
<tr><td>31</td><td>Nevada</td><td>8,439</td><td>0.79%</td><td>28</td><td>Massachusetts</td><td>11,796</td><td>1.10%</td></tr>
<tr><td>45</td><td>New Hampshire</td><td>2,062</td><td>0.19%</td><td>29</td><td>Arkansas</td><td>9,407</td><td>0.88%</td></tr>
<tr><td>12</td><td>New Jersey</td><td>27,490</td><td>2.56%</td><td>30</td><td>Oregon</td><td>8,661</td><td>0.81%</td></tr>
<tr><td>36</td><td>New Mexico</td><td>4,724</td><td>0.44%</td><td>31</td><td>Nevada</td><td>8,439</td><td>0.79%</td></tr>
<tr><td>3</td><td>New York</td><td>69,709</td><td>6.48%</td><td>32</td><td>Kansas</td><td>7,756</td><td>0.72%</td></tr>
<tr><td>10</td><td>North Carolina</td><td>30,647</td><td>2.85%</td><td>33</td><td>Iowa</td><td>6,342</td><td>0.59%</td></tr>
<tr><td>50</td><td>North Dakota</td><td>722</td><td>0.07%</td><td>34</td><td>Minnesota</td><td>5,158</td><td>0.48%</td></tr>
<tr><td>5</td><td>Ohio</td><td>46,174</td><td>4.30%</td><td>35</td><td>Delaware</td><td>5,110</td><td>0.48%</td></tr>
<tr><td>19</td><td>Oklahoma</td><td>19,593</td><td>1.82%</td><td>36</td><td>New Mexico</td><td>4,724</td><td>0.44%</td></tr>
<tr><td>30</td><td>Oregon</td><td>8,661</td><td>0.81%</td><td>37</td><td>Hawaii</td><td>4,011</td><td>0.37%</td></tr>
<tr><td>9</td><td>Pennsylvania</td><td>34,537</td><td>3.21%</td><td>38</td><td>Utah</td><td>3,972</td><td>0.37%</td></tr>
<tr><td>42</td><td>Rhode Island</td><td>3,271</td><td>0.30%</td><td>39</td><td>Idaho</td><td>3,832</td><td>0.36%</td></tr>
<tr><td>18</td><td>South Carolina</td><td>20,446</td><td>1.90%</td><td>40</td><td>Alaska</td><td>3,716</td><td>0.35%</td></tr>
<tr><td>46</td><td>South Dakota</td><td>2,059</td><td>0.19%</td><td>41</td><td>Nebraska</td><td>3,287</td><td>0.31%</td></tr>
<tr><td>21</td><td>Tennessee</td><td>15,626</td><td>1.45%</td><td>42</td><td>Rhode Island</td><td>3,271</td><td>0.30%</td></tr>
<tr><td>2</td><td>Texas</td><td>132,383</td><td>12.31%</td><td>43</td><td>West Virginia</td><td>2,749</td><td>0.26%</td></tr>
<tr><td>38</td><td>Utah</td><td>3,972</td><td>0.37%</td><td>44</td><td>Montana</td><td>2,293</td><td>0.21%</td></tr>
<tr><td>49</td><td>Vermont</td><td>1,119</td><td>0.10%</td><td>45</td><td>New Hampshire</td><td>2,062</td><td>0.19%</td></tr>
<tr><td>11</td><td>Virginia</td><td>27,655</td><td>2.57%</td><td>46</td><td>South Dakota</td><td>2,059</td><td>0.19%</td></tr>
<tr><td>26</td><td>Washington</td><td>12,527</td><td>1.17%</td><td>47</td><td>Wyoming</td><td>1,499</td><td>0.14%</td></tr>
<tr><td>43</td><td>West Virginia</td><td>2,749</td><td>0.26%</td><td>48</td><td>Maine</td><td>1,426</td><td>0.13%</td></tr>
<tr><td>24</td><td>Wisconsin</td><td>12,991</td><td>1.21%</td><td>49</td><td>Vermont</td><td>1,119</td><td>0.10%</td></tr>
<tr><td>47</td><td>Wyoming</td><td>1,499</td><td>0.14%</td><td>50</td><td>North Dakota</td><td>722</td><td>0.07%</td></tr>
<tr><td></td><td></td><td></td><td></td><td></td><td>District of Columbia</td><td>9,376</td><td>0.87%</td></tr>
</table>

Source: U.S. Department of Justice, Bureau of Justice Statistics
    "Prison and Jail Inmates at Midyear 1997 (January 1998, NCJ-167247)
*As of December 31, 1996. Totals reflect all prisoners, including those sentenced to a year or less and those unsentenced. National total does not include 105,544 prisoners under federal jurisdiction. State and federal prisoners combined total 1,180,520.

State Prisoners Sentenced to More than One Year in 1996

National Total = 1,049,372 State Prisoners*

ALPHA ORDER					RANK ORDER			
RANK	STATE	PRISONERS	% of USA		RANK	STATE	PRISONERS	% of USA
16	Alabama	21,108	2.01%		1	California	144,386	13.76%
42	Alaska	2,311	0.22%		2	Texas	132,383	12.62%
15	Arizona	21,603	2.06%		3	New York	69,709	6.64%
29	Arkansas	8,992	0.86%		4	Florida	63,746	6.07%
1	California	144,386	13.76%		5	Ohio	46,174	4.40%
25	Colorado	12,438	1.19%		6	Michigan	42,349	4.04%
28	Connecticut	10,301	0.98%		7	Illinois	38,852	3.70%
39	Delaware	3,119	0.30%		8	Pennsylvania	34,531	3.29%
4	Florida	63,746	6.07%		9	Georgia	34,328	3.27%
9	Georgia	34,328	3.27%		10	North Carolina	27,945	2.66%
40	Hawaii	2,954	0.28%		11	New Jersey	27,490	2.62%
37	Idaho	3,834	0.37%		12	Virginia	27,062	2.58%
7	Illinois	38,852	3.70%		13	Louisiana	26,779	2.55%
20	Indiana	16,801	1.60%		14	Missouri	21,999	2.10%
33	Iowa	6,342	0.60%		15	Arizona	21,603	2.06%
31	Kansas	7,756	0.74%		16	Alabama	21,108	2.01%
23	Kentucky	12,910	1.23%		17	Maryland	20,980	2.00%
13	Louisiana	26,779	2.55%		18	South Carolina	19,758	1.88%
48	Maine	1,401	0.13%		19	Oklahoma	19,593	1.87%
17	Maryland	20,980	2.00%		20	Indiana	16,801	1.60%
27	Massachusetts	10,903	1.04%		21	Tennessee	15,626	1.49%
6	Michigan	42,349	4.04%		22	Mississippi	13,576	1.29%
34	Minnesota	5,158	0.49%		23	Kentucky	12,910	1.23%
22	Mississippi	13,576	1.29%		24	Washington	12,518	1.19%
14	Missouri	21,999	2.10%		25	Colorado	12,438	1.19%
43	Montana	2,073	0.20%		26	Wisconsin	11,928	1.14%
38	Nebraska	3,212	0.31%		27	Massachusetts	10,903	1.04%
30	Nevada	8,215	0.78%		28	Connecticut	10,301	0.98%
44	New Hampshire	2,071	0.20%		29	Arkansas	8,992	0.86%
11	New Jersey	27,490	2.62%		30	Nevada	8,215	0.78%
35	New Mexico	4,506	0.43%		31	Kansas	7,756	0.74%
3	New York	69,709	6.64%		32	Oregon	7,316	0.70%
10	North Carolina	27,945	2.66%		33	Iowa	6,342	0.60%
50	North Dakota	650	0.06%		34	Minnesota	5,158	0.49%
5	Ohio	46,174	4.40%		35	New Mexico	4,506	0.43%
19	Oklahoma	19,593	1.87%		36	Utah	3,913	0.37%
32	Oregon	7,316	0.70%		37	Idaho	3,834	0.37%
8	Pennsylvania	34,531	3.29%		38	Nebraska	3,212	0.31%
46	Rhode Island	2,030	0.19%		39	Delaware	3,119	0.30%
18	South Carolina	19,758	1.88%		40	Hawaii	2,954	0.28%
45	South Dakota	2,064	0.20%		41	West Virginia	2,730	0.26%
21	Tennessee	15,626	1.49%		42	Alaska	2,311	0.22%
2	Texas	132,383	12.62%		43	Montana	2,073	0.20%
36	Utah	3,913	0.37%		44	New Hampshire	2,071	0.20%
49	Vermont	807	0.08%		45	South Dakota	2,064	0.20%
12	Virginia	27,062	2.58%		46	Rhode Island	2,030	0.19%
24	Washington	12,518	1.19%		47	Wyoming	1,483	0.14%
41	West Virginia	2,730	0.26%		48	Maine	1,401	0.13%
26	Wisconsin	11,928	1.14%		49	Vermont	807	0.08%
47	Wyoming	1,483	0.14%		50	North Dakota	650	0.06%
						District of Columbia	8,659	0.83%

Source: U.S. Department of Justice, Bureau of Justice Statistics
"Prisoners in 1996" (June 1997, NCJ-164619)
*Advance figures as of December 31, 1996. Does not include 88,815 prisoners under federal jurisdiction sentenced to more than one year. State and federal prisoners sentenced to more than one year total 1,138,187.

Female Prisoners in State Correctional Institutions in 1996

National Total = 67,030 State Female Prisoners*

ALPHA ORDER

RANK	STATE	PRISONERS	% of USA
16	Alabama	1,357	2.02%
38	Alaska	269	0.40%
13	Arizona	1,519	2.27%
31	Arkansas	548	0.82%
1	California	10,248	15.29%
24	Colorado	845	1.26%
19	Connecticut	1,133	1.69%
35	Delaware	379	0.57%
4	Florida	3,302	4.93%
7	Georgia	2,239	3.34%
34	Hawaii	385	0.57%
37	Idaho	273	0.41%
6	Illinois	2,249	3.36%
21	Indiana	1,008	1.50%
33	Iowa	470	0.70%
32	Kansas	476	0.71%
25	Kentucky	820	1.22%
12	Louisiana	1,562	2.33%
49	Maine	39	0.06%
20	Maryland	1,055	1.57%
26	Massachusetts	747	1.11%
9	Michigan	1,920	2.86%
39	Minnesota	234	0.35%
22	Mississippi	941	1.40%
15	Missouri	1,464	2.18%
45	Montana	117	0.17%
41	Nebraska	228	0.34%
29	Nevada	607	0.91%
47	New Hampshire	106	0.16%
17	New Jersey	1,281	1.91%
36	New Mexico	378	0.56%
3	New York	3,728	5.56%
10	North Carolina	1,870	2.79%
48	North Dakota	45	0.07%
5	Ohio	2,805	4.18%
8	Oklahoma	1,940	2.89%
30	Oregon	571	0.85%
14	Pennsylvania	1,476	2.20%
40	Rhode Island	229	0.34%
18	South Carolina	1,202	1.79%
44	South Dakota	142	0.21%
27	Tennessee	688	1.03%
2	Texas	9,933	14.82%
42	Utah	210	0.31%
50	Vermont	32	0.05%
11	Virginia	1,687	2.52%
23	Washington	920	1.37%
43	West Virginia	148	0.22%
28	Wisconsin	663	0.99%
46	Wyoming	110	0.16%

RANK ORDER

RANK	STATE	PRISONERS	% of USA
1	California	10,248	15.29%
2	Texas	9,933	14.82%
3	New York	3,728	5.56%
4	Florida	3,302	4.93%
5	Ohio	2,805	4.18%
6	Illinois	2,249	3.36%
7	Georgia	2,239	3.34%
8	Oklahoma	1,940	2.89%
9	Michigan	1,920	2.86%
10	North Carolina	1,870	2.79%
11	Virginia	1,687	2.52%
12	Louisiana	1,562	2.33%
13	Arizona	1,519	2.27%
14	Pennsylvania	1,476	2.20%
15	Missouri	1,464	2.18%
16	Alabama	1,357	2.02%
17	New Jersey	1,281	1.91%
18	South Carolina	1,202	1.79%
19	Connecticut	1,133	1.69%
20	Maryland	1,055	1.57%
21	Indiana	1,008	1.50%
22	Mississippi	941	1.40%
23	Washington	920	1.37%
24	Colorado	845	1.26%
25	Kentucky	820	1.22%
26	Massachusetts	747	1.11%
27	Tennessee	688	1.03%
28	Wisconsin	663	0.99%
29	Nevada	607	0.91%
30	Oregon	571	0.85%
31	Arkansas	548	0.82%
32	Kansas	476	0.71%
33	Iowa	470	0.70%
34	Hawaii	385	0.57%
35	Delaware	379	0.57%
36	New Mexico	378	0.56%
37	Idaho	273	0.41%
38	Alaska	269	0.40%
39	Minnesota	234	0.35%
40	Rhode Island	229	0.34%
41	Nebraska	228	0.34%
42	Utah	210	0.31%
43	West Virginia	148	0.22%
44	South Dakota	142	0.21%
45	Montana	117	0.17%
46	Wyoming	110	0.16%
47	New Hampshire	106	0.16%
48	North Dakota	45	0.07%
49	Maine	39	0.06%
50	Vermont	32	0.05%
	District of Columbia	432	0.64%

Source: U.S. Department of Justice, Bureau of Justice Statistics
        "Prisoners in 1996" (June 1997, NCJ-164619)
*As of December 31, 1996. Does not include 7,700 female prisoners under federal jurisdiction. State and federal female prisoners total 74,730.

Female State Prisoner Incarceration Rate in 1996

National Rate = 47 State Female Prisoners per 100,000 Female Population*

ALPHA ORDER

RANK	STATE	RATE
8	Alabama	58
15	Alaska	46
5	Arizona	63
21	Arkansas	41
6	California	60
20	Colorado	43
30	Connecticut	36
18	Delaware	44
18	Florida	44
10	Georgia	56
12	Hawaii	52
15	Idaho	46
28	Illinois	37
32	Indiana	33
34	Iowa	32
30	Kansas	36
21	Kentucky	41
4	Louisiana	69
50	Maine	5
28	Maryland	37
44	Massachusetts	15
24	Michigan	39
48	Minnesota	10
6	Mississippi	60
11	Missouri	53
36	Montana	26
36	Nebraska	26
3	Nevada	76
43	New Hampshire	18
35	New Jersey	31
24	New Mexico	39
23	New York	40
24	North Carolina	39
47	North Dakota	12
13	Ohio	49
1	Oklahoma	115
41	Oregon	22
39	Pennsylvania	24
46	Rhode Island	14
9	South Carolina	57
27	South Dakota	38
38	Tennessee	25
2	Texas	102
42	Utah	21
49	Vermont	7
14	Virginia	47
32	Washington	33
44	West Virginia	15
39	Wisconsin	24
15	Wyoming	46

RANK ORDER

RANK	STATE	RATE
1	Oklahoma	115
2	Texas	102
3	Nevada	76
4	Louisiana	69
5	Arizona	63
6	California	60
6	Mississippi	60
8	Alabama	58
9	South Carolina	57
10	Georgia	56
11	Missouri	53
12	Hawaii	52
13	Ohio	49
14	Virginia	47
15	Alaska	46
15	Idaho	46
15	Wyoming	46
18	Delaware	44
18	Florida	44
20	Colorado	43
21	Arkansas	41
21	Kentucky	41
23	New York	40
24	Michigan	39
24	New Mexico	39
24	North Carolina	39
27	South Dakota	38
28	Illinois	37
28	Maryland	37
30	Connecticut	36
30	Kansas	36
32	Indiana	33
32	Washington	33
34	Iowa	32
35	New Jersey	31
36	Montana	26
36	Nebraska	26
38	Tennessee	25
39	Pennsylvania	24
39	Wisconsin	24
41	Oregon	22
42	Utah	21
43	New Hampshire	18
44	Massachusetts	15
44	West Virginia	15
46	Rhode Island	14
47	North Dakota	12
48	Minnesota	10
49	Vermont	7
50	Maine	5

District of Columbia   119

Source: U.S. Department of Justice, Bureau of Justice Statistics
       "Prisoners in 1996" (June 1997, NCJ-164619)
*As of December 31, 1996. Rate is for female prisoners sentenced to more than one year. National rate does not include federal female inmates. Federal female incarceration rate is four federal female prisoners per 100,000 female population. The combined federal/state female incarceration rate is 51 female prisoners per 100,000 female population.

Female Prisoners in State Correctional Institutions
As a Percent of All State Prisoners in 1996
National Percent = 6.2% of State Prisoners are Female*

ALPHA ORDER   RANK ORDER

RANK	STATE	PERCENT		RANK	STATE	PERCENT
25	Alabama	6.2		1	Oklahoma	9.9
10	Alaska	7.3		2	Hawaii	9.6
18	Arizona	6.7		3	New Mexico	8.0
33	Arkansas	5.8		4	Connecticut	7.5
15	California	6.9		4	Texas	7.5
17	Colorado	6.8		6	Delaware	7.4
4	Connecticut	7.5		6	Iowa	7.4
6	Delaware	7.4		6	Nevada	7.4
40	Florida	5.2		6	Wyoming	7.4
22	Georgia	6.4		10	Alaska	7.3
2	Hawaii	9.6		10	Washington	7.3
12	Idaho	7.1		12	Idaho	7.1
33	Illinois	5.8		13	Nebraska	7.0
31	Indiana	5.9		13	Rhode Island	7.0
6	Iowa	7.4		15	California	6.9
27	Kansas	6.1		15	South Dakota	6.9
22	Kentucky	6.4		17	Colorado	6.8
33	Louisiana	5.8		18	Arizona	6.7
50	Maine	2.6		18	Missouri	6.7
43	Maryland	4.8		20	Mississippi	6.6
24	Massachusetts	6.3		20	Oregon	6.6
45	Michigan	4.5		22	Georgia	6.4
45	Minnesota	4.5		22	Kentucky	6.4
20	Mississippi	6.6		24	Massachusetts	6.3
18	Missouri	6.7		25	Alabama	6.2
36	Montana	5.6		25	North Dakota	6.2
13	Nebraska	7.0		27	Kansas	6.1
6	Nevada	7.4		27	North Carolina	6.1
42	New Hampshire	5.1		27	Ohio	6.1
44	New Jersey	4.7		27	Virginia	6.1
3	New Mexico	8.0		31	Indiana	5.9
38	New York	5.3		31	South Carolina	5.9
27	North Carolina	6.1		33	Arkansas	5.8
25	North Dakota	6.2		33	Illinois	5.8
27	Ohio	6.1		33	Louisiana	5.8
1	Oklahoma	9.9		36	Montana	5.6
20	Oregon	6.6		37	West Virginia	5.4
48	Pennsylvania	4.3		38	New York	5.3
13	Rhode Island	7.0		38	Utah	5.3
31	South Carolina	5.9		40	Florida	5.2
15	South Dakota	6.9		40	Wisconsin	5.2
47	Tennessee	4.4		42	New Hampshire	5.1
4	Texas	7.5		43	Maryland	4.8
38	Utah	5.3		44	New Jersey	4.7
49	Vermont	2.8		45	Michigan	4.5
27	Virginia	6.1		45	Minnesota	4.5
10	Washington	7.3		47	Tennessee	4.4
37	West Virginia	5.4		48	Pennsylvania	4.3
40	Wisconsin	5.2		49	Vermont	2.8
6	Wyoming	7.4		50	Maine	2.6
					District of Columbia	4.6

Source: U.S. Department of Justice, Bureau of Justice Statistics
   "Prisoners in 1996" (June 1997, NCJ-164619)
*As of December 31, 1996. Rate does not include federal female inmates. Federal female inmates constitute 7.3% of federal inmates. The federal/state combined rate is 6.3%.

Percent Change in Female State Prisoner Population: 1995 to 1996

National Percent Change = 9.7% Increase*

ALPHA ORDER			RANK ORDER		
RANK	STATE	PERCENT CHANGE	RANK	STATE	PERCENT CHANGE
36	Alabama	4.8	1	North Dakota	55.2
22	Alaska	10.7	2	Rhode Island	45.9
33	Arizona	6.1	3	New Mexico	36.0
45	Arkansas	(1.1)	4	Wisconsin	32.1
20	California	12.8	5	Utah	30.4
12	Colorado	18.5	6	Idaho	28.8
13	Connecticut	16.2	7	Texas	25.2
32	Delaware	6.2	8	Missouri	24.7
49	Florida	(9.8)	9	Hawaii	23.4
24	Georgia	10.0	10	Oregon	22.8
9	Hawaii	23.4	11	Mississippi	19.0
6	Idaho	28.8	12	Colorado	18.5
41	Illinois	2.4	13	Connecticut	16.2
19	Indiana	13.0	14	Washington	16.0
23	Iowa	10.6	15	South Carolina	15.0
34	Kansas	6.0	16	West Virginia	14.7
21	Kentucky	11.7	17	Nevada	14.5
25	Louisiana	9.7	18	Massachusetts	13.9
26	Maine	8.3	19	Indiana	13.0
48	Maryland	(2.2)	20	California	12.8
18	Massachusetts	13.9	21	Kentucky	11.7
38	Michigan	4.2	22	Alaska	10.7
28	Minnesota	7.8	23	Iowa	10.6
11	Mississippi	19.0	24	Georgia	10.0
8	Missouri	24.7	25	Louisiana	9.7
37	Montana	4.5	26	Maine	8.3
27	Nebraska	8.1	27	Nebraska	8.1
17	Nevada	14.5	28	Minnesota	7.8
44	New Hampshire	(0.9)	29	South Dakota	7.6
47	New Jersey	(2.0)	30	Oklahoma	6.9
3	New Mexico	36.0	31	North Carolina	6.7
40	New York	3.1	32	Delaware	6.2
31	North Carolina	6.7	33	Arizona	6.1
1	North Dakota	55.2	34	Kansas	6.0
43	Ohio	0.4	35	Tennessee	5.2
30	Oklahoma	6.9	36	Alabama	4.8
10	Oregon	22.8	37	Montana	4.5
46	Pennsylvania	(1.7)	38	Michigan	4.2
2	Rhode Island	45.9	39	Wyoming	3.8
15	South Carolina	15.0	40	New York	3.1
29	South Dakota	7.6	41	Illinois	2.4
35	Tennessee	5.2	42	Virginia	1.7
7	Texas	25.2	43	Ohio	0.4
5	Utah	30.4	44	New Hampshire	(0.9)
50	Vermont	(27.3)	45	Arkansas	(1.1)
42	Virginia	1.7	46	Pennsylvania	(1.7)
14	Washington	16.0	47	New Jersey	(2.0)
16	West Virginia	14.7	48	Maryland	(2.2)
4	Wisconsin	32.1	49	Florida	(9.8)
39	Wyoming	3.8	50	Vermont	(27.3)
				District of Columbia	(12.6)

Source: U.S. Department of Justice, Bureau of Justice Statistics
"Prisoners in 1996" (June 1997, NCJ-164619)

As of December 31, 1996. Rate does not include federal female inmates. Federal female inmates increased by 4.1%. The combined federal/state female prison population grew by 9.1%.

White Prisoners in State Correctional Institutions in 1995

National Total = 394,760 White State Prisoners*

ALPHA ORDER

RANK	STATE	PRISONERS	% of USA
21	Alabama	7,131	1.81%
42	Alaska	1,749	0.44%
6	Arizona	16,891	4.28%
29	Arkansas	4,290	1.09%
1	California	40,203	10.18%
17	Colorado	7,899	2.00%
32	Connecticut	3,845	0.97%
44	Delaware	1,555	0.39%
4	Florida	26,217	6.64%
8	Georgia	11,011	2.79%
49	Hawaii	689	0.17%
36	Idaho	2,695	0.68%
14	Illinois	9,196	2.33%
12	Indiana	9,215	2.33%
30	Iowa	4,113	1.04%
31	Kansas	4,111	1.04%
19	Kentucky	7,617	1.93%
24	Louisiana	5,694	1.44%
46	Maine	1,334	0.34%
26	Maryland	4,776	1.21%
27	Massachusetts	4,600	1.17%
7	Michigan	16,875	4.27%
37	Minnesota	2,471	0.63%
34	Mississippi	3,206	0.81%
10	Missouri	9,856	2.50%
43	Montana	1,610	0.41%
39	Nebraska	1,973	0.50%
28	Nevada	4,364	1.11%
40	New Hampshire	1,872	0.47%
18	New Jersey	7,648	1.94%
33	New Mexico	3,259	0.83%
3	New York	29,498	7.47%
13	North Carolina	9,197	2.33%
50	North Dakota	473	0.12%
5	Ohio	19,756	5.00%
11	Oklahoma	9,769	2.47%
22	Oregon	5,974	1.51%
9	Pennsylvania	10,820	2.74%
41	Rhode Island	1,849	0.47%
23	South Carolina	5,865	1.49%
45	South Dakota	1,355	0.34%
20	Tennessee	7,342	1.86%
2	Texas	34,990	8.86%
35	Utah	2,958	0.75%
47	Vermont	1,264	0.32%
15	Virginia	8,705	2.21%
16	Washington	8,202	2.08%
38	West Virginia	2,082	0.53%
25	Wisconsin	5,498	1.39%
48	Wyoming	1,071	0.27%

RANK ORDER

RANK	STATE	PRISONERS	% of USA
1	California	40,203	10.18%
2	Texas	34,990	8.86%
3	New York	29,498	7.47%
4	Florida	26,217	6.64%
5	Ohio	19,756	5.00%
6	Arizona	16,891	4.28%
7	Michigan	16,875	4.27%
8	Georgia	11,011	2.79%
9	Pennsylvania	10,820	2.74%
10	Missouri	9,856	2.50%
11	Oklahoma	9,769	2.47%
12	Indiana	9,215	2.33%
13	North Carolina	9,197	2.33%
14	Illinois	9,196	2.33%
15	Virginia	8,705	2.21%
16	Washington	8,202	2.08%
17	Colorado	7,899	2.00%
18	New Jersey	7,648	1.94%
19	Kentucky	7,617	1.93%
20	Tennessee	7,342	1.86%
21	Alabama	7,131	1.81%
22	Oregon	5,974	1.51%
23	South Carolina	5,865	1.49%
24	Louisiana	5,694	1.44%
25	Wisconsin	5,498	1.39%
26	Maryland	4,776	1.21%
27	Massachusetts	4,600	1.17%
28	Nevada	4,364	1.11%
29	Arkansas	4,290	1.09%
30	Iowa	4,113	1.04%
31	Kansas	4,111	1.04%
32	Connecticut	3,845	0.97%
33	New Mexico	3,259	0.83%
34	Mississippi	3,206	0.81%
35	Utah	2,958	0.75%
36	Idaho	2,695	0.68%
37	Minnesota	2,471	0.63%
38	West Virginia	2,082	0.53%
39	Nebraska	1,973	0.50%
40	New Hampshire	1,872	0.47%
41	Rhode Island	1,849	0.47%
42	Alaska	1,749	0.44%
43	Montana	1,610	0.41%
44	Delaware	1,555	0.39%
45	South Dakota	1,355	0.34%
46	Maine	1,334	0.34%
47	Vermont	1,264	0.32%
48	Wyoming	1,071	0.27%
49	Hawaii	689	0.17%
50	North Dakota	473	0.12%
	District of Columbia	127	0.03%

Source: U.S. Department of Justice, Bureau of Justice Statistics
    "Correctional Populations in the United States, 1995" (May 1997, NCJ-163916)
*As of December 31, 1995. National total does not include 60,261 white federal prisoners.

White State Prisoner Incarceration Rate in 1995

National Rate = 181 White State Prisoners per 100,000 White Population*

ALPHA ORDER

RANK	STATE	RATE
9	Alabama	229
2	Alaska	381
1	Arizona	441
20	Arkansas	208
36	California	159
10	Colorado	228
40	Connecticut	133
5	Delaware	273
11	Florida	222
15	Georgia	218
30	Hawaii	174
6	Idaho	238
47	Illinois	96
28	Indiana	175
38	Iowa	150
28	Kansas	175
16	Kentucky	215
26	Louisiana	197
45	Maine	109
39	Maryland	137
48	Massachusetts	84
18	Michigan	211
50	Minnesota	57
27	Mississippi	189
17	Missouri	212
25	Montana	199
41	Nebraska	128
4	Nevada	328
35	New Hampshire	166
42	New Jersey	119
12	New Mexico	221
19	New York	210
33	North Carolina	169
49	North Dakota	78
21	Ohio	203
3	Oklahoma	359
23	Oregon	202
46	Pennsylvania	101
24	Rhode Island	201
7	South Carolina	233
21	South Dakota	203
32	Tennessee	170
14	Texas	219
37	Utah	158
13	Vermont	220
31	Virginia	171
34	Washington	168
42	West Virginia	119
44	Wisconsin	116
8	Wyoming	232

RANK ORDER

RANK	STATE	RATE
1	Arizona	441
2	Alaska	381
3	Oklahoma	359
4	Nevada	328
5	Delaware	273
6	Idaho	238
7	South Carolina	233
8	Wyoming	232
9	Alabama	229
10	Colorado	228
11	Florida	222
12	New Mexico	221
13	Vermont	220
14	Texas	219
15	Georgia	218
16	Kentucky	215
17	Missouri	212
18	Michigan	211
19	New York	210
20	Arkansas	208
21	Ohio	203
21	South Dakota	203
23	Oregon	202
24	Rhode Island	201
25	Montana	199
26	Louisiana	197
27	Mississippi	189
28	Indiana	175
28	Kansas	175
30	Hawaii	174
31	Virginia	171
32	Tennessee	170
33	North Carolina	169
34	Washington	168
35	New Hampshire	166
36	California	159
37	Utah	158
38	Iowa	150
39	Maryland	137
40	Connecticut	133
41	Nebraska	128
42	New Jersey	119
42	West Virginia	119
44	Wisconsin	116
45	Maine	109
46	Pennsylvania	101
47	Illinois	96
48	Massachusetts	84
49	North Dakota	78
50	Minnesota	57

District of Columbia 69

Source: Morgan Quitno Press using data from U.S. Department of Justice, Bureau of Justice Statistics
    "Correctional Populations in the United States, 1995" (May 1997, NCJ-163916)
*As of December 31, 1995. National rate does not include 60,261 white federal prisoners. Federal rate is 28 white
prisoners per 100,000 white population. The combined federal/state rate is 209 white prisoners per 100,000 white
population.

White Prisoners in State Correctional Institutions
As a Percent of All Prisoners in 1995
National Percent = 38.5% White*

ALPHA ORDER

RANK	STATE	PERCENT
35	Alabama	34.4
26	Alaska	49.7
9	Arizona	79.1
29	Arkansas	45.6
42	California	29.6
14	Colorado	71.4
45	Connecticut	26.0
37	Delaware	32.4
32	Florida	41.0
38	Georgia	32.1
50	Hawaii	19.4
6	Idaho	81.0
47	Illinois	24.4
21	Indiana	57.1
16	Iowa	69.6
20	Kansas	58.3
19	Kentucky	63.2
48	Louisiana	22.6
2	Maine	95.6
49	Maryland	22.3
34	Massachusetts	39.4
32	Michigan	41.0
25	Minnesota	51.0
46	Mississippi	25.3
24	Missouri	51.5
7	Montana	80.5
17	Nebraska	64.2
22	Nevada	56.6
3	New Hampshire	92.9
43	New Jersey	28.3
8	New Mexico	79.9
31	New York	43.1
40	North Carolina	31.4
10	North Dakota	77.8
30	Ohio	44.2
23	Oklahoma	53.8
12	Oregon	75.8
36	Pennsylvania	33.4
18	Rhode Island	63.7
41	South Carolina	29.9
13	South Dakota	73.6
28	Tennessee	48.3
44	Texas	27.4
4	Utah	85.7
1	Vermont	98.8
39	Virginia	31.8
15	Washington	70.7
5	West Virginia	82.9
27	Wisconsin	49.1
11	Wyoming	76.8

RANK ORDER

RANK	STATE	PERCENT
1	Vermont	98.8
2	Maine	95.6
3	New Hampshire	92.9
4	Utah	85.7
5	West Virginia	82.9
6	Idaho	81.0
7	Montana	80.5
8	New Mexico	79.9
9	Arizona	79.1
10	North Dakota	77.8
11	Wyoming	76.8
12	Oregon	75.8
13	South Dakota	73.6
14	Colorado	71.4
15	Washington	70.7
16	Iowa	69.6
17	Nebraska	64.2
18	Rhode Island	63.7
19	Kentucky	63.2
20	Kansas	58.3
21	Indiana	57.1
22	Nevada	56.6
23	Oklahoma	53.8
24	Missouri	51.5
25	Minnesota	51.0
26	Alaska	49.7
27	Wisconsin	49.1
28	Tennessee	48.3
29	Arkansas	45.6
30	Ohio	44.2
31	New York	43.1
32	Florida	41.0
32	Michigan	41.0
34	Massachusetts	39.4
35	Alabama	34.4
36	Pennsylvania	33.4
37	Delaware	32.4
38	Georgia	32.1
39	Virginia	31.8
40	North Carolina	31.4
41	South Carolina	29.9
42	California	29.6
43	New Jersey	28.3
44	Texas	27.4
45	Connecticut	26.0
46	Mississippi	25.3
47	Illinois	24.4
48	Louisiana	22.6
49	Maryland	22.3
50	Hawaii	19.4
	District of Columbia	1.3

Source: Morgan Quitno Press using data from U.S. Department of Justice, Bureau of Justice Statistics
    "Correctional Populations in the United States, 1995" (May 1997, NCJ-163916)
*As of December 31, 1995. National percent does not include white federal prisoners. Federal prison population
is 60.1% white. Combined state and federal percentage is 40.4% white.

Black Prisoners in State Correctional Institutions in 1995

National Total = 506,950 Black State Prisoners*

ALPHA ORDER						RANK ORDER			

RANK	STATE	PRISONERS	% of USA		RANK	STATE	PRISONERS	% of USA
16	Alabama	13,531	2.67%		1	Texas	60,006	11.84%
39	Alaska	481	0.09%		2	California	42,461	8.38%
26	Arizona	3,388	0.67%		3	New York	36,911	7.28%
24	Arkansas	5,096	1.01%		4	Florida	36,407	7.18%
2	California	42,461	8.38%		5	Illinois	24,636	4.86%
30	Colorado	2,744	0.54%		6	Ohio	24,356	4.80%
20	Connecticut	6,857	1.35%		7	Georgia	23,151	4.57%
27	Delaware	3,157	0.62%		8	Michigan	22,940	4.53%
4	Florida	36,407	7.18%		9	Louisiana	19,448	3.84%
7	Georgia	23,151	4.57%		10	North Carolina	19,166	3.78%
42	Hawaii	164	0.03%		11	Virginia	18,516	3.65%
46	Idaho	55	0.01%		12	Pennsylvania	18,359	3.62%
5	Illinois	24,636	4.86%		13	New Jersey	17,545	3.46%
21	Indiana	6,846	1.35%		14	Maryland	16,637	3.28%
34	Iowa	1,481	0.29%		15	South Carolina	13,641	2.69%
29	Kansas	2,779	0.55%		16	Alabama	13,531	2.67%
25	Kentucky	4,416	0.87%		17	Mississippi	9,388	1.85%
9	Louisiana	19,448	3.84%		18	Missouri	9,197	1.81%
48	Maine	30	0.01%		19	Tennessee	7,798	1.54%
14	Maryland	16,637	3.28%		20	Connecticut	6,857	1.35%
28	Massachusetts	2,835	0.56%		21	Indiana	6,846	1.35%
8	Michigan	22,940	4.53%		22	Oklahoma	6,546	1.29%
33	Minnesota	1,705	0.34%		23	Wisconsin	5,371	1.06%
17	Mississippi	9,388	1.85%		24	Arkansas	5,096	1.01%
18	Missouri	9,197	1.81%		25	Kentucky	4,416	0.87%
47	Montana	37	0.01%		26	Arizona	3,388	0.67%
37	Nebraska	979	0.19%		27	Delaware	3,157	0.62%
32	Nevada	2,117	0.42%		28	Massachusetts	2,835	0.56%
43	New Hampshire	129	0.03%		29	Kansas	2,779	0.55%
13	New Jersey	17,545	3.46%		30	Colorado	2,744	0.54%
38	New Mexico	490	0.10%		31	Washington	2,703	0.53%
3	New York	36,911	7.28%		32	Nevada	2,117	0.42%
10	North Carolina	19,166	3.78%		33	Minnesota	1,705	0.34%
49	North Dakota	18	0.00%		34	Iowa	1,481	0.29%
6	Ohio	24,356	4.80%		35	Rhode Island	1,009	0.20%
22	Oklahoma	6,546	1.29%		36	Oregon	999	0.20%
36	Oregon	999	0.20%		37	Nebraska	979	0.19%
12	Pennsylvania	18,359	3.62%		38	New Mexico	490	0.10%
35	Rhode Island	1,009	0.20%		39	Alaska	481	0.09%
15	South Carolina	13,641	2.69%		40	West Virginia	427	0.08%
45	South Dakota	69	0.01%		41	Utah	295	0.06%
19	Tennessee	7,798	1.54%		42	Hawaii	164	0.03%
1	Texas	60,006	11.84%		43	New Hampshire	129	0.03%
41	Utah	295	0.06%		44	Wyoming	73	0.01%
50	Vermont	15	0.00%		45	South Dakota	69	0.01%
11	Virginia	18,516	3.65%		46	Idaho	55	0.01%
31	Washington	2,703	0.53%		47	Montana	37	0.01%
40	West Virginia	427	0.08%		48	Maine	30	0.01%
23	Wisconsin	5,371	1.06%		49	North Dakota	18	0.00%
44	Wyoming	73	0.01%		50	Vermont	15	0.00%
						District of Columbia	9,545	1.88%

Source: U.S. Department of Justice, Bureau of Justice Statistics
"Correctional Populations in the United States, 1995" (May 1997, NCJ-163916)
As of December 31, 1995. National total does not include 37,055 black federal prisoners.

Black State Prisoner Incarceration Rate in 1995

National Rate = 1,532 Black State Prisoners per 100,000 Black Population*

ALPHA ORDER

RANK ORDER

RANK	STATE	RATE		RANK	STATE	RATE
35	Alabama	1,236		1	Iowa	2,730
8	Alaska	2,021		2	Texas	2,613
6	Arizona	2,303		3	Oklahoma	2,608
33	Arkansas	1,281		4	Delaware	2,382
15	California	1,796		5	Connecticut	2,321
18	Colorado	1,702		6	Arizona	2,303
5	Connecticut	2,321		7	Rhode Island	2,182
4	Delaware	2,382		8	Alaska	2,021
17	Florida	1,724		9	Ohio	1,948
41	Georgia	1,145		10	Wisconsin	1,931
48	Hawaii	469		11	Nevada	1,888
44	Idaho	881		12	Utah	1,840
32	Illinois	1,371		13	Wyoming	1,827
28	Indiana	1,448		14	Kansas	1,822
1	Iowa	2,730		15	California	1,796
14	Kansas	1,822		16	Oregon	1,787
22	Kentucky	1,589		17	Florida	1,724
30	Louisiana	1,408		18	Colorado	1,702
47	Maine	554		19	South Dakota	1,690
34	Maryland	1,238		20	New Hampshire	1,688
45	Massachusetts	763		21	Michigan	1,685
21	Michigan	1,685		22	Kentucky	1,589
31	Minnesota	1,386		23	Pennsylvania	1,585
42	Mississippi	960		24	Missouri	1,558
24	Missouri	1,558		25	Nebraska	1,539
39	Montana	1,175		26	New Jersey	1,533
25	Nebraska	1,539		27	Washington	1,478
11	Nevada	1,888		28	Indiana	1,448
20	New Hampshire	1,688		29	Virginia	1,419
26	New Jersey	1,533		30	Louisiana	1,408
38	New Mexico	1,183		31	Minnesota	1,386
40	New York	1,158		32	Illinois	1,371
37	North Carolina	1,197		33	Arkansas	1,281
50	North Dakota	460		34	Maryland	1,238
9	Ohio	1,948		35	Alabama	1,236
3	Oklahoma	2,608		36	South Carolina	1,230
16	Oregon	1,787		37	North Carolina	1,197
23	Pennsylvania	1,585		38	New Mexico	1,183
7	Rhode Island	2,182		39	Montana	1,175
36	South Carolina	1,230		40	New York	1,158
19	South Dakota	1,690		41	Georgia	1,145
43	Tennessee	908		42	Mississippi	960
2	Texas	2,613		43	Tennessee	908
12	Utah	1,840		44	Idaho	881
49	Vermont	464		45	Massachusetts	763
29	Virginia	1,419		46	West Virginia	741
27	Washington	1,478		47	Maine	554
46	West Virginia	741		48	Hawaii	469
10	Wisconsin	1,931		49	Vermont	464
13	Wyoming	1,827		50	North Dakota	460
					District of Columbia	2,714

Source: Morgan Quitno Press using data from U.S. Department of Justice, Bureau of Justice Statistics
"Correctional Populations in the United States, 1995" (May 1997, NCJ-163916)
*As of December 31, 1995. National rate does not include 37,055 black federal prisoners. Federal rate is 112
black prisoners per 100,000 black population. The combined federal/state rate is 1,644 black prisoners per
100,000 black population.

Black Prisoners in State Correctional Institutions
As a Percent of All Prisoners in 1995
National Percent = 49.4% Black*

ALPHA ORDER

ALPHA ORDER

RANK ORDER

RANK	STATE	PERCENT		RANK	STATE	PERCENT
10	Alabama	65.3		1	Maryland	77.6
38	Alaska	13.7		2	Louisiana	77.2
37	Arizona	15.9		3	Mississippi	74.0
16	Arkansas	54.1		4	South Carolina	69.6
30	California	31.3		5	Georgia	67.6
33	Colorado	24.8		6	Virginia	67.5
22	Connecticut	46.3		7	Delaware	65.7
7	Delaware	65.7		8	North Carolina	65.5
12	Florida	57.0		9	Illinois	65.4
5	Georgia	67.6		10	Alabama	65.3
44	Hawaii	4.6		11	New Jersey	64.8
49	Idaho	1.7		12	Florida	57.0
9	Illinois	65.4		13	Pennsylvania	56.6
23	Indiana	42.5		14	Michigan	55.8
32	Iowa	25.1		15	Ohio	54.5
24	Kansas	39.4		16	Arkansas	54.1
25	Kentucky	36.6		17	New York	53.9
2	Louisiana	77.2		18	Tennessee	51.3
47	Maine	2.1		19	Missouri	48.1
1	Maryland	77.6		20	Wisconsin	48.0
34	Massachusetts	24.3		21	Texas	47.0
14	Michigan	55.8		22	Connecticut	46.3
27	Minnesota	35.2		23	Indiana	42.5
3	Mississippi	74.0		24	Kansas	39.4
19	Missouri	48.1		25	Kentucky	36.6
48	Montana	1.9		26	Oklahoma	36.1
29	Nebraska	31.8		27	Minnesota	35.2
31	Nevada	27.4		28	Rhode Island	34.8
42	New Hampshire	6.4		29	Nebraska	31.8
11	New Jersey	64.8		30	California	31.3
40	New Mexico	12.0		31	Nevada	27.4
17	New York	53.9		32	Iowa	25.1
8	North Carolina	65.5		33	Colorado	24.8
46	North Dakota	3.0		34	Massachusetts	24.3
15	Ohio	54.5		35	Washington	23.3
26	Oklahoma	36.1		36	West Virginia	17.0
39	Oregon	12.7		37	Arizona	15.9
13	Pennsylvania	56.6		38	Alaska	13.7
28	Rhode Island	34.8		39	Oregon	12.7
4	South Carolina	69.6		40	New Mexico	12.0
45	South Dakota	3.7		41	Utah	8.5
18	Tennessee	51.3		42	New Hampshire	6.4
21	Texas	47.0		43	Wyoming	5.2
41	Utah	8.5		44	Hawaii	4.6
50	Vermont	1.2		45	South Dakota	3.7
6	Virginia	67.5		46	North Dakota	3.0
35	Washington	23.3		47	Maine	2.1
36	West Virginia	17.0		48	Montana	1.9
20	Wisconsin	48.0		49	Idaho	1.7
43	Wyoming	5.2		50	Vermont	1.2
					District of Columbia	97.4

*Source: Morgan Quitno Press using data from U.S. Department of Justice, Bureau of Justice Statistics
"Correctional Populations in the United States, 1995" (May 1997, NCJ-163916)*
*As of December 31, 1995. National percent does not include black federal prisoners. Federal prison population
is 37.0% black. Combined state and federal percentage is 48.3% black.*

Prisoners Under Sentence of Death in 1996

National Total = 3,208 State Prisoners*

	ALPHA ORDER				RANK ORDER		
RANK	STATE	PRISONERS	% of USA	RANK	STATE	PRISONERS	% of USA
8	Alabama	151	4.71%	1	California	454	14.15%
NA	Alaska**	NA	NA	2	Texas	438	13.65%
10	Arizona	121	3.77%	3	Florida	373	11.63%
20	Arkansas	40	1.25%	4	Pennsylvania	203	6.33%
1	California	454	14.15%	5	Ohio	170	5.30%
31	Colorado	5	0.16%	6	Illinois	161	5.02%
32	Connecticut	4	0.12%	6	North Carolina	161	5.02%
25	Delaware	11	0.34%	8	Alabama	151	4.71%
3	Florida	373	11.63%	9	Oklahoma	133	4.15%
11	Georgia	96	2.99%	10	Arizona	121	3.77%
NA	Hawaii**	NA	NA	11	Georgia	96	2.99%
24	Idaho	18	0.56%	12	Missouri	93	2.90%
6	Illinois	161	5.02%	13	Tennessee	91	2.84%
19	Indiana	45	1.40%	14	Nevada	81	2.52%
NA	Iowa**	NA	NA	15	South Carolina	68	2.12%
35	Kansas	0	0.00%	16	Louisiana	63	1.96%
21	Kentucky	29	0.90%	17	Mississippi	57	1.78%
16	Louisiana	63	1.96%	18	Virginia	49	1.53%
NA	Maine**	NA	NA	19	Indiana	45	1.40%
23	Maryland	19	0.59%	20	Arkansas	40	1.25%
NA	Massachusetts**	NA	NA	21	Kentucky	29	0.90%
NA	Michigan**	NA	NA	22	Oregon	20	0.62%
NA	Minnesota**	NA	NA	23	Maryland	19	0.59%
17	Mississippi	57	1.78%	24	Idaho	18	0.56%
12	Missouri	93	2.90%	25	Delaware	11	0.34%
30	Montana	7	0.22%	25	Nebraska	11	0.34%
25	Nebraska	11	0.34%	25	New Jersey	11	0.34%
14	Nevada	81	2.52%	25	Washington	11	0.34%
35	New Hampshire	0	0.00%	29	Utah	9	0.28%
25	New Jersey	11	0.34%	30	Montana	7	0.22%
32	New Mexico	4	0.12%	31	Colorado	5	0.16%
35	New York	0	0.00%	32	Connecticut	4	0.12%
6	North Carolina	161	5.02%	32	New Mexico	4	0.12%
NA	North Dakota**	NA	NA	34	South Dakota	1	0.03%
5	Ohio	170	5.30%	35	Kansas	0	0.00%
9	Oklahoma	133	4.15%	35	New Hampshire	0	0.00%
22	Oregon	20	0.62%	35	New York	0	0.00%
4	Pennsylvania	203	6.33%	35	Wyoming	0	0.00%
NA	Rhode Island**	NA	NA	NA	Alaska**	NA	NA
15	South Carolina	68	2.12%	NA	Hawaii**	NA	NA
34	South Dakota	1	0.03%	NA	Iowa**	NA	NA
13	Tennessee	91	2.84%	NA	Maine**	NA	NA
2	Texas	438	13.65%	NA	Massachusetts**	NA	NA
29	Utah	9	0.28%	NA	Michigan**	NA	NA
NA	Vermont**	NA	NA	NA	Minnesota**	NA	NA
18	Virginia	49	1.53%	NA	North Dakota**	NA	NA
25	Washington	11	0.34%	NA	Rhode Island**	NA	NA
NA	West Virginia**	NA	NA	NA	Vermont**	NA	NA
NA	Wisconsin**	NA	NA	NA	West Virginia**	NA	NA
35	Wyoming	0	0.00%	NA	Wisconsin**	NA	NA
					District of Columbia**	NA	NA

Source: U.S. Department of Justice, Bureau of Justice Statistics
    "Capital Punishment 1996" (Bulletin, December 1997, NCJ-167031)
*As of December 31, 1996. Does not include 11 federal prisoners under sentence of death. There were 45 executions in 1996.
**No death penalty as of 12/31/96.

Male Prisoners Under Sentence of Death in 1996

National Total = 3,159 Male State Prisoners*

ALPHA ORDER

ALPHA ORDER

RANK ORDER

RANK	STATE	PRISONERS	% of USA
8	Alabama	147	4.65%
NA	Alaska**	NA	NA
10	Arizona	120	3.80%
20	Arkansas	40	1.27%
1	California	446	14.12%
31	Colorado	5	0.16%
32	Connecticut	4	0.13%
25	Delaware	11	0.35%
3	Florida	367	11.62%
11	Georgia	96	3.04%
NA	Hawaii**	NA	NA
24	Idaho	17	0.54%
7	Illinois	157	4.97%
19	Indiana	45	1.42%
NA	Iowa**	NA	NA
35	Kansas	0	0.00%
21	Kentucky	29	0.92%
16	Louisiana	63	1.99%
NA	Maine**	NA	NA
23	Maryland	19	0.60%
NA	Massachusetts**	NA	NA
NA	Michigan**	NA	NA
NA	Minnesota**	NA	NA
17	Mississippi	55	1.74%
12	Missouri	91	2.88%
30	Montana	7	0.22%
25	Nebraska	11	0.35%
14	Nevada	80	2.53%
35	New Hampshire	0	0.00%
25	New Jersey	11	0.35%
32	New Mexico	4	0.13%
35	New York	0	0.00%
6	North Carolina	158	5.00%
NA	North Dakota**	NA	NA
5	Ohio	170	5.38%
9	Oklahoma	129	4.08%
22	Oregon	20	0.63%
4	Pennsylvania	198	6.27%
NA	Rhode Island**	NA	NA
15	South Carolina	68	2.15%
34	South Dakota	1	0.03%
13	Tennessee	89	2.82%
2	Texas	432	13.68%
29	Utah	9	0.28%
NA	Vermont**	NA	NA
18	Virginia	49	1.55%
25	Washington	11	0.35%
NA	West Virginia**	NA	NA
NA	Wisconsin**	NA	NA
35	Wyoming	0	0.00%

RANK	STATE	PRISONERS	% of USA
1	California	446	14.12%
2	Texas	432	13.68%
3	Florida	367	11.62%
4	Pennsylvania	198	6.27%
5	Ohio	170	5.38%
6	North Carolina	158	5.00%
7	Illinois	157	4.97%
8	Alabama	147	4.65%
9	Oklahoma	129	4.08%
10	Arizona	120	3.80%
11	Georgia	96	3.04%
12	Missouri	91	2.88%
13	Tennessee	89	2.82%
14	Nevada	80	2.53%
15	South Carolina	68	2.15%
16	Louisiana	63	1.99%
17	Mississippi	55	1.74%
18	Virginia	49	1.55%
19	Indiana	45	1.42%
20	Arkansas	40	1.27%
21	Kentucky	29	0.92%
22	Oregon	20	0.63%
23	Maryland	19	0.60%
24	Idaho	17	0.54%
25	Delaware	11	0.35%
25	Nebraska	11	0.35%
25	New Jersey	11	0.35%
25	Washington	11	0.35%
29	Utah	9	0.28%
30	Montana	7	0.22%
31	Colorado	5	0.16%
32	Connecticut	4	0.13%
32	New Mexico	4	0.13%
34	South Dakota	1	0.03%
35	Kansas	0	0.00%
35	New Hampshire	0	0.00%
35	New York	0	0.00%
35	Wyoming	0	0.00%
NA	Alaska**	NA	NA
NA	Hawaii**	NA	NA
NA	Iowa**	NA	NA
NA	Maine**	NA	NA
NA	Massachusetts**	NA	NA
NA	Michigan**	NA	NA
NA	Minnesota**	NA	NA
NA	North Dakota**	NA	NA
NA	Rhode Island**	NA	NA
NA	Vermont**	NA	NA
NA	West Virginia**	NA	NA
NA	Wisconsin**	NA	NA
	District of Columbia**	NA	NA

Source: Morgan Quitno Press using data from U.S. Department of Justice, Bureau of Justice Statistics
   "Capital Punishment 1996" (Bulletin, December 1997, NCJ-167031)
*As of December 31, 1996. Does not include 11 male federal prisoners under sentence of death. There were 45 executions in 1996. All were male.
**No death penalty as of 12/31/96.

Female Prisoners Under Sentence of Death in 1996

National Total = 49 Female State Prisoners*

<table>
<tr><td colspan="4">ALPHA ORDER</td><td colspan="4">RANK ORDER</td></tr>
<tr><td>RANK</td><td>STATE</td><td>PRISONERS</td><td>% of USA</td><td>RANK</td><td>STATE</td><td>PRISONERS</td><td>% of USA</td></tr>
<tr><td>5</td><td>Alabama</td><td>4</td><td>8.16%</td><td>1</td><td>California</td><td>8</td><td>16.33%</td></tr>
<tr><td>NA</td><td>Alaska**</td><td>NA</td><td>NA</td><td>2</td><td>Florida</td><td>6</td><td>12.24%</td></tr>
<tr><td>12</td><td>Arizona</td><td>1</td><td>2.04%</td><td>2</td><td>Texas</td><td>6</td><td>12.24%</td></tr>
<tr><td>15</td><td>Arkansas</td><td>0</td><td>0.00%</td><td>4</td><td>Pennsylvania</td><td>5</td><td>10.20%</td></tr>
<tr><td>1</td><td>California</td><td>8</td><td>16.33%</td><td>5</td><td>Alabama</td><td>4</td><td>8.16%</td></tr>
<tr><td>15</td><td>Colorado</td><td>0</td><td>0.00%</td><td>5</td><td>Illinois</td><td>4</td><td>8.16%</td></tr>
<tr><td>15</td><td>Connecticut</td><td>0</td><td>0.00%</td><td>5</td><td>Oklahoma</td><td>4</td><td>8.16%</td></tr>
<tr><td>15</td><td>Delaware</td><td>0</td><td>0.00%</td><td>8</td><td>North Carolina</td><td>3</td><td>6.12%</td></tr>
<tr><td>2</td><td>Florida</td><td>6</td><td>12.24%</td><td>9</td><td>Mississippi</td><td>2</td><td>4.08%</td></tr>
<tr><td>15</td><td>Georgia</td><td>0</td><td>0.00%</td><td>9</td><td>Missouri</td><td>2</td><td>4.08%</td></tr>
<tr><td>NA</td><td>Hawaii**</td><td>NA</td><td>NA</td><td>9</td><td>Tennessee</td><td>2</td><td>4.08%</td></tr>
<tr><td>12</td><td>Idaho</td><td>1</td><td>2.04%</td><td>12</td><td>Arizona</td><td>1</td><td>2.04%</td></tr>
<tr><td>5</td><td>Illinois</td><td>4</td><td>8.16%</td><td>12</td><td>Idaho</td><td>1</td><td>2.04%</td></tr>
<tr><td>15</td><td>Indiana</td><td>0</td><td>0.00%</td><td>12</td><td>Nevada</td><td>1</td><td>2.04%</td></tr>
<tr><td>NA</td><td>Iowa**</td><td>NA</td><td>NA</td><td>15</td><td>Arkansas</td><td>0</td><td>0.00%</td></tr>
<tr><td>15</td><td>Kansas</td><td>0</td><td>0.00%</td><td>15</td><td>Colorado</td><td>0</td><td>0.00%</td></tr>
<tr><td>15</td><td>Kentucky</td><td>0</td><td>0.00%</td><td>15</td><td>Connecticut</td><td>0</td><td>0.00%</td></tr>
<tr><td>15</td><td>Louisiana</td><td>0</td><td>0.00%</td><td>15</td><td>Delaware</td><td>0</td><td>0.00%</td></tr>
<tr><td>NA</td><td>Maine**</td><td>NA</td><td>NA</td><td>15</td><td>Georgia</td><td>0</td><td>0.00%</td></tr>
<tr><td>15</td><td>Maryland</td><td>0</td><td>0.00%</td><td>15</td><td>Indiana</td><td>0</td><td>0.00%</td></tr>
<tr><td>NA</td><td>Massachusetts**</td><td>NA</td><td>NA</td><td>15</td><td>Kansas</td><td>0</td><td>0.00%</td></tr>
<tr><td>NA</td><td>Michigan**</td><td>NA</td><td>NA</td><td>15</td><td>Kentucky</td><td>0</td><td>0.00%</td></tr>
<tr><td>NA</td><td>Minnesota**</td><td>NA</td><td>NA</td><td>15</td><td>Louisiana</td><td>0</td><td>0.00%</td></tr>
<tr><td>9</td><td>Mississippi</td><td>2</td><td>4.08%</td><td>15</td><td>Maryland</td><td>0</td><td>0.00%</td></tr>
<tr><td>9</td><td>Missouri</td><td>2</td><td>4.08%</td><td>15</td><td>Montana</td><td>0</td><td>0.00%</td></tr>
<tr><td>15</td><td>Montana</td><td>0</td><td>0.00%</td><td>15</td><td>Nebraska</td><td>0</td><td>0.00%</td></tr>
<tr><td>15</td><td>Nebraska</td><td>0</td><td>0.00%</td><td>15</td><td>New Hampshire</td><td>0</td><td>0.00%</td></tr>
<tr><td>12</td><td>Nevada</td><td>1</td><td>2.04%</td><td>15</td><td>New Jersey</td><td>0</td><td>0.00%</td></tr>
<tr><td>15</td><td>New Hampshire</td><td>0</td><td>0.00%</td><td>15</td><td>New Mexico</td><td>0</td><td>0.00%</td></tr>
<tr><td>15</td><td>New Jersey</td><td>0</td><td>0.00%</td><td>15</td><td>New York</td><td>0</td><td>0.00%</td></tr>
<tr><td>15</td><td>New Mexico</td><td>0</td><td>0.00%</td><td>15</td><td>Ohio</td><td>0</td><td>0.00%</td></tr>
<tr><td>15</td><td>New York</td><td>0</td><td>0.00%</td><td>15</td><td>Oregon</td><td>0</td><td>0.00%</td></tr>
<tr><td>8</td><td>North Carolina</td><td>3</td><td>6.12%</td><td>15</td><td>South Carolina</td><td>0</td><td>0.00%</td></tr>
<tr><td>NA</td><td>North Dakota**</td><td>NA</td><td>NA</td><td>15</td><td>South Dakota</td><td>0</td><td>0.00%</td></tr>
<tr><td>15</td><td>Ohio</td><td>0</td><td>0.00%</td><td>15</td><td>Utah</td><td>0</td><td>0.00%</td></tr>
<tr><td>5</td><td>Oklahoma</td><td>4</td><td>8.16%</td><td>15</td><td>Virginia</td><td>0</td><td>0.00%</td></tr>
<tr><td>15</td><td>Oregon</td><td>0</td><td>0.00%</td><td>15</td><td>Washington</td><td>0</td><td>0.00%</td></tr>
<tr><td>4</td><td>Pennsylvania</td><td>5</td><td>10.20%</td><td>15</td><td>Wyoming</td><td>0</td><td>0.00%</td></tr>
<tr><td>NA</td><td>Rhode Island**</td><td>NA</td><td>NA</td><td>NA</td><td>Alaska**</td><td>NA</td><td>NA</td></tr>
<tr><td>15</td><td>South Carolina</td><td>0</td><td>0.00%</td><td>NA</td><td>Hawaii**</td><td>NA</td><td>NA</td></tr>
<tr><td>15</td><td>South Dakota</td><td>0</td><td>0.00%</td><td>NA</td><td>Iowa**</td><td>NA</td><td>NA</td></tr>
<tr><td>9</td><td>Tennessee</td><td>2</td><td>4.08%</td><td>NA</td><td>Maine**</td><td>NA</td><td>NA</td></tr>
<tr><td>2</td><td>Texas</td><td>6</td><td>12.24%</td><td>NA</td><td>Massachusetts**</td><td>NA</td><td>NA</td></tr>
<tr><td>15</td><td>Utah</td><td>0</td><td>0.00%</td><td>NA</td><td>Michigan**</td><td>NA</td><td>NA</td></tr>
<tr><td>NA</td><td>Vermont**</td><td>NA</td><td>NA</td><td>NA</td><td>Minnesota**</td><td>NA</td><td>NA</td></tr>
<tr><td>15</td><td>Virginia</td><td>0</td><td>0.00%</td><td>NA</td><td>North Dakota**</td><td>NA</td><td>NA</td></tr>
<tr><td>15</td><td>Washington</td><td>0</td><td>0.00%</td><td>NA</td><td>Rhode Island**</td><td>NA</td><td>NA</td></tr>
<tr><td>NA</td><td>West Virginia**</td><td>NA</td><td>NA</td><td>NA</td><td>Vermont**</td><td>NA</td><td>NA</td></tr>
<tr><td>NA</td><td>Wisconsin**</td><td>NA</td><td>NA</td><td>NA</td><td>West Virginia**</td><td>NA</td><td>NA</td></tr>
<tr><td>15</td><td>Wyoming</td><td>0</td><td>0.00%</td><td>NA</td><td>Wisconsin**</td><td>NA</td><td>NA</td></tr>
<tr><td></td><td></td><td></td><td></td><td></td><td>District of Columbia**</td><td>NA</td><td>NA</td></tr>
</table>

Source: U.S. Department of Justice, Bureau of Justice Statistics
  "Capital Punishment 1996" (Bulletin, December 1997, NCJ-167031)
*As of December 31, 1996. There were no federal female prisoners under sentence of death. There were 45 executions in 1996, none of whom was female.
**No death penalty as of 12/31/96.

Percent of Prisoners Under Sentence of Death Who Are Female: 1996

National Percent = 1.5% of State Death Sentence Prisoners*

ALPHA ORDER

RANK ORDER

RANK	STATE	PERCENT		RANK	STATE	PERCENT
4	Alabama	2.6		1	Idaho	5.6
NA	Alaska**	NA		2	Mississippi	3.5
14	Arizona	0.8		3	Oklahoma	3.0
15	Arkansas	0.0		4	Alabama	2.6
10	California	1.8		5	Illinois	2.5
15	Colorado	0.0		5	Pennsylvania	2.5
15	Connecticut	0.0		7	Missouri	2.2
15	Delaware	0.0		7	Tennessee	2.2
11	Florida	1.6		9	North Carolina	1.9
15	Georgia	0.0		10	California	1.8
NA	Hawaii**	NA		11	Florida	1.6
1	Idaho	5.6		12	Texas	1.4
5	Illinois	2.5		13	Nevada	1.2
15	Indiana	0.0		14	Arizona	0.8
NA	Iowa**	NA		15	Arkansas	0.0
15	Kansas	0.0		15	Colorado	0.0
15	Kentucky	0.0		15	Connecticut	0.0
15	Louisiana	0.0		15	Delaware	0.0
NA	Maine**	NA		15	Georgia	0.0
15	Maryland	0.0		15	Indiana	0.0
NA	Massachusetts**	NA		15	Kansas	0.0
NA	Michigan**	NA		15	Kentucky	0.0
NA	Minnesota**	NA		15	Louisiana	0.0
2	Mississippi	3.5		15	Maryland	0.0
7	Missouri	2.2		15	Montana	0.0
15	Montana	0.0		15	Nebraska	0.0
15	Nebraska	0.0		15	New Hampshire	0.0
13	Nevada	1.2		15	New Jersey	0.0
15	New Hampshire	0.0		15	New Mexico	0.0
15	New Jersey	0.0		15	New York	0.0
15	New Mexico	0.0		15	Ohio	0.0
15	New York	0.0		15	Oregon	0.0
9	North Carolina	1.9		15	South Carolina	0.0
NA	North Dakota**	NA		15	South Dakota	0.0
15	Ohio	0.0		15	Utah	0.0
3	Oklahoma	3.0		15	Virginia	0.0
15	Oregon	0.0		15	Washington	0.0
5	Pennsylvania	2.5		15	Wyoming	0.0
NA	Rhode Island**	NA		NA	Alaska**	NA
15	South Carolina	0.0		NA	Hawaii**	NA
15	South Dakota	0.0		NA	Iowa**	NA
7	Tennessee	2.2		NA	Maine**	NA
12	Texas	1.4		NA	Massachusetts**	NA
15	Utah	0.0		NA	Michigan**	NA
NA	Vermont**	NA		NA	Minnesota**	NA
15	Virginia	0.0		NA	North Dakota**	NA
15	Washington	0.0		NA	Rhode Island**	NA
NA	West Virginia**	NA		NA	Vermont**	NA
NA	Wisconsin**	NA		NA	West Virginia**	NA
15	Wyoming	0.0		NA	Wisconsin**	NA
					District of Columbia**	NA

Source: Morgan Quitno Press using data from U.S. Department of Justice, Bureau of Justice Statistics
    "Capital Punishment 1996" (Bulletin, December 1997, NCJ-167031)
*As of December 31, 1996. There were no federal female prisoners under sentence of death. There were 45 executions in 1996, none of whom was female.
**No death penalty as of 12/31/96.

White Prisoners Under Sentence of Death in 1996

National Total = 1,817 White State Prisoners*

ALPHA ORDER				RANK ORDER			
RANK	STATE	PRISONERS	% of USA	RANK	STATE	PRISONERS	% of USA
5	Alabama	89	4.90%	1	California	272	14.97%
NA	Alaska**	NA	NA	2	Texas	263	14.47%
4	Arizona	101	5.56%	3	Florida	235	12.93%
19	Arkansas	22	1.21%	4	Arizona	101	5.56%
1	California	272	14.97%	5	Alabama	89	4.90%
32	Colorado	3	0.17%	6	Ohio	85	4.68%
33	Connecticut	1	0.06%	7	Oklahoma	80	4.40%
28	Delaware	5	0.28%	8	North Carolina	77	4.24%
3	Florida	235	12.93%	9	Pennsylvania	71	3.91%
12	Georgia	55	3.03%	10	Tennessee	63	3.47%
NA	Hawaii**	NA	NA	11	Illinois	61	3.36%
23	Idaho	18	0.99%	12	Georgia	55	3.03%
11	Illinois	61	3.36%	13	Missouri	50	2.75%
15	Indiana	30	1.65%	14	Nevada	48	2.64%
NA	Iowa**	NA	NA	15	Indiana	30	1.65%
35	Kansas	0	0.00%	15	South Carolina	30	1.65%
19	Kentucky	22	1.21%	17	Mississippi	26	1.43%
19	Louisiana	22	1.21%	18	Virginia	24	1.32%
NA	Maine**	NA	NA	19	Arkansas	22	1.21%
30	Maryland	4	0.22%	19	Kentucky	22	1.21%
NA	Massachusetts**	NA	NA	19	Louisiana	22	1.21%
NA	Michigan**	NA	NA	22	Oregon	19	1.05%
NA	Minnesota**	NA	NA	23	Idaho	18	0.99%
17	Mississippi	26	1.43%	24	Washington	10	0.55%
13	Missouri	50	2.75%	25	Nebraska	8	0.44%
27	Montana	6	0.33%	26	Utah	7	0.39%
25	Nebraska	8	0.44%	27	Montana	6	0.33%
14	Nevada	48	2.64%	28	Delaware	5	0.28%
35	New Hampshire	0	0.00%	28	New Jersey	5	0.28%
28	New Jersey	5	0.28%	30	Maryland	4	0.22%
30	New Mexico	4	0.22%	30	New Mexico	4	0.22%
35	New York	0	0.00%	32	Colorado	3	0.17%
8	North Carolina	77	4.24%	33	Connecticut	1	0.06%
NA	North Dakota**	NA	NA	33	South Dakota	1	0.06%
6	Ohio	85	4.68%	35	Kansas	0	0.00%
7	Oklahoma	80	4.40%	35	New Hampshire	0	0.00%
22	Oregon	19	1.05%	35	New York	0	0.00%
9	Pennsylvania	71	3.91%	35	Wyoming	0	0.00%
NA	Rhode Island**	NA	NA	NA	Alaska**	NA	NA
15	South Carolina	30	1.65%	NA	Hawaii**	NA	NA
33	South Dakota	1	0.06%	NA	Iowa**	NA	NA
10	Tennessee	63	3.47%	NA	Maine**	NA	NA
2	Texas	263	14.47%	NA	Massachusetts**	NA	NA
26	Utah	7	0.39%	NA	Michigan**	NA	NA
NA	Vermont**	NA	NA	NA	Minnesota**	NA	NA
18	Virginia	24	1.32%	NA	North Dakota**	NA	NA
24	Washington	10	0.55%	NA	Rhode Island**	NA	NA
NA	West Virginia**	NA	NA	NA	Vermont**	NA	NA
NA	Wisconsin**	NA	NA	NA	West Virginia**	NA	NA
35	Wyoming	0	0.00%	NA	Wisconsin**	NA	NA
				NA	District of Columbia**	NA	NA

Source: U.S. Department of Justice, Bureau of Justice Statistics
"Capital Punishment 1996" (Bulletin, December 1997, NCJ-167031)
As of December 31, 1996. Does not include three white federal prisoners under sentence of death. There were 45 executions in 1996, 31 of whom were white prisoners.
**No death penalty as of 12/31/96.*

70

Percent of Prisoners Under Sentence of Death Who Are White: 1996

National Percent = 56.6% of State Death Sentence Prisoners*

RANK	STATE	PERCENT
19	Alabama	58.9
NA	Alaska**	NA
7	Arizona	83.5
21	Arkansas	55.0
17	California	59.9
15	Colorado	60.0
33	Connecticut	25.0
27	Delaware	45.5
13	Florida	63.0
20	Georgia	57.3
NA	Hawaii**	NA
1	Idaho	100.0
30	Illinois	37.9
12	Indiana	66.7
NA	Iowa**	NA
35	Kansas	0.0
9	Kentucky	75.9
32	Louisiana	34.9
NA	Maine**	NA
34	Maryland	21.1
NA	Massachusetts**	NA
NA	Michigan**	NA
NA	Minnesota**	NA
26	Mississippi	45.6
22	Missouri	53.8
6	Montana	85.7
10	Nebraska	72.7
18	Nevada	59.3
35	New Hampshire	0.0
27	New Jersey	45.5
1	New Mexico	100.0
35	New York	0.0
25	North Carolina	47.8
NA	North Dakota**	NA
23	Ohio	50.0
14	Oklahoma	60.2
4	Oregon	95.0
31	Pennsylvania	35.0
NA	Rhode Island**	NA
29	South Carolina	44.1
1	South Dakota	100.0
11	Tennessee	69.2
15	Texas	60.0
8	Utah	77.8
NA	Vermont**	NA
24	Virginia	49.0
5	Washington	90.9
NA	West Virginia**	NA
NA	Wisconsin**	NA
35	Wyoming	0.0

RANK	STATE	PERCENT
1	Idaho	100.0
1	New Mexico	100.0
1	South Dakota	100.0
4	Oregon	95.0
5	Washington	90.9
6	Montana	85.7
7	Arizona	83.5
8	Utah	77.8
9	Kentucky	75.9
10	Nebraska	72.7
11	Tennessee	69.2
12	Indiana	66.7
13	Florida	63.0
14	Oklahoma	60.2
15	Colorado	60.0
15	Texas	60.0
17	California	59.9
18	Nevada	59.3
19	Alabama	58.9
20	Georgia	57.3
21	Arkansas	55.0
22	Missouri	53.8
23	Ohio	50.0
24	Virginia	49.0
25	North Carolina	47.8
26	Mississippi	45.6
27	Delaware	45.5
27	New Jersey	45.5
29	South Carolina	44.1
30	Illinois	37.9
31	Pennsylvania	35.0
32	Louisiana	34.9
33	Connecticut	25.0
34	Maryland	21.1
35	Kansas	0.0
35	New Hampshire	0.0
35	New York	0.0
35	Wyoming	0.0
NA	Alaska**	NA
NA	Hawaii**	NA
NA	Iowa**	NA
NA	Maine**	NA
NA	Massachusetts**	NA
NA	Michigan**	NA
NA	Minnesota**	NA
NA	North Dakota**	NA
NA	Rhode Island**	NA
NA	Vermont**	NA
NA	West Virginia**	NA
NA	Wisconsin**	NA
	District of Columbia**	NA

Source: Morgan Quitno Press using data from U.S. Department of Justice, Bureau of Justice Statistics
    "Capital Punishment 1996" (Bulletin, December 1997, NCJ-167031)
*As of December 31, 1996. Does not include three white federal prisoners under sentence of death. There were
45 executions in 1996, 31 of whom were white prisoners.
**No death penalty as of 12/31/96.

Black Prisoners Under Sentence of Death in 1996

National Total = 1,341 Black State Prisoners*

ALPHA ORDER					RANK ORDER			
RANK	STATE		PRISONERS	% of USA	RANK	STATE	PRISONERS	% of USA
8	Alabama		61	4.55%	1	California	171	12.75%
NA	Alaska**		NA	NA	1	Texas	171	12.75%
21	Arizona		14	1.04%	3	Florida	138	10.29%
18	Arkansas		18	1.34%	4	Pennsylvania	125	9.32%
1	California		171	12.75%	5	Illinois	100	7.46%
26	Colorado		2	0.15%	6	Ohio	84	6.26%
25	Connecticut		3	0.22%	7	North Carolina	81	6.04%
23	Delaware		6	0.45%	8	Alabama	61	4.55%
3	Florida		138	10.29%	9	Missouri	43	3.21%
11	Georgia		41	3.06%	10	Oklahoma	42	3.13%
NA	Hawaii**		NA	NA	11	Georgia	41	3.06%
30	Idaho		0	0.00%	11	Louisiana	41	3.06%
5	Illinois		100	7.46%	13	South Carolina	38	2.83%
19	Indiana		15	1.12%	14	Nevada	32	2.39%
NA	Iowa**		NA	NA	15	Mississippi	31	2.31%
30	Kansas		0	0.00%	16	Tennessee	26	1.94%
22	Kentucky		7	0.52%	17	Virginia	25	1.86%
11	Louisiana		41	3.06%	18	Arkansas	18	1.34%
NA	Maine**		NA	NA	19	Indiana	15	1.12%
19	Maryland		15	1.12%	19	Maryland	15	1.12%
NA	Massachusetts**		NA	NA	21	Arizona	14	1.04%
NA	Michigan**		NA	NA	22	Kentucky	7	0.52%
NA	Minnesota**		NA	NA	23	Delaware	6	0.45%
15	Mississippi		31	2.31%	23	New Jersey	6	0.45%
9	Missouri		43	3.21%	25	Connecticut	3	0.22%
30	Montana		0	0.00%	26	Colorado	2	0.15%
26	Nebraska		2	0.15%	26	Nebraska	2	0.15%
14	Nevada		32	2.39%	26	Utah	2	0.15%
30	New Hampshire		0	0.00%	29	Washington	1	0.07%
23	New Jersey		6	0.45%	30	Idaho	0	0.00%
30	New Mexico		0	0.00%	30	Kansas	0	0.00%
30	New York		0	0.00%	30	Montana	0	0.00%
7	North Carolina		81	6.04%	30	New Hampshire	0	0.00%
NA	North Dakota**		NA	NA	30	New Mexico	0	0.00%
6	Ohio		84	6.26%	30	New York	0	0.00%
10	Oklahoma		42	3.13%	30	Oregon	0	0.00%
30	Oregon		0	0.00%	30	South Dakota	0	0.00%
4	Pennsylvania		125	9.32%	30	Wyoming	0	0.00%
NA	Rhode Island**		NA	NA	NA	Alaska**	NA	NA
13	South Carolina		38	2.83%	NA	Hawaii**	NA	NA
30	South Dakota		0	0.00%	NA	Iowa**	NA	NA
16	Tennessee		26	1.94%	NA	Maine**	NA	NA
1	Texas		171	12.75%	NA	Massachusetts**	NA	NA
26	Utah		2	0.15%	NA	Michigan**	NA	NA
NA	Vermont**		NA	NA	NA	Minnesota**	NA	NA
17	Virginia		25	1.86%	NA	North Dakota**	NA	NA
29	Washington		1	0.07%	NA	Rhode Island**	NA	NA
NA	West Virginia**		NA	NA	NA	Vermont**	NA	NA
NA	Wisconsin**		NA	NA	NA	West Virginia**	NA	NA
30	Wyoming		0	0.00%	NA	Wisconsin**	NA	NA
						District of Columbia**	NA	NA

Source: U.S. Department of Justice, Bureau of Justice Statistics
  "Capital Punishment 1996" (Bulletin, December 1997, NCJ-167031)
*As of December 31, 1996. Does not include eight black federal prisoners under sentence of death. There were
45 executions in 1996, 14 of whom were black prisoners.
**No death penalty as of 12/31/96.

Percent of Prisoners Under Sentence of Death Who Are Black: 1996

National Percent = 41.8% of State Death Sentence Prisoners*

ALPHA ORDER				RANK ORDER		
RANK	STATE	PERCENT		RANK	STATE	PERCENT
16	Alabama	40.4		1	Maryland	78.9
NA	Alaska**	NA		2	Connecticut	75.0
28	Arizona	11.6		3	Louisiana	65.1
14	Arkansas	45.0		4	Illinois	62.1
20	California	37.7		5	Pennsylvania	61.6
17	Colorado	40.0		6	South Carolina	55.9
2	Connecticut	75.0		7	Delaware	54.5
7	Delaware	54.5		7	New Jersey	54.5
21	Florida	37.0		9	Mississippi	54.4
15	Georgia	42.7		10	Virginia	51.0
NA	Hawaii**	NA		11	North Carolina	50.3
30	Idaho	0.0		12	Ohio	49.4
4	Illinois	62.1		13	Missouri	46.2
22	Indiana	33.3		14	Arkansas	45.0
NA	Iowa**	NA		15	Georgia	42.7
30	Kansas	0.0		16	Alabama	40.4
25	Kentucky	24.1		17	Colorado	40.0
3	Louisiana	65.1		18	Nevada	39.5
NA	Maine**	NA		19	Texas	39.0
1	Maryland	78.9		20	California	37.7
NA	Massachusetts**	NA		21	Florida	37.0
NA	Michigan**	NA		22	Indiana	33.3
NA	Minnesota**	NA		23	Oklahoma	31.6
9	Mississippi	54.4		24	Tennessee	28.6
13	Missouri	46.2		25	Kentucky	24.1
30	Montana	0.0		26	Utah	22.2
27	Nebraska	18.2		27	Nebraska	18.2
18	Nevada	39.5		28	Arizona	11.6
30	New Hampshire	0.0		29	Washington	9.1
7	New Jersey	54.5		30	Idaho	0.0
30	New Mexico	0.0		30	Kansas	0.0
30	New York	0.0		30	Montana	0.0
11	North Carolina	50.3		30	New Hampshire	0.0
NA	North Dakota**	NA		30	New Mexico	0.0
12	Ohio	49.4		30	New York	0.0
23	Oklahoma	31.6		30	Oregon	0.0
30	Oregon	0.0		30	South Dakota	0.0
5	Pennsylvania	61.6		30	Wyoming	0.0
NA	Rhode Island**	NA		NA	Alaska**	NA
6	South Carolina	55.9		NA	Hawaii**	NA
30	South Dakota	0.0		NA	Iowa**	NA
24	Tennessee	28.6		NA	Maine**	NA
19	Texas	39.0		NA	Massachusetts**	NA
26	Utah	22.2		NA	Michigan**	NA
NA	Vermont**	NA		NA	Minnesota**	NA
10	Virginia	51.0		NA	North Dakota**	NA
29	Washington	9.1		NA	Rhode Island**	NA
NA	West Virginia**	NA		NA	Vermont**	NA
NA	Wisconsin**	NA		NA	West Virginia**	NA
30	Wyoming	0.0		NA	Wisconsin**	NA
					District of Columbia**	NA

Source: Morgan Quitno Press using data from U.S. Department of Justice, Bureau of Justice Statistics
    "Capital Punishment 1996" (Bulletin, December 1997, NCJ-167031)
*As of December 31, 1996. Does not include eight black federal prisoners under sentence of death. There were
45 executions in 1996, 14 of whom were black prisoners.
**No death penalty as of 12/31/96.

Prisoners Executed: 1930 to 1996

National Total = 4,217 Prisoners*

ALPHA ORDER

RANK	STATE	EXECUTIONS	% of USA
12	Alabama	148	3.51%
43	Alaska	0	0.00%
25	Arizona	44	1.04%
13	Arkansas	130	3.08%
4	California	296	7.02%
23	Colorado	47	1.11%
29	Connecticut	21	0.50%
30	Delaware	20	0.47%
6	Florida	208	4.93%
2	Georgia	388	9.20%
43	Hawaii	0	0.00%
39	Idaho	4	0.09%
16	Illinois	98	2.32%
24	Indiana	45	1.07%
32	Iowa	18	0.43%
34	Kansas	15	0.36%
15	Kentucky	103	2.44%
10	Louisiana	156	3.70%
43	Maine	0	0.00%
20	Maryland	69	1.64%
28	Massachusetts	27	0.64%
43	Michigan	0	0.00%
43	Minnesota	0	0.00%
9	Mississippi	158	3.75%
18	Missouri	85	2.02%
37	Montana	7	0.17%
38	Nebraska	6	0.14%
27	Nevada	35	0.83%
41	New Hampshire	1	0.02%
19	New Jersey	74	1.75%
35	New Mexico	8	0.19%
3	New York	329	7.80%
5	North Carolina	271	6.43%
43	North Dakota	0	0.00%
8	Ohio	172	4.08%
21	Oklahoma	68	1.61%
30	Oregon	20	0.47%
11	Pennsylvania	154	3.65%
43	Rhode Island	0	0.00%
7	South Carolina	173	4.10%
41	South Dakota	1	0.02%
17	Tennessee	93	2.21%
1	Texas	404	9.58%
32	Utah	18	0.43%
39	Vermont	4	0.09%
14	Virginia	129	3.06%
22	Washington	49	1.16%
26	West Virginia	40	0.95%
43	Wisconsin	0	0.00%
35	Wyoming	8	0.19%

RANK ORDER

RANK	STATE	EXECUTIONS	% of USA
1	Texas	404	9.58%
2	Georgia	388	9.20%
3	New York	329	7.80%
4	California	296	7.02%
5	North Carolina	271	6.43%
6	Florida	208	4.93%
7	South Carolina	173	4.10%
8	Ohio	172	4.08%
9	Mississippi	158	3.75%
10	Louisiana	156	3.70%
11	Pennsylvania	154	3.65%
12	Alabama	148	3.51%
13	Arkansas	130	3.08%
14	Virginia	129	3.06%
15	Kentucky	103	2.44%
16	Illinois	98	2.32%
17	Tennessee	93	2.21%
18	Missouri	85	2.02%
19	New Jersey	74	1.75%
20	Maryland	69	1.64%
21	Oklahoma	68	1.61%
22	Washington	49	1.16%
23	Colorado	47	1.11%
24	Indiana	45	1.07%
25	Arizona	44	1.04%
26	West Virginia	40	0.95%
27	Nevada	35	0.83%
28	Massachusetts	27	0.64%
29	Connecticut	21	0.50%
30	Delaware	20	0.47%
30	Oregon	20	0.47%
32	Iowa	18	0.43%
32	Utah	18	0.43%
34	Kansas	15	0.36%
35	New Mexico	8	0.19%
35	Wyoming	8	0.19%
37	Montana	7	0.17%
38	Nebraska	6	0.14%
39	Idaho	4	0.09%
39	Vermont	4	0.09%
41	New Hampshire	1	0.02%
41	South Dakota	1	0.02%
43	Alaska	0	0.00%
43	Hawaii	0	0.00%
43	Maine	0	0.00%
43	Michigan	0	0.00%
43	Minnesota	0	0.00%
43	North Dakota	0	0.00%
43	Rhode Island	0	0.00%
43	Wisconsin	0	0.00%
	District of Columbia	40	0.95%

Source: U.S. Department of Justice, Bureau of Justice Statistics
  "Capital Punishment 1996" (Bulletin, December 1997, NCJ-167031)
*Includes 33 executions by the federal government. Does not include 160 executions carried out under military
authority. There were no executions from 1968 to 1976.

Prisoners Executed: 1977 to 1996

National Total = 358 Prisoners*

ALPHA ORDER

RANK	STATE	EXECUTIONS	% of USA
7	Alabama	13	3.63%
28	Alaska	0	0.00%
14	Arizona	6	1.68%
8	Arkansas	12	3.35%
17	California	4	1.12%
28	Colorado	0	0.00%
28	Connecticut	0	0.00%
10	Delaware	8	2.23%
2	Florida	38	10.61%
6	Georgia	22	6.15%
28	Hawaii	0	0.00%
23	Idaho	1	0.28%
10	Illinois	8	2.23%
17	Indiana	4	1.12%
28	Iowa	0	0.00%
28	Kansas	0	0.00%
28	Kentucky	0	0.00%
4	Louisiana	23	6.42%
28	Maine	0	0.00%
23	Maryland	1	0.28%
28	Massachusetts	0	0.00%
28	Michigan	0	0.00%
28	Minnesota	0	0.00%
17	Mississippi	4	1.12%
4	Missouri	23	6.42%
23	Montana	1	0.28%
20	Nebraska	2	0.56%
14	Nevada	6	1.68%
28	New Hampshire	0	0.00%
28	New Jersey	0	0.00%
28	New Mexico	0	0.00%
28	New York	0	0.00%
10	North Carolina	8	2.23%
28	North Dakota	0	0.00%
28	Ohio	0	0.00%
10	Oklahoma	8	2.23%
23	Oregon	1	0.28%
20	Pennsylvania	2	0.56%
28	Rhode Island	0	0.00%
9	South Carolina	11	3.07%
28	South Dakota	0	0.00%
28	Tennessee	0	0.00%
1	Texas	107	29.89%
16	Utah	5	1.40%
28	Vermont	0	0.00%
3	Virginia	37	10.34%
20	Washington	2	0.56%
28	West Virginia	0	0.00%
28	Wisconsin	0	0.00%
23	Wyoming	1	0.28%

RANK ORDER

RANK	STATE	EXECUTIONS	% of USA
1	Texas	107	29.89%
2	Florida	38	10.61%
3	Virginia	37	10.34%
4	Louisiana	23	6.42%
4	Missouri	23	6.42%
6	Georgia	22	6.15%
7	Alabama	13	3.63%
8	Arkansas	12	3.35%
9	South Carolina	11	3.07%
10	Delaware	8	2.23%
10	Illinois	8	2.23%
10	North Carolina	8	2.23%
10	Oklahoma	8	2.23%
14	Arizona	6	1.68%
14	Nevada	6	1.68%
16	Utah	5	1.40%
17	California	4	1.12%
17	Indiana	4	1.12%
17	Mississippi	4	1.12%
20	Nebraska	2	0.56%
20	Pennsylvania	2	0.56%
20	Washington	2	0.56%
23	Idaho	1	0.28%
23	Maryland	1	0.28%
23	Montana	1	0.28%
23	Oregon	1	0.28%
23	Wyoming	1	0.28%
28	Alaska	0	0.00%
28	Colorado	0	0.00%
28	Connecticut	0	0.00%
28	Hawaii	0	0.00%
28	Iowa	0	0.00%
28	Kansas	0	0.00%
28	Kentucky	0	0.00%
28	Maine	0	0.00%
28	Massachusetts	0	0.00%
28	Michigan	0	0.00%
28	Minnesota	0	0.00%
28	New Hampshire	0	0.00%
28	New Jersey	0	0.00%
28	New Mexico	0	0.00%
28	New York	0	0.00%
28	North Dakota	0	0.00%
28	Ohio	0	0.00%
28	Rhode Island	0	0.00%
28	South Dakota	0	0.00%
28	Tennessee	0	0.00%
28	Vermont	0	0.00%
28	West Virginia	0	0.00%
28	Wisconsin	0	0.00%
	District of Columbia	0	0.00%

Source: U.S. Department of Justice, Bureau of Justice Statistics
    "Capital Punishment 1996" (Bulletin, December 1997, NCJ-167031)
*As of December 31, 1996. All executions since 1977 have been for murder. In this time period, there have been no executions by the federal government. The most common method of executions was lethal injection (216) followed by electrocution (128), lethal gas (9), hanging (3) and firing squad (2).

Prisoners Sentenced to Death: 1973 to 1996

National Total = 5,864 Death Sentences*

ALPHA ORDER				RANK ORDER			
RANK	STATE	SENTENCES	% of USA	RANK	STATE	SENTENCES	% of USA
8	Alabama	262	4.47%	1	Florida	759	12.94%
NA	Alaska**	NA	NA	2	Texas	701	11.95%
11	Arizona	202	3.44%	3	California	611	10.42%
20	Arkansas	82	1.40%	4	North Carolina	413	7.04%
3	California	611	10.42%	5	Ohio	316	5.39%
31	Colorado	16	0.27%	6	Pennsylvania	274	4.67%
34	Connecticut	6	0.10%	7	Oklahoma	267	4.55%
26	Delaware	32	0.55%	8	Alabama	262	4.47%
1	Florida	759	12.94%	9	Georgia	258	4.40%
9	Georgia	258	4.40%	10	Illinois	249	4.25%
NA	Hawaii**	NA	NA	11	Arizona	202	3.44%
25	Idaho	34	0.58%	12	Tennessee	170	2.90%
10	Illinois	249	4.25%	13	Louisiana	162	2.76%
19	Indiana	85	1.45%	14	South Carolina	146	2.49%
NA	Iowa**	NA	NA	15	Mississippi	145	2.47%
39	Kansas	0	0.00%	16	Missouri	135	2.30%
21	Kentucky	60	1.02%	17	Nevada	113	1.93%
13	Louisiana	162	2.76%	18	Virginia	103	1.76%
NA	Maine**	NA	NA	19	Indiana	85	1.45%
22	Maryland	45	0.77%	20	Arkansas	82	1.40%
35	Massachusetts	4	0.07%	21	Kentucky	60	1.02%
NA	Michigan**	NA	NA	22	Maryland	45	0.77%
NA	Minnesota**	NA	NA	23	New Jersey	43	0.73%
15	Mississippi	145	2.47%	24	Oregon	39	0.67%
16	Missouri	135	2.30%	25	Idaho	34	0.58%
32	Montana	15	0.26%	26	Delaware	32	0.55%
30	Nebraska	23	0.39%	27	Washington	28	0.48%
17	Nevada	113	1.93%	28	New Mexico	26	0.44%
39	New Hampshire	0	0.00%	29	Utah	24	0.41%
23	New Jersey	43	0.73%	30	Nebraska	23	0.39%
28	New Mexico	26	0.44%	31	Colorado	16	0.27%
36	New York	3	0.05%	32	Montana	15	0.26%
4	North Carolina	413	7.04%	33	Wyoming	9	0.15%
NA	North Dakota**	NA	NA	34	Connecticut	6	0.10%
5	Ohio	316	5.39%	35	Massachusetts	4	0.07%
7	Oklahoma	267	4.55%	36	New York	3	0.05%
24	Oregon	39	0.67%	37	Rhode Island	2	0.03%
6	Pennsylvania	274	4.67%	37	South Dakota	2	0.03%
37	Rhode Island	2	0.03%	39	Kansas	0	0.00%
14	South Carolina	146	2.49%	39	New Hampshire	0	0.00%
37	South Dakota	2	0.03%	NA	Alaska**	NA	NA
12	Tennessee	170	2.90%	NA	Hawaii**	NA	NA
2	Texas	701	11.95%	NA	Iowa**	NA	NA
29	Utah	24	0.41%	NA	Maine**	NA	NA
NA	Vermont**	NA	NA	NA	Michigan**	NA	NA
18	Virginia	103	1.76%	NA	Minnesota**	NA	NA
27	Washington	28	0.48%	NA	North Dakota**	NA	NA
NA	West Virginia**	NA	NA	NA	Vermont**	NA	NA
NA	Wisconsin**	NA	NA	NA	West Virginia**	NA	NA
33	Wyoming	9	0.15%	NA	Wisconsin**	NA	NA
				District of Columbia**		NA	NA

Source: U.S. Department of Justice, Bureau of Justice Statistics
"Capital Punishment 1996" (Bulletin, December 1997, NCJ-167031)
*As of December 31, 1996. Does not includes 13 federal prisoners sentenced to death.
**Not applicable.

Death Sentences Overturned or Commuted: 1973 to 1996

National Total = 2,118 Sentences*

ALPHA ORDER				RANK ORDER			
RANK	STATE	SENTENCES	% of USA	RANK	STATE	SENTENCES	% of USA
8	Alabama	90	4.25%	1	Florida	324	15.30%
NA	Alaska**	NA	NA	2	North Carolina	239	11.28%
12	Arizona	68	3.21%	3	Texas	142	6.70%
17	Arkansas	29	1.37%	4	Ohio	140	6.61%
6	California	128	6.04%	5	Georgia	131	6.19%
29	Colorado	10	0.47%	6	California	128	6.04%
36	Connecticut	2	0.09%	7	Oklahoma	120	5.67%
27	Delaware	13	0.61%	8	Alabama	90	4.25%
1	Florida	324	15.30%	9	Mississippi	80	3.78%
5	Georgia	131	6.19%	10	Tennessee	73	3.45%
NA	Hawaii**	NA	NA	11	Louisiana	72	3.40%
24	Idaho	14	0.66%	12	Arizona	68	3.21%
13	Illinois	66	3.12%	13	Illinois	66	3.12%
16	Indiana	33	1.56%	14	South Carolina	64	3.02%
NA	Iowa**	NA	NA	15	Pennsylvania	61	2.88%
39	Kansas	0	0.00%	16	Indiana	33	1.56%
17	Kentucky	29	1.37%	17	Arkansas	29	1.37%
11	Louisiana	72	3.40%	17	Kentucky	29	1.37%
NA	Maine**	NA	NA	19	Maryland	24	1.13%
19	Maryland	24	1.13%	20	Nevada	22	1.04%
34	Massachusetts	4	0.19%	20	New Jersey	22	1.04%
NA	Michigan**	NA	NA	22	New Mexico	21	0.99%
NA	Minnesota**	NA	NA	23	Oregon	18	0.85%
9	Mississippi	80	3.78%	24	Idaho	14	0.66%
24	Missouri	14	0.66%	24	Missouri	14	0.66%
32	Montana	7	0.33%	24	Washington	14	0.66%
31	Nebraska	8	0.38%	27	Delaware	13	0.61%
20	Nevada	22	1.04%	27	Virginia	13	0.61%
39	New Hampshire	0	0.00%	29	Colorado	10	0.47%
20	New Jersey	22	1.04%	29	Utah	10	0.47%
22	New Mexico	21	0.99%	31	Nebraska	8	0.38%
35	New York	3	0.14%	32	Montana	7	0.33%
2	North Carolina	239	11.28%	32	Wyoming	7	0.33%
NA	North Dakota**	NA	NA	34	Massachusetts	4	0.19%
4	Ohio	140	6.61%	35	New York	3	0.14%
7	Oklahoma	120	5.67%	36	Connecticut	2	0.09%
23	Oregon	18	0.85%	36	Rhode Island	2	0.09%
15	Pennsylvania	61	2.88%	38	South Dakota	1	0.05%
36	Rhode Island	2	0.09%	39	Kansas	0	0.00%
14	South Carolina	64	3.02%	39	New Hampshire	0	0.00%
38	South Dakota	1	0.05%	NA	Alaska**	NA	NA
10	Tennessee	73	3.45%	NA	Hawaii**	NA	NA
3	Texas	142	6.70%	NA	Iowa**	NA	NA
29	Utah	10	0.47%	NA	Maine**	NA	NA
NA	Vermont**	NA	NA	NA	Michigan**	NA	NA
27	Virginia	13	0.61%	NA	Minnesota**	NA	NA
24	Washington	14	0.66%	NA	North Dakota**	NA	NA
NA	West Virginia**	NA	NA	NA	Vermont**	NA	NA
NA	Wisconsin**	NA	NA	NA	West Virginia**	NA	NA
32	Wyoming	7	0.33%	NA	Wisconsin**	NA	NA
					District of Columbia**	NA	NA

Source: U.S. Department of Justice, Bureau of Justice Statistics
"Capital Punishment 1996" (Bulletin, December 1997, NCJ-167031)
*As of December 31, 1996. Does not includes two federal prisoners whose sentences were overturned.
**Not applicable.

77

Percent of Death Penalty Sentences Overturned or Commuted: 1973 to 1996

National Percent = 36.1% of Sentences*

ALPHA ORDER

RANK	STATE	PERCENT		RANK	STATE	PERCENT
29	Alabama	34.4		1	Massachusetts	100.0
NA	Alaska**	NA		1	New York	100.0
30	Arizona	33.7		1	Rhode Island	100.0
27	Arkansas	35.4		4	New Mexico	80.8
34	California	20.9		5	Wyoming	77.8
6	Colorado	62.5		6	Colorado	62.5
31	Connecticut	33.3		7	North Carolina	57.9
25	Delaware	40.6		8	Mississippi	55.2
22	Florida	42.7		9	Maryland	53.3
11	Georgia	50.8		10	New Jersey	51.2
NA	Hawaii**	NA		11	Georgia	50.8
24	Idaho	41.2		12	South Dakota	50.0
32	Illinois	26.5		12	Washington	50.0
26	Indiana	38.8		14	Kentucky	48.3
NA	Iowa**	NA		15	Montana	46.7
39	Kansas	0.0		16	Oregon	46.2
14	Kentucky	48.3		17	Oklahoma	44.9
18	Louisiana	44.4		18	Louisiana	44.4
NA	Maine**	NA		19	Ohio	44.3
9	Maryland	53.3		20	South Carolina	43.8
1	Massachusetts	100.0		21	Tennessee	42.9
NA	Michigan**	NA		22	Florida	42.7
NA	Minnesota**	NA		23	Utah	41.7
8	Mississippi	55.2		24	Idaho	41.2
38	Missouri	10.4		25	Delaware	40.6
15	Montana	46.7		26	Indiana	38.8
28	Nebraska	34.8		27	Arkansas	35.4
36	Nevada	19.5		28	Nebraska	34.8
39	New Hampshire	0.0		29	Alabama	34.4
10	New Jersey	51.2		30	Arizona	33.7
4	New Mexico	80.8		31	Connecticut	33.3
1	New York	100.0		32	Illinois	26.5
7	North Carolina	57.9		33	Pennsylvania	22.3
NA	North Dakota**	NA		34	California	20.9
19	Ohio	44.3		35	Texas	20.3
17	Oklahoma	44.9		36	Nevada	19.5
16	Oregon	46.2		37	Virginia	12.6
33	Pennsylvania	22.3		38	Missouri	10.4
1	Rhode Island	100.0		39	Kansas	0.0
20	South Carolina	43.8		39	New Hampshire	0.0
12	South Dakota	50.0		NA	Alaska**	NA
21	Tennessee	42.9		NA	Hawaii**	NA
35	Texas	20.3		NA	Iowa**	NA
23	Utah	41.7		NA	Maine**	NA
NA	Vermont**	NA		NA	Michigan**	NA
37	Virginia	12.6		NA	Minnesota**	NA
12	Washington	50.0		NA	North Dakota**	NA
NA	West Virginia**	NA		NA	Vermont**	NA
NA	Wisconsin**	NA		NA	West Virginia**	NA
5	Wyoming	77.8		NA	Wisconsin**	NA
					District of Columbia**	NA

Source: Morgan Quitno Press using data from U.S. Department of Justice, Bureau of Justice Statistics
   "Capital Punishment 1996" (Bulletin, December 1997, NCJ-167031)
*As of December 31, 1996. Does not includes two federal prisoners whose sentences were overturned.
**Not applicable.

Sentenced Prisoners Admitted to State Correctional Institutions in 1995

National Total = 535,355 Prisoners Admitted*

<u>ALPHA ORDER</u>

RANK	STATE	ADMISSIONS	% of USA
16	Alabama	8,913	1.66%
37	Alaska	1,999	0.37%
17	Arizona	8,748	1.63%
26	Arkansas	5,280	0.99%
1	California	116,613	21.78%
25	Colorado	5,334	1.00%
40	Connecticut	1,504	0.28%
41	Delaware	1,327	0.25%
4	Florida	26,335	4.92%
8	Georgia	15,407	2.88%
38	Hawaii	1,806	0.34%
35	Idaho	2,356	0.44%
5	Illinois	24,371	4.55%
18	Indiana	8,344	1.56%
30	Iowa	4,072	0.76%
28	Kansas	4,129	0.77%
22	Kentucky	6,968	1.30%
10	Louisiana	12,884	2.41%
47	Maine	713	0.13%
15	Maryland	9,681	1.81%
29	Massachusetts	4,106	0.77%
11	Michigan	12,697	2.37%
33	Minnesota	3,322	0.62%
27	Mississippi	5,091	0.95%
12	Missouri	11,808	2.21%
46	Montana	844	0.16%
39	Nebraska	1,677	0.31%
31	Nevada	3,920	0.73%
44	New Hampshire	968	0.18%
9	New Jersey	15,020	2.81%
36	New Mexico	2,346	0.44%
3	New York	34,688	6.48%
7	North Carolina	19,734	3.69%
50	North Dakota	478	0.09%
6	Ohio	22,678	4.24%
20	Oklahoma	7,726	1.44%
32	Oregon	3,698	0.69%
14	Pennsylvania	11,053	2.06%
45	Rhode Island	890	0.17%
19	South Carolina	8,304	1.55%
43	South Dakota	978	0.18%
21	Tennessee	7,083	1.32%
2	Texas	55,432	10.35%
34	Utah	2,401	0.45%
49	Vermont	570	0.11%
13	Virginia	11,490	2.15%
24	Washington	6,169	1.15%
42	West Virginia	1,116	0.21%
23	Wisconsin	6,943	1.30%
48	Wyoming	628	0.12%

<u>RANK ORDER</u>

RANK	STATE	ADMISSIONS	% of USA
1	California	116,613	21.78%
2	Texas	55,432	10.35%
3	New York	34,688	6.48%
4	Florida	26,335	4.92%
5	Illinois	24,371	4.55%
6	Ohio	22,678	4.24%
7	North Carolina	19,734	3.69%
8	Georgia	15,407	2.88%
9	New Jersey	15,020	2.81%
10	Louisiana	12,884	2.41%
11	Michigan	12,697	2.37%
12	Missouri	11,808	2.21%
13	Virginia	11,490	2.15%
14	Pennsylvania	11,053	2.06%
15	Maryland	9,681	1.81%
16	Alabama	8,913	1.66%
17	Arizona	8,748	1.63%
18	Indiana	8,344	1.56%
19	South Carolina	8,304	1.55%
20	Oklahoma	7,726	1.44%
21	Tennessee	7,083	1.32%
22	Kentucky	6,968	1.30%
23	Wisconsin	6,943	1.30%
24	Washington	6,169	1.15%
25	Colorado	5,334	1.00%
26	Arkansas	5,280	0.99%
27	Mississippi	5,091	0.95%
28	Kansas	4,129	0.77%
29	Massachusetts	4,106	0.77%
30	Iowa	4,072	0.76%
31	Nevada	3,920	0.73%
32	Oregon	3,698	0.69%
33	Minnesota	3,322	0.62%
34	Utah	2,401	0.45%
35	Idaho	2,356	0.44%
36	New Mexico	2,346	0.44%
37	Alaska	1,999	0.37%
38	Hawaii	1,806	0.34%
39	Nebraska	1,677	0.31%
40	Connecticut	1,504	0.28%
41	Delaware	1,327	0.25%
42	West Virginia	1,116	0.21%
43	South Dakota	978	0.18%
44	New Hampshire	968	0.18%
45	Rhode Island	890	0.17%
46	Montana	844	0.16%
47	Maine	713	0.13%
48	Wyoming	628	0.12%
49	Vermont	570	0.11%
50	North Dakota	478	0.09%
	District of Columbia	4,713	0.88%

*Source: U.S. Department of Justice, Bureau of Justice Statistics
"Correctional Populations in the United States, 1995" (May 1997, NCJ-163916)
Includes sentenced prisoners admitted because of new court commitments, parole violators returned, escapees returned and others. Does not include 27,369 new federal commitments.

Sentenced Prisoners Admitted to State Correctional Institutions Through New Court Commitments in 1995
National Total = 337,492 New Prisoners*

ALPHA ORDER

RANK ORDER

RANK	STATE	PRISONERS	% of USA	RANK	STATE	PRISONERS	% of USA
17	Alabama	6,627	1.96%	1	California	45,459	13.47%
35	Alaska	1,320	0.39%	2	Texas	36,844	10.92%
16	Arizona	6,831	2.02%	3	New York	22,980	6.81%
27	Arkansas	3,577	1.06%	4	Florida	18,576	5.50%
1	California	45,459	13.47%	5	Ohio	18,533	5.49%
26	Colorado	3,798	1.13%	6	Illinois	18,405	5.45%
43	Connecticut	723	0.21%	7	North Carolina	13,344	3.95%
40	Delaware	830	0.25%	8	Georgia	11,769	3.49%
4	Florida	18,576	5.50%	9	New Jersey	9,747	2.89%
8	Georgia	11,769	3.49%	10	Virginia	9,494	2.81%
42	Hawaii	781	0.23%	11	Maryland	8,126	2.41%
34	Idaho	1,696	0.50%	12	Michigan	7,694	2.28%
6	Illinois	18,405	5.45%	13	Indiana	7,592	2.25%
13	Indiana	7,592	2.25%	14	Missouri	7,417	2.20%
31	Iowa	2,432	0.72%	15	Oklahoma	6,942	2.06%
29	Kansas	2,652	0.79%	16	Arizona	6,831	2.02%
22	Kentucky	4,974	1.47%	17	Alabama	6,627	1.96%
18	Louisiana	6,171	1.83%	18	Louisiana	6,171	1.83%
47	Maine	460	0.14%	19	Pennsylvania	6,073	1.80%
11	Maryland	8,126	2.41%	20	South Carolina	5,600	1.66%
30	Massachusetts	2,435	0.72%	21	Washington	5,294	1.57%
12	Michigan	7,694	2.28%	22	Kentucky	4,974	1.47%
32	Minnesota	2,358	0.70%	23	Mississippi	4,533	1.34%
23	Mississippi	4,533	1.34%	24	Wisconsin	4,476	1.33%
14	Missouri	7,417	2.20%	25	Tennessee	4,064	1.20%
50	Montana	386	0.11%	26	Colorado	3,798	1.13%
36	Nebraska	1,295	0.38%	27	Arkansas	3,577	1.06%
28	Nevada	3,110	0.92%	28	Nevada	3,110	0.92%
44	New Hampshire	658	0.19%	29	Kansas	2,652	0.79%
9	New Jersey	9,747	2.89%	30	Massachusetts	2,435	0.72%
38	New Mexico	1,260	0.37%	31	Iowa	2,432	0.72%
3	New York	22,980	6.81%	32	Minnesota	2,358	0.70%
7	North Carolina	13,344	3.95%	33	Oregon	1,796	0.53%
49	North Dakota	395	0.12%	34	Idaho	1,696	0.50%
5	Ohio	18,533	5.49%	35	Alaska	1,320	0.39%
15	Oklahoma	6,942	2.06%	36	Nebraska	1,295	0.38%
33	Oregon	1,796	0.53%	37	Utah	1,262	0.37%
19	Pennsylvania	6,073	1.80%	38	New Mexico	1,260	0.37%
45	Rhode Island	583	0.17%	39	West Virginia	1,021	0.30%
20	South Carolina	5,600	1.66%	40	Delaware	830	0.25%
41	South Dakota	783	0.23%	41	South Dakota	783	0.23%
25	Tennessee	4,064	1.20%	42	Hawaii	781	0.23%
2	Texas	36,844	10.92%	43	Connecticut	723	0.21%
37	Utah	1,262	0.37%	44	New Hampshire	658	0.19%
48	Vermont	411	0.12%	45	Rhode Island	583	0.17%
10	Virginia	9,494	2.81%	46	Wyoming	525	0.16%
21	Washington	5,294	1.57%	47	Maine	460	0.14%
39	West Virginia	1,021	0.30%	48	Vermont	411	0.12%
24	Wisconsin	4,476	1.33%	49	North Dakota	395	0.12%
46	Wyoming	525	0.16%	50	Montana	386	0.11%
					District of Columbia	3,380	1.00%

Source: U.S. Department of Justice, Bureau of Justice Statistics
"Correctional Populations in the United States, 1995" (May 1997, NCJ-163916)
*Does not include 23,972 new federal court commitments.

Parole Violators Returned to State Prisons in 1995

National Total = 175,726 Prisoners*

ALPHA ORDER

RANK	STATE	PRISONERS	% of USA
17	Alabama	1,894	1.08%
34	Alaska	676	0.38%
19	Arizona	1,831	1.04%
21	Arkansas	1,614	0.92%
1	California	70,259	39.98%
26	Colorado	1,081	0.62%
37	Connecticut	523	0.30%
40	Delaware	339	0.19%
4	Florida	6,785	3.86%
11	Georgia	3,457	1.97%
29	Hawaii	1,022	0.58%
36	Idaho	589	0.34%
8	Illinois	4,948	2.82%
33	Indiana	691	0.39%
31	Iowa	886	0.50%
23	Kansas	1,410	0.80%
18	Kentucky	1,847	1.05%
5	Louisiana	6,303	3.59%
45	Maine	245	0.14%
22	Maryland	1,435	0.82%
28	Massachusetts	1,023	0.58%
13	Michigan	2,807	1.60%
30	Minnesota	964	0.55%
42	Mississippi	285	0.16%
14	Missouri	2,739	1.56%
38	Montana	453	0.26%
39	Nebraska	348	0.20%
35	Nevada	642	0.37%
41	New Hampshire	296	0.17%
7	New Jersey	5,157	2.93%
27	New Mexico	1,036	0.59%
3	New York	7,782	4.43%
6	North Carolina	5,801	3.30%
50	North Dakota	77	0.04%
10	Ohio	4,118	2.34%
43	Oklahoma	271	0.15%
20	Oregon	1,724	0.98%
9	Pennsylvania	4,409	2.51%
44	Rhode Island	258	0.15%
15	South Carolina	2,413	1.37%
46	South Dakota	180	0.10%
12	Tennessee	2,902	1.65%
2	Texas	16,027	9.12%
25	Utah	1,130	0.64%
47	Vermont	115	0.07%
16	Virginia	1,996	1.14%
32	Washington	706	0.40%
49	West Virginia	86	0.05%
24	Wisconsin	1,363	0.78%
48	Wyoming	91	0.05%

RANK ORDER

RANK	STATE	PRISONERS	% of USA
1	California	70,259	39.98%
2	Texas	16,027	9.12%
3	New York	7,782	4.43%
4	Florida	6,785	3.86%
5	Louisiana	6,303	3.59%
6	North Carolina	5,801	3.30%
7	New Jersey	5,157	2.93%
8	Illinois	4,948	2.82%
9	Pennsylvania	4,409	2.51%
10	Ohio	4,118	2.34%
11	Georgia	3,457	1.97%
12	Tennessee	2,902	1.65%
13	Michigan	2,807	1.60%
14	Missouri	2,739	1.56%
15	South Carolina	2,413	1.37%
16	Virginia	1,996	1.14%
17	Alabama	1,894	1.08%
18	Kentucky	1,847	1.05%
19	Arizona	1,831	1.04%
20	Oregon	1,724	0.98%
21	Arkansas	1,614	0.92%
22	Maryland	1,435	0.82%
23	Kansas	1,410	0.80%
24	Wisconsin	1,363	0.78%
25	Utah	1,130	0.64%
26	Colorado	1,081	0.62%
27	New Mexico	1,036	0.59%
28	Massachusetts	1,023	0.58%
29	Hawaii	1,022	0.58%
30	Minnesota	964	0.55%
31	Iowa	886	0.50%
32	Washington	706	0.40%
33	Indiana	691	0.39%
34	Alaska	676	0.38%
35	Nevada	642	0.37%
36	Idaho	589	0.34%
37	Connecticut	523	0.30%
38	Montana	453	0.26%
39	Nebraska	348	0.20%
40	Delaware	339	0.19%
41	New Hampshire	296	0.17%
42	Mississippi	285	0.16%
43	Oklahoma	271	0.15%
44	Rhode Island	258	0.15%
45	Maine	245	0.14%
46	South Dakota	180	0.10%
47	Vermont	115	0.07%
48	Wyoming	91	0.05%
49	West Virginia	86	0.05%
50	North Dakota	77	0.04%
	District of Columbia	692	0.39%

Source: U.S. Department of Justice, Bureau of Justice Statistics
   "Correctional Populations in the United States, 1995" (May 1997, NCJ-163916)
*Includes other conditional release violators. Does not include 2,915 federal parole violators returned to prison.

Escapees Returned to State Prisons in 1995

National Total = 10,716 Prisoners*

RANK	STATE	PRISONERS	% of USA
12	Alabama	194	1.81%
44	Alaska	3	0.03%
25	Arizona	45	0.42%
33	Arkansas	17	0.16%
8	California	386	3.60%
7	Colorado	420	3.92%
10	Connecticut	249	2.32%
23	Delaware	52	0.49%
9	Florida	298	2.78%
22	Georgia	81	0.76%
44	Hawaii	3	0.03%
43	Idaho	4	0.04%
2	Illinois	1,002	9.35%
32	Indiana	18	0.17%
5	Iowa	562	5.24%
30	Kansas	24	0.22%
17	Kentucky	107	1.00%
19	Louisiana	92	0.86%
39	Maine	8	0.07%
18	Maryland	102	0.95%
31	Massachusetts	21	0.20%
3	Michigan	943	8.80%
46	Minnesota	0	0.00%
24	Mississippi	49	0.46%
4	Missouri	832	7.76%
46	Montana	0	0.00%
26	Nebraska	34	0.32%
20	Nevada	87	0.81%
34	New Hampshire	14	0.13%
16	New Jersey	116	1.08%
29	New Mexico	29	0.27%
1	New York	3,172	29.60%
11	North Carolina	207	1.93%
42	North Dakota	6	0.06%
35	Ohio	12	0.11%
6	Oklahoma	513	4.79%
15	Oregon	126	1.18%
46	Pennsylvania	0	0.00%
26	Rhode Island	34	0.32%
13	South Carolina	150	1.40%
36	South Dakota	10	0.09%
21	Tennessee	84	0.78%
39	Texas	8	0.07%
39	Utah	8	0.07%
28	Vermont	32	0.30%
46	Virginia	0	0.00%
14	Washington	148	1.38%
37	West Virginia	9	0.08%
46	Wisconsin	0	0.00%
37	Wyoming	9	0.08%

RANK	STATE	PRISONERS	% of USA
1	New York	3,172	29.60%
2	Illinois	1,002	9.35%
3	Michigan	943	8.80%
4	Missouri	832	7.76%
5	Iowa	562	5.24%
6	Oklahoma	513	4.79%
7	Colorado	420	3.92%
8	California	386	3.60%
9	Florida	298	2.78%
10	Connecticut	249	2.32%
11	North Carolina	207	1.93%
12	Alabama	194	1.81%
13	South Carolina	150	1.40%
14	Washington	148	1.38%
15	Oregon	126	1.18%
16	New Jersey	116	1.08%
17	Kentucky	107	1.00%
18	Maryland	102	0.95%
19	Louisiana	92	0.86%
20	Nevada	87	0.81%
21	Tennessee	84	0.78%
22	Georgia	81	0.76%
23	Delaware	52	0.49%
24	Mississippi	49	0.46%
25	Arizona	45	0.42%
26	Nebraska	34	0.32%
26	Rhode Island	34	0.32%
28	Vermont	32	0.30%
29	New Mexico	29	0.27%
30	Kansas	24	0.22%
31	Massachusetts	21	0.20%
32	Indiana	18	0.17%
33	Arkansas	17	0.16%
34	New Hampshire	14	0.13%
35	Ohio	12	0.11%
36	South Dakota	10	0.09%
37	West Virginia	9	0.08%
37	Wyoming	9	0.08%
39	Maine	8	0.07%
39	Texas	8	0.07%
39	Utah	8	0.07%
42	North Dakota	6	0.06%
43	Idaho	4	0.04%
44	Alaska	3	0.03%
44	Hawaii	3	0.03%
46	Minnesota	0	0.00%
46	Montana	0	0.00%
46	Pennsylvania	0	0.00%
46	Virginia	0	0.00%
46	Wisconsin	0	0.00%
	District of Columbia	396	3.70%

Source: U.S. Department of Justice, Bureau of Justice Statistics
"Correctional Populations in the United States, 1995" (May 1997, NCJ-163916)
*Includes AWOLs returned. Federal data were not reported.

Prisoners Released from State Correctional Institutions in 1995

National Total = 469,255 Prisoners*

ALPHA ORDER

RANK	STATE	PRISONERS	% of USA
15	Alabama	7,857	1.67%
36	Alaska	1,896	0.40%
16	Arizona	7,462	1.59%
26	Arkansas	4,700	1.00%
1	California	106,438	22.68%
25	Colorado	4,988	1.06%
39	Connecticut	1,586	0.34%
41	Delaware	1,194	0.25%
6	Florida	19,626	4.18%
8	Georgia	13,759	2.93%
38	Hawaii	1,608	0.34%
37	Idaho	1,846	0.39%
4	Illinois	23,244	4.95%
18	Indiana	7,214	1.54%
28	Iowa	3,603	0.77%
29	Kansas	3,446	0.73%
22	Kentucky	5,974	1.27%
11	Louisiana	11,753	2.50%
46	Maine	764	0.16%
14	Maryland	9,085	1.94%
27	Massachusetts	4,265	0.91%
10	Michigan	12,086	2.58%
33	Minnesota	3,051	0.65%
29	Mississippi	3,446	0.73%
13	Missouri	10,572	2.25%
47	Montana	609	0.13%
40	Nebraska	1,338	0.29%
31	Nevada	3,200	0.68%
42	New Hampshire	978	0.21%
9	New Jersey	12,586	2.68%
35	New Mexico	1,954	0.42%
3	New York	32,949	7.02%
7	North Carolina	14,866	3.17%
50	North Dakota	435	0.09%
5	Ohio	19,923	4.25%
21	Oklahoma	6,206	1.32%
32	Oregon	3,118	0.66%
19	Pennsylvania	6,951	1.48%
44	Rhode Island	913	0.19%
17	South Carolina	7,457	1.59%
45	South Dakota	846	0.18%
20	Tennessee	6,278	1.34%
2	Texas	45,861	9.77%
34	Utah	2,001	0.43%
48	Vermont	503	0.11%
12	Virginia	11,022	2.35%
24	Washington	5,394	1.15%
43	West Virginia	965	0.21%
23	Wisconsin	5,745	1.22%
49	Wyoming	450	0.10%

RANK ORDER

RANK	STATE	PRISONERS	% of USA
1	California	106,438	22.68%
2	Texas	45,861	9.77%
3	New York	32,949	7.02%
4	Illinois	23,244	4.95%
5	Ohio	19,923	4.25%
6	Florida	19,626	4.18%
7	North Carolina	14,866	3.17%
8	Georgia	13,759	2.93%
9	New Jersey	12,586	2.68%
10	Michigan	12,086	2.58%
11	Louisiana	11,753	2.50%
12	Virginia	11,022	2.35%
13	Missouri	10,572	2.25%
14	Maryland	9,085	1.94%
15	Alabama	7,857	1.67%
16	Arizona	7,462	1.59%
17	South Carolina	7,457	1.59%
18	Indiana	7,214	1.54%
19	Pennsylvania	6,951	1.48%
20	Tennessee	6,278	1.34%
21	Oklahoma	6,206	1.32%
22	Kentucky	5,974	1.27%
23	Wisconsin	5,745	1.22%
24	Washington	5,394	1.15%
25	Colorado	4,988	1.06%
26	Arkansas	4,700	1.00%
27	Massachusetts	4,265	0.91%
28	Iowa	3,603	0.77%
29	Kansas	3,446	0.73%
29	Mississippi	3,446	0.73%
31	Nevada	3,200	0.68%
32	Oregon	3,118	0.66%
33	Minnesota	3,051	0.65%
34	Utah	2,001	0.43%
35	New Mexico	1,954	0.42%
36	Alaska	1,896	0.40%
37	Idaho	1,846	0.39%
38	Hawaii	1,608	0.34%
39	Connecticut	1,586	0.34%
40	Nebraska	1,338	0.29%
41	Delaware	1,194	0.25%
42	New Hampshire	978	0.21%
43	West Virginia	965	0.21%
44	Rhode Island	913	0.19%
45	South Dakota	846	0.18%
46	Maine	764	0.16%
47	Montana	609	0.13%
48	Vermont	503	0.11%
49	Wyoming	450	0.10%
50	North Dakota	435	0.09%
	District of Columbia	5,244	1.12%

Source: U.S. Department of Justice, Bureau of Justice Statistics
   "Correctional Populations in the United States, 1995" (May 1997, NCJ-163916)
*Includes conditional releases, unconditional releases, escapees, out on appeal, deaths and other releases. Does not include 22,603 federal prisoners released.

State Prisoners Released with Conditions in 1995

National Total = 370,736 Prisoners*

ALPHA ORDER

ALPHA ORDER

RANK	STATE	PRISONERS	% of USA
21	Alabama	4,340	1.17%
34	Alaska	1,536	0.41%
16	Arizona	6,629	1.79%
22	Arkansas	3,705	1.00%
1	California	98,561	26.59%
27	Colorado	2,998	0.81%
38	Connecticut	1,173	0.32%
44	Delaware	543	0.15%
13	Florida	7,973	2.15%
7	Georgia	9,979	2.69%
36	Hawaii	1,421	0.38%
33	Idaho	1,600	0.43%
4	Illinois	21,439	5.78%
15	Indiana	6,697	1.81%
26	Iowa	3,059	0.83%
24	Kansas	3,218	0.87%
25	Kentucky	3,142	0.85%
6	Louisiana	11,092	2.99%
47	Maine	427	0.12%
14	Maryland	7,946	2.14%
39	Massachusetts	1,124	0.30%
10	Michigan	9,078	2.45%
29	Minnesota	2,769	0.75%
32	Mississippi	1,606	0.43%
11	Missouri	8,949	2.41%
46	Montana	476	0.13%
42	Nebraska	718	0.19%
35	Nevada	1,515	0.41%
41	New Hampshire	809	0.22%
9	New Jersey	9,344	2.52%
37	New Mexico	1,194	0.32%
3	New York	26,895	7.25%
5	North Carolina	12,905	3.48%
49	North Dakota	313	0.08%
12	Ohio	8,262	2.23%
30	Oklahoma	2,675	0.72%
28	Oregon	2,973	0.80%
17	Pennsylvania	5,604	1.51%
40	Rhode Island	852	0.23%
20	South Carolina	4,673	1.26%
45	South Dakota	507	0.14%
19	Tennessee	4,704	1.27%
2	Texas	42,055	11.34%
31	Utah	1,808	0.49%
48	Vermont	397	0.11%
8	Virginia	9,562	2.58%
23	Washington	3,380	0.91%
43	West Virginia	634	0.17%
18	Wisconsin	4,873	1.31%
50	Wyoming	263	0.07%

RANK ORDER

RANK	STATE	PRISONERS	% of USA
1	California	98,561	26.59%
2	Texas	42,055	11.34%
3	New York	26,895	7.25%
4	Illinois	21,439	5.78%
5	North Carolina	12,905	3.48%
6	Louisiana	11,092	2.99%
7	Georgia	9,979	2.69%
8	Virginia	9,562	2.58%
9	New Jersey	9,344	2.52%
10	Michigan	9,078	2.45%
11	Missouri	8,949	2.41%
12	Ohio	8,262	2.23%
13	Florida	7,973	2.15%
14	Maryland	7,946	2.14%
15	Indiana	6,697	1.81%
16	Arizona	6,629	1.79%
17	Pennsylvania	5,604	1.51%
18	Wisconsin	4,873	1.31%
19	Tennessee	4,704	1.27%
20	South Carolina	4,673	1.26%
21	Alabama	4,340	1.17%
22	Arkansas	3,705	1.00%
23	Washington	3,380	0.91%
24	Kansas	3,218	0.87%
25	Kentucky	3,142	0.85%
26	Iowa	3,059	0.83%
27	Colorado	2,998	0.81%
28	Oregon	2,973	0.80%
29	Minnesota	2,769	0.75%
30	Oklahoma	2,675	0.72%
31	Utah	1,808	0.49%
32	Mississippi	1,606	0.43%
33	Idaho	1,600	0.43%
34	Alaska	1,536	0.41%
35	Nevada	1,515	0.41%
36	Hawaii	1,421	0.38%
37	New Mexico	1,194	0.32%
38	Connecticut	1,173	0.32%
39	Massachusetts	1,124	0.30%
40	Rhode Island	852	0.23%
41	New Hampshire	809	0.22%
42	Nebraska	718	0.19%
43	West Virginia	634	0.17%
44	Delaware	543	0.15%
45	South Dakota	507	0.14%
46	Montana	476	0.13%
47	Maine	427	0.12%
48	Vermont	397	0.11%
49	North Dakota	313	0.08%
50	Wyoming	263	0.07%
	District of Columbia	2,341	0.63%

Source: U.S. Department of Justice, Bureau of Justice Statistics
"Correctional Populations in the United States, 1995" (May 1997, NCJ-163916)
Released on parole, probation, supervised mandatory release or other conditions. Does not include 3,747 federal prisoners released with conditions.

State Prisoners Released Conditionally as a Percent of All Releases in 1995

National Percent = 79.0% of Prisoners Released*

ALPHA ORDER				RANK ORDER		
RANK	STATE	PERCENT		RANK	STATE	PERCENT
41	Alabama	55.2		1	Oregon	95.3
22	Alaska	81.0		2	Louisiana	94.4
11	Arizona	88.8		3	Kansas	93.4
25	Arkansas	78.8		4	Rhode Island	93.3
6	California	92.6		5	Indiana	92.8
37	Colorado	60.1		6	California	92.6
30	Connecticut	74.0		7	Illinois	92.2
46	Delaware	45.5		8	Texas	91.7
49	Florida	40.6		9	Minnesota	90.8
31	Georgia	72.5		10	Utah	90.4
12	Hawaii	88.4		11	Arizona	88.8
16	Idaho	86.7		12	Hawaii	88.4
7	Illinois	92.2		13	Maryland	87.5
5	Indiana	92.8		14	North Carolina	86.8
17	Iowa	84.9		14	Virginia	86.8
3	Kansas	93.4		16	Idaho	86.7
43	Kentucky	52.6		17	Iowa	84.9
2	Louisiana	94.4		18	Wisconsin	84.8
40	Maine	55.9		19	Missouri	84.6
13	Maryland	87.5		20	New Hampshire	82.7
50	Massachusetts	26.4		21	New York	81.6
27	Michigan	75.1		22	Alaska	81.0
9	Minnesota	90.8		23	Pennsylvania	80.6
45	Mississippi	46.6		24	Vermont	78.9
19	Missouri	84.6		25	Arkansas	78.8
26	Montana	78.2		26	Montana	78.2
42	Nebraska	53.7		27	Michigan	75.1
44	Nevada	47.3		28	Tennessee	74.9
20	New Hampshire	82.7		29	New Jersey	74.2
29	New Jersey	74.2		30	Connecticut	74.0
36	New Mexico	61.1		31	Georgia	72.5
21	New York	81.6		32	North Dakota	72.0
14	North Carolina	86.8		33	West Virginia	65.7
32	North Dakota	72.0		34	South Carolina	62.7
48	Ohio	41.5		34	Washington	62.7
47	Oklahoma	43.1		36	New Mexico	61.1
1	Oregon	95.3		37	Colorado	60.1
23	Pennsylvania	80.6		38	South Dakota	59.9
4	Rhode Island	93.3		39	Wyoming	58.4
34	South Carolina	62.7		40	Maine	55.9
38	South Dakota	59.9		41	Alabama	55.2
28	Tennessee	74.9		42	Nebraska	53.7
8	Texas	91.7		43	Kentucky	52.6
10	Utah	90.4		44	Nevada	47.3
24	Vermont	78.9		45	Mississippi	46.6
14	Virginia	86.8		46	Delaware	45.5
34	Washington	62.7		47	Oklahoma	43.1
33	West Virginia	65.7		48	Ohio	41.5
18	Wisconsin	84.8		49	Florida	40.6
39	Wyoming	58.4		50	Massachusetts	26.4
					District of Columbia	44.6

Source: Morgan Quitno Press using data from U.S. Department of Justice, Bureau of Justice Statistics
"Correctional Populations in the United States, 1995" (May 1997, NCJ-163916)
*Released on parole, probation, supervised mandatory release or other conditions. Does not include federal prisoners released with conditions. Federal percent is 16.6% of releases. The combined state and federal percent is 76.1% of prisoners released are released with conditions.

State Prisoners Released on Parole in 1995

National Total = 147,139 Prisoners*

RANK	STATE	PRISONERS	% of USA
20	Alabama	2,246	1.53%
44	Alaska	64	0.04%
25	Arizona	1,271	0.86%
13	Arkansas	3,354	2.28%
49	California	0	0.00%
18	Colorado	2,535	1.72%
39	Connecticut	185	0.13%
45	Delaware	39	0.03%
42	Florida	124	0.08%
6	Georgia	8,660	5.89%
31	Hawaii	666	0.45%
33	Idaho	659	0.45%
46	Illinois	33	0.02%
49	Indiana	0	0.00%
23	Iowa	1,608	1.09%
16	Kansas	2,882	1.96%
19	Kentucky	2,439	1.66%
21	Louisiana	1,901	1.29%
47	Maine	4	0.00%
10	Maryland	3,971	2.70%
26	Massachusetts	1,124	0.76%
4	Michigan	9,078	6.17%
47	Minnesota	4	0.00%
28	Mississippi	860	0.58%
8	Missouri	5,374	3.65%
37	Montana	346	0.24%
30	Nebraska	718	0.49%
24	Nevada	1,515	1.03%
29	New Hampshire	728	0.49%
5	New Jersey	8,832	6.00%
27	New Mexico	1,098	0.75%
1	New York	22,418	15.24%
3	North Carolina	12,905	8.77%
40	North Dakota	178	0.12%
9	Ohio	4,370	2.97%
32	Oklahoma	661	0.45%
15	Oregon	2,973	2.02%
7	Pennsylvania	5,604	3.81%
35	Rhode Island	475	0.32%
14	South Carolina	3,315	2.25%
36	South Dakota	438	0.30%
17	Tennessee	2,758	1.87%
2	Texas	17,149	11.65%
22	Utah	1,808	1.23%
38	Vermont	207	0.14%
12	Virginia	3,505	2.38%
43	Washington	120	0.08%
34	West Virginia	576	0.39%
11	Wisconsin	3,937	2.68%
41	Wyoming	161	0.11%

RANK	STATE	PRISONERS	% of USA
1	New York	22,418	15.24%
2	Texas	17,149	11.65%
3	North Carolina	12,905	8.77%
4	Michigan	9,078	6.17%
5	New Jersey	8,832	6.00%
6	Georgia	8,660	5.89%
7	Pennsylvania	5,604	3.81%
8	Missouri	5,374	3.65%
9	Ohio	4,370	2.97%
10	Maryland	3,971	2.70%
11	Wisconsin	3,937	2.68%
12	Virginia	3,505	2.38%
13	Arkansas	3,354	2.28%
14	South Carolina	3,315	2.25%
15	Oregon	2,973	2.02%
16	Kansas	2,882	1.96%
17	Tennessee	2,758	1.87%
18	Colorado	2,535	1.72%
19	Kentucky	2,439	1.66%
20	Alabama	2,246	1.53%
21	Louisiana	1,901	1.29%
22	Utah	1,808	1.23%
23	Iowa	1,608	1.09%
24	Nevada	1,515	1.03%
25	Arizona	1,271	0.86%
26	Massachusetts	1,124	0.76%
27	New Mexico	1,098	0.75%
28	Mississippi	860	0.58%
29	New Hampshire	728	0.49%
30	Nebraska	718	0.49%
31	Hawaii	666	0.45%
32	Oklahoma	661	0.45%
33	Idaho	659	0.45%
34	West Virginia	576	0.39%
35	Rhode Island	475	0.32%
36	South Dakota	438	0.30%
37	Montana	346	0.24%
38	Vermont	207	0.14%
39	Connecticut	185	0.13%
40	North Dakota	178	0.12%
41	Wyoming	161	0.11%
42	Florida	124	0.08%
43	Washington	120	0.08%
44	Alaska	64	0.04%
45	Delaware	39	0.03%
46	Illinois	33	0.02%
47	Maine	4	0.00%
47	Minnesota	4	0.00%
49	California	0	0.00%
49	Indiana	0	0.00%
	District of Columbia	1,263	0.86%

Source: U.S. Department of Justice, Bureau of Justice Statistics
  "Correctional Populations in the United States, 1995" (May 1997, NCJ-163916)
Does not include 2,185 federal prisoners released on parole.

State Prisoners Released on Probation in 1995

National Total = 26,576 Prisoners*

RANK	STATE	PRISONERS	% of USA
5	Alabama	2,094	7.88%
11	Alaska	851	3.20%
26	Arizona	72	0.27%
29	Arkansas	0	0.00%
29	California	0	0.00%
20	Colorado	188	0.71%
29	Connecticut	0	0.00%
29	Delaware	0	0.00%
2	Florida	2,781	10.46%
28	Georgia	47	0.18%
12	Hawaii	753	2.83%
10	Idaho	941	3.54%
29	Illinois	0	0.00%
1	Indiana	3,430	12.91%
15	Iowa	509	1.92%
21	Kansas	141	0.53%
14	Kentucky	703	2.65%
18	Louisiana	366	1.38%
16	Maine	413	1.55%
29	Maryland	0	0.00%
29	Massachusetts	0	0.00%
29	Michigan	0	0.00%
29	Minnesota	0	0.00%
13	Mississippi	746	2.81%
4	Missouri	2,641	9.94%
22	Montana	130	0.49%
29	Nebraska	0	0.00%
29	Nevada	0	0.00%
25	New Hampshire	81	0.30%
29	New Jersey	0	0.00%
29	New Mexico	0	0.00%
29	New York	0	0.00%
29	North Carolina	0	0.00%
23	North Dakota	127	0.48%
3	Ohio	2,648	9.96%
6	Oklahoma	1,811	6.81%
29	Oregon	0	0.00%
29	Pennsylvania	0	0.00%
17	Rhode Island	371	1.40%
9	South Carolina	1,356	5.10%
29	South Dakota	0	0.00%
8	Tennessee	1,446	5.44%
7	Texas	1,580	5.95%
29	Utah	0	0.00%
19	Vermont	190	0.71%
29	Virginia	0	0.00%
29	Washington	0	0.00%
27	West Virginia	58	0.22%
29	Wisconsin	0	0.00%
24	Wyoming	102	0.38%

RANK	STATE	PRISONERS	% of USA
1	Indiana	3,430	12.91%
2	Florida	2,781	10.46%
3	Ohio	2,648	9.96%
4	Missouri	2,641	9.94%
5	Alabama	2,094	7.88%
6	Oklahoma	1,811	6.81%
7	Texas	1,580	5.95%
8	Tennessee	1,446	5.44%
9	South Carolina	1,356	5.10%
10	Idaho	941	3.54%
11	Alaska	851	3.20%
12	Hawaii	753	2.83%
13	Mississippi	746	2.81%
14	Kentucky	703	2.65%
15	Iowa	509	1.92%
16	Maine	413	1.55%
17	Rhode Island	371	1.40%
18	Louisiana	366	1.38%
19	Vermont	190	0.71%
20	Colorado	188	0.71%
21	Kansas	141	0.53%
22	Montana	130	0.49%
23	North Dakota	127	0.48%
24	Wyoming	102	0.38%
25	New Hampshire	81	0.30%
26	Arizona	72	0.27%
27	West Virginia	58	0.22%
28	Georgia	47	0.18%
29	Arkansas	0	0.00%
29	California	0	0.00%
29	Connecticut	0	0.00%
29	Delaware	0	0.00%
29	Illinois	0	0.00%
29	Maryland	0	0.00%
29	Massachusetts	0	0.00%
29	Michigan	0	0.00%
29	Minnesota	0	0.00%
29	Nebraska	0	0.00%
29	Nevada	0	0.00%
29	New Jersey	0	0.00%
29	New Mexico	0	0.00%
29	New York	0	0.00%
29	North Carolina	0	0.00%
29	Oregon	0	0.00%
29	Pennsylvania	0	0.00%
29	South Dakota	0	0.00%
29	Utah	0	0.00%
29	Virginia	0	0.00%
29	Washington	0	0.00%
29	Wisconsin	0	0.00%
	District of Columbia	0	0.00%

Source: U.S. Department of Justice, Bureau of Justice Statistics
"Correctional Populations in the United States, 1995" (May 1997, NCJ-163916)
*Does not include 16 federal prisoners released on probation.

State Prisoners Released on Supervised Mandatory Release in 1995

National Total = 177,402 Prisoners*

ALPHA ORDER

RANK ORDER

RANK	STATE	PRISONERS	% of USA	RANK	STATE	PRISONERS	% of USA
17	Alabama	0	0.00%	1	California	98,561	55.56%
14	Alaska	267	0.15%	2	Texas	23,326	13.15%
15	Arizona	102	0.06%	3	Illinois	21,406	12.07%
17	Arkansas	0	0.00%	4	Louisiana	8,825	4.97%
1	California	98,561	55.56%	5	Virginia	6,057	3.41%
13	Colorado	275	0.16%	6	New York	4,477	2.52%
17	Connecticut	0	0.00%	7	Maryland	3,963	2.23%
12	Delaware	504	0.28%	8	Indiana	3,267	1.84%
17	Florida	0	0.00%	9	Washington	3,260	1.84%
17	Georgia	0	0.00%	10	Minnesota	2,107	1.19%
17	Hawaii	0	0.00%	11	Wisconsin	936	0.53%
17	Idaho	0	0.00%	12	Delaware	504	0.28%
3	Illinois	21,406	12.07%	13	Colorado	275	0.16%
8	Indiana	3,267	1.84%	14	Alaska	267	0.15%
17	Iowa	0	0.00%	15	Arizona	102	0.06%
17	Kansas	0	0.00%	16	South Dakota	69	0.04%
17	Kentucky	0	0.00%	17	Alabama	0	0.00%
4	Louisiana	8,825	4.97%	17	Arkansas	0	0.00%
17	Maine	0	0.00%	17	Connecticut	0	0.00%
7	Maryland	3,963	2.23%	17	Florida	0	0.00%
17	Massachusetts	0	0.00%	17	Georgia	0	0.00%
17	Michigan	0	0.00%	17	Hawaii	0	0.00%
10	Minnesota	2,107	1.19%	17	Idaho	0	0.00%
17	Mississippi	0	0.00%	17	Iowa	0	0.00%
17	Missouri	0	0.00%	17	Kansas	0	0.00%
17	Montana	0	0.00%	17	Kentucky	0	0.00%
17	Nebraska	0	0.00%	17	Maine	0	0.00%
17	Nevada	0	0.00%	17	Massachusetts	0	0.00%
17	New Hampshire	0	0.00%	17	Michigan	0	0.00%
17	New Jersey	0	0.00%	17	Mississippi	0	0.00%
17	New Mexico	0	0.00%	17	Missouri	0	0.00%
6	New York	4,477	2.52%	17	Montana	0	0.00%
17	North Carolina	0	0.00%	17	Nebraska	0	0.00%
17	North Dakota	0	0.00%	17	Nevada	0	0.00%
17	Ohio	0	0.00%	17	New Hampshire	0	0.00%
17	Oklahoma	0	0.00%	17	New Jersey	0	0.00%
17	Oregon	0	0.00%	17	New Mexico	0	0.00%
17	Pennsylvania	0	0.00%	17	North Carolina	0	0.00%
17	Rhode Island	0	0.00%	17	North Dakota	0	0.00%
17	South Carolina	0	0.00%	17	Ohio	0	0.00%
16	South Dakota	69	0.04%	17	Oklahoma	0	0.00%
17	Tennessee	0	0.00%	17	Oregon	0	0.00%
2	Texas	23,326	13.15%	17	Pennsylvania	0	0.00%
17	Utah	0	0.00%	17	Rhode Island	0	0.00%
17	Vermont	0	0.00%	17	South Carolina	0	0.00%
5	Virginia	6,057	3.41%	17	Tennessee	0	0.00%
9	Washington	3,260	1.84%	17	Utah	0	0.00%
17	West Virginia	0	0.00%	17	Vermont	0	0.00%
11	Wisconsin	936	0.53%	17	West Virginia	0	0.00%
17	Wyoming	0	0.00%	17	Wyoming	0	0.00%
					District of Columbia	0	0.00%

Source: U.S. Department of Justice, Bureau of Justice Statistics
"Correctional Populations in the United States, 1995" (May 1997, NCJ-163916)
*Does not include 1,546 federal prisoners released on supervised mandatory release.

State Prisoners Released Unconditionally in 1995

National Total = 70,027 Prisoners*

ALPHA ORDER					RANK ORDER			
RANK	STATE	PRISONERS	% of USA		RANK	STATE	PRISONERS	% of USA
3	Alabama	3,084	4.40%		1	Ohio	11,510	16.44%
33	Alaska	333	0.48%		2	Florida	10,923	15.60%
30	Arizona	451	0.64%		3	Alabama	3,084	4.40%
23	Arkansas	713	1.02%		4	Georgia	2,983	4.26%
17	California	1,335	1.91%		5	Oklahoma	2,933	4.19%
15	Colorado	1,452	2.07%		6	New Jersey	2,912	4.16%
39	Connecticut	189	0.27%		7	Kentucky	2,617	3.74%
28	Delaware	461	0.66%		8	South Carolina	2,341	3.34%
2	Florida	10,923	15.60%		9	Massachusetts	2,226	3.18%
4	Georgia	2,983	4.26%		10	Washington	1,816	2.59%
44	Hawaii	146	0.21%		11	Mississippi	1,768	2.52%
38	Idaho	238	0.34%		12	North Carolina	1,688	2.41%
27	Illinois	541	0.77%		13	Nevada	1,570	2.24%
29	Indiana	458	0.65%		14	New York	1,517	2.17%
32	Iowa	418	0.60%		15	Colorado	1,452	2.07%
39	Kansas	189	0.27%		16	Texas	1,404	2.00%
7	Kentucky	2,617	3.74%		17	California	1,335	1.91%
31	Louisiana	446	0.64%		18	Tennessee	1,309	1.87%
35	Maine	314	0.45%		19	Pennsylvania	1,088	1.55%
20	Maryland	937	1.34%		20	Maryland	937	1.34%
9	Massachusetts	2,226	3.18%		21	Virginia	929	1.33%
22	Michigan	846	1.21%		22	Michigan	846	1.21%
37	Minnesota	273	0.39%		23	Arkansas	713	1.02%
11	Mississippi	1,768	2.52%		24	New Mexico	693	0.99%
26	Missouri	542	0.77%		25	Nebraska	577	0.82%
45	Montana	122	0.17%		26	Missouri	542	0.77%
25	Nebraska	577	0.82%		27	Illinois	541	0.77%
13	Nevada	1,570	2.24%		28	Delaware	461	0.66%
42	New Hampshire	154	0.22%		29	Indiana	458	0.65%
6	New Jersey	2,912	4.16%		30	Arizona	451	0.64%
24	New Mexico	693	0.99%		31	Louisiana	446	0.64%
14	New York	1,517	2.17%		32	Iowa	418	0.60%
12	North Carolina	1,688	2.41%		33	Alaska	333	0.48%
46	North Dakota	115	0.16%		34	South Dakota	318	0.45%
1	Ohio	11,510	16.44%		35	Maine	314	0.45%
5	Oklahoma	2,933	4.19%		36	West Virginia	304	0.43%
49	Oregon	10	0.01%		37	Minnesota	273	0.39%
19	Pennsylvania	1,088	1.55%		38	Idaho	238	0.34%
50	Rhode Island	7	0.01%		39	Connecticut	189	0.27%
8	South Carolina	2,341	3.34%		39	Kansas	189	0.27%
34	South Dakota	318	0.45%		41	Utah	164	0.23%
18	Tennessee	1,309	1.87%		42	New Hampshire	154	0.22%
16	Texas	1,404	2.00%		43	Wyoming	150	0.21%
41	Utah	164	0.23%		44	Hawaii	146	0.21%
47	Vermont	106	0.15%		45	Montana	122	0.17%
21	Virginia	929	1.33%		46	North Dakota	115	0.16%
10	Washington	1,816	2.59%		47	Vermont	106	0.15%
36	West Virginia	304	0.43%		48	Wisconsin	99	0.14%
48	Wisconsin	99	0.14%		49	Oregon	10	0.01%
43	Wyoming	150	0.21%		50	Rhode Island	7	0.01%
						District of Columbia	2,308	3.30%

Source: U.S. Department of Justice, Bureau of Justice Statistics
   "Correctional Populations in the United States, 1995" (May 1997, NCJ-163916)
*Does not include 18,054 federal prisoners released without conditions.

State Prisoners Released Unconditionally as a Percent of All Releases in 1995

National Percent = 14.9% of Released Prisoners*

ALPHA ORDER

RANK	STATE	PERCENT
10	Alabama	39.3
25	Alaska	17.6
40	Arizona	6.0
28	Arkansas	15.2
48	California	1.3
18	Colorado	29.1
30	Connecticut	11.9
11	Delaware	38.6
2	Florida	55.7
21	Georgia	21.7
34	Hawaii	9.1
29	Idaho	12.9
46	Illinois	2.3
39	Indiana	6.3
31	Iowa	11.6
41	Kansas	5.5
7	Kentucky	43.8
44	Louisiana	3.8
9	Maine	41.1
33	Maryland	10.3
3	Massachusetts	52.2
38	Michigan	7.0
35	Minnesota	8.9
4	Mississippi	51.3
42	Missouri	5.1
24	Montana	20.0
8	Nebraska	43.1
5	Nevada	49.1
26	New Hampshire	15.7
20	New Jersey	23.1
13	New Mexico	35.5
43	New York	4.6
32	North Carolina	11.4
19	North Dakota	26.4
1	Ohio	57.8
6	Oklahoma	47.3
50	Oregon	0.3
26	Pennsylvania	15.7
49	Rhode Island	0.8
17	South Carolina	31.4
12	South Dakota	37.6
23	Tennessee	20.9
45	Texas	3.1
37	Utah	8.2
22	Vermont	21.1
36	Virginia	8.4
14	Washington	33.7
16	West Virginia	31.5
47	Wisconsin	1.7
15	Wyoming	33.3

RANK ORDER

RANK	STATE	PERCENT
1	Ohio	57.8
2	Florida	55.7
3	Massachusetts	52.2
4	Mississippi	51.3
5	Nevada	49.1
6	Oklahoma	47.3
7	Kentucky	43.8
8	Nebraska	43.1
9	Maine	41.1
10	Alabama	39.3
11	Delaware	38.6
12	South Dakota	37.6
13	New Mexico	35.5
14	Washington	33.7
15	Wyoming	33.3
16	West Virginia	31.5
17	South Carolina	31.4
18	Colorado	29.1
19	North Dakota	26.4
20	New Jersey	23.1
21	Georgia	21.7
22	Vermont	21.1
23	Tennessee	20.9
24	Montana	20.0
25	Alaska	17.6
26	New Hampshire	15.7
26	Pennsylvania	15.7
28	Arkansas	15.2
29	Idaho	12.9
30	Connecticut	11.9
31	Iowa	11.6
32	North Carolina	11.4
33	Maryland	10.3
34	Hawaii	9.1
35	Minnesota	8.9
36	Virginia	8.4
37	Utah	8.2
38	Michigan	7.0
39	Indiana	6.3
40	Arizona	6.0
41	Kansas	5.5
42	Missouri	5.1
43	New York	4.6
44	Louisiana	3.8
45	Texas	3.1
46	Illinois	2.3
47	Wisconsin	1.7
48	California	1.3
49	Rhode Island	0.8
50	Oregon	0.3
	District of Columbia	44.0

Source: Morgan Quitno Press using data from U.S. Department of Justice, Bureau of Justice Statistics
   "Correctional Populations in the United States, 1995" (May 1997, NCJ-163916)
*Does not include federal prisoners released without conditions. Federal percent is 79.9% of releases. The
combined state and federal percent is 18.1% of prisoners released are released without conditions.

State Prisoners Released on Appeal or Bond in 1995

National Total = 678 Prisoners*

ALPHA ORDER

RANK	STATE	PRISONERS	% of USA
2	Alabama	93	13.72%
19	Alaska	2	0.29%
24	Arizona	0	0.00%
7	Arkansas	21	3.10%
24	California	0	0.00%
14	Colorado	14	2.06%
21	Connecticut	1	0.15%
24	Delaware	0	0.00%
24	Florida	0	0.00%
24	Georgia	0	0.00%
24	Hawaii	0	0.00%
24	Idaho	0	0.00%
10	Illinois	18	2.65%
24	Indiana	0	0.00%
4	Iowa	40	5.90%
18	Kansas	5	0.74%
24	Kentucky	0	0.00%
24	Louisiana	0	0.00%
17	Maine	7	1.03%
24	Maryland	0	0.00%
24	Massachusetts	0	0.00%
11	Michigan	16	2.36%
24	Minnesota	0	0.00%
24	Mississippi	0	0.00%
12	Missouri	15	2.21%
24	Montana	0	0.00%
24	Nebraska	0	0.00%
19	Nevada	2	0.29%
21	New Hampshire	1	0.15%
3	New Jersey	62	9.14%
24	New Mexico	0	0.00%
1	New York	198	29.20%
24	North Carolina	0	0.00%
24	North Dakota	0	0.00%
9	Ohio	20	2.95%
24	Oklahoma	0	0.00%
6	Oregon	24	3.54%
5	Pennsylvania	26	3.83%
16	Rhode Island	9	1.33%
15	South Carolina	12	1.77%
21	South Dakota	1	0.15%
24	Tennessee	0	0.00%
24	Texas	0	0.00%
12	Utah	15	2.21%
24	Vermont	0	0.00%
24	Virginia	0	0.00%
7	Washington	21	3.10%
24	West Virginia	0	0.00%
24	Wisconsin	0	0.00%
24	Wyoming	0	0.00%

RANK ORDER

RANK	STATE	PRISONERS	% of USA
1	New York	198	29.20%
2	Alabama	93	13.72%
3	New Jersey	62	9.14%
4	Iowa	40	5.90%
5	Pennsylvania	26	3.83%
6	Oregon	24	3.54%
7	Arkansas	21	3.10%
7	Washington	21	3.10%
9	Ohio	20	2.95%
10	Illinois	18	2.65%
11	Michigan	16	2.36%
12	Missouri	15	2.21%
12	Utah	15	2.21%
14	Colorado	14	2.06%
15	South Carolina	12	1.77%
16	Rhode Island	9	1.33%
17	Maine	7	1.03%
18	Kansas	5	0.74%
19	Alaska	2	0.29%
19	Nevada	2	0.29%
21	Connecticut	1	0.15%
21	New Hampshire	1	0.15%
21	South Dakota	1	0.15%
24	Arizona	0	0.00%
24	California	0	0.00%
24	Delaware	0	0.00%
24	Florida	0	0.00%
24	Georgia	0	0.00%
24	Hawaii	0	0.00%
24	Idaho	0	0.00%
24	Indiana	0	0.00%
24	Kentucky	0	0.00%
24	Louisiana	0	0.00%
24	Maryland	0	0.00%
24	Massachusetts	0	0.00%
24	Minnesota	0	0.00%
24	Mississippi	0	0.00%
24	Montana	0	0.00%
24	Nebraska	0	0.00%
24	New Mexico	0	0.00%
24	North Carolina	0	0.00%
24	North Dakota	0	0.00%
24	Oklahoma	0	0.00%
24	Tennessee	0	0.00%
24	Texas	0	0.00%
24	Vermont	0	0.00%
24	Virginia	0	0.00%
24	West Virginia	0	0.00%
24	Wisconsin	0	0.00%
24	Wyoming	0	0.00%
	District of Columbia	55	8.11%

Source: U.S. Department of Justice, Bureau of Justice Statistics
    "Correctional Populations in the United States, 1995" (May 1997, NCJ-163916)
*Numbers of federal prisoners released on appeal or bond were not available.

State Prisoners Escaped in 1995

National Total = 10,874 Prisoners*

ALPHA ORDER

RANK	STATE	PRISONERS	% of USA
10	Alabama	187	1.72%
46	Alaska	2	0.02%
24	Arizona	30	0.28%
33	Arkansas	12	0.11%
5	California	648	5.96%
7	Colorado	363	3.34%
14	Connecticut	125	1.15%
36	Delaware	10	0.09%
8	Florida	297	2.73%
21	Georgia	80	0.74%
45	Hawaii	3	0.03%
40	Idaho	7	0.06%
4	Illinois	947	8.71%
31	Indiana	15	0.14%
37	Iowa	9	0.08%
29	Kansas	21	0.19%
15	Kentucky	117	1.08%
19	Louisiana	83	0.76%
38	Maine	8	0.07%
16	Maryland	95	0.87%
22	Massachusetts	34	0.31%
2	Michigan	1,507	13.86%
47	Minnesota	0	0.00%
27	Mississippi	22	0.20%
3	Missouri	995	9.15%
47	Montana	0	0.00%
24	Nebraska	30	0.28%
18	Nevada	88	0.81%
34	New Hampshire	11	0.10%
13	New Jersey	131	1.20%
22	New Mexico	34	0.31%
1	New York	3,296	30.31%
9	North Carolina	202	1.86%
42	North Dakota	6	0.06%
32	Ohio	14	0.13%
6	Oklahoma	532	4.89%
17	Oregon	90	0.83%
42	Pennsylvania	6	0.06%
27	Rhode Island	22	0.20%
11	South Carolina	158	1.45%
40	South Dakota	7	0.06%
20	Tennessee	82	0.75%
34	Texas	11	0.10%
38	Utah	8	0.07%
47	Vermont	0	0.00%
44	Virginia	4	0.04%
12	Washington	154	1.42%
30	West Virginia	20	0.18%
47	Wisconsin	0	0.00%
26	Wyoming	26	0.24%

RANK ORDER

RANK	STATE	PRISONERS	% of USA
1	New York	3,296	30.31%
2	Michigan	1,507	13.86%
3	Missouri	995	9.15%
4	Illinois	947	8.71%
5	California	648	5.96%
6	Oklahoma	532	4.89%
7	Colorado	363	3.34%
8	Florida	297	2.73%
9	North Carolina	202	1.86%
10	Alabama	187	1.72%
11	South Carolina	158	1.45%
12	Washington	154	1.42%
13	New Jersey	131	1.20%
14	Connecticut	125	1.15%
15	Kentucky	117	1.08%
16	Maryland	95	0.87%
17	Oregon	90	0.83%
18	Nevada	88	0.81%
19	Louisiana	83	0.76%
20	Tennessee	82	0.75%
21	Georgia	80	0.74%
22	Massachusetts	34	0.31%
22	New Mexico	34	0.31%
24	Arizona	30	0.28%
24	Nebraska	30	0.28%
26	Wyoming	26	0.24%
27	Mississippi	22	0.20%
27	Rhode Island	22	0.20%
29	Kansas	21	0.19%
30	West Virginia	20	0.18%
31	Indiana	15	0.14%
32	Ohio	14	0.13%
33	Arkansas	12	0.11%
34	New Hampshire	11	0.10%
34	Texas	11	0.10%
36	Delaware	10	0.09%
37	Iowa	9	0.08%
38	Maine	8	0.07%
38	Utah	8	0.07%
40	Idaho	7	0.06%
40	South Dakota	7	0.06%
42	North Dakota	6	0.06%
42	Pennsylvania	6	0.06%
44	Virginia	4	0.04%
45	Hawaii	3	0.03%
46	Alaska	2	0.02%
47	Minnesota	0	0.00%
47	Montana	0	0.00%
47	Vermont	0	0.00%
47	Wisconsin	0	0.00%
	District of Columbia	325	2.99%

Source: U.S. Department of Justice, Bureau of Justice Statistics
"Correctional Populations in the United States, 1995" (May 1997, NCJ-163916)
*Includes AWOLs. Numbers of escaped federal prisoners were not available.

State Prisoner Deaths in 1995

National Total = 3,133 Prisoners

ALPHA ORDER

RANK ORDER

RANK	STATE	DEATHS	% of USA		RANK	STATE	DEATHS	% of USA
11	Alabama	88	2.81%		1	Texas	399	12.74%
43	Alaska	5	0.16%		2	New York	396	12.64%
18	Arizona	58	1.85%		3	California	262	8.36%
26	Arkansas	26	0.83%		4	Florida	254	8.11%
3	California	262	8.36%		5	New Jersey	137	4.37%
27	Colorado	25	0.80%		6	Georgia	127	4.05%
22	Connecticut	42	1.34%		7	Pennsylvania	122	3.89%
36	Delaware	9	0.29%		8	Ohio	114	3.64%
4	Florida	254	8.11%		9	Michigan	104	3.32%
6	Georgia	127	4.05%		10	Illinois	103	3.29%
34	Hawaii	11	0.35%		11	Alabama	88	2.81%
46	Idaho	1	0.03%		12	Virginia	83	2.65%
10	Illinois	103	3.29%		13	North Carolina	69	2.20%
21	Indiana	44	1.40%		14	Louisiana	68	2.17%
36	Iowa	9	0.29%		15	Oklahoma	66	2.11%
31	Kansas	13	0.41%		16	Tennessee	64	2.04%
25	Kentucky	29	0.93%		17	South Carolina	63	2.01%
14	Louisiana	68	2.17%		18	Arizona	58	1.85%
49	Maine	0	0.00%		19	Maryland	54	1.72%
19	Maryland	54	1.72%		20	Missouri	53	1.69%
24	Massachusetts	34	1.09%		21	Indiana	44	1.40%
9	Michigan	104	3.32%		22	Connecticut	42	1.34%
36	Minnesota	9	0.29%		22	Mississippi	42	1.34%
22	Mississippi	42	1.34%		24	Massachusetts	34	1.09%
20	Missouri	53	1.69%		25	Kentucky	29	0.93%
34	Montana	11	0.35%		26	Arkansas	26	0.83%
31	Nebraska	13	0.41%		27	Colorado	25	0.80%
27	Nevada	25	0.80%		27	Nevada	25	0.80%
45	New Hampshire	2	0.06%		29	Washington	23	0.73%
5	New Jersey	137	4.37%		30	Oregon	21	0.67%
39	New Mexico	8	0.26%		31	Kansas	13	0.41%
2	New York	396	12.64%		31	Nebraska	13	0.41%
13	North Carolina	69	2.20%		31	Wisconsin	13	0.41%
46	North Dakota	1	0.03%		34	Hawaii	11	0.35%
8	Ohio	114	3.64%		34	Montana	11	0.35%
15	Oklahoma	66	2.11%		36	Delaware	9	0.29%
30	Oregon	21	0.67%		36	Iowa	9	0.29%
7	Pennsylvania	122	3.89%		36	Minnesota	9	0.29%
40	Rhode Island	7	0.22%		39	New Mexico	8	0.26%
17	South Carolina	63	2.01%		40	Rhode Island	7	0.22%
43	South Dakota	5	0.16%		40	West Virginia	7	0.22%
16	Tennessee	64	2.04%		42	Utah	6	0.19%
1	Texas	399	12.74%		43	Alaska	5	0.16%
42	Utah	6	0.19%		43	South Dakota	5	0.16%
49	Vermont	0	0.00%		45	New Hampshire	2	0.06%
12	Virginia	83	2.65%		46	Idaho	1	0.03%
29	Washington	23	0.73%		46	North Dakota	1	0.03%
40	West Virginia	7	0.22%		46	Wyoming	1	0.03%
31	Wisconsin	13	0.41%		49	Maine	0	0.00%
46	Wyoming	1	0.03%		49	Vermont	0	0.00%
						District of Columbia	7	0.22%

Source: U.S. Department of Justice, Bureau of Justice Statistics
"HIV in Prisons and Jails, 1995" (Bulletin, April 1997, NCJ-164260)

Death Rate of State Prisoners in 1995

National Rate = 311 State Prisoner Deaths per 100,000 Inmates

ALPHA ORDER

RANK	STATE	RATE
5	Alabama	438
44	Alaska	154
24	Arizona	277
19	Arkansas	286
36	California	199
33	Colorado	232
20	Connecticut	280
37	Delaware	194
7	Florida	410
10	Georgia	372
15	Hawaii	307
48	Idaho	31
26	Illinois	273
20	Indiana	280
43	Iowa	158
40	Kansas	188
32	Kentucky	243
27	Louisiana	270
49	Maine	0
30	Maryland	252
17	Massachusetts	296
31	Michigan	251
39	Minnesota	189
11	Mississippi	337
20	Missouri	280
1	Montana	581
4	Nebraska	464
12	Nevada	334
46	New Hampshire	97
3	New Jersey	535
37	New Mexico	194
2	New York	578
29	North Carolina	257
42	North Dakota	164
28	Ohio	262
9	Oklahoma	375
20	Oregon	280
8	Pennsylvania	409
34	Rhode Island	223
13	South Carolina	323
25	South Dakota	275
6	Tennessee	429
14	Texas	314
41	Utah	183
49	Vermont	0
16	Virginia	304
35	Washington	202
18	West Virginia	287
45	Wisconsin	122
47	Wyoming	76

RANK ORDER

RANK	STATE	RATE
1	Montana	581
2	New York	578
3	New Jersey	535
4	Nebraska	464
5	Alabama	438
6	Tennessee	429
7	Florida	410
8	Pennsylvania	409
9	Oklahoma	375
10	Georgia	372
11	Mississippi	337
12	Nevada	334
13	South Carolina	323
14	Texas	314
15	Hawaii	307
16	Virginia	304
17	Massachusetts	296
18	West Virginia	287
19	Arkansas	286
20	Connecticut	280
20	Indiana	280
20	Missouri	280
20	Oregon	280
24	Arizona	277
25	South Dakota	275
26	Illinois	273
27	Louisiana	270
28	Ohio	262
29	North Carolina	257
30	Maryland	252
31	Michigan	251
32	Kentucky	243
33	Colorado	232
34	Rhode Island	223
35	Washington	202
36	California	199
37	Delaware	194
37	New Mexico	194
39	Minnesota	189
40	Kansas	188
41	Utah	183
42	North Dakota	164
43	Iowa	158
44	Alaska	154
45	Wisconsin	122
46	New Hampshire	97
47	Wyoming	76
48	Idaho	31
49	Maine	0
49	Vermont	0
	District of Columbia	67

Source: U.S. Department of Justice, Bureau of Justice Statistics
   "HIV in Prisons and Jails, 1995" (Bulletin, April 1997, NCJ-164260)

State Prisoner Deaths by Illness or Other Natural Causes in 1995

National Total = 1,605 Deaths*

ALPHA ORDER

RANK ORDER

RANK	STATE	DEATHS	% of USA		RANK	STATE	DEATHS	% of USA
NA	Alabama**	NA	NA		1	Texas	273	17.01%
40	Alaska	3	0.19%		2	California	130	8.10%
11	Arizona	49	3.05%		3	New York	106	6.60%
23	Arkansas	18	1.12%		4	Michigan	95	5.92%
2	California	130	8.10%		5	Florida	87	5.42%
27	Colorado	15	0.93%		6	Ohio	81	5.05%
25	Connecticut	16	1.00%		7	South Carolina	62	3.86%
33	Delaware	8	0.50%		8	Georgia	57	3.55%
5	Florida	87	5.42%		9	Illinois	55	3.43%
8	Georgia	57	3.55%		10	Pennsylvania	54	3.36%
35	Hawaii	6	0.37%		11	Arizona	49	3.05%
42	Idaho	1	0.06%		12	Virginia	48	2.99%
9	Illinois	55	3.43%		13	Tennessee	46	2.87%
14	Indiana	40	2.49%		14	Indiana	40	2.49%
33	Iowa	8	0.50%		15	North Carolina	37	2.31%
29	Kansas	12	0.75%		16	Oklahoma	35	2.18%
19	Kentucky	27	1.68%		17	Mississippi	32	1.99%
NA	Louisiana**	NA	NA		18	Missouri	30	1.87%
45	Maine	0	0.00%		19	Kentucky	27	1.68%
21	Maryland	25	1.56%		20	New Jersey	26	1.62%
24	Massachusetts	17	1.06%		21	Maryland	25	1.56%
4	Michigan	95	5.92%		22	Washington	19	1.18%
37	Minnesota	5	0.31%		23	Arkansas	18	1.12%
17	Mississippi	32	1.99%		24	Massachusetts	17	1.06%
18	Missouri	30	1.87%		25	Connecticut	16	1.00%
32	Montana	9	0.56%		25	Oregon	16	1.00%
29	Nebraska	12	0.75%		27	Colorado	15	0.93%
27	Nevada	15	0.93%		27	Nevada	15	0.93%
45	New Hampshire	0	0.00%		29	Kansas	12	0.75%
20	New Jersey	26	1.62%		29	Nebraska	12	0.75%
NA	New Mexico**	NA	NA		31	Wisconsin	10	0.62%
3	New York	106	6.60%		32	Montana	9	0.56%
15	North Carolina	37	2.31%		33	Delaware	8	0.50%
42	North Dakota	1	0.06%		33	Iowa	8	0.50%
6	Ohio	81	5.05%		35	Hawaii	6	0.37%
16	Oklahoma	35	2.18%		35	West Virginia	6	0.37%
25	Oregon	16	1.00%		37	Minnesota	5	0.31%
10	Pennsylvania	54	3.36%		37	Rhode Island	5	0.31%
37	Rhode Island	5	0.31%		39	Utah	4	0.25%
7	South Carolina	62	3.86%		40	Alaska	3	0.19%
40	South Dakota	3	0.19%		40	South Dakota	3	0.19%
13	Tennessee	46	2.87%		42	Idaho	1	0.06%
1	Texas	273	17.01%		42	North Dakota	1	0.06%
39	Utah	4	0.25%		42	Wyoming	1	0.06%
45	Vermont	0	0.00%		45	Maine	0	0.00%
12	Virginia	48	2.99%		45	New Hampshire	0	0.00%
22	Washington	19	1.18%		45	Vermont	0	0.00%
35	West Virginia	6	0.37%		NA	Alabama**	NA	NA
31	Wisconsin	10	0.62%		NA	Louisiana**	NA	NA
42	Wyoming	1	0.06%		NA	New Mexico**	NA	NA
						District of Columbia**	NA	NA

Source: U.S. Department of Justice, Bureau of Justice Statistics
   "Correctional Populations in the United States, 1995" (May 1997, NCJ-163916)
*Excludes AIDS. Federal data were not reported.
**Not available.

Deaths of State Prisoners by Illness or Other Natural Causes
As a Percent of All Prison Deaths in 1995
National Percent = 51.2% of Deaths*

ALPHA ORDER			RANK ORDER		
RANK	STATE	PERCENT	RANK	STATE	PERCENT
NA	Alabama**	NA	1	Idaho	100.0
25	Alaska	60.0	1	North Dakota	100.0
13	Arizona	84.5	1	Wyoming	100.0
22	Arkansas	69.2	4	South Carolina	93.9
37	California	49.6	5	Kentucky	93.1
25	Colorado	60.0	6	Kansas	92.3
41	Connecticut	38.1	6	Nebraska	92.3
10	Delaware	88.9	8	Michigan	91.3
42	Florida	34.3	9	Indiana	90.9
39	Georgia	44.9	10	Delaware	88.9
32	Hawaii	54.5	10	Iowa	88.9
1	Idaho	100.0	12	West Virginia	85.7
34	Illinois	53.4	13	Arizona	84.5
9	Indiana	90.9	14	Washington	82.6
10	Iowa	88.9	15	Montana	81.8
6	Kansas	92.3	16	Wisconsin	76.9
5	Kentucky	93.1	17	Mississippi	76.2
NA	Louisiana**	NA	17	Oregon	76.2
45	Maine	0.0	19	Tennessee	71.9
38	Maryland	46.3	20	Rhode Island	71.4
36	Massachusetts	50.0	21	Ohio	71.1
8	Michigan	91.3	22	Arkansas	69.2
31	Minnesota	55.6	23	Texas	68.4
17	Mississippi	76.2	24	Utah	66.7
30	Missouri	56.6	25	Alaska	60.0
15	Montana	81.8	25	Colorado	60.0
6	Nebraska	92.3	25	Nevada	60.0
25	Nevada	60.0	25	South Dakota	60.0
45	New Hampshire	0.0	29	Virginia	57.8
44	New Jersey	19.0	30	Missouri	56.6
NA	New Mexico**	NA	31	Minnesota	55.6
43	New York	26.8	32	Hawaii	54.5
33	North Carolina	53.6	33	North Carolina	53.6
1	North Dakota	100.0	34	Illinois	53.4
21	Ohio	71.1	35	Oklahoma	53.0
35	Oklahoma	53.0	36	Massachusetts	50.0
17	Oregon	76.2	37	California	49.6
40	Pennsylvania	44.3	38	Maryland	46.3
20	Rhode Island	71.4	39	Georgia	44.9
4	South Carolina	93.9	40	Pennsylvania	44.3
25	South Dakota	60.0	41	Connecticut	38.1
19	Tennessee	71.9	42	Florida	34.3
23	Texas	68.4	43	New York	26.8
24	Utah	66.7	44	New Jersey	19.0
45	Vermont	0.0	45	Maine	0.0
29	Virginia	57.8	45	New Hampshire	0.0
14	Washington	82.6	45	Vermont	0.0
12	West Virginia	85.7	NA	Alabama**	NA
16	Wisconsin	76.9	NA	Louisiana**	NA
1	Wyoming	100.0	NA	New Mexico**	NA
				District of Columbia**	NA

Source: Morgan Quitno Press using data from U.S. Department of Justice, Bureau of Justice Statistics
   "Correctional Populations in the United States, 1995" (May 1997, NCJ-163916)

*Excludes AIDS.
**Not available.

Deaths of State Prisoners by AIDS in 1995

National Total = 1,010 Deaths

ALPHA ORDER

RANK	STATE	DEATHS	% of USA
15	Alabama	20	1.98%
32	Alaska	0	0.00%
32	Arizona	0	0.00%
28	Arkansas	1	0.10%
3	California	91	9.01%
18	Colorado	6	0.59%
13	Connecticut	24	2.38%
32	Delaware	0	0.00%
2	Florida	150	14.85%
6	Georgia	50	4.95%
28	Hawaii	1	0.10%
32	Idaho	0	0.00%
9	Illinois	31	3.07%
28	Indiana	1	0.10%
32	Iowa	0	0.00%
32	Kansas	0	0.00%
26	Kentucky	2	0.20%
NA	Louisiana*	NA	NA
32	Maine	0	0.00%
12	Maryland	25	2.48%
16	Massachusetts	14	1.39%
NA	Michigan*	NA	NA
28	Minnesota	1	0.10%
20	Mississippi	5	0.50%
22	Missouri	4	0.40%
32	Montana	0	0.00%
32	Nebraska	0	0.00%
18	Nevada	6	0.59%
26	New Hampshire	2	0.20%
5	New Jersey	66	6.53%
32	New Mexico	0	0.00%
1	New York	258	25.54%
10	North Carolina	28	2.77%
32	North Dakota	0	0.00%
14	Ohio	23	2.28%
22	Oklahoma	4	0.40%
20	Oregon	5	0.50%
7	Pennsylvania	38	3.76%
32	Rhode Island	0	0.00%
8	South Carolina	34	3.37%
32	South Dakota	0	0.00%
17	Tennessee	12	1.19%
4	Texas	74	7.33%
32	Utah	0	0.00%
32	Vermont	0	0.00%
11	Virginia	27	2.67%
22	Washington	4	0.40%
32	West Virginia	0	0.00%
25	Wisconsin	3	0.30%
32	Wyoming	0	0.00%

RANK ORDER

RANK	STATE	DEATHS	% of USA
1	New York	258	25.54%
2	Florida	150	14.85%
3	California	91	9.01%
4	Texas	74	7.33%
5	New Jersey	66	6.53%
6	Georgia	50	4.95%
7	Pennsylvania	38	3.76%
8	South Carolina	34	3.37%
9	Illinois	31	3.07%
10	North Carolina	28	2.77%
11	Virginia	27	2.67%
12	Maryland	25	2.48%
13	Connecticut	24	2.38%
14	Ohio	23	2.28%
15	Alabama	20	1.98%
16	Massachusetts	14	1.39%
17	Tennessee	12	1.19%
18	Colorado	6	0.59%
18	Nevada	6	0.59%
20	Mississippi	5	0.50%
20	Oregon	5	0.50%
22	Missouri	4	0.40%
22	Oklahoma	4	0.40%
22	Washington	4	0.40%
25	Wisconsin	3	0.30%
26	Kentucky	2	0.20%
26	New Hampshire	2	0.20%
28	Arkansas	1	0.10%
28	Hawaii	1	0.10%
28	Indiana	1	0.10%
28	Minnesota	1	0.10%
32	Alaska	0	0.00%
32	Arizona	0	0.00%
32	Delaware	0	0.00%
32	Idaho	0	0.00%
32	Iowa	0	0.00%
32	Kansas	0	0.00%
32	Maine	0	0.00%
32	Montana	0	0.00%
32	Nebraska	0	0.00%
32	New Mexico	0	0.00%
32	North Dakota	0	0.00%
32	Rhode Island	0	0.00%
32	South Dakota	0	0.00%
32	Utah	0	0.00%
32	Vermont	0	0.00%
32	West Virginia	0	0.00%
32	Wyoming	0	0.00%
NA	Louisiana*	NA	NA
NA	Michigan*	NA	NA
	District of Columbia*	NA	NA

Source: U.S. Department of Justice, Bureau of Justice Statistics
"HIV in Prisons and Jails, 1995" (Bulletin, April 1997, NCJ-164260)
*Not available.

AIDS-Related Death Rate for State Prisoners in 1995

National Rate = 109 State Prisoner Deaths per 100,000 Inmates

ALPHA ORDER				RANK ORDER		
RANK	**STATE**	**RATE**		**RANK**	**STATE**	**RATE**
11	Alabama	100		1	New York	376
32	Alaska	0		2	New Jersey	258
32	Arizona	0		3	Florida	242
30	Arkansas	11		4	South Carolina	175
17	California	69		5	Connecticut	160
20	Colorado	56		6	Georgia	147
5	Connecticut	160		7	Pennsylvania	127
32	Delaware	0		8	Massachusetts	122
3	Florida	242		9	Maryland	117
6	Georgia	147		10	North Carolina	104
24	Hawaii	28		11	Alabama	100
32	Idaho	0		12	Virginia	99
14	Illinois	82		13	New Hampshire	97
31	Indiana	6		14	Illinois	82
32	Iowa	0		15	Nevada	80
32	Kansas	0		15	Tennessee	80
29	Kentucky	17		17	California	69
NA	Louisiana*	NA		18	Oregon	67
32	Maine	0		19	Texas	58
9	Maryland	117		20	Colorado	56
8	Massachusetts	122		21	Ohio	53
NA	Michigan*	NA		22	Mississippi	40
27	Minnesota	21		23	Washington	35
22	Mississippi	40		24	Hawaii	28
27	Missouri	21		24	Wisconsin	28
32	Montana	0		26	Oklahoma	23
32	Nebraska	0		27	Minnesota	21
15	Nevada	80		27	Missouri	21
13	New Hampshire	97		29	Kentucky	17
2	New Jersey	258		30	Arkansas	11
32	New Mexico	0		31	Indiana	6
1	New York	376		32	Alaska	0
10	North Carolina	104		32	Arizona	0
32	North Dakota	0		32	Delaware	0
21	Ohio	53		32	Idaho	0
26	Oklahoma	23		32	Iowa	0
18	Oregon	67		32	Kansas	0
7	Pennsylvania	127		32	Maine	0
32	Rhode Island	0		32	Montana	0
4	South Carolina	175		32	Nebraska	0
32	South Dakota	0		32	New Mexico	0
15	Tennessee	80		32	North Dakota	0
19	Texas	58		32	Rhode Island	0
32	Utah	0		32	South Dakota	0
32	Vermont	0		32	Utah	0
12	Virginia	99		32	Vermont	0
23	Washington	35		32	West Virginia	0
32	West Virginia	0		32	Wyoming	0
24	Wisconsin	28		NA	Louisiana*	NA
32	Wyoming	0		NA	Michigan*	NA
					District of Columbia*	NA

*Source: U.S. Department of Justice, Bureau of Justice Statistics
    "HIV in Prisons and Jails, 1995" (Bulletin, April 1997, NCJ-164260)*
Not available.

Deaths of State Prisoners by AIDS as a Percent of All Prison Deaths in 1995

National Percent = 34.2% of Deaths

ALPHA ORDER				RANK ORDER		
RANK	STATE	PERCENT		RANK	STATE	PERCENT
19	Alabama	22.7		1	New Hampshire	100.0
32	Alaska	0.0		2	New York	65.2
32	Arizona	0.0		3	Florida	59.1
30	Arkansas	3.8		4	Connecticut	57.1
11	California	34.7		5	South Carolina	54.0
15	Colorado	24.0		6	New Jersey	48.2
4	Connecticut	57.1		7	Maryland	46.3
32	Delaware	0.0		8	Massachusetts	41.2
3	Florida	59.1		9	North Carolina	40.6
10	Georgia	39.4		10	Georgia	39.4
26	Hawaii	9.1		11	California	34.7
32	Idaho	0.0		12	Virginia	32.5
14	Illinois	30.1		13	Pennsylvania	31.1
31	Indiana	2.3		14	Illinois	30.1
32	Iowa	0.0		15	Colorado	24.0
32	Kansas	0.0		15	Nevada	24.0
28	Kentucky	6.9		17	Oregon	23.8
NA	Louisiana*	NA		18	Wisconsin	23.1
32	Maine	0.0		19	Alabama	22.7
7	Maryland	46.3		20	Ohio	20.2
8	Massachusetts	41.2		21	Tennessee	18.8
NA	Michigan*	NA		22	Texas	18.5
25	Minnesota	11.1		23	Washington	17.4
24	Mississippi	11.9		24	Mississippi	11.9
27	Missouri	7.5		25	Minnesota	11.1
32	Montana	0.0		26	Hawaii	9.1
32	Nebraska	0.0		27	Missouri	7.5
15	Nevada	24.0		28	Kentucky	6.9
1	New Hampshire	100.0		29	Oklahoma	6.1
6	New Jersey	48.2		30	Arkansas	3.8
32	New Mexico	0.0		31	Indiana	2.3
2	New York	65.2		32	Alaska	0.0
9	North Carolina	40.6		32	Arizona	0.0
32	North Dakota	0.0		32	Delaware	0.0
20	Ohio	20.2		32	Idaho	0.0
29	Oklahoma	6.1		32	Iowa	0.0
17	Oregon	23.8		32	Kansas	0.0
13	Pennsylvania	31.1		32	Maine	0.0
32	Rhode Island	0.0		32	Montana	0.0
5	South Carolina	54.0		32	Nebraska	0.0
32	South Dakota	0.0		32	New Mexico	0.0
21	Tennessee	18.8		32	North Dakota	0.0
22	Texas	18.5		32	Rhode Island	0.0
32	Utah	0.0		32	South Dakota	0.0
32	Vermont	0.0		32	Utah	0.0
12	Virginia	32.5		32	Vermont	0.0
23	Washington	17.4		32	West Virginia	0.0
32	West Virginia	0.0		32	Wyoming	0.0
18	Wisconsin	23.1		NA	Louisiana*	NA
32	Wyoming	0.0		NA	Michigan*	NA
					District of Columbia*	NA

Source: U.S. Department of Justice, Bureau of Justice Statistics
    "HIV in Prisons and Jails, 1995" (Bulletin, April 1997, NCJ-164260)
*Not available.

State Prisoners Known to be Positive for HIV Infection/AIDS in 1995

National Total = 23,404 Inmates*

<table>
<tr><td colspan="4">ALPHA ORDER</td><td colspan="4">RANK ORDER</td></tr>
<tr><td>RANK</td><td>STATE</td><td>INMATES</td><td>% of USA</td><td>RANK</td><td>STATE</td><td>INMATES</td><td>% of USA</td></tr>
<tr><td>17</td><td>Alabama</td><td>222</td><td>0.95%</td><td>1</td><td>New York</td><td>9,500</td><td>40.59%</td></tr>
<tr><td>43</td><td>Alaska</td><td>5</td><td>0.02%</td><td>2</td><td>Florida</td><td>2,193</td><td>9.37%</td></tr>
<tr><td>20</td><td>Arizona</td><td>140</td><td>0.60%</td><td>3</td><td>Texas</td><td>1,890</td><td>8.08%</td></tr>
<tr><td>29</td><td>Arkansas</td><td>83</td><td>0.35%</td><td>4</td><td>California</td><td>1,042</td><td>4.45%</td></tr>
<tr><td>4</td><td>California</td><td>1,042</td><td>4.45%</td><td>5</td><td>New Jersey</td><td>847</td><td>3.62%</td></tr>
<tr><td>27</td><td>Colorado</td><td>93</td><td>0.40%</td><td>6</td><td>Georgia</td><td>828</td><td>3.54%</td></tr>
<tr><td>7</td><td>Connecticut</td><td>755</td><td>3.23%</td><td>7</td><td>Connecticut</td><td>755</td><td>3.23%</td></tr>
<tr><td>24</td><td>Delaware</td><td>122</td><td>0.52%</td><td>8</td><td>Maryland</td><td>724</td><td>3.09%</td></tr>
<tr><td>2</td><td>Florida</td><td>2,193</td><td>9.37%</td><td>9</td><td>Pennsylvania</td><td>590</td><td>2.52%</td></tr>
<tr><td>6</td><td>Georgia</td><td>828</td><td>3.54%</td><td>10</td><td>Illinois</td><td>583</td><td>2.49%</td></tr>
<tr><td>40</td><td>Hawaii</td><td>12</td><td>0.05%</td><td>11</td><td>North Carolina</td><td>526</td><td>2.25%</td></tr>
<tr><td>41</td><td>Idaho</td><td>11</td><td>0.05%</td><td>12</td><td>Massachusetts</td><td>409</td><td>1.75%</td></tr>
<tr><td>10</td><td>Illinois</td><td>583</td><td>2.49%</td><td>13</td><td>South Carolina</td><td>380</td><td>1.62%</td></tr>
<tr><td>NA</td><td>Indiana**</td><td>NA</td><td>NA</td><td>14</td><td>Michigan</td><td>379</td><td>1.62%</td></tr>
<tr><td>38</td><td>Iowa</td><td>20</td><td>0.09%</td><td>15</td><td>Ohio</td><td>346</td><td>1.48%</td></tr>
<tr><td>36</td><td>Kansas</td><td>24</td><td>0.10%</td><td>16</td><td>Louisiana</td><td>314</td><td>1.34%</td></tr>
<tr><td>32</td><td>Kentucky</td><td>41</td><td>0.18%</td><td>17</td><td>Alabama</td><td>222</td><td>0.95%</td></tr>
<tr><td>16</td><td>Louisiana</td><td>314</td><td>1.34%</td><td>18</td><td>Missouri</td><td>173</td><td>0.74%</td></tr>
<tr><td>45</td><td>Maine</td><td>4</td><td>0.02%</td><td>19</td><td>Nevada</td><td>147</td><td>0.63%</td></tr>
<tr><td>8</td><td>Maryland</td><td>724</td><td>3.09%</td><td>20</td><td>Arizona</td><td>140</td><td>0.60%</td></tr>
<tr><td>12</td><td>Massachusetts</td><td>409</td><td>1.75%</td><td>21</td><td>Mississippi</td><td>138</td><td>0.59%</td></tr>
<tr><td>14</td><td>Michigan</td><td>379</td><td>1.62%</td><td>22</td><td>Virginia</td><td>134</td><td>0.57%</td></tr>
<tr><td>31</td><td>Minnesota</td><td>46</td><td>0.20%</td><td>23</td><td>Rhode Island</td><td>126</td><td>0.54%</td></tr>
<tr><td>21</td><td>Mississippi</td><td>138</td><td>0.59%</td><td>24</td><td>Delaware</td><td>122</td><td>0.52%</td></tr>
<tr><td>18</td><td>Missouri</td><td>173</td><td>0.74%</td><td>25</td><td>Tennessee</td><td>120</td><td>0.51%</td></tr>
<tr><td>45</td><td>Montana</td><td>4</td><td>0.02%</td><td>26</td><td>Oklahoma</td><td>115</td><td>0.49%</td></tr>
<tr><td>39</td><td>Nebraska</td><td>19</td><td>0.08%</td><td>27</td><td>Colorado</td><td>93</td><td>0.40%</td></tr>
<tr><td>19</td><td>Nevada</td><td>147</td><td>0.63%</td><td>28</td><td>Washington</td><td>92</td><td>0.39%</td></tr>
<tr><td>33</td><td>New Hampshire</td><td>31</td><td>0.13%</td><td>29</td><td>Arkansas</td><td>83</td><td>0.35%</td></tr>
<tr><td>5</td><td>New Jersey</td><td>847</td><td>3.62%</td><td>30</td><td>Wisconsin</td><td>72</td><td>0.31%</td></tr>
<tr><td>36</td><td>New Mexico</td><td>24</td><td>0.10%</td><td>31</td><td>Minnesota</td><td>46</td><td>0.20%</td></tr>
<tr><td>1</td><td>New York</td><td>9,500</td><td>40.59%</td><td>32</td><td>Kentucky</td><td>41</td><td>0.18%</td></tr>
<tr><td>11</td><td>North Carolina</td><td>526</td><td>2.25%</td><td>33</td><td>New Hampshire</td><td>31</td><td>0.13%</td></tr>
<tr><td>48</td><td>North Dakota</td><td>2</td><td>0.01%</td><td>33</td><td>Utah</td><td>31</td><td>0.13%</td></tr>
<tr><td>15</td><td>Ohio</td><td>346</td><td>1.48%</td><td>35</td><td>Oregon</td><td>29</td><td>0.12%</td></tr>
<tr><td>26</td><td>Oklahoma</td><td>115</td><td>0.49%</td><td>36</td><td>Kansas</td><td>24</td><td>0.10%</td></tr>
<tr><td>35</td><td>Oregon</td><td>29</td><td>0.12%</td><td>36</td><td>New Mexico</td><td>24</td><td>0.10%</td></tr>
<tr><td>9</td><td>Pennsylvania</td><td>590</td><td>2.52%</td><td>38</td><td>Iowa</td><td>20</td><td>0.09%</td></tr>
<tr><td>23</td><td>Rhode Island</td><td>126</td><td>0.54%</td><td>39</td><td>Nebraska</td><td>19</td><td>0.08%</td></tr>
<tr><td>13</td><td>South Carolina</td><td>380</td><td>1.62%</td><td>40</td><td>Hawaii</td><td>12</td><td>0.05%</td></tr>
<tr><td>47</td><td>South Dakota</td><td>3</td><td>0.01%</td><td>41</td><td>Idaho</td><td>11</td><td>0.05%</td></tr>
<tr><td>25</td><td>Tennessee</td><td>120</td><td>0.51%</td><td>42</td><td>West Virginia</td><td>10</td><td>0.04%</td></tr>
<tr><td>3</td><td>Texas</td><td>1,890</td><td>8.08%</td><td>43</td><td>Alaska</td><td>5</td><td>0.02%</td></tr>
<tr><td>33</td><td>Utah</td><td>31</td><td>0.13%</td><td>43</td><td>Wyoming</td><td>5</td><td>0.02%</td></tr>
<tr><td>49</td><td>Vermont</td><td>0</td><td>0.00%</td><td>45</td><td>Maine</td><td>4</td><td>0.02%</td></tr>
<tr><td>22</td><td>Virginia</td><td>134</td><td>0.57%</td><td>45</td><td>Montana</td><td>4</td><td>0.02%</td></tr>
<tr><td>28</td><td>Washington</td><td>92</td><td>0.39%</td><td>47</td><td>South Dakota</td><td>3</td><td>0.01%</td></tr>
<tr><td>42</td><td>West Virginia</td><td>10</td><td>0.04%</td><td>48</td><td>North Dakota</td><td>2</td><td>0.01%</td></tr>
<tr><td>30</td><td>Wisconsin</td><td>72</td><td>0.31%</td><td>49</td><td>Vermont</td><td>0</td><td>0.00%</td></tr>
<tr><td>43</td><td>Wyoming</td><td>5</td><td>0.02%</td><td>NA</td><td>Indiana**</td><td>NA</td><td>NA</td></tr>
<tr><td></td><td></td><td></td><td></td><td></td><td>District of Columbia**</td><td>NA</td><td>NA</td></tr>
</table>

Source: U.S. Department of Justice, Bureau of Justice Statistics
"HIV in Prisons and Jails, 1995" (Bulletin, April 1997, NCJ-164260)
*Does not include 822 positive federal inmates.
**Not available.

State Prisoners Known to be Positive for HIV Infection/AIDS As a Percent of Total Prison Population in 1995
National Percent = 2.4% of State Prisoners*

ALPHA ORDER

RANK	STATE	PERCENT
19	Alabama	1.1
46	Alaska	0.2
31	Arizona	0.7
20	Arkansas	1.0
26	California	0.8
20	Colorado	1.0
2	Connecticut	5.1
8	Delaware	2.5
6	Florida	3.4
9	Georgia	2.4
36	Hawaii	0.4
36	Idaho	0.4
15	Illinois	1.5
NA	Indiana**	NA
42	Iowa	0.3
42	Kansas	0.3
36	Kentucky	0.4
13	Louisiana	1.8
42	Maine	0.3
6	Maryland	3.4
4	Massachusetts	3.9
23	Michigan	0.9
20	Minnesota	1.0
18	Mississippi	1.4
23	Missouri	0.9
46	Montana	0.2
32	Nebraska	0.6
11	Nevada	1.9
15	New Hampshire	1.5
5	New Jersey	3.7
32	New Mexico	0.6
1	New York	13.9
11	North Carolina	1.9
42	North Dakota	0.3
26	Ohio	0.8
26	Oklahoma	0.8
36	Oregon	0.4
13	Pennsylvania	1.8
3	Rhode Island	4.4
10	South Carolina	2.0
46	South Dakota	0.2
23	Tennessee	0.9
15	Texas	1.5
26	Utah	0.8
49	Vermont	0.0
32	Virginia	0.6
26	Washington	0.8
36	West Virginia	0.4
32	Wisconsin	0.6
36	Wyoming	0.4

RANK ORDER

RANK	STATE	PERCENT
1	New York	13.9
2	Connecticut	5.1
3	Rhode Island	4.4
4	Massachusetts	3.9
5	New Jersey	3.7
6	Florida	3.4
6	Maryland	3.4
8	Delaware	2.5
9	Georgia	2.4
10	South Carolina	2.0
11	Nevada	1.9
11	North Carolina	1.9
13	Louisiana	1.8
13	Pennsylvania	1.8
15	Illinois	1.5
15	New Hampshire	1.5
15	Texas	1.5
18	Mississippi	1.4
19	Alabama	1.1
20	Arkansas	1.0
20	Colorado	1.0
20	Minnesota	1.0
23	Michigan	0.9
23	Missouri	0.9
23	Tennessee	0.9
26	California	0.8
26	Ohio	0.8
26	Oklahoma	0.8
26	Utah	0.8
26	Washington	0.8
31	Arizona	0.7
32	Nebraska	0.6
32	New Mexico	0.6
32	Virginia	0.6
32	Wisconsin	0.6
36	Hawaii	0.4
36	Idaho	0.4
36	Kentucky	0.4
36	Oregon	0.4
36	West Virginia	0.4
36	Wyoming	0.4
42	Iowa	0.3
42	Kansas	0.3
42	Maine	0.3
42	North Dakota	0.3
46	Alaska	0.2
46	Montana	0.2
46	South Dakota	0.2
49	Vermont	0.0
NA	Indiana**	NA
	District of Columbia**	NA

Source: U.S. Department of Justice, Bureau of Justice Statistics
    "HIV in Prisons and Jails, 1995" (Bulletin, April 1997, NCJ-164260)
*Federal rate is 0.9%, combined state and federal rate is 2.3%.
**Not available.

Deaths of State Prisoners by Suicide in 1995

National Total = 160 Suicides

RANK	STATE	SUICIDES	% of USA
NA	Alabama*	NA	NA
15	Alaska	2	1.25%
15	Arizona	2	1.25%
15	Arkansas	2	1.25%
1	California	25	15.63%
25	Colorado	1	0.63%
15	Connecticut	2	1.25%
33	Delaware	0	0.00%
11	Florida	4	2.50%
4	Georgia	10	6.25%
12	Hawaii	3	1.88%
33	Idaho	0	0.00%
9	Illinois	6	3.75%
15	Indiana	2	1.25%
25	Iowa	1	0.63%
33	Kansas	0	0.00%
33	Kentucky	0	0.00%
NA	Louisiana*	NA	NA
33	Maine	0	0.00%
33	Maryland	0	0.00%
12	Massachusetts	3	1.88%
7	Michigan	8	5.00%
15	Minnesota	2	1.25%
12	Mississippi	3	1.88%
15	Missouri	2	1.25%
33	Montana	0	0.00%
25	Nebraska	1	0.63%
15	Nevada	2	1.25%
33	New Hampshire	0	0.00%
9	New Jersey	6	3.75%
NA	New Mexico*	NA	NA
4	New York	10	6.25%
25	North Carolina	1	0.63%
33	North Dakota	0	0.00%
4	Ohio	10	6.25%
8	Oklahoma	7	4.38%
33	Oregon	0	0.00%
3	Pennsylvania	15	9.38%
25	Rhode Island	1	0.63%
25	South Carolina	1	0.63%
15	South Dakota	2	1.25%
25	Tennessee	1	0.63%
2	Texas	19	11.88%
25	Utah	1	0.63%
33	Vermont	0	0.00%
15	Virginia	2	1.25%
33	Washington	0	0.00%
33	West Virginia	0	0.00%
33	Wisconsin	0	0.00%
33	Wyoming	0	0.00%

RANK	STATE	SUICIDES	% of USA
1	California	25	15.63%
2	Texas	19	11.88%
3	Pennsylvania	15	9.38%
4	Georgia	10	6.25%
4	New York	10	6.25%
4	Ohio	10	6.25%
7	Michigan	8	5.00%
8	Oklahoma	7	4.38%
9	Illinois	6	3.75%
9	New Jersey	6	3.75%
11	Florida	4	2.50%
12	Hawaii	3	1.88%
12	Massachusetts	3	1.88%
12	Mississippi	3	1.88%
15	Alaska	2	1.25%
15	Arizona	2	1.25%
15	Arkansas	2	1.25%
15	Connecticut	2	1.25%
15	Indiana	2	1.25%
15	Minnesota	2	1.25%
15	Missouri	2	1.25%
15	Nevada	2	1.25%
15	South Dakota	2	1.25%
15	Virginia	2	1.25%
25	Colorado	1	0.63%
25	Iowa	1	0.63%
25	Nebraska	1	0.63%
25	North Carolina	1	0.63%
25	Rhode Island	1	0.63%
25	South Carolina	1	0.63%
25	Tennessee	1	0.63%
25	Utah	1	0.63%
33	Delaware	0	0.00%
33	Idaho	0	0.00%
33	Kansas	0	0.00%
33	Kentucky	0	0.00%
33	Maine	0	0.00%
33	Maryland	0	0.00%
33	Montana	0	0.00%
33	New Hampshire	0	0.00%
33	North Dakota	0	0.00%
33	Oregon	0	0.00%
33	Vermont	0	0.00%
33	Washington	0	0.00%
33	West Virginia	0	0.00%
33	Wisconsin	0	0.00%
33	Wyoming	0	0.00%
NA	Alabama*	NA	NA
NA	Louisiana*	NA	NA
NA	New Mexico*	NA	NA
	District of Columbia	3	1.88%

Source: U.S. Department of Justice, Bureau of Justice Statistics
"Correctional Populations in the United States, 1995" (May 1997, NCJ-163916)
*Not available.

Deaths of State Prisoners by Suicide as a Percent of All Prison Deaths in 1995

National Percent = 5.1% of Deaths

<table>
<tr><td colspan="3">ALPHA ORDER</td><td colspan="3">RANK ORDER</td></tr>
<tr><td>RANK</td><td>STATE</td><td>PERCENT</td><td>RANK</td><td>STATE</td><td>PERCENT</td></tr>
<tr><td>NA</td><td>Alabama*</td><td>NA</td><td>1</td><td>Alaska</td><td>40.0</td></tr>
<tr><td>1</td><td>Alaska</td><td>40.0</td><td>1</td><td>South Dakota</td><td>40.0</td></tr>
<tr><td>26</td><td>Arizona</td><td>3.4</td><td>3</td><td>Hawaii</td><td>27.3</td></tr>
<tr><td>15</td><td>Arkansas</td><td>7.7</td><td>4</td><td>Minnesota</td><td>22.2</td></tr>
<tr><td>10</td><td>California</td><td>9.5</td><td>5</td><td>Utah</td><td>16.7</td></tr>
<tr><td>24</td><td>Colorado</td><td>4.0</td><td>6</td><td>Rhode Island</td><td>14.3</td></tr>
<tr><td>20</td><td>Connecticut</td><td>4.8</td><td>7</td><td>Pennsylvania</td><td>12.3</td></tr>
<tr><td>33</td><td>Delaware</td><td>0.0</td><td>8</td><td>Iowa</td><td>11.1</td></tr>
<tr><td>29</td><td>Florida</td><td>1.6</td><td>9</td><td>Oklahoma</td><td>10.6</td></tr>
<tr><td>14</td><td>Georgia</td><td>7.9</td><td>10</td><td>California</td><td>9.5</td></tr>
<tr><td>3</td><td>Hawaii</td><td>27.3</td><td>11</td><td>Massachusetts</td><td>8.8</td></tr>
<tr><td>33</td><td>Idaho</td><td>0.0</td><td>11</td><td>Ohio</td><td>8.8</td></tr>
<tr><td>19</td><td>Illinois</td><td>5.8</td><td>13</td><td>Nevada</td><td>8.0</td></tr>
<tr><td>22</td><td>Indiana</td><td>4.5</td><td>14</td><td>Georgia</td><td>7.9</td></tr>
<tr><td>8</td><td>Iowa</td><td>11.1</td><td>15</td><td>Arkansas</td><td>7.7</td></tr>
<tr><td>33</td><td>Kansas</td><td>0.0</td><td>15</td><td>Michigan</td><td>7.7</td></tr>
<tr><td>33</td><td>Kentucky</td><td>0.0</td><td>15</td><td>Nebraska</td><td>7.7</td></tr>
<tr><td>NA</td><td>Louisiana*</td><td>NA</td><td>18</td><td>Mississippi</td><td>7.1</td></tr>
<tr><td>33</td><td>Maine</td><td>0.0</td><td>19</td><td>Illinois</td><td>5.8</td></tr>
<tr><td>33</td><td>Maryland</td><td>0.0</td><td>20</td><td>Connecticut</td><td>4.8</td></tr>
<tr><td>11</td><td>Massachusetts</td><td>8.8</td><td>20</td><td>Texas</td><td>4.8</td></tr>
<tr><td>15</td><td>Michigan</td><td>7.7</td><td>22</td><td>Indiana</td><td>4.5</td></tr>
<tr><td>4</td><td>Minnesota</td><td>22.2</td><td>23</td><td>New Jersey</td><td>4.4</td></tr>
<tr><td>18</td><td>Mississippi</td><td>7.1</td><td>24</td><td>Colorado</td><td>4.0</td></tr>
<tr><td>25</td><td>Missouri</td><td>3.8</td><td>25</td><td>Missouri</td><td>3.8</td></tr>
<tr><td>33</td><td>Montana</td><td>0.0</td><td>26</td><td>Arizona</td><td>3.4</td></tr>
<tr><td>15</td><td>Nebraska</td><td>7.7</td><td>27</td><td>New York</td><td>2.5</td></tr>
<tr><td>13</td><td>Nevada</td><td>8.0</td><td>28</td><td>Virginia</td><td>2.4</td></tr>
<tr><td>33</td><td>New Hampshire</td><td>0.0</td><td>29</td><td>Florida</td><td>1.6</td></tr>
<tr><td>23</td><td>New Jersey</td><td>4.4</td><td>29</td><td>Tennessee</td><td>1.6</td></tr>
<tr><td>NA</td><td>New Mexico*</td><td>NA</td><td>31</td><td>South Carolina</td><td>1.5</td></tr>
<tr><td>27</td><td>New York</td><td>2.5</td><td>32</td><td>North Carolina</td><td>1.4</td></tr>
<tr><td>32</td><td>North Carolina</td><td>1.4</td><td>33</td><td>Delaware</td><td>0.0</td></tr>
<tr><td>33</td><td>North Dakota</td><td>0.0</td><td>33</td><td>Idaho</td><td>0.0</td></tr>
<tr><td>11</td><td>Ohio</td><td>8.8</td><td>33</td><td>Kansas</td><td>0.0</td></tr>
<tr><td>9</td><td>Oklahoma</td><td>10.6</td><td>33</td><td>Kentucky</td><td>0.0</td></tr>
<tr><td>33</td><td>Oregon</td><td>0.0</td><td>33</td><td>Maine</td><td>0.0</td></tr>
<tr><td>7</td><td>Pennsylvania</td><td>12.3</td><td>33</td><td>Maryland</td><td>0.0</td></tr>
<tr><td>6</td><td>Rhode Island</td><td>14.3</td><td>33</td><td>Montana</td><td>0.0</td></tr>
<tr><td>31</td><td>South Carolina</td><td>1.5</td><td>33</td><td>New Hampshire</td><td>0.0</td></tr>
<tr><td>1</td><td>South Dakota</td><td>40.0</td><td>33</td><td>North Dakota</td><td>0.0</td></tr>
<tr><td>29</td><td>Tennessee</td><td>1.6</td><td>33</td><td>Oregon</td><td>0.0</td></tr>
<tr><td>20</td><td>Texas</td><td>4.8</td><td>33</td><td>Vermont</td><td>0.0</td></tr>
<tr><td>5</td><td>Utah</td><td>16.7</td><td>33</td><td>Washington</td><td>0.0</td></tr>
<tr><td>33</td><td>Vermont</td><td>0.0</td><td>33</td><td>West Virginia</td><td>0.0</td></tr>
<tr><td>28</td><td>Virginia</td><td>2.4</td><td>33</td><td>Wisconsin</td><td>0.0</td></tr>
<tr><td>33</td><td>Washington</td><td>0.0</td><td>33</td><td>Wyoming</td><td>0.0</td></tr>
<tr><td>33</td><td>West Virginia</td><td>0.0</td><td>NA</td><td>Alabama*</td><td>NA</td></tr>
<tr><td>33</td><td>Wisconsin</td><td>0.0</td><td>NA</td><td>Louisiana*</td><td>NA</td></tr>
<tr><td>33</td><td>Wyoming</td><td>0.0</td><td>NA</td><td>New Mexico*</td><td>NA</td></tr>
<tr><td></td><td></td><td></td><td></td><td>District of Columbia</td><td>42.9</td></tr>
</table>

Source: Morgan Quitno Press using data from U.S. Department of Justice, Bureau of Justice Statistics
    "Correctional Populations in the United States, 1995" (May 1997, NCJ-163916)
*Not available.

Adults Under State Correctional Supervision in 1993

National Total = 4,711,500 Adults*

ALPHA ORDER

RANK	STATE	ADULTS	% of USA
22	Alabama	66,400	1.41%
47	Alaska	6,600	0.14%
24	Arizona	65,700	1.39%
30	Arkansas	31,900	0.68%
2	California	557,000	11.82%
27	Colorado	53,400	1.13%
25	Connecticut	64,900	1.38%
35	Delaware	20,600	0.44%
3	Florida	302,800	6.43%
5	Georgia	216,400	4.59%
39	Hawaii	14,500	0.31%
43	Idaho	9,600	0.20%
10	Illinois	148,700	3.16%
14	Indiana	108,400	2.30%
33	Iowa	22,800	0.48%
29	Kansas	39,700	0.84%
31	Kentucky	31,000	0.66%
16	Louisiana	78,800	1.67%
41	Maine	10,800	0.23%
13	Maryland	123,300	2.62%
18	Massachusetts	69,400	1.47%
7	Michigan	205,400	4.36%
15	Minnesota	83,900	1.78%
32	Mississippi	25,000	0.53%
20	Missouri	67,700	1.44%
46	Montana	7,000	0.15%
37	Nebraska	19,500	0.41%
34	Nevada	21,400	0.45%
45	New Hampshire	7,700	0.16%
8	New Jersey	180,600	3.83%
38	New Mexico	15,400	0.33%
4	New York	301,400	6.40%
12	North Carolina	134,400	2.85%
50	North Dakota	2,900	0.06%
9	Ohio	157,100	3.33%
28	Oklahoma	44,300	0.94%
26	Oregon	61,900	1.31%
6	Pennsylvania	205,500	4.36%
36	Rhode Island	19,700	0.42%
21	South Carolina	67,103	1.42%
47	South Dakota	6,600	0.14%
17	Tennessee	78,000	1.66%
1	Texas	620,000	13.16%
39	Utah	14,500	0.31%
44	Vermont	7,800	0.17%
19	Virginia	67,900	1.44%
11	Washington	135,600	2.88%
42	West Virginia	10,600	0.22%
23	Wisconsin	66,300	1.41%
49	Wyoming	4,900	0.10%

RANK ORDER

RANK	STATE	ADULTS	% of USA
1	Texas	620,000	13.16%
2	California	557,000	11.82%
3	Florida	302,800	6.43%
4	New York	301,400	6.40%
5	Georgia	216,400	4.59%
6	Pennsylvania	205,500	4.36%
7	Michigan	205,400	4.36%
8	New Jersey	180,600	3.83%
9	Ohio	157,100	3.33%
10	Illinois	148,700	3.16%
11	Washington	135,600	2.88%
12	North Carolina	134,400	2.85%
13	Maryland	123,300	2.62%
14	Indiana	108,400	2.30%
15	Minnesota	83,900	1.78%
16	Louisiana	78,800	1.67%
17	Tennessee	78,000	1.66%
18	Massachusetts	69,400	1.47%
19	Virginia	67,900	1.44%
20	Missouri	67,700	1.44%
21	South Carolina	67,103	1.42%
22	Alabama	66,400	1.41%
23	Wisconsin	66,300	1.41%
24	Arizona	65,700	1.39%
25	Connecticut	64,900	1.38%
26	Oregon	61,900	1.31%
27	Colorado	53,400	1.13%
28	Oklahoma	44,300	0.94%
29	Kansas	39,700	0.84%
30	Arkansas	31,900	0.68%
31	Kentucky	31,000	0.66%
32	Mississippi	25,000	0.53%
33	Iowa	22,800	0.48%
34	Nevada	21,400	0.45%
35	Delaware	20,600	0.44%
36	Rhode Island	19,700	0.42%
37	Nebraska	19,500	0.41%
38	New Mexico	15,400	0.33%
39	Hawaii	14,500	0.31%
39	Utah	14,500	0.31%
41	Maine	10,800	0.23%
42	West Virginia	10,600	0.22%
43	Idaho	9,600	0.20%
44	Vermont	7,800	0.17%
45	New Hampshire	7,700	0.16%
46	Montana	7,000	0.15%
47	Alaska	6,600	0.14%
47	South Dakota	6,600	0.14%
49	Wyoming	4,900	0.10%
50	North Dakota	2,900	0.06%
	District of Columbia	29,000	0.62%

Source: U.S. Department of Justice, Bureau of Justice Statistics
    "Correctional Populations in the United States, 1993" (October 1995, NCJ-156241)
*Includes adults in prison or jail, on probation or parole. Does not include 168,000 adults under federal correctional supervision.

Percent of Population Under State Correctional Supervision in 1993

National Percent = 2.5% of Adult Population*

RANK	STATE	PERCENT		RANK	STATE	PERCENT
22	Alabama	2.1		1	Texas	4.8
35	Alaska	1.6		2	Georgia	4.3
18	Arizona	2.3		3	Delaware	3.9
28	Arkansas	1.8		4	Washington	3.5
16	California	2.5		5	Maryland	3.3
24	Colorado	2.0		6	Michigan	3.0
10	Connecticut	2.6		6	New Jersey	3.0
3	Delaware	3.9		8	Florida	2.9
8	Florida	2.9		9	Oregon	2.8
2	Georgia	4.3		10	Connecticut	2.6
32	Hawaii	1.7		10	Indiana	2.6
40	Idaho	1.3		10	Louisiana	2.6
32	Illinois	1.7		10	Minnesota	2.6
10	Indiana	2.6		10	North Carolina	2.6
46	Iowa	1.1		10	Rhode Island	2.6
19	Kansas	2.2		16	California	2.5
46	Kentucky	1.1		16	South Carolina	2.5
10	Louisiana	2.6		18	Arizona	2.3
43	Maine	1.2		19	Kansas	2.2
5	Maryland	3.3		19	New York	2.2
36	Massachusetts	1.5		19	Pennsylvania	2.2
6	Michigan	3.0		22	Alabama	2.1
10	Minnesota	2.6		22	Nevada	2.1
40	Mississippi	1.3		24	Colorado	2.0
28	Missouri	1.8		24	Tennessee	2.0
43	Montana	1.2		26	Ohio	1.9
32	Nebraska	1.7		26	Oklahoma	1.9
22	Nevada	2.1		28	Arkansas	1.8
48	New Hampshire	0.9		28	Missouri	1.8
6	New Jersey	3.0		28	Vermont	1.8
38	New Mexico	1.4		28	Wisconsin	1.8
19	New York	2.2		32	Hawaii	1.7
10	North Carolina	2.6		32	Illinois	1.7
50	North Dakota	0.6		32	Nebraska	1.7
26	Ohio	1.9		35	Alaska	1.6
26	Oklahoma	1.9		36	Massachusetts	1.5
9	Oregon	2.8		36	Wyoming	1.5
19	Pennsylvania	2.2		38	New Mexico	1.4
10	Rhode Island	2.6		38	Virginia	1.4
16	South Carolina	2.5		40	Idaho	1.3
40	South Dakota	1.3		40	Mississippi	1.3
24	Tennessee	2.0		40	South Dakota	1.3
1	Texas	4.8		43	Maine	1.2
43	Utah	1.2		43	Montana	1.2
28	Vermont	1.8		43	Utah	1.2
38	Virginia	1.4		46	Iowa	1.1
4	Washington	3.5		46	Kentucky	1.1
49	West Virginia	0.8		48	New Hampshire	0.9
28	Wisconsin	1.8		49	West Virginia	0.8
36	Wyoming	1.5		50	North Dakota	0.6
					District of Columbia	6.3

ALPHA ORDER / RANK ORDER

Source: U.S. Department of Justice, Bureau of Justice Statistics
  "Correctional Populations in the United States, 1993" (October 1995, NCJ-156241)
Includes adults in prison or jail, on probation or parole. Does not include adults under federal correctional supervision. Federal percent is 0.1% making a combined state and federal percent of 2.6% of adult population is under state or federal correctional supervision.

Adults on State Probation in 1996

National Total = 3,146,062 Adults*

<table>
<tr><td colspan="4">ALPHA ORDER</td><td colspan="4">RANK ORDER</td></tr>
<tr><td>RANK</td><td>STATE</td><td>ADULTS</td><td>% of USA</td><td>RANK</td><td>STATE</td><td>ADULTS</td><td>% of USA</td></tr>
<tr><td>24</td><td>Alabama</td><td>38,764</td><td>1.23%</td><td>1</td><td>Texas</td><td>425,789</td><td>13.53%</td></tr>
<tr><td>47</td><td>Alaska</td><td>3,760</td><td>0.12%</td><td>2</td><td>California</td><td>292,019</td><td>9.28%</td></tr>
<tr><td>20</td><td>Arizona</td><td>43,190</td><td>1.37%</td><td>3</td><td>Florida</td><td>249,479</td><td>7.93%</td></tr>
<tr><td>29</td><td>Arkansas</td><td>24,033</td><td>0.76%</td><td>4</td><td>New York</td><td>180,580</td><td>5.74%</td></tr>
<tr><td>2</td><td>California</td><td>292,019</td><td>9.28%</td><td>5</td><td>Michigan</td><td>148,595</td><td>4.72%</td></tr>
<tr><td>23</td><td>Colorado</td><td>41,212</td><td>1.31%</td><td>6</td><td>Georgia</td><td>144,157</td><td>4.58%</td></tr>
<tr><td>16</td><td>Connecticut</td><td>55,978</td><td>1.78%</td><td>7</td><td>New Jersey</td><td>125,881</td><td>4.00%</td></tr>
<tr><td>31</td><td>Delaware</td><td>16,528</td><td>0.53%</td><td>8</td><td>Washington</td><td>125,317</td><td>3.98%</td></tr>
<tr><td>3</td><td>Florida</td><td>249,479</td><td>7.93%</td><td>9</td><td>Illinois</td><td>115,503</td><td>3.67%</td></tr>
<tr><td>6</td><td>Georgia</td><td>144,157</td><td>4.58%</td><td>10</td><td>Pennsylvania</td><td>110,532</td><td>3.51%</td></tr>
<tr><td>35</td><td>Hawaii</td><td>14,238</td><td>0.45%</td><td>11</td><td>Ohio</td><td>102,755</td><td>3.27%</td></tr>
<tr><td>43</td><td>Idaho</td><td>5,855</td><td>0.19%</td><td>12</td><td>North Carolina</td><td>102,483</td><td>3.26%</td></tr>
<tr><td>9</td><td>Illinois</td><td>115,503</td><td>3.67%</td><td>13</td><td>Indiana</td><td>99,590</td><td>3.17%</td></tr>
<tr><td>13</td><td>Indiana</td><td>99,590</td><td>3.17%</td><td>14</td><td>Minnesota</td><td>88,039</td><td>2.80%</td></tr>
<tr><td>33</td><td>Iowa</td><td>15,384</td><td>0.49%</td><td>15</td><td>Maryland</td><td>70,553</td><td>2.24%</td></tr>
<tr><td>32</td><td>Kansas</td><td>15,732</td><td>0.50%</td><td>16</td><td>Connecticut</td><td>55,978</td><td>1.78%</td></tr>
<tr><td>36</td><td>Kentucky</td><td>11,689</td><td>0.37%</td><td>17</td><td>Wisconsin</td><td>51,669</td><td>1.64%</td></tr>
<tr><td>26</td><td>Louisiana</td><td>35,375</td><td>1.12%</td><td>18</td><td>Massachusetts</td><td>44,858</td><td>1.43%</td></tr>
<tr><td>42</td><td>Maine</td><td>7,696</td><td>0.24%</td><td>19</td><td>Missouri</td><td>44,644</td><td>1.42%</td></tr>
<tr><td>15</td><td>Maryland</td><td>70,553</td><td>2.24%</td><td>20</td><td>Arizona</td><td>43,190</td><td>1.37%</td></tr>
<tr><td>18</td><td>Massachusetts</td><td>44,858</td><td>1.43%</td><td>21</td><td>Oregon</td><td>42,292</td><td>1.34%</td></tr>
<tr><td>5</td><td>Michigan</td><td>148,595</td><td>4.72%</td><td>22</td><td>South Carolina</td><td>42,082</td><td>1.34%</td></tr>
<tr><td>14</td><td>Minnesota</td><td>88,039</td><td>2.80%</td><td>23</td><td>Colorado</td><td>41,212</td><td>1.31%</td></tr>
<tr><td>37</td><td>Mississippi</td><td>9,999</td><td>0.32%</td><td>24</td><td>Alabama</td><td>38,764</td><td>1.23%</td></tr>
<tr><td>19</td><td>Missouri</td><td>44,644</td><td>1.42%</td><td>25</td><td>Tennessee</td><td>37,401</td><td>1.19%</td></tr>
<tr><td>45</td><td>Montana</td><td>4,473</td><td>0.14%</td><td>26</td><td>Louisiana</td><td>35,375</td><td>1.12%</td></tr>
<tr><td>34</td><td>Nebraska</td><td>14,503</td><td>0.46%</td><td>27</td><td>Virginia</td><td>29,620</td><td>0.94%</td></tr>
<tr><td>38</td><td>Nevada</td><td>9,760</td><td>0.31%</td><td>28</td><td>Oklahoma</td><td>28,090</td><td>0.89%</td></tr>
<tr><td>46</td><td>New Hampshire</td><td>4,414</td><td>0.14%</td><td>29</td><td>Arkansas</td><td>24,033</td><td>0.76%</td></tr>
<tr><td>7</td><td>New Jersey</td><td>125,881</td><td>4.00%</td><td>30</td><td>Rhode Island</td><td>20,446</td><td>0.65%</td></tr>
<tr><td>40</td><td>New Mexico</td><td>8,928</td><td>0.28%</td><td>31</td><td>Delaware</td><td>16,528</td><td>0.53%</td></tr>
<tr><td>4</td><td>New York</td><td>180,580</td><td>5.74%</td><td>32</td><td>Kansas</td><td>15,732</td><td>0.50%</td></tr>
<tr><td>12</td><td>North Carolina</td><td>102,483</td><td>3.26%</td><td>33</td><td>Iowa</td><td>15,384</td><td>0.49%</td></tr>
<tr><td>50</td><td>North Dakota</td><td>2,521</td><td>0.08%</td><td>34</td><td>Nebraska</td><td>14,503</td><td>0.46%</td></tr>
<tr><td>11</td><td>Ohio</td><td>102,755</td><td>3.27%</td><td>35</td><td>Hawaii</td><td>14,238</td><td>0.45%</td></tr>
<tr><td>28</td><td>Oklahoma</td><td>28,090</td><td>0.89%</td><td>36</td><td>Kentucky</td><td>11,689</td><td>0.37%</td></tr>
<tr><td>21</td><td>Oregon</td><td>42,292</td><td>1.34%</td><td>37</td><td>Mississippi</td><td>9,999</td><td>0.32%</td></tr>
<tr><td>10</td><td>Pennsylvania</td><td>110,532</td><td>3.51%</td><td>38</td><td>Nevada</td><td>9,760</td><td>0.31%</td></tr>
<tr><td>30</td><td>Rhode Island</td><td>20,446</td><td>0.65%</td><td>39</td><td>Utah</td><td>9,111</td><td>0.29%</td></tr>
<tr><td>22</td><td>South Carolina</td><td>42,082</td><td>1.34%</td><td>40</td><td>New Mexico</td><td>8,928</td><td>0.28%</td></tr>
<tr><td>48</td><td>South Dakota</td><td>3,484</td><td>0.11%</td><td>41</td><td>Vermont</td><td>8,220</td><td>0.26%</td></tr>
<tr><td>25</td><td>Tennessee</td><td>37,401</td><td>1.19%</td><td>42</td><td>Maine</td><td>7,696</td><td>0.24%</td></tr>
<tr><td>1</td><td>Texas</td><td>425,789</td><td>13.53%</td><td>43</td><td>Idaho</td><td>5,855</td><td>0.19%</td></tr>
<tr><td>39</td><td>Utah</td><td>9,111</td><td>0.29%</td><td>44</td><td>West Virginia</td><td>5,669</td><td>0.18%</td></tr>
<tr><td>41</td><td>Vermont</td><td>8,220</td><td>0.26%</td><td>45</td><td>Montana</td><td>4,473</td><td>0.14%</td></tr>
<tr><td>27</td><td>Virginia</td><td>29,620</td><td>0.94%</td><td>46</td><td>New Hampshire</td><td>4,414</td><td>0.14%</td></tr>
<tr><td>8</td><td>Washington</td><td>125,317</td><td>3.98%</td><td>47</td><td>Alaska</td><td>3,760</td><td>0.12%</td></tr>
<tr><td>44</td><td>West Virginia</td><td>5,669</td><td>0.18%</td><td>48</td><td>South Dakota</td><td>3,484</td><td>0.11%</td></tr>
<tr><td>17</td><td>Wisconsin</td><td>51,669</td><td>1.64%</td><td>49</td><td>Wyoming</td><td>3,432</td><td>0.11%</td></tr>
<tr><td>49</td><td>Wyoming</td><td>3,432</td><td>0.11%</td><td>50</td><td>North Dakota</td><td>2,521</td><td>0.08%</td></tr>
<tr><td></td><td></td><td></td><td></td><td></td><td>District of Columbia</td><td>9,740</td><td>0.31%</td></tr>
</table>

Source: U.S. Department of Justice, Bureau of Justice Statistics
   "Probation and Parole Population Reached Almost 3.9 Million Last Year" (Press Release, August 14, 1997)
*As of December 31, 1996. Does not include 34,301 adults on federal probation.

Rate of Adults on State Probation in 1996

National Rate = 1,603 Adults on State Probation per 100,000 Adult Population*

ALPHA ORDER

RANK	STATE	RATE
26	Alabama	1,213
35	Alaska	890
22	Arizona	1,318
23	Arkansas	1,299
24	California	1,269
18	Colorado	1,459
9	Connecticut	2,261
3	Delaware	3,012
8	Florida	2,273
5	Georgia	2,669
16	Hawaii	1,623
41	Idaho	696
20	Illinois	1,329
7	Indiana	2,294
40	Iowa	721
36	Kansas	835
50	Kentucky	401
30	Louisiana	1,135
38	Maine	815
13	Maryland	1,864
33	Massachusetts	960
10	Michigan	2,106
6	Minnesota	2,581
47	Mississippi	510
31	Missouri	1,126
42	Montana	692
28	Nebraska	1,199
37	Nevada	823
48	New Hampshire	509
11	New Jersey	2,098
39	New Mexico	737
21	New York	1,323
12	North Carolina	1,867
46	North Dakota	531
25	Ohio	1,234
29	Oklahoma	1,161
15	Oregon	1,766
27	Pennsylvania	1,206
4	Rhode Island	2,708
17	South Carolina	1,524
44	South Dakota	660
34	Tennessee	936
1	Texas	3,113
43	Utah	689
14	Vermont	1,860
45	Virginia	587
2	Washington	3,059
49	West Virginia	404
19	Wisconsin	1,354
32	Wyoming	986

RANK ORDER

RANK	STATE	RATE
1	Texas	3,113
2	Washington	3,059
3	Delaware	3,012
4	Rhode Island	2,708
5	Georgia	2,669
6	Minnesota	2,581
7	Indiana	2,294
8	Florida	2,273
9	Connecticut	2,261
10	Michigan	2,106
11	New Jersey	2,098
12	North Carolina	1,867
13	Maryland	1,864
14	Vermont	1,860
15	Oregon	1,766
16	Hawaii	1,623
17	South Carolina	1,524
18	Colorado	1,459
19	Wisconsin	1,354
20	Illinois	1,329
21	New York	1,323
22	Arizona	1,318
23	Arkansas	1,299
24	California	1,269
25	Ohio	1,234
26	Alabama	1,213
27	Pennsylvania	1,206
28	Nebraska	1,199
29	Oklahoma	1,161
30	Louisiana	1,135
31	Missouri	1,126
32	Wyoming	986
33	Massachusetts	960
34	Tennessee	936
35	Alaska	890
36	Kansas	835
37	Nevada	823
38	Maine	815
39	New Mexico	737
40	Iowa	721
41	Idaho	696
42	Montana	692
43	Utah	689
44	South Dakota	660
45	Virginia	587
46	North Dakota	531
47	Mississippi	510
48	New Hampshire	509
49	West Virginia	404
50	Kentucky	401
	District of Columbia	2,246

Source: U.S. Department of Justice, Bureau of Justice Statistics
    "Probation and Parole Population Reached Almost 3.9 Million Last Year" (Press Release, August 14, 1997)
*As of December 31, 1996. Federal rate is 17 adults on probation per 100,000 adult population.

Adults on State Parole in 1996

National Total = 645,576 Adults*

ALPHA ORDER				RANK ORDER			
RANK	STATE	ADULTS	% of USA	RANK	STATE	ADULTS	% of USA
21	Alabama	5,213	0.81%	1	Texas	112,594	17.44%
46	Alaska	553	0.09%	2	California	97,063	15.04%
25	Arizona	3,785	0.59%	3	Pennsylvania	75,013	11.62%
22	Arkansas	5,143	0.80%	4	New York	57,137	8.85%
2	California	97,063	15.04%	5	New Jersey	41,547	6.44%
27	Colorado	3,294	0.51%	6	Illinois	30,064	4.66%
36	Connecticut	1,083	0.17%	7	Georgia	21,146	3.28%
38	Delaware	1,033	0.16%	8	Louisiana	20,998	3.25%
15	Florida	9,243	1.43%	9	Maryland	16,246	2.52%
7	Georgia	21,146	3.28%	10	Oregon	15,800	2.45%
33	Hawaii	1,733	0.27%	11	Michigan	14,609	2.26%
43	Idaho	692	0.11%	12	North Carolina	12,358	1.91%
6	Illinois	30,064	4.66%	13	Missouri	12,197	1.89%
26	Indiana	3,575	0.55%	14	Virginia	9,918	1.54%
31	Iowa	2,200	0.34%	15	Florida	9,243	1.43%
19	Kansas	6,004	0.93%	16	Tennessee	8,934	1.38%
24	Kentucky	4,621	0.72%	17	Wisconsin	8,121	1.26%
8	Louisiana	20,998	3.25%	18	Ohio	6,331	0.98%
50	Maine	57	0.01%	19	Kansas	6,004	0.93%
9	Maryland	16,246	2.52%	20	South Carolina	5,367	0.83%
23	Massachusetts	4,836	0.75%	21	Alabama	5,213	0.81%
11	Michigan	14,609	2.26%	22	Arkansas	5,143	0.80%
30	Minnesota	2,377	0.37%	23	Massachusetts	4,836	0.75%
34	Mississippi	1,513	0.23%	24	Kentucky	4,621	0.72%
13	Missouri	12,197	1.89%	25	Arizona	3,785	0.59%
40	Montana	771	0.12%	26	Indiana	3,575	0.55%
42	Nebraska	706	0.11%	27	Colorado	3,294	0.51%
28	Nevada	3,216	0.50%	28	Nevada	3,216	0.50%
37	New Hampshire	1,066	0.17%	29	Utah	2,975	0.46%
5	New Jersey	41,547	6.44%	30	Minnesota	2,377	0.37%
35	New Mexico	1,426	0.22%	31	Iowa	2,200	0.34%
4	New York	57,137	8.85%	32	Oklahoma	2,159	0.33%
12	North Carolina	12,358	1.91%	33	Hawaii	1,733	0.27%
49	North Dakota	104	0.02%	34	Mississippi	1,513	0.23%
18	Ohio	6,331	0.98%	35	New Mexico	1,426	0.22%
32	Oklahoma	2,159	0.33%	36	Connecticut	1,083	0.17%
10	Oregon	15,800	2.45%	37	New Hampshire	1,066	0.17%
3	Pennsylvania	75,013	11.62%	38	Delaware	1,033	0.16%
44	Rhode Island	575	0.09%	39	West Virginia	869	0.13%
20	South Carolina	5,367	0.83%	40	Montana	771	0.12%
41	South Dakota	725	0.11%	41	South Dakota	725	0.11%
16	Tennessee	8,934	1.38%	42	Nebraska	706	0.11%
1	Texas	112,594	17.44%	43	Idaho	692	0.11%
29	Utah	2,975	0.46%	44	Rhode Island	575	0.09%
47	Vermont	542	0.08%	45	Washington	560	0.09%
14	Virginia	9,918	1.54%	46	Alaska	553	0.09%
45	Washington	560	0.09%	47	Vermont	542	0.08%
39	West Virginia	869	0.13%	48	Wyoming	364	0.06%
17	Wisconsin	8,121	1.26%	49	North Dakota	104	0.02%
48	Wyoming	364	0.06%	50	Maine	57	0.01%
					District of Columbia	7,120	1.10%

Source: U.S. Department of Justice, Bureau of Justice Statistics
   "Probation and Parole Population Reached Almost 3.9 Million Last Year" (Press Release, August 14, 1997)
*As of December 31, 1996. Does not include 59,133 adults on federal parole.

Rate of Adults on State Parole in 1996

National Rate = 329 Adults on State Parole per 100,000 Adult Population*

ALPHA ORDER

RANK	STATE	RATE
24	Alabama	163
27	Alaska	131
33	Arizona	115
13	Arkansas	278
7	California	422
32	Colorado	117
47	Connecticut	44
23	Delaware	188
38	Florida	84
9	Georgia	392
20	Hawaii	198
39	Idaho	82
10	Illinois	346
39	Indiana	82
36	Iowa	103
11	Kansas	319
25	Kentucky	159
4	Louisiana	674
50	Maine	6
6	Maryland	429
35	Massachusetts	104
19	Michigan	207
44	Minnesota	70
41	Mississippi	77
12	Missouri	308
30	Montana	119
46	Nebraska	58
14	Nevada	271
28	New Hampshire	123
3	New Jersey	692
31	New Mexico	118
8	New York	419
15	North Carolina	225
48	North Dakota	22
42	Ohio	76
37	Oklahoma	89
5	Oregon	660
2	Pennsylvania	819
42	Rhode Island	76
22	South Carolina	194
26	South Dakota	137
17	Tennessee	223
1	Texas	823
15	Utah	225
28	Vermont	123
21	Virginia	197
49	Washington	14
45	West Virginia	62
18	Wisconsin	213
34	Wyoming	105

RANK ORDER

RANK	STATE	RATE
1	Texas	823
2	Pennsylvania	819
3	New Jersey	692
4	Louisiana	674
5	Oregon	660
6	Maryland	429
7	California	422
8	New York	419
9	Georgia	392
10	Illinois	346
11	Kansas	319
12	Missouri	308
13	Arkansas	278
14	Nevada	271
15	North Carolina	225
15	Utah	225
17	Tennessee	223
18	Wisconsin	213
19	Michigan	207
20	Hawaii	198
21	Virginia	197
22	South Carolina	194
23	Delaware	188
24	Alabama	163
25	Kentucky	159
26	South Dakota	137
27	Alaska	131
28	New Hampshire	123
28	Vermont	123
30	Montana	119
31	New Mexico	118
32	Colorado	117
33	Arizona	115
34	Wyoming	105
35	Massachusetts	104
36	Iowa	103
37	Oklahoma	89
38	Florida	84
39	Idaho	82
39	Indiana	82
41	Mississippi	77
42	Ohio	76
42	Rhode Island	76
44	Minnesota	70
45	West Virginia	62
46	Nebraska	58
47	Connecticut	44
48	North Dakota	22
49	Washington	14
50	Maine	6
	District of Columbia	1,642

Source: U.S. Department of Justice, Bureau of Justice Statistics
"Probation and Parole Population Reached Almost 3.9 Million Last Year" (Press Release, August 14, 1997)
*As of December 31, 1996. Federal rate is 30 adults on parole per 100,000 adult population.

State and Local Government Employees in Corrections in 1995

National Total = 614,975 Employees*

RANK	STATE	EMPLOYEES	% of USA
28	Alabama	6,760	1.10%
44	Alaska	1,296	0.21%
14	Arizona	12,324	2.00%
33	Arkansas	4,627	0.75%
1	California	70,854	11.52%
27	Colorado	7,108	1.16%
25	Connecticut	7,443	1.21%
40	Delaware	1,840	0.30%
4	Florida	44,315	7.21%
5	Georgia	25,355	4.12%
39	Hawaii	2,131	0.35%
38	Idaho	2,342	0.38%
8	Illinois	21,757	3.54%
18	Indiana	10,116	1.64%
35	Iowa	3,234	0.53%
30	Kansas	5,510	0.90%
24	Kentucky	7,507	1.22%
20	Louisiana	9,377	1.52%
41	Maine	1,818	0.30%
13	Maryland	13,125	2.13%
16	Massachusetts	11,097	1.80%
9	Michigan	21,226	3.45%
26	Minnesota	7,161	1.16%
32	Mississippi	4,731	0.77%
21	Missouri	8,984	1.46%
46	Montana	1,170	0.19%
37	Nebraska	2,728	0.44%
34	Nevada	4,181	0.68%
43	New Hampshire	1,543	0.25%
11	New Jersey	16,125	2.62%
31	New Mexico	5,187	0.84%
3	New York	58,067	9.44%
12	North Carolina	15,922	2.59%
50	North Dakota	717	0.12%
7	Ohio	22,215	3.61%
23	Oklahoma	8,875	1.44%
29	Oregon	5,708	0.93%
6	Pennsylvania	23,498	3.82%
42	Rhode Island	1,655	0.27%
19	South Carolina	10,075	1.64%
47	South Dakota	1,001	0.16%
15	Tennessee	11,332	1.84%
2	Texas	63,917	10.39%
36	Utah	3,196	0.52%
48	Vermont	868	0.14%
10	Virginia	18,926	3.08%
17	Washington	10,944	1.78%
45	West Virginia	1,204	0.20%
22	Wisconsin	8,888	1.45%
49	Wyoming	810	0.13%

RANK	STATE	EMPLOYEES	% of USA
1	California	70,854	11.52%
2	Texas	63,917	10.39%
3	New York	58,067	9.44%
4	Florida	44,315	7.21%
5	Georgia	25,355	4.12%
6	Pennsylvania	23,498	3.82%
7	Ohio	22,215	3.61%
8	Illinois	21,757	3.54%
9	Michigan	21,226	3.45%
10	Virginia	18,926	3.08%
11	New Jersey	16,125	2.62%
12	North Carolina	15,922	2.59%
13	Maryland	13,125	2.13%
14	Arizona	12,324	2.00%
15	Tennessee	11,332	1.84%
16	Massachusetts	11,097	1.80%
17	Washington	10,944	1.78%
18	Indiana	10,116	1.64%
19	South Carolina	10,075	1.64%
20	Louisiana	9,377	1.52%
21	Missouri	8,984	1.46%
22	Wisconsin	8,888	1.45%
23	Oklahoma	8,875	1.44%
24	Kentucky	7,507	1.22%
25	Connecticut	7,443	1.21%
26	Minnesota	7,161	1.16%
27	Colorado	7,108	1.16%
28	Alabama	6,760	1.10%
29	Oregon	5,708	0.93%
30	Kansas	5,510	0.90%
31	New Mexico	5,187	0.84%
32	Mississippi	4,731	0.77%
33	Arkansas	4,627	0.75%
34	Nevada	4,181	0.68%
35	Iowa	3,234	0.53%
36	Utah	3,196	0.52%
37	Nebraska	2,728	0.44%
38	Idaho	2,342	0.38%
39	Hawaii	2,131	0.35%
40	Delaware	1,840	0.30%
41	Maine	1,818	0.30%
42	Rhode Island	1,655	0.27%
43	New Hampshire	1,543	0.25%
44	Alaska	1,296	0.21%
45	West Virginia	1,204	0.20%
46	Montana	1,170	0.19%
47	South Dakota	1,001	0.16%
48	Vermont	868	0.14%
49	Wyoming	810	0.13%
50	North Dakota	717	0.12%
	District of Columbia	4,185	0.68%

Source: U.S. Bureau of the Census, Governments Division
"1995 State and Local Government Employment" (http://www.census.gov/govs/www/apes95sl.html)
*Full-time equivalent as of October 1995.

State and Local Government Employees in Corrections as a Percent of All State and Local Government Employees in 1995
National Percent = 4.4% of Employees*

ALPHA ORDER				RANK ORDER		
RANK	STATE	PERCENT		RANK	STATE	PERCENT
39	Alabama	2.7		1	Florida	6.3
37	Alaska	2.8		2	Georgia	5.7
5	Arizona	5.6		2	Nevada	5.7
28	Arkansas	3.4		2	Texas	5.7
9	California	4.8		5	Arizona	5.6
26	Colorado	3.5		6	Maryland	5.2
13	Connecticut	4.5		6	New York	5.2
13	Delaware	4.5		6	Virginia	5.2
1	Florida	6.3		9	California	4.8
2	Georgia	5.7		10	New Mexico	4.7
31	Hawaii	3.3		10	South Carolina	4.7
26	Idaho	3.5		12	Michigan	4.6
21	Illinois	3.7		13	Connecticut	4.5
31	Indiana	3.3		13	Delaware	4.5
48	Iowa	1.9		13	Oklahoma	4.5
31	Kansas	3.3		13	Pennsylvania	4.5
24	Kentucky	3.6		17	Tennessee	4.2
24	Louisiana	3.6		18	North Carolina	4.0
39	Maine	2.7		19	Ohio	3.9
6	Maryland	5.2		19	Washington	3.9
21	Massachusetts	3.7		21	Illinois	3.7
12	Michigan	4.6		21	Massachusetts	3.7
39	Minnesota	2.7		21	New Jersey	3.7
39	Mississippi	2.7		24	Kentucky	3.6
31	Missouri	3.3		24	Louisiana	3.6
46	Montana	2.1		26	Colorado	3.5
43	Nebraska	2.6		26	Idaho	3.5
2	Nevada	5.7		28	Arkansas	3.4
37	New Hampshire	2.8		28	Oregon	3.4
21	New Jersey	3.7		28	Rhode Island	3.4
10	New Mexico	4.7		31	Hawaii	3.3
6	New York	5.2		31	Indiana	3.3
18	North Carolina	4.0		31	Kansas	3.3
48	North Dakota	1.9		31	Missouri	3.3
19	Ohio	3.9		31	Wisconsin	3.3
13	Oklahoma	4.5		36	Utah	3.0
28	Oregon	3.4		37	Alaska	2.8
13	Pennsylvania	4.5		37	New Hampshire	2.8
28	Rhode Island	3.4		39	Alabama	2.7
10	South Carolina	4.7		39	Maine	2.7
45	South Dakota	2.5		39	Minnesota	2.7
17	Tennessee	4.2		39	Mississippi	2.7
2	Texas	5.7		43	Nebraska	2.6
36	Utah	3.0		43	Vermont	2.6
43	Vermont	2.6		45	South Dakota	2.5
6	Virginia	5.2		46	Montana	2.1
19	Washington	3.9		46	Wyoming	2.1
50	West Virginia	1.3		48	Iowa	1.9
31	Wisconsin	3.3		48	North Dakota	1.9
46	Wyoming	2.1		50	West Virginia	1.3
					District of Columbia	8.9

Source: Morgan Quitno Press using data from U.S. Bureau of the Census, Governments Division
   "1995 State and Local Government Employment" (http://www.census.gov/govs/www/apes95sl.html)
*Full-time equivalent as of October 1995.

State Government Employees in Corrections in 1995

National Total = 409,208 Employees*

<table>
<tr><td colspan="4">ALPHA ORDER</td><td colspan="4">RANK ORDER</td></tr>
<tr><td>RANK</td><td>STATE</td><td>EMPLOYEES</td><td>% of USA</td><td>RANK</td><td>STATE</td><td>EMPLOYEES</td><td>% of USA</td></tr>
<tr><td>26</td><td>Alabama</td><td>4,323</td><td>1.06%</td><td>1</td><td>California</td><td>43,064</td><td>10.52%</td></tr>
<tr><td>42</td><td>Alaska</td><td>1,255</td><td>0.31%</td><td>2</td><td>Texas</td><td>43,000</td><td>10.51%</td></tr>
<tr><td>16</td><td>Arizona</td><td>7,573</td><td>1.85%</td><td>3</td><td>New York</td><td>33,855</td><td>8.27%</td></tr>
<tr><td>31</td><td>Arkansas</td><td>3,391</td><td>0.83%</td><td>4</td><td>Florida</td><td>31,062</td><td>7.59%</td></tr>
<tr><td>1</td><td>California</td><td>43,064</td><td>10.52%</td><td>5</td><td>Georgia</td><td>19,111</td><td>4.67%</td></tr>
<tr><td>27</td><td>Colorado</td><td>4,210</td><td>1.03%</td><td>6</td><td>Michigan</td><td>16,474</td><td>4.03%</td></tr>
<tr><td>17</td><td>Connecticut</td><td>7,443</td><td>1.82%</td><td>7</td><td>Ohio</td><td>14,684</td><td>3.59%</td></tr>
<tr><td>39</td><td>Delaware</td><td>1,840</td><td>0.45%</td><td>8</td><td>Illinois</td><td>13,621</td><td>3.33%</td></tr>
<tr><td>4</td><td>Florida</td><td>31,062</td><td>7.59%</td><td>9</td><td>Pennsylvania</td><td>12,806</td><td>3.13%</td></tr>
<tr><td>5</td><td>Georgia</td><td>19,111</td><td>4.67%</td><td>10</td><td>Virginia</td><td>12,736</td><td>3.11%</td></tr>
<tr><td>37</td><td>Hawaii</td><td>2,131</td><td>0.52%</td><td>11</td><td>North Carolina</td><td>12,367</td><td>3.02%</td></tr>
<tr><td>41</td><td>Idaho</td><td>1,546</td><td>0.38%</td><td>12</td><td>Maryland</td><td>10,596</td><td>2.59%</td></tr>
<tr><td>8</td><td>Illinois</td><td>13,621</td><td>3.33%</td><td>13</td><td>New Jersey</td><td>8,993</td><td>2.20%</td></tr>
<tr><td>23</td><td>Indiana</td><td>6,273</td><td>1.53%</td><td>14</td><td>South Carolina</td><td>8,076</td><td>1.97%</td></tr>
<tr><td>36</td><td>Iowa</td><td>2,326</td><td>0.57%</td><td>15</td><td>Oklahoma</td><td>7,824</td><td>1.91%</td></tr>
<tr><td>30</td><td>Kansas</td><td>3,589</td><td>0.88%</td><td>16</td><td>Arizona</td><td>7,573</td><td>1.85%</td></tr>
<tr><td>25</td><td>Kentucky</td><td>5,284</td><td>1.29%</td><td>17</td><td>Connecticut</td><td>7,443</td><td>1.82%</td></tr>
<tr><td>20</td><td>Louisiana</td><td>6,789</td><td>1.66%</td><td>18</td><td>Washington</td><td>7,398</td><td>1.81%</td></tr>
<tr><td>43</td><td>Maine</td><td>1,206</td><td>0.29%</td><td>19</td><td>Tennessee</td><td>7,033</td><td>1.72%</td></tr>
<tr><td>12</td><td>Maryland</td><td>10,596</td><td>2.59%</td><td>20</td><td>Louisiana</td><td>6,789</td><td>1.66%</td></tr>
<tr><td>24</td><td>Massachusetts</td><td>6,098</td><td>1.49%</td><td>21</td><td>Missouri</td><td>6,652</td><td>1.63%</td></tr>
<tr><td>6</td><td>Michigan</td><td>16,474</td><td>4.03%</td><td>22</td><td>Wisconsin</td><td>6,502</td><td>1.59%</td></tr>
<tr><td>32</td><td>Minnesota</td><td>3,378</td><td>0.83%</td><td>23</td><td>Indiana</td><td>6,273</td><td>1.53%</td></tr>
<tr><td>29</td><td>Mississippi</td><td>3,696</td><td>0.90%</td><td>24</td><td>Massachusetts</td><td>6,098</td><td>1.49%</td></tr>
<tr><td>21</td><td>Missouri</td><td>6,652</td><td>1.63%</td><td>25</td><td>Kentucky</td><td>5,284</td><td>1.29%</td></tr>
<tr><td>46</td><td>Montana</td><td>824</td><td>0.20%</td><td>26</td><td>Alabama</td><td>4,323</td><td>1.06%</td></tr>
<tr><td>38</td><td>Nebraska</td><td>1,950</td><td>0.48%</td><td>27</td><td>Colorado</td><td>4,210</td><td>1.03%</td></tr>
<tr><td>33</td><td>Nevada</td><td>2,896</td><td>0.71%</td><td>28</td><td>New Mexico</td><td>3,932</td><td>0.96%</td></tr>
<tr><td>44</td><td>New Hampshire</td><td>1,042</td><td>0.25%</td><td>29</td><td>Mississippi</td><td>3,696</td><td>0.90%</td></tr>
<tr><td>13</td><td>New Jersey</td><td>8,993</td><td>2.20%</td><td>30</td><td>Kansas</td><td>3,589</td><td>0.88%</td></tr>
<tr><td>28</td><td>New Mexico</td><td>3,932</td><td>0.96%</td><td>31</td><td>Arkansas</td><td>3,391</td><td>0.83%</td></tr>
<tr><td>3</td><td>New York</td><td>33,855</td><td>8.27%</td><td>32</td><td>Minnesota</td><td>3,378</td><td>0.83%</td></tr>
<tr><td>11</td><td>North Carolina</td><td>12,367</td><td>3.02%</td><td>33</td><td>Nevada</td><td>2,896</td><td>0.71%</td></tr>
<tr><td>49</td><td>North Dakota</td><td>514</td><td>0.13%</td><td>34</td><td>Oregon</td><td>2,873</td><td>0.70%</td></tr>
<tr><td>7</td><td>Ohio</td><td>14,684</td><td>3.59%</td><td>35</td><td>Utah</td><td>2,502</td><td>0.61%</td></tr>
<tr><td>15</td><td>Oklahoma</td><td>7,824</td><td>1.91%</td><td>36</td><td>Iowa</td><td>2,326</td><td>0.57%</td></tr>
<tr><td>34</td><td>Oregon</td><td>2,873</td><td>0.70%</td><td>37</td><td>Hawaii</td><td>2,131</td><td>0.52%</td></tr>
<tr><td>9</td><td>Pennsylvania</td><td>12,806</td><td>3.13%</td><td>38</td><td>Nebraska</td><td>1,950</td><td>0.48%</td></tr>
<tr><td>40</td><td>Rhode Island</td><td>1,655</td><td>0.40%</td><td>39</td><td>Delaware</td><td>1,840</td><td>0.45%</td></tr>
<tr><td>14</td><td>South Carolina</td><td>8,076</td><td>1.97%</td><td>40</td><td>Rhode Island</td><td>1,655</td><td>0.40%</td></tr>
<tr><td>48</td><td>South Dakota</td><td>666</td><td>0.16%</td><td>41</td><td>Idaho</td><td>1,546</td><td>0.38%</td></tr>
<tr><td>19</td><td>Tennessee</td><td>7,033</td><td>1.72%</td><td>42</td><td>Alaska</td><td>1,255</td><td>0.31%</td></tr>
<tr><td>2</td><td>Texas</td><td>43,000</td><td>10.51%</td><td>43</td><td>Maine</td><td>1,206</td><td>0.29%</td></tr>
<tr><td>35</td><td>Utah</td><td>2,502</td><td>0.61%</td><td>44</td><td>New Hampshire</td><td>1,042</td><td>0.25%</td></tr>
<tr><td>45</td><td>Vermont</td><td>868</td><td>0.21%</td><td>45</td><td>Vermont</td><td>868</td><td>0.21%</td></tr>
<tr><td>10</td><td>Virginia</td><td>12,736</td><td>3.11%</td><td>46</td><td>Montana</td><td>824</td><td>0.20%</td></tr>
<tr><td>18</td><td>Washington</td><td>7,398</td><td>1.81%</td><td>47</td><td>West Virginia</td><td>796</td><td>0.19%</td></tr>
<tr><td>47</td><td>West Virginia</td><td>796</td><td>0.19%</td><td>48</td><td>South Dakota</td><td>666</td><td>0.16%</td></tr>
<tr><td>22</td><td>Wisconsin</td><td>6,502</td><td>1.59%</td><td>49</td><td>North Dakota</td><td>514</td><td>0.13%</td></tr>
<tr><td>50</td><td>Wyoming</td><td>485</td><td>0.12%</td><td>50</td><td>Wyoming</td><td>485</td><td>0.12%</td></tr>
<tr><td></td><td></td><td></td><td></td><td></td><td>District of Columbia**</td><td>NA</td><td>NA</td></tr>
</table>

Source: U.S. Bureau of the Census, Governments Division
    "1995 State Government Employment" (http://www.census.gov/govs/www/apes95.html)
*Full-time equivalent as of October 1995. These are updated numbers to reflect changes in Georgia's and Maine's total.
**Not applicable.

State Government Employees in Corrections
As a Percent of All State Government Employees in 1995
National Percent = 10.3% of Employees*

ALPHA ORDER

RANK ORDER

RANK	STATE	PERCENT		RANK	STATE	PERCENT
42	Alabama	5.3		1	Florida	17.8
39	Alaska	5.7		2	Georgia	16.7
7	Arizona	13.0		3	Texas	16.0
33	Arkansas	7.1		4	Nevada	14.1
8	California	12.7		5	Maryland	13.1
29	Colorado	7.3		5	New York	13.1
9	Connecticut	11.8		7	Arizona	13.0
19	Delaware	8.4		8	California	12.7
1	Florida	17.8		9	Connecticut	11.8
2	Georgia	16.7		10	Michigan	11.7
48	Hawaii	4.1		11	Oklahoma	11.6
27	Idaho	7.4		12	Virginia	11.0
17	Illinois	9.7		13	North Carolina	10.8
33	Indiana	7.1		14	Ohio	10.3
47	Iowa	4.4		14	South Carolina	10.3
25	Kansas	7.5		16	Wisconsin	10.1
31	Kentucky	7.2		17	Illinois	9.7
29	Louisiana	7.3		18	New Mexico	9.3
39	Maine	5.7		19	Delaware	8.4
5	Maryland	13.1		19	Missouri	8.4
25	Massachusetts	7.5		19	Pennsylvania	8.4
10	Michigan	11.7		22	Tennessee	8.3
44	Minnesota	4.6		23	Rhode Island	8.2
27	Mississippi	7.4		24	Washington	7.7
19	Missouri	8.4		25	Kansas	7.5
44	Montana	4.6		25	Massachusetts	7.5
36	Nebraska	6.6		27	Idaho	7.4
4	Nevada	14.1		27	Mississippi	7.4
37	New Hampshire	6.2		29	Colorado	7.3
31	New Jersey	7.2		29	Louisiana	7.3
18	New Mexico	9.3		31	Kentucky	7.2
5	New York	13.1		31	New Jersey	7.2
13	North Carolina	10.8		33	Arkansas	7.1
49	North Dakota	3.1		33	Indiana	7.1
14	Ohio	10.3		35	Vermont	6.9
11	Oklahoma	11.6		36	Nebraska	6.6
41	Oregon	5.5		37	New Hampshire	6.2
19	Pennsylvania	8.4		38	Utah	6.0
23	Rhode Island	8.2		39	Alaska	5.7
14	South Carolina	10.3		39	Maine	5.7
43	South Dakota	4.7		41	Oregon	5.5
22	Tennessee	8.3		42	Alabama	5.3
3	Texas	16.0		43	South Dakota	4.7
38	Utah	6.0		44	Minnesota	4.6
35	Vermont	6.9		44	Montana	4.6
12	Virginia	11.0		46	Wyoming	4.5
24	Washington	7.7		47	Iowa	4.4
50	West Virginia	2.3		48	Hawaii	4.1
16	Wisconsin	10.1		49	North Dakota	3.1
46	Wyoming	4.5		50	West Virginia	2.3
					District of Columbia**	NA

Source: Morgan Quitno Press using data from U.S. Bureau of the Census, Governments Division
   "1995 State Government Employment" (http://www.census.gov/govs/www/apes95.html)
*Full-time equivalent as of October 1995. These are updated numbers to reflect changes in Georgia's and Maine's total.
**Not applicable.

State Correctional Officers in 1996

National Total = 211,199 Officers*

ALPHA ORDER					RANK ORDER			
RANK	STATE		OFFICERS	% of USA	RANK	STATE	OFFICERS	% of USA
25	Alabama		2,235	1.05%	1	Texas	26,873	12.68%
40	Alaska		718	0.34%	2	New York**	20,099	9.48%
13	Arizona		5,332	2.52%	3	California	17,938	8.46%
27	Arkansas		1,974	0.93%	4	Florida**	14,226	6.71%
3	California		17,938	8.46%	5	North Carolina	10,083	4.76%
26	Colorado		2,146	1.01%	6	Michigan**	9,145	4.31%
14	Connecticut		4,335	2.04%	7	Georgia**	7,932	3.74%
37	Delaware**		911	0.43%	8	Ohio	7,398	3.49%
4	Florida**		14,226	6.71%	9	Illinois**	7,321	3.45%
7	Georgia**		7,932	3.74%	10	Pennsylvania	6,811	3.21%
36	Hawaii		1,000	0.47%	11	Virginia**	5,595	2.64%
42	Idaho**		669	0.32%	12	New Jersey**	5,367	2.53%
9	Illinois**		7,321	3.45%	13	Arizona	5,332	2.52%
16	Indiana**		4,006	1.89%	14	Connecticut	4,335	2.04%
34	Iowa**		1,236	0.58%	15	Maryland**	4,219	1.99%
29	Kansas		1,791	0.84%	16	Indiana**	4,006	1.89%
30	Kentucky		1,771	0.84%	17	Louisiana	3,946	1.86%
17	Louisiana		3,946	1.86%	18	Missouri	3,931	1.85%
44	Maine**		611	0.29%	19	South Carolina**	3,471	1.64%
15	Maryland**		4,219	1.99%	20	Massachusetts**	3,271	1.54%
20	Massachusetts**		3,271	1.54%	21	Tennessee**	3,122	1.47%
6	Michigan**		9,145	4.31%	22	Wisconsin	2,906	1.37%
31	Minnesota		1,412	0.67%	23	Mississippi	2,629	1.24%
23	Mississippi		2,629	1.24%	24	Washington	2,527	1.19%
18	Missouri		3,931	1.85%	25	Alabama	2,235	1.05%
49	Montana**		222	0.10%	26	Colorado	2,146	1.01%
43	Nebraska		643	0.30%	27	Arkansas	1,974	0.93%
32	Nevada		1,333	0.63%	28	Oklahoma	1,881	0.89%
45	New Hampshire		493	0.23%	29	Kansas	1,791	0.84%
12	New Jersey**		5,367	2.53%	30	Kentucky	1,771	0.84%
35	New Mexico		1,181	0.56%	31	Minnesota	1,412	0.67%
2	New York**		20,099	9.48%	32	Nevada	1,333	0.63%
5	North Carolina		10,083	4.76%	33	Oregon	1,280	0.60%
50	North Dakota		139	0.07%	34	Iowa**	1,236	0.58%
8	Ohio		7,398	3.49%	35	New Mexico	1,181	0.56%
28	Oklahoma		1,881	0.89%	36	Hawaii	1,000	0.47%
33	Oregon		1,280	0.60%	37	Delaware**	911	0.43%
10	Pennsylvania		6,811	3.21%	38	Rhode Island	875	0.41%
38	Rhode Island		875	0.41%	39	Utah	813	0.38%
19	South Carolina**		3,471	1.64%	40	Alaska	718	0.34%
47	South Dakota		322	0.15%	41	West Virginia	692	0.33%
21	Tennessee**		3,122	1.47%	42	Idaho**	669	0.32%
1	Texas		26,873	12.68%	43	Nebraska	643	0.30%
39	Utah		813	0.38%	44	Maine**	611	0.29%
46	Vermont		396	0.19%	45	New Hampshire	493	0.23%
11	Virginia**		5,595	2.64%	46	Vermont	396	0.19%
24	Washington		2,527	1.19%	47	South Dakota	322	0.15%
41	West Virginia		692	0.33%	48	Wyoming**	241	0.11%
22	Wisconsin		2,906	1.37%	49	Montana**	222	0.10%
48	Wyoming**		241	0.11%	50	North Dakota	139	0.07%
						District of Columbia**	2,531	1.19%

Source: American Correctional Association (Lanham, MD)
"1997 Directory of Juvenile and Adult Correctional Departments, Institutions, Agencies and Paroling Authorities"
As of June 30, 1996. Total does not include 12,090 federal correctional officers.
**These states' figures are as of June 30, 1995.*

Male Correctional Officers in Adult Systems in 1996

National Total = 167,522 Male Officers*

ALPHA ORDER					RANK ORDER			

RANK	STATE	OFFICERS	% of USA		RANK	STATE	OFFICERS	% of USA
23	Alabama	1,721	1.03%		1	Texas	19,197	11.46%
39	Alaska	588	0.35%		2	New York**	18,600	11.10%
13	Arizona	4,217	2.52%		3	California	14,574	8.70%
29	Arkansas	1,388	0.83%		4	Florida**	10,513	6.28%
3	California	14,574	8.70%		5	North Carolina	7,920	4.73%
24	Colorado	1,679	1.00%		6	Michigan**	7,261	4.33%
14	Connecticut	3,655	2.18%		7	Georgia**	6,472	3.86%
37	Delaware**	783	0.47%		8	Illinois**	6,423	3.83%
4	Florida**	10,513	6.28%		9	Pennsylvania	6,266	3.74%
7	Georgia**	6,472	3.86%		10	Ohio	5,784	3.45%
35	Hawaii	874	0.52%		11	New Jersey**	4,675	2.79%
40	Idaho**	569	0.34%		12	Virginia**	4,410	2.63%
8	Illinois**	6,423	3.83%		13	Arizona	4,217	2.52%
17	Indiana**	3,098	1.85%		14	Connecticut	3,655	2.18%
32	Iowa**	1,056	0.63%		15	Maryland**	3,315	1.98%
27	Kansas	1,488	0.89%		16	Missouri	3,195	1.91%
28	Kentucky	1,455	0.87%		17	Indiana**	3,098	1.85%
18	Louisiana	3,024	1.81%		18	Louisiana	3,024	1.81%
42	Maine**	547	0.33%		19	South Carolina**	2,506	1.50%
15	Maryland**	3,315	1.98%		20	Tennessee**	2,501	1.49%
NA	Massachusetts***	NA	NA		21	Wisconsin	2,365	1.41%
6	Michigan**	7,261	4.33%		22	Washington	2,039	1.22%
34	Minnesota	1,006	0.60%		23	Alabama	1,721	1.03%
26	Mississippi	1,506	0.90%		24	Colorado	1,679	1.00%
16	Missouri	3,195	1.91%		25	Oklahoma	1,603	0.96%
47	Montana**	200	0.12%		26	Mississippi	1,506	0.90%
43	Nebraska	523	0.31%		27	Kansas	1,488	0.89%
30	Nevada	1,131	0.68%		28	Kentucky	1,455	0.87%
44	New Hampshire	444	0.27%		29	Arkansas	1,388	0.83%
11	New Jersey**	4,675	2.79%		30	Nevada	1,131	0.68%
31	New Mexico	1,097	0.65%		31	New Mexico	1,097	0.65%
2	New York**	18,600	11.10%		32	Iowa**	1,056	0.63%
5	North Carolina	7,920	4.73%		33	Oregon	1,052	0.63%
49	North Dakota	113	0.07%		34	Minnesota	1,006	0.60%
10	Ohio	5,784	3.45%		35	Hawaii	874	0.52%
25	Oklahoma	1,603	0.96%		36	Rhode Island	811	0.48%
33	Oregon	1,052	0.63%		37	Delaware**	783	0.47%
9	Pennsylvania	6,266	3.74%		38	Utah	740	0.44%
36	Rhode Island	811	0.48%		39	Alaska	588	0.35%
19	South Carolina**	2,506	1.50%		40	Idaho**	569	0.34%
46	South Dakota	253	0.15%		41	West Virginia	560	0.33%
20	Tennessee**	2,501	1.49%		42	Maine**	547	0.33%
1	Texas	19,197	11.46%		43	Nebraska	523	0.31%
38	Utah	740	0.44%		44	New Hampshire	444	0.27%
45	Vermont	344	0.21%		45	Vermont	344	0.21%
12	Virginia**	4,410	2.63%		46	South Dakota	253	0.15%
22	Washington	2,039	1.22%		47	Montana**	200	0.12%
41	West Virginia	560	0.33%		47	Wyoming**	200	0.12%
21	Wisconsin	2,365	1.41%		49	North Dakota	113	0.07%
47	Wyoming**	200	0.12%		NA	Massachusetts***	NA	NA
						District of Columbia**	1,781	1.06%

Source: American Correctional Association (Lanham, MD)
  "1997 Directory of Juvenile and Adult Correctional Departments, Institutions, Agencies and Paroling Authorities"
*As of June 30, 1996. Total does not include 10,676 male federal correctional officers.
**These states' figures are as of June 30, 1995.
***Not available.

Female Correctional Officers in Adult Systems in 1996

National Total = 41,159 Female Officers*

RANK	STATE	OFFICERS	% of USA		RANK	STATE	OFFICERS	% of USA
24	Alabama	514	1.25%		1	Texas	7,649	18.58%
34	Alaska	130	0.32%		2	Florida**	3,713	9.02%
11	Arizona	1,115	2.71%		3	California	3,364	8.17%
21	Arkansas	586	1.42%		4	North Carolina	2,163	5.26%
3	California	3,364	8.17%		5	Michigan**	1,884	4.58%
26	Colorado	467	1.13%		6	Ohio	1,614	3.92%
19	Connecticut	680	1.65%		7	New York**	1,499	3.64%
35	Delaware**	128	0.31%		8	Georgia**	1,460	3.55%
2	Florida**	3,713	9.02%		9	Virginia**	1,185	2.88%
8	Georgia**	1,460	3.55%		10	Mississippi	1,123	2.73%
36	Hawaii	126	0.31%		11	Arizona	1,115	2.71%
39	Idaho**	100	0.24%		12	South Carolina**	965	2.34%
16	Illinois**	898	2.18%		13	Louisiana	922	2.24%
14	Indiana**	908	2.21%		14	Indiana**	908	2.21%
33	Iowa**	180	0.44%		15	Maryland**	904	2.20%
29	Kansas	303	0.74%		16	Illinois**	898	2.18%
28	Kentucky	315	0.77%		17	Missouri	736	1.79%
13	Louisiana	922	2.24%		18	New Jersey**	692	1.68%
43	Maine**	64	0.16%		19	Connecticut	680	1.65%
15	Maryland**	904	2.20%		20	Tennessee**	621	1.51%
NA	Massachusetts***	NA	NA		21	Arkansas	586	1.42%
5	Michigan**	1,884	4.58%		22	Pennsylvania	545	1.32%
27	Minnesota	406	0.99%		23	Wisconsin	541	1.31%
10	Mississippi	1,123	2.73%		24	Alabama	514	1.25%
17	Missouri	736	1.79%		25	Washington	488	1.19%
49	Montana**	22	0.05%		26	Colorado	467	1.13%
37	Nebraska	120	0.29%		27	Minnesota	406	0.99%
32	Nevada	202	0.49%		28	Kentucky	315	0.77%
45	New Hampshire	49	0.12%		29	Kansas	303	0.74%
18	New Jersey**	692	1.68%		30	Oklahoma	278	0.68%
41	New Mexico	84	0.20%		31	Oregon	228	0.55%
7	New York**	1,499	3.64%		32	Nevada	202	0.49%
4	North Carolina	2,163	5.26%		33	Iowa**	180	0.44%
48	North Dakota	26	0.06%		34	Alaska	130	0.32%
6	Ohio	1,614	3.92%		35	Delaware**	128	0.31%
30	Oklahoma	278	0.68%		36	Hawaii	126	0.31%
31	Oregon	228	0.55%		37	Nebraska	120	0.29%
22	Pennsylvania	545	1.32%		38	Utah	103	0.25%
43	Rhode Island	64	0.16%		39	Idaho**	100	0.24%
12	South Carolina**	965	2.34%		40	West Virginia	92	0.22%
42	South Dakota	70	0.17%		41	New Mexico	84	0.20%
20	Tennessee**	621	1.51%		42	South Dakota	70	0.17%
1	Texas	7,649	18.58%		43	Maine**	64	0.16%
38	Utah	103	0.25%		43	Rhode Island	64	0.16%
46	Vermont	42	0.10%		45	New Hampshire	49	0.12%
9	Virginia**	1,185	2.88%		46	Vermont	42	0.10%
25	Washington	488	1.19%		47	Wyoming**	41	0.10%
40	West Virginia	92	0.22%		48	North Dakota	26	0.06%
23	Wisconsin	541	1.31%		49	Montana**	22	0.05%
47	Wyoming**	41	0.10%		NA	Massachusetts***	NA	NA
						District of Columbia**	750	1.82%

Source: American Correctional Association (Lanham, MD)
"1997 Directory of Juvenile and Adult Correctional Departments, Institutions, Agencies and Paroling Authorities"
*As of June 30, 1996. Total does not include 1,414 female federal correctional officers.
**These states' figures are as of June 30, 1995.
***Not available.

State Prisoners per Correctional Officer in 1996

National Rate = 4.64 Prisoners per Officer*

RANK	STATE	RATE
NA	Alabama***	NA
NA	Alaska***	NA
21	Arizona	4.3
9	Arkansas	5.8
3	California	7.3
25	Colorado	4.0
37	Connecticut	3.0
NA	Delaware***	NA
11	Florida**	5.6
21	Georgia**	4.3
36	Hawaii	3.2
14	Idaho**	5.0
20	Illinois**	4.4
25	Indiana**	4.0
NA	Iowa***	NA
23	Kansas	4.2
10	Kentucky	5.7
35	Louisiana	3.3
42	Maine**	2.3
8	Maryland**	5.9
33	Massachusetts**	3.4
14	Michigan**	5.0
32	Minnesota	3.6
30	Mississippi	3.8
12	Missouri	5.3
1	Montana**	10.8
16	Nebraska	4.9
29	Nevada	3.9
24	New Hampshire	4.1
31	New Jersey**	3.7
25	New Mexico	4.0
37	New York**	3.0
40	North Carolina	2.8
7	North Dakota	6.0
6	Ohio	6.1
2	Oklahoma	7.6
4	Oregon	6.5
19	Pennsylvania	4.5
NA	Rhode Island***	NA
13	South Carolina**	5.1
4	South Dakota	6.5
25	Tennessee**	4.0
17	Texas	4.6
NA	Utah***	NA
41	Vermont	2.5
33	Virginia**	3.4
17	Washington	4.6
37	West Virginia	3.0
NA	Wisconsin***	NA
NA	Wyoming***	NA

RANK	STATE	RATE
1	Montana**	10.8
2	Oklahoma	7.6
3	California	7.3
4	Oregon	6.5
4	South Dakota	6.5
6	Ohio	6.1
7	North Dakota	6.0
8	Maryland**	5.9
9	Arkansas	5.8
10	Kentucky	5.7
11	Florida**	5.6
12	Missouri	5.3
13	South Carolina**	5.1
14	Idaho**	5.0
14	Michigan**	5.0
16	Nebraska	4.9
17	Texas	4.6
17	Washington	4.6
19	Pennsylvania	4.5
20	Illinois**	4.4
21	Arizona	4.3
21	Georgia**	4.3
23	Kansas	4.2
24	New Hampshire	4.1
25	Colorado	4.0
25	Indiana**	4.0
25	New Mexico	4.0
25	Tennessee**	4.0
29	Nevada	3.9
30	Mississippi	3.8
31	New Jersey**	3.7
32	Minnesota	3.6
33	Massachusetts**	3.4
33	Virginia**	3.4
35	Louisiana	3.3
36	Hawaii	3.2
37	Connecticut	3.0
37	New York**	3.0
37	West Virginia	3.0
40	North Carolina	2.8
41	Vermont	2.5
42	Maine**	2.3
NA	Alabama***	NA
NA	Alaska***	NA
NA	Delaware***	NA
NA	Iowa***	NA
NA	Rhode Island***	NA
NA	Utah***	NA
NA	Wisconsin***	NA
NA	Wyoming***	NA
	District of Columbia**	3.9

Source: American Correctional Association (Lanham, MD)
  "1997 Directory of Juvenile and Adult Correctional Departments, Institutions, Agencies and Paroling Authorities"
*As of June 30, 1996. National rate does not include federal or District of Columbia prisoner to officer rate.
Federal rate is 7.6 prisoners per officer.
**These states' figures are as of June 30, 1995.
***Not available.

Turnover Rate of Correctional Officers in Adult Systems in 1996

National Rate = 11.88%*

ALPHA ORDER				RANK ORDER		
RANK	STATE	TURNOVER RATE		RANK	STATE	TURNOVER RATE
NA	Alabama***	NA		1	South Dakota	26.7
30	Alaska	8.2		2	Arkansas	26.4
8	Arizona	18.2		3	Louisiana	25.0
2	Arkansas	26.4		4	South Carolina**	23.2
37	California	4.5		5	Kentucky	23.0
23	Colorado	10.4		6	Georgia**	20.0
34	Connecticut	6.0		7	Nebraska	18.4
NA	Delaware***	NA		8	Arizona	18.2
22	Florida**	10.7		9	New Mexico	17.6
6	Georgia**	20.0		10	Kansas	16.9
33	Hawaii	6.1		11	Missouri	15.2
20	Idaho**	11.5		12	Tennessee**	14.0
37	Illinois**	4.5		12	Utah	14.0
NA	Indiana***	NA		12	Virginia**	14.0
21	Iowa**	11.0		15	Vermont	12.8
10	Kansas	16.9		16	Ohio	12.7
5	Kentucky	23.0		17	Oklahoma	12.2
3	Louisiana	25.0		18	Texas	12.0
NA	Maine***	NA		19	North Carolina	11.7
24	Maryland**	10.0		20	Idaho**	11.5
NA	Massachusetts***	NA		21	Iowa**	11.0
35	Michigan**	5.0		22	Florida**	10.7
28	Minnesota	8.5		23	Colorado	10.4
NA	Mississippi***	NA		24	Maryland**	10.0
11	Missouri	15.2		24	West Virginia	10.0
NA	Montana***	NA		26	New Hampshire	9.0
7	Nebraska	18.4		27	Oregon	8.8
39	Nevada	4.4		28	Minnesota	8.5
26	New Hampshire	9.0		29	New Jersey**	8.4
29	New Jersey**	8.4		30	Alaska	8.2
9	New Mexico	17.6		31	Wisconsin	7.0
42	New York**	2.3		32	Washington	6.7
19	North Carolina	11.7		33	Hawaii	6.1
35	North Dakota	5.0		34	Connecticut	6.0
16	Ohio	12.7		35	Michigan**	5.0
17	Oklahoma	12.2		35	North Dakota	5.0
27	Oregon	8.8		37	California	4.5
41	Pennsylvania	3.0		37	Illinois**	4.5
40	Rhode Island	4.0		39	Nevada	4.4
4	South Carolina**	23.2		40	Rhode Island	4.0
1	South Dakota	26.7		41	Pennsylvania	3.0
12	Tennessee**	14.0		42	New York**	2.3
18	Texas	12.0		NA	Alabama***	NA
12	Utah	14.0		NA	Delaware***	NA
15	Vermont	12.8		NA	Indiana***	NA
12	Virginia**	14.0		NA	Maine***	NA
32	Washington	6.7		NA	Massachusetts***	NA
24	West Virginia	10.0		NA	Mississippi***	NA
31	Wisconsin	7.0		NA	Montana***	NA
NA	Wyoming***	NA		NA	Wyoming***	NA
					District of Columbia**	9.8

Source: American Correctional Association (Lanham, MD)
  "1997 Directory of Juvenile and Adult Correctional Departments, Institutions, Agencies and Paroling Authorities"
*As of June 30, 1996. National rate does not include federal or District of Columbia turnover rate. Federal turnover rate is 6.7%.
**These states' figures are as of June 30, 1995.
***Not available.

118

Jail and Detention Centers in 1993

National Total = 3,304 Jails*

ALPHA ORDER

RANK	STATE	JAILS	% of USA
4	Alabama	129	3.90%
45	Alaska	5	0.15%
34	Arizona	33	1.00%
19	Arkansas	83	2.51%
3	California	136	4.12%
26	Colorado	61	1.85%
NA	Connecticut**	NA	NA
NA	Delaware**	NA	NA
9	Florida	100	3.03%
2	Georgia	202	6.11%
NA	Hawaii**	NA	NA
32	Idaho	39	1.18%
14	Illinois	93	2.81%
18	Indiana	88	2.66%
16	Iowa	90	2.72%
11	Kansas	96	2.91%
20	Kentucky	81	2.45%
11	Louisiana	96	2.91%
43	Maine	15	0.45%
34	Maryland	33	1.00%
41	Massachusetts	20	0.61%
17	Michigan	89	2.69%
23	Minnesota	75	2.27%
13	Mississippi	95	2.88%
5	Missouri	127	3.84%
29	Montana	44	1.33%
25	Nebraska	64	1.94%
41	Nevada	20	0.61%
44	New Hampshire	11	0.33%
37	New Jersey	25	0.76%
33	New Mexico	34	1.03%
22	New York	78	2.36%
8	North Carolina	104	3.15%
37	North Dakota	25	0.76%
6	Ohio	120	3.63%
9	Oklahoma	100	3.03%
30	Oregon	43	1.30%
21	Pennsylvania	79	2.39%
NA	Rhode Island**	NA	NA
28	South Carolina	55	1.66%
36	South Dakota	28	0.85%
7	Tennessee	111	3.36%
1	Texas	267	8.08%
37	Utah	25	0.76%
NA	Vermont**	NA	NA
14	Virginia	93	2.81%
27	Washington	56	1.69%
31	West Virginia	41	1.24%
24	Wisconsin	72	2.18%
40	Wyoming	22	0.67%

RANK ORDER

RANK	STATE	JAILS	% of USA
1	Texas	267	8.08%
2	Georgia	202	6.11%
3	California	136	4.12%
4	Alabama	129	3.90%
5	Missouri	127	3.84%
6	Ohio	120	3.63%
7	Tennessee	111	3.36%
8	North Carolina	104	3.15%
9	Florida	100	3.03%
9	Oklahoma	100	3.03%
11	Kansas	96	2.91%
11	Louisiana	96	2.91%
13	Mississippi	95	2.88%
14	Illinois	93	2.81%
14	Virginia	93	2.81%
16	Iowa	90	2.72%
17	Michigan	89	2.69%
18	Indiana	88	2.66%
19	Arkansas	83	2.51%
20	Kentucky	81	2.45%
21	Pennsylvania	79	2.39%
22	New York	78	2.36%
23	Minnesota	75	2.27%
24	Wisconsin	72	2.18%
25	Nebraska	64	1.94%
26	Colorado	61	1.85%
27	Washington	56	1.69%
28	South Carolina	55	1.66%
29	Montana	44	1.33%
30	Oregon	43	1.30%
31	West Virginia	41	1.24%
32	Idaho	39	1.18%
33	New Mexico	34	1.03%
34	Arizona	33	1.00%
34	Maryland	33	1.00%
36	South Dakota	28	0.85%
37	New Jersey	25	0.76%
37	North Dakota	25	0.76%
37	Utah	25	0.76%
40	Wyoming	22	0.67%
41	Massachusetts	20	0.61%
41	Nevada	20	0.61%
43	Maine	15	0.45%
44	New Hampshire	11	0.33%
45	Alaska	5	0.15%
NA	Connecticut**	NA	NA
NA	Delaware**	NA	NA
NA	Hawaii**	NA	NA
NA	Rhode Island**	NA	NA
NA	Vermont**	NA	NA
	District of Columbia	1	0.03%

*Source: U.S. Department of Justice, Bureau of Justice Statistics
    "Jail and Jail Inmates 1993-94" (Bulletin, April 1995, NCJ-151651)*
As of July 1, 1993.   Jails are locally operated correctional facilities that confine persons before or after adjudication. Inmates sentenced to jail usually have a sentence of a year or less.
**These states have combined state and local jail systems and are excluded from this count.*

Local Jail Populations as a Percent of Highest Capacity in 1993

National Percent = 96.8% of Highest Capacity*

ALPHA ORDER				RANK ORDER		
RANK	STATE	PERCENT		RANK	STATE	PERCENT
36	Alabama	76.0		1	Virginia	160.4
44	Alaska	47.7		2	South Carolina	123.8
11	Arizona	97.8		3	New Jersey	119.8
29	Arkansas	83.4		4	Texas	114.9
5	California	112.8		5	California	112.8
14	Colorado	93.5		6	Massachusetts	105.8
NA	Connecticut**	NA		7	Washington	101.6
NA	Delaware**	NA		8	Pennsylvania	100.9
28	Florida	84.0		9	Maryland	98.9
19	Georgia	89.7		10	Ohio	98.0
NA	Hawaii**	NA		11	Arizona	97.8
24	Idaho	88.1		12	Indiana	97.1
13	Illinois	96.1		13	Illinois	96.1
12	Indiana	97.1		14	Colorado	93.5
35	Iowa	76.4		15	New Mexico	91.3
30	Kansas	82.7		16	Michigan	90.8
18	Kentucky	90.3		17	Mississippi	90.6
31	Louisiana	81.7		18	Kentucky	90.3
38	Maine	71.4		19	Georgia	89.7
9	Maryland	98.9		20	Wisconsin	89.5
6	Massachusetts	105.8		21	Tennessee	89.4
16	Michigan	90.8		22	West Virginia	88.4
32	Minnesota	78.3		23	North Carolina	88.3
17	Mississippi	90.6		24	Idaho	88.1
34	Missouri	77.4		25	New York	85.7
41	Montana	59.7		26	Utah	84.8
40	Nebraska	64.0		27	Oregon	84.3
33	Nevada	78.2		28	Florida	84.0
39	New Hampshire	67.2		29	Arkansas	83.4
3	New Jersey	119.8		30	Kansas	82.7
15	New Mexico	91.3		31	Louisiana	81.7
25	New York	85.7		32	Minnesota	78.3
23	North Carolina	88.3		33	Nevada	78.2
45	North Dakota	42.8		34	Missouri	77.4
10	Ohio	98.0		35	Iowa	76.4
37	Oklahoma	74.9		36	Alabama	76.0
27	Oregon	84.3		37	Oklahoma	74.9
8	Pennsylvania	100.9		38	Maine	71.4
NA	Rhode Island**	NA		39	New Hampshire	67.2
2	South Carolina	123.8		40	Nebraska	64.0
42	South Dakota	53.9		41	Montana	59.7
21	Tennessee	89.4		42	South Dakota	53.9
4	Texas	114.9		43	Wyoming	51.5
26	Utah	84.8		44	Alaska	47.7
NA	Vermont**	NA		45	North Dakota	42.8
1	Virginia	160.4		NA	Connecticut**	NA
7	Washington	101.6		NA	Delaware**	NA
22	West Virginia	88.4		NA	Hawaii**	NA
20	Wisconsin	89.5		NA	Rhode Island**	NA
43	Wyoming	51.5		NA	Vermont**	NA
					District of Columbia	121.2

Source: U.S. Department of Justice, Bureau of Justice Statistics
  "Jail and Jail Inmates 1993-94" (Bulletin, April 1995, NCJ-151651)
As of July 1, 1993. Jails are locally operated correctional facilities that confine persons before or after adjudication. Inmates sentenced to jail usually have a sentence of a year or less.
**These states have combined state and local jail systems and are excluded from this count.*

Inmates in Local Jails in 1993

National Total = 459,804 Inmates*

RANK	STATE	INMATES	% of USA
21	Alabama	7,072	1.54%
45	Alaska	31	0.01%
20	Arizona	7,231	1.57%
32	Arkansas	2,846	0.62%
1	California	69,298	15.07%
23	Colorado	6,316	1.37%
NA	Connecticut**	NA	NA
NA	Delaware**	NA	NA
3	Florida	34,183	7.43%
5	Georgia	22,663	4.93%
NA	Hawaii**	NA	NA
38	Idaho	1,485	0.32%
10	Illinois	14,549	3.16%
16	Indiana	8,297	1.80%
37	Iowa	1,602	0.35%
33	Kansas	2,797	0.61%
22	Kentucky	6,813	1.48%
7	Louisiana	16,208	3.52%
40	Maine	704	0.15%
14	Maryland	9,358	2.04%
18	Massachusetts	7,878	1.71%
12	Michigan	12,479	2.71%
29	Minnesota	3,654	0.79%
26	Mississippi	4,851	1.06%
25	Missouri	5,030	1.09%
41	Montana	680	0.15%
36	Nebraska	1,680	0.37%
31	Nevada	2,987	0.65%
39	New Hampshire	1,127	0.25%
8	New Jersey	15,122	3.29%
30	New Mexico	3,058	0.67%
4	New York	29,809	6.48%
15	North Carolina	8,939	1.94%
44	North Dakota	361	0.08%
13	Ohio	11,695	2.54%
27	Oklahoma	4,102	0.89%
28	Oregon	3,777	0.82%
6	Pennsylvania	19,231	4.18%
NA	Rhode Island**	NA	NA
24	South Carolina	5,713	1.24%
42	South Dakota	623	0.14%
11	Tennessee	14,375	3.13%
2	Texas	55,395	12.05%
34	Utah	1,895	0.41%
NA	Vermont**	NA	NA
9	Virginia	14,623	3.18%
19	Washington	7,435	1.62%
35	West Virginia	1,771	0.39%
17	Wisconsin	7,879	1.71%
43	Wyoming	495	0.11%

RANK	STATE	INMATES	% of USA
1	California	69,298	15.07%
2	Texas	55,395	12.05%
3	Florida	34,183	7.43%
4	New York	29,809	6.48%
5	Georgia	22,663	4.93%
6	Pennsylvania	19,231	4.18%
7	Louisiana	16,208	3.52%
8	New Jersey	15,122	3.29%
9	Virginia	14,623	3.18%
10	Illinois	14,549	3.16%
11	Tennessee	14,375	3.13%
12	Michigan	12,479	2.71%
13	Ohio	11,695	2.54%
14	Maryland	9,358	2.04%
15	North Carolina	8,939	1.94%
16	Indiana	8,297	1.80%
17	Wisconsin	7,879	1.71%
18	Massachusetts	7,878	1.71%
19	Washington	7,435	1.62%
20	Arizona	7,231	1.57%
21	Alabama	7,072	1.54%
22	Kentucky	6,813	1.48%
23	Colorado	6,316	1.37%
24	South Carolina	5,713	1.24%
25	Missouri	5,030	1.09%
26	Mississippi	4,851	1.06%
27	Oklahoma	4,102	0.89%
28	Oregon	3,777	0.82%
29	Minnesota	3,654	0.79%
30	New Mexico	3,058	0.67%
31	Nevada	2,987	0.65%
32	Arkansas	2,846	0.62%
33	Kansas	2,797	0.61%
34	Utah	1,895	0.41%
35	West Virginia	1,771	0.39%
36	Nebraska	1,680	0.37%
37	Iowa	1,602	0.35%
38	Idaho	1,485	0.32%
39	New Hampshire	1,127	0.25%
40	Maine	704	0.15%
41	Montana	680	0.15%
42	South Dakota	623	0.14%
43	Wyoming	495	0.11%
44	North Dakota	361	0.08%
45	Alaska	31	0.01%
NA	Connecticut**	NA	NA
NA	Delaware**	NA	NA
NA	Hawaii**	NA	NA
NA	Rhode Island**	NA	NA
NA	Vermont**	NA	NA
	District of Columbia	1,687	0.37%

Source: U.S. Department of Justice, Bureau of Justice Statistics
   "Jail and Jail Inmates 1993-94" (Bulletin, April 1995, NCJ-151651)
*As of July 1, 1993. Jails are locally operated correctional facilities that confine persons before or after adjudication. Inmates sentenced to jail usually have a sentence of a year or less.
**These states have combined state and local jail systems and are excluded from this count.

Operating Costs per Inmate in Local Jails: 1993

National Average = $14,667 Per Inmate*

ALPHA ORDER				RANK ORDER		
RANK	STATE	PER INMATE		RANK	STATE	PER INMATE
42	Alabama	$8,297		1	New York	$29,297
NA	Alaska**	NA		2	Massachusetts	27,531
39	Arizona	8,552		3	Oregon	24,345
34	Arkansas	11,201		4	Minnesota	24,238
25	California	14,134		5	Nevada	23,367
9	Colorado	19,177		6	New Hampshire	22,993
NA	Connecticut**	NA		7	Maine	21,200
NA	Delaware**	NA		8	Wyoming	20,130
13	Florida	17,530		9	Colorado	19,177
35	Georgia	10,259		10	Kansas	18,972
NA	Hawaii**	NA		11	Ohio	18,152
31	Idaho	11,676		12	North Dakota	17,607
26	Illinois	13,766		13	Florida	17,530
36	Indiana	10,255		14	Iowa	17,399
14	Iowa	17,399		15	New Jersey	17,259
10	Kansas	18,972		16	Maryland	16,812
33	Kentucky	11,416		17	Michigan	16,451
41	Louisiana	8,404		18	Pennsylvania	16,448
7	Maine	21,200		19	Utah	16,129
16	Maryland	16,812		20	Virginia	15,872
2	Massachusetts	27,531		21	Washington	15,331
17	Michigan	16,451		22	Nebraska	15,198
4	Minnesota	24,238		23	Wisconsin	15,057
44	Mississippi	7,014		24	Missouri	14,575
24	Missouri	14,575		25	California	14,134
28	Montana	13,121		26	Illinois	13,766
22	Nebraska	15,198		27	New Mexico	13,273
5	Nevada	23,367		28	Montana	13,121
6	New Hampshire	22,993		29	South Dakota	13,109
15	New Jersey	17,259		30	North Carolina	12,620
27	New Mexico	13,273		31	Idaho	11,676
1	New York	29,297		32	West Virginia	11,474
30	North Carolina	12,620		33	Kentucky	11,416
12	North Dakota	17,607		34	Arkansas	11,201
11	Ohio	18,152		35	Georgia	10,259
37	Oklahoma	9,397		36	Indiana	10,255
3	Oregon	24,345		37	Oklahoma	9,397
18	Pennsylvania	16,448		38	Texas	9,304
NA	Rhode Island**	NA		39	Arizona	8,552
40	South Carolina	8,438		40	South Carolina	8,438
29	South Dakota	13,109		41	Louisiana	8,404
43	Tennessee	7,675		42	Alabama	8,297
38	Texas	9,304		43	Tennessee	7,675
19	Utah	16,129		44	Mississippi	7,014
NA	Vermont**	NA		NA	Alaska**	NA
20	Virginia	15,872		NA	Connecticut**	NA
21	Washington	15,331		NA	Delaware**	NA
32	West Virginia	11,474		NA	Hawaii**	NA
23	Wisconsin	15,057		NA	Rhode Island**	NA
8	Wyoming	20,130		NA	Vermont**	NA
					District of Columbia**	NA

Source: U.S. Department of Justice, Bureau of Justice Statistics
    "Jail and Jail Inmates 1993-94" (Bulletin, April 1995, NCJ-151651)
As of July 1, 1993. The cost (excluding capital outlays) to keep one jail inmate incarcerated for a year. Jails are locally operated correctional facilities that confine persons before or after adjudication. Inmates sentenced to jail usually have a sentence of a year or less.
**These states have combined state and local jail systems and are excluded from this count.*

Male Inmates in Local Jails in 1993

National Total = 415,161 Male Inmates*

<table>
<tr><td colspan="4"><u>ALPHA ORDER</u></td><td colspan="4"><u>RANK ORDER</u></td></tr>
<tr><td>RANK</td><td>STATE</td><td>INMATES</td><td>% of USA</td><td>RANK</td><td>STATE</td><td>INMATES</td><td>% of USA</td></tr>
<tr><td>20</td><td>Alabama</td><td>6,485</td><td>1.56%</td><td>1</td><td>California</td><td>61,646</td><td>14.85%</td></tr>
<tr><td>45</td><td>Alaska</td><td>30</td><td>0.01%</td><td>2</td><td>Texas</td><td>48,806</td><td>11.76%</td></tr>
<tr><td>21</td><td>Arizona</td><td>6,471</td><td>1.56%</td><td>3</td><td>Florida</td><td>30,500</td><td>7.35%</td></tr>
<tr><td>31</td><td>Arkansas</td><td>2,632</td><td>0.63%</td><td>4</td><td>New York</td><td>27,156</td><td>6.54%</td></tr>
<tr><td>1</td><td>California</td><td>61,646</td><td>14.85%</td><td>5</td><td>Georgia</td><td>20,943</td><td>5.04%</td></tr>
<tr><td>23</td><td>Colorado</td><td>5,787</td><td>1.39%</td><td>6</td><td>Pennsylvania</td><td>17,597</td><td>4.24%</td></tr>
<tr><td>NA</td><td>Connecticut**</td><td>NA</td><td>NA</td><td>7</td><td>Louisiana</td><td>14,800</td><td>3.56%</td></tr>
<tr><td>NA</td><td>Delaware**</td><td>NA</td><td>NA</td><td>8</td><td>New Jersey</td><td>14,035</td><td>3.38%</td></tr>
<tr><td>3</td><td>Florida</td><td>30,500</td><td>7.35%</td><td>9</td><td>Illinois</td><td>13,482</td><td>3.25%</td></tr>
<tr><td>5</td><td>Georgia</td><td>20,943</td><td>5.04%</td><td>10</td><td>Tennessee</td><td>13,048</td><td>3.14%</td></tr>
<tr><td>NA</td><td>Hawaii**</td><td>NA</td><td>NA</td><td>11</td><td>Virginia</td><td>13,042</td><td>3.14%</td></tr>
<tr><td>38</td><td>Idaho</td><td>1,383</td><td>0.33%</td><td>12</td><td>Michigan</td><td>11,395</td><td>2.74%</td></tr>
<tr><td>9</td><td>Illinois</td><td>13,482</td><td>3.25%</td><td>13</td><td>Ohio</td><td>10,332</td><td>2.49%</td></tr>
<tr><td>16</td><td>Indiana</td><td>7,653</td><td>1.84%</td><td>14</td><td>Maryland</td><td>8,524</td><td>2.05%</td></tr>
<tr><td>37</td><td>Iowa</td><td>1,477</td><td>0.36%</td><td>15</td><td>North Carolina</td><td>7,800</td><td>1.88%</td></tr>
<tr><td>33</td><td>Kansas</td><td>2,520</td><td>0.61%</td><td>16</td><td>Indiana</td><td>7,653</td><td>1.84%</td></tr>
<tr><td>22</td><td>Kentucky</td><td>6,198</td><td>1.49%</td><td>17</td><td>Massachusetts</td><td>7,522</td><td>1.81%</td></tr>
<tr><td>7</td><td>Louisiana</td><td>14,800</td><td>3.56%</td><td>18</td><td>Wisconsin</td><td>7,169</td><td>1.73%</td></tr>
<tr><td>40</td><td>Maine</td><td>658</td><td>0.16%</td><td>19</td><td>Washington</td><td>6,663</td><td>1.60%</td></tr>
<tr><td>14</td><td>Maryland</td><td>8,524</td><td>2.05%</td><td>20</td><td>Alabama</td><td>6,485</td><td>1.56%</td></tr>
<tr><td>17</td><td>Massachusetts</td><td>7,522</td><td>1.81%</td><td>21</td><td>Arizona</td><td>6,471</td><td>1.56%</td></tr>
<tr><td>12</td><td>Michigan</td><td>11,395</td><td>2.74%</td><td>22</td><td>Kentucky</td><td>6,198</td><td>1.49%</td></tr>
<tr><td>29</td><td>Minnesota</td><td>3,395</td><td>0.82%</td><td>23</td><td>Colorado</td><td>5,787</td><td>1.39%</td></tr>
<tr><td>26</td><td>Mississippi</td><td>4,459</td><td>1.07%</td><td>24</td><td>South Carolina</td><td>5,242</td><td>1.26%</td></tr>
<tr><td>25</td><td>Missouri</td><td>4,572</td><td>1.10%</td><td>25</td><td>Missouri</td><td>4,572</td><td>1.10%</td></tr>
<tr><td>41</td><td>Montana</td><td>604</td><td>0.15%</td><td>26</td><td>Mississippi</td><td>4,459</td><td>1.07%</td></tr>
<tr><td>36</td><td>Nebraska</td><td>1,545</td><td>0.37%</td><td>27</td><td>Oklahoma</td><td>3,589</td><td>0.86%</td></tr>
<tr><td>32</td><td>Nevada</td><td>2,593</td><td>0.62%</td><td>28</td><td>Oregon</td><td>3,441</td><td>0.83%</td></tr>
<tr><td>39</td><td>New Hampshire</td><td>990</td><td>0.24%</td><td>29</td><td>Minnesota</td><td>3,395</td><td>0.82%</td></tr>
<tr><td>8</td><td>New Jersey</td><td>14,035</td><td>3.38%</td><td>30</td><td>New Mexico</td><td>2,772</td><td>0.67%</td></tr>
<tr><td>30</td><td>New Mexico</td><td>2,772</td><td>0.67%</td><td>31</td><td>Arkansas</td><td>2,632</td><td>0.63%</td></tr>
<tr><td>4</td><td>New York</td><td>27,156</td><td>6.54%</td><td>32</td><td>Nevada</td><td>2,593</td><td>0.62%</td></tr>
<tr><td>15</td><td>North Carolina</td><td>7,800</td><td>1.88%</td><td>33</td><td>Kansas</td><td>2,520</td><td>0.61%</td></tr>
<tr><td>44</td><td>North Dakota</td><td>327</td><td>0.08%</td><td>34</td><td>Utah</td><td>1,715</td><td>0.41%</td></tr>
<tr><td>13</td><td>Ohio</td><td>10,332</td><td>2.49%</td><td>35</td><td>West Virginia</td><td>1,653</td><td>0.40%</td></tr>
<tr><td>27</td><td>Oklahoma</td><td>3,589</td><td>0.86%</td><td>36</td><td>Nebraska</td><td>1,545</td><td>0.37%</td></tr>
<tr><td>28</td><td>Oregon</td><td>3,441</td><td>0.83%</td><td>37</td><td>Iowa</td><td>1,477</td><td>0.36%</td></tr>
<tr><td>6</td><td>Pennsylvania</td><td>17,597</td><td>4.24%</td><td>38</td><td>Idaho</td><td>1,383</td><td>0.33%</td></tr>
<tr><td>NA</td><td>Rhode Island**</td><td>NA</td><td>NA</td><td>39</td><td>New Hampshire</td><td>990</td><td>0.24%</td></tr>
<tr><td>24</td><td>South Carolina</td><td>5,242</td><td>1.26%</td><td>40</td><td>Maine</td><td>658</td><td>0.16%</td></tr>
<tr><td>42</td><td>South Dakota</td><td>557</td><td>0.13%</td><td>41</td><td>Montana</td><td>604</td><td>0.15%</td></tr>
<tr><td>10</td><td>Tennessee</td><td>13,048</td><td>3.14%</td><td>42</td><td>South Dakota</td><td>557</td><td>0.13%</td></tr>
<tr><td>2</td><td>Texas</td><td>48,806</td><td>11.76%</td><td>43</td><td>Wyoming</td><td>444</td><td>0.11%</td></tr>
<tr><td>34</td><td>Utah</td><td>1,715</td><td>0.41%</td><td>44</td><td>North Dakota</td><td>327</td><td>0.08%</td></tr>
<tr><td>NA</td><td>Vermont**</td><td>NA</td><td>NA</td><td>45</td><td>Alaska</td><td>30</td><td>0.01%</td></tr>
<tr><td>11</td><td>Virginia</td><td>13,042</td><td>3.14%</td><td>NA</td><td>Connecticut**</td><td>NA</td><td>NA</td></tr>
<tr><td>19</td><td>Washington</td><td>6,663</td><td>1.60%</td><td>NA</td><td>Delaware**</td><td>NA</td><td>NA</td></tr>
<tr><td>35</td><td>West Virginia</td><td>1,653</td><td>0.40%</td><td>NA</td><td>Hawaii**</td><td>NA</td><td>NA</td></tr>
<tr><td>18</td><td>Wisconsin</td><td>7,169</td><td>1.73%</td><td>NA</td><td>Rhode Island**</td><td>NA</td><td>NA</td></tr>
<tr><td>43</td><td>Wyoming</td><td>444</td><td>0.11%</td><td>NA</td><td>Vermont**</td><td>NA</td><td>NA</td></tr>
<tr><td></td><td></td><td></td><td></td><td></td><td>District of Columbia</td><td>1,509</td><td>0.36%</td></tr>
</table>

Source: U.S. Department of Justice, Bureau of Justice Statistics
   "Correctional Populations in the United States, 1993" (October 1995, NCJ-156241)
*As of July 1, 1993. Jails are locally operated correctional facilities that confine persons before or after
adjudication. Inmates sentenced to jail usually have a sentence of a year or less.
**These states have combined state and local jail systems and are excluded from this count.

Female Inmates in Local Jails in 1993

National Total = 44,184 Female Inmates*

RANK	STATE	INMATES	% of USA
20	Alabama	587	1.33%
45	Alaska	1	0.00%
16	Arizona	760	1.72%
33	Arkansas	214	0.48%
1	California	7,652	17.32%
22	Colorado	529	1.20%
NA	Connecticut**	NA	NA
NA	Delaware**	NA	NA
3	Florida	3,683	8.34%
5	Georgia	1,720	3.89%
NA	Hawaii**	NA	NA
39	Idaho	102	0.23%
13	Illinois	1,067	2.41%
19	Indiana	644	1.46%
37	Iowa	125	0.28%
31	Kansas	277	0.63%
21	Kentucky	547	1.24%
8	Louisiana	1,408	3.19%
43	Maine	46	0.10%
14	Maryland	834	1.89%
28	Massachusetts	356	0.81%
12	Michigan	1,084	2.45%
32	Minnesota	259	0.59%
27	Mississippi	392	0.89%
25	Missouri	458	1.04%
40	Montana	76	0.17%
36	Nebraska	135	0.31%
26	Nevada	394	0.89%
35	New Hampshire	137	0.31%
11	New Jersey	1,087	2.46%
30	New Mexico	286	0.65%
4	New York	2,653	6.00%
17	North Carolina	748	1.69%
44	North Dakota	34	0.08%
9	Ohio	1,363	3.08%
23	Oklahoma	513	1.16%
29	Oregon	336	0.76%
6	Pennsylvania	1,634	3.70%
NA	Rhode Island**	NA	NA
24	South Carolina	471	1.07%
41	South Dakota	66	0.15%
10	Tennessee	1,327	3.00%
2	Texas	6,589	14.91%
34	Utah	180	0.41%
NA	Vermont**	NA	NA
7	Virginia	1,581	3.58%
15	Washington	772	1.75%
38	West Virginia	118	0.27%
18	Wisconsin	710	1.61%
42	Wyoming	51	0.12%

RANK	STATE	INMATES	% of USA
1	California	7,652	17.32%
2	Texas	6,589	14.91%
3	Florida	3,683	8.34%
4	New York	2,653	6.00%
5	Georgia	1,720	3.89%
6	Pennsylvania	1,634	3.70%
7	Virginia	1,581	3.58%
8	Louisiana	1,408	3.19%
9	Ohio	1,363	3.08%
10	Tennessee	1,327	3.00%
11	New Jersey	1,087	2.46%
12	Michigan	1,084	2.45%
13	Illinois	1,067	2.41%
14	Maryland	834	1.89%
15	Washington	772	1.75%
16	Arizona	760	1.72%
17	North Carolina	748	1.69%
18	Wisconsin	710	1.61%
19	Indiana	644	1.46%
20	Alabama	587	1.33%
21	Kentucky	547	1.24%
22	Colorado	529	1.20%
23	Oklahoma	513	1.16%
24	South Carolina	471	1.07%
25	Missouri	458	1.04%
26	Nevada	394	0.89%
27	Mississippi	392	0.89%
28	Massachusetts	356	0.81%
29	Oregon	336	0.76%
30	New Mexico	286	0.65%
31	Kansas	277	0.63%
32	Minnesota	259	0.59%
33	Arkansas	214	0.48%
34	Utah	180	0.41%
35	New Hampshire	137	0.31%
36	Nebraska	135	0.31%
37	Iowa	125	0.28%
38	West Virginia	118	0.27%
39	Idaho	102	0.23%
40	Montana	76	0.17%
41	South Dakota	66	0.15%
42	Wyoming	51	0.12%
43	Maine	46	0.10%
44	North Dakota	34	0.08%
45	Alaska	1	0.00%
NA	Connecticut**	NA	NA
NA	Delaware**	NA	NA
NA	Hawaii**	NA	NA
NA	Rhode Island**	NA	NA
NA	Vermont**	NA	NA
	District of Columbia	178	0.40%

Source: U.S. Department of Justice, Bureau of Justice Statistics
   "Correctional Populations in the United States, 1993" (October 1995, NCJ-156241)
*As of July 1, 1993. Jails are locally operated correctional facilities that confine persons before or after
adjudication. Inmates sentenced to jail usually have a sentence of a year or less.
**These states have combined state and local jail systems and are excluded from this count.

White Inmates in Local Jails in 1993

National Total = 153,999 White Inmates*

ALPHA ORDER

ALPHA ORDER

RANK	STATE	INMATES	% of USA
24	Alabama	2,147	1.39%
45	Alaska	15	0.01%
18	Arizona	2,980	1.94%
29	Arkansas	1,379	0.90%
1	California	18,471	11.99%
23	Colorado	2,299	1.49%
NA	Connecticut**	NA	NA
NA	Delaware**	NA	NA
3	Florida	14,030	9.11%
7	Georgia	5,368	3.49%
NA	Hawaii**	NA	NA
37	Idaho	832	0.54%
15	Illinois	3,800	2.47%
10	Indiana	4,718	3.06%
34	Iowa	1,016	0.66%
28	Kansas	1,497	0.97%
14	Kentucky	3,812	2.48%
19	Louisiana	2,654	1.72%
39	Maine	577	0.37%
17	Maryland	3,000	1.95%
16	Massachusetts	3,099	2.01%
6	Michigan	5,424	3.52%
24	Minnesota	2,147	1.39%
35	Mississippi	972	0.63%
26	Missouri	2,039	1.32%
41	Montana	408	0.26%
36	Nebraska	928	0.60%
33	Nevada	1,209	0.79%
38	New Hampshire	594	0.39%
21	New Jersey	2,471	1.60%
40	New Mexico	479	0.31%
5	New York	6,419	4.17%
20	North Carolina	2,494	1.62%
44	North Dakota	241	0.16%
12	Ohio	4,126	2.68%
27	Oklahoma	1,899	1.23%
22	Oregon	2,350	1.53%
4	Pennsylvania	8,054	5.23%
NA	Rhode Island**	NA	NA
32	South Carolina	1,248	0.81%
42	South Dakota	376	0.24%
8	Tennessee	5,296	3.44%
2	Texas	16,863	10.95%
31	Utah	1,264	0.82%
NA	Vermont**	NA	NA
11	Virginia	4,659	3.03%
9	Washington	4,735	3.07%
30	West Virginia	1,325	0.86%
13	Wisconsin	3,915	2.54%
43	Wyoming	364	0.24%

RANK ORDER

RANK	STATE	INMATES	% of USA
1	California	18,471	11.99%
2	Texas	16,863	10.95%
3	Florida	14,030	9.11%
4	Pennsylvania	8,054	5.23%
5	New York	6,419	4.17%
6	Michigan	5,424	3.52%
7	Georgia	5,368	3.49%
8	Tennessee	5,296	3.44%
9	Washington	4,735	3.07%
10	Indiana	4,718	3.06%
11	Virginia	4,659	3.03%
12	Ohio	4,126	2.68%
13	Wisconsin	3,915	2.54%
14	Kentucky	3,812	2.48%
15	Illinois	3,800	2.47%
16	Massachusetts	3,099	2.01%
17	Maryland	3,000	1.95%
18	Arizona	2,980	1.94%
19	Louisiana	2,654	1.72%
20	North Carolina	2,494	1.62%
21	New Jersey	2,471	1.60%
22	Oregon	2,350	1.53%
23	Colorado	2,299	1.49%
24	Alabama	2,147	1.39%
24	Minnesota	2,147	1.39%
26	Missouri	2,039	1.32%
27	Oklahoma	1,899	1.23%
28	Kansas	1,497	0.97%
29	Arkansas	1,379	0.90%
30	West Virginia	1,325	0.86%
31	Utah	1,264	0.82%
32	South Carolina	1,248	0.81%
33	Nevada	1,209	0.79%
34	Iowa	1,016	0.66%
35	Mississippi	972	0.63%
36	Nebraska	928	0.60%
37	Idaho	832	0.54%
38	New Hampshire	594	0.39%
39	Maine	577	0.37%
40	New Mexico	479	0.31%
41	Montana	408	0.26%
42	South Dakota	376	0.24%
43	Wyoming	364	0.24%
44	North Dakota	241	0.16%
45	Alaska	15	0.01%
NA	Connecticut**	NA	NA
NA	Delaware**	NA	NA
NA	Hawaii**	NA	NA
NA	Rhode Island**	NA	NA
NA	Vermont**	NA	NA
	District of Columbia***	NA	NA

Source: U.S. Department of Justice, Bureau of Justice Statistics
"Correctional Populations in the United States, 1993" (October 1995, NCJ-156241)
*As of July 1, 1993. Jails are locally operated correctional facilities that confine persons before or after adjudication. Inmates sentenced to jail usually have a sentence of a year or less.
**These states have combined state and local jail systems and are excluded from this count.
***Not available.

White Inmates in Local Jails as a Percent of All Inmates in 1993

National Percent = 33.49% of Inmates*

ALPHA ORDER				RANK ORDER		
RANK	STATE	PERCENT		RANK	STATE	PERCENT
35	Alabama	30.36		1	Maine	81.96
20	Alaska	48.39		2	West Virginia	74.82
24	Arizona	41.21		3	Wyoming	73.54
19	Arkansas	48.45		4	North Dakota	66.76
37	California	26.65		5	Utah	66.70
30	Colorado	36.40		6	Washington	63.69
NA	Connecticut**	NA		7	Iowa	63.42
NA	Delaware**	NA		8	Oregon	62.22
25	Florida	41.04		9	South Dakota	60.35
39	Georgia	23.69		10	Montana	60.00
NA	Hawaii**	NA		11	Minnesota	58.76
13	Idaho	56.03		12	Indiana	56.86
38	Illinois	26.12		13	Idaho	56.03
12	Indiana	56.86		14	Kentucky	55.95
7	Iowa	63.42		15	Nebraska	55.24
16	Kansas	53.52		16	Kansas	53.52
14	Kentucky	55.95		17	New Hampshire	52.71
43	Louisiana	16.37		18	Wisconsin	49.69
1	Maine	81.96		19	Arkansas	48.45
32	Maryland	32.06		20	Alaska	48.39
28	Massachusetts	39.34		21	Oklahoma	46.29
22	Michigan	43.47		22	Michigan	43.47
11	Minnesota	58.76		23	Pennsylvania	41.88
42	Mississippi	20.04		24	Arizona	41.21
26	Missouri	40.54		25	Florida	41.04
10	Montana	60.00		26	Missouri	40.54
15	Nebraska	55.24		27	Nevada	40.48
27	Nevada	40.48		28	Massachusetts	39.34
17	New Hampshire	52.71		29	Tennessee	36.84
44	New Jersey	16.34		30	Colorado	36.40
45	New Mexico	15.66		31	Ohio	35.28
41	New York	21.53		32	Maryland	32.06
36	North Carolina	27.90		33	Virginia	31.86
4	North Dakota	66.76		34	Texas	30.44
31	Ohio	35.28		35	Alabama	30.36
21	Oklahoma	46.29		36	North Carolina	27.90
8	Oregon	62.22		37	California	26.65
23	Pennsylvania	41.88		38	Illinois	26.12
NA	Rhode Island**	NA		39	Georgia	23.69
40	South Carolina	21.84		40	South Carolina	21.84
9	South Dakota	60.35		41	New York	21.53
29	Tennessee	36.84		42	Mississippi	20.04
34	Texas	30.44		43	Louisiana	16.37
5	Utah	66.70		44	New Jersey	16.34
NA	Vermont**	NA		45	New Mexico	15.66
33	Virginia	31.86		NA	Connecticut**	NA
6	Washington	63.69		NA	Delaware**	NA
2	West Virginia	74.82		NA	Hawaii**	NA
18	Wisconsin	49.69		NA	Rhode Island**	NA
3	Wyoming	73.54		NA	Vermont**	NA
					District of Columbia***	NA

Source: Morgan Quitno Press using data from U.S. Department of Justice, Bureau of Justice Statistics
  "Correctional Populations in the United States, 1993" (October 1995, NCJ-156241)
*As of July 1, 1993. Jails are locally operated correctional facilities that confine persons before or after
adjudication. Inmates sentenced to jail usually have a sentence of a year or less.
**These states have combined state and local jail systems and are excluded from this count.
***Not available.

Black Inmates in Local Jails in 1993

National Total = 173,193 Black Inmates*

ALPHA ORDER

RANK	STATE	INMATES	% of USA
15	Alabama	3,922	2.26%
45	Alaska	0	0.00%
27	Arizona	921	0.53%
25	Arkansas	1,246	0.72%
3	California	13,887	8.02%
31	Colorado	473	0.27%
NA	Connecticut**	NA	NA
NA	Delaware**	NA	NA
2	Florida	16,426	9.48%
4	Georgia	12,764	7.37%
NA	Hawaii**	NA	NA
41	Idaho	13	0.01%
6	Illinois	8,822	5.09%
23	Indiana	1,650	0.95%
34	Iowa	306	0.18%
28	Kansas	792	0.46%
22	Kentucky	1,810	1.05%
10	Louisiana	6,435	3.72%
42	Maine	11	0.01%
11	Maryland	6,165	3.56%
20	Massachusetts	2,246	1.30%
14	Michigan	4,658	2.69%
29	Minnesota	783	0.45%
18	Mississippi	2,650	1.53%
21	Missouri	2,208	1.27%
40	Montana	14	0.01%
32	Nebraska	415	0.24%
30	Nevada	636	0.37%
42	New Hampshire	11	0.01%
12	New Jersey	5,656	3.27%
37	New Mexico	142	0.08%
5	New York	12,114	6.99%
13	North Carolina	5,443	3.14%
44	North Dakota	10	0.01%
16	Ohio	3,548	2.05%
26	Oklahoma	1,151	0.66%
33	Oregon	389	0.22%
8	Pennsylvania	8,511	4.91%
NA	Rhode Island**	NA	NA
17	South Carolina	3,331	1.92%
38	South Dakota	22	0.01%
7	Tennessee	8,590	4.96%
1	Texas	20,925	12.08%
36	Utah	148	0.09%
NA	Vermont**	NA	NA
9	Virginia	8,183	4.72%
24	Washington	1,299	0.75%
35	West Virginia	217	0.13%
19	Wisconsin	2,587	1.49%
39	Wyoming	20	0.01%

RANK ORDER

RANK	STATE	INMATES	% of USA
1	Texas	20,925	12.08%
2	Florida	16,426	9.48%
3	California	13,887	8.02%
4	Georgia	12,764	7.37%
5	New York	12,114	6.99%
6	Illinois	8,822	5.09%
7	Tennessee	8,590	4.96%
8	Pennsylvania	8,511	4.91%
9	Virginia	8,183	4.72%
10	Louisiana	6,435	3.72%
11	Maryland	6,165	3.56%
12	New Jersey	5,656	3.27%
13	North Carolina	5,443	3.14%
14	Michigan	4,658	2.69%
15	Alabama	3,922	2.26%
16	Ohio	3,548	2.05%
17	South Carolina	3,331	1.92%
18	Mississippi	2,650	1.53%
19	Wisconsin	2,587	1.49%
20	Massachusetts	2,246	1.30%
21	Missouri	2,208	1.27%
22	Kentucky	1,810	1.05%
23	Indiana	1,650	0.95%
24	Washington	1,299	0.75%
25	Arkansas	1,246	0.72%
26	Oklahoma	1,151	0.66%
27	Arizona	921	0.53%
28	Kansas	792	0.46%
29	Minnesota	783	0.45%
30	Nevada	636	0.37%
31	Colorado	473	0.27%
32	Nebraska	415	0.24%
33	Oregon	389	0.22%
34	Iowa	306	0.18%
35	West Virginia	217	0.13%
36	Utah	148	0.09%
37	New Mexico	142	0.08%
38	South Dakota	22	0.01%
39	Wyoming	20	0.01%
40	Montana	14	0.01%
41	Idaho	13	0.01%
42	Maine	11	0.01%
42	New Hampshire	11	0.01%
44	North Dakota	10	0.01%
45	Alaska	0	0.00%
NA	Connecticut**	NA	NA
NA	Delaware**	NA	NA
NA	Hawaii**	NA	NA
NA	Rhode Island**	NA	NA
NA	Vermont**	NA	NA
	District of Columbia***	NA	NA

Source: U.S. Department of Justice, Bureau of Justice Statistics
    "Correctional Populations in the United States, 1993" (October 1995, NCJ-156241)
*As of July 1, 1993. Jails are locally operated correctional facilities that confine persons before or after
adjudication. Inmates sentenced to jail usually have a sentence of a year or less.
**These states have combined state and local jail systems and are excluded from this count.
***Not available.

Black Inmates in Local Jails as a Percent of All Inmates in 1993

National Percent = 37.67% of Inmates*

ALPHA ORDER				RANK ORDER		
RANK	STATE	PERCENT		RANK	STATE	PERCENT
8	Alabama	55.46		1	Maryland	65.88
45	Alaska	0.00		2	North Carolina	60.89
32	Arizona	12.74		3	Illinois	60.64
13	Arkansas	43.78		4	Tennessee	59.76
28	California	20.04		5	South Carolina	58.31
36	Colorado	7.49		6	Georgia	56.32
NA	Connecticut**	NA		7	Virginia	55.96
NA	Delaware**	NA		8	Alabama	55.46
10	Florida	48.05		9	Mississippi	54.63
6	Georgia	56.32		10	Florida	48.05
NA	Hawaii**	NA		11	Pennsylvania	44.26
44	Idaho	0.88		12	Missouri	43.90
3	Illinois	60.64		13	Arkansas	43.78
29	Indiana	19.89		14	New York	40.64
30	Iowa	19.10		15	Louisiana	39.70
22	Kansas	28.32		16	Texas	37.77
24	Kentucky	26.57		17	New Jersey	37.40
15	Louisiana	39.70		18	Michigan	37.33
42	Maine	1.56		19	Wisconsin	32.83
1	Maryland	65.88		20	Ohio	30.34
21	Massachusetts	28.51		21	Massachusetts	28.51
18	Michigan	37.33		22	Kansas	28.32
26	Minnesota	21.43		23	Oklahoma	28.06
9	Mississippi	54.63		24	Kentucky	26.57
12	Missouri	43.90		25	Nebraska	24.70
41	Montana	2.06		26	Minnesota	21.43
25	Nebraska	24.70		27	Nevada	21.29
27	Nevada	21.29		28	California	20.04
43	New Hampshire	0.98		29	Indiana	19.89
17	New Jersey	37.40		30	Iowa	19.10
37	New Mexico	4.64		31	Washington	17.47
14	New York	40.64		32	Arizona	12.74
2	North Carolina	60.89		33	West Virginia	12.25
40	North Dakota	2.77		34	Oregon	10.30
20	Ohio	30.34		35	Utah	7.81
23	Oklahoma	28.06		36	Colorado	7.49
34	Oregon	10.30		37	New Mexico	4.64
11	Pennsylvania	44.26		38	Wyoming	4.04
NA	Rhode Island**	NA		39	South Dakota	3.53
5	South Carolina	58.31		40	North Dakota	2.77
39	South Dakota	3.53		41	Montana	2.06
4	Tennessee	59.76		42	Maine	1.56
16	Texas	37.77		43	New Hampshire	0.98
35	Utah	7.81		44	Idaho	0.88
NA	Vermont**	NA		45	Alaska	0.00
7	Virginia	55.96		NA	Connecticut**	NA
31	Washington	17.47		NA	Delaware**	NA
33	West Virginia	12.25		NA	Hawaii**	NA
19	Wisconsin	32.83		NA	Rhode Island**	NA
38	Wyoming	4.04		NA	Vermont**	NA
					District of Columbia***	NA

*Source: Morgan Quitno Press using data from U.S. Department of Justice, Bureau of Justice Statistics
"Correctional Populations in the United States, 1993" (October 1995, NCJ-156241)*
*As of July 1, 1993. Jails are locally operated correctional facilities that confine persons before or after
adjudication. Inmates sentenced to jail usually have a sentence of a year or less.*
***These states have combined state and local jail systems and are excluded from this count.*
****Not available.*

Hispanic Inmates in Local Jails in 1993

National Total = 58,947 Hispanic Inmates*

ALPHA ORDER					RANK ORDER			
RANK	STATE		INMATES	% of USA	RANK	STATE	INMATES	% of USA
35	Alabama		47	0.08%	1	California	22,110	37.51%
45	Alaska		3	0.01%	2	Texas	11,729	19.90%
5	Arizona		1,872	3.18%	3	New York	6,483	11.00%
39	Arkansas		31	0.05%	4	Florida	2,764	4.69%
1	California		22,110	37.51%	5	Arizona	1,872	3.18%
12	Colorado		860	1.46%	6	New Jersey	1,809	3.07%
NA	Connecticut**		NA	NA	7	Pennsylvania	1,596	2.71%
NA	Delaware**		NA	NA	8	Massachusetts	1,324	2.25%
4	Florida		2,764	4.69%	9	Illinois	1,274	2.16%
20	Georgia		254	0.43%	10	New Mexico	1,229	2.08%
NA	Hawaii**		NA	NA	11	Washington	891	1.51%
18	Idaho		262	0.44%	12	Colorado	860	1.46%
9	Illinois		1,274	2.16%	13	Michigan	577	0.98%
28	Indiana		162	0.27%	14	Oregon	413	0.70%
32	Iowa		71	0.12%	15	Utah	351	0.60%
23	Kansas		204	0.35%	16	Virginia	287	0.49%
30	Kentucky		80	0.14%	17	Wisconsin	272	0.46%
24	Louisiana		190	0.32%	18	Idaho	262	0.44%
43	Maine		7	0.01%	19	Oklahoma	260	0.44%
24	Maryland		190	0.32%	20	Georgia	254	0.43%
8	Massachusetts		1,324	2.25%	21	Nevada	252	0.43%
13	Michigan		577	0.98%	22	Ohio	221	0.37%
27	Minnesota		166	0.28%	23	Kansas	204	0.35%
37	Mississippi		41	0.07%	24	Louisiana	190	0.32%
31	Missouri		75	0.13%	24	Maryland	190	0.32%
38	Montana		40	0.07%	26	Nebraska	176	0.30%
26	Nebraska		176	0.30%	27	Minnesota	166	0.28%
21	Nevada		252	0.43%	28	Indiana	162	0.27%
40	New Hampshire		23	0.04%	29	North Carolina	150	0.25%
6	New Jersey		1,809	3.07%	30	Kentucky	80	0.14%
10	New Mexico		1,229	2.08%	31	Missouri	75	0.13%
3	New York		6,483	11.00%	32	Iowa	71	0.12%
29	North Carolina		150	0.25%	33	Wyoming	58	0.10%
40	North Dakota		23	0.04%	34	Tennessee	56	0.10%
22	Ohio		221	0.37%	35	Alabama	47	0.08%
19	Oklahoma		260	0.44%	36	South Carolina	43	0.07%
14	Oregon		413	0.70%	37	Mississippi	41	0.07%
7	Pennsylvania		1,596	2.71%	38	Montana	40	0.07%
NA	Rhode Island**		NA	NA	39	Arkansas	31	0.05%
36	South Carolina		43	0.07%	40	New Hampshire	23	0.04%
44	South Dakota		6	0.01%	40	North Dakota	23	0.04%
34	Tennessee		56	0.10%	42	West Virginia	11	0.02%
2	Texas		11,729	19.90%	43	Maine	7	0.01%
15	Utah		351	0.60%	44	South Dakota	6	0.01%
NA	Vermont**		NA	NA	45	Alaska	3	0.01%
16	Virginia		287	0.49%	NA	Connecticut**	NA	NA
11	Washington		891	1.51%	NA	Delaware**	NA	NA
42	West Virginia		11	0.02%	NA	Hawaii**	NA	NA
17	Wisconsin		272	0.46%	NA	Rhode Island**	NA	NA
33	Wyoming		58	0.10%	NA	Vermont**	NA	NA
						District of Columbia***	NA	NA

Source: U.S. Department of Justice, Bureau of Justice Statistics
   "Correctional Populations in the United States, 1993" (October 1995, NCJ-156241)
*As of July 1, 1993. Jails are locally operated correctional facilities that confine persons before or after adjudication. Inmates sentenced to jail usually have a sentence of a year or less.
**These states have combined state and local jail systems and are excluded from this count.
***Not available.

Hispanic Inmates in Local Jails as a Percent of All Inmates in 1993

National Percent = 12.82% of Inmates*

ALPHA ORDER

RANK ORDER

RANK	STATE	PERCENT		RANK	STATE	PERCENT
43	Alabama	0.66		1	New Mexico	40.19
15	Alaska	9.68		2	California	31.91
3	Arizona	25.89		3	Arizona	25.89
38	Arkansas	1.09		4	New York	21.75
2	California	31.91		5	Texas	21.17
9	Colorado	13.62		6	Utah	18.52
NA	Connecticut**	NA		7	Idaho	17.64
NA	Delaware**	NA		8	Massachusetts	16.81
19	Florida	8.09		9	Colorado	13.62
37	Georgia	1.12		10	Washington	11.98
NA	Hawaii**	NA		11	New Jersey	11.96
7	Idaho	17.64		12	Wyoming	11.72
16	Illinois	8.76		13	Oregon	10.93
31	Indiana	1.95		14	Nebraska	10.48
26	Iowa	4.43		15	Alaska	9.68
20	Kansas	7.29		16	Illinois	8.76
35	Kentucky	1.17		17	Nevada	8.44
35	Louisiana	1.17		18	Pennsylvania	8.30
39	Maine	0.99		19	Florida	8.09
29	Maryland	2.03		20	Kansas	7.29
8	Massachusetts	16.81		21	North Dakota	6.37
24	Michigan	4.62		22	Oklahoma	6.34
25	Minnesota	4.54		23	Montana	5.88
41	Mississippi	0.85		24	Michigan	4.62
34	Missouri	1.49		25	Minnesota	4.54
23	Montana	5.88		26	Iowa	4.43
14	Nebraska	10.48		27	Wisconsin	3.45
17	Nevada	8.44		28	New Hampshire	2.04
28	New Hampshire	2.04		29	Maryland	2.03
11	New Jersey	11.96		30	Virginia	1.96
1	New Mexico	40.19		31	Indiana	1.95
4	New York	21.75		32	Ohio	1.89
33	North Carolina	1.68		33	North Carolina	1.68
21	North Dakota	6.37		34	Missouri	1.49
32	Ohio	1.89		35	Kentucky	1.17
22	Oklahoma	6.34		35	Louisiana	1.17
13	Oregon	10.93		37	Georgia	1.12
18	Pennsylvania	8.30		38	Arkansas	1.09
NA	Rhode Island**	NA		39	Maine	0.99
42	South Carolina	0.75		40	South Dakota	0.96
40	South Dakota	0.96		41	Mississippi	0.85
45	Tennessee	0.39		42	South Carolina	0.75
5	Texas	21.17		43	Alabama	0.66
6	Utah	18.52		44	West Virginia	0.62
NA	Vermont**	NA		45	Tennessee	0.39
30	Virginia	1.96		NA	Connecticut**	NA
10	Washington	11.98		NA	Delaware**	NA
44	West Virginia	0.62		NA	Hawaii**	NA
27	Wisconsin	3.45		NA	Rhode Island**	NA
12	Wyoming	11.72		NA	Vermont**	NA
					District of Columbia***	NA

Source: Morgan Quitno Press using data from U.S. Department of Justice, Bureau of Justice Statistics
    "Correctional Populations in the United States, 1993" (October 1995, NCJ-156241)
*As of July 1, 1993. Jails are locally operated correctional facilities that confine persons before or after adjudication. Inmates sentenced to jail usually have a sentence of a year or less.
**These states have combined state and local jail systems and are excluded from this count.
***Not available.

Correctional Officers in Local Jails in 1993

National Total = 117,900 Officers*

ALPHA ORDER

RANK	STATE	OFFICERS	% of USA
23	Alabama	1,301	1.10%
45	Alaska	24	0.02%
21	Arizona	1,489	1.26%
29	Arkansas	854	0.72%
3	California	10,389	8.81%
17	Colorado	1,843	1.56%
NA	Connecticut**	NA	NA
NA	Delaware**	NA	NA
4	Florida	8,547	7.25%
7	Georgia	3,815	3.24%
NA	Hawaii**	NA	NA
39	Idaho	410	0.35%
6	Illinois	3,843	3.26%
18	Indiana	1,582	1.34%
31	Iowa	812	0.69%
28	Kansas	977	0.83%
22	Kentucky	1,412	1.20%
15	Louisiana	2,132	1.81%
37	Maine	490	0.42%
14	Maryland	2,272	1.93%
13	Massachusetts	2,851	2.42%
12	Michigan	2,939	2.49%
24	Minnesota	1,248	1.06%
33	Mississippi	753	0.64%
25	Missouri	1,093	0.93%
44	Montana	208	0.18%
34	Nebraska	709	0.60%
35	Nevada	549	0.47%
40	New Hampshire	259	0.22%
11	New Jersey	3,065	2.60%
32	New Mexico	786	0.67%
1	New York	12,824	10.88%
16	North Carolina	2,123	1.80%
41	North Dakota	233	0.20%
8	Ohio	3,557	3.02%
30	Oklahoma	820	0.70%
27	Oregon	1,019	0.86%
5	Pennsylvania	4,937	4.19%
NA	Rhode Island**	NA	NA
26	South Carolina	1,046	0.89%
43	South Dakota	220	0.19%
9	Tennessee	3,258	2.76%
2	Texas	11,304	9.59%
36	Utah	499	0.42%
NA	Vermont**	NA	NA
10	Virginia	3,103	2.63%
19	Washington	1,581	1.34%
38	West Virginia	483	0.41%
20	Wisconsin	1,545	1.31%
42	Wyoming	223	0.19%

RANK ORDER

RANK	STATE	OFFICERS	% of USA
1	New York	12,824	10.88%
2	Texas	11,304	9.59%
3	California	10,389	8.81%
4	Florida	8,547	7.25%
5	Pennsylvania	4,937	4.19%
6	Illinois	3,843	3.26%
7	Georgia	3,815	3.24%
8	Ohio	3,557	3.02%
9	Tennessee	3,258	2.76%
10	Virginia	3,103	2.63%
11	New Jersey	3,065	2.60%
12	Michigan	2,939	2.49%
13	Massachusetts	2,851	2.42%
14	Maryland	2,272	1.93%
15	Louisiana	2,132	1.81%
16	North Carolina	2,123	1.80%
17	Colorado	1,843	1.56%
18	Indiana	1,582	1.34%
19	Washington	1,581	1.34%
20	Wisconsin	1,545	1.31%
21	Arizona	1,489	1.26%
22	Kentucky	1,412	1.20%
23	Alabama	1,301	1.10%
24	Minnesota	1,248	1.06%
25	Missouri	1,093	0.93%
26	South Carolina	1,046	0.89%
27	Oregon	1,019	0.86%
28	Kansas	977	0.83%
29	Arkansas	854	0.72%
30	Oklahoma	820	0.70%
31	Iowa	812	0.69%
32	New Mexico	786	0.67%
33	Mississippi	753	0.64%
34	Nebraska	709	0.60%
35	Nevada	549	0.47%
36	Utah	499	0.42%
37	Maine	490	0.42%
38	West Virginia	483	0.41%
39	Idaho	410	0.35%
40	New Hampshire	259	0.22%
41	North Dakota	233	0.20%
42	Wyoming	223	0.19%
43	South Dakota	220	0.19%
44	Montana	208	0.18%
45	Alaska	24	0.02%
NA	Connecticut**	NA	NA
NA	Delaware**	NA	NA
NA	Hawaii**	NA	NA
NA	Rhode Island**	NA	NA
NA	Vermont**	NA	NA
	District of Columbia	512	0.43%

Source: U.S. Department of Justice, Bureau of Justice Statistics
     "Correctional Populations in the United States, 1993" (October 1995, NCJ-156241)
*National total includes estimates for units that did not provide data. Includes 113,300 full-time and 4,600 part-time officers.
**These states have combined state and local jail systems and are excluded from this count.

131

Number of Local Jail Inmates per Correctional Officer in 1993

National Rate = 3.9 Inmates per Officer*

ALPHA ORDER				RANK ORDER		
RANK	STATE	RATE		RANK	STATE	RATE
6	Alabama	4.8		1	California	6.6
NA	Alaska**	NA		2	Mississippi	5.7
7	Arizona	4.7		3	Nevada	5.3
28	Arkansas	3.2		4	Georgia	5.1
1	California	6.6		4	Indiana	5.1
33	Colorado	2.8		6	Alabama	4.8
NA	Connecticut**	NA		7	Arizona	4.7
NA	Delaware**	NA		7	Washington	4.7
22	Florida	3.5		9	Louisiana	4.6
4	Georgia	5.1		9	Texas	4.6
NA	Hawaii**	NA		9	Wisconsin	4.6
24	Idaho	3.4		12	South Carolina	4.3
20	Illinois	3.6		12	Virginia	4.3
4	Indiana	5.1		14	Kentucky	4.2
41	Iowa	2.0		14	Tennessee	4.2
34	Kansas	2.7		16	Maryland	4.1
14	Kentucky	4.2		17	North Carolina	4.0
9	Louisiana	4.6		18	Michigan	3.9
44	Maine	1.4		19	Utah	3.8
16	Maryland	4.1		20	Illinois	3.6
38	Massachusetts	2.5		20	Oklahoma	3.6
18	Michigan	3.9		22	Florida	3.5
34	Minnesota	2.7		22	New Jersey	3.5
2	Mississippi	5.7		24	Idaho	3.4
25	Missouri	3.3		25	Missouri	3.3
32	Montana	2.9		25	New Mexico	3.3
39	Nebraska	2.2		25	Oregon	3.3
3	Nevada	5.3		28	Arkansas	3.2
36	New Hampshire	2.6		28	West Virginia	3.2
22	New Jersey	3.5		30	Ohio	3.1
25	New Mexico	3.3		31	Pennsylvania	3.0
41	New York	2.0		32	Montana	2.9
17	North Carolina	4.0		33	Colorado	2.8
43	North Dakota	1.5		34	Kansas	2.7
30	Ohio	3.1		34	Minnesota	2.7
20	Oklahoma	3.6		36	New Hampshire	2.6
25	Oregon	3.3		36	South Dakota	2.6
31	Pennsylvania	3.0		38	Massachusetts	2.5
NA	Rhode Island**	NA		39	Nebraska	2.2
12	South Carolina	4.3		39	Wyoming	2.2
36	South Dakota	2.6		41	Iowa	2.0
14	Tennessee	4.2		41	New York	2.0
9	Texas	4.6		43	North Dakota	1.5
19	Utah	3.8		44	Maine	1.4
NA	Vermont**	NA		NA	Alaska**	NA
12	Virginia	4.3		NA	Connecticut**	NA
7	Washington	4.7		NA	Delaware**	NA
28	West Virginia	3.2		NA	Hawaii**	NA
9	Wisconsin	4.6		NA	Rhode Island**	NA
39	Wyoming	2.2		NA	Vermont**	NA
					District of Columbia	3.3

Source: U.S. Department of Justice, Bureau of Justice Statistics
"Correctional Populations in the United States, 1993" (October 1995, NCJ-156241)
*Inmate-to-staff ratios were calculated by dividing the reported number of inmates by the reported number of staff.
**These states have combined state and local jail systems and are excluded from this count.

III. DRUGS AND ALCOHOL

Alcohol and Other Drug Treatment Units in 1995

National Total = 7,064 Units*

ALPHA ORDER					RANK ORDER			
RANK	STATE		UNITS	% of USA	RANK	STATE	UNITS	% of USA
37	Alabama		38	0.54%	1	California	889	12.58%
31	Alaska		56	0.79%	2	Pennsylvania	773	10.94%
25	Arizona		69	0.98%	3	New York	722	10.22%
43	Arkansas		25	0.35%	4	Ohio	529	7.49%
1	California		889	12.58%	5	Texas	347	4.91%
14	Colorado		141	2.00%	6	Illinois	312	4.42%
16	Connecticut		126	1.78%	7	Michigan	251	3.55%
41	Delaware		29	0.41%	8	Massachusetts	248	3.51%
NA	Florida**		NA	NA	9	Virginia	217	3.07%
19	Georgia		95	1.34%	10	Kentucky	201	2.85%
45	Hawaii		22	0.31%	11	Washington	167	2.36%
23	Idaho		71	1.01%	12	New Jersey	153	2.17%
6	Illinois		312	4.42%	13	Wisconsin	142	2.01%
27	Indiana		65	0.92%	14	Colorado	141	2.00%
40	Iowa		35	0.50%	15	Maryland	132	1.87%
32	Kansas		53	0.75%	16	Connecticut	126	1.78%
10	Kentucky		201	2.85%	16	Nebraska	126	1.78%
20	Louisiana		89	1.26%	18	Oregon	101	1.43%
28	Maine		62	0.88%	19	Georgia	95	1.34%
15	Maryland		132	1.87%	20	Louisiana	89	1.26%
8	Massachusetts		248	3.51%	21	Missouri	79	1.12%
7	Michigan		251	3.55%	22	Mississippi	77	1.09%
NA	Minnesota**		NA	NA	23	Idaho	71	1.01%
22	Mississippi		77	1.09%	24	Utah	70	0.99%
21	Missouri		79	1.12%	25	Arizona	69	0.98%
44	Montana		24	0.34%	25	New Mexico	69	0.98%
16	Nebraska		126	1.78%	27	Indiana	65	0.92%
35	Nevada		44	0.62%	28	Maine	62	0.88%
38	New Hampshire		36	0.51%	29	Oklahoma	61	0.86%
12	New Jersey		153	2.17%	30	Tennessee	60	0.85%
25	New Mexico		69	0.98%	31	Alaska	56	0.79%
3	New York		722	10.22%	32	Kansas	53	0.75%
35	North Carolina		44	0.62%	33	Rhode Island	45	0.64%
47	North Dakota		8	0.11%	33	South Dakota	45	0.64%
4	Ohio		529	7.49%	35	Nevada	44	0.62%
29	Oklahoma		61	0.86%	35	North Carolina	44	0.62%
18	Oregon		101	1.43%	37	Alabama	38	0.54%
2	Pennsylvania		773	10.94%	38	New Hampshire	36	0.51%
33	Rhode Island		45	0.64%	38	South Carolina	36	0.51%
38	South Carolina		36	0.51%	40	Iowa	35	0.50%
33	South Dakota		45	0.64%	41	Delaware	29	0.41%
30	Tennessee		60	0.85%	41	West Virginia	29	0.41%
5	Texas		347	4.91%	43	Arkansas	25	0.35%
24	Utah		70	0.99%	44	Montana	24	0.34%
46	Vermont		20	0.28%	45	Hawaii	22	0.31%
9	Virginia		217	3.07%	46	Vermont	20	0.28%
11	Washington		167	2.36%	47	North Dakota	8	0.11%
41	West Virginia		29	0.41%	NA	Florida**	NA	NA
13	Wisconsin		142	2.01%	NA	Minnesota**	NA	NA
NA	Wyoming**		NA	NA	NA	Wyoming**	NA	NA
						District of Columbia	31	0.44%

Source: U.S. Department of Health and Human Services, Substance Abuse and Mental Health Services Administration
"State Resources and Services Related to Alcohol and Other Drug Problems-Fiscal Year 1995" (July 1997)
*Does not include 44 units in U.S. territories. Data are only from treatment units that received at least some funds administered by a state's alcohol/drug agency in fiscal year 1995.
**Not available.

Alcohol and Other Drug Treatment Admissions in 1995

National Total = 1,876,363 Admissions*

ALPHA ORDER

RANK	STATE	ADMISSIONS	% of USA
31	Alabama	14,782	0.79%
38	Alaska	9,098	0.48%
25	Arizona	22,149	1.18%
32	Arkansas	13,950	0.74%
1	California	190,496	10.15%
12	Colorado	52,684	2.81%
17	Connecticut	42,716	2.28%
41	Delaware	6,842	0.36%
4	Florida	104,571	5.57%
10	Georgia	60,788	3.24%
46	Hawaii	4,483	0.24%
45	Idaho	5,521	0.29%
3	Illinois	121,552	6.48%
21	Indiana	27,663	1.47%
24	Iowa	23,986	1.28%
28	Kansas	19,142	1.02%
27	Kentucky	19,692	1.05%
22	Louisiana	27,259	1.45%
39	Maine	9,052	0.48%
19	Maryland	34,454	1.84%
5	Massachusetts	99,864	5.32%
6	Michigan	84,795	4.52%
NA	Minnesota**	NA	NA
33	Mississippi	13,702	0.73%
20	Missouri	33,960	1.81%
44	Montana	5,707	0.30%
26	Nebraska	21,438	1.14%
43	Nevada	6,481	0.35%
47	New Hampshire	3,888	0.21%
13	New Jersey	50,704	2.70%
34	New Mexico	12,840	0.68%
2	New York	156,172	8.32%
14	North Carolina	50,578	2.70%
48	North Dakota	3,277	0.17%
7	Ohio	74,123	3.95%
40	Oklahoma	7,690	0.41%
15	Oregon	46,456	2.48%
9	Pennsylvania	68,659	3.66%
36	Rhode Island	11,204	0.60%
23	South Carolina	26,728	1.42%
35	South Dakota	12,379	0.66%
37	Tennessee	10,670	0.57%
11	Texas	56,039	2.99%
29	Utah	16,624	0.89%
42	Vermont	6,735	0.36%
18	Virginia	35,799	1.91%
16	Washington	45,764	2.44%
30	West Virginia	15,972	0.85%
8	Wisconsin	72,689	3.87%
NA	Wyoming**	NA	NA

RANK ORDER

RANK	STATE	ADMISSIONS	% of USA
1	California	190,496	10.15%
2	New York	156,172	8.32%
3	Illinois	121,552	6.48%
4	Florida	104,571	5.57%
5	Massachusetts	99,864	5.32%
6	Michigan	84,795	4.52%
7	Ohio	74,123	3.95%
8	Wisconsin	72,689	3.87%
9	Pennsylvania	68,659	3.66%
10	Georgia	60,788	3.24%
11	Texas	56,039	2.99%
12	Colorado	52,684	2.81%
13	New Jersey	50,704	2.70%
14	North Carolina	50,578	2.70%
15	Oregon	46,456	2.48%
16	Washington	45,764	2.44%
17	Connecticut	42,716	2.28%
18	Virginia	35,799	1.91%
19	Maryland	34,454	1.84%
20	Missouri	33,960	1.81%
21	Indiana	27,663	1.47%
22	Louisiana	27,259	1.45%
23	South Carolina	26,728	1.42%
24	Iowa	23,986	1.28%
25	Arizona	22,149	1.18%
26	Nebraska	21,438	1.14%
27	Kentucky	19,692	1.05%
28	Kansas	19,142	1.02%
29	Utah	16,624	0.89%
30	West Virginia	15,972	0.85%
31	Alabama	14,782	0.79%
32	Arkansas	13,950	0.74%
33	Mississippi	13,702	0.73%
34	New Mexico	12,840	0.68%
35	South Dakota	12,379	0.66%
36	Rhode Island	11,204	0.60%
37	Tennessee	10,670	0.57%
38	Alaska	9,098	0.48%
39	Maine	9,052	0.48%
40	Oklahoma	7,690	0.41%
41	Delaware	6,842	0.36%
42	Vermont	6,735	0.36%
43	Nevada	6,481	0.35%
44	Montana	5,707	0.30%
45	Idaho	5,521	0.29%
46	Hawaii	4,483	0.24%
47	New Hampshire	3,888	0.21%
48	North Dakota	3,277	0.17%
NA	Minnesota**	NA	NA
NA	Wyoming**	NA	NA
	District of Columbia	14,546	0.78%

Source: U.S. Department of Health and Human Services, Substance Abuse and Mental Health Services Administration "State Resources and Services Related to Alcohol and Other Drug Problems-Fiscal Year 1995" (July 1997)
*Does not include 22,638 admissions in U.S. territories. Data are only from treatment units that received at least some funds administered by a state's alcohol/drug agency in fiscal year 1995. National total is only for reporting states.
**Not available.

134

Male Admissions to Alcohol and Other Drug Treatment Programs in 1995

National Total = 1,290,044 Admissions*

ALPHA ORDER					RANK ORDER			
RANK	STATE	ADMISSIONS	% of USA		RANK	STATE	ADMISSIONS	% of USA
33	Alabama	9,937	0.77%		1	California	121,168	9.39%
39	Alaska	6,242	0.48%		2	New York	116,952	9.07%
25	Arizona	15,070	1.17%		3	Illinois	85,465	6.62%
31	Arkansas	10,836	0.84%		4	Massachusetts	71,868	5.57%
1	California	121,168	9.39%		5	Michigan	59,252	4.59%
13	Colorado	36,251	2.81%		6	Wisconsin	52,716	4.09%
17	Connecticut	30,665	2.38%		7	Ohio	52,026	4.03%
42	Delaware	4,898	0.38%		8	Pennsylvania	49,605	3.85%
9	Florida	43,863	3.40%		9	Florida	43,863	3.40%
10	Georgia	42,901	3.33%		10	Georgia	42,901	3.33%
46	Hawaii	2,940	0.23%		11	Texas	41,392	3.21%
45	Idaho	3,767	0.29%		12	North Carolina	36,815	2.85%
3	Illinois	85,465	6.62%		13	Colorado	36,251	2.81%
22	Indiana	19,858	1.54%		14	New Jersey	35,504	2.75%
23	Iowa	17,501	1.36%		15	Oregon	31,216	2.42%
27	Kansas	14,044	1.09%		16	Washington	30,900	2.40%
26	Kentucky	14,355	1.11%		17	Connecticut	30,665	2.38%
28	Louisiana	13,444	1.04%		18	Virginia	24,774	1.92%
38	Maine	6,789	0.53%		19	Missouri	23,933	1.86%
20	Maryland	23,811	1.85%		20	Maryland	23,811	1.85%
4	Massachusetts	71,868	5.57%		21	South Carolina	20,451	1.59%
5	Michigan	59,252	4.59%		22	Indiana	19,858	1.54%
NA	Minnesota**	NA	NA		23	Iowa	17,501	1.36%
32	Mississippi	10,706	0.83%		24	Nebraska	16,822	1.30%
19	Missouri	23,933	1.86%		25	Arizona	15,070	1.17%
44	Montana	3,910	0.30%		26	Kentucky	14,355	1.11%
24	Nebraska	16,822	1.30%		27	Kansas	14,044	1.09%
43	Nevada	4,260	0.33%		28	Louisiana	13,444	1.04%
47	New Hampshire	2,876	0.22%		29	West Virginia	12,579	0.98%
14	New Jersey	35,504	2.75%		30	Utah	12,221	0.95%
34	New Mexico	9,272	0.72%		31	Arkansas	10,836	0.84%
2	New York	116,952	9.07%		32	Mississippi	10,706	0.83%
12	North Carolina	36,815	2.85%		33	Alabama	9,937	0.77%
48	North Dakota	2,259	0.18%		34	New Mexico	9,272	0.72%
7	Ohio	52,026	4.03%		35	South Dakota	8,927	0.69%
40	Oklahoma	5,002	0.39%		36	Tennessee	7,611	0.59%
15	Oregon	31,216	2.42%		37	Rhode Island	7,306	0.57%
8	Pennsylvania	49,605	3.85%		38	Maine	6,789	0.53%
37	Rhode Island	7,306	0.57%		39	Alaska	6,242	0.48%
21	South Carolina	20,451	1.59%		40	Oklahoma	5,002	0.39%
35	South Dakota	8,927	0.69%		41	Vermont	4,952	0.38%
36	Tennessee	7,611	0.59%		42	Delaware	4,898	0.38%
11	Texas	41,392	3.21%		43	Nevada	4,260	0.33%
30	Utah	12,221	0.95%		44	Montana	3,910	0.30%
41	Vermont	4,952	0.38%		45	Idaho	3,767	0.29%
18	Virginia	24,774	1.92%		46	Hawaii	2,940	0.23%
16	Washington	30,900	2.40%		47	New Hampshire	2,876	0.22%
29	West Virginia	12,579	0.98%		48	North Dakota	2,259	0.18%
6	Wisconsin	52,716	4.09%		NA	Minnesota**	NA	NA
NA	Wyoming**	NA	NA		NA	Wyoming**	NA	NA
						District of Columbia	10,132	0.79%

Source: U.S. Department of Health and Human Services, Substance Abuse and Mental Health Services Administration
"State Resources and Services Related to Alcohol and Other Drug Problems-Fiscal Year 1995" (July 1997)
*Does not include 20,696 male admissions in U.S. territories. Data are only from treatment units that received at least some funds administered by a state's alcohol/drug agency in fiscal year 1995. An additional 58,931 admissions were not reported by sex. National total is only for reporting states.
**Not available.

135

Male Admissions to Alcohol and Drug Treatment Programs
As a Percent of All Admissions in 1995
National Percent = 68.8% Males*

ALPHA ORDER

RANK	STATE	PERCENT
40	Alabama	67.2
35	Alaska	68.6
38	Arizona	68.0
4	Arkansas	77.7
46	California	63.6
34	Colorado	68.8
21	Connecticut	71.8
23	Delaware	71.6
48	Florida	41.9
25	Georgia	70.6
43	Hawaii	65.6
37	Idaho	68.2
27	Illinois	70.3
21	Indiana	71.8
13	Iowa	73.0
12	Kansas	73.4
14	Kentucky	72.9
47	Louisiana	49.3
6	Maine	75.0
32	Maryland	69.1
20	Massachusetts	72.0
30	Michigan	69.9
NA	Minnesota**	NA
3	Mississippi	78.1
26	Missouri	70.5
36	Montana	68.5
2	Nebraska	78.5
42	Nevada	65.7
8	New Hampshire	74.0
29	New Jersey	70.0
17	New Mexico	72.2
7	New York	74.9
15	North Carolina	72.8
33	North Dakota	68.9
28	Ohio	70.2
45	Oklahoma	65.0
40	Oregon	67.2
17	Pennsylvania	72.2
44	Rhode Island	65.2
5	South Carolina	76.5
19	South Dakota	72.1
24	Tennessee	71.3
9	Texas	73.9
10	Utah	73.5
10	Vermont	73.5
31	Virginia	69.2
39	Washington	67.5
1	West Virginia	78.8
16	Wisconsin	72.5
NA	Wyoming**	NA

RANK ORDER

RANK	STATE	PERCENT
1	West Virginia	78.8
2	Nebraska	78.5
3	Mississippi	78.1
4	Arkansas	77.7
5	South Carolina	76.5
6	Maine	75.0
7	New York	74.9
8	New Hampshire	74.0
9	Texas	73.9
10	Utah	73.5
10	Vermont	73.5
12	Kansas	73.4
13	Iowa	73.0
14	Kentucky	72.9
15	North Carolina	72.8
16	Wisconsin	72.5
17	New Mexico	72.2
17	Pennsylvania	72.2
19	South Dakota	72.1
20	Massachusetts	72.0
21	Connecticut	71.8
21	Indiana	71.8
23	Delaware	71.6
24	Tennessee	71.3
25	Georgia	70.6
26	Missouri	70.5
27	Illinois	70.3
28	Ohio	70.2
29	New Jersey	70.0
30	Michigan	69.9
31	Virginia	69.2
32	Maryland	69.1
33	North Dakota	68.9
34	Colorado	68.8
35	Alaska	68.6
36	Montana	68.5
37	Idaho	68.2
38	Arizona	68.0
39	Washington	67.5
40	Alabama	67.2
40	Oregon	67.2
42	Nevada	65.7
43	Hawaii	65.6
44	Rhode Island	65.2
45	Oklahoma	65.0
46	California	63.6
47	Louisiana	49.3
48	Florida	41.9
NA	Minnesota**	NA
NA	Wyoming**	NA

District of Columbia   69.7

Source: Morgan Quitno Press using data from U.S. Department of Health and Human Services, Substance Abuse and Mental Health Services Administration

"State Resources and Services Related to Alcohol and Other Drug Problems-Fiscal Year 1995" (July 1997)
*Does not include admissions in U.S. territories. Data are only from treatment units that received at least some funds administered by a state's alcohol/drug agency in fiscal year 1995. An additional 58,931 admissions were not reported by sex. **Not available.

Female Admissions to Alcohol and Other Drug Treatment Programs in 1995

National Total = 527,388 Female Admissions*

ALPHA ORDER					RANK ORDER			
RANK	STATE	ADMISSIONS	% of USA		RANK	STATE	ADMISSIONS	% of USA
31	Alabama	3,711	0.70%		1	California	69,328	13.15%
38	Alaska	2,856	0.54%		2	New York	39,220	7.44%
22	Arizona	7,079	1.34%		3	Illinois	36,087	6.84%
35	Arkansas	3,114	0.59%		4	Massachusetts	27,996	5.31%
1	California	69,328	13.15%		5	Michigan	25,523	4.84%
17	Colorado	11,261	2.14%		6	Ohio	22,097	4.19%
16	Connecticut	12,051	2.29%		7	Wisconsin	19,973	3.79%
42	Delaware	1,944	0.37%		8	Pennsylvania	19,054	3.61%
9	Florida	18,248	3.46%		9	Florida	18,248	3.46%
10	Georgia	17,887	3.39%		10	Georgia	17,887	3.39%
46	Hawaii	1,539	0.29%		11	Oregon	15,240	2.89%
45	Idaho	1,754	0.33%		12	New Jersey	15,200	2.88%
3	Illinois	36,087	6.84%		13	Washington	14,864	2.82%
21	Indiana	7,805	1.48%		14	Texas	14,642	2.78%
23	Iowa	6,485	1.23%		15	North Carolina	13,727	2.60%
26	Kansas	5,098	0.97%		16	Connecticut	12,051	2.29%
25	Kentucky	5,337	1.01%		17	Colorado	11,261	2.14%
29	Louisiana	4,240	0.80%		18	Virginia	11,025	2.09%
39	Maine	2,263	0.43%		19	Maryland	10,643	2.02%
19	Maryland	10,643	2.02%		20	Missouri	10,027	1.90%
4	Massachusetts	27,996	5.31%		21	Indiana	7,805	1.48%
5	Michigan	25,523	4.84%		22	Arizona	7,079	1.34%
NA	Minnesota**	NA	NA		23	Iowa	6,485	1.23%
37	Mississippi	2,996	0.57%		24	South Carolina	6,277	1.19%
20	Missouri	10,027	1.90%		25	Kentucky	5,337	1.01%
43	Montana	1,797	0.34%		26	Kansas	5,098	0.97%
27	Nebraska	4,610	0.87%		27	Nebraska	4,610	0.87%
40	Nevada	2,221	0.42%		28	Utah	4,375	0.83%
48	New Hampshire	1,012	0.19%		29	Louisiana	4,240	0.80%
12	New Jersey	15,200	2.88%		30	Rhode Island	3,898	0.74%
32	New Mexico	3,568	0.68%		31	Alabama	3,711	0.70%
2	New York	39,220	7.44%		32	New Mexico	3,568	0.68%
15	North Carolina	13,727	2.60%		33	South Dakota	3,452	0.65%
47	North Dakota	1,018	0.19%		34	West Virginia	3,393	0.64%
6	Ohio	22,097	4.19%		35	Arkansas	3,114	0.59%
41	Oklahoma	2,205	0.42%		36	Tennessee	3,059	0.58%
11	Oregon	15,240	2.89%		37	Mississippi	2,996	0.57%
8	Pennsylvania	19,054	3.61%		38	Alaska	2,856	0.54%
30	Rhode Island	3,898	0.74%		39	Maine	2,263	0.43%
24	South Carolina	6,277	1.19%		40	Nevada	2,221	0.42%
33	South Dakota	3,452	0.65%		41	Oklahoma	2,205	0.42%
36	Tennessee	3,059	0.58%		42	Delaware	1,944	0.37%
14	Texas	14,642	2.78%		43	Montana	1,797	0.34%
28	Utah	4,375	0.83%		44	Vermont	1,775	0.34%
44	Vermont	1,775	0.34%		45	Idaho	1,754	0.33%
18	Virginia	11,025	2.09%		46	Hawaii	1,539	0.29%
13	Washington	14,864	2.82%		47	North Dakota	1,018	0.19%
34	West Virginia	3,393	0.64%		48	New Hampshire	1,012	0.19%
7	Wisconsin	19,973	3.79%		NA	Minnesota**	NA	NA
NA	Wyoming**	NA	NA		NA	Wyoming**	NA	NA
						District of Columbia	4,414	0.84%

Source: U.S. Department of Health and Human Services, Substance Abuse and Mental Health Services Administration
"State Resources and Services Related to Alcohol and Other Drug Problems-Fiscal Year 1995" (July 1997)
*Does not include 1,942 female admissions in U.S. territories. Data are only from treatment units that received at least some funds administered by a state's alcohol/drug agency in fiscal year 1995. An additional 58,931 admissions were not reported by sex. National total is only for reporting states.
**Not available.

Female Admissions to Alcohol and Other Drug Treatment Programs
As a Percent of All Admissions in 1995
National Percent = 28.1% Female*

ALPHA ORDER				RANK ORDER		
RANK	STATE	PERCENT		RANK	STATE	PERCENT
38	Alabama	25.1		1	California	36.4
10	Alaska	31.4		2	Rhode Island	34.8
7	Arizona	32.0		3	Hawaii	34.3
42	Arkansas	22.3		3	Nevada	34.3
1	California	36.4		5	Oregon	32.8
45	Colorado	21.4		6	Washington	32.5
23	Connecticut	28.2		7	Arizona	32.0
22	Delaware	28.4		8	Idaho	31.8
47	Florida	17.5		9	Montana	31.5
19	Georgia	29.4		10	Alaska	31.4
3	Hawaii	34.3		11	North Dakota	31.1
8	Idaho	31.8		12	Maryland	30.9
17	Illinois	29.7		13	Virginia	30.8
23	Indiana	28.2		14	Michigan	30.1
32	Iowa	27.0		15	New Jersey	30.0
33	Kansas	26.6		16	Ohio	29.8
30	Kentucky	27.1		17	Illinois	29.7
48	Louisiana	15.6		18	Missouri	29.5
40	Maine	25.0		19	Georgia	29.4
12	Maryland	30.9		20	Oklahoma	28.7
25	Massachusetts	28.0		20	Tennessee	28.7
14	Michigan	30.1		22	Delaware	28.4
NA	Minnesota**	NA		23	Connecticut	28.2
43	Mississippi	21.9		23	Indiana	28.2
18	Missouri	29.5		25	Massachusetts	28.0
9	Montana	31.5		26	South Dakota	27.9
44	Nebraska	21.5		27	New Mexico	27.8
3	Nevada	34.3		27	Pennsylvania	27.8
37	New Hampshire	26.0		29	Wisconsin	27.5
15	New Jersey	30.0		30	Kentucky	27.1
27	New Mexico	27.8		30	North Carolina	27.1
38	New York	25.1		32	Iowa	27.0
30	North Carolina	27.1		33	Kansas	26.6
11	North Dakota	31.1		34	Vermont	26.4
16	Ohio	29.8		35	Utah	26.3
20	Oklahoma	28.7		36	Texas	26.1
5	Oregon	32.8		37	New Hampshire	26.0
27	Pennsylvania	27.8		38	Alabama	25.1
2	Rhode Island	34.8		38	New York	25.1
41	South Carolina	23.5		40	Maine	25.0
26	South Dakota	27.9		41	South Carolina	23.5
20	Tennessee	28.7		42	Arkansas	22.3
36	Texas	26.1		43	Mississippi	21.9
35	Utah	26.3		44	Nebraska	21.5
34	Vermont	26.4		45	Colorado	21.4
13	Virginia	30.8		46	West Virginia	21.2
6	Washington	32.5		47	Florida	17.5
46	West Virginia	21.2		48	Louisiana	15.6
29	Wisconsin	27.5		NA	Minnesota**	NA
NA	Wyoming**	NA		NA	Wyoming**	NA
					District of Columbia	30.3

Source: Morgan Quitno Press using data from U.S. Department of Health and Human Services, Substance Abuse and Mental Health Services Administration
"State Resources and Services Related to Alcohol and Other Drug Problems-Fiscal Year 1995" (July 1997)
*Does not include admissions in U.S. territories. Data are only from treatment units that received at least some funds administered by a state's alcohol/drug agency in fiscal year 1995. An additional 58,931 admissions were not reported by sex. **Not available.

White Admissions to Alcohol and Other Drug Treatment Programs in 1995

National Total = 1,062,509 White Admissions*

ALPHA ORDER

RANK	STATE	ADMISSIONS	% of USA
35	Alabama	7,594	0.71%
43	Alaska	4,135	0.39%
28	Arizona	13,300	1.25%
30	Arkansas	9,262	0.87%
1	California	98,410	9.26%
13	Colorado	28,885	2.72%
16	Connecticut	23,495	2.21%
45	Delaware	3,790	0.36%
10	Florida	36,636	3.45%
12	Georgia	33,008	3.11%
48	Hawaii	1,827	0.17%
40	Idaho	4,763	0.45%
7	Illinois	42,543	4.00%
21	Indiana	18,484	1.74%
19	Iowa	21,330	2.01%
27	Kansas	13,323	1.25%
23	Kentucky	16,698	1.57%
34	Louisiana	8,035	0.76%
31	Maine	8,755	0.82%
22	Maryland	17,466	1.64%
3	Massachusetts	68,602	6.46%
5	Michigan	55,289	5.20%
NA	Minnesota**	NA	NA
38	Mississippi	6,098	0.57%
18	Missouri	22,215	2.09%
42	Montana	4,329	0.41%
25	Nebraska	15,055	1.42%
41	Nevada	4,597	0.43%
46	New Hampshire	3,697	0.35%
15	New Jersey	24,450	2.30%
44	New Mexico	3,944	0.37%
2	New York	72,649	6.84%
14	North Carolina	26,408	2.49%
47	North Dakota	2,416	0.23%
6	Ohio	48,801	4.59%
39	Oklahoma	5,144	0.48%
9	Oregon	37,347	3.51%
8	Pennsylvania	39,006	3.67%
33	Rhode Island	8,458	0.80%
24	South Carolina	15,495	1.46%
32	South Dakota	8,718	0.82%
36	Tennessee	7,258	0.68%
17	Texas	23,064	2.17%
29	Utah	12,319	1.16%
37	Vermont	6,466	0.61%
20	Virginia	19,764	1.86%
11	Washington	33,449	3.15%
26	West Virginia	14,751	1.39%
4	Wisconsin	60,545	5.70%
NA	Wyoming**	NA	NA

RANK ORDER

RANK	STATE	ADMISSIONS	% of USA
1	California	98,410	9.26%
2	New York	72,649	6.84%
3	Massachusetts	68,602	6.46%
4	Wisconsin	60,545	5.70%
5	Michigan	55,289	5.20%
6	Ohio	48,801	4.59%
7	Illinois	42,543	4.00%
8	Pennsylvania	39,006	3.67%
9	Oregon	37,347	3.51%
10	Florida	36,636	3.45%
11	Washington	33,449	3.15%
12	Georgia	33,008	3.11%
13	Colorado	28,885	2.72%
14	North Carolina	26,408	2.49%
15	New Jersey	24,450	2.30%
16	Connecticut	23,495	2.21%
17	Texas	23,064	2.17%
18	Missouri	22,215	2.09%
19	Iowa	21,330	2.01%
20	Virginia	19,764	1.86%
21	Indiana	18,484	1.74%
22	Maryland	17,466	1.64%
23	Kentucky	16,698	1.57%
24	South Carolina	15,495	1.46%
25	Nebraska	15,055	1.42%
26	West Virginia	14,751	1.39%
27	Kansas	13,323	1.25%
28	Arizona	13,300	1.25%
29	Utah	12,319	1.16%
30	Arkansas	9,262	0.87%
31	Maine	8,755	0.82%
32	South Dakota	8,718	0.82%
33	Rhode Island	8,458	0.80%
34	Louisiana	8,035	0.76%
35	Alabama	7,594	0.71%
36	Tennessee	7,258	0.68%
37	Vermont	6,466	0.61%
38	Mississippi	6,098	0.57%
39	Oklahoma	5,144	0.48%
40	Idaho	4,763	0.45%
41	Nevada	4,597	0.43%
42	Montana	4,329	0.41%
43	Alaska	4,135	0.39%
44	New Mexico	3,944	0.37%
45	Delaware	3,790	0.36%
46	New Hampshire	3,697	0.35%
47	North Dakota	2,416	0.23%
48	Hawaii	1,827	0.17%
NA	Minnesota**	NA	NA
NA	Wyoming**	NA	NA
	District of Columbia	436	0.04%

Source: U.S. Department of Health and Human Services, Substance Abuse and Mental Health Services Administration
"State Resources and Services Related to Alcohol and Other Drug Problems-Fiscal Year 1995" (July 1997)
*Data are only from treatment units that received at least some funds administered by a state's alcohol/drug agency
in fiscal year 1995. An additional 95,039 admissions were not reported by race.*
***Not available.*

139

White Admissions to Alcohol and Other Drug Treatment Programs
As a Percent of All Admissions in 1995
National Percent = 56.6% of Admissions*

ALPHA ORDER

RANK	STATE	PERCENT
37	Alabama	51.4
41	Alaska	45.4
27	Arizona	60.0
23	Arkansas	66.4
36	California	51.7
33	Colorado	54.8
32	Connecticut	55.0
30	Delaware	55.4
45	Florida	35.0
34	Georgia	54.3
44	Hawaii	40.8
6	Idaho	86.3
45	Illinois	35.0
22	Indiana	66.8
5	Iowa	88.9
18	Kansas	69.6
7	Kentucky	84.8
48	Louisiana	29.5
1	Maine	96.7
38	Maryland	50.7
19	Massachusetts	68.7
26	Michigan	65.2
NA	Minnesota**	NA
42	Mississippi	44.5
25	Missouri	65.4
10	Montana	75.9
17	Nebraska	70.2
15	Nevada	70.9
3	New Hampshire	95.1
39	New Jersey	48.2
47	New Mexico	30.7
40	New York	46.5
35	North Carolina	52.2
13	North Dakota	73.7
24	Ohio	65.8
21	Oklahoma	66.9
9	Oregon	80.4
29	Pennsylvania	56.8
11	Rhode Island	75.5
28	South Carolina	58.0
16	South Dakota	70.4
20	Tennessee	68.0
43	Texas	41.2
12	Utah	74.1
2	Vermont	96.0
31	Virginia	55.2
14	Washington	73.1
4	West Virginia	92.4
8	Wisconsin	83.3
NA	Wyoming**	NA

RANK ORDER

RANK	STATE	PERCENT
1	Maine	96.7
2	Vermont	96.0
3	New Hampshire	95.1
4	West Virginia	92.4
5	Iowa	88.9
6	Idaho	86.3
7	Kentucky	84.8
8	Wisconsin	83.3
9	Oregon	80.4
10	Montana	75.9
11	Rhode Island	75.5
12	Utah	74.1
13	North Dakota	73.7
14	Washington	73.1
15	Nevada	70.9
16	South Dakota	70.4
17	Nebraska	70.2
18	Kansas	69.6
19	Massachusetts	68.7
20	Tennessee	68.0
21	Oklahoma	66.9
22	Indiana	66.8
23	Arkansas	66.4
24	Ohio	65.8
25	Missouri	65.4
26	Michigan	65.2
27	Arizona	60.0
28	South Carolina	58.0
29	Pennsylvania	56.8
30	Delaware	55.4
31	Virginia	55.2
32	Connecticut	55.0
33	Colorado	54.8
34	Georgia	54.3
35	North Carolina	52.2
36	California	51.7
37	Alabama	51.4
38	Maryland	50.7
39	New Jersey	48.2
40	New York	46.5
41	Alaska	45.4
42	Mississippi	44.5
43	Texas	41.2
44	Hawaii	40.8
45	Florida	35.0
45	Illinois	35.0
47	New Mexico	30.7
48	Louisiana	29.5
NA	Minnesota**	NA
NA	Wyoming**	NA
	District of Columbia	3.0

Source: Morgan Quitno Press using data from U.S. Department of Health and Human Services, Substance Abuse and Mental Health Services Administration
"State Resources and Services Related to Alcohol and Other Drug Problems-Fiscal Year 1995" (July 1997)
Data are only from treatment units that received at least some funds administered by a state's alcohol/drug agency in fiscal year 1995. An additional 95,039 admissions were not reported by race.
Not available.

140

Black Admissions to Alcohol and Other Drug Treatment Programs in 1995

National Total = 493,101 Black Admissions*

ALPHA ORDER

RANK	STATE	ADMISSIONS	% of USA
22	Alabama	5,882	1.19%
39	Alaska	376	0.08%
32	Arizona	1,719	0.35%
24	Arkansas	4,516	0.92%
3	California	37,274	7.56%
25	Colorado	4,260	0.86%
15	Connecticut	11,890	2.41%
29	Delaware	2,737	0.56%
8	Florida	19,698	3.99%
4	Georgia	27,240	5.52%
41	Hawaii	160	0.03%
47	Idaho	44	0.01%
2	Illinois	51,315	10.41%
19	Indiana	8,093	1.64%
33	Iowa	1,674	0.34%
26	Kansas	3,485	0.71%
30	Kentucky	2,690	0.55%
18	Louisiana	9,488	1.92%
45	Maine	77	0.02%
12	Maryland	15,940	3.23%
13	Massachusetts	15,656	3.18%
5	Michigan	26,267	5.33%
NA	Minnesota**	NA	NA
21	Mississippi	7,505	1.52%
16	Missouri	11,225	2.28%
46	Montana	52	0.01%
31	Nebraska	2,514	0.51%
37	Nevada	945	0.19%
43	New Hampshire	99	0.02%
11	New Jersey	17,975	3.65%
40	New Mexico	272	0.06%
1	New York	57,204	11.60%
7	North Carolina	22,297	4.52%
48	North Dakota	10	0.00%
6	Ohio	23,531	4.77%
36	Oklahoma	1,083	0.22%
28	Oregon	2,797	0.57%
10	Pennsylvania	18,001	3.65%
34	Rhode Island	1,230	0.25%
17	South Carolina	10,943	2.22%
42	South Dakota	159	0.03%
27	Tennessee	3,122	0.63%
9	Texas	18,721	3.80%
38	Utah	569	0.12%
44	Vermont	80	0.02%
14	Virginia	14,734	2.99%
23	Washington	4,803	0.97%
35	West Virginia	1,121	0.23%
20	Wisconsin	7,909	1.60%
NA	Wyoming**	NA	NA

RANK ORDER

RANK	STATE	ADMISSIONS	% of USA
1	New York	57,204	11.60%
2	Illinois	51,315	10.41%
3	California	37,274	7.56%
4	Georgia	27,240	5.52%
5	Michigan	26,267	5.33%
6	Ohio	23,531	4.77%
7	North Carolina	22,297	4.52%
8	Florida	19,698	3.99%
9	Texas	18,721	3.80%
10	Pennsylvania	18,001	3.65%
11	New Jersey	17,975	3.65%
12	Maryland	15,940	3.23%
13	Massachusetts	15,656	3.18%
14	Virginia	14,734	2.99%
15	Connecticut	11,890	2.41%
16	Missouri	11,225	2.28%
17	South Carolina	10,943	2.22%
18	Louisiana	9,488	1.92%
19	Indiana	8,093	1.64%
20	Wisconsin	7,909	1.60%
21	Mississippi	7,505	1.52%
22	Alabama	5,882	1.19%
23	Washington	4,803	0.97%
24	Arkansas	4,516	0.92%
25	Colorado	4,260	0.86%
26	Kansas	3,485	0.71%
27	Tennessee	3,122	0.63%
28	Oregon	2,797	0.57%
29	Delaware	2,737	0.56%
30	Kentucky	2,690	0.55%
31	Nebraska	2,514	0.51%
32	Arizona	1,719	0.35%
33	Iowa	1,674	0.34%
34	Rhode Island	1,230	0.25%
35	West Virginia	1,121	0.23%
36	Oklahoma	1,083	0.22%
37	Nevada	945	0.19%
38	Utah	569	0.12%
39	Alaska	376	0.08%
40	New Mexico	272	0.06%
41	Hawaii	160	0.03%
42	South Dakota	159	0.03%
43	New Hampshire	99	0.02%
44	Vermont	80	0.02%
45	Maine	77	0.02%
46	Montana	52	0.01%
47	Idaho	44	0.01%
48	North Dakota	10	0.00%
NA	Minnesota**	NA	NA
NA	Wyoming**	NA	NA
	District of Columbia	13,719	2.78%

Source: U.S. Department of Health and Human Services, Substance Abuse and Mental Health Services Administration
"State Resources and Services Related to Alcohol and Other Drug Problems-Fiscal Year 1995" (July 1997)
*Data are only from treatment units that received at least some funds administered by a state's alcohol/drug agency
in fiscal year 1995. An additional 95,039 admissions were not reported by race.
**Not available.

Black Admissions to Alcohol and Other Drug Treatment Programs
As a Percent of All Admissions in 1995
National Percent = 26.3% of Admissions*

ALPHA ORDER				RANK ORDER		
RANK	STATE	PERCENT		RANK	STATE	PERCENT
9	Alabama	39.8		1	Mississippi	54.8
38	Alaska	4.1		2	Maryland	46.3
34	Arizona	7.8		3	Georgia	44.8
15	Arkansas	32.4		4	North Carolina	44.1
22	California	19.6		5	Illinois	42.2
33	Colorado	8.1		6	Virginia	41.2
20	Connecticut	27.8		7	South Carolina	40.9
8	Delaware	40.0		8	Delaware	40.0
23	Florida	18.8		9	Alabama	39.8
3	Georgia	44.8		10	New York	36.6
39	Hawaii	3.6		11	New Jersey	35.5
47	Idaho	0.8		12	Louisiana	34.8
5	Illinois	42.2		13	Texas	33.4
18	Indiana	29.3		14	Missouri	33.1
35	Iowa	7.0		15	Arkansas	32.4
24	Kansas	18.2		16	Ohio	31.7
28	Kentucky	13.7		17	Michigan	31.0
12	Louisiana	34.8		18	Indiana	29.3
45	Maine	0.9		18	Tennessee	29.3
2	Maryland	46.3		20	Connecticut	27.8
25	Massachusetts	15.7		21	Pennsylvania	26.2
17	Michigan	31.0		22	California	19.6
NA	Minnesota**	NA		23	Florida	18.8
1	Mississippi	54.8		24	Kansas	18.2
14	Missouri	33.1		25	Massachusetts	15.7
45	Montana	0.9		26	Nevada	14.6
29	Nebraska	11.7		27	Oklahoma	14.1
26	Nevada	14.6		28	Kentucky	13.7
41	New Hampshire	2.5		29	Nebraska	11.7
11	New Jersey	35.5		30	Rhode Island	11.0
42	New Mexico	2.1		31	Wisconsin	10.9
10	New York	36.6		32	Washington	10.5
4	North Carolina	44.1		33	Colorado	8.1
48	North Dakota	0.3		34	Arizona	7.8
16	Ohio	31.7		35	Iowa	7.0
27	Oklahoma	14.1		35	West Virginia	7.0
37	Oregon	6.0		37	Oregon	6.0
21	Pennsylvania	26.2		38	Alaska	4.1
30	Rhode Island	11.0		39	Hawaii	3.6
7	South Carolina	40.9		40	Utah	3.4
43	South Dakota	1.3		41	New Hampshire	2.5
18	Tennessee	29.3		42	New Mexico	2.1
13	Texas	33.4		43	South Dakota	1.3
40	Utah	3.4		44	Vermont	1.2
44	Vermont	1.2		45	Maine	0.9
6	Virginia	41.2		45	Montana	0.9
32	Washington	10.5		47	Idaho	0.8
35	West Virginia	7.0		48	North Dakota	0.3
31	Wisconsin	10.9		NA	Minnesota**	NA
NA	Wyoming**	NA		NA	Wyoming**	NA
					District of Columbia	94.3

Source: Morgan Quitno Press using data from U.S. Department of Health and Human Services, Substance Abuse
   and Mental Health Services Administration
   "State Resources and Services Related to Alcohol and Other Drug Problems-Fiscal Year 1995" (July 1997)
*Data are only from treatment units that received at least some funds administered by a state's alcohol/drug agency
in fiscal year 1995. An additional 95,039 admissions were not reported by race.
**Not available.

Hispanic Admissions to Alcohol and Other Drug Treatment Programs in 1995

National Total = 124,079 Hispanic Admissions*

ALPHA ORDER					RANK ORDER			
RANK	STATE	ADMISSIONS	% of USA		RANK	STATE	ADMISSIONS	% of USA
NA	Alabama**	NA	NA		1	California	45,678	36.81%
NA	Alaska**	NA	NA		2	New York	23,369	18.83%
8	Arizona	4,842	3.90%		3	Massachusetts	12,517	10.09%
20	Arkansas	106	0.09%		4	New Jersey	7,678	6.19%
1	California	45,678	36.81%		5	Connecticut	7,023	5.66%
NA	Colorado**	NA	NA		6	Illinois	6,786	5.47%
5	Connecticut	7,023	5.66%		7	New Mexico	6,181	4.98%
NA	Delaware**	NA	NA		8	Arizona	4,842	3.90%
NA	Florida**	NA	NA		9	Pennsylvania	2,292	1.85%
17	Georgia	178	0.14%		10	Kansas	1,734	1.40%
NA	Hawaii**	NA	NA		11	Utah	1,725	1.39%
NA	Idaho**	NA	NA		12	Wisconsin	1,234	0.99%
6	Illinois	6,786	5.47%		13	Rhode Island	995	0.80%
15	Indiana	309	0.25%		14	Nevada	567	0.46%
NA	Iowa**	NA	NA		15	Indiana	309	0.25%
10	Kansas	1,734	1.40%		16	Maryland	183	0.15%
21	Kentucky	100	0.08%		17	Georgia	178	0.14%
24	Louisiana	0	0.00%		18	Montana	147	0.12%
NA	Maine**	NA	NA		19	South Dakota	114	0.09%
16	Maryland	183	0.15%		20	Arkansas	106	0.09%
3	Massachusetts	12,517	10.09%		21	Kentucky	100	0.08%
NA	Michigan**	NA	NA		22	Missouri	98	0.08%
NA	Minnesota**	NA	NA		23	Vermont	22	0.02%
24	Mississippi	0	0.00%		24	Louisiana	0	0.00%
22	Missouri	98	0.08%		24	Mississippi	0	0.00%
18	Montana	147	0.12%		24	Nebraska	0	0.00%
24	Nebraska	0	0.00%		24	North Carolina	0	0.00%
14	Nevada	567	0.46%		24	North Dakota	0	0.00%
NA	New Hampshire**	NA	NA		24	Oklahoma	0	0.00%
4	New Jersey	7,678	6.19%		24	West Virginia	0	0.00%
7	New Mexico	6,181	4.98%		NA	Alabama**	NA	NA
2	New York	23,369	18.83%		NA	Alaska**	NA	NA
24	North Carolina	0	0.00%		NA	Colorado**	NA	NA
24	North Dakota	0	0.00%		NA	Delaware**	NA	NA
NA	Ohio**	NA	NA		NA	Florida**	NA	NA
24	Oklahoma	0	0.00%		NA	Hawaii**	NA	NA
NA	Oregon**	NA	NA		NA	Idaho**	NA	NA
9	Pennsylvania	2,292	1.85%		NA	Iowa**	NA	NA
13	Rhode Island	995	0.80%		NA	Maine**	NA	NA
NA	South Carolina**	NA	NA		NA	Michigan**	NA	NA
19	South Dakota	114	0.09%		NA	Minnesota**	NA	NA
NA	Tennessee**	NA	NA		NA	New Hampshire**	NA	NA
NA	Texas**	NA	NA		NA	Ohio**	NA	NA
11	Utah	1,725	1.39%		NA	Oregon**	NA	NA
23	Vermont	22	0.02%		NA	South Carolina**	NA	NA
NA	Virginia**	NA	NA		NA	Tennessee**	NA	NA
NA	Washington**	NA	NA		NA	Texas**	NA	NA
24	West Virginia	0	0.00%		NA	Virginia**	NA	NA
12	Wisconsin	1,234	0.99%		NA	Washington**	NA	NA
NA	Wyoming**	NA	NA		NA	Wyoming**	NA	NA
						District of Columbia	201	0.16%

Source: U.S. Department of Health and Human Services, Substance Abuse and Mental Health Services Administration "State Resources and Services Related to Alcohol and Other Drug Problems-Fiscal Year 1995" (July 1997)
Does not include 22,581 Hispanic admissions in U.S. territories. Data are only from treatment units that received at least some funds administered by a state's alcohol/drug agency in fiscal year 1995. An additional 95,039 admissions were not reported by race.
**Not available.*

Hispanic Admissions to Alcohol and Other Drug Treatment Programs
As a Percent of All Admissions in 1995
National Percent = 6.6% of Admissions*

ALPHA ORDER

RANK ORDER

RANK	STATE	PERCENT	RANK	STATE	PERCENT
NA	Alabama**	NA	1	New Mexico	48.1
NA	Alaska**	NA	2	California	24.0
3	Arizona	21.9	3	Arizona	21.9
18	Arkansas	0.8	4	Connecticut	16.4
2	California	24.0	5	New Jersey	15.1
NA	Colorado**	NA	6	New York	15.0
4	Connecticut	16.4	7	Massachusetts	12.5
NA	Delaware**	NA	8	Utah	10.4
NA	Florida**	NA	9	Kansas	9.1
21	Georgia	0.3	10	Rhode Island	8.9
NA	Hawaii**	NA	11	Nevada	8.7
NA	Idaho**	NA	12	Illinois	5.6
12	Illinois	5.6	13	Pennsylvania	3.3
16	Indiana	1.1	14	Montana	2.6
NA	Iowa**	NA	15	Wisconsin	1.7
9	Kansas	9.1	16	Indiana	1.1
19	Kentucky	0.5	17	South Dakota	0.9
24	Louisiana	0.0	18	Arkansas	0.8
NA	Maine**	NA	19	Kentucky	0.5
19	Maryland	0.5	19	Maryland	0.5
7	Massachusetts	12.5	21	Georgia	0.3
NA	Michigan**	NA	21	Missouri	0.3
NA	Minnesota**	NA	21	Vermont	0.3
24	Mississippi	0.0	24	Louisiana	0.0
21	Missouri	0.3	24	Mississippi	0.0
14	Montana	2.6	24	Nebraska	0.0
24	Nebraska	0.0	24	North Carolina	0.0
11	Nevada	8.7	24	North Dakota	0.0
NA	New Hampshire**	NA	24	Oklahoma	0.0
5	New Jersey	15.1	24	West Virginia	0.0
1	New Mexico	48.1	NA	Alabama**	NA
6	New York	15.0	NA	Alaska**	NA
24	North Carolina	0.0	NA	Colorado**	NA
24	North Dakota	0.0	NA	Delaware**	NA
NA	Ohio**	NA	NA	Florida**	NA
24	Oklahoma	0.0	NA	Hawaii**	NA
NA	Oregon**	NA	NA	Idaho**	NA
13	Pennsylvania	3.3	NA	Iowa**	NA
10	Rhode Island	8.9	NA	Maine**	NA
NA	South Carolina**	NA	NA	Michigan**	NA
17	South Dakota	0.9	NA	Minnesota**	NA
NA	Tennessee**	NA	NA	New Hampshire**	NA
NA	Texas**	NA	NA	Ohio**	NA
8	Utah	10.4	NA	Oregon**	NA
21	Vermont	0.3	NA	South Carolina**	NA
NA	Virginia**	NA	NA	Tennessee**	NA
NA	Washington**	NA	NA	Texas**	NA
24	West Virginia	0.0	NA	Virginia**	NA
15	Wisconsin	1.7	NA	Washington**	NA
NA	Wyoming**	NA	NA	Wyoming**	NA

District of Columbia 1.4

Source: Morgan Quitno Press using data from U.S. Department of Health and Human Services, Substance Abuse and Mental Health Services Administration
"State Resources and Services Related to Alcohol and Other Drug Problems-Fiscal Year 1995" (July 1997)
*Data are only from treatment units that received at least some funds administered by a state's alcohol/drug agency in fiscal year 1995. An additional 95,039 admissions were not reported by race.
**Not available.

Expenditures for State-Supported Alcohol and Other Drug Abuse Services: 1995

National Total = $4,032,786,784*

ALPHA ORDER					RANK ORDER			
RANK	STATE	EXPENDITURES	% of USA		RANK	STATE	EXPENDITURES	% of USA
32	Alabama	$22,694,860	0.56%		1	New York	$840,056,882	20.83%
33	Alaska	22,450,175	0.56%		2	California	544,851,000	13.51%
26	Arizona	32,458,699	0.80%		3	Pennsylvania	223,120,406	5.53%
37	Arkansas	15,264,992	0.38%		4	Illinois	204,960,979	5.08%
2	California	544,851,000	13.51%		5	Florida	192,020,229	4.76%
20	Colorado	51,124,582	1.27%		6	Ohio	177,308,445	4.40%
9	Connecticut	102,525,662	2.54%		7	Texas	174,713,730	4.33%
44	Delaware	8,887,347	0.22%		8	Michigan	151,573,606	3.76%
5	Florida	192,020,229	4.76%		9	Connecticut	102,525,662	2.54%
16	Georgia	69,501,022	1.72%		10	New Jersey	102,089,567	2.53%
35	Hawaii	17,841,224	0.44%		11	Virginia	89,194,350	2.21%
47	Idaho	6,781,249	0.17%		12	Oregon	82,778,742	2.05%
4	Illinois	204,960,979	5.08%		13	Maryland	76,283,076	1.89%
19	Indiana	52,527,820	1.30%		14	Massachusetts	76,212,460	1.89%
21	Iowa	50,111,156	1.24%		15	Washington	72,165,460	1.79%
34	Kansas	18,156,687	0.45%		16	Georgia	69,501,022	1.72%
28	Kentucky	25,715,370	0.64%		17	North Carolina	60,466,422	1.50%
25	Louisiana	34,964,571	0.87%		18	Wisconsin	59,067,626	1.46%
38	Maine	15,232,636	0.38%		19	Indiana	52,527,820	1.30%
13	Maryland	76,283,076	1.89%		20	Colorado	51,124,582	1.27%
14	Massachusetts	76,212,460	1.89%		21	Iowa	50,111,156	1.24%
8	Michigan	151,573,606	3.76%		22	South Carolina	45,362,123	1.12%
NA	Minnesota**	NA	NA		23	Missouri	44,744,508	1.11%
40	Mississippi	14,915,278	0.37%		24	Utah	36,816,506	0.91%
23	Missouri	44,744,508	1.11%		25	Louisiana	34,964,571	0.87%
42	Montana	12,263,980	0.30%		26	Arizona	32,458,699	0.80%
39	Nebraska	15,085,068	0.37%		27	Tennessee	28,812,282	0.71%
43	Nevada	10,564,331	0.26%		28	Kentucky	25,715,370	0.64%
46	New Hampshire	7,290,076	0.18%		29	Rhode Island	24,044,163	0.60%
10	New Jersey	102,089,567	2.53%		30	New Mexico	23,833,597	0.59%
30	New Mexico	23,833,597	0.59%		31	Oklahoma	23,480,541	0.58%
1	New York	840,056,882	20.83%		32	Alabama	22,694,860	0.56%
17	North Carolina	60,466,422	1.50%		33	Alaska	22,450,175	0.56%
48	North Dakota	4,213,000	0.10%		34	Kansas	18,156,687	0.45%
6	Ohio	177,308,445	4.40%		35	Hawaii	17,841,224	0.44%
31	Oklahoma	23,480,541	0.58%		36	West Virginia	17,350,261	0.43%
12	Oregon	82,778,742	2.05%		37	Arkansas	15,264,992	0.38%
3	Pennsylvania	223,120,406	5.53%		38	Maine	15,232,636	0.38%
29	Rhode Island	24,044,163	0.60%		39	Nebraska	15,085,068	0.37%
22	South Carolina	45,362,123	1.12%		40	Mississippi	14,915,278	0.37%
41	South Dakota	12,892,649	0.32%		41	South Dakota	12,892,649	0.32%
27	Tennessee	28,812,282	0.71%		42	Montana	12,263,980	0.30%
7	Texas	174,713,730	4.33%		43	Nevada	10,564,331	0.26%
24	Utah	36,816,506	0.91%		44	Delaware	8,887,347	0.22%
45	Vermont	7,542,924	0.19%		45	Vermont	7,542,924	0.19%
11	Virginia	89,194,350	2.21%		46	New Hampshire	7,290,076	0.18%
15	Washington	72,165,460	1.79%		47	Idaho	6,781,249	0.17%
36	West Virginia	17,350,261	0.43%		48	North Dakota	4,213,000	0.10%
18	Wisconsin	59,067,626	1.46%		NA	Minnesota**	NA	NA
NA	Wyoming**	NA	NA		NA	Wyoming**	NA	NA
						District of Columbia	30,474,465	0.76%

Source: U.S. Department of Health and Human Services, Substance Abuse and Mental Health Services Administration
"State Resources and Services Related to Alcohol and Other Drug Problems-Fiscal Year 1995" (July 1997)
*Funds for treatment and prevention programs as well as "other" costs (e.g. administration, capital construction and research.) Total does not include $49,009,302 in U.S. territories.
**Not available.

Per Capita Expenditures for State-Supported Alcohol and Other Drug Abuse Services in 1995
National Per Capita = $15.35*

ALPHA ORDER			RANK ORDER		
RANK	STATE	PER CAPITA	RANK	STATE	PER CAPITA
48	Alabama	$5.32	1	New York	$46.29
2	Alaska	37.31	2	Alaska	37.31
37	Arizona	7.53	3	Connecticut	31.38
44	Arkansas	6.15	4	Oregon	26.34
11	California	17.26	5	Rhode Island	24.29
18	Colorado	13.66	6	Utah	18.65
3	Connecticut	31.38	7	Pennsylvania	18.52
25	Delaware	12.42	8	Iowa	17.64
19	Florida	13.54	9	South Dakota	17.54
29	Georgia	9.66	10	Illinois	17.38
15	Hawaii	15.13	11	California	17.26
45	Idaho	5.82	12	Ohio	15.93
10	Illinois	17.38	13	Michigan	15.70
33	Indiana	9.08	14	Maryland	15.17
8	Iowa	17.64	15	Hawaii	15.13
39	Kansas	7.07	16	New Mexico	14.13
41	Kentucky	6.67	17	Montana	14.12
36	Louisiana	8.08	18	Colorado	13.66
26	Maine	12.34	19	Florida	13.54
14	Maryland	15.17	20	Virginia	13.51
24	Massachusetts	12.58	21	Washington	13.28
13	Michigan	15.70	22	Vermont	12.94
NA	Minnesota**	NA	23	New Jersey	12.83
46	Mississippi	5.54	24	Massachusetts	12.58
35	Missouri	8.40	25	Delaware	12.42
17	Montana	14.12	26	Maine	12.34
32	Nebraska	9.22	27	South Carolina	12.32
40	Nevada	6.91	28	Wisconsin	11.55
43	New Hampshire	6.36	29	Georgia	9.66
23	New Jersey	12.83	30	West Virginia	9.52
16	New Mexico	14.13	31	Texas	9.32
1	New York	46.29	32	Nebraska	9.22
34	North Carolina	8.41	33	Indiana	9.08
42	North Dakota	6.57	34	North Carolina	8.41
12	Ohio	15.93	35	Missouri	8.40
38	Oklahoma	7.18	36	Louisiana	8.08
4	Oregon	26.34	37	Arizona	7.53
7	Pennsylvania	18.52	38	Oklahoma	7.18
5	Rhode Island	24.29	39	Kansas	7.07
27	South Carolina	12.32	40	Nevada	6.91
9	South Dakota	17.54	41	Kentucky	6.67
47	Tennessee	5.50	42	North Dakota	6.57
31	Texas	9.32	43	New Hampshire	6.36
6	Utah	18.65	44	Arkansas	6.15
22	Vermont	12.94	45	Idaho	5.82
20	Virginia	13.51	46	Mississippi	5.54
21	Washington	13.28	47	Tennessee	5.50
30	West Virginia	9.52	48	Alabama	5.32
28	Wisconsin	11.55	NA	Minnesota**	NA
NA	Wyoming**	NA	NA	Wyoming**	NA
				District of Columbia	55.18

Source: Morgan Quitno Press using data from U.S. Department of Health and Human Services, Substance Abuse and Mental Health Services Administration
  "State Resources and Services Related to Alcohol and Other Drug Problems-Fiscal Year 1995" (July 1997)
*Funds for treatment and prevention programs as well as "other" costs (e.g. administration, capital construction and research.) National per capita does not include expenditures in U.S. territories.
**Not available.

Expenditures for State-Supported Alcohol and Other Drug Abuse Treatment Programs in 1995
National Total = $3,179,369,701*

ALPHA ORDER

ALPHA ORDER

RANK	STATE	EXPENDITURES	% of USA
33	Alabama	$17,644,108	0.55%
27	Alaska	21,156,174	0.67%
26	Arizona	27,847,817	0.88%
38	Arkansas	11,900,546	0.37%
2	California	362,879,000	11.41%
18	Colorado	44,267,973	1.39%
9	Connecticut	89,533,115	2.82%
43	Delaware	7,797,288	0.25%
3	Florida	178,522,719	5.62%
13	Georgia	63,861,566	2.01%
36	Hawaii	13,766,703	0.43%
47	Idaho	4,597,259	0.14%
4	Illinois	177,595,268	5.59%
19	Indiana	43,195,735	1.36%
21	Iowa	39,769,960	1.25%
35	Kansas	14,323,206	0.45%
28	Kentucky	20,982,223	0.66%
24	Louisiana	29,878,770	0.94%
42	Maine	8,995,047	0.28%
14	Maryland	63,032,310	1.98%
12	Massachusetts	66,353,841	2.09%
8	Michigan	118,015,662	3.71%
NA	Minnesota**	NA	NA
37	Mississippi	11,972,336	0.38%
22	Missouri	37,855,303	1.19%
40	Montana	11,196,526	0.35%
39	Nebraska	11,634,884	0.37%
44	Nevada	7,120,951	0.22%
46	New Hampshire	5,317,451	0.17%
10	New Jersey	86,592,262	2.72%
30	New Mexico	18,232,995	0.57%
1	New York	678,399,295	21.34%
15	North Carolina	53,416,441	1.68%
48	North Dakota	3,787,000	0.12%
6	Ohio	134,404,251	4.23%
29	Oklahoma	18,442,305	0.58%
20	Oregon	40,527,240	1.27%
5	Pennsylvania	177,347,885	5.58%
32	Rhode Island	18,064,415	0.57%
23	South Carolina	35,053,946	1.10%
41	South Dakota	9,531,053	0.30%
31	Tennessee	18,091,874	0.57%
7	Texas	124,247,222	3.91%
25	Utah	28,276,967	0.89%
45	Vermont	6,011,659	0.19%
11	Virginia	77,888,617	2.45%
16	Washington	51,246,222	1.61%
34	West Virginia	15,313,725	0.48%
17	Wisconsin	46,539,757	1.46%
NA	Wyoming**	NA	NA

RANK ORDER

RANK	STATE	EXPENDITURES	% of USA
1	New York	$678,399,295	21.34%
2	California	362,879,000	11.41%
3	Florida	178,522,719	5.62%
4	Illinois	177,595,268	5.59%
5	Pennsylvania	177,347,885	5.58%
6	Ohio	134,404,251	4.23%
7	Texas	124,247,222	3.91%
8	Michigan	118,015,662	3.71%
9	Connecticut	89,533,115	2.82%
10	New Jersey	86,592,262	2.72%
11	Virginia	77,888,617	2.45%
12	Massachusetts	66,353,841	2.09%
13	Georgia	63,861,566	2.01%
14	Maryland	63,032,310	1.98%
15	North Carolina	53,416,441	1.68%
16	Washington	51,246,222	1.61%
17	Wisconsin	46,539,757	1.46%
18	Colorado	44,267,973	1.39%
19	Indiana	43,195,735	1.36%
20	Oregon	40,527,240	1.27%
21	Iowa	39,769,960	1.25%
22	Missouri	37,855,303	1.19%
23	South Carolina	35,053,946	1.10%
24	Louisiana	29,878,770	0.94%
25	Utah	28,276,967	0.89%
26	Arizona	27,847,817	0.88%
27	Alaska	21,156,174	0.67%
28	Kentucky	20,982,223	0.66%
29	Oklahoma	18,442,305	0.58%
30	New Mexico	18,232,995	0.57%
31	Tennessee	18,091,874	0.57%
32	Rhode Island	18,064,415	0.57%
33	Alabama	17,644,108	0.55%
34	West Virginia	15,313,725	0.48%
35	Kansas	14,323,206	0.45%
36	Hawaii	13,766,703	0.43%
37	Mississippi	11,972,336	0.38%
38	Arkansas	11,900,546	0.37%
39	Nebraska	11,634,884	0.37%
40	Montana	11,196,526	0.35%
41	South Dakota	9,531,053	0.30%
42	Maine	8,995,047	0.28%
43	Delaware	7,797,288	0.25%
44	Nevada	7,120,951	0.22%
45	Vermont	6,011,659	0.19%
46	New Hampshire	5,317,451	0.17%
47	Idaho	4,597,259	0.14%
48	North Dakota	3,787,000	0.12%
NA	Minnesota**	NA	NA
NA	Wyoming**	NA	NA
	District of Columbia	26,940,829	0.85%

Source: U.S. Department of Health and Human Services, Substance Abuse and Mental Health Services Administration "State Resources and Services Related to Alcohol and Other Drug Problems-Fiscal Year 1995" (July 1997)
*Total does not include $24,502,015 in U.S. territories.
**Not available.

Expenditures per Alcohol and Other Drug Treatment Admission in 1995

National Rate = $1,694 in Treatment Expenditures per Admission*

ALPHA ORDER

RANK ORDER

RANK	STATE	RATE	RANK	STATE	RATE
26	Alabama	$1,194	1	New York	$4,344
5	Alaska	2,325	2	Hawaii	3,071
25	Arizona	1,257	3	Pennsylvania	2,583
41	Arkansas	853	4	Oklahoma	2,398
10	California	1,905	5	Alaska	2,325
42	Colorado	840	6	Texas	2,217
8	Connecticut	2,096	7	Virginia	2,176
28	Delaware	1,140	8	Connecticut	2,096
14	Florida	1,707	9	Montana	1,962
35	Georgia	1,051	10	California	1,905
2	Hawaii	3,071	11	Maryland	1,829
43	Idaho	833	12	Ohio	1,813
20	Illinois	1,461	13	New Jersey	1,708
19	Indiana	1,561	14	Florida	1,707
17	Iowa	1,658	15	Utah	1,701
45	Kansas	748	16	Tennessee	1,696
33	Kentucky	1,066	17	Iowa	1,658
32	Louisiana	1,096	18	Rhode Island	1,612
36	Maine	994	19	Indiana	1,561
11	Maryland	1,829	20	Illinois	1,461
46	Massachusetts	664	21	New Mexico	1,420
22	Michigan	1,392	22	Michigan	1,392
NA	Minnesota**	NA	23	New Hampshire	1,368
39	Mississippi	874	24	South Carolina	1,312
30	Missouri	1,115	25	Arizona	1,257
9	Montana	1,962	26	Alabama	1,194
48	Nebraska	543	27	North Dakota	1,156
31	Nevada	1,099	28	Delaware	1,140
23	New Hampshire	1,368	29	Washington	1,120
13	New Jersey	1,708	30	Missouri	1,115
21	New Mexico	1,420	31	Nevada	1,099
1	New York	4,344	32	Louisiana	1,096
34	North Carolina	1,056	33	Kentucky	1,066
27	North Dakota	1,156	34	North Carolina	1,056
12	Ohio	1,813	35	Georgia	1,051
4	Oklahoma	2,398	36	Maine	994
40	Oregon	872	37	West Virginia	959
3	Pennsylvania	2,583	38	Vermont	893
18	Rhode Island	1,612	39	Mississippi	874
24	South Carolina	1,312	40	Oregon	872
44	South Dakota	770	41	Arkansas	853
16	Tennessee	1,696	42	Colorado	840
6	Texas	2,217	43	Idaho	833
15	Utah	1,701	44	South Dakota	770
38	Vermont	893	45	Kansas	748
7	Virginia	2,176	46	Massachusetts	664
29	Washington	1,120	47	Wisconsin	640
37	West Virginia	959	48	Nebraska	543
47	Wisconsin	640	NA	Minnesota**	NA
NA	Wyoming**	NA	NA	Wyoming**	NA
				District of Columbia	1,852

Source: Morgan Quitno Press using data from U.S. Department of Health and Human Services, Substance Abuse
and Mental Health Services Administration
"State Resources and Services Related to Alcohol and Other Drug Problems-Fiscal Year 1994" (March 1996)
*Does not include admissions in U.S. territories. Data are only from treatment units that received at least some
funds administered by a state's alcohol/drug agency in fiscal year 1995.
**Not available.

Per Capita Expenditures for State-Supported Alcohol and Other Drug Abuse Treatment Programs in 1995
National Per Capita = $12.10*

ALPHA ORDER

RANK	STATE	PER CAPITA
46	Alabama	$4.14
2	Alaska	35.16
37	Arizona	6.46
42	Arkansas	4.80
19	California	11.50
16	Colorado	11.83
3	Connecticut	27.41
21	Delaware	10.89
12	Florida	12.59
28	Georgia	8.88
18	Hawaii	11.68
47	Idaho	3.95
5	Illinois	15.06
30	Indiana	7.46
8	Iowa	14.00
40	Kansas	5.57
41	Kentucky	5.44
35	Louisiana	6.90
32	Maine	7.29
13	Maryland	12.54
20	Massachusetts	10.95
14	Michigan	12.22
NA	Minnesota**	NA
45	Mississippi	4.45
33	Missouri	7.11
10	Montana	12.89
33	Nebraska	7.11
43	Nevada	4.66
44	New Hampshire	4.64
22	New Jersey	10.88
23	New Mexico	10.81
1	New York	37.39
31	North Carolina	7.43
38	North Dakota	5.90
15	Ohio	12.07
39	Oklahoma	5.64
10	Oregon	12.89
6	Pennsylvania	14.72
4	Rhode Island	18.25
25	South Carolina	9.52
9	South Dakota	12.97
48	Tennessee	3.46
36	Texas	6.63
7	Utah	14.32
24	Vermont	10.31
17	Virginia	11.80
26	Washington	9.43
29	West Virginia	8.41
27	Wisconsin	9.10
NA	Wyoming**	NA

RANK ORDER

RANK	STATE	PER CAPITA
1	New York	$37.39
2	Alaska	35.16
3	Connecticut	27.41
4	Rhode Island	18.25
5	Illinois	15.06
6	Pennsylvania	14.72
7	Utah	14.32
8	Iowa	14.00
9	South Dakota	12.97
10	Montana	12.89
10	Oregon	12.89
12	Florida	12.59
13	Maryland	12.54
14	Michigan	12.22
15	Ohio	12.07
16	Colorado	11.83
17	Virginia	11.80
18	Hawaii	11.68
19	California	11.50
20	Massachusetts	10.95
21	Delaware	10.89
22	New Jersey	10.88
23	New Mexico	10.81
24	Vermont	10.31
25	South Carolina	9.52
26	Washington	9.43
27	Wisconsin	9.10
28	Georgia	8.88
29	West Virginia	8.41
30	Indiana	7.46
31	North Carolina	7.43
32	Maine	7.29
33	Missouri	7.11
33	Nebraska	7.11
35	Louisiana	6.90
36	Texas	6.63
37	Arizona	6.46
38	North Dakota	5.90
39	Oklahoma	5.64
40	Kansas	5.57
41	Kentucky	5.44
42	Arkansas	4.80
43	Nevada	4.66
44	New Hampshire	4.64
45	Mississippi	4.45
46	Alabama	4.14
47	Idaho	3.95
48	Tennessee	3.46
NA	Minnesota**	NA
NA	Wyoming**	NA
	District of Columbia	48.78

Source: Morgan Quitno Press using data from U.S. Department of Health and Human Services, Substance Abuse and Mental Health Services Administration
"State Resources and Services Related to Alcohol and Other Drug Problems-Fiscal Year 1995" (July 1997)
*National per capita does not include expenditures in U.S. territories.
**Not available.

Expenditures for State-Supported Alcohol and Other Drug Abuse Prevention Programs in 1995
National Total = $576,142,644*

ALPHA ORDER

ALPHA ORDER

RANK	STATE	EXPENDITURES	% of USA
33	Alabama	$3,642,937	0.63%
46	Alaska	943,605	0.16%
32	Arizona	3,882,555	0.67%
38	Arkansas	2,326,465	0.40%
1	California	119,152,000	20.68%
31	Colorado	3,956,240	0.69%
18	Connecticut	7,456,762	1.29%
43	Delaware	1,064,899	0.18%
13	Florida	9,830,077	1.71%
22	Georgia	5,639,456	0.98%
35	Hawaii	2,629,038	0.46%
44	Idaho	1,013,273	0.18%
8	Illinois	17,928,187	3.11%
16	Indiana	7,984,381	1.39%
10	Iowa	10,341,196	1.79%
36	Kansas	2,591,227	0.45%
27	Kentucky	4,733,147	0.82%
30	Louisiana	4,006,535	0.70%
25	Maine	5,155,423	0.89%
19	Maryland	7,060,626	1.23%
15	Massachusetts	8,140,164	1.41%
6	Michigan	24,201,032	4.20%
NA	Minnesota**	NA	NA
40	Mississippi	1,997,767	0.35%
23	Missouri	5,341,447	0.93%
47	Montana	646,625	0.11%
37	Nebraska	2,587,590	0.45%
39	Nevada	2,117,379	0.37%
42	New Hampshire	1,355,911	0.24%
9	New Jersey	12,020,819	2.09%
28	New Mexico	4,310,717	0.75%
2	New York	106,321,122	18.45%
20	North Carolina	7,049,981	1.22%
48	North Dakota	426,000	0.07%
4	Ohio	28,884,391	5.01%
29	Oklahoma	4,230,534	0.73%
7	Oregon	19,536,178	3.39%
5	Pennsylvania	24,728,681	4.29%
24	Rhode Island	5,304,590	0.92%
14	South Carolina	9,594,501	1.67%
34	South Dakota	2,787,324	0.48%
21	Tennessee	6,591,154	1.14%
3	Texas	39,626,828	6.88%
17	Utah	7,724,756	1.34%
45	Vermont	954,933	0.17%
12	Virginia	9,888,321	1.72%
26	Washington	5,020,210	0.87%
41	West Virginia	1,512,363	0.26%
11	Wisconsin	10,079,205	1.75%
NA	Wyoming**	NA	NA

RANK ORDER

RANK	STATE	EXPENDITURES	% of USA
1	California	$119,152,000	20.68%
2	New York	106,321,122	18.45%
3	Texas	39,626,828	6.88%
4	Ohio	28,884,391	5.01%
5	Pennsylvania	24,728,681	4.29%
6	Michigan	24,201,032	4.20%
7	Oregon	19,536,178	3.39%
8	Illinois	17,928,187	3.11%
9	New Jersey	12,020,819	2.09%
10	Iowa	10,341,196	1.79%
11	Wisconsin	10,079,205	1.75%
12	Virginia	9,888,321	1.72%
13	Florida	9,830,077	1.71%
14	South Carolina	9,594,501	1.67%
15	Massachusetts	8,140,164	1.41%
16	Indiana	7,984,381	1.39%
17	Utah	7,724,756	1.34%
18	Connecticut	7,456,762	1.29%
19	Maryland	7,060,626	1.23%
20	North Carolina	7,049,981	1.22%
21	Tennessee	6,591,154	1.14%
22	Georgia	5,639,456	0.98%
23	Missouri	5,341,447	0.93%
24	Rhode Island	5,304,590	0.92%
25	Maine	5,155,423	0.89%
26	Washington	5,020,210	0.87%
27	Kentucky	4,733,147	0.82%
28	New Mexico	4,310,717	0.75%
29	Oklahoma	4,230,534	0.73%
30	Louisiana	4,006,535	0.70%
31	Colorado	3,956,240	0.69%
32	Arizona	3,882,555	0.67%
33	Alabama	3,642,937	0.63%
34	South Dakota	2,787,324	0.48%
35	Hawaii	2,629,038	0.46%
36	Kansas	2,591,227	0.45%
37	Nebraska	2,587,590	0.45%
38	Arkansas	2,326,465	0.40%
39	Nevada	2,117,379	0.37%
40	Mississippi	1,997,767	0.35%
41	West Virginia	1,512,363	0.26%
42	New Hampshire	1,355,911	0.24%
43	Delaware	1,064,899	0.18%
44	Idaho	1,013,273	0.18%
45	Vermont	954,933	0.17%
46	Alaska	943,605	0.16%
47	Montana	646,625	0.11%
48	North Dakota	426,000	0.07%
NA	Minnesota**	NA	NA
NA	Wyoming**	NA	NA
	District of Columbia	1,824,092	0.32%

Source: U.S. Department of Health and Human Services, Substance Abuse and Mental Health Services Administration "State Resources and Services Related to Alcohol and Other Drug Problems-Fiscal Year 1995" (July 1997)
*Total does not include $7,056,729 in U.S. territories.
**Not available.

Per Capita Expenditures for State-Supported Alcohol and Other Drug Abuse Prevention Programs in 1995
National Per Capita = $2.19*

ALPHA ORDER				RANK ORDER		
RANK	STATE	PER CAPITA		RANK	STATE	PER CAPITA
42	Alabama	$0.85		1	Oregon	$6.22
20	Alaska	1.57		2	New York	5.86
40	Arizona	0.90		3	Rhode Island	5.36
37	Arkansas	0.94		4	Maine	4.18
7	California	3.78		5	Utah	3.91
33	Colorado	1.06		6	South Dakota	3.79
13	Connecticut	2.28		7	California	3.78
24	Delaware	1.49		8	Iowa	3.64
47	Florida	0.69		9	South Carolina	2.60
44	Georgia	0.78		10	Ohio	2.59
14	Hawaii	2.23		11	New Mexico	2.56
41	Idaho	0.87		12	Michigan	2.51
21	Illinois	1.52		13	Connecticut	2.28
26	Indiana	1.38		14	Hawaii	2.23
8	Iowa	3.64		15	Texas	2.11
34	Kansas	1.01		16	Pennsylvania	2.05
31	Kentucky	1.23		17	Wisconsin	1.97
38	Louisiana	0.93		18	Vermont	1.64
4	Maine	4.18		19	Nebraska	1.58
25	Maryland	1.40		20	Alaska	1.57
28	Massachusetts	1.34		21	Illinois	1.52
12	Michigan	2.51		22	New Jersey	1.51
NA	Minnesota**	NA		23	Virginia	1.50
45	Mississippi	0.74		24	Delaware	1.49
35	Missouri	1.00		25	Maryland	1.40
45	Montana	0.74		26	Indiana	1.38
19	Nebraska	1.58		26	Nevada	1.38
26	Nevada	1.38		28	Massachusetts	1.34
32	New Hampshire	1.18		29	Oklahoma	1.29
22	New Jersey	1.51		30	Tennessee	1.26
11	New Mexico	2.56		31	Kentucky	1.23
2	New York	5.86		32	New Hampshire	1.18
36	North Carolina	0.98		33	Colorado	1.06
48	North Dakota	0.66		34	Kansas	1.01
10	Ohio	2.59		35	Missouri	1.00
29	Oklahoma	1.29		36	North Carolina	0.98
1	Oregon	6.22		37	Arkansas	0.94
16	Pennsylvania	2.05		38	Louisiana	0.93
3	Rhode Island	5.36		39	Washington	0.92
9	South Carolina	2.60		40	Arizona	0.90
6	South Dakota	3.79		41	Idaho	0.87
30	Tennessee	1.26		42	Alabama	0.85
15	Texas	2.11		43	West Virginia	0.83
5	Utah	3.91		44	Georgia	0.78
18	Vermont	1.64		45	Mississippi	0.74
23	Virginia	1.50		45	Montana	0.74
39	Washington	0.92		47	Florida	0.69
43	West Virginia	0.83		48	North Dakota	0.66
17	Wisconsin	1.97		NA	Minnesota**	NA
NA	Wyoming**	NA		NA	Wyoming**	NA
					District of Columbia	3.30

Source: Morgan Quitno Press using data from U.S. Department of Health and Human Services, Substance Abuse and Mental Health Services Administration
"State Resources and Services Related to Alcohol and Other Drug Problems-Fiscal Year 1995" (July 1997)
*National per capita does not include expenditures in U.S. territories.
**Not available.

151

IV. FINANCE

State and Local Government Expenditures for Justice Activities in 1994

National Total = $88,792,165,000*

RANK	STATE	EXPENDITURES	% of USA		RANK	STATE	EXPENDITURES	% of USA
26	Alabama	$957,770,000	1.08%		1	California	$14,861,043,000	16.74%
38	Alaska	407,394,000	0.46%		2	New York	9,296,867,000	10.47%
17	Arizona	1,548,243,000	1.74%		3	Texas	6,063,918,000	6.83%
35	Arkansas	450,189,000	0.51%		4	Florida	5,733,744,000	6.46%
1	California	14,861,043,000	16.74%		5	Illinois	3,749,101,000	4.22%
23	Colorado	1,169,921,000	1.32%		6	Pennsylvania	3,357,153,000	3.78%
21	Connecticut	1,209,036,000	1.36%		7	Ohio	3,335,253,000	3.76%
44	Delaware	243,947,000	0.27%		8	New Jersey	3,326,202,000	3.75%
4	Florida	5,733,744,000	6.46%		9	Michigan	3,319,778,000	3.74%
11	Georgia	2,066,837,000	2.33%		10	North Carolina	2,086,120,000	2.35%
36	Hawaii	436,112,000	0.49%		11	Georgia	2,066,837,000	2.33%
42	Idaho	283,145,000	0.32%		12	Massachusetts	1,952,076,000	2.20%
5	Illinois	3,749,101,000	4.22%		13	Virginia	1,921,475,000	2.16%
22	Indiana	1,185,865,000	1.34%		14	Maryland	1,904,317,000	2.14%
32	Iowa	624,839,000	0.70%		15	Washington	1,765,053,000	1.99%
30	Kansas	667,377,000	0.75%		16	Wisconsin	1,603,488,000	1.81%
28	Kentucky	757,581,000	0.85%		17	Arizona	1,548,243,000	1.74%
20	Louisiana	1,222,427,000	1.38%		18	Tennessee	1,266,438,000	1.43%
45	Maine	240,940,000	0.27%		19	Minnesota	1,263,847,000	1.42%
14	Maryland	1,904,317,000	2.14%		20	Louisiana	1,222,427,000	1.38%
12	Massachusetts	1,952,076,000	2.20%		21	Connecticut	1,209,036,000	1.36%
9	Michigan	3,319,778,000	3.74%		22	Indiana	1,185,865,000	1.34%
19	Minnesota	1,263,847,000	1.42%		23	Colorado	1,169,921,000	1.32%
37	Mississippi	414,024,000	0.47%		24	Missouri	1,151,584,000	1.30%
24	Missouri	1,151,584,000	1.30%		25	Oregon	989,267,000	1.11%
46	Montana	203,619,000	0.23%		26	Alabama	957,770,000	1.08%
39	Nebraska	342,002,000	0.39%		27	South Carolina	913,261,000	1.03%
31	Nevada	659,300,000	0.74%		28	Kentucky	757,581,000	0.85%
41	New Hampshire	289,767,000	0.33%		29	Oklahoma	691,118,000	0.78%
8	New Jersey	3,326,202,000	3.75%		30	Kansas	667,377,000	0.75%
33	New Mexico	528,343,000	0.60%		31	Nevada	659,300,000	0.74%
2	New York	9,296,867,000	10.47%		32	Iowa	624,839,000	0.70%
10	North Carolina	2,086,120,000	2.35%		33	New Mexico	528,343,000	0.60%
50	North Dakota	93,790,000	0.11%		34	Utah	468,520,000	0.53%
7	Ohio	3,335,253,000	3.76%		35	Arkansas	450,189,000	0.51%
29	Oklahoma	691,118,000	0.78%		36	Hawaii	436,112,000	0.49%
25	Oregon	989,267,000	1.11%		37	Mississippi	414,024,000	0.47%
6	Pennsylvania	3,357,153,000	3.78%		38	Alaska	407,394,000	0.46%
40	Rhode Island	333,273,000	0.38%		39	Nebraska	342,002,000	0.39%
27	South Carolina	913,261,000	1.03%		40	Rhode Island	333,273,000	0.38%
47	South Dakota	151,321,000	0.17%		41	New Hampshire	289,767,000	0.33%
18	Tennessee	1,266,438,000	1.43%		42	Idaho	283,145,000	0.32%
3	Texas	6,063,918,000	6.83%		43	West Virginia	273,986,000	0.31%
34	Utah	468,520,000	0.53%		44	Delaware	243,947,000	0.27%
49	Vermont	122,176,000	0.14%		45	Maine	240,940,000	0.27%
13	Virginia	1,921,475,000	2.16%		46	Montana	203,619,000	0.23%
15	Washington	1,765,053,000	1.99%		47	South Dakota	151,321,000	0.17%
43	West Virginia	273,986,000	0.31%		48	Wyoming	148,244,000	0.17%
16	Wisconsin	1,603,488,000	1.81%		49	Vermont	122,176,000	0.14%
48	Wyoming	148,244,000	0.17%		50	North Dakota	93,790,000	0.11%
						District of Columbia	741,074,000	0.83%

Source: Morgan Quitno Press using data from U.S. Bureau of the Census
   "Government Finances: 1993-1994" (1997) (http://www.census.gov/govs/www/esti94.html)
*Direct Expenditures. Includes Police Protection, Corrections and Judicial and Legal Services.

Per Capita State & Local Government Expenditures for Justice Activities: 1994

National Per Capita = $341.12*

ALPHA ORDER			RANK ORDER		
RANK	**STATE**	**PER CAPITA**	**RANK**	**STATE**	**PER CAPITA**
37	Alabama	$226.30	1	Alaska	$678.13
1	Alaska	678.13	2	New York	512.12
8	Arizona	373.18	3	California	473.75
47	Arkansas	183.67	4	Nevada	451.91
3	California	473.75	5	New Jersey	420.45
18	Colorado	319.92	6	Florida	410.85
10	Connecticut	369.78	7	Maryland	381.73
12	Delaware	345.30	8	Arizona	373.18
6	Florida	410.85	9	Hawaii	371.92
26	Georgia	293.21	10	Connecticut	369.78
9	Hawaii	371.92	11	Michigan	346.54
33	Idaho	249.38	12	Delaware	345.30
19	Illinois	319.42	13	Rhode Island	335.29
44	Indiana	206.54	14	Washington	330.58
38	Iowa	220.85	15	Texas	329.83
30	Kansas	261.32	16	Massachusetts	323.79
45	Kentucky	198.11	17	Oregon	320.29
27	Louisiana	283.82	18	Colorado	319.92
46	Maine	194.98	19	Illinois	319.42
7	Maryland	381.73	20	New Mexico	319.06
16	Massachusetts	323.79	21	Wisconsin	315.96
11	Michigan	346.54	22	Wyoming	312.07
29	Minnesota	276.71	23	Ohio	300.60
48	Mississippi	155.47	24	North Carolina	295.40
39	Missouri	218.05	25	Virginia	293.91
36	Montana	238.17	26	Georgia	293.21
42	Nebraska	210.78	27	Louisiana	283.82
4	Nevada	451.91	28	Pennsylvania	278.76
31	New Hampshire	255.56	29	Minnesota	276.71
5	New Jersey	420.45	30	Kansas	261.32
20	New Mexico	319.06	31	New Hampshire	255.56
2	New York	512.12	32	South Carolina	249.96
24	North Carolina	295.40	33	Idaho	249.38
50	North Dakota	146.65	34	Tennessee	245.53
23	Ohio	300.60	35	Utah	242.94
40	Oklahoma	212.76	36	Montana	238.17
17	Oregon	320.29	37	Alabama	226.30
28	Pennsylvania	278.76	38	Iowa	220.85
13	Rhode Island	335.29	39	Missouri	218.05
32	South Carolina	249.96	40	Oklahoma	212.76
43	South Dakota	207.40	41	Vermont	211.01
34	Tennessee	245.53	42	Nebraska	210.78
15	Texas	329.83	43	South Dakota	207.40
35	Utah	242.94	44	Indiana	206.54
41	Vermont	211.01	45	Kentucky	198.11
25	Virginia	293.91	46	Maine	194.98
14	Washington	330.58	47	Arkansas	183.67
49	West Virginia	150.64	48	Mississippi	155.47
21	Wisconsin	315.96	49	West Virginia	150.64
22	Wyoming	312.07	50	North Dakota	146.65
				District of Columbia	1,309.52

Source: Morgan Quitno Press using data from U.S. Bureau of the Census
"Government Finances: 1993-1994" (1997) (http://www.census.gov/govs/www/esti94.html)
*Direct Expenditures. Includes Police Protection, Corrections and Judicial and Legal Services.

153

State and Local Government Expenditures for Justice Activities
As a Percent of All Direct General Expenditures in 1994
National Percent = 8.3% of Direct General Expenditures*

RANK	STATE	PERCENT
34	Alabama	6.5
31	Alaska	6.6
4	Arizona	10.3
38	Arkansas	6.0
2	California	10.7
15	Colorado	7.8
22	Connecticut	7.3
16	Delaware	7.7
1	Florida	11.0
13	Georgia	7.9
31	Hawaii	6.6
19	Idaho	7.5
8	Illinois	8.5
43	Indiana	5.6
43	Iowa	5.6
28	Kansas	6.9
38	Kentucky	6.0
22	Louisiana	7.3
47	Maine	4.9
5	Maryland	9.7
28	Massachusetts	6.9
9	Michigan	8.4
41	Minnesota	5.7
48	Mississippi	4.8
27	Missouri	7.1
37	Montana	6.2
45	Nebraska	5.5
3	Nevada	10.5
34	New Hampshire	6.5
7	New Jersey	8.7
16	New Mexico	7.7
11	New York	8.2
9	North Carolina	8.4
50	North Dakota	3.6
13	Ohio	7.9
34	Oklahoma	6.5
16	Oregon	7.7
26	Pennsylvania	7.2
20	Rhode Island	7.4
31	South Carolina	6.6
41	South Dakota	5.7
20	Tennessee	7.4
6	Texas	9.5
30	Utah	6.8
46	Vermont	5.0
11	Virginia	8.2
22	Washington	7.3
49	West Virginia	4.0
22	Wisconsin	7.3
40	Wyoming	5.8

RANK	STATE	PERCENT
1	Florida	11.0
2	California	10.7
3	Nevada	10.5
4	Arizona	10.3
5	Maryland	9.7
6	Texas	9.5
7	New Jersey	8.7
8	Illinois	8.5
9	Michigan	8.4
9	North Carolina	8.4
11	New York	8.2
11	Virginia	8.2
13	Georgia	7.9
13	Ohio	7.9
15	Colorado	7.8
16	Delaware	7.7
16	New Mexico	7.7
16	Oregon	7.7
19	Idaho	7.5
20	Rhode Island	7.4
20	Tennessee	7.4
22	Connecticut	7.3
22	Louisiana	7.3
22	Washington	7.3
22	Wisconsin	7.3
26	Pennsylvania	7.2
27	Missouri	7.1
28	Kansas	6.9
28	Massachusetts	6.9
30	Utah	6.8
31	Alaska	6.6
31	Hawaii	6.6
31	South Carolina	6.6
34	Alabama	6.5
34	New Hampshire	6.5
34	Oklahoma	6.5
37	Montana	6.2
38	Arkansas	6.0
38	Kentucky	6.0
40	Wyoming	5.8
41	Minnesota	5.7
41	South Dakota	5.7
43	Indiana	5.6
43	Iowa	5.6
45	Nebraska	5.5
46	Vermont	5.0
47	Maine	4.9
48	Mississippi	4.8
49	West Virginia	4.0
50	North Dakota	3.6
	District of Columbia	16.2

Source: Morgan Quitno Press using data from U.S. Bureau of the Census
"Government Finances: 1993-1994" (1997) (http://www.census.gov/govs/www/esti94.html)
*Includes Police Protection, Corrections and Judicial and Legal Services.

State Government Expenditures for Justice Activities in 1994

National Total = $33,495,311,000*

ALPHA ORDER

RANK	STATE	EXPENDITURES	% of USA
24	Alabama	$425,140,000	1.27%
30	Alaska	300,856,000	0.90%
18	Arizona	515,701,000	1.54%
36	Arkansas	205,059,000	0.61%
1	California	4,403,619,000	13.15%
22	Colorado	446,948,000	1.33%
15	Connecticut	773,064,000	2.31%
39	Delaware	169,700,000	0.51%
4	Florida	1,940,216,000	5.79%
13	Georgia	819,796,000	2.45%
34	Hawaii	228,375,000	0.68%
44	Idaho	132,338,000	0.40%
9	Illinois	1,113,435,000	3.32%
20	Indiana	473,146,000	1.41%
31	Iowa	296,264,000	0.88%
32	Kansas	295,005,000	0.88%
25	Kentucky	423,053,000	1.26%
21	Louisiana	460,909,000	1.38%
45	Maine	119,894,000	0.36%
11	Maryland	1,042,664,000	3.11%
12	Massachusetts	950,277,000	2.84%
5	Michigan	1,376,428,000	4.11%
28	Minnesota	384,046,000	1.15%
40	Mississippi	167,712,000	0.50%
26	Missouri	414,353,000	1.24%
46	Montana	95,922,000	0.29%
42	Nebraska	142,574,000	0.43%
38	Nevada	189,635,000	0.57%
43	New Hampshire	141,928,000	0.42%
10	New Jersey	1,093,784,000	3.27%
33	New Mexico	276,859,000	0.83%
2	New York	3,192,341,000	9.53%
6	North Carolina	1,184,442,000	3.54%
50	North Dakota	31,323,000	0.09%
8	Ohio	1,116,489,000	3.33%
29	Oklahoma	347,180,000	1.04%
27	Oregon	411,478,000	1.23%
7	Pennsylvania	1,178,720,000	3.52%
37	Rhode Island	204,230,000	0.61%
23	South Carolina	444,959,000	1.33%
48	South Dakota	76,744,000	0.23%
19	Tennessee	500,674,000	1.49%
3	Texas	2,521,284,000	7.53%
35	Utah	211,353,000	0.63%
47	Vermont	89,340,000	0.27%
14	Virginia	819,399,000	2.45%
16	Washington	611,980,000	1.83%
41	West Virginia	146,661,000	0.44%
17	Wisconsin	525,318,000	1.57%
49	Wyoming	62,696,000	0.19%

RANK ORDER

RANK	STATE	EXPENDITURES	% of USA
1	California	$4,403,619,000	13.15%
2	New York	3,192,341,000	9.53%
3	Texas	2,521,284,000	7.53%
4	Florida	1,940,216,000	5.79%
5	Michigan	1,376,428,000	4.11%
6	North Carolina	1,184,442,000	3.54%
7	Pennsylvania	1,178,720,000	3.52%
8	Ohio	1,116,489,000	3.33%
9	Illinois	1,113,435,000	3.32%
10	New Jersey	1,093,784,000	3.27%
11	Maryland	1,042,664,000	3.11%
12	Massachusetts	950,277,000	2.84%
13	Georgia	819,796,000	2.45%
14	Virginia	819,399,000	2.45%
15	Connecticut	773,064,000	2.31%
16	Washington	611,980,000	1.83%
17	Wisconsin	525,318,000	1.57%
18	Arizona	515,701,000	1.54%
19	Tennessee	500,674,000	1.49%
20	Indiana	473,146,000	1.41%
21	Louisiana	460,909,000	1.38%
22	Colorado	446,948,000	1.33%
23	South Carolina	444,959,000	1.33%
24	Alabama	425,140,000	1.27%
25	Kentucky	423,053,000	1.26%
26	Missouri	414,353,000	1.24%
27	Oregon	411,478,000	1.23%
28	Minnesota	384,046,000	1.15%
29	Oklahoma	347,180,000	1.04%
30	Alaska	300,856,000	0.90%
31	Iowa	296,264,000	0.88%
32	Kansas	295,005,000	0.88%
33	New Mexico	276,859,000	0.83%
34	Hawaii	228,375,000	0.68%
35	Utah	211,353,000	0.63%
36	Arkansas	205,059,000	0.61%
37	Rhode Island	204,230,000	0.61%
38	Nevada	189,635,000	0.57%
39	Delaware	169,700,000	0.51%
40	Mississippi	167,712,000	0.50%
41	West Virginia	146,661,000	0.44%
42	Nebraska	142,574,000	0.43%
43	New Hampshire	141,928,000	0.42%
44	Idaho	132,338,000	0.40%
45	Maine	119,894,000	0.36%
46	Montana	95,922,000	0.29%
47	Vermont	89,340,000	0.27%
48	South Dakota	76,744,000	0.23%
49	Wyoming	62,696,000	0.19%
50	North Dakota	31,323,000	0.09%
	District of Columbia**	NA	NA

Source: Morgan Quitno Press using data from U.S. Bureau of the Census
   "Government Finances: 1993-1994" (1997) (http://www.census.gov/govs/www/esti94.html)
*Direct Expenditures. Includes Police Protection, Corrections and Judicial and Legal Services.
**Not applicable.

Per Capita State Government Expenditures for Justice Activities in 1994

National Per Capita = $128.68*

ALPHA ORDER

RANK ORDER

RANK	STATE	PER CAPITA		RANK	STATE	PER CAPITA
38	Alabama	$100.45		1	Alaska	$500.79
1	Alaska	500.79		2	Delaware	240.20
22	Arizona	124.30		3	Connecticut	236.44
45	Arkansas	83.66		4	Maryland	209.01
13	California	140.38		5	Rhode Island	205.47
23	Colorado	122.22		6	Hawaii	194.76
3	Connecticut	236.44		7	New York	175.85
2	Delaware	240.20		8	North Carolina	167.72
14	Florida	139.03		9	New Mexico	167.19
26	Georgia	116.30		10	Massachusetts	157.62
6	Hawaii	194.76		11	Vermont	154.30
25	Idaho	116.56		12	Michigan	143.68
42	Illinois	94.86		13	California	140.38
46	Indiana	82.41		14	Florida	139.03
35	Iowa	104.72		15	New Jersey	138.26
27	Kansas	115.51		16	Texas	137.14
30	Kentucky	110.63		17	Oregon	133.22
32	Louisiana	107.01		18	Wyoming	131.98
41	Maine	97.02		19	Nevada	129.98
4	Maryland	209.01		20	Virginia	125.34
10	Massachusetts	157.62		21	New Hampshire	125.17
12	Michigan	143.68		22	Arizona	124.30
44	Minnesota	84.08		23	Colorado	122.22
49	Mississippi	62.98		24	South Carolina	121.79
48	Missouri	78.46		25	Idaho	116.56
29	Montana	112.20		26	Georgia	116.30
43	Nebraska	87.87		27	Kansas	115.51
19	Nevada	129.98		28	Washington	114.62
21	New Hampshire	125.17		29	Montana	112.20
15	New Jersey	138.26		30	Kentucky	110.63
9	New Mexico	167.19		31	Utah	109.59
7	New York	175.85		32	Louisiana	107.01
8	North Carolina	167.72		33	Oklahoma	106.88
50	North Dakota	48.98		34	South Dakota	105.18
37	Ohio	100.63		35	Iowa	104.72
33	Oklahoma	106.88		36	Wisconsin	103.51
17	Oregon	133.22		37	Ohio	100.63
39	Pennsylvania	97.87		38	Alabama	100.45
5	Rhode Island	205.47		39	Pennsylvania	97.87
24	South Carolina	121.79		40	Tennessee	97.07
34	South Dakota	105.18		41	Maine	97.02
40	Tennessee	97.07		42	Illinois	94.86
16	Texas	137.14		43	Nebraska	87.87
31	Utah	109.59		44	Minnesota	84.08
11	Vermont	154.30		45	Arkansas	83.66
20	Virginia	125.34		46	Indiana	82.41
28	Washington	114.62		47	West Virginia	80.63
47	West Virginia	80.63		48	Missouri	78.46
36	Wisconsin	103.51		49	Mississippi	62.98
18	Wyoming	131.98		50	North Dakota	48.98
					District of Columbia**	NA

Source: Morgan Quitno Press using data from U.S. Bureau of the Census
    "Government Finances: 1993-1994" (1997) (http://www.census.gov/govs/www/esti94.html)
*Direct Expenditures. Includes Police Protection, Corrections and Judicial and Legal Services.
**Not applicable.

State Government Expenditures for Justice Activities
As a Percent of All Direct General Expenditures in 1994
National Percent = 7.3% of Direct General Expenditures*

RANK ORDER

RANK	STATE	PERCENT		RANK	STATE	PERCENT
35	Alabama	5.6		1	Maryland	11.6
14	Alaska	7.5		2	North Carolina	10.7
8	Arizona	8.7		3	Florida	10.2
43	Arkansas	5.0		4	Texas	9.6
5	California	9.4		5	California	9.4
7	Colorado	8.8		6	Nevada	8.9
9	Connecticut	8.6		7	Colorado	8.8
9	Delaware	8.6		8	Arizona	8.7
3	Florida	10.2		9	Connecticut	8.6
20	Georgia	7.3		9	Delaware	8.6
45	Hawaii	4.5		11	Michigan	8.1
15	Idaho	7.4		12	New York	7.9
30	Illinois	6.0		12	Virginia	7.9
44	Indiana	4.9		14	Alaska	7.5
33	Iowa	5.8		15	Idaho	7.4
15	Kansas	7.4		15	Kansas	7.4
25	Kentucky	6.1		15	New Mexico	7.4
41	Louisiana	5.2		15	Oregon	7.4
47	Maine	4.4		15	Rhode Island	7.4
1	Maryland	11.6		20	Georgia	7.3
31	Massachusetts	5.9		21	Oklahoma	7.2
11	Michigan	8.1		22	New Jersey	6.8
45	Minnesota	4.5		23	Utah	6.2
48	Mississippi	4.1		23	Wisconsin	6.2
35	Missouri	5.6		25	Kentucky	6.1
35	Montana	5.6		25	Ohio	6.1
42	Nebraska	5.1		25	South Carolina	6.1
6	Nevada	8.9		25	Tennessee	6.1
33	New Hampshire	5.8		25	Vermont	6.1
22	New Jersey	6.8		30	Illinois	6.0
15	New Mexico	7.4		31	Massachusetts	5.9
12	New York	7.9		31	Wyoming	5.9
2	North Carolina	10.7		33	Iowa	5.8
50	North Dakota	2.1		33	New Hampshire	5.8
25	Ohio	6.1		35	Alabama	5.6
21	Oklahoma	7.2		35	Missouri	5.6
15	Oregon	7.4		35	Montana	5.6
38	Pennsylvania	5.4		38	Pennsylvania	5.4
15	Rhode Island	7.4		38	Washington	5.4
25	South Carolina	6.1		40	South Dakota	5.3
40	South Dakota	5.3		41	Louisiana	5.2
25	Tennessee	6.1		42	Nebraska	5.1
4	Texas	9.6		43	Arkansas	5.0
23	Utah	6.2		44	Indiana	4.9
25	Vermont	6.1		45	Hawaii	4.5
12	Virginia	7.9		45	Minnesota	4.5
38	Washington	5.4		47	Maine	4.4
49	West Virginia	3.7		48	Mississippi	4.1
23	Wisconsin	6.2		49	West Virginia	3.7
31	Wyoming	5.9		50	North Dakota	2.1
					District of Columbia**	NA

Source: Morgan Quitno Press using data from U.S. Bureau of the Census
    "Government Finances: 1993-1994" (1997) (http://www.census.gov/govs/www/esti94.html)
*Includes Police Protection, Corrections and Judicial and Legal Services.
**Not applicable.

Local Government Expenditures for Justice Activities in 1994

National Total = $55,296,854,000*

ALPHA ORDER

RANK	STATE	EXPENDITURES	% of USA
25	Alabama	$532,630,000	0.96%
45	Alaska	106,538,000	0.19%
14	Arizona	1,032,542,000	1.87%
36	Arkansas	245,130,000	0.44%
1	California	10,457,424,000	18.91%
22	Colorado	722,973,000	1.31%
28	Connecticut	435,972,000	0.79%
48	Delaware	74,247,000	0.13%
3	Florida	3,793,528,000	6.86%
10	Georgia	1,247,041,000	2.26%
37	Hawaii	207,737,000	0.38%
39	Idaho	150,807,000	0.27%
5	Illinois	2,635,666,000	4.77%
23	Indiana	712,719,000	1.29%
32	Iowa	328,575,000	0.59%
29	Kansas	372,372,000	0.67%
31	Kentucky	334,528,000	0.60%
20	Louisiana	761,518,000	1.38%
43	Maine	121,046,000	0.22%
18	Maryland	861,653,000	1.56%
15	Massachusetts	1,001,799,000	1.81%
9	Michigan	1,943,350,000	3.51%
17	Minnesota	879,801,000	1.59%
35	Mississippi	246,312,000	0.45%
21	Missouri	737,231,000	1.33%
44	Montana	107,697,000	0.19%
38	Nebraska	199,428,000	0.36%
26	Nevada	469,665,000	0.85%
40	New Hampshire	147,839,000	0.27%
6	New Jersey	2,232,418,000	4.04%
34	New Mexico	251,484,000	0.45%
2	New York	6,104,526,000	11.04%
16	North Carolina	901,678,000	1.63%
49	North Dakota	62,467,000	0.11%
7	Ohio	2,218,764,000	4.01%
30	Oklahoma	343,938,000	0.62%
24	Oregon	577,789,000	1.04%
8	Pennsylvania	2,178,433,000	3.94%
41	Rhode Island	129,043,000	0.23%
27	South Carolina	468,302,000	0.85%
47	South Dakota	74,577,000	0.13%
19	Tennessee	765,764,000	1.38%
4	Texas	3,542,634,000	6.41%
33	Utah	257,167,000	0.47%
50	Vermont	32,836,000	0.06%
12	Virginia	1,102,076,000	1.99%
11	Washington	1,153,073,000	2.09%
42	West Virginia	127,325,000	0.23%
13	Wisconsin	1,078,170,000	1.95%
46	Wyoming	85,548,000	0.15%

RANK ORDER

RANK	STATE	EXPENDITURES	% of USA
1	California	$10,457,424,000	18.91%
2	New York	6,104,526,000	11.04%
3	Florida	3,793,528,000	6.86%
4	Texas	3,542,634,000	6.41%
5	Illinois	2,635,666,000	4.77%
6	New Jersey	2,232,418,000	4.04%
7	Ohio	2,218,764,000	4.01%
8	Pennsylvania	2,178,433,000	3.94%
9	Michigan	1,943,350,000	3.51%
10	Georgia	1,247,041,000	2.26%
11	Washington	1,153,073,000	2.09%
12	Virginia	1,102,076,000	1.99%
13	Wisconsin	1,078,170,000	1.95%
14	Arizona	1,032,542,000	1.87%
15	Massachusetts	1,001,799,000	1.81%
16	North Carolina	901,678,000	1.63%
17	Minnesota	879,801,000	1.59%
18	Maryland	861,653,000	1.56%
19	Tennessee	765,764,000	1.38%
20	Louisiana	761,518,000	1.38%
21	Missouri	737,231,000	1.33%
22	Colorado	722,973,000	1.31%
23	Indiana	712,719,000	1.29%
24	Oregon	577,789,000	1.04%
25	Alabama	532,630,000	0.96%
26	Nevada	469,665,000	0.85%
27	South Carolina	468,302,000	0.85%
28	Connecticut	435,972,000	0.79%
29	Kansas	372,372,000	0.67%
30	Oklahoma	343,938,000	0.62%
31	Kentucky	334,528,000	0.60%
32	Iowa	328,575,000	0.59%
33	Utah	257,167,000	0.47%
34	New Mexico	251,484,000	0.45%
35	Mississippi	246,312,000	0.45%
36	Arkansas	245,130,000	0.44%
37	Hawaii	207,737,000	0.38%
38	Nebraska	199,428,000	0.36%
39	Idaho	150,807,000	0.27%
40	New Hampshire	147,839,000	0.27%
41	Rhode Island	129,043,000	0.23%
42	West Virginia	127,325,000	0.23%
43	Maine	121,046,000	0.22%
44	Montana	107,697,000	0.19%
45	Alaska	106,538,000	0.19%
46	Wyoming	85,548,000	0.15%
47	South Dakota	74,577,000	0.13%
48	Delaware	74,247,000	0.13%
49	North Dakota	62,467,000	0.11%
50	Vermont	32,836,000	0.06%
	District of Columbia	741,074,000	1.34%

Source: Morgan Quitno Press using data from U.S. Bureau of the Census "Government Finances: 1993-1994" (1997) (http://www.census.gov/govs/www/esti94.html)

**Direct Expenditures. Includes Police Protection, Corrections and Judicial and Legal Services.*

Per Capita Local Government Expenditures for Justice Activities in 1994

National Total = $212.44*

ALPHA ORDER				RANK ORDER		
RANK	STATE	PER CAPITA		RANK	STATE	PER CAPITA
37	Alabama	$125.85		1	New York	$336.27
18	Alaska	177.34		2	California	333.37
6	Arizona	248.88		3	Nevada	321.93
44	Arkansas	100.01		4	New Jersey	282.19
2	California	333.37		5	Florida	271.83
12	Colorado	197.70		6	Arizona	248.88
30	Connecticut	133.34		7	Illinois	224.55
42	Delaware	105.09		8	Washington	215.96
5	Florida	271.83		9	Wisconsin	212.45
20	Georgia	176.91		10	Michigan	202.86
19	Hawaii	177.16		11	Ohio	199.98
31	Idaho	132.83		12	Colorado	197.70
7	Illinois	224.55		13	Texas	192.69
38	Indiana	124.13		14	Minnesota	192.63
40	Iowa	116.14		15	Oregon	187.07
27	Kansas	145.81		16	Pennsylvania	180.89
48	Kentucky	87.48		17	Wyoming	180.09
21	Louisiana	176.81		18	Alaska	177.34
45	Maine	97.95		19	Hawaii	177.16
22	Maryland	172.72		20	Georgia	176.91
24	Massachusetts	166.17		21	Louisiana	176.81
10	Michigan	202.86		22	Maryland	172.72
14	Minnesota	192.63		23	Virginia	168.57
47	Mississippi	92.49		24	Massachusetts	166.17
28	Missouri	139.59		25	New Mexico	151.87
36	Montana	125.97		26	Tennessee	148.46
39	Nebraska	122.91		27	Kansas	145.81
3	Nevada	321.93		28	Missouri	139.59
32	New Hampshire	130.39		29	Utah	133.35
4	New Jersey	282.19		30	Connecticut	133.34
25	New Mexico	151.87		31	Idaho	132.83
1	New York	336.27		32	New Hampshire	130.39
35	North Carolina	127.68		33	Rhode Island	129.82
46	North Dakota	97.67		34	South Carolina	128.17
11	Ohio	199.98		35	North Carolina	127.68
41	Oklahoma	105.88		36	Montana	125.97
15	Oregon	187.07		37	Alabama	125.85
16	Pennsylvania	180.89		38	Indiana	124.13
33	Rhode Island	129.82		39	Nebraska	122.91
34	South Carolina	128.17		40	Iowa	116.14
43	South Dakota	102.21		41	Oklahoma	105.88
26	Tennessee	148.46		42	Delaware	105.09
13	Texas	192.69		43	South Dakota	102.21
29	Utah	133.35		44	Arkansas	100.01
50	Vermont	56.71		45	Maine	97.95
23	Virginia	168.57		46	North Dakota	97.67
8	Washington	215.96		47	Mississippi	92.49
49	West Virginia	70.00		48	Kentucky	87.48
9	Wisconsin	212.45		49	West Virginia	70.00
17	Wyoming	180.09		50	Vermont	56.71
					District of Columbia	1,309.52

Source: Morgan Quitno Press using data from U.S. Bureau of the Census
  "Government Finances: 1993-1994" (1997) (http://www.census.gov/govs/www/esti94.html)
*Direct Expenditures. Includes Police Protection, Corrections and Judicial and Legal Services.

Local Government Expenditures for Justice Activities
As a Percent of All Direct General Expenditures in 1994
National Percent = 9.0% of Direct General Expenditures*

ALPHA ORDER

RANK	STATE	PERCENT
25	Alabama	7.4
48	Alaska	5.0
2	Arizona	11.4
26	Arkansas	7.3
2	California	11.4
26	Colorado	7.3
43	Connecticut	5.7
36	Delaware	6.2
2	Florida	11.4
15	Georgia	8.4
1	Hawaii	13.6
24	Idaho	7.6
6	Illinois	10.3
36	Indiana	6.2
46	Iowa	5.4
33	Kansas	6.5
40	Kentucky	5.8
8	Louisiana	9.6
45	Maine	5.5
20	Maryland	8.1
19	Massachusetts	8.2
13	Michigan	8.7
33	Minnesota	6.5
46	Mississippi	5.4
15	Missouri	8.4
32	Montana	6.8
40	Nebraska	5.8
5	Nevada	11.3
26	New Hampshire	7.3
7	New Jersey	10.2
21	New Mexico	8.0
18	New York	8.3
33	North Carolina	6.5
44	North Dakota	5.6
9	Ohio	9.4
39	Oklahoma	6.0
23	Oregon	7.9
12	Pennsylvania	8.8
26	Rhode Island	7.3
31	South Carolina	7.2
38	South Dakota	6.1
14	Tennessee	8.5
9	Texas	9.4
26	Utah	7.3
50	Vermont	3.4
15	Virginia	8.4
11	Washington	8.9
49	West Virginia	4.5
21	Wisconsin	8.0
40	Wyoming	5.8

RANK ORDER

RANK	STATE	PERCENT
1	Hawaii	13.6
2	Arizona	11.4
2	California	11.4
2	Florida	11.4
5	Nevada	11.3
6	Illinois	10.3
7	New Jersey	10.2
8	Louisiana	9.6
9	Ohio	9.4
9	Texas	9.4
11	Washington	8.9
12	Pennsylvania	8.8
13	Michigan	8.7
14	Tennessee	8.5
15	Georgia	8.4
15	Missouri	8.4
15	Virginia	8.4
18	New York	8.3
19	Massachusetts	8.2
20	Maryland	8.1
21	New Mexico	8.0
21	Wisconsin	8.0
23	Oregon	7.9
24	Idaho	7.6
25	Alabama	7.4
26	Arkansas	7.3
26	Colorado	7.3
26	New Hampshire	7.3
26	Rhode Island	7.3
26	Utah	7.3
31	South Carolina	7.2
32	Montana	6.8
33	Kansas	6.5
33	Minnesota	6.5
33	North Carolina	6.5
36	Delaware	6.2
36	Indiana	6.2
38	South Dakota	6.1
39	Oklahoma	6.0
40	Kentucky	5.8
40	Nebraska	5.8
40	Wyoming	5.8
43	Connecticut	5.7
44	North Dakota	5.6
45	Maine	5.5
46	Iowa	5.4
46	Mississippi	5.4
48	Alaska	5.0
49	West Virginia	4.5
50	Vermont	3.4

District of Columbia	16.2

Source: Morgan Quitno Press using data from U.S. Bureau of the Census
   "Government Finances: 1993-1994" (1997) (http://www.census.gov/govs/www/esti94.html)
*Includes Police Protection, Corrections and Judicial and Legal Services.
**Not applicable.

State and Local Government Expenditures for Police Protection in 1994

National Total = $38,644,615,000*

RANK	STATE	EXPENDITURES	% of USA
25	Alabama	$463,166,000	1.20%
40	Alaska	144,345,000	0.37%
17	Arizona	660,202,000	1.71%
36	Arkansas	205,671,000	0.53%
1	California	6,278,604,000	16.25%
21	Colorado	548,898,000	1.42%
24	Connecticut	506,199,000	1.31%
45	Delaware	102,518,000	0.27%
3	Florida	2,621,022,000	6.78%
12	Georgia	832,313,000	2.15%
37	Hawaii	181,358,000	0.47%
42	Idaho	133,333,000	0.35%
5	Illinois	1,989,004,000	5.15%
23	Indiana	524,197,000	1.36%
31	Iowa	300,406,000	0.78%
29	Kansas	320,287,000	0.83%
30	Kentucky	316,142,000	0.82%
19	Louisiana	614,447,000	1.59%
44	Maine	108,192,000	0.28%
15	Maryland	751,983,000	1.95%
10	Massachusetts	901,449,000	2.33%
8	Michigan	1,367,132,000	3.54%
20	Minnesota	589,208,000	1.52%
34	Mississippi	219,188,000	0.57%
18	Missouri	620,024,000	1.60%
46	Montana	88,670,000	0.23%
38	Nebraska	161,306,000	0.42%
32	Nevada	284,045,000	0.74%
41	New Hampshire	135,054,000	0.35%
6	New Jersey	1,624,864,000	4.20%
33	New Mexico	244,246,000	0.63%
2	New York	3,956,232,000	10.24%
11	North Carolina	848,506,000	2.20%
50	North Dakota	46,108,000	0.12%
7	Ohio	1,433,542,000	3.71%
28	Oklahoma	330,140,000	0.85%
26	Oregon	439,415,000	1.14%
9	Pennsylvania	1,317,443,000	3.41%
39	Rhode Island	146,737,000	0.38%
27	South Carolina	378,022,000	0.98%
47	South Dakota	67,938,000	0.18%
22	Tennessee	538,993,000	1.39%
4	Texas	2,222,275,000	5.75%
35	Utah	215,437,000	0.56%
49	Vermont	55,463,000	0.14%
13	Virginia	825,656,000	2.14%
16	Washington	728,238,000	1.88%
43	West Virginia	115,902,000	0.30%
14	Wisconsin	791,893,000	2.05%
48	Wyoming	67,834,000	0.18%

RANK	STATE	EXPENDITURES	% of USA
1	California	$6,278,604,000	16.25%
2	New York	3,956,232,000	10.24%
3	Florida	2,621,022,000	6.78%
4	Texas	2,222,275,000	5.75%
5	Illinois	1,989,004,000	5.15%
6	New Jersey	1,624,864,000	4.20%
7	Ohio	1,433,542,000	3.71%
8	Michigan	1,367,132,000	3.54%
9	Pennsylvania	1,317,443,000	3.41%
10	Massachusetts	901,449,000	2.33%
11	North Carolina	848,506,000	2.20%
12	Georgia	832,313,000	2.15%
13	Virginia	825,656,000	2.14%
14	Wisconsin	791,893,000	2.05%
15	Maryland	751,983,000	1.95%
16	Washington	728,238,000	1.88%
17	Arizona	660,202,000	1.71%
18	Missouri	620,024,000	1.60%
19	Louisiana	614,447,000	1.59%
20	Minnesota	589,208,000	1.52%
21	Colorado	548,898,000	1.42%
22	Tennessee	538,993,000	1.39%
23	Indiana	524,197,000	1.36%
24	Connecticut	506,199,000	1.31%
25	Alabama	463,166,000	1.20%
26	Oregon	439,415,000	1.14%
27	South Carolina	378,022,000	0.98%
28	Oklahoma	330,140,000	0.85%
29	Kansas	320,287,000	0.83%
30	Kentucky	316,142,000	0.82%
31	Iowa	300,406,000	0.78%
32	Nevada	284,045,000	0.74%
33	New Mexico	244,246,000	0.63%
34	Mississippi	219,188,000	0.57%
35	Utah	215,437,000	0.56%
36	Arkansas	205,671,000	0.53%
37	Hawaii	181,358,000	0.47%
38	Nebraska	161,306,000	0.42%
39	Rhode Island	146,737,000	0.38%
40	Alaska	144,345,000	0.37%
41	New Hampshire	135,054,000	0.35%
42	Idaho	133,333,000	0.35%
43	West Virginia	115,902,000	0.30%
44	Maine	108,192,000	0.28%
45	Delaware	102,518,000	0.27%
46	Montana	88,670,000	0.23%
47	South Dakota	67,938,000	0.18%
48	Wyoming	67,834,000	0.18%
49	Vermont	55,463,000	0.14%
50	North Dakota	46,108,000	0.12%
	District of Columbia	281,368,000	0.73%

Source: Morgan Quitno Press using data from U.S. Bureau of the Census
    "Government Finances: 1993-1994" (1997) (http://www.census.gov/govs/www/esti94.html)
*Direct Expenditures.

Per Capita State & Local Government Expenditures for Police Protection: 1994

National Per Capita = $148.47*

RANK	STATE	PER CAPITA
34	Alabama	$109.43
1	Alaska	240.27
8	Arizona	159.13
46	Arkansas	83.91
4	California	200.16
13	Colorado	150.10
10	Connecticut	154.82
17	Delaware	145.11
6	Florida	187.81
30	Georgia	118.08
11	Hawaii	154.66
31	Idaho	117.43
7	Illinois	169.46
44	Indiana	91.30
36	Iowa	106.18
26	Kansas	125.41
47	Kentucky	82.67
20	Louisiana	142.66
45	Maine	87.55
12	Maryland	150.74
14	Massachusetts	149.52
19	Michigan	142.71
24	Minnesota	129.00
48	Mississippi	82.30
32	Missouri	117.40
38	Montana	103.71
41	Nebraska	99.41
5	Nevada	194.70
29	New Hampshire	119.11
3	New Jersey	205.39
16	New Mexico	147.50
2	New York	217.93
28	North Carolina	120.15
49	North Dakota	72.09
23	Ohio	129.20
40	Oklahoma	101.63
21	Oregon	142.27
35	Pennsylvania	109.39
15	Rhode Island	147.62
39	South Carolina	103.47
43	South Dakota	93.11
37	Tennessee	104.50
27	Texas	120.87
33	Utah	111.71
42	Vermont	95.79
25	Virginia	126.29
22	Washington	136.39
50	West Virginia	63.72
9	Wisconsin	156.04
18	Wyoming	142.80

RANK	STATE	PER CAPITA
1	Alaska	$240.27
2	New York	217.93
3	New Jersey	205.39
4	California	200.16
5	Nevada	194.70
6	Florida	187.81
7	Illinois	169.46
8	Arizona	159.13
9	Wisconsin	156.04
10	Connecticut	154.82
11	Hawaii	154.66
12	Maryland	150.74
13	Colorado	150.10
14	Massachusetts	149.52
15	Rhode Island	147.62
16	New Mexico	147.50
17	Delaware	145.11
18	Wyoming	142.80
19	Michigan	142.71
20	Louisiana	142.66
21	Oregon	142.27
22	Washington	136.39
23	Ohio	129.20
24	Minnesota	129.00
25	Virginia	126.29
26	Kansas	125.41
27	Texas	120.87
28	North Carolina	120.15
29	New Hampshire	119.11
30	Georgia	118.08
31	Idaho	117.43
32	Missouri	117.40
33	Utah	111.71
34	Alabama	109.43
35	Pennsylvania	109.39
36	Iowa	106.18
37	Tennessee	104.50
38	Montana	103.71
39	South Carolina	103.47
40	Oklahoma	101.63
41	Nebraska	99.41
42	Vermont	95.79
43	South Dakota	93.11
44	Indiana	91.30
45	Maine	87.55
46	Arkansas	83.91
47	Kentucky	82.67
48	Mississippi	82.30
49	North Dakota	72.09
50	West Virginia	63.72
	District of Columbia	497.19

Source: Morgan Quitno Press using data from U.S. Bureau of the Census
   "Government Finances: 1993-1994" (1997) (http://www.census.gov/govs/www/esti94.html)
*Direct Expenditures.

State and Local Government Expenditures for Police Protection
As a Percent of All Direct General Expenditures in 1994
National Percent = 3.6% of Direct General Expenditures

ALPHA ORDER

RANK	STATE	PERCENT
26	Alabama	3.1
46	Alaska	2.3
5	Arizona	4.4
33	Arkansas	2.8
2	California	4.5
9	Colorado	3.7
30	Connecticut	3.0
22	Delaware	3.2
1	Florida	5.0
22	Georgia	3.2
35	Hawaii	2.7
12	Idaho	3.5
2	Illinois	4.5
43	Indiana	2.5
35	Iowa	2.7
21	Kansas	3.3
43	Kentucky	2.5
10	Louisiana	3.6
48	Maine	2.2
7	Maryland	3.8
22	Massachusetts	3.2
12	Michigan	3.5
35	Minnesota	2.7
43	Mississippi	2.5
7	Missouri	3.8
35	Montana	2.7
41	Nebraska	2.6
2	Nevada	4.5
30	New Hampshire	3.0
6	New Jersey	4.3
12	New Mexico	3.5
12	New York	3.5
18	North Carolina	3.4
49	North Dakota	1.8
18	Ohio	3.4
26	Oklahoma	3.1
18	Oregon	3.4
33	Pennsylvania	2.8
22	Rhode Island	3.2
35	South Carolina	2.7
41	South Dakota	2.6
26	Tennessee	3.1
12	Texas	3.5
26	Utah	3.1
46	Vermont	2.3
12	Virginia	3.5
30	Washington	3.0
50	West Virginia	1.7
10	Wisconsin	3.6
35	Wyoming	2.7

RANK ORDER

RANK	STATE	PERCENT
1	Florida	5.0
2	California	4.5
2	Illinois	4.5
2	Nevada	4.5
5	Arizona	4.4
6	New Jersey	4.3
7	Maryland	3.8
7	Missouri	3.8
9	Colorado	3.7
10	Louisiana	3.6
10	Wisconsin	3.6
12	Idaho	3.5
12	Michigan	3.5
12	New Mexico	3.5
12	New York	3.5
12	Texas	3.5
12	Virginia	3.5
18	North Carolina	3.4
18	Ohio	3.4
18	Oregon	3.4
21	Kansas	3.3
22	Delaware	3.2
22	Georgia	3.2
22	Massachusetts	3.2
22	Rhode Island	3.2
26	Alabama	3.1
26	Oklahoma	3.1
26	Tennessee	3.1
26	Utah	3.1
30	Connecticut	3.0
30	New Hampshire	3.0
30	Washington	3.0
33	Arkansas	2.8
33	Pennsylvania	2.8
35	Hawaii	2.7
35	Iowa	2.7
35	Minnesota	2.7
35	Montana	2.7
35	South Carolina	2.7
35	Wyoming	2.7
41	Nebraska	2.6
41	South Dakota	2.6
43	Indiana	2.5
43	Kentucky	2.5
43	Mississippi	2.5
46	Alaska	2.3
46	Vermont	2.3
48	Maine	2.2
49	North Dakota	1.8
50	West Virginia	1.7

	District of Columbia	6.1

Source: Morgan Quitno Press using data from U.S. Bureau of the Census
"Government Finances: 1993-1994" (1997) (http://www.census.gov/govs/www/esti94.html)

State Government Expenditures for Police Protection in 1994

National Total = $5,324,906,000*

ALPHA ORDER

RANK	STATE	EXPENDITURES	% of USA
24	Alabama	$75,131,000	1.41%
31	Alaska	48,505,000	0.91%
20	Arizona	95,867,000	1.80%
33	Arkansas	43,215,000	0.81%
1	California	778,391,000	14.62%
30	Colorado	50,218,000	0.94%
18	Connecticut	99,807,000	1.87%
37	Delaware	35,620,000	0.67%
5	Florida	218,409,000	4.10%
14	Georgia	115,128,000	2.16%
50	Hawaii	5,922,000	0.11%
38	Idaho	34,150,000	0.64%
7	Illinois	213,495,000	4.01%
16	Indiana	113,181,000	2.13%
28	Iowa	51,218,000	0.96%
35	Kansas	40,692,000	0.76%
23	Kentucky	89,833,000	1.69%
19	Louisiana	96,903,000	1.82%
42	Maine	27,112,000	0.51%
12	Maryland	147,348,000	2.77%
10	Massachusetts	177,644,000	3.34%
8	Michigan	201,287,000	3.78%
26	Minnesota	68,216,000	1.28%
34	Mississippi	40,981,000	0.77%
22	Missouri	90,475,000	1.70%
46	Montana	19,218,000	0.36%
40	Nebraska	32,965,000	0.62%
41	Nevada	32,766,000	0.62%
44	New Hampshire	24,659,000	0.46%
6	New Jersey	213,798,000	4.02%
29	New Mexico	50,582,000	0.95%
2	New York	323,713,000	6.08%
9	North Carolina	189,260,000	3.55%
49	North Dakota	6,668,000	0.13%
11	Ohio	160,792,000	3.02%
32	Oklahoma	47,758,000	0.90%
21	Oregon	93,498,000	1.76%
3	Pennsylvania	306,178,000	5.75%
43	Rhode Island	25,255,000	0.47%
17	South Carolina	102,494,000	1.92%
47	South Dakota	15,756,000	0.30%
25	Tennessee	73,319,000	1.38%
4	Texas	231,667,000	4.35%
36	Utah	36,480,000	0.69%
45	Vermont	24,528,000	0.46%
13	Virginia	145,210,000	2.73%
15	Washington	114,688,000	2.15%
39	West Virginia	33,456,000	0.63%
27	Wisconsin	51,501,000	0.97%
48	Wyoming	9,949,000	0.19%

RANK ORDER

RANK	STATE	EXPENDITURES	% of USA
1	California	$778,391,000	14.62%
2	New York	323,713,000	6.08%
3	Pennsylvania	306,178,000	5.75%
4	Texas	231,667,000	4.35%
5	Florida	218,409,000	4.10%
6	New Jersey	213,798,000	4.02%
7	Illinois	213,495,000	4.01%
8	Michigan	201,287,000	3.78%
9	North Carolina	189,260,000	3.55%
10	Massachusetts	177,644,000	3.34%
11	Ohio	160,792,000	3.02%
12	Maryland	147,348,000	2.77%
13	Virginia	145,210,000	2.73%
14	Georgia	115,128,000	2.16%
15	Washington	114,688,000	2.15%
16	Indiana	113,181,000	2.13%
17	South Carolina	102,494,000	1.92%
18	Connecticut	99,807,000	1.87%
19	Louisiana	96,903,000	1.82%
20	Arizona	95,867,000	1.80%
21	Oregon	93,498,000	1.76%
22	Missouri	90,475,000	1.70%
23	Kentucky	89,833,000	1.69%
24	Alabama	75,131,000	1.41%
25	Tennessee	73,319,000	1.38%
26	Minnesota	68,216,000	1.28%
27	Wisconsin	51,501,000	0.97%
28	Iowa	51,218,000	0.96%
29	New Mexico	50,582,000	0.95%
30	Colorado	50,218,000	0.94%
31	Alaska	48,505,000	0.91%
32	Oklahoma	47,758,000	0.90%
33	Arkansas	43,215,000	0.81%
34	Mississippi	40,981,000	0.77%
35	Kansas	40,692,000	0.76%
36	Utah	36,480,000	0.69%
37	Delaware	35,620,000	0.67%
38	Idaho	34,150,000	0.64%
39	West Virginia	33,456,000	0.63%
40	Nebraska	32,965,000	0.62%
41	Nevada	32,766,000	0.62%
42	Maine	27,112,000	0.51%
43	Rhode Island	25,255,000	0.47%
44	New Hampshire	24,659,000	0.46%
45	Vermont	24,528,000	0.46%
46	Montana	19,218,000	0.36%
47	South Dakota	15,756,000	0.30%
48	Wyoming	9,949,000	0.19%
49	North Dakota	6,668,000	0.13%
50	Hawaii	5,922,000	0.11%
	District of Columbia**	NA	NA

Source: U.S. Bureau of the Census
    "Government Finances: 1993-1994" (1997) (http://www.census.gov/govs/www/esti94.html)
*Direct Expenditures.
**Not applicable.

Per Capita State Government Expenditures for Police Protection in 1994

National Per Capita = $20.46*

ALPHA ORDER

RANK	STATE	PER CAPITA
35	Alabama	$17.75
1	Alaska	80.74
17	Arizona	23.11
36	Arkansas	17.63
15	California	24.81
46	Colorado	13.73
5	Connecticut	30.53
2	Delaware	50.42
40	Florida	15.65
38	Georgia	16.33
50	Hawaii	5.05
7	Idaho	30.08
32	Illinois	18.19
29	Indiana	19.71
33	Iowa	18.10
39	Kansas	15.93
16	Kentucky	23.49
18	Louisiana	22.50
22	Maine	21.94
8	Maryland	29.54
9	Massachusetts	29.47
26	Michigan	21.01
42	Minnesota	14.94
41	Mississippi	15.39
37	Missouri	17.13
19	Montana	22.48
28	Nebraska	20.32
20	Nevada	22.46
23	New Hampshire	21.75
11	New Jersey	27.03
4	New Mexico	30.55
34	New York	17.83
12	North Carolina	26.80
48	North Dakota	10.43
44	Ohio	14.49
43	Oklahoma	14.70
6	Oregon	30.27
13	Pennsylvania	25.42
14	Rhode Island	25.41
10	South Carolina	28.05
24	South Dakota	21.59
45	Tennessee	14.21
47	Texas	12.60
30	Utah	18.92
3	Vermont	42.36
21	Virginia	22.21
25	Washington	21.48
31	West Virginia	18.39
49	Wisconsin	10.15
27	Wyoming	20.94

RANK ORDER

RANK	STATE	PER CAPITA
1	Alaska	$80.74
2	Delaware	50.42
3	Vermont	42.36
4	New Mexico	30.55
5	Connecticut	30.53
6	Oregon	30.27
7	Idaho	30.08
8	Maryland	29.54
9	Massachusetts	29.47
10	South Carolina	28.05
11	New Jersey	27.03
12	North Carolina	26.80
13	Pennsylvania	25.42
14	Rhode Island	25.41
15	California	24.81
16	Kentucky	23.49
17	Arizona	23.11
18	Louisiana	22.50
19	Montana	22.48
20	Nevada	22.46
21	Virginia	22.21
22	Maine	21.94
23	New Hampshire	21.75
24	South Dakota	21.59
25	Washington	21.48
26	Michigan	21.01
27	Wyoming	20.94
28	Nebraska	20.32
29	Indiana	19.71
30	Utah	18.92
31	West Virginia	18.39
32	Illinois	18.19
33	Iowa	18.10
34	New York	17.83
35	Alabama	17.75
36	Arkansas	17.63
37	Missouri	17.13
38	Georgia	16.33
39	Kansas	15.93
40	Florida	15.65
41	Mississippi	15.39
42	Minnesota	14.94
43	Oklahoma	14.70
44	Ohio	14.49
45	Tennessee	14.21
46	Colorado	13.73
47	Texas	12.60
48	North Dakota	10.43
49	Wisconsin	10.15
50	Hawaii	5.05
	District of Columbia**	NA

Source: Morgan Quitno Press using data from U.S. Bureau of the Census
    "Government Finances: 1993-1994" (1997) (http://www.census.gov/govs/www/esti94.html)
*Direct Expenditures.
**Not applicable.

State Government Expenditures for Police Protection
As a Percent of All Direct General Expenditures in 1994
National Percent = 1.2% of Direct General Expenditures

RANK	STATE	PERCENT
30	Alabama	1.0
16	Alaska	1.2
7	Arizona	1.6
22	Arkansas	1.1
3	California	1.7
30	Colorado	1.0
22	Connecticut	1.1
2	Delaware	1.8
16	Florida	1.2
30	Georgia	1.0
50	Hawaii	0.1
1	Idaho	1.9
22	Illinois	1.1
16	Indiana	1.2
30	Iowa	1.0
30	Kansas	1.0
13	Kentucky	1.3
22	Louisiana	1.1
30	Maine	1.0
7	Maryland	1.6
22	Massachusetts	1.1
16	Michigan	1.2
45	Minnesota	0.8
30	Mississippi	1.0
16	Missouri	1.2
22	Montana	1.1
16	Nebraska	1.2
9	Nevada	1.5
30	New Hampshire	1.0
13	New Jersey	1.3
13	New Mexico	1.3
45	New York	0.8
3	North Carolina	1.7
49	North Dakota	0.5
40	Ohio	0.9
30	Oklahoma	1.0
3	Oregon	1.7
10	Pennsylvania	1.4
40	Rhode Island	0.9
10	South Carolina	1.4
22	South Dakota	1.1
40	Tennessee	0.9
40	Texas	0.9
22	Utah	1.1
3	Vermont	1.7
10	Virginia	1.4
30	Washington	1.0
45	West Virginia	0.8
48	Wisconsin	0.6
40	Wyoming	0.9

RANK	STATE	PERCENT
1	Idaho	1.9
2	Delaware	1.8
3	California	1.7
3	North Carolina	1.7
3	Oregon	1.7
3	Vermont	1.7
7	Arizona	1.6
7	Maryland	1.6
9	Nevada	1.5
10	Pennsylvania	1.4
10	South Carolina	1.4
10	Virginia	1.4
13	Kentucky	1.3
13	New Jersey	1.3
13	New Mexico	1.3
16	Alaska	1.2
16	Florida	1.2
16	Indiana	1.2
16	Michigan	1.2
16	Missouri	1.2
16	Nebraska	1.2
22	Arkansas	1.1
22	Connecticut	1.1
22	Illinois	1.1
22	Louisiana	1.1
22	Massachusetts	1.1
22	Montana	1.1
22	South Dakota	1.1
22	Utah	1.1
30	Alabama	1.0
30	Colorado	1.0
30	Georgia	1.0
30	Iowa	1.0
30	Kansas	1.0
30	Maine	1.0
30	Mississippi	1.0
30	New Hampshire	1.0
30	Oklahoma	1.0
30	Washington	1.0
40	Ohio	0.9
40	Rhode Island	0.9
40	Tennessee	0.9
40	Texas	0.9
40	Wyoming	0.9
45	Minnesota	0.8
45	New York	0.8
45	West Virginia	0.8
48	Wisconsin	0.6
49	North Dakota	0.5
50	Hawaii	0.1
	District of Columbia*	NA

Source: Morgan Quitno Press using data from U.S. Bureau of the Census
"Government Finances: 1993-1994" (1997) (http://www.census.gov/govs/www/esti94.html)
Not applicable.

Local Government Expenditures for Police Protection in 1994

National Total = $33,319,709,000*

ALPHA ORDER			
RANK	STATE	EXPENDITURES	% of USA
25	Alabama	$388,035,000	1.16%
42	Alaska	95,840,000	0.29%
17	Arizona	564,335,000	1.69%
37	Arkansas	162,456,000	0.49%
1	California	5,500,213,000	16.51%
21	Colorado	498,680,000	1.50%
24	Connecticut	406,392,000	1.22%
46	Delaware	66,898,000	0.20%
3	Florida	2,402,613,000	7.21%
12	Georgia	717,185,000	2.15%
36	Hawaii	175,436,000	0.53%
41	Idaho	99,183,000	0.30%
5	Illinois	1,775,509,000	5.33%
23	Indiana	411,016,000	1.23%
31	Iowa	249,188,000	0.75%
28	Kansas	279,595,000	0.84%
32	Kentucky	226,309,000	0.68%
20	Louisiana	517,544,000	1.55%
44	Maine	81,080,000	0.24%
16	Maryland	604,635,000	1.81%
11	Massachusetts	723,805,000	2.17%
8	Michigan	1,165,845,000	3.50%
19	Minnesota	520,992,000	1.56%
35	Mississippi	178,207,000	0.53%
18	Missouri	529,549,000	1.59%
45	Montana	69,452,000	0.21%
38	Nebraska	128,341,000	0.39%
30	Nevada	251,279,000	0.75%
40	New Hampshire	110,395,000	0.33%
6	New Jersey	1,411,066,000	4.23%
33	New Mexico	193,664,000	0.58%
2	New York	3,632,519,000	10.90%
14	North Carolina	659,246,000	1.98%
49	North Dakota	39,440,000	0.12%
7	Ohio	1,272,750,000	3.82%
27	Oklahoma	282,382,000	0.85%
26	Oregon	345,917,000	1.04%
9	Pennsylvania	1,011,265,000	3.04%
39	Rhode Island	121,482,000	0.36%
29	South Carolina	275,528,000	0.83%
48	South Dakota	52,182,000	0.16%
22	Tennessee	465,674,000	1.40%
4	Texas	1,990,608,000	5.97%
34	Utah	178,957,000	0.54%
50	Vermont	30,935,000	0.09%
13	Virginia	680,446,000	2.04%
15	Washington	613,550,000	1.84%
43	West Virginia	82,446,000	0.25%
10	Wisconsin	740,392,000	2.22%
47	Wyoming	57,885,000	0.17%

RANK ORDER			
RANK	STATE	EXPENDITURES	% of USA
1	California	$5,500,213,000	16.51%
2	New York	3,632,519,000	10.90%
3	Florida	2,402,613,000	7.21%
4	Texas	1,990,608,000	5.97%
5	Illinois	1,775,509,000	5.33%
6	New Jersey	1,411,066,000	4.23%
7	Ohio	1,272,750,000	3.82%
8	Michigan	1,165,845,000	3.50%
9	Pennsylvania	1,011,265,000	3.04%
10	Wisconsin	740,392,000	2.22%
11	Massachusetts	723,805,000	2.17%
12	Georgia	717,185,000	2.15%
13	Virginia	680,446,000	2.04%
14	North Carolina	659,246,000	1.98%
15	Washington	613,550,000	1.84%
16	Maryland	604,635,000	1.81%
17	Arizona	564,335,000	1.69%
18	Missouri	529,549,000	1.59%
19	Minnesota	520,992,000	1.56%
20	Louisiana	517,544,000	1.55%
21	Colorado	498,680,000	1.50%
22	Tennessee	465,674,000	1.40%
23	Indiana	411,016,000	1.23%
24	Connecticut	406,392,000	1.22%
25	Alabama	388,035,000	1.16%
26	Oregon	345,917,000	1.04%
27	Oklahoma	282,382,000	0.85%
28	Kansas	279,595,000	0.84%
29	South Carolina	275,528,000	0.83%
30	Nevada	251,279,000	0.75%
31	Iowa	249,188,000	0.75%
32	Kentucky	226,309,000	0.68%
33	New Mexico	193,664,000	0.58%
34	Utah	178,957,000	0.54%
35	Mississippi	178,207,000	0.53%
36	Hawaii	175,436,000	0.53%
37	Arkansas	162,456,000	0.49%
38	Nebraska	128,341,000	0.39%
39	Rhode Island	121,482,000	0.36%
40	New Hampshire	110,395,000	0.33%
41	Idaho	99,183,000	0.30%
42	Alaska	95,840,000	0.29%
43	West Virginia	82,446,000	0.25%
44	Maine	81,080,000	0.24%
45	Montana	69,452,000	0.21%
46	Delaware	66,898,000	0.20%
47	Wyoming	57,885,000	0.17%
48	South Dakota	52,182,000	0.16%
49	North Dakota	39,440,000	0.12%
50	Vermont	30,935,000	0.09%
	District of Columbia	281,368,000	0.84%

Source: U.S. Bureau of the Census
    "Government Finances: 1993-1994" (1997) (http://www.census.gov/govs/www/esti94.html)
*Direct Expenditures.

Per Capita Local Government Expenditures for Police Protection in 1994

National Per Capita = $128.01*

ALPHA ORDER

RANK	STATE	PER CAPITA
33	Alabama	$91.68
6	Alaska	159.53
11	Arizona	136.02
45	Arkansas	66.28
3	California	175.34
10	Colorado	136.37
12	Connecticut	124.29
30	Delaware	94.69
5	Florida	172.16
27	Georgia	101.74
8	Hawaii	149.61
36	Idaho	87.36
7	Illinois	151.27
42	Indiana	71.59
35	Iowa	88.08
24	Kansas	109.48
48	Kentucky	59.18
17	Louisiana	120.16
46	Maine	65.61
16	Maryland	121.20
18	Massachusetts	120.06
15	Michigan	121.70
22	Minnesota	114.07
44	Mississippi	66.92
28	Missouri	100.27
39	Montana	81.24
40	Nebraska	79.10
4	Nevada	172.24
29	New Hampshire	97.36
2	New Jersey	178.37
19	New Mexico	116.95
1	New York	200.10
31	North Carolina	93.35
47	North Dakota	61.67
21	Ohio	114.71
37	Oklahoma	86.93
23	Oregon	112.00
38	Pennsylvania	83.97
13	Rhode Island	122.22
41	South Carolina	75.41
43	South Dakota	71.52
34	Tennessee	90.28
25	Texas	108.27
32	Utah	92.79
49	Vermont	53.43
26	Virginia	104.08
20	Washington	114.91
50	West Virginia	45.33
9	Wisconsin	145.89
14	Wyoming	121.85

RANK ORDER

RANK	STATE	PER CAPITA
1	New York	$200.10
2	New Jersey	178.37
3	California	175.34
4	Nevada	172.24
5	Florida	172.16
6	Alaska	159.53
7	Illinois	151.27
8	Hawaii	149.61
9	Wisconsin	145.89
10	Colorado	136.37
11	Arizona	136.02
12	Connecticut	124.29
13	Rhode Island	122.22
14	Wyoming	121.85
15	Michigan	121.70
16	Maryland	121.20
17	Louisiana	120.16
18	Massachusetts	120.06
19	New Mexico	116.95
20	Washington	114.91
21	Ohio	114.71
22	Minnesota	114.07
23	Oregon	112.00
24	Kansas	109.48
25	Texas	108.27
26	Virginia	104.08
27	Georgia	101.74
28	Missouri	100.27
29	New Hampshire	97.36
30	Delaware	94.69
31	North Carolina	93.35
32	Utah	92.79
33	Alabama	91.68
34	Tennessee	90.28
35	Iowa	88.08
36	Idaho	87.36
37	Oklahoma	86.93
38	Pennsylvania	83.97
39	Montana	81.24
40	Nebraska	79.10
41	South Carolina	75.41
42	Indiana	71.59
43	South Dakota	71.52
44	Mississippi	66.92
45	Arkansas	66.28
46	Maine	65.61
47	North Dakota	61.67
48	Kentucky	59.18
49	Vermont	53.43
50	West Virginia	45.33
	District of Columbia	497.19

Source: Morgan Quitno Press using data from U.S. Bureau of the Census
  "Government Finances: 1993-1994" (1997) (http://www.census.gov/govs/www/esti94.html)
*Direct Expenditures.

Local Government Expenditures for Police Protection
As a Percent of All Direct General Expenditures in 1994
National Percent = 5.4% of Direct General Expenditures

ALPHA ORDER

RANK	STATE	PERCENT
17	Alabama	5.4
35	Alaska	4.5
7	Arizona	6.2
30	Arkansas	4.8
10	California	6.0
25	Colorado	5.0
19	Connecticut	5.3
14	Delaware	5.6
2	Florida	7.2
30	Georgia	4.8
1	Hawaii	11.5
25	Idaho	5.0
3	Illinois	6.9
47	Indiana	3.6
39	Iowa	4.1
28	Kansas	4.9
41	Kentucky	3.9
5	Louisiana	6.5
45	Maine	3.7
13	Maryland	5.7
12	Massachusetts	5.9
21	Michigan	5.2
41	Minnesota	3.9
41	Mississippi	3.9
10	Missouri	6.0
36	Montana	4.4
45	Nebraska	3.7
9	Nevada	6.1
15	New Hampshire	5.5
6	New Jersey	6.4
7	New Mexico	6.2
25	New York	5.0
30	North Carolina	4.8
48	North Dakota	3.5
17	Ohio	5.4
28	Oklahoma	4.9
34	Oregon	4.7
39	Pennsylvania	4.1
3	Rhode Island	6.9
37	South Carolina	4.3
37	South Dakota	4.3
21	Tennessee	5.2
19	Texas	5.3
24	Utah	5.1
49	Vermont	3.2
21	Virginia	5.2
30	Washington	4.8
50	West Virginia	2.9
15	Wisconsin	5.5
41	Wyoming	3.9

RANK ORDER

RANK	STATE	PERCENT
1	Hawaii	11.5
2	Florida	7.2
3	Illinois	6.9
3	Rhode Island	6.9
5	Louisiana	6.5
6	New Jersey	6.4
7	Arizona	6.2
7	New Mexico	6.2
9	Nevada	6.1
10	California	6.0
10	Missouri	6.0
12	Massachusetts	5.9
13	Maryland	5.7
14	Delaware	5.6
15	New Hampshire	5.5
15	Wisconsin	5.5
17	Alabama	5.4
17	Ohio	5.4
19	Connecticut	5.3
19	Texas	5.3
21	Michigan	5.2
21	Tennessee	5.2
21	Virginia	5.2
24	Utah	5.1
25	Colorado	5.0
25	Idaho	5.0
25	New York	5.0
28	Kansas	4.9
28	Oklahoma	4.9
30	Arkansas	4.8
30	Georgia	4.8
30	North Carolina	4.8
30	Washington	4.8
34	Oregon	4.7
35	Alaska	4.5
36	Montana	4.4
37	South Carolina	4.3
37	South Dakota	4.3
39	Iowa	4.1
39	Pennsylvania	4.1
41	Kentucky	3.9
41	Minnesota	3.9
41	Mississippi	3.9
41	Wyoming	3.9
45	Maine	3.7
45	Nebraska	3.7
47	Indiana	3.6
48	North Dakota	3.5
49	Vermont	3.2
50	West Virginia	2.9

	District of Columbia	6.1

Source: Morgan Quitno Press using data from U.S. Bureau of the Census
"Government Finances: 1993-1994" (1997) (http://www.census.gov/govs/www/esti94.html)

State and Local Government Expenditures for Corrections in 1994

National Total = $32,270,340,000*

ALPHA ORDER

RANK	STATE	EXPENDITURES	% of USA
27	Alabama	$290,041,000	0.90%
36	Alaska	138,422,000	0.43%
16	Arizona	522,969,000	1.62%
33	Arkansas	165,881,000	0.51%
1	California	5,330,417,000	16.47%
23	Colorado	388,398,000	1.20%
19	Connecticut	465,293,000	1.44%
43	Delaware	84,344,000	0.26%
4	Florida	2,026,881,000	6.26%
10	Georgia	927,932,000	2.87%
39	Hawaii	109,208,000	0.34%
41	Idaho	89,400,000	0.28%
8	Illinois	1,090,298,000	3.37%
20	Indiana	443,078,000	1.37%
34	Iowa	159,755,000	0.49%
31	Kansas	208,192,000	0.64%
28	Kentucky	277,397,000	0.86%
22	Louisiana	389,024,000	1.20%
42	Maine	87,683,000	0.27%
12	Maryland	801,022,000	2.47%
14	Massachusetts	658,997,000	2.04%
6	Michigan	1,276,829,000	3.94%
24	Minnesota	366,514,000	1.13%
37	Mississippi	117,958,000	0.36%
26	Missouri	327,246,000	1.01%
47	Montana	48,197,000	0.15%
38	Nebraska	111,691,000	0.35%
29	Nevada	245,310,000	0.76%
44	New Hampshire	78,361,000	0.24%
9	New Jersey	986,229,000	3.05%
32	New Mexico	189,138,000	0.58%
2	New York	3,526,962,000	10.90%
11	North Carolina	901,703,000	2.79%
50	North Dakota	24,617,000	0.08%
7	Ohio	1,139,231,000	3.52%
30	Oklahoma	223,812,000	0.69%
25	Oregon	337,639,000	1.04%
5	Pennsylvania	1,281,651,000	3.96%
40	Rhode Island	104,160,000	0.32%
21	South Carolina	410,399,000	1.27%
46	South Dakota	52,010,000	0.16%
17	Tennessee	484,582,000	1.50%
3	Texas	2,870,516,000	8.87%
35	Utah	150,980,000	0.47%
49	Vermont	30,246,000	0.09%
13	Virginia	770,869,000	2.38%
15	Washington	656,154,000	2.03%
45	West Virginia	77,748,000	0.24%
18	Wisconsin	473,503,000	1.46%
48	Wyoming	43,597,000	0.13%

RANK ORDER

RANK	STATE	EXPENDITURES	% of USA
1	California	$5,330,417,000	16.47%
2	New York	3,526,962,000	10.90%
3	Texas	2,870,516,000	8.87%
4	Florida	2,026,881,000	6.26%
5	Pennsylvania	1,281,651,000	3.96%
6	Michigan	1,276,829,000	3.94%
7	Ohio	1,139,231,000	3.52%
8	Illinois	1,090,298,000	3.37%
9	New Jersey	986,229,000	3.05%
10	Georgia	927,932,000	2.87%
11	North Carolina	901,703,000	2.79%
12	Maryland	801,022,000	2.47%
13	Virginia	770,869,000	2.38%
14	Massachusetts	658,997,000	2.04%
15	Washington	656,154,000	2.03%
16	Arizona	522,969,000	1.62%
17	Tennessee	484,582,000	1.50%
18	Wisconsin	473,503,000	1.46%
19	Connecticut	465,293,000	1.44%
20	Indiana	443,078,000	1.37%
21	South Carolina	410,399,000	1.27%
22	Louisiana	389,024,000	1.20%
23	Colorado	388,398,000	1.20%
24	Minnesota	366,514,000	1.13%
25	Oregon	337,639,000	1.04%
26	Missouri	327,246,000	1.01%
27	Alabama	290,041,000	0.90%
28	Kentucky	277,397,000	0.86%
29	Nevada	245,310,000	0.76%
30	Oklahoma	223,812,000	0.69%
31	Kansas	208,192,000	0.64%
32	New Mexico	189,138,000	0.58%
33	Arkansas	165,881,000	0.51%
34	Iowa	159,755,000	0.49%
35	Utah	150,980,000	0.47%
36	Alaska	138,422,000	0.43%
37	Mississippi	117,958,000	0.36%
38	Nebraska	111,691,000	0.35%
39	Hawaii	109,208,000	0.34%
40	Rhode Island	104,160,000	0.32%
41	Idaho	89,400,000	0.28%
42	Maine	87,683,000	0.27%
43	Delaware	84,344,000	0.26%
44	New Hampshire	78,361,000	0.24%
45	West Virginia	77,748,000	0.24%
46	South Dakota	52,010,000	0.16%
47	Montana	48,197,000	0.15%
48	Wyoming	43,597,000	0.13%
49	Vermont	30,246,000	0.09%
50	North Dakota	24,617,000	0.08%
	District of Columbia	307,856,000	0.95%

Source: Morgan Quitno Press using data from U.S. Bureau of the Census
"Government Finances: 1993-1994" (1997) (http://www.census.gov/govs/www/esti94.html)
*Direct Expenditures.

Per Capita State and Local Government Expenditures for Corrections in 1994

National Per Capita = $123.98*

ALPHA ORDER

RANK	STATE	PER CAPITA
42	Alabama	$68.53
1	Alaska	230.41
12	Arizona	126.05
43	Arkansas	67.68
3	California	169.93
22	Colorado	106.21
8	Connecticut	142.31
15	Delaware	119.39
7	Florida	145.24
10	Georgia	131.64
27	Hawaii	93.13
33	Idaho	78.74
28	Illinois	92.89
35	Indiana	77.17
45	Iowa	56.47
31	Kansas	81.52
36	Kentucky	72.54
30	Louisiana	90.32
38	Maine	70.96
5	Maryland	160.57
20	Massachusetts	109.31
9	Michigan	133.28
32	Minnesota	80.25
48	Mississippi	44.29
44	Missouri	61.96
46	Montana	56.37
41	Nebraska	68.84
4	Nevada	168.15
39	New Hampshire	69.11
13	New Jersey	124.66
17	New Mexico	114.22
2	New York	194.28
11	North Carolina	127.68
50	North Dakota	38.49
24	Ohio	102.68
40	Oklahoma	68.90
19	Oregon	109.32
21	Pennsylvania	106.42
23	Rhode Island	104.79
18	South Carolina	112.33
37	South Dakota	71.28
25	Tennessee	93.95
6	Texas	156.13
34	Utah	78.29
47	Vermont	52.24
16	Virginia	117.91
14	Washington	122.89
49	West Virginia	42.75
26	Wisconsin	93.30
29	Wyoming	91.78

RANK ORDER

RANK	STATE	PER CAPITA
1	Alaska	$230.41
2	New York	194.28
3	California	169.93
4	Nevada	168.15
5	Maryland	160.57
6	Texas	156.13
7	Florida	145.24
8	Connecticut	142.31
9	Michigan	133.28
10	Georgia	131.64
11	North Carolina	127.68
12	Arizona	126.05
13	New Jersey	124.66
14	Washington	122.89
15	Delaware	119.39
16	Virginia	117.91
17	New Mexico	114.22
18	South Carolina	112.33
19	Oregon	109.32
20	Massachusetts	109.31
21	Pennsylvania	106.42
22	Colorado	106.21
23	Rhode Island	104.79
24	Ohio	102.68
25	Tennessee	93.95
26	Wisconsin	93.30
27	Hawaii	93.13
28	Illinois	92.89
29	Wyoming	91.78
30	Louisiana	90.32
31	Kansas	81.52
32	Minnesota	80.25
33	Idaho	78.74
34	Utah	78.29
35	Indiana	77.17
36	Kentucky	72.54
37	South Dakota	71.28
38	Maine	70.96
39	New Hampshire	69.11
40	Oklahoma	68.90
41	Nebraska	68.84
42	Alabama	68.53
43	Arkansas	67.68
44	Missouri	61.96
45	Iowa	56.47
46	Montana	56.37
47	Vermont	52.24
48	Mississippi	44.29
49	West Virginia	42.75
50	North Dakota	38.49

District of Columbia — 544.00

Source: Morgan Quitno Press using data from U.S. Bureau of the Census
   "Government Finances: 1993-1994" (1997) (http://www.census.gov/govs/www/esti94.html)
*Direct Expenditures.

State and Local Government Expenditures for Corrections
As a Percent of All Direct General Expenditures in 1994
National Percent = 3.0% of Direct General Expenditures

ALPHA ORDER				RANK ORDER		
RANK	STATE	PERCENT		RANK	STATE	PERCENT
36	Alabama	2.0		1	Texas	4.5
28	Alaska	2.2		2	Maryland	4.1
8	Arizona	3.5		3	Florida	3.9
28	Arkansas	2.2		3	Nevada	3.9
5	California	3.8		5	California	3.8
20	Colorado	2.6		6	Georgia	3.6
13	Connecticut	2.8		6	North Carolina	3.6
15	Delaware	2.7		8	Arizona	3.5
3	Florida	3.9		9	Virginia	3.3
6	Georgia	3.6		10	Michigan	3.2
44	Hawaii	1.6		11	New York	3.1
24	Idaho	2.4		12	South Carolina	3.0
23	Illinois	2.5		13	Connecticut	2.8
33	Indiana	2.1		13	Tennessee	2.8
46	Iowa	1.4		15	Delaware	2.7
33	Kansas	2.1		15	New Mexico	2.7
28	Kentucky	2.2		15	Ohio	2.7
25	Louisiana	2.3		15	Pennsylvania	2.7
39	Maine	1.8		15	Washington	2.7
2	Maryland	4.1		20	Colorado	2.6
25	Massachusetts	2.3		20	New Jersey	2.6
10	Michigan	3.2		20	Oregon	2.6
42	Minnesota	1.7		23	Illinois	2.5
46	Mississippi	1.4		24	Idaho	2.4
36	Missouri	2.0		25	Louisiana	2.3
45	Montana	1.5		25	Massachusetts	2.3
39	Nebraska	1.8		25	Rhode Island	2.3
3	Nevada	3.9		28	Alaska	2.2
39	New Hampshire	1.8		28	Arkansas	2.2
20	New Jersey	2.6		28	Kentucky	2.2
15	New Mexico	2.7		28	Utah	2.2
11	New York	3.1		28	Wisconsin	2.2
6	North Carolina	3.6		33	Indiana	2.1
50	North Dakota	1.0		33	Kansas	2.1
15	Ohio	2.7		33	Oklahoma	2.1
33	Oklahoma	2.1		36	Alabama	2.0
20	Oregon	2.6		36	Missouri	2.0
15	Pennsylvania	2.7		36	South Dakota	2.0
25	Rhode Island	2.3		39	Maine	1.8
12	South Carolina	3.0		39	Nebraska	1.8
36	South Dakota	2.0		39	New Hampshire	1.8
13	Tennessee	2.8		42	Minnesota	1.7
1	Texas	4.5		42	Wyoming	1.7
28	Utah	2.2		44	Hawaii	1.6
48	Vermont	1.2		45	Montana	1.5
9	Virginia	3.3		46	Iowa	1.4
15	Washington	2.7		46	Mississippi	1.4
49	West Virginia	1.1		48	Vermont	1.2
28	Wisconsin	2.2		49	West Virginia	1.1
42	Wyoming	1.7		50	North Dakota	1.0
					District of Columbia	6.7

Source: Morgan Quitno Press using data from U.S. Bureau of the Census
"Government Finances: 1993-1994" (1997) (http://www.census.gov/govs/www/esti94.html)

State Government Expenditures for Corrections in 1994

National Total = $21,266,053,000*

ALPHA ORDER

RANK	STATE	EXPENDITURES	% of USA
25	Alabama	$213,003,000	1.00%
32	Alaska	138,149,000	0.65%
17	Arizona	345,456,000	1.62%
34	Arkansas	129,618,000	0.61%
1	California	3,312,414,000	15.58%
22	Colorado	275,494,000	1.30%
14	Connecticut	465,293,000	2.19%
40	Delaware	84,344,000	0.40%
4	Florida	1,246,462,000	5.86%
11	Georgia	648,496,000	3.05%
37	Hawaii	109,208,000	0.51%
42	Idaho	69,022,000	0.32%
8	Illinois	703,866,000	3.31%
21	Indiana	305,458,000	1.44%
35	Iowa	124,973,000	0.59%
30	Kansas	167,693,000	0.79%
28	Kentucky	191,630,000	0.90%
23	Louisiana	271,316,000	1.28%
44	Maine	55,693,000	0.26%
10	Maryland	675,981,000	3.18%
16	Massachusetts	425,089,000	2.00%
5	Michigan	1,014,909,000	4.77%
27	Minnesota	198,013,000	0.93%
39	Mississippi	97,899,000	0.46%
24	Missouri	219,720,000	1.03%
47	Montana	40,586,000	0.19%
41	Nebraska	79,018,000	0.37%
33	Nevada	135,695,000	0.64%
45	New Hampshire	53,309,000	0.25%
12	New Jersey	631,055,000	2.97%
31	New Mexico	142,792,000	0.67%
3	New York	1,805,428,000	8.49%
7	North Carolina	707,663,000	3.33%
50	North Dakota	17,004,000	0.08%
6	Ohio	824,029,000	3.87%
26	Oklahoma	207,573,000	0.98%
29	Oregon	173,337,000	0.82%
9	Pennsylvania	678,457,000	3.19%
38	Rhode Island	104,160,000	0.49%
20	South Carolina	307,319,000	1.45%
46	South Dakota	41,089,000	0.19%
18	Tennessee	328,157,000	1.54%
2	Texas	2,005,863,000	9.43%
36	Utah	114,362,000	0.54%
49	Vermont	30,243,000	0.14%
13	Virginia	506,696,000	2.38%
15	Washington	442,070,000	2.08%
43	West Virginia	56,811,000	0.27%
19	Wisconsin	313,366,000	1.47%
48	Wyoming	30,772,000	0.14%

RANK ORDER

RANK	STATE	EXPENDITURES	% of USA
1	California	$3,312,414,000	15.58%
2	Texas	2,005,863,000	9.43%
3	New York	1,805,428,000	8.49%
4	Florida	1,246,462,000	5.86%
5	Michigan	1,014,909,000	4.77%
6	Ohio	824,029,000	3.87%
7	North Carolina	707,663,000	3.33%
8	Illinois	703,866,000	3.31%
9	Pennsylvania	678,457,000	3.19%
10	Maryland	675,981,000	3.18%
11	Georgia	648,496,000	3.05%
12	New Jersey	631,055,000	2.97%
13	Virginia	506,696,000	2.38%
14	Connecticut	465,293,000	2.19%
15	Washington	442,070,000	2.08%
16	Massachusetts	425,089,000	2.00%
17	Arizona	345,456,000	1.62%
18	Tennessee	328,157,000	1.54%
19	Wisconsin	313,366,000	1.47%
20	South Carolina	307,319,000	1.45%
21	Indiana	305,458,000	1.44%
22	Colorado	275,494,000	1.30%
23	Louisiana	271,316,000	1.28%
24	Missouri	219,720,000	1.03%
25	Alabama	213,003,000	1.00%
26	Oklahoma	207,573,000	0.98%
27	Minnesota	198,013,000	0.93%
28	Kentucky	191,630,000	0.90%
29	Oregon	173,337,000	0.82%
30	Kansas	167,693,000	0.79%
31	New Mexico	142,792,000	0.67%
32	Alaska	138,149,000	0.65%
33	Nevada	135,695,000	0.64%
34	Arkansas	129,618,000	0.61%
35	Iowa	124,973,000	0.59%
36	Utah	114,362,000	0.54%
37	Hawaii	109,208,000	0.51%
38	Rhode Island	104,160,000	0.49%
39	Mississippi	97,899,000	0.46%
40	Delaware	84,344,000	0.40%
41	Nebraska	79,018,000	0.37%
42	Idaho	69,022,000	0.32%
43	West Virginia	56,811,000	0.27%
44	Maine	55,693,000	0.26%
45	New Hampshire	53,309,000	0.25%
46	South Dakota	41,089,000	0.19%
47	Montana	40,586,000	0.19%
48	Wyoming	30,772,000	0.14%
49	Vermont	30,243,000	0.14%
50	North Dakota	17,004,000	0.08%
	District of Columbia**	NA	NA

Source: U.S. Bureau of the Census
"Government Finances: 1993-1994" (1997) (http://www.census.gov/govs/www/esti94.html)
*Direct Expenditures.
**Not applicable.

Per Capita State Government Expenditures for Corrections in 1994

National Per Capita = $81.70*

ALPHA ORDER				RANK ORDER		
RANK	STATE	PER CAPITA		RANK	STATE	PER CAPITA
39	Alabama	$50.33		1	Alaska	$229.96
1	Alaska	229.96		2	Connecticut	142.31
17	Arizona	83.27		3	Maryland	135.51
37	Arkansas	52.88		4	Delaware	119.39
7	California	105.60		5	Texas	109.10
21	Colorado	75.33		6	Michigan	105.94
2	Connecticut	142.31		7	California	105.60
4	Delaware	119.39		8	Rhode Island	104.79
14	Florida	89.32		9	North Carolina	100.21
13	Georgia	92.00		10	New York	99.45
11	Hawaii	93.13		11	Hawaii	93.13
30	Idaho	60.79		12	Nevada	93.01
31	Illinois	59.97		13	Georgia	92.00
36	Indiana	53.20		14	Florida	89.32
45	Iowa	44.17		15	New Mexico	86.23
24	Kansas	65.66		16	South Carolina	84.11
40	Kentucky	50.11		17	Arizona	83.27
28	Louisiana	62.99		18	Washington	82.80
44	Maine	45.07		19	New Jersey	79.77
3	Maryland	135.51		20	Virginia	77.50
23	Massachusetts	70.51		21	Colorado	75.33
6	Michigan	105.94		22	Ohio	74.27
46	Minnesota	43.35		23	Massachusetts	70.51
48	Mississipoi	36.76		24	Kansas	65.66
47	Missouri	41.60		25	Wyoming	64.78
42	Montana	47.47		26	Oklahoma	63.90
41	Nebraska	48.70		27	Tennessee	63.62
12	Nevada	93.01		28	Louisiana	62.99
43	New Hampshire	47.02		29	Wisconsin	61.75
19	New Jersey	79.77		30	Idaho	60.79
15	New Mexico	86.23		31	Illinois	59.97
10	New York	99.45		32	Utah	59.30
9	North Carolina	100.21		33	Pennsylvania	56.34
50	North Dakota	26.59		34	South Dakota	56.32
22	Ohio	74.27		35	Oregon	56.12
26	Oklahoma	63.90		36	Indiana	53.20
35	Oregon	56.12		37	Arkansas	52.88
33	Pennsylvania	56.34		38	Vermont	52.23
8	Rhode Island	104.79		39	Alabama	50.33
16	South Carolina	84.11		40	Kentucky	50.11
34	South Dakota	56.32		41	Nebraska	48.70
27	Tennessee	63.62		42	Montana	47.47
5	Texas	109.10		43	New Hampshire	47.02
32	Utah	59.30		44	Maine	45.07
38	Vermont	52.23		45	Iowa	44.17
20	Virginia	77.50		46	Minnesota	43.35
18	Washington	82.80		47	Missouri	41.60
49	West Virginia	31.23		48	Mississippi	36.76
29	Wisconsin	61.75		49	West Virginia	31.23
25	Wyoming	64.78		50	North Dakota	26.59
					District of Columbia**	NA

Source: Morgan Quitno Press using data from U.S. Bureau of the Census
  "Government Finances: 1993-1994" (1997) (http://www.census.gov/govs/www/esti94.html)
Direct Expenditures.
**Not applicable.*

State Government Expenditures for Corrections
As a Percent of All Direct General Expenditures in 1994
National Percent = 4.6% of Direct General Expenditures

RANK	STATE	PERCENT
37	Alabama	2.8
27	Alaska	3.4
8	Arizona	5.8
29	Arkansas	3.2
3	California	7.1
10	Colorado	5.4
11	Connecticut	5.2
15	Delaware	4.3
4	Florida	6.6
8	Georgia	5.8
46	Hawaii	2.1
20	Idaho	3.9
23	Illinois	3.8
30	Indiana	3.1
41	Iowa	2.5
17	Kansas	4.2
39	Kentucky	2.7
33	Louisiana	3.0
46	Maine	2.1
2	Maryland	7.5
39	Massachusetts	2.7
7	Michigan	6.0
44	Minnesota	2.3
42	Mississippi	2.4
33	Missouri	3.0
42	Montana	2.4
37	Nebraska	2.8
5	Nevada	6.4
45	New Hampshire	2.2
20	New Jersey	3.9
23	New Mexico	3.8
13	New York	4.5
5	North Carolina	6.4
50	North Dakota	1.2
13	Ohio	4.5
15	Oklahoma	4.3
30	Oregon	3.1
30	Pennsylvania	3.1
23	Rhode Island	3.8
17	South Carolina	4.2
35	South Dakota	2.9
19	Tennessee	4.0
1	Texas	7.6
27	Utah	3.4
46	Vermont	2.1
12	Virginia	4.9
20	Washington	3.9
49	West Virginia	1.4
26	Wisconsin	3.7
35	Wyoming	2.9

RANK	STATE	PERCENT
1	Texas	7.6
2	Maryland	7.5
3	California	7.1
4	Florida	6.6
5	Nevada	6.4
5	North Carolina	6.4
7	Michigan	6.0
8	Arizona	5.8
8	Georgia	5.8
10	Colorado	5.4
11	Connecticut	5.2
12	Virginia	4.9
13	New York	4.5
13	Ohio	4.5
15	Delaware	4.3
15	Oklahoma	4.3
17	Kansas	4.2
17	South Carolina	4.2
19	Tennessee	4.0
20	Idaho	3.9
20	New Jersey	3.9
20	Washington	3.9
23	Illinois	3.8
23	New Mexico	3.8
23	Rhode Island	3.8
26	Wisconsin	3.7
27	Alaska	3.4
27	Utah	3.4
29	Arkansas	3.2
30	Indiana	3.1
30	Oregon	3.1
30	Pennsylvania	3.1
33	Louisiana	3.0
33	Missouri	3.0
35	South Dakota	2.9
35	Wyoming	2.9
37	Alabama	2.8
37	Nebraska	2.8
39	Kentucky	2.7
39	Massachusetts	2.7
41	Iowa	2.5
42	Mississippi	2.4
42	Montana	2.4
44	Minnesota	2.3
45	New Hampshire	2.2
46	Hawaii	2.1
46	Maine	2.1
46	Vermont	2.1
49	West Virginia	1.4
50	North Dakota	1.2

District of Columbia*	NA

Source: Morgan Quitno Press using data from U.S. Bureau of the Census
 "Government Finances: 1993-1994" (1997) (http://www.census.gov/govs/www/esti94.html)
*Not applicable.

Local Government Expenditures for Corrections in 1994

National Total = $11,004,287,000*

ALPHA ORDER					RANK ORDER			

RANK	STATE	EXPENDITURES	% of USA		RANK	STATE	EXPENDITURES	% of USA
28	Alabama	$77,038,000	0.70%		1	California	$2,018,003,000	18.34%
45	Alaska	273,000	0.00%		2	New York	1,721,534,000	15.64%
15	Arizona	177,513,000	1.61%		3	Texas	864,653,000	7.86%
32	Arkansas	36,263,000	0.33%		4	Florida	780,419,000	7.09%
1	California	2,018,003,000	18.34%		5	Pennsylvania	603,194,000	5.48%
23	Colorado	112,904,000	1.03%		6	Illinois	386,432,000	3.51%
47	Connecticut	0	0.00%		7	New Jersey	355,174,000	3.23%
47	Delaware	0	0.00%		8	Ohio	315,202,000	2.86%
4	Florida	780,419,000	7.09%		9	Georgia	279,436,000	2.54%
9	Georgia	279,436,000	2.54%		10	Virginia	264,173,000	2.40%
47	Hawaii	0	0.00%		11	Michigan	261,920,000	2.38%
38	Idaho	20,378,000	0.19%		12	Massachusetts	233,908,000	2.13%
6	Illinois	386,432,000	3.51%		13	Washington	214,084,000	1.95%
20	Indiana	137,620,000	1.25%		14	North Carolina	194,040,000	1.76%
33	Iowa	34,782,000	0.32%		15	Arizona	177,513,000	1.61%
30	Kansas	40,499,000	0.37%		16	Minnesota	168,501,000	1.53%
27	Kentucky	85,767,000	0.78%		17	Oregon	164,302,000	1.49%
22	Louisiana	117,708,000	1.07%		18	Wisconsin	160,137,000	1.46%
35	Maine	31,990,000	0.29%		19	Tennessee	156,425,000	1.42%
21	Maryland	125,041,000	1.14%		20	Indiana	137,620,000	1.25%
12	Massachusetts	233,908,000	2.13%		21	Maryland	125,041,000	1.14%
11	Michigan	261,920,000	2.38%		22	Louisiana	117,708,000	1.07%
16	Minnesota	168,501,000	1.53%		23	Colorado	112,904,000	1.03%
39	Mississippi	20,059,000	0.18%		24	Nevada	109,615,000	1.00%
25	Missouri	107,526,000	0.98%		25	Missouri	107,526,000	0.98%
44	Montana	7,611,000	0.07%		26	South Carolina	103,080,000	0.94%
34	Nebraska	32,673,000	0.30%		27	Kentucky	85,767,000	0.78%
24	Nevada	109,615,000	1.00%		28	Alabama	77,038,000	0.70%
36	New Hampshire	25,052,000	0.23%		29	New Mexico	46,346,000	0.42%
7	New Jersey	355,174,000	3.23%		30	Kansas	40,499,000	0.37%
29	New Mexico	46,346,000	0.42%		31	Utah	36,618,000	0.33%
2	New York	1,721,534,000	15.64%		32	Arkansas	36,263,000	0.33%
14	North Carolina	194,040,000	1.76%		33	Iowa	34,782,000	0.32%
43	North Dakota	7,613,000	0.07%		34	Nebraska	32,673,000	0.30%
8	Ohio	315,202,000	2.86%		35	Maine	31,990,000	0.29%
40	Oklahoma	16,239,000	0.15%		36	New Hampshire	25,052,000	0.23%
17	Oregon	164,302,000	1.49%		37	West Virginia	20,937,000	0.19%
5	Pennsylvania	603,194,000	5.48%		38	Idaho	20,378,000	0.19%
47	Rhode Island	0	0.00%		39	Mississippi	20,059,000	0.18%
26	South Carolina	103,080,000	0.94%		40	Oklahoma	16,239,000	0.15%
42	South Dakota	10,921,000	0.10%		41	Wyoming	12,825,000	0.12%
19	Tennessee	156,425,000	1.42%		42	South Dakota	10,921,000	0.10%
3	Texas	864,653,000	7.86%		43	North Dakota	7,613,000	0.07%
31	Utah	36,618,000	0.33%		44	Montana	7,611,000	0.07%
46	Vermont	3,000	0.00%		45	Alaska	273,000	0.00%
10	Virginia	264,173,000	2.40%		46	Vermont	3,000	0.00%
13	Washington	214,084,000	1.95%		47	Connecticut	0	0.00%
37	West Virginia	20,937,000	0.19%		47	Delaware	0	0.00%
18	Wisconsin	160,137,000	1.46%		47	Hawaii	0	0.00%
41	Wyoming	12,825,000	0.12%		47	Rhode Island	0	0.00%
						District of Columbia	307,856,000	2.80%

Source: U.S. Bureau of the Census
  "Government Finances: 1993-1994" (1997) (http://www.census.gov/govs/www/esti94.html)
*Direct Expenditures.

Per Capita Local Government Expenditures for Corrections in 1994

National Per Capita = $42.28*

ALPHA ORDER

RANK	STATE	PER CAPITA
34	Alabama	$18.20
45	Alaska	0.45
9	Arizona	42.79
38	Arkansas	14.79
3	California	64.33
17	Colorado	30.87
47	Connecticut	0.00
47	Delaware	0.00
4	Florida	55.92
12	Georgia	39.64
47	Hawaii	0.00
35	Idaho	17.95
15	Illinois	32.92
28	Indiana	23.97
39	Iowa	12.29
36	Kansas	15.86
29	Kentucky	22.43
24	Louisiana	27.33
26	Maine	25.89
27	Maryland	25.07
13	Massachusetts	38.80
23	Michigan	27.34
14	Minnesota	36.89
43	Mississippi	7.53
31	Missouri	20.36
42	Montana	8.90
32	Nebraska	20.14
2	Nevada	75.14
30	New Hampshire	22.09
8	New Jersey	44.90
21	New Mexico	27.99
1	New York	94.83
22	North Carolina	27.48
40	North Dakota	11.90
19	Ohio	28.41
44	Oklahoma	5.00
5	Oregon	53.20
6	Pennsylvania	50.09
47	Rhode Island	0.00
20	South Carolina	28.21
37	South Dakota	14.97
18	Tennessee	30.33
7	Texas	47.03
33	Utah	18.99
46	Vermont	0.01
10	Virginia	40.41
11	Washington	40.10
41	West Virginia	11.51
16	Wisconsin	31.55
25	Wyoming	27.00

RANK ORDER

RANK	STATE	PER CAPITA
1	New York	$94.83
2	Nevada	75.14
3	California	64.33
4	Florida	55.92
5	Oregon	53.20
6	Pennsylvania	50.09
7	Texas	47.03
8	New Jersey	44.90
9	Arizona	42.79
10	Virginia	40.41
11	Washington	40.10
12	Georgia	39.64
13	Massachusetts	38.80
14	Minnesota	36.89
15	Illinois	32.92
16	Wisconsin	31.55
17	Colorado	30.87
18	Tennessee	30.33
19	Ohio	28.41
20	South Carolina	28.21
21	New Mexico	27.99
22	North Carolina	27.48
23	Michigan	27.34
24	Louisiana	27.33
25	Wyoming	27.00
26	Maine	25.89
27	Maryland	25.07
28	Indiana	23.97
29	Kentucky	22.43
30	New Hampshire	22.09
31	Missouri	20.36
32	Nebraska	20.14
33	Utah	18.99
34	Alabama	18.20
35	Idaho	17.95
36	Kansas	15.86
37	South Dakota	14.97
38	Arkansas	14.79
39	Iowa	12.29
40	North Dakota	11.90
41	West Virginia	11.51
42	Montana	8.90
43	Mississippi	7.53
44	Oklahoma	5.00
45	Alaska	0.45
46	Vermont	0.01
47	Connecticut	0.00
47	Delaware	0.00
47	Hawaii	0.00
47	Rhode Island	0.00
	District of Columbia	544.00

Source: Morgan Quitno Press using data from U.S. Bureau of the Census
    "Government Finances: 1993-1994" (1997) (http://www.census.gov/govs/www/esti94.html)
*Direct Expenditures.

Local Government Expenditures for Corrections
As a Percent of All Direct General Expenditures in 1994
National Percent = 1.8% of Direct General Expenditures

RANK	STATE	PERCENT
30	Alabama	1.1
45	Alaska	0.0
8	Arizona	2.0
30	Arkansas	1.1
6	California	2.2
30	Colorado	1.1
45	Connecticut	0.0
45	Delaware	0.0
4	Florida	2.3
10	Georgia	1.9
45	Hawaii	0.0
33	Idaho	1.0
16	Illinois	1.5
23	Indiana	1.2
41	Iowa	0.6
38	Kansas	0.7
16	Kentucky	1.5
16	Louisiana	1.5
20	Maine	1.4
23	Maryland	1.2
10	Massachusetts	1.9
23	Michigan	1.2
23	Minnesota	1.2
43	Mississippi	0.4
23	Missouri	1.2
42	Montana	0.5
33	Nebraska	1.0
1	Nevada	2.6
23	New Hampshire	1.2
14	New Jersey	1.6
16	New Mexico	1.5
2	New York	2.4
20	North Carolina	1.4
38	North Dakota	0.7
22	Ohio	1.3
44	Oklahoma	0.3
6	Oregon	2.2
2	Pennsylvania	2.4
45	Rhode Island	0.0
14	South Carolina	1.6
36	South Dakota	0.9
12	Tennessee	1.7
4	Texas	2.3
33	Utah	1.0
45	Vermont	0.0
8	Virginia	2.0
12	Washington	1.7
38	West Virginia	0.7
23	Wisconsin	1.2
36	Wyoming	0.9

RANK	STATE	PERCENT
1	Nevada	2.6
2	New York	2.4
2	Pennsylvania	2.4
4	Florida	2.3
4	Texas	2.3
6	California	2.2
6	Oregon	2.2
8	Arizona	2.0
8	Virginia	2.0
10	Georgia	1.9
10	Massachusetts	1.9
12	Tennessee	1.7
12	Washington	1.7
14	New Jersey	1.6
14	South Carolina	1.6
16	Illinois	1.5
16	Kentucky	1.5
16	Louisiana	1.5
16	New Mexico	1.5
20	Maine	1.4
20	North Carolina	1.4
22	Ohio	1.3
23	Indiana	1.2
23	Maryland	1.2
23	Michigan	1.2
23	Minnesota	1.2
23	Missouri	1.2
23	New Hampshire	1.2
23	Wisconsin	1.2
30	Alabama	1.1
30	Arkansas	1.1
30	Colorado	1.1
33	Idaho	1.0
33	Nebraska	1.0
33	Utah	1.0
36	South Dakota	0.9
36	Wyoming	0.9
38	Kansas	0.7
38	North Dakota	0.7
38	West Virginia	0.7
41	Iowa	0.6
42	Montana	0.5
43	Mississippi	0.4
44	Oklahoma	0.3
45	Alaska	0.0
45	Connecticut	0.0
45	Delaware	0.0
45	Hawaii	0.0
45	Rhode Island	0.0
45	Vermont	0.0
	District of Columbia	6.7

Source: Morgan Quitno Press using data from U.S. Bureau of the Census
"Government Finances: 1993-1994" (1997) (http://www.census.gov/govs/www/esti94.html)

State and Local Government Expenditures for Judicial and Legal Services: 1994

National Total = $17,877,210,000*

ALPHA ORDER

RANK	STATE	EXPENDITURES	% of USA
25	Alabama	$204,563,000	1.14%
34	Alaska	124,627,000	0.70%
12	Arizona	365,072,000	2.04%
39	Arkansas	78,637,000	0.44%
1	California	3,252,022,000	18.19%
21	Colorado	232,625,000	1.30%
20	Connecticut	237,544,000	1.33%
45	Delaware	57,085,000	0.32%
3	Florida	1,085,841,000	6.07%
18	Georgia	306,592,000	1.71%
29	Hawaii	145,546,000	0.81%
44	Idaho	60,412,000	0.34%
9	Illinois	669,799,000	3.75%
23	Indiana	218,590,000	1.22%
27	Iowa	164,678,000	0.92%
30	Kansas	138,898,000	0.78%
28	Kentucky	164,042,000	0.92%
22	Louisiana	218,956,000	1.22%
46	Maine	45,065,000	0.25%
13	Maryland	351,312,000	1.97%
10	Massachusetts	391,630,000	2.19%
8	Michigan	675,817,000	3.78%
17	Minnesota	308,125,000	1.72%
40	Mississippi	76,878,000	0.43%
26	Missouri	204,314,000	1.14%
43	Montana	66,752,000	0.37%
42	Nebraska	69,005,000	0.39%
32	Nevada	129,945,000	0.73%
41	New Hampshire	76,352,000	0.43%
7	New Jersey	715,109,000	4.00%
36	New Mexico	94,959,000	0.53%
2	New York	1,813,673,000	10.15%
15	North Carolina	335,911,000	1.88%
50	North Dakota	23,065,000	0.13%
5	Ohio	762,480,000	4.27%
31	Oklahoma	137,166,000	0.77%
24	Oregon	212,213,000	1.19%
6	Pennsylvania	758,059,000	4.24%
37	Rhode Island	82,376,000	0.46%
33	South Carolina	124,840,000	0.70%
49	South Dakota	31,373,000	0.18%
19	Tennessee	242,863,000	1.36%
4	Texas	971,127,000	5.43%
35	Utah	102,103,000	0.57%
48	Vermont	36,467,000	0.20%
16	Virginia	324,950,000	1.82%
11	Washington	380,661,000	2.13%
38	West Virginia	80,336,000	0.45%
14	Wisconsin	338,092,000	1.89%
47	Wyoming	36,813,000	0.21%

RANK ORDER

RANK	STATE	EXPENDITURES	% of USA
1	California	$3,252,022,000	18.19%
2	New York	1,813,673,000	10.15%
3	Florida	1,085,841,000	6.07%
4	Texas	971,127,000	5.43%
5	Ohio	762,480,000	4.27%
6	Pennsylvania	758,059,000	4.24%
7	New Jersey	715,109,000	4.00%
8	Michigan	675,817,000	3.78%
9	Illinois	669,799,000	3.75%
10	Massachusetts	391,630,000	2.19%
11	Washington	380,661,000	2.13%
12	Arizona	365,072,000	2.04%
13	Maryland	351,312,000	1.97%
14	Wisconsin	338,092,000	1.89%
15	North Carolina	335,911,000	1.88%
16	Virginia	324,950,000	1.82%
17	Minnesota	308,125,000	1.72%
18	Georgia	306,592,000	1.71%
19	Tennessee	242,863,000	1.36%
20	Connecticut	237,544,000	1.33%
21	Colorado	232,625,000	1.30%
22	Louisiana	218,956,000	1.22%
23	Indiana	218,590,000	1.22%
24	Oregon	212,213,000	1.19%
25	Alabama	204,563,000	1.14%
26	Missouri	204,314,000	1.14%
27	Iowa	164,678,000	0.92%
28	Kentucky	164,042,000	0.92%
29	Hawaii	145,546,000	0.81%
30	Kansas	138,898,000	0.78%
31	Oklahoma	137,166,000	0.77%
32	Nevada	129,945,000	0.73%
33	South Carolina	124,840,000	0.70%
34	Alaska	124,627,000	0.70%
35	Utah	102,103,000	0.57%
36	New Mexico	94,959,000	0.53%
37	Rhode Island	82,376,000	0.46%
38	West Virginia	80,336,000	0.45%
39	Arkansas	78,637,000	0.44%
40	Mississippi	76,878,000	0.43%
41	New Hampshire	76,352,000	0.43%
42	Nebraska	69,005,000	0.39%
43	Montana	66,752,000	0.37%
44	Idaho	60,412,000	0.34%
45	Delaware	57,085,000	0.32%
46	Maine	45,065,000	0.25%
47	Wyoming	36,813,000	0.21%
48	Vermont	36,467,000	0.20%
49	South Dakota	31,373,000	0.18%
50	North Dakota	23,065,000	0.13%
	District of Columbia	151,850,000	0.85%

Source: Morgan Quitno Press using data from U.S. Bureau of the Census
   "Government Finances: 1993-1994" (1997) (http://www.census.gov/govs/www/esti94.html)
*Direct expenditures. Includes Courts, Prosecution and Legal Services and Public Defense.

Per Capita State and Local Government Expenditures
For Judicial and Legal Services in 1994
National Per Capita = $68.68*

RANK	STATE	PER CAPITA
35	Alabama	$48.33
1	Alaska	207.45
7	Arizona	87.99
49	Arkansas	32.08
3	California	103.67
23	Colorado	63.61
13	Connecticut	72.65
9	Delaware	80.80
11	Florida	77.81
39	Georgia	43.49
2	Hawaii	124.12
30	Idaho	53.21
28	Illinois	57.07
45	Indiana	38.07
26	Iowa	58.21
29	Kansas	54.39
41	Kentucky	42.90
33	Louisiana	50.84
46	Maine	36.47
16	Maryland	70.42
22	Massachusetts	64.96
15	Michigan	70.55
19	Minnesota	67.46
50	Mississippi	28.87
44	Missouri	38.69
10	Montana	78.08
42	Nebraska	42.53
6	Nevada	89.07
20	New Hampshire	67.34
5	New Jersey	90.39
27	New Mexico	57.34
4	New York	99.91
36	North Carolina	47.57
47	North Dakota	36.06
17	Ohio	68.72
43	Oklahoma	42.23
18	Oregon	68.71
25	Pennsylvania	62.95
8	Rhode Island	82.87
48	South Carolina	34.17
40	South Dakota	43.00
37	Tennessee	47.09
32	Texas	52.82
31	Utah	52.94
24	Vermont	62.98
34	Virginia	49.70
14	Washington	71.29
38	West Virginia	44.17
21	Wisconsin	66.62
12	Wyoming	77.50

RANK	STATE	PER CAPITA
1	Alaska	$207.45
2	Hawaii	124.12
3	California	103.67
4	New York	99.91
5	New Jersey	90.39
6	Nevada	89.07
7	Arizona	87.99
8	Rhode Island	82.87
9	Delaware	80.80
10	Montana	78.08
11	Florida	77.81
12	Wyoming	77.50
13	Connecticut	72.65
14	Washington	71.29
15	Michigan	70.55
16	Maryland	70.42
17	Ohio	68.72
18	Oregon	68.71
19	Minnesota	67.46
20	New Hampshire	67.34
21	Wisconsin	66.62
22	Massachusetts	64.96
23	Colorado	63.61
24	Vermont	62.98
25	Pennsylvania	62.95
26	Iowa	58.21
27	New Mexico	57.34
28	Illinois	57.07
29	Kansas	54.39
30	Idaho	53.21
31	Utah	52.94
32	Texas	52.82
33	Louisiana	50.84
34	Virginia	49.70
35	Alabama	48.33
36	North Carolina	47.57
37	Tennessee	47.09
38	West Virginia	44.17
39	Georgia	43.49
40	South Dakota	43.00
41	Kentucky	42.90
42	Nebraska	42.53
43	Oklahoma	42.23
44	Missouri	38.69
45	Indiana	38.07
46	Maine	36.47
47	North Dakota	36.06
48	South Carolina	34.17
49	Arkansas	32.08
50	Mississippi	28.87
	District of Columbia	268.33

Source: Morgan Quitno Press using data from U.S. Bureau of the Census
"Government Finances: 1993-1994" (1997) (http://www.census.gov/govs/www/esti94.html)
*Direct expenditures. Includes Courts, Prosecution and Legal Services and Public Defense.

State and Local Government Expenditures for Judicial and Legal Services As a Percent of All Direct General Expenditures in 1994
National Percent = 1.7% of Direct General Expenditures*

ALPHA ORDER

RANK	STATE	PERCENT
27	Alabama	1.4
6	Alaska	2.0
1	Arizona	2.4
44	Arkansas	1.1
2	California	2.3
15	Colorado	1.6
27	Connecticut	1.4
9	Delaware	1.8
4	Florida	2.1
41	Georgia	1.2
3	Hawaii	2.2
15	Idaho	1.6
21	Illinois	1.5
46	Indiana	1.0
21	Iowa	1.5
27	Kansas	1.4
36	Kentucky	1.3
36	Louisiana	1.3
47	Maine	0.9
9	Maryland	1.8
27	Massachusetts	1.4
13	Michigan	1.7
27	Minnesota	1.4
47	Mississippi	0.9
36	Missouri	1.3
6	Montana	2.0
44	Nebraska	1.1
4	Nevada	2.1
13	New Hampshire	1.7
8	New Jersey	1.9
27	New Mexico	1.4
15	New York	1.6
36	North Carolina	1.3
47	North Dakota	0.9
9	Ohio	1.8
36	Oklahoma	1.3
15	Oregon	1.6
15	Pennsylvania	1.6
9	Rhode Island	1.8
47	South Carolina	0.9
41	South Dakota	1.2
27	Tennessee	1.4
21	Texas	1.5
21	Utah	1.5
21	Vermont	1.5
27	Virginia	1.4
15	Washington	1.6
41	West Virginia	1.2
21	Wisconsin	1.5
27	Wyoming	1.4

RANK ORDER

RANK	STATE	PERCENT
1	Arizona	2.4
2	California	2.3
3	Hawaii	2.2
4	Florida	2.1
4	Nevada	2.1
6	Alaska	2.0
6	Montana	2.0
8	New Jersey	1.9
9	Delaware	1.8
9	Maryland	1.8
9	Ohio	1.8
9	Rhode Island	1.8
13	Michigan	1.7
13	New Hampshire	1.7
15	Colorado	1.6
15	Idaho	1.6
15	New York	1.6
15	Oregon	1.6
15	Pennsylvania	1.6
15	Washington	1.6
21	Illinois	1.5
21	Iowa	1.5
21	Texas	1.5
21	Utah	1.5
21	Vermont	1.5
21	Wisconsin	1.5
27	Alabama	1.4
27	Connecticut	1.4
27	Kansas	1.4
27	Massachusetts	1.4
27	Minnesota	1.4
27	New Mexico	1.4
27	Tennessee	1.4
27	Virginia	1.4
27	Wyoming	1.4
36	Kentucky	1.3
36	Louisiana	1.3
36	Missouri	1.3
36	North Carolina	1.3
36	Oklahoma	1.3
41	Georgia	1.2
41	South Dakota	1.2
41	West Virginia	1.2
44	Arkansas	1.1
44	Nebraska	1.1
46	Indiana	1.0
47	Maine	0.9
47	Mississippi	0.9
47	North Dakota	0.9
47	South Carolina	0.9
	District of Columbia	3.3

Source: Morgan Quitno Press using data from U.S. Bureau of the Census
    "Government Finances: 1993-1994" (1997) (http://www.census.gov/govs/www/esti94.html)
*Includes Courts, Prosecution and Legal Services and Public Defense.

State Government Expenditures for Judicial and Legal Services in 1994

National Total = $6,904,352,000*

<table>
<tr><td colspan="4">ALPHA ORDER</td><td colspan="4">RANK ORDER</td></tr>
<tr><td>RANK</td><td>STATE</td><td>EXPENDITURES</td><td>% of USA</td><td>RANK</td><td>STATE</td><td>EXPENDITURES</td><td>% of USA</td></tr>
<tr><td>17</td><td>Alabama</td><td>$137,006,000</td><td>1.98%</td><td>1</td><td>New York</td><td>$1,063,200,000</td><td>15.40%</td></tr>
<tr><td>22</td><td>Alaska</td><td>114,202,000</td><td>1.65%</td><td>2</td><td>Florida</td><td>475,345,000</td><td>6.88%</td></tr>
<tr><td>31</td><td>Arizona</td><td>74,378,000</td><td>1.08%</td><td>3</td><td>Massachusetts</td><td>347,544,000</td><td>5.03%</td></tr>
<tr><td>43</td><td>Arkansas</td><td>32,226,000</td><td>0.47%</td><td>4</td><td>California</td><td>312,814,000</td><td>4.53%</td></tr>
<tr><td>4</td><td>California</td><td>312,814,000</td><td>4.53%</td><td>5</td><td>North Carolina</td><td>287,519,000</td><td>4.16%</td></tr>
<tr><td>19</td><td>Colorado</td><td>121,236,000</td><td>1.76%</td><td>6</td><td>Texas</td><td>283,754,000</td><td>4.11%</td></tr>
<tr><td>9</td><td>Connecticut</td><td>207,964,000</td><td>3.01%</td><td>7</td><td>New Jersey</td><td>248,931,000</td><td>3.61%</td></tr>
<tr><td>38</td><td>Delaware</td><td>49,736,000</td><td>0.72%</td><td>8</td><td>Maryland</td><td>219,335,000</td><td>3.18%</td></tr>
<tr><td>2</td><td>Florida</td><td>475,345,000</td><td>6.88%</td><td>9</td><td>Connecticut</td><td>207,964,000</td><td>3.01%</td></tr>
<tr><td>35</td><td>Georgia</td><td>56,172,000</td><td>0.81%</td><td>10</td><td>Illinois</td><td>196,074,000</td><td>2.84%</td></tr>
<tr><td>23</td><td>Hawaii</td><td>113,245,000</td><td>1.64%</td><td>11</td><td>Pennsylvania</td><td>194,085,000</td><td>2.81%</td></tr>
<tr><td>45</td><td>Idaho</td><td>29,166,000</td><td>0.42%</td><td>12</td><td>Virginia</td><td>167,493,000</td><td>2.43%</td></tr>
<tr><td>10</td><td>Illinois</td><td>196,074,000</td><td>2.84%</td><td>13</td><td>Wisconsin</td><td>160,451,000</td><td>2.32%</td></tr>
<tr><td>37</td><td>Indiana</td><td>54,507,000</td><td>0.79%</td><td>14</td><td>Michigan</td><td>160,232,000</td><td>2.32%</td></tr>
<tr><td>20</td><td>Iowa</td><td>120,073,000</td><td>1.74%</td><td>15</td><td>Oregon</td><td>144,643,000</td><td>2.09%</td></tr>
<tr><td>28</td><td>Kansas</td><td>86,620,000</td><td>1.25%</td><td>16</td><td>Kentucky</td><td>141,590,000</td><td>2.05%</td></tr>
<tr><td>16</td><td>Kentucky</td><td>141,590,000</td><td>2.05%</td><td>17</td><td>Alabama</td><td>137,006,000</td><td>1.98%</td></tr>
<tr><td>26</td><td>Louisiana</td><td>92,690,000</td><td>1.34%</td><td>18</td><td>Ohio</td><td>131,668,000</td><td>1.91%</td></tr>
<tr><td>39</td><td>Maine</td><td>37,089,000</td><td>0.54%</td><td>19</td><td>Colorado</td><td>121,236,000</td><td>1.76%</td></tr>
<tr><td>8</td><td>Maryland</td><td>219,335,000</td><td>3.18%</td><td>20</td><td>Iowa</td><td>120,073,000</td><td>1.74%</td></tr>
<tr><td>3</td><td>Massachusetts</td><td>347,544,000</td><td>5.03%</td><td>21</td><td>Minnesota</td><td>117,817,000</td><td>1.71%</td></tr>
<tr><td>14</td><td>Michigan</td><td>160,232,000</td><td>2.32%</td><td>22</td><td>Alaska</td><td>114,202,000</td><td>1.65%</td></tr>
<tr><td>21</td><td>Minnesota</td><td>117,817,000</td><td>1.71%</td><td>23</td><td>Hawaii</td><td>113,245,000</td><td>1.64%</td></tr>
<tr><td>46</td><td>Mississippi</td><td>28,832,000</td><td>0.42%</td><td>24</td><td>Missouri</td><td>104,158,000</td><td>1.51%</td></tr>
<tr><td>24</td><td>Missouri</td><td>104,158,000</td><td>1.51%</td><td>25</td><td>Tennessee</td><td>99,198,000</td><td>1.44%</td></tr>
<tr><td>40</td><td>Montana</td><td>36,118,000</td><td>0.52%</td><td>26</td><td>Louisiana</td><td>92,690,000</td><td>1.34%</td></tr>
<tr><td>44</td><td>Nebraska</td><td>30,591,000</td><td>0.44%</td><td>27</td><td>Oklahoma</td><td>91,849,000</td><td>1.33%</td></tr>
<tr><td>48</td><td>Nevada</td><td>21,174,000</td><td>0.31%</td><td>28</td><td>Kansas</td><td>86,620,000</td><td>1.25%</td></tr>
<tr><td>32</td><td>New Hampshire</td><td>63,960,000</td><td>0.93%</td><td>29</td><td>New Mexico</td><td>83,485,000</td><td>1.21%</td></tr>
<tr><td>7</td><td>New Jersey</td><td>248,931,000</td><td>3.61%</td><td>30</td><td>Rhode Island</td><td>74,815,000</td><td>1.08%</td></tr>
<tr><td>29</td><td>New Mexico</td><td>83,485,000</td><td>1.21%</td><td>31</td><td>Arizona</td><td>74,378,000</td><td>1.08%</td></tr>
<tr><td>1</td><td>New York</td><td>1,063,200,000</td><td>15.40%</td><td>32</td><td>New Hampshire</td><td>63,960,000</td><td>0.93%</td></tr>
<tr><td>5</td><td>North Carolina</td><td>287,519,000</td><td>4.16%</td><td>33</td><td>Utah</td><td>60,511,000</td><td>0.88%</td></tr>
<tr><td>50</td><td>North Dakota</td><td>7,651,000</td><td>0.11%</td><td>34</td><td>West Virginia</td><td>56,394,000</td><td>0.82%</td></tr>
<tr><td>18</td><td>Ohio</td><td>131,668,000</td><td>1.91%</td><td>35</td><td>Georgia</td><td>56,172,000</td><td>0.81%</td></tr>
<tr><td>27</td><td>Oklahoma</td><td>91,849,000</td><td>1.33%</td><td>36</td><td>Washington</td><td>55,222,000</td><td>0.80%</td></tr>
<tr><td>15</td><td>Oregon</td><td>144,643,000</td><td>2.09%</td><td>37</td><td>Indiana</td><td>54,507,000</td><td>0.79%</td></tr>
<tr><td>11</td><td>Pennsylvania</td><td>194,085,000</td><td>2.81%</td><td>38</td><td>Delaware</td><td>49,736,000</td><td>0.72%</td></tr>
<tr><td>30</td><td>Rhode Island</td><td>74,815,000</td><td>1.08%</td><td>39</td><td>Maine</td><td>37,089,000</td><td>0.54%</td></tr>
<tr><td>41</td><td>South Carolina</td><td>35,146,000</td><td>0.51%</td><td>40</td><td>Montana</td><td>36,118,000</td><td>0.52%</td></tr>
<tr><td>49</td><td>South Dakota</td><td>19,899,000</td><td>0.29%</td><td>41</td><td>South Carolina</td><td>35,146,000</td><td>0.51%</td></tr>
<tr><td>25</td><td>Tennessee</td><td>99,198,000</td><td>1.44%</td><td>42</td><td>Vermont</td><td>34,569,000</td><td>0.50%</td></tr>
<tr><td>6</td><td>Texas</td><td>283,754,000</td><td>4.11%</td><td>43</td><td>Arkansas</td><td>32,226,000</td><td>0.47%</td></tr>
<tr><td>33</td><td>Utah</td><td>60,511,000</td><td>0.88%</td><td>44</td><td>Nebraska</td><td>30,591,000</td><td>0.44%</td></tr>
<tr><td>42</td><td>Vermont</td><td>34,569,000</td><td>0.50%</td><td>45</td><td>Idaho</td><td>29,166,000</td><td>0.42%</td></tr>
<tr><td>12</td><td>Virginia</td><td>167,493,000</td><td>2.43%</td><td>46</td><td>Mississippi</td><td>28,832,000</td><td>0.42%</td></tr>
<tr><td>36</td><td>Washington</td><td>55,222,000</td><td>0.80%</td><td>47</td><td>Wyoming</td><td>21,975,000</td><td>0.32%</td></tr>
<tr><td>34</td><td>West Virginia</td><td>56,394,000</td><td>0.82%</td><td>48</td><td>Nevada</td><td>21,174,000</td><td>0.31%</td></tr>
<tr><td>13</td><td>Wisconsin</td><td>160,451,000</td><td>2.32%</td><td>49</td><td>South Dakota</td><td>19,899,000</td><td>0.29%</td></tr>
<tr><td>47</td><td>Wyoming</td><td>21,975,000</td><td>0.32%</td><td>50</td><td>North Dakota</td><td>7,651,000</td><td>0.11%</td></tr>
<tr><td></td><td></td><td></td><td></td><td></td><td>District of Columbia**</td><td>NA</td><td>NA</td></tr>
</table>

Source: U.S. Bureau of the Census
"Government Finances: 1993-1994" (1997) (http://www.census.gov/govs/www/esti94.html)
*Direct expenditures. Includes Courts, Prosecution and Legal Services and Public Defense.
**Not applicable.

Per Capita State Government Expenditures for Judicial and Legal Services: 1994

National Per Capita = $26.53*

ALPHA ORDER

RANK	STATE	PER CAPITA
21	Alabama	$32.37
1	Alaska	190.09
36	Arizona	17.93
42	Arkansas	13.15
47	California	9.97
20	Colorado	33.15
5	Connecticut	63.61
4	Delaware	70.40
18	Florida	34.06
50	Georgia	7.97
2	Hawaii	96.58
30	Idaho	25.69
38	Illinois	16.71
49	Indiana	9.49
14	Iowa	42.44
19	Kansas	33.92
17	Kentucky	37.03
32	Louisiana	21.52
26	Maine	30.01
13	Maryland	43.97
8	Massachusetts	57.65
37	Michigan	16.73
29	Minnesota	25.80
45	Mississippi	10.83
33	Missouri	19.72
15	Montana	42.25
35	Nebraska	18.85
41	Nevada	14.51
9	New Hampshire	56.41
23	New Jersey	31.47
10	New Mexico	50.42
7	New York	58.57
16	North Carolina	40.71
43	North Dakota	11.96
44	Ohio	11.87
27	Oklahoma	28.28
11	Oregon	46.83
39	Pennsylvania	16.12
3	Rhode Island	75.27
48	South Carolina	9.62
28	South Dakota	27.27
34	Tennessee	19.23
40	Texas	15.43
24	Utah	31.38
6	Vermont	59.70
31	Virginia	25.62
46	Washington	10.34
25	West Virginia	31.01
22	Wisconsin	31.62
12	Wyoming	46.26

RANK ORDER

RANK	STATE	PER CAPITA
1	Alaska	$190.09
2	Hawaii	96.58
3	Rhode Island	75.27
4	Delaware	70.40
5	Connecticut	63.61
6	Vermont	59.70
7	New York	58.57
8	Massachusetts	57.65
9	New Hampshire	56.41
10	New Mexico	50.42
11	Oregon	46.83
12	Wyoming	46.26
13	Maryland	43.97
14	Iowa	42.44
15	Montana	42.25
16	North Carolina	40.71
17	Kentucky	37.03
18	Florida	34.06
19	Kansas	33.92
20	Colorado	33.15
21	Alabama	32.37
22	Wisconsin	31.62
23	New Jersey	31.47
24	Utah	31.38
25	West Virginia	31.01
26	Maine	30.01
27	Oklahoma	28.28
28	South Dakota	27.27
29	Minnesota	25.80
30	Idaho	25.69
31	Virginia	25.62
32	Louisiana	21.52
33	Missouri	19.72
34	Tennessee	19.23
35	Nebraska	18.85
36	Arizona	17.93
37	Michigan	16.73
38	Illinois	16.71
39	Pennsylvania	16.12
40	Texas	15.43
41	Nevada	14.51
42	Arkansas	13.15
43	North Dakota	11.96
44	Ohio	11.87
45	Mississippi	10.83
46	Washington	10.34
47	California	9.97
48	South Carolina	9.62
49	Indiana	9.49
50	Georgia	7.97

District of Columbia**   NA

Source: Morgan Quitno Press using data from U.S. Bureau of the Census
    "Government Finances: 1993-1994" (1997) (http://www.census.gov/govs/www/esti94.html)
*Direct expenditures. Includes Courts, Prosecution and Legal Services and Public Defense.
**Not applicable.

State Government Expenditures for Judicial and Legal Services
As a Percent of All Direct General Expenditures in 1994
National Percent = 1.5% of Direct General Expenditures*

ALPHA ORDER

RANK ORDER

RANK	STATE	PERCENT		RANK	STATE	PERCENT
23	Alabama	1.8		1	Alaska	2.8
1	Alaska	2.8		2	Rhode Island	2.7
33	Arizona	1.2		3	New Hampshire	2.6
42	Arkansas	0.8		3	New York	2.6
43	California	0.7		3	North Carolina	2.6
9	Colorado	2.4		3	Oregon	2.6
13	Connecticut	2.3		7	Delaware	2.5
7	Delaware	2.5		7	Florida	2.5
7	Florida	2.5		9	Colorado	2.4
47	Georgia	0.5		9	Iowa	2.4
14	Hawaii	2.2		9	Maryland	2.4
25	Idaho	1.6		9	Vermont	2.4
35	Illinois	1.1		13	Connecticut	2.3
46	Indiana	0.6		14	Hawaii	2.2
9	Iowa	2.4		14	Kansas	2.2
14	Kansas	2.2		14	Massachusetts	2.2
20	Kentucky	2.0		14	New Mexico	2.2
38	Louisiana	1.0		18	Montana	2.1
28	Maine	1.4		18	Wyoming	2.1
9	Maryland	2.4		20	Kentucky	2.0
14	Massachusetts	2.2		21	Oklahoma	1.9
40	Michigan	0.9		21	Wisconsin	1.9
28	Minnesota	1.4		23	Alabama	1.8
43	Mississippi	0.7		23	Utah	1.8
28	Missouri	1.4		25	Idaho	1.6
18	Montana	2.1		25	Virginia	1.6
35	Nebraska	1.1		27	New Jersey	1.5
38	Nevada	1.0		28	Maine	1.4
3	New Hampshire	2.6		28	Minnesota	1.4
27	New Jersey	1.5		28	Missouri	1.4
14	New Mexico	2.2		28	South Dakota	1.4
3	New York	2.6		28	West Virginia	1.4
3	North Carolina	2.6		33	Arizona	1.2
47	North Dakota	0.5		33	Tennessee	1.2
43	Ohio	0.7		35	Illinois	1.1
21	Oklahoma	1.9		35	Nebraska	1.1
3	Oregon	2.6		35	Texas	1.1
40	Pennsylvania	0.9		38	Louisiana	1.0
2	Rhode Island	2.7		38	Nevada	1.0
47	South Carolina	0.5		40	Michigan	0.9
28	South Dakota	1.4		40	Pennsylvania	0.9
33	Tennessee	1.2		42	Arkansas	0.8
35	Texas	1.1		43	California	0.7
23	Utah	1.8		43	Mississippi	0.7
9	Vermont	2.4		43	Ohio	0.7
25	Virginia	1.6		46	Indiana	0.6
47	Washington	0.5		47	Georgia	0.5
28	West Virginia	1.4		47	North Dakota	0.5
21	Wisconsin	1.9		47	South Carolina	0.5
18	Wyoming	2.1		47	Washington	0.5

District of Columbia**   NA

Source: Morgan Quitno Press using data from U.S. Bureau of the Census
   "Government Finances: 1993-1994" (1997) (http://www.census.gov/govs/www/esti94.html)
Includes Courts, Prosecution and Legal Services and Public Defense.
**Not applicable.*

Local Government Expenditures for Judicial and Legal Services in 1994

National Total = $10,972,858,000*

ALPHA ORDER

RANK	STATE	EXPENDITURES	% of USA
25	Alabama	$67,557,000	0.62%
46	Alaska	10,425,000	0.10%
11	Arizona	290,694,000	2.65%
29	Arkansas	46,411,000	0.42%
1	California	2,939,208,000	26.79%
20	Colorado	111,389,000	1.02%
38	Connecticut	29,580,000	0.27%
49	Delaware	7,349,000	0.07%
5	Florida	610,496,000	5.56%
12	Georgia	250,420,000	2.28%
35	Hawaii	32,301,000	0.29%
36	Idaho	31,246,000	0.28%
8	Illinois	473,725,000	4.32%
15	Indiana	164,083,000	1.50%
31	Iowa	44,605,000	0.41%
26	Kansas	52,278,000	0.48%
40	Kentucky	22,452,000	0.20%
19	Louisiana	126,266,000	1.15%
47	Maine	7,976,000	0.07%
18	Maryland	131,977,000	1.20%
32	Massachusetts	44,086,000	0.40%
7	Michigan	515,585,000	4.70%
13	Minnesota	190,308,000	1.73%
28	Mississippi	48,046,000	0.44%
22	Missouri	100,156,000	0.91%
37	Montana	30,634,000	0.28%
34	Nebraska	38,414,000	0.35%
21	Nevada	108,771,000	0.99%
43	New Hampshire	12,392,000	0.11%
9	New Jersey	466,178,000	4.25%
44	New Mexico	11,474,000	0.10%
2	New York	750,473,000	6.84%
27	North Carolina	48,392,000	0.44%
41	North Dakota	15,414,000	0.14%
4	Ohio	630,812,000	5.75%
30	Oklahoma	45,317,000	0.41%
24	Oregon	67,570,000	0.62%
6	Pennsylvania	563,974,000	5.14%
48	Rhode Island	7,561,000	0.07%
23	South Carolina	89,694,000	0.82%
44	South Dakota	11,474,000	0.10%
17	Tennessee	143,665,000	1.31%
3	Texas	687,373,000	6.26%
33	Utah	41,592,000	0.38%
50	Vermont	1,898,000	0.02%
16	Virginia	157,457,000	1.43%
10	Washington	325,439,000	2.97%
39	West Virginia	23,942,000	0.22%
14	Wisconsin	177,641,000	1.62%
42	Wyoming	14,838,000	0.14%

RANK ORDER

RANK	STATE	EXPENDITURES	% of USA
1	California	$2,939,208,000	26.79%
2	New York	750,473,000	6.84%
3	Texas	687,373,000	6.26%
4	Ohio	630,812,000	5.75%
5	Florida	610,496,000	5.56%
6	Pennsylvania	563,974,000	5.14%
7	Michigan	515,585,000	4.70%
8	Illinois	473,725,000	4.32%
9	New Jersey	466,178,000	4.25%
10	Washington	325,439,000	2.97%
11	Arizona	290,694,000	2.65%
12	Georgia	250,420,000	2.28%
13	Minnesota	190,308,000	1.73%
14	Wisconsin	177,641,000	1.62%
15	Indiana	164,083,000	1.50%
16	Virginia	157,457,000	1.43%
17	Tennessee	143,665,000	1.31%
18	Maryland	131,977,000	1.20%
19	Louisiana	126,266,000	1.15%
20	Colorado	111,389,000	1.02%
21	Nevada	108,771,000	0.99%
22	Missouri	100,156,000	0.91%
23	South Carolina	89,694,000	0.82%
24	Oregon	67,570,000	0.62%
25	Alabama	67,557,000	0.62%
26	Kansas	52,278,000	0.48%
27	North Carolina	48,392,000	0.44%
28	Mississippi	48,046,000	0.44%
29	Arkansas	46,411,000	0.42%
30	Oklahoma	45,317,000	0.41%
31	Iowa	44,605,000	0.41%
32	Massachusetts	44,086,000	0.40%
33	Utah	41,592,000	0.38%
34	Nebraska	38,414,000	0.35%
35	Hawaii	32,301,000	0.29%
36	Idaho	31,246,000	0.28%
37	Montana	30,634,000	0.28%
38	Connecticut	29,580,000	0.27%
39	West Virginia	23,942,000	0.22%
40	Kentucky	22,452,000	0.20%
41	North Dakota	15,414,000	0.14%
42	Wyoming	14,838,000	0.14%
43	New Hampshire	12,392,000	0.11%
44	New Mexico	11,474,000	0.10%
44	South Dakota	11,474,000	0.10%
46	Alaska	10,425,000	0.10%
47	Maine	7,976,000	0.07%
48	Rhode Island	7,561,000	0.07%
49	Delaware	7,349,000	0.07%
50	Vermont	1,898,000	0.02%
	District of Columbia	151,850,000	1.38%

Source: U.S. Bureau of the Census
  "Government Finances: 1993-1994" (1997) (http://www.census.gov/govs/www/esti94.html)
*Direct expenditures. Includes Courts, Prosecution and Legal Services and Public Defense.

Per Capita Local Government Expenditures for Judicial & Legal Services: 1994

National Per Capita = $42.16*

ALPHA ORDER

RANK	STATE	PER CAPITA
36	Alabama	$15.96
35	Alaska	17.35
3	Arizona	70.07
33	Arkansas	18.93
1	California	93.70
18	Colorado	30.46
43	Connecticut	9.05
42	Delaware	10.40
9	Florida	43.75
15	Georgia	35.53
22	Hawaii	27.55
23	Idaho	27.52
12	Illinois	40.36
20	Indiana	28.58
37	Iowa	15.77
31	Kansas	20.47
49	Kentucky	5.87
19	Louisiana	29.32
48	Maine	6.45
24	Maryland	26.46
45	Massachusetts	7.31
7	Michigan	53.82
10	Minnesota	41.67
34	Mississippi	18.04
32	Missouri	18.96
14	Montana	35.83
28	Nebraska	23.67
2	Nevada	74.56
41	New Hampshire	10.93
5	New Jersey	58.93
46	New Mexico	6.93
11	New York	41.34
47	North Carolina	6.85
26	North Dakota	24.10
6	Ohio	56.85
39	Oklahoma	13.95
29	Oregon	21.88
8	Pennsylvania	46.83
44	Rhode Island	7.61
25	South Carolina	24.55
38	South Dakota	15.73
21	Tennessee	27.85
13	Texas	37.39
30	Utah	21.57
50	Vermont	3.28
27	Virginia	24.08
4	Washington	60.95
40	West Virginia	13.16
16	Wisconsin	35.00
17	Wyoming	31.24

RANK ORDER

RANK	STATE	PER CAPITA
1	California	$93.70
2	Nevada	74.56
3	Arizona	70.07
4	Washington	60.95
5	New Jersey	58.93
6	Ohio	56.85
7	Michigan	53.82
8	Pennsylvania	46.83
9	Florida	43.75
10	Minnesota	41.67
11	New York	41.34
12	Illinois	40.36
13	Texas	37.39
14	Montana	35.83
15	Georgia	35.53
16	Wisconsin	35.00
17	Wyoming	31.24
18	Colorado	30.46
19	Louisiana	29.32
20	Indiana	28.58
21	Tennessee	27.85
22	Hawaii	27.55
23	Idaho	27.52
24	Maryland	26.46
25	South Carolina	24.55
26	North Dakota	24.10
27	Virginia	24.08
28	Nebraska	23.67
29	Oregon	21.88
30	Utah	21.57
31	Kansas	20.47
32	Missouri	18.96
33	Arkansas	18.93
34	Mississippi	18.04
35	Alaska	17.35
36	Alabama	15.96
37	Iowa	15.77
38	South Dakota	15.73
39	Oklahoma	13.95
40	West Virginia	13.16
41	New Hampshire	10.93
42	Delaware	10.40
43	Connecticut	9.05
44	Rhode Island	7.61
45	Massachusetts	7.31
46	New Mexico	6.93
47	North Carolina	6.85
48	Maine	6.45
49	Kentucky	5.87
50	Vermont	3.28
	District of Columbia	268.33

Source: Morgan Quitno Press using data from U.S. Bureau of the Census
"Government Finances: 1993-1994" (1997) (http://www.census.gov/govs/www/esti94.html)
*Direct expenditures. Includes Courts, Prosecution and Legal Services and Public Defense.

Local Government Expenditures for Judicial and Legal Services
As a Percent of All Direct General Expenditures in 1994
National Percent = 1.8% of Direct General Expenditures*

ALPHA ORDER

RANK	STATE	PERCENT
33	Alabama	0.9
42	Alaska	0.5
1	Arizona	3.2
18	Arkansas	1.4
1	California	3.2
27	Colorado	1.1
43	Connecticut	0.4
40	Delaware	0.6
11	Florida	1.8
14	Georgia	1.7
8	Hawaii	2.1
15	Idaho	1.6
11	Illinois	1.8
18	Indiana	1.4
39	Iowa	0.7
33	Kansas	0.9
43	Kentucky	0.4
15	Louisiana	1.6
43	Maine	0.4
24	Maryland	1.2
43	Massachusetts	0.4
6	Michigan	2.3
18	Minnesota	1.4
27	Mississippi	1.1
27	Missouri	1.1
10	Montana	1.9
27	Nebraska	1.1
4	Nevada	2.6
40	New Hampshire	0.6
8	New Jersey	2.1
43	New Mexico	0.4
31	New York	1.0
49	North Carolina	0.3
18	North Dakota	1.4
3	Ohio	2.7
37	Oklahoma	0.8
33	Oregon	0.9
6	Pennsylvania	2.3
43	Rhode Island	0.4
18	South Carolina	1.4
33	South Dakota	0.9
15	Tennessee	1.6
11	Texas	1.8
24	Utah	1.2
50	Vermont	0.2
24	Virginia	1.2
5	Washington	2.5
37	West Virginia	0.8
23	Wisconsin	1.3
31	Wyoming	1.0

RANK ORDER

RANK	STATE	PERCENT
1	Arizona	3.2
1	California	3.2
3	Ohio	2.7
4	Nevada	2.6
5	Washington	2.5
6	Michigan	2.3
6	Pennsylvania	2.3
8	Hawaii	2.1
8	New Jersey	2.1
10	Montana	1.9
11	Florida	1.8
11	Illinois	1.8
11	Texas	1.8
14	Georgia	1.7
15	Idaho	1.6
15	Louisiana	1.6
15	Tennessee	1.6
18	Arkansas	1.4
18	Indiana	1.4
18	Minnesota	1.4
18	North Dakota	1.4
18	South Carolina	1.4
23	Wisconsin	1.3
24	Maryland	1.2
24	Utah	1.2
24	Virginia	1.2
27	Colorado	1.1
27	Mississippi	1.1
27	Missouri	1.1
27	Nebraska	1.1
31	New York	1.0
31	Wyoming	1.0
33	Alabama	0.9
33	Kansas	0.9
33	Oregon	0.9
33	South Dakota	0.9
37	Oklahoma	0.8
37	West Virginia	0.8
39	Iowa	0.7
40	Delaware	0.6
40	New Hampshire	0.6
42	Alaska	0.5
43	Connecticut	0.4
43	Kentucky	0.4
43	Maine	0.4
43	Massachusetts	0.4
43	New Mexico	0.4
43	Rhode Island	0.4
49	North Carolina	0.3
50	Vermont	0.2

District of Columbia   3.3

Source: Morgan Quitno Press using data from U.S. Bureau of the Census
"Government Finances: 1993-1994" (1997) (http://www.census.gov/govs/www/esti94.html)
*Includes Courts, Prosecution and Legal Services and Public Defense.

State and Local Government Judicial and Legal Payroll in 1995

National Total = $11,924,751,660*

ALPHA ORDER

RANK ORDER

RANK	STATE	PAYROLL	% of USA		RANK	STATE	PAYROLL	% of USA
23	Alabama	$136,609,260	1.15%		1	California	$1,916,338,068	16.07%
37	Alaska	58,151,856	0.49%		2	New York	1,297,945,668	10.88%
12	Arizona	245,938,836	2.06%		3	Florida	813,111,000	6.82%
38	Arkansas	55,487,316	0.47%		4	New Jersey	690,990,684	5.79%
1	California	1,916,338,068	16.07%		5	Texas	622,286,160	5.22%
19	Colorado	186,187,284	1.56%		6	Illinois	555,710,100	4.66%
26	Connecticut	126,396,336	1.06%		7	Ohio	462,723,648	3.88%
41	Delaware	46,992,924	0.39%		8	Pennsylvania	457,367,124	3.84%
3	Florida	813,111,000	6.82%		9	Michigan	390,378,708	3.27%
13	Georgia	244,023,120	2.05%		10	Washington	264,309,684	2.22%
30	Hawaii	99,645,480	0.84%		11	Massachusetts	256,005,612	2.15%
43	Idaho	45,426,360	0.38%		12	Arizona	245,938,836	2.06%
6	Illinois	555,710,100	4.66%		13	Georgia	244,023,120	2.05%
22	Indiana	142,154,568	1.19%		14	Minnesota	209,025,216	1.75%
29	Iowa	109,295,808	0.92%		15	Maryland	205,762,068	1.73%
32	Kansas	92,129,556	0.77%		16	Virginia	203,910,960	1.71%
25	Kentucky	128,047,236	1.07%		17	North Carolina	197,217,888	1.65%
21	Louisiana	162,227,952	1.36%		18	Wisconsin	192,772,296	1.62%
49	Maine	23,020,140	0.19%		19	Colorado	186,187,284	1.56%
15	Maryland	205,762,068	1.73%		20	Tennessee	163,223,520	1.37%
11	Massachusetts	256,005,612	2.15%		21	Louisiana	162,227,952	1.36%
9	Michigan	390,378,708	3.27%		22	Indiana	142,154,568	1.19%
14	Minnesota	209,025,216	1.75%		23	Alabama	136,609,260	1.15%
35	Mississippi	72,642,252	0.61%		24	Oregon	132,095,664	1.11%
27	Missouri	116,000,448	0.97%		25	Kentucky	128,047,236	1.07%
45	Montana	24,283,176	0.20%		26	Connecticut	126,396,336	1.06%
39	Nebraska	49,630,356	0.42%		27	Missouri	116,000,448	0.97%
28	Nevada	114,713,940	0.96%		28	Nevada	114,713,940	0.96%
44	New Hampshire	29,859,672	0.25%		29	Iowa	109,295,808	0.92%
4	New Jersey	690,990,684	5.79%		30	Hawaii	99,645,480	0.84%
34	New Mexico	75,371,292	0.63%		31	Oklahoma	94,243,584	0.79%
2	New York	1,297,945,668	10.88%		32	Kansas	92,129,556	0.77%
17	North Carolina	197,217,888	1.65%		33	South Carolina	87,819,792	0.74%
47	North Dakota	23,449,176	0.20%		34	New Mexico	75,371,292	0.63%
7	Ohio	462,723,648	3.88%		35	Mississippi	72,642,252	0.61%
31	Oklahoma	94,243,584	0.79%		36	Utah	67,056,696	0.56%
24	Oregon	132,095,664	1.11%		37	Alaska	58,151,856	0.49%
8	Pennsylvania	457,367,124	3.84%		38	Arkansas	55,487,316	0.47%
40	Rhode Island	48,118,512	0.40%		39	Nebraska	49,630,356	0.42%
33	South Carolina	87,819,792	0.74%		40	Rhode Island	48,118,512	0.40%
48	South Dakota	23,225,280	0.19%		41	Delaware	46,992,924	0.39%
20	Tennessee	163,223,520	1.37%		42	West Virginia	46,740,480	0.39%
5	Texas	622,286,160	5.22%		43	Idaho	45,426,360	0.38%
36	Utah	67,056,696	0.56%		44	New Hampshire	29,859,672	0.25%
50	Vermont	18,484,524	0.16%		45	Montana	24,283,176	0.20%
16	Virginia	203,910,960	1.71%		46	Wyoming	23,834,184	0.20%
10	Washington	264,309,684	2.22%		47	North Dakota	23,449,176	0.20%
42	West Virginia	46,740,480	0.39%		48	South Dakota	23,225,280	0.19%
18	Wisconsin	192,772,296	1.62%		49	Maine	23,020,140	0.19%
46	Wyoming	23,834,184	0.20%		50	Vermont	18,484,524	0.16%
						District of Columbia	76,370,196	0.64%

Source: U.S. Bureau of the Census, Governments Division
"1995 State and Local Government Employment" (http://www.census.gov/govs/www/apes95sl.html)
*Twelve times the October 1995 full and part time payroll. Includes court and court related activities (except probation and parole which are part of corrections), court activities of sheriffs' offices, prosecuting attorneys' and public defenders' offices, legal departments and attorneys providing government-wide legal service.

State and Local Government Police Protection Payroll in 1995

National Total = $29,721,280,788*

ALPHA ORDER

RANK	STATE	PAYROLL	% of USA
25	Alabama	$316,179,984	1.06%
41	Alaska	103,855,968	0.35%
18	Arizona	475,795,944	1.60%
34	Arkansas	150,816,096	0.51%
1	California	4,540,096,860	15.28%
22	Colorado	392,179,392	1.32%
19	Connecticut	445,772,820	1.50%
44	Delaware	82,874,736	0.28%
4	Florida	1,797,400,944	6.05%
12	Georgia	586,015,716	1.97%
37	Hawaii	137,704,272	0.46%
42	Idaho	102,618,192	0.35%
3	Illinois	1,860,497,208	6.26%
20	Indiana	405,456,396	1.36%
31	Iowa	211,549,116	0.71%
29	Kansas	226,843,860	0.76%
30	Kentucky	216,768,888	0.73%
24	Louisiana	337,949,256	1.14%
43	Maine	86,218,728	0.29%
11	Maryland	586,045,872	1.97%
10	Massachusetts	735,335,484	2.47%
9	Michigan	920,579,340	3.10%
21	Minnesota	397,646,148	1.34%
33	Mississippi	176,300,196	0.59%
17	Missouri	490,154,832	1.65%
46	Montana	59,009,604	0.20%
38	Nebraska	134,608,272	0.45%
32	Nevada	206,638,200	0.70%
40	New Hampshire	111,408,444	0.37%
6	New Jersey	1,539,200,352	5.18%
36	New Mexico	139,406,604	0.47%
2	New York	3,632,610,312	12.22%
14	North Carolina	562,082,532	1.89%
50	North Dakota	36,806,724	0.12%
8	Ohio	1,075,130,676	3.62%
28	Oklahoma	264,462,984	0.89%
26	Oregon	306,612,192	1.03%
7	Pennsylvania	1,159,610,976	3.90%
39	Rhode Island	121,935,756	0.41%
27	South Carolina	283,304,280	0.95%
49	South Dakota	43,354,188	0.15%
23	Tennessee	383,887,140	1.29%
5	Texas	1,746,122,184	5.87%
35	Utah	148,653,048	0.50%
47	Vermont	48,216,804	0.16%
13	Virginia	577,816,608	1.94%
15	Washington	537,328,572	1.81%
45	West Virginia	81,149,364	0.27%
16	Wisconsin	498,652,128	1.68%
48	Wyoming	46,084,428	0.16%

RANK ORDER

RANK	STATE	PAYROLL	% of USA
1	California	$4,540,096,860	15.28%
2	New York	3,632,610,312	12.22%
3	Illinois	1,860,497,208	6.26%
4	Florida	1,797,400,944	6.05%
5	Texas	1,746,122,184	5.87%
6	New Jersey	1,539,200,352	5.18%
7	Pennsylvania	1,159,610,976	3.90%
8	Ohio	1,075,130,676	3.62%
9	Michigan	920,579,340	3.10%
10	Massachusetts	735,335,484	2.47%
11	Maryland	586,045,872	1.97%
12	Georgia	586,015,716	1.97%
13	Virginia	577,816,608	1.94%
14	North Carolina	562,082,532	1.89%
15	Washington	537,328,572	1.81%
16	Wisconsin	498,652,128	1.68%
17	Missouri	490,154,832	1.65%
18	Arizona	475,795,944	1.60%
19	Connecticut	445,772,820	1.50%
20	Indiana	405,456,396	1.36%
21	Minnesota	397,646,148	1.34%
22	Colorado	392,179,392	1.32%
23	Tennessee	383,887,140	1.29%
24	Louisiana	337,949,256	1.14%
25	Alabama	316,179,984	1.06%
26	Oregon	306,612,192	1.03%
27	South Carolina	283,304,280	0.95%
28	Oklahoma	264,462,984	0.89%
29	Kansas	226,843,860	0.76%
30	Kentucky	216,768,888	0.73%
31	Iowa	211,549,116	0.71%
32	Nevada	206,638,200	0.70%
33	Mississippi	176,300,196	0.59%
34	Arkansas	150,816,096	0.51%
35	Utah	148,653,048	0.50%
36	New Mexico	139,406,604	0.47%
37	Hawaii	137,704,272	0.46%
38	Nebraska	134,608,272	0.45%
39	Rhode Island	121,935,756	0.41%
40	New Hampshire	111,408,444	0.37%
41	Alaska	103,855,968	0.35%
42	Idaho	102,618,192	0.35%
43	Maine	86,218,728	0.29%
44	Delaware	82,874,736	0.28%
45	West Virginia	81,149,364	0.27%
46	Montana	59,009,604	0.20%
47	Vermont	48,216,804	0.16%
48	Wyoming	46,084,428	0.16%
49	South Dakota	43,354,188	0.15%
50	North Dakota	36,806,724	0.12%
	District of Columbia	194,532,168	0.65%

Source: U.S. Bureau of the Census, Governments Division
"1995 State and Local Government Employment" (http://www.census.gov/govs/www/apes95sl.html)
*Twelve times the October 1995 full and part time payroll. Includes all activities concerned with the enforcement of law and order, including coroners' offices, police training academies, investigation bureaus and local jails.

State and Local Government Corrections Payroll in 1995

National Total = $19,443,945,636*

ALPHA ORDER

RANK	STATE	PAYROLL	% of USA
27	Alabama	$179,046,504	0.92%
41	Alaska	58,018,464	0.30%
15	Arizona	327,658,428	1.69%
35	Arkansas	97,267,572	0.50%
1	California	2,919,221,748	15.01%
22	Colorado	241,428,108	1.24%
19	Connecticut	263,064,168	1.35%
42	Delaware	57,044,472	0.29%
4	Florida	1,318,425,780	6.78%
10	Georgia	621,128,820	3.19%
40	Hawaii	61,536,360	0.32%
39	Idaho	61,732,776	0.32%
7	Illinois	741,396,912	3.81%
21	Indiana	249,254,796	1.28%
33	Iowa	100,929,012	0.52%
31	Kansas	144,409,296	0.74%
28	Kentucky	172,818,684	0.89%
24	Louisiana	213,230,148	1.10%
44	Maine	50,443,068	0.26%
12	Maryland	422,674,608	2.17%
13	Massachusetts	382,681,596	1.97%
5	Michigan	797,417,808	4.10%
20	Minnesota	254,291,352	1.31%
34	Mississippi	98,979,600	0.51%
26	Missouri	188,918,436	0.97%
45	Montana	29,358,372	0.15%
38	Nebraska	66,723,744	0.34%
29	Nevada	160,492,728	0.83%
43	New Hampshire	52,194,264	0.27%
9	New Jersey	670,403,772	3.45%
32	New Mexico	141,342,744	0.73%
2	New York	2,463,290,892	12.67%
14	North Carolina	382,080,360	1.97%
50	North Dakota	17,214,744	0.09%
8	Ohio	702,146,580	3.61%
30	Oklahoma	152,703,732	0.79%
25	Oregon	192,517,752	0.99%
6	Pennsylvania	741,553,380	3.81%
36	Rhode Island	89,568,288	0.46%
23	South Carolina	226,021,572	1.16%
46	South Dakota	23,046,996	0.12%
17	Tennessee	276,832,620	1.42%
3	Texas	1,565,311,728	8.05%
37	Utah	88,006,656	0.45%
48	Vermont	21,105,384	0.11%
11	Virginia	548,900,436	2.82%
16	Washington	315,152,688	1.62%
47	West Virginia	22,791,948	0.12%
18	Wisconsin	274,563,528	1.41%
49	Wyoming	18,417,636	0.09%

RANK ORDER

RANK	STATE	PAYROLL	% of USA
1	California	$2,919,221,748	15.01%
2	New York	2,463,290,892	12.67%
3	Texas	1,565,311,728	8.05%
4	Florida	1,318,425,780	6.78%
5	Michigan	797,417,808	4.10%
6	Pennsylvania	741,553,380	3.81%
7	Illinois	741,396,912	3.81%
8	Ohio	702,146,580	3.61%
9	New Jersey	670,403,772	3.45%
10	Georgia	621,128,820	3.19%
11	Virginia	548,900,436	2.82%
12	Maryland	422,674,608	2.17%
13	Massachusetts	382,681,596	1.97%
14	North Carolina	382,080,360	1.97%
15	Arizona	327,658,428	1.69%
16	Washington	315,152,688	1.62%
17	Tennessee	276,832,620	1.42%
18	Wisconsin	274,563,528	1.41%
19	Connecticut	263,064,168	1.35%
20	Minnesota	254,291,352	1.31%
21	Indiana	249,254,796	1.28%
22	Colorado	241,428,108	1.24%
23	South Carolina	226,021,572	1.16%
24	Louisiana	213,230,148	1.10%
25	Oregon	192,517,752	0.99%
26	Missouri	188,918,436	0.97%
27	Alabama	179,046,504	0.92%
28	Kentucky	172,818,684	0.89%
29	Nevada	160,492,728	0.83%
30	Oklahoma	152,703,732	0.79%
31	Kansas	144,409,296	0.74%
32	New Mexico	141,342,744	0.73%
33	Iowa	100,929,012	0.52%
34	Mississippi	98,979,600	0.51%
35	Arkansas	97,267,572	0.50%
36	Rhode Island	89,568,288	0.46%
37	Utah	88,006,656	0.45%
38	Nebraska	66,723,744	0.34%
39	Idaho	61,732,776	0.32%
40	Hawaii	61,536,360	0.32%
41	Alaska	58,018,464	0.30%
42	Delaware	57,044,472	0.29%
43	New Hampshire	52,194,264	0.27%
44	Maine	50,443,068	0.26%
45	Montana	29,358,372	0.15%
46	South Dakota	23,046,996	0.12%
47	West Virginia	22,791,948	0.12%
48	Vermont	21,105,384	0.11%
49	Wyoming	18,417,636	0.09%
50	North Dakota	17,214,744	0.09%
	District of Columbia	179,184,576	0.92%

Source: U.S. Bureau of the Census, Governments Division
  "1995 State and Local Government Employment" (http://www.census.gov/govs/www/apes95sl.html)
Twelve times the October 1995 full and part time payroll. Includes all activities pertaining to the confinement and correction of adults and minors accused or convicted of criminal offenses. Includes any pardon, probation or parole activity.

Base Salary for Justices of States' Highest Courts in 1997

National Average = $101,782

RANK	STATE	SALARY
9	Alabama	115,695
13	Alaska	109,908
15	Arizona	108,816
24	Arkansas	102,633
3	California	131,085
38	Colorado	91,000
11	Connecticut	113,042
10	Delaware	113,700
1	Florida	133,600
8	Georgia	119,529
36	Hawaii	93,780
46	Idaho	83,142
4	Illinois	126,579
21	Indiana	105,000
26	Iowa	100,600
37	Kansas	93,226
34	Kentucky	94,095
28	Louisiana	99,800
41	Maine	88,003
19	Maryland	107,300
16	Massachusetts	107,730
7	Michigan	121,727
33	Minnesota	94,395
39	Mississippi	90,800
20	Missouri	105,717
50	Montana	68,874
31	Nebraska	94,891
42	Nevada	85,000
30	New Hampshire	95,623
2	New Jersey	132,250
45	New Mexico	83,593
5	New York	125,000
27	North Carolina	100,320
48	North Dakota	77,448
18	Ohio	107,350
35	Oklahoma	94,000
40	Oregon	89,600
6	Pennsylvania	122,864
17	Rhode Island	107,535
23	South Carolina	103,850
49	South Dakota	76,468
22	Tennessee	104,676
32	Texas	94,686
29	Utah	98,500
47	Vermont	83,072
12	Virginia	112,044
14	Washington	109,880
42	West Virginia	85,000
25	Wisconsin	100,690
42	Wyoming	85,000

RANK	STATE	SALARY
1	Florida	133,600
2	New Jersey	132,250
3	California	131,085
4	Illinois	126,579
5	New York	125,000
6	Pennsylvania	122,864
7	Michigan	121,727
8	Georgia	119,529
9	Alabama	115,695
10	Delaware	113,700
11	Connecticut	113,042
12	Virginia	112,044
13	Alaska	109,908
14	Washington	109,880
15	Arizona	108,816
16	Massachusetts	107,730
17	Rhode Island	107,535
18	Ohio	107,350
19	Maryland	107,300
20	Missouri	105,717
21	Indiana	105,000
22	Tennessee	104,676
23	South Carolina	103,850
24	Arkansas	102,633
25	Wisconsin	100,690
26	Iowa	100,600
27	North Carolina	100,320
28	Louisiana	99,800
29	Utah	98,500
30	New Hampshire	95,623
31	Nebraska	94,891
32	Texas	94,686
33	Minnesota	94,395
34	Kentucky	94,095
35	Oklahoma	94,000
36	Hawaii	93,780
37	Kansas	93,226
38	Colorado	91,000
39	Mississippi	90,800
40	Oregon	89,600
41	Maine	88,003
42	Nevada	85,000
42	West Virginia	85,000
42	Wyoming	85,000
45	New Mexico	83,593
46	Idaho	83,142
47	Vermont	83,072
48	North Dakota	77,448
49	South Dakota	76,468
50	Montana	68,874

	District of Columbia	141,700

Source: National Center for State Courts
"Survey of Judicial Salaries-Winter 1997" (Volume 22, Number 1)

Base Salary of Judges of Intermediate Appellate Courts in 1997

National Average = $100,406

ALPHA ORDER

RANK	STATE	SALARY
8	Alabama	$114,615
14	Alaska	103,824
11	Arizona	106,225
19	Arkansas	99,388
2	California	122,893
36	Colorado	86,500
12	Connecticut	105,111
NA	Delaware*	NA
3	Florida	120,240
7	Georgia	118,771
32	Hawaii	89,780
38	Idaho	82,142
4	Illinois	119,133
24	Indiana	95,000
22	Iowa	96,700
31	Kansas	89,898
29	Kentucky	90,254
26	Louisiana	94,600
NA	Maine*	NA
15	Maryland	100,300
18	Massachusetts	99,690
9	Michigan	114,007
33	Minnesota	88,945
37	Mississippi	84,000
20	Missouri	98,727
NA	Montana*	NA
30	Nebraska	90,146
NA	Nevada*	NA
NA	New Hampshire*	NA
1	New Jersey	124,200
39	New Mexico	79,413
6	New York	119,000
23	North Carolina	96,140
NA	North Dakota*	NA
16	Ohio	99,950
34	Oklahoma	88,000
35	Oregon	87,600
5	Pennsylvania	119,016
NA	Rhode Island*	NA
21	South Carolina	98,659
NA	South Dakota*	NA
17	Tennessee	99,804
28	Texas	93,435
27	Utah	94,050
NA	Vermont*	NA
10	Virginia	106,442
13	Washington	104,448
NA	West Virginia*	NA
25	Wisconsin	94,804
NA	Wyoming*	NA

RANK ORDER

RANK	STATE	SALARY
1	New Jersey	$124,200
2	California	122,893
3	Florida	120,240
4	Illinois	119,133
5	Pennsylvania	119,016
6	New York	119,000
7	Georgia	118,771
8	Alabama	114,615
9	Michigan	114,007
10	Virginia	106,442
11	Arizona	106,225
12	Connecticut	105,111
13	Washington	104,448
14	Alaska	103,824
15	Maryland	100,300
16	Ohio	99,950
17	Tennessee	99,804
18	Massachusetts	99,690
19	Arkansas	99,388
20	Missouri	98,727
21	South Carolina	98,659
22	Iowa	96,700
23	North Carolina	96,140
24	Indiana	95,000
25	Wisconsin	94,804
26	Louisiana	94,600
27	Utah	94,050
28	Texas	93,435
29	Kentucky	90,254
30	Nebraska	90,146
31	Kansas	89,898
32	Hawaii	89,780
33	Minnesota	88,945
34	Oklahoma	88,000
35	Oregon	87,600
36	Colorado	86,500
37	Mississippi	84,000
38	Idaho	82,142
39	New Mexico	79,413
NA	Delaware*	NA
NA	Maine*	NA
NA	Montana*	NA
NA	Nevada*	NA
NA	New Hampshire*	NA
NA	North Dakota*	NA
NA	Rhode Island*	NA
NA	South Dakota*	NA
NA	Vermont*	NA
NA	West Virginia*	NA
NA	Wyoming*	NA
NA	District of Columbia*	NA

Source: National Center for State Courts
"Survey of Judicial Salaries-Winter 1997" (Volume 22, Number 1)
*No intermediate court.

Base Salaries of Judges of General Trial Courts in 1997

National Average = $91,018

<table>
<tr><th colspan="3">ALPHA ORDER</th><th colspan="3">RANK ORDER</th></tr>
<tr><th>RANK</th><th>STATE</th><th>SALARY</th><th>RANK</th><th>STATE</th><th>SALARY</th></tr>
<tr><td>41</td><td>Alabama</td><td>$80,615</td><td>1</td><td>New Jersey</td><td>$115,000</td></tr>
<tr><td>12</td><td>Alaska</td><td>101,628</td><td>2</td><td>New York</td><td>113,000</td></tr>
<tr><td>11</td><td>Arizona</td><td>103,634</td><td>3</td><td>Illinois</td><td>109,321</td></tr>
<tr><td>18</td><td>Arkansas</td><td>96,137</td><td>4</td><td>Delaware</td><td>108,100</td></tr>
<tr><td>6</td><td>California</td><td>107,390</td><td>5</td><td>Florida</td><td>107,758</td></tr>
<tr><td>35</td><td>Colorado</td><td>82,000</td><td>6</td><td>California</td><td>107,390</td></tr>
<tr><td>13</td><td>Connecticut</td><td>100,411</td><td>7</td><td>Pennsylvania</td><td>106,704</td></tr>
<tr><td>4</td><td>Delaware</td><td>108,100</td><td>8</td><td>Michigan</td><td>104,863</td></tr>
<tr><td>5</td><td>Florida</td><td>107,758</td><td>9</td><td>Virginia</td><td>104,014</td></tr>
<tr><td>10</td><td>Georgia</td><td>103,782</td><td>10</td><td>Georgia</td><td>103,782</td></tr>
<tr><td>30</td><td>Hawaii</td><td>86,780</td><td>11</td><td>Arizona</td><td>103,634</td></tr>
<tr><td>45</td><td>Idaho</td><td>77,926</td><td>12</td><td>Alaska</td><td>101,628</td></tr>
<tr><td>3</td><td>Illinois</td><td>109,321</td><td>13</td><td>Connecticut</td><td>100,411</td></tr>
<tr><td>32</td><td>Indiana</td><td>85,000</td><td>14</td><td>Washington</td><td>99,015</td></tr>
<tr><td>22</td><td>Iowa</td><td>92,000</td><td>15</td><td>South Carolina</td><td>98,659</td></tr>
<tr><td>39</td><td>Kansas</td><td>81,046</td><td>16</td><td>Rhode Island</td><td>96,817</td></tr>
<tr><td>31</td><td>Kentucky</td><td>86,413</td><td>17</td><td>Maryland</td><td>96,500</td></tr>
<tr><td>28</td><td>Louisiana</td><td>89,400</td><td>18</td><td>Arkansas</td><td>96,137</td></tr>
<tr><td>34</td><td>Maine</td><td>83,226</td><td>19</td><td>Massachusetts</td><td>95,710</td></tr>
<tr><td>17</td><td>Maryland</td><td>96,500</td><td>20</td><td>Tennessee</td><td>95,496</td></tr>
<tr><td>19</td><td>Massachusetts</td><td>95,710</td><td>21</td><td>Texas</td><td>92,686</td></tr>
<tr><td>8</td><td>Michigan</td><td>104,863</td><td>22</td><td>Iowa</td><td>92,000</td></tr>
<tr><td>33</td><td>Minnesota</td><td>83,494</td><td>23</td><td>Missouri</td><td>91,463</td></tr>
<tr><td>38</td><td>Mississippi</td><td>81,200</td><td>24</td><td>North Carolina</td><td>90,915</td></tr>
<tr><td>23</td><td>Missouri</td><td>91,463</td><td>25</td><td>Wisconsin</td><td>90,661</td></tr>
<tr><td>50</td><td>Montana</td><td>67,513</td><td>26</td><td>New Hampshire</td><td>89,646</td></tr>
<tr><td>29</td><td>Nebraska</td><td>87,775</td><td>27</td><td>Utah</td><td>89,550</td></tr>
<tr><td>43</td><td>Nevada</td><td>79,000</td><td>28</td><td>Louisiana</td><td>89,400</td></tr>
<tr><td>26</td><td>New Hampshire</td><td>89,646</td><td>29</td><td>Nebraska</td><td>87,775</td></tr>
<tr><td>1</td><td>New Jersey</td><td>115,000</td><td>30</td><td>Hawaii</td><td>86,780</td></tr>
<tr><td>47</td><td>New Mexico</td><td>75,443</td><td>31</td><td>Kentucky</td><td>86,413</td></tr>
<tr><td>2</td><td>New York</td><td>113,000</td><td>32</td><td>Indiana</td><td>85,000</td></tr>
<tr><td>24</td><td>North Carolina</td><td>90,915</td><td>33</td><td>Minnesota</td><td>83,494</td></tr>
<tr><td>48</td><td>North Dakota</td><td>71,472</td><td>34</td><td>Maine</td><td>83,226</td></tr>
<tr><td>40</td><td>Ohio</td><td>80,800</td><td>35</td><td>Colorado</td><td>82,000</td></tr>
<tr><td>35</td><td>Oklahoma</td><td>82,000</td><td>35</td><td>Oklahoma</td><td>82,000</td></tr>
<tr><td>37</td><td>Oregon</td><td>81,600</td><td>37</td><td>Oregon</td><td>81,600</td></tr>
<tr><td>7</td><td>Pennsylvania</td><td>106,704</td><td>38</td><td>Mississippi</td><td>81,200</td></tr>
<tr><td>16</td><td>Rhode Island</td><td>96,817</td><td>39</td><td>Kansas</td><td>81,046</td></tr>
<tr><td>15</td><td>South Carolina</td><td>98,659</td><td>40</td><td>Ohio</td><td>80,800</td></tr>
<tr><td>49</td><td>South Dakota</td><td>71,413</td><td>41</td><td>Alabama</td><td>80,615</td></tr>
<tr><td>20</td><td>Tennessee</td><td>95,496</td><td>42</td><td>West Virginia</td><td>80,000</td></tr>
<tr><td>21</td><td>Texas</td><td>92,686</td><td>43</td><td>Nevada</td><td>79,000</td></tr>
<tr><td>27</td><td>Utah</td><td>89,550</td><td>44</td><td>Vermont</td><td>78,910</td></tr>
<tr><td>44</td><td>Vermont</td><td>78,910</td><td>45</td><td>Idaho</td><td>77,926</td></tr>
<tr><td>9</td><td>Virginia</td><td>104,014</td><td>46</td><td>Wyoming</td><td>77,000</td></tr>
<tr><td>14</td><td>Washington</td><td>99,015</td><td>47</td><td>New Mexico</td><td>75,443</td></tr>
<tr><td>42</td><td>West Virginia</td><td>80,000</td><td>48</td><td>North Dakota</td><td>71,472</td></tr>
<tr><td>25</td><td>Wisconsin</td><td>90,661</td><td>49</td><td>South Dakota</td><td>71,413</td></tr>
<tr><td>46</td><td>Wyoming</td><td>77,000</td><td>50</td><td>Montana</td><td>67,513</td></tr>
<tr><td></td><td></td><td></td><td></td><td>District of Columbia</td><td>133,600</td></tr>
</table>

Source: National Center for State Courts
"Survey of Judicial Salaries-Winter 1997" (Volume 22, Number 1)

V. JUVENILES

V. JUVENILES (continued)

Important Note Regarding Juvenile Arrest Rates

The juvenile arrest rates shown in tables 194 to 247 were calculated by the editors as follows:

The state arrest numbers reported by the FBI are only from those law enforcement agencies that submitted complete arrests reports for 12 months in 1996. Included in the FBI report are population totals of these reporting jurisdictions by state. Using these FBI population figures, we first determined what percentage the FBI numbers represented of each state's total resident population. Next, using 1996 US Census Bureau state estimates for 10 to 17 year olds, we multiplied the percentages derived from the FBI population figures into the Census Bureau's total juvenile population estimates. The resulting juvenile population is the base that was used to determine juvenile arrests per 100,000 juvenile population. The national rate was calculated in the same manner.

Reports from law enforcement agencies in Illinois, Mississippi, Kentucky and Tennessee represented less than half of their state populations. Thus the rates for these states may be somewhat skewed.

Reported Arrests of Juveniles in 1996

National Total = 2,103,658 Reported Arrests*

ALPHA ORDER

RANK	STATE	ARRESTS	% of USA
32	Alabama	18,217	0.87%
44	Alaska	5,791	0.28%
8	Arizona	68,974	3.28%
30	Arkansas	21,473	1.02%
1	California	268,835	12.78%
17	Colorado	40,182	1.91%
25	Connecticut	27,006	1.28%
45	Delaware	5,485	0.26%
NA	Florida**	NA	NA
21	Georgia	34,004	1.62%
33	Hawaii	17,334	0.82%
26	Idaho	24,513	1.17%
9	Illinois	68,630	3.26%
19	Indiana	38,458	1.83%
31	Iowa	19,183	0.91%
NA	Kansas**	NA	NA
41	Kentucky	9,044	0.43%
22	Louisiana	33,272	1.58%
36	Maine	12,801	0.61%
14	Maryland	48,856	2.32%
28	Massachusetts	23,230	1.10%
13	Michigan	51,552	2.45%
10	Minnesota	65,992	3.14%
39	Mississippi	9,486	0.45%
18	Missouri	39,412	1.87%
NA	Montana**	NA	NA
35	Nebraska	14,511	0.69%
29	Nevada	22,092	1.05%
38	New Hampshire	9,610	0.46%
6	New Jersey	84,973	4.04%
34	New Mexico	15,450	0.73%
4	New York	105,731	5.03%
11	North Carolina	56,032	2.66%
43	North Dakota	6,120	0.29%
7	Ohio	81,029	3.85%
23	Oklahoma	30,715	1.46%
16	Oregon	45,755	2.18%
5	Pennsylvania	97,297	4.63%
40	Rhode Island	9,128	0.43%
24	South Carolina	29,729	1.41%
37	South Dakota	10,427	0.50%
27	Tennessee	23,810	1.13%
2	Texas	212,368	10.10%
20	Utah	36,408	1.73%
NA	Vermont**	NA	NA
12	Virginia	55,592	2.64%
15	Washington	47,544	2.26%
42	West Virginia	7,881	0.37%
3	Wisconsin	144,403	6.86%
46	Wyoming	5,323	0.25%

RANK ORDER

RANK	STATE	ARRESTS	% of USA
1	California	268,835	12.78%
2	Texas	212,368	10.10%
3	Wisconsin	144,403	6.86%
4	New York	105,731	5.03%
5	Pennsylvania	97,297	4.63%
6	New Jersey	84,973	4.04%
7	Ohio	81,029	3.85%
8	Arizona	68,974	3.28%
9	Illinois	68,630	3.26%
10	Minnesota	65,992	3.14%
11	North Carolina	56,032	2.66%
12	Virginia	55,592	2.64%
13	Michigan	51,552	2.45%
14	Maryland	48,856	2.32%
15	Washington	47,544	2.26%
16	Oregon	45,755	2.18%
17	Colorado	40,182	1.91%
18	Missouri	39,412	1.87%
19	Indiana	38,458	1.83%
20	Utah	36,408	1.73%
21	Georgia	34,004	1.62%
22	Louisiana	33,272	1.58%
23	Oklahoma	30,715	1.46%
24	South Carolina	29,729	1.41%
25	Connecticut	27,006	1.28%
26	Idaho	24,513	1.17%
27	Tennessee	23,810	1.13%
28	Massachusetts	23,230	1.10%
29	Nevada	22,092	1.05%
30	Arkansas	21,473	1.02%
31	Iowa	19,183	0.91%
32	Alabama	18,217	0.87%
33	Hawaii	17,334	0.82%
34	New Mexico	15,450	0.73%
35	Nebraska	14,511	0.69%
36	Maine	12,801	0.61%
37	South Dakota	10,427	0.50%
38	New Hampshire	9,610	0.46%
39	Mississippi	9,486	0.45%
40	Rhode Island	9,128	0.43%
41	Kentucky	9,044	0.43%
42	West Virginia	7,881	0.37%
43	North Dakota	6,120	0.29%
44	Alaska	5,791	0.28%
45	Delaware	5,485	0.26%
46	Wyoming	5,323	0.25%
NA	Florida**	NA	NA
NA	Kansas**	NA	NA
NA	Montana**	NA	NA
NA	Vermont**	NA	NA
	District of Columbia**	NA	NA

Source: Federal Bureau of Investigation
   "Crime in the United States 1996" (Uniform Crime Reports, October 4, 1997)
*Arrests of youths 17 years and younger by law enforcement agencies submitting complete reports to the F.B.I. for 12 months in 1996. See important note at beginning of this chapter.
**Not available.

Reported Juvenile Arrest Rate in 1996

National Rate = 9,691.2 Reported Arrests per 100,000 Juvenile Population*

ALPHA ORDER

RANK ORDER

RANK	STATE	RATE		RANK	STATE	RATE
45	Alabama	3,874.2		1	Wisconsin	22,751.7
34	Alaska	8,062.2		2	Illinois	21,677.2
4	Arizona	15,050.0		3	South Dakota	15,475.6
37	Arkansas	7,439.6		4	Arizona	15,050.0
36	California	7,730.3		5	Idaho	14,930.3
14	Colorado	12,076.7		6	Oregon	14,305.9
24	Connecticut	10,289.1		7	Delaware	14,074.6
7	Delaware	14,074.6		8	Wyoming	13,536.3
NA	Florida**	NA		9	Hawaii	13,512.2
42	Georgia	6,509.6		10	Nevada	12,952.9
9	Hawaii	13,512.2		11	Utah	12,675.0
5	Idaho	14,930.3		12	Minnesota	12,512.3
2	Illinois	21,677.2		13	North Dakota	12,113.3
26	Indiana	10,008.9		14	Colorado	12,076.7
41	Iowa	6,879.6		15	Mississippi	11,629.6
NA	Kansas**	NA		16	New Mexico	11,575.1
25	Kentucky	10,211.9		17	Maryland	11,201.8
29	Louisiana	9,468.8		18	Ohio	10,843.4
32	Maine	9,047.5		19	Washington	10,810.4
17	Maryland	11,201.8		20	Missouri	10,648.2
44	Massachusetts	4,608.6		21	New Jersey	10,585.3
43	Michigan	5,473.3		22	Tennessee	10,331.9
12	Minnesota	12,512.3		23	Texas	10,312.9
15	Mississippi	11,629.6		24	Connecticut	10,289.1
20	Missouri	10,648.2		25	Kentucky	10,211.9
NA	Montana**	NA		26	Indiana	10,008.9
27	Nebraska	9,694.7		27	Nebraska	9,694.7
10	Nevada	12,952.9		28	Pennsylvania	9,585.3
30	New Hampshire	9,416.7		29	Louisiana	9,468.8
21	New Jersey	10,585.3		30	New Hampshire	9,416.7
16	New Mexico	11,575.1		31	Rhode Island	9,359.7
35	New York	8,006.1		32	Maine	9,047.5
39	North Carolina	7,171.9		33	Virginia	8,436.0
13	North Dakota	12,113.3		34	Alaska	8,062.2
18	Ohio	10,843.4		35	New York	8,006.1
38	Oklahoma	7,422.6		36	California	7,730.3
6	Oregon	14,305.9		37	Arkansas	7,439.6
28	Pennsylvania	9,585.3		38	Oklahoma	7,422.6
31	Rhode Island	9,359.7		39	North Carolina	7,171.9
40	South Carolina	7,169.6		40	South Carolina	7,169.6
3	South Dakota	15,475.6		41	Iowa	6,879.6
22	Tennessee	10,331.9		42	Georgia	6,509.6
23	Texas	10,312.9		43	Michigan	5,473.3
11	Utah	12,675.0		44	Massachusetts	4,608.6
NA	Vermont**	NA		45	Alabama	3,874.2
33	Virginia	8,436.0		46	West Virginia	3,841.5
19	Washington	10,810.4		NA	Florida**	NA
46	West Virginia	3,841.5		NA	Kansas**	NA
1	Wisconsin	22,751.7		NA	Montana**	NA
8	Wyoming	13,536.3		NA	Vermont**	NA

District of Columbia** NA

Source: Morgan Quitno Press using data from Federal Bureau of Investigation
    "Crime in the United States 1996" (Uniform Crime Reports, October 4, 1997)
*By law enforcement agencies submitting complete reports to the F.B.I. for 12 months in 1996. Arrests of youths 17
years and younger divided into population of 10 to 17 year olds. See important note at beginning of this chapter.
**Not available.

Reported Arrests of Juveniles as a Percent of All Arrests in 1996

National Percent = 19.0% of Reported Arrests*

RANK	STATE	PERCENT
46	Alabama	8.5
33	Alaska	16.9
15	Arizona	23.0
45	Arkansas	10.8
32	California	17.1
27	Colorado	18.5
31	Connecticut	17.5
23	Delaware	20.6
NA	Florida**	NA
40	Georgia	13.6
10	Hawaii	26.6
3	Idaho	31.3
17	Illinois	22.7
13	Indiana	23.7
21	Iowa	21.3
NA	Kansas**	NA
34	Kentucky	16.0
26	Louisiana	18.8
14	Maine	23.6
24	Maryland	20.2
35	Massachusetts	14.9
40	Michigan	13.6
5	Minnesota	29.8
28	Mississippi	18.4
38	Missouri	14.5
NA	Montana**	NA
12	Nebraska	24.6
29	Nevada	17.8
9	New Hampshire	27.7
20	New Jersey	21.4
30	New Mexico	17.7
42	New York	12.8
44	North Carolina	11.1
6	North Dakota	28.9
19	Ohio	21.5
25	Oklahoma	20.0
7	Oregon	28.7
8	Pennsylvania	28.1
18	Rhode Island	22.2
39	South Carolina	13.8
1	South Dakota	31.6
36	Tennessee	14.8
22	Texas	20.8
4	Utah	30.2
NA	Vermont**	NA
36	Virginia	14.8
16	Washington	22.8
43	West Virginia	11.2
2	Wisconsin	31.4
11	Wyoming	26.5

RANK	STATE	PERCENT
1	South Dakota	31.6
2	Wisconsin	31.4
3	Idaho	31.3
4	Utah	30.2
5	Minnesota	29.8
6	North Dakota	28.9
7	Oregon	28.7
8	Pennsylvania	28.1
9	New Hampshire	27.7
10	Hawaii	26.6
11	Wyoming	26.5
12	Nebraska	24.6
13	Indiana	23.7
14	Maine	23.6
15	Arizona	23.0
16	Washington	22.8
17	Illinois	22.7
18	Rhode Island	22.2
19	Ohio	21.5
20	New Jersey	21.4
21	Iowa	21.3
22	Texas	20.8
23	Delaware	20.6
24	Maryland	20.2
25	Oklahoma	20.0
26	Louisiana	18.8
27	Colorado	18.5
28	Mississippi	18.4
29	Nevada	17.8
30	New Mexico	17.7
31	Connecticut	17.5
32	California	17.1
33	Alaska	16.9
34	Kentucky	16.0
35	Massachusetts	14.9
36	Tennessee	14.8
36	Virginia	14.8
38	Missouri	14.5
39	South Carolina	13.8
40	Georgia	13.6
40	Michigan	13.6
42	New York	12.8
43	West Virginia	11.2
44	North Carolina	11.1
45	Arkansas	10.8
46	Alabama	8.5
NA	Florida**	NA
NA	Kansas**	NA
NA	Montana**	NA
NA	Vermont**	NA
	District of Columbia**	NA

Source: Morgan Quitno Press using data from Federal Bureau of Investigation
    "Crime in the United States 1996" (Uniform Crime Reports, October 4, 1997)
*Arrests of youths 17 years and younger by law enforcement agencies submitting complete reports to the F.B.I. for 12 months in 1996.
**Not available.

Reported Arrests of Juveniles for Crime Index Offenses in 1996

National Total = 632,762 Reported Arrests*

ALPHA ORDER

RANK	STATE	ARRESTS	% of USA
28	Alabama	7,706	1.22%
41	Alaska	2,574	0.41%
11	Arizona	18,607	2.94%
29	Arkansas	7,349	1.16%
1	California	99,432	15.71%
24	Colorado	10,203	1.61%
25	Connecticut	8,545	1.35%
44	Delaware	2,114	0.33%
NA	Florida**	NA	NA
21	Georgia	11,397	1.80%
35	Hawaii	4,468	0.71%
30	Idaho	7,120	1.13%
16	Illinois	13,669	2.16%
23	Indiana	10,862	1.72%
31	Iowa	6,264	0.99%
NA	Kansas**	NA	NA
37	Kentucky	3,730	0.59%
19	Louisiana	11,708	1.85%
33	Maine	5,090	0.80%
13	Maryland	17,542	2.77%
26	Massachusetts	7,931	1.25%
12	Michigan	18,081	2.86%
9	Minnesota	18,773	2.97%
42	Mississippi	2,392	0.38%
17	Missouri	13,248	2.09%
NA	Montana**	NA	NA
36	Nebraska	4,280	0.68%
32	Nevada	6,077	0.96%
43	New Hampshire	2,361	0.37%
5	New Jersey	22,775	3.60%
34	New Mexico	4,855	0.77%
4	New York	30,697	4.85%
10	North Carolina	18,687	2.95%
45	North Dakota	1,333	0.21%
8	Ohio	19,975	3.16%
18	Oklahoma	12,782	2.02%
15	Oregon	13,810	2.18%
6	Pennsylvania	21,866	3.46%
38	Rhode Island	2,861	0.45%
22	South Carolina	10,999	1.74%
39	South Dakota	2,821	0.45%
27	Tennessee	7,736	1.22%
2	Texas	57,578	9.10%
20	Utah	11,486	1.82%
NA	Vermont**	NA	NA
14	Virginia	15,285	2.42%
7	Washington	20,155	3.19%
40	West Virginia	2,656	0.42%
3	Wisconsin	31,573	4.99%
46	Wyoming	1,309	0.21%

RANK ORDER

RANK	STATE	ARRESTS	% of USA
1	California	99,432	15.71%
2	Texas	57,578	9.10%
3	Wisconsin	31,573	4.99%
4	New York	30,697	4.85%
5	New Jersey	22,775	3.60%
6	Pennsylvania	21,866	3.46%
7	Washington	20,155	3.19%
8	Ohio	19,975	3.16%
9	Minnesota	18,773	2.97%
10	North Carolina	18,687	2.95%
11	Arizona	18,607	2.94%
12	Michigan	18,081	2.86%
13	Maryland	17,542	2.77%
14	Virginia	15,285	2.42%
15	Oregon	13,810	2.18%
16	Illinois	13,669	2.16%
17	Missouri	13,248	2.09%
18	Oklahoma	12,782	2.02%
19	Louisiana	11,708	1.85%
20	Utah	11,486	1.82%
21	Georgia	11,397	1.80%
22	South Carolina	10,999	1.74%
23	Indiana	10,862	1.72%
24	Colorado	10,203	1.61%
25	Connecticut	8,545	1.35%
26	Massachusetts	7,931	1.25%
27	Tennessee	7,736	1.22%
28	Alabama	7,706	1.22%
29	Arkansas	7,349	1.16%
30	Idaho	7,120	1.13%
31	Iowa	6,264	0.99%
32	Nevada	6,077	0.96%
33	Maine	5,090	0.80%
34	New Mexico	4,855	0.77%
35	Hawaii	4,468	0.71%
36	Nebraska	4,280	0.68%
37	Kentucky	3,730	0.59%
38	Rhode Island	2,861	0.45%
39	South Dakota	2,821	0.45%
40	West Virginia	2,656	0.42%
41	Alaska	2,574	0.41%
42	Mississippi	2,392	0.38%
43	New Hampshire	2,361	0.37%
44	Delaware	2,114	0.33%
45	North Dakota	1,333	0.21%
46	Wyoming	1,309	0.21%
NA	Florida**	NA	NA
NA	Kansas**	NA	NA
NA	Montana**	NA	NA
NA	Vermont**	NA	NA
	District of Columbia**	NA	NA

Source: Federal Bureau of Investigation
    "Crime in the United States 1996" (Uniform Crime Reports, October 4, 1997)
*Arrests of youths 17 years and younger by law enforcement agencies submitting complete reports to the F.B.I. for 12 months in 1996. Crime index offenses consist of murder, forcible rape, robbery, aggravated assault, burglary, larceny-theft, motor vehicle theft and arson. See important note at beginning of this chapter.
**Not available.

Reported Juvenile Arrest Rate for Crime Index Offenses in 1996

National Rate = 2,915.0 Reported Arrests per 100,000 Juvenile Population*

ALPHA ORDER				RANK ORDER		
RANK	**STATE**	**RATE**		**RANK**	**STATE**	**RATE**
44	Alabama	1,638.8		1	Delaware	5,424.5
14	Alaska	3,583.5		2	Wisconsin	4,974.5
9	Arizona	4,060.0		3	Washington	4,582.8
35	Arkansas	2,546.2		4	Idaho	4,336.6
28	California	2,859.2		5	Oregon	4,317.9
24	Colorado	3,066.5		6	Illinois	4,317.4
22	Connecticut	3,255.6		7	Kentucky	4,211.7
1	Delaware	5,424.5		8	South Dakota	4,186.9
NA	Florida**	NA		9	Arizona	4,060.0
41	Georgia	2,181.8		10	Maryland	4,022.1
18	Hawaii	3,482.9		11	Utah	3,998.7
4	Idaho	4,336.6		12	New Mexico	3,637.4
6	Illinois	4,317.4		13	Maine	3,597.5
30	Indiana	2,826.9		14	Alaska	3,583.5
40	Iowa	2,246.5		15	Missouri	3,579.3
NA	Kansas**	NA		16	Nevada	3,563.1
7	Kentucky	4,211.7		17	Minnesota	3,559.4
20	Louisiana	3,331.9		18	Hawaii	3,482.9
13	Maine	3,597.5		19	Tennessee	3,356.9
10	Maryland	4,022.1		20	Louisiana	3,331.9
45	Massachusetts	1,573.4		21	Wyoming	3,328.8
43	Michigan	1,919.7		22	Connecticut	3,255.6
17	Minnesota	3,559.4		23	Oklahoma	3,088.9
26	Mississippi	2,932.5		24	Colorado	3,066.5
15	Missouri	3,579.3		25	Rhode Island	2,933.6
NA	Montana**	NA		26	Mississippi	2,932.5
27	Nebraska	2,859.4		27	Nebraska	2,859.4
16	Nevada	3,563.1		28	California	2,859.2
39	New Hampshire	2,313.5		29	New Jersey	2,837.1
29	New Jersey	2,837.1		30	Indiana	2,826.9
12	New Mexico	3,637.4		31	Texas	2,796.1
37	New York	2,324.4		32	Ohio	2,673.1
36	North Carolina	2,391.9		33	South Carolina	2,652.6
34	North Dakota	2,638.4		34	North Dakota	2,638.4
32	Ohio	2,673.1		35	Arkansas	2,546.2
23	Oklahoma	3,088.9		36	North Carolina	2,391.9
5	Oregon	4,317.9		37	New York	2,324.4
42	Pennsylvania	2,154.1		38	Virginia	2,319.5
25	Rhode Island	2,933.6		39	New Hampshire	2,313.5
33	South Carolina	2,652.6		40	Iowa	2,246.5
8	South Dakota	4,186.9		41	Georgia	2,181.8
19	Tennessee	3,356.9		42	Pennsylvania	2,154.1
31	Texas	2,796.1		43	Michigan	1,919.7
11	Utah	3,998.7		44	Alabama	1,638.8
NA	Vermont**	NA		45	Massachusetts	1,573.4
38	Virginia	2,319.5		46	West Virginia	1,294.6
3	Washington	4,582.8		NA	Florida**	NA
46	West Virginia	1,294.6		NA	Kansas**	NA
2	Wisconsin	4,974.5		NA	Montana**	NA
21	Wyoming	3,328.8		NA	Vermont**	NA
					District of Columbia**	NA

Source: Morgan Quitno Press using data from Federal Bureau of Investigation
 "Crime in the United States 1996" (Uniform Crime Reports, October 4, 1997)
*By law enforcement agencies submitting complete reports to the F.B.I. for 12 months in 1996. Arrests of youths 17 years and younger divided into population of 10 to 17 year olds. See important note at beginning of this chapter. Crime index offenses consist of murder, forcible rape, robbery, aggravated assault, burglary, larceny-theft, motor vehicle theft and arson. **Not available.

198

Reported Arrests of Juveniles for Crime Index Offenses
As a Percent of All Such Arrests in 1995
National Percent = 30.8% of Reported Arrests for Crime Index Offenses*

ALPHA ORDER

RANK ORDER

RANK	STATE	PERCENT		RANK	STATE	PERCENT
46	Alabama	20.8		1	Idaho	55.8
14	Alaska	37.7		2	North Dakota	55.0
23	Arizona	32.3		3	South Dakota	50.4
30	Arkansas	28.9		4	Nebraska	49.1
38	California	26.8		5	Utah	48.7
21	Colorado	33.9		6	Minnesota	48.5
34	Connecticut	27.6		7	New Hampshire	48.1
28	Delaware	29.2		8	Wyoming	47.1
NA	Florida**	NA		9	Maine	47.0
40	Georgia	24.1		10	Wisconsin	46.6
15	Hawaii	36.0		11	Oklahoma	43.1
1	Idaho	55.8		12	Washington	42.3
44	Illinois	23.0		13	Iowa	39.0
19	Indiana	34.4		14	Alaska	37.7
13	Iowa	39.0		15	Hawaii	36.0
NA	Kansas**	NA		16	Rhode Island	35.6
27	Kentucky	30.0		17	Oregon	35.1
33	Louisiana	27.9		18	Texas	34.8
9	Maine	47.0		19	Indiana	34.4
22	Maryland	33.4		20	New Mexico	34.3
42	Massachusetts	23.6		21	Colorado	33.9
28	Michigan	29.2		22	Maryland	33.4
6	Minnesota	48.5		23	Arizona	32.3
32	Mississippi	28.4		23	Ohio	32.3
36	Missouri	27.3		25	New Jersey	31.7
NA	Montana**	NA		26	Pennsylvania	30.4
4	Nebraska	49.1		27	Kentucky	30.0
31	Nevada	28.8		28	Delaware	29.2
7	New Hampshire	48.1		28	Michigan	29.2
25	New Jersey	31.7		30	Arkansas	28.9
20	New Mexico	34.3		31	Nevada	28.8
41	New York	23.8		32	Mississippi	28.4
45	North Carolina	21.7		33	Louisiana	27.9
2	North Dakota	55.0		34	Connecticut	27.6
23	Ohio	32.3		34	South Carolina	27.6
11	Oklahoma	43.1		36	Missouri	27.3
17	Oregon	35.1		37	Virginia	27.1
26	Pennsylvania	30.4		38	California	26.8
16	Rhode Island	35.6		39	West Virginia	26.4
34	South Carolina	27.6		40	Georgia	24.1
3	South Dakota	50.4		41	New York	23.8
43	Tennessee	23.4		42	Massachusetts	23.6
18	Texas	34.8		43	Tennessee	23.4
5	Utah	48.7		44	Illinois	23.0
NA	Vermont**	NA		45	North Carolina	21.7
37	Virginia	27.1		46	Alabama	20.8
12	Washington	42.3		NA	Florida**	NA
39	West Virginia	26.4		NA	Kansas**	NA
10	Wisconsin	46.6		NA	Montana**	NA
8	Wyoming	47.1		NA	Vermont**	NA
					District of Columbia**	NA

Source: Morgan Quitno Press using data from Federal Bureau of Investigation
   "Crime in the United States 1996" (Uniform Crime Reports, October 4, 1997)
*Arrests of youths 17 years and younger by law enforcement agencies submitting complete reports to the F.B.I. for
12 months in 1996. Crime index offenses consist of murder, forcible rape, robbery, aggravated assault, burglary,
larceny-theft, motor vehicle theft and arson.
**Not available.

Reported Arrests of Juveniles for Violent Crimes in 1996

National Total = 102,231 Reported Arrests*

ALPHA ORDER

RANK	STATE	ARRESTS	% of USA
25	Alabama	1,021	1.00%
38	Alaska	259	0.25%
13	Arizona	2,083	2.04%
27	Arkansas	874	0.85%
1	California	21,227	20.76%
28	Colorado	799	0.78%
21	Connecticut	1,376	1.35%
36	Delaware	384	0.38%
NA	Florida**	NA	NA
23	Georgia	1,260	1.23%
34	Hawaii	463	0.45%
37	Idaho	381	0.37%
7	Illinois	3,444	3.37%
14	Indiana	1,968	1.93%
31	Iowa	627	0.61%
NA	Kansas**	NA	NA
30	Kentucky	646	0.63%
19	Louisiana	1,679	1.64%
39	Maine	237	0.23%
6	Maryland	3,656	3.58%
11	Massachusetts	2,597	2.54%
10	Michigan	2,946	2.88%
15	Minnesota	1,817	1.78%
40	Mississippi	226	0.22%
17	Missouri	1,751	1.71%
NA	Montana**	NA	NA
43	Nebraska	140	0.14%
32	Nevada	621	0.61%
44	New Hampshire	129	0.13%
4	New Jersey	5,256	5.14%
35	New Mexico	440	0.43%
2	New York	12,953	12.67%
8	North Carolina	3,413	3.34%
46	North Dakota	40	0.04%
9	Ohio	3,188	3.12%
22	Oklahoma	1,314	1.29%
24	Oregon	1,056	1.03%
5	Pennsylvania	4,813	4.71%
33	Rhode Island	474	0.46%
16	South Carolina	1,797	1.76%
41	South Dakota	199	0.19%
26	Tennessee	944	0.92%
3	Texas	7,196	7.04%
29	Utah	760	0.74%
NA	Vermont**	NA	NA
20	Virginia	1,568	1.53%
18	Washington	1,700	1.66%
42	West Virginia	151	0.15%
12	Wisconsin	2,291	2.24%
45	Wyoming	67	0.07%

RANK ORDER

RANK	STATE	ARRESTS	% of USA
1	California	21,227	20.76%
2	New York	12,953	12.67%
3	Texas	7,196	7.04%
4	New Jersey	5,256	5.14%
5	Pennsylvania	4,813	4.71%
6	Maryland	3,656	3.58%
7	Illinois	3,444	3.37%
8	North Carolina	3,413	3.34%
9	Ohio	3,188	3.12%
10	Michigan	2,946	2.88%
11	Massachusetts	2,597	2.54%
12	Wisconsin	2,291	2.24%
13	Arizona	2,083	2.04%
14	Indiana	1,968	1.93%
15	Minnesota	1,817	1.78%
16	South Carolina	1,797	1.76%
17	Missouri	1,751	1.71%
18	Washington	1,700	1.66%
19	Louisiana	1,679	1.64%
20	Virginia	1,568	1.53%
21	Connecticut	1,376	1.35%
22	Oklahoma	1,314	1.29%
23	Georgia	1,260	1.23%
24	Oregon	1,056	1.03%
25	Alabama	1,021	1.00%
26	Tennessee	944	0.92%
27	Arkansas	874	0.85%
28	Colorado	799	0.78%
29	Utah	760	0.74%
30	Kentucky	646	0.63%
31	Iowa	627	0.61%
32	Nevada	621	0.61%
33	Rhode Island	474	0.46%
34	Hawaii	463	0.45%
35	New Mexico	440	0.43%
36	Delaware	384	0.38%
37	Idaho	381	0.37%
38	Alaska	259	0.25%
39	Maine	237	0.23%
40	Mississippi	226	0.22%
41	South Dakota	199	0.19%
42	West Virginia	151	0.15%
43	Nebraska	140	0.14%
44	New Hampshire	129	0.13%
45	Wyoming	67	0.07%
46	North Dakota	40	0.04%
NA	Florida**	NA	NA
NA	Kansas**	NA	NA
NA	Montana**	NA	NA
NA	Vermont**	NA	NA
	District of Columbia**	NA	NA

Source: Federal Bureau of Investigation
     "Crime in the United States 1996" (Uniform Crime Reports, October 4, 1997)
*Arrests of youths 17 years and younger by law enforcement agencies submitting complete reports to the F.B.I. for 12 months in 1996. Violent crimes are offenses of murder, forcible rape, robbery and aggravated assault. See important note at beginning of this chapter.
**Not available.

Reported Juvenile Arrest Rate for Violent Crime in 1996

National Rate = 471.0 Reported Arrests per 100,000 Juvenile Population*

ALPHA ORDER

RANK ORDER

RANK	STATE	RATE		RANK	STATE	RATE
40	Alabama	217.1		1	Illinois	1,087.8
24	Alaska	360.6		2	Delaware	985.3
15	Arizona	454.5		3	New York	980.8
31	Arkansas	302.8		4	Maryland	838.3
7	California	610.4		5	Kentucky	729.4
36	Colorado	240.1		6	New Jersey	654.8
8	Connecticut	524.2		7	California	610.4
2	Delaware	985.3		8	Connecticut	524.2
NA	Florida**	NA		9	Massachusetts	515.2
35	Georgia	241.2		10	Indiana	512.2
23	Hawaii	360.9		11	Rhode Island	486.0
38	Idaho	232.1		12	Louisiana	477.8
1	Illinois	1,087.8		13	Pennsylvania	474.2
10	Indiana	512.2		14	Missouri	473.1
39	Iowa	224.9		15	Arizona	454.5
NA	Kansas**	NA		16	North Carolina	436.9
5	Kentucky	729.4		17	South Carolina	433.4
12	Louisiana	477.8		18	Ohio	426.6
42	Maine	167.5		19	Tennessee	409.6
4	Maryland	838.3		20	Washington	386.5
9	Massachusetts	515.2		21	Nevada	364.1
30	Michigan	312.8		22	Wisconsin	361.0
26	Minnesota	344.5		23	Hawaii	360.9
33	Mississippi	277.1		24	Alaska	360.6
14	Missouri	473.1		25	Texas	349.4
NA	Montana**	NA		26	Minnesota	344.5
44	Nebraska	93.5		27	Oregon	330.2
21	Nevada	364.1		28	New Mexico	329.6
43	New Hampshire	126.4		29	Oklahoma	317.5
6	New Jersey	654.8		30	Michigan	312.8
28	New Mexico	329.6		31	Arkansas	302.8
3	New York	980.8		32	South Dakota	295.4
16	North Carolina	436.9		33	Mississippi	277.1
45	North Dakota	79.2		34	Utah	264.6
18	Ohio	426.6		35	Georgia	241.2
29	Oklahoma	317.5		36	Colorado	240.1
27	Oregon	330.2		37	Virginia	237.9
13	Pennsylvania	474.2		38	Idaho	232.1
11	Rhode Island	486.0		39	Iowa	224.9
17	South Carolina	433.4		40	Alabama	217.1
32	South Dakota	295.4		41	Wyoming	170.4
19	Tennessee	409.6		42	Maine	167.5
25	Texas	349.4		43	New Hampshire	126.4
34	Utah	264.6		44	Nebraska	93.5
NA	Vermont**	NA		45	North Dakota	79.2
37	Virginia	237.9		46	West Virginia	73.6
20	Washington	386.5		NA	Florida**	NA
46	West Virginia	73.6		NA	Kansas**	NA
22	Wisconsin	361.0		NA	Montana**	NA
41	Wyoming	170.4		NA	Vermont**	NA

District of Columbia**   NA

Source: Morgan Quitno Press using data from Federal Bureau of Investigation
   "Crime in the United States 1996" (Uniform Crime Reports, October 4, 1997)
*By law enforcement agencies submitting complete reports to the F.B.I. for 12 months in 1996. Arrests of youths 17 years and younger divided into population of 10 to 17 year olds. See important note at beginning of this chapter. Violent crimes are offenses of murder, forcible rape, robbery and aggravated assault.
**Not available.

Reported Arrests of Juveniles for Violent Crime
As a Percent of All Such Arrests in 1996
National Percent = 18.7% of Reported Arrests for Violent Crime*

ALPHA ORDER

RANK	STATE	PERCENT
46	Alabama	9.3
31	Alaska	17.0
18	Arizona	23.1
33	Arkansas	16.6
39	California	14.5
37	Colorado	15.3
19	Connecticut	21.6
20	Delaware	21.5
NA	Florida**	NA
42	Georgia	12.8
2	Hawaii	31.1
6	Idaho	27.8
7	Illinois	27.2
16	Indiana	23.8
23	Iowa	20.1
NA	Kansas**	NA
36	Kentucky	15.4
32	Louisiana	16.9
8	Maine	26.5
4	Maryland	28.8
26	Massachusetts	18.3
40	Michigan	14.3
5	Minnesota	28.4
35	Mississippi	16.2
28	Missouri	17.7
NA	Montana**	NA
29	Nebraska	17.5
30	Nevada	17.2
15	New Hampshire	23.9
9	New Jersey	26.2
22	New Mexico	20.2
16	New York	23.8
43	North Carolina	12.7
10	North Dakota	26.0
26	Ohio	18.3
23	Oklahoma	20.1
12	Oregon	24.5
14	Pennsylvania	24.4
25	Rhode Island	19.7
38	South Carolina	15.1
3	South Dakota	29.0
44	Tennessee	11.7
21	Texas	21.3
1	Utah	33.9
NA	Vermont**	NA
41	Virginia	13.7
11	Washington	25.9
45	West Virginia	10.9
12	Wisconsin	24.5
34	Wyoming	16.3

RANK ORDER

RANK	STATE	PERCENT
1	Utah	33.9
2	Hawaii	31.1
3	South Dakota	29.0
4	Maryland	28.8
5	Minnesota	28.4
6	Idaho	27.8
7	Illinois	27.2
8	Maine	26.5
9	New Jersey	26.2
10	North Dakota	26.0
11	Washington	25.9
12	Oregon	24.5
12	Wisconsin	24.5
14	Pennsylvania	24.4
15	New Hampshire	23.9
16	Indiana	23.8
16	New York	23.8
18	Arizona	23.1
19	Connecticut	21.6
20	Delaware	21.5
21	Texas	21.3
22	New Mexico	20.2
23	Iowa	20.1
23	Oklahoma	20.1
25	Rhode Island	19.7
26	Massachusetts	18.3
26	Ohio	18.3
28	Missouri	17.7
29	Nebraska	17.5
30	Nevada	17.2
31	Alaska	17.0
32	Louisiana	16.9
33	Arkansas	16.6
34	Wyoming	16.3
35	Mississippi	16.2
36	Kentucky	15.4
37	Colorado	15.3
38	South Carolina	15.1
39	California	14.5
40	Michigan	14.3
41	Virginia	13.7
42	Georgia	12.8
43	North Carolina	12.7
44	Tennessee	11.7
45	West Virginia	10.9
46	Alabama	9.3
NA	Florida**	NA
NA	Kansas**	NA
NA	Montana**	NA
NA	Vermont**	NA

District of Columbia**   NA

Source: Morgan Quitno Press using data from Federal Bureau of Investigation
   "Crime in the United States 1996" (Uniform Crime Reports, October 4, 1997)
*Arrests of youths 17 years and younger by law enforcement agencies submitting complete reports to the F.B.I. for 12 months in 1996. Violent crimes are offenses of murder, forcible rape, robbery and aggravated assault.
**Not available.

Reported Arrests of Juveniles for Murder in 1996

National Total = 2,172 Reported Arrests*

ALPHA ORDER

RANK	STATE	ARRESTS	% of USA
14	Alabama	49	2.26%
36	Alaska	4	0.18%
16	Arizona	45	2.07%
17	Arkansas	39	1.80%
1	California	382	17.59%
25	Colorado	18	0.83%
27	Connecticut	16	0.74%
38	Delaware	3	0.14%
NA	Florida**	NA	NA
25	Georgia	18	0.83%
30	Hawaii	12	0.55%
42	Idaho	1	0.05%
3	Illinois	165	7.60%
28	Indiana	15	0.69%
36	Iowa	4	0.18%
NA	Kansas**	NA	NA
35	Kentucky	7	0.32%
8	Louisiana	72	3.31%
42	Maine	1	0.05%
4	Maryland	147	6.77%
28	Massachusetts	15	0.69%
6	Michigan	113	5.20%
22	Minnesota	27	1.24%
34	Mississippi	8	0.37%
10	Missouri	59	2.72%
NA	Montana**	NA	NA
39	Nebraska	2	0.09%
22	Nevada	27	1.24%
39	New Hampshire	2	0.09%
13	New Jersey	52	2.39%
30	New Mexico	12	0.55%
5	New York	142	6.54%
9	North Carolina	71	3.27%
42	North Dakota	1	0.05%
15	Ohio	48	2.21%
20	Oklahoma	29	1.34%
24	Oregon	20	0.92%
11	Pennsylvania	58	2.67%
42	Rhode Island	1	0.05%
18	South Carolina	36	1.66%
39	South Dakota	2	0.09%
19	Tennessee	31	1.43%
2	Texas	217	9.99%
32	Utah	9	0.41%
NA	Vermont**	NA	NA
12	Virginia	57	2.62%
20	Washington	29	1.34%
32	West Virginia	9	0.41%
7	Wisconsin	96	4.42%
42	Wyoming	1	0.05%

RANK ORDER

RANK	STATE	ARRESTS	% of USA
1	California	382	17.59%
2	Texas	217	9.99%
3	Illinois	165	7.60%
4	Maryland	147	6.77%
5	New York	142	6.54%
6	Michigan	113	5.20%
7	Wisconsin	96	4.42%
8	Louisiana	72	3.31%
9	North Carolina	71	3.27%
10	Missouri	59	2.72%
11	Pennsylvania	58	2.67%
12	Virginia	57	2.62%
13	New Jersey	52	2.39%
14	Alabama	49	2.26%
15	Ohio	48	2.21%
16	Arizona	45	2.07%
17	Arkansas	39	1.80%
18	South Carolina	36	1.66%
19	Tennessee	31	1.43%
20	Oklahoma	29	1.34%
20	Washington	29	1.34%
22	Minnesota	27	1.24%
22	Nevada	27	1.24%
24	Oregon	20	0.92%
25	Colorado	18	0.83%
25	Georgia	18	0.83%
27	Connecticut	16	0.74%
28	Indiana	15	0.69%
28	Massachusetts	15	0.69%
30	Hawaii	12	0.55%
30	New Mexico	12	0.55%
32	Utah	9	0.41%
32	West Virginia	9	0.41%
34	Mississippi	8	0.37%
35	Kentucky	7	0.32%
36	Alaska	4	0.18%
36	Iowa	4	0.18%
38	Delaware	3	0.14%
39	Nebraska	2	0.09%
39	New Hampshire	2	0.09%
39	South Dakota	2	0.09%
42	Idaho	1	0.05%
42	Maine	1	0.05%
42	North Dakota	1	0.05%
42	Rhode Island	1	0.05%
42	Wyoming	1	0.05%
NA	Florida**	NA	NA
NA	Kansas**	NA	NA
NA	Montana**	NA	NA
NA	Vermont**	NA	NA
	District of Columbia**	NA	NA

Source: Federal Bureau of Investigation
    "Crime in the United States 1996" (Uniform Crime Reports, October 4, 1997)
*Arrests of youths 17 years and younger by law enforcement agencies submitting complete reports to the F.B.I. for 12 months in 1996. Includes nonnegligent manslaughter. See important note at beginning of this chapter.
**Not available.

Reported Juvenile Arrest Rate for Murder in 1996

National Rate = 10.0 Reported Arrests per 100,000 Juvenile Population*

ALPHA ORDER

RANK ORDER

RANK	STATE	RATE		RANK	STATE	RATE
13	Alabama	10.4		1	Illinois	52.1
30	Alaska	5.6		2	Maryland	33.7
14	Arizona	9.8		3	Louisiana	20.5
7	Arkansas	13.5		4	Missouri	15.9
10	California	11.0		5	Nevada	15.8
31	Colorado	5.4		6	Wisconsin	15.1
28	Connecticut	6.1		7	Arkansas	13.5
22	Delaware	7.7		7	Tennessee	13.5
NA	Florida**	NA		9	Michigan	12.0
35	Georgia	3.4		10	California	11.0
16	Hawaii	9.4		11	New York	10.8
46	Idaho	0.6		12	Texas	10.5
1	Illinois	52.1		13	Alabama	10.4
34	Indiana	3.9		14	Arizona	9.8
42	Iowa	1.4		14	Mississippi	9.8
NA	Kansas**	NA		16	Hawaii	9.4
21	Kentucky	7.9		17	North Carolina	9.1
3	Louisiana	20.5		18	New Mexico	9.0
45	Maine	0.7		19	South Carolina	8.7
2	Maryland	33.7		20	Virginia	8.6
37	Massachusetts	3.0		21	Kentucky	7.9
9	Michigan	12.0		22	Delaware	7.7
32	Minnesota	5.1		23	Oklahoma	7.0
14	Mississippi	9.8		24	Washington	6.6
4	Missouri	15.9		25	New Jersey	6.5
NA	Montana**	NA		26	Ohio	6.4
43	Nebraska	1.3		27	Oregon	6.3
5	Nevada	15.8		28	Connecticut	6.1
40	New Hampshire	2.0		29	Pennsylvania	5.7
25	New Jersey	6.5		30	Alaska	5.6
18	New Mexico	9.0		31	Colorado	5.4
11	New York	10.8		32	Minnesota	5.1
17	North Carolina	9.1		33	West Virginia	4.4
40	North Dakota	2.0		34	Indiana	3.9
26	Ohio	6.4		35	Georgia	3.4
23	Oklahoma	7.0		36	Utah	3.1
27	Oregon	6.3		37	Massachusetts	3.0
29	Pennsylvania	5.7		37	South Dakota	3.0
44	Rhode Island	1.0		39	Wyoming	2.5
19	South Carolina	8.7		40	New Hampshire	2.0
37	South Dakota	3.0		40	North Dakota	2.0
7	Tennessee	13.5		42	Iowa	1.4
12	Texas	10.5		43	Nebraska	1.3
36	Utah	3.1		44	Rhode Island	1.0
NA	Vermont**	NA		45	Maine	0.7
20	Virginia	8.6		46	Idaho	0.6
24	Washington	6.6		NA	Florida**	NA
33	West Virginia	4.4		NA	Kansas**	NA
6	Wisconsin	15.1		NA	Montana**	NA
39	Wyoming	2.5		NA	Vermont**	NA
					District of Columbia**	NA

Source: Morgan Quitno Press using data from Federal Bureau of Investigation
"Crime in the United States 1996" (Uniform Crime Reports, October 4, 1997)
*By law enforcement agencies submitting complete reports to the F.B.I. for 12 months in 1996. Includes nonnegligent manslaughter. Arrests of youths 17 years and younger divided into population of 10 to 17 year olds. See important note at beginning of this chapter.
**Not available.

Reported Arrests of Juveniles for Murder
As a Percent of All Such Arrests in 1996
National Percent = 15.0% of Reported Arrests for Murder*

ALPHA ORDER

RANK ORDER

RANK	STATE	PERCENT		RANK	STATE	PERCENT
35	Alabama	12.2		1	Hawaii	23.5
26	Alaska	14.3		1	Maryland	23.5
9	Arizona	17.8		3	South Dakota	22.2
11	Arkansas	17.2		4	Illinois	21.5
21	California	15.3		5	Wisconsin	20.1
18	Colorado	15.9		6	Texas	18.8
27	Connecticut	13.9		7	Minnesota	18.6
19	Delaware	15.8		8	Washington	18.5
NA	Florida**	NA		9	Arizona	17.8
44	Georgia	7.3		10	Missouri	17.5
1	Hawaii	23.5		11	Arkansas	17.2
46	Idaho	3.4		11	Louisiana	17.2
4	Illinois	21.5		13	New Hampshire	16.7
35	Indiana	12.2		13	New Mexico	16.7
24	Iowa	14.8		13	North Dakota	16.7
NA	Kansas**	NA		16	West Virginia	16.4
39	Kentucky	10.9		17	Massachusetts	16.1
11	Louisiana	17.2		18	Colorado	15.9
45	Maine	6.7		19	Delaware	15.8
1	Maryland	23.5		20	Nevada	15.5
17	Massachusetts	16.1		21	California	15.3
42	Michigan	9.3		22	Tennessee	15.0
7	Minnesota	18.6		23	New Jersey	14.9
41	Mississippi	9.5		24	Iowa	14.8
10	Missouri	17.5		25	Ohio	14.6
NA	Montana**	NA		26	Alaska	14.3
32	Nebraska	13.3		27	Connecticut	13.9
20	Nevada	15.5		28	Virginia	13.7
13	New Hampshire	16.7		29	Oregon	13.6
23	New Jersey	14.9		29	Utah	13.6
13	New Mexico	16.7		31	Oklahoma	13.4
33	New York	12.5		32	Nebraska	13.3
40	North Carolina	10.2		33	New York	12.5
13	North Dakota	16.7		33	Wyoming	12.5
25	Ohio	14.6		35	Alabama	12.2
31	Oklahoma	13.4		35	Indiana	12.2
29	Oregon	13.6		37	Pennsylvania	11.4
37	Pennsylvania	11.4		38	South Carolina	11.1
43	Rhode Island	7.7		39	Kentucky	10.9
38	South Carolina	11.1		40	North Carolina	10.2
3	South Dakota	22.2		41	Mississippi	9.5
22	Tennessee	15.0		42	Michigan	9.3
6	Texas	18.8		43	Rhode Island	7.7
29	Utah	13.6		44	Georgia	7.3
NA	Vermont**	NA		45	Maine	6.7
28	Virginia	13.7		46	Idaho	3.4
8	Washington	18.5		NA	Florida**	NA
16	West Virginia	16.4		NA	Kansas**	NA
5	Wisconsin	20.1		NA	Montana**	NA
33	Wyoming	12.5		NA	Vermont**	NA
					District of Columbia**	NA

Source: Morgan Quitno Press using data from Federal Bureau of Investigation
"Crime in the United States 1996" (Uniform Crime Reports, October 4, 1997)
*Arrests of youths 17 years and younger by law enforcement agencies submitting complete reports to the F.B.I. for 12 months in 1996. Includes nonnegligent manslaughter.
**Not available.

Reported Arrests of Juveniles for Rape in 1996

National Total = 4,128 Reported Arrests*

ALPHA ORDER

RANK	STATE	ARRESTS	% of USA
25	Alabama	51	1.24%
34	Alaska	18	0.44%
27	Arizona	38	0.92%
20	Arkansas	67	1.62%
1	California	480	11.63%
20	Colorado	67	1.62%
23	Connecticut	62	1.50%
32	Delaware	25	0.61%
NA	Florida**	NA	NA
22	Georgia	63	1.53%
37	Hawaii	16	0.39%
42	Idaho	11	0.27%
7	Illinois	159	3.85%
27	Indiana	38	0.92%
38	Iowa	15	0.36%
NA	Kansas**	NA	NA
38	Kentucky	15	0.36%
16	Louisiana	86	2.08%
34	Maine	18	0.44%
12	Maryland	112	2.71%
17	Massachusetts	85	2.06%
3	Michigan	278	6.73%
9	Minnesota	148	3.59%
36	Mississippi	17	0.41%
13	Missouri	109	2.64%
NA	Montana**	NA	NA
45	Nebraska	6	0.15%
26	Nevada	39	0.94%
32	New Hampshire	25	0.61%
8	New Jersey	155	3.75%
40	New Mexico	14	0.34%
5	New York	236	5.72%
14	North Carolina	92	2.23%
44	North Dakota	7	0.17%
4	Ohio	244	5.91%
19	Oklahoma	70	1.70%
24	Oregon	56	1.36%
6	Pennsylvania	191	4.63%
41	Rhode Island	12	0.29%
17	South Carolina	85	2.06%
31	South Dakota	30	0.73%
30	Tennessee	34	0.82%
2	Texas	439	10.63%
29	Utah	36	0.87%
NA	Vermont**	NA	NA
15	Virginia	89	2.16%
11	Washington	131	3.17%
43	West Virginia	10	0.24%
9	Wisconsin	148	3.59%
46	Wyoming	1	0.02%

RANK ORDER

RANK	STATE	ARRESTS	% of USA
1	California	480	11.63%
2	Texas	439	10.63%
3	Michigan	278	6.73%
4	Ohio	244	5.91%
5	New York	236	5.72%
6	Pennsylvania	191	4.63%
7	Illinois	159	3.85%
8	New Jersey	155	3.75%
9	Minnesota	148	3.59%
9	Wisconsin	148	3.59%
11	Washington	131	3.17%
12	Maryland	112	2.71%
13	Missouri	109	2.64%
14	North Carolina	92	2.23%
15	Virginia	89	2.16%
16	Louisiana	86	2.08%
17	Massachusetts	85	2.06%
17	South Carolina	85	2.06%
19	Oklahoma	70	1.70%
20	Arkansas	67	1.62%
20	Colorado	67	1.62%
22	Georgia	63	1.53%
23	Connecticut	62	1.50%
24	Oregon	56	1.36%
25	Alabama	51	1.24%
26	Nevada	39	0.94%
27	Arizona	38	0.92%
27	Indiana	38	0.92%
29	Utah	36	0.87%
30	Tennessee	34	0.82%
31	South Dakota	30	0.73%
32	Delaware	25	0.61%
32	New Hampshire	25	0.61%
34	Alaska	18	0.44%
34	Maine	18	0.44%
36	Mississippi	17	0.41%
37	Hawaii	16	0.39%
38	Iowa	15	0.36%
38	Kentucky	15	0.36%
40	New Mexico	14	0.34%
41	Rhode Island	12	0.29%
42	Idaho	11	0.27%
43	West Virginia	10	0.24%
44	North Dakota	7	0.17%
45	Nebraska	6	0.15%
46	Wyoming	1	0.02%
NA	Florida**	NA	NA
NA	Kansas**	NA	NA
NA	Montana**	NA	NA
NA	Vermont**	NA	NA
	District of Columbia**	NA	NA

Source: Federal Bureau of Investigation
  "Crime in the United States 1996" (Uniform Crime Reports, October 4, 1997)
*Arrests of youths 17 years and younger by law enforcement agencies submitting complete reports to the F.B.I. for 12 months in 1996. Forcible rape is the carnal knowledge of a female forcibly and against her will. Assaults or attempts to commit rape by force or threat of force are included. However, statutory rape without force and other sex offenses are excluded. See important note at beginning of this chapter. **Not available.

Reported Juvenile Arrest Rate for Rape in 1996

National Rate = 19.0 Arrests per 100,000 Population*

ALPHA ORDER				RANK ORDER		
RANK	STATE	RATE		RANK	STATE	RATE
38	Alabama	10.8		1	Delaware	64.2
10	Alaska	25.1		2	Illinois	50.2
41	Arizona	8.3		3	South Dakota	44.5
15	Arkansas	23.2		4	Ohio	32.7
30	California	13.8		5	Washington	29.8
20	Colorado	20.1		6	Michigan	29.5
13	Connecticut	23.6		7	Missouri	29.4
1	Delaware	64.2		8	Minnesota	28.1
NA	Florida**	NA		9	Maryland	25.7
36	Georgia	12.1		10	Alaska	25.1
33	Hawaii	12.5		11	Louisiana	24.5
42	Idaho	6.7		11	New Hampshire	24.5
2	Illinois	50.2		13	Connecticut	23.6
40	Indiana	9.9		14	Wisconsin	23.3
43	Iowa	5.4		15	Arkansas	23.2
NA	Kansas**	NA		16	Nevada	22.9
25	Kentucky	16.9		17	Texas	21.3
11	Louisiana	24.5		18	Mississippi	20.8
32	Maine	12.7		19	South Carolina	20.5
9	Maryland	25.7		20	Colorado	20.1
25	Massachusetts	16.9		21	New Jersey	19.3
6	Michigan	29.5		22	Pennsylvania	18.8
8	Minnesota	28.1		23	New York	17.9
18	Mississippi	20.8		24	Oregon	17.5
7	Missouri	29.4		25	Kentucky	16.9
NA	Montana**	NA		25	Massachusetts	16.9
45	Nebraska	4.0		25	Oklahoma	16.9
16	Nevada	22.9		28	Tennessee	14.8
11	New Hampshire	24.5		29	North Dakota	13.9
21	New Jersey	19.3		30	California	13.8
39	New Mexico	10.5		31	Virginia	13.5
23	New York	17.9		32	Maine	12.7
37	North Carolina	11.8		33	Hawaii	12.5
29	North Dakota	13.9		33	Utah	12.5
4	Ohio	32.7		35	Rhode Island	12.3
25	Oklahoma	16.9		36	Georgia	12.1
24	Oregon	17.5		37	North Carolina	11.8
22	Pennsylvania	18.8		38	Alabama	10.8
35	Rhode Island	12.3		39	New Mexico	10.5
19	South Carolina	20.5		40	Indiana	9.9
3	South Dakota	44.5		41	Arizona	8.3
28	Tennessee	14.8		42	Idaho	6.7
17	Texas	21.3		43	Iowa	5.4
33	Utah	12.5		44	West Virginia	4.9
NA	Vermont**	NA		45	Nebraska	4.0
31	Virginia	13.5		46	Wyoming	2.5
5	Washington	29.8		NA	Florida**	NA
44	West Virginia	4.9		NA	Kansas**	NA
14	Wisconsin	23.3		NA	Montana**	NA
46	Wyoming	2.5		NA	Vermont**	NA
					District of Columbia**	NA

Source: Morgan Quitno Press using data from Federal Bureau of Investigation
    "Crime in the United States 1996" (Uniform Crime Reports, October 4, 1997)
*By law enforcement agencies submitting complete reports to the F.B.I. for 12 months in 1996. Arrests of youths 17 years and younger divided into population of 10 to 17 year olds. See important note at beginning of this chapter. Forcible rape is the carnal knowledge of a female forcibly and against her will. Assaults or attempts to commit rape by force or threat of force are included. **Not available.

Reported Arrests of Juveniles for Rape
As a Percent of All Such Arrests in 1996
National Percent = 17.0% of Reported Arrests for Rape*

ALPHA ORDER

RANK	STATE	PERCENT
42	Alabama	11.2
24	Alaska	15.9
28	Arizona	15.1
28	Arkansas	15.1
27	California	15.3
31	Colorado	14.8
10	Connecticut	20.1
23	Delaware	16.1
NA	Florida**	NA
24	Georgia	15.9
38	Hawaii	12.5
36	Idaho	13.3
1	Illinois	34.8
8	Indiana	21.3
12	Iowa	19.5
NA	Kansas**	NA
37	Kentucky	12.8
13	Louisiana	19.3
4	Maine	24.0
17	Maryland	18.4
32	Massachusetts	14.6
21	Michigan	16.6
15	Minnesota	18.9
33	Mississippi	13.8
18	Missouri	17.6
NA	Montana**	NA
45	Nebraska	7.3
35	Nevada	13.4
4	New Hampshire	24.0
20	New Jersey	17.0
22	New Mexico	16.5
28	New York	15.1
39	North Carolina	11.9
3	North Dakota	28.0
7	Ohio	21.9
26	Oklahoma	15.7
16	Oregon	18.8
19	Pennsylvania	17.4
40	Rhode Island	11.3
34	South Carolina	13.6
2	South Dakota	33.7
43	Tennessee	10.1
14	Texas	19.0
6	Utah	23.4
NA	Vermont**	NA
40	Virginia	11.3
10	Washington	20.1
44	West Virginia	8.5
9	Wisconsin	21.2
46	Wyoming	5.6

RANK ORDER

RANK	STATE	PERCENT
1	Illinois	34.8
2	South Dakota	33.7
3	North Dakota	28.0
4	Maine	24.0
4	New Hampshire	24.0
6	Utah	23.4
7	Ohio	21.9
8	Indiana	21.3
9	Wisconsin	21.2
10	Connecticut	20.1
10	Washington	20.1
12	Iowa	19.5
13	Louisiana	19.3
14	Texas	19.0
15	Minnesota	18.9
16	Oregon	18.8
17	Maryland	18.4
18	Missouri	17.6
19	Pennsylvania	17.4
20	New Jersey	17.0
21	Michigan	16.6
22	New Mexico	16.5
23	Delaware	16.1
24	Alaska	15.9
24	Georgia	15.9
26	Oklahoma	15.7
27	California	15.3
28	Arizona	15.1
28	Arkansas	15.1
28	New York	15.1
31	Colorado	14.8
32	Massachusetts	14.6
33	Mississippi	13.8
34	South Carolina	13.6
35	Nevada	13.4
36	Idaho	13.3
37	Kentucky	12.8
38	Hawaii	12.5
39	North Carolina	11.9
40	Rhode Island	11.3
40	Virginia	11.3
42	Alabama	11.2
43	Tennessee	10.1
44	West Virginia	8.5
45	Nebraska	7.3
46	Wyoming	5.6
NA	Florida**	NA
NA	Kansas**	NA
NA	Montana**	NA
NA	Vermont**	NA

District of Columbia**   NA

Source: Morgan Quitno Press using data from Federal Bureau of Investigation
    "Crime in the United States 1996" (Uniform Crime Reports, October 4, 1997)
*Arrests of youths 17 years and younger by law enforcement agencies submitting complete reports to the F.B.I. for 12 months in 1996. Forcible rape is the carnal knowledge of a female forcibly and against her will. Assaults or attempts to commit rape by force or threat of force are included. However, statutory rape without force and other sex offenses are excluded. **Not available.

Reported Arrests of Juveniles for Robbery in 1996

National Total = 39,037 Reported Arrests*

ALPHA ORDER

RANK	STATE	ARRESTS	% of USA
20	Alabama	401	1.03%
40	Alaska	54	0.14%
17	Arizona	470	1.20%
27	Arkansas	272	0.70%
2	California	8,558	21.92%
31	Colorado	195	0.50%
18	Connecticut	432	1.11%
33	Delaware	106	0.27%
NA	Florida**	NA	NA
21	Georgia	378	0.97%
26	Hawaii	299	0.77%
42	Idaho	45	0.12%
8	Illinois	1,201	3.08%
30	Indiana	206	0.53%
36	Iowa	84	0.22%
NA	Kansas**	NA	NA
29	Kentucky	219	0.56%
25	Louisiana	320	0.82%
35	Maine	88	0.23%
6	Maryland	1,403	3.59%
14	Massachusetts	570	1.46%
10	Michigan	863	2.21%
15	Minnesota	551	1.41%
37	Mississippi	82	0.21%
12	Missouri	651	1.67%
NA	Montana**	NA	NA
43	Nebraska	41	0.11%
24	Nevada	323	0.83%
39	New Hampshire	60	0.15%
4	New Jersey	2,113	5.41%
34	New Mexico	97	0.25%
1	New York	8,796	22.53%
9	North Carolina	979	2.51%
46	North Dakota	3	0.01%
7	Ohio	1,302	3.34%
21	Oklahoma	378	0.97%
23	Oregon	343	0.88%
5	Pennsylvania	1,986	5.09%
38	Rhode Island	65	0.17%
19	South Carolina	415	1.06%
44	South Dakota	37	0.09%
28	Tennessee	244	0.63%
3	Texas	2,291	5.87%
32	Utah	152	0.39%
NA	Vermont**	NA	NA
13	Virginia	637	1.63%
16	Washington	471	1.21%
41	West Virginia	47	0.12%
11	Wisconsin	803	2.06%
45	Wyoming	6	0.02%

RANK ORDER

RANK	STATE	ARRESTS	% of USA
1	New York	8,796	22.53%
2	California	8,558	21.92%
3	Texas	2,291	5.87%
4	New Jersey	2,113	5.41%
5	Pennsylvania	1,986	5.09%
6	Maryland	1,403	3.59%
7	Ohio	1,302	3.34%
8	Illinois	1,201	3.08%
9	North Carolina	979	2.51%
10	Michigan	863	2.21%
11	Wisconsin	803	2.06%
12	Missouri	651	1.67%
13	Virginia	637	1.63%
14	Massachusetts	570	1.46%
15	Minnesota	551	1.41%
16	Washington	471	1.21%
17	Arizona	470	1.20%
18	Connecticut	432	1.11%
19	South Carolina	415	1.06%
20	Alabama	401	1.03%
21	Georgia	378	0.97%
21	Oklahoma	378	0.97%
23	Oregon	343	0.88%
24	Nevada	323	0.83%
25	Louisiana	320	0.82%
26	Hawaii	299	0.77%
27	Arkansas	272	0.70%
28	Tennessee	244	0.63%
29	Kentucky	219	0.56%
30	Indiana	206	0.53%
31	Colorado	195	0.50%
32	Utah	152	0.39%
33	Delaware	106	0.27%
34	New Mexico	97	0.25%
35	Maine	88	0.23%
36	Iowa	84	0.22%
37	Mississippi	82	0.21%
38	Rhode Island	65	0.17%
39	New Hampshire	60	0.15%
40	Alaska	54	0.14%
41	West Virginia	47	0.12%
42	Idaho	45	0.12%
43	Nebraska	41	0.11%
44	South Dakota	37	0.09%
45	Wyoming	6	0.02%
46	North Dakota	3	0.01%
NA	Florida**	NA	NA
NA	Kansas**	NA	NA
NA	Montana**	NA	NA
NA	Vermont**	NA	NA
	District of Columbia**	NA	NA

Source: Federal Bureau of Investigation
    "Crime in the United States 1996" (Uniform Crime Reports, October 4, 1997)
*Arrests of youths 17 years and younger by law enforcement agencies submitting complete reports to the F.B.I. for 12 months in 1996. Robbery is the taking or attempting to take anything of value by force or threat of force. See important note at beginning of this chapter. **Not available.

Reported Juvenile Arrest Rate for Robbery in 1996

National Rate = 179.8 Reported Arrests per 100,000 Juvenile Population*

ALPHA ORDER

RANK	STATE	RATE
30	Alabama	85.3
31	Alaska	75.2
22	Arizona	102.6
26	Arkansas	94.2
7	California	246.1
37	Colorado	58.6
13	Connecticut	164.6
4	Delaware	272.0
NA	Florida**	NA
33	Georgia	72.4
8	Hawaii	233.1
42	Idaho	27.4
2	Illinois	379.3
39	Indiana	53.6
41	Iowa	30.1
NA	Kansas**	NA
6	Kentucky	247.3
29	Louisiana	91.1
35	Maine	62.2
3	Maryland	321.7
16	Massachusetts	113.1
27	Michigan	91.6
21	Minnesota	104.5
23	Mississippi	100.5
11	Missouri	175.9
NA	Montana**	NA
42	Nebraska	27.4
10	Nevada	189.4
36	New Hampshire	58.8
5	New Jersey	263.2
32	New Mexico	72.7
1	New York	666.0
15	North Carolina	125.3
46	North Dakota	5.9
12	Ohio	174.2
28	Oklahoma	91.3
18	Oregon	107.2
9	Pennsylvania	195.7
34	Rhode Island	66.7
24	South Carolina	100.1
38	South Dakota	54.9
20	Tennessee	105.9
17	Texas	111.3
40	Utah	52.9
NA	Vermont**	NA
25	Virginia	96.7
19	Washington	107.1
44	West Virginia	22.9
14	Wisconsin	126.5
45	Wyoming	15.3

RANK ORDER

RANK	STATE	RATE
1	New York	666.0
2	Illinois	379.3
3	Maryland	321.7
4	Delaware	272.0
5	New Jersey	263.2
6	Kentucky	247.3
7	California	246.1
8	Hawaii	233.1
9	Pennsylvania	195.7
10	Nevada	189.4
11	Missouri	175.9
12	Ohio	174.2
13	Connecticut	164.6
14	Wisconsin	126.5
15	North Carolina	125.3
16	Massachusetts	113.1
17	Texas	111.3
18	Oregon	107.2
19	Washington	107.1
20	Tennessee	105.9
21	Minnesota	104.5
22	Arizona	102.6
23	Mississippi	100.5
24	South Carolina	100.1
25	Virginia	96.7
26	Arkansas	94.2
27	Michigan	91.6
28	Oklahoma	91.3
29	Louisiana	91.1
30	Alabama	85.3
31	Alaska	75.2
32	New Mexico	72.7
33	Georgia	72.4
34	Rhode Island	66.7
35	Maine	62.2
36	New Hampshire	58.8
37	Colorado	58.6
38	South Dakota	54.9
39	Indiana	53.6
40	Utah	52.9
41	Iowa	30.1
42	Idaho	27.4
42	Nebraska	27.4
44	West Virginia	22.9
45	Wyoming	15.3
46	North Dakota	5.9
NA	Florida**	NA
NA	Kansas**	NA
NA	Montana**	NA
NA	Vermont**	NA
	District of Columbia**	NA

Source: Morgan Quitno Press using data from Federal Bureau of Investigation
    "Crime in the United States 1996" (Uniform Crime Reports, October 4, 1997)
*By law enforcement agencies submitting complete reports to the F.B.I. for 12 months in 1996. Arrests of youths 17 years and younger divided into population of 10 to 17 year olds. See important note at beginning of this chapter. Robbery is the taking or attempting to take anything of value by force or threat of force.
**Not available.

Reported Arrests of Juveniles for Robbery
As a Percent of All Such Arrests in 1996
National Percent = 32.1% of Reported Arrests for Robbery*

ALPHA ORDER

RANK	STATE	PERCENT
45	Alabama	19.6
18	Alaska	32.9
27	Arizona	29.1
26	Arkansas	29.5
15	California	33.7
17	Colorado	33.1
30	Connecticut	26.8
31	Delaware	26.7
NA	Florida**	NA
44	Georgia	20.2
4	Hawaii	44.1
8	Idaho	38.5
12	Illinois	36.6
37	Indiana	24.2
24	Iowa	29.8
NA	Kansas**	NA
35	Kentucky	24.7
41	Louisiana	23.3
2	Maine	46.6
14	Maryland	35.0
20	Massachusetts	32.6
40	Michigan	23.7
5	Minnesota	39.9
32	Mississippi	25.9
33	Missouri	25.8
NA	Montana**	NA
19	Nebraska	32.8
41	Nevada	23.3
3	New Hampshire	45.8
11	New Jersey	37.4
28	New Mexico	28.6
13	New York	36.3
36	North Carolina	24.3
29	North Dakota	27.3
22	Ohio	32.0
6	Oklahoma	39.2
34	Oregon	25.5
25	Pennsylvania	29.7
23	Rhode Island	31.3
39	South Carolina	23.9
1	South Dakota	58.7
43	Tennessee	21.1
21	Texas	32.3
9	Utah	37.7
NA	Vermont**	NA
37	Virginia	24.2
10	Washington	37.6
46	West Virginia	17.3
7	Wisconsin	39.1
16	Wyoming	33.3

RANK ORDER

RANK	STATE	PERCENT
1	South Dakota	58.7
2	Maine	46.6
3	New Hampshire	45.8
4	Hawaii	44.1
5	Minnesota	39.9
6	Oklahoma	39.2
7	Wisconsin	39.1
8	Idaho	38.5
9	Utah	37.7
10	Washington	37.6
11	New Jersey	37.4
12	Illinois	36.6
13	New York	36.3
14	Maryland	35.0
15	California	33.7
16	Wyoming	33.3
17	Colorado	33.1
18	Alaska	32.9
19	Nebraska	32.8
20	Massachusetts	32.6
21	Texas	32.3
22	Ohio	32.0
23	Rhode Island	31.3
24	Iowa	29.8
25	Pennsylvania	29.7
26	Arkansas	29.5
27	Arizona	29.1
28	New Mexico	28.6
29	North Dakota	27.3
30	Connecticut	26.8
31	Delaware	26.7
32	Mississippi	25.9
33	Missouri	25.8
34	Oregon	25.5
35	Kentucky	24.7
36	North Carolina	24.3
37	Indiana	24.2
37	Virginia	24.2
39	South Carolina	23.9
40	Michigan	23.7
41	Louisiana	23.3
41	Nevada	23.3
43	Tennessee	21.1
44	Georgia	20.2
45	Alabama	19.6
46	West Virginia	17.3
NA	Florida**	NA
NA	Kansas**	NA
NA	Montana**	NA
NA	Vermont**	NA
	District of Columbia**	NA

Source: Morgan Quitno Press using data from Federal Bureau of Investigation
    "Crime in the United States 1996" (Uniform Crime Reports, October 4, 1997)
*Arrests of youths 17 years and younger by law enforcement agencies submitting complete reports to the F.B.I. for
12 months in 1996. Robbery is the taking or attempting to take anything of value by force or threat of force.
**Not available.

211

Reported Arrests of Juveniles for Aggravated Assault in 1996

National Total = 56,894 Reported Arrests*

ALPHA ORDER

RANK	STATE	ARRESTS	% of USA
28	Alabama	520	0.91%
37	Alaska	183	0.32%
13	Arizona	1,530	2.69%
30	Arkansas	496	0.87%
1	California	11,807	20.75%
29	Colorado	519	0.91%
20	Connecticut	866	1.52%
35	Delaware	250	0.44%
NA	Florida**	NA	NA
22	Georgia	801	1.41%
38	Hawaii	136	0.24%
33	Idaho	324	0.57%
9	Illinois	1,919	3.37%
10	Indiana	1,709	3.00%
27	Iowa	524	0.92%
NA	Kansas**	NA	NA
31	Kentucky	405	0.71%
16	Louisiana	1,201	2.11%
39	Maine	130	0.23%
7	Maryland	1,994	3.50%
8	Massachusetts	1,927	3.39%
11	Michigan	1,692	2.97%
17	Minnesota	1,091	1.92%
41	Mississippi	119	0.21%
19	Missouri	932	1.64%
NA	Montana**	NA	NA
42	Nebraska	91	0.16%
36	Nevada	232	0.41%
45	New Hampshire	42	0.07%
4	New Jersey	2,936	5.16%
34	New Mexico	317	0.56%
3	New York	3,779	6.64%
6	North Carolina	2,271	3.99%
46	North Dakota	29	0.05%
12	Ohio	1,594	2.80%
21	Oklahoma	837	1.47%
24	Oregon	637	1.12%
5	Pennsylvania	2,578	4.53%
32	Rhode Island	396	0.70%
14	South Carolina	1,261	2.22%
39	South Dakota	130	0.23%
25	Tennessee	635	1.12%
2	Texas	4,249	7.47%
26	Utah	563	0.99%
NA	Vermont**	NA	NA
23	Virginia	785	1.38%
18	Washington	1,069	1.88%
43	West Virginia	85	0.15%
15	Wisconsin	1,244	2.19%
44	Wyoming	59	0.10%

RANK ORDER

RANK	STATE	ARRESTS	% of USA
1	California	11,807	20.75%
2	Texas	4,249	7.47%
3	New York	3,779	6.64%
4	New Jersey	2,936	5.16%
5	Pennsylvania	2,578	4.53%
6	North Carolina	2,271	3.99%
7	Maryland	1,994	3.50%
8	Massachusetts	1,927	3.39%
9	Illinois	1,919	3.37%
10	Indiana	1,709	3.00%
11	Michigan	1,692	2.97%
12	Ohio	1,594	2.80%
13	Arizona	1,530	2.69%
14	South Carolina	1,261	2.22%
15	Wisconsin	1,244	2.19%
16	Louisiana	1,201	2.11%
17	Minnesota	1,091	1.92%
18	Washington	1,069	1.88%
19	Missouri	932	1.64%
20	Connecticut	866	1.52%
21	Oklahoma	837	1.47%
22	Georgia	801	1.41%
23	Virginia	785	1.38%
24	Oregon	637	1.12%
25	Tennessee	635	1.12%
26	Utah	563	0.99%
27	Iowa	524	0.92%
28	Alabama	520	0.91%
29	Colorado	519	0.91%
30	Arkansas	496	0.87%
31	Kentucky	405	0.71%
32	Rhode Island	396	0.70%
33	Idaho	324	0.57%
34	New Mexico	317	0.56%
35	Delaware	250	0.44%
36	Nevada	232	0.41%
37	Alaska	183	0.32%
38	Hawaii	136	0.24%
39	Maine	130	0.23%
39	South Dakota	130	0.23%
41	Mississippi	119	0.21%
42	Nebraska	91	0.16%
43	West Virginia	85	0.15%
44	Wyoming	59	0.10%
45	New Hampshire	42	0.07%
46	North Dakota	29	0.05%
NA	Florida**	NA	NA
NA	Kansas**	NA	NA
NA	Montana**	NA	NA
NA	Vermont**	NA	NA
	District of Columbia**	NA	NA

Source: Federal Bureau of Investigation
    "Crime in the United States 1996" (Uniform Crime Reports, October 4, 1997)
*Arrests of youths 17 years and younger by law enforcement agencies submitting complete reports to the F.B.I. for 12 months in 1996. Aggravated assault is an attack for the purpose of inflicting severe bodily injury. See important note at beginning of this chapter.
**Not available.

Reported Juvenile Arrest Rate for Aggravated Assault in 1996

National Rate = 262.1 Reported Arrests per 100,000 Juvenile Population*

ALPHA ORDER

RANK ORDER

RANK	STATE	RATE	RANK	STATE	RATE
40	Alabama	110.6	1	Delaware	641.5
17	Alaska	254.8	2	Illinois	606.1
11	Arizona	333.8	3	Kentucky	457.3
33	Arkansas	171.8	4	Maryland	457.2
10	California	339.5	5	Indiana	444.8
34	Colorado	156.0	6	Rhode Island	406.1
12	Connecticut	329.9	7	Massachusetts	382.3
1	Delaware	641.5	8	New Jersey	365.7
NA	Florida**	NA	9	Louisiana	341.8
35	Georgia	153.3	10	California	339.5
41	Hawaii	106.0	11	Arizona	333.8
27	Idaho	197.3	12	Connecticut	329.9
2	Illinois	606.1	13	South Carolina	304.1
5	Indiana	444.8	14	North Carolina	290.7
31	Iowa	187.9	15	New York	286.2
NA	Kansas**	NA	16	Tennessee	275.5
3	Kentucky	457.3	17	Alaska	254.8
9	Louisiana	341.8	18	Pennsylvania	254.0
42	Maine	91.9	19	Missouri	251.8
4	Maryland	457.2	20	Washington	243.1
7	Massachusetts	382.3	21	New Mexico	237.5
32	Michigan	179.6	22	Ohio	213.3
23	Minnesota	206.9	23	Minnesota	206.9
37	Mississippi	145.9	24	Texas	206.3
19	Missouri	251.8	25	Oklahoma	202.3
NA	Montana**	NA	26	Oregon	199.2
43	Nebraska	60.8	27	Idaho	197.3
38	Nevada	136.0	28	Utah	196.0
46	New Hampshire	41.2	28	Wisconsin	196.0
8	New Jersey	365.7	30	South Dakota	192.9
21	New Mexico	237.5	31	Iowa	187.9
15	New York	286.2	32	Michigan	179.6
14	North Carolina	290.7	33	Arkansas	171.8
44	North Dakota	57.4	34	Colorado	156.0
22	Ohio	213.3	35	Georgia	153.3
25	Oklahoma	202.3	36	Wyoming	150.0
26	Oregon	199.2	37	Mississippi	145.9
18	Pennsylvania	254.0	38	Nevada	136.0
6	Rhode Island	406.1	39	Virginia	119.1
13	South Carolina	304.1	40	Alabama	110.6
30	South Dakota	192.9	41	Hawaii	106.0
16	Tennessee	275.5	42	Maine	91.9
24	Texas	206.3	43	Nebraska	60.8
28	Utah	196.0	44	North Dakota	57.4
NA	Vermont**	NA	45	West Virginia	41.4
39	Virginia	119.1	46	New Hampshire	41.2
20	Washington	243.1	NA	Florida**	NA
45	West Virginia	41.4	NA	Kansas**	NA
28	Wisconsin	196.0	NA	Montana**	NA
36	Wyoming	150.0	NA	Vermont**	NA
				District of Columbia**	NA

Source: Morgan Quitno Press using data from Federal Bureau of Investigation
   "Crime in the United States 1996" (Uniform Crime Reports, October 4, 1997)
*By law enforcement agencies submitting complete reports to the F.B.I. for 12 months in 1996. Arrests of youths 17 years and younger divided into population of 10 to 17 year olds. See important note at beginning of this chapter. Aggravated assault is an attack for the purpose of inflicting severe bodily injury.
**Not available.

213

Reported Arrests of Juveniles for Aggravated Assault
As a Percent of All Such Arrests in 1996
National Percent = 14.7% of Reported Arrests for Aggravated Assault*

ALPHA ORDER

RANK ORDER

RANK	STATE	PERCENT		RANK	STATE	PERCENT
46	Alabama	6.4		1	Utah	34.7
28	Alaska	15.1		2	Idaho	28.3
13	Arizona	22.2		3	Maryland	26.7
34	Arkansas	13.5		3	Minnesota	26.7
43	California	10.3		5	North Dakota	25.9
38	Colorado	12.8		6	Oregon	25.3
18	Connecticut	20.0		7	South Dakota	24.8
16	Delaware	20.5		8	Indiana	24.0
NA	Florida**	NA		9	Washington	23.8
40	Georgia	11.0		10	Illinois	23.5
14	Hawaii	21.6		11	Pennsylvania	22.5
2	Idaho	28.3		12	New Jersey	22.4
10	Illinois	23.5		13	Arizona	22.2
8	Indiana	24.0		14	Hawaii	21.6
19	Iowa	19.2		15	Maine	21.1
NA	Kansas**	NA		16	Delaware	20.5
37	Kentucky	13.0		17	Wisconsin	20.4
27	Louisiana	15.5		18	Connecticut	20.0
15	Maine	21.1		19	Iowa	19.2
3	Maryland	26.7		20	Rhode Island	19.0
24	Massachusetts	16.3		21	New Mexico	18.8
39	Michigan	12.1		22	Texas	18.3
3	Minnesota	26.7		23	Oklahoma	17.1
32	Mississippi	13.7		24	Massachusetts	16.3
29	Missouri	14.6		25	Wyoming	16.1
NA	Montana**	NA		26	Nebraska	15.7
26	Nebraska	15.7		27	Louisiana	15.5
36	Nevada	13.2		28	Alaska	15.1
30	New Hampshire	14.4		29	Missouri	14.6
12	New Jersey	22.4		30	New Hampshire	14.4
21	New Mexico	18.8		31	New York	13.8
31	New York	13.8		32	Mississippi	13.7
41	North Carolina	10.6		32	South Carolina	13.7
5	North Dakota	25.9		34	Arkansas	13.5
35	Ohio	13.4		35	Ohio	13.4
23	Oklahoma	17.1		36	Nevada	13.2
6	Oregon	25.3		37	Kentucky	13.0
11	Pennsylvania	22.5		38	Colorado	12.8
20	Rhode Island	19.0		39	Michigan	12.1
32	South Carolina	13.7		40	Georgia	11.0
7	South Dakota	24.8		41	North Carolina	10.6
44	Tennessee	9.9		42	Virginia	10.4
22	Texas	18.3		43	California	10.3
1	Utah	34.7		44	Tennessee	9.9
NA	Vermont**	NA		45	West Virginia	9.0
42	Virginia	10.4		46	Alabama	6.4
9	Washington	23.8		NA	Florida**	NA
45	West Virginia	9.0		NA	Kansas**	NA
17	Wisconsin	20.4		NA	Montana**	NA
25	Wyoming	16.1		NA	Vermont**	NA
					District of Columbia**	NA

Source: Morgan Quitno Press using data from Federal Bureau of Investigation
 "Crime in the United States 1996" (Uniform Crime Reports, October 4, 1997)
*Arrests of youths 17 years and younger by law enforcement agencies submitting complete reports to the F.B.I. for
12 months in 1996. Aggravated assault is an attack for the purpose of inflicting severe bodily injury.
**Not available.

Reported Arrests of Juveniles for Property Crime in 1996

National Total = 530,531 Reported Arrests*

<table>
<tr><td colspan="4">ALPHA ORDER</td><td colspan="4">RANK ORDER</td></tr>
<tr><th>RANK</th><th>STATE</th><th>ARRESTS</th><th>% of USA</th><th>RANK</th><th>STATE</th><th>ARRESTS</th><th>% of USA</th></tr>
<tr><td>28</td><td>Alabama</td><td>6,685</td><td>1.26%</td><td>1</td><td>California</td><td>78,205</td><td>14.74%</td></tr>
<tr><td>41</td><td>Alaska</td><td>2,315</td><td>0.44%</td><td>2</td><td>Texas</td><td>50,382</td><td>9.50%</td></tr>
<tr><td>10</td><td>Arizona</td><td>16,524</td><td>3.11%</td><td>3</td><td>Wisconsin</td><td>29,282</td><td>5.52%</td></tr>
<tr><td>29</td><td>Arkansas</td><td>6,475</td><td>1.22%</td><td>4</td><td>Washington</td><td>18,455</td><td>3.48%</td></tr>
<tr><td>1</td><td>California</td><td>78,205</td><td>14.74%</td><td>5</td><td>New York</td><td>17,744</td><td>3.34%</td></tr>
<tr><td>22</td><td>Colorado</td><td>9,404</td><td>1.77%</td><td>6</td><td>New Jersey</td><td>17,519</td><td>3.30%</td></tr>
<tr><td>25</td><td>Connecticut</td><td>7,169</td><td>1.35%</td><td>7</td><td>Pennsylvania</td><td>17,053</td><td>3.21%</td></tr>
<tr><td>44</td><td>Delaware</td><td>1,730</td><td>0.33%</td><td>8</td><td>Minnesota</td><td>16,956</td><td>3.20%</td></tr>
<tr><td>NA</td><td>Florida**</td><td>NA</td><td>NA</td><td>9</td><td>Ohio</td><td>16,787</td><td>3.16%</td></tr>
<tr><td>20</td><td>Georgia</td><td>10,137</td><td>1.91%</td><td>10</td><td>Arizona</td><td>16,524</td><td>3.11%</td></tr>
<tr><td>36</td><td>Hawaii</td><td>4,005</td><td>0.75%</td><td>11</td><td>North Carolina</td><td>15,274</td><td>2.88%</td></tr>
<tr><td>27</td><td>Idaho</td><td>6,739</td><td>1.27%</td><td>12</td><td>Michigan</td><td>15,135</td><td>2.85%</td></tr>
<tr><td>19</td><td>Illinois</td><td>10,225</td><td>1.93%</td><td>13</td><td>Maryland</td><td>13,886</td><td>2.62%</td></tr>
<tr><td>24</td><td>Indiana</td><td>8,894</td><td>1.68%</td><td>14</td><td>Virginia</td><td>13,717</td><td>2.59%</td></tr>
<tr><td>30</td><td>Iowa</td><td>5,637</td><td>1.06%</td><td>15</td><td>Oregon</td><td>12,754</td><td>2.40%</td></tr>
<tr><td>NA</td><td>Kansas**</td><td>NA</td><td>NA</td><td>16</td><td>Missouri</td><td>11,497</td><td>2.17%</td></tr>
<tr><td>37</td><td>Kentucky</td><td>3,084</td><td>0.58%</td><td>17</td><td>Oklahoma</td><td>11,468</td><td>2.16%</td></tr>
<tr><td>21</td><td>Louisiana</td><td>10,029</td><td>1.89%</td><td>18</td><td>Utah</td><td>10,726</td><td>2.02%</td></tr>
<tr><td>33</td><td>Maine</td><td>4,853</td><td>0.91%</td><td>19</td><td>Illinois</td><td>10,225</td><td>1.93%</td></tr>
<tr><td>13</td><td>Maryland</td><td>13,886</td><td>2.62%</td><td>20</td><td>Georgia</td><td>10,137</td><td>1.91%</td></tr>
<tr><td>32</td><td>Massachusetts</td><td>5,334</td><td>1.01%</td><td>21</td><td>Louisiana</td><td>10,029</td><td>1.89%</td></tr>
<tr><td>12</td><td>Michigan</td><td>15,135</td><td>2.85%</td><td>22</td><td>Colorado</td><td>9,404</td><td>1.77%</td></tr>
<tr><td>8</td><td>Minnesota</td><td>16,956</td><td>3.20%</td><td>23</td><td>South Carolina</td><td>9,202</td><td>1.73%</td></tr>
<tr><td>43</td><td>Mississippi</td><td>2,166</td><td>0.41%</td><td>24</td><td>Indiana</td><td>8,894</td><td>1.68%</td></tr>
<tr><td>16</td><td>Missouri</td><td>11,497</td><td>2.17%</td><td>25</td><td>Connecticut</td><td>7,169</td><td>1.35%</td></tr>
<tr><td>NA</td><td>Montana**</td><td>NA</td><td>NA</td><td>26</td><td>Tennessee</td><td>6,792</td><td>1.28%</td></tr>
<tr><td>35</td><td>Nebraska</td><td>4,140</td><td>0.78%</td><td>27</td><td>Idaho</td><td>6,739</td><td>1.27%</td></tr>
<tr><td>31</td><td>Nevada</td><td>5,456</td><td>1.03%</td><td>28</td><td>Alabama</td><td>6,685</td><td>1.26%</td></tr>
<tr><td>42</td><td>New Hampshire</td><td>2,232</td><td>0.42%</td><td>29</td><td>Arkansas</td><td>6,475</td><td>1.22%</td></tr>
<tr><td>6</td><td>New Jersey</td><td>17,519</td><td>3.30%</td><td>30</td><td>Iowa</td><td>5,637</td><td>1.06%</td></tr>
<tr><td>34</td><td>New Mexico</td><td>4,415</td><td>0.83%</td><td>31</td><td>Nevada</td><td>5,456</td><td>1.03%</td></tr>
<tr><td>5</td><td>New York</td><td>17,744</td><td>3.34%</td><td>32</td><td>Massachusetts</td><td>5,334</td><td>1.01%</td></tr>
<tr><td>11</td><td>North Carolina</td><td>15,274</td><td>2.88%</td><td>33</td><td>Maine</td><td>4,853</td><td>0.91%</td></tr>
<tr><td>45</td><td>North Dakota</td><td>1,293</td><td>0.24%</td><td>34</td><td>New Mexico</td><td>4,415</td><td>0.83%</td></tr>
<tr><td>9</td><td>Ohio</td><td>16,787</td><td>3.16%</td><td>35</td><td>Nebraska</td><td>4,140</td><td>0.78%</td></tr>
<tr><td>17</td><td>Oklahoma</td><td>11,468</td><td>2.16%</td><td>36</td><td>Hawaii</td><td>4,005</td><td>0.75%</td></tr>
<tr><td>15</td><td>Oregon</td><td>12,754</td><td>2.40%</td><td>37</td><td>Kentucky</td><td>3,084</td><td>0.58%</td></tr>
<tr><td>7</td><td>Pennsylvania</td><td>17,053</td><td>3.21%</td><td>38</td><td>South Dakota</td><td>2,622</td><td>0.49%</td></tr>
<tr><td>40</td><td>Rhode Island</td><td>2,387</td><td>0.45%</td><td>39</td><td>West Virginia</td><td>2,505</td><td>0.47%</td></tr>
<tr><td>23</td><td>South Carolina</td><td>9,202</td><td>1.73%</td><td>40</td><td>Rhode Island</td><td>2,387</td><td>0.45%</td></tr>
<tr><td>38</td><td>South Dakota</td><td>2,622</td><td>0.49%</td><td>41</td><td>Alaska</td><td>2,315</td><td>0.44%</td></tr>
<tr><td>26</td><td>Tennessee</td><td>6,792</td><td>1.28%</td><td>42</td><td>New Hampshire</td><td>2,232</td><td>0.42%</td></tr>
<tr><td>2</td><td>Texas</td><td>50,382</td><td>9.50%</td><td>43</td><td>Mississippi</td><td>2,166</td><td>0.41%</td></tr>
<tr><td>18</td><td>Utah</td><td>10,726</td><td>2.02%</td><td>44</td><td>Delaware</td><td>1,730</td><td>0.33%</td></tr>
<tr><td>NA</td><td>Vermont**</td><td>NA</td><td>NA</td><td>45</td><td>North Dakota</td><td>1,293</td><td>0.24%</td></tr>
<tr><td>14</td><td>Virginia</td><td>13,717</td><td>2.59%</td><td>46</td><td>Wyoming</td><td>1,242</td><td>0.23%</td></tr>
<tr><td>4</td><td>Washington</td><td>18,455</td><td>3.48%</td><td>NA</td><td>Florida**</td><td>NA</td><td>NA</td></tr>
<tr><td>39</td><td>West Virginia</td><td>2,505</td><td>0.47%</td><td>NA</td><td>Kansas**</td><td>NA</td><td>NA</td></tr>
<tr><td>3</td><td>Wisconsin</td><td>29,282</td><td>5.52%</td><td>NA</td><td>Montana**</td><td>NA</td><td>NA</td></tr>
<tr><td>46</td><td>Wyoming</td><td>1,242</td><td>0.23%</td><td>NA</td><td>Vermont**</td><td>NA</td><td>NA</td></tr>
<tr><td></td><td></td><td></td><td></td><td></td><td>District of Columbia**</td><td>NA</td><td>NA</td></tr>
</table>

Source: Federal Bureau of Investigation
   "Crime in the United States 1996" (Uniform Crime Reports, October 4, 1997)
*Arrests of youths 17 years and younger by law enforcement agencies submitting complete reports to the F.B.I. for 12 months in 1996. Property crimes are offenses of burglary, larceny-theft, motor vehicle theft and arson. See important note at beginning of this chapter.
**Not available.

Reported Juvenile Arrest Rate for Property Crime in 1996

National Rate = 2,444.1 Reported Arrests per 100,000 Juvenile Population*

RANK	STATE	RATE
43	Alabama	1,421.7
13	Alaska	3,222.9
8	Arizona	3,605.5
33	Arkansas	2,243.3
31	California	2,248.8
22	Colorado	2,826.4
25	Connecticut	2,731.3
2	Delaware	4,439.2
NA	Florida**	NA
40	Georgia	1,940.6
18	Hawaii	3,122.0
4	Idaho	4,104.6
12	Illinois	3,229.6
30	Indiana	2,314.7
38	Iowa	2,021.6
NA	Kansas**	NA
9	Kentucky	3,482.3
21	Louisiana	2,854.1
10	Maine	3,430.0
16	Maryland	3,183.8
46	Massachusetts	1,058.2
42	Michigan	1,606.9
14	Minnesota	3,214.9
26	Mississippi	2,655.5
19	Missouri	3,106.2
NA	Montana**	NA
24	Nebraska	2,765.9
15	Nevada	3,198.9
35	New Hampshire	2,187.1
36	New Jersey	2,182.4
11	New Mexico	3,307.7
44	New York	1,343.6
39	North Carolina	1,955.0
27	North Dakota	2,559.2
32	Ohio	2,246.5
23	Oklahoma	2,771.4
5	Oregon	3,987.7
41	Pennsylvania	1,680.0
28	Rhode Island	2,447.6
34	South Carolina	2,219.2
6	South Dakota	3,891.5
20	Tennessee	2,947.3
29	Texas	2,446.6
7	Utah	3,734.1
NA	Vermont**	NA
37	Virginia	2,081.5
3	Washington	4,196.3
45	West Virginia	1,221.0
1	Wisconsin	4,613.6
17	Wyoming	3,158.4

RANK	STATE	RATE
1	Wisconsin	4,613.6
2	Delaware	4,439.2
3	Washington	4,196.3
4	Idaho	4,104.6
5	Oregon	3,987.7
6	South Dakota	3,891.5
7	Utah	3,734.1
8	Arizona	3,605.5
9	Kentucky	3,482.3
10	Maine	3,430.0
11	New Mexico	3,307.7
12	Illinois	3,229.6
13	Alaska	3,222.9
14	Minnesota	3,214.9
15	Nevada	3,198.9
16	Maryland	3,183.8
17	Wyoming	3,158.4
18	Hawaii	3,122.0
19	Missouri	3,106.2
20	Tennessee	2,947.3
21	Louisiana	2,854.1
22	Colorado	2,826.4
23	Oklahoma	2,771.4
24	Nebraska	2,765.9
25	Connecticut	2,731.3
26	Mississippi	2,655.5
27	North Dakota	2,559.2
28	Rhode Island	2,447.6
29	Texas	2,446.6
30	Indiana	2,314.7
31	California	2,248.8
32	Ohio	2,246.5
33	Arkansas	2,243.3
34	South Carolina	2,219.2
35	New Hampshire	2,187.1
36	New Jersey	2,182.4
37	Virginia	2,081.5
38	Iowa	2,021.6
39	North Carolina	1,955.0
40	Georgia	1,940.6
41	Pennsylvania	1,680.0
42	Michigan	1,606.9
43	Alabama	1,421.7
44	New York	1,343.6
45	West Virginia	1,221.0
46	Massachusetts	1,058.2
NA	Florida**	NA
NA	Kansas**	NA
NA	Montana**	NA
NA	Vermont**	NA
	District of Columbia**	NA

Source: Morgan Quitno Press using data from Federal Bureau of Investigation
   "Crime in the United States 1996" (Uniform Crime Reports, October 4, 1997)
*By law enforcement agencies submitting complete reports to the F.B.I. for 12 months in 1996. Arrests of youths 17 years and younger divided into population of 10 to 17 year olds. See important note at beginning of this chapter. Property crimes are offenses of burglary, larceny-theft, motor vehicle theft and arson.
**Not available.

Reported Arrests of Juveniles for Property Crime
As a Percent of All Such Arrests in 1996
National Percent = 35.2% of Reported Arrests for Property Crime*

ALPHA ORDER

RANK	STATE	PERCENT
44	Alabama	25.7
13	Alaska	43.6
27	Arizona	34.0
31	Arkansas	32.1
25	California	34.9
18	Colorado	37.8
38	Connecticut	29.2
32	Delaware	31.7
NA	Florida**	NA
42	Georgia	27.0
22	Hawaii	36.7
1	Idaho	59.1
46	Illinois	21.9
17	Indiana	38.2
14	Iowa	43.5
NA	Kansas**	NA
20	Kentucky	37.5
33	Louisiana	31.4
11	Maine	48.8
25	Maryland	34.9
40	Massachusetts	27.5
22	Michigan	36.7
4	Minnesota	52.5
35	Mississippi	30.8
37	Missouri	29.8
NA	Montana**	NA
6	Nebraska	52.3
34	Nevada	31.2
7	New Hampshire	51.0
28	New Jersey	33.9
21	New Mexico	36.8
45	New York	23.8
43	North Carolina	25.9
2	North Dakota	57.0
18	Ohio	37.8
10	Oklahoma	49.6
24	Oregon	36.4
30	Pennsylvania	32.8
15	Rhode Island	42.3
29	South Carolina	33.0
3	South Dakota	53.3
41	Tennessee	27.2
16	Texas	38.3
8	Utah	50.3
NA	Vermont**	NA
36	Virginia	30.6
12	Washington	44.9
39	West Virginia	28.9
9	Wisconsin	50.1
5	Wyoming	52.4

RANK ORDER

RANK	STATE	PERCENT
1	Idaho	59.1
2	North Dakota	57.0
3	South Dakota	53.3
4	Minnesota	52.5
5	Wyoming	52.4
6	Nebraska	52.3
7	New Hampshire	51.0
8	Utah	50.3
9	Wisconsin	50.1
10	Oklahoma	49.6
11	Maine	48.8
12	Washington	44.9
13	Alaska	43.6
14	Iowa	43.5
15	Rhode Island	42.3
16	Texas	38.3
17	Indiana	38.2
18	Colorado	37.8
18	Ohio	37.8
20	Kentucky	37.5
21	New Mexico	36.8
22	Hawaii	36.7
22	Michigan	36.7
24	Oregon	36.4
25	California	34.9
25	Maryland	34.9
27	Arizona	34.0
28	New Jersey	33.9
29	South Carolina	33.0
30	Pennsylvania	32.8
31	Arkansas	32.1
32	Delaware	31.7
33	Louisiana	31.4
34	Nevada	31.2
35	Mississippi	30.8
36	Virginia	30.6
37	Missouri	29.8
38	Connecticut	29.2
39	West Virginia	28.9
40	Massachusetts	27.5
41	Tennessee	27.2
42	Georgia	27.0
43	North Carolina	25.9
44	Alabama	25.7
45	New York	23.8
46	Illinois	21.9
NA	Florida**	NA
NA	Kansas**	NA
NA	Montana**	NA
NA	Vermont**	NA
	District of Columbia**	NA

Source: Morgan Quitno Press using data from Federal Bureau of Investigation
    "Crime in the United States 1996" (Uniform Crime Reports, October 4, 1997)
*Arrests of youths 17 years and younger by law enforcement agencies submitting complete reports to the F.B.I. for
12 months in 1996. Property crimes are offenses of burglary, larceny-theft, motor vehicle theft and arson.
**Not available.

Reported Arrests of Juveniles for Burglary in 1996

National Total = 97,809 Reported Arrests*

ALPHA ORDER					RANK ORDER			
RANK	STATE		ARRESTS	% of USA	RANK	STATE	ARRESTS	% of USA
28	Alabama		1,051	1.07%	1	California	22,111	22.61%
37	Alaska		486	0.50%	2	Texas	9,649	9.87%
10	Arizona		2,772	2.83%	3	North Carolina	3,925	4.01%
25	Arkansas		1,244	1.27%	4	Wisconsin	3,674	3.76%
1	California		22,111	22.61%	5	New Jersey	3,238	3.31%
27	Colorado		1,069	1.09%	6	New York	3,203	3.27%
21	Connecticut		1,483	1.52%	7	Pennsylvania	3,032	3.10%
44	Delaware		253	0.26%	8	Ohio	2,912	2.98%
NA	Florida**		NA	NA	9	Washington	2,846	2.91%
16	Georgia		2,012	2.06%	10	Arizona	2,772	2.83%
36	Hawaii		496	0.51%	11	Michigan	2,762	2.82%
32	Idaho		858	0.88%	12	Maryland	2,633	2.69%
24	Illinois		1,265	1.29%	13	Louisiana	2,178	2.23%
30	Indiana		961	0.98%	13	South Carolina	2,178	2.23%
33	Iowa		852	0.87%	15	Virginia	2,087	2.13%
NA	Kansas**		NA	NA	16	Georgia	2,012	2.06%
34	Kentucky		620	0.63%	17	Oklahoma	1,909	1.95%
13	Louisiana		2,178	2.23%	18	Minnesota	1,815	1.86%
26	Maine		1,095	1.12%	19	Oregon	1,665	1.70%
12	Maryland		2,633	2.69%	20	Missouri	1,524	1.56%
22	Massachusetts		1,416	1.45%	21	Connecticut	1,483	1.52%
11	Michigan		2,762	2.82%	22	Massachusetts	1,416	1.45%
18	Minnesota		1,815	1.86%	23	Nevada	1,333	1.36%
35	Mississippi		617	0.63%	24	Illinois	1,265	1.29%
20	Missouri		1,524	1.56%	25	Arkansas	1,244	1.27%
NA	Montana**		NA	NA	26	Maine	1,095	1.12%
39	Nebraska		484	0.49%	27	Colorado	1,069	1.09%
23	Nevada		1,333	1.36%	28	Alabama	1,051	1.07%
43	New Hampshire		277	0.28%	29	Utah	981	1.00%
5	New Jersey		3,238	3.31%	30	Indiana	961	0.98%
38	New Mexico		485	0.50%	31	Tennessee	895	0.92%
6	New York		3,203	3.27%	32	Idaho	858	0.88%
3	North Carolina		3,925	4.01%	33	Iowa	852	0.87%
45	North Dakota		137	0.14%	34	Kentucky	620	0.63%
8	Ohio		2,912	2.98%	35	Mississippi	617	0.63%
17	Oklahoma		1,909	1.95%	36	Hawaii	496	0.51%
19	Oregon		1,665	1.70%	37	Alaska	486	0.50%
7	Pennsylvania		3,032	3.10%	38	New Mexico	485	0.50%
41	Rhode Island		394	0.40%	39	Nebraska	484	0.49%
13	South Carolina		2,178	2.23%	40	West Virginia	472	0.48%
42	South Dakota		369	0.38%	41	Rhode Island	394	0.40%
31	Tennessee		895	0.92%	42	South Dakota	369	0.38%
2	Texas		9,649	9.87%	43	New Hampshire	277	0.28%
29	Utah		981	1.00%	44	Delaware	253	0.26%
NA	Vermont**		NA	NA	45	North Dakota	137	0.14%
15	Virginia		2,087	2.13%	46	Wyoming	91	0.09%
9	Washington		2,846	2.91%	NA	Florida**	NA	NA
40	West Virginia		472	0.48%	NA	Kansas**	NA	NA
4	Wisconsin		3,674	3.76%	NA	Montana**	NA	NA
46	Wyoming		91	0.09%	NA	Vermont**	NA	NA
						District of Columbia**	NA	NA

Source: Federal Bureau of Investigation
   "Crime in the United States 1996" (Uniform Crime Reports, October 4, 1997)
*Arrests of youths 17 years and younger by law enforcement agencies submitting complete reports to the F.B.I. for 12 months in 1996. Burglary is the unlawful entry of a structure to commit a felony or theft. Attempts are included. See important note at beginning of this chapter.
**Not available.

Reported Juvenile Arrest Rate for Burglary in 1996

National Rate = 450.6 Reported Arrests per 100,000 Juvenile Population*

ALPHA ORDER

RANK	STATE	RATE
46	Alabama	223.5
5	Alaska	676.6
10	Arizona	604.8
21	Arkansas	431.0
8	California	635.8
34	Colorado	321.3
13	Connecticut	565.0
6	Delaware	649.2
NA	Florida**	NA
29	Georgia	385.2
28	Hawaii	386.6
16	Idaho	522.6
25	Illinois	399.6
42	Indiana	250.1
36	Iowa	305.6
NA	Kansas**	NA
4	Kentucky	700.1
9	Louisiana	619.8
2	Maine	773.9
11	Maryland	603.7
39	Massachusetts	280.9
38	Michigan	293.2
31	Minnesota	344.1
3	Mississippi	756.4
22	Missouri	411.7
NA	Montana**	NA
33	Nebraska	323.4
1	Nevada	781.6
40	New Hampshire	271.4
24	New Jersey	403.4
30	New Mexico	363.4
43	New York	242.5
18	North Carolina	502.4
41	North Dakota	271.2
26	Ohio	389.7
20	Oklahoma	461.3
17	Oregon	520.6
37	Pennsylvania	298.7
23	Rhode Island	404.0
15	South Carolina	525.3
14	South Dakota	547.7
27	Tennessee	388.4
19	Texas	468.6
32	Utah	341.5
NA	Vermont**	NA
35	Virginia	316.7
7	Washington	647.1
45	West Virginia	230.1
12	Wisconsin	578.9
44	Wyoming	231.4

RANK ORDER

RANK	STATE	RATE
1	Nevada	781.6
2	Maine	773.9
3	Mississippi	756.4
4	Kentucky	700.1
5	Alaska	676.6
6	Delaware	649.2
7	Washington	647.1
8	California	635.8
9	Louisiana	619.8
10	Arizona	604.8
11	Maryland	603.7
12	Wisconsin	578.9
13	Connecticut	565.0
14	South Dakota	547.7
15	South Carolina	525.3
16	Idaho	522.6
17	Oregon	520.6
18	North Carolina	502.4
19	Texas	468.6
20	Oklahoma	461.3
21	Arkansas	431.0
22	Missouri	411.7
23	Rhode Island	404.0
24	New Jersey	403.4
25	Illinois	399.6
26	Ohio	389.7
27	Tennessee	388.4
28	Hawaii	386.6
29	Georgia	385.2
30	New Mexico	363.4
31	Minnesota	344.1
32	Utah	341.5
33	Nebraska	323.4
34	Colorado	321.3
35	Virginia	316.7
36	Iowa	305.6
37	Pennsylvania	298.7
38	Michigan	293.2
39	Massachusetts	280.9
40	New Hampshire	271.4
41	North Dakota	271.2
42	Indiana	250.1
43	New York	242.5
44	Wyoming	231.4
45	West Virginia	230.1
46	Alabama	223.5
NA	Florida**	NA
NA	Kansas**	NA
NA	Montana**	NA
NA	Vermont**	NA
	District of Columbia**	NA

Source: Morgan Quitno Press using data from Federal Bureau of Investigation
    "Crime in the United States 1996" (Uniform Crime Reports, October 4, 1997)
*By law enforcement agencies submitting complete reports to the F.B.I. for 12 months in 1996. Arrests of youths 17 years and younger divided into population of 10 to 17 year olds. See important note at beginning of this chapter. Burglary is the unlawful entry of a structure to commit a felony or theft. Attempts are included.
**Not available.

219

Reported Arrests of Juveniles for Burglary
As a Percent of All Such Arrests in 1996
National Percent = 37.0% of Reported Burglary Arrests*

RANK	STATE	PERCENT
44	Alabama	27.3
2	Alaska	57.0
14	Arizona	46.4
20	Arkansas	38.4
25	California	36.2
16	Colorado	43.3
29	Connecticut	35.3
38	Delaware	31.9
NA	Florida**	NA
31	Georgia	33.9
26	Hawaii	35.9
1	Idaho	58.2
42	Illinois	29.1
22	Indiana	36.8
12	Iowa	47.3
NA	Kansas**	NA
23	Kentucky	36.5
27	Louisiana	35.5
6	Maine	52.2
32	Maryland	33.8
35	Massachusetts	32.5
27	Michigan	35.5
11	Minnesota	49.1
32	Mississippi	33.8
40	Missouri	30.4
NA	Montana**	NA
7	Nebraska	50.3
38	Nevada	31.9
7	New Hampshire	50.3
29	New Jersey	35.3
18	New Mexico	40.1
46	New York	24.2
45	North Carolina	25.4
3	North Dakota	54.4
19	Ohio	39.3
15	Oklahoma	44.9
17	Oregon	42.9
34	Pennsylvania	33.7
23	Rhode Island	36.5
21	South Carolina	37.6
10	South Dakota	49.4
43	Tennessee	28.3
13	Texas	46.5
5	Utah	52.7
NA	Vermont**	NA
37	Virginia	32.0
7	Washington	50.3
41	West Virginia	29.6
4	Wisconsin	53.9
36	Wyoming	32.4

RANK	STATE	PERCENT
1	Idaho	58.2
2	Alaska	57.0
3	North Dakota	54.4
4	Wisconsin	53.9
5	Utah	52.7
6	Maine	52.2
7	Nebraska	50.3
7	New Hampshire	50.3
7	Washington	50.3
10	South Dakota	49.4
11	Minnesota	49.1
12	Iowa	47.3
13	Texas	46.5
14	Arizona	46.4
15	Oklahoma	44.9
16	Colorado	43.3
17	Oregon	42.9
18	New Mexico	40.1
19	Ohio	39.3
20	Arkansas	38.4
21	South Carolina	37.6
22	Indiana	36.8
23	Kentucky	36.5
23	Rhode Island	36.5
25	California	36.2
26	Hawaii	35.9
27	Louisiana	35.5
27	Michigan	35.5
29	Connecticut	35.3
29	New Jersey	35.3
31	Georgia	33.9
32	Maryland	33.8
32	Mississippi	33.8
34	Pennsylvania	33.7
35	Massachusetts	32.5
36	Wyoming	32.4
37	Virginia	32.0
38	Delaware	31.9
38	Nevada	31.9
40	Missouri	30.4
41	West Virginia	29.6
42	Illinois	29.1
43	Tennessee	28.3
44	Alabama	27.3
45	North Carolina	25.4
46	New York	24.2
NA	Florida**	NA
NA	Kansas**	NA
NA	Montana**	NA
NA	Vermont**	NA
	District of Columbia**	NA

Source: Morgan Quitno Press using data from Federal Bureau of Investigation
"Crime in the United States 1996" (Uniform Crime Reports, October 4, 1997)
*Arrests of youths 17 years and younger by law enforcement agencies submitting complete reports to the F.B.I. for 12 months in 1996. Burglary is the unlawful entry of a structure to commit a felony or theft. Attempts are included.
**Not available.

Reported Arrests of Juveniles for Larceny and Theft in 1996

National Total = 370,607 Reported Arrests*

ALPHA ORDER

RANK	STATE	ARRESTS	% of USA
26	Alabama	5,195	1.40%
42	Alaska	1,658	0.45%
8	Arizona	11,935	3.22%
28	Arkansas	4,898	1.32%
1	California	42,822	11.55%
19	Colorado	7,678	2.07%
29	Connecticut	4,873	1.31%
44	Delaware	1,382	0.37%
NA	Florida**	NA	NA
20	Georgia	7,360	1.99%
36	Hawaii	3,050	0.82%
25	Idaho	5,422	1.46%
24	Illinois	5,933	1.60%
22	Indiana	6,821	1.84%
30	Iowa	4,273	1.15%
NA	Kansas**	NA	NA
38	Kentucky	1,963	0.53%
21	Louisiana	7,318	1.97%
33	Maine	3,415	0.92%
17	Maryland	8,240	2.22%
35	Massachusetts	3,300	0.89%
11	Michigan	10,752	2.90%
5	Minnesota	12,958	3.50%
43	Mississippi	1,441	0.39%
15	Missouri	8,740	2.36%
NA	Montana**	NA	NA
34	Nebraska	3,334	0.90%
32	Nevada	3,631	0.98%
39	New Hampshire	1,826	0.49%
6	New Jersey	12,846	3.47%
31	New Mexico	3,689	1.00%
7	New York	12,731	3.44%
12	North Carolina	10,288	2.78%
46	North Dakota	1,046	0.28%
9	Ohio	11,583	3.13%
18	Oklahoma	7,965	2.15%
14	Oregon	9,712	2.62%
10	Pennsylvania	10,993	2.97%
41	Rhode Island	1,707	0.46%
23	South Carolina	6,425	1.73%
37	South Dakota	2,070	0.56%
27	Tennessee	5,091	1.37%
2	Texas	35,835	9.67%
16	Utah	8,685	2.34%
NA	Vermont**	NA	NA
13	Virginia	10,069	2.72%
4	Washington	14,355	3.87%
40	West Virginia	1,790	0.48%
3	Wisconsin	22,426	6.05%
45	Wyoming	1,083	0.29%

RANK ORDER

RANK	STATE	ARRESTS	% of USA
1	California	42,822	11.55%
2	Texas	35,835	9.67%
3	Wisconsin	22,426	6.05%
4	Washington	14,355	3.87%
5	Minnesota	12,958	3.50%
6	New Jersey	12,846	3.47%
7	New York	12,731	3.44%
8	Arizona	11,935	3.22%
9	Ohio	11,583	3.13%
10	Pennsylvania	10,993	2.97%
11	Michigan	10,752	2.90%
12	North Carolina	10,288	2.78%
13	Virginia	10,069	2.72%
14	Oregon	9,712	2.62%
15	Missouri	8,740	2.36%
16	Utah	8,685	2.34%
17	Maryland	8,240	2.22%
18	Oklahoma	7,965	2.15%
19	Colorado	7,678	2.07%
20	Georgia	7,360	1.99%
21	Louisiana	7,318	1.97%
22	Indiana	6,821	1.84%
23	South Carolina	6,425	1.73%
24	Illinois	5,933	1.60%
25	Idaho	5,422	1.46%
26	Alabama	5,195	1.40%
27	Tennessee	5,091	1.37%
28	Arkansas	4,898	1.32%
29	Connecticut	4,873	1.31%
30	Iowa	4,273	1.15%
31	New Mexico	3,689	1.00%
32	Nevada	3,631	0.98%
33	Maine	3,415	0.92%
34	Nebraska	3,334	0.90%
35	Massachusetts	3,300	0.89%
36	Hawaii	3,050	0.82%
37	South Dakota	2,070	0.56%
38	Kentucky	1,963	0.53%
39	New Hampshire	1,826	0.49%
40	West Virginia	1,790	0.48%
41	Rhode Island	1,707	0.46%
42	Alaska	1,658	0.45%
43	Mississippi	1,441	0.39%
44	Delaware	1,382	0.37%
45	Wyoming	1,083	0.29%
46	North Dakota	1,046	0.28%
NA	Florida**	NA	NA
NA	Kansas**	NA	NA
NA	Montana**	NA	NA
NA	Vermont**	NA	NA
	District of Columbia**	NA	NA

Source: Federal Bureau of Investigation
   "Crime in the United States 1996" (Uniform Crime Reports, October 4, 1997)
*Arrests of youths 17 years and younger by law enforcement agencies submitting complete reports to the F.B.I. for 12 months in 1996. Larceny and theft is the unlawful taking of property without use of force, violence or fraud. Attempts are included. Motor vehicle thefts are excluded. See important note at beginning of this chapter.
**Not available.

221

Reported Arrest Rate for Juveniles for Larceny and Theft in 1996

National Rate = 1,707.3 Reported Arrests per 100,000 Juvenile Population*

<table>
<tr><td colspan="3">ALPHA ORDER</td><td colspan="3">RANK ORDER</td></tr>
<tr><th>RANK</th><th>STATE</th><th>RATE</th><th>RANK</th><th>STATE</th><th>RATE</th></tr>
<tr><td>42</td><td>Alabama</td><td>1,104.8</td><td>1</td><td>Delaware</td><td>3,546.2</td></tr>
<tr><td>15</td><td>Alaska</td><td>2,308.3</td><td>2</td><td>Wisconsin</td><td>3,533.4</td></tr>
<tr><td>10</td><td>Arizona</td><td>2,604.2</td><td>3</td><td>Idaho</td><td>3,302.4</td></tr>
<tr><td>32</td><td>Arkansas</td><td>1,697.0</td><td>4</td><td>Washington</td><td>3,264.0</td></tr>
<tr><td>40</td><td>California</td><td>1,231.3</td><td>5</td><td>South Dakota</td><td>3,072.3</td></tr>
<tr><td>16</td><td>Colorado</td><td>2,307.6</td><td>6</td><td>Oregon</td><td>3,036.6</td></tr>
<tr><td>26</td><td>Connecticut</td><td>1,856.6</td><td>7</td><td>Utah</td><td>3,023.6</td></tr>
<tr><td>1</td><td>Delaware</td><td>3,546.2</td><td>8</td><td>New Mexico</td><td>2,763.8</td></tr>
<tr><td>NA</td><td>Florida**</td><td>NA</td><td>9</td><td>Wyoming</td><td>2,754.0</td></tr>
<tr><td>38</td><td>Georgia</td><td>1,409.0</td><td>10</td><td>Arizona</td><td>2,604.2</td></tr>
<tr><td>13</td><td>Hawaii</td><td>2,377.5</td><td>11</td><td>Minnesota</td><td>2,456.9</td></tr>
<tr><td>3</td><td>Idaho</td><td>3,302.4</td><td>12</td><td>Maine</td><td>2,413.6</td></tr>
<tr><td>25</td><td>Illinois</td><td>1,874.0</td><td>13</td><td>Hawaii</td><td>2,377.5</td></tr>
<tr><td>28</td><td>Indiana</td><td>1,775.2</td><td>14</td><td>Missouri</td><td>2,361.3</td></tr>
<tr><td>36</td><td>Iowa</td><td>1,532.4</td><td>15</td><td>Alaska</td><td>2,308.3</td></tr>
<tr><td>NA</td><td>Kansas**</td><td>NA</td><td>16</td><td>Colorado</td><td>2,307.6</td></tr>
<tr><td>18</td><td>Kentucky</td><td>2,216.5</td><td>17</td><td>Nebraska</td><td>2,227.4</td></tr>
<tr><td>21</td><td>Louisiana</td><td>2,082.6</td><td>18</td><td>Kentucky</td><td>2,216.5</td></tr>
<tr><td>12</td><td>Maine</td><td>2,413.6</td><td>19</td><td>Tennessee</td><td>2,209.1</td></tr>
<tr><td>24</td><td>Maryland</td><td>1,889.3</td><td>20</td><td>Nevada</td><td>2,128.9</td></tr>
<tr><td>46</td><td>Massachusetts</td><td>654.7</td><td>21</td><td>Louisiana</td><td>2,082.6</td></tr>
<tr><td>41</td><td>Michigan</td><td>1,141.5</td><td>22</td><td>North Dakota</td><td>2,070.3</td></tr>
<tr><td>11</td><td>Minnesota</td><td>2,456.9</td><td>23</td><td>Oklahoma</td><td>1,924.8</td></tr>
<tr><td>29</td><td>Mississippi</td><td>1,766.6</td><td>24</td><td>Maryland</td><td>1,889.3</td></tr>
<tr><td>14</td><td>Missouri</td><td>2,361.3</td><td>25</td><td>Illinois</td><td>1,874.0</td></tr>
<tr><td>NA</td><td>Montana**</td><td>NA</td><td>26</td><td>Connecticut</td><td>1,856.6</td></tr>
<tr><td>17</td><td>Nebraska</td><td>2,227.4</td><td>27</td><td>New Hampshire</td><td>1,789.3</td></tr>
<tr><td>20</td><td>Nevada</td><td>2,128.9</td><td>28</td><td>Indiana</td><td>1,775.2</td></tr>
<tr><td>27</td><td>New Hampshire</td><td>1,789.3</td><td>29</td><td>Mississippi</td><td>1,766.6</td></tr>
<tr><td>33</td><td>New Jersey</td><td>1,600.3</td><td>30</td><td>Rhode Island</td><td>1,750.3</td></tr>
<tr><td>8</td><td>New Mexico</td><td>2,763.8</td><td>31</td><td>Texas</td><td>1,740.2</td></tr>
<tr><td>44</td><td>New York</td><td>964.0</td><td>32</td><td>Arkansas</td><td>1,697.0</td></tr>
<tr><td>39</td><td>North Carolina</td><td>1,316.8</td><td>33</td><td>New Jersey</td><td>1,600.3</td></tr>
<tr><td>22</td><td>North Dakota</td><td>2,070.3</td><td>34</td><td>Ohio</td><td>1,550.1</td></tr>
<tr><td>34</td><td>Ohio</td><td>1,550.1</td><td>35</td><td>South Carolina</td><td>1,549.5</td></tr>
<tr><td>23</td><td>Oklahoma</td><td>1,924.8</td><td>36</td><td>Iowa</td><td>1,532.4</td></tr>
<tr><td>6</td><td>Oregon</td><td>3,036.6</td><td>37</td><td>Virginia</td><td>1,528.0</td></tr>
<tr><td>43</td><td>Pennsylvania</td><td>1,083.0</td><td>38</td><td>Georgia</td><td>1,409.0</td></tr>
<tr><td>30</td><td>Rhode Island</td><td>1,750.3</td><td>39</td><td>North Carolina</td><td>1,316.8</td></tr>
<tr><td>35</td><td>South Carolina</td><td>1,549.5</td><td>40</td><td>California</td><td>1,231.3</td></tr>
<tr><td>5</td><td>South Dakota</td><td>3,072.3</td><td>41</td><td>Michigan</td><td>1,141.5</td></tr>
<tr><td>19</td><td>Tennessee</td><td>2,209.1</td><td>42</td><td>Alabama</td><td>1,104.8</td></tr>
<tr><td>31</td><td>Texas</td><td>1,740.2</td><td>43</td><td>Pennsylvania</td><td>1,083.0</td></tr>
<tr><td>7</td><td>Utah</td><td>3,023.6</td><td>44</td><td>New York</td><td>964.0</td></tr>
<tr><td>NA</td><td>Vermont**</td><td>NA</td><td>45</td><td>West Virginia</td><td>872.5</td></tr>
<tr><td>37</td><td>Virginia</td><td>1,528.0</td><td>46</td><td>Massachusetts</td><td>654.7</td></tr>
<tr><td>4</td><td>Washington</td><td>3,264.0</td><td>NA</td><td>Florida**</td><td>NA</td></tr>
<tr><td>45</td><td>West Virginia</td><td>872.5</td><td>NA</td><td>Kansas**</td><td>NA</td></tr>
<tr><td>2</td><td>Wisconsin</td><td>3,533.4</td><td>NA</td><td>Montana**</td><td>NA</td></tr>
<tr><td>9</td><td>Wyoming</td><td>2,754.0</td><td>NA</td><td>Vermont**</td><td>NA</td></tr>
<tr><td></td><td></td><td></td><td></td><td>District of Columbia**</td><td>NA</td></tr>
</table>

Source: Morgan Quitno Press using data from Federal Bureau of Investigation
 "Crime in the United States 1996" (Uniform Crime Reports, October 4, 1997)
*By law enforcement agencies submitting complete reports to the F.B.I. for 12 months in 1996. Arrests of youths 17
years and younger divided into population of 10 to 17 year olds. See important note at beginning of this chapter.
Larceny and theft is the unlawful taking of property without use of force, violence or fraud. Attempts are included.
Motor vehicle thefts are excluded. **Not available.

Reported Arrests of Juveniles for Larceny and Theft
As a Percent of All Such Arrests in 1996
National Percent = 33.8% of Reported Larceny and Theft Arrests*

ALPHA ORDER

RANK ORDER

RANK	STATE	PERCENT		RANK	STATE	PERCENT
41	Alabama	25.4		1	Idaho	59.0
14	Alaska	41.6		2	North Dakota	57.1
32	Arizona	30.4		3	Wyoming	55.3
34	Arkansas	30.3		4	South Dakota	52.9
25	California	32.9		5	Minnesota	52.1
18	Colorado	37.1		6	Nebraska	51.9
39	Connecticut	26.2		7	New Hampshire	50.5
29	Delaware	30.9		8	Oklahoma	49.7
NA	Florida**	NA		9	Utah	48.7
43	Georgia	25.0		10	Wisconsin	48.6
16	Hawaii	38.0		11	Maine	47.6
1	Idaho	59.0		12	Rhode Island	43.3
46	Illinois	17.7		13	Washington	43.1
17	Indiana	37.5		14	Alaska	41.6
14	Iowa	41.6		14	Iowa	41.6
NA	Kansas**	NA		16	Hawaii	38.0
20	Kentucky	36.0		17	Indiana	37.5
35	Louisiana	30.2		18	Colorado	37.1
11	Maine	47.6		19	New Mexico	36.4
27	Maryland	31.6		20	Kentucky	36.0
44	Massachusetts	24.8		20	Michigan	36.0
20	Michigan	36.0		22	Texas	35.8
5	Minnesota	52.1		23	Ohio	35.6
32	Mississippi	30.4		24	Oregon	35.4
36	Missouri	29.2		25	California	32.9
NA	Montana**	NA		26	New Jersey	32.2
6	Nebraska	51.9		27	Maryland	31.6
28	Nevada	31.0		28	Nevada	31.0
7	New Hampshire	50.5		29	Delaware	30.9
26	New Jersey	32.2		29	Pennsylvania	30.9
19	New Mexico	36.4		29	South Carolina	30.9
45	New York	23.6		32	Arizona	30.4
42	North Carolina	25.2		32	Mississippi	30.4
2	North Dakota	57.1		34	Arkansas	30.3
23	Ohio	35.6		35	Louisiana	30.2
8	Oklahoma	49.7		36	Missouri	29.2
24	Oregon	35.4		37	Virginia	29.1
29	Pennsylvania	30.9		38	West Virginia	27.9
12	Rhode Island	43.3		39	Connecticut	26.2
29	South Carolina	30.9		40	Tennessee	26.0
4	South Dakota	52.9		41	Alabama	25.4
40	Tennessee	26.0		42	North Carolina	25.2
22	Texas	35.8		43	Georgia	25.0
9	Utah	48.7		44	Massachusetts	24.8
NA	Vermont**	NA		45	New York	23.6
37	Virginia	29.1		46	Illinois	17.7
13	Washington	43.1		NA	Florida**	NA
38	West Virginia	27.9		NA	Kansas**	NA
10	Wisconsin	48.6		NA	Montana**	NA
3	Wyoming	55.3		NA	Vermont**	NA
					District of Columbia**	NA

Source: Morgan Quitno Press using data from Federal Bureau of Investigation
    "Crime in the United States 1996" (Uniform Crime Reports, October 4, 1997)
*Arrests of youths 17 years and younger by law enforcement agencies submitting complete reports to the F.B.I. for
12 months in 1996. Larceny and theft is the unlawful taking of property without use of force, violence or fraud.
Attempts are included. Motor vehicle thefts are excluded.
**Not available.

Reported Arrests of Juveniles for Motor Vehicle Theft in 1996

National Total = 54,813 Reported Arrests*

ALPHA ORDER					RANK ORDER			
RANK	STATE	ARRESTS	% of USA		RANK	STATE	ARRESTS	% of USA
31	Alabama	404	0.74%		1	California	11,912	21.73%
40	Alaska	153	0.28%		2	Texas	4,360	7.95%
10	Arizona	1,554	2.84%		3	Illinois	2,965	5.41%
34	Arkansas	292	0.53%		4	Wisconsin	2,857	5.21%
1	California	11,912	21.73%		5	Maryland	2,818	5.14%
27	Colorado	467	0.85%		6	Pennsylvania	2,676	4.88%
22	Connecticut	718	1.31%		7	Minnesota	1,995	3.64%
43	Delaware	92	0.17%		8	Ohio	1,976	3.60%
NA	Florida**	NA	NA		9	New York	1,634	2.98%
23	Georgia	693	1.26%		10	Arizona	1,554	2.84%
28	Hawaii	452	0.82%		11	Michigan	1,409	2.57%
33	Idaho	359	0.65%		12	Virginia	1,349	2.46%
3	Illinois	2,965	5.41%		13	Oklahoma	1,319	2.41%
18	Indiana	992	1.81%		14	New Jersey	1,140	2.08%
32	Iowa	387	0.71%		15	Oregon	1,113	2.03%
NA	Kansas**	NA	NA		16	Missouri	1,095	2.00%
26	Kentucky	481	0.88%		17	Washington	1,055	1.92%
29	Louisiana	445	0.81%		18	Indiana	992	1.81%
36	Maine	250	0.46%		19	Utah	931	1.70%
5	Maryland	2,818	5.14%		20	North Carolina	860	1.57%
24	Massachusetts	569	1.04%		21	Tennessee	736	1.34%
11	Michigan	1,409	2.57%		22	Connecticut	718	1.31%
7	Minnesota	1,995	3.64%		23	Georgia	693	1.26%
45	Mississippi	86	0.16%		24	Massachusetts	569	1.04%
16	Missouri	1,095	2.00%		25	South Carolina	515	0.94%
NA	Montana**	NA	NA		26	Kentucky	481	0.88%
35	Nebraska	256	0.47%		27	Colorado	467	0.85%
30	Nevada	420	0.77%		28	Hawaii	452	0.82%
44	New Hampshire	90	0.16%		29	Louisiana	445	0.81%
14	New Jersey	1,140	2.08%		30	Nevada	420	0.77%
39	New Mexico	211	0.38%		31	Alabama	404	0.74%
9	New York	1,634	2.98%		32	Iowa	387	0.71%
20	North Carolina	860	1.57%		33	Idaho	359	0.65%
42	North Dakota	101	0.18%		34	Arkansas	292	0.53%
8	Ohio	1,976	3.60%		35	Nebraska	256	0.47%
13	Oklahoma	1,319	2.41%		36	Maine	250	0.46%
15	Oregon	1,113	2.03%		37	Rhode Island	218	0.40%
6	Pennsylvania	2,676	4.88%		37	West Virginia	218	0.40%
37	Rhode Island	218	0.40%		39	New Mexico	211	0.38%
25	South Carolina	515	0.94%		40	Alaska	153	0.28%
41	South Dakota	133	0.24%		41	South Dakota	133	0.24%
21	Tennessee	736	1.34%		42	North Dakota	101	0.18%
2	Texas	4,360	7.95%		43	Delaware	92	0.17%
19	Utah	931	1.70%		44	New Hampshire	90	0.16%
NA	Vermont**	NA	NA		45	Mississippi	86	0.16%
12	Virginia	1,349	2.46%		46	Wyoming	57	0.10%
17	Washington	1,055	1.92%		NA	Florida**	NA	NA
37	West Virginia	218	0.40%		NA	Kansas**	NA	NA
4	Wisconsin	2,857	5.21%		NA	Montana**	NA	NA
46	Wyoming	57	0.10%		NA	Vermont**	NA	NA
						District of Columbia**	NA	NA

Source: Federal Bureau of Investigation
"Crime in the United States 1996" (Uniform Crime Reports, October 4, 1997)
*Arrests of youths 17 years and younger by law enforcement agencies submitting complete reports to the F.B.I. for 12 months in 1996. Motor vehicle theft includes the theft or attempted theft of a self-propelled vehicle. Excludes motorboats, construction equipment, airplanes and farming equipment. See important note at beginning of this chapter. **Not available.*

Reported Arrest Rate of Juveniles for Motor Vehicle Theft in 1996

National Rate = 252.5 Reported Arrests per 100,000 Juvenile Population*

ALPHA ORDER			RANK ORDER		
RANK	STATE	RATE	RANK	STATE	RATE
46	Alabama	85.9	1	Illinois	936.5
23	Alaska	213.0	2	Maryland	646.1
9	Arizona	339.1	3	Kentucky	543.1
44	Arkansas	101.2	4	Wisconsin	450.1
8	California	342.5	5	Minnesota	378.3
34	Colorado	140.4	6	Hawaii	352.3
14	Connecticut	273.6	7	Oregon	348.0
20	Delaware	236.1	8	California	342.5
NA	Florida**	NA	9	Arizona	339.1
36	Georgia	132.7	10	Utah	324.1
6	Hawaii	352.3	11	Tennessee	319.4
22	Idaho	218.7	12	Oklahoma	318.8
1	Illinois	936.5	13	Missouri	295.8
17	Indiana	258.2	14	Connecticut	273.6
35	Iowa	138.8	15	Ohio	264.4
NA	Kansas**	NA	16	Pennsylvania	263.6
3	Kentucky	543.1	17	Indiana	258.2
37	Louisiana	126.6	18	Nevada	246.3
28	Maine	176.7	19	Washington	239.9
2	Maryland	646.1	20	Delaware	236.1
40	Massachusetts	112.9	21	Rhode Island	223.5
31	Michigan	149.6	22	Idaho	218.7
5	Minnesota	378.3	23	Alaska	213.0
43	Mississippi	105.4	24	Texas	211.7
13	Missouri	295.8	25	Virginia	204.7
NA	Montana**	NA	26	North Dakota	199.9
29	Nebraska	171.0	27	South Dakota	197.4
18	Nevada	246.3	28	Maine	176.7
45	New Hampshire	88.2	29	Nebraska	171.0
33	New Jersey	142.0	30	New Mexico	158.1
30	New Mexico	158.1	31	Michigan	149.6
39	New York	123.7	32	Wyoming	144.9
41	North Carolina	110.1	33	New Jersey	142.0
26	North Dakota	199.9	34	Colorado	140.4
15	Ohio	264.4	35	Iowa	138.8
12	Oklahoma	318.8	36	Georgia	132.7
7	Oregon	348.0	37	Louisiana	126.6
16	Pennsylvania	263.6	38	South Carolina	124.2
21	Rhode Island	223.5	39	New York	123.7
38	South Carolina	124.2	40	Massachusetts	112.9
27	South Dakota	197.4	41	North Carolina	110.1
11	Tennessee	319.4	42	West Virginia	106.3
24	Texas	211.7	43	Mississippi	105.4
10	Utah	324.1	44	Arkansas	101.2
NA	Vermont**	NA	45	New Hampshire	88.2
25	Virginia	204.7	46	Alabama	85.9
19	Washington	239.9	NA	Florida**	NA
42	West Virginia	106.3	NA	Kansas**	NA
4	Wisconsin	450.1	NA	Montana**	NA
32	Wyoming	144.9	NA	Vermont**	NA
				District of Columbia**	NA

Source: Morgan Quitno Press using data from Federal Bureau of Investigation
  "Crime in the United States 1996" (Uniform Crime Reports, October 4, 1997)
*By law enforcement agencies submitting complete reports to the F.B.I. for 12 months in 1996. Arrests of youths 17
years and younger divided into population of 10 to 17 year olds. See important note at beginning of this chapter.
Motor vehicle theft includes the theft or attempted theft of a self-propelled vehicle. Excludes motorboats,
construction equipment, airplanes and farming equipment. **Not available.

Reported Arrests of Juveniles for Motor Vehicle Theft
As a Percent of All Such Arrests in 1996
National Percent = 41.5% of Reported Motor Vehicle Theft Arrests*

ALPHA ORDER

RANK ORDER

RANK	STATE	PERCENT
44	Alabama	25.5
39	Alaska	33.8
15	Arizona	50.0
21	Arkansas	46.2
30	California	38.7
38	Colorado	33.9
23	Connecticut	45.0
16	Delaware	49.5
NA	Florida**	NA
32	Georgia	36.1
42	Hawaii	30.7
3	Idaho	59.5
36	Illinois	34.6
25	Indiana	43.5
10	Iowa	56.5
NA	Kansas**	NA
20	Kentucky	46.3
41	Louisiana	32.6
18	Maine	47.6
14	Maryland	51.0
31	Massachusetts	36.6
19	Michigan	47.0
7	Minnesota	57.5
46	Mississippi	20.7
40	Missouri	33.1
NA	Montana**	NA
6	Nebraska	58.6
43	Nevada	28.8
5	New Hampshire	58.8
12	New Jersey	52.5
34	New Mexico	34.8
45	New York	23.6
33	North Carolina	36.0
4	North Dakota	59.4
13	Ohio	51.5
11	Oklahoma	54.6
36	Oregon	34.6
28	Pennsylvania	39.6
26	Rhode Island	43.3
21	South Carolina	46.2
1	South Dakota	68.9
34	Tennessee	34.8
24	Texas	44.0
2	Utah	65.0
NA	Vermont**	NA
27	Virginia	41.2
9	Washington	57.0
29	West Virginia	38.9
7	Wisconsin	57.5
17	Wyoming	47.9

RANK	STATE	PERCENT
1	South Dakota	68.9
2	Utah	65.0
3	Idaho	59.5
4	North Dakota	59.4
5	New Hampshire	58.8
6	Nebraska	58.6
7	Minnesota	57.5
7	Wisconsin	57.5
9	Washington	57.0
10	Iowa	56.5
11	Oklahoma	54.6
12	New Jersey	52.5
13	Ohio	51.5
14	Maryland	51.0
15	Arizona	50.0
16	Delaware	49.5
17	Wyoming	47.9
18	Maine	47.6
19	Michigan	47.0
20	Kentucky	46.3
21	Arkansas	46.2
21	South Carolina	46.2
23	Connecticut	45.0
24	Texas	44.0
25	Indiana	43.5
26	Rhode Island	43.3
27	Virginia	41.2
28	Pennsylvania	39.6
29	West Virginia	38.9
30	California	38.7
31	Massachusetts	36.6
32	Georgia	36.1
33	North Carolina	36.0
34	New Mexico	34.8
34	Tennessee	34.8
36	Illinois	34.6
36	Oregon	34.6
38	Colorado	33.9
39	Alaska	33.8
40	Missouri	33.1
41	Louisiana	32.6
42	Hawaii	30.7
43	Nevada	28.8
44	Alabama	25.5
45	New York	23.6
46	Mississippi	20.7
NA	Florida**	NA
NA	Kansas**	NA
NA	Montana**	NA
NA	Vermont**	NA

District of Columbia**   NA

Source: Morgan Quitno Press using data from Federal Bureau of Investigation
   "Crime in the United States 1996" (Uniform Crime Reports, October 4, 1997)
*Arrests of youths 17 years and younger by law enforcement agencies submitting complete reports to the F.B.I. for 12 months in 1996. Motor vehicle theft includes the theft or attempted theft of a self-propelled vehicle. Excludes motorboats, construction equipment, airplanes and farming equipment.
**Not available.

Reported Arrests of Juveniles for Arson in 1996

National Total = 7,302 Reported Arrests*

ALPHA ORDER

RANK	STATE	ARRESTS	% of USA
37	Alabama	35	0.48%
42	Alaska	18	0.25%
9	Arizona	263	3.60%
35	Arkansas	41	0.56%
1	California	1,360	18.63%
15	Colorado	190	2.60%
23	Connecticut	95	1.30%
46	Delaware	3	0.04%
NA	Florida**	NA	NA
27	Georgia	72	0.99%
45	Hawaii	7	0.10%
22	Idaho	100	1.37%
32	Illinois	62	0.85%
21	Indiana	120	1.64%
20	Iowa	125	1.71%
NA	Kansas**	NA	NA
41	Kentucky	20	0.27%
25	Louisiana	88	1.21%
24	Maine	93	1.27%
14	Maryland	195	2.67%
34	Massachusetts	49	0.67%
10	Michigan	212	2.90%
16	Minnesota	188	2.57%
40	Mississippi	22	0.30%
18	Missouri	138	1.89%
NA	Montana**	NA	NA
31	Nebraska	66	0.90%
27	Nevada	72	0.99%
36	New Hampshire	39	0.53%
6	New Jersey	295	4.04%
38	New Mexico	30	0.41%
17	New York	176	2.41%
12	North Carolina	201	2.75%
44	North Dakota	9	0.12%
5	Ohio	316	4.33%
7	Oklahoma	275	3.77%
8	Oregon	264	3.62%
3	Pennsylvania	352	4.82%
30	Rhode Island	68	0.93%
26	South Carolina	84	1.15%
33	South Dakota	50	0.68%
29	Tennessee	70	0.96%
2	Texas	538	7.37%
19	Utah	129	1.77%
NA	Vermont**	NA	NA
10	Virginia	212	2.90%
13	Washington	199	2.73%
39	West Virginia	25	0.34%
4	Wisconsin	325	4.45%
43	Wyoming	11	0.15%

RANK ORDER

RANK	STATE	ARRESTS	% of USA
1	California	1,360	18.63%
2	Texas	538	7.37%
3	Pennsylvania	352	4.82%
4	Wisconsin	325	4.45%
5	Ohio	316	4.33%
6	New Jersey	295	4.04%
7	Oklahoma	275	3.77%
8	Oregon	264	3.62%
9	Arizona	263	3.60%
10	Michigan	212	2.90%
10	Virginia	212	2.90%
12	North Carolina	201	2.75%
13	Washington	199	2.73%
14	Maryland	195	2.67%
15	Colorado	190	2.60%
16	Minnesota	188	2.57%
17	New York	176	2.41%
18	Missouri	138	1.89%
19	Utah	129	1.77%
20	Iowa	125	1.71%
21	Indiana	120	1.64%
22	Idaho	100	1.37%
23	Connecticut	95	1.30%
24	Maine	93	1.27%
25	Louisiana	88	1.21%
26	South Carolina	84	1.15%
27	Georgia	72	0.99%
27	Nevada	72	0.99%
29	Tennessee	70	0.96%
30	Rhode Island	68	0.93%
31	Nebraska	66	0.90%
32	Illinois	62	0.85%
33	South Dakota	50	0.68%
34	Massachusetts	49	0.67%
35	Arkansas	41	0.56%
36	New Hampshire	39	0.53%
37	Alabama	35	0.48%
38	New Mexico	30	0.41%
39	West Virginia	25	0.34%
40	Mississippi	22	0.30%
41	Kentucky	20	0.27%
42	Alaska	18	0.25%
43	Wyoming	11	0.15%
44	North Dakota	9	0.12%
45	Hawaii	7	0.10%
46	Delaware	3	0.04%
NA	Florida**	NA	NA
NA	Kansas**	NA	NA
NA	Montana**	NA	NA
NA	Vermont**	NA	NA
	District of Columbia**	NA	NA

Source: Federal Bureau of Investigation
   "Crime in the United States 1996" (Uniform Crime Reports, October 4, 1997)
*Arrests of youths 17 years and younger by law enforcement agencies submitting complete reports to the F.B.I. for 12 months in 1996. Arson is the willful burning of or attempt to burn a building, vehicle or another's personal property. See important note at beginning of this chapter.
**Not available.

Reported Juvenile Arrest Rate for Arson in 1996

National Rate = 33.6 Reported Arrests per 100,000 Juvenile Population*

ALPHA ORDER

RANK ORDER

RANK	STATE	RATE		RANK	STATE	RATE
45	Alabama	7.4		1	Oregon	82.5
31	Alaska	25.1		2	South Dakota	74.2
7	Arizona	57.4		3	Rhode Island	69.7
39	Arkansas	14.2		4	Oklahoma	66.5
17	California	39.1		5	Maine	65.7
8	Colorado	57.1		6	Idaho	60.9
21	Connecticut	36.2		7	Arizona	57.4
44	Delaware	7.7		8	Colorado	57.1
NA	Florida**	NA		9	Wisconsin	51.2
40	Georgia	13.8		10	Washington	45.2
46	Hawaii	5.5		11	Utah	44.9
6	Idaho	60.9		12	Iowa	44.8
37	Illinois	19.6		13	Maryland	44.7
25	Indiana	31.2		14	Nebraska	44.1
12	Iowa	44.8		15	Ohio	42.3
NA	Kansas**	NA		16	Nevada	42.2
33	Kentucky	22.6		17	California	39.1
32	Louisiana	25.0		18	New Hampshire	38.2
5	Maine	65.7		19	Missouri	37.3
13	Maryland	44.7		20	New Jersey	36.7
43	Massachusetts	9.7		21	Connecticut	36.2
34	Michigan	22.5		22	Minnesota	35.6
22	Minnesota	35.6		23	Pennsylvania	34.7
28	Mississippi	27.0		24	Virginia	32.2
19	Missouri	37.3		25	Indiana	31.2
NA	Montana**	NA		26	Tennessee	30.4
14	Nebraska	44.1		27	Wyoming	28.0
16	Nevada	42.2		28	Mississippi	27.0
18	New Hampshire	38.2		29	Texas	26.1
20	New Jersey	36.7		30	North Carolina	25.7
34	New Mexico	22.5		31	Alaska	25.1
41	New York	13.3		32	Louisiana	25.0
30	North Carolina	25.7		33	Kentucky	22.6
38	North Dakota	17.8		34	Michigan	22.5
15	Ohio	42.3		34	New Mexico	22.5
4	Oklahoma	66.5		36	South Carolina	20.3
1	Oregon	82.5		37	Illinois	19.6
23	Pennsylvania	34.7		38	North Dakota	17.8
3	Rhode Island	69.7		39	Arkansas	14.2
36	South Carolina	20.3		40	Georgia	13.8
2	South Dakota	74.2		41	New York	13.3
26	Tennessee	30.4		42	West Virginia	12.2
29	Texas	26.1		43	Massachusetts	9.7
11	Utah	44.9		44	Delaware	7.7
NA	Vermont**	NA		45	Alabama	7.4
24	Virginia	32.2		46	Hawaii	5.5
10	Washington	45.2		NA	Florida**	NA
42	West Virginia	12.2		NA	Kansas**	NA
9	Wisconsin	51.2		NA	Montana**	NA
27	Wyoming	28.0		NA	Vermont**	NA
					District of Columbia**	NA

Source: Morgan Quitno Press using data from Federal Bureau of Investigation
 "Crime in the United States 1996" (Uniform Crime Reports, October 4, 1997)
*By law enforcement agencies submitting complete reports to the F.B.I. for 12 months in 1996. Arrests of youths 17 years and younger divided into population of 10 to 17 year olds. See important note at beginning of this chapter. Arson is the willful burning of or attempt to burn a building, vehicle or another's personal property.
**Not available.

Reported Arrests of Juveniles for Arson
As a Percent of All Such Arrests in 1996
National Percent = 53.1% of Reported Arson Arrests*

ALPHA ORDER

RANK	STATE	PERCENT
45	Alabama	23.5
15	Alaska	64.3
10	Arizona	67.6
40	Arkansas	35.0
21	California	60.8
11	Colorado	67.4
26	Connecticut	52.8
41	Delaware	33.3
NA	Florida**	NA
43	Georgia	28.8
46	Hawaii	20.0
3	Idaho	77.5
39	Illinois	35.6
18	Indiana	61.5
9	Iowa	67.9
NA	Kansas**	NA
29	Kentucky	51.3
32	Louisiana	43.6
14	Maine	64.6
25	Maryland	54.3
37	Massachusetts	38.9
42	Michigan	31.4
13	Minnesota	65.7
27	Mississippi	52.4
34	Missouri	39.3
NA	Montana**	NA
5	Nebraska	72.5
6	Nevada	70.6
4	New Hampshire	76.5
24	New Jersey	54.4
7	New Mexico	69.8
36	New York	39.0
33	North Carolina	39.6
8	North Dakota	69.2
28	Ohio	51.9
19	Oklahoma	61.4
22	Oregon	57.4
30	Pennsylvania	48.6
20	Rhode Island	61.3
37	South Carolina	38.9
1	South Dakota	82.0
35	Tennessee	39.1
23	Texas	55.3
12	Utah	66.8
NA	Vermont**	NA
31	Virginia	46.9
16	Washington	63.6
44	West Virginia	24.3
17	Wisconsin	63.0
2	Wyoming	78.6

RANK ORDER

RANK	STATE	PERCENT
1	South Dakota	82.0
2	Wyoming	78.6
3	Idaho	77.5
4	New Hampshire	76.5
5	Nebraska	72.5
6	Nevada	70.6
7	New Mexico	69.8
8	North Dakota	69.2
9	Iowa	67.9
10	Arizona	67.6
11	Colorado	67.4
12	Utah	66.8
13	Minnesota	65.7
14	Maine	64.6
15	Alaska	64.3
16	Washington	63.6
17	Wisconsin	63.0
18	Indiana	61.5
19	Oklahoma	61.4
20	Rhode Island	61.3
21	California	60.8
22	Oregon	57.4
23	Texas	55.3
24	New Jersey	54.4
25	Maryland	54.3
26	Connecticut	52.8
27	Mississippi	52.4
28	Ohio	51.9
29	Kentucky	51.3
30	Pennsylvania	48.6
31	Virginia	46.9
32	Louisiana	43.6
33	North Carolina	39.6
34	Missouri	39.3
35	Tennessee	39.1
36	New York	39.0
37	Massachusetts	38.9
37	South Carolina	38.9
39	Illinois	35.6
40	Arkansas	35.0
41	Delaware	33.3
42	Michigan	31.4
43	Georgia	28.8
44	West Virginia	24.3
45	Alabama	23.5
46	Hawaii	20.0
NA	Florida**	NA
NA	Kansas**	NA
NA	Montana**	NA
NA	Vermont**	NA
	District of Columbia**	NA

Source: Morgan Quitno Press using data from Federal Bureau of Investigation
    "Crime in the United States 1996" (Uniform Crime Reports, October 4, 1997)
*Arrests of youths 17 years and younger by law enforcement agencies submitting complete reports to the F.B.I. for
12 months in 1996. Arson is the willful burning of or attempt to burn a building, vehicle or another's personal
property.
**Not available.

Reported Arrests of Juveniles for Weapons Violations in 1996

National Total = 39,363 Reported Arrests*

ALPHA ORDER			
RANK	STATE	ARRESTS	% of USA
24	Alabama	477	1.21%
38	Alaska	118	0.30%
14	Arizona	878	2.23%
28	Arkansas	367	0.93%
1	California	8,855	22.50%
18	Colorado	574	1.46%
23	Connecticut	486	1.23%
39	Delaware	89	0.23%
NA	Florida**	NA	NA
19	Georgia	572	1.45%
43	Hawaii	77	0.20%
32	Idaho	239	0.61%
5	Illinois	1,907	4.84%
30	Indiana	312	0.79%
42	Iowa	86	0.22%
NA	Kansas**	NA	NA
34	Kentucky	158	0.40%
21	Louisiana	500	1.27%
39	Maine	89	0.23%
9	Maryland	1,284	3.26%
31	Massachusetts	307	0.78%
13	Michigan	1,050	2.67%
11	Minnesota	1,116	2.84%
37	Mississippi	132	0.34%
15	Missouri	742	1.89%
NA	Montana**	NA	NA
35	Nebraska	152	0.39%
27	Nevada	421	1.07%
46	New Hampshire	17	0.04%
6	New Jersey	1,827	4.64%
29	New Mexico	331	0.84%
4	New York	2,002	5.09%
7	North Carolina	1,485	3.77%
45	North Dakota	32	0.08%
12	Ohio	1,087	2.76%
25	Oklahoma	449	1.14%
22	Oregon	487	1.24%
8	Pennsylvania	1,306	3.32%
33	Rhode Island	218	0.55%
16	South Carolina	722	1.83%
41	South Dakota	87	0.22%
26	Tennessee	444	1.13%
2	Texas	3,108	7.90%
20	Utah	551	1.40%
NA	Vermont**	NA	NA
10	Virginia	1,195	3.04%
17	Washington	637	1.62%
36	West Virginia	142	0.36%
3	Wisconsin	2,214	5.62%
44	Wyoming	34	0.09%

RANK ORDER			
RANK	STATE	ARRESTS	% of USA
1	California	8,855	22.50%
2	Texas	3,108	7.90%
3	Wisconsin	2,214	5.62%
4	New York	2,002	5.09%
5	Illinois	1,907	4.84%
6	New Jersey	1,827	4.64%
7	North Carolina	1,485	3.77%
8	Pennsylvania	1,306	3.32%
9	Maryland	1,284	3.26%
10	Virginia	1,195	3.04%
11	Minnesota	1,116	2.84%
12	Ohio	1,087	2.76%
13	Michigan	1,050	2.67%
14	Arizona	878	2.23%
15	Missouri	742	1.89%
16	South Carolina	722	1.83%
17	Washington	637	1.62%
18	Colorado	574	1.46%
19	Georgia	572	1.45%
20	Utah	551	1.40%
21	Louisiana	500	1.27%
22	Oregon	487	1.24%
23	Connecticut	486	1.23%
24	Alabama	477	1.21%
25	Oklahoma	449	1.14%
26	Tennessee	444	1.13%
27	Nevada	421	1.07%
28	Arkansas	367	0.93%
29	New Mexico	331	0.84%
30	Indiana	312	0.79%
31	Massachusetts	307	0.78%
32	Idaho	239	0.61%
33	Rhode Island	218	0.55%
34	Kentucky	158	0.40%
35	Nebraska	152	0.39%
36	West Virginia	142	0.36%
37	Mississippi	132	0.34%
38	Alaska	118	0.30%
39	Delaware	89	0.23%
39	Maine	89	0.23%
41	South Dakota	87	0.22%
42	Iowa	86	0.22%
43	Hawaii	77	0.20%
44	Wyoming	34	0.09%
45	North Dakota	32	0.08%
46	New Hampshire	17	0.04%
NA	Florida**	NA	NA
NA	Kansas**	NA	NA
NA	Montana**	NA	NA
NA	Vermont**	NA	NA
	District of Columbia**	NA	NA

Source: Federal Bureau of Investigation
   "Crime in the United States 1996" (Uniform Crime Reports, October 4, 1997)
*Arrests of youths 17 years and younger by law enforcement agencies submitting complete reports to the F.B.I. for 12 months in 1996. Weapons violations include illegal carrying and possession. See important note at beginning of this chapter.
**Not available.

Reported Arrest Rate of Juveniles for Weapons Violations in 1996

National Rate = 181.3 Reported Arrests per 100,000 Juvenile Population*

ALPHA ORDER

RANK	STATE	RATE
37	Alabama	101.4
21	Alaska	164.3
14	Arizona	191.6
32	Arkansas	127.2
4	California	254.6
20	Colorado	172.5
16	Connecticut	185.2
7	Delaware	228.4
NA	Florida**	NA
34	Georgia	109.5
44	Hawaii	60.0
26	Idaho	145.6
1	Illinois	602.3
39	Indiana	81.2
45	Iowa	30.8
NA	Kansas**	NA
18	Kentucky	178.4
29	Louisiana	142.3
42	Maine	62.9
3	Maryland	294.4
43	Massachusetts	60.9
33	Michigan	111.5
10	Minnesota	211.6
22	Mississippi	161.8
11	Missouri	200.5
NA	Montana**	NA
36	Nebraska	101.5
6	Nevada	246.8
46	New Hampshire	16.7
8	New Jersey	227.6
5	New Mexico	248.0
24	New York	151.6
15	North Carolina	190.1
41	North Dakota	63.3
27	Ohio	145.5
35	Oklahoma	108.5
23	Oregon	152.3
31	Pennsylvania	128.7
9	Rhode Island	223.5
19	South Carolina	174.1
30	South Dakota	129.1
12	Tennessee	192.7
25	Texas	150.9
13	Utah	191.8
NA	Vermont**	NA
17	Virginia	181.3
28	Washington	144.8
40	West Virginia	69.2
2	Wisconsin	348.8
38	Wyoming	86.5

RANK ORDER

RANK	STATE	RATE
1	Illinois	602.3
2	Wisconsin	348.8
3	Maryland	294.4
4	California	254.6
5	New Mexico	248.0
6	Nevada	246.8
7	Delaware	228.4
8	New Jersey	227.6
9	Rhode Island	223.5
10	Minnesota	211.6
11	Missouri	200.5
12	Tennessee	192.7
13	Utah	191.8
14	Arizona	191.6
15	North Carolina	190.1
16	Connecticut	185.2
17	Virginia	181.3
18	Kentucky	178.4
19	South Carolina	174.1
20	Colorado	172.5
21	Alaska	164.3
22	Mississippi	161.8
23	Oregon	152.3
24	New York	151.6
25	Texas	150.9
26	Idaho	145.6
27	Ohio	145.5
28	Washington	144.8
29	Louisiana	142.3
30	South Dakota	129.1
31	Pennsylvania	128.7
32	Arkansas	127.2
33	Michigan	111.5
34	Georgia	109.5
35	Oklahoma	108.5
36	Nebraska	101.5
37	Alabama	101.4
38	Wyoming	86.5
39	Indiana	81.2
40	West Virginia	69.2
41	North Dakota	63.3
42	Maine	62.9
43	Massachusetts	60.9
44	Hawaii	60.0
45	Iowa	30.8
46	New Hampshire	16.7
NA	Florida**	NA
NA	Kansas**	NA
NA	Montana**	NA
NA	Vermont**	NA
	District of Columbia**	NA

Source: Morgan Quitno Press using data from Federal Bureau of Investigation
   "Crime in the United States 1996" (Uniform Crime Reports, October 4, 1997)
*By law enforcement agencies submitting complete reports to the F.B.I. for 12 months in 1996. Arrests of youths 17
years and younger divided into population of 10 to 17 year olds. See important note at beginning of this chapter.
Weapons violations include illegal carrying and possession.
**Not available.

231

Reported Arrests of Juveniles for Weapons Violations
As a Percent of All Such Arrests in 1996
National Percent = 24.4% of Reported Arrests for Weapons Violations*

ALPHA ORDER

RANK	STATE	PERCENT
31	Alabama	20.0
21	Alaska	24.1
28	Arizona	22.1
43	Arkansas	14.5
16	California	28.3
27	Colorado	22.6
18	Connecticut	25.6
17	Delaware	26.0
NA	Florida**	NA
32	Georgia	19.4
35	Hawaii	17.8
10	Idaho	34.0
13	Illinois	30.6
36	Indiana	17.7
44	Iowa	14.3
NA	Kansas**	NA
38	Kentucky	16.4
20	Louisiana	24.6
15	Maine	28.7
12	Maryland	31.9
23	Massachusetts	23.7
40	Michigan	16.0
5	Minnesota	41.9
14	Mississippi	30.1
41	Missouri	15.7
NA	Montana**	NA
22	Nebraska	23.9
30	Nevada	21.3
45	New Hampshire	13.5
11	New Jersey	32.1
6	New Mexico	38.9
32	New York	19.4
34	North Carolina	18.6
3	North Dakota	42.7
24	Ohio	23.0
37	Oklahoma	17.4
29	Oregon	21.7
7	Pennsylvania	36.6
4	Rhode Island	42.4
25	South Carolina	22.9
1	South Dakota	47.8
42	Tennessee	14.6
25	Texas	22.9
2	Utah	44.0
NA	Vermont**	NA
38	Virginia	16.4
19	Washington	25.5
46	West Virginia	10.6
9	Wisconsin	34.9
7	Wyoming	36.6

RANK ORDER

RANK	STATE	PERCENT
1	South Dakota	47.8
2	Utah	44.0
3	North Dakota	42.7
4	Rhode Island	42.4
5	Minnesota	41.9
6	New Mexico	38.9
7	Pennsylvania	36.6
7	Wyoming	36.6
9	Wisconsin	34.9
10	Idaho	34.0
11	New Jersey	32.1
12	Maryland	31.9
13	Illinois	30.6
14	Mississippi	30.1
15	Maine	28.7
16	California	28.3
17	Delaware	26.0
18	Connecticut	25.6
19	Washington	25.5
20	Louisiana	24.6
21	Alaska	24.1
22	Nebraska	23.9
23	Massachusetts	23.7
24	Ohio	23.0
25	South Carolina	22.9
25	Texas	22.9
27	Colorado	22.6
28	Arizona	22.1
29	Oregon	21.7
30	Nevada	21.3
31	Alabama	20.0
32	Georgia	19.4
32	New York	19.4
34	North Carolina	18.6
35	Hawaii	17.8
36	Indiana	17.7
37	Oklahoma	17.4
38	Kentucky	16.4
38	Virginia	16.4
40	Michigan	16.0
41	Missouri	15.7
42	Tennessee	14.6
43	Arkansas	14.5
44	Iowa	14.3
45	New Hampshire	13.5
46	West Virginia	10.6
NA	Florida**	NA
NA	Kansas**	NA
NA	Montana**	NA
NA	Vermont**	NA

District of Columbia**   NA

*Source: Morgan Quitno Press using data from Federal Bureau of Investigation
    "Crime in the United States 1996" (Uniform Crime Reports, October 4, 1997)*
*Arrests of youths 17 years and younger by law enforcement agencies submitting complete reports to the F.B.I. for 12 months in 1996.   Weapons violations include illegal carrying and possession.
**Not available.

Reported Arrests of Juveniles for Driving Under the Influence in 1996

National Total = 12,814 Reported Arrests*

ALPHA ORDER

RANK	STATE	ARRESTS	% of USA
23	Alabama	185	1.44%
40	Alaska	61	0.48%
9	Arizona	432	3.37%
15	Arkansas	286	2.23%
1	California	1,806	14.09%
5	Colorado	537	4.19%
34	Connecticut	112	0.87%
46	Delaware	0	0.00%
NA	Florida**	NA	NA
7	Georgia	510	3.98%
37	Hawaii	67	0.52%
14	Idaho	303	2.36%
43	Illinois	27	0.21%
33	Indiana	123	0.96%
17	Iowa	268	2.09%
NA	Kansas**	NA	NA
41	Kentucky	51	0.40%
31	Louisiana	131	1.02%
27	Maine	153	1.19%
28	Maryland	148	1.15%
30	Massachusetts	144	1.12%
4	Michigan	676	5.28%
8	Minnesota	506	3.95%
38	Mississippi	63	0.49%
21	Missouri	241	1.88%
NA	Montana**	NA	NA
16	Nebraska	284	2.22%
36	Nevada	76	0.59%
35	New Hampshire	94	0.73%
20	New Jersey	258	2.01%
18	New Mexico	261	2.04%
26	New York	158	1.23%
2	North Carolina	1,020	7.96%
44	North Dakota	26	0.20%
13	Ohio	307	2.40%
11	Oklahoma	348	2.72%
19	Oregon	260	2.03%
10	Pennsylvania	350	2.73%
45	Rhode Island	24	0.19%
25	South Carolina	170	1.33%
38	South Dakota	63	0.49%
32	Tennessee	130	1.01%
3	Texas	689	5.38%
23	Utah	185	1.44%
NA	Vermont**	NA	NA
11	Virginia	348	2.72%
21	Washington	241	1.88%
29	West Virginia	145	1.13%
6	Wisconsin	512	4.00%
42	Wyoming	35	0.27%

RANK ORDER

RANK	STATE	ARRESTS	% of USA
1	California	1,806	14.09%
2	North Carolina	1,020	7.96%
3	Texas	689	5.38%
4	Michigan	676	5.28%
5	Colorado	537	4.19%
6	Wisconsin	512	4.00%
7	Georgia	510	3.98%
8	Minnesota	506	3.95%
9	Arizona	432	3.37%
10	Pennsylvania	350	2.73%
11	Oklahoma	348	2.72%
11	Virginia	348	2.72%
13	Ohio	307	2.40%
14	Idaho	303	2.36%
15	Arkansas	286	2.23%
16	Nebraska	284	2.22%
17	Iowa	268	2.09%
18	New Mexico	261	2.04%
19	Oregon	260	2.03%
20	New Jersey	258	2.01%
21	Missouri	241	1.88%
21	Washington	241	1.88%
23	Alabama	185	1.44%
23	Utah	185	1.44%
25	South Carolina	170	1.33%
26	New York	158	1.23%
27	Maine	153	1.19%
28	Maryland	148	1.15%
29	West Virginia	145	1.13%
30	Massachusetts	144	1.12%
31	Louisiana	131	1.02%
32	Tennessee	130	1.01%
33	Indiana	123	0.96%
34	Connecticut	112	0.87%
35	New Hampshire	94	0.73%
36	Nevada	76	0.59%
37	Hawaii	67	0.52%
38	Mississippi	63	0.49%
38	South Dakota	63	0.49%
40	Alaska	61	0.48%
41	Kentucky	51	0.40%
42	Wyoming	35	0.27%
43	Illinois	27	0.21%
44	North Dakota	26	0.20%
45	Rhode Island	24	0.19%
46	Delaware	0	0.00%
NA	Florida**	NA	NA
NA	Kansas**	NA	NA
NA	Montana**	NA	NA
NA	Vermont**	NA	NA
	District of Columbia**	NA	NA

Source: Federal Bureau of Investigation
      "Crime in the United States 1996" (Uniform Crime Reports, October 4, 1997)
*Arrests of youths 17 years and younger by law enforcement agencies submitting complete reports to the F.B.I. for 12 months in 1996. Includes driving any vehicle while drunk or under the influence of liquor or narcotics. See important note at beginning of this chapter.
**Not available.

233

Reported Juvenile Arrest Rate for Driving Under the Influence in 1996

National Rate = 59.0 Reported Arrests per 100,000 Juvenile Population*

ALPHA ORDER

RANK	STATE	RATE
35	Alabama	39.3
15	Alaska	84.9
11	Arizona	94.3
7	Arkansas	99.1
29	California	51.9
4	Colorado	161.4
32	Connecticut	42.7
46	Delaware	0.0
NA	Florida**	NA
8	Georgia	97.6
28	Hawaii	52.2
3	Idaho	184.6
45	Illinois	8.5
41	Indiana	32.0
9	Iowa	96.1
NA	Kansas**	NA
24	Kentucky	57.6
36	Louisiana	37.3
6	Maine	108.1
38	Maryland	33.9
42	Massachusetts	28.6
20	Michigan	71.8
10	Minnesota	95.9
19	Mississippi	77.2
22	Missouri	65.1
NA	Montana**	NA
2	Nebraska	189.7
31	Nevada	44.6
13	New Hampshire	92.1
40	New Jersey	32.1
1	New Mexico	195.5
44	New York	12.0
5	North Carolina	130.6
30	North Dakota	51.5
33	Ohio	41.1
16	Oklahoma	84.1
17	Oregon	81.3
37	Pennsylvania	34.5
43	Rhode Island	24.6
34	South Carolina	41.0
12	South Dakota	93.5
25	Tennessee	56.4
39	Texas	33.5
23	Utah	64.4
NA	Vermont**	NA
27	Virginia	52.8
26	Washington	54.8
21	West Virginia	70.7
18	Wisconsin	80.7
14	Wyoming	89.0

RANK ORDER

RANK	STATE	RATE
1	New Mexico	195.5
2	Nebraska	189.7
3	Idaho	184.6
4	Colorado	161.4
5	North Carolina	130.6
6	Maine	108.1
7	Arkansas	99.1
8	Georgia	97.6
9	Iowa	96.1
10	Minnesota	95.9
11	Arizona	94.3
12	South Dakota	93.5
13	New Hampshire	92.1
14	Wyoming	89.0
15	Alaska	84.9
16	Oklahoma	84.1
17	Oregon	81.3
18	Wisconsin	80.7
19	Mississippi	77.2
20	Michigan	71.8
21	West Virginia	70.7
22	Missouri	65.1
23	Utah	64.4
24	Kentucky	57.6
25	Tennessee	56.4
26	Washington	54.8
27	Virginia	52.8
28	Hawaii	52.2
29	California	51.9
30	North Dakota	51.5
31	Nevada	44.6
32	Connecticut	42.7
33	Ohio	41.1
34	South Carolina	41.0
35	Alabama	39.3
36	Louisiana	37.3
37	Pennsylvania	34.5
38	Maryland	33.9
39	Texas	33.5
40	New Jersey	32.1
41	Indiana	32.0
42	Massachusetts	28.6
43	Rhode Island	24.6
44	New York	12.0
45	Illinois	8.5
46	Delaware	0.0
NA	Florida**	NA
NA	Kansas**	NA
NA	Montana**	NA
NA	Vermont**	NA
	District of Columbia**	NA

Source: Morgan Quitno Press using data from Federal Bureau of Investigation
"Crime in the United States 1996" (Uniform Crime Reports, October 4, 1997)
By law enforcement agencies submitting complete reports to the F.B.I. for 12 months in 1996. Arrests of youths 17 years and younger divided into population of 10 to 17 year olds. See important note at beginning of this chapter. Includes driving any vehicle while drunk or under the influence of liquor or narcotics.
***Not available.*

Reported Arrests of Juveniles for Driving Under the Influence
As a Percent of All Such Arrests in 1996
National Percent = 1.3% of Reported Arrests for Driving Under the Influence*

ALPHA ORDER

RANK	STATE	PERCENT
36	Alabama	1.0
18	Alaska	1.4
22	Arizona	1.3
12	Arkansas	1.5
38	California	0.9
8	Colorado	1.8
28	Connecticut	1.2
46	Delaware	0.0
NA	Florida**	NA
9	Georgia	1.6
18	Hawaii	1.4
2	Idaho	2.7
38	Illinois	0.9
43	Indiana	0.8
4	Iowa	2.2
NA	Kansas**	NA
28	Kentucky	1.2
28	Louisiana	1.2
6	Maine	1.9
43	Maryland	0.8
38	Massachusetts	0.9
12	Michigan	1.5
12	Minnesota	1.5
33	Mississippi	1.1
12	Missouri	1.5
NA	Montana**	NA
1	Nebraska	3.3
36	Nevada	1.0
6	New Hampshire	1.9
33	New Jersey	1.1
5	New Mexico	2.1
45	New York	0.7
18	North Carolina	1.4
22	North Dakota	1.3
22	Ohio	1.3
9	Oklahoma	1.6
22	Oregon	1.3
28	Pennsylvania	1.2
22	Rhode Island	1.3
33	South Carolina	1.1
12	South Dakota	1.5
38	Tennessee	0.9
38	Texas	0.9
3	Utah	2.5
NA	Vermont**	NA
28	Virginia	1.2
9	Washington	1.6
12	West Virginia	1.5
18	Wisconsin	1.4
22	Wyoming	1.3

RANK ORDER

RANK	STATE	PERCENT
1	Nebraska	3.3
2	Idaho	2.7
3	Utah	2.5
4	Iowa	2.2
5	New Mexico	2.1
6	Maine	1.9
6	New Hampshire	1.9
8	Colorado	1.8
9	Georgia	1.6
9	Oklahoma	1.6
9	Washington	1.6
12	Arkansas	1.5
12	Michigan	1.5
12	Minnesota	1.5
12	Missouri	1.5
12	South Dakota	1.5
12	West Virginia	1.5
18	Alaska	1.4
18	Hawaii	1.4
18	North Carolina	1.4
18	Wisconsin	1.4
22	Arizona	1.3
22	North Dakota	1.3
22	Ohio	1.3
22	Oregon	1.3
22	Rhode Island	1.3
22	Wyoming	1.3
28	Connecticut	1.2
28	Kentucky	1.2
28	Louisiana	1.2
28	Pennsylvania	1.2
28	Virginia	1.2
33	Mississippi	1.1
33	New Jersey	1.1
33	South Carolina	1.1
36	Alabama	1.0
36	Nevada	1.0
38	California	0.9
38	Illinois	0.9
38	Massachusetts	0.9
38	Tennessee	0.9
38	Texas	0.9
43	Indiana	0.8
43	Maryland	0.8
45	New York	0.7
46	Delaware	0.0
NA	Florida**	NA
NA	Kansas**	NA
NA	Montana**	NA
NA	Vermont**	NA

District of Columbia**   NA

Source: Morgan Quitno Press using data from Federal Bureau of Investigation
    "Crime in the United States 1996" (Uniform Crime Reports, October 4, 1997)
*Arrests of youths 17 years and younger by law enforcement agencies submitting complete reports to the F.B.I. for
12 months in 1996. Includes driving any vehicle while drunk or under the influence of liquor or narcotics.
**Not available.

Reported Arrests of Juveniles for Drug Abuse Violations in 1996

National Total = 158,447 Reported Arrests*

ALPHA ORDER

RANK	STATE	ARRESTS	% of USA
28	Alabama	1,475	0.93%
44	Alaska	379	0.24%
7	Arizona	5,094	3.21%
30	Arkansas	1,291	0.81%
1	California	24,393	15.40%
24	Colorado	2,034	1.28%
15	Connecticut	3,012	1.90%
42	Delaware	439	0.28%
NA	Florida**	NA	NA
19	Georgia	2,651	1.67%
34	Hawaii	772	0.49%
32	Idaho	861	0.54%
4	Illinois	11,056	6.98%
25	Indiana	1,853	1.17%
36	Iowa	749	0.47%
NA	Kansas**	NA	NA
33	Kentucky	808	0.51%
22	Louisiana	2,197	1.39%
37	Maine	727	0.46%
6	Maryland	7,983	5.04%
18	Massachusetts	2,814	1.78%
12	Michigan	3,845	2.43%
14	Minnesota	3,215	2.03%
35	Mississippi	764	0.48%
17	Missouri	2,816	1.78%
NA	Montana**	NA	NA
38	Nebraska	685	0.43%
31	Nevada	1,238	0.78%
40	New Hampshire	570	0.36%
5	New Jersey	10,240	6.46%
29	New Mexico	1,363	0.86%
2	New York	13,477	8.51%
10	North Carolina	4,326	2.73%
46	North Dakota	142	0.09%
9	Ohio	4,738	2.99%
27	Oklahoma	1,604	1.01%
20	Oregon	2,400	1.51%
11	Pennsylvania	4,186	2.64%
39	Rhode Island	581	0.37%
16	South Carolina	2,904	1.83%
41	South Dakota	448	0.28%
26	Tennessee	1,611	1.02%
3	Texas	13,425	8.47%
23	Utah	2,044	1.29%
NA	Vermont**	NA	NA
13	Virginia	3,493	2.20%
21	Washington	2,338	1.48%
43	West Virginia	424	0.27%
8	Wisconsin	4,759	3.00%
45	Wyoming	223	0.14%

RANK ORDER

RANK	STATE	ARRESTS	% of USA
1	California	24,393	15.40%
2	New York	13,477	8.51%
3	Texas	13,425	8.47%
4	Illinois	11,056	6.98%
5	New Jersey	10,240	6.46%
6	Maryland	7,983	5.04%
7	Arizona	5,094	3.21%
8	Wisconsin	4,759	3.00%
9	Ohio	4,738	2.99%
10	North Carolina	4,326	2.73%
11	Pennsylvania	4,186	2.64%
12	Michigan	3,845	2.43%
13	Virginia	3,493	2.20%
14	Minnesota	3,215	2.03%
15	Connecticut	3,012	1.90%
16	South Carolina	2,904	1.83%
17	Missouri	2,816	1.78%
18	Massachusetts	2,814	1.78%
19	Georgia	2,651	1.67%
20	Oregon	2,400	1.51%
21	Washington	2,338	1.48%
22	Louisiana	2,197	1.39%
23	Utah	2,044	1.29%
24	Colorado	2,034	1.28%
25	Indiana	1,853	1.17%
26	Tennessee	1,611	1.02%
27	Oklahoma	1,604	1.01%
28	Alabama	1,475	0.93%
29	New Mexico	1,363	0.86%
30	Arkansas	1,291	0.81%
31	Nevada	1,238	0.78%
32	Idaho	861	0.54%
33	Kentucky	808	0.51%
34	Hawaii	772	0.49%
35	Mississippi	764	0.48%
36	Iowa	749	0.47%
37	Maine	727	0.46%
38	Nebraska	685	0.43%
39	Rhode Island	581	0.37%
40	New Hampshire	570	0.36%
41	South Dakota	448	0.28%
42	Delaware	439	0.28%
43	West Virginia	424	0.27%
44	Alaska	379	0.24%
45	Wyoming	223	0.14%
46	North Dakota	142	0.09%
NA	Florida**	NA	NA
NA	Kansas**	NA	NA
NA	Montana**	NA	NA
NA	Vermont**	NA	NA
	District of Columbia**	NA	NA

Source: Federal Bureau of Investigation
   "Crime in the United States 1996" (Uniform Crime Reports, October 4, 1997)
*Arrests of youths 17 years and younger by law enforcement agencies submitting complete reports to the F.B.I. for 12 months in 1996. Includes offenses relating to possession, sale, use, growing and manufacturing of narcotic drugs. See important note at beginning of this chapter.
**Not available.

Reported Arrest Rate of Juveniles for Drug Abuse Violations in 1996

National Rate = 729.9 Reported Arrests per 100,000 Juvenile Population*

ALPHA ORDER

RANK	STATE	RATE
43	Alabama	313.7
33	Alaska	527.6
6	Arizona	1,111.5
39	Arkansas	447.3
16	California	701.4
23	Colorado	611.3
4	Connecticut	1,147.6
5	Delaware	1,126.5
NA	Florida**	NA
36	Georgia	507.5
25	Hawaii	601.8
34	Idaho	524.4
1	Illinois	3,492.1
37	Indiana	482.3
45	Iowa	268.6
NA	Kansas**	NA
10	Kentucky	912.3
22	Louisiana	625.2
35	Maine	513.8
2	Maryland	1,830.4
29	Massachusetts	558.3
41	Michigan	408.2
24	Minnesota	609.6
9	Mississippi	936.6
11	Missouri	760.8
NA	Montana**	NA
38	Nebraska	457.6
14	Nevada	725.9
28	New Hampshire	558.5
3	New Jersey	1,275.6
7	New Mexico	1,021.2
8	New York	1,020.5
30	North Carolina	553.7
44	North Dakota	281.1
21	Ohio	634.0
42	Oklahoma	387.6
12	Oregon	750.4
40	Pennsylvania	412.4
26	Rhode Island	595.8
17	South Carolina	700.3
19	South Dakota	664.9
18	Tennessee	699.1
20	Texas	651.9
15	Utah	711.6
NA	Vermont**	NA
32	Virginia	530.1
31	Washington	531.6
46	West Virginia	206.7
13	Wisconsin	749.8
27	Wyoming	567.1

RANK ORDER

RANK	STATE	RATE
1	Illinois	3,492.1
2	Maryland	1,830.4
3	New Jersey	1,275.6
4	Connecticut	1,147.6
5	Delaware	1,126.5
6	Arizona	1,111.5
7	New Mexico	1,021.2
8	New York	1,020.5
9	Mississippi	936.6
10	Kentucky	912.3
11	Missouri	760.8
12	Oregon	750.4
13	Wisconsin	749.8
14	Nevada	725.9
15	Utah	711.6
16	California	701.4
17	South Carolina	700.3
18	Tennessee	699.1
19	South Dakota	664.9
20	Texas	651.9
21	Ohio	634.0
22	Louisiana	625.2
23	Colorado	611.3
24	Minnesota	609.6
25	Hawaii	601.8
26	Rhode Island	595.8
27	Wyoming	567.1
28	New Hampshire	558.5
29	Massachusetts	558.3
30	North Carolina	553.7
31	Washington	531.6
32	Virginia	530.1
33	Alaska	527.6
34	Idaho	524.4
35	Maine	513.8
36	Georgia	507.5
37	Indiana	482.3
38	Nebraska	457.6
39	Arkansas	447.3
40	Pennsylvania	412.4
41	Michigan	408.2
42	Oklahoma	387.6
43	Alabama	313.7
44	North Dakota	281.1
45	Iowa	268.6
46	West Virginia	206.7
NA	Florida**	NA
NA	Kansas**	NA
NA	Montana**	NA
NA	Vermont**	NA
	District of Columbia**	NA

Source: Morgan Quitno Press using data from Federal Bureau of Investigation
    "Crime in the United States 1996" (Uniform Crime Reports, October 4, 1997)
*By law enforcement agencies submitting complete reports to the F.B.I. for 12 months in 1996. Arrests of youths 17 years and younger divided into population of 10 to 17 year olds. See important note at beginning of this chapter. Includes offenses relating to possession, sale, use, growing and manufacturing of narcotic drugs.
**Not available.

Reported Arrests of Juveniles for Drug Abuse Violations
As a Percent of All Such Arrests in 1996
National Percent = 14.0% of Reported Drug Abuse Violation Arrests*

ALPHA ORDER				RANK ORDER		
RANK	STATE	PERCENT		RANK	STATE	PERCENT
43	Alabama	10.1		1	Wyoming	25.9
5	Alaska	23.4		2	South Dakota	25.1
12	Arizona	20.9		3	Delaware	24.9
41	Arkansas	11.1		4	Maryland	24.2
46	California	9.6		5	Alaska	23.4
25	Colorado	15.7		6	Minnesota	22.9
17	Connecticut	18.3		7	Wisconsin	22.4
3	Delaware	24.9		8	Hawaii	22.2
NA	Florida**	NA		8	North Dakota	22.2
42	Georgia	10.8		10	New Mexico	22.0
8	Hawaii	22.2		11	Idaho	21.6
11	Idaho	21.6		12	Arizona	20.9
12	Illinois	20.9		12	Illinois	20.9
21	Indiana	16.8		14	New Hampshire	20.7
39	Iowa	11.4		15	Maine	19.2
NA	Kansas**	NA		16	Utah	18.4
36	Kentucky	12.1		17	Connecticut	18.3
28	Louisiana	14.7		17	New Jersey	18.3
15	Maine	19.2		19	Mississippi	18.0
4	Maryland	24.2		20	Texas	17.1
34	Massachusetts	12.6		21	Indiana	16.8
38	Michigan	11.5		22	Nebraska	16.6
6	Minnesota	22.9		23	Pennsylvania	16.4
19	Mississippi	18.0		24	Washington	15.9
35	Missouri	12.4		25	Colorado	15.7
NA	Montana**	NA		26	Oregon	15.5
22	Nebraska	16.6		27	Rhode Island	15.4
30	Nevada	14.1		28	Louisiana	14.7
14	New Hampshire	20.7		29	Ohio	14.3
17	New Jersey	18.3		30	Nevada	14.1
10	New Mexico	22.0		31	South Carolina	13.9
44	New York	10.0		32	Tennessee	12.9
36	North Carolina	12.1		33	Virginia	12.8
8	North Dakota	22.2		34	Massachusetts	12.6
29	Ohio	14.3		35	Missouri	12.4
40	Oklahoma	11.2		36	Kentucky	12.1
26	Oregon	15.5		36	North Carolina	12.1
23	Pennsylvania	16.4		38	Michigan	11.5
27	Rhode Island	15.4		39	Iowa	11.4
31	South Carolina	13.9		40	Oklahoma	11.2
2	South Dakota	25.1		41	Arkansas	11.1
32	Tennessee	12.9		42	Georgia	10.8
20	Texas	17.1		43	Alabama	10.1
16	Utah	18.4		44	New York	10.0
NA	Vermont**	NA		45	West Virginia	9.8
33	Virginia	12.8		46	California	9.6
24	Washington	15.9		NA	Florida**	NA
45	West Virginia	9.8		NA	Kansas**	NA
7	Wisconsin	22.4		NA	Montana**	NA
1	Wyoming	25.9		NA	Vermont**	NA
					District of Columbia**	NA

Source: Morgan Quitno Press using data from Federal Bureau of Investigation
   "Crime in the United States 1996" (Uniform Crime Reports, October 4, 1997)
*Arrests of youths 17 years and younger by law enforcement agencies submitting complete reports to the F.B.I. for 12 months in 1996. Includes offenses relating to possession, sale, use, growing and manufacturing of narcotic drugs.
**Not available.

Reported Arrests of Juveniles for Sex Offenses in 1996

National Total = 12,660 Reported Arrests*

<table>
<tr><td colspan="4">ALPHA ORDER</td><td colspan="4">RANK ORDER</td></tr>
<tr><td>RANK</td><td>STATE</td><td>ARRESTS</td><td>% of USA</td><td>RANK</td><td>STATE</td><td>ARRESTS</td><td>% of USA</td></tr>
<tr><td>40</td><td>Alabama</td><td>33</td><td>0.26%</td><td>1</td><td>California</td><td>2,245</td><td>17.73%</td></tr>
<tr><td>29</td><td>Alaska</td><td>77</td><td>0.61%</td><td>2</td><td>Wisconsin</td><td>1,529</td><td>12.08%</td></tr>
<tr><td>12</td><td>Arizona</td><td>334</td><td>2.64%</td><td>3</td><td>Texas</td><td>889</td><td>7.02%</td></tr>
<tr><td>28</td><td>Arkansas</td><td>79</td><td>0.62%</td><td>4</td><td>New York</td><td>811</td><td>6.41%</td></tr>
<tr><td>1</td><td>California</td><td>2,245</td><td>17.73%</td><td>5</td><td>Pennsylvania</td><td>458</td><td>3.62%</td></tr>
<tr><td>19</td><td>Colorado</td><td>254</td><td>2.01%</td><td>6</td><td>New Jersey</td><td>435</td><td>3.44%</td></tr>
<tr><td>22</td><td>Connecticut</td><td>187</td><td>1.48%</td><td>7</td><td>Virginia</td><td>377</td><td>2.98%</td></tr>
<tr><td>37</td><td>Delaware</td><td>55</td><td>0.43%</td><td>8</td><td>Maryland</td><td>371</td><td>2.93%</td></tr>
<tr><td>NA</td><td>Florida**</td><td>NA</td><td>NA</td><td>9</td><td>Michigan</td><td>349</td><td>2.76%</td></tr>
<tr><td>13</td><td>Georgia</td><td>332</td><td>2.62%</td><td>10</td><td>Ohio</td><td>338</td><td>2.67%</td></tr>
<tr><td>31</td><td>Hawaii</td><td>74</td><td>0.58%</td><td>11</td><td>Missouri</td><td>337</td><td>2.66%</td></tr>
<tr><td>27</td><td>Idaho</td><td>95</td><td>0.75%</td><td>12</td><td>Arizona</td><td>334</td><td>2.64%</td></tr>
<tr><td>15</td><td>Illinois</td><td>295</td><td>2.33%</td><td>13</td><td>Georgia</td><td>332</td><td>2.62%</td></tr>
<tr><td>24</td><td>Indiana</td><td>131</td><td>1.03%</td><td>14</td><td>North Carolina</td><td>315</td><td>2.49%</td></tr>
<tr><td>38</td><td>Iowa</td><td>44</td><td>0.35%</td><td>15</td><td>Illinois</td><td>295</td><td>2.33%</td></tr>
<tr><td>NA</td><td>Kansas**</td><td>NA</td><td>NA</td><td>15</td><td>Utah</td><td>295</td><td>2.33%</td></tr>
<tr><td>42</td><td>Kentucky</td><td>26</td><td>0.21%</td><td>17</td><td>Oregon</td><td>290</td><td>2.29%</td></tr>
<tr><td>23</td><td>Louisiana</td><td>176</td><td>1.39%</td><td>18</td><td>Washington</td><td>258</td><td>2.04%</td></tr>
<tr><td>29</td><td>Maine</td><td>77</td><td>0.61%</td><td>19</td><td>Colorado</td><td>254</td><td>2.01%</td></tr>
<tr><td>8</td><td>Maryland</td><td>371</td><td>2.93%</td><td>20</td><td>Minnesota</td><td>210</td><td>1.66%</td></tr>
<tr><td>32</td><td>Massachusetts</td><td>62</td><td>0.49%</td><td>21</td><td>South Carolina</td><td>207</td><td>1.64%</td></tr>
<tr><td>9</td><td>Michigan</td><td>349</td><td>2.76%</td><td>22</td><td>Connecticut</td><td>187</td><td>1.48%</td></tr>
<tr><td>20</td><td>Minnesota</td><td>210</td><td>1.66%</td><td>23</td><td>Louisiana</td><td>176</td><td>1.39%</td></tr>
<tr><td>36</td><td>Mississippi</td><td>56</td><td>0.44%</td><td>24</td><td>Indiana</td><td>131</td><td>1.03%</td></tr>
<tr><td>11</td><td>Missouri</td><td>337</td><td>2.66%</td><td>25</td><td>Oklahoma</td><td>124</td><td>0.98%</td></tr>
<tr><td>NA</td><td>Montana**</td><td>NA</td><td>NA</td><td>26</td><td>Nevada</td><td>123</td><td>0.97%</td></tr>
<tr><td>34</td><td>Nebraska</td><td>57</td><td>0.45%</td><td>27</td><td>Idaho</td><td>95</td><td>0.75%</td></tr>
<tr><td>26</td><td>Nevada</td><td>123</td><td>0.97%</td><td>28</td><td>Arkansas</td><td>79</td><td>0.62%</td></tr>
<tr><td>39</td><td>New Hampshire</td><td>38</td><td>0.30%</td><td>29</td><td>Alaska</td><td>77</td><td>0.61%</td></tr>
<tr><td>6</td><td>New Jersey</td><td>435</td><td>3.44%</td><td>29</td><td>Maine</td><td>77</td><td>0.61%</td></tr>
<tr><td>45</td><td>New Mexico</td><td>16</td><td>0.13%</td><td>31</td><td>Hawaii</td><td>74</td><td>0.58%</td></tr>
<tr><td>4</td><td>New York</td><td>811</td><td>6.41%</td><td>32</td><td>Massachusetts</td><td>62</td><td>0.49%</td></tr>
<tr><td>14</td><td>North Carolina</td><td>315</td><td>2.49%</td><td>33</td><td>Rhode Island</td><td>59</td><td>0.47%</td></tr>
<tr><td>41</td><td>North Dakota</td><td>27</td><td>0.21%</td><td>34</td><td>Nebraska</td><td>57</td><td>0.45%</td></tr>
<tr><td>10</td><td>Ohio</td><td>338</td><td>2.67%</td><td>34</td><td>Tennessee</td><td>57</td><td>0.45%</td></tr>
<tr><td>25</td><td>Oklahoma</td><td>124</td><td>0.98%</td><td>36</td><td>Mississippi</td><td>56</td><td>0.44%</td></tr>
<tr><td>17</td><td>Oregon</td><td>290</td><td>2.29%</td><td>37</td><td>Delaware</td><td>55</td><td>0.43%</td></tr>
<tr><td>5</td><td>Pennsylvania</td><td>458</td><td>3.62%</td><td>38</td><td>Iowa</td><td>44</td><td>0.35%</td></tr>
<tr><td>33</td><td>Rhode Island</td><td>59</td><td>0.47%</td><td>39</td><td>New Hampshire</td><td>38</td><td>0.30%</td></tr>
<tr><td>21</td><td>South Carolina</td><td>207</td><td>1.64%</td><td>40</td><td>Alabama</td><td>33</td><td>0.26%</td></tr>
<tr><td>44</td><td>South Dakota</td><td>22</td><td>0.17%</td><td>41</td><td>North Dakota</td><td>27</td><td>0.21%</td></tr>
<tr><td>34</td><td>Tennessee</td><td>57</td><td>0.45%</td><td>42</td><td>Kentucky</td><td>26</td><td>0.21%</td></tr>
<tr><td>3</td><td>Texas</td><td>889</td><td>7.02%</td><td>43</td><td>West Virginia</td><td>24</td><td>0.19%</td></tr>
<tr><td>15</td><td>Utah</td><td>295</td><td>2.33%</td><td>44</td><td>South Dakota</td><td>22</td><td>0.17%</td></tr>
<tr><td>NA</td><td>Vermont**</td><td>NA</td><td>NA</td><td>45</td><td>New Mexico</td><td>16</td><td>0.13%</td></tr>
<tr><td>7</td><td>Virginia</td><td>377</td><td>2.98%</td><td>46</td><td>Wyoming</td><td>12</td><td>0.09%</td></tr>
<tr><td>18</td><td>Washington</td><td>258</td><td>2.04%</td><td>NA</td><td>Florida**</td><td>NA</td><td>NA</td></tr>
<tr><td>43</td><td>West Virginia</td><td>24</td><td>0.19%</td><td>NA</td><td>Kansas**</td><td>NA</td><td>NA</td></tr>
<tr><td>2</td><td>Wisconsin</td><td>1,529</td><td>12.08%</td><td>NA</td><td>Montana**</td><td>NA</td><td>NA</td></tr>
<tr><td>46</td><td>Wyoming</td><td>12</td><td>0.09%</td><td>NA</td><td>Vermont**</td><td>NA</td><td>NA</td></tr>
<tr><td></td><td></td><td></td><td></td><td></td><td>District of Columbia**</td><td>NA</td><td>NA</td></tr>
</table>

Source: Federal Bureau of Investigation
"Crime in the United States 1996" (Uniform Crime Reports, October 4, 1997)
*Arrests of youths 17 years and younger by law enforcement agencies submitting complete reports to the F.B.I. for 12 months in 1996. Excludes forcible rape, prostitution and commercialized vice. Includes statutory rape and offenses against chastity, common decency, morals and the like. See important note at beginning of this chapter.
**Not available.

Reported Arrest Rate of Juveniles for Sex Offenses in 1996

National Rate = 58.3 Reported Arrests per 100,000 Population*

ALPHA ORDER				RANK ORDER		
RANK	STATE	RATE		RANK	STATE	RATE
46	Alabama	7.0		1	Wisconsin	240.9
3	Alaska	107.2		2	Delaware	141.1
10	Arizona	72.9		3	Alaska	107.2
40	Arkansas	27.4		4	Utah	102.7
14	California	64.6		5	Illinois	93.2
9	Colorado	76.3		6	Missouri	91.0
12	Connecticut	71.2		7	Oregon	90.7
2	Delaware	141.1		8	Maryland	85.1
NA	Florida**	NA		9	Colorado	76.3
15	Georgia	63.6		10	Arizona	72.9
20	Hawaii	57.7		11	Nevada	72.1
19	Idaho	57.9		12	Connecticut	71.2
5	Illinois	93.2		13	Mississippi	68.7
35	Indiana	34.1		14	California	64.6
42	Iowa	15.8		15	Georgia	63.6
NA	Kansas**	NA		16	New York	61.4
39	Kentucky	29.4		17	Rhode Island	60.5
25	Louisiana	50.1		18	Washington	58.7
22	Maine	54.4		19	Idaho	57.9
8	Maryland	85.1		20	Hawaii	57.7
43	Massachusetts	12.3		21	Virginia	57.2
34	Michigan	37.1		22	Maine	54.4
31	Minnesota	39.8		23	New Jersey	54.2
13	Mississippi	68.7		24	North Dakota	53.4
6	Missouri	91.0		25	Louisiana	50.1
NA	Montana**	NA		26	South Carolina	49.9
32	Nebraska	38.1		27	Ohio	45.2
11	Nevada	72.1		28	Pennsylvania	45.1
33	New Hampshire	37.2		29	Texas	43.2
23	New Jersey	54.2		30	North Carolina	40.3
44	New Mexico	12.0		31	Minnesota	39.8
16	New York	61.4		32	Nebraska	38.1
30	North Carolina	40.3		33	New Hampshire	37.2
24	North Dakota	53.4		34	Michigan	37.1
27	Ohio	45.2		35	Indiana	34.1
38	Oklahoma	30.0		36	South Dakota	32.7
7	Oregon	90.7		37	Wyoming	30.5
28	Pennsylvania	45.1		38	Oklahoma	30.0
17	Rhode Island	60.5		39	Kentucky	29.4
26	South Carolina	49.9		40	Arkansas	27.4
36	South Dakota	32.7		41	Tennessee	24.7
41	Tennessee	24.7		42	Iowa	15.8
29	Texas	43.2		43	Massachusetts	12.3
4	Utah	102.7		44	New Mexico	12.0
NA	Vermont**	NA		45	West Virginia	11.7
21	Virginia	57.2		46	Alabama	7.0
18	Washington	58.7		NA	Florida**	NA
45	West Virginia	11.7		NA	Kansas**	NA
1	Wisconsin	240.9		NA	Montana**	NA
37	Wyoming	30.5		NA	Vermont**	NA
					District of Columbia**	NA

Source: Morgan Quitno Press using data from Federal Bureau of Investigation
    "Crime in the United States 1996" (Uniform Crime Reports, October 4, 1997)
*By law enforcement agencies submitting complete reports to the F.B.I. for 12 months in 1996. Arrests of youths 17 years and younger divided into population of 10 to 17 year olds. See important note at beginning of this chapter. Excludes forcible rape, prostitution and commercialized vice. Includes statutory rape and offenses against chastity, common decency, morals and the like. **Not available.

Reported Arrests of Juveniles for Sex Offenses
As a Percent of All Such Arrests in 1996
National Percent = 17.9% of Reported Sex Offenses Arrests*

ALPHA ORDER

RANK	STATE	PERCENT
44	Alabama	8.1
9	Alaska	24.6
35	Arizona	14.9
31	Arkansas	15.8
36	California	14.3
14	Colorado	20.9
6	Connecticut	27.3
8	Delaware	25.7
NA	Florida**	NA
21	Georgia	18.1
15	Hawaii	20.2
4	Idaho	29.1
37	Illinois	13.8
32	Indiana	15.1
18	Iowa	18.8
NA	Kansas**	NA
43	Kentucky	10.0
22	Louisiana	17.2
11	Maine	24.1
7	Maryland	26.4
46	Massachusetts	6.3
19	Michigan	18.4
5	Minnesota	28.3
17	Mississippi	19.7
23	Missouri	16.9
NA	Montana**	NA
20	Nebraska	18.2
41	Nevada	12.1
32	New Hampshire	15.1
13	New Jersey	22.0
42	New Mexico	11.3
28	New York	16.0
39	North Carolina	12.4
2	North Dakota	32.5
27	Ohio	16.1
38	Oklahoma	12.6
12	Oregon	22.3
16	Pennsylvania	19.8
30	Rhode Island	15.9
10	South Carolina	24.2
23	South Dakota	16.9
40	Tennessee	12.2
25	Texas	16.6
3	Utah	30.5
NA	Vermont**	NA
26	Virginia	16.2
34	Washington	15.0
45	West Virginia	7.3
1	Wisconsin	38.8
28	Wyoming	16.0

RANK ORDER

RANK	STATE	PERCENT
1	Wisconsin	38.8
2	North Dakota	32.5
3	Utah	30.5
4	Idaho	29.1
5	Minnesota	28.3
6	Connecticut	27.3
7	Maryland	26.4
8	Delaware	25.7
9	Alaska	24.6
10	South Carolina	24.2
11	Maine	24.1
12	Oregon	22.3
13	New Jersey	22.0
14	Colorado	20.9
15	Hawaii	20.2
16	Pennsylvania	19.8
17	Mississippi	19.7
18	Iowa	18.8
19	Michigan	18.4
20	Nebraska	18.2
21	Georgia	18.1
22	Louisiana	17.2
23	Missouri	16.9
23	South Dakota	16.9
25	Texas	16.6
26	Virginia	16.2
27	Ohio	16.1
28	New York	16.0
28	Wyoming	16.0
30	Rhode Island	15.9
31	Arkansas	15.8
32	Indiana	15.1
32	New Hampshire	15.1
34	Washington	15.0
35	Arizona	14.9
36	California	14.3
37	Illinois	13.8
38	Oklahoma	12.6
39	North Carolina	12.4
40	Tennessee	12.2
41	Nevada	12.1
42	New Mexico	11.3
43	Kentucky	10.0
44	Alabama	8.1
45	West Virginia	7.3
46	Massachusetts	6.3
NA	Florida**	NA
NA	Kansas**	NA
NA	Montana**	NA
NA	Vermont**	NA

District of Columbia**   NA

Source: Morgan Quitno Press using data from Federal Bureau of Investigation
   "Crime in the United States 1996" (Uniform Crime Reports, October 4, 1997)
*Arrests of youths 17 years and younger by law enforcement agencies submitting complete reports to the F.B.I. for 12 months in 1996. Excludes forcible rape, prostitution and commercialized vice. Includes statutory rape and offenses against chastity, common decency, morals and the like.
**Not available.

241

Reported Arrests of Juveniles for Prostitution and Commercialized Vice in 1996

National Total = 1,104 Reported Arrests*

ALPHA ORDER					RANK ORDER			
RANK	STATE		ARRESTS	% of USA	RANK	STATE	ARRESTS	% of USA
38	Alabama		2	0.18%	1	California	290	26.27%
35	Alaska		3	0.27%	2	New York	100	9.06%
5	Arizona		42	3.80%	3	Illinois	93	8.42%
26	Arkansas		7	0.63%	4	Texas	66	5.98%
1	California		290	26.27%	5	Arizona	42	3.80%
38	Colorado		2	0.18%	6	Michigan	39	3.53%
28	Connecticut		6	0.54%	7	Massachusetts	32	2.90%
42	Delaware		1	0.09%	7	Missouri	32	2.90%
NA	Florida**		NA	NA	7	Washington	32	2.90%
26	Georgia		7	0.63%	10	Minnesota	29	2.63%
30	Hawaii		5	0.45%	11	Maryland	28	2.54%
42	Idaho		1	0.09%	11	Utah	28	2.54%
3	Illinois		93	8.42%	13	Nevada	27	2.45%
23	Indiana		8	0.72%	14	Pennsylvania	26	2.36%
34	Iowa		4	0.36%	14	Wisconsin	26	2.36%
NA	Kansas**		NA	NA	16	Ohio	25	2.26%
23	Kentucky		8	0.72%	17	New Jersey	20	1.81%
30	Louisiana		5	0.45%	17	Oregon	20	1.81%
30	Maine		5	0.45%	19	South Carolina	19	1.72%
11	Maryland		28	2.54%	20	Oklahoma	14	1.27%
7	Massachusetts		32	2.90%	21	North Carolina	12	1.09%
6	Michigan		39	3.53%	22	New Mexico	9	0.82%
10	Minnesota		29	2.63%	23	Indiana	8	0.72%
35	Mississippi		3	0.27%	23	Kentucky	8	0.72%
7	Missouri		32	2.90%	23	Virginia	8	0.72%
NA	Montana**		NA	NA	26	Arkansas	7	0.63%
46	Nebraska		0	0.00%	26	Georgia	7	0.63%
13	Nevada		27	2.45%	28	Connecticut	6	0.54%
38	New Hampshire		2	0.18%	28	Tennessee	6	0.54%
17	New Jersey		20	1.81%	30	Hawaii	5	0.45%
22	New Mexico		9	0.82%	30	Louisiana	5	0.45%
2	New York		100	9.06%	30	Maine	5	0.45%
21	North Carolina		12	1.09%	30	Rhode Island	5	0.45%
38	North Dakota		2	0.18%	34	Iowa	4	0.36%
16	Ohio		25	2.26%	35	Alaska	3	0.27%
20	Oklahoma		14	1.27%	35	Mississippi	3	0.27%
17	Oregon		20	1.81%	35	West Virginia	3	0.27%
14	Pennsylvania		26	2.36%	38	Alabama	2	0.18%
30	Rhode Island		5	0.45%	38	Colorado	2	0.18%
19	South Carolina		19	1.72%	38	New Hampshire	2	0.18%
42	South Dakota		1	0.09%	38	North Dakota	2	0.18%
28	Tennessee		6	0.54%	42	Delaware	1	0.09%
4	Texas		66	5.98%	42	Idaho	1	0.09%
11	Utah		28	2.54%	42	South Dakota	1	0.09%
NA	Vermont**		NA	NA	42	Wyoming	1	0.09%
23	Virginia		8	0.72%	46	Nebraska	0	0.00%
7	Washington		32	2.90%	NA	Florida**	NA	NA
35	West Virginia		3	0.27%	NA	Kansas**	NA	NA
14	Wisconsin		26	2.36%	NA	Montana**	NA	NA
42	Wyoming		1	0.09%	NA	Vermont**	NA	NA
						District of Columbia**	NA	NA

Source: Federal Bureau of Investigation
   "Crime in the United States 1996" (Uniform Crime Reports, October 4, 1997)
*Arrests of youths 17 years and younger by law enforcement agencies submitting complete reports to the F.B.I. for 12 months in 1996. Includes keeping a bawdy house, procuring or transporting women for immoral purposes. Attempts are included. See important note at beginning of this chapter.
**Not available.

Reported Juvenile Arrest Rate for Prostitution and Commercialized Vice in 1996

National Rate = 5.1 Reported Arrests per 100,000 Juvenile Population*

ALPHA ORDER

RANK ORDER

RANK	STATE	RATE		RANK	STATE	RATE
45	Alabama	0.4		1	Illinois	29.4
17	Alaska	4.2		2	Nevada	15.8
4	Arizona	9.2		3	Utah	9.7
32	Arkansas	2.4		4	Arizona	9.2
7	California	8.3		5	Kentucky	9.0
43	Colorado	0.6		6	Missouri	8.6
33	Connecticut	2.3		7	California	8.3
27	Delaware	2.6		8	New York	7.6
NA	Florida**	NA		9	Washington	7.3
41	Georgia	1.3		10	New Mexico	6.7
21	Hawaii	3.9		11	Maryland	6.4
43	Idaho	0.6		12	Massachusetts	6.3
1	Illinois	29.4		12	Oregon	6.3
34	Indiana	2.1		14	Minnesota	5.5
39	Iowa	1.4		15	Rhode Island	5.1
NA	Kansas**	NA		16	South Carolina	4.6
5	Kentucky	9.0		17	Alaska	4.2
39	Louisiana	1.4		18	Michigan	4.1
23	Maine	3.5		18	Wisconsin	4.1
11	Maryland	6.4		20	North Dakota	4.0
12	Massachusetts	6.3		21	Hawaii	3.9
18	Michigan	4.1		22	Mississippi	3.7
14	Minnesota	5.5		23	Maine	3.5
22	Mississippi	3.7		24	Oklahoma	3.4
6	Missouri	8.6		25	Ohio	3.3
NA	Montana**	NA		26	Texas	3.2
46	Nebraska	0.0		27	Delaware	2.6
2	Nevada	15.8		27	Pennsylvania	2.6
35	New Hampshire	2.0		27	Tennessee	2.6
30	New Jersey	2.5		30	New Jersey	2.5
10	New Mexico	6.7		30	Wyoming	2.5
8	New York	7.6		32	Arkansas	2.4
36	North Carolina	1.5		33	Connecticut	2.3
20	North Dakota	4.0		34	Indiana	2.1
25	Ohio	3.3		35	New Hampshire	2.0
24	Oklahoma	3.4		36	North Carolina	1.5
12	Oregon	6.3		36	South Dakota	1.5
27	Pennsylvania	2.6		36	West Virginia	1.5
15	Rhode Island	5.1		39	Iowa	1.4
16	South Carolina	4.6		39	Louisiana	1.4
36	South Dakota	1.5		41	Georgia	1.3
27	Tennessee	2.6		42	Virginia	1.2
26	Texas	3.2		43	Colorado	0.6
3	Utah	9.7		43	Idaho	0.6
NA	Vermont**	NA		45	Alabama	0.4
42	Virginia	1.2		46	Nebraska	0.0
9	Washington	7.3		NA	Florida**	NA
36	West Virginia	1.5		NA	Kansas**	NA
18	Wisconsin	4.1		NA	Montana**	NA
30	Wyoming	2.5		NA	Vermont**	NA
					District of Columbia**	NA

Source: Morgan Quitno Press using data from Federal Bureau of Investigation
    "Crime in the United States 1996" (Uniform Crime Reports, October 4, 1997)
*By law enforcement agencies submitting complete reports to the F.B.I. for 12 months in 1996. Arrests of youths 17
years and younger divided into population of 10 to 17 year olds. See important note at beginning of this chapter.
Includes keeping a bawdy house, procuring or transporting women for immoral purposes. Attempts are included.
**Not available.

Reported Arrests of Juveniles for Prostitution and Commercialized Vice
As a Percent of All Such Arrests in 1996
National Percent = 1.4% of Reported Prostitution/Commercialized Vice Arrests*

<u>ALPHA ORDER</u>

<u>RANK ORDER</u>

RANK	STATE	PERCENT		RANK	STATE	PERCENT
39	Alabama	0.8		1	North Dakota	100.0
22	Alaska	1.6		2	Wyoming	33.3
19	Arizona	1.7		3	Mississippi	15.8
11	Arkansas	3.0		4	Idaho	14.3
19	California	1.7		5	Maine	10.6
45	Colorado	0.2		6	Oklahoma	7.5
31	Connecticut	1.1		7	South Dakota	6.3
41	Delaware	0.7		8	Washington	4.1
NA	Florida**	NA		9	Utah	3.6
12	Georgia	2.5		10	New Hampshire	3.2
26	Hawaii	1.3		11	Arkansas	3.0
4	Idaho	14.3		12	Georgia	2.5
28	Illinois	1.2		12	Minnesota	2.5
43	Indiana	0.6		12	New Mexico	2.5
22	Iowa	1.6		15	Oregon	2.2
NA	Kansas**	NA		16	Kentucky	2.1
16	Kentucky	2.1		17	Missouri	1.9
24	Louisiana	1.4		17	South Carolina	1.9
5	Maine	10.6		19	Arizona	1.7
19	Maryland	1.7		19	California	1.7
28	Massachusetts	1.2		19	Maryland	1.7
31	Michigan	1.1		22	Alaska	1.6
12	Minnesota	2.5		22	Iowa	1.6
3	Mississippi	15.8		24	Louisiana	1.4
17	Missouri	1.9		24	West Virginia	1.4
NA	Montana**	NA		26	Hawaii	1.3
46	Nebraska	0.0		26	North Carolina	1.3
39	Nevada	0.8		28	Illinois	1.2
10	New Hampshire	3.2		28	Massachusetts	1.2
35	New Jersey	0.9		28	Wisconsin	1.2
12	New Mexico	2.5		31	Connecticut	1.1
31	New York	1.1		31	Michigan	1.1
26	North Carolina	1.3		31	New York	1.1
1	North Dakota	100.0		31	Texas	1.1
35	Ohio	0.9		35	New Jersey	0.9
6	Oklahoma	7.5		35	Ohio	0.9
15	Oregon	2.2		35	Pennsylvania	0.9
35	Pennsylvania	0.9		35	Rhode Island	0.9
35	Rhode Island	0.9		39	Alabama	0.8
17	South Carolina	1.9		39	Nevada	0.8
7	South Dakota	6.3		41	Delaware	0.7
44	Tennessee	0.5		41	Virginia	0.7
31	Texas	1.1		43	Indiana	0.6
9	Utah	3.6		44	Tennessee	0.5
NA	Vermont**	NA		45	Colorado	0.2
41	Virginia	0.7		46	Nebraska	0.0
8	Washington	4.1		NA	Florida**	NA
24	West Virginia	1.4		NA	Kansas**	NA
28	Wisconsin	1.2		NA	Montana**	NA
2	Wyoming	33.3		NA	Vermont**	NA
					District of Columbia**	NA

Source: Morgan Quitno Press using data from Federal Bureau of Investigation
*   "Crime in the United States 1996" (Uniform Crime Reports, October 4, 1997)*
Arrests of youths 17 years and younger by law enforcement agencies submitting complete reports to the F.B.I. for 12 months in 1996. Includes keeping a bawdy house, procuring or transporting women for immoral purposes. Attempts are included.
***Not available.*

244

Reported Arrests of Juveniles for Offenses Against Families & Children in 1996

National Total = 5,850 Reported Arrests*

RANK	STATE	ARRESTS	% of USA
24	Alabama	45	0.77%
45	Alaska	3	0.05%
8	Arizona	167	2.85%
25	Arkansas	41	0.70%
37	California	15	0.26%
26	Colorado	40	0.68%
9	Connecticut	158	2.70%
43	Delaware	4	0.07%
NA	Florida**	NA	NA
14	Georgia	120	2.05%
10	Hawaii	149	2.55%
28	Idaho	35	0.60%
29	Illinois	34	0.58%
3	Indiana	290	4.96%
41	Iowa	7	0.12%
NA	Kansas**	NA	NA
42	Kentucky	5	0.09%
11	Louisiana	133	2.27%
43	Maine	4	0.07%
20	Maryland	80	1.37%
7	Massachusetts	199	3.40%
40	Michigan	8	0.14%
31	Minnesota	30	0.51%
30	Mississippi	33	0.56%
13	Missouri	125	2.14%
NA	Montana**	NA	NA
34	Nebraska	19	0.32%
15	Nevada	113	1.93%
46	New Hampshire	0	0.00%
32	New Jersey	27	0.46%
12	New Mexico	127	2.17%
4	New York	246	4.21%
18	North Carolina	87	1.49%
23	North Dakota	49	0.84%
1	Ohio	2,038	34.84%
16	Oklahoma	101	1.73%
34	Oregon	19	0.32%
21	Pennsylvania	77	1.32%
17	Rhode Island	93	1.59%
33	South Carolina	23	0.39%
19	South Dakota	83	1.42%
27	Tennessee	37	0.63%
5	Texas	222	3.79%
22	Utah	61	1.04%
NA	Vermont**	NA	NA
6	Virginia	204	3.49%
36	Washington	18	0.31%
39	West Virginia	10	0.17%
2	Wisconsin	460	7.86%
38	Wyoming	11	0.19%

RANK	STATE	ARRESTS	% of USA
1	Ohio	2,038	34.84%
2	Wisconsin	460	7.86%
3	Indiana	290	4.96%
4	New York	246	4.21%
5	Texas	222	3.79%
6	Virginia	204	3.49%
7	Massachusetts	199	3.40%
8	Arizona	167	2.85%
9	Connecticut	158	2.70%
10	Hawaii	149	2.55%
11	Louisiana	133	2.27%
12	New Mexico	127	2.17%
13	Missouri	125	2.14%
14	Georgia	120	2.05%
15	Nevada	113	1.93%
16	Oklahoma	101	1.73%
17	Rhode Island	93	1.59%
18	North Carolina	87	1.49%
19	South Dakota	83	1.42%
20	Maryland	80	1.37%
21	Pennsylvania	77	1.32%
22	Utah	61	1.04%
23	North Dakota	49	0.84%
24	Alabama	45	0.77%
25	Arkansas	41	0.70%
26	Colorado	40	0.68%
27	Tennessee	37	0.63%
28	Idaho	35	0.60%
29	Illinois	34	0.58%
30	Mississippi	33	0.56%
31	Minnesota	30	0.51%
32	New Jersey	27	0.46%
33	South Carolina	23	0.39%
34	Nebraska	19	0.32%
34	Oregon	19	0.32%
36	Washington	18	0.31%
37	California	15	0.26%
38	Wyoming	11	0.19%
39	West Virginia	10	0.17%
40	Michigan	8	0.14%
41	Iowa	7	0.12%
42	Kentucky	5	0.09%
43	Delaware	4	0.07%
43	Maine	4	0.07%
45	Alaska	3	0.05%
46	New Hampshire	0	0.00%
NA	Florida**	NA	NA
NA	Kansas**	NA	NA
NA	Montana**	NA	NA
NA	Vermont**	NA	NA
	District of Columbia**	NA	NA

Source: Federal Bureau of Investigation
   "Crime in the United States 1996" (Uniform Crime Reports, October 4, 1997)
*Arrests of youths 17 years and younger by law enforcement agencies submitting complete reports to the F.B.I. for 12 months in 1996. Includes nonsupport, neglect, desertion or abuse of family and children. See important note at beginning of this chapter.
**Not available.

Reported Juvenile Arrest Rate for Offenses Against Families & Children in 1996

National Rate = 26.9 Reported Arrests per 100,000 Juvenile Population*

<table>
<tr><td colspan="3">ALPHA ORDER</td><td colspan="3">RANK ORDER</td></tr>
<tr><td>RANK</td><td>STATE</td><td>RATE</td><td>RANK</td><td>STATE</td><td>RATE</td></tr>
<tr><td>32</td><td>Alabama</td><td>9.6</td><td>1</td><td>Ohio</td><td>272.7</td></tr>
<tr><td>39</td><td>Alaska</td><td>4.2</td><td>2</td><td>South Dakota</td><td>123.2</td></tr>
<tr><td>14</td><td>Arizona</td><td>36.4</td><td>3</td><td>Hawaii</td><td>116.1</td></tr>
<tr><td>25</td><td>Arkansas</td><td>14.2</td><td>4</td><td>North Dakota</td><td>97.0</td></tr>
<tr><td>45</td><td>California</td><td>0.4</td><td>5</td><td>Rhode Island</td><td>95.4</td></tr>
<tr><td>27</td><td>Colorado</td><td>12.0</td><td>6</td><td>New Mexico</td><td>95.1</td></tr>
<tr><td>10</td><td>Connecticut</td><td>60.2</td><td>7</td><td>Indiana</td><td>75.5</td></tr>
<tr><td>31</td><td>Delaware</td><td>10.3</td><td>8</td><td>Wisconsin</td><td>72.5</td></tr>
<tr><td>NA</td><td>Florida**</td><td>NA</td><td>9</td><td>Nevada</td><td>66.3</td></tr>
<tr><td>19</td><td>Georgia</td><td>23.0</td><td>10</td><td>Connecticut</td><td>60.2</td></tr>
<tr><td>3</td><td>Hawaii</td><td>116.1</td><td>11</td><td>Mississippi</td><td>40.5</td></tr>
<tr><td>20</td><td>Idaho</td><td>21.3</td><td>12</td><td>Massachusetts</td><td>39.5</td></tr>
<tr><td>30</td><td>Illinois</td><td>10.7</td><td>13</td><td>Louisiana</td><td>37.9</td></tr>
<tr><td>7</td><td>Indiana</td><td>75.5</td><td>14</td><td>Arizona</td><td>36.4</td></tr>
<tr><td>43</td><td>Iowa</td><td>2.5</td><td>15</td><td>Missouri</td><td>33.8</td></tr>
<tr><td>NA</td><td>Kansas**</td><td>NA</td><td>16</td><td>Virginia</td><td>31.0</td></tr>
<tr><td>36</td><td>Kentucky</td><td>5.6</td><td>17</td><td>Wyoming</td><td>28.0</td></tr>
<tr><td>13</td><td>Louisiana</td><td>37.9</td><td>18</td><td>Oklahoma</td><td>24.4</td></tr>
<tr><td>42</td><td>Maine</td><td>2.8</td><td>19</td><td>Georgia</td><td>23.0</td></tr>
<tr><td>23</td><td>Maryland</td><td>18.3</td><td>20</td><td>Idaho</td><td>21.3</td></tr>
<tr><td>12</td><td>Massachusetts</td><td>39.5</td><td>21</td><td>Utah</td><td>21.2</td></tr>
<tr><td>44</td><td>Michigan</td><td>0.8</td><td>22</td><td>New York</td><td>18.6</td></tr>
<tr><td>35</td><td>Minnesota</td><td>5.7</td><td>23</td><td>Maryland</td><td>18.3</td></tr>
<tr><td>11</td><td>Mississippi</td><td>40.5</td><td>24</td><td>Tennessee</td><td>16.1</td></tr>
<tr><td>15</td><td>Missouri</td><td>33.8</td><td>25</td><td>Arkansas</td><td>14.2</td></tr>
<tr><td>NA</td><td>Montana**</td><td>NA</td><td>26</td><td>Nebraska</td><td>12.7</td></tr>
<tr><td>26</td><td>Nebraska</td><td>12.7</td><td>27</td><td>Colorado</td><td>12.0</td></tr>
<tr><td>9</td><td>Nevada</td><td>66.3</td><td>28</td><td>North Carolina</td><td>11.1</td></tr>
<tr><td>46</td><td>New Hampshire</td><td>0.0</td><td>29</td><td>Texas</td><td>10.8</td></tr>
<tr><td>41</td><td>New Jersey</td><td>3.4</td><td>30</td><td>Illinois</td><td>10.7</td></tr>
<tr><td>6</td><td>New Mexico</td><td>95.1</td><td>31</td><td>Delaware</td><td>10.3</td></tr>
<tr><td>22</td><td>New York</td><td>18.6</td><td>32</td><td>Alabama</td><td>9.6</td></tr>
<tr><td>28</td><td>North Carolina</td><td>11.1</td><td>33</td><td>Pennsylvania</td><td>7.6</td></tr>
<tr><td>4</td><td>North Dakota</td><td>97.0</td><td>34</td><td>Oregon</td><td>5.9</td></tr>
<tr><td>1</td><td>Ohio</td><td>272.7</td><td>35</td><td>Minnesota</td><td>5.7</td></tr>
<tr><td>18</td><td>Oklahoma</td><td>24.4</td><td>36</td><td>Kentucky</td><td>5.6</td></tr>
<tr><td>34</td><td>Oregon</td><td>5.9</td><td>37</td><td>South Carolina</td><td>5.5</td></tr>
<tr><td>33</td><td>Pennsylvania</td><td>7.6</td><td>38</td><td>West Virginia</td><td>4.9</td></tr>
<tr><td>5</td><td>Rhode Island</td><td>95.4</td><td>39</td><td>Alaska</td><td>4.2</td></tr>
<tr><td>37</td><td>South Carolina</td><td>5.5</td><td>40</td><td>Washington</td><td>4.1</td></tr>
<tr><td>2</td><td>South Dakota</td><td>123.2</td><td>41</td><td>New Jersey</td><td>3.4</td></tr>
<tr><td>24</td><td>Tennessee</td><td>16.1</td><td>42</td><td>Maine</td><td>2.8</td></tr>
<tr><td>29</td><td>Texas</td><td>10.8</td><td>43</td><td>Iowa</td><td>2.5</td></tr>
<tr><td>21</td><td>Utah</td><td>21.2</td><td>44</td><td>Michigan</td><td>0.8</td></tr>
<tr><td>NA</td><td>Vermont**</td><td>NA</td><td>45</td><td>California</td><td>0.4</td></tr>
<tr><td>16</td><td>Virginia</td><td>31.0</td><td>46</td><td>New Hampshire</td><td>0.0</td></tr>
<tr><td>40</td><td>Washington</td><td>4.1</td><td>NA</td><td>Florida**</td><td>NA</td></tr>
<tr><td>38</td><td>West Virginia</td><td>4.9</td><td>NA</td><td>Kansas**</td><td>NA</td></tr>
<tr><td>8</td><td>Wisconsin</td><td>72.5</td><td>NA</td><td>Montana**</td><td>NA</td></tr>
<tr><td>17</td><td>Wyoming</td><td>28.0</td><td>NA</td><td>Vermont**</td><td>NA</td></tr>
<tr><td></td><td></td><td></td><td></td><td>District of Columbia**</td><td>NA</td></tr>
</table>

Source: Morgan Quitno Press using data from Federal Bureau of Investigation
"Crime in the United States 1996" (Uniform Crime Reports, October 4, 1997)
By law enforcement agencies submitting complete reports to the F.B.I. for 12 months in 1996. Arrests of youths 17 years and younger divided into population of 10 to 17 year olds. See important note at beginning of this chapter. Includes nonsupport, neglect, desertion or abuse of family and children.
***Not available.*

Reported Arrests of Juveniles for Offenses Against Families and Children
As a Percent of All Such Arrests in 1996
National Percent = 5.6% of Offenses Against Families and Children Arrests*

<table>
<tr><td colspan="3">ALPHA ORDER</td><td colspan="3">RANK ORDER</td></tr>
<tr><td>RANK</td><td>STATE</td><td>PERCENT</td><td>RANK</td><td>STATE</td><td>PERCENT</td></tr>
<tr><td>26</td><td>Alabama</td><td>3.9</td><td>1</td><td>North Dakota</td><td>73.1</td></tr>
<tr><td>37</td><td>Alaska</td><td>1.9</td><td>2</td><td>South Dakota</td><td>31.2</td></tr>
<tr><td>11</td><td>Arizona</td><td>8.7</td><td>3</td><td>Indiana</td><td>24.8</td></tr>
<tr><td>32</td><td>Arkansas</td><td>3.4</td><td>4</td><td>New York</td><td>21.2</td></tr>
<tr><td>36</td><td>California</td><td>2.2</td><td>5</td><td>Rhode Island</td><td>20.4</td></tr>
<tr><td>35</td><td>Colorado</td><td>2.4</td><td>6</td><td>Louisiana</td><td>11.6</td></tr>
<tr><td>16</td><td>Connecticut</td><td>7.8</td><td>7</td><td>Wisconsin</td><td>11.3</td></tr>
<tr><td>25</td><td>Delaware</td><td>4.0</td><td>8</td><td>Nevada</td><td>10.5</td></tr>
<tr><td>NA</td><td>Florida**</td><td>NA</td><td>9</td><td>Oklahoma</td><td>9.2</td></tr>
<tr><td>28</td><td>Georgia</td><td>3.7</td><td>10</td><td>Ohio</td><td>8.9</td></tr>
<tr><td>14</td><td>Hawaii</td><td>8.0</td><td>11</td><td>Arizona</td><td>8.7</td></tr>
<tr><td>13</td><td>Idaho</td><td>8.1</td><td>12</td><td>Wyoming</td><td>8.6</td></tr>
<tr><td>20</td><td>Illinois</td><td>6.3</td><td>13</td><td>Idaho</td><td>8.1</td></tr>
<tr><td>3</td><td>Indiana</td><td>24.8</td><td>14</td><td>Hawaii</td><td>8.0</td></tr>
<tr><td>34</td><td>Iowa</td><td>2.7</td><td>15</td><td>Pennsylvania</td><td>7.9</td></tr>
<tr><td>NA</td><td>Kansas**</td><td>NA</td><td>16</td><td>Connecticut</td><td>7.8</td></tr>
<tr><td>43</td><td>Kentucky</td><td>0.6</td><td>17</td><td>New Mexico</td><td>7.4</td></tr>
<tr><td>6</td><td>Louisiana</td><td>11.6</td><td>18</td><td>Virginia</td><td>6.9</td></tr>
<tr><td>39</td><td>Maine</td><td>1.8</td><td>19</td><td>Massachusetts</td><td>6.4</td></tr>
<tr><td>28</td><td>Maryland</td><td>3.7</td><td>20</td><td>Illinois</td><td>6.3</td></tr>
<tr><td>19</td><td>Massachusetts</td><td>6.4</td><td>21</td><td>Texas</td><td>4.6</td></tr>
<tr><td>44</td><td>Michigan</td><td>0.3</td><td>22</td><td>Utah</td><td>4.4</td></tr>
<tr><td>23</td><td>Minnesota</td><td>4.2</td><td>23</td><td>Minnesota</td><td>4.2</td></tr>
<tr><td>27</td><td>Mississippi</td><td>3.8</td><td>24</td><td>Missouri</td><td>4.1</td></tr>
<tr><td>24</td><td>Missouri</td><td>4.1</td><td>25</td><td>Delaware</td><td>4.0</td></tr>
<tr><td>NA</td><td>Montana**</td><td>NA</td><td>26</td><td>Alabama</td><td>3.9</td></tr>
<tr><td>37</td><td>Nebraska</td><td>1.9</td><td>27</td><td>Mississippi</td><td>3.8</td></tr>
<tr><td>8</td><td>Nevada</td><td>10.5</td><td>28</td><td>Georgia</td><td>3.7</td></tr>
<tr><td>46</td><td>New Hampshire</td><td>0.0</td><td>28</td><td>Maryland</td><td>3.7</td></tr>
<tr><td>45</td><td>New Jersey</td><td>0.2</td><td>28</td><td>Tennessee</td><td>3.7</td></tr>
<tr><td>17</td><td>New Mexico</td><td>7.4</td><td>28</td><td>Washington</td><td>3.7</td></tr>
<tr><td>4</td><td>New York</td><td>21.2</td><td>32</td><td>Arkansas</td><td>3.4</td></tr>
<tr><td>42</td><td>North Carolina</td><td>1.2</td><td>33</td><td>Oregon</td><td>3.0</td></tr>
<tr><td>1</td><td>North Dakota</td><td>73.1</td><td>34</td><td>Iowa</td><td>2.7</td></tr>
<tr><td>10</td><td>Ohio</td><td>8.9</td><td>35</td><td>Colorado</td><td>2.4</td></tr>
<tr><td>9</td><td>Oklahoma</td><td>9.2</td><td>36</td><td>California</td><td>2.2</td></tr>
<tr><td>33</td><td>Oregon</td><td>3.0</td><td>37</td><td>Alaska</td><td>1.9</td></tr>
<tr><td>15</td><td>Pennsylvania</td><td>7.9</td><td>37</td><td>Nebraska</td><td>1.9</td></tr>
<tr><td>5</td><td>Rhode Island</td><td>20.4</td><td>39</td><td>Maine</td><td>1.8</td></tr>
<tr><td>40</td><td>South Carolina</td><td>1.6</td><td>40</td><td>South Carolina</td><td>1.6</td></tr>
<tr><td>2</td><td>South Dakota</td><td>31.2</td><td>41</td><td>West Virginia</td><td>1.3</td></tr>
<tr><td>28</td><td>Tennessee</td><td>3.7</td><td>42</td><td>North Carolina</td><td>1.2</td></tr>
<tr><td>21</td><td>Texas</td><td>4.6</td><td>43</td><td>Kentucky</td><td>0.6</td></tr>
<tr><td>22</td><td>Utah</td><td>4.4</td><td>44</td><td>Michigan</td><td>0.3</td></tr>
<tr><td>NA</td><td>Vermont**</td><td>NA</td><td>45</td><td>New Jersey</td><td>0.2</td></tr>
<tr><td>18</td><td>Virginia</td><td>6.9</td><td>46</td><td>New Hampshire</td><td>0.0</td></tr>
<tr><td>28</td><td>Washington</td><td>3.7</td><td>NA</td><td>Florida**</td><td>NA</td></tr>
<tr><td>41</td><td>West Virginia</td><td>1.3</td><td>NA</td><td>Kansas**</td><td>NA</td></tr>
<tr><td>7</td><td>Wisconsin</td><td>11.3</td><td>NA</td><td>Montana**</td><td>NA</td></tr>
<tr><td>12</td><td>Wyoming</td><td>8.6</td><td>NA</td><td>Vermont**</td><td>NA</td></tr>
<tr><td></td><td></td><td></td><td></td><td>District of Columbia**</td><td>NA</td></tr>
</table>

Source: Morgan Quitno Press using data from Federal Bureau of Investigation
   "Crime in the United States 1996" (Uniform Crime Reports, October 4, 1997)
*Arrests of youths 17 years and younger by law enforcement agencies submitting complete reports to the F.B.I. for 12 months in 1996. Includes nonsupport, neglect, desertion or abuse of family and children.
**Not available.

Juveniles in Public Facilities in 1995

National Total = 69,075 Juveniles*

ALPHA ORDER

RANK	STATE	JUVENILES	% of USA
21	Alabama	908	1.31%
40	Alaska	223	0.32%
16	Arizona	1,083	1.57%
38	Arkansas	275	0.40%
1	California	19,567	28.33%
25	Colorado	776	1.12%
35	Connecticut	371	0.54%
41	Delaware	164	0.24%
5	Florida	2,674	3.87%
7	Georgia	2,337	3.38%
48	Hawaii	101	0.15%
44	Idaho	154	0.22%
6	Illinois	2,641	3.82%
12	Indiana	1,704	2.47%
32	Iowa	461	0.67%
23	Kansas	808	1.17%
30	Kentucky	593	0.86%
13	Louisiana	1,509	2.18%
36	Maine	369	0.53%
26	Maryland	715	1.04%
37	Massachusetts	331	0.48%
11	Michigan	1,778	2.57%
24	Minnesota	803	1.16%
29	Mississippi	641	0.93%
19	Missouri	1,037	1.50%
46	Montana	140	0.20%
33	Nebraska	419	0.61%
28	Nevada	660	0.96%
47	New Hampshire	125	0.18%
9	New Jersey	1,999	2.89%
27	New Mexico	662	0.96%
4	New York	2,862	4.14%
18	North Carolina	1,051	1.52%
49	North Dakota	97	0.14%
2	Ohio	3,551	5.14%
34	Oklahoma	392	0.57%
22	Oregon	902	1.31%
14	Pennsylvania	1,487	2.15%
43	Rhode Island	155	0.22%
17	South Carolina	1,062	1.54%
39	South Dakota	261	0.38%
20	Tennessee	974	1.41%
3	Texas	3,505	5.07%
31	Utah	465	0.67%
50	Vermont	24	0.03%
8	Virginia	2,211	3.20%
10	Washington	1,870	2.71%
45	West Virginia	148	0.21%
15	Wisconsin	1,450	2.10%
41	Wyoming	164	0.24%

RANK ORDER

RANK	STATE	JUVENILES	% of USA
1	California	19,567	28.33%
2	Ohio	3,551	5.14%
3	Texas	3,505	5.07%
4	New York	2,862	4.14%
5	Florida	2,674	3.87%
6	Illinois	2,641	3.82%
7	Georgia	2,337	3.38%
8	Virginia	2,211	3.20%
9	New Jersey	1,999	2.89%
10	Washington	1,870	2.71%
11	Michigan	1,778	2.57%
12	Indiana	1,704	2.47%
13	Louisiana	1,509	2.18%
14	Pennsylvania	1,487	2.15%
15	Wisconsin	1,450	2.10%
16	Arizona	1,083	1.57%
17	South Carolina	1,062	1.54%
18	North Carolina	1,051	1.52%
19	Missouri	1,037	1.50%
20	Tennessee	974	1.41%
21	Alabama	908	1.31%
22	Oregon	902	1.31%
23	Kansas	808	1.17%
24	Minnesota	803	1.16%
25	Colorado	776	1.12%
26	Maryland	715	1.04%
27	New Mexico	662	0.96%
28	Nevada	660	0.96%
29	Mississippi	641	0.93%
30	Kentucky	593	0.86%
31	Utah	465	0.67%
32	Iowa	461	0.67%
33	Nebraska	419	0.61%
34	Oklahoma	392	0.57%
35	Connecticut	371	0.54%
36	Maine	369	0.53%
37	Massachusetts	331	0.48%
38	Arkansas	275	0.40%
39	South Dakota	261	0.38%
40	Alaska	223	0.32%
41	Delaware	164	0.24%
41	Wyoming	164	0.24%
43	Rhode Island	155	0.22%
44	Idaho	154	0.22%
45	West Virginia	148	0.21%
46	Montana	140	0.20%
47	New Hampshire	125	0.18%
48	Hawaii	101	0.15%
49	North Dakota	97	0.14%
50	Vermont	24	0.03%
	District of Columbia	251	0.36%

Source: U.S. Department of Justice, Office of Juvenile Justice and Delinquency Prevention
"States at a Glance: Juveniles in Public Facilities, 1995" (Fact Sheet #69, November 1997)
*Juveniles in residential custody on February 15, 1995. Includes 66,236 held because of delinquent offenses (offenses that would also be illegal if they were adults), 1,785 for status offenses (offenses that would not be illegal if they were adult, such as truancy), 889 for other offenses and 165 whose offenses were unknown.

Rate of Juveniles in Public Facilities in 1995

National Rate = 100.8 Juveniles per 100,000 Population Under 18*

<u>ALPHA ORDER</u>

RANK	STATE	RATE
24	Alabama	84.2
12	Alaska	119.6
19	Arizona	95.1
46	Arkansas	42.1
1	California	223.1
26	Colorado	79.3
42	Connecticut	46.9
21	Delaware	93.1
25	Florida	79.7
10	Georgia	121.6
48	Hawaii	33.1
44	Idaho	44.7
23	Illinois	84.5
14	Indiana	114.4
34	Iowa	63.7
13	Kansas	117.7
36	Kentucky	61.1
8	Louisiana	122.3
9	Maine	122.1
40	Maryland	56.2
49	Massachusetts	23.3
29	Michigan	70.3
33	Minnesota	64.8
22	Mississippi	84.6
27	Missouri	75.0
37	Montana	60.0
20	Nebraska	95.0
2	Nevada	166.1
45	New Hampshire	42.6
18	New Jersey	101.7
4	New Mexico	133.3
35	New York	63.2
38	North Carolina	58.4
39	North Dakota	57.2
7	Ohio	124.6
43	Oklahoma	44.8
15	Oregon	113.1
41	Pennsylvania	51.4
31	Rhode Island	65.9
16	South Carolina	112.8
6	South Dakota	127.2
28	Tennessee	74.3
32	Texas	65.3
30	Utah	68.8
50	Vermont	16.4
3	Virginia	136.7
5	Washington	131.9
47	West Virginia	34.8
17	Wisconsin	108.0
11	Wyoming	121.5

<u>RANK ORDER</u>

RANK	STATE	RATE
1	California	223.1
2	Nevada	166.1
3	Virginia	136.7
4	New Mexico	133.3
5	Washington	131.9
6	South Dakota	127.2
7	Ohio	124.6
8	Louisiana	122.3
9	Maine	122.1
10	Georgia	121.6
11	Wyoming	121.5
12	Alaska	119.6
13	Kansas	117.7
14	Indiana	114.4
15	Oregon	113.1
16	South Carolina	112.8
17	Wisconsin	108.0
18	New Jersey	101.7
19	Arizona	95.1
20	Nebraska	95.0
21	Delaware	93.1
22	Mississippi	84.6
23	Illinois	84.5
24	Alabama	84.2
25	Florida	79.7
26	Colorado	79.3
27	Missouri	75.0
28	Tennessee	74.3
29	Michigan	70.3
30	Utah	68.8
31	Rhode Island	65.9
32	Texas	65.3
33	Minnesota	64.8
34	Iowa	63.7
35	New York	63.2
36	Kentucky	61.1
37	Montana	60.0
38	North Carolina	58.4
39	North Dakota	57.2
40	Maryland	56.2
41	Pennsylvania	51.4
42	Connecticut	46.9
43	Oklahoma	44.8
44	Idaho	44.7
45	New Hampshire	42.6
46	Arkansas	42.1
47	West Virginia	34.8
48	Hawaii	33.1
49	Massachusetts	23.3
50	Vermont	16.4
	District of Columbia	222.5

Source: Morgan Quitno Press using data from U.S. Dept. of Justice, Office of Juvenile Justice and Delinquency Prevention
"States at a Glance: Juveniles in Public Facilities, 1995" (Fact Sheet #69, November 1997)
*Juveniles in residential custody on February 15, 1995. Includes 66,236 held because of delinquent offenses
(offenses that would also be illegal if they were adults), 1,785 for status offenses (offenses that would not be
illegal if they were adult, such as truancy), 889 for other offenses and 165 whose offenses were unknown.

Public Juvenile Facilities Administered by State and Local Governments in 1993

National Total = 1,025 Facilities*

RANK	STATE	FACILITIES	% of USA
19	Alabama	16	1.56%
39	Alaska	5	0.49%
23	Arizona	14	1.37%
30	Arkansas	10	0.98%
1	California	103	10.05%
32	Colorado	9	0.88%
40	Connecticut	4	0.39%
42	Delaware	3	0.29%
6	Florida	49	4.78%
13	Georgia	28	2.73%
45	Hawaii	2	0.20%
42	Idaho	3	0.29%
17	Illinois	19	1.85%
11	Indiana	31	3.02%
25	Iowa	13	1.27%
25	Kansas	13	1.27%
14	Kentucky	27	2.63%
22	Louisiana	15	1.46%
48	Maine	1	0.10%
25	Maryland	13	1.27%
30	Massachusetts	10	0.98%
9	Michigan	43	4.20%
18	Minnesota	18	1.76%
32	Mississippi	9	0.88%
8	Missouri	45	4.39%
36	Montana	6	0.59%
40	Nebraska	4	0.39%
32	Nevada	9	0.88%
45	New Hampshire	2	0.20%
7	New Jersey	46	4.49%
23	New Mexico	14	1.37%
2	New York	65	6.34%
15	North Carolina	24	2.34%
42	North Dakota	3	0.29%
3	Ohio	62	6.05%
19	Oklahoma	16	1.56%
25	Oregon	13	1.27%
10	Pennsylvania	34	3.32%
48	Rhode Island	1	0.10%
32	South Carolina	9	0.88%
36	South Dakota	6	0.59%
16	Tennessee	23	2.24%
5	Texas	55	5.37%
19	Utah	16	1.56%
48	Vermont	1	0.10%
4	Virginia	58	5.66%
12	Washington	30	2.93%
36	West Virginia	6	0.59%
25	Wisconsin	13	1.27%
45	Wyoming	2	0.20%

RANK	STATE	FACILITIES	% of USA
1	California	103	10.05%
2	New York	65	6.34%
3	Ohio	62	6.05%
4	Virginia	58	5.66%
5	Texas	55	5.37%
6	Florida	49	4.78%
7	New Jersey	46	4.49%
8	Missouri	45	4.39%
9	Michigan	43	4.20%
10	Pennsylvania	34	3.32%
11	Indiana	31	3.02%
12	Washington	30	2.93%
13	Georgia	28	2.73%
14	Kentucky	27	2.63%
15	North Carolina	24	2.34%
16	Tennessee	23	2.24%
17	Illinois	19	1.85%
18	Minnesota	18	1.76%
19	Alabama	16	1.56%
19	Oklahoma	16	1.56%
19	Utah	16	1.56%
22	Louisiana	15	1.46%
23	Arizona	14	1.37%
23	New Mexico	14	1.37%
25	Iowa	13	1.27%
25	Kansas	13	1.27%
25	Maryland	13	1.27%
25	Oregon	13	1.27%
25	Wisconsin	13	1.27%
30	Arkansas	10	0.98%
30	Massachusetts	10	0.98%
32	Colorado	9	0.88%
32	Mississippi	9	0.88%
32	Nevada	9	0.88%
32	South Carolina	9	0.88%
36	Montana	6	0.59%
36	South Dakota	6	0.59%
36	West Virginia	6	0.59%
39	Alaska	5	0.49%
40	Connecticut	4	0.39%
40	Nebraska	4	0.39%
42	Delaware	3	0.29%
42	Idaho	3	0.29%
42	North Dakota	3	0.29%
45	Hawaii	2	0.20%
45	New Hampshire	2	0.20%
45	Wyoming	2	0.20%
48	Maine	1	0.10%
48	Rhode Island	1	0.10%
48	Vermont	1	0.10%
	District of Columbia	4	0.39%

Source: U.S. Department of Justice, Office of Juvenile Justice and Delinquency Prevention
    "Juveniles in Public Facilities, 1993" (Fact Sheet #25, May 1995)
*Public facilities available to hold delinquent and status offenders.

Admissions of Juveniles to Alcohol and Other Drug Treatment Programs in 1995

National Total = 121,149 Juvenile Admissions*

<u>ALPHA ORDER</u>

RANK	STATE	ADMISSIONS	% of USA
31	Alabama	1,054	0.87%
34	Alaska	681	0.56%
46	Arizona	51	0.04%
30	Arkansas	1,070	0.88%
2	California	9,950	8.21%
12	Colorado	3,683	3.04%
39	Connecticut	509	0.42%
47	Delaware	14	0.01%
1	Florida	11,140	9.20%
20	Georgia	1,830	1.51%
29	Hawaii	1,118	0.92%
26	Idaho	1,225	1.01%
5	Illinois	6,986	5.77%
33	Indiana	773	0.64%
14	Iowa	3,029	2.50%
23	Kansas	1,635	1.35%
27	Kentucky	1,202	0.99%
28	Louisiana	1,155	0.95%
35	Maine	583	0.48%
8	Maryland	5,145	4.25%
17	Massachusetts	2,396	1.98%
9	Michigan	4,495	3.71%
NA	Minnesota**	NA	NA
36	Mississippi	570	0.47%
24	Missouri	1,552	1.28%
45	Montana	270	0.22%
19	Nebraska	1,910	1.58%
43	Nevada	343	0.28%
40	New Hampshire	424	0.35%
15	New Jersey	2,884	2.38%
41	New Mexico	389	0.32%
4	New York	8,714	7.19%
16	North Carolina	2,733	2.26%
44	North Dakota	326	0.27%
3	Ohio	8,799	7.26%
42	Oklahoma	344	0.28%
10	Oregon	4,338	3.58%
6	Pennsylvania	6,495	5.36%
37	Rhode Island	563	0.46%
25	South Carolina	1,541	1.27%
18	South Dakota	2,058	1.70%
NA	Tennessee**	NA	NA
13	Texas	3,115	2.57%
22	Utah	1,682	1.39%
38	Vermont	537	0.44%
21	Virginia	1,807	1.49%
7	Washington	5,353	4.42%
32	West Virginia	795	0.66%
11	Wisconsin	3,799	3.14%
NA	Wyoming**	NA	NA

<u>RANK ORDER</u>

RANK	STATE	ADMISSIONS	% of USA
1	Florida	11,140	9.20%
2	California	9,950	8.21%
3	Ohio	8,799	7.26%
4	New York	8,714	7.19%
5	Illinois	6,986	5.77%
6	Pennsylvania	6,495	5.36%
7	Washington	5,353	4.42%
8	Maryland	5,145	4.25%
9	Michigan	4,495	3.71%
10	Oregon	4,338	3.58%
11	Wisconsin	3,799	3.14%
12	Colorado	3,683	3.04%
13	Texas	3,115	2.57%
14	Iowa	3,029	2.50%
15	New Jersey	2,884	2.38%
16	North Carolina	2,733	2.26%
17	Massachusetts	2,396	1.98%
18	South Dakota	2,058	1.70%
19	Nebraska	1,910	1.58%
20	Georgia	1,830	1.51%
21	Virginia	1,807	1.49%
22	Utah	1,682	1.39%
23	Kansas	1,635	1.35%
24	Missouri	1,552	1.28%
25	South Carolina	1,541	1.27%
26	Idaho	1,225	1.01%
27	Kentucky	1,202	0.99%
28	Louisiana	1,155	0.95%
29	Hawaii	1,118	0.92%
30	Arkansas	1,070	0.88%
31	Alabama	1,054	0.87%
32	West Virginia	795	0.66%
33	Indiana	773	0.64%
34	Alaska	681	0.56%
35	Maine	583	0.48%
36	Mississippi	570	0.47%
37	Rhode Island	563	0.46%
38	Vermont	537	0.44%
39	Connecticut	509	0.42%
40	New Hampshire	424	0.35%
41	New Mexico	389	0.32%
42	Oklahoma	344	0.28%
43	Nevada	343	0.28%
44	North Dakota	326	0.27%
45	Montana	270	0.22%
46	Arizona	51	0.04%
47	Delaware	14	0.01%
NA	Minnesota**	NA	NA
NA	Tennessee**	NA	NA
NA	Wyoming**	NA	NA
	District of Columbia	84	0.07%

Source: U.S. Department of Health and Human Services, Substance Abuse and Mental Health Services Administration "State Resources and Services Related to Alcohol and Other Drug Problems-Fiscal Year 1995" (July 1997)
Youths 17 years and younger. Does not include 2,361 admissions of juveniles in U.S. territories. Data are only from treatment units that received at least some funds administered by a state's alcohol/drug agency in fiscal year 1995. An additional 87,857 admissions were not reported by age.
***Not available.**

Admissions of Juveniles to Alcohol and Other Drug Treatment Programs
As a Percent of All Admissions in 1995
National Percent = 6.5% of Admissions*

ALPHA ORDER				RANK ORDER		
RANK	STATE	PERCENT		RANK	STATE	PERCENT
19	Alabama	7.1		1	Hawaii	24.9
18	Alaska	7.5		2	Idaho	22.2
46	Arizona	0.2		3	South Dakota	16.6
17	Arkansas	7.7		4	Maryland	14.9
31	California	5.2		5	Iowa	12.6
20	Colorado	7.0		6	Ohio	11.9
45	Connecticut	1.2		7	Washington	11.7
46	Delaware	0.2		8	New Hampshire	10.9
9	Florida	10.7		9	Florida	10.7
41	Georgia	3.0		10	Utah	10.1
1	Hawaii	24.9		11	North Dakota	9.9
2	Idaho	22.2		12	Pennsylvania	9.5
24	Illinois	5.7		13	Oregon	9.3
43	Indiana	2.8		14	Nebraska	8.9
5	Iowa	12.6		15	Kansas	8.5
15	Kansas	8.5		16	Vermont	8.0
22	Kentucky	6.1		17	Arkansas	7.7
39	Louisiana	4.2		18	Alaska	7.5
21	Maine	6.4		19	Alabama	7.1
4	Maryland	14.9		20	Colorado	7.0
44	Massachusetts	2.4		21	Maine	6.4
29	Michigan	5.3		22	Kentucky	6.1
NA	Minnesota**	NA		23	South Carolina	5.8
39	Mississippi	4.2		24	Illinois	5.7
37	Missouri	4.6		24	New Jersey	5.7
36	Montana	4.7		26	New York	5.6
14	Nebraska	8.9		26	Texas	5.6
29	Nevada	5.3		28	North Carolina	5.4
8	New Hampshire	10.9		29	Michigan	5.3
24	New Jersey	5.7		29	Nevada	5.3
41	New Mexico	3.0		31	California	5.2
26	New York	5.6		31	Wisconsin	5.2
28	North Carolina	5.4		33	Rhode Island	5.0
11	North Dakota	9.9		33	Virginia	5.0
6	Ohio	11.9		33	West Virginia	5.0
38	Oklahoma	4.5		36	Montana	4.7
13	Oregon	9.3		37	Missouri	4.6
12	Pennsylvania	9.5		38	Oklahoma	4.5
33	Rhode Island	5.0		39	Louisiana	4.2
23	South Carolina	5.8		39	Mississippi	4.2
3	South Dakota	16.6		41	Georgia	3.0
NA	Tennessee**	NA		41	New Mexico	3.0
26	Texas	5.6		43	Indiana	2.8
10	Utah	10.1		44	Massachusetts	2.4
16	Vermont	8.0		45	Connecticut	1.2
33	Virginia	5.0		46	Arizona	0.2
7	Washington	11.7		46	Delaware	0.2
33	West Virginia	5.0		NA	Minnesota**	NA
31	Wisconsin	5.2		NA	Tennessee**	NA
NA	Wyoming**	NA		NA	Wyoming**	NA
					District of Columbia	0.6

Source: Morgan Quitno Press using data from U.S. Department of Health and Human Services, Substance Abuse and Mental Health Services Administration
"State Resources and Services Related to Alcohol and Other Drug Problems-Fiscal Year 1995" (July 1997)
*Youths 17 years and younger. Does not include admissions in U.S. territories. Data are only from treatment units that received at least some funds administered by a state's alcohol/drug agency in fiscal year 1995. An additional 87,857 admissions were not reported by age. **Not available.

Victims of Child Abuse and Neglect in 1995

National Total = 1,110,000 Children*

ALPHA ORDER

RANK	STATE	CHILDREN	% of USA
16	Alabama	18,120	1.63%
32	Alaska	8,142	0.73%
12	Arizona	25,154	2.27%
31	Arkansas	8,169	0.74%
1	California	166,418	14.99%
34	Colorado	7,602	0.68%
13	Connecticut	23,762	2.14%
45	Delaware	2,300	0.21%
2	Florida	77,976	7.02%
5	Georgia	57,250	5.16%
43	Hawaii	2,635	0.24%
23	Idaho	10,743	0.97%
6	Illinois	49,217	4.43%
14	Indiana	22,493	2.03%
26	Iowa	9,967	0.90%
42	Kansas	3,264	0.29%
10	Kentucky	28,630	2.58%
19	Louisiana	14,194	1.28%
37	Maine	4,628	0.42%
NA	Maryland**	NA	NA
11	Massachusetts	25,375	2.29%
15	Michigan	21,165	1.91%
25	Minnesota	10,142	0.91%
36	Mississippi	5,588	0.50%
17	Missouri	17,764	1.60%
39	Montana	4,194	0.38%
40	Nebraska	3,510	0.32%
33	Nevada	7,791	0.70%
48	New Hampshire	1,059	0.10%
27	New Jersey	9,279	0.84%
30	New Mexico	8,842	0.80%
4	New York	57,699	5.20%
9	North Carolina	30,935	2.79%
41	North Dakota	3,340	0.30%
3	Ohio	58,416	5.26%
21	Oklahoma	11,700	1.05%
28	Oregon	8,991	0.81%
35	Pennsylvania	6,891	0.62%
38	Rhode Island	4,437	0.40%
22	South Carolina	11,439	1.03%
44	South Dakota	2,526	0.23%
20	Tennessee	12,166	1.10%
7	Texas	46,768	4.21%
29	Utah	8,848	0.80%
47	Vermont	1,122	0.10%
24	Virginia	10,416	0.94%
8	Washington	44,893	4.04%
NA	West Virginia**	NA	NA
18	Wisconsin	17,118	1.54%
46	Wyoming	1,508	0.14%

RANK ORDER

RANK	STATE	CHILDREN	% of USA
1	California	166,418	14.99%
2	Florida	77,976	7.02%
3	Ohio	58,416	5.26%
4	New York	57,699	5.20%
5	Georgia	57,250	5.16%
6	Illinois	49,217	4.43%
7	Texas	46,768	4.21%
8	Washington	44,893	4.04%
9	North Carolina	30,935	2.79%
10	Kentucky	28,630	2.58%
11	Massachusetts	25,375	2.29%
12	Arizona	25,154	2.27%
13	Connecticut	23,762	2.14%
14	Indiana	22,493	2.03%
15	Michigan	21,165	1.91%
16	Alabama	18,120	1.63%
17	Missouri	17,764	1.60%
18	Wisconsin	17,118	1.54%
19	Louisiana	14,194	1.28%
20	Tennessee	12,166	1.10%
21	Oklahoma	11,700	1.05%
22	South Carolina	11,439	1.03%
23	Idaho	10,743	0.97%
24	Virginia	10,416	0.94%
25	Minnesota	10,142	0.91%
26	Iowa	9,967	0.90%
27	New Jersey	9,279	0.84%
28	Oregon	8,991	0.81%
29	Utah	8,848	0.80%
30	New Mexico	8,842	0.80%
31	Arkansas	8,169	0.74%
32	Alaska	8,142	0.73%
33	Nevada	7,791	0.70%
34	Colorado	7,602	0.68%
35	Pennsylvania	6,891	0.62%
36	Mississippi	5,588	0.50%
37	Maine	4,628	0.42%
38	Rhode Island	4,437	0.40%
39	Montana	4,194	0.38%
40	Nebraska	3,510	0.32%
41	North Dakota	3,340	0.30%
42	Kansas	3,264	0.29%
43	Hawaii	2,635	0.24%
44	South Dakota	2,526	0.23%
45	Delaware	2,300	0.21%
46	Wyoming	1,508	0.14%
47	Vermont	1,122	0.10%
48	New Hampshire	1,059	0.10%
NA	Maryland**	NA	NA
NA	West Virginia**	NA	NA
	District of Columbia**	NA	NA

*Source: U.S. Department of Health and Human Services, National Center on Child Abuse and Neglect
"Child Maltreatment 1995: Reports from the States to the National Center on Child Abuse and Neglect"
*State-substantiated incidents. There were reports of 2,960,000 children abused leading to 1,110,000 cases confirmed. Fifty-two percent of maltreated children suffered neglect, 25% physical abuse, 13% sexual abuse, 5% emotional maltreatment, 3% medical neglect and 14% other forms of maltreatment. More than half of the abused or neglected children were 7 years old or younger, with about 26% younger than four years old. **Not available.*

Rate of Child Abuse and Neglect in 1995

National Rate = 15.7 Abused Children per 1,000 Population Under 18*

ALPHA ORDER

RANK	STATE	RATE
20	Alabama	14.7
1	Alaska	37.9
8	Arizona	20.7
29	Arkansas	11.8
15	California	18.1
40	Colorado	7.5
6	Connecticut	27.3
24	Delaware	12.8
7	Florida	22.2
4	Georgia	29.5
36	Hawaii	8.3
2	Idaho	33.6
19	Illinois	15.7
17	Indiana	16.0
29	Iowa	11.8
46	Kansas	4.7
5	Kentucky	28.2
28	Louisiana	12.0
18	Maine	15.8
NA	Maryland**	NA
16	Massachusetts	17.4
38	Michigan	7.8
39	Minnesota	7.7
42	Mississippi	7.3
22	Missouri	14.5
14	Montana	18.9
41	Nebraska	7.4
10	Nevada	19.5
47	New Hampshire	3.7
45	New Jersey	4.8
21	New Mexico	14.6
27	New York	12.1
9	North Carolina	20.1
12	North Dakota	19.0
11	Ohio	19.4
23	Oklahoma	13.9
34	Oregon	10.7
48	Pennsylvania	2.3
12	Rhode Island	19.0
32	South Carolina	10.9
25	South Dakota	12.6
36	Tennessee	8.3
35	Texas	8.6
26	Utah	12.4
44	Vermont	6.9
43	Virginia	7.0
3	Washington	32.0
NA	West Virginia**	NA
33	Wisconsin	10.8
31	Wyoming	11.3

RANK ORDER

RANK	STATE	RATE
1	Alaska	37.9
2	Idaho	33.6
3	Washington	32.0
4	Georgia	29.5
5	Kentucky	28.2
6	Connecticut	27.3
7	Florida	22.2
8	Arizona	20.7
9	North Carolina	20.1
10	Nevada	19.5
11	Ohio	19.4
12	North Dakota	19.0
12	Rhode Island	19.0
14	Montana	18.9
15	California	18.1
16	Massachusetts	17.4
17	Indiana	16.0
18	Maine	15.8
19	Illinois	15.7
20	Alabama	14.7
21	New Mexico	14.6
22	Missouri	14.5
23	Oklahoma	13.9
24	Delaware	12.8
25	South Dakota	12.6
26	Utah	12.4
27	New York	12.1
28	Louisiana	12.0
29	Arkansas	11.8
29	Iowa	11.8
31	Wyoming	11.3
32	South Carolina	10.9
33	Wisconsin	10.8
34	Oregon	10.7
35	Texas	8.6
36	Hawaii	8.3
36	Tennessee	8.3
38	Michigan	7.8
39	Minnesota	7.7
40	Colorado	7.5
41	Nebraska	7.4
42	Mississippi	7.3
43	Virginia	7.0
44	Vermont	6.9
45	New Jersey	4.8
46	Kansas	4.7
47	New Hampshire	3.7
48	Pennsylvania	2.3
NA	Maryland**	NA
NA	West Virginia**	NA
	District of Columbia**	NA

Source: U.S. Department of Health and Human Services, National Center on Child Abuse and Neglect "Child Maltreatment 1995: Reports from the States to the National Center on Child Abuse and Neglect"
*State-substantiated incidents. The median rate for states reporting is 12.6 children. Fifty-two percent of maltreated children suffered neglect, 25% physical abuse, 13% sexual abuse, 5% emotional maltreatment, 3% medical neglect and 14% other forms of maltreatment. More than half of the abused or neglected children were 7 years old or younger, with about 26% younger than four years old. **Not available.*

Physically Abused Children in 1995

National Total = 244,427 Children*

<u>ALPHA ORDER</u>

RANK	STATE	CHILDREN	% of USA
10	Alabama	6,389	2.61%
30	Alaska	1,955	0.80%
8	Arizona	7,907	3.23%
32	Arkansas	1,877	0.77%
1	California	51,756	21.17%
28	Colorado	2,257	0.92%
16	Connecticut	3,977	1.63%
45	Delaware	387	0.16%
2	Florida	15,687	6.42%
7	Georgia	10,092	4.13%
43	Hawaii	703	0.29%
18	Idaho	3,656	1.50%
12	Illinois	5,313	2.17%
15	Indiana	4,581	1.87%
19	Iowa	3,525	1.44%
41	Kansas	838	0.34%
9	Kentucky	7,265	2.97%
23	Louisiana	3,075	1.26%
42	Maine	721	0.29%
NA	Maryland**	NA	NA
11	Massachusetts	6,166	2.52%
14	Michigan	4,671	1.91%
21	Minnesota	3,238	1.32%
34	Mississippi	1,715	0.70%
20	Missouri	3,432	1.40%
37	Montana	1,326	0.54%
39	Nebraska	983	0.40%
35	Nevada	1,420	0.58%
47	New Hampshire	309	0.13%
25	New Jersey	2,803	1.15%
29	New Mexico	2,136	0.87%
5	New York	13,853	5.67%
36	North Carolina	1,408	0.58%
40	North Dakota	916	0.37%
4	Ohio	14,370	5.88%
17	Oklahoma	3,835	1.57%
33	Oregon	1,727	0.71%
22	Pennsylvania	3,236	1.32%
38	Rhode Island	1,325	0.54%
26	South Carolina	2,660	1.09%
44	South Dakota	542	0.22%
27	Tennessee	2,517	1.03%
3	Texas	14,772	6.04%
31	Utah	1,948	0.80%
48	Vermont	301	0.12%
24	Virginia	2,807	1.15%
6	Washington	12,780	5.23%
NA	West Virginia**	NA	NA
13	Wisconsin	4,929	2.02%
46	Wyoming	341	0.14%

<u>RANK ORDER</u>

RANK	STATE	CHILDREN	% of USA
1	California	51,756	21.17%
2	Florida	15,687	6.42%
3	Texas	14,772	6.04%
4	Ohio	14,370	5.88%
5	New York	13,853	5.67%
6	Washington	12,780	5.23%
7	Georgia	10,092	4.13%
8	Arizona	7,907	3.23%
9	Kentucky	7,265	2.97%
10	Alabama	6,389	2.61%
11	Massachusetts	6,166	2.52%
12	Illinois	5,313	2.17%
13	Wisconsin	4,929	2.02%
14	Michigan	4,671	1.91%
15	Indiana	4,581	1.87%
16	Connecticut	3,977	1.63%
17	Oklahoma	3,835	1.57%
18	Idaho	3,656	1.50%
19	Iowa	3,525	1.44%
20	Missouri	3,432	1.40%
21	Minnesota	3,238	1.32%
22	Pennsylvania	3,236	1.32%
23	Louisiana	3,075	1.26%
24	Virginia	2,807	1.15%
25	New Jersey	2,803	1.15%
26	South Carolina	2,660	1.09%
27	Tennessee	2,517	1.03%
28	Colorado	2,257	0.92%
29	New Mexico	2,136	0.87%
30	Alaska	1,955	0.80%
31	Utah	1,948	0.80%
32	Arkansas	1,877	0.77%
33	Oregon	1,727	0.71%
34	Mississippi	1,715	0.70%
35	Nevada	1,420	0.58%
36	North Carolina	1,408	0.58%
37	Montana	1,326	0.54%
38	Rhode Island	1,325	0.54%
39	Nebraska	983	0.40%
40	North Dakota	916	0.37%
41	Kansas	838	0.34%
42	Maine	721	0.29%
43	Hawaii	703	0.29%
44	South Dakota	542	0.22%
45	Delaware	387	0.16%
46	Wyoming	341	0.14%
47	New Hampshire	309	0.13%
48	Vermont	301	0.12%
NA	Maryland**	NA	NA
NA	West Virginia**	NA	NA
	District of Columbia**	NA	NA

Source: U.S. Department of Health and Human Services, National Center on Child Abuse and Neglect
"Child Maltreatment 1995: Reports from the States to the National Center on Child Abuse and Neglect"
*State-substantiated incidents. National total is for reporting states only. Fifty-two percent of maltreated children suffered neglect, 25% physical abuse, 13% sexual abuse, 5% emotional maltreatment, 3% medical neglect and 14% other forms of maltreatment. More than half of the abused or neglected children were 7 years old or younger, with about 26% younger than four years old. **Not available.

Rate of Physically Abused Children in 1995

National Rate = 3.6 Physically Abused Children per 1,000 Population Under 18*

ALPHA ORDER

RANK	STATE	RATE
9	Alabama	5.2
2	Alaska	9.1
5	Arizona	6.5
24	Arkansas	2.7
8	California	5.6
33	Colorado	2.2
13	Connecticut	4.6
33	Delaware	2.2
15	Florida	4.5
9	Georgia	5.2
33	Hawaii	2.2
1	Idaho	11.4
41	Illinois	1.7
20	Indiana	3.3
16	Iowa	4.2
45	Kansas	1.2
4	Kentucky	7.2
28	Louisiana	2.6
29	Maine	2.5
NA	Maryland**	NA
16	Massachusetts	4.2
41	Michigan	1.7
29	Minnesota	2.5
33	Mississippi	2.2
23	Missouri	2.8
6	Montana	6.0
37	Nebraska	2.1
18	Nevada	3.6
46	New Hampshire	1.1
44	New Jersey	1.4
19	New Mexico	3.5
22	New York	2.9
48	North Carolina	0.9
9	North Dakota	5.2
12	Ohio	4.8
13	Oklahoma	4.6
37	Oregon	2.1
46	Pennsylvania	1.1
7	Rhode Island	5.7
29	South Carolina	2.5
24	South Dakota	2.7
41	Tennessee	1.7
24	Texas	2.7
24	Utah	2.7
39	Vermont	1.9
39	Virginia	1.9
2	Washington	9.1
NA	West Virginia**	NA
21	Wisconsin	3.1
29	Wyoming	2.5

RANK ORDER

RANK	STATE	RATE
1	Idaho	11.4
2	Alaska	9.1
2	Washington	9.1
4	Kentucky	7.2
5	Arizona	6.5
6	Montana	6.0
7	Rhode Island	5.7
8	California	5.6
9	Alabama	5.2
9	Georgia	5.2
9	North Dakota	5.2
12	Ohio	4.8
13	Connecticut	4.6
13	Oklahoma	4.6
15	Florida	4.5
16	Iowa	4.2
16	Massachusetts	4.2
18	Nevada	3.6
19	New Mexico	3.5
20	Indiana	3.3
21	Wisconsin	3.1
22	New York	2.9
23	Missouri	2.8
24	Arkansas	2.7
24	South Dakota	2.7
24	Texas	2.7
24	Utah	2.7
28	Louisiana	2.6
29	Maine	2.5
29	Minnesota	2.5
29	South Carolina	2.5
29	Wyoming	2.5
33	Colorado	2.2
33	Delaware	2.2
33	Hawaii	2.2
33	Mississippi	2.2
37	Nebraska	2.1
37	Oregon	2.1
39	Vermont	1.9
39	Virginia	1.9
41	Illinois	1.7
41	Michigan	1.7
41	Tennessee	1.7
44	New Jersey	1.4
45	Kansas	1.2
46	New Hampshire	1.1
46	Pennsylvania	1.1
48	North Carolina	0.9
NA	Maryland**	NA
NA	West Virginia**	NA
	District of Columbia**	NA

Source: U.S. Department of Health and Human Services, National Center on Child Abuse and Neglect
"Child Maltreatment 1995: Reports from the States to the National Center on Child Abuse and Neglect"
*State-substantiated incidents for reporting states. The median rate for states reporting is 2.7 children. Fifty-two percent of maltreated children suffered neglect, 25% physical abuse, 13% sexual abuse, 5% emotional maltreatment, 3% medical neglect and 14% other forms of maltreatment. More than half of the abused or neglected children were 7 years old or younger, with about 26% younger than four years old. **Not available.*

Sexually Abused Children in 1995

National Total = 126,032 Children*

ALPHA ORDER

RANK	STATE	CHILDREN	% of USA
11	Alabama	3,798	3.01%
32	Alaska	868	0.69%
23	Arizona	1,567	1.24%
26	Arkansas	1,222	0.97%
1	California	26,128	20.73%
28	Colorado	1,160	0.92%
NA	Connecticut**	NA	NA
45	Delaware	200	0.16%
4	Florida	7,114	5.64%
7	Georgia	5,308	4.21%
44	Hawaii	240	0.19%
17	Idaho	2,020	1.60%
8	Illinois	4,593	3.64%
10	Indiana	4,164	3.30%
25	Iowa	1,382	1.10%
31	Kansas	957	0.76%
15	Kentucky	2,315	1.84%
29	Louisiana	1,008	0.80%
37	Maine	426	0.34%
NA	Maryland**	NA	NA
24	Massachusetts	1,516	1.20%
19	Michigan	1,775	1.41%
30	Minnesota	980	0.78%
34	Mississippi	704	0.56%
13	Missouri	2,923	2.32%
38	Montana	422	0.33%
39	Nebraska	406	0.32%
42	Nevada	310	0.25%
41	New Hampshire	328	0.26%
33	New Jersey	833	0.66%
35	New Mexico	639	0.51%
9	New York	4,273	3.39%
21	North Carolina	1,611	1.28%
NA	North Dakota**	NA	NA
2	Ohio	10,154	8.06%
18	Oklahoma	1,897	1.51%
22	Oregon	1,587	1.26%
12	Pennsylvania	3,100	2.46%
40	Rhode Island	403	0.32%
27	South Carolina	1,201	0.95%
43	South Dakota	283	0.22%
14	Tennessee	2,657	2.11%
3	Texas	7,343	5.83%
16	Utah	2,089	1.66%
36	Vermont	563	0.45%
20	Virginia	1,616	1.28%
6	Washington	5,784	4.59%
NA	West Virginia**	NA	NA
5	Wisconsin	6,014	4.77%
46	Wyoming	151	0.12%

RANK ORDER

RANK	STATE	CHILDREN	% of USA
1	California	26,128	20.73%
2	Ohio	10,154	8.06%
3	Texas	7,343	5.83%
4	Florida	7,114	5.64%
5	Wisconsin	6,014	4.77%
6	Washington	5,784	4.59%
7	Georgia	5,308	4.21%
8	Illinois	4,593	3.64%
9	New York	4,273	3.39%
10	Indiana	4,164	3.30%
11	Alabama	3,798	3.01%
12	Pennsylvania	3,100	2.46%
13	Missouri	2,923	2.32%
14	Tennessee	2,657	2.11%
15	Kentucky	2,315	1.84%
16	Utah	2,089	1.66%
17	Idaho	2,020	1.60%
18	Oklahoma	1,897	1.51%
19	Michigan	1,775	1.41%
20	Virginia	1,616	1.28%
21	North Carolina	1,611	1.28%
22	Oregon	1,587	1.26%
23	Arizona	1,567	1.24%
24	Massachusetts	1,516	1.20%
25	Iowa	1,382	1.10%
26	Arkansas	1,222	0.97%
27	South Carolina	1,201	0.95%
28	Colorado	1,160	0.92%
29	Louisiana	1,008	0.80%
30	Minnesota	980	0.78%
31	Kansas	957	0.76%
32	Alaska	868	0.69%
33	New Jersey	833	0.66%
34	Mississippi	704	0.56%
35	New Mexico	639	0.51%
36	Vermont	563	0.45%
37	Maine	426	0.34%
38	Montana	422	0.33%
39	Nebraska	406	0.32%
40	Rhode Island	403	0.32%
41	New Hampshire	328	0.26%
42	Nevada	310	0.25%
43	South Dakota	283	0.22%
44	Hawaii	240	0.19%
45	Delaware	200	0.16%
46	Wyoming	151	0.12%
NA	Connecticut**	NA	NA
NA	Maryland**	NA	NA
NA	North Dakota**	NA	NA
NA	West Virginia**	NA	NA
	District of Columbia**	NA	NA

Source: U.S. Department of Health and Human Services, National Center on Child Abuse and Neglect
"Child Maltreatment 1995: Reports from the States to the National Center on Child Abuse and Neglect"
*State-substantiated incidents. National total is for reporting states only. Fifty-two percent of maltreated children suffered neglect, 25% physical abuse, 13% sexual abuse, 5% emotional maltreatment, 3% medical neglect and 14% other forms of maltreatment. More than half of the abused or neglected children were 7 years old or younger, with about 26% younger than four years old. **Not available.

Rate of Sexually Abused Children in 1995

National Rate = 1.8 Sexually Abused Children per 1,000 Population Under 18*

ALPHA ORDER			RANK ORDER		
RANK	STATE	RATE	RANK	STATE	RATE
7	Alabama	3.1	1	Idaho	6.3
3	Alaska	4.0	2	Washington	4.1
26	Arizona	1.3	3	Alaska	4.0
18	Arkansas	1.8	4	Wisconsin	3.8
10	California	2.8	5	Vermont	3.5
28	Colorado	1.1	6	Ohio	3.4
NA	Connecticut**	NA	7	Alabama	3.1
28	Delaware	1.1	8	Indiana	3.0
15	Florida	2.0	9	Utah	2.9
11	Georgia	2.7	10	California	2.8
42	Hawaii	0.8	11	Georgia	2.7
1	Idaho	6.3	12	Missouri	2.4
22	Illinois	1.5	13	Kentucky	2.3
8	Indiana	3.0	13	Oklahoma	2.3
21	Iowa	1.6	15	Florida	2.0
24	Kansas	1.4	16	Montana	1.9
13	Kentucky	2.3	16	Oregon	1.9
38	Louisiana	0.9	18	Arkansas	1.8
22	Maine	1.5	18	Tennessee	1.8
NA	Maryland**	NA	20	Rhode Island	1.7
35	Massachusetts	1.0	21	Iowa	1.6
44	Michigan	0.7	22	Illinois	1.5
44	Minnesota	0.7	22	Maine	1.5
38	Mississippi	0.9	24	Kansas	1.4
12	Missouri	2.4	24	South Dakota	1.4
16	Montana	1.9	26	Arizona	1.3
38	Nebraska	0.9	26	Texas	1.3
42	Nevada	0.8	28	Colorado	1.1
28	New Hampshire	1.1	28	Delaware	1.1
46	New Jersey	0.4	28	New Hampshire	1.1
28	New Mexico	1.1	28	New Mexico	1.1
38	New York	0.9	28	South Carolina	1.1
35	North Carolina	1.0	28	Virginia	1.1
NA	North Dakota**	NA	28	Wyoming	1.1
6	Ohio	3.4	35	Massachusetts	1.0
13	Oklahoma	2.3	35	North Carolina	1.0
16	Oregon	1.9	35	Pennsylvania	1.0
35	Pennsylvania	1.0	38	Louisiana	0.9
20	Rhode Island	1.7	38	Mississippi	0.9
28	South Carolina	1.1	38	Nebraska	0.9
24	South Dakota	1.4	38	New York	0.9
18	Tennessee	1.8	42	Hawaii	0.8
26	Texas	1.3	42	Nevada	0.8
9	Utah	2.9	44	Michigan	0.7
5	Vermont	3.5	44	Minnesota	0.7
28	Virginia	1.1	46	New Jersey	0.4
2	Washington	4.1	NA	Connecticut**	NA
NA	West Virginia**	NA	NA	Maryland**	NA
4	Wisconsin	3.8	NA	North Dakota**	NA
28	Wyoming	1.1	NA	West Virginia**	NA
				District of Columbia**	NA

Source: U.S. Department of Health and Human Services, National Center on Child Abuse and Neglect
"Child Maltreatment 1995: Reports from the States to the National Center on Child Abuse and Neglect"
*State-substantiated incidents for reporting states. The median rate for states reporting is 1.4 children. Fifty-two percent of maltreated children suffered neglect, 25% physical abuse, 13% sexual abuse, 5% emotional maltreatment, 3% medical neglect and 14% other forms of maltreatment. More than half of the abused or neglected children were 7 years old or younger, with about 26% younger than four years old. **Not available.

Neglected Children in 1995

National Total = 518,348 Children*

ALPHA ORDER

RANK	STATE	CHILDREN	% of USA
19	Alabama	9,095	1.75%
31	Alaska	3,589	0.69%
13	Arizona	12,553	2.42%
37	Arkansas	1,931	0.37%
1	California	79,714	15.38%
28	Colorado	4,769	0.92%
15	Connecticut	11,483	2.22%
43	Delaware	766	0.15%
2	Florida	38,895	7.50%
3	Georgia	34,087	6.58%
44	Hawaii	755	0.15%
29	Idaho	4,473	0.86%
10	Illinois	18,433	3.56%
14	Indiana	12,510	2.41%
24	Iowa	6,069	1.17%
42	Kansas	808	0.16%
11	Kentucky	17,651	3.41%
18	Louisiana	9,494	1.83%
40	Maine	1,634	0.32%
NA	Maryland**	NA	NA
8	Massachusetts	20,283	3.91%
12	Michigan	13,608	2.63%
22	Minnesota	6,302	1.22%
33	Mississippi	3,167	0.61%
17	Missouri	9,786	1.89%
35	Montana	2,392	0.46%
36	Nebraska	2,245	0.43%
27	Nevada	4,801	0.93%
46	New Hampshire	579	0.11%
30	New Jersey	3,606	0.70%
25	New Mexico	6,067	1.17%
7	New York	23,528	4.54%
5	North Carolina	26,500	5.11%
38	North Dakota	1,832	0.35%
4	Ohio	32,147	6.20%
16	Oklahoma	10,460	2.02%
32	Oregon	3,178	0.61%
48	Pennsylvania	124	0.02%
34	Rhode Island	3,048	0.59%
20	South Carolina	7,355	1.42%
39	South Dakota	1,781	0.34%
26	Tennessee	4,851	0.94%
6	Texas	25,914	5.00%
41	Utah	1,625	0.31%
47	Vermont	325	0.06%
21	Virginia	7,037	1.36%
9	Washington	20,187	3.89%
NA	West Virginia**	NA	NA
23	Wisconsin	6,220	1.20%
45	Wyoming	691	0.13%

RANK ORDER

RANK	STATE	CHILDREN	% of USA
1	California	79,714	15.38%
2	Florida	38,895	7.50%
3	Georgia	34,087	6.58%
4	Ohio	32,147	6.20%
5	North Carolina	26,500	5.11%
6	Texas	25,914	5.00%
7	New York	23,528	4.54%
8	Massachusetts	20,283	3.91%
9	Washington	20,187	3.89%
10	Illinois	18,433	3.56%
11	Kentucky	17,651	3.41%
12	Michigan	13,608	2.63%
13	Arizona	12,553	2.42%
14	Indiana	12,510	2.41%
15	Connecticut	11,483	2.22%
16	Oklahoma	10,460	2.02%
17	Missouri	9,786	1.89%
18	Louisiana	9,494	1.83%
19	Alabama	9,095	1.75%
20	South Carolina	7,355	1.42%
21	Virginia	7,037	1.36%
22	Minnesota	6,302	1.22%
23	Wisconsin	6,220	1.20%
24	Iowa	6,069	1.17%
25	New Mexico	6,067	1.17%
26	Tennessee	4,851	0.94%
27	Nevada	4,801	0.93%
28	Colorado	4,769	0.92%
29	Idaho	4,473	0.86%
30	New Jersey	3,606	0.70%
31	Alaska	3,589	0.69%
32	Oregon	3,178	0.61%
33	Mississippi	3,167	0.61%
34	Rhode Island	3,048	0.59%
35	Montana	2,392	0.46%
36	Nebraska	2,245	0.43%
37	Arkansas	1,931	0.37%
38	North Dakota	1,832	0.35%
39	South Dakota	1,781	0.34%
40	Maine	1,634	0.32%
41	Utah	1,625	0.31%
42	Kansas	808	0.16%
43	Delaware	766	0.15%
44	Hawaii	755	0.15%
45	Wyoming	691	0.13%
46	New Hampshire	579	0.11%
47	Vermont	325	0.06%
48	Pennsylvania	124	0.02%
NA	Maryland**	NA	NA
NA	West Virginia**	NA	NA
	District of Columbia**	NA	NA

Source: U.S. Department of Health and Human Services, National Center on Child Abuse and Neglect
"Child Maltreatment 1995: Reports from the States to the National Center on Child Abuse and Neglect"
*State-substantiated incidents. National total is for reporting states only. Fifty-two percent of maltreated children suffered neglect, 25% physical abuse, 13% sexual abuse, 5% emotional maltreatment, 3% medical neglect and 14% other forms of maltreatment. More than half of the abused or neglected children were 7 years old or younger, with about 26% younger than four years old. **Not available.*

Rate of Neglected Children in 1995

National Rate = 7.5 Neglected Children per 1,000 Population Under 18*

ALPHA ORDER

RANK	STATE	RATE
23	Alabama	7.4
4	Alaska	16.7
16	Arizona	10.3
41	Arkansas	2.8
20	California	8.7
34	Colorado	4.7
8	Connecticut	13.2
36	Delaware	4.3
12	Florida	11.1
1	Georgia	17.6
42	Hawaii	2.4
6	Idaho	14.0
26	Illinois	5.9
18	Indiana	8.9
24	Iowa	7.2
47	Kansas	1.2
2	Kentucky	17.4
21	Louisiana	8.1
27	Maine	5.6
NA	Maryland**	NA
7	Massachusetts	13.9
29	Michigan	5.0
31	Minnesota	4.8
37	Mississippi	4.1
22	Missouri	8.0
13	Montana	10.8
34	Nebraska	4.7
11	Nevada	12.0
44	New Hampshire	2.0
46	New Jersey	1.9
17	New Mexico	10.0
30	New York	4.9
3	North Carolina	17.2
15	North Dakota	10.4
14	Ohio	10.7
10	Oklahoma	12.5
39	Oregon	3.8
48	Pennsylvania	0.0
9	Rhode Island	13.0
25	South Carolina	7.0
18	South Dakota	8.9
40	Tennessee	3.3
31	Texas	4.8
43	Utah	2.3
44	Vermont	2.0
31	Virginia	4.8
5	Washington	14.4
NA	West Virginia**	NA
38	Wisconsin	3.9
28	Wyoming	5.2

RANK ORDER

RANK	STATE	RATE
1	Georgia	17.6
2	Kentucky	17.4
3	North Carolina	17.2
4	Alaska	16.7
5	Washington	14.4
6	Idaho	14.0
7	Massachusetts	13.9
8	Connecticut	13.2
9	Rhode Island	13.0
10	Oklahoma	12.5
11	Nevada	12.0
12	Florida	11.1
13	Montana	10.8
14	Ohio	10.7
15	North Dakota	10.4
16	Arizona	10.3
17	New Mexico	10.0
18	Indiana	8.9
18	South Dakota	8.9
20	California	8.7
21	Louisiana	8.1
22	Missouri	8.0
23	Alabama	7.4
24	Iowa	7.2
25	South Carolina	7.0
26	Illinois	5.9
27	Maine	5.6
28	Wyoming	5.2
29	Michigan	5.0
30	New York	4.9
31	Minnesota	4.8
31	Texas	4.8
31	Virginia	4.8
34	Colorado	4.7
34	Nebraska	4.7
36	Delaware	4.3
37	Mississippi	4.1
38	Wisconsin	3.9
39	Oregon	3.8
40	Tennessee	3.3
41	Arkansas	2.8
42	Hawaii	2.4
43	Utah	2.3
44	New Hampshire	2.0
44	Vermont	2.0
46	New Jersey	1.9
47	Kansas	1.2
48	Pennsylvania	0.0
NA	Maryland**	NA
NA	West Virginia**	NA
	District of Columbia**	NA

Source: U.S. Department of Health and Human Services, National Center on Child Abuse and Neglect
"Child Maltreatment 1995: Reports from the States to the National Center on Child Abuse and Neglect"
*State-substantiated incidents for reporting states. The median rate for states reporting is 7.0 children. Fifty-two percent of maltreated children suffered neglect, 25% physical abuse, 13% sexual abuse, 5% emotional maltreatment, 3% medical neglect and 14% other forms of maltreatment. More than half of the abused or neglected children were 7 years old or younger, with about 26% younger than four years old. **Not available.*

Child Abuse and Neglect Fatalities in 1995

National Total = 996 Fatalities*

ALPHA ORDER					RANK ORDER			
RANK	**STATE**		**DEATHS**	**% of USA**	**RANK**	**STATE**	**DEATHS**	**% of USA**
13	Alabama		26	2.61%	1	Texas	96	9.64%
NA	Alaska**		NA	NA	2	Illinois	89	8.94%
18	Arizona		16	1.61%	3	Florida	68	6.83%
38	Arkansas		3	0.30%	3	New York	68	6.83%
5	California		66	6.63%	5	California	66	6.63%
16	Colorado		23	2.31%	6	Pennsylvania	61	6.12%
33	Connecticut		5	0.50%	7	Missouri	43	4.32%
31	Delaware		6	0.60%	8	Oregon	36	3.61%
3	Florida		68	6.83%	9	Oklahoma	34	3.41%
18	Georgia		16	1.61%	9	Tennessee	34	3.41%
31	Hawaii		6	0.60%	11	Indiana	29	2.91%
22	Idaho		15	1.51%	12	New Jersey	28	2.81%
2	Illinois		89	8.94%	13	Alabama	26	2.61%
11	Indiana		29	2.91%	14	Kentucky	24	2.41%
25	Iowa		13	1.31%	14	Virginia	24	2.41%
35	Kansas		4	0.40%	16	Colorado	23	2.31%
14	Kentucky		24	2.41%	17	North Carolina	17	1.71%
18	Louisiana		16	1.61%	18	Arizona	16	1.61%
40	Maine		2	0.20%	18	Georgia	16	1.61%
NA	Maryland**		NA	NA	18	Louisiana	16	1.61%
27	Massachusetts		9	0.90%	18	Wisconsin	16	1.61%
NA	Michigan**		NA	NA	22	Idaho	15	1.51%
23	Minnesota		14	1.41%	23	Minnesota	14	1.41%
26	Mississippi		12	1.20%	23	Utah	14	1.41%
7	Missouri		43	4.32%	25	Iowa	13	1.31%
44	Montana		0	0.00%	26	Mississippi	12	1.20%
43	Nebraska		1	0.10%	27	Massachusetts	9	0.90%
35	Nevada		4	0.40%	27	Washington	9	0.90%
33	New Hampshire		5	0.50%	29	New Mexico	7	0.70%
12	New Jersey		28	2.81%	29	South Carolina	7	0.70%
29	New Mexico		7	0.70%	31	Delaware	6	0.60%
3	New York		68	6.83%	31	Hawaii	6	0.60%
17	North Carolina		17	1.71%	33	Connecticut	5	0.50%
40	North Dakota		2	0.20%	33	New Hampshire	5	0.50%
NA	Ohio**		NA	NA	35	Kansas	4	0.40%
9	Oklahoma		34	3.41%	35	Nevada	4	0.40%
8	Oregon		36	3.61%	35	Rhode Island	4	0.40%
6	Pennsylvania		61	6.12%	38	Arkansas	3	0.30%
35	Rhode Island		4	0.40%	38	Wyoming	3	0.30%
29	South Carolina		7	0.70%	40	Maine	2	0.20%
40	South Dakota		2	0.20%	40	North Dakota	2	0.20%
9	Tennessee		34	3.41%	40	South Dakota	2	0.20%
1	Texas		96	9.64%	43	Nebraska	1	0.10%
23	Utah		14	1.41%	44	Montana	0	0.00%
44	Vermont		0	0.00%	44	Vermont	0	0.00%
14	Virginia		24	2.41%	NA	Alaska**	NA	NA
27	Washington		9	0.90%	NA	Maryland**	NA	NA
NA	West Virginia**		NA	NA	NA	Michigan**	NA	NA
18	Wisconsin		16	1.61%	NA	Ohio**	NA	NA
38	Wyoming		3	0.30%	NA	West Virginia**	NA	NA
						District of Columbia**	NA	NA

Source: U.S. Department of Health and Human Services, National Center on Child Abuse and Neglect
"Child Maltreatment 1995: Reports from the States to the National Center on Child Abuse and Neglect"
*State-substantiated incidents. There were reports of 2,960,000 children abused leading to 1,110,000 cases confirmed. Fifty-two percent of maltreated children suffered neglect, 25% physical abuse, 13% sexual abuse, 5% emotional maltreatment, 3% medical neglect and 14% other forms of maltreatment. More than half of the abused or neglected children were 7 years old or younger, with about 26% younger than four years old. **Not available.

Rate of Child Abuse and Neglect Fatalities in 1995

National Rate = 1.6 Fatalities per 100,000 Population Under 18*

ALPHA ORDER

RANK	STATE	RATE
11	Alabama	2.1
NA	Alaska**	NA
26	Arizona	1.3
42	Arkansas	0.4
35	California	0.7
8	Colorado	2.3
38	Connecticut	0.6
5	Delaware	3.4
15	Florida	1.9
34	Georgia	0.8
15	Hawaii	1.9
1	Idaho	4.7
6	Illinois	2.8
11	Indiana	2.1
22	Iowa	1.5
38	Kansas	0.6
7	Kentucky	2.4
23	Louisiana	1.4
35	Maine	0.7
NA	Maryland**	NA
38	Massachusetts	0.6
NA	Michigan**	NA
28	Minnesota	1.1
20	Mississippi	1.6
4	Missouri	3.5
44	Montana	0.0
43	Nebraska	0.2
31	Nevada	1.0
18	New Hampshire	1.7
23	New Jersey	1.4
27	New Mexico	1.2
23	New York	1.4
28	North Carolina	1.1
28	North Dakota	1.1
NA	Ohio**	NA
3	Oklahoma	4.0
2	Oregon	4.3
13	Pennsylvania	2.0
18	Rhode Island	1.7
35	South Carolina	0.7
31	South Dakota	1.0
8	Tennessee	2.3
17	Texas	1.8
13	Utah	2.0
44	Vermont	0.0
20	Virginia	1.6
38	Washington	0.6
NA	West Virginia**	NA
31	Wisconsin	1.0
10	Wyoming	2.2

RANK ORDER

RANK	STATE	RATE
1	Idaho	4.7
2	Oregon	4.3
3	Oklahoma	4.0
4	Missouri	3.5
5	Delaware	3.4
6	Illinois	2.8
7	Kentucky	2.4
8	Colorado	2.3
8	Tennessee	2.3
10	Wyoming	2.2
11	Alabama	2.1
11	Indiana	2.1
13	Pennsylvania	2.0
13	Utah	2.0
15	Florida	1.9
15	Hawaii	1.9
17	Texas	1.8
18	New Hampshire	1.7
18	Rhode Island	1.7
20	Mississippi	1.6
20	Virginia	1.6
22	Iowa	1.5
23	Louisiana	1.4
23	New Jersey	1.4
23	New York	1.4
26	Arizona	1.3
27	New Mexico	1.2
28	Minnesota	1.1
28	North Carolina	1.1
28	North Dakota	1.1
31	Nevada	1.0
31	South Dakota	1.0
31	Wisconsin	1.0
34	Georgia	0.8
35	California	0.7
35	Maine	0.7
35	South Carolina	0.7
38	Connecticut	0.6
38	Kansas	0.6
38	Massachusetts	0.6
38	Washington	0.6
42	Arkansas	0.4
43	Nebraska	0.2
44	Montana	0.0
44	Vermont	0.0
NA	Alaska**	NA
NA	Maryland**	NA
NA	Michigan**	NA
NA	Ohio**	NA
NA	West Virginia**	NA
	District of Columbia**	NA

Source: U.S. Department of Health and Human Services, National Center on Child Abuse and Neglect
"Child Maltreatment 1995: Reports from the States to the National Center on Child Abuse and Neglect"
*State-substantiated incidents for reporting states. Fifty-two percent of maltreated children suffered neglect, 25% physical abuse, 13% sexual abuse, 5% emotional maltreatment, 3% medical neglect and 14% other forms of maltreatment. More than half of the abused or neglected children were 7 years old or younger, with about 26% younger than four years old. **Not available.*

VI. LAW ENFORCEMENT

Federal Law Enforcement Officers in 1996

National Total = 74,493 Officers*

ALPHA ORDER					RANK ORDER			
RANK	STATE	OFFICERS	% of USA		RANK	STATE	OFFICERS	% of USA
25	Alabama	696	0.93%		1	California	10,469	14.05%
38	Alaska	325	0.44%		2	Texas	8,836	11.86%
7	Arizona	2,608	3.50%		3	New York	6,556	8.80%
36	Arkansas	351	0.47%		4	Florida	4,980	6.69%
1	California	10,469	14.05%		5	Pennsylvania	2,853	3.83%
12	Colorado	1,442	1.94%		6	Illinois	2,652	3.56%
33	Connecticut	412	0.55%		7	Arizona	2,608	3.50%
46	Delaware	149	0.20%		8	New Jersey	1,997	2.68%
4	Florida	4,980	6.69%		9	Virginia	1,891	2.54%
10	Georgia	1,869	2.51%		10	Georgia	1,869	2.51%
28	Hawaii	511	0.69%		11	Michigan	1,541	2.07%
43	Idaho	178	0.24%		12	Colorado	1,442	1.94%
6	Illinois	2,652	3.56%		13	Washington	1,246	1.67%
27	Indiana	629	0.84%		14	Louisiana	1,178	1.58%
47	Iowa	133	0.18%		15	Maryland	1,142	1.53%
34	Kansas	390	0.52%		16	Missouri	1,100	1.48%
21	Kentucky	851	1.14%		17	Massachusetts	1,053	1.41%
14	Louisiana	1,178	1.58%		18	North Carolina	972	1.30%
40	Maine	284	0.38%		19	Tennessee	935	1.26%
15	Maryland	1,142	1.53%		20	Ohio	883	1.19%
17	Massachusetts	1,053	1.41%		21	Kentucky	851	1.14%
11	Michigan	1,541	2.07%		22	Minnesota	804	1.08%
22	Minnesota	804	1.08%		23	New Mexico	775	1.04%
39	Mississippi	305	0.41%		24	Oklahoma	757	1.02%
16	Missouri	1,100	1.48%		25	Alabama	696	0.93%
37	Montana	330	0.44%		26	Oregon	649	0.87%
42	Nebraska	206	0.28%		27	Indiana	629	0.84%
31	Nevada	459	0.62%		28	Hawaii	511	0.69%
50	New Hampshire	58	0.08%		29	South Carolina	486	0.65%
8	New Jersey	1,997	2.68%		29	West Virginia	486	0.65%
23	New Mexico	775	1.04%		31	Nevada	459	0.62%
3	New York	6,556	8.80%		32	Wisconsin	421	0.57%
18	North Carolina	972	1.30%		33	Connecticut	412	0.55%
41	North Dakota	226	0.30%		34	Kansas	390	0.52%
20	Ohio	883	1.19%		35	Utah	376	0.50%
24	Oklahoma	757	1.02%		36	Arkansas	351	0.47%
26	Oregon	649	0.87%		37	Montana	330	0.44%
5	Pennsylvania	2,853	3.83%		38	Alaska	325	0.44%
49	Rhode Island	94	0.13%		39	Mississippi	305	0.41%
29	South Carolina	486	0.65%		40	Maine	284	0.38%
45	South Dakota	155	0.21%		41	North Dakota	226	0.30%
19	Tennessee	935	1.26%		42	Nebraska	206	0.28%
2	Texas	8,836	11.86%		43	Idaho	178	0.24%
35	Utah	376	0.50%		44	Vermont	162	0.22%
44	Vermont	162	0.22%		45	South Dakota	155	0.21%
9	Virginia	1,891	2.54%		46	Delaware	149	0.20%
13	Washington	1,246	1.67%		47	Iowa	133	0.18%
29	West Virginia	486	0.65%		47	Wyoming	133	0.18%
32	Wisconsin	421	0.57%		49	Rhode Island	94	0.13%
47	Wyoming	133	0.18%		50	New Hampshire	58	0.08%
						District of Columbia	6,508	8.74%

Source: U.S. Department of Justice, Bureau of Justice Statistics
"Federal Law Enforcement Officers, 1996" (NCJ-164617, January 1998)
*Full-time officers authorized to carry firearms and make arrests. Includes F.B.I., Customs Service, Immigration and Naturalization Service, I.R.S., Postal Inspection, Drug Enforcement Administration, Secret Service, National Park Service, Bureau of Alcohol, Tobacco and Firearms, Capitol Police, U.S. Courts, Federal Bureau of Prisons, Tennessee Valley Authority, and U.S. Forest Service.

Rate of Federal Law Enforcement Officers in 1996

National Rate = 28 Officers per 100,000 Population*

ALPHA ORDER			RANK ORDER		
RANK	STATE	RATE	RANK	STATE	RATE
35	Alabama	16	1	Arizona	59
2	Alaska	54	2	Alaska	54
1	Arizona	59	3	Texas	46
39	Arkansas	14	4	New Mexico	45
11	California	33	5	Hawaii	43
6	Colorado	38	6	Colorado	38
40	Connecticut	13	6	Montana	38
27	Delaware	21	8	New York	36
9	Florida	35	9	Florida	35
18	Georgia	25	9	North Dakota	35
5	Hawaii	43	11	California	33
37	Idaho	15	12	Nevada	29
25	Illinois	22	13	Vermont	28
44	Indiana	11	13	Virginia	28
49	Iowa	5	13	Wyoming	28
37	Kansas	15	16	Louisiana	27
25	Kentucky	22	16	West Virginia	27
16	Louisiana	27	18	Georgia	25
21	Maine	23	18	New Jersey	25
21	Maryland	23	20	Pennsylvania	24
33	Massachusetts	17	21	Maine	23
35	Michigan	16	21	Maryland	23
33	Minnesota	17	21	Oklahoma	23
44	Mississippi	11	21	Washington	23
27	Missouri	21	25	Illinois	22
6	Montana	38	25	Kentucky	22
43	Nebraska	12	27	Delaware	21
12	Nevada	29	27	Missouri	21
49	New Hampshire	5	27	South Dakota	21
18	New Jersey	25	30	Oregon	20
4	New Mexico	45	31	Utah	19
8	New York	36	32	Tennessee	18
40	North Carolina	13	33	Massachusetts	17
9	North Dakota	35	33	Minnesota	17
47	Ohio	8	35	Alabama	16
21	Oklahoma	23	35	Michigan	16
30	Oregon	20	37	Idaho	15
20	Pennsylvania	24	37	Kansas	15
46	Rhode Island	9	39	Arkansas	14
40	South Carolina	13	40	Connecticut	13
27	South Dakota	21	40	North Carolina	13
32	Tennessee	18	40	South Carolina	13
3	Texas	46	43	Nebraska	12
31	Utah	19	44	Indiana	11
13	Vermont	28	44	Mississippi	11
13	Virginia	28	46	Rhode Island	9
21	Washington	23	47	Ohio	8
16	West Virginia	27	47	Wisconsin	8
47	Wisconsin	8	49	Iowa	5
13	Wyoming	28	49	New Hampshire	5
				District of Columbia	1,198

Source: U.S. Department of Justice, Bureau of Justice Statistics
   "Federal Law Enforcement Officers, 1996" (NCJ-164617, January 1998)
*Full-time officers authorized to carry firearms and make arrests. Includes F.B.I., Customs Service, Immigration and Naturalization Service, I.R.S., Postal Inspection, Drug Enforcement Administration, Secret Service, National Park Service, Bureau of Alcohol, Tobacco and Firearms, Capitol Police, U.S. Courts, Federal Bureau of Prisons, Tennessee Valley Authority, and U.S. Forest Service.

State and Local Justice System Employment in 1995

National Total = 1,724,927 Employees*

ALPHA ORDER

RANK	STATE	EMPLOYEES	% of USA
25	Alabama	21,894	1.27%
45	Alaska	4,296	0.25%
15	Arizona	32,282	1.87%
32	Arkansas	12,996	0.75%
1	California	199,819	11.58%
23	Colorado	22,508	1.30%
27	Connecticut	20,723	1.20%
44	Delaware	5,301	0.31%
4	Florida	115,783	6.71%
10	Georgia	54,506	3.16%
38	Hawaii	8,118	0.47%
39	Idaho	7,166	0.42%
5	Illinois	80,619	4.67%
17	Indiana	30,411	1.76%
33	Iowa	12,868	0.75%
30	Kansas	16,262	0.94%
28	Kentucky	20,014	1.16%
20	Louisiana	29,172	1.69%
43	Maine	5,327	0.31%
14	Maryland	35,011	2.03%
13	Massachusetts	36,183	2.10%
9	Michigan	55,039	3.19%
24	Minnesota	22,196	1.29%
31	Mississippi	14,805	0.86%
16	Missouri	30,461	1.77%
46	Montana	4,141	0.24%
37	Nebraska	8,458	0.49%
35	Nevada	11,577	0.67%
42	New Hampshire	5,558	0.32%
7	New Jersey	68,714	3.98%
34	New Mexico	12,416	0.72%
2	New York	162,219	9.40%
11	North Carolina	41,811	2.42%
49	North Dakota	2,791	0.16%
8	Ohio	68,005	3.94%
26	Oklahoma	21,704	1.26%
29	Oregon	17,009	0.99%
6	Pennsylvania	70,322	4.08%
41	Rhode Island	5,805	0.34%
22	South Carolina	24,067	1.40%
47	South Dakota	3,337	0.19%
18	Tennessee	29,984	1.74%
3	Texas	141,399	8.20%
36	Utah	9,842	0.57%
50	Vermont	2,697	0.16%
12	Virginia	41,260	2.39%
19	Washington	29,915	1.73%
40	West Virginia	6,188	0.36%
21	Wisconsin	28,253	1.64%
48	Wyoming	3,184	0.18%

RANK ORDER

RANK	STATE	EMPLOYEES	% of USA
1	California	199,819	11.58%
2	New York	162,219	9.40%
3	Texas	141,399	8.20%
4	Florida	115,783	6.71%
5	Illinois	80,619	4.67%
6	Pennsylvania	70,322	4.08%
7	New Jersey	68,714	3.98%
8	Ohio	68,005	3.94%
9	Michigan	55,039	3.19%
10	Georgia	54,506	3.16%
11	North Carolina	41,811	2.42%
12	Virginia	41,260	2.39%
13	Massachusetts	36,183	2.10%
14	Maryland	35,011	2.03%
15	Arizona	32,282	1.87%
16	Missouri	30,461	1.77%
17	Indiana	30,411	1.76%
18	Tennessee	29,984	1.74%
19	Washington	29,915	1.73%
20	Louisiana	29,172	1.69%
21	Wisconsin	28,253	1.64%
22	South Carolina	24,067	1.40%
23	Colorado	22,508	1.30%
24	Minnesota	22,196	1.29%
25	Alabama	21,894	1.27%
26	Oklahoma	21,704	1.26%
27	Connecticut	20,723	1.20%
28	Kentucky	20,014	1.16%
29	Oregon	17,009	0.99%
30	Kansas	16,262	0.94%
31	Mississippi	14,805	0.86%
32	Arkansas	12,996	0.75%
33	Iowa	12,868	0.75%
34	New Mexico	12,416	0.72%
35	Nevada	11,577	0.67%
36	Utah	9,842	0.57%
37	Nebraska	8,458	0.49%
38	Hawaii	8,118	0.47%
39	Idaho	7,166	0.42%
40	West Virginia	6,188	0.36%
41	Rhode Island	5,805	0.34%
42	New Hampshire	5,558	0.32%
43	Maine	5,327	0.31%
44	Delaware	5,301	0.31%
45	Alaska	4,296	0.25%
46	Montana	4,141	0.24%
47	South Dakota	3,337	0.19%
48	Wyoming	3,184	0.18%
49	North Dakota	2,791	0.16%
50	Vermont	2,697	0.16%
	District of Columbia	10,511	0.61%

Source: Morgan Quitno Press using data from U.S. Bureau of the Census, Governments Division
    "1995 State and Local Government Employment" (http://www.census.gov/govs/www/apes95sl.html)
*Full-time equivalent as of October 1995. Includes police, courts, prosecution, public defense and corrections.

Rate of State and Local Justice System Employment in 1995

National Rate = 65.7 Employees per 10,000 Population*

ALPHA ORDER

RANK	STATE	RATE
40	Alabama	51.5
10	Alaska	71.3
7	Arizona	75.0
37	Arkansas	52.3
20	California	63.3
24	Colorado	60.2
18	Connecticut	63.5
8	Delaware	74.0
3	Florida	81.6
4	Georgia	75.6
12	Hawaii	69.0
22	Idaho	61.5
13	Illinois	68.5
36	Indiana	52.5
47	Iowa	45.3
19	Kansas	63.4
38	Kentucky	51.9
14	Louisiana	67.2
49	Maine	43.1
11	Maryland	69.4
25	Massachusetts	59.6
29	Michigan	57.8
43	Minnesota	48.1
33	Mississippi	54.9
30	Missouri	57.3
44	Montana	47.6
39	Nebraska	51.6
4	Nevada	75.6
42	New Hampshire	48.4
2	New Jersey	86.5
9	New Mexico	73.5
1	New York	89.2
28	North Carolina	58.0
48	North Dakota	43.5
23	Ohio	61.1
16	Oklahoma	66.3
35	Oregon	54.0
27	Pennsylvania	58.3
26	Rhode Island	58.5
17	South Carolina	65.7
46	South Dakota	45.7
31	Tennessee	57.1
6	Texas	75.2
41	Utah	50.2
45	Vermont	46.0
21	Virginia	62.4
33	Washington	54.9
50	West Virginia	33.9
32	Wisconsin	55.3
15	Wyoming	66.4

RANK ORDER

RANK	STATE	RATE
1	New York	89.2
2	New Jersey	86.5
3	Florida	81.6
4	Georgia	75.6
4	Nevada	75.6
6	Texas	75.2
7	Arizona	75.0
8	Delaware	74.0
9	New Mexico	73.5
10	Alaska	71.3
11	Maryland	69.4
12	Hawaii	69.0
13	Illinois	68.5
14	Louisiana	67.2
15	Wyoming	66.4
16	Oklahoma	66.3
17	South Carolina	65.7
18	Connecticut	63.5
19	Kansas	63.4
20	California	63.3
21	Virginia	62.4
22	Idaho	61.5
23	Ohio	61.1
24	Colorado	60.2
25	Massachusetts	59.6
26	Rhode Island	58.5
27	Pennsylvania	58.3
28	North Carolina	58.0
29	Michigan	57.8
30	Missouri	57.3
31	Tennessee	57.1
32	Wisconsin	55.3
33	Mississippi	54.9
33	Washington	54.9
35	Oregon	54.0
36	Indiana	52.5
37	Arkansas	52.3
38	Kentucky	51.9
39	Nebraska	51.6
40	Alabama	51.5
41	Utah	50.2
42	New Hampshire	48.4
43	Minnesota	48.1
44	Montana	47.6
45	Vermont	46.0
46	South Dakota	45.7
47	Iowa	45.3
48	North Dakota	43.5
49	Maine	43.1
50	West Virginia	33.9

District of Columbia   189.6

Source: Morgan Quitno Press using data from U.S. Bureau of the Census, Governments Division
"1995 State and Local Government Employment" (http://www.census.gov/govs/www/apes95sl.html)
Full-time equivalent as of October 1995. Includes police, courts, prosecution, public defense and corrections.

State and Local Judicial and Legal System Employment in 1995

National Total = 331,196 Employees*

RANK	STATE	EMPLOYEES	% of USA
25	Alabama	4,243	1.28%
43	Alaska	1,228	0.37%
11	Arizona	7,207	2.18%
36	Arkansas	2,076	0.63%
1	California	38,481	11.62%
24	Colorado	4,792	1.45%
27	Connecticut	3,655	1.10%
41	Delaware	1,461	0.44%
3	Florida	22,799	6.88%
10	Georgia	8,000	2.42%
33	Hawaii	2,696	0.81%
40	Idaho	1,490	0.45%
7	Illinois	15,742	4.75%
17	Indiana	5,855	1.77%
31	Iowa	3,001	0.91%
30	Kansas	3,200	0.97%
23	Kentucky	4,801	1.45%
14	Louisiana	6,359	1.92%
49	Maine	691	0.21%
15	Maryland	6,158	1.86%
12	Massachusetts	6,766	2.04%
9	Michigan	10,475	3.16%
20	Minnesota	5,166	1.56%
34	Mississippi	2,560	0.77%
19	Missouri	5,194	1.57%
45	Montana	841	0.25%
39	Nebraska	1,590	0.48%
32	Nevada	2,724	0.82%
44	New Hampshire	972	0.29%
5	New Jersey	20,404	6.16%
35	New Mexico	2,274	0.69%
2	New York	27,559	8.32%
16	North Carolina	6,062	1.83%
48	North Dakota	736	0.22%
6	Ohio	16,155	4.88%
28	Oklahoma	3,281	0.99%
26	Oregon	3,904	1.18%
8	Pennsylvania	15,338	4.63%
42	Rhode Island	1,271	0.38%
29	South Carolina	3,222	0.97%
47	South Dakota	762	0.23%
22	Tennessee	5,090	1.54%
4	Texas	20,688	6.25%
37	Utah	1,983	0.60%
50	Vermont	551	0.17%
18	Virginia	5,624	1.70%
13	Washington	6,561	1.98%
38	West Virginia	1,744	0.53%
21	Wisconsin	5,164	1.56%
46	Wyoming	764	0.23%

RANK	STATE	EMPLOYEES	% of USA
1	California	38,481	11.62%
2	New York	27,559	8.32%
3	Florida	22,799	6.88%
4	Texas	20,688	6.25%
5	New Jersey	20,404	6.16%
6	Ohio	16,155	4.88%
7	Illinois	15,742	4.75%
8	Pennsylvania	15,338	4.63%
9	Michigan	10,475	3.16%
10	Georgia	8,000	2.42%
11	Arizona	7,207	2.18%
12	Massachusetts	6,766	2.04%
13	Washington	6,561	1.98%
14	Louisiana	6,359	1.92%
15	Maryland	6,158	1.86%
16	North Carolina	6,062	1.83%
17	Indiana	5,855	1.77%
18	Virginia	5,624	1.70%
19	Missouri	5,194	1.57%
20	Minnesota	5,166	1.56%
21	Wisconsin	5,164	1.56%
22	Tennessee	5,090	1.54%
23	Kentucky	4,801	1.45%
24	Colorado	4,792	1.45%
25	Alabama	4,243	1.28%
26	Oregon	3,904	1.18%
27	Connecticut	3,655	1.10%
28	Oklahoma	3,281	0.99%
29	South Carolina	3,222	0.97%
30	Kansas	3,200	0.97%
31	Iowa	3,001	0.91%
32	Nevada	2,724	0.82%
33	Hawaii	2,696	0.81%
34	Mississippi	2,560	0.77%
35	New Mexico	2,274	0.69%
36	Arkansas	2,076	0.63%
37	Utah	1,983	0.60%
38	West Virginia	1,744	0.53%
39	Nebraska	1,590	0.48%
40	Idaho	1,490	0.45%
41	Delaware	1,461	0.44%
42	Rhode Island	1,271	0.38%
43	Alaska	1,228	0.37%
44	New Hampshire	972	0.29%
45	Montana	841	0.25%
46	Wyoming	764	0.23%
47	South Dakota	762	0.23%
48	North Dakota	736	0.22%
49	Maine	691	0.21%
50	Vermont	551	0.17%
	District of Columbia	1,836	0.55%

Source: U.S. Bureau of the Census, Governments Division
   "1995 State and Local Government Employment" (http://www.census.gov/govs/www/apes95sl.html)
*Full-time equivalent as of October 1995. Includes courts, prosecution and public defense.

Rate of State and Local Judicial and Legal System Employment in 1995

National Rate = 12.6 Employees per 10,000 Population*

ALPHA ORDER

RANK	STATE	RATE
36	Alabama	10.0
3	Alaska	20.4
6	Arizona	16.7
48	Arkansas	8.4
21	California	12.2
14	Colorado	12.8
25	Connecticut	11.2
3	Delaware	20.4
7	Florida	16.1
27	Georgia	11.1
2	Hawaii	22.9
14	Idaho	12.8
13	Illinois	13.4
33	Indiana	10.1
31	Iowa	10.6
18	Kansas	12.5
19	Kentucky	12.4
10	Louisiana	14.7
50	Maine	5.6
21	Maryland	12.2
27	Massachusetts	11.1
29	Michigan	11.0
25	Minnesota	11.2
43	Mississippi	9.5
38	Missouri	9.8
39	Montana	9.7
39	Nebraska	9.7
5	Nevada	17.8
46	New Hampshire	8.5
1	New Jersey	25.7
12	New Mexico	13.5
9	New York	15.2
48	North Carolina	8.4
24	North Dakota	11.5
11	Ohio	14.5
36	Oklahoma	10.0
19	Oregon	12.4
17	Pennsylvania	12.7
14	Rhode Island	12.8
45	South Carolina	8.8
32	South Dakota	10.4
39	Tennessee	9.7
29	Texas	11.0
33	Utah	10.1
44	Vermont	9.4
46	Virginia	8.5
23	Washington	12.0
42	West Virginia	9.6
33	Wisconsin	10.1
8	Wyoming	15.9

RANK ORDER

RANK	STATE	RATE
1	New Jersey	25.7
2	Hawaii	22.9
3	Alaska	20.4
3	Delaware	20.4
5	Nevada	17.8
6	Arizona	16.7
7	Florida	16.1
8	Wyoming	15.9
9	New York	15.2
10	Louisiana	14.7
11	Ohio	14.5
12	New Mexico	13.5
13	Illinois	13.4
14	Colorado	12.8
14	Idaho	12.8
14	Rhode Island	12.8
17	Pennsylvania	12.7
18	Kansas	12.5
19	Kentucky	12.4
19	Oregon	12.4
21	California	12.2
21	Maryland	12.2
23	Washington	12.0
24	North Dakota	11.5
25	Connecticut	11.2
25	Minnesota	11.2
27	Georgia	11.1
27	Massachusetts	11.1
29	Michigan	11.0
29	Texas	11.0
31	Iowa	10.6
32	South Dakota	10.4
33	Indiana	10.1
33	Utah	10.1
33	Wisconsin	10.1
36	Alabama	10.0
36	Oklahoma	10.0
38	Missouri	9.8
39	Montana	9.7
39	Nebraska	9.7
39	Tennessee	9.7
42	West Virginia	9.6
43	Mississippi	9.5
44	Vermont	9.4
45	South Carolina	8.8
46	New Hampshire	8.5
46	Virginia	8.5
48	Arkansas	8.4
48	North Carolina	8.4
50	Maine	5.6
	District of Columbia	33.1

Source: U.S. Bureau of the Census, Governments Division
"1995 State and Local Government Employment" (http://www.census.gov/govs/www/apes95sl.html)
*Full-time equivalent as of October 1995. Includes courts, prosecution and public defense.

State and Local Police Officers in 1995

National Total = 585,156 Officers*

RANK	STATE	OFFICERS	% of USA
22	Alabama	8,427	1.44%
46	Alaska	1,193	0.20%
21	Arizona	8,637	1.48%
33	Arkansas	4,841	0.83%
2	California	63,713	10.89%
23	Colorado	8,039	1.37%
25	Connecticut	7,445	1.27%
44	Delaware	1,460	0.25%
5	Florida	32,156	5.50%
10	Georgia	16,084	2.75%
39	Hawaii	2,542	0.43%
40	Idaho	2,325	0.40%
4	Illinois	32,274	5.52%
17	Indiana	10,473	1.79%
32	Iowa	4,959	0.85%
31	Kansas	5,365	0.92%
28	Kentucky	5,549	0.95%
18	Louisiana	10,433	1.78%
43	Maine	2,155	0.37%
14	Maryland	12,671	2.17%
12	Massachusetts	15,165	2.59%
9	Michigan	18,389	3.14%
26	Minnesota	7,397	1.26%
29	Mississippi	5,490	0.94%
15	Missouri	11,544	1.97%
45	Montana	1,455	0.25%
37	Nebraska	3,060	0.52%
36	Nevada	3,159	0.54%
41	New Hampshire	2,291	0.39%
7	New Jersey	22,628	3.87%
34	New Mexico	3,556	0.61%
1	New York	66,280	11.33%
11	North Carolina	15,846	2.71%
49	North Dakota	1,008	0.17%
8	Ohio	22,022	3.76%
27	Oklahoma	6,872	1.17%
30	Oregon	5,412	0.92%
6	Pennsylvania	24,814	4.24%
42	Rhode Island	2,254	0.39%
24	South Carolina	7,998	1.37%
47	South Dakota	1,190	0.20%
19	Tennessee	10,362	1.77%
3	Texas	41,976	7.17%
35	Utah	3,171	0.54%
50	Vermont	897	0.15%
13	Virginia	12,816	2.19%
20	Washington	8,874	1.52%
38	West Virginia	2,545	0.43%
16	Wisconsin	11,095	1.90%
48	Wyoming	1,095	0.19%

RANK	STATE	OFFICERS	% of USA
1	New York	66,280	11.33%
2	California	63,713	10.89%
3	Texas	41,976	7.17%
4	Illinois	32,274	5.52%
5	Florida	32,156	5.50%
6	Pennsylvania	24,814	4.24%
7	New Jersey	22,628	3.87%
8	Ohio	22,022	3.76%
9	Michigan	18,389	3.14%
10	Georgia	16,084	2.75%
11	North Carolina	15,846	2.71%
12	Massachusetts	15,165	2.59%
13	Virginia	12,816	2.19%
14	Maryland	12,671	2.17%
15	Missouri	11,544	1.97%
16	Wisconsin	11,095	1.90%
17	Indiana	10,473	1.79%
18	Louisiana	10,433	1.78%
19	Tennessee	10,362	1.77%
20	Washington	8,874	1.52%
21	Arizona	8,637	1.48%
22	Alabama	8,427	1.44%
23	Colorado	8,039	1.37%
24	South Carolina	7,998	1.37%
25	Connecticut	7,445	1.27%
26	Minnesota	7,397	1.26%
27	Oklahoma	6,872	1.17%
28	Kentucky	5,549	0.95%
29	Mississippi	5,490	0.94%
30	Oregon	5,412	0.92%
31	Kansas	5,365	0.92%
32	Iowa	4,959	0.85%
33	Arkansas	4,841	0.83%
34	New Mexico	3,556	0.61%
35	Utah	3,171	0.54%
36	Nevada	3,159	0.54%
37	Nebraska	3,060	0.52%
38	West Virginia	2,545	0.43%
39	Hawaii	2,542	0.43%
40	Idaho	2,325	0.40%
41	New Hampshire	2,291	0.39%
42	Rhode Island	2,254	0.39%
43	Maine	2,155	0.37%
44	Delaware	1,460	0.25%
45	Montana	1,455	0.25%
46	Alaska	1,193	0.20%
47	South Dakota	1,190	0.20%
48	Wyoming	1,095	0.19%
49	North Dakota	1,008	0.17%
50	Vermont	897	0.15%
	District of Columbia	3,754	0.64%

Source: U.S. Bureau of the Census, Governments Division
"1995 State and Local Government Employment" (http://www.census.gov/govs/www/apes95sl.html)
*Full-time equivalent as of October 1995. Does not include employees of police departments who are not officers.

Rate of State and Local Police Officers in 1995

National Rate = 22.3 Officers per 10,000 Population*

<table>
<tr><td colspan="3">ALPHA ORDER</td><td colspan="3">RANK ORDER</td></tr>
<tr><td>RANK</td><td>STATE</td><td>RATE</td><td>RANK</td><td>STATE</td><td>RATE</td></tr>
<tr><td>30</td><td>Alabama</td><td>19.8</td><td>1</td><td>New York</td><td>36.4</td></tr>
<tr><td>30</td><td>Alaska</td><td>19.8</td><td>2</td><td>New Jersey</td><td>28.5</td></tr>
<tr><td>27</td><td>Arizona</td><td>20.1</td><td>3</td><td>Illinois</td><td>27.4</td></tr>
<tr><td>34</td><td>Arkansas</td><td>19.5</td><td>4</td><td>Maryland</td><td>25.1</td></tr>
<tr><td>26</td><td>California</td><td>20.2</td><td>5</td><td>Massachusetts</td><td>25.0</td></tr>
<tr><td>18</td><td>Colorado</td><td>21.5</td><td>6</td><td>Louisiana</td><td>24.0</td></tr>
<tr><td>8</td><td>Connecticut</td><td>22.8</td><td>7</td><td>Wyoming</td><td>22.9</td></tr>
<tr><td>24</td><td>Delaware</td><td>20.4</td><td>8</td><td>Connecticut</td><td>22.8</td></tr>
<tr><td>9</td><td>Florida</td><td>22.7</td><td>9</td><td>Florida</td><td>22.7</td></tr>
<tr><td>11</td><td>Georgia</td><td>22.3</td><td>9</td><td>Rhode Island</td><td>22.7</td></tr>
<tr><td>17</td><td>Hawaii</td><td>21.6</td><td>11</td><td>Georgia</td><td>22.3</td></tr>
<tr><td>29</td><td>Idaho</td><td>19.9</td><td>11</td><td>Texas</td><td>22.3</td></tr>
<tr><td>3</td><td>Illinois</td><td>27.4</td><td>13</td><td>North Carolina</td><td>22.0</td></tr>
<tr><td>38</td><td>Indiana</td><td>18.1</td><td>14</td><td>South Carolina</td><td>21.8</td></tr>
<tr><td>39</td><td>Iowa</td><td>17.4</td><td>15</td><td>Missouri</td><td>21.7</td></tr>
<tr><td>21</td><td>Kansas</td><td>20.9</td><td>15</td><td>Wisconsin</td><td>21.7</td></tr>
<tr><td>49</td><td>Kentucky</td><td>14.4</td><td>17</td><td>Hawaii</td><td>21.6</td></tr>
<tr><td>6</td><td>Louisiana</td><td>24.0</td><td>18</td><td>Colorado</td><td>21.5</td></tr>
<tr><td>39</td><td>Maine</td><td>17.4</td><td>19</td><td>New Mexico</td><td>21.0</td></tr>
<tr><td>4</td><td>Maryland</td><td>25.1</td><td>19</td><td>Oklahoma</td><td>21.0</td></tr>
<tr><td>5</td><td>Massachusetts</td><td>25.0</td><td>21</td><td>Kansas</td><td>20.9</td></tr>
<tr><td>36</td><td>Michigan</td><td>19.3</td><td>22</td><td>Nevada</td><td>20.6</td></tr>
<tr><td>46</td><td>Minnesota</td><td>16.0</td><td>22</td><td>Pennsylvania</td><td>20.6</td></tr>
<tr><td>24</td><td>Mississippi</td><td>20.4</td><td>24</td><td>Delaware</td><td>20.4</td></tr>
<tr><td>15</td><td>Missouri</td><td>21.7</td><td>24</td><td>Mississippi</td><td>20.4</td></tr>
<tr><td>42</td><td>Montana</td><td>16.7</td><td>26</td><td>California</td><td>20.2</td></tr>
<tr><td>37</td><td>Nebraska</td><td>18.7</td><td>27</td><td>Arizona</td><td>20.1</td></tr>
<tr><td>22</td><td>Nevada</td><td>20.6</td><td>28</td><td>New Hampshire</td><td>20.0</td></tr>
<tr><td>28</td><td>New Hampshire</td><td>20.0</td><td>29</td><td>Idaho</td><td>19.9</td></tr>
<tr><td>2</td><td>New Jersey</td><td>28.5</td><td>30</td><td>Alabama</td><td>19.8</td></tr>
<tr><td>19</td><td>New Mexico</td><td>21.0</td><td>30</td><td>Alaska</td><td>19.8</td></tr>
<tr><td>1</td><td>New York</td><td>36.4</td><td>30</td><td>Ohio</td><td>19.8</td></tr>
<tr><td>13</td><td>North Carolina</td><td>22.0</td><td>33</td><td>Tennessee</td><td>19.7</td></tr>
<tr><td>47</td><td>North Dakota</td><td>15.7</td><td>34</td><td>Arkansas</td><td>19.5</td></tr>
<tr><td>30</td><td>Ohio</td><td>19.8</td><td>35</td><td>Virginia</td><td>19.4</td></tr>
<tr><td>19</td><td>Oklahoma</td><td>21.0</td><td>36</td><td>Michigan</td><td>19.3</td></tr>
<tr><td>41</td><td>Oregon</td><td>17.2</td><td>37</td><td>Nebraska</td><td>18.7</td></tr>
<tr><td>22</td><td>Pennsylvania</td><td>20.6</td><td>38</td><td>Indiana</td><td>18.1</td></tr>
<tr><td>9</td><td>Rhode Island</td><td>22.7</td><td>39</td><td>Iowa</td><td>17.4</td></tr>
<tr><td>14</td><td>South Carolina</td><td>21.8</td><td>39</td><td>Maine</td><td>17.4</td></tr>
<tr><td>43</td><td>South Dakota</td><td>16.3</td><td>41</td><td>Oregon</td><td>17.2</td></tr>
<tr><td>33</td><td>Tennessee</td><td>19.7</td><td>42</td><td>Montana</td><td>16.7</td></tr>
<tr><td>11</td><td>Texas</td><td>22.3</td><td>43</td><td>South Dakota</td><td>16.3</td></tr>
<tr><td>45</td><td>Utah</td><td>16.2</td><td>43</td><td>Washington</td><td>16.3</td></tr>
<tr><td>48</td><td>Vermont</td><td>15.3</td><td>45</td><td>Utah</td><td>16.2</td></tr>
<tr><td>35</td><td>Virginia</td><td>19.4</td><td>46</td><td>Minnesota</td><td>16.0</td></tr>
<tr><td>43</td><td>Washington</td><td>16.3</td><td>47</td><td>North Dakota</td><td>15.7</td></tr>
<tr><td>50</td><td>West Virginia</td><td>13.9</td><td>48</td><td>Vermont</td><td>15.3</td></tr>
<tr><td>15</td><td>Wisconsin</td><td>21.7</td><td>49</td><td>Kentucky</td><td>14.4</td></tr>
<tr><td>7</td><td>Wyoming</td><td>22.9</td><td>50</td><td>West Virginia</td><td>13.9</td></tr>
<tr><td></td><td></td><td></td><td></td><td>District of Columbia</td><td>67.7</td></tr>
</table>

Source: U.S. Bureau of the Census, Governments Division
   "1995 State and Local Government Employment" (http://www.census.gov/govs/www/apes95sl.html)
*Full-time equivalent as of October 1995. Does not include employees of police departments who are not officers.

Law Enforcement Agencies in 1992

National Total = 17,358 Agencies*

ALPHA ORDER

RANK	STATE	AGENCIES	% of USA
18	Alabama	377	2.17%
46	Alaska	48	0.28%
43	Arizona	102	0.59%
26	Arkansas	277	1.60%
11	California	493	2.84%
32	Colorado	218	1.26%
37	Connecticut	133	0.77%
48	Delaware	42	0.24%
20	Florida	371	2.14%
8	Georgia	540	3.11%
50	Hawaii	6	0.03%
42	Idaho	112	0.65%
4	Illinois	894	5.15%
14	Indiana	448	2.58%
15	Iowa	427	2.46%
22	Kansas	345	1.99%
18	Kentucky	377	2.17%
21	Louisiana	348	2.00%
35	Maine	142	0.82%
39	Maryland	124	0.71%
17	Massachusetts	388	2.24%
6	Michigan	578	3.33%
13	Minnesota	456	2.63%
25	Mississippi	297	1.71%
5	Missouri	594	3.42%
40	Montana	119	0.69%
29	Nebraska	247	1.42%
49	Nevada	35	0.20%
30	New Hampshire	228	1.31%
9	New Jersey	534	3.08%
41	New Mexico	115	0.66%
6	New York	578	3.33%
12	North Carolina	458	2.64%
36	North Dakota	134	0.77%
3	Ohio	908	5.23%
16	Oklahoma	410	2.36%
33	Oregon	183	1.05%
2	Pennsylvania	1,167	6.72%
46	Rhode Island	48	0.28%
27	South Carolina	255	1.47%
34	South Dakota	171	0.99%
24	Tennessee	326	1.88%
1	Texas	1,712	9.86%
38	Utah	127	0.73%
45	Vermont	73	0.42%
23	Virginia	327	1.88%
28	Washington	252	1.45%
30	West Virginia	228	1.31%
10	Wisconsin	506	2.92%
44	Wyoming	77	0.44%

RANK ORDER

RANK	STATE	AGENCIES	% of USA
1	Texas	1,712	9.86%
2	Pennsylvania	1,167	6.72%
3	Ohio	908	5.23%
4	Illinois	894	5.15%
5	Missouri	594	3.42%
6	Michigan	578	3.33%
6	New York	578	3.33%
8	Georgia	540	3.11%
9	New Jersey	534	3.08%
10	Wisconsin	506	2.92%
11	California	493	2.84%
12	North Carolina	458	2.64%
13	Minnesota	456	2.63%
14	Indiana	448	2.58%
15	Iowa	427	2.46%
16	Oklahoma	410	2.36%
17	Massachusetts	388	2.24%
18	Alabama	377	2.17%
18	Kentucky	377	2.17%
20	Florida	371	2.14%
21	Louisiana	348	2.00%
22	Kansas	345	1.99%
23	Virginia	327	1.88%
24	Tennessee	326	1.88%
25	Mississippi	297	1.71%
26	Arkansas	277	1.60%
27	South Carolina	255	1.47%
28	Washington	252	1.45%
29	Nebraska	247	1.42%
30	New Hampshire	228	1.31%
30	West Virginia	228	1.31%
32	Colorado	218	1.26%
33	Oregon	183	1.05%
34	South Dakota	171	0.99%
35	Maine	142	0.82%
36	North Dakota	134	0.77%
37	Connecticut	133	0.77%
38	Utah	127	0.73%
39	Maryland	124	0.71%
40	Montana	119	0.69%
41	New Mexico	115	0.66%
42	Idaho	112	0.65%
43	Arizona	102	0.59%
44	Wyoming	77	0.44%
45	Vermont	73	0.42%
46	Alaska	48	0.28%
46	Rhode Island	48	0.28%
48	Delaware	42	0.24%
49	Nevada	35	0.20%
50	Hawaii	6	0.03%
	District of Columbia	3	0.02%

Source: U.S. Department of Justice, Bureau of Justice Statistics
"Census of State and Local Law Enforcement Agencies, 1992" (Bulletin, July 1993, NCJ-142972)
*Includes state and local police, sheriffs' departments and special police agencies.

Population per Law Enforcement Agency in 1992

National Rate = 14,695 Population per Agency*

ALPHA ORDER			RANK ORDER		
RANK	STATE	RATE	RANK	STATE	RATE
29	Alabama	10,971	1	Hawaii	193,333
27	Alaska	12,229	2	California	62,611
5	Arizona	37,569	3	Maryland	39,581
39	Arkansas	8,661	4	Nevada	37,914
2	California	62,611	5	Arizona	37,569
15	Colorado	15,917	6	Florida	36,356
8	Connecticut	24,669	7	New York	31,348
12	Delaware	16,405	8	Connecticut	24,669
6	Florida	36,356	9	Rhode Island	20,938
25	Georgia	12,502	10	Washington	20,381
1	Hawaii	193,333	11	Virginia	19,502
35	Idaho	9,527	12	Delaware	16,405
23	Illinois	13,010	13	Michigan	16,327
24	Indiana	12,638	14	Oregon	16,268
45	Iowa	6,585	15	Colorado	15,917
43	Kansas	7,313	16	Massachusetts	15,459
32	Kentucky	9,960	17	Tennessee	15,411
26	Louisiana	12,319	18	North Carolina	14,941
38	Maine	8,697	19	New Jersey	14,586
3	Maryland	39,581	20	Utah	14,276
16	Massachusetts	15,459	21	South Carolina	14,129
13	Michigan	16,327	22	New Mexico	13,748
34	Minnesota	9,825	23	Illinois	13,010
36	Mississippi	8,801	24	Indiana	12,638
37	Missouri	8,742	25	Georgia	12,502
44	Montana	6,924	26	Louisiana	12,319
46	Nebraska	6,502	27	Alaska	12,229
4	Nevada	37,914	28	Ohio	12,132
48	New Hampshire	4,873	29	Alabama	10,971
19	New Jersey	14,586	30	Texas	10,313
22	New Mexico	13,748	31	Pennsylvania	10,290
7	New York	31,348	32	Kentucky	9,960
18	North Carolina	14,941	33	Wisconsin	9,895
49	North Dakota	4,746	34	Minnesota	9,825
28	Ohio	12,132	35	Idaho	9,527
41	Oklahoma	7,834	36	Mississippi	8,801
14	Oregon	16,268	37	Missouri	8,742
31	Pennsylvania	10,290	38	Maine	8,697
9	Rhode Island	20,938	39	Arkansas	8,661
21	South Carolina	14,129	40	West Virginia	7,947
50	South Dakota	4,158	41	Oklahoma	7,834
17	Tennessee	15,411	42	Vermont	7,808
30	Texas	10,313	43	Kansas	7,313
20	Utah	14,276	44	Montana	6,924
42	Vermont	7,808	45	Iowa	6,585
11	Virginia	19,502	46	Nebraska	6,502
10	Washington	20,381	47	Wyoming	6,052
40	West Virginia	7,947	48	New Hampshire	4,873
33	Wisconsin	9,895	49	North Dakota	4,746
47	Wyoming	6,052	50	South Dakota	4,158
				District of Columbia	196,333

Source: Morgan Quitno Press using data from U.S. Department of Justice, Bureau of Justice Statistics
"Census of State and Local Law Enforcement Agencies, 1992" (Bulletin, July 1993, NCJ-142972)
*Includes state and local police, sheriffs' departments and special police agencies.

Law Enforcement Agencies per 1,000 Square Miles in 1992

National Rate = 4.58 Agencies per 1,000 Square Miles*

ALPHA ORDER				RANK ORDER		
RANK	STATE	RATE		RANK	STATE	RATE
24	Alabama	7.19		1	New Jersey	61.22
50	Alaska	0.07		2	Massachusetts	36.76
45	Arizona	0.89		3	Rhode Island	31.07
32	Arkansas	5.21		4	Pennsylvania	25.34
37	California	3.01		5	New Hampshire	24.38
39	Colorado	2.09		6	Connecticut	23.99
6	Connecticut	23.99		7	Ohio	20.26
8	Delaware	16.87		8	Delaware	16.87
30	Florida	5.64		9	Illinois	15.44
15	Georgia	9.08		10	Indiana	12.30
48	Hawaii	0.55		11	New York	10.61
43	Idaho	1.34		12	Maryland	9.99
9	Illinois	15.44		13	West Virginia	9.41
10	Indiana	12.30		14	Kentucky	9.33
22	Iowa	7.59		15	Georgia	9.08
33	Kansas	4.19		16	Missouri	8.52
14	Kentucky	9.33		17	North Carolina	8.51
25	Louisiana	6.71		18	South Carolina	7.97
34	Maine	4.01		19	Tennessee	7.74
12	Maryland	9.99		20	Wisconsin	7.72
2	Massachusetts	36.76		21	Virginia	7.65
28	Michigan	5.97		22	Iowa	7.59
31	Minnesota	5.24		22	Vermont	7.59
27	Mississippi	6.13		24	Alabama	7.19
16	Missouri	8.52		25	Louisiana	6.71
46	Montana	0.81		26	Texas	6.37
36	Nebraska	3.19		27	Mississippi	6.13
49	Nevada	0.32		28	Michigan	5.97
5	New Hampshire	24.38		29	Oklahoma	5.87
1	New Jersey	61.22		30	Florida	5.64
44	New Mexico	0.95		31	Minnesota	5.24
11	New York	10.61		32	Arkansas	5.21
17	North Carolina	8.51		33	Kansas	4.19
40	North Dakota	1.90		34	Maine	4.01
7	Ohio	20.26		35	Washington	3.53
29	Oklahoma	5.87		36	Nebraska	3.19
41	Oregon	1.86		37	California	3.01
4	Pennsylvania	25.34		38	South Dakota	2.22
3	Rhode Island	31.07		39	Colorado	2.09
18	South Carolina	7.97		40	North Dakota	1.90
38	South Dakota	2.22		41	Oregon	1.86
19	Tennessee	7.74		42	Utah	1.50
26	Texas	6.37		43	Idaho	1.34
42	Utah	1.50		44	New Mexico	0.95
22	Vermont	7.59		45	Arizona	0.89
21	Virginia	7.65		46	Montana	0.81
35	Washington	3.53		47	Wyoming	0.79
13	West Virginia	9.41		48	Hawaii	0.55
20	Wisconsin	7.72		49	Nevada	0.32
47	Wyoming	0.79		50	Alaska	0.07
					District of Columbia**	NA

Source: Morgan Quitno Press using data from U.S. Department of Justice, Bureau of Justice Statistics
   "Census of State and Local Law Enforcement Agencies, 1992" (Bulletin, July 1993, NCJ-142972)
*Includes state and local police, sheriffs' departments and special police agencies.
**The District of Columbia has three agencies for its 68 square miles.

Full-Time Sworn Officers in Law Enforcement Agencies in 1992

National Total = 603,954 Officers*

<table>
<tr><td colspan="4"><u>ALPHA ORDER</u></td><td colspan="4"><u>RANK ORDER</u></td></tr>
<tr><td>RANK</td><td>STATE</td><td>OFFICERS</td><td>% of USA</td><td>RANK</td><td>STATE</td><td>OFFICERS</td><td>% of USA</td></tr>
<tr><td>20</td><td>Alabama</td><td>8,771</td><td>1.45%</td><td>1</td><td>New York</td><td>68,208</td><td>11.29%</td></tr>
<tr><td>49</td><td>Alaska</td><td>1,057</td><td>0.18%</td><td>2</td><td>California</td><td>65,797</td><td>10.89%</td></tr>
<tr><td>23</td><td>Arizona</td><td>7,900</td><td>1.31%</td><td>3</td><td>Texas</td><td>41,349</td><td>6.85%</td></tr>
<tr><td>33</td><td>Arkansas</td><td>4,475</td><td>0.74%</td><td>4</td><td>Illinois</td><td>35,674</td><td>5.91%</td></tr>
<tr><td>2</td><td>California</td><td>65,797</td><td>10.89%</td><td>5</td><td>Florida</td><td>32,879</td><td>5.44%</td></tr>
<tr><td>21</td><td>Colorado</td><td>8,726</td><td>1.44%</td><td>6</td><td>New Jersey</td><td>26,688</td><td>4.42%</td></tr>
<tr><td>25</td><td>Connecticut</td><td>7,639</td><td>1.26%</td><td>7</td><td>Pennsylvania</td><td>23,700</td><td>3.92%</td></tr>
<tr><td>44</td><td>Delaware</td><td>1,572</td><td>0.26%</td><td>8</td><td>Ohio</td><td>20,929</td><td>3.47%</td></tr>
<tr><td>5</td><td>Florida</td><td>32,879</td><td>5.44%</td><td>9</td><td>Michigan</td><td>19,642</td><td>3.25%</td></tr>
<tr><td>10</td><td>Georgia</td><td>16,792</td><td>2.78%</td><td>10</td><td>Georgia</td><td>16,792</td><td>2.78%</td></tr>
<tr><td>38</td><td>Hawaii</td><td>2,783</td><td>0.46%</td><td>11</td><td>Virginia</td><td>16,365</td><td>2.71%</td></tr>
<tr><td>42</td><td>Idaho</td><td>2,157</td><td>0.36%</td><td>12</td><td>Massachusetts</td><td>16,014</td><td>2.65%</td></tr>
<tr><td>4</td><td>Illinois</td><td>35,674</td><td>5.91%</td><td>13</td><td>Louisiana</td><td>15,049</td><td>2.49%</td></tr>
<tr><td>19</td><td>Indiana</td><td>10,038</td><td>1.66%</td><td>14</td><td>North Carolina</td><td>14,586</td><td>2.42%</td></tr>
<tr><td>31</td><td>Iowa</td><td>4,703</td><td>0.78%</td><td>15</td><td>Maryland</td><td>12,601</td><td>2.09%</td></tr>
<tr><td>29</td><td>Kansas</td><td>5,631</td><td>0.93%</td><td>16</td><td>Wisconsin</td><td>11,594</td><td>1.92%</td></tr>
<tr><td>28</td><td>Kentucky</td><td>6,085</td><td>1.01%</td><td>17</td><td>Missouri</td><td>11,266</td><td>1.87%</td></tr>
<tr><td>13</td><td>Louisiana</td><td>15,049</td><td>2.49%</td><td>18</td><td>Tennessee</td><td>10,379</td><td>1.72%</td></tr>
<tr><td>41</td><td>Maine</td><td>2,267</td><td>0.38%</td><td>19</td><td>Indiana</td><td>10,038</td><td>1.66%</td></tr>
<tr><td>15</td><td>Maryland</td><td>12,601</td><td>2.09%</td><td>20</td><td>Alabama</td><td>8,771</td><td>1.45%</td></tr>
<tr><td>12</td><td>Massachusetts</td><td>16,014</td><td>2.65%</td><td>21</td><td>Colorado</td><td>8,726</td><td>1.44%</td></tr>
<tr><td>9</td><td>Michigan</td><td>19,642</td><td>3.25%</td><td>22</td><td>Washington</td><td>8,192</td><td>1.36%</td></tr>
<tr><td>26</td><td>Minnesota</td><td>7,365</td><td>1.22%</td><td>23</td><td>Arizona</td><td>7,900</td><td>1.31%</td></tr>
<tr><td>32</td><td>Mississippi</td><td>4,675</td><td>0.77%</td><td>24</td><td>South Carolina</td><td>7,752</td><td>1.28%</td></tr>
<tr><td>17</td><td>Missouri</td><td>11,266</td><td>1.87%</td><td>25</td><td>Connecticut</td><td>7,639</td><td>1.26%</td></tr>
<tr><td>45</td><td>Montana</td><td>1,410</td><td>0.23%</td><td>26</td><td>Minnesota</td><td>7,365</td><td>1.22%</td></tr>
<tr><td>35</td><td>Nebraska</td><td>3,084</td><td>0.51%</td><td>27</td><td>Oklahoma</td><td>6,458</td><td>1.07%</td></tr>
<tr><td>36</td><td>Nevada</td><td>3,052</td><td>0.51%</td><td>28</td><td>Kentucky</td><td>6,085</td><td>1.01%</td></tr>
<tr><td>43</td><td>New Hampshire</td><td>2,139</td><td>0.35%</td><td>29</td><td>Kansas</td><td>5,631</td><td>0.93%</td></tr>
<tr><td>6</td><td>New Jersey</td><td>26,688</td><td>4.42%</td><td>30</td><td>Oregon</td><td>5,495</td><td>0.91%</td></tr>
<tr><td>34</td><td>New Mexico</td><td>3,420</td><td>0.57%</td><td>31</td><td>Iowa</td><td>4,703</td><td>0.78%</td></tr>
<tr><td>1</td><td>New York</td><td>68,208</td><td>11.29%</td><td>32</td><td>Mississippi</td><td>4,675</td><td>0.77%</td></tr>
<tr><td>14</td><td>North Carolina</td><td>14,586</td><td>2.42%</td><td>33</td><td>Arkansas</td><td>4,475</td><td>0.74%</td></tr>
<tr><td>48</td><td>North Dakota</td><td>1,060</td><td>0.18%</td><td>34</td><td>New Mexico</td><td>3,420</td><td>0.57%</td></tr>
<tr><td>8</td><td>Ohio</td><td>20,929</td><td>3.47%</td><td>35</td><td>Nebraska</td><td>3,084</td><td>0.51%</td></tr>
<tr><td>27</td><td>Oklahoma</td><td>6,458</td><td>1.07%</td><td>36</td><td>Nevada</td><td>3,052</td><td>0.51%</td></tr>
<tr><td>30</td><td>Oregon</td><td>5,495</td><td>0.91%</td><td>37</td><td>Utah</td><td>2,979</td><td>0.49%</td></tr>
<tr><td>7</td><td>Pennsylvania</td><td>23,700</td><td>3.92%</td><td>38</td><td>Hawaii</td><td>2,783</td><td>0.46%</td></tr>
<tr><td>40</td><td>Rhode Island</td><td>2,389</td><td>0.40%</td><td>39</td><td>West Virginia</td><td>2,622</td><td>0.43%</td></tr>
<tr><td>24</td><td>South Carolina</td><td>7,752</td><td>1.28%</td><td>40</td><td>Rhode Island</td><td>2,389</td><td>0.40%</td></tr>
<tr><td>47</td><td>South Dakota</td><td>1,145</td><td>0.19%</td><td>41</td><td>Maine</td><td>2,267</td><td>0.38%</td></tr>
<tr><td>18</td><td>Tennessee</td><td>10,379</td><td>1.72%</td><td>42</td><td>Idaho</td><td>2,157</td><td>0.36%</td></tr>
<tr><td>3</td><td>Texas</td><td>41,349</td><td>6.85%</td><td>43</td><td>New Hampshire</td><td>2,139</td><td>0.35%</td></tr>
<tr><td>37</td><td>Utah</td><td>2,979</td><td>0.49%</td><td>44</td><td>Delaware</td><td>1,572</td><td>0.26%</td></tr>
<tr><td>50</td><td>Vermont</td><td>978</td><td>0.16%</td><td>45</td><td>Montana</td><td>1,410</td><td>0.23%</td></tr>
<tr><td>11</td><td>Virginia</td><td>16,365</td><td>2.71%</td><td>46</td><td>Wyoming</td><td>1,210</td><td>0.20%</td></tr>
<tr><td>22</td><td>Washington</td><td>8,192</td><td>1.36%</td><td>47</td><td>South Dakota</td><td>1,145</td><td>0.19%</td></tr>
<tr><td>39</td><td>West Virginia</td><td>2,622</td><td>0.43%</td><td>48</td><td>North Dakota</td><td>1,060</td><td>0.18%</td></tr>
<tr><td>16</td><td>Wisconsin</td><td>11,594</td><td>1.92%</td><td>49</td><td>Alaska</td><td>1,057</td><td>0.18%</td></tr>
<tr><td>46</td><td>Wyoming</td><td>1,210</td><td>0.20%</td><td>50</td><td>Vermont</td><td>978</td><td>0.16%</td></tr>
<tr><td></td><td></td><td></td><td></td><td></td><td>District of Columbia</td><td>5,213</td><td>0.86%</td></tr>
</table>

Source: U.S. Department of Justice, Bureau of Justice Statistics
   "Census of State and Local Law Enforcement Agencies, 1992" (Bulletin, July 1993, NCJ-142972)
*Includes state and local police, sheriffs' departments and special police agencies.

Percent of Full-Time Law Enforcement Agency Employees
Who are Sworn Officers: 1992
National Rate = 71.81% of Employees are Sworn Officers*

ALPHA ORDER

RANK ORDER

RANK	STATE	PERCENT	RANK	STATE	PERCENT
29	Alabama	70.07	1	Louisiana	86.64
44	Alaska	64.26	2	Pennsylvania	83.67
50	Arizona	59.65	3	Rhode Island	82.64
40	Arkansas	65.59	4	Connecticut	82.35
41	California	65.42	5	New Jersey	81.40
31	Colorado	69.48	6	New York	80.08
4	Connecticut	82.35	7	Hawaii	80.02
8	Delaware	78.36	8	Delaware	78.36
48	Florida	60.87	9	Illinois	77.23
33	Georgia	68.49	10	South Carolina	76.76
7	Hawaii	80.02	11	Kentucky	76.55
20	Idaho	73.82	12	Virginia	76.28
9	Illinois	77.23	13	Wisconsin	75.88
36	Indiana	67.21	14	Massachusetts	75.61
15	Iowa	75.16	15	Iowa	75.16
27	Kansas	71.90	16	Maryland	74.69
11	Kentucky	76.55	17	Michigan	74.47
1	Louisiana	86.64	18	North Carolina	74.29
34	Maine	68.43	19	New Hampshire	73.91
16	Maryland	74.69	20	Idaho	73.82
14	Massachusetts	75.61	21	Vermont	73.59
17	Michigan	74.47	22	Nebraska	73.53
25	Minnesota	72.41	23	Missouri	73.30
30	Mississippi	69.89	24	North Dakota	73.15
23	Missouri	73.30	25	Minnesota	72.41
38	Montana	66.48	26	South Dakota	71.92
22	Nebraska	73.53	27	Kansas	71.90
47	Nevada	61.13	28	Ohio	70.43
19	New Hampshire	73.91	29	Alabama	70.07
5	New Jersey	81.40	30	Mississippi	69.89
32	New Mexico	68.99	31	Colorado	69.48
6	New York	80.08	32	New Mexico	68.99
18	North Carolina	74.29	33	Georgia	68.49
24	North Dakota	73.15	34	Maine	68.43
28	Ohio	70.43	35	Oklahoma	67.59
35	Oklahoma	67.59	36	Indiana	67.21
39	Oregon	66.13	37	West Virginia	67.02
2	Pennsylvania	83.67	38	Montana	66.48
3	Rhode Island	82.64	39	Oregon	66.13
10	South Carolina	76.76	40	Arkansas	65.59
26	South Dakota	71.92	41	California	65.42
45	Tennessee	63.48	42	Texas	64.36
42	Texas	64.36	43	Washington	64.34
46	Utah	61.64	44	Alaska	64.26
21	Vermont	73.59	45	Tennessee	63.48
12	Virginia	76.28	46	Utah	61.64
43	Washington	64.34	47	Nevada	61.13
37	West Virginia	67.02	48	Florida	60.87
13	Wisconsin	75.88	49	Wyoming	60.02
49	Wyoming	60.02	50	Arizona	59.65

	District of Columbia	84.43

Source: Morgan Quitno Press using data from U.S. Department of Justice, Bureau of Justice Statistics
"Census of State and Local Law Enforcement Agencies, 1992" (Bulletin, July 1993, NCJ-142972)
*Includes state and local police, sheriffs' departments and special police agencies.

Rate of Full-Time Sworn Officers in Law Enforcement Agencies in 1992

National Rate = 23.68 Officers per 10,000 Population*

ALPHA ORDER

RANK ORDER

RANK	STATE	RATE		RANK	STATE	RATE
25	Alabama	21.21		1	New York	37.64
38	Alaska	18.01		2	Louisiana	35.10
28	Arizona	20.62		3	New Jersey	34.26
35	Arkansas	18.65		4	Illinois	30.67
23	California	21.32		5	Massachusetts	26.70
9	Colorado	25.15		6	Wyoming	25.97
15	Connecticut	23.28		7	Maryland	25.67
18	Delaware	22.82		8	Virginia	25.66
11	Florida	24.38		9	Colorado	25.15
10	Georgia	24.87		10	Georgia	24.87
12	Hawaii	23.99		11	Florida	24.38
29	Idaho	20.22		12	Hawaii	23.99
4	Illinois	30.67		13	Rhode Island	23.77
40	Indiana	17.73		14	Texas	23.42
43	Iowa	16.72		15	Connecticut	23.28
19	Kansas	22.32		16	Wisconsin	23.16
47	Kentucky	16.21		17	Nevada	23.00
2	Louisiana	35.10		18	Delaware	22.82
37	Maine	18.36		19	Kansas	22.32
7	Maryland	25.67		20	Missouri	21.69
5	Massachusetts	26.70		21	New Mexico	21.63
26	Michigan	20.81		22	South Carolina	21.52
45	Minnesota	16.44		23	California	21.32
39	Mississippi	17.88		23	North Carolina	21.32
20	Missouri	21.69		25	Alabama	21.21
42	Montana	17.11		26	Michigan	20.81
33	Nebraska	19.20		27	Tennessee	20.66
17	Nevada	23.00		28	Arizona	20.62
32	New Hampshire	19.25		29	Idaho	20.22
3	New Jersey	34.26		30	Oklahoma	20.11
21	New Mexico	21.63		31	Pennsylvania	19.74
1	New York	37.64		32	New Hampshire	19.25
23	North Carolina	21.32		33	Nebraska	19.20
44	North Dakota	16.67		34	Ohio	19.00
34	Ohio	19.00		35	Arkansas	18.65
30	Oklahoma	20.11		36	Oregon	18.46
36	Oregon	18.46		37	Maine	18.36
31	Pennsylvania	19.74		38	Alaska	18.01
13	Rhode Island	23.77		39	Mississippi	17.88
22	South Carolina	21.52		40	Indiana	17.73
48	South Dakota	16.10		41	Vermont	17.16
27	Tennessee	20.66		42	Montana	17.11
14	Texas	23.42		43	Iowa	16.72
46	Utah	16.43		44	North Dakota	16.67
41	Vermont	17.16		45	Minnesota	16.44
8	Virginia	25.66		46	Utah	16.43
49	Washington	15.95		47	Kentucky	16.21
50	West Virginia	14.47		48	South Dakota	16.10
16	Wisconsin	23.16		49	Washington	15.95
6	Wyoming	25.97		50	West Virginia	14.47
					District of Columbia	88.51

Source: Morgan Quitno Press using data from U.S. Department of Justice, Bureau of Justice Statistics
"Census of State and Local Law Enforcement Agencies, 1992" (Bulletin, July 1993, NCJ-142972)
*Includes state and local police, sheriffs' departments and special police agencies.

Full-Time Sworn Law Enforcement Officers per 1,000 Square Miles in 1992

National Rate = 159 Officers per 1,000 Square Miles*

<u>ALPHA ORDER</u>

<u>RANK</u> <u>STATE</u> <u>RATE</u>

<u>RANK ORDER</u>

<u>RANK</u> <u>STATE</u> <u>RATE</u>

RANK	STATE	RATE	RANK	STATE	RATE
24	Alabama	167	1	New Jersey	3,060
50	Alaska	2	2	Rhode Island	1,546
37	Arizona	69	3	Massachusetts	1,517
34	Arkansas	84	4	Connecticut	1,378
12	California	402	5	New York	1,252
34	Colorado	84	6	Maryland	1,016
4	Connecticut	1,378	7	Delaware	632
7	Delaware	632	8	Illinois	616
10	Florida	500	9	Pennsylvania	515
15	Georgia	282	10	Florida	500
18	Hawaii	255	11	Ohio	467
45	Idaho	26	12	California	402
8	Illinois	616	13	Virginia	383
16	Indiana	276	14	Louisiana	290
34	Iowa	84	15	Georgia	282
38	Kansas	68	16	Indiana	276
27	Kentucky	151	17	North Carolina	271
14	Louisiana	290	18	Hawaii	255
39	Maine	64	19	Tennessee	246
6	Maryland	1,016	20	South Carolina	242
3	Massachusetts	1,517	21	New Hampshire	229
22	Michigan	203	22	Michigan	203
33	Minnesota	85	23	Wisconsin	177
31	Mississippi	97	24	Alabama	167
25	Missouri	162	25	Missouri	162
49	Montana	10	26	Texas	154
41	Nebraska	40	27	Kentucky	151
43	Nevada	28	28	Washington	115
21	New Hampshire	229	29	West Virginia	108
1	New Jersey	3,060	30	Vermont	102
43	New Mexico	28	31	Mississippi	97
5	New York	1,252	32	Oklahoma	92
17	North Carolina	271	33	Minnesota	85
46	North Dakota	15	34	Arkansas	84
11	Ohio	467	34	Colorado	84
32	Oklahoma	92	34	Iowa	84
40	Oregon	56	37	Arizona	69
9	Pennsylvania	515	38	Kansas	68
2	Rhode Island	1,546	39	Maine	64
20	South Carolina	242	40	Oregon	56
46	South Dakota	15	41	Nebraska	40
19	Tennessee	246	42	Utah	35
26	Texas	154	43	Nevada	28
42	Utah	35	43	New Mexico	28
30	Vermont	102	45	Idaho	26
13	Virginia	383	46	North Dakota	15
28	Washington	115	46	South Dakota	15
29	West Virginia	108	48	Wyoming	12
23	Wisconsin	177	49	Montana	10
48	Wyoming	12	50	Alaska	2
				District of Columbia**	NA

Source: Morgan Quitno Press using data from U.S. Department of Justice, Bureau of Justice Statistics "Census of State and Local Law Enforcement Agencies, 1992" (Bulletin, July 1993, NCJ-142972)
*Includes state and local police, sheriffs' departments and special police agencies.
**The District of Columbia has 5,213 sworn officers for its 68 square miles.

Full-Time Employees in Law Enforcement Agencies in 1992

National Total = 841,099 Employees*

<u>ALPHA ORDER</u>

RANK	STATE	EMPLOYEES	% of USA
23	Alabama	12,517	1.49%
47	Alaska	1,645	0.20%
20	Arizona	13,243	1.57%
31	Arkansas	6,823	0.81%
1	California	100,582	11.96%
22	Colorado	12,559	1.49%
27	Connecticut	9,276	1.10%
46	Delaware	2,006	0.24%
4	Florida	54,011	6.42%
10	Georgia	24,516	2.91%
39	Hawaii	3,478	0.41%
41	Idaho	2,922	0.35%
5	Illinois	46,189	5.49%
19	Indiana	14,935	1.78%
33	Iowa	6,257	0.74%
30	Kansas	7,832	0.93%
29	Kentucky	7,949	0.95%
14	Louisiana	17,370	2.07%
40	Maine	3,313	0.39%
15	Maryland	16,871	2.01%
12	Massachusetts	21,181	2.52%
9	Michigan	26,375	3.14%
24	Minnesota	10,171	1.21%
32	Mississippi	6,689	0.80%
17	Missouri	15,370	1.83%
44	Montana	2,121	0.25%
37	Nebraska	4,194	0.50%
34	Nevada	4,993	0.59%
42	New Hampshire	2,894	0.34%
6	New Jersey	32,785	3.90%
35	New Mexico	4,957	0.59%
2	New York	85,177	10.13%
13	North Carolina	19,633	2.33%
49	North Dakota	1,449	0.17%
7	Ohio	29,718	3.53%
26	Oklahoma	9,554	1.14%
28	Oregon	8,310	0.99%
8	Pennsylvania	28,326	3.37%
43	Rhode Island	2,891	0.34%
25	South Carolina	10,099	1.20%
48	South Dakota	1,592	0.19%
16	Tennessee	16,349	1.94%
3	Texas	64,247	7.64%
36	Utah	4,833	0.57%
50	Vermont	1,329	0.16%
11	Virginia	21,454	2.55%
21	Washington	12,733	1.51%
38	West Virginia	3,912	0.47%
18	Wisconsin	15,279	1.82%
45	Wyoming	2,016	0.24%

<u>RANK ORDER</u>

RANK	STATE	EMPLOYEES	% of USA
1	California	100,582	11.96%
2	New York	85,177	10.13%
3	Texas	64,247	7.64%
4	Florida	54,011	6.42%
5	Illinois	46,189	5.49%
6	New Jersey	32,785	3.90%
7	Ohio	29,718	3.53%
8	Pennsylvania	28,326	3.37%
9	Michigan	26,375	3.14%
10	Georgia	24,516	2.91%
11	Virginia	21,454	2.55%
12	Massachusetts	21,181	2.52%
13	North Carolina	19,633	2.33%
14	Louisiana	17,370	2.07%
15	Maryland	16,871	2.01%
16	Tennessee	16,349	1.94%
17	Missouri	15,370	1.83%
18	Wisconsin	15,279	1.82%
19	Indiana	14,935	1.78%
20	Arizona	13,243	1.57%
21	Washington	12,733	1.51%
22	Colorado	12,559	1.49%
23	Alabama	12,517	1.49%
24	Minnesota	10,171	1.21%
25	South Carolina	10,099	1.20%
26	Oklahoma	9,554	1.14%
27	Connecticut	9,276	1.10%
28	Oregon	8,310	0.99%
29	Kentucky	7,949	0.95%
30	Kansas	7,832	0.93%
31	Arkansas	6,823	0.81%
32	Mississippi	6,689	0.80%
33	Iowa	6,257	0.74%
34	Nevada	4,993	0.59%
35	New Mexico	4,957	0.59%
36	Utah	4,833	0.57%
37	Nebraska	4,194	0.50%
38	West Virginia	3,912	0.47%
39	Hawaii	3,478	0.41%
40	Maine	3,313	0.39%
41	Idaho	2,922	0.35%
42	New Hampshire	2,894	0.34%
43	Rhode Island	2,891	0.34%
44	Montana	2,121	0.25%
45	Wyoming	2,016	0.24%
46	Delaware	2,006	0.24%
47	Alaska	1,645	0.20%
48	South Dakota	1,592	0.19%
49	North Dakota	1,449	0.17%
50	Vermont	1,329	0.16%
	District of Columbia	6,174	0.73%

Source: U.S. Department of Justice, Bureau of Justice Statistics
"Census of State and Local Law Enforcement Agencies, 1992" (Bulletin, July 1993, NCJ-142972)
*Includes state and local police, sheriffs' departments and special police agencies.

Full-Time Employees in Law Enforcement Agencies per 10,000 Population: 1992

National Rate = 32.97 Employees per 10,000 Population*

ALPHA ORDER

RANK ORDER

RANK	STATE	RATE		RANK	STATE	RATE
20	Alabama	30.26		1	New York	47.01
30	Alaska	28.02		2	Wyoming	43.26
12	Arizona	34.56		3	New Jersey	42.09
27	Arkansas	28.44		4	Louisiana	40.52
15	California	32.59		5	Florida	40.04
10	Colorado	36.19		6	Illinois	39.71
28	Connecticut	28.27		7	Nevada	37.63
24	Delaware	29.11		8	Texas	36.39
5	Florida	40.04		9	Georgia	36.31
9	Georgia	36.31		10	Colorado	36.19
21	Hawaii	29.98		11	Massachusetts	35.31
33	Idaho	27.39		12	Arizona	34.56
6	Illinois	39.71		13	Maryland	34.37
37	Indiana	26.38		14	Virginia	33.64
48	Iowa	22.25		15	California	32.59
18	Kansas	31.04		16	Tennessee	32.54
50	Kentucky	21.17		17	New Mexico	31.35
4	Louisiana	40.52		18	Kansas	31.04
35	Maine	26.83		19	Wisconsin	30.52
13	Maryland	34.37		20	Alabama	30.26
11	Massachusetts	35.31		21	Hawaii	29.98
31	Michigan	27.95		22	Oklahoma	29.74
46	Minnesota	22.70		23	Missouri	29.60
41	Mississippi	25.59		24	Delaware	29.11
23	Missouri	29.60		25	Rhode Island	28.77
40	Montana	25.74		26	North Carolina	28.69
38	Nebraska	26.11		27	Arkansas	28.44
7	Nevada	37.63		28	Connecticut	28.27
39	New Hampshire	26.05		29	South Carolina	28.03
3	New Jersey	42.09		30	Alaska	28.02
17	New Mexico	31.35		31	Michigan	27.95
1	New York	47.01		32	Oregon	27.91
26	North Carolina	28.69		33	Idaho	27.39
45	North Dakota	22.78		34	Ohio	26.98
34	Ohio	26.98		35	Maine	26.83
22	Oklahoma	29.74		36	Utah	26.66
32	Oregon	27.91		37	Indiana	26.38
43	Pennsylvania	23.59		38	Nebraska	26.11
25	Rhode Island	28.77		39	New Hampshire	26.05
29	South Carolina	28.03		40	Montana	25.74
47	South Dakota	22.39		41	Mississippi	25.59
16	Tennessee	32.54		42	Washington	24.79
8	Texas	36.39		43	Pennsylvania	23.59
36	Utah	26.66		44	Vermont	23.32
44	Vermont	23.32		45	North Dakota	22.78
14	Virginia	33.64		46	Minnesota	22.70
42	Washington	24.79		47	South Dakota	22.39
49	West Virginia	21.59		48	Iowa	22.25
19	Wisconsin	30.52		49	West Virginia	21.59
2	Wyoming	43.26		50	Kentucky	21.17
					District of Columbia	104.82

Source: Morgan Quitno Press using data from U.S. Department of Justice, Bureau of Justice Statistics
"Census of State and Local Law Enforcement Agencies, 1992" (Bulletin, July 1993, NCJ-142972)
*Includes state and local police, sheriffs' departments and special police agencies.

Full-Time Sworn Officers in State Police Departments in 1992

National Total = 52,980 Officers*

ALPHA ORDER

RANK	STATE	OFFICERS	% of USA
26	Alabama	629	1.19%
42	Alaska	260	0.49%
15	Arizona	1,100	2.08%
34	Arkansas	484	0.91%
1	California	6,062	11.44%
33	Colorado	493	0.93%
19	Connecticut	905	1.71%
28	Delaware	505	0.95%
11	Florida	1,605	3.03%
24	Georgia	777	1.47%
50	Hawaii	0	0.00%
45	Idaho	192	0.36%
8	Illinois	1,977	3.73%
16	Indiana	1,097	2.07%
37	Iowa	410	0.77%
27	Kansas	604	1.14%
18	Kentucky	960	1.81%
25	Louisiana	714	1.35%
39	Maine	332	0.63%
9	Maryland	1,700	3.21%
6	Massachusetts	2,070	3.91%
7	Michigan	2,019	3.81%
30	Minnesota	501	0.95%
31	Mississippi	499	0.94%
21	Missouri	883	1.67%
44	Montana	200	0.38%
29	Nebraska	502	0.95%
40	Nevada	306	0.58%
43	New Hampshire	250	0.47%
5	New Jersey	2,572	4.85%
36	New Mexico	425	0.80%
3	New York	4,013	7.57%
13	North Carolina	1,260	2.38%
49	North Dakota	125	0.24%
12	Ohio	1,292	2.44%
22	Oklahoma	786	1.48%
19	Oregon	905	1.71%
2	Pennsylvania	4,075	7.69%
46	Rhode Island	165	0.31%
14	South Carolina	1,193	2.25%
48	South Dakota	151	0.29%
23	Tennessee	782	1.48%
4	Texas	2,789	5.26%
38	Utah	365	0.69%
41	Vermont	285	0.54%
10	Virginia	1,606	3.03%
17	Washington	1,032	1.95%
35	West Virginia	468	0.88%
32	Wisconsin	498	0.94%
47	Wyoming	157	0.30%

RANK ORDER

RANK	STATE	OFFICERS	% of USA
1	California	6,062	11.44%
2	Pennsylvania	4,075	7.69%
3	New York	4,013	7.57%
4	Texas	2,789	5.26%
5	New Jersey	2,572	4.85%
6	Massachusetts	2,070	3.91%
7	Michigan	2,019	3.81%
8	Illinois	1,977	3.73%
9	Maryland	1,700	3.21%
10	Virginia	1,606	3.03%
11	Florida	1,605	3.03%
12	Ohio	1,292	2.44%
13	North Carolina	1,260	2.38%
14	South Carolina	1,193	2.25%
15	Arizona	1,100	2.08%
16	Indiana	1,097	2.07%
17	Washington	1,032	1.95%
18	Kentucky	960	1.81%
19	Connecticut	905	1.71%
19	Oregon	905	1.71%
21	Missouri	883	1.67%
22	Oklahoma	786	1.48%
23	Tennessee	782	1.48%
24	Georgia	777	1.47%
25	Louisiana	714	1.35%
26	Alabama	629	1.19%
27	Kansas	604	1.14%
28	Delaware	505	0.95%
29	Nebraska	502	0.95%
30	Minnesota	501	0.95%
31	Mississippi	499	0.94%
32	Wisconsin	498	0.94%
33	Colorado	493	0.93%
34	Arkansas	484	0.91%
35	West Virginia	468	0.88%
36	New Mexico	425	0.80%
37	Iowa	410	0.77%
38	Utah	365	0.69%
39	Maine	332	0.63%
40	Nevada	306	0.58%
41	Vermont	285	0.54%
42	Alaska	260	0.49%
43	New Hampshire	250	0.47%
44	Montana	200	0.38%
45	Idaho	192	0.36%
46	Rhode Island	165	0.31%
47	Wyoming	157	0.30%
48	South Dakota	151	0.29%
49	North Dakota	125	0.24%
50	Hawaii	0	0.00%
	District of Columbia	0	0.00%

Source: U.S. Department of Justice, Bureau of Justice Statistics
"Census of State and Local Law Enforcement Agencies, 1992" (Bulletin, July 1993, NCJ-142972)
*All states except Hawaii and the District of Columbia have a state police department.

Percent of Full-Time State Police Department Employees
Who are Sworn Officers: 1992
National Rate = 67.43% of Employees*

ALPHA ORDER

RANK ORDER

RANK	STATE	PERCENT		RANK	STATE	PERCENT
47	Alabama	49.1		1	South Carolina	100.0
39	Alaska	59.2		2	Utah	92.4
30	Arizona	68.3		3	South Dakota	89.4
24	Arkansas	71.3		4	Iowa	89.3
31	California	68.2		5	New York	85.7
23	Colorado	71.7		6	Rhode Island	81.3
29	Connecticut	68.5		7	Massachusetts	80.3
19	Delaware	73.5		8	Oregon	79.0
14	Florida	76.2		9	North Carolina	78.7
49	Georgia	40.9		10	Nebraska	78.1
NA	Hawaii**	NA		11	Pennsylvania	77.9
15	Idaho	75.6		12	New Mexico	77.0
37	Illinois	59.9		13	Montana	76.3
35	Indiana	62.9		14	Florida	76.2
4	Iowa	89.3		15	Idaho	75.6
17	Kansas	73.6		16	Wisconsin	74.9
40	Kentucky	58.0		17	Kansas	73.6
28	Louisiana	68.5		18	New Hampshire	73.5
22	Maine	72.2		19	Delaware	73.5
25	Maryland	70.8		20	Virginia	72.8
7	Massachusetts	80.3		21	New Jersey	72.5
26	Michigan	69.3		22	Maine	72.2
27	Minnesota	69.3		23	Colorado	71.7
38	Mississippi	59.6		24	Arkansas	71.3
48	Missouri	48.2		25	Maryland	70.8
13	Montana	76.3		26	Michigan	69.3
10	Nebraska	78.1		27	Minnesota	69.3
33	Nevada	66.7		28	Louisiana	68.5
18	New Hampshire	73.5		29	Connecticut	68.5
21	New Jersey	72.5		30	Arizona	68.3
12	New Mexico	77.0		31	California	68.2
5	New York	85.7		32	Vermont	66.9
9	North Carolina	78.7		33	Nevada	66.7
36	North Dakota	62.8		34	West Virginia	63.8
42	Ohio	55.0		35	Indiana	62.9
41	Oklahoma	55.9		36	North Dakota	62.8
8	Oregon	79.0		37	Illinois	59.9
11	Pennsylvania	77.9		38	Mississippi	59.6
6	Rhode Island	81.3		39	Alaska	59.2
1	South Carolina	100.0		40	Kentucky	58.0
3	South Dakota	89.4		41	Oklahoma	55.9
44	Tennessee	50.7		42	Ohio	55.0
45	Texas	49.8		43	Wyoming	51.0
2	Utah	92.4		44	Tennessee	50.7
32	Vermont	66.9		45	Texas	49.8
20	Virginia	72.8		45	Washington	49.8
45	Washington	49.8		47	Alabama	49.1
34	West Virginia	63.8		48	Missouri	48.2
16	Wisconsin	74.9		49	Georgia	40.9
43	Wyoming	51.0		NA	Hawaii**	NA
					District of Columbia**	NA

Source: Morgan Quitno Press using data from U.S. Department of Justice, Bureau of Justice Statistics
"Census of State and Local Law Enforcement Agencies, 1992" (Bulletin, July 1993, NCJ-142972)
*All states except Hawaii and the District of Columbia have a state police department.
**Not available.

Rate of Full-Time Sworn Officers in State Police Departments in 1992

National Rate = 2.08 Officers per 10,000 Population*

<table>
<tr><td colspan="3">ALPHA ORDER</td><td colspan="3">RANK ORDER</td></tr>
<tr><td>RANK</td><td>STATE</td><td>RATE</td><td>RANK</td><td>STATE</td><td>RATE</td></tr>
<tr><td>42</td><td>Alabama</td><td>1.52</td><td>1</td><td>Delaware</td><td>7.33</td></tr>
<tr><td>3</td><td>Alaska</td><td>4.43</td><td>2</td><td>Vermont</td><td>5.00</td></tr>
<tr><td>12</td><td>Arizona</td><td>2.87</td><td>3</td><td>Alaska</td><td>4.43</td></tr>
<tr><td>27</td><td>Arkansas</td><td>2.02</td><td>4</td><td>Maryland</td><td>3.46</td></tr>
<tr><td>31</td><td>California</td><td>1.96</td><td>5</td><td>Massachusetts</td><td>3.45</td></tr>
<tr><td>44</td><td>Colorado</td><td>1.42</td><td>6</td><td>Pennsylvania</td><td>3.39</td></tr>
<tr><td>13</td><td>Connecticut</td><td>2.76</td><td>7</td><td>Wyoming</td><td>3.37</td></tr>
<tr><td>1</td><td>Delaware</td><td>7.33</td><td>8</td><td>South Carolina</td><td>3.31</td></tr>
<tr><td>45</td><td>Florida</td><td>1.19</td><td>9</td><td>New Jersey</td><td>3.30</td></tr>
<tr><td>47</td><td>Georgia</td><td>1.15</td><td>10</td><td>Nebraska</td><td>3.13</td></tr>
<tr><td>50</td><td>Hawaii</td><td>0.00</td><td>11</td><td>Oregon</td><td>3.04</td></tr>
<tr><td>35</td><td>Idaho</td><td>1.80</td><td>12</td><td>Arizona</td><td>2.87</td></tr>
<tr><td>36</td><td>Illinois</td><td>1.70</td><td>13</td><td>Connecticut</td><td>2.76</td></tr>
<tr><td>32</td><td>Indiana</td><td>1.94</td><td>14</td><td>Maine</td><td>2.69</td></tr>
<tr><td>43</td><td>Iowa</td><td>1.46</td><td>14</td><td>New Mexico</td><td>2.69</td></tr>
<tr><td>21</td><td>Kansas</td><td>2.39</td><td>16</td><td>West Virginia</td><td>2.58</td></tr>
<tr><td>17</td><td>Kentucky</td><td>2.56</td><td>17</td><td>Kentucky</td><td>2.56</td></tr>
<tr><td>38</td><td>Louisiana</td><td>1.67</td><td>18</td><td>Virginia</td><td>2.52</td></tr>
<tr><td>14</td><td>Maine</td><td>2.69</td><td>19</td><td>Oklahoma</td><td>2.45</td></tr>
<tr><td>4</td><td>Maryland</td><td>3.46</td><td>20</td><td>Montana</td><td>2.43</td></tr>
<tr><td>5</td><td>Massachusetts</td><td>3.45</td><td>21</td><td>Kansas</td><td>2.39</td></tr>
<tr><td>25</td><td>Michigan</td><td>2.14</td><td>22</td><td>Nevada</td><td>2.31</td></tr>
<tr><td>48</td><td>Minnesota</td><td>1.12</td><td>23</td><td>New Hampshire</td><td>2.25</td></tr>
<tr><td>33</td><td>Mississippi</td><td>1.91</td><td>24</td><td>New York</td><td>2.21</td></tr>
<tr><td>36</td><td>Missouri</td><td>1.70</td><td>25</td><td>Michigan</td><td>2.14</td></tr>
<tr><td>20</td><td>Montana</td><td>2.43</td><td>26</td><td>South Dakota</td><td>2.12</td></tr>
<tr><td>10</td><td>Nebraska</td><td>3.13</td><td>27</td><td>Arkansas</td><td>2.02</td></tr>
<tr><td>22</td><td>Nevada</td><td>2.31</td><td>28</td><td>Utah</td><td>2.01</td></tr>
<tr><td>23</td><td>New Hampshire</td><td>2.25</td><td>28</td><td>Washington</td><td>2.01</td></tr>
<tr><td>9</td><td>New Jersey</td><td>3.30</td><td>30</td><td>North Dakota</td><td>1.97</td></tr>
<tr><td>14</td><td>New Mexico</td><td>2.69</td><td>31</td><td>California</td><td>1.96</td></tr>
<tr><td>24</td><td>New York</td><td>2.21</td><td>32</td><td>Indiana</td><td>1.94</td></tr>
<tr><td>34</td><td>North Carolina</td><td>1.84</td><td>33</td><td>Mississippi</td><td>1.91</td></tr>
<tr><td>30</td><td>North Dakota</td><td>1.97</td><td>34</td><td>North Carolina</td><td>1.84</td></tr>
<tr><td>46</td><td>Ohio</td><td>1.17</td><td>35</td><td>Idaho</td><td>1.80</td></tr>
<tr><td>19</td><td>Oklahoma</td><td>2.45</td><td>36</td><td>Illinois</td><td>1.70</td></tr>
<tr><td>11</td><td>Oregon</td><td>3.04</td><td>36</td><td>Missouri</td><td>1.70</td></tr>
<tr><td>6</td><td>Pennsylvania</td><td>3.39</td><td>38</td><td>Louisiana</td><td>1.67</td></tr>
<tr><td>39</td><td>Rhode Island</td><td>1.64</td><td>39</td><td>Rhode Island</td><td>1.64</td></tr>
<tr><td>8</td><td>South Carolina</td><td>3.31</td><td>40</td><td>Texas</td><td>1.58</td></tr>
<tr><td>26</td><td>South Dakota</td><td>2.12</td><td>41</td><td>Tennessee</td><td>1.56</td></tr>
<tr><td>41</td><td>Tennessee</td><td>1.56</td><td>42</td><td>Alabama</td><td>1.52</td></tr>
<tr><td>40</td><td>Texas</td><td>1.58</td><td>43</td><td>Iowa</td><td>1.46</td></tr>
<tr><td>28</td><td>Utah</td><td>2.01</td><td>44</td><td>Colorado</td><td>1.42</td></tr>
<tr><td>2</td><td>Vermont</td><td>5.00</td><td>45</td><td>Florida</td><td>1.19</td></tr>
<tr><td>18</td><td>Virginia</td><td>2.52</td><td>46</td><td>Ohio</td><td>1.17</td></tr>
<tr><td>28</td><td>Washington</td><td>2.01</td><td>47</td><td>Georgia</td><td>1.15</td></tr>
<tr><td>16</td><td>West Virginia</td><td>2.58</td><td>48</td><td>Minnesota</td><td>1.12</td></tr>
<tr><td>49</td><td>Wisconsin</td><td>0.99</td><td>49</td><td>Wisconsin</td><td>0.99</td></tr>
<tr><td>7</td><td>Wyoming</td><td>3.37</td><td>50</td><td>Hawaii</td><td>0.00</td></tr>
<tr><td></td><td></td><td></td><td></td><td>District of Columbia</td><td>0.00</td></tr>
</table>

Source: Morgan Quitno Press using data from U.S. Department of Justice, Bureau of Justice Statistics
"Census of State and Local Law Enforcement Agencies, 1992" (Bulletin, July 1993, NCJ-142972)
*All states except Hawaii and the District of Columbia have a state police department.

State Government Law Enforcement Officers in 1996

National Total = 61,837 Officers*

ALPHA ORDER				RANK ORDER			
RANK	STATE	OFFICERS	% of USA	RANK	STATE	OFFICERS	% of USA
28	Alabama	745	1.20%	1	California	7,457	12.06%
42	Alaska	317	0.51%	2	Pennsylvania	4,332	7.01%
19	Arizona	992	1.60%	3	New York	4,017	6.50%
34	Arkansas	513	0.83%	4	Texas	2,797	4.52%
1	California	7,457	12.06%	5	New Jersey	2,650	4.29%
21	Colorado	971	1.57%	6	Maryland	2,619	4.24%
20	Connecticut	986	1.59%	7	Illinois	2,580	4.17%
31	Delaware	650	1.05%	8	Massachusetts	2,304	3.73%
13	Florida	1,696	2.74%	9	Michigan	2,136	3.45%
12	Georgia	1,858	3.00%	10	North Carolina	2,027	3.28%
50	Hawaii	0	0.00%	11	Virginia	1,947	3.15%
46	Idaho	221	0.36%	12	Georgia	1,858	3.00%
7	Illinois	2,580	4.17%	13	Florida	1,696	2.74%
17	Indiana	1,244	2.01%	14	South Carolina	1,355	2.19%
32	Iowa	614	0.99%	15	Kentucky	1,354	2.19%
30	Kansas	664	1.07%	16	Ohio	1,352	2.19%
15	Kentucky	1,354	2.19%	17	Indiana	1,244	2.01%
24	Louisiana	859	1.39%	18	Missouri	1,056	1.71%
41	Maine	341	0.55%	19	Arizona	992	1.60%
6	Maryland	2,619	4.24%	20	Connecticut	986	1.59%
8	Massachusetts	2,304	3.73%	21	Colorado	971	1.57%
9	Michigan	2,136	3.45%	22	Washington	922	1.49%
36	Minnesota	474	0.77%	23	Tennessee	865	1.40%
33	Mississippi	523	0.85%	24	Louisiana	859	1.39%
18	Missouri	1,056	1.71%	25	Oregon	824	1.33%
39	Montana	390	0.63%	26	Oklahoma	795	1.29%
35	Nebraska	486	0.79%	27	West Virginia	765	1.24%
40	Nevada	356	0.58%	28	Alabama	745	1.20%
43	New Hampshire	287	0.46%	29	Wisconsin	723	1.17%
5	New Jersey	2,650	4.29%	30	Kansas	664	1.07%
37	New Mexico	435	0.70%	31	Delaware	650	1.05%
3	New York	4,017	6.50%	32	Iowa	614	0.99%
10	North Carolina	2,027	3.28%	33	Mississippi	523	0.85%
49	North Dakota	117	0.19%	34	Arkansas	513	0.83%
16	Ohio	1,352	2.19%	35	Nebraska	486	0.79%
26	Oklahoma	795	1.29%	36	Minnesota	474	0.77%
25	Oregon	824	1.33%	37	New Mexico	435	0.70%
2	Pennsylvania	4,332	7.01%	38	Utah	404	0.65%
45	Rhode Island	239	0.39%	39	Montana	390	0.63%
14	South Carolina	1,355	2.19%	40	Nevada	356	0.58%
48	South Dakota	145	0.23%	41	Maine	341	0.55%
23	Tennessee	865	1.40%	42	Alaska	317	0.51%
4	Texas	2,797	4.52%	43	New Hampshire	287	0.46%
38	Utah	404	0.65%	44	Vermont	282	0.46%
44	Vermont	282	0.46%	45	Rhode Island	239	0.39%
11	Virginia	1,947	3.15%	46	Idaho	221	0.36%
22	Washington	922	1.49%	47	Wyoming	151	0.24%
27	West Virginia	765	1.24%	48	South Dakota	145	0.23%
29	Wisconsin	723	1.17%	49	North Dakota	117	0.19%
47	Wyoming	151	0.24%	50	Hawaii	0	0.00%
					District of Columbia	0	0.00%

Source: Federal Bureau of Investigation
"Crime in the United States 1996" (Uniform Crime Reports, October 4, 1997)
*Includes state police agencies and other agencies with law enforcement powers. Hawaii and the District of Columbia do not have a state police agency.

Male State Government Law Enforcement Officers in 1996

National Total = 57,684 Male Officers*

<table>
<tr><td colspan="4">ALPHA ORDER</td><td colspan="4">RANK ORDER</td></tr>
<tr><th>RANK</th><th>STATE</th><th>OFFICERS</th><th>% of USA</th><th>RANK</th><th>STATE</th><th>OFFICERS</th><th>% of USA</th></tr>
<tr><td>28</td><td>Alabama</td><td>727</td><td>1.26%</td><td>1</td><td>California</td><td>6,726</td><td>11.66%</td></tr>
<tr><td>42</td><td>Alaska</td><td>299</td><td>0.52%</td><td>2</td><td>Pennsylvania</td><td>4,161</td><td>7.21%</td></tr>
<tr><td>19</td><td>Arizona</td><td>926</td><td>1.61%</td><td>3</td><td>New York</td><td>3,702</td><td>6.42%</td></tr>
<tr><td>34</td><td>Arkansas</td><td>491</td><td>0.85%</td><td>4</td><td>Texas</td><td>2,669</td><td>4.63%</td></tr>
<tr><td>1</td><td>California</td><td>6,726</td><td>11.66%</td><td>5</td><td>New Jersey</td><td>2,574</td><td>4.46%</td></tr>
<tr><td>21</td><td>Colorado</td><td>908</td><td>1.57%</td><td>6</td><td>Illinois</td><td>2,372</td><td>4.11%</td></tr>
<tr><td>20</td><td>Connecticut</td><td>921</td><td>1.60%</td><td>7</td><td>Maryland</td><td>2,322</td><td>4.03%</td></tr>
<tr><td>31</td><td>Delaware</td><td>597</td><td>1.03%</td><td>8</td><td>Massachusetts</td><td>2,079</td><td>3.60%</td></tr>
<tr><td>13</td><td>Florida</td><td>1,511</td><td>2.62%</td><td>9</td><td>North Carolina</td><td>1,942</td><td>3.37%</td></tr>
<tr><td>12</td><td>Georgia</td><td>1,717</td><td>2.98%</td><td>10</td><td>Virginia</td><td>1,861</td><td>3.23%</td></tr>
<tr><td>50</td><td>Hawaii</td><td>0</td><td>0.00%</td><td>11</td><td>Michigan</td><td>1,849</td><td>3.21%</td></tr>
<tr><td>46</td><td>Idaho</td><td>211</td><td>0.37%</td><td>12</td><td>Georgia</td><td>1,717</td><td>2.98%</td></tr>
<tr><td>6</td><td>Illinois</td><td>2,372</td><td>4.11%</td><td>13</td><td>Florida</td><td>1,511</td><td>2.62%</td></tr>
<tr><td>17</td><td>Indiana</td><td>1,182</td><td>2.05%</td><td>14</td><td>Kentucky</td><td>1,309</td><td>2.27%</td></tr>
<tr><td>32</td><td>Iowa</td><td>581</td><td>1.01%</td><td>15</td><td>South Carolina</td><td>1,256</td><td>2.18%</td></tr>
<tr><td>29</td><td>Kansas</td><td>648</td><td>1.12%</td><td>16</td><td>Ohio</td><td>1,241</td><td>2.15%</td></tr>
<tr><td>14</td><td>Kentucky</td><td>1,309</td><td>2.27%</td><td>17</td><td>Indiana</td><td>1,182</td><td>2.05%</td></tr>
<tr><td>23</td><td>Louisiana</td><td>839</td><td>1.45%</td><td>18</td><td>Missouri</td><td>1,023</td><td>1.77%</td></tr>
<tr><td>41</td><td>Maine</td><td>324</td><td>0.56%</td><td>19</td><td>Arizona</td><td>926</td><td>1.61%</td></tr>
<tr><td>7</td><td>Maryland</td><td>2,322</td><td>4.03%</td><td>20</td><td>Connecticut</td><td>921</td><td>1.60%</td></tr>
<tr><td>8</td><td>Massachusetts</td><td>2,079</td><td>3.60%</td><td>21</td><td>Colorado</td><td>908</td><td>1.57%</td></tr>
<tr><td>11</td><td>Michigan</td><td>1,849</td><td>3.21%</td><td>22</td><td>Washington</td><td>881</td><td>1.53%</td></tr>
<tr><td>36</td><td>Minnesota</td><td>443</td><td>0.77%</td><td>23</td><td>Louisiana</td><td>839</td><td>1.45%</td></tr>
<tr><td>33</td><td>Mississippi</td><td>515</td><td>0.89%</td><td>24</td><td>Tennessee</td><td>815</td><td>1.41%</td></tr>
<tr><td>18</td><td>Missouri</td><td>1,023</td><td>1.77%</td><td>25</td><td>Oklahoma</td><td>783</td><td>1.36%</td></tr>
<tr><td>39</td><td>Montana</td><td>372</td><td>0.64%</td><td>26</td><td>Oregon</td><td>766</td><td>1.33%</td></tr>
<tr><td>35</td><td>Nebraska</td><td>466</td><td>0.81%</td><td>27</td><td>West Virginia</td><td>747</td><td>1.29%</td></tr>
<tr><td>40</td><td>Nevada</td><td>333</td><td>0.58%</td><td>28</td><td>Alabama</td><td>727</td><td>1.26%</td></tr>
<tr><td>44</td><td>New Hampshire</td><td>260</td><td>0.45%</td><td>29</td><td>Kansas</td><td>648</td><td>1.12%</td></tr>
<tr><td>5</td><td>New Jersey</td><td>2,574</td><td>4.46%</td><td>30</td><td>Wisconsin</td><td>638</td><td>1.11%</td></tr>
<tr><td>37</td><td>New Mexico</td><td>423</td><td>0.73%</td><td>31</td><td>Delaware</td><td>597</td><td>1.03%</td></tr>
<tr><td>3</td><td>New York</td><td>3,702</td><td>6.42%</td><td>32</td><td>Iowa</td><td>581</td><td>1.01%</td></tr>
<tr><td>9</td><td>North Carolina</td><td>1,942</td><td>3.37%</td><td>33</td><td>Mississippi</td><td>515</td><td>0.89%</td></tr>
<tr><td>49</td><td>North Dakota</td><td>114</td><td>0.20%</td><td>34</td><td>Arkansas</td><td>491</td><td>0.85%</td></tr>
<tr><td>16</td><td>Ohio</td><td>1,241</td><td>2.15%</td><td>35</td><td>Nebraska</td><td>466</td><td>0.81%</td></tr>
<tr><td>25</td><td>Oklahoma</td><td>783</td><td>1.36%</td><td>36</td><td>Minnesota</td><td>443</td><td>0.77%</td></tr>
<tr><td>26</td><td>Oregon</td><td>766</td><td>1.33%</td><td>37</td><td>New Mexico</td><td>423</td><td>0.73%</td></tr>
<tr><td>2</td><td>Pennsylvania</td><td>4,161</td><td>7.21%</td><td>38</td><td>Utah</td><td>381</td><td>0.66%</td></tr>
<tr><td>45</td><td>Rhode Island</td><td>219</td><td>0.38%</td><td>39</td><td>Montana</td><td>372</td><td>0.64%</td></tr>
<tr><td>15</td><td>South Carolina</td><td>1,256</td><td>2.18%</td><td>40</td><td>Nevada</td><td>333</td><td>0.58%</td></tr>
<tr><td>48</td><td>South Dakota</td><td>143</td><td>0.25%</td><td>41</td><td>Maine</td><td>324</td><td>0.56%</td></tr>
<tr><td>24</td><td>Tennessee</td><td>815</td><td>1.41%</td><td>42</td><td>Alaska</td><td>299</td><td>0.52%</td></tr>
<tr><td>4</td><td>Texas</td><td>2,669</td><td>4.63%</td><td>43</td><td>Vermont</td><td>267</td><td>0.46%</td></tr>
<tr><td>38</td><td>Utah</td><td>381</td><td>0.66%</td><td>44</td><td>New Hampshire</td><td>260</td><td>0.45%</td></tr>
<tr><td>43</td><td>Vermont</td><td>267</td><td>0.46%</td><td>45</td><td>Rhode Island</td><td>219</td><td>0.38%</td></tr>
<tr><td>10</td><td>Virginia</td><td>1,861</td><td>3.23%</td><td>46</td><td>Idaho</td><td>211</td><td>0.37%</td></tr>
<tr><td>22</td><td>Washington</td><td>881</td><td>1.53%</td><td>47</td><td>Wyoming</td><td>150</td><td>0.26%</td></tr>
<tr><td>27</td><td>West Virginia</td><td>747</td><td>1.29%</td><td>48</td><td>South Dakota</td><td>143</td><td>0.25%</td></tr>
<tr><td>30</td><td>Wisconsin</td><td>638</td><td>1.11%</td><td>49</td><td>North Dakota</td><td>114</td><td>0.20%</td></tr>
<tr><td>47</td><td>Wyoming</td><td>150</td><td>0.26%</td><td>50</td><td>Hawaii</td><td>0</td><td>0.00%</td></tr>
<tr><td></td><td></td><td></td><td></td><td></td><td>District of Columbia</td><td>0</td><td>0.00%</td></tr>
</table>

Source: Federal Bureau of Investigation
"Crime in the United States 1996" (Uniform Crime Reports, October 4, 1997)
*Includes state police agencies and other agencies with law enforcement powers. Hawaii and the District of Columbia do not have a state police agency.

Female State Government Law Enforcement Officers in 1996

National Total = 4,153 Female Officers*

ALPHA ORDER

RANK	STATE	OFFICERS	% of USA
36	Alabama	18	0.43%
36	Alaska	18	0.43%
17	Arizona	66	1.59%
32	Arkansas	22	0.53%
1	California	731	17.60%
19	Colorado	63	1.52%
18	Connecticut	65	1.57%
22	Delaware	53	1.28%
7	Florida	185	4.45%
9	Georgia	141	3.40%
50	Hawaii	0	0.00%
45	Idaho	10	0.24%
6	Illinois	208	5.01%
20	Indiana	62	1.49%
26	Iowa	33	0.79%
41	Kansas	16	0.39%
24	Kentucky	45	1.08%
33	Louisiana	20	0.48%
40	Maine	17	0.41%
3	Maryland	297	7.15%
5	Massachusetts	225	5.42%
4	Michigan	287	6.91%
28	Minnesota	31	0.75%
46	Mississippi	8	0.19%
26	Missouri	33	0.79%
36	Montana	18	0.43%
33	Nebraska	20	0.48%
30	Nevada	23	0.55%
29	New Hampshire	27	0.65%
16	New Jersey	76	1.83%
43	New Mexico	12	0.29%
2	New York	315	7.58%
14	North Carolina	85	2.05%
47	North Dakota	3	0.07%
11	Ohio	111	2.67%
43	Oklahoma	12	0.29%
21	Oregon	58	1.40%
8	Pennsylvania	171	4.12%
33	Rhode Island	20	0.48%
12	South Carolina	99	2.38%
48	South Dakota	2	0.05%
23	Tennessee	50	1.20%
10	Texas	128	3.08%
30	Utah	23	0.55%
42	Vermont	15	0.36%
13	Virginia	86	2.07%
25	Washington	41	0.99%
36	West Virginia	18	0.43%
14	Wisconsin	85	2.05%
49	Wyoming	1	0.02%

RANK ORDER

RANK	STATE	OFFICERS	% of USA
1	California	731	17.60%
2	New York	315	7.58%
3	Maryland	297	7.15%
4	Michigan	287	6.91%
5	Massachusetts	225	5.42%
6	Illinois	208	5.01%
7	Florida	185	4.45%
8	Pennsylvania	171	4.12%
9	Georgia	141	3.40%
10	Texas	128	3.08%
11	Ohio	111	2.67%
12	South Carolina	99	2.38%
13	Virginia	86	2.07%
14	North Carolina	85	2.05%
14	Wisconsin	85	2.05%
16	New Jersey	76	1.83%
17	Arizona	66	1.59%
18	Connecticut	65	1.57%
19	Colorado	63	1.52%
20	Indiana	62	1.49%
21	Oregon	58	1.40%
22	Delaware	53	1.28%
23	Tennessee	50	1.20%
24	Kentucky	45	1.08%
25	Washington	41	0.99%
26	Iowa	33	0.79%
26	Missouri	33	0.79%
28	Minnesota	31	0.75%
29	New Hampshire	27	0.65%
30	Nevada	23	0.55%
30	Utah	23	0.55%
32	Arkansas	22	0.53%
33	Louisiana	20	0.48%
33	Nebraska	20	0.48%
33	Rhode Island	20	0.48%
36	Alabama	18	0.43%
36	Alaska	18	0.43%
36	Montana	18	0.43%
36	West Virginia	18	0.43%
40	Maine	17	0.41%
41	Kansas	16	0.39%
42	Vermont	15	0.36%
43	New Mexico	12	0.29%
43	Oklahoma	12	0.29%
45	Idaho	10	0.24%
46	Mississippi	8	0.19%
47	North Dakota	3	0.07%
48	South Dakota	2	0.05%
49	Wyoming	1	0.02%
50	Hawaii	0	0.00%
	District of Columbia	0	0.00%

Source: Federal Bureau of Investigation
"Crime in the United States 1996" (Uniform Crime Reports, October 4, 1997)
*Includes state police agencies and other agencies with law enforcement powers. Hawaii and the District of Columbia do not have a state police agency.

Female State Government Law Enforcement Officers
As a Percent of All Officers: 1996
National Percent = 6.7% of Officers*

ALPHA ORDER

RANK ORDER

RANK	STATE	PERCENT	RANK	STATE	PERCENT
42	Alabama	2.4	1	Michigan	13.4
22	Alaska	5.7	2	Wisconsin	11.8
16	Arizona	6.7	3	Maryland	11.3
33	Arkansas	4.3	4	Florida	10.9
5	California	9.8	5	California	9.8
18	Colorado	6.5	5	Massachusetts	9.8
17	Connecticut	6.6	7	New Hampshire	9.4
9	Delaware	8.2	8	Rhode Island	8.4
4	Florida	10.9	9	Delaware	8.2
13	Georgia	7.6	9	Ohio	8.2
NA	Hawaii**	NA	11	Illinois	8.1
30	Idaho	4.5	12	New York	7.8
11	Illinois	8.1	13	Georgia	7.6
26	Indiana	5.0	14	South Carolina	7.3
24	Iowa	5.4	15	Oregon	7.0
42	Kansas	2.4	16	Arizona	6.7
37	Kentucky	3.3	17	Connecticut	6.6
45	Louisiana	2.3	18	Colorado	6.5
26	Maine	5.0	18	Minnesota	6.5
3	Maryland	11.3	18	Nevada	6.5
5	Massachusetts	9.8	21	Tennessee	5.8
1	Michigan	13.4	22	Alaska	5.7
18	Minnesota	6.5	22	Utah	5.7
46	Mississippi	1.5	24	Iowa	5.4
38	Missouri	3.1	25	Vermont	5.3
28	Montana	4.6	26	Indiana	5.0
35	Nebraska	4.1	26	Maine	5.0
18	Nevada	6.5	28	Montana	4.6
7	New Hampshire	9.4	28	Texas	4.6
39	New Jersey	2.9	30	Idaho	4.5
40	New Mexico	2.8	31	Virginia	4.4
12	New York	7.8	31	Washington	4.4
34	North Carolina	4.2	33	Arkansas	4.3
41	North Dakota	2.6	34	North Carolina	4.2
9	Ohio	8.2	35	Nebraska	4.1
46	Oklahoma	1.5	36	Pennsylvania	3.9
15	Oregon	7.0	37	Kentucky	3.3
36	Pennsylvania	3.9	38	Missouri	3.1
8	Rhode Island	8.4	39	New Jersey	2.9
14	South Carolina	7.3	40	New Mexico	2.8
48	South Dakota	1.4	41	North Dakota	2.6
21	Tennessee	5.8	42	Alabama	2.4
28	Texas	4.6	42	Kansas	2.4
22	Utah	5.7	42	West Virginia	2.4
25	Vermont	5.3	45	Louisiana	2.3
31	Virginia	4.4	46	Mississippi	1.5
31	Washington	4.4	46	Oklahoma	1.5
42	West Virginia	2.4	48	South Dakota	1.4
2	Wisconsin	11.8	49	Wyoming	0.7
49	Wyoming	0.7	NA	Hawaii**	NA
				District of Columbia**	NA

Source: Morgan Quitno Press using data from Federal Bureau of Investigation
    "Crime in the United States 1996" (Uniform Crime Reports, October 4, 1997)
*Includes state police agencies and other agencies with law enforcement powers.
**Hawaii and the District of Columbia do not have a state police agency.

Local Police Departments in 1992

National Total = 12,502 Departments*

ALPHA ORDER

RANK	STATE	DEPARTMENTS	% of USA
18	Alabama	285	2.28%
46	Alaska	43	0.34%
40	Arizona	75	0.60%
28	Arkansas	185	1.48%
12	California	341	2.73%
32	Colorado	140	1.12%
35	Connecticut	108	0.86%
48	Delaware	33	0.26%
18	Florida	285	2.28%
11	Georgia	343	2.74%
50	Hawaii	4	0.03%
42	Idaho	66	0.53%
3	Illinois	748	5.98%
14	Indiana	336	2.69%
16	Iowa	321	2.57%
22	Kansas	221	1.77%
21	Kentucky	240	1.92%
20	Louisiana	256	2.05%
34	Maine	119	0.95%
38	Maryland	78	0.62%
12	Massachusetts	341	2.73%
6	Michigan	474	3.79%
10	Minnesota	359	2.87%
26	Mississippi	189	1.51%
7	Missouri	463	3.70%
43	Montana	59	0.47%
31	Nebraska	149	1.19%
49	Nevada	14	0.11%
23	New Hampshire	214	1.71%
5	New Jersey	488	3.90%
41	New Mexico	72	0.58%
7	New York	463	3.70%
15	North Carolina	332	2.66%
39	North Dakota	76	0.61%
2	Ohio	776	6.21%
17	Oklahoma	312	2.50%
33	Oregon	137	1.10%
1	Pennsylvania	1,049	8.39%
47	Rhode Island	39	0.31%
27	South Carolina	188	1.50%
36	South Dakota	102	0.82%
24	Tennessee	211	1.69%
4	Texas	632	5.06%
37	Utah	84	0.67%
44	Vermont	57	0.46%
29	Virginia	167	1.34%
25	Washington	202	1.62%
30	West Virginia	158	1.26%
9	Wisconsin	417	3.34%
45	Wyoming	50	0.40%

RANK ORDER

RANK	STATE	DEPARTMENTS	% of USA
1	Pennsylvania	1,049	8.39%
2	Ohio	776	6.21%
3	Illinois	748	5.98%
4	Texas	632	5.06%
5	New Jersey	488	3.90%
6	Michigan	474	3.79%
7	Missouri	463	3.70%
7	New York	463	3.70%
9	Wisconsin	417	3.34%
10	Minnesota	359	2.87%
11	Georgia	343	2.74%
12	California	341	2.73%
12	Massachusetts	341	2.73%
14	Indiana	336	2.69%
15	North Carolina	332	2.66%
16	Iowa	321	2.57%
17	Oklahoma	312	2.50%
18	Alabama	285	2.28%
18	Florida	285	2.28%
20	Louisiana	256	2.05%
21	Kentucky	240	1.92%
22	Kansas	221	1.77%
23	New Hampshire	214	1.71%
24	Tennessee	211	1.69%
25	Washington	202	1.62%
26	Mississippi	189	1.51%
27	South Carolina	188	1.50%
28	Arkansas	185	1.48%
29	Virginia	167	1.34%
30	West Virginia	158	1.26%
31	Nebraska	149	1.19%
32	Colorado	140	1.12%
33	Oregon	137	1.10%
34	Maine	119	0.95%
35	Connecticut	108	0.86%
36	South Dakota	102	0.82%
37	Utah	84	0.67%
38	Maryland	78	0.62%
39	North Dakota	76	0.61%
40	Arizona	75	0.60%
41	New Mexico	72	0.58%
42	Idaho	66	0.53%
43	Montana	59	0.47%
44	Vermont	57	0.46%
45	Wyoming	50	0.40%
46	Alaska	43	0.34%
47	Rhode Island	39	0.31%
48	Delaware	33	0.26%
49	Nevada	14	0.11%
50	Hawaii	4	0.03%
	District of Columbia	1	0.01%

Source: U.S. Department of Justice, Bureau of Justice Statistics
   "Census of State and Local Law Enforcement Agencies, 1992" (Bulletin, July 1993, NCJ-142972)
*Includes consolidated police-sheriffs' departments.

Full-Time Officers in Local Police Departments in 1992

National Total = 373,061 Officers*

ALPHA ORDER				RANK ORDER			
RANK	STATE	OFFICERS	% of USA	RANK	STATE	OFFICERS	% of USA
20	Alabama	5,640	1.51%	1	New York	45,822	12.28%
45	Alaska	677	0.18%	2	California	33,191	8.90%
22	Arizona	5,209	1.40%	3	Illinois	24,988	6.70%
34	Arkansas	2,494	0.67%	4	Texas	24,576	6.59%
2	California	33,191	8.90%	5	New Jersey	19,221	5.15%
23	Colorado	4,787	1.28%	6	Florida	18,037	4.83%
18	Connecticut	6,068	1.63%	7	Pennsylvania	17,256	4.63%
44	Delaware	887	0.24%	8	Ohio	14,668	3.93%
6	Florida	18,037	4.83%	9	Michigan	13,027	3.49%
11	Georgia	9,404	2.52%	10	Massachusetts	12,087	3.24%
33	Hawaii	2,690	0.72%	11	Georgia	9,404	2.52%
43	Idaho	921	0.25%	12	Maryland	8,273	2.22%
3	Illinois	24,988	6.70%	13	Virginia	8,205	2.20%
19	Indiana	5,992	1.61%	14	North Carolina	8,023	2.15%
30	Iowa	2,863	0.77%	15	Missouri	7,921	2.12%
29	Kansas	3,189	0.85%	16	Wisconsin	7,184	1.93%
27	Kentucky	3,804	1.02%	17	Tennessee	6,214	1.67%
21	Louisiana	5,548	1.49%	18	Connecticut	6,068	1.63%
41	Maine	1,399	0.38%	19	Indiana	5,992	1.61%
12	Maryland	8,273	2.22%	20	Alabama	5,640	1.51%
10	Massachusetts	12,087	3.24%	21	Louisiana	5,548	1.49%
9	Michigan	13,027	3.49%	22	Arizona	5,209	1.40%
25	Minnesota	4,580	1.23%	23	Colorado	4,787	1.28%
32	Mississippi	2,745	0.74%	24	Washington	4,704	1.26%
15	Missouri	7,921	2.12%	25	Minnesota	4,580	1.23%
49	Montana	568	0.15%	26	Oklahoma	4,529	1.21%
38	Nebraska	1,720	0.46%	27	Kentucky	3,804	1.02%
37	Nevada	1,795	0.48%	28	South Carolina	3,481	0.93%
39	New Hampshire	1,717	0.46%	29	Kansas	3,189	0.85%
5	New Jersey	19,221	5.15%	30	Iowa	2,863	0.77%
35	New Mexico	2,092	0.56%	31	Oregon	2,782	0.75%
1	New York	45,822	12.28%	32	Mississippi	2,745	0.74%
14	North Carolina	8,023	2.15%	33	Hawaii	2,690	0.72%
50	North Dakota	538	0.14%	34	Arkansas	2,494	0.67%
8	Ohio	14,668	3.93%	35	New Mexico	2,092	0.56%
26	Oklahoma	4,529	1.21%	36	Rhode Island	2,024	0.54%
31	Oregon	2,782	0.75%	37	Nevada	1,795	0.48%
7	Pennsylvania	17,256	4.63%	38	Nebraska	1,720	0.46%
36	Rhode Island	2,024	0.54%	39	New Hampshire	1,717	0.46%
28	South Carolina	3,481	0.93%	40	Utah	1,546	0.41%
46	South Dakota	648	0.17%	41	Maine	1,399	0.38%
17	Tennessee	6,214	1.67%	42	West Virginia	1,260	0.34%
4	Texas	24,576	6.59%	43	Idaho	921	0.25%
40	Utah	1,546	0.41%	44	Delaware	887	0.24%
47	Vermont	594	0.16%	45	Alaska	677	0.18%
13	Virginia	8,205	2.20%	46	South Dakota	648	0.17%
24	Washington	4,704	1.26%	47	Vermont	594	0.16%
42	West Virginia	1,260	0.34%	48	Wyoming	584	0.16%
16	Wisconsin	7,184	1.93%	49	Montana	568	0.15%
48	Wyoming	584	0.16%	50	North Dakota	538	0.14%
					District of Columbia	4,889	1.31%

Source: U.S. Department of Justice, Bureau of Justice Statistics
"Census of State and Local Law Enforcement Agencies, 1992" (Bulletin, July 1993, NCJ-142972)
*Includes consolidated police-sheriffs' departments.

Percent of Full-Time Local Police Department Employees Who Are Sworn Officers: 1992
National Percent = 78.33% of Employees*

ALPHA ORDER				RANK ORDER		
RANK	STATE	PERCENT		RANK	STATE	PERCENT
31	Alabama	77.31		1	Pennsylvania	86.68
49	Alaska	63.21		2	Massachusetts	85.02
44	Arizona	72.57		3	Delaware	84.72
32	Arkansas	76.46		4	New Jersey	84.33
46	California	70.70		5	Connecticut	83.86
42	Colorado	74.27		6	Michigan	83.31
5	Connecticut	83.86		7	Minnesota	83.18
3	Delaware	84.72		8	West Virginia	82.51
47	Florida	70.46		9	Rhode Island	82.41
40	Georgia	75.09		10	Iowa	82.36
25	Hawaii	79.49		11	Utah	82.15
23	Idaho	80.02		12	Louisiana	82.07
18	Illinois	80.68		13	North Carolina	81.83
33	Indiana	76.20		14	Ohio	81.78
10	Iowa	82.36		15	Wisconsin	81.68
36	Kansas	75.66		16	Maryland	81.46
20	Kentucky	80.58		17	New York	81.24
12	Louisiana	82.07		18	Illinois	80.68
26	Maine	79.22		19	South Dakota	80.60
16	Maryland	81.46		20	Kentucky	80.58
2	Massachusetts	85.02		21	South Carolina	80.52
6	Michigan	83.31		22	Nebraska	80.11
7	Minnesota	83.18		23	Idaho	80.02
37	Mississippi	75.56		24	North Dakota	79.82
33	Missouri	76.20		25	Hawaii	79.49
30	Montana	77.49		26	Maine	79.22
22	Nebraska	80.11		27	Vermont	78.99
50	Nevada	56.54		28	New Hampshire	78.37
28	New Hampshire	78.37		29	Virginia	77.93
4	New Jersey	84.33		30	Montana	77.49
48	New Mexico	69.66		31	Alabama	77.31
17	New York	81.24		32	Arkansas	76.46
13	North Carolina	81.83		33	Indiana	76.20
24	North Dakota	79.82		33	Missouri	76.20
14	Ohio	81.78		35	Tennessee	75.74
39	Oklahoma	75.13		36	Kansas	75.66
45	Oregon	71.65		37	Mississippi	75.56
1	Pennsylvania	86.68		38	Washington	75.31
9	Rhode Island	82.41		39	Oklahoma	75.13
21	South Carolina	80.52		40	Georgia	75.09
19	South Dakota	80.60		41	Texas	74.34
35	Tennessee	75.74		42	Colorado	74.27
41	Texas	74.34		43	Wyoming	73.09
11	Utah	82.15		44	Arizona	72.57
27	Vermont	78.99		45	Oregon	71.65
29	Virginia	77.93		46	California	70.70
38	Washington	75.31		47	Florida	70.46
8	West Virginia	82.51		48	New Mexico	69.66
15	Wisconsin	81.68		49	Alaska	63.21
43	Wyoming	73.09		50	Nevada	56.54
					District of Columbia	85.03

Source: Morgan Quitno Press using data from U.S. Department of Justice, Bureau of Justice Statistics "Census of State and Local Law Enforcement Agencies, 1992" (Bulletin, July 1993, NCJ-142972)
*Includes consolidated police-sheriffs' departments.

Rate of Full-Time Officers in Local Police Departments in 1992

National Rate = 14.63 Officers per 10,000 Population*

RANK	STATE	RATE	RANK	STATE	RATE
18	Alabama	13.64	1	New York	25.29
31	Alaska	11.53	2	New Jersey	24.68
19	Arizona	13.59	3	Hawaii	23.19
38	Arkansas	10.40	4	Illinois	21.48
33	California	10.75	5	Massachusetts	20.15
16	Colorado	13.80	6	Rhode Island	20.14
7	Connecticut	18.49	7	Connecticut	18.49
25	Delaware	12.87	8	Maryland	16.86
21	Florida	13.37	9	New Hampshire	15.45
14	Georgia	13.93	10	Missouri	15.25
3	Hawaii	23.19	11	Pennsylvania	14.37
46	Idaho	8.63	12	Wisconsin	14.35
4	Illinois	21.48	13	Oklahoma	14.10
35	Indiana	10.58	14	Georgia	13.93
40	Iowa	10.18	15	Texas	13.92
27	Kansas	12.64	16	Colorado	13.80
41	Kentucky	10.13	16	Michigan	13.80
24	Louisiana	12.94	18	Alabama	13.64
32	Maine	11.33	19	Arizona	13.59
8	Maryland	16.86	20	Nevada	13.53
5	Massachusetts	20.15	21	Florida	13.37
16	Michigan	13.80	22	Ohio	13.32
39	Minnesota	10.22	23	New Mexico	13.23
36	Mississippi	10.50	24	Louisiana	12.94
10	Missouri	15.25	25	Delaware	12.87
50	Montana	6.89	25	Virginia	12.87
34	Nebraska	10.71	27	Kansas	12.64
20	Nevada	13.53	28	Wyoming	12.53
9	New Hampshire	15.45	29	Tennessee	12.37
2	New Jersey	24.68	30	North Carolina	11.72
23	New Mexico	13.23	31	Alaska	11.53
1	New York	25.29	32	Maine	11.33
30	North Carolina	11.72	33	California	10.75
48	North Dakota	8.46	34	Nebraska	10.71
22	Ohio	13.32	35	Indiana	10.58
13	Oklahoma	14.10	36	Mississippi	10.50
43	Oregon	9.34	37	Vermont	10.42
11	Pennsylvania	14.37	38	Arkansas	10.40
6	Rhode Island	20.14	39	Minnesota	10.22
42	South Carolina	9.66	40	Iowa	10.18
45	South Dakota	9.11	41	Kentucky	10.13
29	Tennessee	12.37	42	South Carolina	9.66
15	Texas	13.92	43	Oregon	9.34
47	Utah	8.53	44	Washington	9.16
37	Vermont	10.42	45	South Dakota	9.11
25	Virginia	12.87	46	Idaho	8.63
44	Washington	9.16	47	Utah	8.53
49	West Virginia	6.95	48	North Dakota	8.46
12	Wisconsin	14.35	49	West Virginia	6.95
28	Wyoming	12.53	50	Montana	6.89
				District of Columbia	83.01

Source: Morgan Quitno Press using data from U.S. Department of Justice, Bureau of Justice Statistics
  "Census of State and Local Law Enforcement Agencies, 1992" (Bulletin, July 1993, NCJ-142972)
*Includes consolidated police-sheriffs' departments.

Full-Time Employees in Local Police Departments in 1992

National Total = 476,261 Employees*

<table>
<thead>
<tr><th colspan="4">ALPHA ORDER</th><th colspan="4">RANK ORDER</th></tr>
<tr><th>RANK</th><th>STATE</th><th>EMPLOYEES</th><th>% of USA</th><th>RANK</th><th>STATE</th><th>EMPLOYEES</th><th>% of USA</th></tr>
</thead>
<tbody>
<tr><td>19</td><td>Alabama</td><td>7,295</td><td>1.53%</td><td>1</td><td>New York</td><td>56,406</td><td>11.84%</td></tr>
<tr><td>44</td><td>Alaska</td><td>1,071</td><td>0.22%</td><td>2</td><td>California</td><td>46,947</td><td>9.86%</td></tr>
<tr><td>21</td><td>Arizona</td><td>7,178</td><td>1.51%</td><td>3</td><td>Texas</td><td>33,059</td><td>6.94%</td></tr>
<tr><td>34</td><td>Arkansas</td><td>3,262</td><td>0.68%</td><td>4</td><td>Illinois</td><td>30,971</td><td>6.50%</td></tr>
<tr><td>2</td><td>California</td><td>46,947</td><td>9.86%</td><td>5</td><td>Florida</td><td>25,598</td><td>5.37%</td></tr>
<tr><td>23</td><td>Colorado</td><td>6,445</td><td>1.35%</td><td>6</td><td>New Jersey</td><td>22,793</td><td>4.79%</td></tr>
<tr><td>20</td><td>Connecticut</td><td>7,236</td><td>1.52%</td><td>7</td><td>Pennsylvania</td><td>19,907</td><td>4.18%</td></tr>
<tr><td>45</td><td>Delaware</td><td>1,047</td><td>0.22%</td><td>8</td><td>Ohio</td><td>17,936</td><td>3.77%</td></tr>
<tr><td>5</td><td>Florida</td><td>25,598</td><td>5.37%</td><td>9</td><td>Michigan</td><td>15,636</td><td>3.28%</td></tr>
<tr><td>11</td><td>Georgia</td><td>12,524</td><td>2.63%</td><td>10</td><td>Massachusetts</td><td>14,217</td><td>2.99%</td></tr>
<tr><td>33</td><td>Hawaii</td><td>3,384</td><td>0.71%</td><td>11</td><td>Georgia</td><td>12,524</td><td>2.63%</td></tr>
<tr><td>43</td><td>Idaho</td><td>1,151</td><td>0.24%</td><td>12</td><td>Virginia</td><td>10,529</td><td>2.21%</td></tr>
<tr><td>4</td><td>Illinois</td><td>30,971</td><td>6.50%</td><td>13</td><td>Missouri</td><td>10,395</td><td>2.18%</td></tr>
<tr><td>18</td><td>Indiana</td><td>7,864</td><td>1.65%</td><td>14</td><td>Maryland</td><td>10,156</td><td>2.13%</td></tr>
<tr><td>32</td><td>Iowa</td><td>3,476</td><td>0.73%</td><td>15</td><td>North Carolina</td><td>9,805</td><td>2.06%</td></tr>
<tr><td>29</td><td>Kansas</td><td>4,215</td><td>0.89%</td><td>16</td><td>Wisconsin</td><td>8,795</td><td>1.85%</td></tr>
<tr><td>27</td><td>Kentucky</td><td>4,721</td><td>0.99%</td><td>17</td><td>Tennessee</td><td>8,204</td><td>1.72%</td></tr>
<tr><td>22</td><td>Louisiana</td><td>6,760</td><td>1.42%</td><td>18</td><td>Indiana</td><td>7,864</td><td>1.65%</td></tr>
<tr><td>41</td><td>Maine</td><td>1,766</td><td>0.37%</td><td>19</td><td>Alabama</td><td>7,295</td><td>1.53%</td></tr>
<tr><td>14</td><td>Maryland</td><td>10,156</td><td>2.13%</td><td>20</td><td>Connecticut</td><td>7,236</td><td>1.52%</td></tr>
<tr><td>10</td><td>Massachusetts</td><td>14,217</td><td>2.99%</td><td>21</td><td>Arizona</td><td>7,178</td><td>1.51%</td></tr>
<tr><td>9</td><td>Michigan</td><td>15,636</td><td>3.28%</td><td>22</td><td>Louisiana</td><td>6,760</td><td>1.42%</td></tr>
<tr><td>26</td><td>Minnesota</td><td>5,506</td><td>1.16%</td><td>23</td><td>Colorado</td><td>6,445</td><td>1.35%</td></tr>
<tr><td>31</td><td>Mississippi</td><td>3,633</td><td>0.76%</td><td>24</td><td>Washington</td><td>6,246</td><td>1.31%</td></tr>
<tr><td>13</td><td>Missouri</td><td>10,395</td><td>2.18%</td><td>25</td><td>Oklahoma</td><td>6,028</td><td>1.27%</td></tr>
<tr><td>49</td><td>Montana</td><td>733</td><td>0.15%</td><td>26</td><td>Minnesota</td><td>5,506</td><td>1.16%</td></tr>
<tr><td>39</td><td>Nebraska</td><td>2,147</td><td>0.45%</td><td>27</td><td>Kentucky</td><td>4,721</td><td>0.99%</td></tr>
<tr><td>35</td><td>Nevada</td><td>3,175</td><td>0.67%</td><td>28</td><td>South Carolina</td><td>4,323</td><td>0.91%</td></tr>
<tr><td>38</td><td>New Hampshire</td><td>2,191</td><td>0.46%</td><td>29</td><td>Kansas</td><td>4,215</td><td>0.89%</td></tr>
<tr><td>6</td><td>New Jersey</td><td>22,793</td><td>4.79%</td><td>30</td><td>Oregon</td><td>3,883</td><td>0.82%</td></tr>
<tr><td>36</td><td>New Mexico</td><td>3,003</td><td>0.63%</td><td>31</td><td>Mississippi</td><td>3,633</td><td>0.76%</td></tr>
<tr><td>1</td><td>New York</td><td>56,406</td><td>11.84%</td><td>32</td><td>Iowa</td><td>3,476</td><td>0.73%</td></tr>
<tr><td>15</td><td>North Carolina</td><td>9,805</td><td>2.06%</td><td>33</td><td>Hawaii</td><td>3,384</td><td>0.71%</td></tr>
<tr><td>50</td><td>North Dakota</td><td>674</td><td>0.14%</td><td>34</td><td>Arkansas</td><td>3,262</td><td>0.68%</td></tr>
<tr><td>8</td><td>Ohio</td><td>17,936</td><td>3.77%</td><td>35</td><td>Nevada</td><td>3,175</td><td>0.67%</td></tr>
<tr><td>25</td><td>Oklahoma</td><td>6,028</td><td>1.27%</td><td>36</td><td>New Mexico</td><td>3,003</td><td>0.63%</td></tr>
<tr><td>30</td><td>Oregon</td><td>3,883</td><td>0.82%</td><td>37</td><td>Rhode Island</td><td>2,456</td><td>0.52%</td></tr>
<tr><td>7</td><td>Pennsylvania</td><td>19,907</td><td>4.18%</td><td>38</td><td>New Hampshire</td><td>2,191</td><td>0.46%</td></tr>
<tr><td>37</td><td>Rhode Island</td><td>2,456</td><td>0.52%</td><td>39</td><td>Nebraska</td><td>2,147</td><td>0.45%</td></tr>
<tr><td>28</td><td>South Carolina</td><td>4,323</td><td>0.91%</td><td>40</td><td>Utah</td><td>1,882</td><td>0.40%</td></tr>
<tr><td>46</td><td>South Dakota</td><td>804</td><td>0.17%</td><td>41</td><td>Maine</td><td>1,766</td><td>0.37%</td></tr>
<tr><td>17</td><td>Tennessee</td><td>8,204</td><td>1.72%</td><td>42</td><td>West Virginia</td><td>1,527</td><td>0.32%</td></tr>
<tr><td>3</td><td>Texas</td><td>33,059</td><td>6.94%</td><td>43</td><td>Idaho</td><td>1,151</td><td>0.24%</td></tr>
<tr><td>40</td><td>Utah</td><td>1,882</td><td>0.40%</td><td>44</td><td>Alaska</td><td>1,071</td><td>0.22%</td></tr>
<tr><td>48</td><td>Vermont</td><td>752</td><td>0.16%</td><td>45</td><td>Delaware</td><td>1,047</td><td>0.22%</td></tr>
<tr><td>12</td><td>Virginia</td><td>10,529</td><td>2.21%</td><td>46</td><td>South Dakota</td><td>804</td><td>0.17%</td></tr>
<tr><td>24</td><td>Washington</td><td>6,246</td><td>1.31%</td><td>47</td><td>Wyoming</td><td>799</td><td>0.17%</td></tr>
<tr><td>42</td><td>West Virginia</td><td>1,527</td><td>0.32%</td><td>48</td><td>Vermont</td><td>752</td><td>0.16%</td></tr>
<tr><td>16</td><td>Wisconsin</td><td>8,795</td><td>1.85%</td><td>49</td><td>Montana</td><td>733</td><td>0.15%</td></tr>
<tr><td>47</td><td>Wyoming</td><td>799</td><td>0.17%</td><td>50</td><td>North Dakota</td><td>674</td><td>0.14%</td></tr>
<tr><td></td><td></td><td></td><td></td><td></td><td>District of Columbia</td><td>5,750</td><td>1.21%</td></tr>
</tbody>
</table>

Source: U.S. Department of Justice, Bureau of Justice Statistics
"Census of State and Local Law Enforcement Agencies, 1992" (Bulletin, July 1993, NCJ-142972)
*Includes consolidated police-sheriffs' departments.

Sheriffs' Departments in 1992

National Total = 3,086 Departments*

RANK	STATE	DEPARTMENTS	% of USA		RANK	STATE	DEPARTMENTS	% of USA
20	Alabama	67	2.17%		1	Texas	255	8.26%
49	Alaska	0	0.00%		2	Georgia	159	5.15%
42	Arizona	15	0.49%		3	Virginia	125	4.05%
18	Arkansas	75	2.43%		4	Kentucky	120	3.89%
26	California	58	1.88%		5	Missouri	114	3.69%
25	Colorado	63	2.04%		6	Kansas	105	3.40%
46	Connecticut	8	0.26%		7	Illinois	102	3.31%
48	Delaware	3	0.10%		8	North Carolina	100	3.24%
23	Florida	65	2.11%		9	Iowa	99	3.21%
2	Georgia	159	5.15%		10	Tennessee	95	3.08%
49	Hawaii	0	0.00%		11	Nebraska	93	3.01%
32	Idaho	44	1.43%		12	Indiana	91	2.95%
7	Illinois	102	3.31%		13	Ohio	88	2.85%
12	Indiana	91	2.95%		14	Minnesota	87	2.82%
9	Iowa	99	3.21%		15	Michigan	83	2.69%
6	Kansas	105	3.40%		16	Mississippi	82	2.66%
4	Kentucky	120	3.89%		17	Oklahoma	77	2.50%
24	Louisiana	64	2.07%		18	Arkansas	75	2.43%
40	Maine	16	0.52%		19	Wisconsin	72	2.33%
37	Maryland	24	0.78%		20	Alabama	67	2.17%
43	Massachusetts	14	0.45%		21	Pennsylvania	66	2.14%
15	Michigan	83	2.69%		21	South Dakota	66	2.14%
14	Minnesota	87	2.82%		23	Florida	65	2.11%
16	Mississippi	82	2.66%		24	Louisiana	64	2.07%
5	Missouri	114	3.69%		25	Colorado	63	2.04%
28	Montana	55	1.78%		26	California	58	1.88%
11	Nebraska	93	3.01%		27	New York	57	1.85%
40	Nevada	16	0.52%		28	Montana	55	1.78%
45	New Hampshire	10	0.32%		28	West Virginia	55	1.78%
39	New Jersey	21	0.68%		30	North Dakota	53	1.72%
35	New Mexico	33	1.07%		31	South Carolina	46	1.49%
27	New York	57	1.85%		32	Idaho	44	1.43%
8	North Carolina	100	3.24%		33	Washington	39	1.26%
30	North Dakota	53	1.72%		34	Oregon	36	1.17%
13	Ohio	88	2.85%		35	New Mexico	33	1.07%
17	Oklahoma	77	2.50%		36	Utah	29	0.94%
34	Oregon	36	1.17%		37	Maryland	24	0.78%
21	Pennsylvania	66	2.14%		38	Wyoming	23	0.75%
47	Rhode Island	4	0.13%		39	New Jersey	21	0.68%
31	South Carolina	46	1.49%		40	Maine	16	0.52%
21	South Dakota	66	2.14%		40	Nevada	16	0.52%
10	Tennessee	95	3.08%		42	Arizona	15	0.49%
1	Texas	255	8.26%		43	Massachusetts	14	0.45%
36	Utah	29	0.94%		43	Vermont	14	0.45%
43	Vermont	14	0.45%		45	New Hampshire	10	0.32%
3	Virginia	125	4.05%		46	Connecticut	8	0.26%
33	Washington	39	1.26%		47	Rhode Island	4	0.13%
28	West Virginia	55	1.78%		48	Delaware	3	0.10%
19	Wisconsin	72	2.33%		49	Alaska	0	0.00%
38	Wyoming	23	0.75%		49	Hawaii	0	0.00%
						District of Columbia	0	0.00%

ALPHA ORDER / RANK ORDER

Source: U.S. Department of Justice, Bureau of Justice Statistics
"Census of State and Local Law Enforcement Agencies, 1992" (Bulletin, July 1993, NCJ-142972)
*Sheriffs' departments generally operate at the county level.

Full-Time Sworn Officers in Sheriffs' Departments in 1992

National Total = 136,542 Officers*

<u>ALPHA ORDER</u>

RANK	STATE	OFFICERS	% of USA
20	Alabama	1,902	1.39%
49	Alaska	0	0.00%
24	Arizona	1,427	1.05%
30	Arkansas	1,054	0.77%
1	California	22,552	16.52%
14	Colorado	3,042	2.23%
41	Connecticut	418	0.31%
48	Delaware	22	0.02%
2	Florida	11,805	8.65%
6	Georgia	5,852	4.29%
49	Hawaii	0	0.00%
32	Idaho	1,032	0.76%
5	Illinois	7,845	5.75%
17	Indiana	2,389	1.75%
27	Iowa	1,217	0.89%
23	Kansas	1,546	1.13%
31	Kentucky	1,041	0.76%
4	Louisiana	8,217	6.02%
42	Maine	367	0.27%
25	Maryland	1,348	0.99%
26	Massachusetts	1,264	0.93%
10	Michigan	3,954	2.90%
21	Minnesota	1,887	1.38%
28	Mississippi	1,107	0.81%
19	Missouri	2,071	1.52%
39	Montana	595	0.44%
37	Nebraska	769	0.56%
35	Nevada	808	0.59%
46	New Hampshire	104	0.08%
12	New Jersey	3,833	2.81%
36	New Mexico	792	0.58%
8	New York	5,039	3.69%
9	North Carolina	4,596	3.37%
43	North Dakota	348	0.25%
11	Ohio	3,870	2.83%
33	Oklahoma	842	0.62%
22	Oregon	1,691	1.24%
29	Pennsylvania	1,076	0.79%
45	Rhode Island	124	0.09%
16	South Carolina	2,494	1.83%
44	South Dakota	338	0.25%
15	Tennessee	2,866	2.10%
3	Texas	9,876	7.23%
34	Utah	818	0.60%
47	Vermont	78	0.06%
7	Virginia	5,590	4.09%
18	Washington	2,228	1.63%
38	West Virginia	651	0.48%
13	Wisconsin	3,309	2.42%
40	Wyoming	448	0.33%

<u>RANK ORDER</u>

RANK	STATE	OFFICERS	% of USA
1	California	22,552	16.52%
2	Florida	11,805	8.65%
3	Texas	9,876	7.23%
4	Louisiana	8,217	6.02%
5	Illinois	7,845	5.75%
6	Georgia	5,852	4.29%
7	Virginia	5,590	4.09%
8	New York	5,039	3.69%
9	North Carolina	4,596	3.37%
10	Michigan	3,954	2.90%
11	Ohio	3,870	2.83%
12	New Jersey	3,833	2.81%
13	Wisconsin	3,309	2.42%
14	Colorado	3,042	2.23%
15	Tennessee	2,866	2.10%
16	South Carolina	2,494	1.83%
17	Indiana	2,389	1.75%
18	Washington	2,228	1.63%
19	Missouri	2,071	1.52%
20	Alabama	1,902	1.39%
21	Minnesota	1,887	1.38%
22	Oregon	1,691	1.24%
23	Kansas	1,546	1.13%
24	Arizona	1,427	1.05%
25	Maryland	1,348	0.99%
26	Massachusetts	1,264	0.93%
27	Iowa	1,217	0.89%
28	Mississippi	1,107	0.81%
29	Pennsylvania	1,076	0.79%
30	Arkansas	1,054	0.77%
31	Kentucky	1,041	0.76%
32	Idaho	1,032	0.76%
33	Oklahoma	842	0.62%
34	Utah	818	0.60%
35	Nevada	808	0.59%
36	New Mexico	792	0.58%
37	Nebraska	769	0.56%
38	West Virginia	651	0.48%
39	Montana	595	0.44%
40	Wyoming	448	0.33%
41	Connecticut	418	0.31%
42	Maine	367	0.27%
43	North Dakota	348	0.25%
44	South Dakota	338	0.25%
45	Rhode Island	124	0.09%
46	New Hampshire	104	0.08%
47	Vermont	78	0.06%
48	Delaware	22	0.02%
49	Alaska	0	0.00%
49	Hawaii	0	0.00%
	District of Columbia	0	0.00%

Source: U.S. Department of Justice, Bureau of Justice Statistics
"Census of State and Local Law Enforcement Agencies, 1992" (Bulletin, July 1993, NCJ-142972)
*Sheriffs' departments generally operate at the county level.

Percent of Full-Time Sheriffs' Department Employees
Who Are Sworn Officers: 1992
National Percent = 60.59% of Employees*

<u>ALPHA ORDER</u>

<u>RANK ORDER</u>

RANK	STATE	PERCENT	RANK	STATE	PERCENT
24	Alabama	59.96	1	Rhode Island	99.20
NA	Alaska**	NA	2	Connecticut	98.35
48	Arizona	34.01	3	Louisiana	92.44
29	Arkansas	57.00	4	Kentucky	91.24
23	California	62.22	5	Virginia	85.34
16	Colorado	67.41	6	New Jersey	81.45
2	Connecticut	98.35	7	Missouri	79.08
31	Delaware	55.00	8	Pennsylvania	74.05
43	Florida	48.33	9	South Carolina	72.86
12	Georgia	69.82	10	Illinois	72.52
NA	Hawaii**	NA	11	Nevada	70.75
15	Idaho	68.71	12	Georgia	69.82
10	Illinois	72.52	13	Wisconsin	69.63
37	Indiana	51.92	14	North Dakota	69.18
25	Iowa	59.14	15	Idaho	68.71
20	Kansas	64.50	16	Colorado	67.41
4	Kentucky	91.24	17	New Hampshire	65.82
3	Louisiana	92.44	18	Vermont	65.55
46	Maine	40.96	19	North Carolina	64.65
36	Maryland	52.95	20	Kansas	64.50
47	Massachusetts	34.97	21	New Mexico	63.82
27	Michigan	57.63	22	Mississippi	62.61
33	Minnesota	54.44	23	California	62.22
22	Mississippi	62.61	24	Alabama	59.96
7	Missouri	79.08	25	Iowa	59.14
28	Montana	57.54	26	Nebraska	59.02
26	Nebraska	59.02	27	Michigan	57.63
11	Nevada	70.75	28	Montana	57.54
17	New Hampshire	65.82	29	Arkansas	57.00
6	New Jersey	81.45	30	South Dakota	56.05
21	New Mexico	63.82	31	Delaware	55.00
35	New York	54.28	32	Washington	54.47
19	North Carolina	64.65	33	Minnesota	54.44
14	North Dakota	69.18	34	Oregon	54.43
39	Ohio	51.45	35	New York	54.28
41	Oklahoma	48.50	36	Maryland	52.95
34	Oregon	54.43	37	Indiana	51.92
8	Pennsylvania	74.05	38	Texas	51.77
1	Rhode Island	99.20	39	Ohio	51.45
9	South Carolina	72.86	40	Wyoming	51.20
30	South Dakota	56.05	41	Oklahoma	48.50
42	Tennessee	48.35	42	Tennessee	48.35
38	Texas	51.77	43	Florida	48.33
44	Utah	47.86	44	Utah	47.86
18	Vermont	65.55	45	West Virginia	47.41
5	Virginia	85.34	46	Maine	40.96
32	Washington	54.47	47	Massachusetts	34.97
45	West Virginia	47.41	48	Arizona	34.01
13	Wisconsin	69.63	NA	Alaska**	NA
40	Wyoming	51.20	NA	Hawaii**	NA
				District of Columbia**	NA

Source: Morgan Quitno Press using data from U.S. Department of Justice, Bureau of Justice Statistics
"Census of State and Local Law Enforcement Agencies, 1992" (Bulletin, July 1993, NCJ-142972)
*Sheriffs' departments generally operate at the county level.
**Not applicable.

Rate of Full-Time Sworn Officers in Sheriffs' Departments in 1992

National Rate = 5.35 Officers per 10,000 Population*

ALPHA ORDER

RANK ORDER

RANK	STATE	RATE
24	Alabama	4.60
49	Alaska	0.00
34	Arizona	3.72
26	Arkansas	4.39
8	California	7.31
4	Colorado	8.77
44	Connecticut	1.27
48	Delaware	0.32
6	Florida	8.75
7	Georgia	8.67
49	Hawaii	0.00
2	Idaho	9.67
11	Illinois	6.74
30	Indiana	4.22
28	Iowa	4.33
14	Kansas	6.13
39	Kentucky	2.77
1	Louisiana	19.17
37	Maine	2.97
40	Maryland	2.75
42	Massachusetts	2.11
32	Michigan	4.19
31	Minnesota	4.21
29	Mississippi	4.23
33	Missouri	3.99
9	Montana	7.22
22	Nebraska	4.79
15	Nevada	6.09
46	New Hampshire	0.94
21	New Jersey	4.92
20	New Mexico	5.01
38	New York	2.78
12	North Carolina	6.72
19	North Dakota	5.47
36	Ohio	3.51
41	Oklahoma	2.62
17	Oregon	5.68
47	Pennsylvania	0.90
45	Rhode Island	1.23
10	South Carolina	6.92
23	South Dakota	4.75
16	Tennessee	5.70
18	Texas	5.59
25	Utah	4.51
43	Vermont	1.37
4	Virginia	8.77
27	Washington	4.34
35	West Virginia	3.59
13	Wisconsin	6.61
3	Wyoming	9.61

RANK	STATE	RATE
1	Louisiana	19.17
2	Idaho	9.67
3	Wyoming	9.61
4	Colorado	8.77
4	Virginia	8.77
6	Florida	8.75
7	Georgia	8.67
8	California	7.31
9	Montana	7.22
10	South Carolina	6.92
11	Illinois	6.74
12	North Carolina	6.72
13	Wisconsin	6.61
14	Kansas	6.13
15	Nevada	6.09
16	Tennessee	5.70
17	Oregon	5.68
18	Texas	5.59
19	North Dakota	5.47
20	New Mexico	5.01
21	New Jersey	4.92
22	Nebraska	4.79
23	South Dakota	4.75
24	Alabama	4.60
25	Utah	4.51
26	Arkansas	4.39
27	Washington	4.34
28	Iowa	4.33
29	Mississippi	4.23
30	Indiana	4.22
31	Minnesota	4.21
32	Michigan	4.19
33	Missouri	3.99
34	Arizona	3.72
35	West Virginia	3.59
36	Ohio	3.51
37	Maine	2.97
38	New York	2.78
39	Kentucky	2.77
40	Maryland	2.75
41	Oklahoma	2.62
42	Massachusetts	2.11
43	Vermont	1.37
44	Connecticut	1.27
45	Rhode Island	1.23
46	New Hampshire	0.94
47	Pennsylvania	0.90
48	Delaware	0.32
49	Alaska	0.00
49	Hawaii	0.00
	District of Columbia	0.00

Source: Morgan Quitno Press using data from U.S. Department of Justice, Bureau of Justice Statistics
"Census of State and Local Law Enforcement Agencies, 1992" (Bulletin, July 1993, NCJ-142972)
*Sheriffs' departments generally operate at the county level.

Full-Time Employees in Sheriffs' Departments in 1992

National Total = 225,342 Employees*

<table>
<tr><td colspan="4">ALPHA ORDER</td><td colspan="4">RANK ORDER</td></tr>
<tr><td>RANK</td><td>STATE</td><td>EMPLOYEES</td><td>% of USA</td><td>RANK</td><td>STATE</td><td>EMPLOYEES</td><td>% of USA</td></tr>
<tr><td>22</td><td>Alabama</td><td>3,172</td><td>1.41%</td><td>1</td><td>California</td><td>36,243</td><td>16.08%</td></tr>
<tr><td>49</td><td>Alaska</td><td>0</td><td>0.00%</td><td>2</td><td>Florida</td><td>24,426</td><td>10.84%</td></tr>
<tr><td>17</td><td>Arizona</td><td>4,196</td><td>1.86%</td><td>3</td><td>Texas</td><td>19,077</td><td>8.47%</td></tr>
<tr><td>28</td><td>Arkansas</td><td>1,849</td><td>0.82%</td><td>4</td><td>Illinois</td><td>10,817</td><td>4.80%</td></tr>
<tr><td>1</td><td>California</td><td>36,243</td><td>16.08%</td><td>5</td><td>New York</td><td>9,284</td><td>4.12%</td></tr>
<tr><td>16</td><td>Colorado</td><td>4,513</td><td>2.00%</td><td>6</td><td>Louisiana</td><td>8,889</td><td>3.94%</td></tr>
<tr><td>44</td><td>Connecticut</td><td>425</td><td>0.19%</td><td>7</td><td>Georgia</td><td>8,381</td><td>3.72%</td></tr>
<tr><td>48</td><td>Delaware</td><td>40</td><td>0.02%</td><td>8</td><td>Ohio</td><td>7,522</td><td>3.34%</td></tr>
<tr><td>2</td><td>Florida</td><td>24,426</td><td>10.84%</td><td>9</td><td>North Carolina</td><td>7,109</td><td>3.15%</td></tr>
<tr><td>7</td><td>Georgia</td><td>8,381</td><td>3.72%</td><td>10</td><td>Michigan</td><td>6,861</td><td>3.04%</td></tr>
<tr><td>49</td><td>Hawaii</td><td>0</td><td>0.00%</td><td>11</td><td>Virginia</td><td>6,550</td><td>2.91%</td></tr>
<tr><td>32</td><td>Idaho</td><td>1,502</td><td>0.67%</td><td>12</td><td>Tennessee</td><td>5,927</td><td>2.63%</td></tr>
<tr><td>4</td><td>Illinois</td><td>10,817</td><td>4.80%</td><td>13</td><td>Wisconsin</td><td>4,752</td><td>2.11%</td></tr>
<tr><td>15</td><td>Indiana</td><td>4,601</td><td>2.04%</td><td>14</td><td>New Jersey</td><td>4,706</td><td>2.09%</td></tr>
<tr><td>27</td><td>Iowa</td><td>2,058</td><td>0.91%</td><td>15</td><td>Indiana</td><td>4,601</td><td>2.04%</td></tr>
<tr><td>26</td><td>Kansas</td><td>2,397</td><td>1.06%</td><td>16</td><td>Colorado</td><td>4,513</td><td>2.00%</td></tr>
<tr><td>38</td><td>Kentucky</td><td>1,141</td><td>0.51%</td><td>17</td><td>Arizona</td><td>4,196</td><td>1.86%</td></tr>
<tr><td>6</td><td>Louisiana</td><td>8,889</td><td>3.94%</td><td>18</td><td>Washington</td><td>4,090</td><td>1.82%</td></tr>
<tr><td>40</td><td>Maine</td><td>896</td><td>0.40%</td><td>19</td><td>Massachusetts</td><td>3,615</td><td>1.60%</td></tr>
<tr><td>25</td><td>Maryland</td><td>2,546</td><td>1.13%</td><td>20</td><td>Minnesota</td><td>3,466</td><td>1.54%</td></tr>
<tr><td>19</td><td>Massachusetts</td><td>3,615</td><td>1.60%</td><td>21</td><td>South Carolina</td><td>3,423</td><td>1.52%</td></tr>
<tr><td>10</td><td>Michigan</td><td>6,861</td><td>3.04%</td><td>22</td><td>Alabama</td><td>3,172</td><td>1.41%</td></tr>
<tr><td>20</td><td>Minnesota</td><td>3,466</td><td>1.54%</td><td>23</td><td>Oregon</td><td>3,107</td><td>1.38%</td></tr>
<tr><td>29</td><td>Mississippi</td><td>1,768</td><td>0.78%</td><td>24</td><td>Missouri</td><td>2,619</td><td>1.16%</td></tr>
<tr><td>24</td><td>Missouri</td><td>2,619</td><td>1.16%</td><td>25</td><td>Maryland</td><td>2,546</td><td>1.13%</td></tr>
<tr><td>39</td><td>Montana</td><td>1,034</td><td>0.46%</td><td>26</td><td>Kansas</td><td>2,397</td><td>1.06%</td></tr>
<tr><td>35</td><td>Nebraska</td><td>1,303</td><td>0.58%</td><td>27</td><td>Iowa</td><td>2,058</td><td>0.91%</td></tr>
<tr><td>37</td><td>Nevada</td><td>1,142</td><td>0.51%</td><td>28</td><td>Arkansas</td><td>1,849</td><td>0.82%</td></tr>
<tr><td>45</td><td>New Hampshire</td><td>158</td><td>0.07%</td><td>29</td><td>Mississippi</td><td>1,768</td><td>0.78%</td></tr>
<tr><td>14</td><td>New Jersey</td><td>4,706</td><td>2.09%</td><td>30</td><td>Oklahoma</td><td>1,736</td><td>0.77%</td></tr>
<tr><td>36</td><td>New Mexico</td><td>1,241</td><td>0.55%</td><td>31</td><td>Utah</td><td>1,709</td><td>0.76%</td></tr>
<tr><td>5</td><td>New York</td><td>9,284</td><td>4.12%</td><td>32</td><td>Idaho</td><td>1,502</td><td>0.67%</td></tr>
<tr><td>9</td><td>North Carolina</td><td>7,109</td><td>3.15%</td><td>33</td><td>Pennsylvania</td><td>1,453</td><td>0.64%</td></tr>
<tr><td>43</td><td>North Dakota</td><td>503</td><td>0.22%</td><td>34</td><td>West Virginia</td><td>1,373</td><td>0.61%</td></tr>
<tr><td>8</td><td>Ohio</td><td>7,522</td><td>3.34%</td><td>35</td><td>Nebraska</td><td>1,303</td><td>0.58%</td></tr>
<tr><td>30</td><td>Oklahoma</td><td>1,736</td><td>0.77%</td><td>36</td><td>New Mexico</td><td>1,241</td><td>0.55%</td></tr>
<tr><td>23</td><td>Oregon</td><td>3,107</td><td>1.38%</td><td>37</td><td>Nevada</td><td>1,142</td><td>0.51%</td></tr>
<tr><td>33</td><td>Pennsylvania</td><td>1,453</td><td>0.64%</td><td>38</td><td>Kentucky</td><td>1,141</td><td>0.51%</td></tr>
<tr><td>46</td><td>Rhode Island</td><td>125</td><td>0.06%</td><td>39</td><td>Montana</td><td>1,034</td><td>0.46%</td></tr>
<tr><td>21</td><td>South Carolina</td><td>3,423</td><td>1.52%</td><td>40</td><td>Maine</td><td>896</td><td>0.40%</td></tr>
<tr><td>42</td><td>South Dakota</td><td>603</td><td>0.27%</td><td>41</td><td>Wyoming</td><td>875</td><td>0.39%</td></tr>
<tr><td>12</td><td>Tennessee</td><td>5,927</td><td>2.63%</td><td>42</td><td>South Dakota</td><td>603</td><td>0.27%</td></tr>
<tr><td>3</td><td>Texas</td><td>19,077</td><td>8.47%</td><td>43</td><td>North Dakota</td><td>503</td><td>0.22%</td></tr>
<tr><td>31</td><td>Utah</td><td>1,709</td><td>0.76%</td><td>44</td><td>Connecticut</td><td>425</td><td>0.19%</td></tr>
<tr><td>47</td><td>Vermont</td><td>119</td><td>0.05%</td><td>45</td><td>New Hampshire</td><td>158</td><td>0.07%</td></tr>
<tr><td>11</td><td>Virginia</td><td>6,550</td><td>2.91%</td><td>46</td><td>Rhode Island</td><td>125</td><td>0.06%</td></tr>
<tr><td>18</td><td>Washington</td><td>4,090</td><td>1.82%</td><td>47</td><td>Vermont</td><td>119</td><td>0.05%</td></tr>
<tr><td>34</td><td>West Virginia</td><td>1,373</td><td>0.61%</td><td>48</td><td>Delaware</td><td>40</td><td>0.02%</td></tr>
<tr><td>13</td><td>Wisconsin</td><td>4,752</td><td>2.11%</td><td>49</td><td>Alaska</td><td>0</td><td>0.00%</td></tr>
<tr><td>41</td><td>Wyoming</td><td>875</td><td>0.39%</td><td>49</td><td>Hawaii</td><td>0</td><td>0.00%</td></tr>
<tr><td></td><td></td><td></td><td></td><td></td><td>District of Columbia</td><td>0</td><td>0.00%</td></tr>
</table>

Source: U.S. Department of Justice, Bureau of Justice Statistics
"Census of State and Local Law Enforcement Agencies, 1992" (Bulletin, July 1993, NCJ-142972)
Sheriffs' departments generally operate at the county level.

Special Police Agencies in 1992

National Total = 1,721 Agencies*

ALPHA ORDER				RANK ORDER			
RANK	STATE	AGENCIES	% of USA	RANK	STATE	AGENCIES	% of USA
13	Alabama	24	1.39%	1	Texas**	824	47.88%
39	Alaska	4	0.23%	2	California	93	5.40%
31	Arizona	11	0.64%	3	New York	57	3.31%
23	Arkansas	16	0.93%	4	Pennsylvania	51	2.96%
2	California	93	5.40%	5	Illinois	43	2.50%
28	Colorado	14	0.81%	5	Ohio	43	2.50%
23	Connecticut	16	0.93%	7	Georgia	37	2.15%
38	Delaware	5	0.29%	8	Virginia	34	1.98%
16	Florida	20	1.16%	9	Massachusetts	32	1.86%
7	Georgia	37	2.15%	10	Louisiana	27	1.57%
47	Hawaii	2	0.12%	11	Mississippi	25	1.45%
49	Idaho	1	0.06%	11	North Carolina	25	1.45%
5	Illinois	43	2.50%	13	Alabama	24	1.39%
16	Indiana	20	1.16%	13	New Jersey	24	1.39%
36	Iowa	6	0.35%	15	Maryland	21	1.22%
22	Kansas	18	1.05%	16	Florida	20	1.16%
23	Kentucky	16	0.93%	16	Indiana	20	1.16%
10	Louisiana	27	1.57%	16	Michigan	20	1.16%
36	Maine	6	0.35%	16	Oklahoma	20	1.16%
15	Maryland	21	1.22%	16	South Carolina	20	1.16%
9	Massachusetts	32	1.86%	21	Tennessee	19	1.10%
16	Michigan	20	1.16%	22	Kansas	18	1.05%
33	Minnesota	9	0.52%	23	Arkansas	16	0.93%
11	Mississippi	25	1.45%	23	Connecticut	16	0.93%
23	Missouri	16	0.93%	23	Kentucky	16	0.93%
39	Montana	4	0.23%	23	Missouri	16	0.93%
39	Nebraska	4	0.23%	23	Wisconsin	16	0.93%
39	Nevada	4	0.23%	28	Colorado	14	0.81%
45	New Hampshire	3	0.17%	28	West Virginia	14	0.81%
13	New Jersey	24	1.39%	30	Utah	13	0.76%
33	New Mexico	9	0.52%	31	Arizona	11	0.64%
3	New York	57	3.31%	32	Washington	10	0.58%
11	North Carolina	25	1.45%	33	Minnesota	9	0.52%
39	North Dakota	4	0.23%	33	New Mexico	9	0.52%
5	Ohio	43	2.50%	33	Oregon	9	0.52%
16	Oklahoma	20	1.16%	36	Iowa	6	0.35%
33	Oregon	9	0.52%	36	Maine	6	0.35%
4	Pennsylvania	51	2.96%	38	Delaware	5	0.29%
39	Rhode Island	4	0.23%	39	Alaska	4	0.23%
16	South Carolina	20	1.16%	39	Montana	4	0.23%
47	South Dakota	2	0.12%	39	Nebraska	4	0.23%
21	Tennessee	19	1.10%	39	Nevada	4	0.23%
1	Texas**	824	47.88%	39	North Dakota	4	0.23%
30	Utah	13	0.76%	39	Rhode Island	4	0.23%
49	Vermont	1	0.06%	45	New Hampshire	3	0.17%
8	Virginia	34	1.98%	45	Wyoming	3	0.17%
32	Washington	10	0.58%	47	Hawaii	2	0.12%
28	West Virginia	14	0.81%	47	South Dakota	2	0.12%
23	Wisconsin	16	0.93%	49	Idaho	1	0.06%
45	Wyoming	3	0.17%	49	Vermont	1	0.06%
					District of Columbia	2	0.12%

Source: U.S. Department of Justice, Bureau of Justice Statistics
   "Census of State and Local Law Enforcement Agencies, 1992" (Bulletin, July 1993, NCJ-142972)
*Agencies with special jurisdictions or special enforcement responsibilities.
**Texas' total includes 751 county constable offices.

Full-Time Sworn Officers in Special Police Departments in 1992

National Total = 41,371 Officers*

<u>ALPHA ORDER</u>

RANK	STATE	OFFICERS	% of USA
15	Alabama	600	1.45%
38	Alaska	120	0.29%
35	Arizona	164	0.40%
21	Arkansas	443	1.07%
3	California	3,992	9.65%
22	Colorado	404	0.98%
30	Connecticut	248	0.60%
36	Delaware	158	0.38%
4	Florida	1,432	3.46%
11	Georgia	759	1.83%
41	Hawaii	93	0.22%
49	Idaho	12	0.03%
10	Illinois	864	2.09%
19	Indiana	560	1.35%
33	Iowa	213	0.51%
27	Kansas	292	0.71%
28	Kentucky	280	0.68%
18	Louisiana	570	1.38%
34	Maine	169	0.41%
6	Maryland	1,280	3.09%
16	Massachusetts	593	1.43%
13	Michigan	642	1.55%
23	Minnesota	397	0.96%
25	Mississippi	324	0.78%
24	Missouri	391	0.95%
46	Montana	47	0.11%
41	Nebraska	93	0.22%
37	Nevada	143	0.35%
44	New Hampshire	68	0.16%
8	New Jersey	1,062	2.57%
40	New Mexico	111	0.27%
1	New York	13,334	32.23%
12	North Carolina	707	1.71%
45	North Dakota	49	0.12%
7	Ohio	1,099	2.66%
26	Oklahoma	301	0.73%
39	Oregon	117	0.28%
5	Pennsylvania	1,293	3.13%
43	Rhode Island	76	0.18%
17	South Carolina	584	1.41%
50	South Dakota	8	0.02%
20	Tennessee	517	1.25%
2	Texas**	4,108	9.93%
29	Utah	250	0.60%
47	Vermont	21	0.05%
9	Virginia	964	2.33%
32	Washington	228	0.55%
31	West Virginia	243	0.59%
14	Wisconsin	603	1.46%
47	Wyoming	21	0.05%

<u>RANK ORDER</u>

RANK	STATE	OFFICERS	% of USA
1	New York	13,334	32.23%
2	Texas**	4,108	9.93%
3	California	3,992	9.65%
4	Florida	1,432	3.46%
5	Pennsylvania	1,293	3.13%
6	Maryland	1,280	3.09%
7	Ohio	1,099	2.66%
8	New Jersey	1,062	2.57%
9	Virginia	964	2.33%
10	Illinois	864	2.09%
11	Georgia	759	1.83%
12	North Carolina	707	1.71%
13	Michigan	642	1.55%
14	Wisconsin	603	1.46%
15	Alabama	600	1.45%
16	Massachusetts	593	1.43%
17	South Carolina	584	1.41%
18	Louisiana	570	1.38%
19	Indiana	560	1.35%
20	Tennessee	517	1.25%
21	Arkansas	443	1.07%
22	Colorado	404	0.98%
23	Minnesota	397	0.96%
24	Missouri	391	0.95%
25	Mississippi	324	0.78%
26	Oklahoma	301	0.73%
27	Kansas	292	0.71%
28	Kentucky	280	0.68%
29	Utah	250	0.60%
30	Connecticut	248	0.60%
31	West Virginia	243	0.59%
32	Washington	228	0.55%
33	Iowa	213	0.51%
34	Maine	169	0.41%
35	Arizona	164	0.40%
36	Delaware	158	0.38%
37	Nevada	143	0.35%
38	Alaska	120	0.29%
39	Oregon	117	0.28%
40	New Mexico	111	0.27%
41	Hawaii	93	0.22%
41	Nebraska	93	0.22%
43	Rhode Island	76	0.18%
44	New Hampshire	68	0.16%
45	North Dakota	49	0.12%
46	Montana	47	0.11%
47	Vermont	21	0.05%
47	Wyoming	21	0.05%
49	Idaho	12	0.03%
50	South Dakota	8	0.02%
	District of Columbia	324	0.78%

Source: U.S. Department of Justice, Bureau of Justice Statistics
     "Census of State and Local Law Enforcement Agencies, 1992" (Bulletin, July 1993, NCJ-142972)
*Agencies with special jurisdictions or special enforcement responsibilities.
**Texas' total includes 751 county constable offices with 1,723 sworn constable office employees..

Percent of Full-Time Special Police Department Employees
Who Are Sworn Officers: 1992
National Percent = 67.90% of Employees*

ALPHA ORDER

RANK ORDER

RANK	STATE	PERCENT	RANK	STATE	PERCENT
14	Alabama	78.02	1	Hawaii	98.94
4	Alaska	88.89	2	Nebraska	92.08
34	Arizona	63.57	3	New York	90.08
48	Arkansas	42.88	4	Alaska	88.89
44	California	46.98	5	Maine	88.48
47	Colorado	44.25	6	West Virginia	87.41
7	Connecticut	84.35	7	Connecticut	84.35
27	Delaware	68.10	8	Louisiana	83.95
18	Florida	76.13	9	Minnesota	83.40
46	Georgia	44.36	10	Iowa	80.68
1	Hawaii	98.94	11	Idaho	80.00
11	Idaho	80.00	12	Illinois	78.47
12	Illinois	78.47	13	Oklahoma	78.39
15	Indiana	77.24	14	Alabama	78.02
10	Iowa	80.68	15	Indiana	77.24
21	Kansas	73.18	16	Massachusetts	77.01
33	Kentucky	64.67	17	Tennessee	76.59
8	Louisiana	83.95	18	Florida	76.13
5	Maine	88.48	19	Missouri	74.76
22	Maryland	72.36	20	Pennsylvania	74.57
16	Massachusetts	77.01	21	Kansas	73.18
30	Michigan	66.53	22	Maryland	72.36
9	Minnesota	83.40	23	Mississippi	72.00
23	Mississippi	72.00	24	Rhode Island	71.03
19	Missouri	74.76	25	Washington	70.59
41	Montana	51.09	26	New Mexico	68.94
2	Nebraska	92.08	27	Delaware	68.10
31	Nevada	65.90	28	North Dakota	67.12
49	New Hampshire	33.17	29	Oregon	66.86
38	New Jersey	61.18	30	Michigan	66.53
26	New Mexico	68.94	31	Nevada	65.90
3	New York	90.08	32	Vermont	65.63
35	North Carolina	63.29	33	Kentucky	64.67
28	North Dakota	67.12	34	Arizona	63.57
39	Ohio	57.48	35	North Carolina	63.29
13	Oklahoma	78.39	36	Texas**	63.14
29	Oregon	66.86	37	Wyoming	61.76
20	Pennsylvania	74.57	38	New Jersey	61.18
24	Rhode Island	71.03	39	Ohio	57.48
42	South Carolina	50.34	40	Wisconsin	56.51
43	South Dakota	50.00	41	Montana	51.09
17	Tennessee	76.59	42	South Carolina	50.34
36	Texas**	63.14	43	South Dakota	50.00
50	Utah	29.52	44	California	46.98
32	Vermont	65.63	45	Virginia	44.44
45	Virginia	44.44	46	Georgia	44.36
25	Washington	70.59	47	Colorado	44.25
6	West Virginia	87.41	48	Arkansas	42.88
40	Wisconsin	56.51	49	New Hampshire	33.17
37	Wyoming	61.76	50	Utah	29.52
				District of Columbia	76.42

Source: Morgan Quitno Press using data from U.S. Department of Justice, Bureau of Justice Statistics
   "Census of State and Local Law Enforcement Agencies, 1992" (Bulletin, July 1993, NCJ-142972)
*Agencies with special jurisdictions or special enforcement responsibilities.
**Texas' total includes 751 county constable offices with 1,723 sworn constable office employees..

Rate of Full-Time Sworn Officers in Special Police Departments in 1992

National Rate = 1.62 Officers per 10,000 Population*

ALPHA ORDER

RANK	STATE	RATE
9	Alabama	1.45
5	Alaska	2.04
46	Arizona	0.43
6	Arkansas	1.85
15	California	1.29
18	Colorado	1.16
33	Connecticut	0.76
4	Delaware	2.29
23	Florida	1.06
20	Georgia	1.12
31	Hawaii	0.80
49	Idaho	0.11
38	Illinois	0.74
27	Indiana	0.99
33	Iowa	0.76
18	Kansas	1.16
36	Kentucky	0.75
14	Louisiana	1.33
11	Maine	1.37
2	Maryland	2.61
27	Massachusetts	0.99
40	Michigan	0.68
30	Minnesota	0.89
16	Mississippi	1.24
36	Missouri	0.75
43	Montana	0.57
42	Nebraska	0.58
21	Nevada	1.08
41	New Hampshire	0.61
12	New Jersey	1.36
39	New Mexico	0.70
1	New York	7.36
24	North Carolina	1.03
32	North Dakota	0.77
26	Ohio	1.00
29	Oklahoma	0.94
47	Oregon	0.39
21	Pennsylvania	1.08
33	Rhode Island	0.76
7	South Carolina	1.62
49	South Dakota	0.11
24	Tennessee	1.03
3	Texas**	2.33
10	Utah	1.38
48	Vermont	0.37
8	Virginia	1.51
45	Washington	0.44
13	West Virginia	1.34
17	Wisconsin	1.20
44	Wyoming	0.45

RANK ORDER

RANK	STATE	RATE
1	New York	7.36
2	Maryland	2.61
3	Texas**	2.33
4	Delaware	2.29
5	Alaska	2.04
6	Arkansas	1.85
7	South Carolina	1.62
8	Virginia	1.51
9	Alabama	1.45
10	Utah	1.38
11	Maine	1.37
12	New Jersey	1.36
13	West Virginia	1.34
14	Louisiana	1.33
15	California	1.29
16	Mississippi	1.24
17	Wisconsin	1.20
18	Colorado	1.16
18	Kansas	1.16
20	Georgia	1.12
21	Nevada	1.08
21	Pennsylvania	1.08
23	Florida	1.06
24	North Carolina	1.03
24	Tennessee	1.03
26	Ohio	1.00
27	Indiana	0.99
27	Massachusetts	0.99
29	Oklahoma	0.94
30	Minnesota	0.89
31	Hawaii	0.80
32	North Dakota	0.77
33	Connecticut	0.76
33	Iowa	0.76
33	Rhode Island	0.76
36	Kentucky	0.75
36	Missouri	0.75
38	Illinois	0.74
39	New Mexico	0.70
40	Michigan	0.68
41	New Hampshire	0.61
42	Nebraska	0.58
43	Montana	0.57
44	Wyoming	0.45
45	Washington	0.44
46	Arizona	0.43
47	Oregon	0.39
48	Vermont	0.37
49	Idaho	0.11
49	South Dakota	0.11
	District of Columbia	5.50

Source: Morgan Quitno Press using data from U.S. Department of Justice, Bureau of Justice Statistics "Census of State and Local Law Enforcement Agencies, 1992" (Bulletin, July 1993, NCJ-142972)
*Agencies with special jurisdictions or special enforcement responsibilities.
**Texas' total includes 751 county constable offices with 1,723 sworn constable office employees..

Full-Time Employees in Special Police Departments in 1992

National Total = 60,926 Employees*

ALPHA ORDER					RANK ORDER			
RANK	STATE	EMPLOYEES	% of USA		RANK	STATE	EMPLOYEES	% of USA
20	Alabama	769	1.26%		1	New York	14,803	24.30%
41	Alaska	135	0.22%		2	California	8,498	13.95%
34	Arizona	258	0.42%		3	Texas**	6,506	10.68%
15	Arkansas	1,033	1.70%		4	Virginia	2,169	3.56%
2	California	8,498	13.95%		5	Ohio	1,912	3.14%
17	Colorado	913	1.50%		6	Florida	1,881	3.09%
31	Connecticut	294	0.48%		7	Maryland	1,769	2.90%
35	Delaware	232	0.38%		8	New Jersey	1,736	2.85%
6	Florida	1,881	3.09%		9	Pennsylvania	1,734	2.85%
10	Georgia	1,711	2.81%		10	Georgia	1,711	2.81%
44	Hawaii	94	0.15%		11	South Carolina	1,160	1.90%
50	Idaho	15	0.02%		12	North Carolina	1,117	1.83%
13	Illinois	1,101	1.81%		13	Illinois	1,101	1.81%
21	Indiana	725	1.19%		14	Wisconsin	1,067	1.75%
33	Iowa	264	0.43%		15	Arkansas	1,033	1.70%
28	Kansas	399	0.65%		16	Michigan	965	1.58%
27	Kentucky	433	0.71%		17	Colorado	913	1.50%
22	Louisiana	679	1.11%		18	Utah	847	1.39%
38	Maine	191	0.31%		19	Massachusetts	770	1.26%
7	Maryland	1,769	2.90%		20	Alabama	769	1.26%
19	Massachusetts	770	1.26%		21	Indiana	725	1.19%
16	Michigan	965	1.58%		22	Louisiana	679	1.11%
25	Minnesota	476	0.78%		23	Tennessee	675	1.11%
26	Mississippi	450	0.74%		24	Missouri	523	0.86%
24	Missouri	523	0.86%		25	Minnesota	476	0.78%
45	Montana	92	0.15%		26	Mississippi	450	0.74%
43	Nebraska	101	0.17%		27	Kentucky	433	0.71%
36	Nevada	217	0.36%		28	Kansas	399	0.65%
37	New Hampshire	205	0.34%		29	Oklahoma	384	0.63%
8	New Jersey	1,736	2.85%		30	Washington	323	0.53%
40	New Mexico	161	0.26%		31	Connecticut	294	0.48%
1	New York	14,803	24.30%		32	West Virginia	278	0.46%
12	North Carolina	1,117	1.83%		33	Iowa	264	0.43%
46	North Dakota	73	0.12%		34	Arizona	258	0.42%
5	Ohio	1,912	3.14%		35	Delaware	232	0.38%
29	Oklahoma	384	0.63%		36	Nevada	217	0.36%
39	Oregon	175	0.29%		37	New Hampshire	205	0.34%
9	Pennsylvania	1,734	2.85%		38	Maine	191	0.31%
42	Rhode Island	107	0.18%		39	Oregon	175	0.29%
11	South Carolina	1,160	1.90%		40	New Mexico	161	0.26%
49	South Dakota	16	0.03%		41	Alaska	135	0.22%
23	Tennessee	675	1.11%		42	Rhode Island	107	0.18%
3	Texas**	6,506	10.68%		43	Nebraska	101	0.17%
18	Utah	847	1.39%		44	Hawaii	94	0.15%
48	Vermont	32	0.05%		45	Montana	92	0.15%
4	Virginia	2,169	3.56%		46	North Dakota	73	0.12%
30	Washington	323	0.53%		47	Wyoming	34	0.06%
32	West Virginia	278	0.46%		48	Vermont	32	0.05%
14	Wisconsin	1,067	1.75%		49	South Dakota	16	0.03%
47	Wyoming	34	0.06%		50	Idaho	15	0.02%
						District of Columbia	424	0.70%

Source: U.S. Department of Justice, Bureau of Justice Statistics
   "Census of State and Local Law Enforcement Agencies, 1992" (Bulletin, July 1993, NCJ-142972)
*Agencies with special jurisdictions or special enforcement responsibilities.
**Texas' total includes 751 county constable offices with 1,723 sworn constable office employees..

Law Enforcement Officers Feloniously Killed in 1995

National Total = 71 Officers*

ALPHA ORDER

RANK	STATE	OFFICERS	% of USA
9	Alabama	2	2.82%
28	Alaska	0	0.00%
3	Arizona	5	7.04%
4	Arkansas	3	4.23%
1	California	11	15.49%
4	Colorado	3	4.23%
28	Connecticut	0	0.00%
28	Delaware	0	0.00%
9	Florida	2	2.82%
9	Georgia	2	2.82%
28	Hawaii	0	0.00%
28	Idaho	0	0.00%
9	Illinois	2	2.82%
28	Indiana	0	0.00%
28	Iowa	0	0.00%
9	Kansas	2	2.82%
28	Kentucky	0	0.00%
4	Louisiana	3	4.23%
28	Maine	0	0.00%
9	Maryland	2	2.82%
20	Massachusetts	1	1.41%
20	Michigan	1	1.41%
28	Minnesota	0	0.00%
20	Mississippi	1	1.41%
28	Missouri	0	0.00%
28	Montana	0	0.00%
20	Nebraska	1	1.41%
9	Nevada	2	2.82%
28	New Hampshire	0	0.00%
4	New Jersey	3	4.23%
28	New Mexico	0	0.00%
9	New York	2	2.82%
9	North Carolina	2	2.82%
28	North Dakota	0	0.00%
20	Ohio	1	1.41%
2	Oklahoma	8	11.27%
28	Oregon	0	0.00%
9	Pennsylvania	2	2.82%
28	Rhode Island	0	0.00%
28	South Carolina	0	0.00%
28	South Dakota	0	0.00%
4	Tennessee	3	4.23%
9	Texas	2	2.82%
28	Utah	0	0.00%
28	Vermont	0	0.00%
28	Virginia	0	0.00%
20	Washington	1	1.41%
28	West Virginia	0	0.00%
20	Wisconsin	1	1.41%
20	Wyoming	1	1.41%

RANK ORDER

RANK	STATE	OFFICERS	% of USA
1	California	11	15.49%
2	Oklahoma	8	11.27%
3	Arizona	5	7.04%
4	Arkansas	3	4.23%
4	Colorado	3	4.23%
4	Louisiana	3	4.23%
4	New Jersey	3	4.23%
4	Tennessee	3	4.23%
9	Alabama	2	2.82%
9	Florida	2	2.82%
9	Georgia	2	2.82%
9	Illinois	2	2.82%
9	Kansas	2	2.82%
9	Maryland	2	2.82%
9	Nevada	2	2.82%
9	New York	2	2.82%
9	North Carolina	2	2.82%
9	Pennsylvania	2	2.82%
9	Texas	2	2.82%
20	Massachusetts	1	1.41%
20	Michigan	1	1.41%
20	Mississippi	1	1.41%
20	Nebraska	1	1.41%
20	Ohio	1	1.41%
20	Washington	1	1.41%
20	Wisconsin	1	1.41%
20	Wyoming	1	1.41%
28	Alaska	0	0.00%
28	Connecticut	0	0.00%
28	Delaware	0	0.00%
28	Hawaii	0	0.00%
28	Idaho	0	0.00%
28	Indiana	0	0.00%
28	Iowa	0	0.00%
28	Kentucky	0	0.00%
28	Maine	0	0.00%
28	Minnesota	0	0.00%
28	Missouri	0	0.00%
28	Montana	0	0.00%
28	New Hampshire	0	0.00%
28	New Mexico	0	0.00%
28	North Dakota	0	0.00%
28	Oregon	0	0.00%
28	Rhode Island	0	0.00%
28	South Carolina	0	0.00%
28	South Dakota	0	0.00%
28	Utah	0	0.00%
28	Vermont	0	0.00%
28	Virginia	0	0.00%
28	West Virginia	0	0.00%
	District of Columbia	2	2.82%

Source: Federal Bureau of Investigation
    "Law Enforcement Officers Killed and Assaulted 1995"

*Total does not include two officers killed in Puerto Rico and one officer killed in the Mariana Islands in 1995.
Fifty-seven additional officers were killed in accidents occurring while performing official duties.

Law Enforcement Officers Feloniously Killed: 1986 to 1995

National Total = 653 Officers*

ALPHA ORDER					RANK ORDER			
RANK	STATE		OFFICERS	% of USA	RANK	STATE	OFFICERS	% of USA
19	Alabama		13	1.99%	1	Texas	64	9.80%
33	Alaska		4	0.61%	2	California	63	9.65%
8	Arizona		22	3.37%	3	Florida	43	6.58%
26	Arkansas		9	1.38%	4	New York	39	5.97%
2	California		63	9.65%	5	Georgia	28	4.29%
16	Colorado		14	2.14%	6	Illinois	26	3.98%
36	Connecticut		3	0.46%	6	Michigan	26	3.98%
47	Delaware		0	0.00%	8	Arizona	22	3.37%
3	Florida		43	6.58%	8	Mississippi	22	3.37%
5	Georgia		28	4.29%	10	Pennsylvania	21	3.22%
36	Hawaii		3	0.46%	11	Louisiana	18	2.76%
36	Idaho		3	0.46%	12	Missouri	17	2.60%
6	Illinois		26	3.98%	12	North Carolina	17	2.60%
22	Indiana		12	1.84%	14	Kentucky	15	2.30%
47	Iowa		0	0.00%	14	Virginia	15	2.30%
30	Kansas		6	0.92%	16	Colorado	14	2.14%
14	Kentucky		15	2.30%	16	Ohio	14	2.14%
11	Louisiana		18	2.76%	16	South Carolina	14	2.14%
41	Maine		2	0.31%	19	Alabama	13	1.99%
23	Maryland		10	1.53%	19	Oklahoma	13	1.99%
23	Massachusetts		10	1.53%	19	Tennessee	13	1.99%
6	Michigan		26	3.98%	22	Indiana	12	1.84%
26	Minnesota		9	1.38%	23	Maryland	10	1.53%
8	Mississippi		22	3.37%	23	Massachusetts	10	1.53%
12	Missouri		17	2.60%	23	Wisconsin	10	1.53%
33	Montana		4	0.61%	26	Arkansas	9	1.38%
33	Nebraska		4	0.61%	26	Minnesota	9	1.38%
32	Nevada		5	0.77%	28	New Jersey	8	1.23%
43	New Hampshire		1	0.15%	28	New Mexico	8	1.23%
28	New Jersey		8	1.23%	30	Kansas	6	0.92%
28	New Mexico		8	1.23%	30	Washington	6	0.92%
4	New York		39	5.97%	32	Nevada	5	0.77%
12	North Carolina		17	2.60%	33	Alaska	4	0.61%
43	North Dakota		1	0.15%	33	Montana	4	0.61%
16	Ohio		14	2.14%	33	Nebraska	4	0.61%
19	Oklahoma		13	1.99%	36	Connecticut	3	0.46%
41	Oregon		2	0.31%	36	Hawaii	3	0.46%
10	Pennsylvania		21	3.22%	36	Idaho	3	0.46%
43	Rhode Island		1	0.15%	36	Utah	3	0.46%
16	South Carolina		14	2.14%	36	West Virginia	3	0.46%
47	South Dakota		0	0.00%	41	Maine	2	0.31%
19	Tennessee		13	1.99%	41	Oregon	2	0.31%
1	Texas		64	9.80%	43	New Hampshire	1	0.15%
36	Utah		3	0.46%	43	North Dakota	1	0.15%
47	Vermont		0	0.00%	43	Rhode Island	1	0.15%
14	Virginia		15	2.30%	43	Wyoming	1	0.15%
30	Washington		6	0.92%	47	Delaware	0	0.00%
36	West Virginia		3	0.46%	47	Iowa	0	0.00%
23	Wisconsin		10	1.53%	47	South Dakota	0	0.00%
43	Wyoming		1	0.15%	47	Vermont	0	0.00%
						District of Columbia	8	1.23%

Source: Federal Bureau of Investigation
"Law Enforcement Officers Killed and Assaulted 1995"
*Total does not include 53 officers killed in U.S. territories (50 officers killed in Puerto Rico, one in American Samoa, one in the U.S. Virgin Islands and one in the Mariana Islands). An additional 660 officers were killed in accidents occurring while performing official duties. Twenty of these accident victims were in U.S. territories or abroad.

U.S. District Judges in 1996

National Total = 647 Judges*

ALPHA ORDER

RANK	STATE	JUDGES	% of USA
15	Alabama	13	2.01%
41	Alaska	3	0.46%
25	Arizona	8	1.24%
25	Arkansas	8	1.24%
1	California	56	8.66%
29	Colorado	7	1.08%
25	Connecticut	8	1.24%
37	Delaware	4	0.62%
5	Florida	31	4.79%
10	Georgia	18	2.78%
37	Hawaii	4	0.62%
48	Idaho	2	0.31%
6	Illinois	30	4.64%
20	Indiana	10	1.55%
34	Iowa	5	0.77%
31	Kansas	6	0.93%
22	Kentucky	9	1.39%
7	Louisiana	22	3.40%
41	Maine	3	0.46%
20	Maryland	10	1.55%
15	Massachusetts	13	2.01%
9	Michigan	19	2.94%
29	Minnesota	7	1.08%
22	Mississippi	9	1.39%
12	Missouri	14	2.16%
41	Montana	3	0.46%
37	Nebraska	4	0.62%
37	Nevada	4	0.62%
41	New Hampshire	3	0.46%
11	New Jersey	17	2.63%
34	New Mexico	5	0.77%
2	New York	52	8.04%
17	North Carolina	11	1.70%
48	North Dakota	2	0.31%
8	Ohio	20	3.09%
17	Oklahoma	11	1.70%
31	Oregon	6	0.93%
4	Pennsylvania	39	6.03%
41	Rhode Island	3	0.46%
22	South Carolina	9	1.39%
41	South Dakota	3	0.46%
12	Tennessee	14	2.16%
3	Texas	47	7.26%
34	Utah	5	0.77%
48	Vermont	2	0.31%
12	Virginia	14	2.16%
17	Washington	11	1.70%
25	West Virginia	8	1.24%
31	Wisconsin	6	0.93%
41	Wyoming	3	0.46%

RANK ORDER

RANK	STATE	JUDGES	% of USA
1	California	56	8.66%
2	New York	52	8.04%
3	Texas	47	7.26%
4	Pennsylvania	39	6.03%
5	Florida	31	4.79%
6	Illinois	30	4.64%
7	Louisiana	22	3.40%
8	Ohio	20	3.09%
9	Michigan	19	2.94%
10	Georgia	18	2.78%
11	New Jersey	17	2.63%
12	Missouri	14	2.16%
12	Tennessee	14	2.16%
12	Virginia	14	2.16%
15	Alabama	13	2.01%
15	Massachusetts	13	2.01%
17	North Carolina	11	1.70%
17	Oklahoma	11	1.70%
17	Washington	11	1.70%
20	Indiana	10	1.55%
20	Maryland	10	1.55%
22	Kentucky	9	1.39%
22	Mississippi	9	1.39%
22	South Carolina	9	1.39%
25	Arizona	8	1.24%
25	Arkansas	8	1.24%
25	Connecticut	8	1.24%
25	West Virginia	8	1.24%
29	Colorado	7	1.08%
29	Minnesota	7	1.08%
31	Kansas	6	0.93%
31	Oregon	6	0.93%
31	Wisconsin	6	0.93%
34	Iowa	5	0.77%
34	New Mexico	5	0.77%
34	Utah	5	0.77%
37	Delaware	4	0.62%
37	Hawaii	4	0.62%
37	Nebraska	4	0.62%
37	Nevada	4	0.62%
41	Alaska	3	0.46%
41	Maine	3	0.46%
41	Montana	3	0.46%
41	New Hampshire	3	0.46%
41	Rhode Island	3	0.46%
41	South Dakota	3	0.46%
41	Wyoming	3	0.46%
48	Idaho	2	0.31%
48	North Dakota	2	0.31%
48	Vermont	2	0.31%
	District of Columbia	15	2.32%

Source: Administrative Office of the United States Courts
    "1996 Federal Court Management Statistics" (March 1997)
*Total includes 11 judgeships in U.S. territories.

Rate of U.S. District Judges in 1996

National Rate = 0.24 Judges per 100,000 Population*

ALPHA ORDER				RANK ORDER		
RANK	STATE	RATE		RANK	STATE	RATE
15	Alabama	0.30		1	Wyoming	0.62
4	Alaska	0.49		2	Delaware	0.55
41	Arizona	0.18		3	Louisiana	0.51
12	Arkansas	0.32		4	Alaska	0.49
41	California	0.18		5	West Virginia	0.44
41	Colorado	0.18		6	South Dakota	0.41
26	Connecticut	0.24		7	Hawaii	0.34
2	Delaware	0.55		7	Montana	0.34
33	Florida	0.22		7	Vermont	0.34
26	Georgia	0.24		10	Mississippi	0.33
7	Hawaii	0.34		10	Oklahoma	0.33
46	Idaho	0.17		12	Arkansas	0.32
22	Illinois	0.25		12	Pennsylvania	0.32
46	Indiana	0.17		14	North Dakota	0.31
41	Iowa	0.18		15	Alabama	0.30
31	Kansas	0.23		15	Rhode Island	0.30
31	Kentucky	0.23		17	New Mexico	0.29
3	Louisiana	0.51		17	New York	0.29
26	Maine	0.24		19	Missouri	0.26
37	Maryland	0.20		19	New Hampshire	0.26
34	Massachusetts	0.21		19	Tennessee	0.26
37	Michigan	0.20		22	Illinois	0.25
48	Minnesota	0.15		22	Nevada	0.25
10	Mississippi	0.33		22	Texas	0.25
19	Missouri	0.26		22	Utah	0.25
7	Montana	0.34		26	Connecticut	0.24
26	Nebraska	0.24		26	Georgia	0.24
22	Nevada	0.25		26	Maine	0.24
19	New Hampshire	0.26		26	Nebraska	0.24
34	New Jersey	0.21		26	South Carolina	0.24
17	New Mexico	0.29		31	Kansas	0.23
17	New York	0.29		31	Kentucky	0.23
48	North Carolina	0.15		33	Florida	0.22
14	North Dakota	0.31		34	Massachusetts	0.21
41	Ohio	0.18		34	New Jersey	0.21
10	Oklahoma	0.33		34	Virginia	0.21
40	Oregon	0.19		37	Maryland	0.20
12	Pennsylvania	0.32		37	Michigan	0.20
15	Rhode Island	0.30		37	Washington	0.20
26	South Carolina	0.24		40	Oregon	0.19
6	South Dakota	0.41		41	Arizona	0.18
19	Tennessee	0.26		41	California	0.18
22	Texas	0.25		41	Colorado	0.18
22	Utah	0.25		41	Iowa	0.18
7	Vermont	0.34		41	Ohio	0.18
34	Virginia	0.21		46	Idaho	0.17
37	Washington	0.20		46	Indiana	0.17
5	West Virginia	0.44		48	Minnesota	0.15
50	Wisconsin	0.12		48	North Carolina	0.15
1	Wyoming	0.62		50	Wisconsin	0.12
					District of Columbia	2.76

Source: Morgan Quitno Press using data from Administrative Office of the United States Courts
  "1996 Federal Court Management Statistics" (March 1997)
*National rate does not include judgeships or population in U.S. territories.

Felony Criminal Cases Filed in U.S. District Court in 1996

National Total = 34,729 Felony Criminal Cases*

ALPHA ORDER					RANK ORDER			
RANK	STATE		CASES	% of USA	RANK	STATE	CASES	% of USA
15	Alabama		630	1.81%	1	California	4,565	13.14%
50	Alaska		61	0.18%	2	Texas	4,010	11.55%
5	Arizona		1,243	3.58%	3	Florida	2,532	7.29%
25	Arkansas		390	1.12%	4	New York	2,523	7.26%
1	California		4,565	13.14%	5	Arizona	1,243	3.58%
22	Colorado		495	1.43%	6	Pennsylvania	1,111	3.20%
40	Connecticut		207	0.60%	7	Virginia	964	2.78%
49	Delaware		80	0.23%	8	Illinois	837	2.41%
3	Florida		2,532	7.29%	9	Michigan	809	2.33%
11	Georgia		755	2.17%	10	North Carolina	804	2.32%
41	Hawaii		197	0.57%	11	Georgia	755	2.17%
48	Idaho		89	0.26%	12	Ohio	703	2.02%
8	Illinois		837	2.41%	13	Washington	696	2.00%
30	Indiana		333	0.96%	14	New Mexico	633	1.82%
28	Iowa		358	1.03%	15	Alabama	630	1.81%
36	Kansas		252	0.73%	16	New Jersey	626	1.80%
23	Kentucky		480	1.38%	17	Tennessee	618	1.78%
20	Louisiana		546	1.57%	18	Missouri	601	1.73%
43	Maine		144	0.41%	18	Oregon	601	1.73%
26	Maryland		383	1.10%	20	Louisiana	546	1.57%
29	Massachusetts		357	1.03%	21	South Carolina	512	1.47%
9	Michigan		809	2.33%	22	Colorado	495	1.43%
38	Minnesota		234	0.67%	23	Kentucky	480	1.38%
33	Mississippi		284	0.82%	24	Oklahoma	398	1.15%
18	Missouri		601	1.73%	25	Arkansas	390	1.12%
37	Montana		244	0.70%	26	Maryland	383	1.10%
39	Nebraska		231	0.67%	27	South Dakota	369	1.06%
31	Nevada		316	0.91%	28	Iowa	358	1.03%
44	New Hampshire		133	0.38%	29	Massachusetts	357	1.03%
16	New Jersey		626	1.80%	30	Indiana	333	0.96%
14	New Mexico		633	1.82%	31	Nevada	316	0.91%
4	New York		2,523	7.26%	32	West Virginia	288	0.83%
10	North Carolina		804	2.32%	33	Mississippi	284	0.82%
42	North Dakota		187	0.54%	34	Wisconsin	277	0.80%
12	Ohio		703	2.02%	35	Utah	270	0.78%
24	Oklahoma		398	1.15%	36	Kansas	252	0.73%
18	Oregon		601	1.73%	37	Montana	244	0.70%
6	Pennsylvania		1,111	3.20%	38	Minnesota	234	0.67%
45	Rhode Island		95	0.27%	39	Nebraska	231	0.67%
21	South Carolina		512	1.47%	40	Connecticut	207	0.60%
27	South Dakota		369	1.06%	41	Hawaii	197	0.57%
17	Tennessee		618	1.78%	42	North Dakota	187	0.54%
2	Texas		4,010	11.55%	43	Maine	144	0.41%
35	Utah		270	0.78%	44	New Hampshire	133	0.38%
45	Vermont		95	0.27%	45	Rhode Island	95	0.27%
7	Virginia		964	2.78%	45	Vermont	95	0.27%
13	Washington		696	2.00%	47	Wyoming	92	0.26%
32	West Virginia		288	0.83%	48	Idaho	89	0.26%
34	Wisconsin		277	0.80%	49	Delaware	80	0.23%
47	Wyoming		92	0.26%	50	Alaska	61	0.18%
						District of Columbia	418	1.20%

Source: Morgan Quitno Press using data from Administrative Office of the United States Courts
"1996 Federal Court Management Statistics" (March 1997)
*National total includes 653 cases in U.S. territories. Does not include transfers from one district to another.

Felony Criminal Cases Filed per U.S. District Judge in 1996

National Rate = 54 Felony Criminal Cases per Judge*

ALPHA ORDER

RANK ORDER

RANK	STATE	RATE
23	Alabama	48
49	Alaska	20
1	Arizona	155
20	Arkansas	49
7	California	82
13	Colorado	71
47	Connecticut	26
49	Delaware	20
7	Florida	82
32	Georgia	42
20	Hawaii	49
27	Idaho	45
44	Illinois	28
39	Indiana	33
12	Iowa	72
32	Kansas	42
19	Kentucky	53
48	Louisiana	25
23	Maine	48
34	Maryland	38
46	Massachusetts	27
30	Michigan	43
39	Minnesota	33
41	Mississippi	32
30	Missouri	43
9	Montana	81
16	Nebraska	58
10	Nevada	79
28	New Hampshire	44
35	New Jersey	37
2	New Mexico	127
20	New York	49
11	North Carolina	73
5	North Dakota	94
38	Ohio	35
36	Oklahoma	36
4	Oregon	100
44	Pennsylvania	28
41	Rhode Island	32
17	South Carolina	57
3	South Dakota	123
28	Tennessee	44
6	Texas	85
18	Utah	54
23	Vermont	48
14	Virginia	69
15	Washington	63
36	West Virginia	36
26	Wisconsin	46
43	Wyoming	31

RANK	STATE	RATE
1	Arizona	155
2	New Mexico	127
3	South Dakota	123
4	Oregon	100
5	North Dakota	94
6	Texas	85
7	California	82
7	Florida	82
9	Montana	81
10	Nevada	79
11	North Carolina	73
12	Iowa	72
13	Colorado	71
14	Virginia	69
15	Washington	63
16	Nebraska	58
17	South Carolina	57
18	Utah	54
19	Kentucky	53
20	Arkansas	49
20	Hawaii	49
20	New York	49
23	Alabama	48
23	Maine	48
23	Vermont	48
26	Wisconsin	46
27	Idaho	45
28	New Hampshire	44
28	Tennessee	44
30	Michigan	43
30	Missouri	43
32	Georgia	42
32	Kansas	42
34	Maryland	38
35	New Jersey	37
36	Oklahoma	36
36	West Virginia	36
38	Ohio	35
39	Indiana	33
39	Minnesota	33
41	Mississippi	32
41	Rhode Island	32
43	Wyoming	31
44	Illinois	28
44	Pennsylvania	28
46	Massachusetts	27
47	Connecticut	26
48	Louisiana	25
49	Alaska	20
49	Delaware	20
	District of Columbia	28

Source: Morgan Quitno Press using data from Administrative Office of the United States Courts
"1996 Federal Court Management Statistics" (March 1997)
*National rate includes cases and judges in U.S. territories. Does not include transfers from one district to another.

Median Length of Federal Criminal Cases in 1996

National Median = 6.8 Months*

ALPHA ORDER

RANK	STATE	MONTHS
40	Alabama	5.6
40	Alaska	5.6
38	Arizona	5.7
33	Arkansas	6.2
35	California	6.1
47	Colorado	5.3
3	Connecticut	10.5
44	Delaware	5.5
25	Florida	6.7
17	Georgia	7.7
22	Hawaii	7.2
30	Idaho	6.4
7	Illinois	8.8
9	Indiana	8.5
18	Iowa	7.6
10	Kansas	8.4
29	Kentucky	6.6
30	Louisiana	6.4
38	Maine	5.7
12	Maryland	8.2
1	Massachusetts	11.8
16	Michigan	7.9
25	Minnesota	6.7
25	Mississippi	6.7
6	Missouri	8.9
18	Montana	7.6
5	Nebraska	9.9
8	Nevada	8.7
18	New Hampshire	7.6
15	New Jersey	8.0
21	New Mexico	7.3
2	New York	10.6
12	North Carolina	8.2
50	North Dakota	4.5
25	Ohio	6.7
48	Oklahoma	5.0
37	Oregon	5.9
14	Pennsylvania	8.1
32	Rhode Island	6.3
23	South Carolina	7.0
40	South Dakota	5.6
11	Tennessee	8.3
44	Texas	5.5
33	Utah	6.2
4	Vermont	10.2
35	Virginia	6.1
48	Washington	5.0
23	West Virginia	7.0
46	Wisconsin	5.4
40	Wyoming	5.6

RANK ORDER

RANK	STATE	MONTHS
1	Massachusetts	11.8
2	New York	10.6
3	Connecticut	10.5
4	Vermont	10.2
5	Nebraska	9.9
6	Missouri	8.9
7	Illinois	8.8
8	Nevada	8.7
9	Indiana	8.5
10	Kansas	8.4
11	Tennessee	8.3
12	Maryland	8.2
12	North Carolina	8.2
14	Pennsylvania	8.1
15	New Jersey	8.0
16	Michigan	7.9
17	Georgia	7.7
18	Iowa	7.6
18	Montana	7.6
18	New Hampshire	7.6
21	New Mexico	7.3
22	Hawaii	7.2
23	South Carolina	7.0
23	West Virginia	7.0
25	Florida	6.7
25	Minnesota	6.7
25	Mississippi	6.7
25	Ohio	6.7
29	Kentucky	6.6
30	Idaho	6.4
30	Louisiana	6.4
32	Rhode Island	6.3
33	Arkansas	6.2
33	Utah	6.2
35	California	6.1
35	Virginia	6.1
37	Oregon	5.9
38	Arizona	5.7
38	Maine	5.7
40	Alabama	5.6
40	Alaska	5.6
40	South Dakota	5.6
40	Wyoming	5.6
44	Delaware	5.5
44	Texas	5.5
46	Wisconsin	5.4
47	Colorado	5.3
48	Oklahoma	5.0
48	Washington	5.0
50	North Dakota	4.5

	District of Columbia	6.1

Source: Morgan Quitno Press using data from Administrative Office of the United States Courts
    "1996 Federal Court Management Statistics" (March 1997)
*Felony criminal cases. National rate includes cases U.S. territories. Does not include transfers from one district to another.

Authorized Wiretaps in 1996

National Total = 568 State Authorized Wiretaps*

<table>
<tr><td colspan="4">ALPHA ORDER</td><td colspan="4">RANK ORDER</td></tr>
<tr><td>RANK</td><td>STATE</td><td>WIRETAPS</td><td>% of USA</td><td>RANK</td><td>STATE</td><td>WIRETAPS</td><td>% of USA</td></tr>
<tr><td>NA</td><td>Alabama**</td><td>NA</td><td>NA</td><td>1</td><td>New York</td><td>246</td><td>43.31%</td></tr>
<tr><td>NA</td><td>Alaska**</td><td>NA</td><td>NA</td><td>2</td><td>New Jersey</td><td>103</td><td>18.13%</td></tr>
<tr><td>11</td><td>Arizona</td><td>5</td><td>0.88%</td><td>3</td><td>Florida</td><td>68</td><td>11.97%</td></tr>
<tr><td>NA</td><td>Arkansas**</td><td>NA</td><td>NA</td><td>4</td><td>Pennsylvania</td><td>53</td><td>9.33%</td></tr>
<tr><td>8</td><td>California</td><td>12</td><td>2.11%</td><td>5</td><td>Texas</td><td>16</td><td>2.82%</td></tr>
<tr><td>12</td><td>Colorado</td><td>4</td><td>0.70%</td><td>6</td><td>Nevada</td><td>15</td><td>2.64%</td></tr>
<tr><td>24</td><td>Connecticut</td><td>0</td><td>0.00%</td><td>7</td><td>Minnesota</td><td>14</td><td>2.46%</td></tr>
<tr><td>24</td><td>Delaware</td><td>0</td><td>0.00%</td><td>8</td><td>California</td><td>12</td><td>2.11%</td></tr>
<tr><td>3</td><td>Florida</td><td>68</td><td>11.97%</td><td>9</td><td>Georgia</td><td>6</td><td>1.06%</td></tr>
<tr><td>9</td><td>Georgia</td><td>6</td><td>1.06%</td><td>9</td><td>Maryland</td><td>6</td><td>1.06%</td></tr>
<tr><td>24</td><td>Hawaii</td><td>0</td><td>0.00%</td><td>11</td><td>Arizona</td><td>5</td><td>0.88%</td></tr>
<tr><td>24</td><td>Idaho</td><td>0</td><td>0.00%</td><td>12</td><td>Colorado</td><td>4</td><td>0.70%</td></tr>
<tr><td>24</td><td>Illinois</td><td>0</td><td>0.00%</td><td>12</td><td>Mississippi</td><td>4</td><td>0.70%</td></tr>
<tr><td>24</td><td>Indiana</td><td>0</td><td>0.00%</td><td>12</td><td>Oklahoma</td><td>4</td><td>0.70%</td></tr>
<tr><td>17</td><td>Iowa</td><td>1</td><td>0.18%</td><td>15</td><td>Nebraska</td><td>3</td><td>0.53%</td></tr>
<tr><td>17</td><td>Kansas</td><td>1</td><td>0.18%</td><td>16</td><td>Utah</td><td>2</td><td>0.35%</td></tr>
<tr><td>NA</td><td>Kentucky**</td><td>NA</td><td>NA</td><td>17</td><td>Iowa</td><td>1</td><td>0.18%</td></tr>
<tr><td>24</td><td>Louisiana</td><td>0</td><td>0.00%</td><td>17</td><td>Kansas</td><td>1</td><td>0.18%</td></tr>
<tr><td>NA</td><td>Maine**</td><td>NA</td><td>NA</td><td>17</td><td>Massachusetts</td><td>1</td><td>0.18%</td></tr>
<tr><td>9</td><td>Maryland</td><td>6</td><td>1.06%</td><td>17</td><td>New Mexico</td><td>1</td><td>0.18%</td></tr>
<tr><td>17</td><td>Massachusetts</td><td>1</td><td>0.18%</td><td>17</td><td>North Carolina</td><td>1</td><td>0.18%</td></tr>
<tr><td>NA</td><td>Michigan**</td><td>NA</td><td>NA</td><td>17</td><td>Virginia</td><td>1</td><td>0.18%</td></tr>
<tr><td>7</td><td>Minnesota</td><td>14</td><td>2.46%</td><td>17</td><td>Washington</td><td>1</td><td>0.18%</td></tr>
<tr><td>12</td><td>Mississippi</td><td>4</td><td>0.70%</td><td>24</td><td>Connecticut</td><td>0</td><td>0.00%</td></tr>
<tr><td>24</td><td>Missouri</td><td>0</td><td>0.00%</td><td>24</td><td>Delaware</td><td>0</td><td>0.00%</td></tr>
<tr><td>NA</td><td>Montana**</td><td>NA</td><td>NA</td><td>24</td><td>Hawaii</td><td>0</td><td>0.00%</td></tr>
<tr><td>15</td><td>Nebraska</td><td>3</td><td>0.53%</td><td>24</td><td>Idaho</td><td>0</td><td>0.00%</td></tr>
<tr><td>6</td><td>Nevada</td><td>15</td><td>2.64%</td><td>24</td><td>Illinois</td><td>0</td><td>0.00%</td></tr>
<tr><td>24</td><td>New Hampshire</td><td>0</td><td>0.00%</td><td>24</td><td>Indiana</td><td>0</td><td>0.00%</td></tr>
<tr><td>2</td><td>New Jersey</td><td>103</td><td>18.13%</td><td>24</td><td>Louisiana</td><td>0</td><td>0.00%</td></tr>
<tr><td>17</td><td>New Mexico</td><td>1</td><td>0.18%</td><td>24</td><td>Missouri</td><td>0</td><td>0.00%</td></tr>
<tr><td>1</td><td>New York</td><td>246</td><td>43.31%</td><td>24</td><td>New Hampshire</td><td>0</td><td>0.00%</td></tr>
<tr><td>17</td><td>North Carolina</td><td>1</td><td>0.18%</td><td>24</td><td>North Dakota</td><td>0</td><td>0.00%</td></tr>
<tr><td>24</td><td>North Dakota</td><td>0</td><td>0.00%</td><td>24</td><td>Ohio</td><td>0</td><td>0.00%</td></tr>
<tr><td>24</td><td>Ohio</td><td>0</td><td>0.00%</td><td>24</td><td>Oregon</td><td>0</td><td>0.00%</td></tr>
<tr><td>12</td><td>Oklahoma</td><td>4</td><td>0.70%</td><td>24</td><td>Rhode Island</td><td>0</td><td>0.00%</td></tr>
<tr><td>24</td><td>Oregon</td><td>0</td><td>0.00%</td><td>24</td><td>South Dakota</td><td>0</td><td>0.00%</td></tr>
<tr><td>4</td><td>Pennsylvania</td><td>53</td><td>9.33%</td><td>24</td><td>Tennessee</td><td>0</td><td>0.00%</td></tr>
<tr><td>24</td><td>Rhode Island</td><td>0</td><td>0.00%</td><td>24</td><td>West Virginia</td><td>0</td><td>0.00%</td></tr>
<tr><td>NA</td><td>South Carolina**</td><td>NA</td><td>NA</td><td>24</td><td>Wisconsin</td><td>0</td><td>0.00%</td></tr>
<tr><td>24</td><td>South Dakota</td><td>0</td><td>0.00%</td><td>24</td><td>Wyoming</td><td>0</td><td>0.00%</td></tr>
<tr><td>24</td><td>Tennessee</td><td>0</td><td>0.00%</td><td>NA</td><td>Alabama**</td><td>NA</td><td>NA</td></tr>
<tr><td>5</td><td>Texas</td><td>16</td><td>2.82%</td><td>NA</td><td>Alaska**</td><td>NA</td><td>NA</td></tr>
<tr><td>16</td><td>Utah</td><td>2</td><td>0.35%</td><td>NA</td><td>Arkansas**</td><td>NA</td><td>NA</td></tr>
<tr><td>NA</td><td>Vermont**</td><td>NA</td><td>NA</td><td>NA</td><td>Kentucky**</td><td>NA</td><td>NA</td></tr>
<tr><td>17</td><td>Virginia</td><td>1</td><td>0.18%</td><td>NA</td><td>Maine**</td><td>NA</td><td>NA</td></tr>
<tr><td>17</td><td>Washington</td><td>1</td><td>0.18%</td><td>NA</td><td>Michigan**</td><td>NA</td><td>NA</td></tr>
<tr><td>24</td><td>West Virginia</td><td>0</td><td>0.00%</td><td>NA</td><td>Montana**</td><td>NA</td><td>NA</td></tr>
<tr><td>24</td><td>Wisconsin</td><td>0</td><td>0.00%</td><td>NA</td><td>South Carolina**</td><td>NA</td><td>NA</td></tr>
<tr><td>24</td><td>Wyoming</td><td>0</td><td>0.00%</td><td>NA</td><td>Vermont**</td><td>NA</td><td>NA</td></tr>
<tr><td></td><td></td><td></td><td></td><td></td><td>District of Columbia</td><td>0</td><td>0.00%</td></tr>
</table>

Source: Administrative Office of the United States Courts
"1996 Wiretap Report" (April 1997)
*Total does not include 581 wiretaps authorized under federal statute.
**No state statute authorizing wiretaps.

VII. OFFENSES

VII. OFFENSES (continued)

369 Aggravated Assault Rate in 1996
370 Percent Change in Aggravated Assault Rate: 1995 to 1996
371 Aggravated Assaults with Firearms in 1996
372 Aggravated Assault Rate with Firearms in 1996
373 Percent of Aggravated Assaults Involving Firearms in 1996
374 Aggravated Assaults with Knives or Cutting Instruments in 1996
375 Percent of Aggravated Assaults Involving Knives or Cutting Instruments in 1996
376 Aggravated Assaults with Blunt Objects and Other Dangerous Weapons in 1996
377 Percent of Aggravated assaults Involving Blunt Objects and Other Dangerous Weapons in 1996
378 Aggravated Assaults Committed with Hands, Fists or Feet in 1996
379 Percent of Aggravated Assaults Committed with Hands, Fists or Feet in 1996
380 Property Crimes in 1996
381 Average Time Between Property Crimes in 1996
382 Property Crimes per Square Mile in 1996
383 Percent Change in Number of Property Crimes: 1995 to 1996
384 Property Crime Rate in 1996
385 Percent Change in Property Crime Rate: 1995 to 1996
386 Burglaries in 1996
387 Average Time Between Burglaries in 1996
388 Percent Change in Number of Burglaries: 1995 to 1996
389 Burglary Rate in 1996
390 Percent Change in Burglary Rate: 1995 to 1996
391 Larcenies and Thefts in 1996
392 Average Time Between Larcenies and Thefts in 1996
393 Percent Change in Number of Larcenies and Thefts: 1995 to 1996
394 Larceny and Theft Rate in 1996
395 Percent Change in Larceny and Theft Rate: 1995 to 1996
396 Motor Vehicle Thefts in 1996
397 Average Time Between Motor Vehicle Thefts in 1996
398 Percent Change in Number of Motor Vehicle Thefts: 1995 to 1996
399 Motor Vehicle Theft Rate in 1996
400 Percent Change in Motor Vehicle Theft Rate: 1995 to 1996

Urban/Rural Crime

401 Crimes in Urban Areas in 1996
402 Urban Crime Rate in 1996
403 Percent of Crimes Occurring in Urban Areas in 1996
404 Crimes in Rural Areas in 1996
405 Rural Crime Rate in 1996
406 Percent of Crimes Occurring in Rural Areas in 1996
407 Violent Crimes in Urban Areas in 1996
408 Urban Violent Crime Rate in 1996
409 Percent of Violent Crimes Occurring in Urban Areas in 1996
410 Violent Crimes in Rural Areas in 1996
411 Rural Violent Crime Rate in 1996
412 Percent of Violent Crimes Occurring in Rural Areas in 1996
413 Murders in Urban Areas in 1996
414 Urban Murder Rate in 1996
415 Percent of Murders Occurring in Urban Areas in 1996
416 Murders in Rural Areas in 1996
417 Rural Murder Rate in 1996
418 Percent of Murders Occurring in Rural Areas in 1996
419 Rapes in Urban Areas in 1996
420 Urban Rape Rate in 1996
421 Percent of Rapes Occurring in Urban Areas in 1996
422 Rapes in Rural Areas in 1996
423 Rural Rape Rate in 1996

VII. OFFENSES (continued)

VII. OFFENSES (continued)

Crimes in 1996

National Total = 13,473,614 Crimes*

ALPHA ORDER

RANK	STATE	CRIMES	% of USA
23	Alabama	205,962	1.53%
45	Alaska	33,084	0.25%
13	Arizona	312,927	2.32%
33	Arkansas	117,951	0.88%
1	California	1,660,131	12.32%
25	Colorado	195,681	1.45%
28	Connecticut	138,414	1.03%
44	Delaware	35,488	0.26%
3	Florida	1,079,623	8.01%
8	Georgia	463,952	3.44%
37	Hawaii	77,961	0.58%
39	Idaho	47,709	0.35%
5	Illinois	629,762	4.67%
19	Indiana	262,742	1.95%
35	Iowa	104,067	0.77%
31	Kansas	120,414	0.89%
29	Kentucky	122,979	0.91%
15	Louisiana	297,556	2.21%
41	Maine	42,189	0.31%
14	Maryland	307,461	2.28%
20	Massachusetts	233,758	1.73%
7	Michigan	490,971	3.64%
22	Minnesota	207,891	1.54%
30	Mississippi	122,842	0.91%
17	Missouri	272,450	2.02%
43	Montana	39,499	0.29%
38	Nebraska	73,292	0.54%
36	Nevada	96,052	0.71%
46	New Hampshire	32,809	0.24%
11	New Jersey	346,116	2.57%
34	New Mexico	113,097	0.84%
4	New York	751,456	5.58%
10	North Carolina	404,684	3.00%
50	North Dakota	17,189	0.13%
6	Ohio	497,831	3.69%
27	Oklahoma	186,602	1.38%
26	Oregon	192,132	1.43%
9	Pennsylvania	409,004	3.04%
42	Rhode Island	39,536	0.29%
21	South Carolina	229,861	1.71%
47	South Dakota	21,740	0.16%
16	Tennessee	289,904	2.15%
2	Texas	1,092,002	8.10%
32	Utah	119,717	0.89%
49	Vermont	17,687	0.13%
18	Virginia	264,882	1.97%
12	Washington	326,968	2.43%
40	West Virginia	45,346	0.34%
24	Wisconsin	197,182	1.46%
48	Wyoming	20,462	0.15%

RANK ORDER

RANK	STATE	CRIMES	% of USA
1	California	1,660,131	12.32%
2	Texas	1,092,002	8.10%
3	Florida	1,079,623	8.01%
4	New York	751,456	5.58%
5	Illinois	629,762	4.67%
6	Ohio	497,831	3.69%
7	Michigan	490,971	3.64%
8	Georgia	463,952	3.44%
9	Pennsylvania	409,004	3.04%
10	North Carolina	404,684	3.00%
11	New Jersey	346,116	2.57%
12	Washington	326,968	2.43%
13	Arizona	312,927	2.32%
14	Maryland	307,461	2.28%
15	Louisiana	297,556	2.21%
16	Tennessee	289,904	2.15%
17	Missouri	272,450	2.02%
18	Virginia	264,882	1.97%
19	Indiana	262,742	1.95%
20	Massachusetts	233,758	1.73%
21	South Carolina	229,861	1.71%
22	Minnesota	207,891	1.54%
23	Alabama	205,962	1.53%
24	Wisconsin	197,182	1.46%
25	Colorado	195,681	1.45%
26	Oregon	192,132	1.43%
27	Oklahoma	186,602	1.38%
28	Connecticut	138,414	1.03%
29	Kentucky	122,979	0.91%
30	Mississippi	122,842	0.91%
31	Kansas	120,414	0.89%
32	Utah	119,717	0.89%
33	Arkansas	117,951	0.88%
34	New Mexico	113,097	0.84%
35	Iowa	104,067	0.77%
36	Nevada	96,052	0.71%
37	Hawaii	77,961	0.58%
38	Nebraska	73,292	0.54%
39	Idaho	47,709	0.35%
40	West Virginia	45,346	0.34%
41	Maine	42,189	0.31%
42	Rhode Island	39,536	0.29%
43	Montana	39,499	0.29%
44	Delaware	35,488	0.26%
45	Alaska	33,084	0.25%
46	New Hampshire	32,809	0.24%
47	South Dakota	21,740	0.16%
48	Wyoming	20,462	0.15%
49	Vermont	17,687	0.13%
50	North Dakota	17,189	0.13%
	District of Columbia	64,599	0.48%

Source: Federal Bureau of Investigation
"Crime in the United States 1996" (Uniform Crime Reports, October 4, 1997)
*Includes murder, rape, robbery, aggravated assault, burglary, larceny-theft and motor vehicle theft.

Average Time Between Crimes in 1996

National Rate = A Crime Occurs Every 2 Seconds*

ALPHA ORDER

RANK	STATE	MINUTES.SECONDS
28	Alabama	2.34
6	Alaska	15.56
38	Arizona	1.41
18	Arkansas	4.28
50	California	0.19
26	Colorado	2.41
23	Connecticut	3.49
7	Delaware	14.51
48	Florida	0.29
43	Georgia	1.08
14	Hawaii	6.46
12	Idaho	11.03
46	Illinois	0.50
32	Indiana	2.01
16	Iowa	5.04
20	Kansas	4.23
21	Kentucky	4.17
36	Louisiana	1.46
10	Maine	12.29
37	Maryland	1.43
31	Massachusetts	2.15
44	Michigan	1.04
29	Minnesota	2.32
21	Mississippi	4.17
34	Missouri	1.56
8	Montana	13.20
13	Nebraska	7.11
15	Nevada	5.29
5	New Hampshire	16.04
40	New Jersey	1.31
17	New Mexico	4.40
47	New York	0.42
41	North Carolina	1.18
1	North Dakota	30.40
44	Ohio	1.04
24	Oklahoma	2.49
25	Oregon	2.44
42	Pennsylvania	1.17
8	Rhode Island	13.20
30	South Carolina	2.17
4	South Dakota	24.14
35	Tennessee	1.49
48	Texas	0.29
19	Utah	4.24
2	Vermont	29.48
33	Virginia	1.59
39	Washington	1.37
11	West Virginia	11.37
27	Wisconsin	2.40
3	Wyoming	25.46

RANK ORDER

RANK	STATE	MINUTES.SECONDS
1	North Dakota	30.40
2	Vermont	29.48
3	Wyoming	25.46
4	South Dakota	24.14
5	New Hampshire	16.04
6	Alaska	15.56
7	Delaware	14.51
8	Montana	13.20
8	Rhode Island	13.20
10	Maine	12.29
11	West Virginia	11.37
12	Idaho	11.03
13	Nebraska	7.11
14	Hawaii	6.46
15	Nevada	5.29
16	Iowa	5.04
17	New Mexico	4.40
18	Arkansas	4.28
19	Utah	4.24
20	Kansas	4.23
21	Kentucky	4.17
21	Mississippi	4.17
23	Connecticut	3.49
24	Oklahoma	2.49
25	Oregon	2.44
26	Colorado	2.41
27	Wisconsin	2.40
28	Alabama	2.34
29	Minnesota	2.32
30	South Carolina	2.17
31	Massachusetts	2.15
32	Indiana	2.01
33	Virginia	1.59
34	Missouri	1.56
35	Tennessee	1.49
36	Louisiana	1.46
37	Maryland	1.43
38	Arizona	1.41
39	Washington	1.37
40	New Jersey	1.31
41	North Carolina	1.18
42	Pennsylvania	1.17
43	Georgia	1.08
44	Michigan	1.04
44	Ohio	1.04
46	Illinois	0.50
47	New York	0.42
48	Florida	0.29
48	Texas	0.29
50	California	0.19
	District of Columbia	8.10

Source: Morgan Quitno Press using data from Federal Bureau of Investigation
"Crime in the United States 1996" (Uniform Crime Reports, October 4, 1997)
*Includes murder, rape, robbery, aggravated assault, burglary, larceny-theft and motor vehicle theft.

Crimes per Square Mile in 1996

National Rate = 3.6 Crimes per Square Mile*

ALPHA ORDER

RANK ORDER

RANK	STATE	RATE
24	Alabama	3.9
50	Alaska	0.1
29	Arizona	2.7
33	Arkansas	2.2
12	California	10.4
35	Colorado	1.9
4	Connecticut	25.0
7	Delaware	14.8
6	Florida	18.0
14	Georgia	7.9
9	Hawaii	12.1
45	Idaho	0.6
11	Illinois	10.9
17	Indiana	7.2
37	Iowa	1.8
39	Kansas	1.5
27	Kentucky	3.0
20	Louisiana	6.0
41	Maine	1.3
4	Maryland	25.0
3	Massachusetts	25.3
21	Michigan	5.1
32	Minnesota	2.4
31	Mississippi	2.5
24	Missouri	3.9
46	Montana	0.3
42	Nebraska	0.9
42	Nevada	0.9
26	New Hampshire	3.5
1	New Jersey	42.1
42	New Mexico	0.9
8	New York	13.9
15	North Carolina	7.7
48	North Dakota	0.2
10	Ohio	11.1
29	Oklahoma	2.7
34	Oregon	2.0
13	Pennsylvania	8.9
2	Rhode Island	32.1
16	South Carolina	7.4
46	South Dakota	0.3
18	Tennessee	6.9
23	Texas	4.1
40	Utah	1.4
37	Vermont	1.8
19	Virginia	6.3
22	Washington	4.6
35	West Virginia	1.9
27	Wisconsin	3.0
48	Wyoming	0.2

RANK	STATE	RATE
1	New Jersey	42.1
2	Rhode Island	32.1
3	Massachusetts	25.3
4	Connecticut	25.0
4	Maryland	25.0
6	Florida	18.0
7	Delaware	14.8
8	New York	13.9
9	Hawaii	12.1
10	Ohio	11.1
11	Illinois	10.9
12	California	10.4
13	Pennsylvania	8.9
14	Georgia	7.9
15	North Carolina	7.7
16	South Carolina	7.4
17	Indiana	7.2
18	Tennessee	6.9
19	Virginia	6.3
20	Louisiana	6.0
21	Michigan	5.1
22	Washington	4.6
23	Texas	4.1
24	Alabama	3.9
24	Missouri	3.9
26	New Hampshire	3.5
27	Kentucky	3.0
27	Wisconsin	3.0
29	Arizona	2.7
29	Oklahoma	2.7
31	Mississippi	2.5
32	Minnesota	2.4
33	Arkansas	2.2
34	Oregon	2.0
35	Colorado	1.9
35	West Virginia	1.9
37	Iowa	1.8
37	Vermont	1.8
39	Kansas	1.5
40	Utah	1.4
41	Maine	1.3
42	Nebraska	0.9
42	Nevada	0.9
42	New Mexico	0.9
45	Idaho	0.6
46	Montana	0.3
46	South Dakota	0.3
48	North Dakota	0.2
48	Wyoming	0.2
50	Alaska	0.1
	District of Columbia	950.0

Source: Morgan Quitno Press using data from Federal Bureau of Investigation
   "Crime in the United States 1996" (Uniform Crime Reports, October 4, 1997)
*Includes murder, rape, robbery, aggravated assault, burglary, larceny-theft and motor vehicle theft.

Percent Change in Number of Crimes: 1995 to 1996

National Percent Change = 2.8% Decrease*

ALPHA ORDER				RANK ORDER		
RANK	STATE	PERCENT CHANGE		RANK	STATE	PERCENT CHANGE
18	Alabama	(0.1)		1	New Hampshire	7.6
35	Alaska	(4.8)		2	Georgia	7.3
46	Arizona	(9.7)		3	New Mexico	4.4
11	Arkansas	1.2		4	Maine	3.5
47	California	(9.9)		5	South Carolina	3.2
30	Colorado	(3.2)		6	Tennessee	2.9
39	Connecticut	(6.1)		7	Louisiana	2.7
33	Delaware	(4.1)		8	Texas	2.6
23	Florida	(1.0)		9	Oklahoma	1.7
2	Georgia	7.3		10	Ohio	1.3
44	Hawaii	(8.8)		11	Arkansas	1.2
41	Idaho	(6.8)		12	Mississippi	0.9
27	Illinois	(2.4)		12	West Virginia	0.9
26	Indiana	(2.2)		14	Pennsylvania	0.7
48	Iowa	(10.7)		14	Utah	0.7
31	Kansas	(3.9)		16	Minnesota	0.3
36	Kentucky	(4.9)		16	Virginia	0.3
7	Louisiana	2.7		18	Alabama	(0.1)
4	Maine	3.5		18	Missouri	(0.1)
29	Maryland	(3.1)		20	North Carolina	(0.3)
49	Massachusetts	(11.4)		21	Michigan	(0.8)
21	Michigan	(0.8)		22	Wisconsin	(0.9)
16	Minnesota	0.3		23	Florida	(1.0)
12	Mississippi	0.9		24	Wyoming	(1.3)
18	Missouri	(0.1)		25	Nebraska	(1.5)
37	Montana	(5.4)		26	Indiana	(2.2)
25	Nebraska	(1.5)		27	Illinois	(2.4)
34	Nevada	(4.6)		28	South Dakota	(2.6)
1	New Hampshire	7.6		29	Maryland	(3.1)
43	New Jersey	(7.4)		30	Colorado	(3.2)
3	New Mexico	4.4		31	Kansas	(3.9)
45	New York	(9.1)		32	Washington	(4.0)
20	North Carolina	(0.3)		33	Delaware	(4.1)
40	North Dakota	(6.4)		34	Nevada	(4.6)
10	Ohio	1.3		35	Alaska	(4.8)
9	Oklahoma	1.7		36	Kentucky	(4.9)
41	Oregon	(6.8)		37	Montana	(5.4)
14	Pennsylvania	0.7		38	Rhode Island	(5.9)
38	Rhode Island	(5.9)		39	Connecticut	(6.1)
5	South Carolina	3.2		40	North Dakota	(6.4)
28	South Dakota	(2.6)		41	Idaho	(6.8)
6	Tennessee	2.9		41	Oregon	(6.8)
8	Texas	2.6		43	New Jersey	(7.4)
14	Utah	0.7		44	Hawaii	(8.8)
50	Vermont	(11.9)		45	New York	(9.1)
16	Virginia	0.3		46	Arizona	(9.7)
32	Washington	(4.0)		47	California	(9.9)
12	West Virginia	0.9		48	Iowa	(10.7)
22	Wisconsin	(0.9)		49	Massachusetts	(11.4)
24	Wyoming	(1.3)		50	Vermont	(11.9)
					District of Columbia	(4.2)

Source: Federal Bureau of Investigation
   "Crime in the United States 1996" (Uniform Crime Reports, October 4, 1997)
*Includes murder, rape, robbery, aggravated assault, burglary, larceny-theft and motor vehicle theft.

Crime Rate in 1996

National Rate = 5,078.9 Crimes per 100,000 Population*

ALPHA ORDER

RANK ORDER

RANK	STATE	RATE	RANK	STATE	RATE
24	Alabama	4,820.1	1	Florida	7,497.4
16	Alaska	5,450.4	2	Arizona	7,067.0
2	Arizona	7,067.0	3	Louisiana	6,838.8
25	Arkansas	4,699.2	4	New Mexico	6,602.3
19	California	5,207.8	5	Hawaii	6,584.5
20	Colorado	5,118.5	6	Georgia	6,309.7
35	Connecticut	4,227.7	7	South Carolina	6,214.1
23	Delaware	4,894.9	8	Maryland	6,061.9
1	Florida	7,497.4	9	Oregon	5,996.6
6	Georgia	6,309.7	10	Nevada	5,992.0
5	Hawaii	6,584.5	11	Utah	5,985.9
37	Idaho	4,012.5	12	Washington	5,909.4
18	Illinois	5,315.8	13	Texas	5,708.9
28	Indiana	4,498.2	14	Oklahoma	5,652.9
42	Iowa	3,648.9	15	North Carolina	5,526.2
26	Kansas	4,681.7	16	Alaska	5,450.4
45	Kentucky	3,166.3	17	Tennessee	5,449.3
3	Louisiana	6,838.8	18	Illinois	5,315.8
43	Maine	3,394.1	19	California	5,207.8
8	Maryland	6,061.9	20	Colorado	5,118.5
40	Massachusetts	3,837.1	21	Michigan	5,117.5
21	Michigan	5,117.5	22	Missouri	5,084.0
30	Minnesota	4,463.1	23	Delaware	4,894.9
27	Mississippi	4,522.9	24	Alabama	4,820.1
22	Missouri	5,084.0	25	Arkansas	4,699.2
29	Montana	4,493.6	26	Kansas	4,681.7
32	Nebraska	4,436.6	27	Mississippi	4,522.9
10	Nevada	5,992.0	28	Indiana	4,498.2
48	New Hampshire	2,823.5	29	Montana	4,493.6
33	New Jersey	4,332.9	30	Minnesota	4,463.1
4	New Mexico	6,602.3	31	Ohio	4,455.7
36	New York	4,132.3	32	Nebraska	4,436.6
15	North Carolina	5,526.2	33	New Jersey	4,332.9
49	North Dakota	2,669.1	34	Wyoming	4,254.1
31	Ohio	4,455.7	35	Connecticut	4,227.7
14	Oklahoma	5,652.9	36	New York	4,132.3
9	Oregon	5,996.6	37	Idaho	4,012.5
44	Pennsylvania	3,392.5	38	Rhode Island	3,993.5
38	Rhode Island	3,993.5	39	Virginia	3,968.3
7	South Carolina	6,214.1	40	Massachusetts	3,837.1
47	South Dakota	2,969.9	41	Wisconsin	3,821.4
17	Tennessee	5,449.3	42	Iowa	3,648.9
13	Texas	5,708.9	43	Maine	3,394.1
11	Utah	5,985.9	44	Pennsylvania	3,392.5
46	Vermont	3,002.9	45	Kentucky	3,166.3
39	Virginia	3,968.3	46	Vermont	3,002.9
12	Washington	5,909.4	47	South Dakota	2,969.9
50	West Virginia	2,483.4	48	New Hampshire	2,823.5
41	Wisconsin	3,821.4	49	North Dakota	2,669.1
34	Wyoming	4,254.1	50	West Virginia	2,483.4
				District of Columbia	11,896.7

Source: Federal Bureau of Investigation
"Crime in the United States 1996" (Uniform Crime Reports, October 4, 1997)
*Includes murder, rape, robbery, aggravated assault, burglary, larceny-theft and motor vehicle theft.

Percent Change in Crime Rate: 1995 to 1996

National Percent Change = 3.7% Decrease*

ALPHA ORDER

RANK	STATE	PERCENT CHANGE
16	Alabama	(0.6)
33	Alaska	(5.3)
50	Arizona	(14.0)
13	Arkansas	0.2
46	California	(10.7)
31	Colorado	(5.1)
37	Connecticut	(6.1)
31	Delaware	(5.1)
26	Florida	(2.7)
2	Georgia	5.1
41	Hawaii	(8.5)
43	Idaho	(8.8)
25	Illinois	(2.6)
27	Indiana	(2.9)
47	Iowa	(11.0)
30	Kansas	(4.2)
34	Kentucky	(5.5)
6	Louisiana	2.4
3	Maine	3.3
29	Maryland	(3.7)
48	Massachusetts	(11.6)
19	Michigan	(1.3)
18	Minnesota	(0.8)
13	Mississippi	0.2
17	Missouri	(0.7)
38	Montana	(6.3)
24	Nebraska	(2.4)
44	Nevada	(8.9)
1	New Hampshire	6.3
40	New Jersey	(7.9)
4	New Mexico	2.7
45	New York	(9.4)
23	North Carolina	(2.0)
39	North Dakota	(6.9)
8	Ohio	1.1
9	Oklahoma	1.0
42	Oregon	(8.6)
11	Pennsylvania	0.8
36	Rhode Island	(5.9)
5	South Carolina	2.5
28	South Dakota	(3.0)
7	Tennessee	1.6
12	Texas	0.4
21	Utah	(1.7)
49	Vermont	(12.5)
15	Virginia	(0.5)
35	Washington	(5.7)
9	West Virginia	1.0
21	Wisconsin	(1.7)
20	Wyoming	(1.5)

RANK ORDER

RANK	STATE	PERCENT CHANGE
1	New Hampshire	6.3
2	Georgia	5.1
3	Maine	3.3
4	New Mexico	2.7
5	South Carolina	2.5
6	Louisiana	2.4
7	Tennessee	1.6
8	Ohio	1.1
9	Oklahoma	1.0
9	West Virginia	1.0
11	Pennsylvania	0.8
12	Texas	0.4
13	Arkansas	0.2
13	Mississippi	0.2
15	Virginia	(0.5)
16	Alabama	(0.6)
17	Missouri	(0.7)
18	Minnesota	(0.8)
19	Michigan	(1.3)
20	Wyoming	(1.5)
21	Utah	(1.7)
21	Wisconsin	(1.7)
23	North Carolina	(2.0)
24	Nebraska	(2.4)
25	Illinois	(2.6)
26	Florida	(2.7)
27	Indiana	(2.9)
28	South Dakota	(3.0)
29	Maryland	(3.7)
30	Kansas	(4.2)
31	Colorado	(5.1)
31	Delaware	(5.1)
33	Alaska	(5.3)
34	Kentucky	(5.5)
35	Washington	(5.7)
36	Rhode Island	(5.9)
37	Connecticut	(6.1)
38	Montana	(6.3)
39	North Dakota	(6.9)
40	New Jersey	(7.9)
41	Hawaii	(8.5)
42	Oregon	(8.6)
43	Idaho	(8.8)
44	Nevada	(8.9)
45	New York	(9.4)
46	California	(10.7)
47	Iowa	(11.0)
48	Massachusetts	(11.6)
49	Vermont	(12.5)
50	Arizona	(14.0)
	District of Columbia	(2.3)

Source: Federal Bureau of Investigation
   "Crime in the United States 1996" (Uniform Crime Reports, October 4, 1997)
*Includes murder, rape, robbery, aggravated assault, burglary, larceny-theft and motor vehicle theft.

Violent Crimes in 1996

National Total = 1,682,278 Violent Crimes*

ALPHA ORDER

RANK	STATE	CRIMES	% of USA
20	Alabama	24,159	1.44%
39	Alaska	4,417	0.26%
19	Arizona	27,963	1.66%
30	Arkansas	13,161	0.78%
1	California	274,996	16.35%
25	Colorado	15,463	0.92%
28	Connecticut	13,490	0.80%
38	Delaware	4,845	0.29%
2	Florida	151,350	9.00%
10	Georgia	46,966	2.79%
42	Hawaii	3,322	0.20%
43	Idaho	3,177	0.19%
5	Illinois	104,985	6.24%
18	Indiana	31,366	1.86%
35	Iowa	7,771	0.46%
34	Kansas	10,642	0.63%
33	Kentucky	12,448	0.74%
14	Louisiana	40,426	2.40%
44	Maine	1,553	0.09%
9	Maryland	47,230	2.81%
15	Massachusetts	39,122	2.33%
6	Michigan	60,951	3.62%
24	Minnesota	15,782	0.94%
29	Mississippi	13,261	0.79%
17	Missouri	31,669	1.88%
45	Montana	1,415	0.08%
36	Nebraska	7,182	0.43%
32	Nevada	13,005	0.77%
46	New Hampshire	1,373	0.08%
12	New Jersey	42,459	2.52%
27	New Mexico	14,399	0.86%
3	New York	132,206	7.86%
11	North Carolina	43,068	2.56%
50	North Dakota	541	0.03%
8	Ohio	47,896	2.85%
23	Oklahoma	19,710	1.17%
26	Oregon	14,837	0.88%
7	Pennsylvania	52,140	3.10%
41	Rhode Island	3,437	0.20%
16	South Carolina	36,875	2.19%
47	South Dakota	1,297	0.08%
13	Tennessee	41,175	2.45%
4	Texas	123,270	7.33%
37	Utah	6,638	0.39%
49	Vermont	714	0.04%
22	Virginia	22,782	1.35%
21	Washington	23,857	1.42%
40	West Virginia	3,836	0.23%
31	Wisconsin	13,039	0.78%
48	Wyoming	1,201	0.07%

RANK ORDER

RANK	STATE	CRIMES	% of USA
1	California	274,996	16.35%
2	Florida	151,350	9.00%
3	New York	132,206	7.86%
4	Texas	123,270	7.33%
5	Illinois	104,985	6.24%
6	Michigan	60,951	3.62%
7	Pennsylvania	52,140	3.10%
8	Ohio	47,896	2.85%
9	Maryland	47,230	2.81%
10	Georgia	46,966	2.79%
11	North Carolina	43,068	2.56%
12	New Jersey	42,459	2.52%
13	Tennessee	41,175	2.45%
14	Louisiana	40,426	2.40%
15	Massachusetts	39,122	2.33%
16	South Carolina	36,875	2.19%
17	Missouri	31,669	1.88%
18	Indiana	31,366	1.86%
19	Arizona	27,963	1.66%
20	Alabama	24,159	1.44%
21	Washington	23,857	1.42%
22	Virginia	22,782	1.35%
23	Oklahoma	19,710	1.17%
24	Minnesota	15,782	0.94%
25	Colorado	15,463	0.92%
26	Oregon	14,837	0.88%
27	New Mexico	14,399	0.86%
28	Connecticut	13,490	0.80%
29	Mississippi	13,261	0.79%
30	Arkansas	13,161	0.78%
31	Wisconsin	13,039	0.78%
32	Nevada	13,005	0.77%
33	Kentucky	12,448	0.74%
34	Kansas	10,642	0.63%
35	Iowa	7,771	0.46%
36	Nebraska	7,182	0.43%
37	Utah	6,638	0.39%
38	Delaware	4,845	0.29%
39	Alaska	4,417	0.26%
40	West Virginia	3,836	0.23%
41	Rhode Island	3,437	0.20%
42	Hawaii	3,322	0.20%
43	Idaho	3,177	0.19%
44	Maine	1,553	0.09%
45	Montana	1,415	0.08%
46	New Hampshire	1,373	0.08%
47	South Dakota	1,297	0.08%
48	Wyoming	1,201	0.07%
49	Vermont	714	0.04%
50	North Dakota	541	0.03%
	District of Columbia	13,411	0.80%

Source: Federal Bureau of Investigation
    "Crime in the United States 1996" (Uniform Crime Reports, October 4, 1997)
*Violent crimes are offenses of murder, forcible rape, robbery and aggravated assault.

Average Time Between Violent Crimes in 1996

National Rate = A Violent Crime Occurs Every 19 Seconds*

ALPHA ORDER				RANK ORDER		
RANK	STATE	MINUTES.SECONDS		RANK	STATE	MINUTES.SECONDS
31	Alabama	21.49		1	North Dakota	974.12
12	Alaska	119.19		2	Vermont	738.09
32	Arizona	18.51		3	Wyoming	438.50
21	Arkansas	40.03		4	South Dakota	406.21
50	California	1.55		5	New Hampshire	383.52
26	Colorado	34.05		6	Montana	372.28
23	Connecticut	39.04		7	Maine	339.22
13	Delaware	108.47		8	Idaho	165.53
49	Florida	3.29		9	Hawaii	158.39
41	Georgia	11.13		10	Rhode Island	153.20
9	Hawaii	158.39		11	West Virginia	137.23
8	Idaho	165.53		12	Alaska	119.19
46	Illinois	5.01		13	Delaware	108.47
33	Indiana	16.48		14	Utah	79.24
16	Iowa	67.49		15	Nebraska	73.23
17	Kansas	49.31		16	Iowa	67.49
18	Kentucky	42.20		17	Kansas	49.31
37	Louisiana	13.02		18	Kentucky	42.20
7	Maine	339.22		19	Nevada	40.32
42	Maryland	11.10		20	Wisconsin	40.25
36	Massachusetts	13.28		21	Arkansas	40.03
45	Michigan	8.39		22	Mississippi	39.44
27	Minnesota	33.24		23	Connecticut	39.04
22	Mississippi	39.44		24	New Mexico	36.36
34	Missouri	16.38		25	Oregon	35.31
6	Montana	372.28		26	Colorado	34.05
15	Nebraska	73.23		27	Minnesota	33.24
19	Nevada	40.32		28	Oklahoma	26.44
5	New Hampshire	383.52		29	Virginia	23.08
39	New Jersey	12.25		30	Washington	22.05
24	New Mexico	36.36		31	Alabama	21.49
48	New York	3.59		32	Arizona	18.51
40	North Carolina	12.14		33	Indiana	16.48
1	North Dakota	974.12		34	Missouri	16.38
43	Ohio	11.00		35	South Carolina	14.17
28	Oklahoma	26.44		36	Massachusetts	13.28
25	Oregon	35.31		37	Louisiana	13.02
44	Pennsylvania	10.07		38	Tennessee	12.48
10	Rhode Island	153.20		39	New Jersey	12.25
35	South Carolina	14.17		40	North Carolina	12.14
4	South Dakota	406.21		41	Georgia	11.13
38	Tennessee	12.48		42	Maryland	11.10
47	Texas	4.17		43	Ohio	11.00
14	Utah	79.24		44	Pennsylvania	10.07
2	Vermont	738.09		45	Michigan	8.39
29	Virginia	23.08		46	Illinois	5.01
30	Washington	22.05		47	Texas	4.17
11	West Virginia	137.23		48	New York	3.59
20	Wisconsin	40.25		49	Florida	3.29
3	Wyoming	438.50		50	California	1.55
					District of Columbia	39.18

Source: Morgan Quitno Press using data from Federal Bureau of Investigation
    "Crime in the United States 1996" (Uniform Crime Reports, October 4, 1997)
*Violent crimes are offenses of murder, forcible rape, robbery and aggravated assault.

Violent Crimes per Square Mile in 1996

National Rate = 0.5 Violent Crimes per Square Mile*

ALPHA ORDER

RANK	STATE	RATE
20	Alabama	0.5
44	Alaska	0.0
29	Arizona	0.2
29	Arkansas	0.2
10	California	1.7
35	Colorado	0.1
6	Connecticut	2.4
8	Delaware	2.0
5	Florida	2.5
16	Georgia	0.8
20	Hawaii	0.5
44	Idaho	0.0
9	Illinois	1.8
15	Indiana	0.9
35	Iowa	0.1
35	Kansas	0.1
25	Kentucky	0.3
16	Louisiana	0.8
44	Maine	0.0
3	Maryland	3.8
2	Massachusetts	4.2
19	Michigan	0.6
29	Minnesota	0.2
25	Mississippi	0.3
20	Missouri	0.5
44	Montana	0.0
35	Nebraska	0.1
35	Nevada	0.1
35	New Hampshire	0.1
1	New Jersey	5.2
35	New Mexico	0.1
6	New York	2.4
16	North Carolina	0.8
44	North Dakota	0.0
12	Ohio	1.1
25	Oklahoma	0.3
29	Oregon	0.2
12	Pennsylvania	1.1
4	Rhode Island	2.8
11	South Carolina	1.2
44	South Dakota	0.0
14	Tennessee	1.0
20	Texas	0.5
35	Utah	0.1
35	Vermont	0.1
20	Virginia	0.5
25	Washington	0.3
29	West Virginia	0.2
29	Wisconsin	0.2
44	Wyoming	0.0

RANK ORDER

RANK	STATE	RATE
1	New Jersey	5.2
2	Massachusetts	4.2
3	Maryland	3.8
4	Rhode Island	2.8
5	Florida	2.5
6	Connecticut	2.4
6	New York	2.4
8	Delaware	2.0
9	Illinois	1.8
10	California	1.7
11	South Carolina	1.2
12	Ohio	1.1
12	Pennsylvania	1.1
14	Tennessee	1.0
15	Indiana	0.9
16	Georgia	0.8
16	Louisiana	0.8
16	North Carolina	0.8
19	Michigan	0.6
20	Alabama	0.5
20	Hawaii	0.5
20	Missouri	0.5
20	Texas	0.5
20	Virginia	0.5
25	Kentucky	0.3
25	Mississippi	0.3
25	Oklahoma	0.3
25	Washington	0.3
29	Arizona	0.2
29	Arkansas	0.2
29	Minnesota	0.2
29	Oregon	0.2
29	West Virginia	0.2
29	Wisconsin	0.2
35	Colorado	0.1
35	Iowa	0.1
35	Kansas	0.1
35	Nebraska	0.1
35	Nevada	0.1
35	New Hampshire	0.1
35	New Mexico	0.1
35	Utah	0.1
35	Vermont	0.1
44	Alaska	0.0
44	Idaho	0.0
44	Maine	0.0
44	Montana	0.0
44	North Dakota	0.0
44	South Dakota	0.0
44	Wyoming	0.0
	District of Columbia	197.2

Source: Morgan Quitno Press using data from Federal Bureau of Investigation
"Crime in the United States 1996" (Uniform Crime Reports, October 4, 1997)
*Violent crimes are offenses of murder, forcible rape, robbery and aggravated assault.

Percent Change in Number of Violent Crimes: 1995 to 1996

National Percent Change = 6.5% Decrease*

ALPHA ORDER

RANK	STATE	PERCENT CHANGE

ALPHA ORDER

RANK	STATE	PERCENT CHANGE
41	Alabama	(10.2)
23	Alaska	(5.1)
31	Arizona	(7.1)
20	Arkansas	(4.2)
39	California	(9.9)
28	Colorado	(6.3)
8	Connecticut	1.5
30	Delaware	(6.8)
11	Florida	(0.2)
13	Georgia	(0.7)
26	Hawaii	(5.3)
49	Idaho	(15.2)
43	Illinois	(10.9)
6	Indiana	3.0
50	Iowa	(22.8)
15	Kansas	(1.4)
46	Kentucky	(11.6)
34	Louisiana	(7.6)
21	Maine	(4.8)
23	Maryland	(5.1)
28	Massachusetts	(6.3)
32	Michigan	(7.2)
19	Minnesota	(3.9)
17	Mississippi	(2.2)
42	Missouri	(10.4)
23	Montana	(5.1)
1	Nebraska	14.9
40	Nevada	(10.1)
2	New Hampshire	4.5
43	New Jersey	(10.9)
3	New Mexico	4.3
47	New York	(13.4)
33	North Carolina	(7.4)
18	North Dakota	(2.7)
45	Ohio	(11.0)
37	Oklahoma	(9.5)
38	Oregon	(9.6)
10	Pennsylvania	1.1
27	Rhode Island	(5.7)
7	South Carolina	2.2
48	South Dakota	(14.3)
8	Tennessee	1.5
14	Texas	(0.8)
4	Utah	3.5
5	Vermont	3.2
21	Virginia	(4.8)
35	Washington	(9.3)
11	West Virginia	(0.2)
36	Wisconsin	(9.4)
16	Wyoming	(1.6)

RANK ORDER

RANK	STATE	PERCENT CHANGE
1	Nebraska	14.9
2	New Hampshire	4.5
3	New Mexico	4.3
4	Utah	3.5
5	Vermont	3.2
6	Indiana	3.0
7	South Carolina	2.2
8	Connecticut	1.5
8	Tennessee	1.5
10	Pennsylvania	1.1
11	Florida	(0.2)
11	West Virginia	(0.2)
13	Georgia	(0.7)
14	Texas	(0.8)
15	Kansas	(1.4)
16	Wyoming	(1.6)
17	Mississippi	(2.2)
18	North Dakota	(2.7)
19	Minnesota	(3.9)
20	Arkansas	(4.2)
21	Maine	(4.8)
21	Virginia	(4.8)
23	Alaska	(5.1)
23	Maryland	(5.1)
23	Montana	(5.1)
26	Hawaii	(5.3)
27	Rhode Island	(5.7)
28	Colorado	(6.3)
28	Massachusetts	(6.3)
30	Delaware	(6.8)
31	Arizona	(7.1)
32	Michigan	(7.2)
33	North Carolina	(7.4)
34	Louisiana	(7.6)
35	Washington	(9.3)
36	Wisconsin	(9.4)
37	Oklahoma	(9.5)
38	Oregon	(9.6)
39	California	(9.9)
40	Nevada	(10.1)
41	Alabama	(10.2)
42	Missouri	(10.4)
43	Illinois	(10.9)
43	New Jersey	(10.9)
45	Ohio	(11.0)
46	Kentucky	(11.6)
47	New York	(13.4)
48	South Dakota	(14.3)
49	Idaho	(15.2)
50	Iowa	(22.8)

District of Columbia   (9.0)

Source: Federal Bureau of Investigation
   "Crime in the United States 1996" (Uniform Crime Reports, October 4, 1997)
*Violent crimes are offenses of murder, forcible rape, robbery and aggravated assault.

Violent Crime Rate in 1996

National Rate = 634.1 Violent Crimes per 100,000 Population*

ALPHA ORDER				RANK ORDER		
RANK	STATE	RATE		RANK	STATE	RATE
21	Alabama	565.4		1	Florida	1,051.0
10	Alaska	727.7		2	South Carolina	996.9
17	Arizona	631.5		3	Maryland	931.2
24	Arkansas	524.3		4	Louisiana	929.1
6	California	862.7		5	Illinois	886.2
33	Colorado	404.5		6	California	862.7
32	Connecticut	412.0		7	New Mexico	840.6
12	Delaware	668.3		8	Nevada	811.3
1	Florida	1,051.0		9	Tennessee	774.0
15	Georgia	638.7		10	Alaska	727.7
39	Hawaii	280.6		11	New York	727.0
41	Idaho	267.2		12	Delaware	668.3
5	Illinois	886.2		13	Texas	644.4
22	Indiana	537.0		14	Massachusetts	642.2
40	Iowa	272.5		15	Georgia	638.7
31	Kansas	413.8		16	Michigan	635.3
38	Kentucky	320.5		17	Arizona	631.5
4	Louisiana	929.1		18	Oklahoma	597.1
47	Maine	124.9		19	Missouri	590.9
3	Maryland	931.2		20	North Carolina	588.1
14	Massachusetts	642.2		21	Alabama	565.4
16	Michigan	635.3		22	Indiana	537.0
36	Minnesota	338.8		23	New Jersey	531.5
25	Mississippi	488.3		24	Arkansas	524.3
19	Missouri	590.9		25	Mississippi	488.3
46	Montana	161.0		26	Oregon	463.1
27	Nebraska	434.7		27	Nebraska	434.7
8	Nevada	811.3		28	Pennsylvania	432.5
49	New Hampshire	118.2		29	Washington	431.2
23	New Jersey	531.5		30	Ohio	428.7
7	New Mexico	840.6		31	Kansas	413.8
11	New York	727.0		32	Connecticut	412.0
20	North Carolina	588.1		33	Colorado	404.5
50	North Dakota	84.0		34	Rhode Island	347.2
30	Ohio	428.7		35	Virginia	341.3
18	Oklahoma	597.1		36	Minnesota	338.8
26	Oregon	463.1		37	Utah	331.9
28	Pennsylvania	432.5		38	Kentucky	320.5
34	Rhode Island	347.2		39	Hawaii	280.6
2	South Carolina	996.9		40	Iowa	272.5
45	South Dakota	177.2		41	Idaho	267.2
9	Tennessee	774.0		42	Wisconsin	252.7
13	Texas	644.4		43	Wyoming	249.7
37	Utah	331.9		44	West Virginia	210.1
48	Vermont	121.2		45	South Dakota	177.2
35	Virginia	341.3		46	Montana	161.0
29	Washington	431.2		47	Maine	124.9
44	West Virginia	210.1		48	Vermont	121.2
42	Wisconsin	252.7		49	New Hampshire	118.2
43	Wyoming	249.7		50	North Dakota	84.0
					District of Columbia	2,469.8

Source: Federal Bureau of Investigation
   "Crime in the United States 1996" (Uniform Crime Reports, October 4, 1997)
*Violent crimes are offenses of murder, forcible rape, robbery and aggravated assault.

Percent Change in Violent Crime Rate: 1995 to 1996

National Percent Change = 7.4% Decrease*

ALPHA ORDER				RANK ORDER		
RANK	STATE	PERCENT CHANGE		RANK	STATE	PERCENT CHANGE
36	Alabama	(10.6)		1	Nebraska	13.8
23	Alaska	(5.6)		2	New Hampshire	3.2
44	Arizona	(11.5)		3	New Mexico	2.6
22	Arkansas	(5.2)		4	Vermont	2.5
37	California	(10.7)		5	Indiana	2.3
32	Colorado	(8.1)		6	Connecticut	1.5
6	Connecticut	1.5		6	South Carolina	1.5
30	Delaware	(7.8)		8	Pennsylvania	1.2
14	Florida	(1.9)		9	Utah	0.9
15	Georgia	(2.8)		10	Tennessee	0.3
21	Hawaii	(5.1)		11	West Virginia	0.0
49	Idaho	(17.0)		12	Kansas	(1.6)
38	Illinois	(11.0)		13	Wyoming	(1.8)
5	Indiana	2.3		14	Florida	(1.9)
50	Iowa	(23.1)		15	Georgia	(2.8)
12	Kansas	(1.6)		16	Mississippi	(2.9)
45	Kentucky	(12.1)		16	Texas	(2.9)
30	Louisiana	(7.8)		18	North Dakota	(3.1)
19	Maine	(4.9)		19	Maine	(4.9)
23	Maryland	(5.6)		19	Minnesota	(4.9)
28	Massachusetts	(6.5)		21	Hawaii	(5.1)
29	Michigan	(7.6)		22	Arkansas	(5.2)
19	Minnesota	(4.9)		23	Alaska	(5.6)
16	Mississippi	(2.9)		23	Maryland	(5.6)
38	Missouri	(11.0)		23	Virginia	(5.6)
27	Montana	(6.1)		26	Rhode Island	(5.7)
1	Nebraska	13.8		27	Montana	(6.1)
47	Nevada	(14.2)		28	Massachusetts	(6.5)
2	New Hampshire	3.2		29	Michigan	(7.6)
42	New Jersey	(11.4)		30	Delaware	(7.8)
3	New Mexico	2.6		30	Louisiana	(7.8)
46	New York	(13.6)		32	Colorado	(8.1)
33	North Carolina	(9.0)		33	North Carolina	(9.0)
18	North Dakota	(3.1)		34	Oklahoma	(10.1)
41	Ohio	(11.2)		34	Wisconsin	(10.1)
34	Oklahoma	(10.1)		36	Alabama	(10.6)
42	Oregon	(11.4)		37	California	(10.7)
8	Pennsylvania	1.2		38	Illinois	(11.0)
26	Rhode Island	(5.7)		38	Missouri	(11.0)
6	South Carolina	1.5		38	Washington	(11.0)
48	South Dakota	(14.6)		41	Ohio	(11.2)
10	Tennessee	0.3		42	New Jersey	(11.4)
16	Texas	(2.9)		42	Oregon	(11.4)
9	Utah	0.9		44	Arizona	(11.5)
4	Vermont	2.5		45	Kentucky	(12.1)
23	Virginia	(5.6)		46	New York	(13.6)
38	Washington	(11.0)		47	Nevada	(14.2)
11	West Virginia	0.0		48	South Dakota	(14.6)
34	Wisconsin	(10.1)		49	Idaho	(17.0)
13	Wyoming	(1.8)		50	Iowa	(23.1)
					District of Columbia	(7.2)

Source: Federal Bureau of Investigation
"Crime in the United States 1996" (Uniform Crime Reports, October 4, 1997)
Violent crimes are offenses of murder, forcible rape, robbery and aggravated assault.

Violent Crimes with Firearms in 1996

National Total = 418,660 Violent Crimes*

ALPHA ORDER					RANK ORDER			
RANK	**STATE**	**CRIMES**	**% of USA**		**RANK**	**STATE**	**CRIMES**	**% of USA**
18	Alabama	7,709	1.84%		1	California	70,039	16.73%
38	Alaska	922	0.22%		2	New York*	37,973	9.07%
16	Arizona	9,112	2.18%		3	Texas	34,753	8.30%
23	Arkansas	4,076	0.97%		4	Illinois	24,890	5.95%
1	California	70,039	16.73%		5	Florida	23,149	5.53%
26	Colorado	3,640	0.87%		6	Michigan	16,963	4.05%
33	Connecticut	2,398	0.57%		7	Maryland	15,806	3.78%
37	Delaware	924	0.22%		8	Georgia	14,761	3.53%
5	Florida	23,149	5.53%		9	Pennsylvania	14,356	3.43%
8	Georgia	14,761	3.53%		10	North Carolina	14,031	3.35%
43	Hawaii	314	0.08%		11	Louisiana	13,965	3.34%
39	Idaho	877	0.21%		12	Tennessee	13,707	3.27%
4	Illinois	24,890	5.95%		13	Ohio	9,925	2.37%
20	Indiana	4,967	1.19%		14	South Carolina	9,733	2.32%
40	Iowa	790	0.19%		15	Missouri	9,448	2.26%
36	Kansas	1,156	0.28%		16	Arizona	9,112	2.18%
31	Kentucky	2,742	0.65%		17	New Jersey	9,051	2.16%
11	Louisiana	13,965	3.34%		18	Alabama	7,709	1.84%
47	Maine	92	0.02%		19	Virginia	5,820	1.39%
7	Maryland	15,806	3.78%		20	Indiana	4,967	1.19%
29	Massachusetts	3,465	0.83%		21	Washington	4,931	1.18%
6	Michigan	16,963	4.05%		22	Oklahoma	4,241	1.01%
28	Minnesota	3,493	0.83%		23	Arkansas	4,076	0.97%
32	Mississippi	2,515	0.60%		24	New Mexico	3,701	0.88%
15	Missouri	9,448	2.26%		25	Nevada	3,644	0.87%
NA	Montana**	NA	NA		26	Colorado	3,640	0.87%
35	Nebraska	1,191	0.28%		27	Wisconsin	3,547	0.85%
25	Nevada	3,644	0.87%		28	Minnesota	3,493	0.83%
46	New Hampshire	120	0.03%		29	Massachusetts	3,465	0.83%
17	New Jersey	9,051	2.16%		30	Oregon	2,931	0.70%
24	New Mexico	3,701	0.88%		31	Kentucky	2,742	0.65%
2	New York*	37,973	9.07%		32	Mississippi	2,515	0.60%
10	North Carolina	14,031	3.35%		33	Connecticut	2,398	0.57%
48	North Dakota	19	0.00%		34	Utah	1,266	0.30%
13	Ohio	9,925	2.37%		35	Nebraska	1,191	0.28%
22	Oklahoma	4,241	1.01%		36	Kansas	1,156	0.28%
30	Oregon	2,931	0.70%		37	Delaware	924	0.22%
9	Pennsylvania	14,356	3.43%		38	Alaska	922	0.22%
42	Rhode Island	438	0.10%		39	Idaho	877	0.21%
14	South Carolina	9,733	2.32%		40	Iowa	790	0.19%
44	South Dakota	198	0.05%		41	West Virginia	684	0.16%
12	Tennessee	13,707	3.27%		42	Rhode Island	438	0.10%
3	Texas	34,753	8.30%		43	Hawaii	314	0.08%
34	Utah	1,266	0.30%		44	South Dakota	198	0.05%
NA	Vermont**	NA	NA		45	Wyoming	133	0.03%
19	Virginia	5,820	1.39%		46	New Hampshire	120	0.03%
21	Washington	4,931	1.18%		47	Maine	92	0.02%
41	West Virginia	684	0.16%		48	North Dakota	19	0.00%
27	Wisconsin	3,547	0.85%		NA	Montana**	NA	NA
45	Wyoming	133	0.03%		NA	Vermont**	NA	NA
						District of Columbia	4,054	0.97%

Source: Morgan Quitno Press using data from Federal Bureau of Investigation "Crime in the United States 1996" (Uniform Crime Reports, October 4, 1997)

*Includes murder, robbery and aggravated assault. Does not include rape. National total reflects only those violent crimes for which the type of weapon was known and reported. There were an additional 196,391 violent crimes (excluding rape) for which the type of weapon was not reported to the F.B.I. New York's number does not include New York City. **Not available.

Violent Crime Rate with Firearms in 1996

National Rate = 202.4 Violent Crimes per 100,000 Population*

ALPHA ORDER

RANK	STATE	RATE
20	Alabama	185.0
23	Alaska	168.8
17	Arizona	218.4
22	Arkansas	171.4
16	California	220.9
30	Colorado	102.6
32	Connecticut	90.8
12	Delaware	249.1
5	Florida	379.1
13	Georgia	231.2
44	Hawaii	26.6
35	Idaho	74.9
2	Illinois	746.5
25	Indiana	146.1
42	Iowa	35.3
NA	Kansas**	NA
11	Kentucky	264.5
4	Louisiana	406.2
46	Maine	7.5
7	Maryland	315.1
36	Massachusetts	69.7
18	Michigan	215.5
34	Minnesota	75.9
8	Mississippi	277.6
14	Missouri	229.8
NA	Montana**	NA
33	Nebraska	77.0
15	Nevada	228.8
45	New Hampshire	13.0
28	New Jersey	113.3
6	New Mexico	365.7
9	New York*	271.1
19	North Carolina	195.5
47	North Dakota	5.3
26	Ohio	141.3
27	Oklahoma	128.5
29	Oregon	103.3
24	Pennsylvania	154.1
39	Rhode Island	44.3
10	South Carolina	266.0
40	South Dakota	39.2
3	Tennessee	481.6
21	Texas	182.2
38	Utah	65.3
NA	Vermont**	NA
1	Virginia	863.9
31	Washington	94.9
41	West Virginia	37.5
37	Wisconsin	69.0
43	Wyoming	33.5

RANK ORDER

RANK	STATE	RATE
1	Virginia	863.9
2	Illinois	746.5
3	Tennessee	481.6
4	Louisiana	406.2
5	Florida	379.1
6	New Mexico	365.7
7	Maryland	315.1
8	Mississippi	277.6
9	New York*	271.1
10	South Carolina	266.0
11	Kentucky	264.5
12	Delaware	249.1
13	Georgia	231.2
14	Missouri	229.8
15	Nevada	228.8
16	California	220.9
17	Arizona	218.4
18	Michigan	215.5
19	North Carolina	195.5
20	Alabama	185.0
21	Texas	182.2
22	Arkansas	171.4
23	Alaska	168.8
24	Pennsylvania	154.1
25	Indiana	146.1
26	Ohio	141.3
27	Oklahoma	128.5
28	New Jersey	113.3
29	Oregon	103.3
30	Colorado	102.6
31	Washington	94.9
32	Connecticut	90.8
33	Nebraska	77.0
34	Minnesota	75.9
35	Idaho	74.9
36	Massachusetts	69.7
37	Wisconsin	69.0
38	Utah	65.3
39	Rhode Island	44.3
40	South Dakota	39.2
41	West Virginia	37.5
42	Iowa	35.3
43	Wyoming	33.5
44	Hawaii	26.6
45	New Hampshire	13.0
46	Maine	7.5
47	North Dakota	5.3
NA	Kansas**	NA
NA	Montana**	NA
NA	Vermont**	NA
	District of Columbia**	NA

Source: Morgan Quitno Press using data from Federal Bureau of Investigation
    "Crime in the United States 1996" (Uniform Crime Reports, October 4, 1997)
*Based only on population of reporting jurisdictions. Includes murder, robbery and aggravated assault. Does not include rape. National rate reflects only those violent crimes for which the type of weapon was known and reported. Illinois and Virginia rates especially affected by number of nonreporting jurisdictions. New York's rate does not include New York City. **Not available.

Percent of Violent Crimes Involving Firearms in 1996

National Percent = 30.1% of Violent Crimes*

ALPHA ORDER				RANK ORDER		
RANK	STATE	PERCENT		RANK	STATE	PERCENT
12	Alabama	34.5		1	Mississippi	45.7
31	Alaska	26.2		2	Tennessee	43.8
6	Arizona	35.8		3	Louisiana	43.0
13	Arkansas	34.2		4	New Mexico	37.0
30	California	26.5		5	Georgia	36.5
25	Colorado	28.1		6	Arizona	35.8
38	Connecticut	22.3		7	Illinois	35.1
29	Delaware	26.7		7	Maryland	35.1
23	Florida	29.0		7	Pennsylvania	35.1
5	Georgia	36.5		10	North Carolina	34.9
45	Hawaii	10.5		11	Missouri	34.7
17	Idaho	31.4		12	Alabama	34.5
7	Illinois	35.1		13	Arkansas	34.2
27	Indiana	27.7		14	Michigan	33.4
44	Iowa	14.0		15	Kansas	32.9
15	Kansas	32.9		16	New York*	31.9
21	Kentucky	29.9		17	Idaho	31.4
3	Louisiana	43.0		18	Ohio	30.8
48	Maine	7.2		19	Nevada	30.3
7	Maryland	35.1		19	Texas	30.3
46	Massachusetts	10.1		21	Kentucky	29.9
14	Michigan	33.4		22	Wisconsin	29.7
28	Minnesota	27.0		23	Florida	29.0
1	Mississippi	45.7		24	Virginia	28.7
11	Missouri	34.7		25	Colorado	28.1
NA	Montana**	NA		26	South Carolina	28.0
40	Nebraska	18.1		27	Indiana	27.7
19	Nevada	30.3		28	Minnesota	27.0
42	New Hampshire	15.3		29	Delaware	26.7
37	New Jersey	22.4		30	California	26.5
4	New Mexico	37.0		31	Alaska	26.2
16	New York*	31.9		32	Washington	24.9
10	North Carolina	34.9		33	Oklahoma	23.4
47	North Dakota	8.6		34	Utah	23.3
18	Ohio	30.8		35	South Dakota	22.9
33	Oklahoma	23.4		36	Oregon	22.7
36	Oregon	22.7		37	New Jersey	22.4
7	Pennsylvania	35.1		38	Connecticut	22.3
43	Rhode Island	14.2		39	West Virginia	19.7
26	South Carolina	28.0		40	Nebraska	18.1
35	South Dakota	22.9		41	Wyoming	15.6
2	Tennessee	43.8		42	New Hampshire	15.3
19	Texas	30.3		43	Rhode Island	14.2
34	Utah	23.3		44	Iowa	14.0
NA	Vermont**	NA		45	Hawaii	10.5
24	Virginia	28.7		46	Massachusetts	10.1
32	Washington	24.9		47	North Dakota	8.6
39	West Virginia	19.7		48	Maine	7.2
22	Wisconsin	29.7		NA	Montana**	NA
41	Wyoming	15.6		NA	Vermont**	NA
					District of Columbia	31.8

Source: Morgan Quitno Press using data from Federal Bureau of Investigation
   "Crime in the United States 1996" (Uniform Crime Reports, October 4, 1997)
*Includes murder, robbery and aggravated assault. Does not include rape. National percent reflects only those violent crimes for which the type of weapon was known and reported. There were an additional 196,391 violent crimes (excluding rape) for which the type of weapon was not reported to the F.B.I. New York's percentage does not include New York city. **Not available.

Bombings in 1995

National Total = 1,941 Bombings*

ALPHA ORDER					RANK ORDER			
RANK	STATE	BOMBINGS	% of USA		RANK	STATE	BOMBINGS	% of USA
37	Alabama	7	0.36%		1	California	354	18.24%
43	Alaska	4	0.21%		2	Florida	175	9.02%
5	Arizona	96	4.95%		3	Illinois	173	8.91%
33	Arkansas	10	0.52%		4	Texas	108	5.56%
1	California	354	18.24%		5	Arizona	96	4.95%
8	Colorado	68	3.50%		6	Ohio	77	3.97%
32	Connecticut	11	0.57%		7	Michigan	74	3.81%
43	Delaware	4	0.21%		8	Colorado	68	3.50%
2	Florida	175	9.02%		9	Maryland	63	3.25%
28	Georgia	16	0.82%		10	New York	61	3.14%
50	Hawaii	0	0.00%		11	Minnesota	57	2.94%
39	Idaho	5	0.26%		12	Utah	43	2.22%
3	Illinois	173	8.91%		13	Virginia	41	2.11%
15	Indiana	36	1.85%		14	Missouri	39	2.01%
20	Iowa	26	1.34%		15	Indiana	36	1.85%
39	Kansas	5	0.26%		15	Washington	36	1.85%
20	Kentucky	26	1.34%		17	Oregon	35	1.80%
28	Louisiana	16	0.82%		18	Pennsylvania	34	1.75%
48	Maine	2	0.10%		19	Tennessee	31	1.60%
9	Maryland	63	3.25%		20	Iowa	26	1.34%
35	Massachusetts	8	0.41%		20	Kentucky	26	1.34%
7	Michigan	74	3.81%		20	North Carolina	26	1.34%
11	Minnesota	57	2.94%		23	New Jersey	25	1.29%
39	Mississippi	5	0.26%		24	Wisconsin	22	1.13%
14	Missouri	39	2.01%		25	Oklahoma	18	0.93%
43	Montana	4	0.21%		26	Nevada	17	0.88%
34	Nebraska	9	0.46%		26	New Mexico	17	0.88%
26	Nevada	17	0.88%		28	Georgia	16	0.82%
43	New Hampshire	4	0.21%		28	Louisiana	16	0.82%
23	New Jersey	25	1.29%		30	North Dakota	14	0.72%
26	New Mexico	17	0.88%		31	South Dakota	12	0.62%
10	New York	61	3.14%		32	Connecticut	11	0.57%
20	North Carolina	26	1.34%		33	Arkansas	10	0.52%
30	North Dakota	14	0.72%		34	Nebraska	9	0.46%
6	Ohio	77	3.97%		35	Massachusetts	8	0.41%
25	Oklahoma	18	0.93%		35	West Virginia	8	0.41%
17	Oregon	35	1.80%		37	Alabama	7	0.36%
18	Pennsylvania	34	1.75%		38	Rhode Island	6	0.31%
38	Rhode Island	6	0.31%		39	Idaho	5	0.26%
39	South Carolina	5	0.26%		39	Kansas	5	0.26%
31	South Dakota	12	0.62%		39	Mississippi	5	0.26%
19	Tennessee	31	1.60%		39	South Carolina	5	0.26%
4	Texas	108	5.56%		43	Alaska	4	0.21%
12	Utah	43	2.22%		43	Delaware	4	0.21%
49	Vermont	1	0.05%		43	Montana	4	0.21%
13	Virginia	41	2.11%		43	New Hampshire	4	0.21%
15	Washington	36	1.85%		43	Wyoming	4	0.21%
35	West Virginia	8	0.41%		48	Maine	2	0.10%
24	Wisconsin	22	1.13%		49	Vermont	1	0.05%
43	Wyoming	4	0.21%		50	Hawaii	0	0.00%
					District of Columbia		3	0.15%

Source: Federal Bureau of Investigation, Bomb Data Center
   "1995 Bombing Incidents" (General Information Bulletin 97-1)
*Includes explosive and incendiary bombings and excludes bombing attempts. Total does not include 25 bombings
in Puerto Rico, 1 in Guam or 1 in the Virgin Islands. There were 193 deaths and 744 injuries from bombings in 1995.
Of this total, 168 deaths were from the bombing of the Alfred P. Murrah Federal Building in Oklahoma City on
April 19, 1995.

Murders in 1996

National Total = 19,645 Murders*

ALPHA ORDER

RANK	STATE	MURDERS	% of USA
15	Alabama	444	2.26%
39	Alaska	45	0.23%
18	Arizona	377	1.92%
26	Arkansas	219	1.11%
1	California	2,916	14.84%
29	Colorado	180	0.92%
32	Connecticut	158	0.80%
43	Delaware	31	0.16%
5	Florida	1,077	5.48%
9	Georgia	630	3.21%
41	Hawaii	40	0.20%
40	Idaho	43	0.22%
4	Illinois	1,179	6.00%
17	Indiana	420	2.14%
37	Iowa	53	0.27%
30	Kansas	170	0.87%
23	Kentucky	228	1.16%
6	Louisiana	762	3.88%
44	Maine	25	0.13%
11	Maryland	588	2.99%
33	Massachusetts	157	0.80%
7	Michigan	722	3.68%
31	Minnesota	167	0.85%
21	Mississippi	301	1.53%
16	Missouri	433	2.20%
42	Montana	34	0.17%
38	Nebraska	48	0.24%
25	Nevada	220	1.12%
46	New Hampshire	20	0.10%
19	New Jersey	338	1.72%
28	New Mexico	197	1.00%
3	New York	1,353	6.89%
10	North Carolina	619	3.15%
48	North Dakota	14	0.07%
12	Ohio	538	2.74%
24	Oklahoma	223	1.14%
34	Oregon	129	0.66%
8	Pennsylvania	686	3.49%
44	Rhode Island	25	0.13%
20	South Carolina	332	1.69%
50	South Dakota	9	0.05%
13	Tennessee	503	2.56%
2	Texas	1,477	7.52%
36	Utah	63	0.32%
49	Vermont	11	0.06%
14	Virginia	500	2.55%
22	Washington	255	1.30%
35	West Virginia	69	0.35%
27	Wisconsin	204	1.04%
47	Wyoming	16	0.08%

RANK ORDER

RANK	STATE	MURDERS	% of USA
1	California	2,916	14.84%
2	Texas	1,477	7.52%
3	New York	1,353	6.89%
4	Illinois	1,179	6.00%
5	Florida	1,077	5.48%
6	Louisiana	762	3.88%
7	Michigan	722	3.68%
8	Pennsylvania	686	3.49%
9	Georgia	630	3.21%
10	North Carolina	619	3.15%
11	Maryland	588	2.99%
12	Ohio	538	2.74%
13	Tennessee	503	2.56%
14	Virginia	500	2.55%
15	Alabama	444	2.26%
16	Missouri	433	2.20%
17	Indiana	420	2.14%
18	Arizona	377	1.92%
19	New Jersey	338	1.72%
20	South Carolina	332	1.69%
21	Mississippi	301	1.53%
22	Washington	255	1.30%
23	Kentucky	228	1.16%
24	Oklahoma	223	1.14%
25	Nevada	220	1.12%
26	Arkansas	219	1.11%
27	Wisconsin	204	1.04%
28	New Mexico	197	1.00%
29	Colorado	180	0.92%
30	Kansas	170	0.87%
31	Minnesota	167	0.85%
32	Connecticut	158	0.80%
33	Massachusetts	157	0.80%
34	Oregon	129	0.66%
35	West Virginia	69	0.35%
36	Utah	63	0.32%
37	Iowa	53	0.27%
38	Nebraska	48	0.24%
39	Alaska	45	0.23%
40	Idaho	43	0.22%
41	Hawaii	40	0.20%
42	Montana	34	0.17%
43	Delaware	31	0.16%
44	Maine	25	0.13%
44	Rhode Island	25	0.13%
46	New Hampshire	20	0.10%
47	Wyoming	16	0.08%
48	North Dakota	14	0.07%
49	Vermont	11	0.06%
50	South Dakota	9	0.05%
	District of Columbia	397	2.02%

Source: Federal Bureau of Investigation
    "Crime in the United States 1996" (Uniform Crime Reports, October 4, 1997)
*Includes nonnegligent manslaughter.

Average Time Between Murders in 1996

National Rate = A Murder Occurs Every 27 Minutes*

ALPHA ORDER

RANK	STATE	HOURS.MINUTES
36	Alabama	19.47
12	Alaska	195.12
33	Arizona	23.18
25	Arkansas	40.07
50	California	3.01
22	Colorado	48.48
19	Connecticut	55.36
8	Delaware	283.21
46	Florida	8.10
42	Georgia	13.56
10	Hawaii	219.36
11	Idaho	204.17
47	Illinois	7.27
34	Indiana	20.55
14	Iowa	165.44
21	Kansas	51.40
28	Kentucky	38.32
45	Louisiana	11.32
6	Maine	351.22
40	Maryland	14.56
18	Massachusetts	55.57
44	Michigan	12.10
20	Minnesota	52.36
30	Mississippi	29.11
35	Missouri	20.17
9	Montana	258.21
13	Nebraska	183.00
26	Nevada	39.56
5	New Hampshire	439.12
32	New Jersey	25.59
23	New Mexico	44.35
48	New York	6.29
41	North Carolina	14.11
3	North Dakota	627.26
39	Ohio	16.20
27	Oklahoma	39.23
17	Oregon	68.05
43	Pennsylvania	12.48
6	Rhode Island	351.22
31	South Carolina	26.28
1	South Dakota	976.00
38	Tennessee	17.28
49	Texas	5.57
15	Utah	139.26
2	Vermont	798.33
37	Virginia	17.34
29	Washington	34.27
16	West Virginia	127.18
24	Wisconsin	43.04
4	Wyoming	549.00

RANK ORDER

RANK	STATE	HOURS.MINUTES
1	South Dakota	976.00
2	Vermont	798.33
3	North Dakota	627.26
4	Wyoming	549.00
5	New Hampshire	439.12
6	Maine	351.22
6	Rhode Island	351.22
8	Delaware	283.21
9	Montana	258.21
10	Hawaii	219.36
11	Idaho	204.17
12	Alaska	195.12
13	Nebraska	183.00
14	Iowa	165.44
15	Utah	139.26
16	West Virginia	127.18
17	Oregon	68.05
18	Massachusetts	55.57
19	Connecticut	55.36
20	Minnesota	52.36
21	Kansas	51.40
22	Colorado	48.48
23	New Mexico	44.35
24	Wisconsin	43.04
25	Arkansas	40.07
26	Nevada	39.56
27	Oklahoma	39.23
28	Kentucky	38.32
29	Washington	34.27
30	Mississippi	29.11
31	South Carolina	26.28
32	New Jersey	25.59
33	Arizona	23.18
34	Indiana	20.55
35	Missouri	20.17
36	Alabama	19.47
37	Virginia	17.34
38	Tennessee	17.28
39	Ohio	16.20
40	Maryland	14.56
41	North Carolina	14.11
42	Georgia	13.56
43	Pennsylvania	12.48
44	Michigan	12.10
45	Louisiana	11.32
46	Florida	8.10
47	Illinois	7.27
48	New York	6.29
49	Texas	5.57
50	California	3.01
	District of Columbia	22.08

Source: Morgan Quitno Press using data from Federal Bureau of Investigation
    "Crime in the United States 1996" (Uniform Crime Reports, October 4, 1997)
*Includes nonnegligent manslaughter.

Percent Change in Number of Murders: 1995 to 1996

National Percent Change = 9.1% Decrease*

ALPHA ORDER				RANK ORDER		
RANK	STATE	PERCENT CHANGE		RANK	STATE	PERCENT CHANGE
20	Alabama	(6.5)		1	North Dakota	133.3
44	Alaska	(18.2)		2	Wyoming	60.0
36	Arizona	(14.1)		3	Nevada	35.0
37	Arkansas	(15.4)		4	New Mexico	33.1
41	California	(17.4)		5	Delaware	24.0
39	Colorado	(16.7)		6	South Carolina	13.7
8	Connecticut	5.3		7	Kansas	6.9
5	Delaware	24.0		8	Connecticut	5.3
9	Florida	3.9		9	Florida	3.9
24	Georgia	(7.8)		9	Iowa	3.9
48	Hawaii	(28.6)		11	Louisiana	3.0
31	Idaho	(10.4)		12	Maine	0.0
18	Illinois	(3.4)		12	Nebraska	0.0
29	Indiana	(9.9)		12	Oregon	0.0
9	Iowa	3.9		15	Virginia	(0.6)
7	Kansas	6.9		16	Maryland	(1.3)
41	Kentucky	(17.4)		17	Montana	(2.9)
11	Louisiana	3.0		18	Illinois	(3.4)
12	Maine	0.0		19	New Hampshire	(4.8)
16	Maryland	(1.3)		20	Alabama	(6.5)
47	Massachusetts	(27.6)		21	Wisconsin	(6.8)
32	Michigan	(10.6)		22	Washington	(7.3)
25	Minnesota	(8.2)		23	Missouri	(7.7)
35	Mississippi	(13.5)		24	Georgia	(7.8)
23	Missouri	(7.7)		25	Minnesota	(8.2)
17	Montana	(2.9)		26	North Carolina	(8.6)
12	Nebraska	0.0		27	Pennsylvania	(9.1)
3	Nevada	35.0		28	Tennessee	(9.7)
19	New Hampshire	(4.8)		29	Indiana	(9.9)
41	New Jersey	(17.4)		30	Ohio	(10.3)
4	New Mexico	33.1		31	Idaho	(10.4)
33	New York	(12.7)		32	Michigan	(10.6)
26	North Carolina	(8.6)		33	New York	(12.7)
1	North Dakota	133.3		34	Texas	(12.8)
30	Ohio	(10.3)		35	Mississippi	(13.5)
50	Oklahoma	(44.3)		36	Arizona	(14.1)
12	Oregon	0.0		37	Arkansas	(15.4)
27	Pennsylvania	(9.1)		37	Vermont	(15.4)
46	Rhode Island	(24.2)		39	Colorado	(16.7)
6	South Carolina	13.7		40	Utah	(17.1)
49	South Dakota	(30.8)		41	California	(17.4)
28	Tennessee	(9.7)		41	Kentucky	(17.4)
34	Texas	(12.8)		41	New Jersey	(17.4)
40	Utah	(17.1)		44	Alaska	(18.2)
37	Vermont	(15.4)		45	West Virginia	(22.5)
15	Virginia	(0.6)		46	Rhode Island	(24.2)
22	Washington	(7.3)		47	Massachusetts	(27.6)
45	West Virginia	(22.5)		48	Hawaii	(28.6)
21	Wisconsin	(6.8)		49	South Dakota	(30.8)
2	Wyoming	60.0		50	Oklahoma	(44.3)
					District of Columbia	10.3

Source: Federal Bureau of Investigation
      "Crime in the United States 1996" (Uniform Crime Reports, October 4, 1997)
*Includes nonnegligent manslaughter.

Murder Rate in 1996

National Rate = 7.4 Murders per 100,000 Population*

ALPHA ORDER

RANK	STATE	RATE
6	Alabama	10.4
20	Alaska	7.4
13	Arizona	8.5
11	Arkansas	8.7
9	California	9.1
29	Colorado	4.7
27	Connecticut	4.8
31	Delaware	4.3
17	Florida	7.5
12	Georgia	8.6
39	Hawaii	3.4
37	Idaho	3.6
7	Illinois	10.0
22	Indiana	7.2
47	Iowa	1.9
24	Kansas	6.6
25	Kentucky	5.9
1	Louisiana	17.5
46	Maine	2.0
3	Maryland	11.6
43	Massachusetts	2.6
17	Michigan	7.5
37	Minnesota	3.6
5	Mississippi	11.1
15	Missouri	8.1
35	Montana	3.9
42	Nebraska	2.9
2	Nevada	13.7
49	New Hampshire	1.7
32	New Jersey	4.2
4	New Mexico	11.5
20	New York	7.4
13	North Carolina	8.5
45	North Dakota	2.2
27	Ohio	4.8
23	Oklahoma	6.8
33	Oregon	4.0
26	Pennsylvania	5.7
44	Rhode Island	2.5
10	South Carolina	9.0
50	South Dakota	1.2
8	Tennessee	9.5
16	Texas	7.7
41	Utah	3.2
47	Vermont	1.9
17	Virginia	7.5
30	Washington	4.6
36	West Virginia	3.8
33	Wisconsin	4.0
40	Wyoming	3.3

RANK ORDER

RANK	STATE	RATE
1	Louisiana	17.5
2	Nevada	13.7
3	Maryland	11.6
4	New Mexico	11.5
5	Mississippi	11.1
6	Alabama	10.4
7	Illinois	10.0
8	Tennessee	9.5
9	California	9.1
10	South Carolina	9.0
11	Arkansas	8.7
12	Georgia	8.6
13	Arizona	8.5
13	North Carolina	8.5
15	Missouri	8.1
16	Texas	7.7
17	Florida	7.5
17	Michigan	7.5
17	Virginia	7.5
20	Alaska	7.4
20	New York	7.4
22	Indiana	7.2
23	Oklahoma	6.8
24	Kansas	6.6
25	Kentucky	5.9
26	Pennsylvania	5.7
27	Connecticut	4.8
27	Ohio	4.8
29	Colorado	4.7
30	Washington	4.6
31	Delaware	4.3
32	New Jersey	4.2
33	Oregon	4.0
33	Wisconsin	4.0
35	Montana	3.9
36	West Virginia	3.8
37	Idaho	3.6
37	Minnesota	3.6
39	Hawaii	3.4
40	Wyoming	3.3
41	Utah	3.2
42	Nebraska	2.9
43	Massachusetts	2.6
44	Rhode Island	2.5
45	North Dakota	2.2
46	Maine	2.0
47	Iowa	1.9
47	Vermont	1.9
49	New Hampshire	1.7
50	South Dakota	1.2
	District of Columbia	73.1

Source: Federal Bureau of Investigation
      "Crime in the United States 1996" (Uniform Crime Reports, October 4, 1997)
*Includes nonnegligent manslaughter.

Percent Change in Murder Rate: 1995 to 1996

National Percent Change = 9.8% Decrease*

Source: Federal Bureau of Investigation
"Crime in the United States 1996" (Uniform Crime Reports, October 4, 1997)
*Includes nonnegligent manslaughter.

ALPHA ORDER

RANK	STATE	PERCENT CHANGE
21	Alabama	(7.1)
42	Alaska	(18.7)
41	Arizona	(18.3)
37	Arkansas	(16.3)
43	California	(18.8)
44	Colorado	(19.0)
9	Connecticut	4.3
5	Delaware	22.9
11	Florida	2.7
24	Georgia	(9.5)
47	Hawaii	(27.7)
32	Idaho	(12.2)
18	Illinois	(2.9)
28	Indiana	(10.0)
8	Iowa	5.6
7	Kansas	6.5
40	Kentucky	(18.1)
10	Louisiana	2.9
12	Maine	0.0
15	Maryland	(1.7)
48	Massachusetts	(27.8)
31	Michigan	(11.8)
22	Minnesota	(7.7)
35	Mississippi	(14.0)
23	Missouri	(8.0)
17	Montana	(2.5)
12	Nebraska	0.0
4	Nevada	28.0
19	New Hampshire	(5.6)
38	New Jersey	(17.6)
3	New Mexico	30.7
33	New York	(12.9)
26	North Carolina	(9.6)
1	North Dakota	144.4
30	Ohio	(11.1)
50	Oklahoma	(44.3)
16	Oregon	(2.4)
24	Pennsylvania	(9.5)
46	Rhode Island	(24.2)
6	South Carolina	13.9
49	South Dakota	(33.3)
29	Tennessee	(10.4)
36	Texas	(14.4)
39	Utah	(17.9)
34	Vermont	(13.6)
14	Virginia	(1.3)
27	Washington	(9.8)
45	West Virginia	(22.4)
20	Wisconsin	(7.0)
2	Wyoming	57.1

RANK ORDER

RANK	STATE	PERCENT CHANGE
1	North Dakota	144.4
2	Wyoming	57.1
3	New Mexico	30.7
4	Nevada	28.0
5	Delaware	22.9
6	South Carolina	13.9
7	Kansas	6.5
8	Iowa	5.6
9	Connecticut	4.3
10	Louisiana	2.9
11	Florida	2.7
12	Maine	0.0
12	Nebraska	0.0
14	Virginia	(1.3)
15	Maryland	(1.7)
16	Oregon	(2.4)
17	Montana	(2.5)
18	Illinois	(2.9)
19	New Hampshire	(5.6)
20	Wisconsin	(7.0)
21	Alabama	(7.1)
22	Minnesota	(7.7)
23	Missouri	(8.0)
24	Georgia	(9.5)
24	Pennsylvania	(9.5)
26	North Carolina	(9.6)
27	Washington	(9.8)
28	Indiana	(10.0)
29	Tennessee	(10.4)
30	Ohio	(11.1)
31	Michigan	(11.8)
32	Idaho	(12.2)
33	New York	(12.9)
34	Vermont	(13.6)
35	Mississippi	(14.0)
36	Texas	(14.4)
37	Arkansas	(16.3)
38	New Jersey	(17.6)
39	Utah	(17.9)
40	Kentucky	(18.1)
41	Arizona	(18.3)
42	Alaska	(18.7)
43	California	(18.8)
44	Colorado	(19.0)
45	West Virginia	(22.4)
46	Rhode Island	(24.2)
47	Hawaii	(27.7)
48	Massachusetts	(27.8)
49	South Dakota	(33.3)
50	Oklahoma	(44.3)
	District of Columbia	12.5

Murders with Firearms in 1996

National Total = 10,733 Murders with Firearms*

ALPHA ORDER

RANK	STATE	MURDERS	% of USA
11	Alabama	308	2.87%
37	Alaska	27	0.25%
14	Arizona	270	2.52%
21	Arkansas	155	1.44%
1	California	2,061	19.20%
29	Colorado	87	0.81%
27	Connecticut	109	1.02%
40	Delaware	15	0.14%
20	Florida	163	1.52%
7	Georgia	445	4.15%
39	Hawaii	16	0.15%
36	Idaho	28	0.26%
3	Illinois	585	5.45%
17	Indiana	200	1.86%
37	Iowa	27	0.25%
NA	Kansas**	NA	NA
22	Kentucky	146	1.36%
4	Louisiana	547	5.10%
43	Maine	11	0.10%
8	Maryland	424	3.95%
31	Massachusetts	75	0.70%
6	Michigan	480	4.47%
32	Minnesota	71	0.66%
23	Mississippi	136	1.27%
15	Missouri	264	2.46%
NA	Montana**	NA	NA
44	Nebraska	9	0.08%
25	Nevada	130	1.21%
44	New Hampshire	9	0.08%
19	New Jersey	164	1.53%
30	New Mexico	76	0.71%
18	New York*	168	1.57%
9	North Carolina	397	3.70%
47	North Dakota	3	0.03%
12	Ohio	300	2.80%
23	Oklahoma	136	1.27%
33	Oregon	59	0.55%
5	Pennsylvania	493	4.59%
42	Rhode Island	13	0.12%
16	South Carolina	224	2.09%
47	South Dakota	3	0.03%
13	Tennessee	279	2.60%
2	Texas	962	8.96%
35	Utah	35	0.33%
46	Vermont	5	0.05%
10	Virginia	322	3.00%
26	Washington	129	1.20%
34	West Virginia	45	0.42%
28	Wisconsin	108	1.01%
41	Wyoming	14	0.13%

RANK ORDER

RANK	STATE	MURDERS	% of USA
1	California	2,061	19.20%
2	Texas	962	8.96%
3	Illinois	585	5.45%
4	Louisiana	547	5.10%
5	Pennsylvania	493	4.59%
6	Michigan	480	4.47%
7	Georgia	445	4.15%
8	Maryland	424	3.95%
9	North Carolina	397	3.70%
10	Virginia	322	3.00%
11	Alabama	308	2.87%
12	Ohio	300	2.80%
13	Tennessee	279	2.60%
14	Arizona	270	2.52%
15	Missouri	264	2.46%
16	South Carolina	224	2.09%
17	Indiana	200	1.86%
18	New York*	168	1.57%
19	New Jersey	164	1.53%
20	Florida	163	1.52%
21	Arkansas	155	1.44%
22	Kentucky	146	1.36%
23	Mississippi	136	1.27%
23	Oklahoma	136	1.27%
25	Nevada	130	1.21%
26	Washington	129	1.20%
27	Connecticut	109	1.02%
28	Wisconsin	108	1.01%
29	Colorado	87	0.81%
30	New Mexico	76	0.71%
31	Massachusetts	75	0.70%
32	Minnesota	71	0.66%
33	Oregon	59	0.55%
34	West Virginia	45	0.42%
35	Utah	35	0.33%
36	Idaho	28	0.26%
37	Alaska	27	0.25%
37	Iowa	27	0.25%
39	Hawaii	16	0.15%
40	Delaware	15	0.14%
41	Wyoming	14	0.13%
42	Rhode Island	13	0.12%
43	Maine	11	0.10%
44	Nebraska	9	0.08%
44	New Hampshire	9	0.08%
46	Vermont	5	0.05%
47	North Dakota	3	0.03%
47	South Dakota	3	0.03%
NA	Kansas**	NA	NA
NA	Montana**	NA	NA
	District of Columbia**	NA	NA

Source: Federal Bureau of Investigation
      "Crime in the United States 1996" (Uniform Crime Reports, October 4, 1997)
*Of the 15,835 murders in 1996 for which supplemental data were received by the F.B.I. There were an additional
3,810 murders for which the type of murder weapon was not reported to the F.B.I. Includes nonnegligent
manslaughter. Numbers are for reporting jurisdictions only. New York's number does not include New York City.
**Not available.

Murder Rate with Firearms in 1996

National Rate = 5.1 Murders per 100,000 Population*

<table>
<tr><td colspan="3">ALPHA ORDER</td><td colspan="3">RANK ORDER</td></tr>
<tr><th>RANK</th><th>STATE</th><th>RATE</th><th>RANK</th><th>STATE</th><th>RATE</th></tr>
<tr><td>9</td><td>Alabama</td><td>7.4</td><td>1</td><td>Illinois</td><td>17.5</td></tr>
<tr><td>21</td><td>Alaska</td><td>4.9</td><td>2</td><td>Louisiana</td><td>15.9</td></tr>
<tr><td>11</td><td>Arizona</td><td>6.5</td><td>3</td><td>Mississippi</td><td>15.0</td></tr>
<tr><td>11</td><td>Arkansas</td><td>6.5</td><td>4</td><td>Kentucky</td><td>14.1</td></tr>
<tr><td>11</td><td>California</td><td>6.5</td><td>5</td><td>Tennessee</td><td>9.8</td></tr>
<tr><td>29</td><td>Colorado</td><td>2.5</td><td>6</td><td>Maryland</td><td>8.5</td></tr>
<tr><td>24</td><td>Connecticut</td><td>4.1</td><td>7</td><td>Nevada</td><td>8.2</td></tr>
<tr><td>26</td><td>Delaware</td><td>4.0</td><td>8</td><td>New Mexico</td><td>7.5</td></tr>
<tr><td>28</td><td>Florida</td><td>2.7</td><td>9</td><td>Alabama</td><td>7.4</td></tr>
<tr><td>10</td><td>Georgia</td><td>7.0</td><td>10</td><td>Georgia</td><td>7.0</td></tr>
<tr><td>40</td><td>Hawaii</td><td>1.4</td><td>11</td><td>Arizona</td><td>6.5</td></tr>
<tr><td>32</td><td>Idaho</td><td>2.4</td><td>11</td><td>Arkansas</td><td>6.5</td></tr>
<tr><td>1</td><td>Illinois</td><td>17.5</td><td>11</td><td>California</td><td>6.5</td></tr>
<tr><td>17</td><td>Indiana</td><td>5.9</td><td>14</td><td>Missouri</td><td>6.4</td></tr>
<tr><td>42</td><td>Iowa</td><td>1.2</td><td>15</td><td>Michigan</td><td>6.1</td></tr>
<tr><td>NA</td><td>Kansas**</td><td>NA</td><td>15</td><td>South Carolina</td><td>6.1</td></tr>
<tr><td>4</td><td>Kentucky</td><td>14.1</td><td>17</td><td>Indiana</td><td>5.9</td></tr>
<tr><td>2</td><td>Louisiana</td><td>15.9</td><td>18</td><td>North Carolina</td><td>5.5</td></tr>
<tr><td>44</td><td>Maine</td><td>0.9</td><td>19</td><td>Pennsylvania</td><td>5.3</td></tr>
<tr><td>6</td><td>Maryland</td><td>8.5</td><td>20</td><td>Texas</td><td>5.0</td></tr>
<tr><td>37</td><td>Massachusetts</td><td>1.5</td><td>21</td><td>Alaska</td><td>4.9</td></tr>
<tr><td>15</td><td>Michigan</td><td>6.1</td><td>22</td><td>Virginia</td><td>4.8</td></tr>
<tr><td>37</td><td>Minnesota</td><td>1.5</td><td>23</td><td>Ohio</td><td>4.3</td></tr>
<tr><td>3</td><td>Mississippi</td><td>15.0</td><td>24</td><td>Connecticut</td><td>4.1</td></tr>
<tr><td>14</td><td>Missouri</td><td>6.4</td><td>24</td><td>Oklahoma</td><td>4.1</td></tr>
<tr><td>NA</td><td>Montana**</td><td>NA</td><td>26</td><td>Delaware</td><td>4.0</td></tr>
<tr><td>47</td><td>Nebraska</td><td>0.6</td><td>27</td><td>Wyoming</td><td>3.5</td></tr>
<tr><td>7</td><td>Nevada</td><td>8.2</td><td>28</td><td>Florida</td><td>2.7</td></tr>
<tr><td>43</td><td>New Hampshire</td><td>1.0</td><td>29</td><td>Colorado</td><td>2.5</td></tr>
<tr><td>33</td><td>New Jersey</td><td>2.1</td><td>29</td><td>Washington</td><td>2.5</td></tr>
<tr><td>8</td><td>New Mexico</td><td>7.5</td><td>29</td><td>West Virginia</td><td>2.5</td></tr>
<tr><td>37</td><td>New York*</td><td>1.5</td><td>32</td><td>Idaho</td><td>2.4</td></tr>
<tr><td>18</td><td>North Carolina</td><td>5.5</td><td>33</td><td>New Jersey</td><td>2.1</td></tr>
<tr><td>45</td><td>North Dakota</td><td>0.8</td><td>33</td><td>Oregon</td><td>2.1</td></tr>
<tr><td>23</td><td>Ohio</td><td>4.3</td><td>33</td><td>Wisconsin</td><td>2.1</td></tr>
<tr><td>24</td><td>Oklahoma</td><td>4.1</td><td>36</td><td>Utah</td><td>1.8</td></tr>
<tr><td>33</td><td>Oregon</td><td>2.1</td><td>37</td><td>Massachusetts</td><td>1.5</td></tr>
<tr><td>19</td><td>Pennsylvania</td><td>5.3</td><td>37</td><td>Minnesota</td><td>1.5</td></tr>
<tr><td>41</td><td>Rhode Island</td><td>1.3</td><td>37</td><td>New York*</td><td>1.5</td></tr>
<tr><td>15</td><td>South Carolina</td><td>6.1</td><td>40</td><td>Hawaii</td><td>1.4</td></tr>
<tr><td>47</td><td>South Dakota</td><td>0.6</td><td>41</td><td>Rhode Island</td><td>1.3</td></tr>
<tr><td>5</td><td>Tennessee</td><td>9.8</td><td>42</td><td>Iowa</td><td>1.2</td></tr>
<tr><td>20</td><td>Texas</td><td>5.0</td><td>43</td><td>New Hampshire</td><td>1.0</td></tr>
<tr><td>36</td><td>Utah</td><td>1.8</td><td>44</td><td>Maine</td><td>0.9</td></tr>
<tr><td>45</td><td>Vermont</td><td>0.8</td><td>45</td><td>North Dakota</td><td>0.8</td></tr>
<tr><td>22</td><td>Virginia</td><td>4.8</td><td>45</td><td>Vermont</td><td>0.8</td></tr>
<tr><td>29</td><td>Washington</td><td>2.5</td><td>47</td><td>Nebraska</td><td>0.6</td></tr>
<tr><td>29</td><td>West Virginia</td><td>2.5</td><td>47</td><td>South Dakota</td><td>0.6</td></tr>
<tr><td>33</td><td>Wisconsin</td><td>2.1</td><td>NA</td><td>Kansas**</td><td>NA</td></tr>
<tr><td>27</td><td>Wyoming</td><td>3.5</td><td>NA</td><td>Montana**</td><td>NA</td></tr>
<tr><td></td><td></td><td></td><td></td><td>District of Columbia**</td><td>NA</td></tr>
</table>

Source: Morgan Quitno Press using data from Federal Bureau of Investigation
   "Crime in the United States 1996" (Uniform Crime Reports, October 4, 1997)
*Of the 15,835 murders in 1996 for which supplemental data were received by the F.B.I. There were an additional 3,810 murders for which the type of murder weapon was not reported to the F.B.I. Includes nonnegligent manslaughter. National and state rates based on population for reporting jurisdictions only. New York's rate does not include New York City. **Not available.

Percent of Murders Involving Firearms in 1996

National Percent = 67.8% of Murders*

ALPHA ORDER			RANK ORDER		
RANK	STATE	PERCENT	RANK	STATE	PERCENT
9	Alabama	72.6	1	Wyoming	87.5
18	Alaska	67.5	2	Louisiana	77.7
5	Arizona	75.2	3	Illinois	76.5
11	Arkansas	71.8	4	Mississippi	76.4
12	California	70.7	5	Arizona	75.2
39	Colorado	51.5	6	Pennsylvania	74.1
14	Connecticut	69.0	7	Maryland	73.4
38	Delaware	51.7	8	Georgia	73.0
28	Florida	62.0	9	Alabama	72.6
8	Georgia	73.0	10	Tennessee	72.5
48	Hawaii	42.1	11	Arkansas	71.8
20	Idaho	66.7	12	California	70.7
3	Illinois	76.5	13	Michigan	69.1
17	Indiana	68.0	14	Connecticut	69.0
29	Iowa	61.4	15	Missouri	68.8
NA	Kansas**	NA	16	South Carolina	68.1
20	Kentucky	66.7	17	Indiana	68.0
2	Louisiana	77.7	18	Alaska	67.5
46	Maine	44.0	19	West Virginia	67.2
7	Maryland	73.4	20	Idaho	66.7
43	Massachusetts	48.4	20	Kentucky	66.7
13	Michigan	69.1	22	Virginia	65.7
36	Minnesota	53.4	23	Ohio	65.4
4	Mississippi	76.4	24	Texas	65.2
15	Missouri	68.8	25	North Carolina	64.6
NA	Montana**	NA	26	Oklahoma	63.6
44	Nebraska	47.4	27	Vermont	62.5
30	Nevada	60.5	28	Florida	62.0
44	New Hampshire	47.4	29	Iowa	61.4
42	New Jersey	49.4	30	Nevada	60.5
33	New Mexico	55.9	31	Utah	56.5
34	New York*	55.1	32	Wisconsin	56.0
25	North Carolina	64.6	33	New Mexico	55.9
47	North Dakota	42.9	34	New York*	55.1
23	Ohio	65.4	35	Washington	54.2
26	Oklahoma	63.6	36	Minnesota	53.4
40	Oregon	50.9	37	Rhode Island	52.0
6	Pennsylvania	74.1	38	Delaware	51.7
37	Rhode Island	52.0	39	Colorado	51.5
16	South Carolina	68.1	40	Oregon	50.9
41	South Dakota	50.0	41	South Dakota	50.0
10	Tennessee	72.5	42	New Jersey	49.4
24	Texas	65.2	43	Massachusetts	48.4
31	Utah	56.5	44	Nebraska	47.4
27	Vermont	62.5	44	New Hampshire	47.4
22	Virginia	65.7	46	Maine	44.0
35	Washington	54.2	47	North Dakota	42.9
19	West Virginia	67.2	48	Hawaii	42.1
32	Wisconsin	56.0	NA	Kansas**	NA
1	Wyoming	87.5	NA	Montana**	NA
				District of Columbia**	NA

Source: Morgan Quitno Press using data from Federal Bureau of Investigation
    "Crime in the United States 1996" (Uniform Crime Reports, October 4, 1997)
*Of the 15,835 murders in 1996 for which supplemental data were received by the F.B.I. There were an additional
3,810 murders for which the type of murder weapon was not reported to the F.B.I. Includes nonnegligent
manslaughter. New York's percentage does not include New York City.
**Not available.

333

Murders with Handguns in 1996

National Total = 8,587 Murders*

ALPHA ORDER					RANK ORDER			

RANK	STATE	MURDERS	% of USA		RANK	STATE	MURDERS	% of USA
10	Alabama	265	3.09%		1	California	1,872	21.80%
33	Alaska	24	0.28%		2	Texas	689	8.02%
14	Arizona	223	2.60%		3	Illinois	513	5.97%
21	Arkansas	116	1.35%		4	Louisiana	453	5.28%
1	California	1,872	21.80%		5	Pennsylvania	438	5.10%
28	Colorado	66	0.77%		6	Maryland	398	4.63%
27	Connecticut	87	1.01%		7	Georgia	378	4.40%
39	Delaware	9	0.10%		8	North Carolina	318	3.70%
NA	Florida**	NA	NA		9	Ohio	270	3.14%
7	Georgia	378	4.40%		10	Alabama	265	3.09%
38	Hawaii	10	0.12%		11	Virginia	250	2.91%
37	Idaho	14	0.16%		12	Tennessee	243	2.83%
3	Illinois	513	5.97%		13	Michigan	225	2.62%
16	Indiana	161	1.87%		14	Arizona	223	2.60%
36	Iowa	21	0.24%		15	Missouri	204	2.38%
NA	Kansas**	NA	NA		16	Indiana	161	1.87%
25	Kentucky	98	1.14%		17	South Carolina	160	1.86%
4	Louisiana	453	5.28%		18	New Jersey	157	1.83%
43	Maine	5	0.06%		19	New York*	125	1.46%
6	Maryland	398	4.63%		20	Nevada	118	1.37%
35	Massachusetts	23	0.27%		21	Arkansas	116	1.35%
13	Michigan	225	2.62%		22	Mississippi	107	1.25%
29	Minnesota	58	0.68%		23	Washington	105	1.22%
22	Mississippi	107	1.25%		24	Oklahoma	99	1.15%
15	Missouri	204	2.38%		25	Kentucky	98	1.14%
NA	Montana**	NA	NA		25	Wisconsin	98	1.14%
42	Nebraska	7	0.08%		27	Connecticut	87	1.01%
20	Nevada	118	1.37%		28	Colorado	66	0.77%
44	New Hampshire	4	0.05%		29	Minnesota	58	0.68%
18	New Jersey	157	1.83%		30	New Mexico	54	0.63%
30	New Mexico	54	0.63%		31	Oregon	50	0.58%
19	New York*	125	1.46%		32	West Virginia	27	0.31%
8	North Carolina	318	3.70%		33	Alaska	24	0.28%
46	North Dakota	1	0.01%		33	Utah	24	0.28%
9	Ohio	270	3.14%		35	Massachusetts	23	0.27%
24	Oklahoma	99	1.15%		36	Iowa	21	0.24%
31	Oregon	50	0.58%		37	Idaho	14	0.16%
5	Pennsylvania	438	5.10%		38	Hawaii	10	0.12%
39	Rhode Island	9	0.10%		39	Delaware	9	0.10%
17	South Carolina	160	1.86%		39	Rhode Island	9	0.10%
47	South Dakota	0	0.00%		41	Wyoming	8	0.09%
12	Tennessee	243	2.83%		42	Nebraska	7	0.08%
2	Texas	689	8.02%		43	Maine	5	0.06%
33	Utah	24	0.28%		44	New Hampshire	4	0.05%
45	Vermont	3	0.03%		45	Vermont	3	0.03%
11	Virginia	250	2.91%		46	North Dakota	1	0.01%
23	Washington	105	1.22%		47	South Dakota	0	0.00%
32	West Virginia	27	0.31%		NA	Florida**	NA	NA
25	Wisconsin	98	1.14%		NA	Kansas**	NA	NA
41	Wyoming	8	0.09%		NA	Montana**	NA	NA
						District of Columbia**	NA	NA

Source: Federal Bureau of Investigation
   "Crime in the United States 1996" (Uniform Crime Reports, October 4, 1997)
*Of the 15,572 murders in 1996 for which supplemental data were received by the F.B.I. There were an additional 3,973 murders for which the type of murder weapon was not reported to the F.B.I. This includes 163 murders in Florida that were reported as murders by firearms but not broken down by type of firearm. New York's number does not include New York City. Murder includes nonnegligent manslaughter. **Not available.*

Murder Rate with Handguns in 1996

National Rate = 4.2 Murders per 100,000 Population*

ALPHA ORDER			RANK ORDER		
RANK	STATE	RATE	RANK	STATE	RATE
8	Alabama	6.4	1	Illinois	15.4
17	Alaska	4.4	2	Louisiana	13.2
11	Arizona	5.3	3	Mississippi	11.8
14	Arkansas	4.9	4	Kentucky	9.5
9	California	5.9	5	Tennessee	8.5
30	Colorado	1.9	6	Maryland	7.9
23	Connecticut	3.3	7	Nevada	7.4
26	Delaware	2.4	8	Alabama	6.4
NA	Florida**	NA	9	California	5.9
9	Georgia	5.9	9	Georgia	5.9
40	Hawaii	0.8	11	Arizona	5.3
35	Idaho	1.2	11	New Mexico	5.3
1	Illinois	15.4	13	Missouri	5.0
15	Indiana	4.7	14	Arkansas	4.9
38	Iowa	0.9	15	Indiana	4.7
NA	Kansas**	NA	15	Pennsylvania	4.7
4	Kentucky	9.5	17	Alaska	4.4
2	Louisiana	13.2	17	North Carolina	4.4
44	Maine	0.4	17	South Carolina	4.4
6	Maryland	7.9	20	Ohio	3.8
41	Massachusetts	0.5	21	Virginia	3.7
25	Michigan	2.9	22	Texas	3.6
34	Minnesota	1.3	23	Connecticut	3.3
3	Mississippi	11.8	24	Oklahoma	3.0
13	Missouri	5.0	25	Michigan	2.9
NA	Montana**	NA	26	Delaware	2.4
41	Nebraska	0.5	27	New Jersey	2.0
7	Nevada	7.4	27	Washington	2.0
44	New Hampshire	0.4	27	Wyoming	2.0
27	New Jersey	2.0	30	Colorado	1.9
11	New Mexico	5.3	30	Wisconsin	1.9
35	New York*	1.2	32	Oregon	1.8
17	North Carolina	4.4	33	West Virginia	1.5
46	North Dakota	0.3	34	Minnesota	1.3
20	Ohio	3.8	35	Idaho	1.2
24	Oklahoma	3.0	35	New York*	1.2
32	Oregon	1.8	35	Utah	1.2
15	Pennsylvania	4.7	38	Iowa	0.9
38	Rhode Island	0.9	38	Rhode Island	0.9
17	South Carolina	4.4	40	Hawaii	0.8
47	South Dakota	0.0	41	Massachusetts	0.5
5	Tennessee	8.5	41	Nebraska	0.5
22	Texas	3.6	41	Vermont	0.5
35	Utah	1.2	44	Maine	0.4
41	Vermont	0.5	44	New Hampshire	0.4
21	Virginia	3.7	46	North Dakota	0.3
27	Washington	2.0	47	South Dakota	0.0
33	West Virginia	1.5	NA	Florida**	NA
30	Wisconsin	1.9	NA	Kansas**	NA
27	Wyoming	2.0	NA	Montana**	NA
				District of Columbia**	NA

Source: Morgan Quitno Press using data from Federal Bureau of Investigation
"Crime in the United States 1996" (Uniform Crime Reports, October 4, 1997)
*Of the 15,572 murders in 1996 for which supplemental data were received by the F.B.I. There were an additional 3,973 murders for which the type of murder weapon was not reported to the F.B.I. This includes 163 murders in Florida that were reported as murders by firearms but not broken down by type of firearm. New York's rate does not include New York City. Murder includes nonnegligent manslaughter. **Not available.

Percent of Murders Involving Handguns in 1996

National Percent = 55.1% of Murders*

RANK	STATE	PERCENT	RANK	STATE	PERCENT
7	Alabama	62.5	1	Maryland	68.9
11	Alaska	60.0	2	Illinois	67.1
8	Arizona	62.1	3	Pennsylvania	65.9
16	Arkansas	53.7	4	Louisiana	64.3
5	California	64.2	5	California	64.2
34	Colorado	39.1	6	Tennessee	63.1
13	Connecticut	55.1	7	Alabama	62.5
41	Delaware	31.0	8	Arizona	62.1
NA	Florida**	NA	9	Georgia	62.0
9	Georgia	62.0	10	Mississippi	60.1
42	Hawaii	26.3	11	Alaska	60.0
39	Idaho	33.3	12	Ohio	58.8
2	Illinois	67.1	13	Connecticut	55.1
15	Indiana	54.8	14	Nevada	54.9
23	Iowa	47.7	15	Indiana	54.8
NA	Kansas**	NA	16	Arkansas	53.7
27	Kentucky	44.7	17	Missouri	53.1
4	Louisiana	64.3	18	North Carolina	51.7
44	Maine	20.0	19	Virginia	51.0
1	Maryland	68.9	20	Wisconsin	50.8
45	Massachusetts	14.8	21	Wyoming	50.0
40	Michigan	32.4	22	South Carolina	48.6
29	Minnesota	43.6	23	Iowa	47.7
10	Mississippi	60.1	24	New Jersey	47.3
17	Missouri	53.1	25	Texas	46.7
NA	Montana**	NA	26	Oklahoma	46.3
37	Nebraska	36.8	27	Kentucky	44.7
14	Nevada	54.9	28	Washington	44.1
43	New Hampshire	21.1	29	Minnesota	43.6
24	New Jersey	47.3	30	Oregon	43.1
33	New Mexico	39.7	31	New York*	41.0
31	New York*	41.0	32	West Virginia	40.3
18	North Carolina	51.7	33	New Mexico	39.7
46	North Dakota	14.3	34	Colorado	39.1
12	Ohio	58.8	35	Utah	38.7
26	Oklahoma	46.3	36	Vermont	37.5
30	Oregon	43.1	37	Nebraska	36.8
3	Pennsylvania	65.9	38	Rhode Island	36.0
38	Rhode Island	36.0	39	Idaho	33.3
22	South Carolina	48.6	40	Michigan	32.4
47	South Dakota	0.0	41	Delaware	31.0
6	Tennessee	63.1	42	Hawaii	26.3
25	Texas	46.7	43	New Hampshire	21.1
35	Utah	38.7	44	Maine	20.0
36	Vermont	37.5	45	Massachusetts	14.8
19	Virginia	51.0	46	North Dakota	14.3
28	Washington	44.1	47	South Dakota	0.0
32	West Virginia	40.3	NA	Florida**	NA
20	Wisconsin	50.8	NA	Kansas**	NA
21	Wyoming	50.0	NA	Montana**	NA
				District of Columbia**	NA

Source: Morgan Quitno Press using data from Federal Bureau of Investigation
"Crime in the United States 1996" (Uniform Crime Reports, October 4, 1997)
*Of the 15,572 murders in 1996 for which supplemental data were received by the F.B.I. There were an additional 3,973 murders for which the type of murder weapon was not reported to the F.B.I. This includes 163 murders in Florida that were reported as murders by firearms but not broken down by type of firearm. New York's rate does not include New York City. Murder includes nonnegligent manslaughter. **Not available.*

Murders with Rifles in 1996

National Total = 545 Murders*

ALPHA ORDER					RANK ORDER			
RANK	STATE	MURDERS	% of USA		RANK	STATE	MURDERS	% of USA
6	Alabama	23	4.22%		1	California	95	17.43%
45	Alaska	0	0.00%		2	Texas	73	13.39%
11	Arizona	16	2.94%		3	Michigan	39	7.16%
12	Arkansas	14	2.57%		4	North Carolina	26	4.77%
1	California	95	17.43%		5	Louisiana	25	4.59%
20	Colorado	7	1.28%		6	Alabama	23	4.22%
31	Connecticut	3	0.55%		7	Georgia	21	3.85%
31	Delaware	3	0.55%		8	Missouri	19	3.49%
NA	Florida**	NA	NA		8	Pennsylvania	19	3.49%
7	Georgia	21	3.85%		10	Virginia	18	3.30%
38	Hawaii	1	0.18%		11	Arizona	16	2.94%
18	Idaho	8	1.47%		12	Arkansas	14	2.57%
28	Illinois	4	0.73%		13	Kentucky	12	2.20%
20	Indiana	7	1.28%		13	New York*	12	2.20%
38	Iowa	1	0.18%		13	Washington	12	2.20%
NA	Kansas**	NA	NA		16	Oklahoma	10	1.83%
13	Kentucky	12	2.20%		17	Tennessee	9	1.65%
5	Louisiana	25	4.59%		18	Idaho	8	1.47%
45	Maine	0	0.00%		18	South Carolina	8	1.47%
31	Maryland	3	0.55%		20	Colorado	7	1.28%
25	Massachusetts	5	0.92%		20	Indiana	7	1.28%
3	Michigan	39	7.16%		20	New Mexico	7	1.28%
25	Minnesota	5	0.92%		20	Ohio	7	1.28%
24	Mississippi	6	1.10%		24	Mississippi	6	1.10%
8	Missouri	19	3.49%		25	Massachusetts	5	0.92%
NA	Montana**	NA	NA		25	Minnesota	5	0.92%
35	Nebraska	2	0.37%		25	West Virginia	5	0.92%
31	Nevada	3	0.55%		28	Illinois	4	0.73%
35	New Hampshire	2	0.37%		28	Wisconsin	4	0.73%
38	New Jersey	1	0.18%		28	Wyoming	4	0.73%
20	New Mexico	7	1.28%		31	Connecticut	3	0.55%
13	New York*	12	2.20%		31	Delaware	3	0.55%
4	North Carolina	26	4.77%		31	Maryland	3	0.55%
38	North Dakota	1	0.18%		31	Nevada	3	0.55%
20	Ohio	7	1.28%		35	Nebraska	2	0.37%
16	Oklahoma	10	1.83%		35	New Hampshire	2	0.37%
38	Oregon	1	0.18%		35	Rhode Island	2	0.37%
8	Pennsylvania	19	3.49%		38	Hawaii	1	0.18%
35	Rhode Island	2	0.37%		38	Iowa	1	0.18%
18	South Carolina	8	1.47%		38	New Jersey	1	0.18%
38	South Dakota	1	0.18%		38	North Dakota	1	0.18%
17	Tennessee	9	1.65%		38	Oregon	1	0.18%
2	Texas	73	13.39%		38	South Dakota	1	0.18%
45	Utah	0	0.00%		38	Vermont	1	0.18%
38	Vermont	1	0.18%		45	Alaska	0	0.00%
10	Virginia	18	3.30%		45	Maine	0	0.00%
13	Washington	12	2.20%		45	Utah	0	0.00%
25	West Virginia	5	0.92%		NA	Florida**	NA	NA
28	Wisconsin	4	0.73%		NA	Kansas**	NA	NA
28	Wyoming	4	0.73%		NA	Montana**	NA	NA
						District of Columbia**	NA	NA

Source: Federal Bureau of Investigation
"Crime in the United States 1996" (Uniform Crime Reports, October 4, 1997)
*Of the 15,572 murders in 1996 for which supplemental data were received by the F.B.I. There were an additional 3,973 murders for which the type of murder weapon was not reported to the F.B.I. This includes 163 murders in Florida that were reported as murders by firearms but not broken down by type of firearm. New York's number does not include New York City. Murder includes nonnegligent manslaughter. **Not available.

337

Percent of Murders Involving Rifles in 1996

National Percent = 3.5% of Murders*

ALPHA ORDER

RANK ORDER

RANK	STATE	PERCENT		RANK	STATE	PERCENT
14	Alabama	5.4		1	Wyoming	25.0
45	Alaska	0.0		2	Idaho	19.0
20	Arizona	4.5		3	South Dakota	16.7
11	Arkansas	6.5		4	North Dakota	14.3
29	California	3.3		5	Vermont	12.5
22	Colorado	4.1		6	Nebraska	10.5
38	Connecticut	1.9		6	New Hampshire	10.5
8	Delaware	10.3		8	Delaware	10.3
NA	Florida**	NA		9	Rhode Island	8.0
27	Georgia	3.4		10	West Virginia	7.5
32	Hawaii	2.6		11	Arkansas	6.5
2	Idaho	19.0		12	Michigan	5.6
42	Illinois	0.5		13	Kentucky	5.5
33	Indiana	2.4		14	Alabama	5.4
35	Iowa	2.3		15	New Mexico	5.1
NA	Kansas**	NA		16	Washington	5.0
13	Kentucky	5.5		17	Missouri	4.9
26	Louisiana	3.6		17	Texas	4.9
45	Maine	0.0		19	Oklahoma	4.7
42	Maryland	0.5		20	Arizona	4.5
30	Massachusetts	3.2		21	North Carolina	4.2
12	Michigan	5.6		22	Colorado	4.1
24	Minnesota	3.8		23	New York*	3.9
27	Mississippi	3.4		24	Minnesota	3.8
17	Missouri	4.9		25	Virginia	3.7
NA	Montana**	NA		26	Louisiana	3.6
6	Nebraska	10.5		27	Georgia	3.4
40	Nevada	1.4		27	Mississippi	3.4
6	New Hampshire	10.5		29	California	3.3
44	New Jersey	0.3		30	Massachusetts	3.2
15	New Mexico	5.1		31	Pennsylvania	2.9
23	New York*	3.9		32	Hawaii	2.6
21	North Carolina	4.2		33	Indiana	2.4
4	North Dakota	14.3		33	South Carolina	2.4
39	Ohio	1.5		35	Iowa	2.3
19	Oklahoma	4.7		35	Tennessee	2.3
41	Oregon	0.9		37	Wisconsin	2.1
31	Pennsylvania	2.9		38	Connecticut	1.9
9	Rhode Island	8.0		39	Ohio	1.5
33	South Carolina	2.4		40	Nevada	1.4
3	South Dakota	16.7		41	Oregon	0.9
35	Tennessee	2.3		42	Illinois	0.5
17	Texas	4.9		42	Maryland	0.5
45	Utah	0.0		44	New Jersey	0.3
5	Vermont	12.5		45	Alaska	0.0
25	Virginia	3.7		45	Maine	0.0
16	Washington	5.0		45	Utah	0.0
10	West Virginia	7.5		NA	Florida**	NA
37	Wisconsin	2.1		NA	Kansas**	NA
1	Wyoming	25.0		NA	Montana**	NA
					District of Columbia**	NA

Source: Morgan Quitno Press using data from Federal Bureau of Investigation
"Crime in the United States 1996" (Uniform Crime Reports, October 4, 1997)

*Of the 15,572 murders in 1996 for which supplemental data were received by the F.B.I. There were an additional 3,973 murders for which the type of murder weapon was not reported to the F.B.I. This includes 163 murders in Florida that were reported as murders by firearms but not broken down by type of firearm. New York's percent does not include New York City. Murder includes nonnegligent manslaughter. **Not available.*

Murders with Shotguns in 1996

National Total = 673 Murders*

ALPHA ORDER					RANK ORDER			
RANK	STATE	MURDERS	% of USA		RANK	STATE	MURDERS	% of USA
12	Alabama	19	2.82%		1	Texas	89	13.22%
34	Alaska	3	0.45%		2	California	86	12.78%
18	Arizona	13	1.93%		3	North Carolina	48	7.13%
14	Arkansas	18	2.67%		4	Michigan	31	4.61%
2	California	86	12.78%		5	Georgia	29	4.31%
26	Colorado	6	0.89%		5	Virginia	29	4.31%
34	Connecticut	3	0.45%		7	South Carolina	25	3.71%
39	Delaware	2	0.30%		8	Louisiana	23	3.42%
NA	Florida**	NA	NA		9	Pennsylvania	22	3.27%
5	Georgia	29	4.31%		10	Oklahoma	21	3.12%
30	Hawaii	4	0.59%		10	Tennessee	21	3.12%
30	Idaho	4	0.59%		12	Alabama	19	2.82%
25	Illinois	7	1.04%		12	New York*	19	2.82%
22	Indiana	10	1.49%		14	Arkansas	18	2.67%
42	Iowa	1	0.15%		15	Kentucky	17	2.53%
NA	Kansas**	NA	NA		16	Maryland	14	2.08%
15	Kentucky	17	2.53%		16	Missouri	14	2.08%
8	Louisiana	23	3.42%		18	Arizona	13	1.93%
28	Maine	5	0.74%		18	New Mexico	13	1.93%
16	Maryland	14	2.08%		20	Ohio	12	1.78%
30	Massachusetts	4	0.59%		21	West Virginia	11	1.63%
4	Michigan	31	4.61%		22	Indiana	10	1.49%
34	Minnesota	3	0.45%		22	Mississippi	10	1.49%
22	Mississippi	10	1.49%		24	Washington	9	1.34%
16	Missouri	14	2.08%		25	Illinois	7	1.04%
NA	Montana**	NA	NA		26	Colorado	6	0.89%
46	Nebraska	0	0.00%		26	Oregon	6	0.89%
28	Nevada	5	0.74%		28	Maine	5	0.74%
34	New Hampshire	3	0.45%		28	Nevada	5	0.74%
39	New Jersey	2	0.30%		30	Hawaii	4	0.59%
18	New Mexico	13	1.93%		30	Idaho	4	0.59%
12	New York*	19	2.82%		30	Massachusetts	4	0.59%
3	North Carolina	48	7.13%		30	Wisconsin	4	0.59%
42	North Dakota	1	0.15%		34	Alaska	3	0.45%
20	Ohio	12	1.78%		34	Connecticut	3	0.45%
10	Oklahoma	21	3.12%		34	Minnesota	3	0.45%
26	Oregon	6	0.89%		34	New Hampshire	3	0.45%
9	Pennsylvania	22	3.27%		34	Utah	3	0.45%
46	Rhode Island	0	0.00%		39	Delaware	2	0.30%
7	South Carolina	25	3.71%		39	New Jersey	2	0.30%
42	South Dakota	1	0.15%		39	Wyoming	2	0.30%
10	Tennessee	21	3.12%		42	Iowa	1	0.15%
1	Texas	89	13.22%		42	North Dakota	1	0.15%
34	Utah	3	0.45%		42	South Dakota	1	0.15%
42	Vermont	1	0.15%		42	Vermont	1	0.15%
5	Virginia	29	4.31%		46	Nebraska	0	0.00%
24	Washington	9	1.34%		46	Rhode Island	0	0.00%
21	West Virginia	11	1.63%		NA	Florida**	NA	NA
30	Wisconsin	4	0.59%		NA	Kansas**	NA	NA
39	Wyoming	2	0.30%		NA	Montana**	NA	NA
						District of Columbia**	NA	NA

Source: Federal Bureau of Investigation
   "Crime in the United States 1996" (Uniform Crime Reports, October 4, 1997)
*Of the 15,572 murders in 1996 for which supplemental data were received by the F.B.I. There were an additional 3,973 murders for which the type of murder weapon was not reported to the F.B.I. This includes 163 murders in Florida that were reported as murders by firearms but not broken down by type of firearm. New York's number does not include New York City. Murder includes nonnegligent manslaughter. **Not available.

Percent of Murders Involving Shotguns in 1996

National Percent = 4.3% of Murders*

RANK	STATE	PERCENT
26	Alabama	4.5
16	Alaska	7.5
29	Arizona	3.6
12	Arkansas	8.3
35	California	2.9
29	Colorado	3.6
43	Connecticut	1.9
17	Delaware	6.9
NA	Florida**	NA
24	Georgia	4.8
8	Hawaii	10.5
11	Idaho	9.5
44	Illinois	0.9
32	Indiana	3.4
39	Iowa	2.3
NA	Kansas**	NA
13	Kentucky	7.8
33	Louisiana	3.3
1	Maine	20.0
38	Maryland	2.4
36	Massachusetts	2.6
26	Michigan	4.5
39	Minnesota	2.3
21	Mississippi	5.6
29	Missouri	3.6
NA	Montana**	NA
46	Nebraska	0.0
39	Nevada	2.3
4	New Hampshire	15.8
45	New Jersey	0.6
10	New Mexico	9.6
18	New York*	6.2
13	North Carolina	7.8
5	North Dakota	14.3
36	Ohio	2.6
9	Oklahoma	9.8
23	Oregon	5.2
33	Pennsylvania	3.3
46	Rhode Island	0.0
15	South Carolina	7.6
2	South Dakota	16.7
22	Tennessee	5.5
19	Texas	6.0
24	Utah	4.8
6	Vermont	12.5
20	Virginia	5.9
28	Washington	3.8
3	West Virginia	16.4
42	Wisconsin	2.1
6	Wyoming	12.5

RANK	STATE	PERCENT
1	Maine	20.0
2	South Dakota	16.7
3	West Virginia	16.4
4	New Hampshire	15.8
5	North Dakota	14.3
6	Vermont	12.5
6	Wyoming	12.5
8	Hawaii	10.5
9	Oklahoma	9.8
10	New Mexico	9.6
11	Idaho	9.5
12	Arkansas	8.3
13	Kentucky	7.8
13	North Carolina	7.8
15	South Carolina	7.6
16	Alaska	7.5
17	Delaware	6.9
18	New York*	6.2
19	Texas	6.0
20	Virginia	5.9
21	Mississippi	5.6
22	Tennessee	5.5
23	Oregon	5.2
24	Georgia	4.8
24	Utah	4.8
26	Alabama	4.5
26	Michigan	4.5
28	Washington	3.8
29	Arizona	3.6
29	Colorado	3.6
29	Missouri	3.6
32	Indiana	3.4
33	Louisiana	3.3
33	Pennsylvania	3.3
35	California	2.9
36	Massachusetts	2.6
36	Ohio	2.6
38	Maryland	2.4
39	Iowa	2.3
39	Minnesota	2.3
39	Nevada	2.3
42	Wisconsin	2.1
43	Connecticut	1.9
44	Illinois	0.9
45	New Jersey	0.6
46	Nebraska	0.0
46	Rhode Island	0.0
NA	Florida**	NA
NA	Kansas**	NA
NA	Montana**	NA
	District of Columbia**	NA

Source: Morgan Quitno Press using data from Federal Bureau of Investigation
"Crime in the United States 1996" (Uniform Crime Reports, October 4, 1997)
*Of the 15,572 murders in 1996 for which supplemental data were received by the F.B.I. There were an additional 3,973 murders for which the type of murder weapon was not reported to the F.B.I. This includes 163 murders in Florida that were reported as murders by firearms but not broken down by type of firearm. New York's percent does not include New York City. Murder includes nonnegligent manslaughter. **Not available.

Murders with Knives or Cutting Instruments in 1996

National Total = 2,141 Murders*

<u>ALPHA ORDER</u>

RANK	STATE	MURDERS	% of USA
12	Alabama	63	2.94%
36	Alaska	6	0.28%
17	Arizona	44	2.06%
28	Arkansas	26	1.21%
1	California	342	15.97%
25	Colorado	36	1.68%
33	Connecticut	17	0.79%
41	Delaware	4	0.19%
20	Florida	39	1.82%
4	Georgia	79	3.69%
38	Hawaii	5	0.23%
38	Idaho	5	0.23%
7	Illinois	72	3.36%
22	Indiana	38	1.77%
38	Iowa	5	0.23%
NA	Kansas**	NA	NA
20	Kentucky	39	1.82%
10	Louisiana	70	3.27%
35	Maine	7	0.33%
11	Maryland	69	3.22%
16	Massachusetts	50	2.34%
4	Michigan	79	3.69%
30	Minnesota	25	1.17%
31	Mississippi	21	0.98%
14	Missouri	54	2.52%
NA	Montana**	NA	NA
44	Nebraska	3	0.14%
24	Nevada	37	1.73%
41	New Hampshire	4	0.19%
13	New Jersey	62	2.90%
26	New Mexico	32	1.49%
7	New York*	72	3.36%
3	North Carolina	82	3.83%
45	North Dakota	2	0.09%
22	Ohio	38	1.77%
27	Oklahoma	28	1.31%
32	Oregon	18	0.84%
9	Pennsylvania	71	3.32%
41	Rhode Island	4	0.19%
18	South Carolina	41	1.91%
45	South Dakota	2	0.09%
15	Tennessee	52	2.43%
2	Texas	235	10.98%
34	Utah	10	0.47%
45	Vermont	2	0.09%
6	Virginia	78	3.64%
19	Washington	40	1.87%
36	West Virginia	6	0.28%
28	Wisconsin	26	1.21%
48	Wyoming	1	0.05%

<u>RANK ORDER</u>

RANK	STATE	MURDERS	% of USA
1	California	342	15.97%
2	Texas	235	10.98%
3	North Carolina	82	3.83%
4	Georgia	79	3.69%
4	Michigan	79	3.69%
6	Virginia	78	3.64%
7	Illinois	72	3.36%
7	New York*	72	3.36%
9	Pennsylvania	71	3.32%
10	Louisiana	70	3.27%
11	Maryland	69	3.22%
12	Alabama	63	2.94%
13	New Jersey	62	2.90%
14	Missouri	54	2.52%
15	Tennessee	52	2.43%
16	Massachusetts	50	2.34%
17	Arizona	44	2.06%
18	South Carolina	41	1.91%
19	Washington	40	1.87%
20	Florida	39	1.82%
20	Kentucky	39	1.82%
22	Indiana	38	1.77%
22	Ohio	38	1.77%
24	Nevada	37	1.73%
25	Colorado	36	1.68%
26	New Mexico	32	1.49%
27	Oklahoma	28	1.31%
28	Arkansas	26	1.21%
28	Wisconsin	26	1.21%
30	Minnesota	25	1.17%
31	Mississippi	21	0.98%
32	Oregon	18	0.84%
33	Connecticut	17	0.79%
34	Utah	10	0.47%
35	Maine	7	0.33%
36	Alaska	6	0.28%
36	West Virginia	6	0.28%
38	Hawaii	5	0.23%
38	Idaho	5	0.23%
38	Iowa	5	0.23%
41	Delaware	4	0.19%
41	New Hampshire	4	0.19%
41	Rhode Island	4	0.19%
44	Nebraska	3	0.14%
45	North Dakota	2	0.09%
45	South Dakota	2	0.09%
45	Vermont	2	0.09%
48	Wyoming	1	0.05%
NA	Kansas**	NA	NA
NA	Montana**	NA	NA
	District of Columbia**	NA	NA

Source: Federal Bureau of Investigation
"Crime in the United States 1996" (Uniform Crime Reports, October 4, 1997)
*Of the 15,835 murders in 1996 for which supplemental data were received by the F.B.I. There were an additional 3,810 murders for which the type of murder weapon was not reported to the F.B.I. Includes nonnegligent manslaughter. Numbers are for reporting jurisdictions only. New York's number does not include New York City.
**Not available.

Percent of Murders Involving Knives or Cutting Instruments in 1996

National Percent = 13.5% of Murders*

<table>
<tr><td colspan="3">ALPHA ORDER</td><td colspan="3">RANK ORDER</td></tr>
<tr><td>RANK</td><td>STATE</td><td>PERCENT</td><td>RANK</td><td>STATE</td><td>PERCENT</td></tr>
<tr><td>22</td><td>Alabama</td><td>14.9</td><td>1</td><td>South Dakota</td><td>33.3</td></tr>
<tr><td>21</td><td>Alaska</td><td>15.0</td><td>2</td><td>Massachusetts</td><td>32.3</td></tr>
<tr><td>34</td><td>Arizona</td><td>12.3</td><td>3</td><td>North Dakota</td><td>28.6</td></tr>
<tr><td>35</td><td>Arkansas</td><td>12.0</td><td>4</td><td>Maine</td><td>28.0</td></tr>
<tr><td>39</td><td>California</td><td>11.7</td><td>5</td><td>Vermont</td><td>25.0</td></tr>
<tr><td>8</td><td>Colorado</td><td>21.3</td><td>6</td><td>New York*</td><td>23.6</td></tr>
<tr><td>42</td><td>Connecticut</td><td>10.8</td><td>7</td><td>New Mexico</td><td>23.5</td></tr>
<tr><td>25</td><td>Delaware</td><td>13.8</td><td>8</td><td>Colorado</td><td>21.3</td></tr>
<tr><td>23</td><td>Florida</td><td>14.8</td><td>9</td><td>New Hampshire</td><td>21.1</td></tr>
<tr><td>31</td><td>Georgia</td><td>13.0</td><td>10</td><td>Minnesota</td><td>18.8</td></tr>
<tr><td>29</td><td>Hawaii</td><td>13.2</td><td>11</td><td>New Jersey</td><td>18.7</td></tr>
<tr><td>36</td><td>Idaho</td><td>11.9</td><td>12</td><td>Kentucky</td><td>17.8</td></tr>
<tr><td>45</td><td>Illinois</td><td>9.4</td><td>13</td><td>Nevada</td><td>17.2</td></tr>
<tr><td>32</td><td>Indiana</td><td>12.9</td><td>14</td><td>Washington</td><td>16.8</td></tr>
<tr><td>40</td><td>Iowa</td><td>11.4</td><td>15</td><td>Utah</td><td>16.1</td></tr>
<tr><td>NA</td><td>Kansas**</td><td>NA</td><td>16</td><td>Rhode Island</td><td>16.0</td></tr>
<tr><td>12</td><td>Kentucky</td><td>17.8</td><td>17</td><td>Texas</td><td>15.9</td></tr>
<tr><td>44</td><td>Louisiana</td><td>9.9</td><td>17</td><td>Virginia</td><td>15.9</td></tr>
<tr><td>4</td><td>Maine</td><td>28.0</td><td>19</td><td>Nebraska</td><td>15.8</td></tr>
<tr><td>36</td><td>Maryland</td><td>11.9</td><td>20</td><td>Oregon</td><td>15.5</td></tr>
<tr><td>2</td><td>Massachusetts</td><td>32.3</td><td>21</td><td>Alaska</td><td>15.0</td></tr>
<tr><td>40</td><td>Michigan</td><td>11.4</td><td>22</td><td>Alabama</td><td>14.9</td></tr>
<tr><td>10</td><td>Minnesota</td><td>18.8</td><td>23</td><td>Florida</td><td>14.8</td></tr>
<tr><td>38</td><td>Mississippi</td><td>11.8</td><td>24</td><td>Missouri</td><td>14.1</td></tr>
<tr><td>24</td><td>Missouri</td><td>14.1</td><td>25</td><td>Delaware</td><td>13.8</td></tr>
<tr><td>NA</td><td>Montana**</td><td>NA</td><td>26</td><td>Tennessee</td><td>13.5</td></tr>
<tr><td>19</td><td>Nebraska</td><td>15.8</td><td>26</td><td>Wisconsin</td><td>13.5</td></tr>
<tr><td>13</td><td>Nevada</td><td>17.2</td><td>28</td><td>North Carolina</td><td>13.3</td></tr>
<tr><td>9</td><td>New Hampshire</td><td>21.1</td><td>29</td><td>Hawaii</td><td>13.2</td></tr>
<tr><td>11</td><td>New Jersey</td><td>18.7</td><td>30</td><td>Oklahoma</td><td>13.1</td></tr>
<tr><td>7</td><td>New Mexico</td><td>23.5</td><td>31</td><td>Georgia</td><td>13.0</td></tr>
<tr><td>6</td><td>New York*</td><td>23.6</td><td>32</td><td>Indiana</td><td>12.9</td></tr>
<tr><td>28</td><td>North Carolina</td><td>13.3</td><td>33</td><td>South Carolina</td><td>12.5</td></tr>
<tr><td>3</td><td>North Dakota</td><td>28.6</td><td>34</td><td>Arizona</td><td>12.3</td></tr>
<tr><td>47</td><td>Ohio</td><td>8.3</td><td>35</td><td>Arkansas</td><td>12.0</td></tr>
<tr><td>30</td><td>Oklahoma</td><td>13.1</td><td>36</td><td>Idaho</td><td>11.9</td></tr>
<tr><td>20</td><td>Oregon</td><td>15.5</td><td>36</td><td>Maryland</td><td>11.9</td></tr>
<tr><td>43</td><td>Pennsylvania</td><td>10.7</td><td>38</td><td>Mississippi</td><td>11.8</td></tr>
<tr><td>16</td><td>Rhode Island</td><td>16.0</td><td>39</td><td>California</td><td>11.7</td></tr>
<tr><td>33</td><td>South Carolina</td><td>12.5</td><td>40</td><td>Iowa</td><td>11.4</td></tr>
<tr><td>1</td><td>South Dakota</td><td>33.3</td><td>40</td><td>Michigan</td><td>11.4</td></tr>
<tr><td>26</td><td>Tennessee</td><td>13.5</td><td>42</td><td>Connecticut</td><td>10.8</td></tr>
<tr><td>17</td><td>Texas</td><td>15.9</td><td>43</td><td>Pennsylvania</td><td>10.7</td></tr>
<tr><td>15</td><td>Utah</td><td>16.1</td><td>44</td><td>Louisiana</td><td>9.9</td></tr>
<tr><td>5</td><td>Vermont</td><td>25.0</td><td>45</td><td>Illinois</td><td>9.4</td></tr>
<tr><td>17</td><td>Virginia</td><td>15.9</td><td>46</td><td>West Virginia</td><td>9.0</td></tr>
<tr><td>14</td><td>Washington</td><td>16.8</td><td>47</td><td>Ohio</td><td>8.3</td></tr>
<tr><td>46</td><td>West Virginia</td><td>9.0</td><td>48</td><td>Wyoming</td><td>6.3</td></tr>
<tr><td>26</td><td>Wisconsin</td><td>13.5</td><td>NA</td><td>Kansas**</td><td>NA</td></tr>
<tr><td>48</td><td>Wyoming</td><td>6.3</td><td>NA</td><td>Montana**</td><td>NA</td></tr>
<tr><td></td><td></td><td></td><td></td><td>District of Columbia**</td><td>NA</td></tr>
</table>

Source: Morgan Quitno Press using data from Federal Bureau of Investigation
    "Crime in the United States 1996" (Uniform Crime Reports, October 4, 1997)
*Of the 15,835 murders in 1996 for which supplemental data were received by the F.B.I. There were an additional 3,810 murders for which the type of murder weapon was not reported to the F.B.I. Includes nonnegligent manslaughter. National and state rates based on population for reporting jurisdictions only. New York's percent does not include New York City. **Not available.

Murders by Hands, Fists or Feet in 1996

National Total = 939 Murders*

ALPHA ORDER				RANK ORDER			
RANK	STATE	MURDERS	% of USA	RANK	STATE	MURDERS	% of USA
19	Alabama	16	1.70%	1	California	156	16.61%
42	Alaska	2	0.21%	2	Texas	84	8.95%
15	Arizona	21	2.24%	3	Illinois	46	4.90%
28	Arkansas	10	1.06%	4	New Jersey	44	4.69%
1	California	156	16.61%	5	North Carolina	39	4.15%
21	Colorado	15	1.60%	6	Ohio	34	3.62%
22	Connecticut	14	1.49%	6	Pennsylvania	34	3.62%
36	Delaware	5	0.53%	6	Virginia	34	3.62%
14	Florida	22	2.34%	9	Tennessee	32	3.41%
10	Georgia	30	3.19%	10	Georgia	30	3.19%
30	Hawaii	9	0.96%	11	Michigan	29	3.09%
37	Idaho	4	0.43%	12	Louisiana	28	2.98%
3	Illinois	46	4.90%	13	New York*	23	2.45%
15	Indiana	21	2.24%	14	Florida	22	2.34%
33	Iowa	6	0.64%	15	Arizona	21	2.24%
NA	Kansas**	NA	NA	15	Indiana	21	2.24%
22	Kentucky	14	1.49%	17	South Carolina	20	2.13%
12	Louisiana	28	2.98%	18	Maryland	18	1.92%
40	Maine	3	0.32%	19	Alabama	16	1.70%
18	Maryland	18	1.92%	19	Oklahoma	16	1.70%
44	Massachusetts	1	0.11%	21	Colorado	15	1.60%
11	Michigan	29	3.09%	22	Connecticut	14	1.49%
22	Minnesota	14	1.49%	22	Kentucky	14	1.49%
33	Mississippi	6	0.64%	22	Minnesota	14	1.49%
25	Missouri	13	1.38%	25	Missouri	13	1.38%
NA	Montana**	NA	NA	25	Nevada	13	1.38%
42	Nebraska	2	0.21%	25	Wisconsin	13	1.38%
25	Nevada	13	1.38%	28	Arkansas	10	1.06%
37	New Hampshire	4	0.43%	28	Oregon	10	1.06%
4	New Jersey	44	4.69%	30	Hawaii	9	0.96%
33	New Mexico	6	0.64%	30	Washington	9	0.96%
13	New York*	23	2.45%	32	Utah	8	0.85%
5	North Carolina	39	4.15%	33	Iowa	6	0.64%
44	North Dakota	1	0.11%	33	Mississippi	6	0.64%
6	Ohio	34	3.62%	33	New Mexico	6	0.64%
19	Oklahoma	16	1.70%	36	Delaware	5	0.53%
28	Oregon	10	1.06%	37	Idaho	4	0.43%
6	Pennsylvania	34	3.62%	37	New Hampshire	4	0.43%
40	Rhode Island	3	0.32%	37	West Virginia	4	0.43%
17	South Carolina	20	2.13%	40	Maine	3	0.32%
44	South Dakota	1	0.11%	40	Rhode Island	3	0.32%
9	Tennessee	32	3.41%	42	Alaska	2	0.21%
2	Texas	84	8.95%	42	Nebraska	2	0.21%
32	Utah	8	0.85%	44	Massachusetts	1	0.11%
44	Vermont	1	0.11%	44	North Dakota	1	0.11%
6	Virginia	34	3.62%	44	South Dakota	1	0.11%
30	Washington	9	0.96%	44	Vermont	1	0.11%
37	West Virginia	4	0.43%	44	Wyoming	1	0.11%
25	Wisconsin	13	1.38%	NA	Kansas**	NA	NA
44	Wyoming	1	0.11%	NA	Montana**	NA	NA
					District of Columbia**	NA	NA

Source: Federal Bureau of Investigation
    "Crime in the United States 1996" (Uniform Crime Reports, October 4, 1997)
*Of the 15,835 murders in 1996 for which supplemental data were received by the F.B.I. There were an additional 3,810 murders for which the type of murder weapon was not reported to the F.B.I. Includes nonnegligent manslaughter. Numbers are for reporting jurisdictions only. New York's number does not include New York City.
**Not available.

Percent of Murders Involving Hands, Fists or Feet in 1996

National Percent = 5.9% of Murders*

<table>
<tr><td colspan="3">ALPHA ORDER</td><td colspan="3">RANK ORDER</td></tr>
<tr><th>RANK</th><th>STATE</th><th>PERCENT</th><th>RANK</th><th>STATE</th><th>PERCENT</th></tr>
<tr><td>43</td><td>Alabama</td><td>3.8</td><td>1</td><td>Hawaii</td><td>23.7</td></tr>
<tr><td>37</td><td>Alaska</td><td>5.0</td><td>2</td><td>New Hampshire</td><td>21.1</td></tr>
<tr><td>33</td><td>Arizona</td><td>5.8</td><td>3</td><td>Delaware</td><td>17.2</td></tr>
<tr><td>39</td><td>Arkansas</td><td>4.6</td><td>4</td><td>South Dakota</td><td>16.7</td></tr>
<tr><td>35</td><td>California</td><td>5.3</td><td>5</td><td>North Dakota</td><td>14.3</td></tr>
<tr><td>15</td><td>Colorado</td><td>8.9</td><td>6</td><td>Iowa</td><td>13.6</td></tr>
<tr><td>15</td><td>Connecticut</td><td>8.9</td><td>7</td><td>New Jersey</td><td>13.3</td></tr>
<tr><td>3</td><td>Delaware</td><td>17.2</td><td>8</td><td>Utah</td><td>12.9</td></tr>
<tr><td>18</td><td>Florida</td><td>8.4</td><td>9</td><td>Vermont</td><td>12.5</td></tr>
<tr><td>38</td><td>Georgia</td><td>4.9</td><td>10</td><td>Maine</td><td>12.0</td></tr>
<tr><td>1</td><td>Hawaii</td><td>23.7</td><td>10</td><td>Rhode Island</td><td>12.0</td></tr>
<tr><td>14</td><td>Idaho</td><td>9.5</td><td>12</td><td>Minnesota</td><td>10.5</td></tr>
<tr><td>30</td><td>Illinois</td><td>6.0</td><td>12</td><td>Nebraska</td><td>10.5</td></tr>
<tr><td>23</td><td>Indiana</td><td>7.1</td><td>14</td><td>Idaho</td><td>9.5</td></tr>
<tr><td>6</td><td>Iowa</td><td>13.6</td><td>15</td><td>Colorado</td><td>8.9</td></tr>
<tr><td>NA</td><td>Kansas**</td><td>NA</td><td>15</td><td>Connecticut</td><td>8.9</td></tr>
<tr><td>26</td><td>Kentucky</td><td>6.4</td><td>17</td><td>Oregon</td><td>8.6</td></tr>
<tr><td>42</td><td>Louisiana</td><td>4.0</td><td>18</td><td>Florida</td><td>8.4</td></tr>
<tr><td>10</td><td>Maine</td><td>12.0</td><td>19</td><td>Tennessee</td><td>8.3</td></tr>
<tr><td>47</td><td>Maryland</td><td>3.1</td><td>20</td><td>New York*</td><td>7.5</td></tr>
<tr><td>48</td><td>Massachusetts</td><td>0.6</td><td>20</td><td>Oklahoma</td><td>7.5</td></tr>
<tr><td>41</td><td>Michigan</td><td>4.2</td><td>22</td><td>Ohio</td><td>7.4</td></tr>
<tr><td>12</td><td>Minnesota</td><td>10.5</td><td>23</td><td>Indiana</td><td>7.1</td></tr>
<tr><td>45</td><td>Mississippi</td><td>3.4</td><td>24</td><td>Virginia</td><td>6.9</td></tr>
<tr><td>45</td><td>Missouri</td><td>3.4</td><td>25</td><td>Wisconsin</td><td>6.7</td></tr>
<tr><td>NA</td><td>Montana**</td><td>NA</td><td>26</td><td>Kentucky</td><td>6.4</td></tr>
<tr><td>12</td><td>Nebraska</td><td>10.5</td><td>27</td><td>North Carolina</td><td>6.3</td></tr>
<tr><td>30</td><td>Nevada</td><td>6.0</td><td>27</td><td>Wyoming</td><td>6.3</td></tr>
<tr><td>2</td><td>New Hampshire</td><td>21.1</td><td>29</td><td>South Carolina</td><td>6.1</td></tr>
<tr><td>7</td><td>New Jersey</td><td>13.3</td><td>30</td><td>Illinois</td><td>6.0</td></tr>
<tr><td>40</td><td>New Mexico</td><td>4.4</td><td>30</td><td>Nevada</td><td>6.0</td></tr>
<tr><td>20</td><td>New York*</td><td>7.5</td><td>30</td><td>West Virginia</td><td>6.0</td></tr>
<tr><td>27</td><td>North Carolina</td><td>6.3</td><td>33</td><td>Arizona</td><td>5.8</td></tr>
<tr><td>5</td><td>North Dakota</td><td>14.3</td><td>34</td><td>Texas</td><td>5.7</td></tr>
<tr><td>22</td><td>Ohio</td><td>7.4</td><td>35</td><td>California</td><td>5.3</td></tr>
<tr><td>20</td><td>Oklahoma</td><td>7.5</td><td>36</td><td>Pennsylvania</td><td>5.1</td></tr>
<tr><td>17</td><td>Oregon</td><td>8.6</td><td>37</td><td>Alaska</td><td>5.0</td></tr>
<tr><td>36</td><td>Pennsylvania</td><td>5.1</td><td>38</td><td>Georgia</td><td>4.9</td></tr>
<tr><td>10</td><td>Rhode Island</td><td>12.0</td><td>39</td><td>Arkansas</td><td>4.6</td></tr>
<tr><td>29</td><td>South Carolina</td><td>6.1</td><td>40</td><td>New Mexico</td><td>4.4</td></tr>
<tr><td>4</td><td>South Dakota</td><td>16.7</td><td>41</td><td>Michigan</td><td>4.2</td></tr>
<tr><td>19</td><td>Tennessee</td><td>8.3</td><td>42</td><td>Louisiana</td><td>4.0</td></tr>
<tr><td>34</td><td>Texas</td><td>5.7</td><td>43</td><td>Alabama</td><td>3.8</td></tr>
<tr><td>8</td><td>Utah</td><td>12.9</td><td>43</td><td>Washington</td><td>3.8</td></tr>
<tr><td>9</td><td>Vermont</td><td>12.5</td><td>45</td><td>Mississippi</td><td>3.4</td></tr>
<tr><td>24</td><td>Virginia</td><td>6.9</td><td>45</td><td>Missouri</td><td>3.4</td></tr>
<tr><td>43</td><td>Washington</td><td>3.8</td><td>47</td><td>Maryland</td><td>3.1</td></tr>
<tr><td>30</td><td>West Virginia</td><td>6.0</td><td>48</td><td>Massachusetts</td><td>0.6</td></tr>
<tr><td>25</td><td>Wisconsin</td><td>6.7</td><td>NA</td><td>Kansas**</td><td>NA</td></tr>
<tr><td>27</td><td>Wyoming</td><td>6.3</td><td>NA</td><td>Montana**</td><td>NA</td></tr>
<tr><td></td><td></td><td></td><td></td><td>District of Columbia**</td><td>NA</td></tr>
</table>

Source: Morgan Quitno Press using data from Federal Bureau of Investigation
   "Crime in the United States 1996" (Uniform Crime Reports, October 4, 1997)
*Of the 15,835 murders in 1996 for which supplemental data were received by the F.B.I. There were an additional 3,810 murders for which the type of murder weapon was not reported to the F.B.I. Includes nonnegligent manslaughter. National and state rates based on population for reporting jurisdictions only. New York's percent does not include New York City. **Not available.

Rapes in 1996

National Total = 95,769 Rapes*

ALPHA ORDER

RANK	STATE	RAPES	% of USA
24	Alabama	1,397	1.46%
40	Alaska	398	0.42%
25	Arizona	1,381	1.44%
31	Arkansas	1,046	1.09%
1	California	10,244	10.70%
21	Colorado	1,765	1.84%
35	Connecticut	755	0.79%
37	Delaware	454	0.47%
3	Florida	7,508	7.84%
11	Georgia	2,357	2.46%
42	Hawaii	326	0.34%
43	Idaho	313	0.33%
7	Illinois	4,051	4.23%
14	Indiana	1,992	2.08%
36	Iowa	561	0.59%
28	Kansas	1,096	1.14%
27	Kentucky	1,230	1.28%
18	Louisiana	1,805	1.88%
46	Maine	260	0.27%
16	Maryland	1,905	1.99%
20	Massachusetts	1,767	1.85%
4	Michigan	5,466	5.71%
12	Minnesota	2,327	2.43%
32	Mississippi	981	1.02%
22	Missouri	1,566	1.64%
47	Montana	238	0.25%
38	Nebraska	447	0.47%
33	Nevada	856	0.89%
39	New Hampshire	404	0.42%
15	New Jersey	1,976	2.06%
29	New Mexico	1,088	1.14%
6	New York	4,174	4.36%
13	North Carolina	2,289	2.39%
49	North Dakota	155	0.16%
5	Ohio	4,617	4.82%
23	Oklahoma	1,545	1.61%
26	Oregon	1,272	1.33%
8	Pennsylvania	3,048	3.18%
45	Rhode Island	287	0.30%
17	South Carolina	1,821	1.90%
44	South Dakota	300	0.31%
10	Tennessee	2,475	2.58%
2	Texas	8,376	8.75%
34	Utah	836	0.87%
48	Vermont	159	0.17%
19	Virginia	1,783	1.86%
9	Washington	2,828	2.95%
41	West Virginia	358	0.37%
30	Wisconsin	1,086	1.13%
50	Wyoming	140	0.15%

RANK ORDER

RANK	STATE	RAPES	% of USA
1	California	10,244	10.70%
2	Texas	8,376	8.75%
3	Florida	7,508	7.84%
4	Michigan	5,466	5.71%
5	Ohio	4,617	4.82%
6	New York	4,174	4.36%
7	Illinois	4,051	4.23%
8	Pennsylvania	3,048	3.18%
9	Washington	2,828	2.95%
10	Tennessee	2,475	2.58%
11	Georgia	2,357	2.46%
12	Minnesota	2,327	2.43%
13	North Carolina	2,289	2.39%
14	Indiana	1,992	2.08%
15	New Jersey	1,976	2.06%
16	Maryland	1,905	1.99%
17	South Carolina	1,821	1.90%
18	Louisiana	1,805	1.88%
19	Virginia	1,783	1.86%
20	Massachusetts	1,767	1.85%
21	Colorado	1,765	1.84%
22	Missouri	1,566	1.64%
23	Oklahoma	1,545	1.61%
24	Alabama	1,397	1.46%
25	Arizona	1,381	1.44%
26	Oregon	1,272	1.33%
27	Kentucky	1,230	1.28%
28	Kansas	1,096	1.14%
29	New Mexico	1,088	1.14%
30	Wisconsin	1,086	1.13%
31	Arkansas	1,046	1.09%
32	Mississippi	981	1.02%
33	Nevada	856	0.89%
34	Utah	836	0.87%
35	Connecticut	755	0.79%
36	Iowa	561	0.59%
37	Delaware	454	0.47%
38	Nebraska	447	0.47%
39	New Hampshire	404	0.42%
40	Alaska	398	0.42%
41	West Virginia	358	0.37%
42	Hawaii	326	0.34%
43	Idaho	313	0.33%
44	South Dakota	300	0.31%
45	Rhode Island	287	0.30%
46	Maine	260	0.27%
47	Montana	238	0.25%
48	Vermont	159	0.17%
49	North Dakota	155	0.16%
50	Wyoming	140	0.15%
	District of Columbia	260	0.27%

Source: Federal Bureau of Investigation
    "Crime in the United States 1996" (Uniform Crime Reports, October 4, 1997)
*Forcible rape is the carnal knowledge of a female forcibly and against her will. Assaults or attempts to commit rape by force or threat of force are included. However, statutory rape without force and other sex offenses are excluded.

Average Time Between Rapes in 1996

National Rate = A Rape Occurs Every 6 Minutes*

RANK	STATE	HOURS.MINUTES
27	Alabama	6.17
11	Alaska	22.04
26	Arizona	6.22
20	Arkansas	8.24
50	California	0.52
30	Colorado	4.59
16	Connecticut	11.38
14	Delaware	19.21
48	Florida	1.10
40	Georgia	3.44
9	Hawaii	26.56
8	Idaho	28.04
44	Illinois	2.10
37	Indiana	4.25
15	Iowa	15.40
23	Kansas	8.01
24	Kentucky	7.08
33	Louisiana	4.52
5	Maine	33.47
35	Maryland	4.37
31	Massachusetts	4.58
47	Michigan	1.37
39	Minnesota	3.46
19	Mississippi	8.57
29	Missouri	5.37
4	Montana	36.55
13	Nebraska	19.39
18	Nevada	10.16
12	New Hampshire	21.44
36	New Jersey	4.27
22	New Mexico	8.04
45	New York	2.06
38	North Carolina	3.50
2	North Dakota	56.40
46	Ohio	1.54
28	Oklahoma	5.41
25	Oregon	6.55
43	Pennsylvania	2.53
6	Rhode Island	30.37
34	South Carolina	4.49
7	South Dakota	29.17
41	Tennessee	3.33
49	Texas	1.03
17	Utah	10.31
3	Vermont	55.15
32	Virginia	4.56
42	Washington	3.07
10	West Virginia	24.32
21	Wisconsin	8.05
1	Wyoming	62.44

RANK	STATE	HOURS.MINUTES
1	Wyoming	62.44
2	North Dakota	56.40
3	Vermont	55.15
4	Montana	36.55
5	Maine	33.47
6	Rhode Island	30.37
7	South Dakota	29.17
8	Idaho	28.04
9	Hawaii	26.56
10	West Virginia	24.32
11	Alaska	22.04
12	New Hampshire	21.44
13	Nebraska	19.39
14	Delaware	19.21
15	Iowa	15.40
16	Connecticut	11.38
17	Utah	10.31
18	Nevada	10.16
19	Mississippi	8.57
20	Arkansas	8.24
21	Wisconsin	8.05
22	New Mexico	8.04
23	Kansas	8.01
24	Kentucky	7.08
25	Oregon	6.55
26	Arizona	6.22
27	Alabama	6.17
28	Oklahoma	5.41
29	Missouri	5.37
30	Colorado	4.59
31	Massachusetts	4.58
32	Virginia	4.56
33	Louisiana	4.52
34	South Carolina	4.49
35	Maryland	4.37
36	New Jersey	4.27
37	Indiana	4.25
38	North Carolina	3.50
39	Minnesota	3.46
40	Georgia	3.44
41	Tennessee	3.33
42	Washington	3.07
43	Pennsylvania	2.53
44	Illinois	2.10
45	New York	2.06
46	Ohio	1.54
47	Michigan	1.37
48	Florida	1.10
49	Texas	1.03
50	California	0.52
	District of Columbia	33.47

Source: Morgan Quitno Press using data from Federal Bureau of Investigation
   "Crime in the United States 1996" (Uniform Crime Reports, October 4, 1997)
*Forcible rape is the carnal knowledge of a female forcibly and against her will. Assaults or attempts to commit rape by force or threat of force are included. However, statutory rape without force and other sex offenses are excluded.

Percent Change in Number of Rapes: 1995 to 1996

National Percent Change = 1.7% Decrease*

ALPHA ORDER				RANK ORDER		
RANK	STATE	PERCENT CHANGE		RANK	STATE	PERCENT CHANGE
12	Alabama	3.5		1	Nebraska	41.0
49	Alaska	(17.9)		2	New Hampshire	21.3
26	Arizona	(2.6)		3	Colorado	19.3
6	Arkansas	13.1		4	Kansas	16.8
31	California	(2.9)		5	New Mexico	14.0
3	Colorado	19.3		6	Arkansas	13.1
27	Connecticut	(2.7)		7	Florida	9.0
50	Delaware	(21.0)		8	Rhode Island	7.5
7	Florida	9.0		9	North Dakota	6.2
38	Georgia	(7.2)		10	Oklahoma	5.7
32	Hawaii	(3.0)		11	South Carolina	4.8
35	Idaho	(5.2)		12	Alabama	3.5
36	Illinois	(6.1)		13	Indiana	3.2
13	Indiana	3.2		14	Montana	3.0
44	Iowa	(9.4)		15	New Jersey	2.5
4	Kansas	16.8		16	Massachusetts	0.5
20	Kentucky	(0.1)		17	South Dakota	0.3
27	Louisiana	(2.7)		18	Utah	0.2
24	Maine	(1.9)		19	Pennsylvania	0.1
46	Maryland	(10.6)		20	Kentucky	(0.1)
16	Massachusetts	0.5		20	Tennessee	(0.1)
39	Michigan	(7.6)		22	Virginia	(0.9)
45	Minnesota	(10.3)		23	North Carolina	(1.3)
37	Mississippi	(6.9)		24	Maine	(1.9)
41	Missouri	(8.5)		25	Texas	(2.2)
14	Montana	3.0		26	Arizona	(2.6)
1	Nebraska	41.0		27	Connecticut	(2.7)
42	Nevada	(8.6)		27	Louisiana	(2.7)
2	New Hampshire	21.3		27	New York	(2.7)
15	New Jersey	2.5		30	Oregon	(2.8)
5	New Mexico	14.0		31	California	(2.9)
27	New York	(2.7)		32	Hawaii	(3.0)
23	North Carolina	(1.3)		33	Vermont	(3.6)
9	North Dakota	6.2		34	Ohio	(4.5)
34	Ohio	(4.5)		35	Idaho	(5.2)
10	Oklahoma	5.7		36	Illinois	(6.1)
30	Oregon	(2.8)		37	Mississippi	(6.9)
19	Pennsylvania	0.1		38	Georgia	(7.2)
8	Rhode Island	7.5		39	Michigan	(7.6)
11	South Carolina	4.8		40	West Virginia	(7.7)
17	South Dakota	0.3		41	Missouri	(8.5)
20	Tennessee	(0.1)		42	Nevada	(8.6)
25	Texas	(2.2)		43	Wisconsin	(9.0)
18	Utah	0.2		44	Iowa	(9.4)
33	Vermont	(3.6)		45	Minnesota	(10.3)
22	Virginia	(0.9)		46	Maryland	(10.6)
47	Washington	(12.0)		47	Washington	(12.0)
40	West Virginia	(7.7)		48	Wyoming	(15.2)
43	Wisconsin	(9.0)		49	Alaska	(17.9)
48	Wyoming	(15.2)		50	Delaware	(21.0)
					District of Columbia	(11.0)

Source: Federal Bureau of Investigation
  "Crime in the United States 1996" (Uniform Crime Reports, October 4, 1997)
*Forcible rape is the carnal knowledge of a female forcibly and against her will. Assaults or attempts to commit rape by force or threat of force are included. However, statutory rape without force and other sex offenses are excluded.

Rape Rate in 1996

National Rate = 36.1 Rapes per 100,000 Population*

ALPHA ORDER				RANK ORDER		
RANK	STATE	RATE		RANK	STATE	RATE
26	Alabama	32.7		1	Alaska	65.6
1	Alaska	65.6		2	New Mexico	63.5
31	Arizona	31.2		3	Delaware	62.6
16	Arkansas	41.7		4	Michigan	57.0
27	California	32.1		5	Nevada	53.4
12	Colorado	46.2		6	Florida	52.1
45	Connecticut	23.1		7	Washington	51.1
3	Delaware	62.6		8	Minnesota	50.0
6	Florida	52.1		9	South Carolina	49.2
27	Georgia	32.1		10	Oklahoma	46.8
36	Hawaii	27.5		11	Tennessee	46.5
41	Idaho	26.3		12	Colorado	46.2
24	Illinois	34.2		13	Texas	43.8
25	Indiana	34.1		14	Kansas	42.6
49	Iowa	19.7		15	Utah	41.8
14	Kansas	42.6		16	Arkansas	41.7
29	Kentucky	31.7		17	Louisiana	41.5
17	Louisiana	41.5		18	Ohio	41.3
48	Maine	20.9		19	South Dakota	41.0
21	Maryland	37.6		20	Oregon	39.7
34	Massachusetts	29.0		21	Maryland	37.6
4	Michigan	57.0		22	Mississippi	36.1
8	Minnesota	50.0		23	New Hampshire	34.8
22	Mississippi	36.1		24	Illinois	34.2
32	Missouri	29.2		25	Indiana	34.1
37	Montana	27.1		26	Alabama	32.7
37	Nebraska	27.1		27	California	32.1
5	Nevada	53.4		27	Georgia	32.1
23	New Hampshire	34.8		29	Kentucky	31.7
43	New Jersey	24.7		30	North Carolina	31.3
2	New Mexico	63.5		31	Arizona	31.2
46	New York	23.0		32	Missouri	29.2
30	North Carolina	31.3		33	Wyoming	29.1
44	North Dakota	24.1		34	Massachusetts	29.0
18	Ohio	41.3		34	Rhode Island	29.0
10	Oklahoma	46.8		36	Hawaii	27.5
20	Oregon	39.7		37	Montana	27.1
42	Pennsylvania	25.3		37	Nebraska	27.1
34	Rhode Island	29.0		39	Vermont	27.0
9	South Carolina	49.2		40	Virginia	26.7
19	South Dakota	41.0		41	Idaho	26.3
11	Tennessee	46.5		42	Pennsylvania	25.3
13	Texas	43.8		43	New Jersey	24.7
15	Utah	41.8		44	North Dakota	24.1
39	Vermont	27.0		45	Connecticut	23.1
40	Virginia	26.7		46	New York	23.0
7	Washington	51.1		47	Wisconsin	21.0
50	West Virginia	19.6		48	Maine	20.9
47	Wisconsin	21.0		49	Iowa	19.7
33	Wyoming	29.1		50	West Virginia	19.6
					District of Columbia	47.9

Source: Federal Bureau of Investigation

"Crime in the United States 1996" (Uniform Crime Reports, October 4, 1997)

*Forcible rape is the carnal knowledge of a female forcibly and against her will. Assaults or attempts to commit rape by force or threat of force are included. However, statutory rape without force and other sex offenses are excluded.

Percent Change in Rape Rate: 1995 to 1996

National Percent Change = 2.7% Decrease*

ALPHA ORDER			RANK ORDER		
RANK	STATE	PERCENT CHANGE	RANK	STATE	PERCENT CHANGE
12	Alabama	3.2	1	Nebraska	39.7
49	Alaska	(18.3)	2	New Hampshire	20.0
35	Arizona	(7.1)	3	Colorado	17.0
6	Arkansas	12.1	4	Kansas	16.4
29	California	(3.9)	5	New Mexico	12.2
3	Colorado	17.0	6	Arkansas	12.1
24	Connecticut	(2.5)	7	Rhode Island	7.4
50	Delaware	(21.9)	8	Florida	7.2
8	Florida	7.2	9	North Dakota	5.7
41	Georgia	(9.1)	10	Oklahoma	4.9
25	Hawaii	(2.8)	11	South Carolina	4.0
36	Idaho	(7.4)	12	Alabama	3.2
34	Illinois	(6.3)	13	Indiana	2.4
13	Indiana	2.4	14	Montana	1.9
42	Iowa	(9.6)	15	New Jersey	1.6
4	Kansas	16.4	16	Pennsylvania	0.4
19	Kentucky	(0.6)	17	Massachusetts	0.0
25	Louisiana	(2.8)	17	South Dakota	0.0
23	Maine	(2.3)	19	Kentucky	(0.6)
44	Maryland	(10.9)	20	Tennessee	(1.3)
17	Massachusetts	0.0	21	Virginia	(1.8)
39	Michigan	(8.1)	22	Utah	(2.1)
45	Minnesota	(11.0)	23	Maine	(2.3)
38	Mississippi	(7.7)	24	Connecticut	(2.5)
40	Missouri	(9.0)	25	Hawaii	(2.8)
14	Montana	1.9	25	Louisiana	(2.8)
1	Nebraska	39.7	25	North Carolina	(2.8)
46	Nevada	(12.7)	28	New York	(3.0)
2	New Hampshire	20.0	29	California	(3.9)
15	New Jersey	1.6	30	Texas	(4.2)
5	New Mexico	12.2	31	Vermont	(4.3)
28	New York	(3.0)	32	Ohio	(4.8)
25	North Carolina	(2.8)	32	Oregon	(4.8)
9	North Dakota	5.7	34	Illinois	(6.3)
32	Ohio	(4.8)	35	Arizona	(7.1)
10	Oklahoma	4.9	36	Idaho	(7.4)
32	Oregon	(4.8)	37	West Virginia	(7.5)
16	Pennsylvania	0.4	38	Mississippi	(7.7)
7	Rhode Island	7.4	39	Michigan	(8.1)
11	South Carolina	4.0	40	Missouri	(9.0)
17	South Dakota	0.0	41	Georgia	(9.1)
20	Tennessee	(1.3)	42	Iowa	(9.6)
30	Texas	(4.2)	43	Wisconsin	(9.9)
22	Utah	(2.1)	44	Maryland	(10.9)
31	Vermont	(4.3)	45	Minnesota	(11.0)
21	Virginia	(1.8)	46	Nevada	(12.7)
47	Washington	(13.7)	47	Washington	(13.7)
37	West Virginia	(7.5)	48	Wyoming	(15.4)
43	Wisconsin	(9.9)	49	Alaska	(18.3)
48	Wyoming	(15.4)	50	Delaware	(21.9)
				District of Columbia	(9.1)

Source: Federal Bureau of Investigation
    "Crime in the United States 1996" (Uniform Crime Reports, October 4, 1997)
Forcible rape is the carnal knowledge of a female forcibly and against her will. Assaults or attempts to commit rape by force or threat of force are included. However, statutory rape without force and other sex offenses are excluded.

Rape Rate per 100,000 Female Population in 1996

National Rate = 70.7 Rapes per 100,000 Females*

ALPHA ORDER				RANK ORDER		
RANK	STATE	RATE		RANK	STATE	RATE
27	Alabama	63.0		1	Alaska	138.3
1	Alaska	138.3		2	New Mexico	125.4
29	Arizona	61.8		3	Delaware	122.2
17	Arkansas	80.7		4	Michigan	111.2
26	California	64.4		5	Nevada	108.9
11	Colorado	91.6		6	Washington	101.8
45	Connecticut	44.9		7	Florida	101.4
3	Delaware	122.2		8	Minnesota	98.6
7	Florida	101.4		9	South Carolina	95.3
28	Georgia	62.5		10	Oklahoma	91.7
36	Hawaii	55.6		11	Colorado	91.6
40	Idaho	52.6		12	Tennessee	90.1
24	Illinois	66.8		13	Texas	86.6
25	Indiana	66.5		14	Kansas	83.9
49	Iowa	38.4		15	Utah	83.3
14	Kansas	83.9		16	South Dakota	80.8
30	Kentucky	61.6		17	Arkansas	80.7
18	Louisiana	80.1		18	Louisiana	80.1
48	Maine	40.9		18	Ohio	80.1
21	Maryland	73.2		20	Oregon	78.5
34	Massachusetts	56.1		21	Maryland	73.2
4	Michigan	111.2		22	Mississippi	69.5
8	Minnesota	98.6		23	New Hampshire	68.5
22	Mississippi	69.5		24	Illinois	66.8
33	Missouri	56.7		25	Indiana	66.5
37	Montana	53.9		26	California	64.4
39	Nebraska	53.0		27	Alabama	63.0
5	Nevada	108.9		28	Georgia	62.5
23	New Hampshire	68.5		29	Arizona	61.8
43	New Jersey	48.1		30	Kentucky	61.6
2	New Mexico	125.4		31	North Carolina	60.8
46	New York	44.3		32	Wyoming	58.6
31	North Carolina	60.8		33	Missouri	56.7
43	North Dakota	48.1		34	Massachusetts	56.1
18	Ohio	80.1		35	Rhode Island	55.9
10	Oklahoma	91.7		36	Hawaii	55.6
20	Oregon	78.5		37	Montana	53.9
42	Pennsylvania	48.8		38	Vermont	53.2
35	Rhode Island	55.9		39	Nebraska	53.0
9	South Carolina	95.3		40	Idaho	52.6
16	South Dakota	80.8		41	Virginia	52.4
12	Tennessee	90.1		42	Pennsylvania	48.8
13	Texas	86.6		43	New Jersey	48.1
15	Utah	83.3		43	North Dakota	48.1
38	Vermont	53.2		45	Connecticut	44.9
41	Virginia	52.4		46	New York	44.3
6	Washington	101.8		47	Wisconsin	41.4
50	West Virginia	37.9		48	Maine	40.9
47	Wisconsin	41.4		49	Iowa	38.4
32	Wyoming	58.6		50	West Virginia	37.9
					District of Columbia	90.0

Source: Morgan Quitno Press using data from Federal Bureau of Investigation
    "Crime in the United States 1996" (Uniform Crime Reports, October 4, 1997)
*Forcible rape is the carnal knowledge of a female forcibly and against her will. Assaults or attempts to commit rape by force or threat of force are included. However, statutory rape without force and other sex offenses are excluded.

Robberies in 1996

National Total = 537,050 Robberies*

ALPHA ORDER

RANK	STATE	ROBBERIES	% of USA
20	Alabama	7,124	1.33%
42	Alaska	710	0.13%
18	Arizona	7,429	1.38%
32	Arkansas	2,864	0.53%
1	California	94,222	17.54%
28	Colorado	3,755	0.70%
23	Connecticut	5,552	1.03%
37	Delaware	1,304	0.24%
3	Florida	41,643	7.75%
11	Georgia	15,100	2.81%
35	Hawaii	1,606	0.30%
46	Idaho	241	0.04%
4	Illinois	33,106	6.16%
19	Indiana	7,249	1.35%
38	Iowa	1,286	0.24%
34	Kansas	2,476	0.46%
30	Kentucky	3,643	0.68%
12	Louisiana	12,036	2.24%
44	Maine	292	0.05%
7	Maryland	19,944	3.71%
17	Massachusetts	7,778	1.45%
10	Michigan	16,907	3.15%
24	Minnesota	5,385	1.00%
29	Mississippi	3,646	0.68%
15	Missouri	9,142	1.70%
45	Montana	261	0.05%
39	Nebraska	1,052	0.20%
26	Nevada	4,931	0.92%
43	New Hampshire	317	0.06%
8	New Jersey	18,838	3.51%
33	New Mexico	2,782	0.52%
2	New York	61,822	11.51%
13	North Carolina	12,001	2.23%
50	North Dakota	71	0.01%
9	Ohio	18,336	3.41%
31	Oklahoma	3,519	0.66%
27	Oregon	3,914	0.73%
6	Pennsylvania	24,240	4.51%
40	Rhode Island	824	0.15%
22	South Carolina	6,361	1.18%
47	South Dakota	138	0.03%
14	Tennessee	11,902	2.22%
5	Texas	32,804	6.11%
36	Utah	1,377	0.26%
49	Vermont	91	0.02%
16	Virginia	8,181	1.52%
21	Washington	6,587	1.23%
41	West Virginia	737	0.14%
25	Wisconsin	4,982	0.93%
48	Wyoming	98	0.02%

RANK ORDER

RANK	STATE	ROBBERIES	% of USA
1	California	94,222	17.54%
2	New York	61,822	11.51%
3	Florida	41,643	7.75%
4	Illinois	33,106	6.16%
5	Texas	32,804	6.11%
6	Pennsylvania	24,240	4.51%
7	Maryland	19,944	3.71%
8	New Jersey	18,838	3.51%
9	Ohio	18,336	3.41%
10	Michigan	16,907	3.15%
11	Georgia	15,100	2.81%
12	Louisiana	12,036	2.24%
13	North Carolina	12,001	2.23%
14	Tennessee	11,902	2.22%
15	Missouri	9,142	1.70%
16	Virginia	8,181	1.52%
17	Massachusetts	7,778	1.45%
18	Arizona	7,429	1.38%
19	Indiana	7,249	1.35%
20	Alabama	7,124	1.33%
21	Washington	6,587	1.23%
22	South Carolina	6,361	1.18%
23	Connecticut	5,552	1.03%
24	Minnesota	5,385	1.00%
25	Wisconsin	4,982	0.93%
26	Nevada	4,931	0.92%
27	Oregon	3,914	0.73%
28	Colorado	3,755	0.70%
29	Mississippi	3,646	0.68%
30	Kentucky	3,643	0.68%
31	Oklahoma	3,519	0.66%
32	Arkansas	2,864	0.53%
33	New Mexico	2,782	0.52%
34	Kansas	2,476	0.46%
35	Hawaii	1,606	0.30%
36	Utah	1,377	0.26%
37	Delaware	1,304	0.24%
38	Iowa	1,286	0.24%
39	Nebraska	1,052	0.20%
40	Rhode Island	824	0.15%
41	West Virginia	737	0.14%
42	Alaska	710	0.13%
43	New Hampshire	317	0.06%
44	Maine	292	0.05%
45	Montana	261	0.05%
46	Idaho	241	0.04%
47	South Dakota	138	0.03%
48	Wyoming	98	0.02%
49	Vermont	91	0.02%
50	North Dakota	71	0.01%
	District of Columbia	6,444	1.20%

Source: Federal Bureau of Investigation
"Crime in the United States 1996" (Uniform Crime Reports, October 4, 1997)
*Robbery is the taking or attempting to take anything of value by force or threat of force.

Average Time Between Robberies in 1996

National Rate = A Robbery Occurs Every 59 Seconds*

ALPHA ORDER			RANK ORDER		
RANK	STATE	HOURS.MINUTES	RANK	STATE	HOURS.MINUTES
31	Alabama	1.14	1	North Dakota	123.43
9	Alaska	12.22	2	Vermont	96.32
33	Arizona	1.11	3	Wyoming	89.38
19	Arkansas	3.04	4	South Dakota	63.39
50	California	0.05	5	Idaho	36.27
23	Colorado	2.20	6	Montana	33.40
28	Connecticut	1.35	7	Maine	30.05
14	Delaware	6.44	8	New Hampshire	27.43
48	Florida	0.13	9	Alaska	12.22
40	Georgia	0.35	10	West Virginia	11.55
16	Hawaii	5.28	11	Rhode Island	10.40
5	Idaho	36.27	12	Nebraska	8.21
46	Illinois	0.16	13	Iowa	6.50
32	Indiana	1.13	14	Delaware	6.44
13	Iowa	6.50	15	Utah	6.23
17	Kansas	3.33	16	Hawaii	5.28
21	Kentucky	2.25	17	Kansas	3.33
37	Louisiana	0.44	18	New Mexico	3.10
7	Maine	30.05	19	Arkansas	3.04
44	Maryland	0.26	20	Oklahoma	2.30
34	Massachusetts	1.08	21	Kentucky	2.25
41	Michigan	0.31	21	Mississippi	2.25
27	Minnesota	1.38	23	Colorado	2.20
21	Mississippi	2.25	24	Oregon	2.14
36	Missouri	0.58	25	Nevada	1.47
6	Montana	33.40	26	Wisconsin	1.46
12	Nebraska	8.21	27	Minnesota	1.38
25	Nevada	1.47	28	Connecticut	1.35
8	New Hampshire	27.43	29	South Carolina	1.23
43	New Jersey	0.28	30	Washington	1.20
18	New Mexico	3.10	31	Alabama	1.14
49	New York	0.08	32	Indiana	1.13
37	North Carolina	0.44	33	Arizona	1.11
1	North Dakota	123.43	34	Massachusetts	1.08
42	Ohio	0.29	35	Virginia	1.04
20	Oklahoma	2.30	36	Missouri	0.58
24	Oregon	2.14	37	Louisiana	0.44
45	Pennsylvania	0.22	37	North Carolina	0.44
11	Rhode Island	10.40	37	Tennessee	0.44
29	South Carolina	1.23	40	Georgia	0.35
4	South Dakota	63.39	41	Michigan	0.31
37	Tennessee	0.44	42	Ohio	0.29
46	Texas	0.16	43	New Jersey	0.28
15	Utah	6.23	44	Maryland	0.26
2	Vermont	96.32	45	Pennsylvania	0.22
35	Virginia	1.04	46	Illinois	0.16
30	Washington	1.20	46	Texas	0.16
10	West Virginia	11.55	48	Florida	0.13
26	Wisconsin	1.46	49	New York	0.08
3	Wyoming	89.38	50	California	0.05
				District of Columbia	1.22

Source: Morgan Quitno Press using data from Federal Bureau of Investigation
"Crime in the United States 1996" (Uniform Crime Reports, October 4, 1997)
*Robbery is the taking or attempting to take anything of value by force or threat of force.

Percent Change in Number of Robberies: 1995 to 1996

National Percent Change = 7.5% Decrease*

ALPHA ORDER

RANK	STATE	PERCENT CHANGE
37	Alabama	(9.8)
49	Alaska	(24.2)
14	Arizona	1.4
32	Arkansas	(8.3)
39	California	(9.9)
7	Colorado	4.2
8	Connecticut	3.9
33	Delaware	(8.5)
20	Florida	(2.0)
13	Georgia	2.2
9	Hawaii	3.4
42	Idaho	(13.6)
46	Illinois	(15.4)
30	Indiana	(7.6)
43	Iowa	(14.7)
40	Kansas	(10.8)
35	Kentucky	(8.9)
11	Louisiana	3.2
41	Maine	(12.6)
26	Maryland	(6.5)
45	Massachusetts	(14.9)
22	Michigan	(5.5)
23	Minnesota	(5.6)
10	Mississippi	3.3
47	Missouri	(15.8)
11	Montana	3.2
18	Nebraska	(1.4)
17	Nevada	(0.7)
16	New Hampshire	1.0
48	New Jersey	(16.2)
4	New Mexico	6.8
43	New York	(14.7)
27	North Carolina	(6.9)
3	North Dakota	10.9
31	Ohio	(8.0)
28	Oklahoma	(7.1)
36	Oregon	(9.6)
5	Pennsylvania	6.0
37	Rhode Island	(9.8)
19	South Carolina	(1.5)
50	South Dakota	(27.0)
14	Tennessee	1.4
21	Texas	(2.6)
6	Utah	5.2
1	Vermont	42.2
25	Virginia	(6.2)
34	Washington	(8.6)
23	West Virginia	(5.6)
29	Wisconsin	(7.5)
2	Wyoming	14.0

RANK ORDER

RANK	STATE	PERCENT CHANGE
1	Vermont	42.2
2	Wyoming	14.0
3	North Dakota	10.9
4	New Mexico	6.8
5	Pennsylvania	6.0
6	Utah	5.2
7	Colorado	4.2
8	Connecticut	3.9
9	Hawaii	3.4
10	Mississippi	3.3
11	Louisiana	3.2
11	Montana	3.2
13	Georgia	2.2
14	Arizona	1.4
14	Tennessee	1.4
16	New Hampshire	1.0
17	Nevada	(0.7)
18	Nebraska	(1.4)
19	South Carolina	(1.5)
20	Florida	(2.0)
21	Texas	(2.6)
22	Michigan	(5.5)
23	Minnesota	(5.6)
23	West Virginia	(5.6)
25	Virginia	(6.2)
26	Maryland	(6.5)
27	North Carolina	(6.9)
28	Oklahoma	(7.1)
29	Wisconsin	(7.5)
30	Indiana	(7.6)
31	Ohio	(8.0)
32	Arkansas	(8.3)
33	Delaware	(8.5)
34	Washington	(8.6)
35	Kentucky	(8.9)
36	Oregon	(9.6)
37	Alabama	(9.8)
37	Rhode Island	(9.8)
39	California	(9.9)
40	Kansas	(10.8)
41	Maine	(12.6)
42	Idaho	(13.6)
43	Iowa	(14.7)
43	New York	(14.7)
45	Massachusetts	(14.9)
46	Illinois	(15.4)
47	Missouri	(15.8)
48	New Jersey	(16.2)
49	Alaska	(24.2)
50	South Dakota	(27.0)

District of Columbia   (6.1)

Source: Federal Bureau of Investigation
  "Crime in the United States 1996" (Uniform Crime Reports, October 4, 1997)
*Robbery is the taking or attempting to take anything of value by force or threat of force.

Robbery Rate in 1996

National Rate = 202.4 Robberies per 100,000 Population*

ALPHA ORDER

RANK	STATE	RATE
19	Alabama	166.7
30	Alaska	117.0
18	Arizona	167.8
32	Arkansas	114.1
4	California	295.6
34	Colorado	98.2
17	Connecticut	169.6
12	Delaware	179.9
5	Florida	289.2
10	Georgia	205.4
23	Hawaii	135.6
47	Idaho	20.3
6	Illinois	279.4
26	Indiana	124.1
41	Iowa	45.1
36	Kansas	96.3
37	Kentucky	93.8
7	Louisiana	276.6
45	Maine	23.5
1	Maryland	393.2
25	Massachusetts	127.7
13	Michigan	176.2
31	Minnesota	115.6
24	Mississippi	134.2
16	Missouri	170.6
43	Montana	29.7
40	Nebraska	63.7
3	Nevada	307.6
44	New Hampshire	27.3
8	New Jersey	235.8
22	New Mexico	162.4
2	New York	340.0
21	North Carolina	163.9
50	North Dakota	11.0
20	Ohio	164.1
33	Oklahoma	106.6
28	Oregon	122.2
11	Pennsylvania	201.1
38	Rhode Island	83.2
14	South Carolina	172.0
48	South Dakota	18.9
9	Tennessee	223.7
15	Texas	171.5
39	Utah	68.9
49	Vermont	15.4
27	Virginia	122.6
29	Washington	119.0
42	West Virginia	40.4
35	Wisconsin	96.6
46	Wyoming	20.4

RANK ORDER

RANK	STATE	RATE
1	Maryland	393.2
2	New York	340.0
3	Nevada	307.6
4	California	295.6
5	Florida	289.2
6	Illinois	279.4
7	Louisiana	276.6
8	New Jersey	235.8
9	Tennessee	223.7
10	Georgia	205.4
11	Pennsylvania	201.1
12	Delaware	179.9
13	Michigan	176.2
14	South Carolina	172.0
15	Texas	171.5
16	Missouri	170.6
17	Connecticut	169.6
18	Arizona	167.8
19	Alabama	166.7
20	Ohio	164.1
21	North Carolina	163.9
22	New Mexico	162.4
23	Hawaii	135.6
24	Mississippi	134.2
25	Massachusetts	127.7
26	Indiana	124.1
27	Virginia	122.6
28	Oregon	122.2
29	Washington	119.0
30	Alaska	117.0
31	Minnesota	115.6
32	Arkansas	114.1
33	Oklahoma	106.6
34	Colorado	98.2
35	Wisconsin	96.6
36	Kansas	96.3
37	Kentucky	93.8
38	Rhode Island	83.2
39	Utah	68.9
40	Nebraska	63.7
41	Iowa	45.1
42	West Virginia	40.4
43	Montana	29.7
44	New Hampshire	27.3
45	Maine	23.5
46	Wyoming	20.4
47	Idaho	20.3
48	South Dakota	18.9
49	Vermont	15.4
50	North Dakota	11.0
	District of Columbia	1,186.7

Source: Federal Bureau of Investigation
"Crime in the United States 1996" (Uniform Crime Reports, October 4, 1997)
**Robbery is the taking or attempting to take anything of value by force or threat of force.*

Percent Change in Robbery Rate: 1995 to 1996

National Percent Change = 8.4% Decrease*

<table>
<tr><td colspan="3">ALPHA ORDER</td><td colspan="3">RANK ORDER</td></tr>
<tr><td>RANK</td><td>STATE</td><td>PERCENT CHANGE</td><td>RANK</td><td>STATE</td><td>PERCENT CHANGE</td></tr>
<tr><td>36</td><td>Alabama</td><td>(10.3)</td><td>1</td><td>Vermont</td><td>41.3</td></tr>
<tr><td>49</td><td>Alaska</td><td>(24.6)</td><td>2</td><td>Wyoming</td><td>14.0</td></tr>
<tr><td>18</td><td>Arizona</td><td>(3.5)</td><td>3</td><td>North Dakota</td><td>10.0</td></tr>
<tr><td>32</td><td>Arkansas</td><td>(9.2)</td><td>4</td><td>Pennsylvania</td><td>6.2</td></tr>
<tr><td>38</td><td>California</td><td>(10.7)</td><td>5</td><td>New Mexico</td><td>5.1</td></tr>
<tr><td>11</td><td>Colorado</td><td>2.1</td><td>6</td><td>Connecticut</td><td>3.9</td></tr>
<tr><td>6</td><td>Connecticut</td><td>3.9</td><td>7</td><td>Hawaii</td><td>3.7</td></tr>
<tr><td>33</td><td>Delaware</td><td>(9.5)</td><td>8</td><td>Louisiana</td><td>3.0</td></tr>
<tr><td>19</td><td>Florida</td><td>(3.6)</td><td>9</td><td>Utah</td><td>2.7</td></tr>
<tr><td>14</td><td>Georgia</td><td>0.1</td><td>10</td><td>Mississippi</td><td>2.5</td></tr>
<tr><td>7</td><td>Hawaii</td><td>3.7</td><td>11</td><td>Colorado</td><td>2.1</td></tr>
<tr><td>45</td><td>Idaho</td><td>(15.4)</td><td>11</td><td>Montana</td><td>2.1</td></tr>
<tr><td>46</td><td>Illinois</td><td>(15.5)</td><td>13</td><td>Tennessee</td><td>0.2</td></tr>
<tr><td>29</td><td>Indiana</td><td>(8.2)</td><td>14</td><td>Georgia</td><td>0.1</td></tr>
<tr><td>42</td><td>Iowa</td><td>(14.9)</td><td>15</td><td>New Hampshire</td><td>(0.4)</td></tr>
<tr><td>39</td><td>Kansas</td><td>(11.0)</td><td>16</td><td>South Carolina</td><td>(2.2)</td></tr>
<tr><td>33</td><td>Kentucky</td><td>(9.5)</td><td>17</td><td>Nebraska</td><td>(2.3)</td></tr>
<tr><td>8</td><td>Louisiana</td><td>3.0</td><td>18</td><td>Arizona</td><td>(3.5)</td></tr>
<tr><td>41</td><td>Maine</td><td>(12.6)</td><td>19</td><td>Florida</td><td>(3.6)</td></tr>
<tr><td>26</td><td>Maryland</td><td>(7.1)</td><td>20</td><td>Texas</td><td>(4.6)</td></tr>
<tr><td>44</td><td>Massachusetts</td><td>(15.1)</td><td>21</td><td>Nevada</td><td>(5.2)</td></tr>
<tr><td>23</td><td>Michigan</td><td>(5.9)</td><td>22</td><td>West Virginia</td><td>(5.4)</td></tr>
<tr><td>24</td><td>Minnesota</td><td>(6.5)</td><td>23</td><td>Michigan</td><td>(5.9)</td></tr>
<tr><td>10</td><td>Mississippi</td><td>2.5</td><td>24</td><td>Minnesota</td><td>(6.5)</td></tr>
<tr><td>47</td><td>Missouri</td><td>(16.4)</td><td>25</td><td>Virginia</td><td>(6.9)</td></tr>
<tr><td>11</td><td>Montana</td><td>2.1</td><td>26</td><td>Maryland</td><td>(7.1)</td></tr>
<tr><td>17</td><td>Nebraska</td><td>(2.3)</td><td>27</td><td>Oklahoma</td><td>(7.8)</td></tr>
<tr><td>21</td><td>Nevada</td><td>(5.2)</td><td>28</td><td>Wisconsin</td><td>(8.1)</td></tr>
<tr><td>15</td><td>New Hampshire</td><td>(0.4)</td><td>29</td><td>Indiana</td><td>(8.2)</td></tr>
<tr><td>48</td><td>New Jersey</td><td>(16.7)</td><td>29</td><td>Ohio</td><td>(8.2)</td></tr>
<tr><td>5</td><td>New Mexico</td><td>5.1</td><td>31</td><td>North Carolina</td><td>(8.5)</td></tr>
<tr><td>42</td><td>New York</td><td>(14.9)</td><td>32</td><td>Arkansas</td><td>(9.2)</td></tr>
<tr><td>31</td><td>North Carolina</td><td>(8.5)</td><td>33</td><td>Delaware</td><td>(9.5)</td></tr>
<tr><td>3</td><td>North Dakota</td><td>10.0</td><td>33</td><td>Kentucky</td><td>(9.5)</td></tr>
<tr><td>29</td><td>Ohio</td><td>(8.2)</td><td>35</td><td>Rhode Island</td><td>(9.9)</td></tr>
<tr><td>27</td><td>Oklahoma</td><td>(7.8)</td><td>36</td><td>Alabama</td><td>(10.3)</td></tr>
<tr><td>40</td><td>Oregon</td><td>(11.4)</td><td>36</td><td>Washington</td><td>(10.3)</td></tr>
<tr><td>4</td><td>Pennsylvania</td><td>6.2</td><td>38</td><td>California</td><td>(10.7)</td></tr>
<tr><td>35</td><td>Rhode Island</td><td>(9.9)</td><td>39</td><td>Kansas</td><td>(11.0)</td></tr>
<tr><td>16</td><td>South Carolina</td><td>(2.2)</td><td>40</td><td>Oregon</td><td>(11.4)</td></tr>
<tr><td>50</td><td>South Dakota</td><td>(27.0)</td><td>41</td><td>Maine</td><td>(12.6)</td></tr>
<tr><td>13</td><td>Tennessee</td><td>0.2</td><td>42</td><td>Iowa</td><td>(14.9)</td></tr>
<tr><td>20</td><td>Texas</td><td>(4.6)</td><td>42</td><td>New York</td><td>(14.9)</td></tr>
<tr><td>9</td><td>Utah</td><td>2.7</td><td>44</td><td>Massachusetts</td><td>(15.1)</td></tr>
<tr><td>1</td><td>Vermont</td><td>41.3</td><td>45</td><td>Idaho</td><td>(15.4)</td></tr>
<tr><td>25</td><td>Virginia</td><td>(6.9)</td><td>46</td><td>Illinois</td><td>(15.5)</td></tr>
<tr><td>36</td><td>Washington</td><td>(10.3)</td><td>47</td><td>Missouri</td><td>(16.4)</td></tr>
<tr><td>22</td><td>West Virginia</td><td>(5.4)</td><td>48</td><td>New Jersey</td><td>(16.7)</td></tr>
<tr><td>28</td><td>Wisconsin</td><td>(8.1)</td><td>49</td><td>Alaska</td><td>(24.6)</td></tr>
<tr><td>2</td><td>Wyoming</td><td>14.0</td><td>50</td><td>South Dakota</td><td>(27.0)</td></tr>
<tr><td></td><td></td><td></td><td></td><td>District of Columbia</td><td>(4.2)</td></tr>
</table>

Source: Federal Bureau of Investigation
"Crime in the United States 1996" (Uniform Crime Reports, October 4, 1997)
*Robbery is the taking or attempting to take anything of value by force or threat of force.

Robberies with Firearms in 1996

National Total = 208,022 Robberies*

ALPHA ORDER				RANK ORDER			
RANK	STATE	ROBBERIES	% of USA	RANK	STATE	ROBBERIES	% of USA
17	Alabama	3,284	1.58%	1	California	37,125	17.85%
39	Alaska	260	0.12%	2	New York	24,102	11.59%
18	Arizona	2,866	1.38%	3	Texas	13,991	6.73%
28	Arkansas	1,342	0.65%	4	Illinois	12,045	5.79%
1	California	37,125	17.85%	5	Maryland	10,365	4.98%
30	Colorado	1,264	0.61%	6	Florida	10,151	4.88%
25	Connecticut	1,665	0.80%	7	Pennsylvania	9,980	4.80%
35	Delaware	461	0.22%	8	Michigan	7,409	3.56%
6	Florida	10,151	4.88%	9	Georgia	7,322	3.52%
9	Georgia	7,322	3.52%	10	Louisiana	7,027	3.38%
42	Hawaii	134	0.06%	11	Tennessee	6,737	3.24%
43	Idaho	83	0.04%	12	Ohio	5,845	2.81%
4	Illinois	12,045	5.79%	13	New Jersey	5,616	2.70%
19	Indiana	2,649	1.27%	14	North Carolina	5,339	2.57%
40	Iowa	235	0.11%	15	Missouri	3,794	1.82%
34	Kansas	563	0.27%	16	Virginia	3,614	1.74%
27	Kentucky	1,355	0.65%	17	Alabama	3,284	1.58%
10	Louisiana	7,027	3.38%	18	Arizona	2,866	1.38%
45	Maine	52	0.02%	19	Indiana	2,649	1.27%
5	Maryland	10,365	4.98%	20	South Carolina	2,613	1.26%
24	Massachusetts	1,720	0.83%	21	Wisconsin	2,500	1.20%
8	Michigan	7,409	3.56%	22	Nevada	2,014	0.97%
26	Minnesota	1,550	0.75%	23	Washington	1,935	0.93%
31	Mississippi	1,216	0.58%	24	Massachusetts	1,720	0.83%
15	Missouri	3,794	1.82%	25	Connecticut	1,665	0.80%
NA	Montana**	NA	NA	26	Minnesota	1,550	0.75%
37	Nebraska	387	0.19%	27	Kentucky	1,355	0.65%
22	Nevada	2,014	0.97%	28	Arkansas	1,342	0.65%
44	New Hampshire	63	0.03%	29	Oklahoma	1,294	0.62%
13	New Jersey	5,616	2.70%	30	Colorado	1,264	0.61%
32	New Mexico	1,207	0.58%	31	Mississippi	1,216	0.58%
2	New York	24,102	11.59%	32	New Mexico	1,207	0.58%
14	North Carolina	5,339	2.57%	33	Oregon	1,126	0.54%
48	North Dakota	2	0.00%	34	Kansas	563	0.27%
12	Ohio	5,845	2.81%	35	Delaware	461	0.22%
29	Oklahoma	1,294	0.62%	36	Utah	454	0.22%
33	Oregon	1,126	0.54%	37	Nebraska	387	0.19%
7	Pennsylvania	9,980	4.80%	38	West Virginia	268	0.13%
41	Rhode Island	177	0.09%	39	Alaska	260	0.12%
20	South Carolina	2,613	1.26%	40	Iowa	235	0.11%
45	South Dakota	52	0.02%	41	Rhode Island	177	0.09%
11	Tennessee	6,737	3.24%	42	Hawaii	134	0.06%
3	Texas	13,991	6.73%	43	Idaho	83	0.04%
36	Utah	454	0.22%	44	New Hampshire	63	0.03%
NA	Vermont**	NA	NA	45	Maine	52	0.02%
16	Virginia	3,614	1.74%	45	South Dakota	52	0.02%
23	Washington	1,935	0.93%	47	Wyoming	23	0.01%
38	West Virginia	268	0.13%	48	North Dakota	2	0.00%
21	Wisconsin	2,500	1.20%	NA	Montana**	NA	NA
47	Wyoming	23	0.01%	NA	Vermont**	NA	NA
				District of Columbia		2,746	1.32%

Source: Federal Bureau of Investigation
"Crime in the United States 1996" (Uniform Crime Reports, October 4, 1997)
Of the 493,772 robberies in 1996 for which supplemental data were received by the F.B.I. There were an additional 43,278 robberies for which the type of weapon was not reported to the F.B.I. Robbery is the taking or attempting to take anything of value by force or threat of force.
***Not available.*

Robbery Rate with Firearms in 1996

National Rate = 100.6 Robberies per 100,000 Population*

RANK	STATE	RATE		RANK	STATE	RATE
20	Alabama	78.8		1	Virginia	564.7
30	Alaska	47.6		2	Illinois	361.3
26	Arizona	68.7		3	Tennessee	236.7
28	Arkansas	56.4		4	Maryland	206.6
14	California	117.1		5	Louisiana	204.4
34	Colorado	35.6		6	New York	171.9
27	Connecticut	63.1		7	Florida	166.2
12	Delaware	124.3		8	Mississippi	134.2
7	Florida	166.2		9	Kentucky	130.7
15	Georgia	114.7		10	Kansas	129.7
41	Hawaii	11.3		11	Nevada	126.4
44	Idaho	7.1		12	Delaware	124.3
2	Illinois	361.3		13	New Mexico	119.3
21	Indiana	77.9		14	California	117.1
42	Iowa	10.5		15	Georgia	114.7
10	Kansas	129.7		16	Pennsylvania	107.1
9	Kentucky	130.7		17	Michigan	94.1
5	Louisiana	204.4		18	Missouri	92.3
47	Maine	4.2		19	Ohio	83.2
4	Maryland	206.6		20	Alabama	78.8
35	Massachusetts	34.6		21	Indiana	77.9
17	Michigan	94.1		22	North Carolina	74.4
36	Minnesota	33.7		23	Texas	73.4
8	Mississippi	134.2		24	South Carolina	71.4
18	Missouri	92.3		25	New Jersey	70.3
NA	Montana**	NA		26	Arizona	68.7
37	Nebraska	25.0		27	Connecticut	63.1
11	Nevada	126.4		28	Arkansas	56.4
45	New Hampshire	6.8		29	Wisconsin	48.6
25	New Jersey	70.3		30	Alaska	47.6
13	New Mexico	119.3		31	Oregon	39.7
6	New York	171.9		32	Oklahoma	39.2
22	North Carolina	74.4		33	Washington	37.2
48	North Dakota	0.6		34	Colorado	35.6
19	Ohio	83.2		35	Massachusetts	34.6
32	Oklahoma	39.2		36	Minnesota	33.7
31	Oregon	39.7		37	Nebraska	25.0
16	Pennsylvania	107.1		38	Utah	23.4
39	Rhode Island	17.9		39	Rhode Island	17.9
24	South Carolina	71.4		40	West Virginia	14.7
43	South Dakota	10.3		41	Hawaii	11.3
3	Tennessee	236.7		42	Iowa	10.5
23	Texas	73.4		43	South Dakota	10.3
38	Utah	23.4		44	Idaho	7.1
NA	Vermont**	NA		45	New Hampshire	6.8
1	Virginia	564.7		46	Wyoming	5.8
33	Washington	37.2		47	Maine	4.2
40	West Virginia	14.7		48	North Dakota	0.6
29	Wisconsin	48.6		NA	Montana**	NA
46	Wyoming	5.8		NA	Vermont**	NA
					District of Columbia	505.7

ALPHA ORDER

RANK ORDER

Source: Morgan Quitno Press using data from Federal Bureau of Investigation
       "Crime in the United States 1996" (Uniform Crime Reports, October 4, 1997)
*Based only on population of reporting jurisdictions. Robbery is the taking or attempting to take anything of value by force or threat of force. National rate reflects only those robberies for which the type of weapon was known and reported. Kansas, Kentucky, Mississippi and Virginia rates especially affected by number of nonreporting jurisdictions. **Not available.

357

Percent of Robberies Involving Firearms in 1996

National Percent = 42.1% of Robberies*

ALPHA ORDER					RANK ORDER		
RANK	STATE	PERCENT			RANK	STATE	PERCENT
11	Alabama	46.5			1	Louisiana	63.1
28	Alaska	38.8			2	Tennessee	61.0
27	Arizona	39.4			3	Mississippi	57.2
9	Arkansas	47.2			4	Maryland	52.1
26	California	39.5			5	Georgia	51.7
34	Colorado	35.5			6	Wisconsin	50.2
33	Connecticut	36.2			7	Indiana	49.4
21	Delaware	41.0			8	New Mexico	48.7
22	Florida	40.9			9	Arkansas	47.2
5	Georgia	51.7			10	Pennsylvania	46.8
48	Hawaii	8.3			11	Alabama	46.5
35	Idaho	34.6			11	Michigan	46.5
18	Illinois	41.9			13	Virginia	45.5
7	Indiana	49.4			14	North Carolina	45.0
43	Iowa	23.4			15	Kentucky	44.0
19	Kansas	41.5			16	Missouri	42.7
15	Kentucky	44.0			16	Texas	42.7
1	Louisiana	63.1			18	Illinois	41.9
46	Maine	18.1			19	Kansas	41.5
4	Maryland	52.1			20	South Carolina	41.2
45	Massachusetts	22.8			21	Delaware	41.0
11	Michigan	46.5			22	Florida	40.9
40	Minnesota	29.8			23	Nevada	40.8
3	Mississippi	57.2			24	New York	40.6
16	Missouri	42.7			24	South Dakota	40.6
NA	Montana**	NA			26	California	39.5
30	Nebraska	37.4			27	Arizona	39.4
23	Nevada	40.8			28	Alaska	38.8
44	New Hampshire	23.2			28	Ohio	38.8
39	New Jersey	29.9			30	Nebraska	37.4
8	New Mexico	48.7			31	Oklahoma	36.8
24	New York	40.6			32	West Virginia	36.4
14	North Carolina	45.0			33	Connecticut	36.2
47	North Dakota	8.7			34	Colorado	35.5
28	Ohio	38.8			35	Idaho	34.6
31	Oklahoma	36.8			36	Utah	34.4
38	Oregon	30.2			37	Washington	31.3
10	Pennsylvania	46.8			38	Oregon	30.2
42	Rhode Island	23.7			39	New Jersey	29.9
20	South Carolina	41.2			40	Minnesota	29.8
24	South Dakota	40.6			41	Wyoming	27.4
2	Tennessee	61.0			42	Rhode Island	23.7
16	Texas	42.7			43	Iowa	23.4
36	Utah	34.4			44	New Hampshire	23.2
NA	Vermont**	NA			45	Massachusetts	22.8
13	Virginia	45.5			46	Maine	18.1
37	Washington	31.3			47	North Dakota	8.7
32	West Virginia	36.4			48	Hawaii	8.3
6	Wisconsin	50.2			NA	Montana**	NA
41	Wyoming	27.4			NA	Vermont**	NA
						District of Columbia	42.6

Source: Morgan Quitno Press using data from Federal Bureau of Investigation
"Crime in the United States 1996" (Uniform Crime Reports, October 4, 1997)
Of the 493,772 robberies in 1996 for which supplemental data were received by the F.B.I. There were an additional 43,278 robberies for which the type of weapon was not reported to the F.B.I. Robbery is the taking or attempting to take anything of value by force or threat of force.
***Not available.*

358

Robberies with Knives or Cutting Instruments in 1996

National Total = 43,199 Robberies*

ALPHA ORDER

RANK	STATE	ROBBERIES	% of USA
18	Alabama	571	1.32%
39	Alaska	71	0.16%
14	Arizona	699	1.62%
32	Arkansas	206	0.48%
1	California	9,109	21.09%
29	Colorado	328	0.76%
24	Connecticut	436	1.01%
40	Delaware	54	0.13%
5	Florida	2,031	4.70%
13	Georgia	777	1.80%
34	Hawaii	125	0.29%
43	Idaho	27	0.06%
3	Illinois	3,065	7.10%
25	Indiana	391	0.91%
36	Iowa	108	0.25%
33	Kansas	129	0.30%
30	Kentucky	312	0.72%
20	Louisiana	549	1.27%
44	Maine	26	0.06%
7	Maryland	1,489	3.45%
8	Massachusetts	1,319	3.05%
10	Michigan	945	2.19%
23	Minnesota	447	1.03%
38	Mississippi	92	0.21%
17	Missouri	573	1.33%
NA	Montana**	NA	NA
35	Nebraska	109	0.25%
21	Nevada	470	1.09%
42	New Hampshire	36	0.08%
6	New Jersey	1,827	4.23%
28	New Mexico	337	0.78%
2	New York	6,515	15.08%
12	North Carolina	822	1.90%
48	North Dakota	7	0.02%
11	Ohio	862	2.00%
31	Oklahoma	308	0.71%
25	Oregon	391	0.91%
9	Pennsylvania	1,295	3.00%
47	Rhode Island	8	0.02%
19	South Carolina	558	1.29%
46	South Dakota	10	0.02%
15	Tennessee	694	1.61%
4	Texas	3,035	7.03%
37	Utah	99	0.23%
NA	Vermont**	NA	NA
22	Virginia	453	1.05%
16	Washington	600	1.39%
41	West Virginia	51	0.12%
27	Wisconsin	371	0.86%
45	Wyoming	16	0.04%

RANK ORDER

RANK	STATE	ROBBERIES	% of USA
1	California	9,109	21.09%
2	New York	6,515	15.08%
3	Illinois	3,065	7.10%
4	Texas	3,035	7.03%
5	Florida	2,031	4.70%
6	New Jersey	1,827	4.23%
7	Maryland	1,489	3.45%
8	Massachusetts	1,319	3.05%
9	Pennsylvania	1,295	3.00%
10	Michigan	945	2.19%
11	Ohio	862	2.00%
12	North Carolina	822	1.90%
13	Georgia	777	1.80%
14	Arizona	699	1.62%
15	Tennessee	694	1.61%
16	Washington	600	1.39%
17	Missouri	573	1.33%
18	Alabama	571	1.32%
19	South Carolina	558	1.29%
20	Louisiana	549	1.27%
21	Nevada	470	1.09%
22	Virginia	453	1.05%
23	Minnesota	447	1.03%
24	Connecticut	436	1.01%
25	Indiana	391	0.91%
25	Oregon	391	0.91%
27	Wisconsin	371	0.86%
28	New Mexico	337	0.78%
29	Colorado	328	0.76%
30	Kentucky	312	0.72%
31	Oklahoma	308	0.71%
32	Arkansas	206	0.48%
33	Kansas	129	0.30%
34	Hawaii	125	0.29%
35	Nebraska	109	0.25%
36	Iowa	108	0.25%
37	Utah	99	0.23%
38	Mississippi	92	0.21%
39	Alaska	71	0.16%
40	Delaware	54	0.13%
41	West Virginia	51	0.12%
42	New Hampshire	36	0.08%
43	Idaho	27	0.06%
44	Maine	26	0.06%
45	Wyoming	16	0.04%
46	South Dakota	10	0.02%
47	Rhode Island	8	0.02%
48	North Dakota	7	0.02%
NA	Montana**	NA	NA
NA	Vermont**	NA	NA
	District of Columbia	446	1.03%

Source: Federal Bureau of Investigation
"Crime in the United States 1996" (Uniform Crime Reports, October 4, 1997)
*Of the 493,772 robberies in 1996 for which supplemental data were received by the F.B.I. There were an additional 43,278 robberies for which the type of weapon was not reported to the F.B.I. Robbery is the taking or attempting to take anything of value by force or threat of force.
**Not available.

Percent of Robberies Involving Knives or Cutting Instruments in 1996

National Percent = 8.7% of Robberies*

ALPHA ORDER			RANK ORDER		
RANK	STATE	PERCENT	RANK	STATE	PERCENT
28	Alabama	8.1	1	North Dakota	30.4
10	Alaska	10.6	2	Wyoming	19.0
17	Arizona	9.6	3	Massachusetts	17.5
35	Arkansas	7.2	4	New Mexico	13.6
14	California	9.7	5	New Hampshire	13.3
22	Colorado	9.2	6	Idaho	11.3
18	Connecticut	9.5	7	New York	11.0
46	Delaware	4.8	8	Illinois	10.7
27	Florida	8.2	8	Iowa	10.7
44	Georgia	5.5	10	Alaska	10.6
29	Hawaii	7.8	11	Nebraska	10.5
6	Idaho	11.3	11	Oregon	10.5
8	Illinois	10.7	13	Kentucky	10.1
34	Indiana	7.3	14	California	9.7
8	Iowa	10.7	14	New Jersey	9.7
18	Kansas	9.5	14	Washington	9.7
13	Kentucky	10.1	17	Arizona	9.6
45	Louisiana	4.9	18	Connecticut	9.5
23	Maine	9.0	18	Kansas	9.5
31	Maryland	7.5	18	Nevada	9.5
3	Massachusetts	17.5	21	Texas	9.3
41	Michigan	5.9	22	Colorado	9.2
26	Minnesota	8.6	23	Maine	9.0
47	Mississippi	4.3	24	Oklahoma	8.8
38	Missouri	6.5	24	South Carolina	8.8
NA	Montana**	NA	26	Minnesota	8.6
11	Nebraska	10.5	27	Florida	8.2
18	Nevada	9.5	28	Alabama	8.1
5	New Hampshire	13.3	29	Hawaii	7.8
14	New Jersey	9.7	29	South Dakota	7.8
4	New Mexico	13.6	31	Maryland	7.5
7	New York	11.0	31	Utah	7.5
36	North Carolina	6.9	33	Wisconsin	7.4
1	North Dakota	30.4	34	Indiana	7.3
42	Ohio	5.7	35	Arkansas	7.2
24	Oklahoma	8.8	36	North Carolina	6.9
11	Oregon	10.5	36	West Virginia	6.9
40	Pennsylvania	6.1	38	Missouri	6.5
48	Rhode Island	1.1	39	Tennessee	6.3
24	South Carolina	8.8	40	Pennsylvania	6.1
29	South Dakota	7.8	41	Michigan	5.9
39	Tennessee	6.3	42	Ohio	5.7
21	Texas	9.3	42	Virginia	5.7
31	Utah	7.5	44	Georgia	5.5
NA	Vermont**	NA	45	Louisiana	4.9
42	Virginia	5.7	46	Delaware	4.8
14	Washington	9.7	47	Mississippi	4.3
36	West Virginia	6.9	48	Rhode Island	1.1
33	Wisconsin	7.4	NA	Montana**	NA
2	Wyoming	19.0	NA	Vermont**	NA
				District of Columbia	6.9

Source: Morgan Quitno Press using data from Federal Bureau of Investigation
    "Crime in the United States 1996" (Uniform Crime Reports, October 4, 1997)
*Of the 493,772 robberies in 1996 for which supplemental data were received by the F.B.I. There were an additional 43,278 robberies for which the type of weapon was not reported to the F.B.I. Robbery is the taking or attempting to take anything of value by force or threat of force.
**Not available.

360

Robberies with Blunt Objects and Other Dangerous Weapons in 1996

National Total = 45,225 Robberies*

<table>
<tr><td colspan="4">ALPHA ORDER</td><td colspan="4">RANK ORDER</td></tr>
<tr><td>RANK</td><td>STATE</td><td>ROBBERIES</td><td>% of USA</td><td>RANK</td><td>STATE</td><td>ROBBERIES</td><td>% of USA</td></tr>
<tr><td>20</td><td>Alabama</td><td>577</td><td>1.28%</td><td>1</td><td>California</td><td>8,609</td><td>19.04%</td></tr>
<tr><td>41</td><td>Alaska</td><td>53</td><td>0.12%</td><td>2</td><td>New York</td><td>5,731</td><td>12.67%</td></tr>
<tr><td>18</td><td>Arizona</td><td>730</td><td>1.61%</td><td>3</td><td>Texas</td><td>3,548</td><td>7.85%</td></tr>
<tr><td>30</td><td>Arkansas</td><td>234</td><td>0.52%</td><td>4</td><td>Michigan</td><td>2,792</td><td>6.17%</td></tr>
<tr><td>1</td><td>California</td><td>8,609</td><td>19.04%</td><td>5</td><td>Illinois</td><td>2,640</td><td>5.84%</td></tr>
<tr><td>21</td><td>Colorado</td><td>506</td><td>1.12%</td><td>6</td><td>Florida</td><td>2,288</td><td>5.06%</td></tr>
<tr><td>25</td><td>Connecticut</td><td>373</td><td>0.82%</td><td>7</td><td>Georgia</td><td>1,651</td><td>3.65%</td></tr>
<tr><td>37</td><td>Delaware</td><td>72</td><td>0.16%</td><td>8</td><td>New Jersey</td><td>1,372</td><td>3.03%</td></tr>
<tr><td>6</td><td>Florida</td><td>2,288</td><td>5.06%</td><td>9</td><td>Maryland</td><td>1,362</td><td>3.01%</td></tr>
<tr><td>7</td><td>Georgia</td><td>1,651</td><td>3.65%</td><td>10</td><td>Ohio</td><td>1,250</td><td>2.76%</td></tr>
<tr><td>43</td><td>Hawaii</td><td>30</td><td>0.07%</td><td>11</td><td>North Carolina</td><td>1,153</td><td>2.55%</td></tr>
<tr><td>42</td><td>Idaho</td><td>32</td><td>0.07%</td><td>12</td><td>Virginia</td><td>1,059</td><td>2.34%</td></tr>
<tr><td>5</td><td>Illinois</td><td>2,640</td><td>5.84%</td><td>13</td><td>Massachusetts</td><td>1,010</td><td>2.23%</td></tr>
<tr><td>26</td><td>Indiana</td><td>344</td><td>0.76%</td><td>14</td><td>Pennsylvania</td><td>979</td><td>2.16%</td></tr>
<tr><td>33</td><td>Iowa</td><td>191</td><td>0.42%</td><td>15</td><td>South Carolina</td><td>789</td><td>1.74%</td></tr>
<tr><td>36</td><td>Kansas</td><td>138</td><td>0.31%</td><td>16</td><td>Missouri</td><td>769</td><td>1.70%</td></tr>
<tr><td>35</td><td>Kentucky</td><td>159</td><td>0.35%</td><td>17</td><td>Tennessee</td><td>736</td><td>1.63%</td></tr>
<tr><td>19</td><td>Louisiana</td><td>621</td><td>1.37%</td><td>18</td><td>Arizona</td><td>730</td><td>1.61%</td></tr>
<tr><td>44</td><td>Maine</td><td>28</td><td>0.06%</td><td>19</td><td>Louisiana</td><td>621</td><td>1.37%</td></tr>
<tr><td>9</td><td>Maryland</td><td>1,362</td><td>3.01%</td><td>20</td><td>Alabama</td><td>577</td><td>1.28%</td></tr>
<tr><td>13</td><td>Massachusetts</td><td>1,010</td><td>2.23%</td><td>21</td><td>Colorado</td><td>506</td><td>1.12%</td></tr>
<tr><td>4</td><td>Michigan</td><td>2,792</td><td>6.17%</td><td>22</td><td>Washington</td><td>499</td><td>1.10%</td></tr>
<tr><td>23</td><td>Minnesota</td><td>436</td><td>0.96%</td><td>23</td><td>Minnesota</td><td>436</td><td>0.96%</td></tr>
<tr><td>32</td><td>Mississippi</td><td>199</td><td>0.44%</td><td>24</td><td>Nevada</td><td>420</td><td>0.93%</td></tr>
<tr><td>16</td><td>Missouri</td><td>769</td><td>1.70%</td><td>25</td><td>Connecticut</td><td>373</td><td>0.82%</td></tr>
<tr><td>NA</td><td>Montana**</td><td>NA</td><td>NA</td><td>26</td><td>Indiana</td><td>344</td><td>0.76%</td></tr>
<tr><td>39</td><td>Nebraska</td><td>61</td><td>0.13%</td><td>27</td><td>Oregon</td><td>326</td><td>0.72%</td></tr>
<tr><td>24</td><td>Nevada</td><td>420</td><td>0.93%</td><td>28</td><td>Wisconsin</td><td>315</td><td>0.70%</td></tr>
<tr><td>45</td><td>New Hampshire</td><td>27</td><td>0.06%</td><td>29</td><td>Oklahoma</td><td>248</td><td>0.55%</td></tr>
<tr><td>8</td><td>New Jersey</td><td>1,372</td><td>3.03%</td><td>30</td><td>Arkansas</td><td>234</td><td>0.52%</td></tr>
<tr><td>34</td><td>New Mexico</td><td>180</td><td>0.40%</td><td>31</td><td>Utah</td><td>210</td><td>0.46%</td></tr>
<tr><td>2</td><td>New York</td><td>5,731</td><td>12.67%</td><td>32</td><td>Mississippi</td><td>199</td><td>0.44%</td></tr>
<tr><td>11</td><td>North Carolina</td><td>1,153</td><td>2.55%</td><td>33</td><td>Iowa</td><td>191</td><td>0.42%</td></tr>
<tr><td>48</td><td>North Dakota</td><td>3</td><td>0.01%</td><td>34</td><td>New Mexico</td><td>180</td><td>0.40%</td></tr>
<tr><td>10</td><td>Ohio</td><td>1,250</td><td>2.76%</td><td>35</td><td>Kentucky</td><td>159</td><td>0.35%</td></tr>
<tr><td>29</td><td>Oklahoma</td><td>248</td><td>0.55%</td><td>36</td><td>Kansas</td><td>138</td><td>0.31%</td></tr>
<tr><td>27</td><td>Oregon</td><td>326</td><td>0.72%</td><td>37</td><td>Delaware</td><td>72</td><td>0.16%</td></tr>
<tr><td>14</td><td>Pennsylvania</td><td>979</td><td>2.16%</td><td>38</td><td>Rhode Island</td><td>64</td><td>0.14%</td></tr>
<tr><td>38</td><td>Rhode Island</td><td>64</td><td>0.14%</td><td>39</td><td>Nebraska</td><td>61</td><td>0.13%</td></tr>
<tr><td>15</td><td>South Carolina</td><td>789</td><td>1.74%</td><td>40</td><td>West Virginia</td><td>54</td><td>0.12%</td></tr>
<tr><td>46</td><td>South Dakota</td><td>11</td><td>0.02%</td><td>41</td><td>Alaska</td><td>53</td><td>0.12%</td></tr>
<tr><td>17</td><td>Tennessee</td><td>736</td><td>1.63%</td><td>42</td><td>Idaho</td><td>32</td><td>0.07%</td></tr>
<tr><td>3</td><td>Texas</td><td>3,548</td><td>7.85%</td><td>43</td><td>Hawaii</td><td>30</td><td>0.07%</td></tr>
<tr><td>31</td><td>Utah</td><td>210</td><td>0.46%</td><td>44</td><td>Maine</td><td>28</td><td>0.06%</td></tr>
<tr><td>NA</td><td>Vermont**</td><td>NA</td><td>NA</td><td>45</td><td>New Hampshire</td><td>27</td><td>0.06%</td></tr>
<tr><td>12</td><td>Virginia</td><td>1,059</td><td>2.34%</td><td>46</td><td>South Dakota</td><td>11</td><td>0.02%</td></tr>
<tr><td>22</td><td>Washington</td><td>499</td><td>1.10%</td><td>47</td><td>Wyoming</td><td>7</td><td>0.02%</td></tr>
<tr><td>40</td><td>West Virginia</td><td>54</td><td>0.12%</td><td>48</td><td>North Dakota</td><td>3</td><td>0.01%</td></tr>
<tr><td>28</td><td>Wisconsin</td><td>315</td><td>0.70%</td><td>NA</td><td>Montana**</td><td>NA</td><td>NA</td></tr>
<tr><td>47</td><td>Wyoming</td><td>7</td><td>0.02%</td><td>NA</td><td>Vermont**</td><td>NA</td><td>NA</td></tr>
<tr><td></td><td></td><td></td><td></td><td></td><td>District of Columbia</td><td>339</td><td>0.75%</td></tr>
</table>

Source: Federal Bureau of Investigation
     "Crime in the United States 1996" (Uniform Crime Reports, October 4, 1997)
*Of the 493,772 robberies in 1996 for which supplemental data were received by the F.B.I. There were an additional 43,278 robberies for which the type of weapon was not reported to the F.B.I. Robbery is the taking or attempting to take anything of value by force or threat of force.
**Not available.

Percent of Robberies Involving Blunt Objects
And Other Dangerous Weapons in 1996
National Percent = 9.2% of Robberies*

ALPHA ORDER

RANK ORDER

RANK	STATE	PERCENT
30	Alabama	8.2
34	Alaska	7.9
13	Arizona	10.0
30	Arkansas	8.2
19	California	9.2
4	Colorado	14.2
32	Connecticut	8.1
41	Delaware	6.4
19	Florida	9.2
10	Georgia	11.7
48	Hawaii	1.9
6	Idaho	13.3
19	Illinois	9.2
41	Indiana	6.4
1	Iowa	19.0
12	Kansas	10.2
46	Kentucky	5.2
45	Louisiana	5.6
15	Maine	9.7
39	Maryland	6.8
5	Massachusetts	13.4
2	Michigan	17.5
27	Minnesota	8.4
18	Mississippi	9.4
22	Missouri	8.7
NA	Montana**	NA
44	Nebraska	5.9
26	Nevada	8.5
13	New Hampshire	10.0
35	New Jersey	7.3
35	New Mexico	7.3
15	New York	9.7
15	North Carolina	9.7
8	North Dakota	13.0
28	Ohio	8.3
38	Oklahoma	7.0
22	Oregon	8.7
47	Pennsylvania	4.6
24	Rhode Island	8.6
9	South Carolina	12.4
24	South Dakota	8.6
40	Tennessee	6.7
11	Texas	10.8
3	Utah	15.9
NA	Vermont**	NA
6	Virginia	13.3
32	Washington	8.1
35	West Virginia	7.3
43	Wisconsin	6.3
28	Wyoming	8.3

RANK	STATE	PERCENT
1	Iowa	19.0
2	Michigan	17.5
3	Utah	15.9
4	Colorado	14.2
5	Massachusetts	13.4
6	Idaho	13.3
6	Virginia	13.3
8	North Dakota	13.0
9	South Carolina	12.4
10	Georgia	11.7
11	Texas	10.8
12	Kansas	10.2
13	Arizona	10.0
13	New Hampshire	10.0
15	Maine	9.7
15	New York	9.7
15	North Carolina	9.7
18	Mississippi	9.4
19	California	9.2
19	Florida	9.2
19	Illinois	9.2
22	Missouri	8.7
22	Oregon	8.7
24	Rhode Island	8.6
24	South Dakota	8.6
26	Nevada	8.5
27	Minnesota	8.4
28	Ohio	8.3
28	Wyoming	8.3
30	Alabama	8.2
30	Arkansas	8.2
32	Connecticut	8.1
32	Washington	8.1
34	Alaska	7.9
35	New Jersey	7.3
35	New Mexico	7.3
35	West Virginia	7.3
38	Oklahoma	7.0
39	Maryland	6.8
40	Tennessee	6.7
41	Delaware	6.4
41	Indiana	6.4
43	Wisconsin	6.3
44	Nebraska	5.9
45	Louisiana	5.6
46	Kentucky	5.2
47	Pennsylvania	4.6
48	Hawaii	1.9
NA	Montana**	NA
NA	Vermont**	NA
	District of Columbia	5.3

Source: Morgan Quitno Press using data from Federal Bureau of Investigation
   "Crime in the United States 1996" (Uniform Crime Reports, October 4, 1997)
*Of the 493,772 robberies in 1996 for which supplemental data were received by the F.B.I. There were an additional 43,278 robberies for which the type of weapon was not reported to the F.B.I. Robbery is the taking or attempting to take anything of value by force or threat of force.
**Not available.

Robberies Committed with Hands, Fists or Feet in 1996

National Total = 197,236 Robberies*

ALPHA ORDER

RANK	STATE	ROBBERIES	% of USA
21	Alabama	2,625	1.33%
42	Alaska	286	0.14%
16	Arizona	2,977	1.51%
32	Arkansas	1,061	0.54%
1	California	39,189	19.86%
29	Colorado	1,465	0.74%
23	Connecticut	2,130	1.08%
36	Delaware	537	0.27%
5	Florida	10,378	5.26%
12	Georgia	4,418	2.24%
30	Hawaii	1,317	0.67%
45	Idaho	98	0.05%
4	Illinois	11,002	5.58%
25	Indiana	1,977	1.00%
40	Iowa	472	0.24%
37	Kansas	526	0.27%
31	Kentucky	1,251	0.63%
17	Louisiana	2,933	1.49%
43	Maine	182	0.09%
9	Maryland	6,675	3.38%
14	Massachusetts	3,493	1.77%
10	Michigan	4,794	2.43%
20	Minnesota	2,770	1.40%
34	Mississippi	618	0.31%
13	Missouri	3,742	1.90%
NA	Montana**	NA	NA
39	Nebraska	478	0.24%
24	Nevada	2,027	1.03%
44	New Hampshire	145	0.07%
6	New Jersey	9,996	5.07%
33	New Mexico	753	0.38%
2	New York	23,019	11.67%
11	North Carolina	4,554	2.31%
48	North Dakota	11	0.01%
8	Ohio	7,124	3.61%
28	Oklahoma	1,669	0.85%
26	Oregon	1,885	0.96%
7	Pennsylvania	9,076	4.60%
38	Rhode Island	499	0.25%
22	South Carolina	2,384	1.21%
46	South Dakota	55	0.03%
18	Tennessee	2,877	1.46%
3	Texas	12,213	6.19%
35	Utah	557	0.28%
NA	Vermont**	NA	NA
19	Virginia	2,821	1.43%
15	Washington	3,157	1.60%
41	West Virginia	364	0.18%
27	Wisconsin	1,795	0.91%
47	Wyoming	38	0.02%

RANK ORDER

RANK	STATE	ROBBERIES	% of USA
1	California	39,189	19.86%
2	New York	23,019	11.67%
3	Texas	12,213	6.19%
4	Illinois	11,002	5.58%
5	Florida	10,378	5.26%
6	New Jersey	9,996	5.07%
7	Pennsylvania	9,076	4.60%
8	Ohio	7,124	3.61%
9	Maryland	6,675	3.38%
10	Michigan	4,794	2.43%
11	North Carolina	4,554	2.31%
12	Georgia	4,418	2.24%
13	Missouri	3,742	1.90%
14	Massachusetts	3,493	1.77%
15	Washington	3,157	1.60%
16	Arizona	2,977	1.51%
17	Louisiana	2,933	1.49%
18	Tennessee	2,877	1.46%
19	Virginia	2,821	1.43%
20	Minnesota	2,770	1.40%
21	Alabama	2,625	1.33%
22	South Carolina	2,384	1.21%
23	Connecticut	2,130	1.08%
24	Nevada	2,027	1.03%
25	Indiana	1,977	1.00%
26	Oregon	1,885	0.96%
27	Wisconsin	1,795	0.91%
28	Oklahoma	1,669	0.85%
29	Colorado	1,465	0.74%
30	Hawaii	1,317	0.67%
31	Kentucky	1,251	0.63%
32	Arkansas	1,061	0.54%
33	New Mexico	753	0.38%
34	Mississippi	618	0.31%
35	Utah	557	0.28%
36	Delaware	537	0.27%
37	Kansas	526	0.27%
38	Rhode Island	499	0.25%
39	Nebraska	478	0.24%
40	Iowa	472	0.24%
41	West Virginia	364	0.18%
42	Alaska	286	0.14%
43	Maine	182	0.09%
44	New Hampshire	145	0.07%
45	Idaho	98	0.05%
46	South Dakota	55	0.03%
47	Wyoming	38	0.02%
48	North Dakota	11	0.01%
NA	Montana**	NA	NA
NA	Vermont**	NA	NA
	District of Columbia	2,913	1.48%

Source: Federal Bureau of Investigation
    "Crime in the United States 1996" (Uniform Crime Reports, October 4, 1997)
*Also called strong-armed robberies. Of the 493,772 robberies in 1996 for which supplemental data were received
by the F.B.I. There were an additional 43,278 robberies for which the type of weapon was not reported to the F.B.I.
Robbery is the taking or attempting to take anything of value by force or threat of force.
**Not available.

Percent of Robberies Committed with Hands, Fists or Feet in 1996

National Percent = 40.0% of Robberies*

<table>
<tr><td colspan="3">ALPHA ORDER</td><td colspan="3">RANK ORDER</td></tr>
<tr><th>RANK</th><th>STATE</th><th>PERCENT</th><th>RANK</th><th>STATE</th><th>PERCENT</th></tr>
<tr><td>37</td><td>Alabama</td><td>37.2</td><td>1</td><td>Hawaii</td><td>82.0</td></tr>
<tr><td>20</td><td>Alaska</td><td>42.7</td><td>2</td><td>Rhode Island</td><td>66.7</td></tr>
<tr><td>28</td><td>Arizona</td><td>40.9</td><td>3</td><td>Maine</td><td>63.2</td></tr>
<tr><td>36</td><td>Arkansas</td><td>37.3</td><td>4</td><td>New Hampshire</td><td>53.5</td></tr>
<tr><td>25</td><td>California</td><td>41.7</td><td>5</td><td>Minnesota</td><td>53.2</td></tr>
<tr><td>26</td><td>Colorado</td><td>41.1</td><td>6</td><td>New Jersey</td><td>53.1</td></tr>
<tr><td>15</td><td>Connecticut</td><td>46.3</td><td>7</td><td>Washington</td><td>51.0</td></tr>
<tr><td>10</td><td>Delaware</td><td>47.8</td><td>8</td><td>Oregon</td><td>50.6</td></tr>
<tr><td>24</td><td>Florida</td><td>41.8</td><td>9</td><td>West Virginia</td><td>49.4</td></tr>
<tr><td>43</td><td>Georgia</td><td>31.2</td><td>10</td><td>Delaware</td><td>47.8</td></tr>
<tr><td>1</td><td>Hawaii</td><td>82.0</td><td>10</td><td>North Dakota</td><td>47.8</td></tr>
<tr><td>29</td><td>Idaho</td><td>40.8</td><td>12</td><td>Oklahoma</td><td>47.4</td></tr>
<tr><td>34</td><td>Illinois</td><td>38.3</td><td>13</td><td>Ohio</td><td>47.2</td></tr>
<tr><td>39</td><td>Indiana</td><td>36.9</td><td>14</td><td>Iowa</td><td>46.9</td></tr>
<tr><td>14</td><td>Iowa</td><td>46.9</td><td>15</td><td>Connecticut</td><td>46.3</td></tr>
<tr><td>31</td><td>Kansas</td><td>38.8</td><td>15</td><td>Massachusetts</td><td>46.3</td></tr>
<tr><td>30</td><td>Kentucky</td><td>40.7</td><td>17</td><td>Nebraska</td><td>46.2</td></tr>
<tr><td>47</td><td>Louisiana</td><td>26.4</td><td>18</td><td>Wyoming</td><td>45.2</td></tr>
<tr><td>3</td><td>Maine</td><td>63.2</td><td>19</td><td>South Dakota</td><td>43.0</td></tr>
<tr><td>42</td><td>Maryland</td><td>33.6</td><td>20</td><td>Alaska</td><td>42.7</td></tr>
<tr><td>15</td><td>Massachusetts</td><td>46.3</td><td>21</td><td>Pennsylvania</td><td>42.6</td></tr>
<tr><td>45</td><td>Michigan</td><td>30.1</td><td>22</td><td>Utah</td><td>42.2</td></tr>
<tr><td>5</td><td>Minnesota</td><td>53.2</td><td>23</td><td>Missouri</td><td>42.1</td></tr>
<tr><td>46</td><td>Mississippi</td><td>29.1</td><td>24</td><td>Florida</td><td>41.8</td></tr>
<tr><td>23</td><td>Missouri</td><td>42.1</td><td>25</td><td>California</td><td>41.7</td></tr>
<tr><td>NA</td><td>Montana**</td><td>NA</td><td>26</td><td>Colorado</td><td>41.1</td></tr>
<tr><td>17</td><td>Nebraska</td><td>46.2</td><td>26</td><td>Nevada</td><td>41.1</td></tr>
<tr><td>26</td><td>Nevada</td><td>41.1</td><td>28</td><td>Arizona</td><td>40.9</td></tr>
<tr><td>4</td><td>New Hampshire</td><td>53.5</td><td>29</td><td>Idaho</td><td>40.8</td></tr>
<tr><td>6</td><td>New Jersey</td><td>53.1</td><td>30</td><td>Kentucky</td><td>40.7</td></tr>
<tr><td>44</td><td>New Mexico</td><td>30.4</td><td>31</td><td>Kansas</td><td>38.8</td></tr>
<tr><td>31</td><td>New York</td><td>38.8</td><td>31</td><td>New York</td><td>38.8</td></tr>
<tr><td>33</td><td>North Carolina</td><td>38.4</td><td>33</td><td>North Carolina</td><td>38.4</td></tr>
<tr><td>10</td><td>North Dakota</td><td>47.8</td><td>34</td><td>Illinois</td><td>38.3</td></tr>
<tr><td>13</td><td>Ohio</td><td>47.2</td><td>35</td><td>South Carolina</td><td>37.6</td></tr>
<tr><td>12</td><td>Oklahoma</td><td>47.4</td><td>36</td><td>Arkansas</td><td>37.3</td></tr>
<tr><td>8</td><td>Oregon</td><td>50.6</td><td>37</td><td>Alabama</td><td>37.2</td></tr>
<tr><td>21</td><td>Pennsylvania</td><td>42.6</td><td>37</td><td>Texas</td><td>37.2</td></tr>
<tr><td>2</td><td>Rhode Island</td><td>66.7</td><td>39</td><td>Indiana</td><td>36.9</td></tr>
<tr><td>35</td><td>South Carolina</td><td>37.6</td><td>40</td><td>Wisconsin</td><td>36.0</td></tr>
<tr><td>19</td><td>South Dakota</td><td>43.0</td><td>41</td><td>Virginia</td><td>35.5</td></tr>
<tr><td>48</td><td>Tennessee</td><td>26.1</td><td>42</td><td>Maryland</td><td>33.6</td></tr>
<tr><td>37</td><td>Texas</td><td>37.2</td><td>43</td><td>Georgia</td><td>31.2</td></tr>
<tr><td>22</td><td>Utah</td><td>42.2</td><td>44</td><td>New Mexico</td><td>30.4</td></tr>
<tr><td>NA</td><td>Vermont**</td><td>NA</td><td>45</td><td>Michigan</td><td>30.1</td></tr>
<tr><td>41</td><td>Virginia</td><td>35.5</td><td>46</td><td>Mississippi</td><td>29.1</td></tr>
<tr><td>7</td><td>Washington</td><td>51.0</td><td>47</td><td>Louisiana</td><td>26.4</td></tr>
<tr><td>9</td><td>West Virginia</td><td>49.4</td><td>48</td><td>Tennessee</td><td>26.1</td></tr>
<tr><td>40</td><td>Wisconsin</td><td>36.0</td><td>NA</td><td>Montana**</td><td>NA</td></tr>
<tr><td>18</td><td>Wyoming</td><td>45.2</td><td>NA</td><td>Vermont**</td><td>NA</td></tr>
<tr><td></td><td></td><td></td><td></td><td>District of Columbia</td><td>45.2</td></tr>
</table>

Source: Morgan Quitno Press using data from Federal Bureau of Investigation
   "Crime in the United States 1996" (Uniform Crime Reports, October 4, 1997)
*Also called strong-armed robberies. Of the 493,772 robberies in 1996 for which supplemental data were received
by the F.B.I. There were an additional 43,278 robberies for which the type of weapon was not reported to the F.B.I.
Robbery is the taking or attempting to take anything of value by force or threat of force.
**Not available.

Bank Robberies in 1996

National Total = 8,024 Robberies*

RANK	STATE	ROBBERIES	% of USA
26	Alabama	83	1.03%
41	Alaska	10	0.12%
9	Arizona	260	3.24%
35	Arkansas	19	0.24%
1	California	2,048	25.52%
13	Colorado	169	2.11%
30	Connecticut	66	0.82%
39	Delaware	15	0.19%
2	Florida	628	7.83%
18	Georgia	145	1.81%
33	Hawaii	33	0.41%
43	Idaho	9	0.11%
10	Illinois	248	3.09%
22	Indiana	116	1.45%
38	Iowa	18	0.22%
31	Kansas	45	0.56%
29	Kentucky	70	0.87%
23	Louisiana	113	1.41%
46	Maine	2	0.02%
6	Maryland	316	3.94%
20	Massachusetts	119	1.48%
5	Michigan	343	4.27%
27	Minnesota	79	0.98%
32	Mississippi	39	0.49%
28	Missouri	75	0.93%
45	Montana	4	0.05%
35	Nebraska	19	0.24%
13	Nevada	169	2.11%
44	New Hampshire	6	0.07%
19	New Jersey	127	1.58%
25	New Mexico	85	1.06%
3	New York	355	4.42%
12	North Carolina	179	2.23%
49	North Dakota	1	0.01%
3	Ohio	355	4.42%
35	Oklahoma	19	0.24%
11	Oregon	241	3.00%
16	Pennsylvania	167	2.08%
40	Rhode Island	11	0.14%
24	South Carolina	95	1.18%
46	South Dakota	2	0.02%
17	Tennessee	161	2.01%
7	Texas	301	3.75%
34	Utah	32	0.40%
50	Vermont	0	0.00%
15	Virginia	168	2.09%
8	Washington	262	3.27%
41	West Virginia	10	0.12%
21	Wisconsin	117	1.46%
46	Wyoming	2	0.02%

RANK	STATE	ROBBERIES	% of USA
1	California	2,048	25.52%
2	Florida	628	7.83%
3	New York	355	4.42%
3	Ohio	355	4.42%
5	Michigan	343	4.27%
6	Maryland	316	3.94%
7	Texas	301	3.75%
8	Washington	262	3.27%
9	Arizona	260	3.24%
10	Illinois	248	3.09%
11	Oregon	241	3.00%
12	North Carolina	179	2.23%
13	Colorado	169	2.11%
13	Nevada	169	2.11%
15	Virginia	168	2.09%
16	Pennsylvania	167	2.08%
17	Tennessee	161	2.01%
18	Georgia	145	1.81%
19	New Jersey	127	1.58%
20	Massachusetts	119	1.48%
21	Wisconsin	117	1.46%
22	Indiana	116	1.45%
23	Louisiana	113	1.41%
24	South Carolina	95	1.18%
25	New Mexico	85	1.06%
26	Alabama	83	1.03%
27	Minnesota	79	0.98%
28	Missouri	75	0.93%
29	Kentucky	70	0.87%
30	Connecticut	66	0.82%
31	Kansas	45	0.56%
32	Mississippi	39	0.49%
33	Hawaii	33	0.41%
34	Utah	32	0.40%
35	Arkansas	19	0.24%
35	Nebraska	19	0.24%
35	Oklahoma	19	0.24%
38	Iowa	18	0.22%
39	Delaware	15	0.19%
40	Rhode Island	11	0.14%
41	Alaska	10	0.12%
41	West Virginia	10	0.12%
43	Idaho	9	0.11%
44	New Hampshire	6	0.07%
45	Montana	4	0.05%
46	Maine	2	0.02%
46	South Dakota	2	0.02%
46	Wyoming	2	0.02%
49	North Dakota	1	0.01%
50	Vermont	0	0.00%
	District of Columbia	68	0.85%

Source: Federal Bureau of Investigation
   "Bank Crime Statistics, Federally Insured Financial Institutions, January 1, 1996 - December 31, 1996"
Does not include 22 robberies in Puerto Rico. In addition, there were 290 bank burglaries, 47 bank larcenies and 40 extortions. Of these 8,383 bank crimes, loot valued at $77,163,480 was taken in 7,704 cases. Of this, $13,556,682 was recovered.

Aggravated Assaults in 1996

National Total = 1,029,814 Aggravated Assaults*

ALPHA ORDER

RANK ORDER

RANK	STATE	ASSAULTS	% of USA		RANK	STATE	ASSAULTS	% of USA
20	Alabama	15,194	1.48%		1	California	167,614	16.28%
38	Alaska	3,264	0.32%		2	Florida	101,122	9.82%
19	Arizona	18,776	1.82%		3	Texas	80,613	7.83%
27	Arkansas	9,032	0.88%		4	Illinois	66,649	6.47%
1	California	167,614	16.28%		5	New York	64,857	6.30%
25	Colorado	9,763	0.95%		6	Michigan	37,856	3.68%
31	Connecticut	7,025	0.68%		7	Massachusetts	29,420	2.86%
39	Delaware	3,056	0.30%		8	Georgia	28,879	2.80%
2	Florida	101,122	9.82%		9	South Carolina	28,361	2.75%
8	Georgia	28,879	2.80%		10	North Carolina	28,159	2.73%
43	Hawaii	1,350	0.13%		11	Tennessee	26,295	2.55%
41	Idaho	2,580	0.25%		12	Louisiana	25,823	2.51%
4	Illinois	66,649	6.47%		13	Maryland	24,793	2.41%
16	Indiana	21,705	2.11%		14	Ohio	24,405	2.37%
35	Iowa	5,871	0.57%		15	Pennsylvania	24,166	2.35%
33	Kansas	6,900	0.67%		16	Indiana	21,705	2.11%
30	Kentucky	7,347	0.71%		17	New Jersey	21,307	2.07%
12	Louisiana	25,823	2.51%		18	Missouri	20,528	1.99%
44	Maine	976	0.09%		19	Arizona	18,776	1.82%
13	Maryland	24,793	2.41%		20	Alabama	15,194	1.48%
7	Massachusetts	29,420	2.86%		21	Oklahoma	14,423	1.40%
6	Michigan	37,856	3.68%		22	Washington	14,187	1.38%
29	Minnesota	7,903	0.77%		23	Virginia	12,318	1.20%
28	Mississippi	8,333	0.81%		24	New Mexico	10,332	1.00%
18	Missouri	20,528	1.99%		25	Colorado	9,763	0.95%
46	Montana	882	0.09%		26	Oregon	9,522	0.92%
36	Nebraska	5,635	0.55%		27	Arkansas	9,032	0.88%
32	Nevada	6,998	0.68%		28	Mississippi	8,333	0.81%
48	New Hampshire	632	0.06%		29	Minnesota	7,903	0.77%
17	New Jersey	21,307	2.07%		30	Kentucky	7,347	0.71%
24	New Mexico	10,332	1.00%		31	Connecticut	7,025	0.68%
5	New York	64,857	6.30%		32	Nevada	6,998	0.68%
10	North Carolina	28,159	2.73%		33	Kansas	6,900	0.67%
50	North Dakota	301	0.03%		34	Wisconsin	6,767	0.66%
14	Ohio	24,405	2.37%		35	Iowa	5,871	0.57%
21	Oklahoma	14,423	1.40%		36	Nebraska	5,635	0.55%
26	Oregon	9,522	0.92%		37	Utah	4,362	0.42%
15	Pennsylvania	24,166	2.35%		38	Alaska	3,264	0.32%
42	Rhode Island	2,301	0.22%		39	Delaware	3,056	0.30%
9	South Carolina	28,361	2.75%		40	West Virginia	2,672	0.26%
47	South Dakota	850	0.08%		41	Idaho	2,580	0.25%
11	Tennessee	26,295	2.55%		42	Rhode Island	2,301	0.22%
3	Texas	80,613	7.83%		43	Hawaii	1,350	0.13%
37	Utah	4,362	0.42%		44	Maine	976	0.09%
49	Vermont	453	0.04%		45	Wyoming	947	0.09%
23	Virginia	12,318	1.20%		46	Montana	882	0.09%
22	Washington	14,187	1.38%		47	South Dakota	850	0.08%
40	West Virginia	2,672	0.26%		48	New Hampshire	632	0.06%
34	Wisconsin	6,767	0.66%		49	Vermont	453	0.04%
45	Wyoming	947	0.09%		50	North Dakota	301	0.03%
						District of Columbia	6,310	0.61%

Source: Federal Bureau of Investigation
    "Crime in the United States 1996" (Uniform Crime Reports, October 4, 1997)
*Aggravated assault is an attack for the purpose of inflicting severe bodily injury.

Average Time Between Aggravated Assaults in 1996

National Rate = An Aggravated Assault Occurs Every 31 Seconds*

ALPHA ORDER

RANK	STATE	MINUTES.SECONDS
31	Alabama	34.41
13	Alaska	161.28
32	Arizona	28.04
24	Arkansas	58.21
50	California	3.08
26	Colorado	53.59
20	Connecticut	75.01
12	Delaware	172.28
49	Florida	5.13
43	Georgia	18.15
8	Hawaii	390.24
10	Idaho	204.17
47	Illinois	7.55
35	Indiana	24.17
16	Iowa	89.46
18	Kansas	76.23
21	Kentucky	71.44
39	Louisiana	20.25
7	Maine	540.00
38	Maryland	21.16
44	Massachusetts	17.55
45	Michigan	13.55
22	Minnesota	66.41
23	Mississippi	63.15
33	Missouri	25.40
5	Montana	597.33
15	Nebraska	93.32
19	Nevada	75.19
3	New Hampshire	833.55
34	New Jersey	24.44
27	New Mexico	51.01
46	New York	8.08
41	North Carolina	18.43
1	North Dakota	1,750.58
37	Ohio	21.36
30	Oklahoma	36.32
25	Oregon	55.21
36	Pennsylvania	21.49
9	Rhode Island	229.03
42	South Carolina	18.35
4	South Dakota	620.03
40	Tennessee	20.02
48	Texas	6.32
14	Utah	120.50
2	Vermont	1,163.26
28	Virginia	42.47
29	Washington	37.09
11	West Virginia	197.15
17	Wisconsin	77.53
6	Wyoming	556.32

RANK ORDER

RANK	STATE	MINUTES.SECONDS
1	North Dakota	1,750.58
2	Vermont	1,163.26
3	New Hampshire	833.55
4	South Dakota	620.03
5	Montana	597.33
6	Wyoming	556.32
7	Maine	540.00
8	Hawaii	390.24
9	Rhode Island	229.03
10	Idaho	204.17
11	West Virginia	197.15
12	Delaware	172.28
13	Alaska	161.28
14	Utah	120.50
15	Nebraska	93.32
16	Iowa	89.46
17	Wisconsin	77.53
18	Kansas	76.23
19	Nevada	75.19
20	Connecticut	75.01
21	Kentucky	71.44
22	Minnesota	66.41
23	Mississippi	63.15
24	Arkansas	58.21
25	Oregon	55.21
26	Colorado	53.59
27	New Mexico	51.01
28	Virginia	42.47
29	Washington	37.09
30	Oklahoma	36.32
31	Alabama	34.41
32	Arizona	28.04
33	Missouri	25.40
34	New Jersey	24.44
35	Indiana	24.17
36	Pennsylvania	21.49
37	Ohio	21.36
38	Maryland	21.16
39	Louisiana	20.25
40	Tennessee	20.02
41	North Carolina	18.43
42	South Carolina	18.35
43	Georgia	18.15
44	Massachusetts	17.55
45	Michigan	13.55
46	New York	8.08
47	Illinois	7.55
48	Texas	6.32
49	Florida	5.13
50	California	3.08
	District of Columbia	83.31

Source: Morgan Quitno Press using data from Federal Bureau of Investigation
    "Crime in the United States 1996" (Uniform Crime Reports, October 4, 1997)
*Aggravated assault is an attack for the purpose of inflicting severe bodily injury.

Percent Change in Number of Aggravated Assaults: 1995 to 1996

National Percent Change = 6.3% Decrease*

RANK	STATE	PERCENT CHANGE		RANK	STATE	PERCENT CHANGE
39	Alabama	(11.5)		1	Nebraska	16.9
6	Alaska	2.7		2	Indiana	7.4
35	Arizona	(10.2)		3	Utah	4.0
24	Arkansas	(4.3)		4	West Virginia	3.4
34	California	(10.1)		5	South Carolina	2.8
42	Colorado	(12.8)		6	Alaska	2.7
11	Connecticut	0.0		7	New Mexico	2.3
22	Delaware	(3.7)		8	Tennessee	2.0
12	Florida	(0.2)		9	Vermont	0.7
16	Georgia	(1.5)		10	Texas	0.3
44	Hawaii	(13.7)		11	Connecticut	0.0
48	Idaho	(16.5)		12	Florida	(0.2)
31	Illinois	(8.9)		13	Kansas	(0.3)
2	Indiana	7.4		14	Minnesota	(0.5)
50	Iowa	(25.6)		15	Wyoming	(1.3)
13	Kansas	(0.3)		16	Georgia	(1.5)
46	Kentucky	(14.3)		17	New Hampshire	(2.2)
41	Louisiana	(12.4)		18	Maine	(3.1)
18	Maine	(3.1)		18	Pennsylvania	(3.1)
21	Maryland	(3.5)		20	Mississippi	(3.4)
23	Massachusetts	(3.9)		21	Maryland	(3.5)
28	Michigan	(7.8)		22	Delaware	(3.7)
14	Minnesota	(0.5)		23	Massachusetts	(3.9)
20	Mississippi	(3.4)		24	Arkansas	(4.3)
29	Missouri	(7.9)		25	Virginia	(4.5)
33	Montana	(9.3)		26	Rhode Island	(5.3)
1	Nebraska	16.9		27	New Jersey	(6.7)
49	Nevada	(16.6)		28	Michigan	(7.8)
17	New Hampshire	(2.2)		29	Missouri	(7.9)
27	New Jersey	(6.7)		30	North Carolina	(8.0)
7	New Mexico	2.3		31	Illinois	(8.9)
42	New York	(12.8)		32	Washington	(9.1)
30	North Carolina	(8.0)		33	Montana	(9.3)
39	North Dakota	(11.5)		34	California	(10.1)
45	Ohio	(14.2)		35	Arizona	(10.2)
36	Oklahoma	(10.5)		36	Oklahoma	(10.5)
36	Oregon	(10.5)		36	Oregon	(10.5)
18	Pennsylvania	(3.1)		38	Wisconsin	(11.0)
26	Rhode Island	(5.3)		39	Alabama	(11.5)
5	South Carolina	2.8		39	North Dakota	(11.5)
47	South Dakota	(16.0)		41	Louisiana	(12.4)
8	Tennessee	2.0		42	Colorado	(12.8)
10	Texas	0.3		42	New York	(12.8)
3	Utah	4.0		44	Hawaii	(13.7)
9	Vermont	0.7		45	Ohio	(14.2)
25	Virginia	(4.5)		46	Kentucky	(14.3)
32	Washington	(9.1)		47	South Dakota	(16.0)
4	West Virginia	3.4		48	Idaho	(16.5)
38	Wisconsin	(11.0)		49	Nevada	(16.6)
15	Wyoming	(1.3)		50	Iowa	(25.6)
					District of Columbia	(12.7)

ALPHA ORDER (left) / RANK ORDER (right)

Source: Federal Bureau of Investigation
   "Crime in the United States 1996" (Uniform Crime Reports, October 4, 1997)
*Aggravated assault is an attack for the purpose of inflicting severe bodily injury.

Aggravated Assault Rate in 1996

National Rate = 388.2 Assaults per 100,000 Population*

ALPHA ORDER				RANK ORDER		
RANK	STATE	RATE		RANK	STATE	RATE
23	Alabama	355.6		1	South Carolina	766.7
6	Alaska	537.7		2	Florida	702.2
13	Arizona	424.0		3	New Mexico	603.2
21	Arkansas	359.8		4	Louisiana	593.5
7	California	525.8		5	Illinois	562.6
30	Colorado	255.4		6	Alaska	537.7
35	Connecticut	214.6		7	California	525.8
14	Delaware	421.5		8	Tennessee	494.3
2	Florida	702.2		9	Maryland	488.8
17	Georgia	392.8		10	Massachusetts	482.9
45	Hawaii	114.0		11	Oklahoma	436.9
34	Idaho	217.0		12	Nevada	436.6
5	Illinois	562.6		13	Arizona	424.0
20	Indiana	371.6		14	Delaware	421.5
36	Iowa	205.9		15	Texas	421.4
27	Kansas	268.3		16	Michigan	394.6
39	Kentucky	189.2		17	Georgia	392.8
4	Louisiana	593.5		18	North Carolina	384.5
47	Maine	78.5		19	Missouri	383.1
9	Maryland	488.8		20	Indiana	371.6
10	Massachusetts	482.9		21	Arkansas	359.8
16	Michigan	394.6		22	New York	356.7
41	Minnesota	169.7		23	Alabama	355.6
25	Mississippi	306.8		24	Nebraska	341.1
19	Missouri	383.1		25	Mississippi	306.8
46	Montana	100.3		26	Oregon	297.2
24	Nebraska	341.1		27	Kansas	268.3
12	Nevada	436.6		28	New Jersey	266.7
49	New Hampshire	54.4		29	Washington	256.4
28	New Jersey	266.7		30	Colorado	255.4
3	New Mexico	603.2		31	Rhode Island	232.4
22	New York	356.7		32	Ohio	218.4
18	North Carolina	384.5		33	Utah	218.1
50	North Dakota	46.7		34	Idaho	217.0
32	Ohio	218.4		35	Connecticut	214.6
11	Oklahoma	436.9		36	Iowa	205.9
26	Oregon	297.2		37	Pennsylvania	200.4
37	Pennsylvania	200.4		38	Wyoming	196.9
31	Rhode Island	232.4		39	Kentucky	189.2
1	South Carolina	766.7		40	Virginia	184.5
44	South Dakota	116.1		41	Minnesota	169.7
8	Tennessee	494.3		42	West Virginia	146.3
15	Texas	421.4		43	Wisconsin	131.1
33	Utah	218.1		44	South Dakota	116.1
48	Vermont	76.9		45	Hawaii	114.0
40	Virginia	184.5		46	Montana	100.3
29	Washington	256.4		47	Maine	78.5
42	West Virginia	146.3		48	Vermont	76.9
43	Wisconsin	131.1		49	New Hampshire	54.4
38	Wyoming	196.9		50	North Dakota	46.7
					District of Columbia	1,162.1

Source: Federal Bureau of Investigation
"Crime in the United States 1996" (Uniform Crime Reports, October 4, 1997)
Aggravated assault is an attack for the purpose of inflicting severe bodily injury.

Percent Change in Aggravated Assault Rate: 1995 to 1996

National Percent Change = 7.2% Decrease*

RANK	STATE (ALPHA ORDER)	PERCENT CHANGE	RANK	STATE (RANK ORDER)	PERCENT CHANGE
37	Alabama	(11.9)	1	Nebraska	15.8
4	Alaska	2.2	2	Indiana	6.7
44	Arizona	(14.5)	3	West Virginia	3.5
24	Arkansas	(5.3)	4	Alaska	2.2
34	California	(10.9)	5	South Carolina	2.1
44	Colorado	(14.5)	6	Utah	1.4
9	Connecticut	0.1	7	Tennessee	0.8
23	Delaware	(4.7)	8	New Mexico	0.7
14	Florida	(1.8)	9	Connecticut	0.1
19	Georgia	(3.5)	10	Vermont	0.0
42	Hawaii	(13.5)	11	Kansas	(0.6)
48	Idaho	(18.3)	12	Minnesota	(1.5)
30	Illinois	(9.0)	12	Wyoming	(1.5)
2	Indiana	6.7	14	Florida	(1.8)
50	Iowa	(25.9)	14	Texas	(1.8)
11	Kansas	(0.6)	16	Pennsylvania	(3.0)
46	Kentucky	(14.8)	17	Maine	(3.2)
40	Louisiana	(12.6)	18	New Hampshire	(3.4)
17	Maine	(3.2)	19	Georgia	(3.5)
20	Maryland	(4.1)	20	Maryland	(4.1)
22	Massachusetts	(4.2)	20	Mississippi	(4.1)
28	Michigan	(8.3)	22	Massachusetts	(4.2)
12	Minnesota	(1.5)	23	Delaware	(4.7)
20	Mississippi	(4.1)	24	Arkansas	(5.3)
29	Missouri	(8.5)	24	Rhode Island	(5.3)
32	Montana	(10.2)	24	Virginia	(5.3)
1	Nebraska	15.8	27	New Jersey	(7.2)
49	Nevada	(20.4)	28	Michigan	(8.3)
18	New Hampshire	(3.4)	29	Missouri	(8.5)
27	New Jersey	(7.2)	30	Illinois	(9.0)
8	New Mexico	0.7	31	North Carolina	(9.6)
41	New York	(13.0)	32	Montana	(10.2)
31	North Carolina	(9.6)	33	Washington	(10.8)
37	North Dakota	(11.9)	34	California	(10.9)
43	Ohio	(14.4)	35	Oklahoma	(11.2)
35	Oklahoma	(11.2)	36	Wisconsin	(11.7)
39	Oregon	(12.3)	37	Alabama	(11.9)
16	Pennsylvania	(3.0)	37	North Dakota	(11.9)
24	Rhode Island	(5.3)	39	Oregon	(12.3)
5	South Carolina	2.1	40	Louisiana	(12.6)
47	South Dakota	(16.4)	41	New York	(13.0)
7	Tennessee	0.8	42	Hawaii	(13.5)
14	Texas	(1.8)	43	Ohio	(14.4)
6	Utah	1.4	44	Arizona	(14.5)
10	Vermont	0.0	44	Colorado	(14.5)
24	Virginia	(5.3)	46	Kentucky	(14.8)
33	Washington	(10.8)	47	South Dakota	(16.4)
3	West Virginia	3.5	48	Idaho	(18.3)
36	Wisconsin	(11.7)	49	Nevada	(20.4)
12	Wyoming	(1.5)	50	Iowa	(25.9)
				District of Columbia	(10.9)

Source: Federal Bureau of Investigation
   "Crime in the United States 1996" (Uniform Crime Reports, October 4, 1997)
*Aggravated assault is an attack for the purpose of inflicting severe bodily injury.

Aggravated Assaults with Firearms in 1996

National Total = 199,910 Aggravated Assaults*

ALPHA ORDER

RANK	STATE	ASSAULTS	% of USA
15	Alabama	4,117	2.06%
36	Alaska	635	0.32%
12	Arizona	5,976	2.99%
21	Arkansas	2,579	1.29%
1	California	30,853	15.43%
23	Colorado	2,289	1.15%
37	Connecticut	624	0.31%
40	Delaware	448	0.22%
4	Florida	12,835	6.42%
8	Georgia	6,994	3.50%
43	Hawaii	164	0.08%
35	Idaho	766	0.38%
5	Illinois	12,260	6.13%
24	Indiana	2,118	1.06%
39	Iowa	528	0.26%
38	Kansas	593	0.30%
30	Kentucky	1,241	0.62%
11	Louisiana	6,391	3.20%
47	Maine	29	0.01%
14	Maryland	5,017	2.51%
28	Massachusetts	1,670	0.84%
6	Michigan	9,074	4.54%
26	Minnesota	1,872	0.94%
31	Mississippi	1,163	0.58%
13	Missouri	5,390	2.70%
NA	Montana**	NA	NA
33	Nebraska	795	0.40%
29	Nevada	1,500	0.75%
46	New Hampshire	48	0.02%
18	New Jersey	3,271	1.64%
22	New Mexico	2,418	1.21%
3	New York	13,703	6.85%
7	North Carolina	8,295	4.15%
48	North Dakota	14	0.01%
17	Ohio	3,780	1.89%
20	Oklahoma	2,811	1.41%
27	Oregon	1,746	0.87%
16	Pennsylvania	3,883	1.94%
42	Rhode Island	248	0.12%
9	South Carolina	6,896	3.45%
44	South Dakota	143	0.07%
10	Tennessee	6,691	3.35%
2	Texas	19,800	9.90%
34	Utah	777	0.39%
NA	Vermont**	NA	NA
25	Virginia	1,884	0.94%
19	Washington	2,867	1.43%
41	West Virginia	371	0.19%
32	Wisconsin	939	0.47%
45	Wyoming	96	0.05%

RANK ORDER

RANK	STATE	ASSAULTS	% of USA
1	California	30,853	15.43%
2	Texas	19,800	9.90%
3	New York	13,703	6.85%
4	Florida	12,835	6.42%
5	Illinois	12,260	6.13%
6	Michigan	9,074	4.54%
7	North Carolina	8,295	4.15%
8	Georgia	6,994	3.50%
9	South Carolina	6,896	3.45%
10	Tennessee	6,691	3.35%
11	Louisiana	6,391	3.20%
12	Arizona	5,976	2.99%
13	Missouri	5,390	2.70%
14	Maryland	5,017	2.51%
15	Alabama	4,117	2.06%
16	Pennsylvania	3,883	1.94%
17	Ohio	3,780	1.89%
18	New Jersey	3,271	1.64%
19	Washington	2,867	1.43%
20	Oklahoma	2,811	1.41%
21	Arkansas	2,579	1.29%
22	New Mexico	2,418	1.21%
23	Colorado	2,289	1.15%
24	Indiana	2,118	1.06%
25	Virginia	1,884	0.94%
26	Minnesota	1,872	0.94%
27	Oregon	1,746	0.87%
28	Massachusetts	1,670	0.84%
29	Nevada	1,500	0.75%
30	Kentucky	1,241	0.62%
31	Mississippi	1,163	0.58%
32	Wisconsin	939	0.47%
33	Nebraska	795	0.40%
34	Utah	777	0.39%
35	Idaho	766	0.38%
36	Alaska	635	0.32%
37	Connecticut	624	0.31%
38	Kansas	593	0.30%
39	Iowa	528	0.26%
40	Delaware	448	0.22%
41	West Virginia	371	0.19%
42	Rhode Island	248	0.12%
43	Hawaii	164	0.08%
44	South Dakota	143	0.07%
45	Wyoming	96	0.05%
46	New Hampshire	48	0.02%
47	Maine	29	0.01%
48	North Dakota	14	0.01%
NA	Montana**	NA	NA
NA	Vermont**	NA	NA
	District of Columbia	1,308	0.65%

Source: Federal Bureau of Investigation
   "Crime in the United States 1996" (Uniform Crime Reports, October 4, 1997)
*Of the 880,511 aggravated assaults in 1996 for which supplemental data were received by the F.B.I. There were an additional 149,303 aggravated assaults for which the type of weapon was not reported to the F.B.I. Aggravated assault is an attack for the purpose of inflicting severe bodily injury.
**Not available.

371

Aggravated Assault Rate with Firearms in 1996

National Rate = 96.7 Aggravated Assaults per 100,000 Population*

ALPHA ORDER				RANK ORDER		
RANK	STATE	RATE		RANK	STATE	RATE
21	Alabama	98.8		1	Illinois	367.7
14	Alaska	116.3		2	Virginia	294.4
8	Arizona	143.2		3	New Mexico	238.9
18	Arkansas	108.5		4	Tennessee	235.1
23	California	97.3		5	Florida	210.2
27	Colorado	64.5		6	South Carolina	188.5
41	Connecticut	23.6		7	Louisiana	185.9
12	Delaware	120.8		8	Arizona	143.2
5	Florida	210.2		9	Kansas	136.6
17	Georgia	109.5		10	Missouri	131.1
45	Hawaii	13.9		11	Mississippi	128.4
26	Idaho	65.4		12	Delaware	120.8
1	Illinois	367.7		13	Kentucky	119.7
28	Indiana	62.3		14	Alaska	116.3
41	Iowa	23.6		15	North Carolina	115.6
9	Kansas	136.6		16	Michigan	115.3
13	Kentucky	119.7		17	Georgia	109.5
7	Louisiana	185.9		18	Arkansas	108.5
48	Maine	2.4		19	Texas	103.8
20	Maryland	100.0		20	Maryland	100.0
37	Massachusetts	33.6		21	Alabama	98.8
16	Michigan	115.3		22	New York	97.7
35	Minnesota	40.7		23	California	97.3
11	Mississippi	128.4		24	Nevada	94.2
10	Missouri	131.1		25	Oklahoma	85.2
NA	Montana**	NA		26	Idaho	65.4
32	Nebraska	51.4		27	Colorado	64.5
24	Nevada	94.2		28	Indiana	62.3
46	New Hampshire	5.2		29	Oregon	61.5
34	New Jersey	40.9		30	Washington	55.2
3	New Mexico	238.9		31	Ohio	53.8
22	New York	97.7		32	Nebraska	51.4
15	North Carolina	115.6		33	Pennsylvania	41.7
47	North Dakota	3.9		34	New Jersey	40.9
31	Ohio	53.8		35	Minnesota	40.7
25	Oklahoma	85.2		36	Utah	40.1
29	Oregon	61.5		37	Massachusetts	33.6
33	Pennsylvania	41.7		38	South Dakota	28.3
39	Rhode Island	25.1		39	Rhode Island	25.1
6	South Carolina	188.5		40	Wyoming	24.2
38	South Dakota	28.3		41	Connecticut	23.6
4	Tennessee	235.1		41	Iowa	23.6
19	Texas	103.8		43	West Virginia	20.3
36	Utah	40.1		44	Wisconsin	18.3
NA	Vermont**	NA		45	Hawaii	13.9
2	Virginia	294.4		46	New Hampshire	5.2
30	Washington	55.2		47	North Dakota	3.9
43	West Virginia	20.3		48	Maine	2.4
44	Wisconsin	18.3		NA	Montana**	NA
40	Wyoming	24.2		NA	Vermont**	NA
					District of Columbia	240.9

Source: Morgan Quitno Press using data from Federal Bureau of Investigation
"Crime in the United States 1996" (Uniform Crime Reports, October 4, 1997)
*Based only on population of reporting jurisdictions. Aggravated assault is an attack for the purpose of inflicting severe bodily injury. National rate reflects only those robberies for which the type of weapon was known and reported. Illinois, Kansas, Kentucky, Mississippi and Virginia rates especially affected by number of nonreporting jurisdictions. **Not available.

Percent of Aggravated Assaults Involving Firearms in 1996

National Percent = 22.7% of Aggravated Assaults*

ALPHA ORDER				RANK ORDER		
RANK	**STATE**	**PERCENT**		**RANK**	**STATE**	**PERCENT**
11	Alabama	27.7		1	Mississippi	36.4
22	Alaska	22.6		2	Tennessee	33.6
3	Arizona	33.5		3	Arizona	33.5
10	Arkansas	29.2		4	New Mexico	32.7
33	California	18.5		5	Louisiana	30.9
15	Colorado	24.8		6	Idaho	30.5
44	Connecticut	10.5		7	Missouri	30.0
29	Delaware	19.5		8	North Carolina	29.9
19	Florida	23.5		9	Illinois	29.7
13	Georgia	27.2		10	Arkansas	29.2
41	Hawaii	12.1		11	Alabama	27.7
6	Idaho	30.5		12	Kansas	27.4
9	Illinois	29.7		13	Georgia	27.2
34	Indiana	17.2		14	Michigan	26.6
42	Iowa	11.5		15	Colorado	24.8
12	Kansas	27.4		16	Minnesota	24.7
25	Kentucky	21.1		17	South Carolina	24.6
5	Louisiana	30.9		17	Texas	24.6
48	Maine	3.0		19	Florida	23.5
27	Maryland	20.4		20	New York	23.0
47	Massachusetts	6.2		21	Ohio	22.7
14	Michigan	26.6		22	Alaska	22.6
16	Minnesota	24.7		23	Nevada	21.8
1	Mississippi	36.4		24	Washington	21.5
7	Missouri	30.0		25	Kentucky	21.1
NA	Montana**	NA		26	Pennsylvania	20.6
37	Nebraska	14.4		27	Maryland	20.4
23	Nevada	21.8		28	South Dakota	19.6
45	New Hampshire	9.8		29	Delaware	19.5
36	New Jersey	15.4		29	Oklahoma	19.5
4	New Mexico	32.7		31	Oregon	19.3
20	New York	23.0		32	Utah	19.2
8	North Carolina	29.9		33	California	18.5
46	North Dakota	7.4		34	Indiana	17.2
21	Ohio	22.7		35	Virginia	15.9
29	Oklahoma	19.5		36	New Jersey	15.4
31	Oregon	19.3		37	Nebraska	14.4
26	Pennsylvania	20.6		38	West Virginia	13.9
43	Rhode Island	10.8		38	Wisconsin	13.9
17	South Carolina	24.6		40	Wyoming	12.7
28	South Dakota	19.6		41	Hawaii	12.1
2	Tennessee	33.6		42	Iowa	11.5
17	Texas	24.6		43	Rhode Island	10.8
32	Utah	19.2		44	Connecticut	10.5
NA	Vermont**	NA		45	New Hampshire	9.8
35	Virginia	15.9		46	North Dakota	7.4
24	Washington	21.5		47	Massachusetts	6.2
38	West Virginia	13.9		48	Maine	3.0
38	Wisconsin	13.9		NA	Montana**	NA
40	Wyoming	12.7		NA	Vermont**	NA
					District of Columbia	20.7

Source: Morgan Quitno Press using data from Federal Bureau of Investigation
"Crime in the United States 1996" (Uniform Crime Reports, October 4, 1997)
Of the 880,511 aggravated assaults in 1996 for which supplemental data were received by the F.B.I. There were an additional 149,303 aggravated assaults for which the type of weapon was not reported to the F.B.I. Aggravated assault is an attack for the purpose of inflicting severe bodily injury.
***Not available.*

Aggravated Assaults with Knives or Cutting Instruments in 1996

National Total = 157,292 Aggravated Assaults*

ALPHA ORDER

RANK	STATE	ASSAULTS	% of USA
19	Alabama	2,635	1.68%
37	Alaska	585	0.37%
18	Arizona	2,664	1.69%
25	Arkansas	1,468	0.93%
1	California	21,269	13.52%
24	Colorado	1,914	1.22%
31	Connecticut	917	0.58%
39	Delaware	466	0.30%
4	Florida	10,431	6.63%
9	Georgia	5,008	3.18%
44	Hawaii	155	0.10%
36	Idaho	601	0.38%
5	Illinois	9,524	6.05%
27	Indiana	1,399	0.89%
32	Iowa	742	0.47%
42	Kansas	338	0.21%
34	Kentucky	667	0.42%
12	Louisiana	3,996	2.54%
46	Maine	128	0.08%
10	Maryland	4,945	3.14%
13	Massachusetts	3,951	2.51%
7	Michigan	6,354	4.04%
23	Minnesota	2,104	1.34%
38	Mississippi	515	0.33%
16	Missouri	3,024	1.92%
NA	Montana**	NA	NA
35	Nebraska	634	0.40%
29	Nevada	1,048	0.67%
47	New Hampshire	84	0.05%
11	New Jersey	4,459	2.83%
28	New Mexico	1,386	0.88%
3	New York	12,018	7.64%
8	North Carolina	5,320	3.38%
48	North Dakota	33	0.02%
15	Ohio	3,262	2.07%
22	Oklahoma	2,201	1.40%
26	Oregon	1,410	0.90%
17	Pennsylvania	2,800	1.78%
40	Rhode Island	418	0.27%
6	South Carolina	6,610	4.20%
43	South Dakota	209	0.13%
14	Tennessee	3,610	2.30%
2	Texas	17,243	10.96%
33	Utah	720	0.46%
NA	Vermont**	NA	NA
21	Virginia	2,354	1.50%
20	Washington	2,498	1.59%
41	West Virginia	413	0.26%
30	Wisconsin	1,026	0.65%
45	Wyoming	135	0.09%

RANK ORDER

RANK	STATE	ASSAULTS	% of USA
1	California	21,269	13.52%
2	Texas	17,243	10.96%
3	New York	12,018	7.64%
4	Florida	10,431	6.63%
5	Illinois	9,524	6.05%
6	South Carolina	6,610	4.20%
7	Michigan	6,354	4.04%
8	North Carolina	5,320	3.38%
9	Georgia	5,008	3.18%
10	Maryland	4,945	3.14%
11	New Jersey	4,459	2.83%
12	Louisiana	3,996	2.54%
13	Massachusetts	3,951	2.51%
14	Tennessee	3,610	2.30%
15	Ohio	3,262	2.07%
16	Missouri	3,024	1.92%
17	Pennsylvania	2,800	1.78%
18	Arizona	2,664	1.69%
19	Alabama	2,635	1.68%
20	Washington	2,498	1.59%
21	Virginia	2,354	1.50%
22	Oklahoma	2,201	1.40%
23	Minnesota	2,104	1.34%
24	Colorado	1,914	1.22%
25	Arkansas	1,468	0.93%
26	Oregon	1,410	0.90%
27	Indiana	1,399	0.89%
28	New Mexico	1,386	0.88%
29	Nevada	1,048	0.67%
30	Wisconsin	1,026	0.65%
31	Connecticut	917	0.58%
32	Iowa	742	0.47%
33	Utah	720	0.46%
34	Kentucky	667	0.42%
35	Nebraska	634	0.40%
36	Idaho	601	0.38%
37	Alaska	585	0.37%
38	Mississippi	515	0.33%
39	Delaware	466	0.30%
40	Rhode Island	418	0.27%
41	West Virginia	413	0.26%
42	Kansas	338	0.21%
43	South Dakota	209	0.13%
44	Hawaii	155	0.10%
45	Wyoming	135	0.09%
46	Maine	128	0.08%
47	New Hampshire	84	0.05%
48	North Dakota	33	0.02%
NA	Montana**	NA	NA
NA	Vermont**	NA	NA
	District of Columbia	1,601	1.02%

Source: Federal Bureau of Investigation
"Crime in the United States 1996" (Uniform Crime Reports, October 4, 1997)
*Of the 880,511 aggravated assaults in 1996 for which supplemental data were received by the F.B.I. There were an additional 149,303 aggravated assaults for which the type of weapon was not reported to the F.B.I. Aggravated assault is an attack for the purpose of inflicting severe bodily injury.
**Not available.

Percent of Aggravated Assaults Involving Knives or Cutting Instruments in 1996

National Percent = 17.9% of Aggravated Assaults*

ALPHA ORDER				RANK ORDER		
RANK	STATE	PERCENT		RANK	STATE	PERCENT
26	Alabama	17.7		1	South Dakota	28.7
8	Alaska	20.8		2	Minnesota	27.7
40	Arizona	14.9		3	Idaho	23.9
30	Arkansas	16.6		4	South Carolina	23.6
44	California	12.7		5	Illinois	23.0
9	Colorado	20.7		6	Texas	21.4
36	Connecticut	15.4		7	New Jersey	20.9
10	Delaware	20.2		8	Alaska	20.8
18	Florida	19.1		9	Colorado	20.7
15	Georgia	19.5		10	Delaware	20.2
45	Hawaii	11.5		10	Maryland	20.2
3	Idaho	23.9		10	New York	20.2
5	Illinois	23.0		13	Virginia	19.9
46	Indiana	11.4		14	Ohio	19.6
31	Iowa	16.1		15	Georgia	19.5
33	Kansas	15.6		16	Louisiana	19.3
46	Kentucky	11.4		17	North Carolina	19.2
16	Louisiana	19.3		18	Florida	19.1
43	Maine	13.3		19	New Mexico	18.8
10	Maryland	20.2		20	Washington	18.7
42	Massachusetts	14.8		21	Michigan	18.6
21	Michigan	18.6		22	Rhode Island	18.2
2	Minnesota	27.7		23	Tennessee	18.1
31	Mississippi	16.1		24	Wyoming	17.9
29	Missouri	16.8		25	Utah	17.8
NA	Montana**	NA		26	Alabama	17.7
46	Nebraska	11.4		27	North Dakota	17.4
38	Nevada	15.2		28	New Hampshire	17.1
28	New Hampshire	17.1		29	Missouri	16.8
7	New Jersey	20.9		30	Arkansas	16.6
19	New Mexico	18.8		31	Iowa	16.1
10	New York	20.2		31	Mississippi	16.1
17	North Carolina	19.2		33	Kansas	15.6
27	North Dakota	17.4		33	Oregon	15.6
14	Ohio	19.6		35	West Virginia	15.5
37	Oklahoma	15.3		36	Connecticut	15.4
33	Oregon	15.6		37	Oklahoma	15.3
40	Pennsylvania	14.9		38	Nevada	15.2
22	Rhode Island	18.2		38	Wisconsin	15.2
4	South Carolina	23.6		40	Arizona	14.9
1	South Dakota	28.7		40	Pennsylvania	14.9
23	Tennessee	18.1		42	Massachusetts	14.8
6	Texas	21.4		43	Maine	13.3
25	Utah	17.8		44	California	12.7
NA	Vermont**	NA		45	Hawaii	11.5
13	Virginia	19.9		46	Indiana	11.4
20	Washington	18.7		46	Kentucky	11.4
35	West Virginia	15.5		46	Nebraska	11.4
38	Wisconsin	15.2		NA	Montana**	NA
24	Wyoming	17.9		NA	Vermont**	NA
					District of Columbia	25.4

Source: Morgan Quitno Press using data from Federal Bureau of Investigation
"Crime in the United States 1996" (Uniform Crime Reports, October 4, 1997)
*Of the 880,511 aggravated assaults in 1996 for which supplemental data were received by the F.B.I. There
were an additional 149,303 aggravated assaults for which the type of weapon was not reported to the F.B.I.
Aggravated assault is an attack for the purpose of inflicting severe bodily injury.
**Not available.

375

Aggravated Assaults with Blunt Objects and Other Dangerous Weapons in 1996

National Total = 294,556 Aggravated Assaults*

<table>
<tr><td colspan="4">ALPHA ORDER</td><td colspan="4">RANK ORDER</td></tr>
<tr><td>RANK</td><td>STATE</td><td>ASSAULTS</td><td>% of USA</td><td>RANK</td><td>STATE</td><td>ASSAULTS</td><td>% of USA</td></tr>
<tr><td>19</td><td>Alabama</td><td>4,431</td><td>1.50%</td><td>1</td><td>California</td><td>51,945</td><td>17.64%</td></tr>
<tr><td>41</td><td>Alaska</td><td>693</td><td>0.24%</td><td>2</td><td>Texas</td><td>26,260</td><td>8.92%</td></tr>
<tr><td>18</td><td>Arizona</td><td>4,868</td><td>1.65%</td><td>3</td><td>Florida</td><td>22,255</td><td>7.56%</td></tr>
<tr><td>29</td><td>Arkansas</td><td>1,993</td><td>0.68%</td><td>4</td><td>New York</td><td>19,374</td><td>6.58%</td></tr>
<tr><td>1</td><td>California</td><td>51,945</td><td>17.64%</td><td>5</td><td>Illinois</td><td>17,589</td><td>5.97%</td></tr>
<tr><td>24</td><td>Colorado</td><td>2,971</td><td>1.01%</td><td>6</td><td>Michigan</td><td>15,334</td><td>5.21%</td></tr>
<tr><td>28</td><td>Connecticut</td><td>1,999</td><td>0.68%</td><td>7</td><td>Massachusetts</td><td>10,892</td><td>3.70%</td></tr>
<tr><td>36</td><td>Delaware</td><td>1,090</td><td>0.37%</td><td>8</td><td>Maryland</td><td>10,590</td><td>3.60%</td></tr>
<tr><td>3</td><td>Florida</td><td>22,255</td><td>7.56%</td><td>9</td><td>South Carolina</td><td>10,274</td><td>3.49%</td></tr>
<tr><td>10</td><td>Georgia</td><td>8,275</td><td>2.81%</td><td>10</td><td>Georgia</td><td>8,275</td><td>2.81%</td></tr>
<tr><td>43</td><td>Hawaii</td><td>292</td><td>0.10%</td><td>11</td><td>North Carolina</td><td>8,032</td><td>2.73%</td></tr>
<tr><td>40</td><td>Idaho</td><td>807</td><td>0.27%</td><td>12</td><td>Louisiana</td><td>6,909</td><td>2.35%</td></tr>
<tr><td>5</td><td>Illinois</td><td>17,589</td><td>5.97%</td><td>13</td><td>New Jersey</td><td>6,659</td><td>2.26%</td></tr>
<tr><td>22</td><td>Indiana</td><td>3,244</td><td>1.10%</td><td>14</td><td>Tennessee</td><td>6,579</td><td>2.23%</td></tr>
<tr><td>35</td><td>Iowa</td><td>1,354</td><td>0.46%</td><td>15</td><td>Missouri</td><td>6,230</td><td>2.12%</td></tr>
<tr><td>37</td><td>Kansas</td><td>1,002</td><td>0.34%</td><td>16</td><td>Ohio</td><td>4,899</td><td>1.66%</td></tr>
<tr><td>33</td><td>Kentucky</td><td>1,501</td><td>0.51%</td><td>17</td><td>Oklahoma</td><td>4,890</td><td>1.66%</td></tr>
<tr><td>12</td><td>Louisiana</td><td>6,909</td><td>2.35%</td><td>18</td><td>Arizona</td><td>4,868</td><td>1.65%</td></tr>
<tr><td>44</td><td>Maine</td><td>258</td><td>0.09%</td><td>19</td><td>Alabama</td><td>4,431</td><td>1.50%</td></tr>
<tr><td>8</td><td>Maryland</td><td>10,590</td><td>3.60%</td><td>20</td><td>Pennsylvania</td><td>4,236</td><td>1.44%</td></tr>
<tr><td>7</td><td>Massachusetts</td><td>10,892</td><td>3.70%</td><td>21</td><td>Washington</td><td>4,161</td><td>1.41%</td></tr>
<tr><td>6</td><td>Michigan</td><td>15,334</td><td>5.21%</td><td>22</td><td>Indiana</td><td>3,244</td><td>1.10%</td></tr>
<tr><td>30</td><td>Minnesota</td><td>1,828</td><td>0.62%</td><td>23</td><td>Virginia</td><td>3,148</td><td>1.07%</td></tr>
<tr><td>39</td><td>Mississippi</td><td>836</td><td>0.28%</td><td>24</td><td>Colorado</td><td>2,971</td><td>1.01%</td></tr>
<tr><td>15</td><td>Missouri</td><td>6,230</td><td>2.12%</td><td>25</td><td>Oregon</td><td>2,932</td><td>1.00%</td></tr>
<tr><td>NA</td><td>Montana**</td><td>NA</td><td>NA</td><td>26</td><td>New Mexico</td><td>2,302</td><td>0.78%</td></tr>
<tr><td>34</td><td>Nebraska</td><td>1,451</td><td>0.49%</td><td>27</td><td>Nevada</td><td>2,244</td><td>0.76%</td></tr>
<tr><td>27</td><td>Nevada</td><td>2,244</td><td>0.76%</td><td>28</td><td>Connecticut</td><td>1,999</td><td>0.68%</td></tr>
<tr><td>47</td><td>New Hampshire</td><td>128</td><td>0.04%</td><td>29</td><td>Arkansas</td><td>1,993</td><td>0.68%</td></tr>
<tr><td>13</td><td>New Jersey</td><td>6,659</td><td>2.26%</td><td>30</td><td>Minnesota</td><td>1,828</td><td>0.62%</td></tr>
<tr><td>26</td><td>New Mexico</td><td>2,302</td><td>0.78%</td><td>31</td><td>Wisconsin</td><td>1,676</td><td>0.57%</td></tr>
<tr><td>4</td><td>New York</td><td>19,374</td><td>6.58%</td><td>32</td><td>Utah</td><td>1,605</td><td>0.54%</td></tr>
<tr><td>11</td><td>North Carolina</td><td>8,032</td><td>2.73%</td><td>33</td><td>Kentucky</td><td>1,501</td><td>0.51%</td></tr>
<tr><td>48</td><td>North Dakota</td><td>82</td><td>0.03%</td><td>34</td><td>Nebraska</td><td>1,451</td><td>0.49%</td></tr>
<tr><td>16</td><td>Ohio</td><td>4,899</td><td>1.66%</td><td>35</td><td>Iowa</td><td>1,354</td><td>0.46%</td></tr>
<tr><td>17</td><td>Oklahoma</td><td>4,890</td><td>1.66%</td><td>36</td><td>Delaware</td><td>1,090</td><td>0.37%</td></tr>
<tr><td>25</td><td>Oregon</td><td>2,932</td><td>1.00%</td><td>37</td><td>Kansas</td><td>1,002</td><td>0.34%</td></tr>
<tr><td>20</td><td>Pennsylvania</td><td>4,236</td><td>1.44%</td><td>38</td><td>Rhode Island</td><td>960</td><td>0.33%</td></tr>
<tr><td>38</td><td>Rhode Island</td><td>960</td><td>0.33%</td><td>39</td><td>Mississippi</td><td>836</td><td>0.28%</td></tr>
<tr><td>9</td><td>South Carolina</td><td>10,274</td><td>3.49%</td><td>40</td><td>Idaho</td><td>807</td><td>0.27%</td></tr>
<tr><td>46</td><td>South Dakota</td><td>178</td><td>0.06%</td><td>41</td><td>Alaska</td><td>693</td><td>0.24%</td></tr>
<tr><td>14</td><td>Tennessee</td><td>6,579</td><td>2.23%</td><td>42</td><td>West Virginia</td><td>507</td><td>0.17%</td></tr>
<tr><td>2</td><td>Texas</td><td>26,260</td><td>8.92%</td><td>43</td><td>Hawaii</td><td>292</td><td>0.10%</td></tr>
<tr><td>32</td><td>Utah</td><td>1,605</td><td>0.54%</td><td>44</td><td>Maine</td><td>258</td><td>0.09%</td></tr>
<tr><td>NA</td><td>Vermont**</td><td>NA</td><td>NA</td><td>45</td><td>Wyoming</td><td>210</td><td>0.07%</td></tr>
<tr><td>23</td><td>Virginia</td><td>3,148</td><td>1.07%</td><td>46</td><td>South Dakota</td><td>178</td><td>0.06%</td></tr>
<tr><td>21</td><td>Washington</td><td>4,161</td><td>1.41%</td><td>47</td><td>New Hampshire</td><td>128</td><td>0.04%</td></tr>
<tr><td>42</td><td>West Virginia</td><td>507</td><td>0.17%</td><td>48</td><td>North Dakota</td><td>82</td><td>0.03%</td></tr>
<tr><td>31</td><td>Wisconsin</td><td>1,676</td><td>0.57%</td><td>NA</td><td>Montana**</td><td>NA</td><td>NA</td></tr>
<tr><td>45</td><td>Wyoming</td><td>210</td><td>0.07%</td><td>NA</td><td>Vermont**</td><td>NA</td><td>NA</td></tr>
<tr><td></td><td></td><td></td><td></td><td></td><td>District of Columbia</td><td>2,583</td><td>0.88%</td></tr>
</table>

Source: Federal Bureau of Investigation
    "Crime in the United States 1996" (Uniform Crime Reports, October 4, 1997)
*Of the 880,511 aggravated assaults in 1996 for which supplemental data were received by the F.B.I. There were an additional 149,303 aggravated assaults for which the type of weapon was not reported to the F.B.I. Aggravated assault is an attack for the purpose of inflicting severe bodily injury.
**Not available.

Percent of Aggravated Assaults Involving Blunt Objects And Other Dangerous Weapons in 1996
National Percent = 33.5% of Aggravated Assaults*

ALPHA ORDER

ALPHA ORDER / RANK ORDER

RANK	STATE	PERCENT	RANK	STATE	PERCENT
28	Alabama	29.8	1	Delaware	47.4
42	Alaska	24.7	2	Kansas	46.4
33	Arizona	27.3	3	Michigan	44.9
45	Arkansas	22.5	4	Maryland	43.2
27	California	31.1	4	North Dakota	43.2
21	Colorado	32.2	6	Illinois	42.6
14	Connecticut	33.5	7	Rhode Island	41.7
1	Delaware	47.4	8	Florida	40.7
8	Florida	40.7	8	Massachusetts	40.7
21	Georgia	32.2	10	Utah	39.7
47	Hawaii	21.6	11	South Carolina	36.6
23	Idaho	32.1	12	Missouri	34.6
6	Illinois	42.6	13	Oklahoma	33.9
36	Indiana	26.4	14	Connecticut	33.5
29	Iowa	29.4	15	Louisiana	33.4
2	Kansas	46.4	16	Tennessee	33.1
40	Kentucky	25.6	17	Nevada	32.6
15	Louisiana	33.4	17	New York	32.6
34	Maine	26.9	17	Texas	32.6
4	Maryland	43.2	20	Oregon	32.4
8	Massachusetts	40.7	21	Colorado	32.2
3	Michigan	44.9	21	Georgia	32.2
44	Minnesota	24.1	23	Idaho	32.1
38	Mississippi	26.1	24	New Jersey	31.3
12	Missouri	34.6	25	New Mexico	31.2
NA	Montana**	NA	25	Washington	31.2
37	Nebraska	26.2	27	California	31.1
17	Nevada	32.6	28	Alabama	29.8
39	New Hampshire	26.0	29	Iowa	29.4
24	New Jersey	31.3	29	Ohio	29.4
25	New Mexico	31.2	31	North Carolina	28.9
17	New York	32.6	32	Wyoming	27.9
31	North Carolina	28.9	33	Arizona	27.3
4	North Dakota	43.2	34	Maine	26.9
29	Ohio	29.4	35	Virginia	26.6
13	Oklahoma	33.9	36	Indiana	26.4
20	Oregon	32.4	37	Nebraska	26.2
45	Pennsylvania	22.5	38	Mississippi	26.1
7	Rhode Island	41.7	39	New Hampshire	26.0
11	South Carolina	36.6	40	Kentucky	25.6
43	South Dakota	24.4	41	Wisconsin	24.8
16	Tennessee	33.1	42	Alaska	24.7
17	Texas	32.6	43	South Dakota	24.4
10	Utah	39.7	44	Minnesota	24.1
NA	Vermont**	NA	45	Arkansas	22.5
35	Virginia	26.6	45	Pennsylvania	22.5
25	Washington	31.2	47	Hawaii	21.6
48	West Virginia	19.0	48	West Virginia	19.0
41	Wisconsin	24.8	NA	Montana**	NA
32	Wyoming	27.9	NA	Vermont**	NA
				District of Columbia	40.9

Source: Morgan Quitno Press using data from Federal Bureau of Investigation
  "Crime in the United States 1996" (Uniform Crime Reports, October 4, 1997)
*Of the 880,511 aggravated assaults in 1996 for which supplemental data were received by the F.B.I. There were an additional 149,303 aggravated assaults for which the type of weapon was not reported to the F.B.I. Aggravated assault is an attack for the purpose of inflicting severe bodily injury.
**Not available.

Aggravated Assaults Committed with Hands, Fists or Feet in 1996

National Total = 228,753 Aggravated Assaults*

ALPHA ORDER

RANK	STATE	ASSAULTS	% of USA
18	Alabama	3,684	1.61%
37	Alaska	895	0.39%
14	Arizona	4,331	1.89%
25	Arkansas	2,805	1.23%
1	California	63,097	27.58%
30	Colorado	2,060	0.90%
28	Connecticut	2,431	1.06%
44	Delaware	298	0.13%
5	Florida	9,093	3.98%
10	Georgia	5,422	2.37%
38	Hawaii	739	0.32%
42	Idaho	338	0.15%
32	Illinois	1,963	0.86%
9	Indiana	5,538	2.42%
31	Iowa	1,976	0.86%
46	Kansas	228	0.10%
27	Kentucky	2,464	1.08%
20	Louisiana	3,382	1.48%
41	Maine	544	0.24%
16	Maryland	3,987	1.74%
4	Massachusetts	10,216	4.47%
19	Michigan	3,405	1.49%
33	Minnesota	1,781	0.78%
39	Mississippi	683	0.30%
21	Missouri	3,342	1.46%
NA	Montana**	NA	NA
26	Nebraska	2,660	1.16%
29	Nevada	2,099	0.92%
45	New Hampshire	232	0.10%
7	New Jersey	6,918	3.02%
35	New Mexico	1,278	0.56%
3	New York	14,416	6.30%
8	North Carolina	6,112	2.67%
48	North Dakota	61	0.03%
11	Ohio	4,714	2.06%
12	Oklahoma	4,521	1.98%
24	Oregon	2,955	1.29%
6	Pennsylvania	7,935	3.47%
40	Rhode Island	675	0.30%
15	South Carolina	4,286	1.87%
47	South Dakota	199	0.09%
23	Tennessee	3,014	1.32%
2	Texas	17,152	7.50%
36	Utah	938	0.41%
NA	Vermont**	NA	NA
13	Virginia	4,437	1.94%
17	Washington	3,820	1.67%
34	West Virginia	1,381	0.60%
22	Wisconsin	3,118	1.36%
43	Wyoming	312	0.14%

RANK ORDER

RANK	STATE	ASSAULTS	% of USA
1	California	63,097	27.58%
2	Texas	17,152	7.50%
3	New York	14,416	6.30%
4	Massachusetts	10,216	4.47%
5	Florida	9,093	3.98%
6	Pennsylvania	7,935	3.47%
7	New Jersey	6,918	3.02%
8	North Carolina	6,112	2.67%
9	Indiana	5,538	2.42%
10	Georgia	5,422	2.37%
11	Ohio	4,714	2.06%
12	Oklahoma	4,521	1.98%
13	Virginia	4,437	1.94%
14	Arizona	4,331	1.89%
15	South Carolina	4,286	1.87%
16	Maryland	3,987	1.74%
17	Washington	3,820	1.67%
18	Alabama	3,684	1.61%
19	Michigan	3,405	1.49%
20	Louisiana	3,382	1.48%
21	Missouri	3,342	1.46%
22	Wisconsin	3,118	1.36%
23	Tennessee	3,014	1.32%
24	Oregon	2,955	1.29%
25	Arkansas	2,805	1.23%
26	Nebraska	2,660	1.16%
27	Kentucky	2,464	1.08%
28	Connecticut	2,431	1.06%
29	Nevada	2,099	0.92%
30	Colorado	2,060	0.90%
31	Iowa	1,976	0.86%
32	Illinois	1,963	0.86%
33	Minnesota	1,781	0.78%
34	West Virginia	1,381	0.60%
35	New Mexico	1,278	0.56%
36	Utah	938	0.41%
37	Alaska	895	0.39%
38	Hawaii	739	0.32%
39	Mississippi	683	0.30%
40	Rhode Island	675	0.30%
41	Maine	544	0.24%
42	Idaho	338	0.15%
43	Wyoming	312	0.14%
44	Delaware	298	0.13%
45	New Hampshire	232	0.10%
46	Kansas	228	0.10%
47	South Dakota	199	0.09%
48	North Dakota	61	0.03%
NA	Montana**	NA	NA
NA	Vermont**	NA	NA
	District of Columbia	818	0.36%

Source: Federal Bureau of Investigation
"Crime in the United States 1996" (Uniform Crime Reports, October 4, 1997)
*Referred to as "personal weapons" by the F.B.I. Of the 880,511 aggravated assaults in 1996 for which supplemental data were received by the F.B.I. There were an additional 149,303 aggravated assaults for which the type of weapon was not reported to the F.B.I. Aggravated assault is an attack for the purpose of inflicting severe bodily injury. **Not available.

Percent of Aggravated Assaults Committed with Hands, Fists or Feet in 1996

National Percent = 26.0% of Aggravated Assaults*

<table>
<tr><td colspan="3">ALPHA ORDER</td><td colspan="3">RANK ORDER</td></tr>
<tr><td>RANK</td><td>STATE</td><td>PERCENT</td><td>RANK</td><td>STATE</td><td>PERCENT</td></tr>
<tr><td>27</td><td>Alabama</td><td>24.8</td><td>1</td><td>Maine</td><td>56.7</td></tr>
<tr><td>19</td><td>Alaska</td><td>31.9</td><td>2</td><td>Hawaii</td><td>54.7</td></tr>
<tr><td>28</td><td>Arizona</td><td>24.3</td><td>3</td><td>West Virginia</td><td>51.7</td></tr>
<tr><td>20</td><td>Arkansas</td><td>31.7</td><td>4</td><td>Nebraska</td><td>48.0</td></tr>
<tr><td>14</td><td>California</td><td>37.7</td><td>5</td><td>New Hampshire</td><td>47.2</td></tr>
<tr><td>32</td><td>Colorado</td><td>22.3</td><td>6</td><td>Wisconsin</td><td>46.1</td></tr>
<tr><td>12</td><td>Connecticut</td><td>40.7</td><td>7</td><td>Indiana</td><td>45.0</td></tr>
<tr><td>45</td><td>Delaware</td><td>12.9</td><td>8</td><td>Iowa</td><td>43.0</td></tr>
<tr><td>39</td><td>Florida</td><td>16.6</td><td>9</td><td>Pennsylvania</td><td>42.1</td></tr>
<tr><td>36</td><td>Georgia</td><td>21.1</td><td>10</td><td>Kentucky</td><td>42.0</td></tr>
<tr><td>2</td><td>Hawaii</td><td>54.7</td><td>11</td><td>Wyoming</td><td>41.4</td></tr>
<tr><td>44</td><td>Idaho</td><td>13.5</td><td>12</td><td>Connecticut</td><td>40.7</td></tr>
<tr><td>48</td><td>Illinois</td><td>4.7</td><td>13</td><td>Massachusetts</td><td>38.2</td></tr>
<tr><td>7</td><td>Indiana</td><td>45.0</td><td>14</td><td>California</td><td>37.7</td></tr>
<tr><td>8</td><td>Iowa</td><td>43.0</td><td>15</td><td>Virginia</td><td>37.5</td></tr>
<tr><td>46</td><td>Kansas</td><td>10.6</td><td>16</td><td>Oregon</td><td>32.7</td></tr>
<tr><td>10</td><td>Kentucky</td><td>42.0</td><td>17</td><td>New Jersey</td><td>32.5</td></tr>
<tr><td>40</td><td>Louisiana</td><td>16.4</td><td>18</td><td>North Dakota</td><td>32.1</td></tr>
<tr><td>1</td><td>Maine</td><td>56.7</td><td>19</td><td>Alaska</td><td>31.9</td></tr>
<tr><td>41</td><td>Maryland</td><td>16.2</td><td>20</td><td>Arkansas</td><td>31.7</td></tr>
<tr><td>13</td><td>Massachusetts</td><td>38.2</td><td>21</td><td>Oklahoma</td><td>31.3</td></tr>
<tr><td>47</td><td>Michigan</td><td>10.0</td><td>22</td><td>Nevada</td><td>30.5</td></tr>
<tr><td>30</td><td>Minnesota</td><td>23.5</td><td>23</td><td>Rhode Island</td><td>29.3</td></tr>
<tr><td>34</td><td>Mississippi</td><td>21.4</td><td>24</td><td>Washington</td><td>28.6</td></tr>
<tr><td>37</td><td>Missouri</td><td>18.6</td><td>25</td><td>Ohio</td><td>28.3</td></tr>
<tr><td>NA</td><td>Montana**</td><td>NA</td><td>26</td><td>South Dakota</td><td>27.3</td></tr>
<tr><td>4</td><td>Nebraska</td><td>48.0</td><td>27</td><td>Alabama</td><td>24.8</td></tr>
<tr><td>22</td><td>Nevada</td><td>30.5</td><td>28</td><td>Arizona</td><td>24.3</td></tr>
<tr><td>5</td><td>New Hampshire</td><td>47.2</td><td>29</td><td>New York</td><td>24.2</td></tr>
<tr><td>17</td><td>New Jersey</td><td>32.5</td><td>30</td><td>Minnesota</td><td>23.5</td></tr>
<tr><td>38</td><td>New Mexico</td><td>17.3</td><td>31</td><td>Utah</td><td>23.2</td></tr>
<tr><td>29</td><td>New York</td><td>24.2</td><td>32</td><td>Colorado</td><td>22.3</td></tr>
<tr><td>33</td><td>North Carolina</td><td>22.0</td><td>33</td><td>North Carolina</td><td>22.0</td></tr>
<tr><td>18</td><td>North Dakota</td><td>32.1</td><td>34</td><td>Mississippi</td><td>21.4</td></tr>
<tr><td>25</td><td>Ohio</td><td>28.3</td><td>35</td><td>Texas</td><td>21.3</td></tr>
<tr><td>21</td><td>Oklahoma</td><td>31.3</td><td>36</td><td>Georgia</td><td>21.1</td></tr>
<tr><td>16</td><td>Oregon</td><td>32.7</td><td>37</td><td>Missouri</td><td>18.6</td></tr>
<tr><td>9</td><td>Pennsylvania</td><td>42.1</td><td>38</td><td>New Mexico</td><td>17.3</td></tr>
<tr><td>23</td><td>Rhode Island</td><td>29.3</td><td>39</td><td>Florida</td><td>16.6</td></tr>
<tr><td>42</td><td>South Carolina</td><td>15.3</td><td>40</td><td>Louisiana</td><td>16.4</td></tr>
<tr><td>26</td><td>South Dakota</td><td>27.3</td><td>41</td><td>Maryland</td><td>16.2</td></tr>
<tr><td>43</td><td>Tennessee</td><td>15.2</td><td>42</td><td>South Carolina</td><td>15.3</td></tr>
<tr><td>35</td><td>Texas</td><td>21.3</td><td>43</td><td>Tennessee</td><td>15.2</td></tr>
<tr><td>31</td><td>Utah</td><td>23.2</td><td>44</td><td>Idaho</td><td>13.5</td></tr>
<tr><td>NA</td><td>Vermont**</td><td>NA</td><td>45</td><td>Delaware</td><td>12.9</td></tr>
<tr><td>15</td><td>Virginia</td><td>37.5</td><td>46</td><td>Kansas</td><td>10.6</td></tr>
<tr><td>24</td><td>Washington</td><td>28.6</td><td>47</td><td>Michigan</td><td>10.0</td></tr>
<tr><td>3</td><td>West Virginia</td><td>51.7</td><td>48</td><td>Illinois</td><td>4.7</td></tr>
<tr><td>6</td><td>Wisconsin</td><td>46.1</td><td>NA</td><td>Montana**</td><td>NA</td></tr>
<tr><td>11</td><td>Wyoming</td><td>41.4</td><td>NA</td><td>Vermont**</td><td>NA</td></tr>
<tr><td></td><td></td><td></td><td></td><td>District of Columbia</td><td>13.0</td></tr>
</table>

Source: Morgan Quitno Press using data from Federal Bureau of Investigation
   "Crime in the United States 1996" (Uniform Crime Reports, October 4, 1997)
*Referred to as "personal weapons" by the F.B.I. Of the 880,511 aggravated assaults in 1996 for which supplemental data were received by the F.B.I. There were an additional 149,303 aggravated assaults for which the type of weapon was not reported to the F.B.I. Aggravated assault is an attack for the purpose of inflicting severe bodily injury. **Not available.

Property Crimes in 1996

National Total = 11,791,336 Property Crimes*

ALPHA ORDER

RANK	STATE	CRIMES	% of USA
24	Alabama	181,803	1.54%
46	Alaska	28,667	0.24%
13	Arizona	284,964	2.42%
33	Arkansas	104,790	0.89%
1	California	1,385,135	11.75%
25	Colorado	180,218	1.53%
28	Connecticut	124,924	1.06%
45	Delaware	30,643	0.26%
3	Florida	928,273	7.87%
8	Georgia	416,986	3.54%
37	Hawaii	74,639	0.63%
39	Idaho	44,532	0.38%
5	Illinois	524,777	4.45%
19	Indiana	231,376	1.96%
35	Iowa	96,296	0.82%
31	Kansas	109,772	0.93%
30	Kentucky	110,531	0.94%
15	Louisiana	257,130	2.18%
41	Maine	40,636	0.34%
14	Maryland	260,231	2.21%
20	Massachusetts	194,636	1.65%
7	Michigan	430,020	3.65%
22	Minnesota	192,109	1.63%
32	Mississippi	109,581	0.93%
18	Missouri	240,781	2.04%
42	Montana	38,084	0.32%
38	Nebraska	66,110	0.56%
36	Nevada	83,047	0.70%
44	New Hampshire	31,436	0.27%
11	New Jersey	303,657	2.58%
34	New Mexico	98,698	0.84%
4	New York	619,250	5.25%
9	North Carolina	361,616	3.07%
50	North Dakota	16,648	0.14%
6	Ohio	449,935	3.82%
27	Oklahoma	166,892	1.42%
26	Oregon	177,295	1.50%
10	Pennsylvania	356,864	3.03%
43	Rhode Island	36,099	0.31%
21	South Carolina	192,986	1.64%
47	South Dakota	20,443	0.17%
16	Tennessee	248,729	2.11%
2	Texas	968,732	8.22%
29	Utah	113,079	0.96%
49	Vermont	16,973	0.14%
17	Virginia	242,100	2.05%
12	Washington	303,111	2.57%
40	West Virginia	41,510	0.35%
23	Wisconsin	184,143	1.56%
48	Wyoming	19,261	0.16%

RANK ORDER

RANK	STATE	CRIMES	% of USA
1	California	1,385,135	11.75%
2	Texas	968,732	8.22%
3	Florida	928,273	7.87%
4	New York	619,250	5.25%
5	Illinois	524,777	4.45%
6	Ohio	449,935	3.82%
7	Michigan	430,020	3.65%
8	Georgia	416,986	3.54%
9	North Carolina	361,616	3.07%
10	Pennsylvania	356,864	3.03%
11	New Jersey	303,657	2.58%
12	Washington	303,111	2.57%
13	Arizona	284,964	2.42%
14	Maryland	260,231	2.21%
15	Louisiana	257,130	2.18%
16	Tennessee	248,729	2.11%
17	Virginia	242,100	2.05%
18	Missouri	240,781	2.04%
19	Indiana	231,376	1.96%
20	Massachusetts	194,636	1.65%
21	South Carolina	192,986	1.64%
22	Minnesota	192,109	1.63%
23	Wisconsin	184,143	1.56%
24	Alabama	181,803	1.54%
25	Colorado	180,218	1.53%
26	Oregon	177,295	1.50%
27	Oklahoma	166,892	1.42%
28	Connecticut	124,924	1.06%
29	Utah	113,079	0.96%
30	Kentucky	110,531	0.94%
31	Kansas	109,772	0.93%
32	Mississippi	109,581	0.93%
33	Arkansas	104,790	0.89%
34	New Mexico	98,698	0.84%
35	Iowa	96,296	0.82%
36	Nevada	83,047	0.70%
37	Hawaii	74,639	0.63%
38	Nebraska	66,110	0.56%
39	Idaho	44,532	0.38%
40	West Virginia	41,510	0.35%
41	Maine	40,636	0.34%
42	Montana	38,084	0.32%
43	Rhode Island	36,099	0.31%
44	New Hampshire	31,436	0.27%
45	Delaware	30,643	0.26%
46	Alaska	28,667	0.24%
47	South Dakota	20,443	0.17%
48	Wyoming	19,261	0.16%
49	Vermont	16,973	0.14%
50	North Dakota	16,648	0.14%
	District of Columbia	51,188	0.43%

Source: Federal Bureau of Investigation
"Crime in the United States 1996" (Uniform Crime Reports, October 4, 1997)
*Property crimes are offenses of burglary, larceny-theft and motor vehicle theft.

Average Time Between Property Crimes in 1996

National Rate = A Property Crime Occurs Every 3 Seconds*

ALPHA ORDER				RANK ORDER		
RANK	STATE	MINUTES.SECONDS		RANK	STATE	MINUTES.SECONDS
27	Alabama	2.54		1	North Dakota	31.40
5	Alaska	18.23		2	Vermont	31.03
38	Arizona	1.51		3	Wyoming	27.22
18	Arkansas	5.02		4	South Dakota	25.47
50	California	0.23		5	Alaska	18.23
26	Colorado	2.55		6	Delaware	17.12
23	Connecticut	4.13		7	New Hampshire	16.46
6	Delaware	17.12		8	Rhode Island	14.36
48	Florida	0.34		9	Montana	13.50
43	Georgia	1.16		10	Maine	12.58
14	Hawaii	7.04		11	West Virginia	12.42
12	Idaho	11.50		12	Idaho	11.50
46	Illinois	1.00		13	Nebraska	7.58
32	Indiana	2.17		14	Hawaii	7.04
16	Iowa	5.28		15	Nevada	6.21
20	Kansas	4.48		16	Iowa	5.28
21	Kentucky	4.46		17	New Mexico	5.20
36	Louisiana	2.03		18	Arkansas	5.02
10	Maine	12.58		19	Mississippi	4.49
37	Maryland	2.02		20	Kansas	4.48
31	Massachusetts	2.43		21	Kentucky	4.46
44	Michigan	1.14		22	Utah	4.40
29	Minnesota	2.44		23	Connecticut	4.13
19	Mississippi	4.49		24	Oklahoma	3.10
33	Missouri	2.11		25	Oregon	2.58
9	Montana	13.50		26	Colorado	2.55
13	Nebraska	7.58		27	Alabama	2.54
15	Nevada	6.21		28	Wisconsin	2.52
7	New Hampshire	16.46		29	Minnesota	2.44
39	New Jersey	1.44		29	South Carolina	2.44
17	New Mexico	5.20		31	Massachusetts	2.43
47	New York	0.51		32	Indiana	2.17
42	North Carolina	1.28		33	Missouri	2.11
1	North Dakota	31.40		33	Virginia	2.11
45	Ohio	1.10		35	Tennessee	2.07
24	Oklahoma	3.10		36	Louisiana	2.03
25	Oregon	2.58		37	Maryland	2.02
41	Pennsylvania	1.29		38	Arizona	1.51
8	Rhode Island	14.36		39	New Jersey	1.44
29	South Carolina	2.44		39	Washington	1.44
4	South Dakota	25.47		41	Pennsylvania	1.29
35	Tennessee	2.07		42	North Carolina	1.28
49	Texas	0.32		43	Georgia	1.16
22	Utah	4.40		44	Michigan	1.14
2	Vermont	31.03		45	Ohio	1.10
33	Virginia	2.11		46	Illinois	1.00
39	Washington	1.44		47	New York	0.51
11	West Virginia	12.42		48	Florida	0.34
28	Wisconsin	2.52		49	Texas	0.32
3	Wyoming	27.22		50	California	0.23
					District of Columbia	10.18

Source: Morgan Quitno Press using data from Federal Bureau of Investigation
    "Crime in the United States 1996" (Uniform Crime Reports, October 4, 1997)
*Property crimes are offenses of burglary, larceny-theft and motor vehicle theft.

Property Crimes per Square Mile in 1996

National Rate = 3.2 Property Crimes per Square Mile*

<table>
<tr><td colspan="3">ALPHA ORDER</td><td colspan="3">RANK ORDER</td></tr>
<tr><td>RANK</td><td>STATE</td><td>RATE</td><td>RANK</td><td>STATE</td><td>RATE</td></tr>
<tr><td>24</td><td>Alabama</td><td>3.5</td><td>1</td><td>New Jersey</td><td>37.0</td></tr>
<tr><td>50</td><td>Alaska</td><td>0.0</td><td>2</td><td>Rhode Island</td><td>29.3</td></tr>
<tr><td>29</td><td>Arizona</td><td>2.5</td><td>3</td><td>Connecticut</td><td>22.5</td></tr>
<tr><td>33</td><td>Arkansas</td><td>2.0</td><td>4</td><td>Maryland</td><td>21.2</td></tr>
<tr><td>12</td><td>California</td><td>8.7</td><td>5</td><td>Massachusetts</td><td>21.1</td></tr>
<tr><td>36</td><td>Colorado</td><td>1.7</td><td>6</td><td>Florida</td><td>15.5</td></tr>
<tr><td>3</td><td>Connecticut</td><td>22.5</td><td>7</td><td>Delaware</td><td>12.8</td></tr>
<tr><td>7</td><td>Delaware</td><td>12.8</td><td>8</td><td>Hawaii</td><td>11.6</td></tr>
<tr><td>6</td><td>Florida</td><td>15.5</td><td>9</td><td>New York</td><td>11.5</td></tr>
<tr><td>14</td><td>Georgia</td><td>7.1</td><td>10</td><td>Ohio</td><td>10.0</td></tr>
<tr><td>8</td><td>Hawaii</td><td>11.6</td><td>11</td><td>Illinois</td><td>9.1</td></tr>
<tr><td>45</td><td>Idaho</td><td>0.5</td><td>12</td><td>California</td><td>8.7</td></tr>
<tr><td>11</td><td>Illinois</td><td>9.1</td><td>13</td><td>Pennsylvania</td><td>7.7</td></tr>
<tr><td>16</td><td>Indiana</td><td>6.4</td><td>14</td><td>Georgia</td><td>7.1</td></tr>
<tr><td>36</td><td>Iowa</td><td>1.7</td><td>15</td><td>North Carolina</td><td>6.9</td></tr>
<tr><td>39</td><td>Kansas</td><td>1.3</td><td>16</td><td>Indiana</td><td>6.4</td></tr>
<tr><td>28</td><td>Kentucky</td><td>2.7</td><td>17</td><td>South Carolina</td><td>6.2</td></tr>
<tr><td>20</td><td>Louisiana</td><td>5.2</td><td>18</td><td>Tennessee</td><td>5.9</td></tr>
<tr><td>41</td><td>Maine</td><td>1.2</td><td>19</td><td>Virginia</td><td>5.7</td></tr>
<tr><td>4</td><td>Maryland</td><td>21.2</td><td>20</td><td>Louisiana</td><td>5.2</td></tr>
<tr><td>5</td><td>Massachusetts</td><td>21.1</td><td>21</td><td>Michigan</td><td>4.4</td></tr>
<tr><td>21</td><td>Michigan</td><td>4.4</td><td>22</td><td>Washington</td><td>4.3</td></tr>
<tr><td>32</td><td>Minnesota</td><td>2.2</td><td>23</td><td>Texas</td><td>3.6</td></tr>
<tr><td>31</td><td>Mississippi</td><td>2.3</td><td>24</td><td>Alabama</td><td>3.5</td></tr>
<tr><td>24</td><td>Missouri</td><td>3.5</td><td>24</td><td>Missouri</td><td>3.5</td></tr>
<tr><td>46</td><td>Montana</td><td>0.3</td><td>26</td><td>New Hampshire</td><td>3.4</td></tr>
<tr><td>42</td><td>Nebraska</td><td>0.9</td><td>27</td><td>Wisconsin</td><td>2.8</td></tr>
<tr><td>43</td><td>Nevada</td><td>0.8</td><td>28</td><td>Kentucky</td><td>2.7</td></tr>
<tr><td>26</td><td>New Hampshire</td><td>3.4</td><td>29</td><td>Arizona</td><td>2.5</td></tr>
<tr><td>1</td><td>New Jersey</td><td>37.0</td><td>30</td><td>Oklahoma</td><td>2.4</td></tr>
<tr><td>43</td><td>New Mexico</td><td>0.8</td><td>31</td><td>Mississippi</td><td>2.3</td></tr>
<tr><td>9</td><td>New York</td><td>11.5</td><td>32</td><td>Minnesota</td><td>2.2</td></tr>
<tr><td>15</td><td>North Carolina</td><td>6.9</td><td>33</td><td>Arkansas</td><td>2.0</td></tr>
<tr><td>48</td><td>North Dakota</td><td>0.2</td><td>34</td><td>Oregon</td><td>1.8</td></tr>
<tr><td>10</td><td>Ohio</td><td>10.0</td><td>34</td><td>Vermont</td><td>1.8</td></tr>
<tr><td>30</td><td>Oklahoma</td><td>2.4</td><td>36</td><td>Colorado</td><td>1.7</td></tr>
<tr><td>34</td><td>Oregon</td><td>1.8</td><td>36</td><td>Iowa</td><td>1.7</td></tr>
<tr><td>13</td><td>Pennsylvania</td><td>7.7</td><td>36</td><td>West Virginia</td><td>1.7</td></tr>
<tr><td>2</td><td>Rhode Island</td><td>29.3</td><td>39</td><td>Kansas</td><td>1.3</td></tr>
<tr><td>17</td><td>South Carolina</td><td>6.2</td><td>39</td><td>Utah</td><td>1.3</td></tr>
<tr><td>46</td><td>South Dakota</td><td>0.3</td><td>41</td><td>Maine</td><td>1.2</td></tr>
<tr><td>18</td><td>Tennessee</td><td>5.9</td><td>42</td><td>Nebraska</td><td>0.9</td></tr>
<tr><td>23</td><td>Texas</td><td>3.6</td><td>43</td><td>Nevada</td><td>0.8</td></tr>
<tr><td>39</td><td>Utah</td><td>1.3</td><td>43</td><td>New Mexico</td><td>0.8</td></tr>
<tr><td>34</td><td>Vermont</td><td>1.8</td><td>45</td><td>Idaho</td><td>0.5</td></tr>
<tr><td>19</td><td>Virginia</td><td>5.7</td><td>46</td><td>Montana</td><td>0.3</td></tr>
<tr><td>22</td><td>Washington</td><td>4.3</td><td>46</td><td>South Dakota</td><td>0.3</td></tr>
<tr><td>36</td><td>West Virginia</td><td>1.7</td><td>48</td><td>North Dakota</td><td>0.2</td></tr>
<tr><td>27</td><td>Wisconsin</td><td>2.8</td><td>48</td><td>Wyoming</td><td>0.2</td></tr>
<tr><td>48</td><td>Wyoming</td><td>0.2</td><td>50</td><td>Alaska</td><td>0.0</td></tr>
<tr><td></td><td></td><td></td><td></td><td>District of Columbia</td><td>752.8</td></tr>
</table>

Source: Morgan Quitno Press using data from Federal Bureau of Investigation
    "Crime in the United States 1996" (Uniform Crime Reports, October 4, 1997)
*Property crimes are offenses of burglary, larceny-theft and motor vehicle theft.

Percent Change in Number of Property Crimes: 1995 to 1996

National Percent Change = 2.3% Decrease*

ALPHA ORDER			RANK ORDER		
RANK	STATE	PERCENT CHANGE	RANK	STATE	PERCENT CHANGE
13	Alabama	1.4	1	Georgia	8.3
36	Alaska	(4.8)	2	New Hampshire	7.8
47	Arizona	(9.9)	3	Louisiana	4.5
11	Arkansas	2.0	4	New Mexico	4.4
47	California	(9.9)	5	Maine	3.8
29	Colorado	(3.0)	6	South Carolina	3.4
42	Connecticut	(6.9)	7	Oklahoma	3.2
32	Delaware	(3.6)	8	Tennessee	3.1
24	Florida	(1.2)	8	Texas	3.1
1	Georgia	8.3	10	Ohio	2.9
45	Hawaii	(8.9)	11	Arkansas	2.0
39	Idaho	(6.1)	12	Missouri	1.5
23	Illinois	(0.5)	13	Alabama	1.4
28	Indiana	(2.9)	14	Mississippi	1.3
46	Iowa	(9.6)	15	West Virginia	1.0
35	Kansas	(4.2)	16	Virginia	0.8
34	Kentucky	(4.1)	17	North Carolina	0.7
3	Louisiana	4.5	18	Minnesota	0.6
5	Maine	3.8	18	Pennsylvania	0.6
27	Maryland	(2.8)	18	Utah	0.6
49	Massachusetts	(12.3)	21	Michigan	0.2
21	Michigan	0.2	22	Wisconsin	(0.3)
18	Minnesota	0.6	23	Illinois	(0.5)
14	Mississippi	1.3	24	Florida	(1.2)
12	Missouri	1.5	25	Wyoming	(1.3)
37	Montana	(5.4)	26	South Dakota	(1.7)
29	Nebraska	(3.0)	27	Maryland	(2.8)
33	Nevada	(3.7)	28	Indiana	(2.9)
2	New Hampshire	7.8	29	Colorado	(3.0)
42	New Jersey	(6.9)	29	Nebraska	(3.0)
4	New Mexico	4.4	31	Washington	(3.5)
44	New York	(8.2)	32	Delaware	(3.6)
17	North Carolina	0.7	33	Nevada	(3.7)
40	North Dakota	(6.6)	34	Kentucky	(4.1)
10	Ohio	2.9	35	Kansas	(4.2)
7	Oklahoma	3.2	36	Alaska	(4.8)
40	Oregon	(6.6)	37	Montana	(5.4)
18	Pennsylvania	0.6	38	Rhode Island	(5.9)
38	Rhode Island	(5.9)	39	Idaho	(6.1)
6	South Carolina	3.4	40	North Dakota	(6.6)
26	South Dakota	(1.7)	40	Oregon	(6.6)
8	Tennessee	3.1	42	Connecticut	(6.9)
8	Texas	3.1	42	New Jersey	(6.9)
18	Utah	0.6	44	New York	(8.2)
50	Vermont	(12.5)	45	Hawaii	(8.9)
16	Virginia	0.8	46	Iowa	(9.6)
31	Washington	(3.5)	47	Arizona	(9.9)
15	West Virginia	1.0	47	California	(9.9)
22	Wisconsin	(0.3)	49	Massachusetts	(12.3)
25	Wyoming	(1.3)	50	Vermont	(12.5)
				District of Columbia	(2.9)

Source: Federal Bureau of Investigation
   "Crime in the United States 1996" (Uniform Crime Reports, October 4, 1997)
*Property crimes are offenses of burglary, larceny-theft and motor vehicle theft.

Property Crime Rate in 1996

National Rate = 4,444.8 Property Crimes per 100,000 Population*

ALPHA ORDER

RANK	STATE	RATE
25	Alabama	4,254.7
16	Alaska	4,722.7
2	Arizona	6,435.5
27	Arkansas	4,174.9
22	California	4,345.1
17	Colorado	4,714.0
34	Connecticut	3,815.6
26	Delaware	4,226.6
1	Florida	6,446.3
6	Georgia	5,671.0
3	Hawaii	6,304.0
36	Idaho	3,745.3
21	Illinois	4,429.6
33	Indiana	3,961.2
41	Iowa	3,376.4
24	Kansas	4,268.0
46	Kentucky	2,845.8
4	Louisiana	5,909.7
42	Maine	3,269.2
12	Maryland	5,130.7
43	Massachusetts	3,194.9
20	Michigan	4,482.2
28	Minnesota	4,124.3
29	Mississippi	4,034.6
19	Missouri	4,493.0
23	Montana	4,332.7
32	Nebraska	4,001.8
11	Nevada	5,180.7
48	New Hampshire	2,705.3
35	New Jersey	3,801.4
5	New Mexico	5,761.7
40	New York	3,405.3
15	North Carolina	4,938.1
49	North Dakota	2,585.1
30	Ohio	4,027.0
14	Oklahoma	5,055.8
8	Oregon	5,533.6
44	Pennsylvania	2,960.1
37	Rhode Island	3,646.4
10	South Carolina	5,217.2
47	South Dakota	2,792.8
18	Tennessee	4,675.4
13	Texas	5,064.5
7	Utah	5,654.0
45	Vermont	2,881.7
38	Virginia	3,627.0
9	Washington	5,478.2
50	West Virginia	2,273.3
39	Wisconsin	3,568.7
31	Wyoming	4,004.4

RANK ORDER

RANK	STATE	RATE
1	Florida	6,446.3
2	Arizona	6,435.5
3	Hawaii	6,304.0
4	Louisiana	5,909.7
5	New Mexico	5,761.7
6	Georgia	5,671.0
7	Utah	5,654.0
8	Oregon	5,533.6
9	Washington	5,478.2
10	South Carolina	5,217.2
11	Nevada	5,180.7
12	Maryland	5,130.7
13	Texas	5,064.5
14	Oklahoma	5,055.8
15	North Carolina	4,938.1
16	Alaska	4,722.7
17	Colorado	4,714.0
18	Tennessee	4,675.4
19	Missouri	4,493.0
20	Michigan	4,482.2
21	Illinois	4,429.6
22	California	4,345.1
23	Montana	4,332.7
24	Kansas	4,268.0
25	Alabama	4,254.7
26	Delaware	4,226.6
27	Arkansas	4,174.9
28	Minnesota	4,124.3
29	Mississippi	4,034.6
30	Ohio	4,027.0
31	Wyoming	4,004.4
32	Nebraska	4,001.8
33	Indiana	3,961.2
34	Connecticut	3,815.6
35	New Jersey	3,801.4
36	Idaho	3,745.3
37	Rhode Island	3,646.4
38	Virginia	3,627.0
39	Wisconsin	3,568.7
40	New York	3,405.3
41	Iowa	3,376.4
42	Maine	3,269.2
43	Massachusetts	3,194.9
44	Pennsylvania	2,960.1
45	Vermont	2,881.7
46	Kentucky	2,845.8
47	South Dakota	2,792.8
48	New Hampshire	2,705.3
49	North Dakota	2,585.1
50	West Virginia	2,273.3
	District of Columbia	9,426.9

Source: Federal Bureau of Investigation

"Crime in the United States 1996" (Uniform Crime Reports, October 4, 1997)
Property crimes are offenses of burglary, larceny-theft and motor vehicle theft.

Percent Change in Property Crime Rate: 1995 to 1996

National Percent Change = 3.2% Decrease*

ALPHA ORDER				RANK ORDER		
RANK	STATE	PERCENT CHANGE		RANK	STATE	PERCENT CHANGE
11	Alabama	0.9		1	New Hampshire	6.5
34	Alaska	(5.2)		2	Georgia	6.1
50	Arizona	(14.2)		3	Louisiana	4.3
11	Arkansas	0.9		4	Maine	3.7
47	California	(10.7)		5	New Mexico	2.7
33	Colorado	(4.9)		5	Ohio	2.7
38	Connecticut	(6.9)		5	South Carolina	2.7
31	Delaware	(4.7)		8	Oklahoma	2.5
26	Florida	(2.8)		9	Tennessee	1.8
2	Georgia	6.1		10	West Virginia	1.1
45	Hawaii	(8.7)		11	Alabama	0.9
42	Idaho	(8.2)		11	Arkansas	0.9
20	Illinois	(0.7)		11	Texas	0.9
28	Indiana	(3.5)		14	Missouri	0.8
46	Iowa	(9.9)		14	Pennsylvania	0.8
30	Kansas	(4.4)		16	Mississippi	0.6
31	Kentucky	(4.7)		17	Virginia	0.0
3	Louisiana	4.3		18	Michigan	(0.3)
4	Maine	3.7		19	Minnesota	(0.4)
27	Maryland	(3.3)		20	Illinois	(0.7)
48	Massachusetts	(12.6)		21	Wisconsin	(1.0)
18	Michigan	(0.3)		22	North Carolina	(1.1)
19	Minnesota	(0.4)		23	Wyoming	(1.5)
16	Mississippi	0.6		24	Utah	(1.9)
14	Missouri	0.8		25	South Dakota	(2.1)
37	Montana	(6.3)		26	Florida	(2.8)
29	Nebraska	(3.9)		27	Maryland	(3.3)
41	Nevada	(8.0)		28	Indiana	(3.5)
1	New Hampshire	6.5		29	Nebraska	(3.9)
40	New Jersey	(7.4)		30	Kansas	(4.4)
5	New Mexico	2.7		31	Delaware	(4.7)
43	New York	(8.4)		31	Kentucky	(4.7)
22	North Carolina	(1.1)		33	Colorado	(4.9)
39	North Dakota	(7.0)		34	Alaska	(5.2)
5	Ohio	2.7		35	Washington	(5.3)
8	Oklahoma	2.5		36	Rhode Island	(5.9)
43	Oregon	(8.4)		37	Montana	(6.3)
14	Pennsylvania	0.8		38	Connecticut	(6.9)
36	Rhode Island	(5.9)		39	North Dakota	(7.0)
5	South Carolina	2.7		40	New Jersey	(7.4)
25	South Dakota	(2.1)		41	Nevada	(8.0)
9	Tennessee	1.8		42	Idaho	(8.2)
11	Texas	0.9		43	New York	(8.4)
24	Utah	(1.9)		43	Oregon	(8.4)
49	Vermont	(13.1)		45	Hawaii	(8.7)
17	Virginia	0.0		46	Iowa	(9.9)
35	Washington	(5.3)		47	California	(10.7)
10	West Virginia	1.1		48	Massachusetts	(12.6)
21	Wisconsin	(1.0)		49	Vermont	(13.1)
23	Wyoming	(1.5)		50	Arizona	(14.2)
					District of Columbia	(0.9)

Source: Federal Bureau of Investigation
"Crime in the United States 1996" (Uniform Crime Reports, October 4, 1997)
Property crimes are offenses of burglary, larceny-theft and motor vehicle theft.

Burglaries in 1996

National Total = 2,501,524 Burglaries*

<u>ALPHA ORDER</u>   <u>RANK ORDER</u>

RANK	STATE	BURGLARIES	% of USA		RANK	STATE	BURGLARIES	% of USA
21	Alabama	42,821	1.71%		1	California	312,212	12.48%
44	Alaska	5,118	0.20%		2	Florida	219,056	8.76%
15	Arizona	55,630	2.22%		3	Texas	204,390	8.17%
32	Arkansas	23,925	0.96%		4	New York	129,828	5.19%
1	California	312,212	12.48%		5	Illinois	108,185	4.32%
25	Colorado	34,436	1.38%		6	North Carolina	98,539	3.94%
29	Connecticut	27,574	1.10%		7	Ohio	93,336	3.73%
43	Delaware	5,830	0.23%		8	Michigan	85,908	3.43%
2	Florida	219,056	8.76%		9	Georgia	81,968	3.28%
9	Georgia	81,968	3.28%		10	Pennsylvania	66,481	2.66%
37	Hawaii	12,781	0.51%		11	New Jersey	63,259	2.53%
41	Idaho	8,431	0.34%		12	Tennessee	61,896	2.47%
5	Illinois	108,185	4.32%		13	Washington	58,512	2.34%
19	Indiana	45,782	1.83%		14	Louisiana	56,379	2.25%
35	Iowa	18,954	0.76%		15	Arizona	55,630	2.22%
31	Kansas	25,239	1.01%		16	Maryland	50,331	2.01%
30	Kentucky	26,736	1.07%		17	Missouri	47,919	1.92%
14	Louisiana	56,379	2.25%		18	South Carolina	47,487	1.90%
40	Maine	9,303	0.37%		19	Indiana	45,782	1.83%
16	Maryland	50,331	2.01%		20	Massachusetts	42,896	1.71%
20	Massachusetts	42,896	1.71%		21	Alabama	42,821	1.71%
8	Michigan	85,908	3.43%		22	Oklahoma	41,447	1.66%
24	Minnesota	35,515	1.42%		23	Virginia	39,255	1.57%
27	Mississippi	30,755	1.23%		24	Minnesota	35,515	1.42%
17	Missouri	47,919	1.92%		25	Colorado	34,436	1.38%
46	Montana	4,908	0.20%		26	Oregon	31,664	1.27%
38	Nebraska	10,152	0.41%		27	Mississippi	30,755	1.23%
34	Nevada	19,558	0.78%		28	Wisconsin	30,356	1.21%
45	New Hampshire	5,063	0.20%		29	Connecticut	27,574	1.10%
11	New Jersey	63,259	2.53%		30	Kentucky	26,736	1.07%
33	New Mexico	23,586	0.94%		31	Kansas	25,239	1.01%
4	New York	129,828	5.19%		32	Arkansas	23,925	0.96%
6	North Carolina	98,539	3.94%		33	New Mexico	23,586	0.94%
50	North Dakota	1,991	0.08%		34	Nevada	19,558	0.78%
7	Ohio	93,336	3.73%		35	Iowa	18,954	0.76%
22	Oklahoma	41,447	1.66%		36	Utah	16,965	0.68%
26	Oregon	31,664	1.27%		37	Hawaii	12,781	0.51%
10	Pennsylvania	66,481	2.66%		38	Nebraska	10,152	0.41%
42	Rhode Island	8,135	0.33%		39	West Virginia	9,979	0.40%
18	South Carolina	47,487	1.90%		40	Maine	9,303	0.37%
47	South Dakota	4,077	0.16%		41	Idaho	8,431	0.34%
12	Tennessee	61,896	2.47%		42	Rhode Island	8,135	0.33%
3	Texas	204,390	8.17%		43	Delaware	5,830	0.23%
36	Utah	16,965	0.68%		44	Alaska	5,118	0.20%
48	Vermont	3,964	0.16%		45	New Hampshire	5,063	0.20%
23	Virginia	39,255	1.57%		46	Montana	4,908	0.20%
13	Washington	58,512	2.34%		47	South Dakota	4,077	0.16%
39	West Virginia	9,979	0.40%		48	Vermont	3,964	0.16%
28	Wisconsin	30,356	1.21%		49	Wyoming	3,184	0.13%
49	Wyoming	3,184	0.13%		50	North Dakota	1,991	0.08%
						District of Columbia	9,828	0.39%

Source: Federal Bureau of Investigation
"Crime in the United States 1996" (Uniform Crime Reports, October 4, 1997)
Burglary is the unlawful entry of a structure to commit a felony or theft. Attempts are included.

Average Time Between Burglaries in 1996

National Rate = A Burglary Occurs Every 13 Seconds*

ALPHA ORDER

RANK	STATE	MINUTES.SECONDS
30	Alabama	12.19
7	Alaska	102.59
36	Arizona	9.28
19	Arkansas	22.02
50	California	1.41
26	Colorado	15.18
22	Connecticut	19.07
8	Delaware	90.24
49	Florida	2.25
42	Georgia	6.26
14	Hawaii	41.14
10	Idaho	62.31
46	Illinois	4.52
32	Indiana	11.31
16	Iowa	27.49
20	Kansas	20.53
21	Kentucky	19.43
37	Louisiana	9.21
11	Maine	56.39
35	Maryland	10.28
31	Massachusetts	12.17
43	Michigan	6.08
27	Minnesota	14.50
24	Mississippi	17.08
34	Missouri	11.00
5	Montana	107.23
13	Nebraska	51.55
17	Nevada	26.57
6	New Hampshire	104.06
40	New Jersey	8.20
18	New Mexico	22.21
47	New York	4.04
45	North Carolina	5.21
1	North Dakota	264.43
44	Ohio	5.39
29	Oklahoma	12.43
25	Oregon	16.38
41	Pennsylvania	7.56
9	Rhode Island	64.47
33	South Carolina	11.06
4	South Dakota	129.16
39	Tennessee	8.31
48	Texas	2.35
15	Utah	31.04
3	Vermont	132.58
28	Virginia	13.26
38	Washington	9.01
12	West Virginia	52.49
23	Wisconsin	17.22
2	Wyoming	165.32

RANK ORDER

RANK	STATE	MINUTES.SECONDS
1	North Dakota	264.43
2	Wyoming	165.32
3	Vermont	132.58
4	South Dakota	129.16
5	Montana	107.23
6	New Hampshire	104.06
7	Alaska	102.59
8	Delaware	90.24
9	Rhode Island	64.47
10	Idaho	62.31
11	Maine	56.39
12	West Virginia	52.49
13	Nebraska	51.55
14	Hawaii	41.14
15	Utah	31.04
16	Iowa	27.49
17	Nevada	26.57
18	New Mexico	22.21
19	Arkansas	22.02
20	Kansas	20.53
21	Kentucky	19.43
22	Connecticut	19.07
23	Wisconsin	17.22
24	Mississippi	17.08
25	Oregon	16.38
26	Colorado	15.18
27	Minnesota	14.50
28	Virginia	13.26
29	Oklahoma	12.43
30	Alabama	12.19
31	Massachusetts	12.17
32	Indiana	11.31
33	South Carolina	11.06
34	Missouri	11.00
35	Maryland	10.28
36	Arizona	9.28
37	Louisiana	9.21
38	Washington	9.01
39	Tennessee	8.31
40	New Jersey	8.20
41	Pennsylvania	7.56
42	Georgia	6.26
43	Michigan	6.08
44	Ohio	5.39
45	North Carolina	5.21
46	Illinois	4.52
47	New York	4.04
48	Texas	2.35
49	Florida	2.25
50	California	1.41
	District of Columbia	53.38

Source: Morgan Quitno Press using data from Federal Bureau of Investigation
"Crime in the United States 1996" (Uniform Crime Reports, October 4, 1997)
*Burglary is the unlawful entry of a structure to commit a felony or theft. Attempts are included.

Percent Change in Number of Burglaries: 1995 to 1996

National Percent Change = 3.6% Decrease*

ALPHA ORDER				RANK ORDER		
RANK	STATE	PERCENT CHANGE		RANK	STATE	PERCENT CHANGE
21	Alabama	(1.8)		1	Utah	8.6
11	Alaska	1.2		2	Wyoming	8.4
37	Arizona	(6.9)		3	Georgia	7.4
27	Arkansas	(3.4)		4	Louisiana	5.4
47	California	(11.8)		5	New Hampshire	5.3
20	Colorado	(1.6)		6	South Dakota	3.4
34	Connecticut	(5.2)		7	Maine	3.2
43	Delaware	(10.2)		8	South Carolina	3.0
10	Florida	1.6		8	Tennessee	3.0
3	Georgia	7.4		10	Florida	1.6
39	Hawaii	(7.6)		11	Alaska	1.2
38	Idaho	(7.0)		12	Texas	0.9
15	Illinois	(0.3)		13	Mississippi	0.8
33	Indiana	(4.0)		14	Ohio	(0.2)
49	Iowa	(12.0)		15	Illinois	(0.3)
40	Kansas	(7.9)		15	Virginia	(0.3)
36	Kentucky	(5.8)		17	Oklahoma	(0.6)
4	Louisiana	5.4		18	Michigan	(1.1)
7	Maine	3.2		19	Washington	(1.3)
35	Maryland	(5.6)		20	Colorado	(1.6)
50	Massachusetts	(13.6)		21	Alabama	(1.8)
18	Michigan	(1.1)		22	Nebraska	(1.9)
27	Minnesota	(3.4)		23	Pennsylvania	(2.0)
13	Mississippi	0.8		24	Montana	(3.0)
32	Missouri	(3.5)		25	Nevada	(3.3)
24	Montana	(3.0)		25	New Mexico	(3.3)
22	Nebraska	(1.9)		27	Arkansas	(3.4)
25	Nevada	(3.3)		27	Minnesota	(3.4)
5	New Hampshire	5.3		27	North Carolina	(3.4)
42	New Jersey	(9.0)		27	West Virginia	(3.4)
25	New Mexico	(3.3)		27	Wisconsin	(3.4)
45	New York	(11.4)		32	Missouri	(3.5)
27	North Carolina	(3.4)		33	Indiana	(4.0)
45	North Dakota	(11.4)		34	Connecticut	(5.2)
14	Ohio	(0.2)		35	Maryland	(5.6)
17	Oklahoma	(0.6)		36	Kentucky	(5.8)
41	Oregon	(8.6)		37	Arizona	(6.9)
23	Pennsylvania	(2.0)		38	Idaho	(7.0)
48	Rhode Island	(11.9)		39	Hawaii	(7.6)
8	South Carolina	3.0		40	Kansas	(7.9)
6	South Dakota	3.4		41	Oregon	(8.6)
8	Tennessee	3.0		42	New Jersey	(9.0)
12	Texas	0.9		43	Delaware	(10.2)
1	Utah	8.6		44	Vermont	(10.9)
44	Vermont	(10.9)		45	New York	(11.4)
15	Virginia	(0.3)		45	North Dakota	(11.4)
19	Washington	(1.3)		47	California	(11.8)
27	West Virginia	(3.4)		48	Rhode Island	(11.9)
27	Wisconsin	(3.4)		49	Iowa	(12.0)
2	Wyoming	8.4		50	Massachusetts	(13.6)
					District of Columbia	(3.5)

Source: Federal Bureau of Investigation
"Crime in the United States 1996" (Uniform Crime Reports, October 4, 1997)
*Burglary is the unlawful entry of a structure to commit a felony or theft. Attempts are included.

Burglary Rate in 1996

National Rate = 943.0 Burglaries per 100,000 Population*

ALPHA ORDER			RANK ORDER		
RANK	STATE	RATE	RANK	STATE	RATE
15	Alabama	1,002.1	1	Florida	1,521.2
26	Alaska	843.2	2	New Mexico	1,376.9
6	Arizona	1,256.3	3	North Carolina	1,345.6
20	Arkansas	953.2	4	Louisiana	1,295.8
19	California	979.4	5	South Carolina	1,283.8
22	Colorado	900.8	6	Arizona	1,256.3
27	Connecticut	842.2	7	Oklahoma	1,255.6
30	Delaware	804.1	8	Nevada	1,220.1
1	Florida	1,521.2	9	Tennessee	1,163.5
11	Georgia	1,114.8	10	Mississippi	1,132.4
12	Hawaii	1,079.5	11	Georgia	1,114.8
36	Idaho	709.1	12	Hawaii	1,079.5
21	Illinois	913.2	13	Texas	1,068.5
32	Indiana	783.8	14	Washington	1,057.5
40	Iowa	664.6	15	Alabama	1,002.1
18	Kansas	981.3	16	Maryland	992.3
38	Kentucky	688.4	17	Oregon	988.3
4	Louisiana	1,295.8	18	Kansas	981.3
34	Maine	748.4	19	California	979.4
16	Maryland	992.3	20	Arkansas	953.2
37	Massachusetts	704.1	21	Illinois	913.2
23	Michigan	895.4	22	Colorado	900.8
33	Minnesota	762.5	23	Michigan	895.4
10	Mississippi	1,132.4	24	Missouri	894.2
24	Missouri	894.2	25	Utah	848.3
45	Montana	558.4	26	Alaska	843.2
42	Nebraska	614.5	27	Connecticut	842.2
8	Nevada	1,220.1	28	Ohio	835.4
49	New Hampshire	435.7	29	Rhode Island	821.7
31	New Jersey	791.9	30	Delaware	804.1
2	New Mexico	1,376.9	31	New Jersey	791.9
35	New York	713.9	32	Indiana	783.8
3	North Carolina	1,345.6	33	Minnesota	762.5
50	North Dakota	309.2	34	Maine	748.4
28	Ohio	835.4	35	New York	713.9
7	Oklahoma	1,255.6	36	Idaho	709.1
17	Oregon	988.3	37	Massachusetts	704.1
47	Pennsylvania	551.4	38	Kentucky	688.4
29	Rhode Island	821.7	39	Vermont	673.0
5	South Carolina	1,283.8	40	Iowa	664.6
46	South Dakota	557.0	41	Wyoming	662.0
9	Tennessee	1,163.5	42	Nebraska	614.5
13	Texas	1,068.5	43	Wisconsin	588.3
25	Utah	848.3	44	Virginia	588.1
39	Vermont	673.0	45	Montana	558.4
44	Virginia	588.1	46	South Dakota	557.0
14	Washington	1,057.5	47	Pennsylvania	551.4
48	West Virginia	546.5	48	West Virginia	546.5
43	Wisconsin	588.3	49	New Hampshire	435.7
41	Wyoming	662.0	50	North Dakota	309.2
				District of Columbia	1,809.9

Source: Federal Bureau of Investigation
  "Crime in the United States 1996" (Uniform Crime Reports, October 4, 1997)
*Burglary is the unlawful entry of a structure to commit a felony or theft. Attempts are included.

Percent Change in Burglary Rate: 1995 to 1996

National Percent Change = 4.5% Decrease*

<u>ALPHA ORDER</u>

RANK	STATE	PERCENT CHANGE
20	Alabama	(2.2)
10	Alaska	0.8
43	Arizona	(11.3)
28	Arkansas	(4.4)
49	California	(12.6)
24	Colorado	(3.6)
33	Connecticut	(5.2)
42	Delaware	(11.2)
12	Florida	(0.1)
3	Georgia	5.2
36	Hawaii	(7.4)
39	Idaho	(9.1)
14	Illinois	(0.5)
30	Indiana	(4.6)
48	Iowa	(12.3)
38	Kansas	(8.2)
35	Kentucky	(6.4)
3	Louisiana	5.2
6	Maine	3.0
34	Maryland	(6.2)
50	Massachusetts	(13.9)
18	Michigan	(1.6)
28	Minnesota	(4.4)
11	Mississippi	0.1
26	Missouri	(4.1)
25	Montana	(4.0)
21	Nebraska	(2.8)
37	Nevada	(7.7)
5	New Hampshire	4.1
40	New Jersey	(9.5)
31	New Mexico	(4.9)
45	New York	(11.7)
32	North Carolina	(5.1)
46	North Dakota	(11.8)
13	Ohio	(0.4)
16	Oklahoma	(1.3)
41	Oregon	(10.4)
19	Pennsylvania	(1.9)
47	Rhode Island	(11.9)
8	South Carolina	2.3
6	South Dakota	3.0
9	Tennessee	1.8
16	Texas	(1.3)
2	Utah	5.9
44	Vermont	(11.6)
15	Virginia	(1.2)
22	Washington	(3.1)
23	West Virginia	(3.3)
26	Wisconsin	(4.1)
1	Wyoming	8.2

<u>RANK ORDER</u>

RANK	STATE	PERCENT CHANGE
1	Wyoming	8.2
2	Utah	5.9
3	Georgia	5.2
3	Louisiana	5.2
5	New Hampshire	4.1
6	Maine	3.0
6	South Dakota	3.0
8	South Carolina	2.3
9	Tennessee	1.8
10	Alaska	0.8
11	Mississippi	0.1
12	Florida	(0.1)
13	Ohio	(0.4)
14	Illinois	(0.5)
15	Virginia	(1.2)
16	Oklahoma	(1.3)
16	Texas	(1.3)
18	Michigan	(1.6)
19	Pennsylvania	(1.9)
20	Alabama	(2.2)
21	Nebraska	(2.8)
22	Washington	(3.1)
23	West Virginia	(3.3)
24	Colorado	(3.6)
25	Montana	(4.0)
26	Missouri	(4.1)
26	Wisconsin	(4.1)
28	Arkansas	(4.4)
28	Minnesota	(4.4)
30	Indiana	(4.6)
31	New Mexico	(4.9)
32	North Carolina	(5.1)
33	Connecticut	(5.2)
34	Maryland	(6.2)
35	Kentucky	(6.4)
36	Hawaii	(7.4)
37	Nevada	(7.7)
38	Kansas	(8.2)
39	Idaho	(9.1)
40	New Jersey	(9.5)
41	Oregon	(10.4)
42	Delaware	(11.2)
43	Arizona	(11.3)
44	Vermont	(11.6)
45	New York	(11.7)
46	North Dakota	(11.8)
47	Rhode Island	(11.9)
48	Iowa	(12.3)
49	California	(12.6)
50	Massachusetts	(13.9)
	District of Columbia	(1.6)

Source: Federal Bureau of Investigation
"Crime in the United States 1996" (Uniform Crime Reports, October 4, 1997)
*Burglary is the unlawful entry of a structure to commit a felony or theft. Attempts are included.

Larcenies and Thefts in 1996

National Total = 7,894,620 Larcenies and Thefts*

ALPHA ORDER					RANK ORDER			
RANK	STATE	LARCENIES	% of USA		RANK	STATE	LARCENIES	% of USA
25	Alabama	123,350	1.56%		1	California	830,457	10.52%
46	Alaska	20,557	0.26%		2	Texas	659,414	8.35%
13	Arizona	188,300	2.39%		3	Florida	605,448	7.67%
32	Arkansas	73,010	0.92%		4	New York	399,522	5.06%
1	California	830,457	10.52%		5	Illinois	358,515	4.54%
22	Colorado	130,576	1.65%		6	Ohio	311,071	3.94%
29	Connecticut	81,328	1.03%		7	Georgia	288,803	3.66%
45	Delaware	21,665	0.27%		8	Michigan	276,909	3.51%
3	Florida	605,448	7.67%		9	Pennsylvania	240,693	3.05%
7	Georgia	288,803	3.66%		10	North Carolina	238,511	3.02%
36	Hawaii	54,701	0.69%		11	Washington	215,706	2.73%
39	Idaho	33,872	0.43%		12	New Jersey	193,961	2.46%
5	Illinois	358,515	4.54%		13	Arizona	188,300	2.39%
18	Indiana	160,777	2.04%		14	Virginia	184,237	2.33%
33	Iowa	71,893	0.91%		15	Maryland	173,817	2.20%
30	Kansas	78,145	0.99%		16	Louisiana	173,271	2.19%
31	Kentucky	73,653	0.93%		17	Missouri	168,870	2.14%
16	Louisiana	173,271	2.19%		18	Indiana	160,777	2.04%
41	Maine	29,557	0.37%		19	Tennessee	152,405	1.93%
15	Maryland	173,817	2.20%		20	Minnesota	138,671	1.76%
26	Massachusetts	119,562	1.51%		21	Wisconsin	135,941	1.72%
8	Michigan	276,909	3.51%		22	Colorado	130,576	1.65%
20	Minnesota	138,671	1.76%		23	South Carolina	129,650	1.64%
34	Mississippi	69,299	0.88%		24	Oregon	128,618	1.63%
17	Missouri	168,870	2.14%		25	Alabama	123,350	1.56%
40	Montana	30,928	0.39%		26	Massachusetts	119,562	1.51%
38	Nebraska	50,315	0.64%		27	Oklahoma	109,506	1.39%
37	Nevada	52,295	0.66%		28	Utah	87,542	1.11%
43	New Hampshire	24,611	0.31%		29	Connecticut	81,328	1.03%
12	New Jersey	193,961	2.46%		30	Kansas	78,145	0.99%
35	New Mexico	65,139	0.83%		31	Kentucky	73,653	0.93%
4	New York	399,522	5.06%		32	Arkansas	73,010	0.92%
10	North Carolina	238,511	3.02%		33	Iowa	71,893	0.91%
49	North Dakota	13,433	0.17%		34	Mississippi	69,299	0.88%
6	Ohio	311,071	3.94%		35	New Mexico	65,139	0.83%
27	Oklahoma	109,506	1.39%		36	Hawaii	54,701	0.69%
24	Oregon	128,618	1.63%		37	Nevada	52,295	0.66%
9	Pennsylvania	240,693	3.05%		38	Nebraska	50,315	0.64%
44	Rhode Island	23,367	0.30%		39	Idaho	33,872	0.43%
23	South Carolina	129,650	1.64%		40	Montana	30,928	0.39%
47	South Dakota	15,532	0.20%		41	Maine	29,557	0.37%
19	Tennessee	152,405	1.93%		42	West Virginia	28,300	0.36%
2	Texas	659,414	8.35%		43	New Hampshire	24,611	0.31%
28	Utah	87,542	1.11%		44	Rhode Island	23,367	0.30%
50	Vermont	12,124	0.15%		45	Delaware	21,665	0.27%
14	Virginia	184,237	2.33%		46	Alaska	20,557	0.26%
11	Washington	215,706	2.73%		47	South Dakota	15,532	0.20%
42	West Virginia	28,300	0.36%		48	Wyoming	15,408	0.20%
21	Wisconsin	135,941	1.72%		49	North Dakota	13,433	0.17%
48	Wyoming	15,408	0.20%		50	Vermont	12,124	0.15%
						District of Columbia	31,385	0.40%

Source: Federal Bureau of Investigation
    "Crime in the United States 1996" (Uniform Crime Reports, October 4, 1997)
*Larceny and theft is the unlawful taking of property without use of force, violence or fraud. Attempts are included.
Motor vehicle thefts are excluded.

Average Time Between Larcenies and Thefts in 1996

National Rate = A Larceny-Theft Occurs Every 4 Seconds*

ALPHA ORDER

RANK	STATE	MINUTES.SECONDS
26	Alabama	4.16
5	Alaska	25.38
38	Arizona	2.48
19	Arkansas	7.13
50	California	0.38
29	Colorado	4.02
22	Connecticut	6.29
6	Delaware	24.20
48	Florida	0.52
44	Georgia	1.49
15	Hawaii	9.38
12	Idaho	15.34
46	Illinois	1.28
33	Indiana	3.17
18	Iowa	7.20
21	Kansas	6.44
20	Kentucky	7.10
35	Louisiana	3.02
10	Maine	17.50
35	Maryland	3.02
25	Massachusetts	4.25
43	Michigan	1.54
31	Minnesota	3.48
17	Mississippi	7.37
34	Missouri	3.07
11	Montana	17.02
13	Nebraska	10.28
14	Nevada	10.05
8	New Hampshire	21.25
39	New Jersey	2.43
16	New Mexico	8.05
47	New York	1.19
41	North Carolina	2.13
2	North Dakota	39.14
45	Ohio	1.41
24	Oklahoma	4.49
27	Oregon	4.06
42	Pennsylvania	2.11
7	Rhode Island	22.33
28	South Carolina	4.04
4	South Dakota	33.56
32	Tennessee	3.28
49	Texas	0.48
23	Utah	6.01
1	Vermont	43.28
37	Virginia	2.52
40	Washington	2.26
9	West Virginia	18.37
30	Wisconsin	3.53
3	Wyoming	34.13

RANK ORDER

RANK	STATE	MINUTES.SECONDS
1	Vermont	43.28
2	North Dakota	39.14
3	Wyoming	34.13
4	South Dakota	33.56
5	Alaska	25.38
6	Delaware	24.20
7	Rhode Island	22.33
8	New Hampshire	21.25
9	West Virginia	18.37
10	Maine	17.50
11	Montana	17.02
12	Idaho	15.34
13	Nebraska	10.28
14	Nevada	10.05
15	Hawaii	9.38
16	New Mexico	8.05
17	Mississippi	7.37
18	Iowa	7.20
19	Arkansas	7.13
20	Kentucky	7.10
21	Kansas	6.44
22	Connecticut	6.29
23	Utah	6.01
24	Oklahoma	4.49
25	Massachusetts	4.25
26	Alabama	4.16
27	Oregon	4.06
28	South Carolina	4.04
29	Colorado	4.02
30	Wisconsin	3.53
31	Minnesota	3.48
32	Tennessee	3.28
33	Indiana	3.17
34	Missouri	3.07
35	Louisiana	3.02
35	Maryland	3.02
37	Virginia	2.52
38	Arizona	2.48
39	New Jersey	2.43
40	Washington	2.26
41	North Carolina	2.13
42	Pennsylvania	2.11
43	Michigan	1.54
44	Georgia	1.49
45	Ohio	1.41
46	Illinois	1.28
47	New York	1.19
48	Florida	0.52
49	Texas	0.48
50	California	0.38

| | District of Columbia | 16.47 |

Source: Morgan Quitno Press using data from Federal Bureau of Investigation
"Crime in the United States 1996" (Uniform Crime Reports, October 4, 1997)
*Larceny and theft is the unlawful taking of property without use of force, violence or fraud. Attempts are included.
Motor vehicle thefts are excluded.

Percent Change in Number of Larcenies and Thefts: 1995 to 1996

National Percent Change = 1.3% Decrease*

ALPHA ORDER				RANK ORDER		
RANK	STATE	PERCENT CHANGE		RANK	STATE	PERCENT CHANGE
14	Alabama	2.0		1	Georgia	9.0
42	Alaska	(6.1)		2	New Hampshire	8.4
48	Arizona	(9.4)		3	New Mexico	6.0
6	Arkansas	4.4		4	Oklahoma	5.6
45	California	(8.0)		5	Ohio	4.5
33	Colorado	(4.1)		6	Arkansas	4.4
43	Connecticut	(6.9)		7	Texas	4.3
30	Delaware	(3.0)		8	Louisiana	4.0
23	Florida	(1.1)		8	Missouri	4.0
1	Georgia	9.0		10	Maine	3.9
47	Hawaii	(8.7)		11	Tennessee	3.6
37	Idaho	(4.7)		12	South Carolina	2.6
20	Illinois	0.4		13	West Virginia	2.1
25	Indiana	(1.7)		14	Alabama	2.0
46	Iowa	(8.6)		14	Mississippi	2.0
22	Kansas	(0.9)		16	Pennsylvania	1.6
35	Kentucky	(4.2)		16	Virginia	1.6
8	Louisiana	4.0		18	North Carolina	1.5
10	Maine	3.9		19	Wisconsin	1.0
28	Maryland	(2.4)		20	Illinois	0.4
49	Massachusetts	(11.8)		21	Minnesota	0.2
24	Michigan	(1.4)		22	Kansas	(0.9)
21	Minnesota	0.2		23	Florida	(1.1)
14	Mississippi	2.0		24	Michigan	(1.4)
8	Missouri	4.0		25	Indiana	(1.7)
38	Montana	(5.7)		26	Utah	(1.9)
31	Nebraska	(3.3)		27	Wyoming	(2.3)
35	Nevada	(4.2)		28	Maryland	(2.4)
2	New Hampshire	8.4		29	South Dakota	(2.8)
40	New Jersey	(6.0)		30	Delaware	(3.0)
3	New Mexico	6.0		31	Nebraska	(3.3)
40	New York	(6.0)		31	Oregon	(3.3)
18	North Carolina	1.5		33	Colorado	(4.1)
43	North Dakota	(6.9)		33	Washington	(4.1)
5	Ohio	4.5		35	Kentucky	(4.2)
4	Oklahoma	5.6		35	Nevada	(4.2)
31	Oregon	(3.3)		37	Idaho	(4.7)
16	Pennsylvania	1.6		38	Montana	(5.7)
38	Rhode Island	(5.7)		38	Rhode Island	(5.7)
12	South Carolina	2.6		40	New Jersey	(6.0)
29	South Dakota	(2.8)		40	New York	(6.0)
11	Tennessee	3.6		42	Alaska	(6.1)
7	Texas	4.3		43	Connecticut	(6.9)
26	Utah	(1.9)		43	North Dakota	(6.9)
50	Vermont	(14.3)		45	California	(8.0)
16	Virginia	1.6		46	Iowa	(8.6)
33	Washington	(4.1)		47	Hawaii	(8.7)
13	West Virginia	2.1		48	Arizona	(9.4)
19	Wisconsin	1.0		49	Massachusetts	(11.8)
27	Wyoming	(2.3)		50	Vermont	(14.3)
					District of Columbia	(2.9)

Source: Federal Bureau of Investigation
   "Crime in the United States 1996" (Uniform Crime Reports, October 4, 1997)
*Larceny and theft is the unlawful taking of property without use of force, violence or fraud. Attempts are included. Motor vehicle thefts are excluded.

Larceny and Theft Rate in 1996

National Rate = 2,975.9 Larcenies and Thefts per 100,000 Population*

ALPHA ORDER				RANK ORDER		
RANK	STATE	RATE		RANK	STATE	RATE
27	Alabama	2,886.7		1	Hawaii	4,620.0
15	Alaska	3,386.7		2	Utah	4,377.1
3	Arizona	4,252.5		3	Arizona	4,252.5
26	Arkansas	2,908.8		4	Florida	4,204.5
35	California	2,605.1		5	Oregon	4,014.3
14	Colorado	3,415.5		6	Louisiana	3,982.3
38	Connecticut	2,484.1		7	Georgia	3,927.7
24	Delaware	2,988.3		8	Washington	3,898.5
4	Florida	4,204.5		9	New Mexico	3,802.6
7	Georgia	3,927.7		10	Montana	3,518.5
1	Hawaii	4,620.0		11	South Carolina	3,505.0
30	Idaho	2,848.8		12	Texas	3,447.4
23	Illinois	3,026.2		13	Maryland	3,427.0
33	Indiana	2,752.6		14	Colorado	3,415.5
37	Iowa	2,520.8		15	Alaska	3,386.7
22	Kansas	3,038.3		16	Oklahoma	3,317.4
49	Kentucky	1,896.3		17	Nevada	3,262.3
6	Louisiana	3,982.3		18	North Carolina	3,257.0
40	Maine	2,377.9		19	Wyoming	3,203.3
13	Maryland	3,427.0		20	Missouri	3,151.1
48	Massachusetts	1,962.6		21	Nebraska	3,045.7
28	Michigan	2,886.3		22	Kansas	3,038.3
25	Minnesota	2,977.1		23	Illinois	3,026.2
36	Mississippi	2,551.5		24	Delaware	2,988.3
20	Missouri	3,151.1		25	Minnesota	2,977.1
10	Montana	3,518.5		26	Arkansas	2,908.8
21	Nebraska	3,045.7		27	Alabama	2,886.7
17	Nevada	3,262.3		28	Michigan	2,886.3
44	New Hampshire	2,118.0		29	Tennessee	2,864.8
39	New Jersey	2,428.2		30	Idaho	2,848.8
9	New Mexico	3,802.6		31	Ohio	2,784.1
42	New York	2,197.0		32	Virginia	2,760.1
18	North Carolina	3,257.0		33	Indiana	2,752.6
45	North Dakota	2,085.9		34	Wisconsin	2,634.5
31	Ohio	2,784.1		35	California	2,605.1
16	Oklahoma	3,317.4		36	Mississippi	2,551.5
5	Oregon	4,014.3		37	Iowa	2,520.8
47	Pennsylvania	1,996.5		38	Connecticut	2,484.1
41	Rhode Island	2,360.3		39	New Jersey	2,428.2
11	South Carolina	3,505.0		40	Maine	2,377.9
43	South Dakota	2,121.9		41	Rhode Island	2,360.3
29	Tennessee	2,864.8		42	New York	2,197.0
12	Texas	3,447.4		43	South Dakota	2,121.9
2	Utah	4,377.1		44	New Hampshire	2,118.0
46	Vermont	2,058.4		45	North Dakota	2,085.9
32	Virginia	2,760.1		46	Vermont	2,058.4
8	Washington	3,898.5		47	Pennsylvania	1,996.5
50	West Virginia	1,549.8		48	Massachusetts	1,962.6
34	Wisconsin	2,634.5		49	Kentucky	1,896.3
19	Wyoming	3,203.3		50	West Virginia	1,549.8
					District of Columbia	5,779.9

Source: Federal Bureau of Investigation
   "Crime in the United States 1996" (Uniform Crime Reports, October 4, 1997)
*Larceny and theft is the unlawful taking of property without use of force, violence or fraud. Attempts are included.
Motor vehicle thefts are excluded.

394

Percent Change in Larceny and Theft Rate: 1995 to 1996

National Percent Change = 2.2% Decrease*

ALPHA ORDER				RANK ORDER		
RANK	STATE	PERCENT CHANGE		RANK	STATE	PERCENT CHANGE
15	Alabama	1.5		1	New Hampshire	7.1
39	Alaska	(6.6)		2	Georgia	6.8
49	Arizona	(13.7)		3	Oklahoma	4.8
8	Arkansas	3.3		4	Ohio	4.3
46	California	(8.8)		5	New Mexico	4.2
36	Colorado	(6.0)		6	Louisiana	3.7
42	Connecticut	(6.9)		6	Maine	3.7
29	Delaware	(4.0)		8	Arkansas	3.3
26	Florida	(2.7)		8	Missouri	3.3
2	Georgia	6.8		10	Tennessee	2.3
44	Hawaii	(8.5)		11	West Virginia	2.2
41	Idaho	(6.8)		12	Texas	2.1
19	Illinois	0.2		13	South Carolina	1.8
24	Indiana	(2.4)		14	Pennsylvania	1.7
47	Iowa	(8.9)		15	Alabama	1.5
22	Kansas	(1.2)		16	Mississippi	1.2
32	Kentucky	(4.8)		17	Virginia	0.7
6	Louisiana	3.7		18	Wisconsin	0.3
6	Maine	3.7		19	Illinois	0.2
27	Maryland	(3.0)		20	North Carolina	(0.2)
48	Massachusetts	(12.1)		21	Minnesota	(0.8)
23	Michigan	(1.8)		22	Kansas	(1.2)
21	Minnesota	(0.8)		23	Michigan	(1.8)
16	Mississippi	1.2		24	Indiana	(2.4)
8	Missouri	3.3		25	Wyoming	(2.5)
40	Montana	(6.7)		26	Florida	(2.7)
30	Nebraska	(4.2)		27	Maryland	(3.0)
44	Nevada	(8.5)		28	South Dakota	(3.2)
1	New Hampshire	7.1		29	Delaware	(4.0)
38	New Jersey	(6.5)		30	Nebraska	(4.2)
5	New Mexico	4.2		31	Utah	(4.3)
37	New York	(6.3)		32	Kentucky	(4.8)
20	North Carolina	(0.2)		33	Oregon	(5.2)
43	North Dakota	(7.3)		34	Rhode Island	(5.7)
4	Ohio	4.3		35	Washington	(5.8)
3	Oklahoma	4.8		36	Colorado	(6.0)
33	Oregon	(5.2)		37	New York	(6.3)
14	Pennsylvania	1.7		38	New Jersey	(6.5)
34	Rhode Island	(5.7)		39	Alaska	(6.6)
13	South Carolina	1.8		40	Montana	(6.7)
28	South Dakota	(3.2)		41	Idaho	(6.8)
10	Tennessee	2.3		42	Connecticut	(6.9)
12	Texas	2.1		43	North Dakota	(7.3)
31	Utah	(4.3)		44	Hawaii	(8.5)
50	Vermont	(14.9)		44	Nevada	(8.5)
17	Virginia	0.7		46	California	(8.8)
35	Washington	(5.8)		47	Iowa	(8.9)
11	West Virginia	2.2		48	Massachusetts	(12.1)
18	Wisconsin	0.3		49	Arizona	(13.7)
25	Wyoming	(2.5)		50	Vermont	(14.9)
					District of Columbia	(0.9)

Source: Federal Bureau of Investigation
    "Crime in the United States 1996" (Uniform Crime Reports, October 4, 1997)
*Larceny and theft is the unlawful taking of property without use of force, violence or fraud. Attempts are included.
Motor vehicle thefts are excluded.

Motor Vehicle Thefts in 1996

National Total = 1,395,192 Motor Vehicle Thefts*

ALPHA ORDER					RANK ORDER			
RANK	STATE	THEFTS	% of USA		RANK	STATE	THEFTS	% of USA
27	Alabama	15,632	1.12%		1	California	242,466	17.38%
42	Alaska	2,992	0.21%		2	Texas	104,928	7.52%
11	Arizona	41,034	2.94%		3	Florida	103,769	7.44%
34	Arkansas	7,855	0.56%		4	New York	89,900	6.44%
1	California	242,466	17.38%		5	Michigan	67,203	4.82%
28	Colorado	15,206	1.09%		6	Illinois	58,077	4.16%
24	Connecticut	16,022	1.15%		7	Pennsylvania	49,690	3.56%
41	Delaware	3,148	0.23%		8	New Jersey	46,437	3.33%
3	Florida	103,769	7.44%		9	Georgia	46,215	3.31%
9	Georgia	46,215	3.31%		10	Ohio	45,528	3.26%
35	Hawaii	7,157	0.51%		11	Arizona	41,034	2.94%
44	Idaho	2,229	0.16%		12	Maryland	36,083	2.59%
6	Illinois	58,077	4.16%		13	Tennessee	34,428	2.47%
17	Indiana	24,817	1.78%		14	Massachusetts	32,178	2.31%
38	Iowa	5,449	0.39%		15	Washington	28,893	2.07%
36	Kansas	6,388	0.46%		16	Louisiana	27,480	1.97%
30	Kentucky	10,142	0.73%		17	Indiana	24,817	1.78%
16	Louisiana	27,480	1.97%		18	North Carolina	24,566	1.76%
45	Maine	1,776	0.13%		19	Missouri	23,992	1.72%
12	Maryland	36,083	2.59%		20	Virginia	18,608	1.33%
14	Massachusetts	32,178	2.31%		21	Minnesota	17,923	1.28%
5	Michigan	67,203	4.82%		22	Wisconsin	17,846	1.28%
21	Minnesota	17,923	1.28%		23	Oregon	17,013	1.22%
32	Mississippi	9,527	0.68%		24	Connecticut	16,022	1.15%
19	Missouri	23,992	1.72%		25	Oklahoma	15,939	1.14%
43	Montana	2,248	0.16%		26	South Carolina	15,849	1.14%
37	Nebraska	5,643	0.40%		27	Alabama	15,632	1.12%
29	Nevada	11,194	0.80%		28	Colorado	15,206	1.09%
46	New Hampshire	1,762	0.13%		29	Nevada	11,194	0.80%
8	New Jersey	46,437	3.33%		30	Kentucky	10,142	0.73%
31	New Mexico	9,973	0.71%		31	New Mexico	9,973	0.71%
4	New York	89,900	6.44%		32	Mississippi	9,527	0.68%
18	North Carolina	24,566	1.76%		33	Utah	8,572	0.61%
47	North Dakota	1,224	0.09%		34	Arkansas	7,855	0.56%
10	Ohio	45,528	3.26%		35	Hawaii	7,157	0.51%
25	Oklahoma	15,939	1.14%		36	Kansas	6,388	0.46%
23	Oregon	17,013	1.22%		37	Nebraska	5,643	0.40%
7	Pennsylvania	49,690	3.56%		38	Iowa	5,449	0.39%
39	Rhode Island	4,597	0.33%		39	Rhode Island	4,597	0.33%
26	South Carolina	15,849	1.14%		40	West Virginia	3,231	0.23%
49	South Dakota	834	0.06%		41	Delaware	3,148	0.23%
13	Tennessee	34,428	2.47%		42	Alaska	2,992	0.21%
2	Texas	104,928	7.52%		43	Montana	2,248	0.16%
33	Utah	8,572	0.61%		44	Idaho	2,229	0.16%
48	Vermont	885	0.06%		45	Maine	1,776	0.13%
20	Virginia	18,608	1.33%		46	New Hampshire	1,762	0.13%
15	Washington	28,893	2.07%		47	North Dakota	1,224	0.09%
40	West Virginia	3,231	0.23%		48	Vermont	885	0.06%
22	Wisconsin	17,846	1.28%		49	South Dakota	834	0.06%
50	Wyoming	669	0.05%		50	Wyoming	669	0.05%
						District of Columbia	9,975	0.71%

Source: Federal Bureau of Investigation
"Crime in the United States 1996" (Uniform Crime Reports, October 4, 1997)
Includes the theft or attempted theft of a self-propelled vehicle. Excludes motorboats, construction equipment, airplanes and farming equipment.

Average Time Between Motor Vehicle Thefts in 1996

National Rate = A Motor Vehicle Theft Occurs Every 23 Seconds*

<table>
<tr><td colspan="3">ALPHA ORDER</td><td colspan="3">RANK ORDER</td></tr>
<tr><td>RANK</td><td>STATE</td><td>MINUTES.SECONDS</td><td>RANK</td><td>STATE</td><td>MINUTES.SECONDS</td></tr>
<tr><td>24</td><td>Alabama</td><td>33.43</td><td>1</td><td>Wyoming</td><td>787.48</td></tr>
<tr><td>9</td><td>Alaska</td><td>176.09</td><td>2</td><td>South Dakota</td><td>631.56</td></tr>
<tr><td>40</td><td>Arizona</td><td>12.50</td><td>3</td><td>Vermont</td><td>595.32</td></tr>
<tr><td>17</td><td>Arkansas</td><td>67.06</td><td>4</td><td>North Dakota</td><td>430.35</td></tr>
<tr><td>50</td><td>California</td><td>2.10</td><td>5</td><td>New Hampshire</td><td>299.07</td></tr>
<tr><td>23</td><td>Colorado</td><td>34.40</td><td>6</td><td>Maine</td><td>296.46</td></tr>
<tr><td>27</td><td>Connecticut</td><td>32.53</td><td>7</td><td>Idaho</td><td>236.27</td></tr>
<tr><td>10</td><td>Delaware</td><td>167.25</td><td>8</td><td>Montana</td><td>234.27</td></tr>
<tr><td>48</td><td>Florida</td><td>5.05</td><td>9</td><td>Alaska</td><td>176.09</td></tr>
<tr><td>42</td><td>Georgia</td><td>11.24</td><td>10</td><td>Delaware</td><td>167.25</td></tr>
<tr><td>16</td><td>Hawaii</td><td>73.38</td><td>11</td><td>West Virginia</td><td>163.07</td></tr>
<tr><td>7</td><td>Idaho</td><td>236.27</td><td>12</td><td>Rhode Island</td><td>114.39</td></tr>
<tr><td>45</td><td>Illinois</td><td>9.04</td><td>13</td><td>Iowa</td><td>96.43</td></tr>
<tr><td>34</td><td>Indiana</td><td>21.14</td><td>14</td><td>Nebraska</td><td>93.24</td></tr>
<tr><td>13</td><td>Iowa</td><td>96.43</td><td>15</td><td>Kansas</td><td>82.30</td></tr>
<tr><td>15</td><td>Kansas</td><td>82.30</td><td>16</td><td>Hawaii</td><td>73.38</td></tr>
<tr><td>21</td><td>Kentucky</td><td>51.58</td><td>17</td><td>Arkansas</td><td>67.06</td></tr>
<tr><td>35</td><td>Louisiana</td><td>19.11</td><td>18</td><td>Utah</td><td>61.29</td></tr>
<tr><td>6</td><td>Maine</td><td>296.46</td><td>19</td><td>Mississippi</td><td>55.19</td></tr>
<tr><td>39</td><td>Maryland</td><td>14.37</td><td>20</td><td>New Mexico</td><td>52.51</td></tr>
<tr><td>37</td><td>Massachusetts</td><td>16.23</td><td>21</td><td>Kentucky</td><td>51.58</td></tr>
<tr><td>46</td><td>Michigan</td><td>7.50</td><td>22</td><td>Nevada</td><td>47.05</td></tr>
<tr><td>30</td><td>Minnesota</td><td>29.25</td><td>23</td><td>Colorado</td><td>34.40</td></tr>
<tr><td>19</td><td>Mississippi</td><td>55.19</td><td>24</td><td>Alabama</td><td>33.43</td></tr>
<tr><td>32</td><td>Missouri</td><td>21.58</td><td>25</td><td>South Carolina</td><td>33.15</td></tr>
<tr><td>8</td><td>Montana</td><td>234.27</td><td>26</td><td>Oklahoma</td><td>33.04</td></tr>
<tr><td>14</td><td>Nebraska</td><td>93.24</td><td>27</td><td>Connecticut</td><td>32.53</td></tr>
<tr><td>22</td><td>Nevada</td><td>47.05</td><td>28</td><td>Oregon</td><td>30.59</td></tr>
<tr><td>5</td><td>New Hampshire</td><td>299.07</td><td>29</td><td>Wisconsin</td><td>29.32</td></tr>
<tr><td>43</td><td>New Jersey</td><td>11.21</td><td>30</td><td>Minnesota</td><td>29.25</td></tr>
<tr><td>20</td><td>New Mexico</td><td>52.51</td><td>31</td><td>Virginia</td><td>28.19</td></tr>
<tr><td>47</td><td>New York</td><td>5.52</td><td>32</td><td>Missouri</td><td>21.58</td></tr>
<tr><td>33</td><td>North Carolina</td><td>21.27</td><td>33</td><td>North Carolina</td><td>21.27</td></tr>
<tr><td>4</td><td>North Dakota</td><td>430.35</td><td>34</td><td>Indiana</td><td>21.14</td></tr>
<tr><td>41</td><td>Ohio</td><td>11.35</td><td>35</td><td>Louisiana</td><td>19.11</td></tr>
<tr><td>26</td><td>Oklahoma</td><td>33.04</td><td>36</td><td>Washington</td><td>18.14</td></tr>
<tr><td>28</td><td>Oregon</td><td>30.59</td><td>37</td><td>Massachusetts</td><td>16.23</td></tr>
<tr><td>44</td><td>Pennsylvania</td><td>10.37</td><td>38</td><td>Tennessee</td><td>15.19</td></tr>
<tr><td>12</td><td>Rhode Island</td><td>114.39</td><td>39</td><td>Maryland</td><td>14.37</td></tr>
<tr><td>25</td><td>South Carolina</td><td>33.15</td><td>40</td><td>Arizona</td><td>12.50</td></tr>
<tr><td>2</td><td>South Dakota</td><td>631.56</td><td>41</td><td>Ohio</td><td>11.35</td></tr>
<tr><td>38</td><td>Tennessee</td><td>15.19</td><td>42</td><td>Georgia</td><td>11.24</td></tr>
<tr><td>49</td><td>Texas</td><td>5.01</td><td>43</td><td>New Jersey</td><td>11.21</td></tr>
<tr><td>18</td><td>Utah</td><td>61.29</td><td>44</td><td>Pennsylvania</td><td>10.37</td></tr>
<tr><td>3</td><td>Vermont</td><td>595.32</td><td>45</td><td>Illinois</td><td>9.04</td></tr>
<tr><td>31</td><td>Virginia</td><td>28.19</td><td>46</td><td>Michigan</td><td>7.50</td></tr>
<tr><td>36</td><td>Washington</td><td>18.14</td><td>47</td><td>New York</td><td>5.52</td></tr>
<tr><td>11</td><td>West Virginia</td><td>163.07</td><td>48</td><td>Florida</td><td>5.05</td></tr>
<tr><td>29</td><td>Wisconsin</td><td>29.32</td><td>49</td><td>Texas</td><td>5.01</td></tr>
<tr><td>1</td><td>Wyoming</td><td>787.48</td><td>50</td><td>California</td><td>2.10</td></tr>
<tr><td></td><td></td><td></td><td></td><td>District of Columbia</td><td>52.50</td></tr>
</table>

Source: Morgan Quitno Press using data from Federal Bureau of Investigation
    "Crime in the United States 1996" (Uniform Crime Reports, October 4, 1997)
*Includes the theft or attempted theft of a self-propelled vehicle. Excludes motorboats, construction equipment, airplanes and farming equipment.

Percent Change in Number of Motor Vehicle Thefts: 1995 to 1996

National Percent Change = 5.2% Decrease*

ALPHA ORDER			RANK ORDER		
RANK	STATE	PERCENT CHANGE	RANK	STATE	PERCENT CHANGE
11	Alabama	6.0	1	New Mexico	15.3
33	Alaska	(5.0)	2	Minnesota	13.9
46	Arizona	(16.0)	3	Utah	12.9
28	Arkansas	(2.8)	4	South Carolina	12.0
44	California	(13.6)	5	Vermont	11.5
17	Colorado	4.7	6	North Carolina	9.9
40	Connecticut	(9.4)	7	Michigan	9.0
11	Delaware	6.0	8	North Dakota	6.6
37	Florida	(6.8)	9	West Virginia	6.3
15	Georgia	5.5	10	Maine	6.2
43	Hawaii	(12.7)	11	Alabama	6.0
48	Idaho	(20.8)	11	Delaware	6.0
36	Illinois	(6.1)	13	Louisiana	5.8
39	Indiana	(8.2)	13	New Hampshire	5.8
45	Iowa	(13.9)	15	Georgia	5.5
50	Kansas	(23.0)	16	Rhode Island	5.3
18	Kentucky	1.4	17	Colorado	4.7
13	Louisiana	5.8	18	Kentucky	1.4
10	Maine	6.2	19	Tennessee	1.0
21	Maryland	(0.3)	20	Texas	0.0
41	Massachusetts	(12.4)	21	Maryland	(0.3)
7	Michigan	9.0	21	Pennsylvania	(0.3)
2	Minnesota	13.9	23	Ohio	(1.6)
26	Mississippi	(2.0)	24	Nebraska	(1.9)
32	Missouri	(4.8)	24	Nevada	(1.9)
35	Montana	(5.9)	26	Mississippi	(2.0)
24	Nebraska	(1.9)	26	Oklahoma	(2.0)
24	Nevada	(1.9)	28	Arkansas	(2.8)
13	New Hampshire	5.8	29	Virginia	(3.9)
38	New Jersey	(7.5)	30	Washington	(4.0)
1	New Mexico	15.3	31	Wisconsin	(4.2)
41	New York	(12.4)	32	Missouri	(4.8)
6	North Carolina	9.9	33	Alaska	(5.0)
8	North Dakota	6.6	34	South Dakota	(5.3)
23	Ohio	(1.6)	35	Montana	(5.9)
26	Oklahoma	(2.0)	36	Illinois	(6.1)
49	Oregon	(22.8)	37	Florida	(6.8)
21	Pennsylvania	(0.3)	38	New Jersey	(7.5)
16	Rhode Island	5.3	39	Indiana	(8.2)
4	South Carolina	12.0	40	Connecticut	(9.4)
34	South Dakota	(5.3)	41	Massachusetts	(12.4)
19	Tennessee	1.0	41	New York	(12.4)
20	Texas	0.0	43	Hawaii	(12.7)
3	Utah	12.9	44	California	(13.6)
5	Vermont	11.5	45	Iowa	(13.9)
29	Virginia	(3.9)	46	Arizona	(16.0)
30	Washington	(4.0)	47	Wyoming	(16.9)
9	West Virginia	6.3	48	Idaho	(20.8)
31	Wisconsin	(4.2)	49	Oregon	(22.8)
47	Wyoming	(16.9)	50	Kansas	(23.0)
				District of Columbia	(2.1)

Source: Federal Bureau of Investigation
    "Crime in the United States 1996" (Uniform Crime Reports, October 4, 1997)
*Includes the theft or attempted theft of a self-propelled vehicle. Excludes motorboats, construction equipment, airplanes and farming equipment.

Motor Vehicle Theft Rate in 1996

National Rate = 525.9 Motor Vehicle Thefts per 100,000 Population*

ALPHA ORDER				RANK ORDER		
RANK	STATE	RATE		RANK	STATE	RATE
32	Alabama	365.8		1	Arizona	926.7
18	Alaska	492.9		2	California	760.6
1	Arizona	926.7		3	Florida	720.6
37	Arkansas	312.9		4	Maryland	711.4
2	California	760.6		5	Michigan	700.5
30	Colorado	397.8		6	Nevada	698.3
20	Connecticut	489.4		7	Tennessee	647.1
24	Delaware	434.2		8	Louisiana	631.6
3	Florida	720.6		9	Georgia	628.5
9	Georgia	628.5		10	Hawaii	604.5
10	Hawaii	604.5		11	New Mexico	582.2
44	Idaho	187.5		12	New Jersey	581.3
19	Illinois	490.2		13	Texas	548.6
27	Indiana	424.9		14	Oregon	531.0
42	Iowa	191.1		15	Massachusetts	528.2
41	Kansas	248.4		16	Washington	522.2
39	Kentucky	261.1		17	New York	494.4
8	Louisiana	631.6		18	Alaska	492.9
48	Maine	142.9		19	Illinois	490.2
4	Maryland	711.4		20	Connecticut	489.4
15	Massachusetts	528.2		21	Oklahoma	482.9
5	Michigan	700.5		22	Rhode Island	464.3
31	Minnesota	384.8		23	Missouri	447.7
33	Mississippi	350.8		24	Delaware	434.2
23	Missouri	447.7		25	Utah	428.6
40	Montana	255.7		26	South Carolina	428.5
35	Nebraska	341.6		27	Indiana	424.9
6	Nevada	698.3		28	Pennsylvania	412.2
46	New Hampshire	151.6		29	Ohio	407.5
12	New Jersey	581.3		30	Colorado	397.8
11	New Mexico	582.2		31	Minnesota	384.8
17	New York	494.4		32	Alabama	365.8
36	North Carolina	335.5		33	Mississippi	350.8
43	North Dakota	190.1		34	Wisconsin	345.9
29	Ohio	407.5		35	Nebraska	341.6
21	Oklahoma	482.9		36	North Carolina	335.5
14	Oregon	531.0		37	Arkansas	312.9
28	Pennsylvania	412.2		38	Virginia	278.8
22	Rhode Island	464.3		39	Kentucky	261.1
26	South Carolina	428.5		40	Montana	255.7
50	South Dakota	113.9		41	Kansas	248.4
7	Tennessee	647.1		42	Iowa	191.1
13	Texas	548.6		43	North Dakota	190.1
25	Utah	428.6		44	Idaho	187.5
47	Vermont	150.3		45	West Virginia	176.9
38	Virginia	278.8		46	New Hampshire	151.6
16	Washington	522.2		47	Vermont	150.3
45	West Virginia	176.9		48	Maine	142.9
34	Wisconsin	345.9		49	Wyoming	139.1
49	Wyoming	139.1		50	South Dakota	113.9
					District of Columbia	1,837.0

Source: Federal Bureau of Investigation
   "Crime in the United States 1996" (Uniform Crime Reports, October 4, 1997)
*Includes the theft or attempted theft of a self-propelled vehicle. Excludes motorboats, construction equipment, airplanes and farming equipment.

Percent Change in Motor Vehicle Theft Rate: 1995 to 1996

National Percent Change = 6.2% Decrease*

RANK	STATE	PERCENT CHANGE
11	Alabama	5.5
31	Alaska	(5.5)
47	Arizona	(20.0)
27	Arkansas	(3.8)
45	California	(14.3)
17	Colorado	2.7
40	Connecticut	(9.4)
14	Delaware	4.8
38	Florida	(8.3)
16	Georgia	3.3
41	Hawaii	(12.5)
48	Idaho	(22.5)
34	Illinois	(6.3)
39	Indiana	(8.8)
44	Iowa	(14.2)
49	Kansas	(23.2)
18	Kentucky	0.7
11	Louisiana	5.5
10	Maine	6.0
21	Maryland	(0.9)
42	Massachusetts	(12.6)
6	Michigan	8.5
2	Minnesota	12.7
24	Mississippi	(2.7)
30	Missouri	(5.4)
36	Montana	(6.9)
26	Nebraska	(2.8)
34	Nevada	(6.3)
15	New Hampshire	4.5
37	New Jersey	(8.0)
1	New Mexico	13.4
42	New York	(12.6)
7	North Carolina	8.0
9	North Dakota	6.1
22	Ohio	(1.8)
24	Oklahoma	(2.7)
50	Oregon	(24.4)
19	Pennsylvania	(0.1)
13	Rhode Island	5.3
3	South Carolina	11.2
33	South Dakota	(5.8)
20	Tennessee	(0.2)
23	Texas	(2.1)
5	Utah	10.2
4	Vermont	10.8
28	Virginia	(4.7)
32	Washington	(5.7)
8	West Virginia	6.4
29	Wisconsin	(4.9)
46	Wyoming	(17.1)

RANK	STATE	PERCENT CHANGE
1	New Mexico	13.4
2	Minnesota	12.7
3	South Carolina	11.2
4	Vermont	10.8
5	Utah	10.2
6	Michigan	8.5
7	North Carolina	8.0
8	West Virginia	6.4
9	North Dakota	6.1
10	Maine	6.0
11	Alabama	5.5
11	Louisiana	5.5
13	Rhode Island	5.3
14	Delaware	4.8
15	New Hampshire	4.5
16	Georgia	3.3
17	Colorado	2.7
18	Kentucky	0.7
19	Pennsylvania	(0.1)
20	Tennessee	(0.2)
21	Maryland	(0.9)
22	Ohio	(1.8)
23	Texas	(2.1)
24	Mississippi	(2.7)
24	Oklahoma	(2.7)
26	Nebraska	(2.8)
27	Arkansas	(3.8)
28	Virginia	(4.7)
29	Wisconsin	(4.9)
30	Missouri	(5.4)
31	Alaska	(5.5)
32	Washington	(5.7)
33	South Dakota	(5.8)
34	Illinois	(6.3)
34	Nevada	(6.3)
36	Montana	(6.9)
37	New Jersey	(8.0)
38	Florida	(8.3)
39	Indiana	(8.8)
40	Connecticut	(9.4)
41	Hawaii	(12.5)
42	Massachusetts	(12.6)
42	New York	(12.6)
44	Iowa	(14.2)
45	California	(14.3)
46	Wyoming	(17.1)
47	Arizona	(20.0)
48	Idaho	(22.5)
49	Kansas	(23.2)
50	Oregon	(24.4)

	District of Columbia	(0.2)

Source: Federal Bureau of Investigation
   "Crime in the United States 1996" (Uniform Crime Reports, October 4, 1997)
Includes the theft or attempted theft of a self-propelled vehicle. Excludes motorboats, construction equipment, airplanes and farming equipment.

Crimes in Urban Areas in 1996

National Urban Total = 12,816,839 Crimes*

ALPHA ORDER					RANK ORDER			
RANK	STATE	CRIMES	% of USA		RANK	STATE	CRIMES	% of USA
19	Alabama	196,222	1.53%		1	California	1,641,423	12.81%
41	Alaska	27,387	0.21%		2	Texas	1,060,432	8.27%
11	Arizona	306,290	2.39%		3	New York	732,684	5.72%
29	Arkansas	104,787	0.82%		4	Ohio	476,744	3.72%
1	California	1,641,423	12.81%		5	Michigan	462,949	3.61%
22	Colorado	188,355	1.47%		6	Georgia	423,422	3.30%
26	Connecticut	134,994	1.05%		7	Pennsylvania	392,055	3.06%
40	Delaware	31,793	0.25%		8	North Carolina	359,143	2.80%
NA	Florida**	NA	NA		9	New Jersey	346,116	2.70%
6	Georgia	423,422	3.30%		10	Washington	309,948	2.42%
34	Hawaii	62,934	0.49%		11	Arizona	306,290	2.39%
35	Idaho	40,048	0.31%		12	Maryland	300,299	2.34%
NA	Illinois**	NA	NA		13	Louisiana	281,160	2.19%
17	Indiana	244,875	1.91%		14	Tennessee	267,418	2.09%
31	Iowa	94,747	0.74%		15	Missouri	256,485	2.00%
NA	Kansas**	NA	NA		16	Virginia	247,824	1.93%
NA	Kentucky**	NA	NA		17	Indiana	244,875	1.91%
13	Louisiana	281,160	2.19%		18	Massachusetts	233,708	1.82%
37	Maine	35,614	0.28%		19	Alabama	196,222	1.53%
12	Maryland	300,299	2.34%		20	South Carolina	195,588	1.53%
18	Massachusetts	233,708	1.82%		21	Minnesota	190,329	1.48%
5	Michigan	462,949	3.61%		22	Colorado	188,355	1.47%
21	Minnesota	190,329	1.48%		23	Wisconsin	180,780	1.41%
28	Mississippi	107,034	0.84%		24	Oregon	178,199	1.39%
15	Missouri	256,485	2.00%		25	Oklahoma	175,428	1.37%
NA	Montana**	NA	NA		26	Connecticut	134,994	1.05%
33	Nebraska	67,511	0.53%		27	Utah	113,992	0.89%
32	Nevada	90,730	0.71%		28	Mississippi	107,034	0.84%
39	New Hampshire	31,903	0.25%		29	Arkansas	104,787	0.82%
9	New Jersey	346,116	2.70%		30	New Mexico	103,719	0.81%
30	New Mexico	103,719	0.81%		31	Iowa	94,747	0.74%
3	New York	732,684	5.72%		32	Nevada	90,730	0.71%
8	North Carolina	359,143	2.80%		33	Nebraska	67,511	0.53%
44	North Dakota	15,154	0.12%		34	Hawaii	62,934	0.49%
4	Ohio	476,744	3.72%		35	Idaho	40,048	0.31%
25	Oklahoma	175,428	1.37%		36	Rhode Island	39,504	0.31%
24	Oregon	178,199	1.39%		37	Maine	35,614	0.28%
7	Pennsylvania	392,055	3.06%		38	West Virginia	35,052	0.27%
36	Rhode Island	39,504	0.31%		39	New Hampshire	31,903	0.25%
20	South Carolina	195,588	1.53%		40	Delaware	31,793	0.25%
42	South Dakota	19,035	0.15%		41	Alaska	27,387	0.21%
14	Tennessee	267,418	2.09%		42	South Dakota	19,035	0.15%
2	Texas	1,060,432	8.27%		43	Wyoming	17,846	0.14%
27	Utah	113,992	0.89%		44	North Dakota	15,154	0.12%
45	Vermont	14,357	0.11%		45	Vermont	14,357	0.11%
16	Virginia	247,824	1.93%		NA	Florida**	NA	NA
10	Washington	309,948	2.42%		NA	Illinois**	NA	NA
38	West Virginia	35,052	0.27%		NA	Kansas**	NA	NA
23	Wisconsin	180,780	1.41%		NA	Kentucky**	NA	NA
43	Wyoming	17,846	0.14%		NA	Montana**	NA	NA
					District of Columbia		64,599	0.50%

Source: Morgan Quitno Press using data from Federal Bureau of Investigation
    "Crime in the United States 1996" (Uniform Crime Reports, October 4, 1997)
*Estimated rates for urban areas, defined by the F.B.I. as Metropolitan Statistical Areas and other cities outside such areas. National total includes those states listed as not available. Includes murder, rape, robbery, aggravated assault, burglary, larceny-theft and motor vehicle theft.
**Not available.

Urban Crime Rate in 1996

National Urban Rate = 5,494.9 Crimes per 100,000 Population*

ALPHA ORDER			RANK ORDER		
RANK	STATE	RATE	RANK	STATE	RATE
20	Alabama	5,621.7	1	Louisiana	7,671.5
9	Alaska	6,585.0	2	Arizona	7,495.8
2	Arizona	7,495.8	3	New Mexico	7,352.6
18	Arkansas	6,148.2	4	Georgia	7,169.9
24	California	5,252.8	5	Hawaii	6,851.7
23	Colorado	5,373.3	6	South Carolina	6,727.1
33	Connecticut	4,382.0	7	Mississippi	6,667.4
28	Delaware	5,030.8	8	Oregon	6,625.8
NA	Florida**	NA	9	Alaska	6,585.0
4	Georgia	7,169.9	10	Oklahoma	6,580.7
5	Hawaii	6,851.7	11	Nevada	6,405.3
26	Idaho	5,049.8	12	Utah	6,382.5
NA	Illinois**	NA	13	North Carolina	6,375.2
25	Indiana	5,119.2	14	Tennessee	6,335.6
31	Iowa	4,818.3	15	Maryland	6,249.5
NA	Kansas**	NA	16	Missouri	6,181.1
NA	Kentucky**	NA	17	Washington	6,170.8
1	Louisiana	7,671.5	18	Arkansas	6,148.2
40	Maine	3,978.1	19	Texas	6,060.4
15	Maryland	6,249.5	20	Alabama	5,621.7
41	Massachusetts	3,843.3	21	Nebraska	5,481.6
22	Michigan	5,422.2	22	Michigan	5,422.2
27	Minnesota	5,032.9	23	Colorado	5,373.3
7	Mississippi	6,667.4	24	California	5,252.8
16	Missouri	6,181.1	25	Indiana	5,119.2
NA	Montana**	NA	26	Idaho	5,049.8
21	Nebraska	5,481.6	27	Minnesota	5,032.9
11	Nevada	6,405.3	28	Delaware	5,030.8
45	New Hampshire	3,153.5	29	Wyoming	5,025.8
35	New Jersey	4,332.9	30	Ohio	4,843.3
3	New Mexico	7,352.6	31	Iowa	4,818.3
37	New York	4,227.9	32	Virginia	4,415.0
13	North Carolina	6,375.2	33	Connecticut	4,382.0
42	North Dakota	3,600.2	34	Wisconsin	4,335.4
30	Ohio	4,843.3	35	New Jersey	4,332.9
10	Oklahoma	6,580.7	36	South Dakota	4,329.3
8	Oregon	6,625.8	37	New York	4,227.9
43	Pennsylvania	3,565.1	38	Vermont	4,119.3
39	Rhode Island	3,990.3	39	Rhode Island	3,990.3
6	South Carolina	6,727.1	40	Maine	3,978.1
36	South Dakota	4,329.3	41	Massachusetts	3,843.3
14	Tennessee	6,335.6	42	North Dakota	3,600.2
19	Texas	6,060.4	43	Pennsylvania	3,565.1
12	Utah	6,382.5	44	West Virginia	3,361.2
38	Vermont	4,119.3	45	New Hampshire	3,153.5
32	Virginia	4,415.0	NA	Florida**	NA
17	Washington	6,170.8	NA	Illinois**	NA
44	West Virginia	3,361.2	NA	Kansas**	NA
34	Wisconsin	4,335.4	NA	Kentucky**	NA
29	Wyoming	5,025.8	NA	Montana**	NA

District of Columbia   11,896.7

Source: Morgan Quitno Press using data from Federal Bureau of Investigation
   "Crime in the United States 1996" (Uniform Crime Reports, October 4, 1997)
Estimated rates for urban areas, defined by the F.B.I. as Metropolitan Statistical Areas and other cities outside such areas. National rate includes those states listed as not available. Includes murder, rape, robbery, aggravated assault, burglary, larceny-theft and motor vehicle theft.
***Not available.*

Percent of Crimes Occurring in Urban Areas in 1996

National Percent = 95.1% of Crimes*

ALPHA ORDER				RANK ORDER		
RANK	STATE	PERCENT		RANK	STATE	PERCENT
14	Alabama	95.3		1	Massachusetts	100.0
42	Alaska	82.8		1	New Jersey	100.0
5	Arizona	97.9		3	Rhode Island	99.9
33	Arkansas	88.8		4	California	98.9
4	California	98.9		5	Arizona	97.9
11	Colorado	96.3		6	Maryland	97.7
7	Connecticut	97.5		7	Connecticut	97.5
32	Delaware	89.6		7	New York	97.5
NA	Florida**	NA		9	New Hampshire	97.2
30	Georgia	91.3		10	Texas	97.1
44	Hawaii	80.7		11	Colorado	96.3
41	Idaho	83.9		12	Pennsylvania	95.9
NA	Illinois**	NA		13	Ohio	95.8
23	Indiana	93.2		14	Alabama	95.3
31	Iowa	91.0		15	Utah	95.2
NA	Kansas**	NA		16	Washington	94.8
NA	Kentucky**	NA		17	Louisiana	94.5
17	Louisiana	94.5		17	Nevada	94.5
40	Maine	84.4		19	Michigan	94.3
6	Maryland	97.7		20	Missouri	94.1
1	Massachusetts	100.0		21	Oklahoma	94.0
19	Michigan	94.3		22	Virginia	93.6
29	Minnesota	91.6		23	Indiana	93.2
38	Mississippi	87.1		24	Oregon	92.7
20	Missouri	94.1		25	Tennessee	92.2
NA	Montana**	NA		26	Nebraska	92.1
26	Nebraska	92.1		27	New Mexico	91.7
17	Nevada	94.5		27	Wisconsin	91.7
9	New Hampshire	97.2		29	Minnesota	91.6
1	New Jersey	100.0		30	Georgia	91.3
27	New Mexico	91.7		31	Iowa	91.0
7	New York	97.5		32	Delaware	89.6
34	North Carolina	88.7		33	Arkansas	88.8
35	North Dakota	88.2		34	North Carolina	88.7
13	Ohio	95.8		35	North Dakota	88.2
21	Oklahoma	94.0		36	South Dakota	87.6
24	Oregon	92.7		37	Wyoming	87.2
12	Pennsylvania	95.9		38	Mississippi	87.1
3	Rhode Island	99.9		39	South Carolina	85.1
39	South Carolina	85.1		40	Maine	84.4
36	South Dakota	87.6		41	Idaho	83.9
25	Tennessee	92.2		42	Alaska	82.8
10	Texas	97.1		43	Vermont	81.2
15	Utah	95.2		44	Hawaii	80.7
43	Vermont	81.2		45	West Virginia	77.3
22	Virginia	93.6		NA	Florida**	NA
16	Washington	94.8		NA	Illinois**	NA
45	West Virginia	77.3		NA	Kansas**	NA
27	Wisconsin	91.7		NA	Kentucky**	NA
37	Wyoming	87.2		NA	Montana**	NA
				District of Columbia		100.0

Source: Morgan Quitno Press using data from Federal Bureau of Investigation
   "Crime in the United States 1996" (Uniform Crime Reports, October 4, 1997)
*Estimated percentages for urban areas, defined by the F.B.I. as Metropolitan Statistical Areas and other cities
outside such areas. National percent includes those states listed as not available. Includes murder, rape, robbery,
aggravated assault, burglary, larceny-theft and motor vehicle theft.
**Not available.

Crimes in Rural Areas in 1996

National Rural Total = 656,775 Crimes*

ALPHA ORDER

RANK	STATE	CRIMES	% of USA
24	Alabama	9,740	1.48%
34	Alaska	5,697	0.87%
30	Arizona	6,637	1.01%
21	Arkansas	13,164	2.00%
9	California	18,708	2.85%
28	Colorado	7,326	1.12%
37	Connecticut	3,420	0.52%
36	Delaware	3,695	0.56%
NA	Florida**	NA	NA
2	Georgia	40,530	6.17%
19	Hawaii	15,027	2.29%
27	Idaho	7,661	1.17%
NA	Illinois**	NA	NA
10	Indiana	17,867	2.72%
26	Iowa	9,320	1.42%
NA	Kansas**	NA	NA
NA	Kentucky**	NA	NA
16	Louisiana	16,396	2.50%
31	Maine	6,575	1.00%
29	Maryland	7,162	1.09%
43	Massachusetts	50	0.01%
5	Michigan	28,022	4.27%
11	Minnesota	17,562	2.67%
18	Mississippi	15,808	2.41%
17	Missouri	15,965	2.43%
NA	Montana**	NA	NA
32	Nebraska	5,781	0.88%
35	Nevada	5,322	0.81%
42	New Hampshire	906	0.14%
45	New Jersey	0	0.00%
25	New Mexico	9,378	1.43%
8	New York	18,772	2.86%
1	North Carolina	45,541	6.93%
41	North Dakota	2,035	0.31%
7	Ohio	21,087	3.21%
22	Oklahoma	11,174	1.70%
20	Oregon	13,933	2.12%
14	Pennsylvania	16,949	2.58%
44	Rhode Island	32	0.00%
3	South Carolina	34,273	5.22%
39	South Dakota	2,705	0.41%
6	Tennessee	22,486	3.42%
4	Texas	31,570	4.81%
33	Utah	5,725	0.87%
38	Vermont	3,330	0.51%
12	Virginia	17,058	2.60%
13	Washington	17,020	2.59%
23	West Virginia	10,294	1.57%
15	Wisconsin	16,402	2.50%
40	Wyoming	2,616	0.40%

RANK ORDER

RANK	STATE	CRIMES	% of USA
1	North Carolina	45,541	6.93%
2	Georgia	40,530	6.17%
3	South Carolina	34,273	5.22%
4	Texas	31,570	4.81%
5	Michigan	28,022	4.27%
6	Tennessee	22,486	3.42%
7	Ohio	21,087	3.21%
8	New York	18,772	2.86%
9	California	18,708	2.85%
10	Indiana	17,867	2.72%
11	Minnesota	17,562	2.67%
12	Virginia	17,058	2.60%
13	Washington	17,020	2.59%
14	Pennsylvania	16,949	2.58%
15	Wisconsin	16,402	2.50%
16	Louisiana	16,396	2.50%
17	Missouri	15,965	2.43%
18	Mississippi	15,808	2.41%
19	Hawaii	15,027	2.29%
20	Oregon	13,933	2.12%
21	Arkansas	13,164	2.00%
22	Oklahoma	11,174	1.70%
23	West Virginia	10,294	1.57%
24	Alabama	9,740	1.48%
25	New Mexico	9,378	1.43%
26	Iowa	9,320	1.42%
27	Idaho	7,661	1.17%
28	Colorado	7,326	1.12%
29	Maryland	7,162	1.09%
30	Arizona	6,637	1.01%
31	Maine	6,575	1.00%
32	Nebraska	5,781	0.88%
33	Utah	5,725	0.87%
34	Alaska	5,697	0.87%
35	Nevada	5,322	0.81%
36	Delaware	3,695	0.56%
37	Connecticut	3,420	0.52%
38	Vermont	3,330	0.51%
39	South Dakota	2,705	0.41%
40	Wyoming	2,616	0.40%
41	North Dakota	2,035	0.31%
42	New Hampshire	906	0.14%
43	Massachusetts	50	0.01%
44	Rhode Island	32	0.00%
45	New Jersey	0	0.00%
NA	Florida**	NA	NA
NA	Illinois**	NA	NA
NA	Kansas**	NA	NA
NA	Kentucky**	NA	NA
NA	Montana**	NA	NA
	District of Columbia	0	0.00%

Source: Federal Bureau of Investigation
"Crime in the United States 1996" (Uniform Crime Reports, October 4, 1997)
*Estimated totals for rural areas, defined by the F.B.I. as other than Metropolitan Statistical Areas and other cities outside such areas. National total includes those states listed as not available. Includes murder, rape, robbery, aggravated assault, burglary, larceny-theft and motor vehicle theft.
**Not available.

Rural Crime Rate in 1996

National Rural Rate = 2,050.2 Crimes per 100,000 Population*

ALPHA ORDER			RANK ORDER		
RANK	STATE	RATE	RANK	STATE	RATE
38	Alabama	1,244.6	1	Hawaii	5,660.3
6	Alaska	2,981.2	2	South Carolina	4,330.0
21	Arizona	1,941.6	3	Delaware	3,971.8
29	Arkansas	1,634.0	4	Washington	3,336.3
7	California	2,973.0	5	New Mexico	3,101.7
16	Colorado	2,306.8	6	Alaska	2,981.2
25	Connecticut	1,768.7	7	California	2,973.0
3	Delaware	3,971.8	8	Nevada	2,853.4
NA	Florida**	NA	9	Georgia	2,800.1
9	Georgia	2,800.1	10	Oregon	2,708.0
1	Hawaii	5,660.3	11	North Carolina	2,695.5
23	Idaho	1,934.9	12	Maryland	2,684.0
NA	Illinois**	NA	13	Utah	2,675.2
27	Indiana	1,689.5	14	Michigan	2,653.7
39	Iowa	1,052.4	15	Louisiana	2,390.1
NA	Kansas**	NA	16	Colorado	2,306.8
NA	Kentucky**	NA	17	New York	2,194.4
15	Louisiana	2,390.1	18	Wyoming	2,077.7
24	Maine	1,890.8	19	Tennessee	2,045.8
12	Maryland	2,684.0	20	Minnesota	2,004.1
43	Massachusetts	451.9	21	Arizona	1,941.6
14	Michigan	2,653.7	22	Texas	1,936.3
20	Minnesota	2,004.1	23	Idaho	1,934.9
33	Mississippi	1,423.3	24	Maine	1,890.8
36	Missouri	1,320.0	25	Connecticut	1,768.7
NA	Montana**	NA	26	Oklahoma	1,759.1
35	Nebraska	1,375.1	27	Indiana	1,689.5
8	Nevada	2,853.4	28	Wisconsin	1,656.6
42	New Hampshire	602.6	29	Arkansas	1,634.0
44	New Jersey	0.0	30	Virginia	1,606.5
5	New Mexico	3,101.7	31	Pennsylvania	1,600.5
17	New York	2,194.4	32	Ohio	1,586.0
11	North Carolina	2,695.5	33	Mississippi	1,423.3
41	North Dakota	912.2	34	Vermont	1,384.8
32	Ohio	1,586.0	35	Nebraska	1,375.1
26	Oklahoma	1,759.1	36	Missouri	1,320.0
10	Oregon	2,708.0	37	West Virginia	1,314.4
31	Pennsylvania	1,600.5	38	Alabama	1,244.6
44	Rhode Island	0.0	39	Iowa	1,052.4
2	South Carolina	4,330.0	40	South Dakota	925.3
40	South Dakota	925.3	41	North Dakota	912.2
19	Tennessee	2,045.8	42	New Hampshire	602.6
22	Texas	1,936.3	43	Massachusetts	451.9
13	Utah	2,675.2	44	New Jersey	0.0
34	Vermont	1,384.8	44	Rhode Island	0.0
30	Virginia	1,606.5	NA	Florida**	NA
4	Washington	3,336.3	NA	Illinois**	NA
37	West Virginia	1,314.4	NA	Kansas**	NA
28	Wisconsin	1,656.6	NA	Kentucky**	NA
18	Wyoming	2,077.7	NA	Montana**	NA
				District of Columbia	0.0

Source: Morgan Quitno Press using data from Federal Bureau of Investigation
    "Crime in the United States 1996" (Uniform Crime Reports, October 4, 1997)
*Estimated rates for rural areas, defined by the F.B.I. as other than Metropolitan Statistical Areas and other cities
outside such areas. National rate includes those states listed as not available. Includes murder, rape, robbery,
aggravated assault, burglary, larceny-theft and motor vehicle theft.
**Not available.

Percent of Crimes Occurring in Rural Areas in 1996

National Percent = 4.9% of Crimes*

<table>
<tr><td colspan="3"><u>ALPHA ORDER</u></td><td colspan="3"><u>RANK ORDER</u></td></tr>
<tr><td>RANK</td><td>STATE</td><td>PERCENT</td><td>RANK</td><td>STATE</td><td>PERCENT</td></tr>
<tr><td>32</td><td>Alabama</td><td>4.7</td><td>1</td><td>West Virginia</td><td>22.7</td></tr>
<tr><td>4</td><td>Alaska</td><td>17.2</td><td>2</td><td>Hawaii</td><td>19.3</td></tr>
<tr><td>41</td><td>Arizona</td><td>2.1</td><td>3</td><td>Vermont</td><td>18.8</td></tr>
<tr><td>13</td><td>Arkansas</td><td>11.2</td><td>4</td><td>Alaska</td><td>17.2</td></tr>
<tr><td>42</td><td>California</td><td>1.1</td><td>5</td><td>Idaho</td><td>16.1</td></tr>
<tr><td>35</td><td>Colorado</td><td>3.7</td><td>6</td><td>Maine</td><td>15.6</td></tr>
<tr><td>38</td><td>Connecticut</td><td>2.5</td><td>7</td><td>South Carolina</td><td>14.9</td></tr>
<tr><td>14</td><td>Delaware</td><td>10.4</td><td>8</td><td>Mississippi</td><td>12.9</td></tr>
<tr><td>NA</td><td>Florida**</td><td>NA</td><td>9</td><td>Wyoming</td><td>12.8</td></tr>
<tr><td>16</td><td>Georgia</td><td>8.7</td><td>10</td><td>South Dakota</td><td>12.4</td></tr>
<tr><td>2</td><td>Hawaii</td><td>19.3</td><td>11</td><td>North Dakota</td><td>11.8</td></tr>
<tr><td>5</td><td>Idaho</td><td>16.1</td><td>12</td><td>North Carolina</td><td>11.3</td></tr>
<tr><td>NA</td><td>Illinois**</td><td>NA</td><td>13</td><td>Arkansas</td><td>11.2</td></tr>
<tr><td>23</td><td>Indiana</td><td>6.8</td><td>14</td><td>Delaware</td><td>10.4</td></tr>
<tr><td>15</td><td>Iowa</td><td>9.0</td><td>15</td><td>Iowa</td><td>9.0</td></tr>
<tr><td>NA</td><td>Kansas**</td><td>NA</td><td>16</td><td>Georgia</td><td>8.7</td></tr>
<tr><td>NA</td><td>Kentucky**</td><td>NA</td><td>17</td><td>Minnesota</td><td>8.4</td></tr>
<tr><td>28</td><td>Louisiana</td><td>5.5</td><td>18</td><td>New Mexico</td><td>8.3</td></tr>
<tr><td>6</td><td>Maine</td><td>15.6</td><td>18</td><td>Wisconsin</td><td>8.3</td></tr>
<tr><td>40</td><td>Maryland</td><td>2.3</td><td>20</td><td>Nebraska</td><td>7.9</td></tr>
<tr><td>44</td><td>Massachusetts</td><td>0.0</td><td>21</td><td>Tennessee</td><td>7.8</td></tr>
<tr><td>27</td><td>Michigan</td><td>5.7</td><td>22</td><td>Oregon</td><td>7.3</td></tr>
<tr><td>17</td><td>Minnesota</td><td>8.4</td><td>23</td><td>Indiana</td><td>6.8</td></tr>
<tr><td>8</td><td>Mississippi</td><td>12.9</td><td>24</td><td>Virginia</td><td>6.4</td></tr>
<tr><td>26</td><td>Missouri</td><td>5.9</td><td>25</td><td>Oklahoma</td><td>6.0</td></tr>
<tr><td>NA</td><td>Montana**</td><td>NA</td><td>26</td><td>Missouri</td><td>5.9</td></tr>
<tr><td>20</td><td>Nebraska</td><td>7.9</td><td>27</td><td>Michigan</td><td>5.7</td></tr>
<tr><td>28</td><td>Nevada</td><td>5.5</td><td>28</td><td>Louisiana</td><td>5.5</td></tr>
<tr><td>37</td><td>New Hampshire</td><td>2.8</td><td>28</td><td>Nevada</td><td>5.5</td></tr>
<tr><td>44</td><td>New Jersey</td><td>0.0</td><td>30</td><td>Washington</td><td>5.2</td></tr>
<tr><td>18</td><td>New Mexico</td><td>8.3</td><td>31</td><td>Utah</td><td>4.8</td></tr>
<tr><td>38</td><td>New York</td><td>2.5</td><td>32</td><td>Alabama</td><td>4.7</td></tr>
<tr><td>12</td><td>North Carolina</td><td>11.3</td><td>33</td><td>Ohio</td><td>4.2</td></tr>
<tr><td>11</td><td>North Dakota</td><td>11.8</td><td>34</td><td>Pennsylvania</td><td>4.1</td></tr>
<tr><td>33</td><td>Ohio</td><td>4.2</td><td>35</td><td>Colorado</td><td>3.7</td></tr>
<tr><td>25</td><td>Oklahoma</td><td>6.0</td><td>36</td><td>Texas</td><td>2.9</td></tr>
<tr><td>22</td><td>Oregon</td><td>7.3</td><td>37</td><td>New Hampshire</td><td>2.8</td></tr>
<tr><td>34</td><td>Pennsylvania</td><td>4.1</td><td>38</td><td>Connecticut</td><td>2.5</td></tr>
<tr><td>43</td><td>Rhode Island</td><td>0.1</td><td>38</td><td>New York</td><td>2.5</td></tr>
<tr><td>7</td><td>South Carolina</td><td>14.9</td><td>40</td><td>Maryland</td><td>2.3</td></tr>
<tr><td>10</td><td>South Dakota</td><td>12.4</td><td>41</td><td>Arizona</td><td>2.1</td></tr>
<tr><td>21</td><td>Tennessee</td><td>7.8</td><td>42</td><td>California</td><td>1.1</td></tr>
<tr><td>36</td><td>Texas</td><td>2.9</td><td>43</td><td>Rhode Island</td><td>0.1</td></tr>
<tr><td>31</td><td>Utah</td><td>4.8</td><td>44</td><td>Massachusetts</td><td>0.0</td></tr>
<tr><td>3</td><td>Vermont</td><td>18.8</td><td>44</td><td>New Jersey</td><td>0.0</td></tr>
<tr><td>24</td><td>Virginia</td><td>6.4</td><td>NA</td><td>Florida**</td><td>NA</td></tr>
<tr><td>30</td><td>Washington</td><td>5.2</td><td>NA</td><td>Illinois**</td><td>NA</td></tr>
<tr><td>1</td><td>West Virginia</td><td>22.7</td><td>NA</td><td>Kansas**</td><td>NA</td></tr>
<tr><td>18</td><td>Wisconsin</td><td>8.3</td><td>NA</td><td>Kentucky**</td><td>NA</td></tr>
<tr><td>9</td><td>Wyoming</td><td>12.8</td><td>NA</td><td>Montana**</td><td>NA</td></tr>
<tr><td></td><td></td><td></td><td></td><td>District of Columbia</td><td>0.0</td></tr>
</table>

Source: Morgan Quitno Press using data from Federal Bureau of Investigation
    "Crime in the United States 1996" (Uniform Crime Reports, October 4, 1997)
*Estimated percentages for rural areas, defined by the F.B.I. as other than Metropolitan Statistical Areas and other cities outside such areas. National percent includes those states listed as not available. Includes murder, rape, robbery, aggravated assault, burglary, larceny-theft and motor vehicle theft.
**Not available.

Violent Crimes in Urban Areas in 1996

National Urban Total = 1,611,175 Violent Crimes*

ALPHA ORDER

RANK	STATE	CRIMES	% of USA
18	Alabama	22,905	1.42%
35	Alaska	3,434	0.21%
17	Arizona	27,079	1.68%
29	Arkansas	11,946	0.74%
1	California	271,965	16.88%
22	Colorado	14,966	0.93%
25	Connecticut	13,043	0.81%
34	Delaware	4,060	0.25%
NA	Florida**	NA	NA
9	Georgia	42,445	2.63%
37	Hawaii	2,834	0.18%
39	Idaho	2,449	0.15%
NA	Illinois**	NA	NA
16	Indiana	29,151	1.81%
31	Iowa	7,269	0.45%
NA	Kansas**	NA	NA
NA	Kentucky**	NA	NA
13	Louisiana	37,246	2.31%
40	Maine	1,372	0.09%
7	Maryland	46,297	2.87%
10	Massachusetts	39,104	2.43%
4	Michigan	58,320	3.62%
23	Minnesota	14,909	0.93%
30	Mississippi	10,336	0.64%
15	Missouri	29,393	1.82%
NA	Montana**	NA	NA
32	Nebraska	6,930	0.43%
27	Nevada	12,379	0.77%
41	New Hampshire	1,287	0.08%
8	New Jersey	42,459	2.64%
26	New Mexico	12,570	0.78%
2	New York	130,041	8.07%
11	North Carolina	38,785	2.41%
45	North Dakota	470	0.03%
6	Ohio	46,752	2.90%
21	Oklahoma	18,156	1.13%
24	Oregon	13,867	0.86%
5	Pennsylvania	50,649	3.14%
36	Rhode Island	3,417	0.21%
14	South Carolina	30,584	1.90%
42	South Dakota	1,150	0.07%
12	Tennessee	38,615	2.40%
3	Texas	119,661	7.43%
33	Utah	6,275	0.39%
44	Vermont	606	0.04%
20	Virginia	21,098	1.31%
19	Washington	22,754	1.41%
38	West Virginia	2,656	0.16%
28	Wisconsin	12,218	0.76%
43	Wyoming	965	0.06%

RANK ORDER

RANK	STATE	CRIMES	% of USA
1	California	271,965	16.88%
2	New York	130,041	8.07%
3	Texas	119,661	7.43%
4	Michigan	58,320	3.62%
5	Pennsylvania	50,649	3.14%
6	Ohio	46,752	2.90%
7	Maryland	46,297	2.87%
8	New Jersey	42,459	2.64%
9	Georgia	42,445	2.63%
10	Massachusetts	39,104	2.43%
11	North Carolina	38,785	2.41%
12	Tennessee	38,615	2.40%
13	Louisiana	37,246	2.31%
14	South Carolina	30,584	1.90%
15	Missouri	29,393	1.82%
16	Indiana	29,151	1.81%
17	Arizona	27,079	1.68%
18	Alabama	22,905	1.42%
19	Washington	22,754	1.41%
20	Virginia	21,098	1.31%
21	Oklahoma	18,156	1.13%
22	Colorado	14,966	0.93%
23	Minnesota	14,909	0.93%
24	Oregon	13,867	0.86%
25	Connecticut	13,043	0.81%
26	New Mexico	12,570	0.78%
27	Nevada	12,379	0.77%
28	Wisconsin	12,218	0.76%
29	Arkansas	11,946	0.74%
30	Mississippi	10,336	0.64%
31	Iowa	7,269	0.45%
32	Nebraska	6,930	0.43%
33	Utah	6,275	0.39%
34	Delaware	4,060	0.25%
35	Alaska	3,434	0.21%
36	Rhode Island	3,417	0.21%
37	Hawaii	2,834	0.18%
38	West Virginia	2,656	0.16%
39	Idaho	2,449	0.15%
40	Maine	1,372	0.09%
41	New Hampshire	1,287	0.08%
42	South Dakota	1,150	0.07%
43	Wyoming	965	0.06%
44	Vermont	606	0.04%
45	North Dakota	470	0.03%
NA	Florida**	NA	NA
NA	Illinois**	NA	NA
NA	Kansas**	NA	NA
NA	Kentucky**	NA	NA
NA	Montana**	NA	NA
	District of Columbia	13,411	0.83%

Source: Morgan Quitno Press using data from Federal Bureau of Investigation
    "Crime in the United States 1996" (Uniform Crime Reports, October 4, 1997)
*Estimated totals for urban areas, defined by the F.B.I. as Metropolitan Statistical Areas and other cities outside such areas. National total includes those states listed as not available. Violent crimes are offenses of murder, forcible rape, robbery and aggravated assault.
**Not available.

Urban Violent Crime Rate in 1996

National Urban Rate = 690.8 Violent Crimes per 100,000 Population*

ALPHA ORDER				RANK ORDER		
RANK	STATE	RATE		RANK	STATE	RATE
18	Alabama	656.2		1	South Carolina	1,051.9
8	Alaska	825.7		2	Louisiana	1,016.3
17	Arizona	662.7		3	Maryland	963.5
12	Arkansas	700.9		4	Tennessee	914.9
7	California	870.3		5	New Mexico	891.1
29	Colorado	426.9		6	Nevada	873.9
30	Connecticut	423.4		7	California	870.3
21	Delaware	642.4		8	Alaska	825.7
NA	Florida**	NA		9	New York	750.4
10	Georgia	718.7		10	Georgia	718.7
37	Hawaii	308.5		11	Missouri	708.3
36	Idaho	308.8		12	Arkansas	700.9
NA	Illinois**	NA		13	North Carolina	688.5
22	Indiana	609.4		14	Texas	683.9
33	Iowa	369.7		15	Michigan	683.1
NA	Kansas**	NA		16	Oklahoma	681.1
NA	Kentucky**	NA		17	Arizona	662.7
2	Louisiana	1,016.3		18	Alabama	656.2
43	Maine	153.3		19	Mississippi	643.9
3	Maryland	963.5		20	Massachusetts	643.1
20	Massachusetts	643.1		21	Delaware	642.4
15	Michigan	683.1		22	Indiana	609.4
31	Minnesota	394.2		23	Nebraska	562.7
19	Mississippi	643.9		24	New Jersey	531.5
11	Missouri	708.3		25	Oregon	515.6
NA	Montana**	NA		26	Ohio	475.0
23	Nebraska	562.7		27	Pennsylvania	460.6
6	Nevada	873.9		28	Washington	453.0
44	New Hampshire	127.2		29	Colorado	426.9
24	New Jersey	531.5		30	Connecticut	423.4
5	New Mexico	891.1		31	Minnesota	394.2
9	New York	750.4		32	Virginia	375.9
13	North Carolina	688.5		33	Iowa	369.7
45	North Dakota	111.7		34	Utah	351.3
26	Ohio	475.0		35	Rhode Island	345.2
16	Oklahoma	681.1		36	Idaho	308.8
25	Oregon	515.6		37	Hawaii	308.5
27	Pennsylvania	460.6		38	Wisconsin	293.0
35	Rhode Island	345.2		39	Wyoming	271.8
1	South Carolina	1,051.9		40	South Dakota	261.6
40	South Dakota	261.6		41	West Virginia	254.7
4	Tennessee	914.9		42	Vermont	173.9
14	Texas	683.9		43	Maine	153.3
34	Utah	351.3		44	New Hampshire	127.2
42	Vermont	173.9		45	North Dakota	111.7
32	Virginia	375.9		NA	Florida**	NA
28	Washington	453.0		NA	Illinois**	NA
41	West Virginia	254.7		NA	Kansas**	NA
38	Wisconsin	293.0		NA	Kentucky**	NA
39	Wyoming	271.8		NA	Montana**	NA
					District of Columbia	2,469.8

Source: Morgan Quitno Press using data from Federal Bureau of Investigation
"Crime in the United States 1996" (Uniform Crime Reports, October 4, 1997)
*Estimated rates for urban areas, defined by the F.B.I. as Metropolitan Statistical Areas and other cities outside such areas. National rate includes those states listed as not available. Violent crimes are offenses of murder, forcible rape, robbery and aggravated assault.
**Not available.

Percent of Violent Crimes Occurring in Urban Areas in 1996

National Percent = 95.8% of Violent Crimes*

ALPHA ORDER

RANK	STATE	PERCENT
17	Alabama	94.8
43	Alaska	77.7
10	Arizona	96.8
30	Arkansas	90.8
4	California	98.9
10	Colorado	96.8
12	Connecticut	96.7
39	Delaware	83.8
NA	Florida**	NA
31	Georgia	90.4
37	Hawaii	85.3
44	Idaho	77.1
NA	Illinois**	NA
25	Indiana	92.9
23	Iowa	93.5
NA	Kansas**	NA
NA	Kentucky**	NA
28	Louisiana	92.1
34	Maine	88.3
6	Maryland	98.0
1	Massachusetts	100.0
14	Michigan	95.7
18	Minnesota	94.5
42	Mississippi	77.9
26	Missouri	92.8
NA	Montana**	NA
13	Nebraska	96.5
16	Nevada	95.2
21	New Hampshire	93.7
1	New Jersey	100.0
35	New Mexico	87.3
5	New York	98.4
32	North Carolina	90.1
36	North Dakota	86.9
7	Ohio	97.6
28	Oklahoma	92.1
23	Oregon	93.5
8	Pennsylvania	97.1
3	Rhode Island	99.4
40	South Carolina	82.9
33	South Dakota	88.7
20	Tennessee	93.8
8	Texas	97.1
18	Utah	94.5
38	Vermont	84.9
27	Virginia	92.6
15	Washington	95.4
45	West Virginia	69.2
21	Wisconsin	93.7
41	Wyoming	80.3

RANK ORDER

RANK	STATE	PERCENT
1	Massachusetts	100.0
1	New Jersey	100.0
3	Rhode Island	99.4
4	California	98.9
5	New York	98.4
6	Maryland	98.0
7	Ohio	97.6
8	Pennsylvania	97.1
8	Texas	97.1
10	Arizona	96.8
10	Colorado	96.8
12	Connecticut	96.7
13	Nebraska	96.5
14	Michigan	95.7
15	Washington	95.4
16	Nevada	95.2
17	Alabama	94.8
18	Minnesota	94.5
18	Utah	94.5
20	Tennessee	93.8
21	New Hampshire	93.7
21	Wisconsin	93.7
23	Iowa	93.5
23	Oregon	93.5
25	Indiana	92.9
26	Missouri	92.8
27	Virginia	92.6
28	Louisiana	92.1
28	Oklahoma	92.1
30	Arkansas	90.8
31	Georgia	90.4
32	North Carolina	90.1
33	South Dakota	88.7
34	Maine	88.3
35	New Mexico	87.3
36	North Dakota	86.9
37	Hawaii	85.3
38	Vermont	84.9
39	Delaware	83.8
40	South Carolina	82.9
41	Wyoming	80.3
42	Mississippi	77.9
43	Alaska	77.7
44	Idaho	77.1
45	West Virginia	69.2
NA	Florida**	NA
NA	Illinois**	NA
NA	Kansas**	NA
NA	Kentucky**	NA
NA	Montana**	NA

	District of Columbia	100.0

Source: Morgan Quitno Press using data from Federal Bureau of Investigation
    "Crime in the United States 1996" (Uniform Crime Reports, October 4, 1997)
*Estimated percentages for urban areas, defined by the F.B.I. as Metropolitan Statistical Areas and other cities
outside such areas. National percent includes those states listed as not available. Violent crimes are offenses of
murder, forcible rape, robbery and aggravated assault.
**Not available.

Violent Crimes in Rural Areas in 1996

National Rural Total = 71,103 Violent Crimes*

ALPHA ORDER

RANK ORDER

RANK	STATE	CRIMES		RANK	STATE	CRIMES
17	Alabama	1,254		1	South Carolina	6,291
22	Alaska	983		2	Georgia	4,521
25	Arizona	884		3	North Carolina	4,283
18	Arkansas	1,215		4	Texas	3,609
6	California	3,031		5	Louisiana	3,180
32	Colorado	497		6	California	3,031
34	Connecticut	447		7	Mississippi	2,925
28	Delaware	785		8	Michigan	2,631
NA	Florida**	NA		9	Tennessee	2,560
2	Georgia	4,521		10	Missouri	2,276
33	Hawaii	488		11	Indiana	2,215
29	Idaho	728		12	New York	2,165
NA	Illinois**	NA		13	New Mexico	1,829
11	Indiana	2,215		14	Virginia	1,684
31	Iowa	502		15	Oklahoma	1,554
NA	Kansas**	NA		16	Pennsylvania	1,491
NA	Kentucky**	NA		17	Alabama	1,254
5	Louisiana	3,180		18	Arkansas	1,215
38	Maine	181		19	West Virginia	1,180
24	Maryland	933		20	Ohio	1,144
44	Massachusetts	18		21	Washington	1,103
8	Michigan	2,631		22	Alaska	983
26	Minnesota	873		23	Oregon	970
7	Mississippi	2,925		24	Maryland	933
10	Missouri	2,276		25	Arizona	884
NA	Montana**	NA		26	Minnesota	873
36	Nebraska	252		27	Wisconsin	821
30	Nevada	626		28	Delaware	785
41	New Hampshire	86		29	Idaho	728
45	New Jersey	0		30	Nevada	626
13	New Mexico	1,829		31	Iowa	502
12	New York	2,165		32	Colorado	497
3	North Carolina	4,283		33	Hawaii	488
42	North Dakota	71		34	Connecticut	447
20	Ohio	1,144		35	Utah	363
15	Oklahoma	1,554		36	Nebraska	252
23	Oregon	970		37	Wyoming	236
16	Pennsylvania	1,491		38	Maine	181
43	Rhode Island	20		39	South Dakota	147
1	South Carolina	6,291		40	Vermont	108
39	South Dakota	147		41	New Hampshire	86
9	Tennessee	2,560		42	North Dakota	71
4	Texas	3,609		43	Rhode Island	20
35	Utah	363		44	Massachusetts	18
40	Vermont	108		45	New Jersey	0
14	Virginia	1,684		NA	Florida**	NA
21	Washington	1,103		NA	Illinois**	NA
19	West Virginia	1,180		NA	Kansas**	NA
27	Wisconsin	821		NA	Kentucky**	NA
37	Wyoming	236		NA	Montana**	NA
					District of Columbia	0

Source: Federal Bureau of Investigation
"Crime in the United States 1996" (Uniform Crime Reports, October 4, 1997)
*Estimated totals for rural areas, defined by the F.B.I. as other than Metropolitan Statistical Areas and other cities outside such areas. National total includes those states listed as not available. Violent crimes are offenses of murder, forcible rape, robbery and aggravated assault.
**Not available.

Rural Violent Crime Rate in 1996

National Rural Rate = 222.0 Violent Crimes per 100,000 Population*

ALPHA ORDER			RANK ORDER		
RANK	STATE	RATE	RANK	STATE	RATE
28	Alabama	160.2	1	Delaware	843.8
4	Alaska	514.4	2	South Carolina	794.8
11	Arizona	258.6	3	New Mexico	604.9
31	Arkansas	150.8	4	Alaska	514.4
5	California	481.7	5	California	481.7
30	Colorado	156.5	6	Louisiana	463.6
17	Connecticut	231.2	7	Maryland	349.6
1	Delaware	843.8	8	Nevada	335.6
NA	Florida**	NA	9	Georgia	312.3
9	Georgia	312.3	10	Mississippi	263.4
25	Hawaii	183.8	11	Arizona	258.6
24	Idaho	183.9	12	North Carolina	253.5
NA	Illinois**	NA	13	New York	253.1
20	Indiana	209.4	14	Michigan	249.2
39	Iowa	56.7	15	Oklahoma	244.6
NA	Kansas**	NA	16	Tennessee	232.9
NA	Kentucky**	NA	17	Connecticut	231.2
6	Louisiana	463.6	18	Texas	221.4
40	Maine	52.1	19	Washington	216.2
7	Maryland	349.6	20	Indiana	209.4
27	Massachusetts	162.7	21	Oregon	188.5
14	Michigan	249.2	22	Missouri	188.2
34	Minnesota	99.6	23	Wyoming	187.4
10	Mississippi	263.4	24	Idaho	183.9
22	Missouri	188.2	25	Hawaii	183.8
NA	Montana**	NA	26	Utah	169.6
37	Nebraska	59.9	27	Massachusetts	162.7
8	Nevada	335.6	28	Alabama	160.2
38	New Hampshire	57.2	29	Virginia	158.6
44	New Jersey	0.0	30	Colorado	156.5
3	New Mexico	604.9	31	Arkansas	150.8
13	New York	253.1	32	West Virginia	150.7
12	North Carolina	253.5	33	Pennsylvania	140.8
43	North Dakota	31.8	34	Minnesota	99.6
35	Ohio	86.0	35	Ohio	86.0
15	Oklahoma	244.6	36	Wisconsin	82.9
21	Oregon	188.5	37	Nebraska	59.9
33	Pennsylvania	140.8	38	New Hampshire	57.2
44	Rhode Island	0.0	39	Iowa	56.7
2	South Carolina	794.8	40	Maine	52.1
41	South Dakota	50.3	41	South Dakota	50.3
16	Tennessee	232.9	42	Vermont	44.9
18	Texas	221.4	43	North Dakota	31.8
26	Utah	169.6	44	New Jersey	0.0
42	Vermont	44.9	44	Rhode Island	0.0
29	Virginia	158.6	NA	Florida**	NA
19	Washington	216.2	NA	Illinois**	NA
32	West Virginia	150.7	NA	Kansas**	NA
36	Wisconsin	82.9	NA	Kentucky**	NA
23	Wyoming	187.4	NA	Montana**	NA
				District of Columbia	0.0

Source: Morgan Quitno Press using data from Federal Bureau of Investigation
   "Crime in the United States 1996" (Uniform Crime Reports, October 4, 1997)
*Estimated rates for rural areas, defined by the F.B.I. as other than Metropolitan Statistical Areas and other cities outside such areas. National rate includes those states listed as not available. Violent crimes are offenses of murder, forcible rape, robbery and aggravated assault.
**Not available.

Percent of Violent Crimes Occurring in Rural Areas in 1996

National Percent = 4.2% of Violent Crimes*

ALPHA ORDER

RANK	STATE	PERCENT
29	Alabama	5.2
3	Alaska	22.3
35	Arizona	3.2
16	Arkansas	9.2
42	California	1.1
35	Colorado	3.2
34	Connecticut	3.3
7	Delaware	16.2
NA	Florida**	NA
15	Georgia	9.6
9	Hawaii	14.7
2	Idaho	22.9
NA	Illinois**	NA
21	Indiana	7.1
22	Iowa	6.5
NA	Kansas**	NA
NA	Kentucky**	NA
17	Louisiana	7.9
12	Maine	11.7
40	Maryland	2.0
44	Massachusetts	0.0
32	Michigan	4.3
27	Minnesota	5.5
4	Mississippi	22.1
20	Missouri	7.2
NA	Montana**	NA
33	Nebraska	3.5
30	Nevada	4.8
24	New Hampshire	6.3
44	New Jersey	0.0
11	New Mexico	12.7
41	New York	1.6
14	North Carolina	9.9
10	North Dakota	13.1
39	Ohio	2.4
17	Oklahoma	7.9
22	Oregon	6.5
37	Pennsylvania	2.9
43	Rhode Island	0.6
6	South Carolina	17.1
13	South Dakota	11.3
26	Tennessee	6.2
37	Texas	2.9
27	Utah	5.5
8	Vermont	15.1
19	Virginia	7.4
31	Washington	4.6
1	West Virginia	30.8
24	Wisconsin	6.3
5	Wyoming	19.7

RANK ORDER

RANK	STATE	PERCENT
1	West Virginia	30.8
2	Idaho	22.9
3	Alaska	22.3
4	Mississippi	22.1
5	Wyoming	19.7
6	South Carolina	17.1
7	Delaware	16.2
8	Vermont	15.1
9	Hawaii	14.7
10	North Dakota	13.1
11	New Mexico	12.7
12	Maine	11.7
13	South Dakota	11.3
14	North Carolina	9.9
15	Georgia	9.6
16	Arkansas	9.2
17	Louisiana	7.9
17	Oklahoma	7.9
19	Virginia	7.4
20	Missouri	7.2
21	Indiana	7.1
22	Iowa	6.5
22	Oregon	6.5
24	New Hampshire	6.3
24	Wisconsin	6.3
26	Tennessee	6.2
27	Minnesota	5.5
27	Utah	5.5
29	Alabama	5.2
30	Nevada	4.8
31	Washington	4.6
32	Michigan	4.3
33	Nebraska	3.5
34	Connecticut	3.3
35	Arizona	3.2
35	Colorado	3.2
37	Pennsylvania	2.9
37	Texas	2.9
39	Ohio	2.4
40	Maryland	2.0
41	New York	1.6
42	California	1.1
43	Rhode Island	0.6
44	Massachusetts	0.0
44	New Jersey	0.0
NA	Florida**	NA
NA	Illinois**	NA
NA	Kansas**	NA
NA	Kentucky**	NA
NA	Montana**	NA
	District of Columbia	0.0

Source: Morgan Quitno Press using data from Federal Bureau of Investigation
    "Crime in the United States 1996" (Uniform Crime Reports, October 4, 1997)
Estimated percentages for rural areas, defined by the F.B.I. as other than Metropolitan Statistical Areas and other cities outside such areas. National percent includes those states listed as not available. Violent crimes are offenses of murder, forcible rape, robbery and aggravated assault.
**Not available.*

Murders in Urban Areas in 1996

National Urban Total = 18,150 Murders*

ALPHA ORDER					RANK ORDER			
RANK	STATE	MURDERS	% of USA		RANK	STATE	MURDERS	% of USA
13	Alabama	420	2.31%		1	California	2,892	15.93%
35	Alaska	30	0.17%		2	Texas	1,376	7.58%
16	Arizona	369	2.03%		3	New York	1,325	7.30%
25	Arkansas	162	0.89%		4	Louisiana	703	3.87%
1	California	2,892	15.93%		5	Michigan	693	3.82%
24	Colorado	169	0.93%		6	Pennsylvania	650	3.58%
28	Connecticut	154	0.85%		7	Maryland	577	3.18%
38	Delaware	23	0.13%		8	Georgia	551	3.04%
NA	Florida**	NA	NA		9	Ohio	517	2.85%
8	Georgia	551	3.04%		10	North Carolina	495	2.73%
36	Hawaii	29	0.16%		11	Tennessee	443	2.44%
39	Idaho	19	0.10%		12	Virginia	442	2.44%
NA	Illinois**	NA	NA		13	Alabama	420	2.31%
14	Indiana	377	2.08%		14	Indiana	377	2.08%
32	Iowa	46	0.25%		15	Missouri	371	2.04%
NA	Kansas**	NA	NA		16	Arizona	369	2.03%
NA	Kentucky**	NA	NA		17	New Jersey	338	1.86%
4	Louisiana	703	3.87%		18	South Carolina	260	1.43%
41	Maine	15	0.08%		19	Mississippi	231	1.27%
7	Maryland	577	3.18%		20	Washington	222	1.22%
27	Massachusetts	157	0.87%		21	Nevada	214	1.18%
5	Michigan	693	3.82%		22	Wisconsin	186	1.02%
29	Minnesota	147	0.81%		23	Oklahoma	181	1.00%
19	Mississippi	231	1.27%		24	Colorado	169	0.93%
15	Missouri	371	2.04%		25	Arkansas	162	0.89%
NA	Montana**	NA	NA		26	New Mexico	158	0.87%
33	Nebraska	45	0.25%		27	Massachusetts	157	0.87%
21	Nevada	214	1.18%		28	Connecticut	154	0.85%
40	New Hampshire	16	0.09%		29	Minnesota	147	0.81%
17	New Jersey	338	1.86%		30	Oregon	114	0.63%
26	New Mexico	158	0.87%		31	Utah	60	0.33%
3	New York	1,325	7.30%		32	Iowa	46	0.25%
10	North Carolina	495	2.73%		33	Nebraska	45	0.25%
42	North Dakota	10	0.06%		34	West Virginia	39	0.21%
9	Ohio	517	2.85%		35	Alaska	30	0.17%
23	Oklahoma	181	1.00%		36	Hawaii	29	0.16%
30	Oregon	114	0.63%		37	Rhode Island	25	0.14%
6	Pennsylvania	650	3.58%		38	Delaware	23	0.13%
37	Rhode Island	25	0.14%		39	Idaho	19	0.10%
18	South Carolina	260	1.43%		40	New Hampshire	16	0.09%
45	South Dakota	3	0.02%		41	Maine	15	0.08%
11	Tennessee	443	2.44%		42	North Dakota	10	0.06%
2	Texas	1,376	7.58%		43	Vermont	6	0.03%
31	Utah	60	0.33%		43	Wyoming	6	0.03%
43	Vermont	6	0.03%		45	South Dakota	3	0.02%
12	Virginia	442	2.44%		NA	Florida**	NA	NA
20	Washington	222	1.22%		NA	Illinois**	NA	NA
34	West Virginia	39	0.21%		NA	Kansas**	NA	NA
22	Wisconsin	186	1.02%		NA	Kentucky**	NA	NA
43	Wyoming	6	0.03%		NA	Montana**	NA	NA
						District of Columbia	397	2.19%

Source: Morgan Quitno Press using data from Federal Bureau of Investigation
  "Crime in the United States 1996" (Uniform Crime Reports, October 4, 1997)
*Estimated totals for urban areas, defined by the F.B.I. as Metropolitan Statistical Areas and other cities outside
such areas. National total includes those states listed as not available. Includes nonnegligent manslaughter.
**Not available.

Urban Murder Rate in 1996

National Urban Rate = 7.8 Murders per 100,000 Population*

ALPHA ORDER

RANK	STATE	RATE
4	Alabama	12.0
20	Alaska	7.2
11	Arizona	9.0
8	Arkansas	9.5
9	California	9.3
25	Colorado	4.8
24	Connecticut	5.0
33	Delaware	3.6
NA	Florida**	NA
9	Georgia	9.3
35	Hawaii	3.2
38	Idaho	2.4
NA	Illinois**	NA
16	Indiana	7.9
40	Iowa	2.3
NA	Kansas**	NA
NA	Kentucky**	NA
1	Louisiana	19.2
41	Maine	1.7
4	Maryland	12.0
36	Massachusetts	2.6
15	Michigan	8.1
30	Minnesota	3.9
3	Mississippi	14.4
12	Missouri	8.9
NA	Montana**	NA
31	Nebraska	3.7
2	Nevada	15.1
44	New Hampshire	1.6
28	New Jersey	4.2
6	New Mexico	11.2
19	New York	7.6
14	North Carolina	8.8
38	North Dakota	2.4
23	Ohio	5.3
21	Oklahoma	6.8
28	Oregon	4.2
22	Pennsylvania	5.9
37	Rhode Island	2.5
12	South Carolina	8.9
45	South Dakota	0.7
7	Tennessee	10.5
16	Texas	7.9
34	Utah	3.4
41	Vermont	1.7
16	Virginia	7.9
27	Washington	4.4
31	West Virginia	3.7
26	Wisconsin	4.5
41	Wyoming	1.7

RANK ORDER

RANK	STATE	RATE
1	Louisiana	19.2
2	Nevada	15.1
3	Mississippi	14.4
4	Alabama	12.0
4	Maryland	12.0
6	New Mexico	11.2
7	Tennessee	10.5
8	Arkansas	9.5
9	California	9.3
9	Georgia	9.3
11	Arizona	9.0
12	Missouri	8.9
12	South Carolina	8.9
14	North Carolina	8.8
15	Michigan	8.1
16	Indiana	7.9
16	Texas	7.9
16	Virginia	7.9
19	New York	7.6
20	Alaska	7.2
21	Oklahoma	6.8
22	Pennsylvania	5.9
23	Ohio	5.3
24	Connecticut	5.0
25	Colorado	4.8
26	Wisconsin	4.5
27	Washington	4.4
28	New Jersey	4.2
28	Oregon	4.2
30	Minnesota	3.9
31	Nebraska	3.7
31	West Virginia	3.7
33	Delaware	3.6
34	Utah	3.4
35	Hawaii	3.2
36	Massachusetts	2.6
37	Rhode Island	2.5
38	Idaho	2.4
38	North Dakota	2.4
40	Iowa	2.3
41	Maine	1.7
41	Vermont	1.7
41	Wyoming	1.7
44	New Hampshire	1.6
45	South Dakota	0.7
NA	Florida**	NA
NA	Illinois**	NA
NA	Kansas**	NA
NA	Kentucky**	NA
NA	Montana**	NA
	District of Columbia	73.1

Source: Morgan Quitno Press using data from Federal Bureau of Investigation
"Crime in the United States 1996" (Uniform Crime Reports, October 4, 1997)
*Estimated rates for urban areas, defined by the F.B.I. as Metropolitan Statistical Areas and other cities outside such areas. National rate includes those states listed as not available. Includes nonnegligent manslaughter.
**Not available.

Percent of Murders Occurring in Urban Areas in 1996

National Percent = 92.4% of Murders*

ALPHA ORDER

RANK	STATE	PERCENT
14	Alabama	94.6
39	Alaska	66.7
6	Arizona	97.9
36	Arkansas	74.0
4	California	99.2
15	Colorado	93.9
8	Connecticut	97.5
35	Delaware	74.2
NA	Florida**	NA
25	Georgia	87.5
37	Hawaii	72.5
43	Idaho	44.2
NA	Illinois**	NA
20	Indiana	89.8
27	Iowa	86.8
NA	Kansas**	NA
NA	Kentucky**	NA
18	Louisiana	92.3
40	Maine	60.0
5	Maryland	98.1
1	Massachusetts	100.0
11	Michigan	96.0
24	Minnesota	88.0
34	Mississippi	76.7
28	Missouri	85.7
NA	Montana**	NA
16	Nebraska	93.8
9	Nevada	97.3
31	New Hampshire	80.0
1	New Jersey	100.0
30	New Mexico	80.2
6	New York	97.9
31	North Carolina	80.0
38	North Dakota	71.4
10	Ohio	96.1
29	Oklahoma	81.2
21	Oregon	88.4
13	Pennsylvania	94.8
1	Rhode Island	100.0
33	South Carolina	78.3
45	South Dakota	33.3
23	Tennessee	88.1
17	Texas	93.2
12	Utah	95.2
42	Vermont	54.5
21	Virginia	88.4
26	Washington	87.1
41	West Virginia	56.5
19	Wisconsin	91.2
44	Wyoming	37.5

RANK ORDER

RANK	STATE	PERCENT
1	Massachusetts	100.0
1	New Jersey	100.0
1	Rhode Island	100.0
4	California	99.2
5	Maryland	98.1
6	Arizona	97.9
6	New York	97.9
8	Connecticut	97.5
9	Nevada	97.3
10	Ohio	96.1
11	Michigan	96.0
12	Utah	95.2
13	Pennsylvania	94.8
14	Alabama	94.6
15	Colorado	93.9
16	Nebraska	93.8
17	Texas	93.2
18	Louisiana	92.3
19	Wisconsin	91.2
20	Indiana	89.8
21	Oregon	88.4
21	Virginia	88.4
23	Tennessee	88.1
24	Minnesota	88.0
25	Georgia	87.5
26	Washington	87.1
27	Iowa	86.8
28	Missouri	85.7
29	Oklahoma	81.2
30	New Mexico	80.2
31	New Hampshire	80.0
31	North Carolina	80.0
33	South Carolina	78.3
34	Mississippi	76.7
35	Delaware	74.2
36	Arkansas	74.0
37	Hawaii	72.5
38	North Dakota	71.4
39	Alaska	66.7
40	Maine	60.0
41	West Virginia	56.5
42	Vermont	54.5
43	Idaho	44.2
44	Wyoming	37.5
45	South Dakota	33.3
NA	Florida**	NA
NA	Illinois**	NA
NA	Kansas**	NA
NA	Kentucky**	NA
NA	Montana**	NA
	District of Columbia	100.0

Source: Morgan Quitno Press using data from Federal Bureau of Investigation
    "Crime in the United States 1996" (Uniform Crime Reports, October 4, 1997)
*Estimated percentages for urban areas, defined by the F.B.I. as Metropolitan Statistical Areas and other cities outside such areas. National percent includes those states listed as not available. Includes nonnegligent manslaughter.
**Not available.

Murders in Rural Areas in 1996

National Rural Total = 1,495 Murders*

ALPHA ORDER				RANK ORDER		
RANK	**STATE**	**MURDERS**		**RANK**	**STATE**	**MURDERS**
19	Alabama	24		1	North Carolina	124
25	Alaska	15		2	Texas	101
32	Arizona	8		3	Georgia	79
10	Arkansas	57		4	South Carolina	72
19	California	24		5	Mississippi	70
27	Colorado	11		6	Missouri	62
38	Connecticut	4		7	Tennessee	60
32	Delaware	8		8	Louisiana	59
NA	Florida**	NA		9	Virginia	58
3	Georgia	79		10	Arkansas	57
27	Hawaii	11		11	Indiana	43
19	Idaho	24		12	Oklahoma	42
NA	Illinois**	NA		13	New Mexico	39
11	Indiana	43		14	Pennsylvania	36
34	Iowa	7		15	Washington	33
NA	Kansas**	NA		16	West Virginia	30
NA	Kentucky**	NA		17	Michigan	29
8	Louisiana	59		18	New York	28
30	Maine	10		19	Alabama	24
27	Maryland	11		19	California	24
43	Massachusetts	0		19	Idaho	24
17	Michigan	29		22	Ohio	21
23	Minnesota	20		23	Minnesota	20
5	Mississippi	70		24	Wisconsin	18
6	Missouri	62		25	Alaska	15
NA	Montana**	NA		25	Oregon	15
41	Nebraska	3		27	Colorado	11
35	Nevada	6		27	Hawaii	11
38	New Hampshire	4		27	Maryland	11
43	New Jersey	0		30	Maine	10
13	New Mexico	39		30	Wyoming	10
18	New York	28		32	Arizona	8
1	North Carolina	124		32	Delaware	8
38	North Dakota	4		34	Iowa	7
22	Ohio	21		35	Nevada	6
12	Oklahoma	42		35	South Dakota	6
25	Oregon	15		37	Vermont	5
14	Pennsylvania	36		38	Connecticut	4
43	Rhode Island	0		38	New Hampshire	4
4	South Carolina	72		38	North Dakota	4
35	South Dakota	6		41	Nebraska	3
7	Tennessee	60		41	Utah	3
2	Texas	101		43	Massachusetts	0
41	Utah	3		43	New Jersey	0
37	Vermont	5		43	Rhode Island	0
9	Virginia	58		NA	Florida**	NA
15	Washington	33		NA	Illinois**	NA
16	West Virginia	30		NA	Kansas**	NA
24	Wisconsin	18		NA	Kentucky**	NA
30	Wyoming	10		NA	Montana**	NA
					District of Columbia	0

Source: Federal Bureau of Investigation
       "Crime in the United States 1996" (Uniform Crime Reports, October 4, 1997)
Estimated totals for rural areas, defined by the F.B.I. as other than Metropolitan Statistical Areas and other cities outside such areas. National total includes those states listed as not available. Includes nonnegligent manslaughter.
**Not available.*

Rural Murder Rate in 1996

National Rural Rate = 4.7 Murders per 100,000 Population*

<u>ALPHA ORDER</u>

<u>RANK ORDER</u>

RANK	STATE	RATE	RANK	STATE	RATE
27	Alabama	3.1	1	New Mexico	12.9
6	Alaska	7.8	2	South Carolina	9.1
32	Arizona	2.3	3	Delaware	8.6
8	Arkansas	7.1	3	Louisiana	8.6
21	California	3.8	5	Wyoming	7.9
23	Colorado	3.5	6	Alaska	7.8
34	Connecticut	2.1	7	North Carolina	7.3
3	Delaware	8.6	8	Arkansas	7.1
NA	Florida**	NA	9	Oklahoma	6.6
14	Georgia	5.5	10	Washington	6.5
18	Hawaii	4.1	11	Mississippi	6.3
13	Idaho	6.1	12	Texas	6.2
NA	Illinois**	NA	13	Idaho	6.1
18	Indiana	4.1	14	Georgia	5.5
41	Iowa	0.8	14	Tennessee	5.5
NA	Kansas**	NA	14	Virginia	5.5
NA	Kentucky**	NA	17	Missouri	5.1
3	Louisiana	8.6	18	Hawaii	4.1
28	Maine	2.9	18	Indiana	4.1
18	Maryland	4.1	18	Maryland	4.1
43	Massachusetts	0.0	21	California	3.8
30	Michigan	2.7	21	West Virginia	3.8
32	Minnesota	2.3	23	Colorado	3.5
11	Mississippi	6.3	24	Pennsylvania	3.4
17	Missouri	5.1	25	New York	3.3
NA	Montana**	NA	26	Nevada	3.2
42	Nebraska	0.7	27	Alabama	3.1
26	Nevada	3.2	28	Maine	2.9
30	New Hampshire	2.7	28	Oregon	2.9
43	New Jersey	0.0	30	Michigan	2.7
1	New Mexico	12.9	30	New Hampshire	2.7
25	New York	3.3	32	Arizona	2.3
7	North Carolina	7.3	32	Minnesota	2.3
37	North Dakota	1.8	34	Connecticut	2.1
39	Ohio	1.6	34	South Dakota	2.1
9	Oklahoma	6.6	34	Vermont	2.1
28	Oregon	2.9	37	North Dakota	1.8
24	Pennsylvania	3.4	37	Wisconsin	1.8
43	Rhode Island	0.0	39	Ohio	1.6
2	South Carolina	9.1	40	Utah	1.4
34	South Dakota	2.1	41	Iowa	0.8
14	Tennessee	5.5	42	Nebraska	0.7
12	Texas	6.2	43	Massachusetts	0.0
40	Utah	1.4	43	New Jersey	0.0
34	Vermont	2.1	43	Rhode Island	0.0
14	Virginia	5.5	NA	Florida**	NA
10	Washington	6.5	NA	Illinois**	NA
21	West Virginia	3.8	NA	Kansas**	NA
37	Wisconsin	1.8	NA	Kentucky**	NA
5	Wyoming	7.9	NA	Montana**	NA
				District of Columbia	0.0

Source: Morgan Quitno Press using data from Federal Bureau of Investigation
    "Crime in the United States 1996" (Uniform Crime Reports, October 4, 1997)
*Estimated rates for rural areas, defined by the F.B.I. as other than Metropolitan Statistical Areas and other cities outside such areas. National rate includes those states listed as not available. Includes nonnegligent manslaughter.
**Not available.

Percent of Murders Occurring in Rural Areas in 1996

National Percent = 7.6% of Murders*

ALPHA ORDER				RANK ORDER		
RANK	STATE	PERCENT		RANK	STATE	PERCENT
32	Alabama	5.4		1	South Dakota	66.7
7	Alaska	33.3		2	Wyoming	62.5
39	Arizona	2.1		3	Idaho	55.8
10	Arkansas	26.0		4	Vermont	45.5
42	California	0.8		5	West Virginia	43.5
31	Colorado	6.1		6	Maine	40.0
38	Connecticut	2.5		7	Alaska	33.3
11	Delaware	25.8		8	North Dakota	28.6
NA	Florida**	NA		9	Hawaii	27.5
21	Georgia	12.5		10	Arkansas	26.0
9	Hawaii	27.5		11	Delaware	25.8
3	Idaho	55.8		12	Mississippi	23.3
NA	Illinois**	NA		13	South Carolina	21.7
26	Indiana	10.2		14	New Hampshire	20.0
19	Iowa	13.2		14	North Carolina	20.0
NA	Kansas**	NA		16	New Mexico	19.8
NA	Kentucky**	NA		17	Oklahoma	18.8
28	Louisiana	7.7		18	Missouri	14.3
6	Maine	40.0		19	Iowa	13.2
41	Maryland	1.9		20	Washington	12.9
43	Massachusetts	0.0		21	Georgia	12.5
35	Michigan	4.0		22	Minnesota	12.0
22	Minnesota	12.0		23	Tennessee	11.9
12	Mississippi	23.3		24	Oregon	11.6
18	Missouri	14.3		24	Virginia	11.6
NA	Montana**	NA		26	Indiana	10.2
30	Nebraska	6.3		27	Wisconsin	8.8
37	Nevada	2.7		28	Louisiana	7.7
14	New Hampshire	20.0		29	Texas	6.8
43	New Jersey	0.0		30	Nebraska	6.3
16	New Mexico	19.8		31	Colorado	6.1
39	New York	2.1		32	Alabama	5.4
14	North Carolina	20.0		33	Pennsylvania	5.2
8	North Dakota	28.6		34	Utah	4.8
36	Ohio	3.9		35	Michigan	4.0
17	Oklahoma	18.8		36	Ohio	3.9
24	Oregon	11.6		37	Nevada	2.7
33	Pennsylvania	5.2		38	Connecticut	2.5
43	Rhode Island	0.0		39	Arizona	2.1
13	South Carolina	21.7		39	New York	2.1
1	South Dakota	66.7		41	Maryland	1.9
23	Tennessee	11.9		42	California	0.8
29	Texas	6.8		43	Massachusetts	0.0
34	Utah	4.8		43	New Jersey	0.0
4	Vermont	45.5		43	Rhode Island	0.0
24	Virginia	11.6		NA	Florida**	NA
20	Washington	12.9		NA	Illinois**	NA
5	West Virginia	43.5		NA	Kansas**	NA
27	Wisconsin	8.8		NA	Kentucky**	NA
2	Wyoming	62.5		NA	Montana**	NA
					District of Columbia	0.0

Source: Morgan Quitno Press using data from Federal Bureau of Investigation
"Crime in the United States 1996" (Uniform Crime Reports, October 4, 1997)
Estimated percentages for rural areas, defined by the F.B.I. as other than Metropolitan Statistical Areas and other cities outside such areas. National percent includes those states listed as not available. Includes nonnegligent manslaughter.
**Not available.*

Rapes in Urban Areas in 1996

National Urban Total = 88,136 Rapes*

ALPHA ORDER

RANK	STATE	RAPES	% of USA
23	Alabama	1,287	1.46%
36	Alaska	281	0.32%
22	Arizona	1,349	1.53%
26	Arkansas	897	1.02%
1	California	10,070	11.43%
16	Colorado	1,703	1.93%
31	Connecticut	734	0.83%
34	Delaware	382	0.43%
NA	Florida**	NA	NA
9	Georgia	2,064	2.34%
41	Hawaii	236	0.27%
40	Idaho	241	0.27%
NA	Illinois**	NA	NA
14	Indiana	1,823	2.07%
32	Iowa	523	0.59%
NA	Kansas**	NA	NA
NA	Kentucky**	NA	NA
17	Louisiana	1,646	1.87%
42	Maine	205	0.23%
13	Maryland	1,829	2.08%
15	Massachusetts	1,767	2.00%
3	Michigan	4,593	5.21%
10	Minnesota	2,015	2.29%
29	Mississippi	807	0.92%
21	Missouri	1,390	1.58%
NA	Montana**	NA	NA
33	Nebraska	416	0.47%
28	Nevada	812	0.92%
34	New Hampshire	382	0.43%
11	New Jersey	1,976	2.24%
27	New Mexico	889	1.01%
5	New York	4,036	4.58%
12	North Carolina	1,935	2.20%
43	North Dakota	138	0.16%
4	Ohio	4,446	5.04%
20	Oklahoma	1,445	1.64%
24	Oregon	1,137	1.29%
6	Pennsylvania	2,770	3.14%
37	Rhode Island	280	0.32%
19	South Carolina	1,504	1.71%
39	South Dakota	260	0.29%
8	Tennessee	2,266	2.57%
2	Texas	8,060	9.14%
30	Utah	775	0.88%
44	Vermont	134	0.15%
18	Virginia	1,595	1.81%
7	Washington	2,615	2.97%
38	West Virginia	267	0.30%
25	Wisconsin	967	1.10%
45	Wyoming	128	0.15%

RANK ORDER

RANK	STATE	RAPES	% of USA
1	California	10,070	11.43%
2	Texas	8,060	9.14%
3	Michigan	4,593	5.21%
4	Ohio	4,446	5.04%
5	New York	4,036	4.58%
6	Pennsylvania	2,770	3.14%
7	Washington	2,615	2.97%
8	Tennessee	2,266	2.57%
9	Georgia	2,064	2.34%
10	Minnesota	2,015	2.29%
11	New Jersey	1,976	2.24%
12	North Carolina	1,935	2.20%
13	Maryland	1,829	2.08%
14	Indiana	1,823	2.07%
15	Massachusetts	1,767	2.00%
16	Colorado	1,703	1.93%
17	Louisiana	1,646	1.87%
18	Virginia	1,595	1.81%
19	South Carolina	1,504	1.71%
20	Oklahoma	1,445	1.64%
21	Missouri	1,390	1.58%
22	Arizona	1,349	1.53%
23	Alabama	1,287	1.46%
24	Oregon	1,137	1.29%
25	Wisconsin	967	1.10%
26	Arkansas	897	1.02%
27	New Mexico	889	1.01%
28	Nevada	812	0.92%
29	Mississippi	807	0.92%
30	Utah	775	0.88%
31	Connecticut	734	0.83%
32	Iowa	523	0.59%
33	Nebraska	416	0.47%
34	Delaware	382	0.43%
34	New Hampshire	382	0.43%
36	Alaska	281	0.32%
37	Rhode Island	280	0.32%
38	West Virginia	267	0.30%
39	South Dakota	260	0.29%
40	Idaho	241	0.27%
41	Hawaii	236	0.27%
42	Maine	205	0.23%
43	North Dakota	138	0.16%
44	Vermont	134	0.15%
45	Wyoming	128	0.15%
NA	Florida**	NA	NA
NA	Illinois**	NA	NA
NA	Kansas**	NA	NA
NA	Kentucky**	NA	NA
NA	Montana**	NA	NA
	District of Columbia	260	0.29%

Source: Morgan Quitno Press using data from Federal Bureau of Investigation
"Crime in the United States 1996" (Uniform Crime Reports, October 4, 1997)
*Estimated totals for urban areas, defined by the F.B.I. as Metropolitan Statistical Areas and other cities outside such areas. National total includes those states listed as not available. Forcible rape is the carnal knowledge of a female forcibly and against her will. Attempts are included. However, statutory rape without force and other sex offenses are excluded. **Not available.

Urban Rape Rate in 1996

National Urban Rate = 37.8 Rapes per 100,000 Population*

RANK	STATE (ALPHA ORDER)	RATE		RANK	STATE (RANK ORDER)	RATE
24	Alabama	36.9		1	Alaska	67.6
1	Alaska	67.6		2	New Mexico	63.0
30	Arizona	33.0		3	Delaware	60.4
10	Arkansas	52.6		4	South Dakota	59.1
32	California	32.2		5	Nevada	57.3
14	Colorado	48.6		6	Oklahoma	54.2
42	Connecticut	23.8		7	Michigan	53.8
3	Delaware	60.4		8	Tennessee	53.7
NA	Florida**	NA		9	Minnesota	53.3
26	Georgia	35.0		10	Arkansas	52.6
38	Hawaii	25.7		11	Washington	52.1
33	Idaho	30.4		12	South Carolina	51.7
NA	Illinois**	NA		13	Mississippi	50.3
21	Indiana	38.1		14	Colorado	48.6
37	Iowa	26.6		15	Texas	46.1
NA	Kansas**	NA		16	Ohio	45.2
NA	Kentucky**	NA		17	Louisiana	44.9
17	Louisiana	44.9		18	Utah	43.4
45	Maine	22.9		19	Oregon	42.3
21	Maryland	38.1		20	Vermont	38.4
34	Massachusetts	29.1		21	Indiana	38.1
7	Michigan	53.8		21	Maryland	38.1
9	Minnesota	53.3		23	New Hampshire	37.8
13	Mississippi	50.3		24	Alabama	36.9
29	Missouri	33.5		25	Wyoming	36.0
NA	Montana**	NA		26	Georgia	35.0
28	Nebraska	33.8		27	North Carolina	34.3
5	Nevada	57.3		28	Nebraska	33.8
23	New Hampshire	37.8		29	Missouri	33.5
41	New Jersey	24.7		30	Arizona	33.0
2	New Mexico	63.0		31	North Dakota	32.8
43	New York	23.3		32	California	32.2
27	North Carolina	34.3		33	Idaho	30.4
31	North Dakota	32.8		34	Massachusetts	29.1
16	Ohio	45.2		35	Virginia	28.4
6	Oklahoma	54.2		36	Rhode Island	28.3
19	Oregon	42.3		37	Iowa	26.6
40	Pennsylvania	25.2		38	Hawaii	25.7
36	Rhode Island	28.3		39	West Virginia	25.6
12	South Carolina	51.7		40	Pennsylvania	25.2
4	South Dakota	59.1		41	New Jersey	24.7
8	Tennessee	53.7		42	Connecticut	23.8
15	Texas	46.1		43	New York	23.3
18	Utah	43.4		44	Wisconsin	23.2
20	Vermont	38.4		45	Maine	22.9
35	Virginia	28.4		NA	Florida**	NA
11	Washington	52.1		NA	Illinois**	NA
39	West Virginia	25.6		NA	Kansas**	NA
44	Wisconsin	23.2		NA	Kentucky**	NA
25	Wyoming	36.0		NA	Montana**	NA
					District of Columbia	47.9

Source: Morgan Quitno Press using data from Federal Bureau of Investigation
"Crime in the United States 1996" (Uniform Crime Reports, October 4, 1997)
*Estimated rates for urban areas, defined by the F.B.I. as Metropolitan Statistical Areas and other cities outside such areas. National rate includes those states listed as not available. Forcible rape is the carnal knowledge of a female forcibly and against her will. Attempts are included. However, statutory rape without force and other sex offenses are excluded. **Not available.

Percent of Rapes Occurring in Urban Areas in 1996

National Percent = 92.0% of Rapes*

ALPHA ORDER				RANK ORDER		
RANK	STATE	PERCENT		RANK	STATE	PERCENT
19	Alabama	92.1		1	Massachusetts	100.0
45	Alaska	70.6		1	New Jersey	100.0
4	Arizona	97.7		3	California	98.3
33	Arkansas	85.8		4	Arizona	97.7
3	California	98.3		5	Rhode Island	97.6
8	Colorado	96.5		6	Connecticut	97.2
6	Connecticut	97.2		7	New York	96.7
36	Delaware	84.1		8	Colorado	96.5
NA	Florida**	NA		9	Ohio	96.3
30	Georgia	87.6		10	Texas	96.2
44	Hawaii	72.4		11	Maryland	96.0
42	Idaho	77.0		12	Nevada	94.9
NA	Illinois**	NA		13	New Hampshire	94.6
21	Indiana	91.5		14	Oklahoma	93.5
15	Iowa	93.2		15	Iowa	93.2
NA	Kansas**	NA		16	Nebraska	93.1
NA	Kentucky**	NA		17	Utah	92.7
23	Louisiana	91.2		18	Washington	92.5
41	Maine	78.8		19	Alabama	92.1
11	Maryland	96.0		20	Tennessee	91.6
1	Massachusetts	100.0		21	Indiana	91.5
37	Michigan	84.0		22	Wyoming	91.4
32	Minnesota	86.6		23	Louisiana	91.2
39	Mississippi	82.3		24	Pennsylvania	90.9
29	Missouri	88.8		25	Virginia	89.5
NA	Montana**	NA		26	Oregon	89.4
16	Nebraska	93.1		27	North Dakota	89.0
12	Nevada	94.9		27	Wisconsin	89.0
13	New Hampshire	94.6		29	Missouri	88.8
1	New Jersey	100.0		30	Georgia	87.6
40	New Mexico	81.7		31	South Dakota	86.7
7	New York	96.7		32	Minnesota	86.6
34	North Carolina	84.5		33	Arkansas	85.8
27	North Dakota	89.0		34	North Carolina	84.5
9	Ohio	96.3		35	Vermont	84.3
14	Oklahoma	93.5		36	Delaware	84.1
26	Oregon	89.4		37	Michigan	84.0
24	Pennsylvania	90.9		38	South Carolina	82.6
5	Rhode Island	97.6		39	Mississippi	82.3
38	South Carolina	82.6		40	New Mexico	81.7
31	South Dakota	86.7		41	Maine	78.8
20	Tennessee	91.6		42	Idaho	77.0
10	Texas	96.2		43	West Virginia	74.6
17	Utah	92.7		44	Hawaii	72.4
35	Vermont	84.3		45	Alaska	70.6
25	Virginia	89.5		NA	Florida**	NA
18	Washington	92.5		NA	Illinois**	NA
43	West Virginia	74.6		NA	Kansas**	NA
27	Wisconsin	89.0		NA	Kentucky**	NA
22	Wyoming	91.4		NA	Montana**	NA
					District of Columbia	100.0

Source: Morgan Quitno Press using data from Federal Bureau of Investigation
    "Crime in the United States 1996" (Uniform Crime Reports, October 4, 1997)
*Estimated percentages for urban areas, defined by the F.B.I. as Metropolitan Statistical Areas and other cities
outside such areas. National percent includes those states listed as not available. Forcible rape is the carnal
knowledge of a female forcibly and against her will. Attempts are included. However, statutory rape without force
and other sex offenses are excluded. **Not available.

Rapes in Rural Areas in 1996

National Rural Total = 7,633 Rapes*

ALPHA ORDER					RANK ORDER			
RANK	STATE		RAPES	% of USA	RANK	STATE	RAPES	% of USA
23	Alabama		110	1.44%	1	Michigan	873	11.44%
22	Alaska		117	1.53%	2	North Carolina	354	4.64%
36	Arizona		32	0.42%	3	South Carolina	317	4.15%
18	Arkansas		149	1.95%	4	Texas	316	4.14%
13	California		174	2.28%	5	Minnesota	312	4.09%
30	Colorado		62	0.81%	6	Georgia	293	3.84%
40	Connecticut		21	0.28%	7	Pennsylvania	278	3.64%
28	Delaware		72	0.94%	8	Washington	213	2.79%
NA	Florida**		NA	NA	9	Tennessee	209	2.74%
6	Georgia		293	3.84%	10	New Mexico	199	2.61%
26	Hawaii		90	1.18%	11	Virginia	188	2.46%
28	Idaho		72	0.94%	12	Missouri	176	2.31%
NA	Illinois**		NA	NA	13	California	174	2.28%
16	Indiana		169	2.21%	13	Mississippi	174	2.28%
35	Iowa		38	0.50%	15	Ohio	171	2.24%
NA	Kansas**		NA	NA	16	Indiana	169	2.21%
NA	Kentucky**		NA	NA	17	Louisiana	159	2.08%
17	Louisiana		159	2.08%	18	Arkansas	149	1.95%
32	Maine		55	0.72%	19	New York	138	1.81%
27	Maryland		76	1.00%	20	Oregon	135	1.77%
44	Massachusetts		0	0.00%	21	Wisconsin	119	1.56%
1	Michigan		873	11.44%	22	Alaska	117	1.53%
5	Minnesota		312	4.09%	23	Alabama	110	1.44%
13	Mississippi		174	2.28%	24	Oklahoma	100	1.31%
12	Missouri		176	2.31%	25	West Virginia	91	1.19%
NA	Montana**		NA	NA	26	Hawaii	90	1.18%
37	Nebraska		31	0.41%	27	Maryland	76	1.00%
33	Nevada		44	0.58%	28	Delaware	72	0.94%
39	New Hampshire		22	0.29%	28	Idaho	72	0.94%
44	New Jersey		0	0.00%	30	Colorado	62	0.81%
10	New Mexico		199	2.61%	31	Utah	61	0.80%
19	New York		138	1.81%	32	Maine	55	0.72%
2	North Carolina		354	4.64%	33	Nevada	44	0.58%
41	North Dakota		17	0.22%	34	South Dakota	40	0.52%
15	Ohio		171	2.24%	35	Iowa	38	0.50%
24	Oklahoma		100	1.31%	36	Arizona	32	0.42%
20	Oregon		135	1.77%	37	Nebraska	31	0.41%
7	Pennsylvania		278	3.64%	38	Vermont	25	0.33%
43	Rhode Island		7	0.09%	39	New Hampshire	22	0.29%
3	South Carolina		317	4.15%	40	Connecticut	21	0.28%
34	South Dakota		40	0.52%	41	North Dakota	17	0.22%
9	Tennessee		209	2.74%	42	Wyoming	12	0.16%
4	Texas		316	4.14%	43	Rhode Island	7	0.09%
31	Utah		61	0.80%	44	Massachusetts	0	0.00%
38	Vermont		25	0.33%	44	New Jersey	0	0.00%
11	Virginia		188	2.46%	NA	Florida**	NA	NA
8	Washington		213	2.79%	NA	Illinois**	NA	NA
25	West Virginia		91	1.19%	NA	Kansas**	NA	NA
21	Wisconsin		119	1.56%	NA	Kentucky**	NA	NA
42	Wyoming		12	0.16%	NA	Montana**	NA	NA
						District of Columbia	0	0.00%

Source: Federal Bureau of Investigation
"Crime in the United States 1996" (Uniform Crime Reports, October 4, 1997)
*Estimated totals for rural areas, defined by the F.B.I. as other than Metropolitan Statistical Areas and other cities outside such areas. National total includes those states listed as not available. Forcible rape is the carnal knowledge of a female forcibly and against her will. Attempts are included. However, statutory rape without force and other sex offenses are excluded. **Not available.

Rural Rape Rate in 1996

National Rural Rate = 23.8 Rapes per 100,000 Population*

ALPHA ORDER				RANK ORDER		
RANK	STATE	RATE		RANK	STATE	RATE
31	Alabama	14.1		1	Michigan	82.7
4	Alaska	61.2		2	Delaware	77.4
39	Arizona	9.4		3	New Mexico	65.8
21	Arkansas	18.5		4	Alaska	61.2
11	California	27.7		5	Washington	41.8
18	Colorado	19.5		6	South Carolina	40.0
36	Connecticut	10.9		7	Minnesota	35.6
2	Delaware	77.4		8	Hawaii	33.9
NA	Florida**	NA		9	Maryland	28.5
17	Georgia	20.2		9	Utah	28.5
8	Hawaii	33.9		11	California	27.7
22	Idaho	18.2		12	Pennsylvania	26.3
NA	Illinois**	NA		13	Oregon	26.2
25	Indiana	16.0		14	Nevada	23.6
42	Iowa	4.3		15	Louisiana	23.2
NA	Kansas**	NA		16	North Carolina	21.0
NA	Kentucky**	NA		17	Georgia	20.2
15	Louisiana	23.2		18	Colorado	19.5
26	Maine	15.8		19	Texas	19.4
9	Maryland	28.5		20	Tennessee	19.0
43	Massachusetts	0.0		21	Arkansas	18.5
1	Michigan	82.7		22	Idaho	18.2
7	Minnesota	35.6		23	Virginia	17.7
27	Mississippi	15.7		24	New York	16.1
29	Missouri	14.6		25	Indiana	16.0
NA	Montana**	NA		26	Maine	15.8
41	Nebraska	7.4		27	Mississippi	15.7
14	Nevada	23.6		27	Oklahoma	15.7
29	New Hampshire	14.6		29	Missouri	14.6
43	New Jersey	0.0		29	New Hampshire	14.6
3	New Mexico	65.8		31	Alabama	14.1
24	New York	16.1		32	South Dakota	13.7
16	North Carolina	21.0		33	Ohio	12.9
40	North Dakota	7.6		34	Wisconsin	12.0
33	Ohio	12.9		35	West Virginia	11.6
27	Oklahoma	15.7		36	Connecticut	10.9
13	Oregon	26.2		37	Vermont	10.4
12	Pennsylvania	26.3		38	Wyoming	9.5
43	Rhode Island	0.0		39	Arizona	9.4
6	South Carolina	40.0		40	North Dakota	7.6
32	South Dakota	13.7		41	Nebraska	7.4
20	Tennessee	19.0		42	Iowa	4.3
19	Texas	19.4		43	Massachusetts	0.0
9	Utah	28.5		43	New Jersey	0.0
37	Vermont	10.4		43	Rhode Island	0.0
23	Virginia	17.7		NA	Florida**	NA
5	Washington	41.8		NA	Illinois**	NA
35	West Virginia	11.6		NA	Kansas**	NA
34	Wisconsin	12.0		NA	Kentucky**	NA
38	Wyoming	9.5		NA	Montana**	NA
					District of Columbia	0.0

Source: Morgan Quitno Press using data from Federal Bureau of Investigation
    "Crime in the United States 1996" (Uniform Crime Reports, October 4, 1997)
*Estimated rates for rural areas, defined by the F.B.I. as other than Metropolitan Statistical Areas and other cities outside such areas. National rate includes those states listed as not available. Forcible rape is the carnal knowledge of a female forcibly and against her will. Attempts are included. However, statutory rape without force and other sex offenses are excluded. **Not available.

423

Percent of Rapes Occurring in Rural Areas in 1996

National Percent = 8.0% of Rapes*

ALPHA ORDER

RANK	STATE	PERCENT
27	Alabama	7.9
1	Alaska	29.4
42	Arizona	2.3
13	Arkansas	14.2
43	California	1.7
38	Colorado	3.5
40	Connecticut	2.8
10	Delaware	15.9
NA	Florida**	NA
16	Georgia	12.4
2	Hawaii	27.6
4	Idaho	23.0
NA	Illinois**	NA
25	Indiana	8.5
31	Iowa	6.8
NA	Kansas**	NA
NA	Kentucky**	NA
23	Louisiana	8.8
5	Maine	21.2
35	Maryland	4.0
44	Massachusetts	0.0
9	Michigan	16.0
14	Minnesota	13.4
7	Mississippi	17.7
17	Missouri	11.2
NA	Montana**	NA
30	Nebraska	6.9
34	Nevada	5.1
33	New Hampshire	5.4
44	New Jersey	0.0
6	New Mexico	18.3
39	New York	3.3
12	North Carolina	15.5
18	North Dakota	11.0
37	Ohio	3.7
32	Oklahoma	6.5
20	Oregon	10.6
22	Pennsylvania	9.1
41	Rhode Island	2.4
8	South Carolina	17.4
15	South Dakota	13.3
26	Tennessee	8.4
36	Texas	3.8
29	Utah	7.3
11	Vermont	15.7
21	Virginia	10.5
28	Washington	7.5
3	West Virginia	25.4
18	Wisconsin	11.0
24	Wyoming	8.6

RANK ORDER

RANK	STATE	PERCENT
1	Alaska	29.4
2	Hawaii	27.6
3	West Virginia	25.4
4	Idaho	23.0
5	Maine	21.2
6	New Mexico	18.3
7	Mississippi	17.7
8	South Carolina	17.4
9	Michigan	16.0
10	Delaware	15.9
11	Vermont	15.7
12	North Carolina	15.5
13	Arkansas	14.2
14	Minnesota	13.4
15	South Dakota	13.3
16	Georgia	12.4
17	Missouri	11.2
18	North Dakota	11.0
18	Wisconsin	11.0
20	Oregon	10.6
21	Virginia	10.5
22	Pennsylvania	9.1
23	Louisiana	8.8
24	Wyoming	8.6
25	Indiana	8.5
26	Tennessee	8.4
27	Alabama	7.9
28	Washington	7.5
29	Utah	7.3
30	Nebraska	6.9
31	Iowa	6.8
32	Oklahoma	6.5
33	New Hampshire	5.4
34	Nevada	5.1
35	Maryland	4.0
36	Texas	3.8
37	Ohio	3.7
38	Colorado	3.5
39	New York	3.3
40	Connecticut	2.8
41	Rhode Island	2.4
42	Arizona	2.3
43	California	1.7
44	Massachusetts	0.0
44	New Jersey	0.0
NA	Florida**	NA
NA	Illinois**	NA
NA	Kansas**	NA
NA	Kentucky**	NA
NA	Montana**	NA
	District of Columbia	0.0

Source: Morgan Quitno Press using data from Federal Bureau of Investigation
      "Crime in the United States 1996" (Uniform Crime Reports, October 4, 1997)
*Estimated percentages for rural areas, defined by the F.B.I. as other than Metropolitan Statistical Areas and other cities outside such areas. National percent includes those states listed as not available. Forcible rape is the carnal knowledge of a female forcibly and against her will. Attempts are included. However, statutory rape without force and other sex offenses are excluded. **Not available.*

Robberies in Urban Areas in 1996

National Urban Total = 531,786 Robberies*

ALPHA ORDER					RANK ORDER			
RANK	STATE	ROBBERIES	% of USA		RANK	STATE	ROBBERIES	% of USA
18	Alabama	7,019	1.32%		1	California	94,048	17.69%
37	Alaska	677	0.13%		2	New York	61,729	11.61%
16	Arizona	7,405	1.39%		3	Texas	32,591	6.13%
29	Arkansas	2,780	0.52%		4	Pennsylvania	24,126	4.54%
1	California	94,048	17.69%		5	Maryland	19,842	3.73%
26	Colorado	3,735	0.70%		6	New Jersey	18,838	3.54%
21	Connecticut	5,519	1.04%		7	Ohio	18,239	3.43%
34	Delaware	1,222	0.23%		8	Michigan	16,815	3.16%
NA	Florida**	NA	NA		9	Georgia	14,709	2.77%
9	Georgia	14,709	2.77%		10	Louisiana	11,897	2.24%
31	Hawaii	1,451	0.27%		11	Tennessee	11,747	2.21%
41	Idaho	216	0.04%		12	North Carolina	11,502	2.16%
NA	Illinois**	NA	NA		13	Missouri	9,051	1.70%
17	Indiana	7,174	1.35%		14	Virginia	7,971	1.50%
33	Iowa	1,277	0.24%		15	Massachusetts	7,778	1.46%
NA	Kansas**	NA	NA		16	Arizona	7,405	1.39%
NA	Kentucky**	NA	NA		17	Indiana	7,174	1.35%
10	Louisiana	11,897	2.24%		18	Alabama	7,019	1.32%
40	Maine	280	0.05%		19	Washington	6,519	1.23%
5	Maryland	19,842	3.73%		20	South Carolina	5,669	1.07%
15	Massachusetts	7,778	1.46%		21	Connecticut	5,519	1.04%
8	Michigan	16,815	3.16%		22	Minnesota	5,348	1.01%
22	Minnesota	5,348	1.01%		23	Wisconsin	4,955	0.93%
28	Mississippi	3,295	0.62%		24	Nevada	4,876	0.92%
13	Missouri	9,051	1.70%		25	Oregon	3,816	0.72%
NA	Montana**	NA	NA		26	Colorado	3,735	0.70%
35	Nebraska	1,043	0.20%		27	Oklahoma	3,469	0.65%
24	Nevada	4,876	0.92%		28	Mississippi	3,295	0.62%
39	New Hampshire	312	0.06%		29	Arkansas	2,780	0.52%
6	New Jersey	18,838	3.54%		30	New Mexico	2,723	0.51%
30	New Mexico	2,723	0.51%		31	Hawaii	1,451	0.27%
2	New York	61,729	11.61%		32	Utah	1,356	0.25%
12	North Carolina	11,502	2.16%		33	Iowa	1,277	0.24%
45	North Dakota	66	0.01%		34	Delaware	1,222	0.23%
7	Ohio	18,239	3.43%		35	Nebraska	1,043	0.20%
27	Oklahoma	3,469	0.65%		36	Rhode Island	823	0.15%
25	Oregon	3,816	0.72%		37	Alaska	677	0.13%
4	Pennsylvania	24,126	4.54%		38	West Virginia	676	0.13%
36	Rhode Island	823	0.15%		39	New Hampshire	312	0.06%
20	South Carolina	5,669	1.07%		40	Maine	280	0.05%
42	South Dakota	129	0.02%		41	Idaho	216	0.04%
11	Tennessee	11,747	2.21%		42	South Dakota	129	0.02%
3	Texas	32,591	6.13%		43	Wyoming	92	0.02%
32	Utah	1,356	0.25%		44	Vermont	88	0.02%
44	Vermont	88	0.02%		45	North Dakota	66	0.01%
14	Virginia	7,971	1.50%		NA	Florida**	NA	NA
19	Washington	6,519	1.23%		NA	Illinois**	NA	NA
38	West Virginia	676	0.13%		NA	Kansas**	NA	NA
23	Wisconsin	4,955	0.93%		NA	Kentucky**	NA	NA
43	Wyoming	92	0.02%		NA	Montana**	NA	NA
						District of Columbia	6,444	1.21%

Source: Morgan Quitno Press using data from Federal Bureau of Investigation
"Crime in the United States 1996" (Uniform Crime Reports, October 4, 1997)
*Estimated totals for urban areas, defined by the F.B.I. as Metropolitan Statistical Areas and other cities outside such areas. National total includes those states listed as not available. Robbery is the taking or attempting to take anything of value by force or threat of force.
**Not available.

Urban Robbery Rate in 1996

National Urban Rate = 228.0 Robberies per 100,000 Population*

ALPHA ORDER

RANK	STATE	RATE
13	Alabama	201.1
23	Alaska	162.8
20	Arizona	181.2
22	Arkansas	163.1
5	California	301.0
33	Colorado	106.5
21	Connecticut	179.2
16	Delaware	193.4
NA	Florida**	NA
7	Georgia	249.1
24	Hawaii	158.0
42	Idaho	27.2
NA	Illinois**	NA
25	Indiana	150.0
37	Iowa	64.9
NA	Kansas**	NA
NA	Kentucky**	NA
4	Louisiana	324.6
39	Maine	31.3
1	Maryland	412.9
31	Massachusetts	127.9
14	Michigan	196.9
28	Minnesota	141.4
11	Mississippi	205.3
10	Missouri	218.1
NA	Montana**	NA
34	Nebraska	84.7
3	Nevada	344.2
40	New Hampshire	30.8
8	New Jersey	235.8
17	New Mexico	193.0
2	New York	356.2
12	North Carolina	204.2
45	North Dakota	15.7
19	Ohio	185.3
29	Oklahoma	130.1
27	Oregon	141.9
9	Pennsylvania	219.4
35	Rhode Island	83.1
15	South Carolina	195.0
41	South Dakota	29.3
6	Tennessee	278.3
18	Texas	186.3
36	Utah	75.9
44	Vermont	25.2
26	Virginia	142.0
30	Washington	129.8
38	West Virginia	64.8
32	Wisconsin	118.8
43	Wyoming	25.9

RANK ORDER

RANK	STATE	RATE
1	Maryland	412.9
2	New York	356.2
3	Nevada	344.2
4	Louisiana	324.6
5	California	301.0
6	Tennessee	278.3
7	Georgia	249.1
8	New Jersey	235.8
9	Pennsylvania	219.4
10	Missouri	218.1
11	Mississippi	205.3
12	North Carolina	204.2
13	Alabama	201.1
14	Michigan	196.9
15	South Carolina	195.0
16	Delaware	193.4
17	New Mexico	193.0
18	Texas	186.3
19	Ohio	185.3
20	Arizona	181.2
21	Connecticut	179.2
22	Arkansas	163.1
23	Alaska	162.8
24	Hawaii	158.0
25	Indiana	150.0
26	Virginia	142.0
27	Oregon	141.9
28	Minnesota	141.4
29	Oklahoma	130.1
30	Washington	129.8
31	Massachusetts	127.9
32	Wisconsin	118.8
33	Colorado	106.5
34	Nebraska	84.7
35	Rhode Island	83.1
36	Utah	75.9
37	Iowa	64.9
38	West Virginia	64.8
39	Maine	31.3
40	New Hampshire	30.8
41	South Dakota	29.3
42	Idaho	27.2
43	Wyoming	25.9
44	Vermont	25.2
45	North Dakota	15.7
NA	Florida**	NA
NA	Illinois**	NA
NA	Kansas**	NA
NA	Kentucky**	NA
NA	Montana**	NA
	District of Columbia	1,186.7

Source: Morgan Quitno Press using data from Federal Bureau of Investigation
"Crime in the United States 1996" (Uniform Crime Reports, October 4, 1997)
*Estimated rates for urban areas, defined by the F.B.I. as Metropolitan Statistical Areas and other cities outside such areas. National rate includes those states listed as not available. Robbery is the taking or attempting to take anything of value by force or threat of force.
**Not available.

Percent of Robberies Occurring in Urban Areas in 1996

National Percent = 99.0% of Robberies*

ALPHA ORDER				RANK ORDER		
RANK	STATE	PERCENT		RANK	STATE	PERCENT
25	Alabama	98.5		1	Massachusetts	100.0
36	Alaska	95.4		1	New Jersey	100.0
6	Arizona	99.7		3	Rhode Island	99.9
32	Arkansas	97.1		4	California	99.8
4	California	99.8		4	New York	99.8
7	Colorado	99.5		6	Arizona	99.7
13	Connecticut	99.4		7	Colorado	99.5
38	Delaware	93.7		7	Maryland	99.5
NA	Florida**	NA		7	Michigan	99.5
30	Georgia	97.4		7	Ohio	99.5
43	Hawaii	90.3		7	Pennsylvania	99.5
44	Idaho	89.6		7	Wisconsin	99.5
NA	Illinois**	NA		13	Connecticut	99.4
18	Indiana	99.0		13	Texas	99.4
15	Iowa	99.3		15	Iowa	99.3
NA	Kansas**	NA		15	Minnesota	99.3
NA	Kentucky**	NA		17	Nebraska	99.1
22	Louisiana	98.8		18	Indiana	99.0
34	Maine	95.9		18	Missouri	99.0
7	Maryland	99.5		18	Washington	99.0
1	Massachusetts	100.0		21	Nevada	98.9
7	Michigan	99.5		22	Louisiana	98.8
15	Minnesota	99.3		23	Tennessee	98.7
42	Mississippi	90.4		24	Oklahoma	98.6
18	Missouri	99.0		25	Alabama	98.5
NA	Montana**	NA		25	Utah	98.5
17	Nebraska	99.1		27	New Hampshire	98.4
21	Nevada	98.9		28	New Mexico	97.9
27	New Hampshire	98.4		29	Oregon	97.5
1	New Jersey	100.0		30	Georgia	97.4
28	New Mexico	97.9		30	Virginia	97.4
4	New York	99.8		32	Arkansas	97.1
35	North Carolina	95.8		33	Vermont	96.7
40	North Dakota	93.0		34	Maine	95.9
7	Ohio	99.5		35	North Carolina	95.8
24	Oklahoma	98.6		36	Alaska	95.4
29	Oregon	97.5		37	Wyoming	93.9
7	Pennsylvania	99.5		38	Delaware	93.7
3	Rhode Island	99.9		39	South Dakota	93.5
45	South Carolina	89.1		40	North Dakota	93.0
39	South Dakota	93.5		41	West Virginia	91.7
23	Tennessee	98.7		42	Mississippi	90.4
13	Texas	99.4		43	Hawaii	90.3
25	Utah	98.5		44	Idaho	89.6
33	Vermont	96.7		45	South Carolina	89.1
30	Virginia	97.4		NA	Florida**	NA
18	Washington	99.0		NA	Illinois**	NA
41	West Virginia	91.7		NA	Kansas**	NA
7	Wisconsin	99.5		NA	Kentucky**	NA
37	Wyoming	93.9		NA	Montana**	NA
					District of Columbia	100.0

Source: Morgan Quitno Press using data from Federal Bureau of Investigation
"Crime in the United States 1996" (Uniform Crime Reports, October 4, 1997)
*Estimated percentages for urban areas, defined by the F.B.I. as Metropolitan Statistical Areas and other cities outside such areas. National percent includes those states listed as not available. Robbery is the taking or attempting to take anything of value by force or threat of force.
**Not available.

Robberies in Rural Areas in 1996

National Rural Total = 5,264 Robberies*

ALPHA ORDER					RANK ORDER			

RANK	STATE	ROBBERIES	% of USA		RANK	STATE	ROBBERIES	% of USA
12	Alabama	105	1.99%		1	South Carolina	692	13.15%
28	Alaska	33	0.63%		2	North Carolina	499	9.48%
32	Arizona	24	0.46%		3	Georgia	391	7.43%
19	Arkansas	84	1.60%		4	Mississippi	351	6.67%
7	California	174	3.31%		5	Texas	213	4.05%
34	Colorado	20	0.38%		6	Virginia	210	3.99%
28	Connecticut	33	0.63%		7	California	174	3.31%
20	Delaware	82	1.56%		8	Hawaii	155	2.94%
NA	Florida**	NA	NA		8	Tennessee	155	2.94%
3	Georgia	391	7.43%		10	Louisiana	139	2.64%
8	Hawaii	155	2.94%		11	Pennsylvania	114	2.17%
31	Idaho	25	0.47%		12	Alabama	105	1.99%
NA	Illinois**	NA	NA		13	Maryland	102	1.94%
21	Indiana	75	1.42%		14	Oregon	98	1.86%
36	Iowa	9	0.17%		15	Ohio	97	1.84%
NA	Kansas**	NA	NA		16	New York	93	1.77%
NA	Kentucky**	NA	NA		17	Michigan	92	1.75%
10	Louisiana	139	2.64%		18	Missouri	91	1.73%
35	Maine	12	0.23%		19	Arkansas	84	1.60%
13	Maryland	102	1.94%		20	Delaware	82	1.56%
44	Massachusetts	0	0.00%		21	Indiana	75	1.42%
17	Michigan	92	1.75%		22	Washington	68	1.29%
27	Minnesota	37	0.70%		23	West Virginia	61	1.16%
4	Mississippi	351	6.67%		24	New Mexico	59	1.12%
18	Missouri	91	1.73%		25	Nevada	55	1.04%
NA	Montana**	NA	NA		26	Oklahoma	50	0.95%
36	Nebraska	9	0.17%		27	Minnesota	37	0.70%
25	Nevada	55	1.04%		28	Alaska	33	0.63%
40	New Hampshire	5	0.09%		28	Connecticut	33	0.63%
44	New Jersey	0	0.00%		30	Wisconsin	27	0.51%
24	New Mexico	59	1.12%		31	Idaho	25	0.47%
16	New York	93	1.77%		32	Arizona	24	0.46%
2	North Carolina	499	9.48%		33	Utah	21	0.40%
40	North Dakota	5	0.09%		34	Colorado	20	0.38%
15	Ohio	97	1.84%		35	Maine	12	0.23%
26	Oklahoma	50	0.95%		36	Iowa	9	0.17%
14	Oregon	98	1.86%		36	Nebraska	9	0.17%
11	Pennsylvania	114	2.17%		36	South Dakota	9	0.17%
43	Rhode Island	1	0.02%		39	Wyoming	6	0.11%
1	South Carolina	692	13.15%		40	New Hampshire	5	0.09%
36	South Dakota	9	0.17%		40	North Dakota	5	0.09%
8	Tennessee	155	2.94%		42	Vermont	3	0.06%
5	Texas	213	4.05%		43	Rhode Island	1	0.02%
33	Utah	21	0.40%		44	Massachusetts	0	0.00%
42	Vermont	3	0.06%		44	New Jersey	0	0.00%
6	Virginia	210	3.99%		NA	Florida**	NA	NA
22	Washington	68	1.29%		NA	Illinois**	NA	NA
23	West Virginia	61	1.16%		NA	Kansas**	NA	NA
30	Wisconsin	27	0.51%		NA	Kentucky**	NA	NA
39	Wyoming	6	0.11%		NA	Montana**	NA	NA
						District of Columbia	0	0.00%

Source: Federal Bureau of Investigation
   "Crime in the United States 1996" (Uniform Crime Reports, October 4, 1997)
*Estimated totals for rural areas, defined by the F.B.I. as other than Metropolitan Statistical Areas and other cities outside such areas. National total includes those states listed as not available. Robbery is the taking or attempting to take anything of value by force or threat of force.
**Not available.

Rural Robbery Rate in 1996

National Rural Rate = 16.4 Robberies per 100,000 Population*

RANK	STATE	RATE
17	Alabama	13.4
14	Alaska	17.3
30	Arizona	7.0
22	Arkansas	10.4
8	California	27.7
31	Colorado	6.3
15	Connecticut	17.1
1	Delaware	88.1
NA	Florida**	NA
9	Georgia	27.0
3	Hawaii	58.4
31	Idaho	6.3
NA	Illinois**	NA
29	Indiana	7.1
42	Iowa	1.0
NA	Kansas**	NA
NA	Kentucky**	NA
10	Louisiana	20.3
35	Maine	3.5
4	Maryland	38.2
43	Massachusetts	0.0
24	Michigan	8.7
34	Minnesota	4.2
5	Mississippi	31.6
27	Missouri	7.5
NA	Montana**	NA
40	Nebraska	2.1
6	Nevada	29.5
36	New Hampshire	3.3
43	New Jersey	0.0
12	New Mexico	19.5
20	New York	10.9
6	North Carolina	29.5
39	North Dakota	2.2
28	Ohio	7.3
25	Oklahoma	7.9
13	Oregon	19.0
21	Pennsylvania	10.8
43	Rhode Island	0.0
2	South Carolina	87.4
37	South Dakota	3.1
16	Tennessee	14.1
19	Texas	13.1
23	Utah	9.8
41	Vermont	1.2
11	Virginia	19.8
18	Washington	13.3
26	West Virginia	7.8
38	Wisconsin	2.7
33	Wyoming	4.8

RANK ORDER

RANK	STATE	RATE
1	Delaware	88.1
2	South Carolina	87.4
3	Hawaii	58.4
4	Maryland	38.2
5	Mississippi	31.6
6	Nevada	29.5
6	North Carolina	29.5
8	California	27.7
9	Georgia	27.0
10	Louisiana	20.3
11	Virginia	19.8
12	New Mexico	19.5
13	Oregon	19.0
14	Alaska	17.3
15	Connecticut	17.1
16	Tennessee	14.1
17	Alabama	13.4
18	Washington	13.3
19	Texas	13.1
20	New York	10.9
21	Pennsylvania	10.8
22	Arkansas	10.4
23	Utah	9.8
24	Michigan	8.7
25	Oklahoma	7.9
26	West Virginia	7.8
27	Missouri	7.5
28	Ohio	7.3
29	Indiana	7.1
30	Arizona	7.0
31	Colorado	6.3
31	Idaho	6.3
33	Wyoming	4.8
34	Minnesota	4.2
35	Maine	3.5
36	New Hampshire	3.3
37	South Dakota	3.1
38	Wisconsin	2.7
39	North Dakota	2.2
40	Nebraska	2.1
41	Vermont	1.2
42	Iowa	1.0
43	Massachusetts	0.0
43	New Jersey	0.0
43	Rhode Island	0.0
NA	Florida**	NA
NA	Illinois**	NA
NA	Kansas**	NA
NA	Kentucky**	NA
NA	Montana**	NA
	District of Columbia	0.0

Source: Morgan Quitno Press using data from Federal Bureau of Investigation
    "Crime in the United States 1996" (Uniform Crime Reports, October 4, 1997)
*Estimated rates for rural areas, defined by the F.B.I. as other than Metropolitan Statistical Areas and other cities
outside such areas. National rate includes those states listed as not available. Robbery is the taking or
attempting to take anything of value by force or threat of force.
**Not available.

Percent of Robberies Occurring in Rural Areas in 1996

National Percent = 1.0% of Robberies*

ALPHA ORDER

RANK	STATE	PERCENT
20	Alabama	1.5
10	Alaska	4.6
40	Arizona	0.3
14	Arkansas	2.9
41	California	0.2
34	Colorado	0.5
32	Connecticut	0.6
8	Delaware	6.3
NA	Florida**	NA
15	Georgia	2.6
3	Hawaii	9.7
2	Idaho	10.4
NA	Illinois**	NA
26	Indiana	1.0
30	Iowa	0.7
NA	Kansas**	NA
NA	Kentucky**	NA
24	Louisiana	1.2
12	Maine	4.1
34	Maryland	0.5
44	Massachusetts	0.0
34	Michigan	0.5
30	Minnesota	0.7
4	Mississippi	9.6
26	Missouri	1.0
NA	Montana**	NA
29	Nebraska	0.9
25	Nevada	1.1
19	New Hampshire	1.6
44	New Jersey	0.0
18	New Mexico	2.1
41	New York	0.2
11	North Carolina	4.2
6	North Dakota	7.0
34	Ohio	0.5
22	Oklahoma	1.4
17	Oregon	2.5
34	Pennsylvania	0.5
43	Rhode Island	0.1
1	South Carolina	10.9
7	South Dakota	6.5
23	Tennessee	1.3
32	Texas	0.6
20	Utah	1.5
13	Vermont	3.3
15	Virginia	2.6
26	Washington	1.0
5	West Virginia	8.3
34	Wisconsin	0.5
9	Wyoming	6.1

RANK ORDER

RANK	STATE	PERCENT
1	South Carolina	10.9
2	Idaho	10.4
3	Hawaii	9.7
4	Mississippi	9.6
5	West Virginia	8.3
6	North Dakota	7.0
7	South Dakota	6.5
8	Delaware	6.3
9	Wyoming	6.1
10	Alaska	4.6
11	North Carolina	4.2
12	Maine	4.1
13	Vermont	3.3
14	Arkansas	2.9
15	Georgia	2.6
15	Virginia	2.6
17	Oregon	2.5
18	New Mexico	2.1
19	New Hampshire	1.6
20	Alabama	1.5
20	Utah	1.5
22	Oklahoma	1.4
23	Tennessee	1.3
24	Louisiana	1.2
25	Nevada	1.1
26	Indiana	1.0
26	Missouri	1.0
26	Washington	1.0
29	Nebraska	0.9
30	Iowa	0.7
30	Minnesota	0.7
32	Connecticut	0.6
32	Texas	0.6
34	Colorado	0.5
34	Maryland	0.5
34	Michigan	0.5
34	Ohio	0.5
34	Pennsylvania	0.5
34	Wisconsin	0.5
40	Arizona	0.3
41	California	0.2
41	New York	0.2
43	Rhode Island	0.1
44	Massachusetts	0.0
44	New Jersey	0.0
NA	Florida**	NA
NA	Illinois**	NA
NA	Kansas**	NA
NA	Kentucky**	NA
NA	Montana**	NA

| | District of Columbia | 0.0 |

Source: Morgan Quitno Press using data from Federal Bureau of Investigation
"Crime in the United States 1996" (Uniform Crime Reports, October 4, 1997)
Estimated percentages for rural areas, defined by the F.B.I. as other than Metropolitan Statistical Areas and other cities outside such areas. National percent includes those states listed as not available. Robbery is the taking or attempting to take anything of value by force or threat of force.
**Not available.*

Aggravated Assaults in Urban Areas in 1996

National Urban Total = 973,103 Aggravated Assaults*

RANK	STATE	ASSAULTS	% of USA		RANK	STATE	ASSAULTS	% of USA
18	Alabama	14,179	1.46%		1	California	164,955	16.95%
34	Alaska	2,446	0.25%		2	Texas	77,634	7.98%
17	Arizona	17,956	1.85%		3	New York	62,951	6.47%
25	Arkansas	8,107	0.83%		4	Michigan	36,219	3.72%
1	California	164,955	16.95%		5	Massachusetts	29,402	3.02%
22	Colorado	9,359	0.96%		6	Georgia	25,121	2.58%
27	Connecticut	6,636	0.68%		7	North Carolina	24,853	2.55%
35	Delaware	2,433	0.25%		8	Tennessee	24,159	2.48%
NA	Florida**	NA	NA		9	Maryland	24,049	2.47%
6	Georgia	25,121	2.58%		10	Ohio	23,550	2.42%
39	Hawaii	1,118	0.11%		11	South Carolina	23,151	2.38%
37	Idaho	1,973	0.20%		12	Pennsylvania	23,103	2.37%
NA	Illinois**	NA	NA		13	Louisiana	23,000	2.36%
15	Indiana	19,777	2.03%		14	New Jersey	21,307	2.19%
32	Iowa	5,423	0.56%		15	Indiana	19,777	2.03%
NA	Kansas**	NA	NA		16	Missouri	18,581	1.91%
NA	Kentucky**	NA	NA		17	Arizona	17,956	1.85%
13	Louisiana	23,000	2.36%		18	Alabama	14,179	1.46%
40	Maine	872	0.09%		19	Washington	13,398	1.38%
9	Maryland	24,049	2.47%		20	Oklahoma	13,061	1.34%
5	Massachusetts	29,402	3.02%		21	Virginia	11,090	1.14%
4	Michigan	36,219	3.72%		22	Colorado	9,359	0.96%
26	Minnesota	7,399	0.76%		23	New Mexico	8,800	0.90%
30	Mississippi	6,003	0.62%		23	Oregon	8,800	0.90%
16	Missouri	18,581	1.91%		25	Arkansas	8,107	0.83%
NA	Montana**	NA	NA		26	Minnesota	7,399	0.76%
31	Nebraska	5,426	0.56%		27	Connecticut	6,636	0.68%
28	Nevada	6,477	0.67%		28	Nevada	6,477	0.67%
43	New Hampshire	577	0.06%		29	Wisconsin	6,110	0.63%
14	New Jersey	21,307	2.19%		30	Mississippi	6,003	0.62%
23	New Mexico	8,800	0.90%		31	Nebraska	5,426	0.56%
3	New York	62,951	6.47%		32	Iowa	5,423	0.56%
7	North Carolina	24,853	2.55%		33	Utah	4,084	0.42%
45	North Dakota	256	0.03%		34	Alaska	2,446	0.25%
10	Ohio	23,550	2.42%		35	Delaware	2,433	0.25%
20	Oklahoma	13,061	1.34%		36	Rhode Island	2,289	0.24%
23	Oregon	8,800	0.90%		37	Idaho	1,973	0.20%
12	Pennsylvania	23,103	2.37%		38	West Virginia	1,674	0.17%
36	Rhode Island	2,289	0.24%		39	Hawaii	1,118	0.11%
11	South Carolina	23,151	2.38%		40	Maine	872	0.09%
41	South Dakota	758	0.08%		41	South Dakota	758	0.08%
8	Tennessee	24,159	2.48%		42	Wyoming	739	0.08%
2	Texas	77,634	7.98%		43	New Hampshire	577	0.06%
33	Utah	4,084	0.42%		44	Vermont	378	0.04%
44	Vermont	378	0.04%		45	North Dakota	256	0.03%
21	Virginia	11,090	1.14%		NA	Florida**	NA	NA
19	Washington	13,398	1.38%		NA	Illinois**	NA	NA
38	West Virginia	1,674	0.17%		NA	Kansas**	NA	NA
29	Wisconsin	6,110	0.63%		NA	Kentucky**	NA	NA
42	Wyoming	739	0.08%		NA	Montana**	NA	NA
						District of Columbia	6,310	0.65%

ALPHA ORDER / RANK ORDER

Source: Morgan Quitno Press using data from Federal Bureau of Investigation
"Crime in the United States 1996" (Uniform Crime Reports, October 4, 1997)
Estimated totals for urban areas, defined by the F.B.I. as Metropolitan Statistical Areas and other cities outside such areas. National total includes those states listed as not available. Aggravated assault is an attack for the purpose of inflicting severe bodily injury.
**Not available.

431

Urban Aggravated Assault Rate in 1996

National Urban Rate = 417.2 Aggravated Assaults per 100,000 Population*

ALPHA ORDER

RANK	STATE	RATE
20	Alabama	406.2
4	Alaska	588.1
16	Arizona	439.4
10	Arkansas	475.7
6	California	527.9
26	Colorado	267.0
33	Connecticut	215.4
21	Delaware	385.0
NA	Florida**	NA
17	Georgia	425.4
41	Hawaii	121.7
29	Idaho	248.8
NA	Illinois**	NA
19	Indiana	413.4
25	Iowa	275.8
NA	Kansas**	NA
NA	Kentucky**	NA
2	Louisiana	627.6
43	Maine	97.4
7	Maryland	500.5
9	Massachusetts	483.5
18	Michigan	424.2
37	Minnesota	195.7
22	Mississippi	373.9
12	Missouri	447.8
NA	Montana**	NA
15	Nebraska	440.6
11	Nevada	457.3
45	New Hampshire	57.0
27	New Jersey	266.7
3	New Mexico	623.8
23	New York	363.3
14	North Carolina	441.2
44	North Dakota	60.8
30	Ohio	239.2
8	Oklahoma	489.9
24	Oregon	327.2
34	Pennsylvania	210.1
31	Rhode Island	231.2
1	South Carolina	796.3
38	South Dakota	172.4
5	Tennessee	572.4
13	Texas	443.7
32	Utah	228.7
42	Vermont	108.5
36	Virginia	197.6
27	Washington	266.7
39	West Virginia	160.5
40	Wisconsin	146.5
35	Wyoming	208.1

RANK ORDER

RANK	STATE	RATE
1	South Carolina	796.3
2	Louisiana	627.6
3	New Mexico	623.8
4	Alaska	588.1
5	Tennessee	572.4
6	California	527.9
7	Maryland	500.5
8	Oklahoma	489.9
9	Massachusetts	483.5
10	Arkansas	475.7
11	Nevada	457.3
12	Missouri	447.8
13	Texas	443.7
14	North Carolina	441.2
15	Nebraska	440.6
16	Arizona	439.4
17	Georgia	425.4
18	Michigan	424.2
19	Indiana	413.4
20	Alabama	406.2
21	Delaware	385.0
22	Mississippi	373.9
23	New York	363.3
24	Oregon	327.2
25	Iowa	275.8
26	Colorado	267.0
27	New Jersey	266.7
27	Washington	266.7
29	Idaho	248.8
30	Ohio	239.2
31	Rhode Island	231.2
32	Utah	228.7
33	Connecticut	215.4
34	Pennsylvania	210.1
35	Wyoming	208.1
36	Virginia	197.6
37	Minnesota	195.7
38	South Dakota	172.4
39	West Virginia	160.5
40	Wisconsin	146.5
41	Hawaii	121.7
42	Vermont	108.5
43	Maine	97.4
44	North Dakota	60.8
45	New Hampshire	57.0
NA	Florida**	NA
NA	Illinois**	NA
NA	Kansas**	NA
NA	Kentucky**	NA
NA	Montana**	NA

District of Columbia   1,162.1

Source: Morgan Quitno Press using data from Federal Bureau of Investigation
        "Crime in the United States 1996" (Uniform Crime Reports, October 4, 1997)
*Estimated rates for urban areas, defined by the F.B.I. as Metropolitan Statistical Areas and other cities outside such areas. National rate includes those states listed as not available. Aggravated assault is an attack for the purpose of inflicting severe bodily injury.
**Not available.

Percent of Aggravated Assaults Occurring in Urban Areas in 1996

National Percent = 94.5% of Aggravated Assaults*

ALPHA ORDER			RANK ORDER		
RANK	STATE	PERCENT	RANK	STATE	PERCENT
18	Alabama	93.3	1	New Jersey	100.0
43	Alaska	74.9	2	Massachusetts	99.9
12	Arizona	95.6	3	Rhode Island	99.5
29	Arkansas	89.8	4	California	98.4
4	California	98.4	5	New York	97.1
10	Colorado	95.9	6	Maryland	97.0
14	Connecticut	94.5	7	Ohio	96.5
40	Delaware	79.6	8	Nebraska	96.3
NA	Florida**	NA	8	Texas	96.3
34	Georgia	87.0	10	Colorado	95.9
38	Hawaii	82.8	11	Michigan	95.7
42	Idaho	76.5	12	Arizona	95.6
NA	Illinois**	NA	12	Pennsylvania	95.6
24	Indiana	91.1	14	Connecticut	94.5
20	Iowa	92.4	15	Washington	94.4
NA	Kansas**	NA	16	Minnesota	93.6
NA	Kentucky**	NA	16	Utah	93.6
32	Louisiana	89.1	18	Alabama	93.3
30	Maine	89.3	19	Nevada	92.6
6	Maryland	97.0	20	Iowa	92.4
2	Massachusetts	99.9	20	Oregon	92.4
11	Michigan	95.7	22	Tennessee	91.9
16	Minnesota	93.6	23	New Hampshire	91.3
44	Mississippi	72.0	24	Indiana	91.1
26	Missouri	90.5	25	Oklahoma	90.6
NA	Montana**	NA	26	Missouri	90.5
8	Nebraska	96.3	27	Wisconsin	90.3
19	Nevada	92.6	28	Virginia	90.0
23	New Hampshire	91.3	29	Arkansas	89.8
1	New Jersey	100.0	30	Maine	89.3
35	New Mexico	85.2	31	South Dakota	89.2
5	New York	97.1	32	Louisiana	89.1
33	North Carolina	88.3	33	North Carolina	88.3
36	North Dakota	85.0	34	Georgia	87.0
7	Ohio	96.5	35	New Mexico	85.2
25	Oklahoma	90.6	36	North Dakota	85.0
20	Oregon	92.4	37	Vermont	83.4
12	Pennsylvania	95.6	38	Hawaii	82.8
3	Rhode Island	99.5	39	South Carolina	81.6
39	South Carolina	81.6	40	Delaware	79.6
31	South Dakota	89.2	41	Wyoming	78.0
22	Tennessee	91.9	42	Idaho	76.5
8	Texas	96.3	43	Alaska	74.9
16	Utah	93.6	44	Mississippi	72.0
37	Vermont	83.4	45	West Virginia	62.6
28	Virginia	90.0	NA	Florida**	NA
15	Washington	94.4	NA	Illinois**	NA
45	West Virginia	62.6	NA	Kansas**	NA
27	Wisconsin	90.3	NA	Kentucky**	NA
41	Wyoming	78.0	NA	Montana**	NA
				District of Columbia	100.0

Source: Morgan Quitno Press using data from Federal Bureau of Investigation
    "Crime in the United States 1996" (Uniform Crime Reports, October 4, 1997)
*Estimated percentages for urban areas, defined by the F.B.I. as Metropolitan Statistical Areas and other cities outside such areas. National percent includes those states listed as not available. Aggravated assault is an attack for the purpose of inflicting severe bodily injury.
**Not available.

Aggravated Assaults in Rural Areas in 1996

National Rural Total = 56,711 Aggravated Assaults*

ALPHA ORDER				RANK ORDER			
RANK	STATE	ASSAULTS	% of USA	RANK	STATE	ASSAULTS	% of USA
17	Alabama	1,015	1.79%	1	South Carolina	5,210	9.19%
22	Alaska	818	1.44%	2	Georgia	3,758	6.63%
21	Arizona	820	1.45%	3	North Carolina	3,306	5.83%
19	Arkansas	925	1.63%	4	Texas	2,979	5.25%
6	California	2,659	4.69%	5	Louisiana	2,823	4.98%
32	Colorado	404	0.71%	6	California	2,659	4.69%
33	Connecticut	389	0.69%	7	Mississippi	2,330	4.11%
27	Delaware	623	1.10%	8	Tennessee	2,136	3.77%
NA	Florida**	NA	NA	9	Missouri	1,947	3.43%
2	Georgia	3,758	6.63%	10	Indiana	1,928	3.40%
35	Hawaii	232	0.41%	11	New York	1,906	3.36%
28	Idaho	607	1.07%	12	Michigan	1,637	2.89%
NA	Illinois**	NA	NA	13	New Mexico	1,532	2.70%
10	Indiana	1,928	3.40%	14	Oklahoma	1,362	2.40%
31	Iowa	448	0.79%	15	Virginia	1,228	2.17%
NA	Kansas**	NA	NA	16	Pennsylvania	1,063	1.87%
NA	Kentucky**	NA	NA	17	Alabama	1,015	1.79%
5	Louisiana	2,823	4.98%	18	West Virginia	998	1.76%
38	Maine	104	0.18%	19	Arkansas	925	1.63%
24	Maryland	744	1.31%	20	Ohio	855	1.51%
43	Massachusetts	18	0.03%	21	Arizona	820	1.45%
12	Michigan	1,637	2.89%	22	Alaska	818	1.44%
30	Minnesota	504	0.89%	23	Washington	789	1.39%
7	Mississippi	2,330	4.11%	24	Maryland	744	1.31%
9	Missouri	1,947	3.43%	25	Oregon	722	1.27%
NA	Montana**	NA	NA	26	Wisconsin	657	1.16%
36	Nebraska	209	0.37%	27	Delaware	623	1.10%
29	Nevada	521	0.92%	28	Idaho	607	1.07%
41	New Hampshire	55	0.10%	29	Nevada	521	0.92%
45	New Jersey	0	0.00%	30	Minnesota	504	0.89%
13	New Mexico	1,532	2.70%	31	Iowa	448	0.79%
11	New York	1,906	3.36%	32	Colorado	404	0.71%
3	North Carolina	3,306	5.83%	33	Connecticut	389	0.69%
42	North Dakota	45	0.08%	34	Utah	278	0.49%
20	Ohio	855	1.51%	35	Hawaii	232	0.41%
14	Oklahoma	1,362	2.40%	36	Nebraska	209	0.37%
25	Oregon	722	1.27%	37	Wyoming	208	0.37%
16	Pennsylvania	1,063	1.87%	38	Maine	104	0.18%
44	Rhode Island	12	0.02%	39	South Dakota	92	0.16%
1	South Carolina	5,210	9.19%	40	Vermont	75	0.13%
39	South Dakota	92	0.16%	41	New Hampshire	55	0.10%
8	Tennessee	2,136	3.77%	42	North Dakota	45	0.08%
4	Texas	2,979	5.25%	43	Massachusetts	18	0.03%
34	Utah	278	0.49%	44	Rhode Island	12	0.02%
40	Vermont	75	0.13%	45	New Jersey	0	0.00%
15	Virginia	1,228	2.17%	NA	Florida**	NA	NA
23	Washington	789	1.39%	NA	Illinois**	NA	NA
18	West Virginia	998	1.76%	NA	Kansas**	NA	NA
26	Wisconsin	657	1.16%	NA	Kentucky**	NA	NA
37	Wyoming	208	0.37%	NA	Montana**	NA	NA
					District of Columbia	0	0.00%

Source: Federal Bureau of Investigation
   "Crime in the United States 1996" (Uniform Crime Reports, October 4, 1997)
*Estimated totals for rural areas, defined by the F.B.I. as other than Metropolitan Statistical Areas and other cities outside such areas. National total includes those states listed as not available. Aggravated assault is an attack for the purpose of inflicting severe bodily injury.
**Not available.

Rural Aggravated Assault Rate in 1996

National Rural Rate = 177.0 Aggravated Assaults per 100,000 Population*

ALPHA ORDER				RANK ORDER		
RANK	STATE	RATE		RANK	STATE	RATE
27	Alabama	129.7		1	Delaware	669.7
4	Alaska	428.1		2	South Carolina	658.2
10	Arizona	239.9		3	New Mexico	506.7
31	Arkansas	114.8		4	Alaska	428.1
5	California	422.6		5	California	422.6
29	Colorado	127.2		6	Louisiana	411.5
14	Connecticut	201.2		7	Nevada	279.3
1	Delaware	669.7		8	Maryland	278.8
NA	Florida**	NA		9	Georgia	259.6
9	Georgia	259.6		10	Arizona	239.9
33	Hawaii	87.4		11	New York	222.8
24	Idaho	153.3		12	Oklahoma	214.4
NA	Illinois**	NA		13	Mississippi	209.8
18	Indiana	182.3		14	Connecticut	201.2
37	Iowa	50.6		15	North Carolina	195.7
NA	Kansas**	NA		16	Tennessee	194.3
NA	Kentucky**	NA		17	Texas	182.7
6	Louisiana	411.5		18	Indiana	182.3
42	Maine	29.9		19	Wyoming	165.2
8	Maryland	278.8		20	Massachusetts	162.7
20	Massachusetts	162.7		21	Missouri	161.0
22	Michigan	155.0		22	Michigan	155.0
36	Minnesota	57.5		23	Washington	154.7
13	Mississippi	209.8		24	Idaho	153.3
21	Missouri	161.0		25	Oregon	140.3
NA	Montana**	NA		26	Utah	129.9
38	Nebraska	49.7		27	Alabama	129.7
7	Nevada	279.3		28	West Virginia	127.4
39	New Hampshire	36.6		29	Colorado	127.2
44	New Jersey	0.0		30	Virginia	115.7
3	New Mexico	506.7		31	Arkansas	114.8
11	New York	222.8		32	Pennsylvania	100.4
15	North Carolina	195.7		33	Hawaii	87.4
43	North Dakota	20.2		34	Wisconsin	66.4
35	Ohio	64.3		35	Ohio	64.3
12	Oklahoma	214.4		36	Minnesota	57.5
25	Oregon	140.3		37	Iowa	50.6
32	Pennsylvania	100.4		38	Nebraska	49.7
44	Rhode Island	0.0		39	New Hampshire	36.6
2	South Carolina	658.2		40	South Dakota	31.5
40	South Dakota	31.5		41	Vermont	31.2
16	Tennessee	194.3		42	Maine	29.9
17	Texas	182.7		43	North Dakota	20.2
26	Utah	129.9		44	New Jersey	0.0
41	Vermont	31.2		44	Rhode Island	0.0
30	Virginia	115.7		NA	Florida**	NA
23	Washington	154.7		NA	Illinois**	NA
28	West Virginia	127.4		NA	Kansas**	NA
34	Wisconsin	66.4		NA	Kentucky**	NA
19	Wyoming	165.2		NA	Montana**	NA
					District of Columbia	0.0

Source: Morgan Quitno Press using data from Federal Bureau of Investigation
     "Crime in the United States 1996" (Uniform Crime Reports, October 4, 1997)
*Estimated rates for rural areas, defined by the F.B.I. as other than Metropolitan Statistical Areas and other cities outside such areas. National rate includes those states listed as not available. Aggravated assault is an attack for the purpose of inflicting severe bodily injury.
**Not available.

Percent of Aggravated Assaults Occurring in Rural Areas in 1996

National Percent = 5.5% of Aggravated Assaults*

ALPHA ORDER				RANK ORDER		
RANK	STATE	PERCENT		RANK	STATE	PERCENT
28	Alabama	6.7		1	West Virginia	37.4
3	Alaska	25.1		2	Mississippi	28.0
33	Arizona	4.4		3	Alaska	25.1
17	Arkansas	10.2		4	Idaho	23.5
42	California	1.6		5	Wyoming	22.0
36	Colorado	4.1		6	Delaware	20.4
32	Connecticut	5.5		7	South Carolina	18.4
6	Delaware	20.4		8	Hawaii	17.2
NA	Florida**	NA		9	Vermont	16.6
12	Georgia	13.0		10	North Dakota	15.0
8	Hawaii	17.2		11	New Mexico	14.8
4	Idaho	23.5		12	Georgia	13.0
NA	Illinois**	NA		13	North Carolina	11.7
22	Indiana	8.9		14	Louisiana	10.9
25	Iowa	7.6		15	South Dakota	10.8
NA	Kansas**	NA		16	Maine	10.7
NA	Kentucky**	NA		17	Arkansas	10.2
14	Louisiana	10.9		18	Virginia	10.0
16	Maine	10.7		19	Wisconsin	9.7
40	Maryland	3.0		20	Missouri	9.5
44	Massachusetts	0.1		21	Oklahoma	9.4
35	Michigan	4.3		22	Indiana	8.9
29	Minnesota	6.4		23	New Hampshire	8.7
2	Mississippi	28.0		24	Tennessee	8.1
20	Missouri	9.5		25	Iowa	7.6
NA	Montana**	NA		25	Oregon	7.6
37	Nebraska	3.7		27	Nevada	7.4
27	Nevada	7.4		28	Alabama	6.7
23	New Hampshire	8.7		29	Minnesota	6.4
45	New Jersey	0.0		29	Utah	6.4
11	New Mexico	14.8		31	Washington	5.6
41	New York	2.9		32	Connecticut	5.5
13	North Carolina	11.7		33	Arizona	4.4
10	North Dakota	15.0		33	Pennsylvania	4.4
39	Ohio	3.5		35	Michigan	4.3
21	Oklahoma	9.4		36	Colorado	4.1
25	Oregon	7.6		37	Nebraska	3.7
33	Pennsylvania	4.4		37	Texas	3.7
43	Rhode Island	0.5		39	Ohio	3.5
7	South Carolina	18.4		40	Maryland	3.0
15	South Dakota	10.8		41	New York	2.9
24	Tennessee	8.1		42	California	1.6
37	Texas	3.7		43	Rhode Island	0.5
29	Utah	6.4		44	Massachusetts	0.1
9	Vermont	16.6		45	New Jersey	0.0
18	Virginia	10.0		NA	Florida**	NA
31	Washington	5.6		NA	Illinois**	NA
1	West Virginia	37.4		NA	Kansas**	NA
19	Wisconsin	9.7		NA	Kentucky**	NA
5	Wyoming	22.0		NA	Montana**	NA
					District of Columbia	0.0

Source: Morgan Quitno Press using data from Federal Bureau of Investigation
    "Crime in the United States 1996" (Uniform Crime Reports, October 4, 1997)
*Estimated percentages for rural areas, defined by the F.B.I. as other than Metropolitan Statistical Areas and other cities outside such areas. National percent includes those states listed as not available. Aggravated assault is an attack for the purpose of inflicting severe bodily injury.
**Not available.

Property Crimes in Urban Areas in 1996

National Urban Total = 11,205,664 Property Crimes*

ALPHA ORDER

RANK	STATE	CRIMES	% of USA
21	Alabama	173,317	1.55%
41	Alaska	23,953	0.21%
11	Arizona	279,211	2.49%
29	Arkansas	92,841	0.83%
1	California	1,369,458	12.22%
20	Colorado	173,389	1.55%
26	Connecticut	121,951	1.09%
40	Delaware	27,733	0.25%
NA	Florida**	NA	NA
6	Georgia	380,977	3.40%
34	Hawaii	60,100	0.54%
35	Idaho	37,599	0.34%
NA	Illinois**	NA	NA
17	Indiana	215,724	1.93%
31	Iowa	87,478	0.78%
NA	Kansas**	NA	NA
NA	Kentucky**	NA	NA
13	Louisiana	243,914	2.18%
37	Maine	34,242	0.31%
12	Maryland	254,002	2.27%
18	Massachusetts	194,604	1.74%
5	Michigan	404,629	3.61%
19	Minnesota	175,420	1.57%
28	Mississippi	96,698	0.86%
15	Missouri	227,092	2.03%
NA	Montana**	NA	NA
33	Nebraska	60,581	0.54%
32	Nevada	78,351	0.70%
39	New Hampshire	30,616	0.27%
9	New Jersey	303,657	2.71%
30	New Mexico	91,149	0.81%
3	New York	602,643	5.38%
8	North Carolina	320,358	2.86%
44	North Dakota	14,684	0.13%
4	Ohio	429,992	3.84%
25	Oklahoma	157,272	1.40%
24	Oregon	164,332	1.47%
7	Pennsylvania	341,406	3.05%
36	Rhode Island	36,087	0.32%
23	South Carolina	165,004	1.47%
42	South Dakota	17,885	0.16%
14	Tennessee	228,803	2.04%
2	Texas	940,771	8.40%
27	Utah	107,717	0.96%
45	Vermont	13,751	0.12%
16	Virginia	226,726	2.02%
10	Washington	287,194	2.56%
38	West Virginia	32,396	0.29%
22	Wisconsin	168,562	1.50%
43	Wyoming	16,881	0.15%

RANK ORDER

RANK	STATE	CRIMES	% of USA
1	California	1,369,458	12.22%
2	Texas	940,771	8.40%
3	New York	602,643	5.38%
4	Ohio	429,992	3.84%
5	Michigan	404,629	3.61%
6	Georgia	380,977	3.40%
7	Pennsylvania	341,406	3.05%
8	North Carolina	320,358	2.86%
9	New Jersey	303,657	2.71%
10	Washington	287,194	2.56%
11	Arizona	279,211	2.49%
12	Maryland	254,002	2.27%
13	Louisiana	243,914	2.18%
14	Tennessee	228,803	2.04%
15	Missouri	227,092	2.03%
16	Virginia	226,726	2.02%
17	Indiana	215,724	1.93%
18	Massachusetts	194,604	1.74%
19	Minnesota	175,420	1.57%
20	Colorado	173,389	1.55%
21	Alabama	173,317	1.55%
22	Wisconsin	168,562	1.50%
23	South Carolina	165,004	1.47%
24	Oregon	164,332	1.47%
25	Oklahoma	157,272	1.40%
26	Connecticut	121,951	1.09%
27	Utah	107,717	0.96%
28	Mississippi	96,698	0.86%
29	Arkansas	92,841	0.83%
30	New Mexico	91,149	0.81%
31	Iowa	87,478	0.78%
32	Nevada	78,351	0.70%
33	Nebraska	60,581	0.54%
34	Hawaii	60,100	0.54%
35	Idaho	37,599	0.34%
36	Rhode Island	36,087	0.32%
37	Maine	34,242	0.31%
38	West Virginia	32,396	0.29%
39	New Hampshire	30,616	0.27%
40	Delaware	27,733	0.25%
41	Alaska	23,953	0.21%
42	South Dakota	17,885	0.16%
43	Wyoming	16,881	0.15%
44	North Dakota	14,684	0.13%
45	Vermont	13,751	0.12%
NA	Florida**	NA	NA
NA	Illinois**	NA	NA
NA	Kansas**	NA	NA
NA	Kentucky**	NA	NA
NA	Montana**	NA	NA
	District of Columbia	51,188	0.46%

Source: Morgan Quitno Press using data from Federal Bureau of Investigation
    "Crime in the United States 1996" (Uniform Crime Reports, October 4, 1997)

*Estimated totals for urban areas, defined by the F.B.I. as Metropolitan Statistical Areas and other cities outside such areas. National total includes those states listed as not available. Property crimes are offenses of burglary, larceny-theft and motor vehicle theft.
**Not available.

Urban Property Crime Rate in 1996

National Urban Rate = 4,804.2 Property Crimes per 100,000 Population*

	ALPHA ORDER			RANK ORDER	
RANK	STATE	RATE	RANK	STATE	RATE
20	Alabama	4,965.5	1	Arizona	6,833.1
10	Alaska	5,759.3	2	Louisiana	6,655.2
1	Arizona	6,833.1	3	Hawaii	6,543.1
16	Arkansas	5,447.3	4	New Mexico	6,461.5
30	California	4,382.4	5	Georgia	6,451.2
21	Colorado	4,946.3	6	Oregon	6,110.2
35	Connecticut	3,958.6	7	Utah	6,031.2
29	Delaware	4,388.3	8	Mississippi	6,023.5
NA	Florida**	NA	9	Oklahoma	5,899.6
5	Georgia	6,451.2	10	Alaska	5,759.3
3	Hawaii	6,543.1	11	Washington	5,717.8
24	Idaho	4,741.0	12	North Carolina	5,686.7
NA	Illinois**	NA	13	South Carolina	5,675.2
27	Indiana	4,509.8	14	Nevada	5,531.4
28	Iowa	4,448.7	15	Missouri	5,472.7
NA	Kansas**	NA	16	Arkansas	5,447.3
NA	Kentucky**	NA	17	Tennessee	5,420.7
2	Louisiana	6,655.2	18	Texas	5,376.6
37	Maine	3,824.8	19	Maryland	5,286.0
19	Maryland	5,286.0	20	Alabama	4,965.5
42	Massachusetts	3,200.2	21	Colorado	4,946.3
25	Michigan	4,739.1	22	Nebraska	4,918.9
26	Minnesota	4,638.6	23	Wyoming	4,754.0
8	Mississippi	6,023.5	24	Idaho	4,741.0
15	Missouri	5,472.7	25	Michigan	4,739.1
NA	Montana**	NA	26	Minnesota	4,638.6
22	Nebraska	4,918.9	27	Indiana	4,509.8
14	Nevada	5,531.4	28	Iowa	4,448.7
45	New Hampshire	3,026.3	29	Delaware	4,388.3
38	New Jersey	3,801.4	30	California	4,382.4
4	New Mexico	6,461.5	31	Ohio	4,368.3
41	New York	3,477.5	32	South Dakota	4,067.8
12	North Carolina	5,686.7	33	Wisconsin	4,042.4
40	North Dakota	3,488.6	34	Virginia	4,039.2
31	Ohio	4,368.3	35	Connecticut	3,958.6
9	Oklahoma	5,899.6	36	Vermont	3,945.4
6	Oregon	6,110.2	37	Maine	3,824.8
44	Pennsylvania	3,104.5	38	New Jersey	3,801.4
39	Rhode Island	3,645.2	39	Rhode Island	3,645.2
13	South Carolina	5,675.2	40	North Dakota	3,488.6
32	South Dakota	4,067.8	41	New York	3,477.5
17	Tennessee	5,420.7	42	Massachusetts	3,200.2
18	Texas	5,376.6	43	West Virginia	3,106.5
7	Utah	6,031.2	44	Pennsylvania	3,104.5
36	Vermont	3,945.4	45	New Hampshire	3,026.3
34	Virginia	4,039.2	NA	Florida**	NA
11	Washington	5,717.8	NA	Illinois**	NA
43	West Virginia	3,106.5	NA	Kansas**	NA
33	Wisconsin	4,042.4	NA	Kentucky**	NA
23	Wyoming	4,754.0	NA	Montana**	NA
				District of Columbia	9,426.9

Source: Morgan Quitno Press using data from Federal Bureau of Investigation
"Crime in the United States 1996" (Uniform Crime Reports, October 4, 1997)
*Estimated rates for urban areas, defined by the F.B.I. as Metropolitan Statistical Areas and other cities outside such areas. National rate includes those states listed as not available. Property crimes are offenses of burglary, larceny-theft and motor vehicle theft.
**Not available.

438

Percent of Property Crimes Occurring in Urban Areas in 1996

National Percent = 95.0% of Property Crimes*

ALPHA ORDER				RANK ORDER		
RANK	STATE	PERCENT		RANK	STATE	PERCENT
14	Alabama	95.3		1	Massachusetts	100.0
42	Alaska	83.6		1	New Jersey	100.0
5	Arizona	98.0		1	Rhode Island	100.0
33	Arkansas	88.6		4	California	98.9
4	California	98.9		5	Arizona	98.0
11	Colorado	96.2		6	Connecticut	97.6
6	Connecticut	97.6		6	Maryland	97.6
32	Delaware	90.5		8	New Hampshire	97.4
NA	Florida**	NA		9	New York	97.3
29	Georgia	91.4		10	Texas	97.1
44	Hawaii	80.5		11	Colorado	96.2
40	Idaho	84.4		12	Pennsylvania	95.7
NA	Illinois**	NA		13	Ohio	95.6
23	Indiana	93.2		14	Alabama	95.3
31	Iowa	90.8		14	Utah	95.3
NA	Kansas**	NA		16	Louisiana	94.9
NA	Kentucky**	NA		17	Washington	94.7
16	Louisiana	94.9		18	Missouri	94.3
41	Maine	84.3		18	Nevada	94.3
6	Maryland	97.6		20	Oklahoma	94.2
1	Massachusetts	100.0		21	Michigan	94.1
21	Michigan	94.1		22	Virginia	93.6
30	Minnesota	91.3		23	Indiana	93.2
35	Mississippi	88.2		24	Oregon	92.7
18	Missouri	94.3		25	New Mexico	92.4
NA	Montana**	NA		26	Tennessee	92.0
27	Nebraska	91.6		27	Nebraska	91.6
18	Nevada	94.3		28	Wisconsin	91.5
8	New Hampshire	97.4		29	Georgia	91.4
1	New Jersey	100.0		30	Minnesota	91.3
25	New Mexico	92.4		31	Iowa	90.8
9	New York	97.3		32	Delaware	90.5
33	North Carolina	88.6		33	Arkansas	88.6
35	North Dakota	88.2		33	North Carolina	88.6
13	Ohio	95.6		35	Mississippi	88.2
20	Oklahoma	94.2		35	North Dakota	88.2
24	Oregon	92.7		37	Wyoming	87.6
12	Pennsylvania	95.7		38	South Dakota	87.5
1	Rhode Island	100.0		39	South Carolina	85.5
39	South Carolina	85.5		40	Idaho	84.4
38	South Dakota	87.5		41	Maine	84.3
26	Tennessee	92.0		42	Alaska	83.6
10	Texas	97.1		43	Vermont	81.0
14	Utah	95.3		44	Hawaii	80.5
43	Vermont	81.0		45	West Virginia	78.0
22	Virginia	93.6		NA	Florida**	NA
17	Washington	94.7		NA	Illinois**	NA
45	West Virginia	78.0		NA	Kansas**	NA
28	Wisconsin	91.5		NA	Kentucky**	NA
37	Wyoming	87.6		NA	Montana**	NA
					District of Columbia	100.0

Source: Morgan Quitno Press using data from Federal Bureau of Investigation
   "Crime in the United States 1996" (Uniform Crime Reports, October 4, 1997)
*Estimated percentages for urban areas, defined by the F.B.I. as Metropolitan Statistical Areas and other cities
outside such areas. National percent includes those states listed as not available. Property crimes are offenses of
burglary, larceny-theft and motor vehicle theft.
**Not available.

Property Crimes in Rural Areas in 1996

National Rural Total = 585,672 Property Crimes*

ALPHA ORDER				RANK ORDER			
RANK	STATE	CRIMES	% of USA	RANK	STATE	CRIMES	% of USA
25	Alabama	8,486	1.45%	1	North Carolina	41,258	7.04%
34	Alaska	4,714	0.80%	2	Georgia	36,009	6.15%
31	Arizona	5,753	0.98%	3	South Carolina	27,982	4.78%
21	Arkansas	11,949	2.04%	4	Texas	27,961	4.77%
11	California	15,677	2.68%	5	Michigan	25,391	4.34%
28	Colorado	6,829	1.17%	6	Ohio	19,943	3.41%
37	Connecticut	2,973	0.51%	7	Tennessee	19,926	3.40%
38	Delaware	2,910	0.50%	8	Minnesota	16,689	2.85%
NA	Florida**	NA	NA	9	New York	16,607	2.84%
2	Georgia	36,009	6.15%	10	Washington	15,917	2.72%
16	Hawaii	14,539	2.48%	11	California	15,677	2.68%
27	Idaho	6,933	1.18%	12	Indiana	15,652	2.67%
NA	Illinois**	NA	NA	13	Wisconsin	15,581	2.66%
12	Indiana	15,652	2.67%	14	Pennsylvania	15,458	2.64%
24	Iowa	8,818	1.51%	15	Virginia	15,374	2.63%
NA	Kansas**	NA	NA	16	Hawaii	14,539	2.48%
NA	Kentucky**	NA	NA	17	Missouri	13,689	2.34%
18	Louisiana	13,216	2.26%	18	Louisiana	13,216	2.26%
29	Maine	6,394	1.09%	19	Oregon	12,963	2.21%
30	Maryland	6,229	1.06%	20	Mississippi	12,883	2.20%
43	Massachusetts	32	0.01%	21	Arkansas	11,949	2.04%
5	Michigan	25,391	4.34%	22	Oklahoma	9,620	1.64%
8	Minnesota	16,689	2.85%	23	West Virginia	9,114	1.56%
20	Mississippi	12,883	2.20%	24	Iowa	8,818	1.51%
17	Missouri	13,689	2.34%	25	Alabama	8,486	1.45%
NA	Montana**	NA	NA	26	New Mexico	7,549	1.29%
32	Nebraska	5,529	0.94%	27	Idaho	6,933	1.18%
35	Nevada	4,696	0.80%	28	Colorado	6,829	1.17%
42	New Hampshire	820	0.14%	29	Maine	6,394	1.09%
45	New Jersey	0	0.00%	30	Maryland	6,229	1.06%
26	New Mexico	7,549	1.29%	31	Arizona	5,753	0.98%
9	New York	16,607	2.84%	32	Nebraska	5,529	0.94%
1	North Carolina	41,258	7.04%	33	Utah	5,362	0.92%
41	North Dakota	1,964	0.34%	34	Alaska	4,714	0.80%
6	Ohio	19,943	3.41%	35	Nevada	4,696	0.80%
22	Oklahoma	9,620	1.64%	36	Vermont	3,222	0.55%
19	Oregon	12,963	2.21%	37	Connecticut	2,973	0.51%
14	Pennsylvania	15,458	2.64%	38	Delaware	2,910	0.50%
44	Rhode Island	12	0.00%	39	South Dakota	2,558	0.44%
3	South Carolina	27,982	4.78%	40	Wyoming	2,380	0.41%
39	South Dakota	2,558	0.44%	41	North Dakota	1,964	0.34%
7	Tennessee	19,926	3.40%	42	New Hampshire	820	0.14%
4	Texas	27,961	4.77%	43	Massachusetts	32	0.01%
33	Utah	5,362	0.92%	44	Rhode Island	12	0.00%
36	Vermont	3,222	0.55%	45	New Jersey	0	0.00%
15	Virginia	15,374	2.63%	NA	Florida**	NA	NA
10	Washington	15,917	2.72%	NA	Illinois**	NA	NA
23	West Virginia	9,114	1.56%	NA	Kansas**	NA	NA
13	Wisconsin	15,581	2.66%	NA	Kentucky**	NA	NA
40	Wyoming	2,380	0.41%	NA	Montana**	NA	NA
					District of Columbia	0	0.00%

Source: Federal Bureau of Investigation
"Crime in the United States 1996" (Uniform Crime Reports, October 4, 1997)
Estimated totals for rural areas, defined by the F.B.I. as other than Metropolitan Statistical Areas and other cities outside such areas. National total includes those states listed as not available. Property crimes are offenses of burglary, larceny-theft and motor vehicle theft.
**Not available.*

Rural Property Crime Rate in 1996

National Rural Rate = 1,828.2 Property Crimes per 100,000 Population*

ALPHA ORDER

RANK ORDER

RANK	STATE	RATE	RANK	STATE	RATE
38	Alabama	1,084.3	1	Hawaii	5,476.5
11	Alaska	2,466.8	2	South Carolina	3,535.2
24	Arizona	1,683.0	3	Delaware	3,128.0
29	Arkansas	1,483.2	4	Washington	3,120.1
9	California	2,491.3	5	Oregon	2,519.5
15	Colorado	2,150.3	6	Nevada	2,517.8
26	Connecticut	1,537.6	7	Utah	2,505.6
3	Delaware	3,128.0	8	New Mexico	2,496.8
NA	Florida**	NA	9	California	2,491.3
10	Georgia	2,487.8	10	Georgia	2,487.8
1	Hawaii	5,476.5	11	Alaska	2,466.8
22	Idaho	1,751.1	12	North Carolina	2,442.0
NA	Illinois**	NA	13	Michigan	2,404.6
30	Indiana	1,480.0	14	Maryland	2,334.3
39	Iowa	995.7	15	Colorado	2,150.3
NA	Kansas**	NA	16	New York	1,941.3
NA	Kentucky**	NA	17	Louisiana	1,926.5
17	Louisiana	1,926.5	18	Minnesota	1,904.5
20	Maine	1,838.7	19	Wyoming	1,890.3
14	Maryland	2,334.3	20	Maine	1,838.7
43	Massachusetts	289.2	21	Tennessee	1,812.9
13	Michigan	2,404.6	22	Idaho	1,751.1
18	Minnesota	1,904.5	23	Texas	1,715.0
36	Mississippi	1,159.9	24	Arizona	1,683.0
37	Missouri	1,131.8	25	Wisconsin	1,573.7
NA	Montana**	NA	26	Connecticut	1,537.6
34	Nebraska	1,315.2	27	Oklahoma	1,514.5
6	Nevada	2,517.8	28	Ohio	1,500.0
42	New Hampshire	545.4	29	Arkansas	1,483.2
44	New Jersey	0.0	30	Indiana	1,480.0
8	New Mexico	2,496.8	31	Pennsylvania	1,459.7
16	New York	1,941.3	32	Virginia	1,447.9
12	North Carolina	2,442.0	33	Vermont	1,339.9
40	North Dakota	880.4	34	Nebraska	1,315.2
28	Ohio	1,500.0	35	West Virginia	1,163.8
27	Oklahoma	1,514.5	36	Mississippi	1,159.9
5	Oregon	2,519.5	37	Missouri	1,131.8
31	Pennsylvania	1,459.7	38	Alabama	1,084.3
44	Rhode Island	0.0	39	Iowa	995.7
2	South Carolina	3,535.2	40	North Dakota	880.4
41	South Dakota	875.1	41	South Dakota	875.1
21	Tennessee	1,812.9	42	New Hampshire	545.4
23	Texas	1,715.0	43	Massachusetts	289.2
7	Utah	2,505.6	44	New Jersey	0.0
33	Vermont	1,339.9	44	Rhode Island	0.0
32	Virginia	1,447.9	NA	Florida**	NA
4	Washington	3,120.1	NA	Illinois**	NA
35	West Virginia	1,163.8	NA	Kansas**	NA
25	Wisconsin	1,573.7	NA	Kentucky**	NA
19	Wyoming	1,890.3	NA	Montana**	NA
				District of Columbia	0.0

Source: Morgan Quitno Press using data from Federal Bureau of Investigation
    "Crime in the United States 1996" (Uniform Crime Reports, October 4, 1997)
*Estimated rates for rural areas, defined by the F.B.I. as other than Metropolitan Statistical Areas and other cities outside such areas. National rate includes those states listed as not available. Property crimes are offenses of burglary, larceny-theft and motor vehicle theft.
**Not available.

Percent of Property Crime Occurring in Rural Areas in 1996

National Percent = 5.0% of Property Crimes*

ALPHA ORDER

RANK	STATE	PERCENT
31	Alabama	4.7
4	Alaska	16.4
41	Arizona	2.0
12	Arkansas	11.4
42	California	1.1
35	Colorado	3.8
39	Connecticut	2.4
14	Delaware	9.5
NA	Florida**	NA
17	Georgia	8.6
2	Hawaii	19.5
6	Idaho	15.6
NA	Illinois**	NA
23	Indiana	6.8
15	Iowa	9.2
NA	Kansas**	NA
NA	Kentucky**	NA
30	Louisiana	5.1
5	Maine	15.7
39	Maryland	2.4
43	Massachusetts	0.0
25	Michigan	5.9
16	Minnesota	8.7
10	Mississippi	11.8
27	Missouri	5.7
NA	Montana**	NA
19	Nebraska	8.4
27	Nevada	5.7
38	New Hampshire	2.6
43	New Jersey	0.0
21	New Mexico	7.6
37	New York	2.7
12	North Carolina	11.4
10	North Dakota	11.8
33	Ohio	4.4
26	Oklahoma	5.8
22	Oregon	7.3
34	Pennsylvania	4.3
43	Rhode Island	0.0
7	South Carolina	14.5
8	South Dakota	12.5
20	Tennessee	8.0
36	Texas	2.9
31	Utah	4.7
3	Vermont	19.0
24	Virginia	6.4
29	Washington	5.3
1	West Virginia	22.0
18	Wisconsin	8.5
9	Wyoming	12.4

RANK ORDER

RANK	STATE	PERCENT
1	West Virginia	22.0
2	Hawaii	19.5
3	Vermont	19.0
4	Alaska	16.4
5	Maine	15.7
6	Idaho	15.6
7	South Carolina	14.5
8	South Dakota	12.5
9	Wyoming	12.4
10	Mississippi	11.8
10	North Dakota	11.8
12	Arkansas	11.4
12	North Carolina	11.4
14	Delaware	9.5
15	Iowa	9.2
16	Minnesota	8.7
17	Georgia	8.6
18	Wisconsin	8.5
19	Nebraska	8.4
20	Tennessee	8.0
21	New Mexico	7.6
22	Oregon	7.3
23	Indiana	6.8
24	Virginia	6.4
25	Michigan	5.9
26	Oklahoma	5.8
27	Missouri	5.7
27	Nevada	5.7
29	Washington	5.3
30	Louisiana	5.1
31	Alabama	4.7
31	Utah	4.7
33	Ohio	4.4
34	Pennsylvania	4.3
35	Colorado	3.8
36	Texas	2.9
37	New York	2.7
38	New Hampshire	2.6
39	Connecticut	2.4
39	Maryland	2.4
41	Arizona	2.0
42	California	1.1
43	Massachusetts	0.0
43	New Jersey	0.0
43	Rhode Island	0.0
NA	Florida**	NA
NA	Illinois**	NA
NA	Kansas**	NA
NA	Kentucky**	NA
NA	Montana**	NA
	District of Columbia	0.0

Source: Morgan Quitno Press using data from Federal Bureau of Investigation
    "Crime in the United States 1996" (Uniform Crime Reports, October 4, 1997)
*Estimated percentages for rural areas, defined by the F.B.I. as other than Metropolitan Statistical Areas and other cities outside such areas. National percent includes those states listed as not available. Property crimes are offenses of burglary, larceny-theft and motor vehicle theft.
**Not available.

Burglaries in Urban Areas in 1996

National Urban Total = 2,302,917 Burglaries*

ALPHA ORDER | | | | RANK ORDER | | |

RANK	STATE	BURGLARIES	% of USA	RANK	STATE	BURGLARIES	% of USA
18	Alabama	39,383	1.71%	1	California	305,995	13.29%
41	Alaska	3,572	0.16%	2	Texas	193,163	8.39%
11	Arizona	53,628	2.33%	3	New York	124,232	5.39%
29	Arkansas	19,815	0.86%	4	Ohio	87,825	3.81%
1	California	305,995	13.29%	5	North Carolina	80,789	3.51%
22	Colorado	32,825	1.43%	6	Michigan	77,330	3.36%
25	Connecticut	26,527	1.15%	7	Georgia	71,212	3.09%
39	Delaware	4,865	0.21%	8	New Jersey	63,259	2.75%
NA	Florida**	NA	NA	9	Pennsylvania	61,228	2.66%
7	Georgia	71,212	3.09%	10	Tennessee	54,356	2.36%
33	Hawaii	9,543	0.41%	11	Arizona	53,628	2.33%
38	Idaho	6,419	0.28%	12	Washington	53,497	2.32%
NA	Illinois**	NA	NA	13	Louisiana	52,526	2.28%
17	Indiana	41,100	1.78%	14	Maryland	48,614	2.11%
31	Iowa	16,126	0.70%	15	Massachusetts	42,887	1.86%
NA	Kansas**	NA	NA	16	Missouri	41,979	1.82%
NA	Kentucky**	NA	NA	17	Indiana	41,100	1.78%
13	Louisiana	52,526	2.28%	18	Alabama	39,383	1.71%
36	Maine	6,755	0.29%	19	South Carolina	38,781	1.68%
14	Maryland	48,614	2.11%	20	Oklahoma	37,238	1.62%
15	Massachusetts	42,887	1.86%	21	Virginia	34,678	1.51%
6	Michigan	77,330	3.36%	22	Colorado	32,825	1.43%
23	Minnesota	30,116	1.31%	23	Minnesota	30,116	1.31%
27	Mississippi	24,383	1.06%	24	Oregon	27,724	1.20%
16	Missouri	41,979	1.82%	25	Connecticut	26,527	1.15%
NA	Montana**	NA	NA	26	Wisconsin	25,193	1.09%
34	Nebraska	8,825	0.38%	27	Mississippi	24,383	1.06%
30	Nevada	18,307	0.79%	28	New Mexico	20,539	0.89%
40	New Hampshire	4,764	0.21%	29	Arkansas	19,815	0.86%
8	New Jersey	63,259	2.75%	30	Nevada	18,307	0.79%
28	New Mexico	20,539	0.89%	31	Iowa	16,126	0.70%
3	New York	124,232	5.39%	32	Utah	15,793	0.69%
5	North Carolina	80,789	3.51%	33	Hawaii	9,543	0.41%
45	North Dakota	1,487	0.06%	34	Nebraska	8,825	0.38%
4	Ohio	87,825	3.81%	35	Rhode Island	8,132	0.35%
20	Oklahoma	37,238	1.62%	36	Maine	6,755	0.29%
24	Oregon	27,724	1.20%	37	West Virginia	6,585	0.29%
9	Pennsylvania	61,228	2.66%	38	Idaho	6,419	0.28%
35	Rhode Island	8,132	0.35%	39	Delaware	4,865	0.21%
19	South Carolina	38,781	1.68%	40	New Hampshire	4,764	0.21%
42	South Dakota	3,182	0.14%	41	Alaska	3,572	0.16%
10	Tennessee	54,356	2.36%	42	South Dakota	3,182	0.14%
2	Texas	193,163	8.39%	43	Vermont	2,708	0.12%
32	Utah	15,793	0.69%	44	Wyoming	2,571	0.11%
43	Vermont	2,708	0.12%	45	North Dakota	1,487	0.06%
21	Virginia	34,678	1.51%	NA	Florida**	NA	NA
12	Washington	53,497	2.32%	NA	Illinois**	NA	NA
37	West Virginia	6,585	0.29%	NA	Kansas**	NA	NA
26	Wisconsin	25,193	1.09%	NA	Kentucky**	NA	NA
44	Wyoming	2,571	0.11%	NA	Montana**	NA	NA
				District of Columbia		9,828	0.43%

Source: Morgan Quitno Press using data from Federal Bureau of Investigation
"Crime in the United States 1996" (Uniform Crime Reports, October 4, 1997)
*Estimated totals for urban areas, defined by the F.B.I. as Metropolitan Statistical Areas and other cities outside such areas. National total includes those states listed as not available. Burglary is the unlawful entry of a structure to commit a felony or theft. Attempts are included.
**Not available.

Urban Burglary Rate in 1996

National Urban Rate = 987.3 Burglaries per 100,000 Population*

ALPHA ORDER

RANK	STATE	RATE
12	Alabama	1,128.3
26	Alaska	858.9
7	Arizona	1,312.4
11	Arkansas	1,162.6
19	California	979.2
20	Colorado	936.4
24	Connecticut	861.1
33	Delaware	769.8
NA	Florida**	NA
10	Georgia	1,205.8
15	Hawaii	1,039.0
29	Idaho	809.4
NA	Illinois**	NA
25	Indiana	859.2
28	Iowa	820.1
NA	Kansas**	NA
NA	Kentucky**	NA
4	Louisiana	1,433.2
34	Maine	754.5
17	Maryland	1,011.7
39	Massachusetts	705.3
21	Michigan	905.7
30	Minnesota	796.4
1	Mississippi	1,518.9
17	Missouri	1,011.7
NA	Montana**	NA
38	Nebraska	716.6
8	Nevada	1,292.4
44	New Hampshire	470.9
31	New Jersey	791.9
2	New Mexico	1,456.0
37	New York	716.9
3	North Carolina	1,434.1
45	North Dakota	353.3
22	Ohio	892.2
5	Oklahoma	1,396.9
16	Oregon	1,030.8
43	Pennsylvania	556.8
27	Rhode Island	821.4
6	South Carolina	1,333.8
36	South Dakota	723.7
9	Tennessee	1,287.8
13	Texas	1,103.9
23	Utah	884.3
32	Vermont	777.0
41	Virginia	617.8
14	Washington	1,065.1
40	West Virginia	631.4
42	Wisconsin	604.2
35	Wyoming	724.0

RANK ORDER

RANK	STATE	RATE
1	Mississippi	1,518.9
2	New Mexico	1,456.0
3	North Carolina	1,434.1
4	Louisiana	1,433.2
5	Oklahoma	1,396.9
6	South Carolina	1,333.8
7	Arizona	1,312.4
8	Nevada	1,292.4
9	Tennessee	1,287.8
10	Georgia	1,205.8
11	Arkansas	1,162.6
12	Alabama	1,128.3
13	Texas	1,103.9
14	Washington	1,065.1
15	Hawaii	1,039.0
16	Oregon	1,030.8
17	Maryland	1,011.7
17	Missouri	1,011.7
19	California	979.2
20	Colorado	936.4
21	Michigan	905.7
22	Ohio	892.2
23	Utah	884.3
24	Connecticut	861.1
25	Indiana	859.2
26	Alaska	858.9
27	Rhode Island	821.4
28	Iowa	820.1
29	Idaho	809.4
30	Minnesota	796.4
31	New Jersey	791.9
32	Vermont	777.0
33	Delaware	769.8
34	Maine	754.5
35	Wyoming	724.0
36	South Dakota	723.7
37	New York	716.9
38	Nebraska	716.6
39	Massachusetts	705.3
40	West Virginia	631.4
41	Virginia	617.8
42	Wisconsin	604.2
43	Pennsylvania	556.8
44	New Hampshire	470.9
45	North Dakota	353.3
NA	Florida**	NA
NA	Illinois**	NA
NA	Kansas**	NA
NA	Kentucky**	NA
NA	Montana**	NA

District of Columbia 1,809.9

Source: Morgan Quitno Press using data from Federal Bureau of Investigation
"Crime in the United States 1996" (Uniform Crime Reports, October 4, 1997)
Estimated rates for urban areas, defined by the F.B.I. as Metropolitan Statistical Areas and other cities outside such areas. National rate includes those states listed as not available. Burglary is the unlawful entry of a structure to commit a felony or theft. Attempts are included.
Not available.

Percent of Burglaries Occurring in Urban Areas in 1996

National Percent = 92.1% of Burglaries*

ALPHA ORDER   RANK ORDER

RANK	STATE	PERCENT		RANK	STATE	PERCENT
17	Alabama	92.0		1	Massachusetts	100.0
43	Alaska	69.8		1	New Jersey	100.0
6	Arizona	96.4		1	Rhode Island	100.0
33	Arkansas	82.8		4	California	98.0
4	California	98.0		5	Maryland	96.6
9	Colorado	95.3		6	Arizona	96.4
7	Connecticut	96.2		7	Connecticut	96.2
31	Delaware	83.4		8	New York	95.7
NA	Florida**	NA		9	Colorado	95.3
27	Georgia	86.9		10	Texas	94.5
40	Hawaii	74.7		11	New Hampshire	94.1
39	Idaho	76.1		11	Ohio	94.1
NA	Illinois**	NA		13	Nevada	93.6
20	Indiana	89.8		14	Louisiana	93.2
29	Iowa	85.1		15	Utah	93.1
NA	Kansas**	NA		16	Pennsylvania	92.1
NA	Kentucky**	NA		17	Alabama	92.0
14	Louisiana	93.2		18	Washington	91.4
42	Maine	72.6		19	Michigan	90.0
5	Maryland	96.6		20	Indiana	89.8
1	Massachusetts	100.0		20	Oklahoma	89.8
19	Michigan	90.0		22	Virginia	88.3
30	Minnesota	84.8		23	Tennessee	87.8
37	Mississippi	79.3		24	Missouri	87.6
24	Missouri	87.6		24	Oregon	87.6
NA	Montana**	NA		26	New Mexico	87.1
27	Nebraska	86.9		27	Georgia	86.9
13	Nevada	93.6		27	Nebraska	86.9
11	New Hampshire	94.1		29	Iowa	85.1
1	New Jersey	100.0		30	Minnesota	84.8
26	New Mexico	87.1		31	Delaware	83.4
8	New York	95.7		32	Wisconsin	83.0
34	North Carolina	82.0		33	Arkansas	82.8
40	North Dakota	74.7		34	North Carolina	82.0
11	Ohio	94.1		35	South Carolina	81.7
20	Oklahoma	89.8		36	Wyoming	80.7
24	Oregon	87.6		37	Mississippi	79.3
16	Pennsylvania	92.1		38	South Dakota	78.0
1	Rhode Island	100.0		39	Idaho	76.1
35	South Carolina	81.7		40	Hawaii	74.7
38	South Dakota	78.0		40	North Dakota	74.7
23	Tennessee	87.8		42	Maine	72.6
10	Texas	94.5		43	Alaska	69.8
15	Utah	93.1		44	Vermont	68.3
44	Vermont	68.3		45	West Virginia	66.0
22	Virginia	88.3		NA	Florida**	NA
18	Washington	91.4		NA	Illinois**	NA
45	West Virginia	66.0		NA	Kansas**	NA
32	Wisconsin	83.0		NA	Kentucky**	NA
36	Wyoming	80.7		NA	Montana**	NA
					District of Columbia	100.0

Source: Morgan Quitno Press using data from Federal Bureau of Investigation
    "Crime in the United States 1996" (Uniform Crime Reports, October 4, 1997)
*Estimated percentages for urban areas, defined by the F.B.I. as Metropolitan Statistical Areas and other cities
outside such areas. National percent includes those states listed as not available. Burglary is the unlawful entry
of a structure to commit a felony or theft. Attempts are included.
**Not available.

445

Burglaries in Rural Areas in 1996

National Rural Total = 198,607 Burglaries*

RANK	STATE	BURGLARIES	% of USA
22	Alabama	3,438	1.73%
32	Alaska	1,546	0.78%
29	Arizona	2,002	1.01%
19	Arkansas	4,110	2.07%
8	California	6,217	3.13%
31	Colorado	1,611	0.81%
37	Connecticut	1,047	0.53%
38	Delaware	965	0.49%
NA	Florida**	NA	NA
3	Georgia	10,756	5.42%
24	Hawaii	3,238	1.63%
28	Idaho	2,012	1.01%
NA	Illinois**	NA	NA
16	Indiana	4,682	2.36%
26	Iowa	2,828	1.42%
NA	Kansas**	NA	NA
NA	Kentucky**	NA	NA
21	Louisiana	3,853	1.94%
27	Maine	2,548	1.28%
30	Maryland	1,717	0.86%
43	Massachusetts	9	0.00%
5	Michigan	8,578	4.32%
12	Minnesota	5,399	2.72%
7	Mississippi	6,372	3.21%
9	Missouri	5,940	2.99%
NA	Montana**	NA	NA
33	Nebraska	1,327	0.67%
35	Nevada	1,251	0.63%
42	New Hampshire	299	0.15%
45	New Jersey	0	0.00%
25	New Mexico	3,047	1.53%
10	New York	5,596	2.82%
1	North Carolina	17,750	8.94%
41	North Dakota	504	0.25%
11	Ohio	5,511	2.77%
18	Oklahoma	4,209	2.12%
20	Oregon	3,940	1.98%
13	Pennsylvania	5,253	2.64%
44	Rhode Island	3	0.00%
4	South Carolina	8,706	4.38%
39	South Dakota	895	0.45%
6	Tennessee	7,540	3.80%
2	Texas	11,227	5.65%
36	Utah	1,172	0.59%
34	Vermont	1,256	0.63%
17	Virginia	4,577	2.30%
15	Washington	5,015	2.53%
23	West Virginia	3,394	1.71%
14	Wisconsin	5,163	2.60%
40	Wyoming	613	0.31%

RANK	STATE	BURGLARIES	% of USA
1	North Carolina	17,750	8.94%
2	Texas	11,227	5.65%
3	Georgia	10,756	5.42%
4	South Carolina	8,706	4.38%
5	Michigan	8,578	4.32%
6	Tennessee	7,540	3.80%
7	Mississippi	6,372	3.21%
8	California	6,217	3.13%
9	Missouri	5,940	2.99%
10	New York	5,596	2.82%
11	Ohio	5,511	2.77%
12	Minnesota	5,399	2.72%
13	Pennsylvania	5,253	2.64%
14	Wisconsin	5,163	2.60%
15	Washington	5,015	2.53%
16	Indiana	4,682	2.36%
17	Virginia	4,577	2.30%
18	Oklahoma	4,209	2.12%
19	Arkansas	4,110	2.07%
20	Oregon	3,940	1.98%
21	Louisiana	3,853	1.94%
22	Alabama	3,438	1.73%
23	West Virginia	3,394	1.71%
24	Hawaii	3,238	1.63%
25	New Mexico	3,047	1.53%
26	Iowa	2,828	1.42%
27	Maine	2,548	1.28%
28	Idaho	2,012	1.01%
29	Arizona	2,002	1.01%
30	Maryland	1,717	0.86%
31	Colorado	1,611	0.81%
32	Alaska	1,546	0.78%
33	Nebraska	1,327	0.67%
34	Vermont	1,256	0.63%
35	Nevada	1,251	0.63%
36	Utah	1,172	0.59%
37	Connecticut	1,047	0.53%
38	Delaware	965	0.49%
39	South Dakota	895	0.45%
40	Wyoming	613	0.31%
41	North Dakota	504	0.25%
42	New Hampshire	299	0.15%
43	Massachusetts	9	0.00%
44	Rhode Island	3	0.00%
45	New Jersey	0	0.00%
NA	Florida**	NA	NA
NA	Illinois**	NA	NA
NA	Kansas**	NA	NA
NA	Kentucky**	NA	NA
NA	Montana**	NA	NA
	District of Columbia	0	0.00%

Source: Federal Bureau of Investigation
"Crime in the United States 1996" (Uniform Crime Reports, October 4, 1997)
Estimated totals for rural areas, defined by the F.B.I. as other than Metropolitan Statistical Areas and other cities outside such areas. National total includes those states listed as not available. Burglary is the unlawful entry of a structure to commit a felony or theft. Attempts are included.
**Not available.*

Rural Burglary Rate in 1996

National Rural Rate = 620.0 Burglaries per 100,000 Population*

ALPHA ORDER				RANK ORDER		
RANK	STATE	RATE		RANK	STATE	RATE
34	Alabama	439.3		1	Hawaii	1,219.7
9	Alaska	809.0		2	South Carolina	1,099.9
20	Arizona	585.7		3	North Carolina	1,050.6
27	Arkansas	510.2		4	Delaware	1,037.3
6	California	988.0		5	New Mexico	1,007.8
29	Colorado	507.3		6	California	988.0
24	Connecticut	541.5		7	Washington	983.0
4	Delaware	1,037.3		8	Michigan	812.4
NA	Florida**	NA		9	Alaska	809.0
11	Georgia	743.1		10	Oregon	765.8
1	Hawaii	1,219.7		11	Georgia	743.1
28	Idaho	508.2		12	Maine	732.7
NA	Illinois**	NA		13	Texas	688.6
33	Indiana	442.7		14	Tennessee	686.0
38	Iowa	319.3		15	Nevada	670.7
NA	Kansas**	NA		16	Oklahoma	662.6
NA	Kentucky**	NA		17	New York	654.1
22	Louisiana	561.7		18	Maryland	643.4
12	Maine	732.7		19	Minnesota	616.1
18	Maryland	643.4		20	Arizona	585.7
43	Massachusetts	81.3		21	Mississippi	573.7
8	Michigan	812.4		22	Louisiana	561.7
19	Minnesota	616.1		23	Utah	547.7
21	Mississippi	573.7		24	Connecticut	541.5
31	Missouri	491.1		25	Vermont	522.3
NA	Montana**	NA		26	Wisconsin	521.5
39	Nebraska	315.6		27	Arkansas	510.2
15	Nevada	670.7		28	Idaho	508.2
42	New Hampshire	198.9		29	Colorado	507.3
44	New Jersey	0.0		30	Pennsylvania	496.0
5	New Mexico	1,007.8		31	Missouri	491.1
17	New York	654.1		32	Wyoming	486.9
3	North Carolina	1,050.6		33	Indiana	442.7
41	North Dakota	225.9		34	Alabama	439.3
37	Ohio	414.5		35	West Virginia	433.4
16	Oklahoma	662.6		36	Virginia	431.1
10	Oregon	765.8		37	Ohio	414.5
30	Pennsylvania	496.0		38	Iowa	319.3
44	Rhode Island	0.0		39	Nebraska	315.6
2	South Carolina	1,099.9		40	South Dakota	306.2
40	South Dakota	306.2		41	North Dakota	225.9
14	Tennessee	686.0		42	New Hampshire	198.9
13	Texas	688.6		43	Massachusetts	81.3
23	Utah	547.7		44	New Jersey	0.0
25	Vermont	522.3		44	Rhode Island	0.0
36	Virginia	431.1		NA	Florida**	NA
7	Washington	983.0		NA	Illinois**	NA
35	West Virginia	433.4		NA	Kansas**	NA
26	Wisconsin	521.5		NA	Kentucky**	NA
32	Wyoming	486.9		NA	Montana**	NA
					District of Columbia	0.0

Source: Morgan Quitno Press using data from Federal Bureau of Investigation
    "Crime in the United States 1996" (Uniform Crime Reports, October 4, 1997)
*Estimated rates for rural areas, defined by the F.B.I. as other than Metropolitan Statistical Areas and other cities outside such areas. National rate includes those states listed as not available. Burglary is the unlawful entry of a structure to commit a felony or theft. Attempts are included.
**Not available.

447

Percent of Burglaries Occurring in Rural Areas in 1996

National Percent = 7.9% of Burglaries*

<table>
<tr><td colspan="3">ALPHA ORDER</td><td colspan="3">RANK ORDER</td></tr>
<tr><td>RANK</td><td>STATE</td><td>PERCENT</td><td>RANK</td><td>STATE</td><td>PERCENT</td></tr>
<tr><td>29</td><td>Alabama</td><td>8.0</td><td>1</td><td>West Virginia</td><td>34.0</td></tr>
<tr><td>3</td><td>Alaska</td><td>30.2</td><td>2</td><td>Vermont</td><td>31.7</td></tr>
<tr><td>40</td><td>Arizona</td><td>3.6</td><td>3</td><td>Alaska</td><td>30.2</td></tr>
<tr><td>13</td><td>Arkansas</td><td>17.2</td><td>4</td><td>Maine</td><td>27.4</td></tr>
<tr><td>42</td><td>California</td><td>2.0</td><td>5</td><td>Hawaii</td><td>25.3</td></tr>
<tr><td>37</td><td>Colorado</td><td>4.7</td><td>5</td><td>North Dakota</td><td>25.3</td></tr>
<tr><td>39</td><td>Connecticut</td><td>3.8</td><td>7</td><td>Idaho</td><td>23.9</td></tr>
<tr><td>15</td><td>Delaware</td><td>16.6</td><td>8</td><td>South Dakota</td><td>22.0</td></tr>
<tr><td>NA</td><td>Florida**</td><td>NA</td><td>9</td><td>Mississippi</td><td>20.7</td></tr>
<tr><td>18</td><td>Georgia</td><td>13.1</td><td>10</td><td>Wyoming</td><td>19.3</td></tr>
<tr><td>5</td><td>Hawaii</td><td>25.3</td><td>11</td><td>South Carolina</td><td>18.3</td></tr>
<tr><td>7</td><td>Idaho</td><td>23.9</td><td>12</td><td>North Carolina</td><td>18.0</td></tr>
<tr><td>NA</td><td>Illinois**</td><td>NA</td><td>13</td><td>Arkansas</td><td>17.2</td></tr>
<tr><td>25</td><td>Indiana</td><td>10.2</td><td>14</td><td>Wisconsin</td><td>17.0</td></tr>
<tr><td>17</td><td>Iowa</td><td>14.9</td><td>15</td><td>Delaware</td><td>16.6</td></tr>
<tr><td>NA</td><td>Kansas**</td><td>NA</td><td>16</td><td>Minnesota</td><td>15.2</td></tr>
<tr><td>NA</td><td>Kentucky**</td><td>NA</td><td>17</td><td>Iowa</td><td>14.9</td></tr>
<tr><td>32</td><td>Louisiana</td><td>6.8</td><td>18</td><td>Georgia</td><td>13.1</td></tr>
<tr><td>4</td><td>Maine</td><td>27.4</td><td>18</td><td>Nebraska</td><td>13.1</td></tr>
<tr><td>41</td><td>Maryland</td><td>3.4</td><td>20</td><td>New Mexico</td><td>12.9</td></tr>
<tr><td>43</td><td>Massachusetts</td><td>0.0</td><td>21</td><td>Missouri</td><td>12.4</td></tr>
<tr><td>27</td><td>Michigan</td><td>10.0</td><td>21</td><td>Oregon</td><td>12.4</td></tr>
<tr><td>16</td><td>Minnesota</td><td>15.2</td><td>23</td><td>Tennessee</td><td>12.2</td></tr>
<tr><td>9</td><td>Mississippi</td><td>20.7</td><td>24</td><td>Virginia</td><td>11.7</td></tr>
<tr><td>21</td><td>Missouri</td><td>12.4</td><td>25</td><td>Indiana</td><td>10.2</td></tr>
<tr><td>NA</td><td>Montana**</td><td>NA</td><td>25</td><td>Oklahoma</td><td>10.2</td></tr>
<tr><td>18</td><td>Nebraska</td><td>13.1</td><td>27</td><td>Michigan</td><td>10.0</td></tr>
<tr><td>33</td><td>Nevada</td><td>6.4</td><td>28</td><td>Washington</td><td>8.6</td></tr>
<tr><td>34</td><td>New Hampshire</td><td>5.9</td><td>29</td><td>Alabama</td><td>8.0</td></tr>
<tr><td>43</td><td>New Jersey</td><td>0.0</td><td>30</td><td>Pennsylvania</td><td>7.9</td></tr>
<tr><td>20</td><td>New Mexico</td><td>12.9</td><td>31</td><td>Utah</td><td>6.9</td></tr>
<tr><td>38</td><td>New York</td><td>4.3</td><td>32</td><td>Louisiana</td><td>6.8</td></tr>
<tr><td>12</td><td>North Carolina</td><td>18.0</td><td>33</td><td>Nevada</td><td>6.4</td></tr>
<tr><td>5</td><td>North Dakota</td><td>25.3</td><td>34</td><td>New Hampshire</td><td>5.9</td></tr>
<tr><td>34</td><td>Ohio</td><td>5.9</td><td>34</td><td>Ohio</td><td>5.9</td></tr>
<tr><td>25</td><td>Oklahoma</td><td>10.2</td><td>36</td><td>Texas</td><td>5.5</td></tr>
<tr><td>21</td><td>Oregon</td><td>12.4</td><td>37</td><td>Colorado</td><td>4.7</td></tr>
<tr><td>30</td><td>Pennsylvania</td><td>7.9</td><td>38</td><td>New York</td><td>4.3</td></tr>
<tr><td>43</td><td>Rhode Island</td><td>0.0</td><td>39</td><td>Connecticut</td><td>3.8</td></tr>
<tr><td>11</td><td>South Carolina</td><td>18.3</td><td>40</td><td>Arizona</td><td>3.6</td></tr>
<tr><td>8</td><td>South Dakota</td><td>22.0</td><td>41</td><td>Maryland</td><td>3.4</td></tr>
<tr><td>23</td><td>Tennessee</td><td>12.2</td><td>42</td><td>California</td><td>2.0</td></tr>
<tr><td>36</td><td>Texas</td><td>5.5</td><td>43</td><td>Massachusetts</td><td>0.0</td></tr>
<tr><td>31</td><td>Utah</td><td>6.9</td><td>43</td><td>New Jersey</td><td>0.0</td></tr>
<tr><td>2</td><td>Vermont</td><td>31.7</td><td>43</td><td>Rhode Island</td><td>0.0</td></tr>
<tr><td>24</td><td>Virginia</td><td>11.7</td><td>NA</td><td>Florida**</td><td>NA</td></tr>
<tr><td>28</td><td>Washington</td><td>8.6</td><td>NA</td><td>Illinois**</td><td>NA</td></tr>
<tr><td>1</td><td>West Virginia</td><td>34.0</td><td>NA</td><td>Kansas**</td><td>NA</td></tr>
<tr><td>14</td><td>Wisconsin</td><td>17.0</td><td>NA</td><td>Kentucky**</td><td>NA</td></tr>
<tr><td>10</td><td>Wyoming</td><td>19.3</td><td>NA</td><td>Montana**</td><td>NA</td></tr>
<tr><td></td><td></td><td></td><td></td><td>District of Columbia</td><td>0.0</td></tr>
</table>

Source: Morgan Quitno Press using data from Federal Bureau of Investigation
    "Crime in the United States 1996" (Uniform Crime Reports, October 4, 1997)
*Estimated percentages for rural areas, defined by the F.B.I. as other than Metropolitan Statistical Areas and other
cities outside such areas. National percent includes those states listed as not available. Burglary is the unlawful
entry of a structure to commit a felony or theft. Attempts are included.
**Not available.

Larcenies and Thefts in Urban Areas in 1996

National Urban Total = 7,547,766 Larcenies and Thefts*

ALPHA ORDER					RANK ORDER			
RANK	STATE	THEFTS	% of USA		RANK	STATE	THEFTS	% of USA
23	Alabama	118,914	1.58%		1	California	822,412	10.90%
41	Alaska	17,839	0.24%		2	Texas	644,274	8.54%
11	Arizona	185,018	2.45%		3	New York	389,078	5.15%
29	Arkansas	66,146	0.88%		4	Ohio	297,804	3.95%
1	California	822,412	10.90%		5	Georgia	266,430	3.53%
20	Colorado	125,819	1.67%		6	Michigan	261,645	3.47%
27	Connecticut	79,654	1.06%		7	Pennsylvania	231,720	3.07%
40	Delaware	19,825	0.26%		8	North Carolina	217,665	2.88%
NA	Florida**	NA	NA		9	Washington	205,759	2.73%
5	Georgia	266,430	3.53%		10	New Jersey	193,961	2.57%
34	Hawaii	44,062	0.58%		11	Arizona	185,018	2.45%
35	Idaho	29,423	0.39%		12	Virginia	174,591	2.31%
NA	Illinois**	NA	NA		13	Maryland	169,597	2.25%
16	Indiana	150,950	2.00%		14	Louisiana	164,444	2.18%
28	Iowa	66,423	0.88%		15	Missouri	162,091	2.15%
NA	Kansas**	NA	NA		16	Indiana	150,950	2.00%
NA	Kentucky**	NA	NA		17	Tennessee	141,612	1.88%
14	Louisiana	164,444	2.18%		18	Minnesota	128,833	1.71%
36	Maine	26,090	0.35%		19	Wisconsin	126,564	1.68%
13	Maryland	169,597	2.25%		20	Colorado	125,819	1.67%
22	Massachusetts	119,541	1.58%		21	Oregon	120,611	1.60%
6	Michigan	261,645	3.47%		22	Massachusetts	119,541	1.58%
18	Minnesota	128,833	1.71%		23	Alabama	118,914	1.58%
30	Mississippi	63,753	0.84%		24	South Carolina	112,592	1.49%
15	Missouri	162,091	2.15%		25	Oklahoma	104,886	1.39%
NA	Montana**	NA	NA		26	Utah	83,686	1.11%
33	Nebraska	46,408	0.61%		27	Connecticut	79,654	1.06%
32	Nevada	49,146	0.65%		28	Iowa	66,423	0.88%
37	New Hampshire	24,134	0.32%		29	Arkansas	66,146	0.88%
10	New Jersey	193,961	2.57%		30	Mississippi	63,753	0.84%
31	New Mexico	61,317	0.81%		31	New Mexico	61,317	0.81%
3	New York	389,078	5.15%		32	Nevada	49,146	0.65%
8	North Carolina	217,665	2.88%		33	Nebraska	46,408	0.61%
44	North Dakota	12,119	0.16%		34	Hawaii	44,062	0.58%
4	Ohio	297,804	3.95%		35	Idaho	29,423	0.39%
25	Oklahoma	104,886	1.39%		36	Maine	26,090	0.35%
21	Oregon	120,611	1.60%		37	New Hampshire	24,134	0.32%
7	Pennsylvania	231,720	3.07%		38	West Virginia	23,548	0.31%
39	Rhode Island	23,359	0.31%		39	Rhode Island	23,359	0.31%
24	South Carolina	112,592	1.49%		40	Delaware	19,825	0.26%
42	South Dakota	14,005	0.19%		41	Alaska	17,839	0.24%
17	Tennessee	141,612	1.88%		42	South Dakota	14,005	0.19%
2	Texas	644,274	8.54%		43	Wyoming	13,750	0.18%
26	Utah	83,686	1.11%		44	North Dakota	12,119	0.16%
45	Vermont	10,285	0.14%		45	Vermont	10,285	0.14%
12	Virginia	174,591	2.31%		NA	Florida**	NA	NA
9	Washington	205,759	2.73%		NA	Illinois**	NA	NA
38	West Virginia	23,548	0.31%		NA	Kansas**	NA	NA
19	Wisconsin	126,564	1.68%		NA	Kentucky**	NA	NA
43	Wyoming	13,750	0.18%		NA	Montana**	NA	NA
						District of Columbia	31,385	0.42%

Source: Morgan Quitno Press using data from Federal Bureau of Investigation
"Crime in the United States 1996" (Uniform Crime Reports, October 4, 1997)
Estimated totals for urban areas, defined by the F.B.I. as Metropolitan Statistical Areas and other cities outside such areas. National total includes those states listed as not available. Larceny and theft is the unlawful taking of property without use of force, violence or fraud. Attempts are included. Motor vehicle thefts are excluded.
**Not available.*

Urban Larceny and Theft Rate in 1996

National Urban Rate = 3,235.9 Larcenies and Thefts per 100,000 Population*

ALPHA ORDER

RANK	STATE	RATE
23	Alabama	3,406.9
8	Alaska	4,289.2
3	Arizona	4,527.9
13	Arkansas	3,881.0
37	California	2,631.8
20	Colorado	3,589.3
38	Connecticut	2,585.6
29	Delaware	3,137.0
NA	Florida**	NA
4	Georgia	4,511.5
1	Hawaii	4,797.1
18	Idaho	3,710.0
NA	Illinois**	NA
28	Indiana	3,155.7
25	Iowa	3,377.9
NA	Kansas**	NA
NA	Kentucky**	NA
5	Louisiana	4,486.9
35	Maine	2,914.2
21	Maryland	3,529.5
45	Massachusetts	1,965.8
31	Michigan	3,064.5
24	Minnesota	3,406.7
10	Mississippi	3,971.3
12	Missouri	3,906.2
NA	Montana**	NA
17	Nebraska	3,768.1
22	Nevada	3,469.6
40	New Hampshire	2,385.6
39	New Jersey	2,428.2
7	New Mexico	4,346.7
43	New York	2,245.2
16	North Carolina	3,863.8
36	North Dakota	2,879.2
33	Ohio	3,025.4
11	Oklahoma	3,934.5
6	Oregon	4,484.5
44	Pennsylvania	2,107.1
41	Rhode Island	2,359.5
14	South Carolina	3,872.5
27	South Dakota	3,185.3
26	Tennessee	3,355.0
19	Texas	3,682.1
2	Utah	4,685.7
34	Vermont	2,950.9
30	Virginia	3,110.4
9	Washington	4,096.5
42	West Virginia	2,258.0
32	Wisconsin	3,035.2
15	Wyoming	3,872.2

RANK ORDER

RANK	STATE	RATE
1	Hawaii	4,797.1
2	Utah	4,685.7
3	Arizona	4,527.9
4	Georgia	4,511.5
5	Louisiana	4,486.9
6	Oregon	4,484.5
7	New Mexico	4,346.7
8	Alaska	4,289.2
9	Washington	4,096.5
10	Mississippi	3,971.3
11	Oklahoma	3,934.5
12	Missouri	3,906.2
13	Arkansas	3,881.0
14	South Carolina	3,872.5
15	Wyoming	3,872.2
16	North Carolina	3,863.8
17	Nebraska	3,768.1
18	Idaho	3,710.0
19	Texas	3,682.1
20	Colorado	3,589.3
21	Maryland	3,529.5
22	Nevada	3,469.6
23	Alabama	3,406.9
24	Minnesota	3,406.7
25	Iowa	3,377.9
26	Tennessee	3,355.0
27	South Dakota	3,185.3
28	Indiana	3,155.7
29	Delaware	3,137.0
30	Virginia	3,110.4
31	Michigan	3,064.5
32	Wisconsin	3,035.2
33	Ohio	3,025.4
34	Vermont	2,950.9
35	Maine	2,914.2
36	North Dakota	2,879.2
37	California	2,631.8
38	Connecticut	2,585.6
39	New Jersey	2,428.2
40	New Hampshire	2,385.6
41	Rhode Island	2,359.5
42	West Virginia	2,258.0
43	New York	2,245.2
44	Pennsylvania	2,107.1
45	Massachusetts	1,965.8
NA	Florida**	NA
NA	Illinois**	NA
NA	Kansas**	NA
NA	Kentucky**	NA
NA	Montana**	NA

District of Columbia   5,779.9

Source: Morgan Quitno Press using data from Federal Bureau of Investigation
  "Crime in the United States 1996" (Uniform Crime Reports, October 4, 1997)
Estimated rates for urban areas, defined by the F.B.I. as Metropolitan Statistical Areas and other cities outside such areas. National rate includes those states listed as not available. Larceny and theft is the unlawful taking of property without use of force, violence or fraud. Attempts are included. Motor vehicle thefts are excluded.
**Not available.

Percent of Larcenies and Thefts Occurring in Urban Areas in 1996

National Percent = 95.6% of Larcenies and Thefts*

ALPHA ORDER

RANK ORDER

RANK	STATE	PERCENT		RANK	STATE	PERCENT
11	Alabama	96.4		1	Massachusetts	100.0
41	Alaska	86.8		1	New Jersey	100.0
5	Arizona	98.3		1	Rhode Island	100.0
35	Arkansas	90.6		4	California	99.0
4	California	99.0		5	Arizona	98.3
11	Colorado	96.4		6	New Hampshire	98.1
7	Connecticut	97.9		7	Connecticut	97.9
33	Delaware	91.5		8	Texas	97.7
NA	Florida**	NA		9	Maryland	97.6
30	Georgia	92.3		10	New York	97.4
45	Hawaii	80.6		11	Alabama	96.4
40	Idaho	86.9		11	Colorado	96.4
NA	Illinois**	NA		13	Pennsylvania	96.3
24	Indiana	93.9		14	Missouri	96.0
29	Iowa	92.4		15	Oklahoma	95.8
NA	Kansas**	NA		16	Ohio	95.7
NA	Kentucky**	NA		17	Utah	95.6
19	Louisiana	94.9		18	Washington	95.4
39	Maine	88.3		19	Louisiana	94.9
9	Maryland	97.6		20	Virginia	94.8
1	Massachusetts	100.0		21	Michigan	94.5
21	Michigan	94.5		22	New Mexico	94.1
27	Minnesota	92.9		23	Nevada	94.0
32	Mississippi	92.0		24	Indiana	93.9
14	Missouri	96.0		25	Oregon	93.8
NA	Montana**	NA		26	Wisconsin	93.1
31	Nebraska	92.2		27	Minnesota	92.9
23	Nevada	94.0		27	Tennessee	92.9
6	New Hampshire	98.1		29	Iowa	92.4
1	New Jersey	100.0		30	Georgia	92.3
22	New Mexico	94.1		31	Nebraska	92.2
10	New York	97.4		32	Mississippi	92.0
34	North Carolina	91.3		33	Delaware	91.5
36	North Dakota	90.2		34	North Carolina	91.3
16	Ohio	95.7		35	Arkansas	90.6
15	Oklahoma	95.8		36	North Dakota	90.2
25	Oregon	93.8		36	South Dakota	90.2
13	Pennsylvania	96.3		38	Wyoming	89.2
1	Rhode Island	100.0		39	Maine	88.3
41	South Carolina	86.8		40	Idaho	86.9
36	South Dakota	90.2		41	Alaska	86.8
27	Tennessee	92.9		41	South Carolina	86.8
8	Texas	97.7		43	Vermont	84.8
17	Utah	95.6		44	West Virginia	83.2
43	Vermont	84.8		45	Hawaii	80.6
20	Virginia	94.8		NA	Florida**	NA
18	Washington	95.4		NA	Illinois**	NA
44	West Virginia	83.2		NA	Kansas**	NA
26	Wisconsin	93.1		NA	Kentucky**	NA
38	Wyoming	89.2		NA	Montana**	NA
					District of Columbia	100.0

Source: Morgan Quitno Press using data from Federal Bureau of Investigation
  "Crime in the United States 1996" (Uniform Crime Reports, October 4, 1997)
*Estimated percentages for urban areas, defined by the F.B.I. as Metropolitan Statistical Areas and other cities outside such areas. National percent includes those states listed as not available. Larceny and theft is the unlawful taking of property without use of force, violence or fraud. Attempts are included. Motor vehicle thefts are excluded.
**Not available.

451

Larcenies and Thefts in Rural Areas in 1996

National Rural Total = 346,854 Larcenies and Thefts*

ALPHA ORDER

RANK	STATE	THEFTS	% of USA
27	Alabama	4,436	1.28%
35	Alaska	2,718	0.78%
33	Arizona	3,282	0.95%
19	Arkansas	6,864	1.98%
17	California	8,045	2.32%
23	Colorado	4,757	1.37%
38	Connecticut	1,674	0.48%
36	Delaware	1,840	0.53%
NA	Florida**	NA	NA
1	Georgia	22,373	6.45%
8	Hawaii	10,639	3.07%
26	Idaho	4,449	1.28%
NA	Illinois**	NA	NA
12	Indiana	9,827	2.83%
22	Iowa	5,470	1.58%
NA	Kansas**	NA	NA
NA	Kentucky**	NA	NA
16	Louisiana	8,827	2.54%
32	Maine	3,467	1.00%
28	Maryland	4,220	1.22%
43	Massachusetts	21	0.01%
4	Michigan	15,264	4.40%
11	Minnesota	9,838	2.84%
21	Mississippi	5,546	1.60%
20	Missouri	6,779	1.95%
NA	Montana**	NA	NA
29	Nebraska	3,907	1.13%
34	Nevada	3,149	0.91%
42	New Hampshire	477	0.14%
45	New Jersey	0	0.00%
31	New Mexico	3,822	1.10%
9	New York	10,444	3.01%
2	North Carolina	20,846	6.01%
41	North Dakota	1,314	0.38%
6	Ohio	13,267	3.82%
25	Oklahoma	4,620	1.33%
18	Oregon	8,007	2.31%
15	Pennsylvania	8,973	2.59%
44	Rhode Island	8	0.00%
3	South Carolina	17,058	4.92%
40	South Dakota	1,527	0.44%
7	Tennessee	10,793	3.11%
5	Texas	15,140	4.36%
30	Utah	3,856	1.11%
37	Vermont	1,839	0.53%
13	Virginia	9,646	2.78%
10	Washington	9,947	2.87%
24	West Virginia	4,752	1.37%
14	Wisconsin	9,377	2.70%
39	Wyoming	1,658	0.48%

RANK ORDER

RANK	STATE	THEFTS	% of USA
1	Georgia	22,373	6.45%
2	North Carolina	20,846	6.01%
3	South Carolina	17,058	4.92%
4	Michigan	15,264	4.40%
5	Texas	15,140	4.36%
6	Ohio	13,267	3.82%
7	Tennessee	10,793	3.11%
8	Hawaii	10,639	3.07%
9	New York	10,444	3.01%
10	Washington	9,947	2.87%
11	Minnesota	9,838	2.84%
12	Indiana	9,827	2.83%
13	Virginia	9,646	2.78%
14	Wisconsin	9,377	2.70%
15	Pennsylvania	8,973	2.59%
16	Louisiana	8,827	2.54%
17	California	8,045	2.32%
18	Oregon	8,007	2.31%
19	Arkansas	6,864	1.98%
20	Missouri	6,779	1.95%
21	Mississippi	5,546	1.60%
22	Iowa	5,470	1.58%
23	Colorado	4,757	1.37%
24	West Virginia	4,752	1.37%
25	Oklahoma	4,620	1.33%
26	Idaho	4,449	1.28%
27	Alabama	4,436	1.28%
28	Maryland	4,220	1.22%
29	Nebraska	3,907	1.13%
30	Utah	3,856	1.11%
31	New Mexico	3,822	1.10%
32	Maine	3,467	1.00%
33	Arizona	3,282	0.95%
34	Nevada	3,149	0.91%
35	Alaska	2,718	0.78%
36	Delaware	1,840	0.53%
37	Vermont	1,839	0.53%
38	Connecticut	1,674	0.48%
39	Wyoming	1,658	0.48%
40	South Dakota	1,527	0.44%
41	North Dakota	1,314	0.38%
42	New Hampshire	477	0.14%
43	Massachusetts	21	0.01%
44	Rhode Island	8	0.00%
45	New Jersey	0	0.00%
NA	Florida**	NA	NA
NA	Illinois**	NA	NA
NA	Kansas**	NA	NA
NA	Kentucky**	NA	NA
NA	Montana**	NA	NA
	District of Columbia	0	0.00%

Source: Federal Bureau of Investigation
   "Crime in the United States 1996" (Uniform Crime Reports, October 4, 1997)
*Estimated totals for rural areas, defined by the F.B.I. as other than Metropolitan Statistical Areas and other cities outside such areas. National total includes those states listed as not available. Larceny and theft is the unlawful taking of property without use of force, violence or fraud. Attempts are included. Motor vehicle thefts are excluded.
**Not available.

Rural Larceny and Theft Rate in 1996

National Rural Rate = 1,082.7 Larcenies and Thefts per 100,000 Population*

RANK	STATE	RATE		RANK	STATE	RATE
38	Alabama	566.8		1	Hawaii	4,007.4
12	Alaska	1,422.3		2	South Carolina	2,155.1
24	Arizona	960.1		3	Delaware	1,977.8
31	Arkansas	852.0		4	Washington	1,949.8
15	California	1,278.5		5	Utah	1,801.9
10	Colorado	1,497.9		6	Nevada	1,688.4
30	Connecticut	865.8		7	Maryland	1,581.5
3	Delaware	1,977.8		8	Oregon	1,556.2
NA	Florida**	NA		9	Georgia	1,545.7
9	Georgia	1,545.7		10	Colorado	1,497.9
1	Hawaii	4,007.4		11	Michigan	1,445.5
19	Idaho	1,123.7		12	Alaska	1,422.3
NA	Illinois**	NA		13	Wyoming	1,316.8
27	Indiana	929.2		14	Louisiana	1,286.7
35	Iowa	617.6		15	California	1,278.5
NA	Kansas**	NA		16	New Mexico	1,264.1
NA	Kentucky**	NA		17	North Carolina	1,233.8
14	Louisiana	1,286.7		18	New York	1,220.9
22	Maine	997.0		19	Idaho	1,123.7
7	Maryland	1,581.5		20	Minnesota	1,122.7
43	Massachusetts	189.8		21	Ohio	997.9
11	Michigan	1,445.5		22	Maine	997.0
20	Minnesota	1,122.7		23	Tennessee	982.0
41	Mississippi	499.3		24	Arizona	960.1
39	Missouri	560.5		25	Wisconsin	947.1
NA	Montana**	NA		26	Nebraska	929.3
26	Nebraska	929.3		27	Indiana	929.2
6	Nevada	1,688.4		28	Texas	928.6
42	New Hampshire	317.3		29	Virginia	908.5
44	New Jersey	0.0		30	Connecticut	865.8
16	New Mexico	1,264.1		31	Arkansas	852.0
18	New York	1,220.9		32	Pennsylvania	847.3
17	North Carolina	1,233.8		33	Vermont	764.8
37	North Dakota	589.0		34	Oklahoma	727.3
21	Ohio	997.9		35	Iowa	617.6
34	Oklahoma	727.3		36	West Virginia	606.8
8	Oregon	1,556.2		37	North Dakota	589.0
32	Pennsylvania	847.3		38	Alabama	566.8
44	Rhode Island	0.0		39	Missouri	560.5
2	South Carolina	2,155.1		40	South Dakota	522.4
40	South Dakota	522.4		41	Mississippi	499.3
23	Tennessee	982.0		42	New Hampshire	317.3
28	Texas	928.6		43	Massachusetts	189.8
5	Utah	1,801.9		44	New Jersey	0.0
33	Vermont	764.8		44	Rhode Island	0.0
29	Virginia	908.5		NA	Florida**	NA
4	Washington	1,949.8		NA	Illinois**	NA
36	West Virginia	606.8		NA	Kansas**	NA
25	Wisconsin	947.1		NA	Kentucky**	NA
13	Wyoming	1,316.8		NA	Montana**	NA
					District of Columbia	0.0

Source: Morgan Quitno Press using data from Federal Bureau of Investigation
"Crime in the United States 1996" (Uniform Crime Reports, October 4, 1997)
*Estimated rates for rural areas, defined by the F.B.I. as other than Metropolitan Statistical Areas and other cities outside such areas. National rate includes those states listed as not available. Larceny and theft is the unlawful taking of property without use of force, violence or fraud. Attempts are included. Motor vehicle thefts are excluded.
**Not available.

Percent of Larcenies and Thefts Occurring in Rural Areas in 1996

National Percent = 4.4% of Larcenies and Thefts*

ALPHA ORDER				RANK ORDER		
RANK	STATE	PERCENT		RANK	STATE	PERCENT
34	Alabama	3.6		1	Hawaii	19.4
4	Alaska	13.2		2	West Virginia	16.8
41	Arizona	1.7		3	Vermont	15.2
11	Arkansas	9.4		4	Alaska	13.2
42	California	1.0		4	South Carolina	13.2
34	Colorado	3.6		6	Idaho	13.1
39	Connecticut	2.1		7	Maine	11.7
13	Delaware	8.5		8	Wyoming	10.8
NA	Florida**	NA		9	North Dakota	9.8
16	Georgia	7.7		9	South Dakota	9.8
1	Hawaii	19.4		11	Arkansas	9.4
6	Idaho	13.1		12	North Carolina	8.7
NA	Illinois**	NA		13	Delaware	8.5
22	Indiana	6.1		14	Mississippi	8.0
17	Iowa	7.6		15	Nebraska	7.8
NA	Kansas**	NA		16	Georgia	7.7
NA	Kentucky**	NA		17	Iowa	7.6
27	Louisiana	5.1		18	Minnesota	7.1
7	Maine	11.7		18	Tennessee	7.1
37	Maryland	2.4		20	Wisconsin	6.9
43	Massachusetts	0.0		21	Oregon	6.2
25	Michigan	5.5		22	Indiana	6.1
18	Minnesota	7.1		23	Nevada	6.0
14	Mississippi	8.0		24	New Mexico	5.9
32	Missouri	4.0		25	Michigan	5.5
NA	Montana**	NA		26	Virginia	5.2
15	Nebraska	7.8		27	Louisiana	5.1
23	Nevada	6.0		28	Washington	4.6
40	New Hampshire	1.9		29	Utah	4.4
43	New Jersey	0.0		30	Ohio	4.3
24	New Mexico	5.9		31	Oklahoma	4.2
36	New York	2.6		32	Missouri	4.0
12	North Carolina	8.7		33	Pennsylvania	3.7
9	North Dakota	9.8		34	Alabama	3.6
30	Ohio	4.3		34	Colorado	3.6
31	Oklahoma	4.2		36	New York	2.6
21	Oregon	6.2		37	Maryland	2.4
33	Pennsylvania	3.7		38	Texas	2.3
43	Rhode Island	0.0		39	Connecticut	2.1
4	South Carolina	13.2		40	New Hampshire	1.9
9	South Dakota	9.8		41	Arizona	1.7
18	Tennessee	7.1		42	California	1.0
38	Texas	2.3		43	Massachusetts	0.0
29	Utah	4.4		43	New Jersey	0.0
3	Vermont	15.2		43	Rhode Island	0.0
26	Virginia	5.2		NA	Florida**	NA
28	Washington	4.6		NA	Illinois**	NA
2	West Virginia	16.8		NA	Kansas**	NA
20	Wisconsin	6.9		NA	Kentucky**	NA
8	Wyoming	10.8		NA	Montana**	NA
					District of Columbia	0.0

Source: Morgan Quitno Press using data from Federal Bureau of Investigation
     "Crime in the United States 1996" (Uniform Crime Reports, October 4, 1997)
*Estimated percentages for rural areas, defined by the F.B.I. as other than Metropolitan Statistical Areas and other cities outside such areas. National percent includes those states listed as not available. Larceny and theft is the unlawful taking of property without use of force, violence or fraud. Attempts are included. Motor vehicle thefts are excluded. **Not available.

Motor Vehicle Thefts in Urban Areas in 1996

National Urban Total = 1,354,981 Motor Vehicle Thefts*

ALPHA ORDER

RANK ORDER

RANK	STATE	THEFTS	% of USA	RANK	STATE	THEFTS	% of USA
24	Alabama	15,020	1.11%	1	California	241,051	17.79%
37	Alaska	2,542	0.19%	2	Texas	103,334	7.63%
9	Arizona	40,565	2.99%	3	New York	89,333	6.59%
31	Arkansas	6,880	0.51%	4	Michigan	65,654	4.85%
1	California	241,051	17.79%	5	Pennsylvania	48,458	3.58%
25	Colorado	14,745	1.09%	6	New Jersey	46,437	3.43%
22	Connecticut	15,770	1.16%	7	Ohio	44,363	3.27%
36	Delaware	3,043	0.22%	8	Georgia	43,335	3.20%
NA	Florida**	NA	NA	9	Arizona	40,565	2.99%
8	Georgia	43,335	3.20%	10	Maryland	35,791	2.64%
32	Hawaii	6,495	0.48%	11	Tennessee	32,835	2.42%
39	Idaho	1,757	0.13%	12	Massachusetts	32,176	2.37%
NA	Illinois**	NA	NA	13	Washington	27,938	2.06%
15	Indiana	23,674	1.75%	14	Louisiana	26,944	1.99%
34	Iowa	4,929	0.36%	15	Indiana	23,674	1.75%
NA	Kansas**	NA	NA	16	Missouri	23,022	1.70%
NA	Kentucky**	NA	NA	17	North Carolina	21,904	1.62%
14	Louisiana	26,944	1.99%	18	Virginia	17,457	1.29%
41	Maine	1,397	0.10%	19	Wisconsin	16,805	1.24%
10	Maryland	35,791	2.64%	20	Minnesota	16,471	1.22%
12	Massachusetts	32,176	2.37%	21	Oregon	15,997	1.18%
4	Michigan	65,654	4.85%	22	Connecticut	15,770	1.16%
20	Minnesota	16,471	1.22%	23	Oklahoma	15,148	1.12%
29	Mississippi	8,562	0.63%	24	Alabama	15,020	1.11%
16	Missouri	23,022	1.70%	25	Colorado	14,745	1.09%
NA	Montana**	NA	NA	26	South Carolina	13,631	1.01%
33	Nebraska	5,348	0.39%	27	Nevada	10,898	0.80%
27	Nevada	10,898	0.80%	28	New Mexico	9,293	0.69%
40	New Hampshire	1,718	0.13%	29	Mississippi	8,562	0.63%
6	New Jersey	46,437	3.43%	30	Utah	8,238	0.61%
28	New Mexico	9,293	0.69%	31	Arkansas	6,880	0.51%
3	New York	89,333	6.59%	32	Hawaii	6,495	0.48%
17	North Carolina	21,904	1.62%	33	Nebraska	5,348	0.39%
42	North Dakota	1,078	0.08%	34	Iowa	4,929	0.36%
7	Ohio	44,363	3.27%	35	Rhode Island	4,596	0.34%
23	Oklahoma	15,148	1.12%	36	Delaware	3,043	0.22%
21	Oregon	15,997	1.18%	37	Alaska	2,542	0.19%
5	Pennsylvania	48,458	3.58%	38	West Virginia	2,263	0.17%
35	Rhode Island	4,596	0.34%	39	Idaho	1,757	0.13%
26	South Carolina	13,631	1.01%	40	New Hampshire	1,718	0.13%
44	South Dakota	698	0.05%	41	Maine	1,397	0.10%
11	Tennessee	32,835	2.42%	42	North Dakota	1,078	0.08%
2	Texas	103,334	7.63%	43	Vermont	758	0.06%
30	Utah	8,238	0.61%	44	South Dakota	698	0.05%
43	Vermont	758	0.06%	45	Wyoming	560	0.04%
18	Virginia	17,457	1.29%	NA	Florida**	NA	NA
13	Washington	27,938	2.06%	NA	Illinois**	NA	NA
38	West Virginia	2,263	0.17%	NA	Kansas**	NA	NA
19	Wisconsin	16,805	1.24%	NA	Kentucky**	NA	NA
45	Wyoming	560	0.04%	NA	Montana**	NA	NA
					District of Columbia	9,975	0.74%

Source: Morgan Quitno Press using data from Federal Bureau of Investigation
   "Crime in the United States 1996" (Uniform Crime Reports, October 4, 1997)
*Estimated totals for urban areas, defined by the F.B.I. as Metropolitan Statistical Areas and other cities outside such areas. National total includes those states listed as not available. Motor vehicle theft includes the theft or attempted theft of a self-propelled vehicle. Excludes motorboats, construction equipment, airplanes and farming equipment. **Not available.

Urban Motor Vehicle Theft Rate in 1996

National Urban Rate = 580.9 Motor Vehicle Thefts per 100,000 Population*

ALPHA ORDER

RANK	STATE	RATE
31	Alabama	430.3
11	Alaska	611.2
1	Arizona	992.7
33	Arkansas	403.7
3	California	771.4
32	Colorado	420.6
21	Connecticut	511.9
23	Delaware	481.5
NA	Florida**	NA
8	Georgia	733.8
9	Hawaii	707.1
39	Idaho	221.5
NA	Illinois**	NA
22	Indiana	494.9
38	Iowa	250.7
NA	Kansas**	NA
NA	Kentucky**	NA
7	Louisiana	735.2
45	Maine	156.0
6	Maryland	744.8
19	Massachusetts	529.1
5	Michigan	769.0
29	Minnesota	435.5
18	Mississippi	533.3
17	Missouri	554.8
NA	Montana**	NA
30	Nebraska	434.2
4	Nevada	769.4
42	New Hampshire	169.8
14	New Jersey	581.3
10	New Mexico	658.8
20	New York	515.5
35	North Carolina	388.8
37	North Dakota	256.1
27	Ohio	450.7
15	Oklahoma	568.2
12	Oregon	594.8
28	Pennsylvania	440.6
25	Rhode Island	464.2
24	South Carolina	468.8
43	South Dakota	158.8
2	Tennessee	777.9
13	Texas	590.6
26	Utah	461.3
40	Vermont	217.5
36	Virginia	311.0
16	Washington	556.2
41	West Virginia	217.0
34	Wisconsin	403.0
44	Wyoming	157.7

RANK ORDER

RANK	STATE	RATE
1	Arizona	992.7
2	Tennessee	777.9
3	California	771.4
4	Nevada	769.4
5	Michigan	769.0
6	Maryland	744.8
7	Louisiana	735.2
8	Georgia	733.8
9	Hawaii	707.1
10	New Mexico	658.8
11	Alaska	611.2
12	Oregon	594.8
13	Texas	590.6
14	New Jersey	581.3
15	Oklahoma	568.2
16	Washington	556.2
17	Missouri	554.8
18	Mississippi	533.3
19	Massachusetts	529.1
20	New York	515.5
21	Connecticut	511.9
22	Indiana	494.9
23	Delaware	481.5
24	South Carolina	468.8
25	Rhode Island	464.2
26	Utah	461.3
27	Ohio	450.7
28	Pennsylvania	440.6
29	Minnesota	435.5
30	Nebraska	434.2
31	Alabama	430.3
32	Colorado	420.6
33	Arkansas	403.7
34	Wisconsin	403.0
35	North Carolina	388.8
36	Virginia	311.0
37	North Dakota	256.1
38	Iowa	250.7
39	Idaho	221.5
40	Vermont	217.5
41	West Virginia	217.0
42	New Hampshire	169.8
43	South Dakota	158.8
44	Wyoming	157.7
45	Maine	156.0
NA	Florida**	NA
NA	Illinois**	NA
NA	Kansas**	NA
NA	Kentucky**	NA
NA	Montana**	NA

District of Columbia   1,837.0

Source: Morgan Quitno Press using data from Federal Bureau of Investigation
     "Crime in the United States 1996" (Uniform Crime Reports, October 4, 1997)
*Estimated rates for urban areas, defined by the F.B.I. as Metropolitan Statistical Areas and other cities outside such areas. National rate includes those states listed as not available. Motor vehicle theft includes the theft or attempted theft of a self-propelled vehicle. Excludes motorboats, construction equipment, airplanes and farming equipment. **Not available.

Percent of Motor Vehicle Thefts Occurring in Urban Areas in 1996

National Percent = 97.1% of Motor Vehicle Thefts*

RANK	STATE	PERCENT		RANK	STATE	PERCENT
19	Alabama	96.1		1	Massachusetts	100.0
40	Alaska	85.0		1	New Jersey	100.0
7	Arizona	98.9		1	Rhode Island	100.0
37	Arkansas	87.6		4	California	99.4
4	California	99.4		4	New York	99.4
16	Colorado	97.0		6	Maryland	99.2
9	Connecticut	98.4		7	Arizona	98.9
17	Delaware	96.7		8	Texas	98.5
NA	Florida**	NA		9	Connecticut	98.4
28	Georgia	93.8		10	Louisiana	98.0
32	Hawaii	90.8		11	Michigan	97.7
43	Idaho	78.8		12	New Hampshire	97.5
NA	Illinois**	NA		12	Pennsylvania	97.5
22	Indiana	95.4		14	Nevada	97.4
33	Iowa	90.5		14	Ohio	97.4
NA	Kansas**	NA		16	Colorado	97.0
NA	Kentucky**	NA		17	Delaware	96.7
10	Louisiana	98.0		17	Washington	96.7
44	Maine	78.7		19	Alabama	96.1
6	Maryland	99.2		19	Utah	96.1
1	Massachusetts	100.0		21	Missouri	96.0
11	Michigan	97.7		22	Indiana	95.4
31	Minnesota	91.9		22	Tennessee	95.4
34	Mississippi	89.9		24	Oklahoma	95.0
21	Missouri	96.0		25	Nebraska	94.8
NA	Montana**	NA		26	Wisconsin	94.2
25	Nebraska	94.8		27	Oregon	94.0
14	Nevada	97.4		28	Georgia	93.8
12	New Hampshire	97.5		28	Virginia	93.8
1	New Jersey	100.0		30	New Mexico	93.2
30	New Mexico	93.2		31	Minnesota	91.9
4	New York	99.4		32	Hawaii	90.8
35	North Carolina	89.2		33	Iowa	90.5
36	North Dakota	88.1		34	Mississippi	89.9
14	Ohio	97.4		35	North Carolina	89.2
24	Oklahoma	95.0		36	North Dakota	88.1
27	Oregon	94.0		37	Arkansas	87.6
12	Pennsylvania	97.5		38	South Carolina	86.0
1	Rhode Island	100.0		39	Vermont	85.6
38	South Carolina	86.0		40	Alaska	85.0
41	South Dakota	83.7		41	South Dakota	83.7
22	Tennessee	95.4		41	Wyoming	83.7
8	Texas	98.5		43	Idaho	78.8
19	Utah	96.1		44	Maine	78.7
39	Vermont	85.6		45	West Virginia	70.0
28	Virginia	93.8		NA	Florida**	NA
17	Washington	96.7		NA	Illinois**	NA
45	West Virginia	70.0		NA	Kansas**	NA
26	Wisconsin	94.2		NA	Kentucky**	NA
41	Wyoming	83.7		NA	Montana**	NA
					District of Columbia	100.0

Source: Morgan Quitno Press using data from Federal Bureau of Investigation
   "Crime in the United States 1996" (Uniform Crime Reports, October 4, 1997)
*Estimated percentages for urban areas, defined by the F.B.I. as Metropolitan Statistical Areas and other cities outside such areas. National percent includes those states listed as not available. Motor vehicle theft includes the theft or attempted theft of a self-propelled vehicle. Excludes motorboats, construction equipment, airplanes and farming equipment. **Not available.

Motor Vehicle Thefts in Rural Areas in 1996

National Rural Total = 40,211 Motor Vehicle Thefts*

ALPHA ORDER

RANK	STATE	THEFTS	% of USA
23	Alabama	612	1.52%
30	Alaska	450	1.12%
28	Arizona	469	1.17%
15	Arkansas	975	2.42%
8	California	1,415	3.52%
29	Colorado	461	1.15%
36	Connecticut	252	0.63%
41	Delaware	105	0.26%
NA	Florida**	NA	NA
1	Georgia	2,880	7.16%
22	Hawaii	662	1.65%
27	Idaho	472	1.17%
NA	Illinois**	NA	NA
12	Indiana	1,143	2.84%
26	Iowa	520	1.29%
NA	Kansas**	NA	NA
NA	Kentucky**	NA	NA
25	Louisiana	536	1.33%
31	Maine	379	0.94%
35	Maryland	292	0.73%
43	Massachusetts	2	0.00%
6	Michigan	1,549	3.85%
7	Minnesota	1,452	3.61%
18	Mississippi	965	2.40%
16	Missouri	970	2.41%
NA	Montana**	NA	NA
34	Nebraska	295	0.73%
33	Nevada	296	0.74%
42	New Hampshire	44	0.11%
45	New Jersey	0	0.00%
21	New Mexico	680	1.69%
24	New York	567	1.41%
2	North Carolina	2,662	6.62%
37	North Dakota	146	0.36%
10	Ohio	1,165	2.90%
20	Oklahoma	791	1.97%
14	Oregon	1,016	2.53%
9	Pennsylvania	1,232	3.06%
44	Rhode Island	1	0.00%
3	South Carolina	2,218	5.52%
38	South Dakota	136	0.34%
5	Tennessee	1,593	3.96%
4	Texas	1,594	3.96%
32	Utah	334	0.83%
39	Vermont	127	0.32%
11	Virginia	1,151	2.86%
19	Washington	955	2.37%
17	West Virginia	968	2.41%
13	Wisconsin	1,041	2.59%
40	Wyoming	109	0.27%

RANK ORDER

RANK	STATE	THEFTS	% of USA
1	Georgia	2,880	7.16%
2	North Carolina	2,662	6.62%
3	South Carolina	2,218	5.52%
4	Texas	1,594	3.96%
5	Tennessee	1,593	3.96%
6	Michigan	1,549	3.85%
7	Minnesota	1,452	3.61%
8	California	1,415	3.52%
9	Pennsylvania	1,232	3.06%
10	Ohio	1,165	2.90%
11	Virginia	1,151	2.86%
12	Indiana	1,143	2.84%
13	Wisconsin	1,041	2.59%
14	Oregon	1,016	2.53%
15	Arkansas	975	2.42%
16	Missouri	970	2.41%
17	West Virginia	968	2.41%
18	Mississippi	965	2.40%
19	Washington	955	2.37%
20	Oklahoma	791	1.97%
21	New Mexico	680	1.69%
22	Hawaii	662	1.65%
23	Alabama	612	1.52%
24	New York	567	1.41%
25	Louisiana	536	1.33%
26	Iowa	520	1.29%
27	Idaho	472	1.17%
28	Arizona	469	1.17%
29	Colorado	461	1.15%
30	Alaska	450	1.12%
31	Maine	379	0.94%
32	Utah	334	0.83%
33	Nevada	296	0.74%
34	Nebraska	295	0.73%
35	Maryland	292	0.73%
36	Connecticut	252	0.63%
37	North Dakota	146	0.36%
38	South Dakota	136	0.34%
39	Vermont	127	0.32%
40	Wyoming	109	0.27%
41	Delaware	105	0.26%
42	New Hampshire	44	0.11%
43	Massachusetts	2	0.00%
44	Rhode Island	1	0.00%
45	New Jersey	0	0.00%
NA	Florida**	NA	NA
NA	Illinois**	NA	NA
NA	Kansas**	NA	NA
NA	Kentucky**	NA	NA
NA	Montana**	NA	NA
	District of Columbia	0	0.00%

Source: Federal Bureau of Investigation
    "Crime in the United States 1996" (Uniform Crime Reports, October 4, 1997)
*Estimated totals for rural areas, defined by the F.B.I. as other than Metropolitan Statistical Areas and other cities outside such areas. National total includes those states listed as not available. Motor vehicle theft includes the theft or attempted theft of a self-propelled vehicle. Excludes motorboats, construction equipment, airplanes and farming equipment. **Not available.

Rural Motor Vehicle Theft Rate in 1996

National Rural Rate = 125.5 Motor Vehicle Thefts per 100,000 Population*

RANK	STATE	RATE
34	Alabama	78.2
3	Alaska	235.5
16	Arizona	137.2
20	Arkansas	121.0
4	California	224.9
14	Colorado	145.2
17	Connecticut	130.3
23	Delaware	112.9
NA	Florida**	NA
6	Georgia	199.0
2	Hawaii	249.4
21	Idaho	119.2
NA	Illinois**	NA
27	Indiana	108.1
39	Iowa	58.7
NA	Kansas**	NA
NA	Kentucky**	NA
35	Louisiana	78.1
25	Maine	109.0
24	Maryland	109.4
43	Massachusetts	18.1
13	Michigan	146.7
9	Minnesota	165.7
31	Mississippi	86.9
33	Missouri	80.2
NA	Montana**	NA
36	Nebraska	70.2
10	Nevada	158.7
42	New Hampshire	29.3
44	New Jersey	0.0
4	New Mexico	224.9
37	New York	66.3
11	North Carolina	157.6
38	North Dakota	65.4
30	Ohio	87.6
18	Oklahoma	124.5
7	Oregon	197.5
22	Pennsylvania	116.3
44	Rhode Island	0.0
1	South Carolina	280.2
41	South Dakota	46.5
15	Tennessee	144.9
29	Texas	97.8
12	Utah	156.1
40	Vermont	52.8
26	Virginia	108.4
8	Washington	187.2
19	West Virginia	123.6
28	Wisconsin	105.1
32	Wyoming	86.6

RANK	STATE	RATE
1	South Carolina	280.2
2	Hawaii	249.4
3	Alaska	235.5
4	California	224.9
4	New Mexico	224.9
6	Georgia	199.0
7	Oregon	197.5
8	Washington	187.2
9	Minnesota	165.7
10	Nevada	158.7
11	North Carolina	157.6
12	Utah	156.1
13	Michigan	146.7
14	Colorado	145.2
15	Tennessee	144.9
16	Arizona	137.2
17	Connecticut	130.3
18	Oklahoma	124.5
19	West Virginia	123.6
20	Arkansas	121.0
21	Idaho	119.2
22	Pennsylvania	116.3
23	Delaware	112.9
24	Maryland	109.4
25	Maine	109.0
26	Virginia	108.4
27	Indiana	108.1
28	Wisconsin	105.1
29	Texas	97.8
30	Ohio	87.6
31	Mississippi	86.9
32	Wyoming	86.6
33	Missouri	80.2
34	Alabama	78.2
35	Louisiana	78.1
36	Nebraska	70.2
37	New York	66.3
38	North Dakota	65.4
39	Iowa	58.7
40	Vermont	52.8
41	South Dakota	46.5
42	New Hampshire	29.3
43	Massachusetts	18.1
44	New Jersey	0.0
44	Rhode Island	0.0
NA	Florida**	NA
NA	Illinois**	NA
NA	Kansas**	NA
NA	Kentucky**	NA
NA	Montana**	NA
	District of Columbia	0.0

Source: Morgan Quitno Press using data from Federal Bureau of Investigation
"Crime in the United States 1996" (Uniform Crime Reports, October 4, 1997)
*Estimated rates for rural areas, defined by the F.B.I. as other than Metropolitan Statistical Areas and other cities outside such areas. National rate includes those states listed as not available. Motor vehicle theft includes the theft or attempted theft of a self-propelled vehicle. Excludes motorboats, construction equipment, airplanes and farming equipment. **Not available.

Percent of Motor Vehicle Thefts Occurring in Rural Areas in 1996

National Percent = 2.9% of Motor Vehicle Thefts*

ALPHA ORDER

RANK	STATE	PERCENT
26	Alabama	3.9
6	Alaska	15.0
39	Arizona	1.1
9	Arkansas	12.4
41	California	0.6
30	Colorado	3.0
37	Connecticut	1.6
28	Delaware	3.3
NA	Florida**	NA
17	Georgia	6.2
14	Hawaii	9.2
3	Idaho	21.2
NA	Illinois**	NA
23	Indiana	4.6
13	Iowa	9.5
NA	Kansas**	NA
NA	Kentucky**	NA
36	Louisiana	2.0
2	Maine	21.3
40	Maryland	0.8
43	Massachusetts	0.0
35	Michigan	2.3
15	Minnesota	8.1
12	Mississippi	10.1
25	Missouri	4.0
NA	Montana**	NA
21	Nebraska	5.2
31	Nevada	2.6
33	New Hampshire	2.5
43	New Jersey	0.0
16	New Mexico	6.8
41	New York	0.6
11	North Carolina	10.8
10	North Dakota	11.9
31	Ohio	2.6
22	Oklahoma	5.0
19	Oregon	6.0
33	Pennsylvania	2.5
43	Rhode Island	0.0
8	South Carolina	14.0
4	South Dakota	16.3
23	Tennessee	4.6
38	Texas	1.5
26	Utah	3.9
7	Vermont	14.4
17	Virginia	6.2
28	Washington	3.3
1	West Virginia	30.0
20	Wisconsin	5.8
4	Wyoming	16.3

RANK ORDER

RANK	STATE	PERCENT
1	West Virginia	30.0
2	Maine	21.3
3	Idaho	21.2
4	South Dakota	16.3
4	Wyoming	16.3
6	Alaska	15.0
7	Vermont	14.4
8	South Carolina	14.0
9	Arkansas	12.4
10	North Dakota	11.9
11	North Carolina	10.8
12	Mississippi	10.1
13	Iowa	9.5
14	Hawaii	9.2
15	Minnesota	8.1
16	New Mexico	6.8
17	Georgia	6.2
17	Virginia	6.2
19	Oregon	6.0
20	Wisconsin	5.8
21	Nebraska	5.2
22	Oklahoma	5.0
23	Indiana	4.6
23	Tennessee	4.6
25	Missouri	4.0
26	Alabama	3.9
26	Utah	3.9
28	Delaware	3.3
28	Washington	3.3
30	Colorado	3.0
31	Nevada	2.6
31	Ohio	2.6
33	New Hampshire	2.5
33	Pennsylvania	2.5
35	Michigan	2.3
36	Louisiana	2.0
37	Connecticut	1.6
38	Texas	1.5
39	Arizona	1.1
40	Maryland	0.8
41	California	0.6
41	New York	0.6
43	Massachusetts	0.0
43	New Jersey	0.0
43	Rhode Island	0.0
NA	Florida**	NA
NA	Illinois**	NA
NA	Kansas**	NA
NA	Kentucky**	NA
NA	Montana**	NA

District of Columbia   0.0

*Source: Morgan Quitno Press using data from Federal Bureau of Investigation
"Crime in the United States 1996" (Uniform Crime Reports, October 4, 1997)
*Estimated percentages for rural areas, defined by the F.B.I. as other than Metropolitan Statistical Areas and other cities outside such areas. National percent includes those states listed as not available. Motor vehicle theft includes the theft or attempted theft of a self-propelled vehicle. Excludes motorboats, construction equipment, airplanes and farming equipment. **Not available.*

Crimes Reported at Universities and Colleges in 1996

National Total = 104,613 Reported Crimes*

<u>ALPHA ORDER</u>

RANK	STATE	CRIMES	% of USA
21	Alabama	1,619	1.55%
40	Alaska	115	0.11%
9	Arizona	3,703	3.54%
26	Arkansas	1,211	1.16%
1	California	15,723	15.03%
15	Colorado	2,329	2.23%
20	Connecticut	1,785	1.71%
35	Delaware	605	0.58%
30	Florida	849	0.81%
5	Georgia	5,165	4.94%
NA	Hawaii**	NA	NA
NA	Idaho**	NA	NA
NA	Illinois**	NA	NA
10	Indiana	3,492	3.34%
25	Iowa	1,241	1.19%
NA	Kansas**	NA	NA
NA	Kentucky**	NA	NA
13	Louisiana	2,754	2.63%
37	Maine	359	0.34%
11	Maryland	3,393	3.24%
8	Massachusetts	3,854	3.68%
3	Michigan	6,650	6.36%
24	Minnesota	1,282	1.23%
29	Mississippi	856	0.82%
28	Missouri	1,186	1.13%
NA	Montana**	NA	NA
31	Nebraska	734	0.70%
36	Nevada	596	0.57%
38	New Hampshire	237	0.23%
12	New Jersey	3,265	3.12%
33	New Mexico	687	0.66%
23	New York	1,373	1.31%
4	North Carolina	5,586	5.34%
NA	North Dakota**	NA	NA
6	Ohio	4,980	4.76%
22	Oklahoma	1,481	1.42%
NA	Oregon**	NA	NA
14	Pennsylvania	2,343	2.24%
34	Rhode Island	641	0.61%
16	South Carolina	2,199	2.10%
41	South Dakota	41	0.04%
27	Tennessee	1,202	1.15%
2	Texas	9,522	9.10%
19	Utah	1,906	1.82%
NA	Vermont**	NA	NA
7	Virginia	4,640	4.44%
18	Washington	1,933	1.85%
32	West Virginia	709	0.68%
17	Wisconsin	2,132	2.04%
39	Wyoming	235	0.22%

<u>RANK ORDER</u>

RANK	STATE	CRIMES	% of USA
1	California	15,723	15.03%
2	Texas	9,522	9.10%
3	Michigan	6,650	6.36%
4	North Carolina	5,586	5.34%
5	Georgia	5,165	4.94%
6	Ohio	4,980	4.76%
7	Virginia	4,640	4.44%
8	Massachusetts	3,854	3.68%
9	Arizona	3,703	3.54%
10	Indiana	3,492	3.34%
11	Maryland	3,393	3.24%
12	New Jersey	3,265	3.12%
13	Louisiana	2,754	2.63%
14	Pennsylvania	2,343	2.24%
15	Colorado	2,329	2.23%
16	South Carolina	2,199	2.10%
17	Wisconsin	2,132	2.04%
18	Washington	1,933	1.85%
19	Utah	1,906	1.82%
20	Connecticut	1,785	1.71%
21	Alabama	1,619	1.55%
22	Oklahoma	1,481	1.42%
23	New York	1,373	1.31%
24	Minnesota	1,282	1.23%
25	Iowa	1,241	1.19%
26	Arkansas	1,211	1.16%
27	Tennessee	1,202	1.15%
28	Missouri	1,186	1.13%
29	Mississippi	856	0.82%
30	Florida	849	0.81%
31	Nebraska	734	0.70%
32	West Virginia	709	0.68%
33	New Mexico	687	0.66%
34	Rhode Island	641	0.61%
35	Delaware	605	0.58%
36	Nevada	596	0.57%
37	Maine	359	0.34%
38	New Hampshire	237	0.23%
39	Wyoming	235	0.22%
40	Alaska	115	0.11%
41	South Dakota	41	0.04%
NA	Hawaii**	NA	NA
NA	Idaho**	NA	NA
NA	Illinois**	NA	NA
NA	Kansas**	NA	NA
NA	Kentucky**	NA	NA
NA	Montana**	NA	NA
NA	North Dakota**	NA	NA
NA	Oregon**	NA	NA
NA	Vermont**	NA	NA
	District of Columbia**	NA	NA

Source: Morgan Quitno Press using data from Federal Bureau of Investigation
     "Crime in the United States 1996" (Uniform Crime Reports, October 4, 1997)
*Includes murder, rape, robbery, aggravated assault, burglary, larceny-theft and motor vehicle theft. Total is only for states shown separately. Many states had incomplete reports.
**Not available.

Crimes Reported at Universities and Colleges as a Percent of All Crimes in 1996

National Percent = 0.86% of Crimes*

ALPHA ORDER			RANK ORDER		
RANK	STATE	PERCENT	RANK	STATE	PERCENT
27	Alabama	0.79	1	Virginia	1.75
38	Alaska	0.35	2	Delaware	1.70
13	Arizona	1.18	3	Massachusetts	1.65
18	Arkansas	1.03	4	Rhode Island	1.62
22	California	0.95	5	Utah	1.59
11	Colorado	1.19	6	West Virginia	1.56
10	Connecticut	1.29	7	North Carolina	1.38
2	Delaware	1.70	8	Michigan	1.35
41	Florida	0.08	9	Indiana	1.33
15	Georgia	1.11	10	Connecticut	1.29
NA	Hawaii**	NA	11	Colorado	1.19
NA	Idaho**	NA	11	Iowa	1.19
NA	Illinois**	NA	13	Arizona	1.18
9	Indiana	1.33	14	Wyoming	1.15
11	Iowa	1.19	15	Georgia	1.11
NA	Kansas**	NA	16	Maryland	1.10
NA	Kentucky**	NA	17	Wisconsin	1.08
24	Louisiana	0.93	18	Arkansas	1.03
26	Maine	0.85	19	Nebraska	1.00
16	Maryland	1.10	19	Ohio	1.00
3	Massachusetts	1.65	21	South Carolina	0.96
8	Michigan	1.35	22	California	0.95
31	Minnesota	0.62	23	New Jersey	0.94
30	Mississippi	0.70	24	Louisiana	0.93
36	Missouri	0.44	25	Texas	0.87
NA	Montana**	NA	26	Maine	0.85
19	Nebraska	1.00	27	Alabama	0.79
31	Nevada	0.62	27	Oklahoma	0.79
29	New Hampshire	0.72	29	New Hampshire	0.72
23	New Jersey	0.94	30	Mississippi	0.70
33	New Mexico	0.61	31	Minnesota	0.62
40	New York	0.18	31	Nevada	0.62
7	North Carolina	1.38	33	New Mexico	0.61
NA	North Dakota**	NA	34	Washington	0.59
19	Ohio	1.00	35	Pennsylvania	0.57
27	Oklahoma	0.79	36	Missouri	0.44
NA	Oregon**	NA	37	Tennessee	0.41
35	Pennsylvania	0.57	38	Alaska	0.35
4	Rhode Island	1.62	39	South Dakota	0.19
21	South Carolina	0.96	40	New York	0.18
39	South Dakota	0.19	41	Florida	0.08
37	Tennessee	0.41	NA	Hawaii**	NA
25	Texas	0.87	NA	Idaho**	NA
5	Utah	1.59	NA	Illinois**	NA
NA	Vermont**	NA	NA	Kansas**	NA
1	Virginia	1.75	NA	Kentucky**	NA
34	Washington	0.59	NA	Montana**	NA
6	West Virginia	1.56	NA	North Dakota**	NA
17	Wisconsin	1.08	NA	Oregon**	NA
14	Wyoming	1.15	NA	Vermont**	NA
				District of Columbia**	NA

Source: Morgan Quitno Press using data from Federal Bureau of Investigation
   "Crime in the United States 1996" (Uniform Crime Reports, October 4, 1997)
*Includes murder, rape, robbery, aggravated assault, burglary, larceny-theft and motor vehicle theft. National
percent is only for states shown separately. Many states had incomplete reports.
**Not available.

Violent Crimes Reported at Universities and Colleges in 1996

National Total = 2,517 Reported Violent Crimes*

ALPHA ORDER					RANK ORDER			
RANK	STATE		CRIMES	% of USA	RANK	STATE	CRIMES	% of USA
18	Alabama		44	1.75%	1	California	386	15.34%
28	Alaska		20	0.79%	2	North Carolina	221	8.78%
9	Arizona		88	3.50%	3	Texas	172	6.83%
16	Arkansas		53	2.11%	4	Virginia	161	6.40%
1	California		386	15.34%	5	Maryland	143	5.68%
17	Colorado		51	2.03%	6	Michigan	142	5.64%
23	Connecticut		32	1.27%	7	Massachusetts	107	4.25%
26	Delaware		22	0.87%	8	New Jersey	105	4.17%
25	Florida		23	0.91%	9	Arizona	88	3.50%
10	Georgia		84	3.34%	10	Georgia	84	3.34%
NA	Hawaii**		NA	NA	11	Ohio	72	2.86%
NA	Idaho**		NA	NA	12	South Carolina	71	2.82%
NA	Illinois**		NA	NA	13	Louisiana	68	2.70%
14	Indiana		59	2.34%	14	Indiana	59	2.34%
28	Iowa		20	0.79%	15	Pennsylvania	56	2.22%
NA	Kansas**		NA	NA	16	Arkansas	53	2.11%
NA	Kentucky**		NA	NA	17	Colorado	51	2.03%
13	Louisiana		68	2.70%	18	Alabama	44	1.75%
37	Maine		6	0.24%	19	Mississippi	34	1.35%
5	Maryland		143	5.68%	19	Nevada	34	1.35%
7	Massachusetts		107	4.25%	19	Oklahoma	34	1.35%
6	Michigan		142	5.64%	22	Utah	33	1.31%
33	Minnesota		16	0.64%	23	Connecticut	32	1.27%
19	Mississippi		34	1.35%	24	Tennessee	31	1.23%
31	Missouri		19	0.75%	25	Florida	23	0.91%
NA	Montana**		NA	NA	26	Delaware	22	0.87%
37	Nebraska		6	0.24%	26	Wisconsin	22	0.87%
19	Nevada		34	1.35%	28	Alaska	20	0.79%
39	New Hampshire		5	0.20%	28	Iowa	20	0.79%
8	New Jersey		105	4.17%	28	New York	20	0.79%
34	New Mexico		13	0.52%	31	Missouri	19	0.75%
28	New York		20	0.79%	31	Washington	19	0.75%
2	North Carolina		221	8.78%	33	Minnesota	16	0.64%
NA	North Dakota**		NA	NA	34	New Mexico	13	0.52%
11	Ohio		72	2.86%	34	Rhode Island	13	0.52%
19	Oklahoma		34	1.35%	36	West Virginia	12	0.48%
NA	Oregon**		NA	NA	37	Maine	6	0.24%
15	Pennsylvania		56	2.22%	37	Nebraska	6	0.24%
34	Rhode Island		13	0.52%	39	New Hampshire	5	0.20%
12	South Carolina		71	2.82%	40	South Dakota	0	0.00%
40	South Dakota		0	0.00%	40	Wyoming	0	0.00%
24	Tennessee		31	1.23%	NA	Hawaii**	NA	NA
3	Texas		172	6.83%	NA	Idaho**	NA	NA
22	Utah		33	1.31%	NA	Illinois**	NA	NA
NA	Vermont**		NA	NA	NA	Kansas**	NA	NA
4	Virginia		161	6.40%	NA	Kentucky**	NA	NA
31	Washington		19	0.75%	NA	Montana**	NA	NA
36	West Virginia		12	0.48%	NA	North Dakota**	NA	NA
26	Wisconsin		22	0.87%	NA	Oregon**	NA	NA
40	Wyoming		0	0.00%	NA	Vermont**	NA	NA
						District of Columbia**	NA	NA

Source: Morgan Quitno Press using data from Federal Bureau of Investigation
   "Crime in the United States 1996" (Uniform Crime Reports, October 4, 1997)
*Includes murder, rape, robbery and aggravated assault. Total is only for states shown separately. Many states had incomplete reports.
**Not available.

Violent Crimes Reported at Universities and Colleges
As a Percent of All Violent Crimes in 1996
National Percent = 0.17% of Violent Crimes*

RANK	STATE	PERCENT	RANK	STATE	PERCENT
23	Alabama	0.18	1	Virginia	0.71
4	Alaska	0.45	2	North Carolina	0.51
11	Arizona	0.31	3	Utah	0.50
6	Arkansas	0.40	4	Alaska	0.45
29	California	0.14	4	Delaware	0.45
10	Colorado	0.33	6	Arkansas	0.40
19	Connecticut	0.24	7	Maine	0.39
4	Delaware	0.45	8	Rhode Island	0.38
38	Florida	0.02	9	New Hampshire	0.36
23	Georgia	0.18	10	Colorado	0.33
NA	Hawaii**	NA	11	Arizona	0.31
NA	Idaho**	NA	11	West Virginia	0.31
NA	Illinois**	NA	13	Maryland	0.30
21	Indiana	0.19	14	Massachusetts	0.27
15	Iowa	0.26	15	Iowa	0.26
NA	Kansas**	NA	15	Mississippi	0.26
NA	Kentucky**	NA	15	Nevada	0.26
25	Louisiana	0.17	18	New Jersey	0.25
7	Maine	0.39	19	Connecticut	0.24
13	Maryland	0.30	20	Michigan	0.23
14	Massachusetts	0.27	21	Indiana	0.19
20	Michigan	0.23	21	South Carolina	0.19
32	Minnesota	0.10	23	Alabama	0.18
15	Mississippi	0.26	23	Georgia	0.18
37	Missouri	0.06	25	Louisiana	0.17
NA	Montana**	NA	25	Oklahoma	0.17
34	Nebraska	0.08	25	Wisconsin	0.17
15	Nevada	0.26	28	Ohio	0.15
9	New Hampshire	0.36	29	California	0.14
18	New Jersey	0.25	29	Texas	0.14
33	New Mexico	0.09	31	Pennsylvania	0.11
38	New York	0.02	32	Minnesota	0.10
2	North Carolina	0.51	33	New Mexico	0.09
NA	North Dakota**	NA	34	Nebraska	0.08
28	Ohio	0.15	34	Tennessee	0.08
25	Oklahoma	0.17	34	Washington	0.08
NA	Oregon**	NA	37	Missouri	0.06
31	Pennsylvania	0.11	38	Florida	0.02
8	Rhode Island	0.38	38	New York	0.02
21	South Carolina	0.19	40	South Dakota	0.00
40	South Dakota	0.00	40	Wyoming	0.00
34	Tennessee	0.08	NA	Hawaii**	NA
29	Texas	0.14	NA	Idaho**	NA
3	Utah	0.50	NA	Illinois**	NA
NA	Vermont**	NA	NA	Kansas**	NA
1	Virginia	0.71	NA	Kentucky**	NA
34	Washington	0.08	NA	Montana**	NA
11	West Virginia	0.31	NA	North Dakota**	NA
25	Wisconsin	0.17	NA	Oregon**	NA
40	Wyoming	0.00	NA	Vermont**	NA
				District of Columbia**	NA

Source: Morgan Quitno Press using data from Federal Bureau of Investigation
    "Crime in the United States 1996" (Uniform Crime Reports, October 4, 1997)

*Includes murder, rape, robbery and aggravated assault. National percent is only for states shown separately.
Many states had incomplete reports.
**Not available.

Property Crimes Reported at Universities and Colleges in 1996

National Total = 102,096 Reported Property Crimes*

ALPHA ORDER

RANK	STATE	CRIMES	% of USA
21	Alabama	1,575	1.54%
40	Alaska	95	0.09%
9	Arizona	3,615	3.54%
28	Arkansas	1,158	1.13%
1	California	15,337	15.02%
15	Colorado	2,278	2.23%
20	Connecticut	1,753	1.72%
35	Delaware	583	0.57%
29	Florida	826	0.81%
5	Georgia	5,081	4.98%
NA	Hawaii**	NA	NA
NA	Idaho**	NA	NA
NA	Illinois**	NA	NA
10	Indiana	3,433	3.36%
25	Iowa	1,221	1.20%
NA	Kansas**	NA	NA
NA	Kentucky**	NA	NA
13	Louisiana	2,686	2.63%
37	Maine	353	0.35%
11	Maryland	3,250	3.18%
8	Massachusetts	3,747	3.67%
3	Michigan	6,508	6.37%
24	Minnesota	1,266	1.24%
30	Mississippi	822	0.81%
27	Missouri	1,167	1.14%
NA	Montana**	NA	NA
31	Nebraska	728	0.71%
36	Nevada	562	0.55%
39	New Hampshire	232	0.23%
12	New Jersey	3,160	3.10%
33	New Mexico	674	0.66%
23	New York	1,353	1.33%
4	North Carolina	5,365	5.25%
NA	North Dakota**	NA	NA
6	Ohio	4,908	4.81%
22	Oklahoma	1,447	1.42%
NA	Oregon**	NA	NA
14	Pennsylvania	2,287	2.24%
34	Rhode Island	628	0.62%
16	South Carolina	2,128	2.08%
41	South Dakota	41	0.04%
26	Tennessee	1,171	1.15%
2	Texas	9,350	9.16%
19	Utah	1,873	1.83%
NA	Vermont**	NA	NA
7	Virginia	4,479	4.39%
18	Washington	1,914	1.87%
32	West Virginia	697	0.68%
17	Wisconsin	2,110	2.07%
38	Wyoming	235	0.23%

RANK ORDER

RANK	STATE	CRIMES	% of USA
1	California	15,337	15.02%
2	Texas	9,350	9.16%
3	Michigan	6,508	6.37%
4	North Carolina	5,365	5.25%
5	Georgia	5,081	4.98%
6	Ohio	4,908	4.81%
7	Virginia	4,479	4.39%
8	Massachusetts	3,747	3.67%
9	Arizona	3,615	3.54%
10	Indiana	3,433	3.36%
11	Maryland	3,250	3.18%
12	New Jersey	3,160	3.10%
13	Louisiana	2,686	2.63%
14	Pennsylvania	2,287	2.24%
15	Colorado	2,278	2.23%
16	South Carolina	2,128	2.08%
17	Wisconsin	2,110	2.07%
18	Washington	1,914	1.87%
19	Utah	1,873	1.83%
20	Connecticut	1,753	1.72%
21	Alabama	1,575	1.54%
22	Oklahoma	1,447	1.42%
23	New York	1,353	1.33%
24	Minnesota	1,266	1.24%
25	Iowa	1,221	1.20%
26	Tennessee	1,171	1.15%
27	Missouri	1,167	1.14%
28	Arkansas	1,158	1.13%
29	Florida	826	0.81%
30	Mississippi	822	0.81%
31	Nebraska	728	0.71%
32	West Virginia	697	0.68%
33	New Mexico	674	0.66%
34	Rhode Island	628	0.62%
35	Delaware	583	0.57%
36	Nevada	562	0.55%
37	Maine	353	0.35%
38	Wyoming	235	0.23%
39	New Hampshire	232	0.23%
40	Alaska	95	0.09%
41	South Dakota	41	0.04%
NA	Hawaii**	NA	NA
NA	Idaho**	NA	NA
NA	Illinois**	NA	NA
NA	Kansas**	NA	NA
NA	Kentucky**	NA	NA
NA	Montana**	NA	NA
NA	North Dakota**	NA	NA
NA	Oregon**	NA	NA
NA	Vermont**	NA	NA
	District of Columbia**	NA	NA

Source: Morgan Quitno Press using data from Federal Bureau of Investigation
   "Crime in the United States 1996" (Uniform Crime Reports, October 4, 1997)
*Includes burglary, larceny-theft and motor vehicle theft. Total is only for states shown separately. Many states had incomplete reports.
**Not available.

Property Crimes at Universities and Colleges
As a Percent of All Property Crimes in 1996
National Percent = 0.96% of Property Crimes*

ALPHA ORDER

RANK	STATE	PERCENT
26	Alabama	0.87
38	Alaska	0.33
11	Arizona	1.27
18	Arkansas	1.11
18	California	1.11
13	Colorado	1.26
10	Connecticut	1.40
2	Delaware	1.90
41	Florida	0.09
15	Georgia	1.22
NA	Hawaii**	NA
NA	Idaho**	NA
NA	Illinois**	NA
8	Indiana	1.48
11	Iowa	1.27
NA	Kansas**	NA
NA	Kentucky**	NA
23	Louisiana	1.04
26	Maine	0.87
14	Maryland	1.25
1	Massachusetts	1.93
7	Michigan	1.51
33	Minnesota	0.66
29	Mississippi	0.75
36	Missouri	0.48
NA	Montana**	NA
20	Nebraska	1.10
31	Nevada	0.68
30	New Hampshire	0.74
23	New Jersey	1.04
31	New Mexico	0.68
39	New York	0.22
8	North Carolina	1.48
NA	North Dakota**	NA
22	Ohio	1.09
26	Oklahoma	0.87
NA	Oregon**	NA
34	Pennsylvania	0.64
4	Rhode Island	1.74
20	South Carolina	1.10
40	South Dakota	0.20
37	Tennessee	0.47
25	Texas	0.97
6	Utah	1.66
NA	Vermont**	NA
3	Virginia	1.85
35	Washington	0.63
5	West Virginia	1.68
17	Wisconsin	1.15
15	Wyoming	1.22

RANK ORDER

RANK	STATE	PERCENT
1	Massachusetts	1.93
2	Delaware	1.90
3	Virginia	1.85
4	Rhode Island	1.74
5	West Virginia	1.68
6	Utah	1.66
7	Michigan	1.51
8	Indiana	1.48
8	North Carolina	1.48
10	Connecticut	1.40
11	Arizona	1.27
11	Iowa	1.27
13	Colorado	1.26
14	Maryland	1.25
15	Georgia	1.22
15	Wyoming	1.22
17	Wisconsin	1.15
18	Arkansas	1.11
18	California	1.11
20	Nebraska	1.10
20	South Carolina	1.10
22	Ohio	1.09
23	Louisiana	1.04
23	New Jersey	1.04
25	Texas	0.97
26	Alabama	0.87
26	Maine	0.87
26	Oklahoma	0.87
29	Mississippi	0.75
30	New Hampshire	0.74
31	Nevada	0.68
31	New Mexico	0.68
33	Minnesota	0.66
34	Pennsylvania	0.64
35	Washington	0.63
36	Missouri	0.48
37	Tennessee	0.47
38	Alaska	0.33
39	New York	0.22
40	South Dakota	0.20
41	Florida	0.09
NA	Hawaii**	NA
NA	Idaho**	NA
NA	Illinois**	NA
NA	Kansas**	NA
NA	Kentucky**	NA
NA	Montana**	NA
NA	North Dakota**	NA
NA	Oregon**	NA
NA	Vermont**	NA
	District of Columbia**	NA

Source: Morgan Quitno Press using data from Federal Bureau of Investigation
"Crime in the United States 1996" (Uniform Crime Reports, October 4, 1997)
*Includes burglary, larceny-theft and motor vehicle theft. National percent is only for states shown separately.
Many states had incomplete reports.
**Not available.

Crimes in 1992

National Total = 14,438,191 Crimes*

	ALPHA ORDER				RANK ORDER		
RANK	STATE	CRIMES	% of USA	RANK	STATE	CRIMES	% of USA
21	Alabama	217,889	1.51%	1	California	2,061,761	14.28%
46	Alaska	32,693	0.23%	2	Texas	1,246,148	8.63%
17	Arizona	269,335	1.87%	3	Florida	1,127,360	7.81%
31	Arkansas	114,233	0.79%	4	New York	1,061,489	7.35%
1	California	2,061,761	14.28%	5	Illinois	670,564	4.64%
24	Colorado	206,770	1.43%	6	Michigan	529,472	3.67%
28	Connecticut	165,787	1.15%	7	Ohio	513,952	3.56%
45	Delaware	33,406	0.23%	8	Georgia	432,430	3.00%
3	Florida	1,127,360	7.81%	9	Pennsylvania	407,431	2.82%
8	Georgia	432,430	3.00%	10	North Carolina	397,047	2.75%
37	Hawaii	70,899	0.49%	11	New Jersey	394,463	2.73%
42	Idaho	42,639	0.30%	12	Washington	317,035	2.20%
5	Illinois	670,564	4.64%	13	Maryland	305,503	2.12%
18	Indiana	265,375	1.84%	14	Massachusetts	300,071	2.08%
33	Iowa	111,275	0.77%	15	Louisiana	280,647	1.94%
29	Kansas	134,222	0.93%	16	Virginia	274,118	1.90%
30	Kentucky	124,799	0.86%	17	Arizona	269,335	1.87%
15	Louisiana	280,647	1.94%	18	Indiana	265,375	1.84%
41	Maine	43,516	0.30%	19	Missouri	264,694	1.83%
13	Maryland	305,503	2.12%	20	Tennessee	258,021	1.79%
14	Massachusetts	300,071	2.08%	21	Alabama	217,889	1.51%
6	Michigan	529,472	3.67%	22	Wisconsin	216,254	1.50%
25	Minnesota	205,664	1.42%	23	South Carolina	212,327	1.47%
32	Mississippi	111,944	0.78%	24	Colorado	206,770	1.43%
19	Missouri	264,694	1.83%	25	Minnesota	205,664	1.42%
43	Montana	37,872	0.26%	26	Oklahoma	174,464	1.21%
38	Nebraska	69,444	0.48%	27	Oregon	173,289	1.20%
36	Nevada	82,324	0.57%	28	Connecticut	165,787	1.15%
44	New Hampshire	34,225	0.24%	29	Kansas	134,222	0.93%
11	New Jersey	394,463	2.73%	30	Kentucky	124,799	0.86%
35	New Mexico	101,723	0.70%	31	Arkansas	114,233	0.79%
4	New York	1,061,489	7.35%	32	Mississippi	111,944	0.78%
10	North Carolina	397,047	2.75%	33	Iowa	111,275	0.77%
50	North Dakota	18,465	0.13%	34	Utah	102,589	0.71%
7	Ohio	513,952	3.56%	35	New Mexico	101,723	0.70%
26	Oklahoma	174,464	1.21%	36	Nevada	82,324	0.57%
27	Oregon	173,289	1.20%	37	Hawaii	70,899	0.49%
9	Pennsylvania	407,431	2.82%	38	Nebraska	69,444	0.48%
40	Rhode Island	46,009	0.32%	39	West Virginia	47,288	0.33%
23	South Carolina	212,327	1.47%	40	Rhode Island	46,009	0.32%
47	South Dakota	21,322	0.15%	41	Maine	43,516	0.30%
20	Tennessee	258,021	1.79%	42	Idaho	42,639	0.30%
2	Texas	1,246,148	8.63%	43	Montana	37,872	0.26%
34	Utah	102,589	0.71%	44	New Hampshire	34,225	0.24%
49	Vermont	19,437	0.13%	45	Delaware	33,406	0.23%
16	Virginia	274,118	1.90%	46	Alaska	32,693	0.23%
12	Washington	317,035	2.20%	47	South Dakota	21,322	0.15%
39	West Virginia	47,288	0.33%	48	Wyoming	21,320	0.15%
22	Wisconsin	216,254	1.50%	49	Vermont	19,437	0.13%
48	Wyoming	21,320	0.15%	50	North Dakota	18,465	0.13%
					District of Columbia	67,187	0.47%

Source: Federal Bureau of Investigation
   "Crime in the United States 1992" (Uniform Crime Reports, October 3, 1993)
*Includes murder, rape, robbery, aggravated assault, burglary, larceny-theft and motor vehicle theft.

Percent Change in Number of Crimes: 1992 to 1996

National Percent Change = 6.7% Decrease*

ALPHA ORDER				RANK ORDER		
RANK	STATE	PERCENT CHANGE		RANK	STATE	PERCENT CHANGE
36	Alabama	(5.5)		1	Nevada	16.7
22	Alaska	1.2		1	Utah	16.7
3	Arizona	16.2		3	Arizona	16.2
17	Arkansas	3.3		4	Tennessee	12.4
48	California	(19.5)		5	Idaho	11.9
35	Colorado	(5.4)		6	New Mexico	11.2
47	Connecticut	(16.5)		7	Oregon	10.9
13	Delaware	6.2		8	Hawaii	10.0
34	Florida	(4.2)		9	Mississippi	9.7
11	Georgia	7.3		10	South Carolina	8.3
8	Hawaii	10.0		11	Georgia	7.3
5	Idaho	11.9		12	Oklahoma	7.0
37	Illinois	(6.1)		13	Delaware	6.2
26	Indiana	(1.0)		14	Louisiana	6.0
38	Iowa	(6.5)		15	Nebraska	5.5
43	Kansas	(10.3)		16	Montana	4.3
27	Kentucky	(1.5)		17	Arkansas	3.3
14	Louisiana	6.0		18	Washington	3.1
28	Maine	(3.0)		19	Missouri	2.9
24	Maryland	0.6		20	South Dakota	2.0
49	Massachusetts	(22.1)		21	North Carolina	1.9
40	Michigan	(7.3)		22	Alaska	1.2
23	Minnesota	1.1		23	Minnesota	1.1
9	Mississippi	9.7		24	Maryland	0.6
19	Missouri	2.9		25	Pennsylvania	0.4
16	Montana	4.3		26	Indiana	(1.0)
15	Nebraska	5.5		27	Kentucky	(1.5)
1	Nevada	16.7		28	Maine	(3.0)
32	New Hampshire	(4.1)		29	Ohio	(3.1)
44	New Jersey	(12.3)		30	Virginia	(3.4)
6	New Mexico	11.2		31	Wyoming	(4.0)
50	New York	(29.2)		32	New Hampshire	(4.1)
21	North Carolina	1.9		32	West Virginia	(4.1)
39	North Dakota	(6.9)		34	Florida	(4.2)
29	Ohio	(3.1)		35	Colorado	(5.4)
12	Oklahoma	7.0		36	Alabama	(5.5)
7	Oregon	10.9		37	Illinois	(6.1)
25	Pennsylvania	0.4		38	Iowa	(6.5)
46	Rhode Island	(14.1)		39	North Dakota	(6.9)
10	South Carolina	8.3		40	Michigan	(7.3)
20	South Dakota	2.0		41	Wisconsin	(8.8)
4	Tennessee	12.4		42	Vermont	(9.0)
45	Texas	(12.4)		43	Kansas	(10.3)
1	Utah	16.7		44	New Jersey	(12.3)
42	Vermont	(9.0)		45	Texas	(12.4)
30	Virginia	(3.4)		46	Rhode Island	(14.1)
18	Washington	3.1		47	Connecticut	(16.5)
32	West Virginia	(4.1)		48	California	(19.5)
41	Wisconsin	(8.8)		49	Massachusetts	(22.1)
31	Wyoming	(4.0)		50	New York	(29.2)
					District of Columbia	(3.9)

Source: Morgan Quitno Press using data from Federal Bureau of Investigation
    "Crime in the United States" (Uniform Crime Reports, 1992 and 1996 editions)
*Includes murder, rape, robbery, aggravated assault, burglary, larceny-theft and motor vehicle theft.

Crime Rate in 1992

National Rate = 5,660.2 Crimes per 100,000 Population*

ALPHA ORDER			RANK ORDER		
RANK	STATE	RATE	RANK	STATE	RATE
23	Alabama	5,268.1	1	Florida	8,358.2
20	Alaska	5,569.5	2	Texas	7,057.9
3	Arizona	7,028.6	3	Arizona	7,028.6
30	Arkansas	4,761.7	4	California	6,679.5
4	California	6,679.5	5	Louisiana	6,546.5
12	Colorado	5,958.8	6	New Mexico	6,434.1
27	Connecticut	5,052.9	7	Georgia	6,405.4
29	Delaware	4,848.5	8	Maryland	6,224.6
1	Florida	8,358.2	9	Nevada	6,203.8
7	Georgia	6,405.4	10	Washington	6,172.8
11	Hawaii	6,112.0	11	Hawaii	6,112.0
41	Idaho	3,996.2	12	Colorado	5,958.8
17	Illinois	5,765.3	13	South Carolina	5,893.1
31	Indiana	4,686.9	14	New York	5,858.4
42	Iowa	3,957.1	15	Oregon	5,820.9
22	Kansas	5,319.9	16	North Carolina	5,802.2
46	Kentucky	3,323.5	17	Illinois	5,765.3
5	Louisiana	6,546.5	18	Utah	5,658.5
43	Maine	3,523.6	19	Michigan	5,610.6
8	Maryland	6,224.6	20	Alaska	5,569.5
28	Massachusetts	5,002.9	21	Oklahoma	5,431.6
19	Michigan	5,610.6	22	Kansas	5,319.9
34	Minnesota	4,590.7	23	Alabama	5,268.1
40	Mississippi	4,282.5	24	Tennessee	5,135.8
25	Missouri	5,097.1	25	Missouri	5,097.1
33	Montana	4,596.1	26	New Jersey	5,064.4
37	Nebraska	4,324.0	27	Connecticut	5,052.9
9	Nevada	6,203.8	28	Massachusetts	5,002.9
47	New Hampshire	3,080.6	29	Delaware	4,848.5
26	New Jersey	5,064.4	30	Arkansas	4,761.7
6	New Mexico	6,434.1	31	Indiana	4,686.9
14	New York	5,858.4	32	Ohio	4,665.5
16	North Carolina	5,802.2	33	Montana	4,596.1
49	North Dakota	2,903.3	34	Minnesota	4,590.7
32	Ohio	4,665.5	35	Rhode Island	4,578.0
21	Oklahoma	5,431.6	36	Wyoming	4,575.1
15	Oregon	5,820.9	37	Nebraska	4,324.0
45	Pennsylvania	3,392.7	38	Wisconsin	4,319.0
35	Rhode Island	4,578.0	39	Virginia	4,298.5
13	South Carolina	5,893.1	40	Mississippi	4,282.5
48	South Dakota	2,998.9	41	Idaho	3,996.2
24	Tennessee	5,135.8	42	Iowa	3,957.1
2	Texas	7,057.9	43	Maine	3,523.6
18	Utah	5,658.5	44	Vermont	3,410.0
44	Vermont	3,410.0	45	Pennsylvania	3,392.7
39	Virginia	4,298.5	46	Kentucky	3,323.5
10	Washington	6,172.8	47	New Hampshire	3,080.6
50	West Virginia	2,609.7	48	South Dakota	2,998.9
38	Wisconsin	4,319.0	49	North Dakota	2,903.3
36	Wyoming	4,575.1	50	West Virginia	2,609.7
				District of Columbia	11,407.0

Source: Federal Bureau of Investigation
   "Crime in the United States 1992" (Uniform Crime Reports, October 3, 1993)
*Includes murder, rape, robbery, aggravated assault, burglary, larceny-theft and motor vehicle theft.

Percent Change in Crime Rate: 1992 to 1996

National Percent Change = 10.3% Decrease*

ALPHA ORDER				RANK ORDER		
RANK	STATE	PERCENT CHANGE		RANK	STATE	PERCENT CHANGE
37	Alabama	(8.5)		1	Hawaii	7.7
19	Alaska	(2.1)		2	Tennessee	6.1
12	Arizona	0.5		3	Utah	5.8
17	Arkansas	(1.3)		4	Mississippi	5.6
48	California	(22.0)		5	South Carolina	5.4
44	Colorado	(14.1)		6	Louisiana	4.5
46	Connecticut	(16.3)		7	Oklahoma	4.1
11	Delaware	1.0		8	Oregon	3.0
39	Florida	(10.3)		9	Nebraska	2.6
18	Georgia	(1.5)		9	New Mexico	2.6
1	Hawaii	7.7		11	Delaware	1.0
13	Idaho	0.4		12	Arizona	0.5
33	Illinois	(7.8)		13	Idaho	0.4
25	Indiana	(4.0)		14	Pennsylvania	0.0
33	Iowa	(7.8)		15	Missouri	(0.3)
42	Kansas	(12.0)		16	South Dakota	(1.0)
28	Kentucky	(4.7)		17	Arkansas	(1.3)
6	Louisiana	4.5		18	Georgia	(1.5)
24	Maine	(3.7)		19	Alaska	(2.1)
21	Maryland	(2.6)		20	Montana	(2.2)
49	Massachusetts	(23.3)		21	Maryland	(2.6)
38	Michigan	(8.8)		22	Minnesota	(2.8)
22	Minnesota	(2.8)		23	Nevada	(3.4)
4	Mississippi	5.6		24	Maine	(3.7)
15	Missouri	(0.3)		25	Indiana	(4.0)
20	Montana	(2.2)		26	Washington	(4.3)
9	Nebraska	2.6		27	Ohio	(4.5)
23	Nevada	(3.4)		28	Kentucky	(4.7)
36	New Hampshire	(8.3)		29	North Carolina	(4.8)
45	New Jersey	(14.4)		29	West Virginia	(4.8)
9	New Mexico	2.6		31	Wyoming	(7.0)
50	New York	(29.5)		32	Virginia	(7.7)
29	North Carolina	(4.8)		33	Illinois	(7.8)
35	North Dakota	(8.1)		33	Iowa	(7.8)
27	Ohio	(4.5)		35	North Dakota	(8.1)
7	Oklahoma	4.1		36	New Hampshire	(8.3)
8	Oregon	3.0		37	Alabama	(8.5)
14	Pennsylvania	0.0		38	Michigan	(8.8)
43	Rhode Island	(12.8)		39	Florida	(10.3)
5	South Carolina	5.4		40	Wisconsin	(11.5)
16	South Dakota	(1.0)		41	Vermont	(11.9)
2	Tennessee	6.1		42	Kansas	(12.0)
47	Texas	(19.1)		43	Rhode Island	(12.8)
3	Utah	5.8		44	Colorado	(14.1)
41	Vermont	(11.9)		45	New Jersey	(14.4)
32	Virginia	(7.7)		46	Connecticut	(16.3)
26	Washington	(4.3)		47	Texas	(19.1)
29	West Virginia	(4.8)		48	California	(22.0)
40	Wisconsin	(11.5)		49	Massachusetts	(23.3)
31	Wyoming	(7.0)		50	New York	(29.5)
					District of Columbia	4.3

*Source: Morgan Quitno Press using data from Federal Bureau of Investigation
"Crime in the United States" (Uniform Crime Reports, 1992 and 1996 editions)
Includes murder, rape, robbery, aggravated assault, burglary, larceny-theft and motor vehicle theft.

Violent Crimes in 1992

National Total = 1,932,274 Violent Crimes*

ALPHA ORDER

RANK	STATE	CRIMES	% of USA
17	Alabama	36,052	1.87%
40	Alaska	3,877	0.20%
21	Arizona	25,706	1.33%
30	Arkansas	13,831	0.72%
1	California	345,624	17.89%
24	Colorado	20,086	1.04%
26	Connecticut	16,252	0.84%
38	Delaware	4,280	0.22%
3	Florida	162,827	8.43%
9	Georgia	49,496	2.56%
43	Hawaii	2,998	0.16%
42	Idaho	3,003	0.16%
5	Illinois	113,664	5.88%
19	Indiana	28,791	1.49%
35	Iowa	7,816	0.40%
32	Kansas	12,888	0.67%
23	Kentucky	20,107	1.04%
14	Louisiana	42,209	2.18%
44	Maine	1,616	0.08%
10	Maryland	49,085	2.54%
12	Massachusetts	46,727	2.42%
6	Michigan	72,672	3.76%
28	Minnesota	15,144	0.78%
33	Mississippi	10,763	0.56%
15	Missouri	38,448	1.99%
46	Montana	1,400	0.07%
36	Nebraska	5,598	0.29%
34	Nevada	9,247	0.48%
47	New Hampshire	1,397	0.07%
11	New Jersey	48,745	2.52%
29	New Mexico	14,781	0.76%
2	New York	203,311	10.52%
13	North Carolina	46,600	2.41%
50	North Dakota	530	0.03%
7	Ohio	57,935	3.00%
25	Oklahoma	20,005	1.04%
27	Oregon	15,189	0.79%
8	Pennsylvania	51,276	2.65%
39	Rhode Island	3,965	0.21%
18	South Carolina	34,029	1.76%
48	South Dakota	1,383	0.07%
16	Tennessee	37,487	1.94%
4	Texas	142,369	7.37%
37	Utah	5,267	0.27%
49	Vermont	624	0.03%
22	Virginia	23,907	1.24%
20	Washington	27,454	1.42%
41	West Virginia	3,833	0.20%
31	Wisconsin	13,806	0.71%
45	Wyoming	1,489	0.08%

RANK ORDER

RANK	STATE	CRIMES	% of USA
1	California	345,624	17.89%
2	New York	203,311	10.52%
3	Florida	162,827	8.43%
4	Texas	142,369	7.37%
5	Illinois	113,664	5.88%
6	Michigan	72,672	3.76%
7	Ohio	57,935	3.00%
8	Pennsylvania	51,276	2.65%
9	Georgia	49,496	2.56%
10	Maryland	49,085	2.54%
11	New Jersey	48,745	2.52%
12	Massachusetts	46,727	2.42%
13	North Carolina	46,600	2.41%
14	Louisiana	42,209	2.18%
15	Missouri	38,448	1.99%
16	Tennessee	37,487	1.94%
17	Alabama	36,052	1.87%
18	South Carolina	34,029	1.76%
19	Indiana	28,791	1.49%
20	Washington	27,454	1.42%
21	Arizona	25,706	1.33%
22	Virginia	23,907	1.24%
23	Kentucky	20,107	1.04%
24	Colorado	20,086	1.04%
25	Oklahoma	20,005	1.04%
26	Connecticut	16,252	0.84%
27	Oregon	15,189	0.79%
28	Minnesota	15,144	0.78%
29	New Mexico	14,781	0.76%
30	Arkansas	13,831	0.72%
31	Wisconsin	13,806	0.71%
32	Kansas	12,888	0.67%
33	Mississippi	10,763	0.56%
34	Nevada	9,247	0.48%
35	Iowa	7,816	0.40%
36	Nebraska	5,598	0.29%
37	Utah	5,267	0.27%
38	Delaware	4,280	0.22%
39	Rhode Island	3,965	0.21%
40	Alaska	3,877	0.20%
41	West Virginia	3,833	0.20%
42	Idaho	3,003	0.16%
43	Hawaii	2,998	0.16%
44	Maine	1,616	0.08%
45	Wyoming	1,489	0.08%
46	Montana	1,400	0.07%
47	New Hampshire	1,397	0.07%
48	South Dakota	1,383	0.07%
49	Vermont	624	0.03%
50	North Dakota	530	0.03%
	District of Columbia	16,685	0.86%

Source: Federal Bureau of Investigation
    "Crime in the United States 1992" (Uniform Crime Reports, October 3, 1993)
*Violent crimes are offenses of murder, forcible rape, robbery and aggravated assault.

Percent Change in Number of Violent Crimes: 1992 to 1996

National Percent Change = 12.9% Decrease*

RANK	STATE	PERCENT CHANGE		RANK	STATE	PERCENT CHANGE
48	Alabama	(33.0)		1	Nevada	40.6
6	Alaska	13.9		2	Nebraska	28.3
11	Arizona	8.8		3	Utah	26.0
28	Arkansas	(4.8)		4	Mississippi	23.2
46	California	(20.4)		5	Vermont	14.4
47	Colorado	(23.0)		6	Alaska	13.9
41	Connecticut	(17.0)		7	Delaware	13.2
7	Delaware	13.2		8	Hawaii	10.8
32	Florida	(7.0)		9	Tennessee	9.8
29	Georgia	(5.1)		10	Indiana	8.9
8	Hawaii	10.8		11	Arizona	8.8
13	Idaho	5.8		12	South Carolina	8.4
33	Illinois	(7.6)		13	Idaho	5.8
10	Indiana	8.9		14	Minnesota	4.2
19	Iowa	(0.6)		15	North Dakota	2.1
43	Kansas	(17.4)		16	Pennsylvania	1.7
50	Kentucky	(38.1)		17	Montana	1.1
26	Louisiana	(4.2)		18	West Virginia	0.1
25	Maine	(3.9)		19	Iowa	(0.6)
24	Maryland	(3.8)		20	Oklahoma	(1.5)
40	Massachusetts	(16.3)		21	New Hampshire	(1.7)
39	Michigan	(16.1)		22	Oregon	(2.3)
14	Minnesota	4.2		23	New Mexico	(2.6)
4	Mississippi	23.2		24	Maryland	(3.8)
44	Missouri	(17.6)		25	Maine	(3.9)
17	Montana	1.1		26	Louisiana	(4.2)
2	Nebraska	28.3		27	Virginia	(4.7)
1	Nevada	40.6		28	Arkansas	(4.8)
21	New Hampshire	(1.7)		29	Georgia	(5.1)
35	New Jersey	(12.9)		30	Wisconsin	(5.6)
23	New Mexico	(2.6)		31	South Dakota	(6.2)
49	New York	(35.0)		32	Florida	(7.0)
33	North Carolina	(7.6)		33	Illinois	(7.6)
15	North Dakota	2.1		33	North Carolina	(7.6)
42	Ohio	(17.3)		35	New Jersey	(12.9)
20	Oklahoma	(1.5)		36	Washington	(13.1)
22	Oregon	(2.3)		37	Rhode Island	(13.3)
16	Pennsylvania	1.7		38	Texas	(13.4)
37	Rhode Island	(13.3)		39	Michigan	(16.1)
12	South Carolina	8.4		40	Massachusetts	(16.3)
31	South Dakota	(6.2)		41	Connecticut	(17.0)
9	Tennessee	9.8		42	Ohio	(17.3)
38	Texas	(13.4)		43	Kansas	(17.4)
3	Utah	26.0		44	Missouri	(17.6)
5	Vermont	14.4		45	Wyoming	(19.3)
27	Virginia	(4.7)		46	California	(20.4)
36	Washington	(13.1)		47	Colorado	(23.0)
18	West Virginia	0.1		48	Alabama	(33.0)
30	Wisconsin	(5.6)		49	New York	(35.0)
45	Wyoming	(19.3)		50	Kentucky	(38.1)
					District of Columbia	(19.6)

Source: Morgan Quitno Press using data from Federal Bureau of Investigation
    "Crime in the United States" (Uniform Crime Reports, 1992 and 1996 editions)
*Violent crimes are offenses of murder, forcible rape, robbery and aggravated assault.

Violent Crime Rate in 1992

National Rate = 757.5 Violent Crimes per 100,000 Population*

ALPHA ORDER			RANK ORDER		
RANK	**STATE**	**RATE**	**RANK**	**STATE**	**RATE**
9	Alabama	871.7	1	Florida	1,207.2
19	Alaska	660.5	2	New York	1,122.1
18	Arizona	670.8	3	California	1,119.7
24	Arkansas	576.5	4	Maryland	1,000.1
3	California	1,119.7	5	Louisiana	984.6
23	Colorado	578.8	6	Illinois	977.3
31	Connecticut	495.3	7	South Carolina	944.5
22	Delaware	621.2	8	New Mexico	934.9
1	Florida	1,207.2	9	Alabama	871.7
15	Georgia	733.2	10	Texas	806.3
43	Hawaii	258.4	11	Massachusetts	779.0
40	Idaho	281.4	12	Michigan	770.1
6	Illinois	977.3	13	Tennessee	746.2
30	Indiana	508.5	14	Missouri	740.4
41	Iowa	278.0	15	Georgia	733.2
28	Kansas	510.8	16	Nevada	696.8
25	Kentucky	535.5	17	North Carolina	681.0
5	Louisiana	984.6	18	Arizona	670.8
47	Maine	130.9	19	Alaska	660.5
4	Maryland	1,000.1	20	New Jersey	625.8
11	Massachusetts	779.0	21	Oklahoma	622.8
12	Michigan	770.1	22	Delaware	621.2
37	Minnesota	338.0	23	Colorado	578.8
33	Mississippi	411.7	24	Arkansas	576.5
14	Missouri	740.4	25	Kentucky	535.5
46	Montana	169.9	26	Washington	534.5
36	Nebraska	348.6	27	Ohio	525.9
16	Nevada	696.8	28	Kansas	510.8
48	New Hampshire	125.7	29	Oregon	510.2
20	New Jersey	625.8	30	Indiana	508.5
8	New Mexico	934.9	31	Connecticut	495.3
2	New York	1,122.1	32	Pennsylvania	427.0
17	North Carolina	681.0	33	Mississippi	411.7
50	North Dakota	83.3	34	Rhode Island	394.5
27	Ohio	525.9	35	Virginia	374.9
21	Oklahoma	622.8	36	Nebraska	348.6
29	Oregon	510.2	37	Minnesota	338.0
32	Pennsylvania	427.0	38	Wyoming	319.5
34	Rhode Island	394.5	39	Utah	290.5
7	South Carolina	944.5	40	Idaho	281.4
45	South Dakota	194.5	41	Iowa	278.0
13	Tennessee	746.2	42	Wisconsin	275.7
10	Texas	806.3	43	Hawaii	258.4
39	Utah	290.5	44	West Virginia	211.5
49	Vermont	109.5	45	South Dakota	194.5
35	Virginia	374.9	46	Montana	169.9
26	Washington	534.5	47	Maine	130.9
44	West Virginia	211.5	48	New Hampshire	125.7
42	Wisconsin	275.7	49	Vermont	109.5
38	Wyoming	319.5	50	North Dakota	83.3
				District of Columbia	2,832.8

Source: Federal Bureau of Investigation
   "Crime in the United States 1992" (Uniform Crime Reports, October 3, 1993)
*Violent crimes are offenses of murder, forcible rape, robbery and aggravated assault.

Percent Change in Violent Crime Rate: 1992 to 1996

National Percent Change = 16.3% Decrease*

ALPHA ORDER				RANK ORDER		
RANK	STATE	PERCENT CHANGE		RANK	STATE	PERCENT CHANGE
48	Alabama	(35.1)		1	Nebraska	24.7
6	Alaska	10.2		2	Mississippi	18.6
22	Arizona	(5.9)		3	Nevada	16.4
28	Arkansas	(9.1)		4	Utah	14.3
46	California	(23.0)		5	Vermont	10.7
47	Colorado	(30.1)		6	Alaska	10.2
37	Connecticut	(16.8)		7	Hawaii	8.6
8	Delaware	7.6		8	Delaware	7.6
33	Florida	(12.9)		9	Indiana	5.6
33	Georgia	(12.9)		10	South Carolina	5.5
7	Hawaii	8.6		11	Tennessee	3.7
19	Idaho	(5.0)		12	Pennsylvania	1.3
30	Illinois	(9.3)		13	North Dakota	0.8
9	Indiana	5.6		14	Minnesota	0.2
16	Iowa	(2.0)		15	West Virginia	(0.7)
41	Kansas	(19.0)		16	Iowa	(2.0)
50	Kentucky	(40.1)		17	Oklahoma	(4.1)
21	Louisiana	(5.6)		18	Maine	(4.6)
18	Maine	(4.6)		19	Idaho	(5.0)
24	Maryland	(6.9)		20	Montana	(5.2)
39	Massachusetts	(17.6)		21	Louisiana	(5.6)
38	Michigan	(17.5)		22	Arizona	(5.9)
14	Minnesota	0.2		23	New Hampshire	(6.0)
2	Mississippi	18.6		24	Maryland	(6.9)
44	Missouri	(20.2)		25	Wisconsin	(8.3)
20	Montana	(5.2)		26	South Dakota	(8.9)
1	Nebraska	24.7		27	Virginia	(9.0)
3	Nevada	16.4		28	Arkansas	(9.1)
23	New Hampshire	(6.0)		29	Oregon	(9.2)
36	New Jersey	(15.1)		30	Illinois	(9.3)
31	New Mexico	(10.1)		31	New Mexico	(10.1)
49	New York	(35.2)		32	Rhode Island	(12.0)
35	North Carolina	(13.6)		33	Florida	(12.9)
13	North Dakota	0.8		33	Georgia	(12.9)
40	Ohio	(18.5)		35	North Carolina	(13.6)
17	Oklahoma	(4.1)		36	New Jersey	(15.1)
29	Oregon	(9.2)		37	Connecticut	(16.8)
12	Pennsylvania	1.3		38	Michigan	(17.5)
32	Rhode Island	(12.0)		39	Massachusetts	(17.6)
10	South Carolina	5.5		40	Ohio	(18.5)
26	South Dakota	(8.9)		41	Kansas	(19.0)
11	Tennessee	3.7		42	Washington	(19.3)
43	Texas	(20.1)		43	Texas	(20.1)
4	Utah	14.3		44	Missouri	(20.2)
5	Vermont	10.7		45	Wyoming	(21.8)
27	Virginia	(9.0)		46	California	(23.0)
42	Washington	(19.3)		47	Colorado	(30.1)
15	West Virginia	(0.7)		48	Alabama	(35.1)
25	Wisconsin	(8.3)		49	New York	(35.2)
45	Wyoming	(21.8)		50	Kentucky	(40.1)
					District of Columbia	(12.8)

Source: Morgan Quitno Press using data from Federal Bureau of Investigation
    "Crime in the United States" (Uniform Crime Reports, 1992 and 1996 editions)
*Violent crimes are offenses of murder, forcible rape, robbery and aggravated assault.

Murders in 1992

National Total = 23,760 Murders*

<table>
<tr><th colspan="4">ALPHA ORDER</th><th colspan="4">RANK ORDER</th></tr>
<tr><th>RANK</th><th>STATE</th><th>MURDERS</th><th>% of USA</th><th>RANK</th><th>STATE</th><th>MURDERS</th><th>% of USA</th></tr>
<tr><td>17</td><td>Alabama</td><td>455</td><td>1.91%</td><td>1</td><td>California</td><td>3,921</td><td>16.50%</td></tr>
<tr><td>38</td><td>Alaska</td><td>44</td><td>0.19%</td><td>2</td><td>New York</td><td>2,397</td><td>10.09%</td></tr>
<tr><td>21</td><td>Arizona</td><td>312</td><td>1.31%</td><td>3</td><td>Texas</td><td>2,239</td><td>9.42%</td></tr>
<tr><td>22</td><td>Arkansas</td><td>259</td><td>1.09%</td><td>4</td><td>Illinois</td><td>1,322</td><td>5.56%</td></tr>
<tr><td>1</td><td>California</td><td>3,921</td><td>16.50%</td><td>5</td><td>Florida</td><td>1,208</td><td>5.08%</td></tr>
<tr><td>25</td><td>Colorado</td><td>216</td><td>0.91%</td><td>6</td><td>Michigan</td><td>938</td><td>3.95%</td></tr>
<tr><td>29</td><td>Connecticut</td><td>166</td><td>0.70%</td><td>7</td><td>Louisiana</td><td>747</td><td>3.14%</td></tr>
<tr><td>43</td><td>Delaware</td><td>32</td><td>0.13%</td><td>8</td><td>Pennsylvania</td><td>746</td><td>3.14%</td></tr>
<tr><td>5</td><td>Florida</td><td>1,208</td><td>5.08%</td><td>9</td><td>Georgia</td><td>741</td><td>3.12%</td></tr>
<tr><td>9</td><td>Georgia</td><td>741</td><td>3.12%</td><td>10</td><td>Ohio</td><td>724</td><td>3.05%</td></tr>
<tr><td>40</td><td>Hawaii</td><td>42</td><td>0.18%</td><td>11</td><td>North Carolina</td><td>723</td><td>3.04%</td></tr>
<tr><td>41</td><td>Idaho</td><td>37</td><td>0.16%</td><td>12</td><td>Maryland</td><td>596</td><td>2.51%</td></tr>
<tr><td>4</td><td>Illinois</td><td>1,322</td><td>5.56%</td><td>13</td><td>Virginia</td><td>564</td><td>2.37%</td></tr>
<tr><td>16</td><td>Indiana</td><td>464</td><td>1.95%</td><td>14</td><td>Missouri</td><td>547</td><td>2.30%</td></tr>
<tr><td>38</td><td>Iowa</td><td>44</td><td>0.19%</td><td>15</td><td>Tennessee</td><td>520</td><td>2.19%</td></tr>
<tr><td>30</td><td>Kansas</td><td>151</td><td>0.64%</td><td>16</td><td>Indiana</td><td>464</td><td>1.95%</td></tr>
<tr><td>25</td><td>Kentucky</td><td>216</td><td>0.91%</td><td>17</td><td>Alabama</td><td>455</td><td>1.91%</td></tr>
<tr><td>7</td><td>Louisiana</td><td>747</td><td>3.14%</td><td>18</td><td>New Jersey</td><td>397</td><td>1.67%</td></tr>
<tr><td>45</td><td>Maine</td><td>21</td><td>0.09%</td><td>19</td><td>South Carolina</td><td>373</td><td>1.57%</td></tr>
<tr><td>12</td><td>Maryland</td><td>596</td><td>2.51%</td><td>20</td><td>Mississippi</td><td>320</td><td>1.35%</td></tr>
<tr><td>27</td><td>Massachusetts</td><td>214</td><td>0.90%</td><td>21</td><td>Arizona</td><td>312</td><td>1.31%</td></tr>
<tr><td>6</td><td>Michigan</td><td>938</td><td>3.95%</td><td>22</td><td>Arkansas</td><td>259</td><td>1.09%</td></tr>
<tr><td>31</td><td>Minnesota</td><td>150</td><td>0.63%</td><td>23</td><td>Washington</td><td>258</td><td>1.09%</td></tr>
<tr><td>20</td><td>Mississippi</td><td>320</td><td>1.35%</td><td>24</td><td>Wisconsin</td><td>218</td><td>0.92%</td></tr>
<tr><td>14</td><td>Missouri</td><td>547</td><td>2.30%</td><td>25</td><td>Colorado</td><td>216</td><td>0.91%</td></tr>
<tr><td>44</td><td>Montana</td><td>24</td><td>0.10%</td><td>25</td><td>Kentucky</td><td>216</td><td>0.91%</td></tr>
<tr><td>36</td><td>Nebraska</td><td>68</td><td>0.29%</td><td>27</td><td>Massachusetts</td><td>214</td><td>0.90%</td></tr>
<tr><td>32</td><td>Nevada</td><td>145</td><td>0.61%</td><td>28</td><td>Oklahoma</td><td>210</td><td>0.88%</td></tr>
<tr><td>46</td><td>New Hampshire</td><td>18</td><td>0.08%</td><td>29</td><td>Connecticut</td><td>166</td><td>0.70%</td></tr>
<tr><td>18</td><td>New Jersey</td><td>397</td><td>1.67%</td><td>30</td><td>Kansas</td><td>151</td><td>0.64%</td></tr>
<tr><td>33</td><td>New Mexico</td><td>141</td><td>0.59%</td><td>31</td><td>Minnesota</td><td>150</td><td>0.63%</td></tr>
<tr><td>2</td><td>New York</td><td>2,397</td><td>10.09%</td><td>32</td><td>Nevada</td><td>145</td><td>0.61%</td></tr>
<tr><td>11</td><td>North Carolina</td><td>723</td><td>3.04%</td><td>33</td><td>New Mexico</td><td>141</td><td>0.59%</td></tr>
<tr><td>48</td><td>North Dakota</td><td>12</td><td>0.05%</td><td>34</td><td>Oregon</td><td>139</td><td>0.59%</td></tr>
<tr><td>10</td><td>Ohio</td><td>724</td><td>3.05%</td><td>35</td><td>West Virginia</td><td>115</td><td>0.48%</td></tr>
<tr><td>28</td><td>Oklahoma</td><td>210</td><td>0.88%</td><td>36</td><td>Nebraska</td><td>68</td><td>0.29%</td></tr>
<tr><td>34</td><td>Oregon</td><td>139</td><td>0.59%</td><td>37</td><td>Utah</td><td>54</td><td>0.23%</td></tr>
<tr><td>8</td><td>Pennsylvania</td><td>746</td><td>3.14%</td><td>38</td><td>Alaska</td><td>44</td><td>0.19%</td></tr>
<tr><td>42</td><td>Rhode Island</td><td>36</td><td>0.15%</td><td>38</td><td>Iowa</td><td>44</td><td>0.19%</td></tr>
<tr><td>19</td><td>South Carolina</td><td>373</td><td>1.57%</td><td>40</td><td>Hawaii</td><td>42</td><td>0.18%</td></tr>
<tr><td>50</td><td>South Dakota</td><td>4</td><td>0.02%</td><td>41</td><td>Idaho</td><td>37</td><td>0.16%</td></tr>
<tr><td>15</td><td>Tennessee</td><td>520</td><td>2.19%</td><td>42</td><td>Rhode Island</td><td>36</td><td>0.15%</td></tr>
<tr><td>3</td><td>Texas</td><td>2,239</td><td>9.42%</td><td>43</td><td>Delaware</td><td>32</td><td>0.13%</td></tr>
<tr><td>37</td><td>Utah</td><td>54</td><td>0.23%</td><td>44</td><td>Montana</td><td>24</td><td>0.10%</td></tr>
<tr><td>48</td><td>Vermont</td><td>12</td><td>0.05%</td><td>45</td><td>Maine</td><td>21</td><td>0.09%</td></tr>
<tr><td>13</td><td>Virginia</td><td>564</td><td>2.37%</td><td>46</td><td>New Hampshire</td><td>18</td><td>0.08%</td></tr>
<tr><td>23</td><td>Washington</td><td>258</td><td>1.09%</td><td>47</td><td>Wyoming</td><td>17</td><td>0.07%</td></tr>
<tr><td>35</td><td>West Virginia</td><td>115</td><td>0.48%</td><td>48</td><td>North Dakota</td><td>12</td><td>0.05%</td></tr>
<tr><td>24</td><td>Wisconsin</td><td>218</td><td>0.92%</td><td>48</td><td>Vermont</td><td>12</td><td>0.05%</td></tr>
<tr><td>47</td><td>Wyoming</td><td>17</td><td>0.07%</td><td>50</td><td>South Dakota</td><td>4</td><td>0.02%</td></tr>
<tr><td></td><td></td><td></td><td></td><td></td><td>District of Columbia</td><td>443</td><td>1.86%</td></tr>
</table>

Source: Federal Bureau of Investigation
   "Crime in the United States 1992" (Uniform Crime Reports, October 3, 1993)
*Includes nonnegligent manslaughter.

Percent Change in Number of Murders: 1992 to 1996

National Percent Change = 17.3% Decrease*

ALPHA ORDER				RANK ORDER		
RANK	STATE	PERCENT CHANGE		RANK	STATE	PERCENT CHANGE
20	Alabama	(2.4)		1	South Dakota	125.0
16	Alaska	2.3		2	Nevada	51.7
5	Arizona	20.8		3	Montana	41.7
39	Arkansas	(15.4)		4	New Mexico	39.7
43	California	(25.6)		5	Arizona	20.8
40	Colorado	(16.7)		6	Iowa	20.5
23	Connecticut	(4.8)		7	Maine	19.0
21	Delaware	(3.1)		8	North Dakota	16.7
32	Florida	(10.8)		8	Utah	16.7
38	Georgia	(15.0)		10	Idaho	16.2
23	Hawaii	(4.8)		11	Kansas	12.6
10	Idaho	16.2		12	Minnesota	11.3
32	Illinois	(10.8)		13	New Hampshire	11.1
31	Indiana	(9.5)		14	Oklahoma	6.2
6	Iowa	20.5		15	Kentucky	5.6
11	Kansas	12.6		16	Alaska	2.3
15	Kentucky	5.6		17	Louisiana	2.0
17	Louisiana	2.0		18	Washington	(1.2)
7	Maine	19.0		19	Maryland	(1.3)
19	Maryland	(1.3)		20	Alabama	(2.4)
45	Massachusetts	(26.6)		21	Delaware	(3.1)
42	Michigan	(23.0)		22	Tennessee	(3.3)
12	Minnesota	11.3		23	Connecticut	(4.8)
25	Mississippi	(5.9)		23	Hawaii	(4.8)
41	Missouri	(20.8)		25	Mississippi	(5.9)
3	Montana	41.7		25	Wyoming	(5.9)
46	Nebraska	(29.4)		27	Wisconsin	(6.4)
2	Nevada	51.7		28	Oregon	(7.2)
13	New Hampshire	11.1		29	Pennsylvania	(8.0)
37	New Jersey	(14.9)		30	Vermont	(8.3)
4	New Mexico	39.7		31	Indiana	(9.5)
50	New York	(43.6)		32	Florida	(10.8)
36	North Carolina	(14.4)		32	Illinois	(10.8)
8	North Dakota	16.7		34	South Carolina	(11.0)
44	Ohio	(25.7)		35	Virginia	(11.3)
14	Oklahoma	6.2		36	North Carolina	(14.4)
28	Oregon	(7.2)		37	New Jersey	(14.9)
29	Pennsylvania	(8.0)		38	Georgia	(15.0)
47	Rhode Island	(30.6)		39	Arkansas	(15.4)
34	South Carolina	(11.0)		40	Colorado	(16.7)
1	South Dakota	125.0		41	Missouri	(20.8)
22	Tennessee	(3.3)		42	Michigan	(23.0)
48	Texas	(34.0)		43	California	(25.6)
8	Utah	16.7		44	Ohio	(25.7)
30	Vermont	(8.3)		45	Massachusetts	(26.6)
35	Virginia	(11.3)		46	Nebraska	(29.4)
18	Washington	(1.2)		47	Rhode Island	(30.6)
49	West Virginia	(40.0)		48	Texas	(34.0)
27	Wisconsin	(6.4)		49	West Virginia	(40.0)
25	Wyoming	(5.9)		50	New York	(43.6)
					District of Columbia	(10.4)

Source: Morgan Quitno Press using data from Federal Bureau of Investigation
    "Crime in the United States" (Uniform Crime Reports, 1992 and 1996 editions)
*Includes nonnegligent manslaughter.

Murder Rate in 1992

National Rate = 9.3 Murders per 100,000 Population*

<u>ALPHA ORDER</u>

RANK	STATE	RATE
8	Alabama	11.0
22	Alaska	7.5
21	Arizona	8.1
11	Arkansas	10.8
3	California	12.7
26	Colorado	6.2
30	Connecticut	5.1
34	Delaware	4.6
17	Florida	9.0
8	Georgia	11.0
37	Hawaii	3.6
41	Idaho	3.5
7	Illinois	11.4
20	Indiana	8.2
48	Iowa	1.6
28	Kansas	6.0
29	Kentucky	5.8
1	Louisiana	17.4
47	Maine	1.7
6	Maryland	12.1
37	Massachusetts	3.6
16	Michigan	9.9
42	Minnesota	3.3
5	Mississippi	12.2
13	Missouri	10.5
44	Montana	2.9
36	Nebraska	4.2
10	Nevada	10.9
48	New Hampshire	1.6
30	New Jersey	5.1
18	New Mexico	8.9
2	New York	13.2
12	North Carolina	10.6
46	North Dakota	1.9
23	Ohio	6.6
24	Oklahoma	6.5
33	Oregon	4.7
26	Pennsylvania	6.2
37	Rhode Island	3.6
14	South Carolina	10.4
50	South Dakota	0.6
14	Tennessee	10.4
3	Texas	12.7
43	Utah	3.0
45	Vermont	2.1
19	Virginia	8.8
32	Washington	5.0
25	West Virginia	6.3
35	Wisconsin	4.4
37	Wyoming	3.6

<u>RANK ORDER</u>

RANK	STATE	RATE
1	Louisiana	17.4
2	New York	13.2
3	California	12.7
3	Texas	12.7
5	Mississippi	12.2
6	Maryland	12.1
7	Illinois	11.4
8	Alabama	11.0
8	Georgia	11.0
10	Nevada	10.9
11	Arkansas	10.8
12	North Carolina	10.6
13	Missouri	10.5
14	South Carolina	10.4
14	Tennessee	10.4
16	Michigan	9.9
17	Florida	9.0
18	New Mexico	8.9
19	Virginia	8.8
20	Indiana	8.2
21	Arizona	8.1
22	Alaska	7.5
23	Ohio	6.6
24	Oklahoma	6.5
25	West Virginia	6.3
26	Colorado	6.2
26	Pennsylvania	6.2
28	Kansas	6.0
29	Kentucky	5.8
30	Connecticut	5.1
30	New Jersey	5.1
32	Washington	5.0
33	Oregon	4.7
34	Delaware	4.6
35	Wisconsin	4.4
36	Nebraska	4.2
37	Hawaii	3.6
37	Massachusetts	3.6
37	Rhode Island	3.6
37	Wyoming	3.6
41	Idaho	3.5
42	Minnesota	3.3
43	Utah	3.0
44	Montana	2.9
45	Vermont	2.1
46	North Dakota	1.9
47	Maine	1.7
48	Iowa	1.6
48	New Hampshire	1.6
50	South Dakota	0.6
	District of Columbia	75.2

Source: Federal Bureau of Investigation
"Crime in the United States 1992" (Uniform Crime Reports, October 3, 1993)
Includes nonnegligent manslaughter.

Percent Change in Murder Rate: 1992 to 1996

National Percent Change = 20.4% Decrease*

RANK	STATE	PERCENT CHANGE
19	Alabama	(5.5)
17	Alaska	(1.3)
12	Arizona	4.9
37	Arkansas	(19.4)
45	California	(28.3)
41	Colorado	(24.2)
21	Connecticut	(5.9)
22	Delaware	(6.5)
35	Florida	(16.7)
39	Georgia	(21.8)
20	Hawaii	(5.6)
14	Idaho	2.9
31	Illinois	(12.3)
30	Indiana	(12.2)
5	Iowa	18.8
8	Kansas	10.0
15	Kentucky	1.7
16	Louisiana	0.6
6	Maine	17.6
18	Maryland	(4.1)
44	Massachusetts	(27.8)
41	Michigan	(24.2)
9	Minnesota	9.1
27	Mississippi	(9.0)
40	Missouri	(22.9)
2	Montana	34.5
47	Nebraska	(31.0)
4	Nevada	25.7
11	New Hampshire	6.3
36	New Jersey	(17.6)
3	New Mexico	29.2
50	New York	(43.9)
38	North Carolina	(19.8)
7	North Dakota	15.8
43	Ohio	(27.3)
13	Oklahoma	4.6
34	Oregon	(14.9)
24	Pennsylvania	(8.1)
46	Rhode Island	(30.6)
32	South Carolina	(13.5)
1	South Dakota	100.0
26	Tennessee	(8.7)
48	Texas	(39.4)
10	Utah	6.7
29	Vermont	(9.5)
33	Virginia	(14.8)
23	Washington	(8.0)
49	West Virginia	(39.7)
28	Wisconsin	(9.1)
25	Wyoming	(8.3)

RANK	STATE	PERCENT CHANGE
1	South Dakota	100.0
2	Montana	34.5
3	New Mexico	29.2
4	Nevada	25.7
5	Iowa	18.8
6	Maine	17.6
7	North Dakota	15.8
8	Kansas	10.0
9	Minnesota	9.1
10	Utah	6.7
11	New Hampshire	6.3
12	Arizona	4.9
13	Oklahoma	4.6
14	Idaho	2.9
15	Kentucky	1.7
16	Louisiana	0.6
17	Alaska	(1.3)
18	Maryland	(4.1)
19	Alabama	(5.5)
20	Hawaii	(5.6)
21	Connecticut	(5.9)
22	Delaware	(6.5)
23	Washington	(8.0)
24	Pennsylvania	(8.1)
25	Wyoming	(8.3)
26	Tennessee	(8.7)
27	Mississippi	(9.0)
28	Wisconsin	(9.1)
29	Vermont	(9.5)
30	Indiana	(12.2)
31	Illinois	(12.3)
32	South Carolina	(13.5)
33	Virginia	(14.8)
34	Oregon	(14.9)
35	Florida	(16.7)
36	New Jersey	(17.6)
37	Arkansas	(19.4)
38	North Carolina	(19.8)
39	Georgia	(21.8)
40	Missouri	(22.9)
41	Colorado	(24.2)
41	Michigan	(24.2)
43	Ohio	(27.3)
44	Massachusetts	(27.8)
45	California	(28.3)
46	Rhode Island	(30.6)
47	Nebraska	(31.0)
48	Texas	(39.4)
49	West Virginia	(39.7)
50	New York	(43.9)
	District of Columbia	(2.8)

Source: Morgan Quitno Press using data from Federal Bureau of Investigation
"Crime in the United States" (Uniform Crime Reports, 1992 and 1996 editions)
*Includes nonnegligent manslaughter.

Rapes in 1992

National Total = 109,062 Rapes*

ALPHA ORDER				RANK ORDER			
RANK	STATE	RAPES	% of USA	RANK	STATE	RAPES	% of USA
22	Alabama	1,704	1.56%	1	California	12,761	11.70%
37	Alaska	579	0.53%	2	Texas	9,437	8.65%
23	Arizona	1,647	1.51%	3	Michigan	7,550	6.92%
31	Arkansas	990	0.91%	4	Florida	7,310	6.70%
1	California	12,761	11.70%	5	Ohio	5,739	5.26%
24	Colorado	1,641	1.50%	6	New York	5,152	4.72%
33	Connecticut	884	0.81%	7	Illinois	4,312	3.95%
36	Delaware	591	0.54%	8	Washington	3,697	3.39%
4	Florida	7,310	6.70%	9	Pennsylvania	3,324	3.05%
10	Georgia	3,057	2.80%	10	Georgia	3,057	2.80%
40	Hawaii	440	0.40%	11	North Carolina	2,455	2.25%
44	Idaho	339	0.31%	12	Indiana	2,398	2.20%
7	Illinois	4,312	3.95%	13	New Jersey	2,392	2.19%
12	Indiana	2,398	2.20%	14	Tennessee	2,377	2.18%
38	Iowa	528	0.48%	15	Maryland	2,278	2.09%
30	Kansas	1,042	0.96%	16	Massachusetts	2,166	1.99%
28	Kentucky	1,209	1.11%	17	South Carolina	2,072	1.90%
21	Louisiana	1,813	1.66%	18	Virginia	2,008	1.84%
46	Maine	294	0.27%	19	Missouri	1,895	1.74%
15	Maryland	2,278	2.09%	20	Minnesota	1,840	1.69%
16	Massachusetts	2,166	1.99%	21	Louisiana	1,813	1.66%
3	Michigan	7,550	6.92%	22	Alabama	1,704	1.56%
20	Minnesota	1,840	1.69%	23	Arizona	1,647	1.51%
29	Mississippi	1,166	1.07%	24	Colorado	1,641	1.50%
19	Missouri	1,895	1.74%	25	Oregon	1,580	1.45%
47	Montana	210	0.19%	26	Oklahoma	1,556	1.43%
39	Nebraska	504	0.46%	27	Wisconsin	1,315	1.21%
34	Nevada	833	0.76%	28	Kentucky	1,209	1.11%
41	New Hampshire	424	0.39%	29	Mississippi	1,166	1.07%
13	New Jersey	2,392	2.19%	30	Kansas	1,042	0.96%
31	New Mexico	990	0.91%	31	Arkansas	990	0.91%
6	New York	5,152	4.72%	31	New Mexico	990	0.91%
11	North Carolina	2,455	2.25%	33	Connecticut	884	0.81%
49	North Dakota	148	0.14%	34	Nevada	833	0.76%
5	Ohio	5,739	5.26%	35	Utah	823	0.75%
26	Oklahoma	1,556	1.43%	36	Delaware	591	0.54%
25	Oregon	1,580	1.45%	37	Alaska	579	0.53%
9	Pennsylvania	3,324	3.05%	38	Iowa	528	0.48%
45	Rhode Island	311	0.29%	39	Nebraska	504	0.46%
17	South Carolina	2,072	1.90%	40	Hawaii	440	0.40%
43	South Dakota	368	0.34%	41	New Hampshire	424	0.39%
14	Tennessee	2,377	2.18%	42	West Virginia	393	0.36%
2	Texas	9,437	8.65%	43	South Dakota	368	0.34%
35	Utah	823	0.75%	44	Idaho	339	0.31%
50	Vermont	142	0.13%	45	Rhode Island	311	0.29%
18	Virginia	2,008	1.84%	46	Maine	294	0.27%
8	Washington	3,697	3.39%	47	Montana	210	0.19%
42	West Virginia	393	0.36%	48	Wyoming	163	0.15%
27	Wisconsin	1,315	1.21%	49	North Dakota	148	0.14%
48	Wyoming	163	0.15%	50	Vermont	142	0.13%
					District of Columbia	215	0.20%

Source: Federal Bureau of Investigation
   "Crime in the United States 1992" (Uniform Crime Reports, October 3, 1993)
*Forcible rape is the carnal knowledge of a female forcibly and against her will. Assaults or attempts to commit rape by force or threat of force are included. However, statutory rape without force and other sex offenses are excluded.

Percent Change in Number of Rapes: 1992 to 1996

National Percent Change = 12.2% Decrease*

<table>
<tr><td colspan="3"><u>ALPHA ORDER</u></td><td colspan="3"><u>RANK ORDER</u></td></tr>
<tr><td>RANK</td><td>STATE</td><td>PERCENT CHANGE</td><td>RANK</td><td>STATE</td><td>PERCENT CHANGE</td></tr>
<tr><td>38</td><td>Alabama</td><td>(18.0)</td><td>1</td><td>Minnesota</td><td>26.5</td></tr>
<tr><td>50</td><td>Alaska</td><td>(31.3)</td><td>2</td><td>Montana</td><td>13.3</td></tr>
<tr><td>32</td><td>Arizona</td><td>(16.2)</td><td>3</td><td>Vermont</td><td>12.0</td></tr>
<tr><td>7</td><td>Arkansas</td><td>5.7</td><td>4</td><td>New Mexico</td><td>9.9</td></tr>
<tr><td>44</td><td>California</td><td>(19.7)</td><td>5</td><td>Colorado</td><td>7.6</td></tr>
<tr><td>5</td><td>Colorado</td><td>7.6</td><td>6</td><td>Iowa</td><td>6.3</td></tr>
<tr><td>30</td><td>Connecticut</td><td>(14.6)</td><td>7</td><td>Arkansas</td><td>5.7</td></tr>
<tr><td>46</td><td>Delaware</td><td>(23.2)</td><td>8</td><td>Kansas</td><td>5.2</td></tr>
<tr><td>12</td><td>Florida</td><td>2.7</td><td>9</td><td>North Dakota</td><td>4.7</td></tr>
<tr><td>45</td><td>Georgia</td><td>(22.9)</td><td>10</td><td>Tennessee</td><td>4.1</td></tr>
<tr><td>48</td><td>Hawaii</td><td>(25.9)</td><td>11</td><td>Nevada</td><td>2.8</td></tr>
<tr><td>20</td><td>Idaho</td><td>(7.7)</td><td>12</td><td>Florida</td><td>2.7</td></tr>
<tr><td>18</td><td>Illinois</td><td>(6.1)</td><td>13</td><td>Kentucky</td><td>1.7</td></tr>
<tr><td>34</td><td>Indiana</td><td>(16.9)</td><td>14</td><td>Utah</td><td>1.6</td></tr>
<tr><td>6</td><td>Iowa</td><td>6.3</td><td>15</td><td>Louisiana</td><td>(0.4)</td></tr>
<tr><td>8</td><td>Kansas</td><td>5.2</td><td>16</td><td>Oklahoma</td><td>(0.7)</td></tr>
<tr><td>13</td><td>Kentucky</td><td>1.7</td><td>17</td><td>New Hampshire</td><td>(4.7)</td></tr>
<tr><td>15</td><td>Louisiana</td><td>(0.4)</td><td>18</td><td>Illinois</td><td>(6.1)</td></tr>
<tr><td>27</td><td>Maine</td><td>(11.6)</td><td>19</td><td>North Carolina</td><td>(6.8)</td></tr>
<tr><td>33</td><td>Maryland</td><td>(16.4)</td><td>20</td><td>Idaho</td><td>(7.7)</td></tr>
<tr><td>39</td><td>Massachusetts</td><td>(18.4)</td><td>20</td><td>Rhode Island</td><td>(7.7)</td></tr>
<tr><td>49</td><td>Michigan</td><td>(27.6)</td><td>22</td><td>Pennsylvania</td><td>(8.3)</td></tr>
<tr><td>1</td><td>Minnesota</td><td>26.5</td><td>23</td><td>West Virginia</td><td>(8.9)</td></tr>
<tr><td>31</td><td>Mississippi</td><td>(15.9)</td><td>24</td><td>Texas</td><td>(11.2)</td></tr>
<tr><td>35</td><td>Missouri</td><td>(17.4)</td><td>24</td><td>Virginia</td><td>(11.2)</td></tr>
<tr><td>2</td><td>Montana</td><td>13.3</td><td>26</td><td>Nebraska</td><td>(11.3)</td></tr>
<tr><td>26</td><td>Nebraska</td><td>(11.3)</td><td>27</td><td>Maine</td><td>(11.6)</td></tr>
<tr><td>11</td><td>Nevada</td><td>2.8</td><td>28</td><td>South Carolina</td><td>(12.1)</td></tr>
<tr><td>17</td><td>New Hampshire</td><td>(4.7)</td><td>29</td><td>Wyoming</td><td>(14.1)</td></tr>
<tr><td>35</td><td>New Jersey</td><td>(17.4)</td><td>30</td><td>Connecticut</td><td>(14.6)</td></tr>
<tr><td>4</td><td>New Mexico</td><td>9.9</td><td>31</td><td>Mississippi</td><td>(15.9)</td></tr>
<tr><td>41</td><td>New York</td><td>(19.0)</td><td>32</td><td>Arizona</td><td>(16.2)</td></tr>
<tr><td>19</td><td>North Carolina</td><td>(6.8)</td><td>33</td><td>Maryland</td><td>(16.4)</td></tr>
<tr><td>9</td><td>North Dakota</td><td>4.7</td><td>34</td><td>Indiana</td><td>(16.9)</td></tr>
<tr><td>43</td><td>Ohio</td><td>(19.6)</td><td>35</td><td>Missouri</td><td>(17.4)</td></tr>
<tr><td>16</td><td>Oklahoma</td><td>(0.7)</td><td>35</td><td>New Jersey</td><td>(17.4)</td></tr>
<tr><td>42</td><td>Oregon</td><td>(19.5)</td><td>35</td><td>Wisconsin</td><td>(17.4)</td></tr>
<tr><td>22</td><td>Pennsylvania</td><td>(8.3)</td><td>38</td><td>Alabama</td><td>(18.0)</td></tr>
<tr><td>20</td><td>Rhode Island</td><td>(7.7)</td><td>39</td><td>Massachusetts</td><td>(18.4)</td></tr>
<tr><td>28</td><td>South Carolina</td><td>(12.1)</td><td>40</td><td>South Dakota</td><td>(18.5)</td></tr>
<tr><td>40</td><td>South Dakota</td><td>(18.5)</td><td>41</td><td>New York</td><td>(19.0)</td></tr>
<tr><td>10</td><td>Tennessee</td><td>4.1</td><td>42</td><td>Oregon</td><td>(19.5)</td></tr>
<tr><td>24</td><td>Texas</td><td>(11.2)</td><td>43</td><td>Ohio</td><td>(19.6)</td></tr>
<tr><td>14</td><td>Utah</td><td>1.6</td><td>44</td><td>California</td><td>(19.7)</td></tr>
<tr><td>3</td><td>Vermont</td><td>12.0</td><td>45</td><td>Georgia</td><td>(22.9)</td></tr>
<tr><td>24</td><td>Virginia</td><td>(11.2)</td><td>46</td><td>Delaware</td><td>(23.2)</td></tr>
<tr><td>47</td><td>Washington</td><td>(23.5)</td><td>47</td><td>Washington</td><td>(23.5)</td></tr>
<tr><td>23</td><td>West Virginia</td><td>(8.9)</td><td>48</td><td>Hawaii</td><td>(25.9)</td></tr>
<tr><td>35</td><td>Wisconsin</td><td>(17.4)</td><td>49</td><td>Michigan</td><td>(27.6)</td></tr>
<tr><td>29</td><td>Wyoming</td><td>(14.1)</td><td>50</td><td>Alaska</td><td>(31.3)</td></tr>
<tr><td></td><td></td><td></td><td></td><td>District of Columbia</td><td>20.9</td></tr>
</table>

Source: Morgan Quitno Press using data from Federal Bureau of Investigation
    "Crime in the United States" (Uniform Crime Reports, 1992 and 1996 editions)
*Forcible rape is the carnal knowledge of a female forcibly and against her will. Assaults or attempts to commit rape by force or threat of force are included. However, statutory rape without force and other sex offenses are excluded.

Rape Rate in 1992

National Rate = 42.8 Rapes per 100,000 Population*

RANK	STATE	RATE
26	Alabama	41.2
1	Alaska	98.6
20	Arizona	43.0
23	Arkansas	41.3
23	California	41.3
14	Colorado	47.3
43	Connecticut	26.9
2	Delaware	85.8
8	Florida	54.2
18	Georgia	45.3
29	Hawaii	37.9
36	Idaho	31.8
30	Illinois	37.1
21	Indiana	42.4
50	Iowa	18.8
23	Kansas	41.3
35	Kentucky	32.2
22	Louisiana	42.3
47	Maine	23.8
16	Maryland	46.4
32	Massachusetts	36.1
3	Michigan	80.0
27	Minnesota	41.1
19	Mississippi	44.6
31	Missouri	36.5
45	Montana	25.5
38	Nebraska	31.4
5	Nevada	62.8
28	New Hampshire	38.2
40	New Jersey	30.7
6	New Mexico	62.6
41	New York	28.4
33	North Carolina	35.9
48	North Dakota	23.3
11	Ohio	52.1
13	Oklahoma	48.4
10	Oregon	53.1
42	Pennsylvania	27.7
39	Rhode Island	30.9
7	South Carolina	57.5
12	South Dakota	51.8
14	Tennessee	47.3
9	Texas	53.4
17	Utah	45.4
46	Vermont	24.9
37	Virginia	31.5
4	Washington	72.0
49	West Virginia	21.7
44	Wisconsin	26.3
34	Wyoming	35.0

RANK	STATE	RATE
1	Alaska	98.6
2	Delaware	85.8
3	Michigan	80.0
4	Washington	72.0
5	Nevada	62.8
6	New Mexico	62.6
7	South Carolina	57.5
8	Florida	54.2
9	Texas	53.4
10	Oregon	53.1
11	Ohio	52.1
12	South Dakota	51.8
13	Oklahoma	48.4
14	Colorado	47.3
14	Tennessee	47.3
16	Maryland	46.4
17	Utah	45.4
18	Georgia	45.3
19	Mississippi	44.6
20	Arizona	43.0
21	Indiana	42.4
22	Louisiana	42.3
23	Arkansas	41.3
23	California	41.3
23	Kansas	41.3
26	Alabama	41.2
27	Minnesota	41.1
28	New Hampshire	38.2
29	Hawaii	37.9
30	Illinois	37.1
31	Missouri	36.5
32	Massachusetts	36.1
33	North Carolina	35.9
34	Wyoming	35.0
35	Kentucky	32.2
36	Idaho	31.8
37	Virginia	31.5
38	Nebraska	31.4
39	Rhode Island	30.9
40	New Jersey	30.7
41	New York	28.4
42	Pennsylvania	27.7
43	Connecticut	26.9
44	Wisconsin	26.3
45	Montana	25.5
46	Vermont	24.9
47	Maine	23.8
48	North Dakota	23.3
49	West Virginia	21.7
50	Iowa	18.8
	District of Columbia	36.5

Source: Federal Bureau of Investigation
   "Crime in the United States 1992" (Uniform Crime Reports, October 3, 1993)
*Forcible rape is the carnal knowledge of a female forcibly and against her will. Assaults or attempts to commit rape by force or threat of force are included. However, statutory rape without force and other sex offenses are excluded.

Percent Change in Rape Rate: 1992 to 1996

National Percent Change = 15.7% Decrease*

RANK	STATE	PERCENT CHANGE
39	Alabama	(20.6)
50	Alaska	(33.5)
45	Arizona	(27.4)
8	Arkansas	1.0
42	California	(22.3)
12	Colorado	(2.3)
24	Connecticut	(14.1)
44	Delaware	(27.0)
14	Florida	(3.9)
49	Georgia	(29.1)
45	Hawaii	(27.4)
29	Idaho	(17.3)
16	Illinois	(7.8)
35	Indiana	(19.6)
4	Iowa	4.8
6	Kansas	3.1
9	Kentucky	(1.6)
11	Louisiana	(1.9)
21	Maine	(12.2)
31	Maryland	(19.0)
36	Massachusetts	(19.7)
47	Michigan	(28.8)
1	Minnesota	21.7
33	Mississippi	(19.1)
37	Missouri	(20.0)
3	Montana	6.3
23	Nebraska	(13.7)
26	Nevada	(15.0)
19	New Hampshire	(8.9)
34	New Jersey	(19.5)
7	New Mexico	1.4
31	New York	(19.0)
22	North Carolina	(12.8)
5	North Dakota	3.4
40	Ohio	(20.7)
13	Oklahoma	(3.3)
43	Oregon	(25.2)
18	Pennsylvania	(8.7)
15	Rhode Island	(6.1)
25	South Carolina	(14.4)
41	South Dakota	(20.8)
10	Tennessee	(1.7)
30	Texas	(18.0)
17	Utah	(7.9)
2	Vermont	8.4
27	Virginia	(15.2)
48	Washington	(29.0)
20	West Virginia	(9.7)
38	Wisconsin	(20.2)
28	Wyoming	(16.9)

RANK	STATE	PERCENT CHANGE
1	Minnesota	21.7
2	Vermont	8.4
3	Montana	6.3
4	Iowa	4.8
5	North Dakota	3.4
6	Kansas	3.1
7	New Mexico	1.4
8	Arkansas	1.0
9	Kentucky	(1.6)
10	Tennessee	(1.7)
11	Louisiana	(1.9)
12	Colorado	(2.3)
13	Oklahoma	(3.3)
14	Florida	(3.9)
15	Rhode Island	(6.1)
16	Illinois	(7.8)
17	Utah	(7.9)
18	Pennsylvania	(8.7)
19	New Hampshire	(8.9)
20	West Virginia	(9.7)
21	Maine	(12.2)
22	North Carolina	(12.8)
23	Nebraska	(13.7)
24	Connecticut	(14.1)
25	South Carolina	(14.4)
26	Nevada	(15.0)
27	Virginia	(15.2)
28	Wyoming	(16.9)
29	Idaho	(17.3)
30	Texas	(18.0)
31	Maryland	(19.0)
31	New York	(19.0)
33	Mississippi	(19.1)
34	New Jersey	(19.5)
35	Indiana	(19.6)
36	Massachusetts	(19.7)
37	Missouri	(20.0)
38	Wisconsin	(20.2)
39	Alabama	(20.6)
40	Ohio	(20.7)
41	South Dakota	(20.8)
42	California	(22.3)
43	Oregon	(25.2)
44	Delaware	(27.0)
45	Arizona	(27.4)
45	Hawaii	(27.4)
47	Michigan	(28.8)
48	Washington	(29.0)
49	Georgia	(29.1)
50	Alaska	(33.5)
	District of Columbia	31.2

Source: Morgan Quitno Press using data from Federal Bureau of Investigation
"Crime in the United States" (Uniform Crime Reports, 1992 and 1996 editions)
Forcible rape is the carnal knowledge of a female forcibly and against her will. Assaults or attempts to commit rape by force or threat of force are included. However, statutory rape without force and other sex offenses are excluded.

Robberies in 1992

National Total = 672,478 Robberies*

ALPHA ORDER					RANK ORDER			
RANK	STATE	ROBBERIES	% of USA		RANK	STATE	ROBBERIES	% of USA
21	Alabama	6,819	1.01%		1	California	130,897	19.46%
42	Alaska	640	0.10%		2	New York	108,154	16.08%
24	Arizona	5,867	0.87%		3	Florida	49,482	7.36%
33	Arkansas	3,011	0.45%		4	Illinois	47,973	7.13%
1	California	130,897	19.46%		5	Texas	44,588	6.63%
29	Colorado	4,180	0.62%		6	New Jersey	22,216	3.30%
20	Connecticut	6,918	1.03%		7	Ohio	21,925	3.26%
37	Delaware	1,042	0.15%		8	Pennsylvania	21,701	3.23%
3	Florida	49,482	7.36%		9	Maryland	21,054	3.13%
11	Georgia	16,863	2.51%		10	Michigan	20,902	3.11%
35	Hawaii	1,151	0.17%		11	Georgia	16,863	2.51%
45	Idaho	229	0.03%		12	North Carolina	12,784	1.90%
4	Illinois	47,973	7.13%		13	Missouri	11,783	1.75%
19	Indiana	6,921	1.03%		14	Louisiana	11,636	1.73%
36	Iowa	1,113	0.17%		15	Massachusetts	11,059	1.64%
30	Kansas	3,277	0.49%		16	Tennessee	10,964	1.63%
31	Kentucky	3,273	0.49%		17	Virginia	8,787	1.31%
14	Louisiana	11,636	1.73%		18	Washington	7,178	1.07%
44	Maine	288	0.04%		19	Indiana	6,921	1.03%
9	Maryland	21,054	3.13%		20	Connecticut	6,918	1.03%
15	Massachusetts	11,059	1.64%		21	Alabama	6,819	1.01%
10	Michigan	20,902	3.11%		22	South Carolina	6,148	0.91%
25	Minnesota	4,906	0.73%		23	Wisconsin	5,997	0.89%
32	Mississippi	3,254	0.48%		24	Arizona	5,867	0.87%
13	Missouri	11,783	1.75%		25	Minnesota	4,906	0.73%
46	Montana	222	0.03%		26	Oregon	4,507	0.67%
40	Nebraska	911	0.14%		27	Nevada	4,397	0.65%
27	Nevada	4,397	0.65%		28	Oklahoma	4,376	0.65%
43	New Hampshire	367	0.05%		29	Colorado	4,180	0.62%
6	New Jersey	22,216	3.30%		30	Kansas	3,277	0.49%
34	New Mexico	2,202	0.33%		31	Kentucky	3,273	0.49%
2	New York	108,154	16.08%		32	Mississippi	3,254	0.48%
12	North Carolina	12,784	1.90%		33	Arkansas	3,011	0.45%
50	North Dakota	50	0.01%		34	New Mexico	2,202	0.33%
7	Ohio	21,925	3.26%		35	Hawaii	1,151	0.17%
28	Oklahoma	4,376	0.65%		36	Iowa	1,113	0.17%
26	Oregon	4,507	0.67%		37	Delaware	1,042	0.15%
8	Pennsylvania	21,701	3.23%		38	Utah	1,014	0.15%
39	Rhode Island	950	0.14%		39	Rhode Island	950	0.14%
22	South Carolina	6,148	0.91%		40	Nebraska	911	0.14%
47	South Dakota	120	0.02%		41	West Virginia	788	0.12%
16	Tennessee	10,964	1.63%		42	Alaska	640	0.10%
5	Texas	44,588	6.63%		43	New Hampshire	367	0.05%
38	Utah	1,014	0.15%		44	Maine	288	0.04%
49	Vermont	51	0.01%		45	Idaho	229	0.03%
17	Virginia	8,787	1.31%		46	Montana	222	0.03%
18	Washington	7,178	1.07%		47	South Dakota	120	0.02%
41	West Virginia	788	0.12%		48	Wyoming	84	0.01%
23	Wisconsin	5,997	0.89%		49	Vermont	51	0.01%
48	Wyoming	84	0.01%		50	North Dakota	50	0.01%
						District of Columbia	7,459	1.11%

Source: Federal Bureau of Investigation
"Crime in the United States 1992" (Uniform Crime Reports, October 3, 1993)
*Robbery is the taking or attempting to take anything of value by force or threat of force.

Percent Change in Number of Robberies: 1992 to 1996

National Percent Change = 20.1% Decrease*

ALPHA ORDER				RANK ORDER		
RANK	**STATE**	**PERCENT CHANGE**		**RANK**	**STATE**	**PERCENT CHANGE**
22	Alabama	4.5		1	Vermont	78.4
17	Alaska	10.9		2	North Dakota	42.0
5	Arizona	26.6		3	Hawaii	39.5
26	Arkansas	(4.9)		4	Utah	35.8
47	California	(28.0)		5	Arizona	26.6
32	Colorado	(10.2)		6	New Mexico	26.3
43	Connecticut	(19.7)		7	Delaware	25.1
7	Delaware	25.1		8	Montana	17.6
38	Florida	(15.8)		9	Wyoming	16.7
33	Georgia	(10.5)		10	Iowa	15.5
3	Hawaii	39.5		10	Nebraska	15.5
20	Idaho	5.2		12	South Dakota	15.0
49	Illinois	(31.0)		13	Nevada	12.1
21	Indiana	4.7		14	Mississippi	12.0
10	Iowa	15.5		15	Pennsylvania	11.7
45	Kansas	(24.4)		16	Kentucky	11.3
16	Kentucky	11.3		17	Alaska	10.9
24	Louisiana	3.4		18	Minnesota	9.8
25	Maine	1.4		19	Tennessee	8.6
27	Maryland	(5.3)		20	Idaho	5.2
48	Massachusetts	(29.7)		21	Indiana	4.7
41	Michigan	(19.1)		22	Alabama	4.5
18	Minnesota	9.8		23	South Carolina	3.5
14	Mississippi	12.0		24	Louisiana	3.4
44	Missouri	(22.4)		25	Maine	1.4
8	Montana	17.6		26	Arkansas	(4.9)
10	Nebraska	15.5		27	Maryland	(5.3)
13	Nevada	12.1		28	North Carolina	(6.1)
36	New Hampshire	(13.6)		29	West Virginia	(6.5)
37	New Jersey	(15.2)		30	Virginia	(6.9)
6	New Mexico	26.3		31	Washington	(8.2)
50	New York	(42.8)		32	Colorado	(10.2)
28	North Carolina	(6.1)		33	Georgia	(10.5)
2	North Dakota	42.0		34	Oregon	(13.2)
39	Ohio	(16.4)		35	Rhode Island	(13.3)
42	Oklahoma	(19.6)		36	New Hampshire	(13.6)
34	Oregon	(13.2)		37	New Jersey	(15.2)
15	Pennsylvania	11.7		38	Florida	(15.8)
35	Rhode Island	(13.3)		39	Ohio	(16.4)
23	South Carolina	3.5		40	Wisconsin	(16.9)
12	South Dakota	15.0		41	Michigan	(19.1)
19	Tennessee	8.6		42	Oklahoma	(19.6)
46	Texas	(26.4)		43	Connecticut	(19.7)
4	Utah	35.8		44	Missouri	(22.4)
1	Vermont	78.4		45	Kansas	(24.4)
30	Virginia	(6.9)		46	Texas	(26.4)
31	Washington	(8.2)		47	California	(28.0)
29	West Virginia	(6.5)		48	Massachusetts	(29.7)
40	Wisconsin	(16.9)		49	Illinois	(31.0)
9	Wyoming	16.7		50	New York	(42.8)
					District of Columbia	(13.6)

Source: Morgan Quitno Press using data from Federal Bureau of Investigation
"Crime in the United States" (Uniform Crime Reports, 1992 and 1996 editions)
*Robbery is the taking or attempting to take anything of value by force or threat of force.

Robbery Rate in 1992

National Rate = 263.6 Robberies per 100,000 Population*

ALPHA ORDER				RANK ORDER		
RANK	**STATE**	**RATE**		**RANK**	**STATE**	**RATE**
20	Alabama	164.9		1	New York	596.9
35	Alaska	109.0		2	Maryland	429.0
21	Arizona	153.1		3	California	424.1
29	Arkansas	125.5		4	Illinois	412.5
3	California	424.1		5	Florida	366.9
32	Colorado	120.5		6	Nevada	331.3
14	Connecticut	210.9		7	New Jersey	285.2
23	Delaware	151.2		8	Louisiana	271.4
5	Florida	366.9		9	Texas	252.5
10	Georgia	249.8		10	Georgia	249.8
36	Hawaii	99.2		11	Missouri	226.9
46	Idaho	21.5		12	Michigan	221.5
4	Illinois	412.5		13	Tennessee	218.2
31	Indiana	122.2		14	Connecticut	210.9
42	Iowa	39.6		15	Ohio	199.0
28	Kansas	129.9		16	North Carolina	186.8
38	Kentucky	87.2		17	Massachusetts	184.4
8	Louisiana	271.4		18	Pennsylvania	180.7
45	Maine	23.3		19	South Carolina	170.6
2	Maryland	429.0		20	Alabama	164.9
17	Massachusetts	184.4		21	Arizona	153.1
12	Michigan	221.5		22	Oregon	151.4
34	Minnesota	109.5		23	Delaware	151.2
30	Mississippi	124.5		24	Washington	139.8
11	Missouri	226.9		25	New Mexico	139.3
44	Montana	26.9		26	Virginia	137.8
39	Nebraska	56.7		27	Oklahoma	136.2
6	Nevada	331.3		28	Kansas	129.9
43	New Hampshire	33.0		29	Arkansas	125.5
7	New Jersey	285.2		30	Mississippi	124.5
25	New Mexico	139.3		31	Indiana	122.2
1	New York	596.9		32	Colorado	120.5
16	North Carolina	186.8		33	Wisconsin	119.8
50	North Dakota	7.9		34	Minnesota	109.5
15	Ohio	199.0		35	Alaska	109.0
27	Oklahoma	136.2		36	Hawaii	99.2
22	Oregon	151.4		37	Rhode Island	94.5
18	Pennsylvania	180.7		38	Kentucky	87.2
37	Rhode Island	94.5		39	Nebraska	56.7
19	South Carolina	170.6		40	Utah	55.9
48	South Dakota	16.9		41	West Virginia	43.5
13	Tennessee	218.2		42	Iowa	39.6
9	Texas	252.5		43	New Hampshire	33.0
40	Utah	55.9		44	Montana	26.9
49	Vermont	8.9		45	Maine	23.3
26	Virginia	137.8		46	Idaho	21.5
24	Washington	139.8		47	Wyoming	18.0
41	West Virginia	43.5		48	South Dakota	16.9
33	Wisconsin	119.8		49	Vermont	8.9
47	Wyoming	18.0		50	North Dakota	7.9
				District of Columbia		1,266.4

Source: Federal Bureau of Investigation
"Crime in the United States 1992" (Uniform Crime Reports, October 3, 1993)
*Robbery is the taking or attempting to take anything of value by force or threat of force.

Percent Change in Robbery Rate: 1992 to 1996

National Percent Change = 23.2% Decrease*

ALPHA ORDER				RANK ORDER		
RANK	STATE	PERCENT CHANGE		RANK	STATE	PERCENT CHANGE
21	Alabama	1.1		1	Vermont	73.0
16	Alaska	7.3		2	North Dakota	39.2
13	Arizona	9.6		3	Hawaii	36.7
28	Arkansas	(9.1)		4	Utah	23.3
46	California	(30.3)		5	Delaware	19.0
37	Colorado	(18.5)		6	New Mexico	16.6
40	Connecticut	(19.6)		7	Iowa	13.9
5	Delaware	19.0		8	Wyoming	13.3
42	Florida	(21.2)		9	Nebraska	12.3
36	Georgia	(17.8)		10	South Dakota	11.8
3	Hawaii	36.7		11	Pennsylvania	11.3
24	Idaho	(5.6)		12	Montana	10.4
49	Illinois	(32.3)		13	Arizona	9.6
20	Indiana	1.6		14	Mississippi	7.8
7	Iowa	13.9		15	Kentucky	7.6
45	Kansas	(25.9)		16	Alaska	7.3
15	Kentucky	7.6		17	Minnesota	5.6
19	Louisiana	1.9		18	Tennessee	2.5
22	Maine	0.9		19	Louisiana	1.9
27	Maryland	(8.3)		20	Indiana	1.6
47	Massachusetts	(30.7)		21	Alabama	1.1
41	Michigan	(20.5)		22	Maine	0.9
17	Minnesota	5.6		23	South Carolina	0.8
14	Mississippi	7.8		24	Idaho	(5.6)
44	Missouri	(24.8)		25	West Virginia	(7.1)
12	Montana	10.4		26	Nevada	(7.2)
9	Nebraska	12.3		27	Maryland	(8.3)
26	Nevada	(7.2)		28	Arkansas	(9.1)
33	New Hampshire	(17.3)		29	Virginia	(11.0)
33	New Jersey	(17.3)		30	Rhode Island	(12.0)
6	New Mexico	16.6		31	North Carolina	(12.3)
50	New York	(43.0)		32	Washington	(14.9)
31	North Carolina	(12.3)		33	New Hampshire	(17.3)
2	North Dakota	39.2		33	New Jersey	(17.3)
35	Ohio	(17.5)		35	Ohio	(17.5)
43	Oklahoma	(21.7)		36	Georgia	(17.8)
38	Oregon	(19.3)		37	Colorado	(18.5)
11	Pennsylvania	11.3		38	Oregon	(19.3)
30	Rhode Island	(12.0)		39	Wisconsin	(19.4)
23	South Carolina	0.8		40	Connecticut	(19.6)
10	South Dakota	11.8		41	Michigan	(20.5)
18	Tennessee	2.5		42	Florida	(21.2)
48	Texas	(32.1)		43	Oklahoma	(21.7)
4	Utah	23.3		44	Missouri	(24.8)
1	Vermont	73.0		45	Kansas	(25.9)
29	Virginia	(11.0)		46	California	(30.3)
32	Washington	(14.9)		47	Massachusetts	(30.7)
25	West Virginia	(7.1)		48	Texas	(32.1)
39	Wisconsin	(19.4)		49	Illinois	(32.3)
8	Wyoming	13.3		50	New York	(43.0)
					District of Columbia	(6.3)

Source: Morgan Quitno Press using data from Federal Bureau of Investigation
"Crime in the United States" (Uniform Crime Reports, 1992 and 1996 editions)
*Robbery is the taking or attempting to take anything of value by force or threat of force.

Aggravated Assaults in 1992

National Total = 1,126,974 Aggravated Assaults*

<u>ALPHA ORDER</u>

RANK	STATE	ASSAULTS	% of USA
12	Alabama	27,074	2.40%
40	Alaska	2,614	0.23%
20	Arizona	17,880	1.59%
27	Arkansas	9,571	0.85%
1	California	198,045	17.57%
23	Colorado	14,049	1.25%
30	Connecticut	8,284	0.74%
39	Delaware	2,615	0.23%
2	Florida	104,827	9.30%
10	Georgia	28,835	2.56%
43	Hawaii	1,365	0.12%
42	Idaho	2,398	0.21%
5	Illinois	60,057	5.33%
19	Indiana	19,008	1.69%
33	Iowa	6,131	0.54%
29	Kansas	8,418	0.75%
22	Kentucky	15,409	1.37%
11	Louisiana	28,013	2.49%
45	Maine	1,013	0.09%
15	Maryland	25,157	2.23%
7	Massachusetts	33,288	2.95%
6	Michigan	43,282	3.84%
31	Minnesota	8,248	0.73%
34	Mississippi	6,023	0.53%
16	Missouri	24,223	2.15%
46	Montana	944	0.08%
35	Nebraska	4,115	0.37%
36	Nevada	3,872	0.34%
48	New Hampshire	588	0.05%
17	New Jersey	23,740	2.11%
26	New Mexico	11,448	1.02%
3	New York	87,608	7.77%
8	North Carolina	30,638	2.72%
50	North Dakota	320	0.03%
9	Ohio	29,547	2.62%
24	Oklahoma	13,863	1.23%
28	Oregon	8,963	0.80%
13	Pennsylvania	25,505	2.26%
38	Rhode Island	2,668	0.24%
14	South Carolina	25,436	2.26%
47	South Dakota	891	0.08%
18	Tennessee	23,626	2.10%
4	Texas	86,105	7.64%
37	Utah	3,376	0.30%
49	Vermont	419	0.04%
25	Virginia	12,548	1.11%
21	Washington	16,321	1.45%
41	West Virginia	2,537	0.23%
32	Wisconsin	6,276	0.56%
44	Wyoming	1,225	0.11%

<u>RANK ORDER</u>

RANK	STATE	ASSAULTS	% of USA
1	California	198,045	17.57%
2	Florida	104,827	9.30%
3	New York	87,608	7.77%
4	Texas	86,105	7.64%
5	Illinois	60,057	5.33%
6	Michigan	43,282	3.84%
7	Massachusetts	33,288	2.95%
8	North Carolina	30,638	2.72%
9	Ohio	29,547	2.62%
10	Georgia	28,835	2.56%
11	Louisiana	28,013	2.49%
12	Alabama	27,074	2.40%
13	Pennsylvania	25,505	2.26%
14	South Carolina	25,436	2.26%
15	Maryland	25,157	2.23%
16	Missouri	24,223	2.15%
17	New Jersey	23,740	2.11%
18	Tennessee	23,626	2.10%
19	Indiana	19,008	1.69%
20	Arizona	17,880	1.59%
21	Washington	16,321	1.45%
22	Kentucky	15,409	1.37%
23	Colorado	14,049	1.25%
24	Oklahoma	13,863	1.23%
25	Virginia	12,548	1.11%
26	New Mexico	11,448	1.02%
27	Arkansas	9,571	0.85%
28	Oregon	8,963	0.80%
29	Kansas	8,418	0.75%
30	Connecticut	8,284	0.74%
31	Minnesota	8,248	0.73%
32	Wisconsin	6,276	0.56%
33	Iowa	6,131	0.54%
34	Mississippi	6,023	0.53%
35	Nebraska	4,115	0.37%
36	Nevada	3,872	0.34%
37	Utah	3,376	0.30%
38	Rhode Island	2,668	0.24%
39	Delaware	2,615	0.23%
40	Alaska	2,614	0.23%
41	West Virginia	2,537	0.23%
42	Idaho	2,398	0.21%
43	Hawaii	1,365	0.12%
44	Wyoming	1,225	0.11%
45	Maine	1,013	0.09%
46	Montana	944	0.08%
47	South Dakota	891	0.08%
48	New Hampshire	588	0.05%
49	Vermont	419	0.04%
50	North Dakota	320	0.03%
	District of Columbia	8,568	0.76%

Source: Federal Bureau of Investigation
"Crime in the United States 1992" (Uniform Crime Reports, October 3, 1993)
Aggravated assault is an attack for the purpose of inflicting severe bodily injury.

Percent Change in Number of Aggravated Assaults: 1992 to 1996

National Percent Change = 8.6% Decrease*

ALPHA ORDER				RANK ORDER		
RANK	STATE	PERCENT CHANGE		RANK	STATE	PERCENT CHANGE
49	Alabama	(43.9)		1	Nevada	80.7
5	Alaska	24.9		2	Mississippi	38.4
17	Arizona	5.0		3	Nebraska	36.9
29	Arkansas	(5.6)		4	Utah	29.2
43	California	(15.4)		5	Alaska	24.9
48	Colorado	(30.5)		6	Delaware	16.9
41	Connecticut	(15.2)		7	Indiana	14.2
6	Delaware	16.9		8	South Carolina	11.5
23	Florida	(3.5)		9	Tennessee	11.3
19	Georgia	0.2		10	Illinois	11.0
20	Hawaii	(1.1)		11	Vermont	8.1
13	Idaho	7.6		12	Wisconsin	7.8
10	Illinois	11.0		13	Idaho	7.6
7	Indiana	14.2		14	New Hampshire	7.5
25	Iowa	(4.2)		15	Oregon	6.2
45	Kansas	(18.0)		16	West Virginia	5.3
50	Kentucky	(52.3)		17	Arizona	5.0
33	Louisiana	(7.8)		18	Oklahoma	4.0
24	Maine	(3.7)		19	Georgia	0.2
21	Maryland	(1.4)		20	Hawaii	(1.1)
37	Massachusetts	(11.6)		21	Maryland	(1.4)
38	Michigan	(12.5)		22	Virginia	(1.8)
25	Minnesota	(4.2)		23	Florida	(3.5)
2	Mississippi	38.4		24	Maine	(3.7)
42	Missouri	(15.3)		25	Iowa	(4.2)
32	Montana	(6.6)		25	Minnesota	(4.2)
3	Nebraska	36.9		27	South Dakota	(4.6)
1	Nevada	80.7		28	Pennsylvania	(5.2)
14	New Hampshire	7.5		29	Arkansas	(5.6)
36	New Jersey	(10.2)		30	North Dakota	(5.9)
35	New Mexico	(9.7)		31	Texas	(6.4)
47	New York	(26.0)		32	Montana	(6.6)
34	North Carolina	(8.1)		33	Louisiana	(7.8)
30	North Dakota	(5.9)		34	North Carolina	(8.1)
44	Ohio	(17.4)		35	New Mexico	(9.7)
18	Oklahoma	4.0		36	New Jersey	(10.2)
15	Oregon	6.2		37	Massachusetts	(11.6)
28	Pennsylvania	(5.2)		38	Michigan	(12.5)
40	Rhode Island	(13.8)		39	Washington	(13.1)
8	South Carolina	11.5		40	Rhode Island	(13.8)
27	South Dakota	(4.6)		41	Connecticut	(15.2)
9	Tennessee	11.3		42	Missouri	(15.3)
31	Texas	(6.4)		43	California	(15.4)
4	Utah	29.2		44	Ohio	(17.4)
11	Vermont	8.1		45	Kansas	(18.0)
22	Virginia	(1.8)		46	Wyoming	(22.7)
39	Washington	(13.1)		47	New York	(26.0)
16	West Virginia	5.3		48	Colorado	(30.5)
12	Wisconsin	7.8		49	Alabama	(43.9)
46	Wyoming	(22.7)		50	Kentucky	(52.3)
					District of Columbia	(26.4)

Source: Morgan Quitno Press using data from Federal Bureau of Investigation
    "Crime in the United States" (Uniform Crime Reports, 1992 and 1996 editions)
*Aggravated assault is an attack for the purpose of inflicting severe bodily injury.

Aggravated Assault Rate in 1992

National Rate = 441.8 Aggravated Assaults per 100,000 Population*

ALPHA ORDER

RANK ORDER

RANK	STATE	RATE		RANK	STATE	RATE
4	Alabama	654.6		1	Florida	777.2
17	Alaska	445.3		2	New Mexico	724.1
13	Arizona	466.6		3	South Carolina	706.0
22	Arkansas	399.0		4	Alabama	654.6
6	California	641.6		5	Louisiana	653.4
21	Colorado	404.9		6	California	641.6
34	Connecticut	252.5		7	Massachusetts	555.0
23	Delaware	379.5		8	Illinois	516.4
1	Florida	777.2		9	Maryland	512.6
19	Georgia	427.1		10	Texas	487.7
45	Hawaii	117.7		11	New York	483.5
36	Idaho	224.7		12	Tennessee	470.3
8	Illinois	516.4		13	Arizona	466.6
24	Indiana	335.7		14	Missouri	466.5
37	Iowa	218.0		15	Michigan	458.6
25	Kansas	333.7		16	North Carolina	447.7
20	Kentucky	410.4		17	Alaska	445.3
5	Louisiana	653.4		18	Oklahoma	431.6
47	Maine	82.0		19	Georgia	427.1
9	Maryland	512.6		20	Kentucky	410.4
7	Massachusetts	555.0		21	Colorado	404.9
15	Michigan	458.6		22	Arkansas	399.0
41	Minnesota	184.1		23	Delaware	379.5
35	Mississippi	230.4		24	Indiana	335.7
14	Missouri	466.5		25	Kansas	333.7
46	Montana	114.6		26	Washington	317.8
33	Nebraska	256.2		27	New Jersey	304.8
29	Nevada	291.8		28	Oregon	301.1
49	New Hampshire	52.9		29	Nevada	291.8
27	New Jersey	304.8		30	Ohio	268.2
2	New Mexico	724.1		31	Rhode Island	265.5
11	New York	483.5		32	Wyoming	262.9
16	North Carolina	447.7		33	Nebraska	256.2
50	North Dakota	50.3		34	Connecticut	252.5
30	Ohio	268.2		35	Mississippi	230.4
18	Oklahoma	431.6		36	Idaho	224.7
28	Oregon	301.1		37	Iowa	218.0
38	Pennsylvania	212.4		38	Pennsylvania	212.4
31	Rhode Island	265.5		39	Virginia	196.8
3	South Carolina	706.0		40	Utah	186.2
43	South Dakota	125.3		41	Minnesota	184.1
12	Tennessee	470.3		42	West Virginia	140.0
10	Texas	487.7		43	South Dakota	125.3
40	Utah	186.2		43	Wisconsin	125.3
48	Vermont	73.5		45	Hawaii	117.7
39	Virginia	196.8		46	Montana	114.6
26	Washington	317.8		47	Maine	82.0
42	West Virginia	140.0		48	Vermont	73.5
43	Wisconsin	125.3		49	New Hampshire	52.9
32	Wyoming	262.9		50	North Dakota	50.3
					District of Columbia	1,454.7

Source: Federal Bureau of Investigation
    "Crime in the United States 1992" (Uniform Crime Reports, October 3, 1993)
*Aggravated assault is an attack for the purpose of inflicting severe bodily injury.

Percent Change in Rate of Aggravated Assaults: 1992 to 1996

National Percent Change = 12.1% Decrease*

ALPHA ORDER

RANK	STATE	PERCENT CHANGE
49	Alabama	(45.7)
4	Alaska	20.8
28	Arizona	(9.1)
31	Arkansas	(9.8)
42	California	(18.0)
48	Colorado	(36.9)
39	Connecticut	(15.0)
6	Delaware	11.1
30	Florida	(9.7)
27	Georgia	(8.0)
17	Hawaii	(3.1)
18	Idaho	(3.4)
8	Illinois	8.9
7	Indiana	10.7
21	Iowa	(5.6)
45	Kansas	(19.6)
50	Kentucky	(53.9)
29	Louisiana	(9.2)
19	Maine	(4.3)
20	Maryland	(4.6)
35	Massachusetts	(13.0)
37	Michigan	(14.0)
26	Minnesota	(7.8)
2	Mississippi	33.2
41	Missouri	(17.9)
32	Montana	(12.5)
3	Nebraska	33.1
1	Nevada	49.6
14	New Hampshire	2.8
32	New Jersey	(12.5)
40	New Mexico	(16.7)
47	New York	(26.2)
38	North Carolina	(14.1)
24	North Dakota	(7.2)
43	Ohio	(18.6)
15	Oklahoma	1.2
16	Oregon	(1.3)
21	Pennsylvania	(5.6)
32	Rhode Island	(12.5)
9	South Carolina	8.6
25	South Dakota	(7.3)
10	Tennessee	5.1
36	Texas	(13.6)
5	Utah	17.1
11	Vermont	4.6
23	Virginia	(6.3)
44	Washington	(19.3)
13	West Virginia	4.5
11	Wisconsin	4.6
46	Wyoming	(25.1)

RANK ORDER

RANK	STATE	PERCENT CHANGE
1	Nevada	49.6
2	Mississippi	33.2
3	Nebraska	33.1
4	Alaska	20.8
5	Utah	17.1
6	Delaware	11.1
7	Indiana	10.7
8	Illinois	8.9
9	South Carolina	8.6
10	Tennessee	5.1
11	Vermont	4.6
11	Wisconsin	4.6
13	West Virginia	4.5
14	New Hampshire	2.8
15	Oklahoma	1.2
16	Oregon	(1.3)
17	Hawaii	(3.1)
18	Idaho	(3.4)
19	Maine	(4.3)
20	Maryland	(4.6)
21	Iowa	(5.6)
21	Pennsylvania	(5.6)
23	Virginia	(6.3)
24	North Dakota	(7.2)
25	South Dakota	(7.3)
26	Minnesota	(7.8)
27	Georgia	(8.0)
28	Arizona	(9.1)
29	Louisiana	(9.2)
30	Florida	(9.7)
31	Arkansas	(9.8)
32	Montana	(12.5)
32	New Jersey	(12.5)
32	Rhode Island	(12.5)
35	Massachusetts	(13.0)
36	Texas	(13.6)
37	Michigan	(14.0)
38	North Carolina	(14.1)
39	Connecticut	(15.0)
40	New Mexico	(16.7)
41	Missouri	(17.9)
42	California	(18.0)
43	Ohio	(18.6)
44	Washington	(19.3)
45	Kansas	(19.6)
46	Wyoming	(25.1)
47	New York	(26.2)
48	Colorado	(36.9)
49	Alabama	(45.7)
50	Kentucky	(53.9)

District of Columbia — (20.1)

Source: Morgan Quitno Press using data from Federal Bureau of Investigation
   "Crime in the United States" (Uniform Crime Reports, 1992 and 1996 editions)
*Aggravated assault is an attack for the purpose of inflicting severe bodily injury.

Property Crimes in 1992

National Total = 12,505,917 Property Crimes*

ALPHA ORDER

RANK	STATE	CRIMES	% of USA
24	Alabama	181,837	1.45%
46	Alaska	28,816	0.23%
16	Arizona	243,629	1.95%
33	Arkansas	100,402	0.80%
1	California	1,716,137	13.72%
23	Colorado	186,684	1.49%
28	Connecticut	149,535	1.20%
45	Delaware	29,126	0.23%
3	Florida	964,533	7.71%
8	Georgia	382,934	3.06%
37	Hawaii	67,901	0.54%
42	Idaho	39,636	0.32%
5	Illinois	556,900	4.45%
18	Indiana	236,584	1.89%
31	Iowa	103,459	0.83%
29	Kansas	121,334	0.97%
30	Kentucky	104,692	0.84%
17	Louisiana	238,438	1.91%
41	Maine	41,900	0.34%
13	Maryland	256,418	2.05%
14	Massachusetts	253,344	2.03%
6	Michigan	456,800	3.65%
22	Minnesota	190,520	1.52%
32	Mississippi	101,181	0.81%
19	Missouri	226,246	1.81%
43	Montana	36,472	0.29%
38	Nebraska	63,846	0.51%
36	Nevada	73,077	0.58%
44	New Hampshire	32,828	0.26%
11	New Jersey	345,718	2.76%
35	New Mexico	86,942	0.70%
4	New York	858,178	6.86%
10	North Carolina	350,447	2.80%
50	North Dakota	17,935	0.14%
7	Ohio	456,017	3.65%
27	Oklahoma	154,459	1.24%
26	Oregon	158,100	1.26%
9	Pennsylvania	356,155	2.85%
40	Rhode Island	42,044	0.34%
25	South Carolina	178,298	1.43%
47	South Dakota	19,939	0.16%
20	Tennessee	220,534	1.76%
2	Texas	1,103,779	8.83%
34	Utah	97,322	0.78%
49	Vermont	18,813	0.15%
15	Virginia	250,211	2.00%
12	Washington	289,581	2.32%
39	West Virginia	43,455	0.35%
21	Wisconsin	202,448	1.62%
48	Wyoming	19,831	0.16%

RANK ORDER

RANK	STATE	CRIMES	% of USA
1	California	1,716,137	13.72%
2	Texas	1,103,779	8.83%
3	Florida	964,533	7.71%
4	New York	858,178	6.86%
5	Illinois	556,900	4.45%
6	Michigan	456,800	3.65%
7	Ohio	456,017	3.65%
8	Georgia	382,934	3.06%
9	Pennsylvania	356,155	2.85%
10	North Carolina	350,447	2.80%
11	New Jersey	345,718	2.76%
12	Washington	289,581	2.32%
13	Maryland	256,418	2.05%
14	Massachusetts	253,344	2.03%
15	Virginia	250,211	2.00%
16	Arizona	243,629	1.95%
17	Louisiana	238,438	1.91%
18	Indiana	236,584	1.89%
19	Missouri	226,246	1.81%
20	Tennessee	220,534	1.76%
21	Wisconsin	202,448	1.62%
22	Minnesota	190,520	1.52%
23	Colorado	186,684	1.49%
24	Alabama	181,837	1.45%
25	South Carolina	178,298	1.43%
26	Oregon	158,100	1.26%
27	Oklahoma	154,459	1.24%
28	Connecticut	149,535	1.20%
29	Kansas	121,334	0.97%
30	Kentucky	104,692	0.84%
31	Iowa	103,459	0.83%
32	Mississippi	101,181	0.81%
33	Arkansas	100,402	0.80%
34	Utah	97,322	0.78%
35	New Mexico	86,942	0.70%
36	Nevada	73,077	0.58%
37	Hawaii	67,901	0.54%
38	Nebraska	63,846	0.51%
39	West Virginia	43,455	0.35%
40	Rhode Island	42,044	0.34%
41	Maine	41,900	0.34%
42	Idaho	39,636	0.32%
43	Montana	36,472	0.29%
44	New Hampshire	32,828	0.26%
45	Delaware	29,126	0.23%
46	Alaska	28,816	0.23%
47	South Dakota	19,939	0.16%
48	Wyoming	19,831	0.16%
49	Vermont	18,813	0.15%
50	North Dakota	17,935	0.14%
	District of Columbia	50,502	0.40%

Source: Federal Bureau of Investigation
     "Crime in the United States 1992" (Uniform Crime Reports, October 3, 1993)
*Property crimes are offenses of burglary, larceny-theft and motor vehicle theft.

Percent Change in Number of Property Crimes: 1992 to 1996

National Percent Change = 5.7% Decrease*

ALPHA ORDER

ALPHA ORDER

RANK	STATE	PERCENT CHANGE	RANK	STATE	PERCENT CHANGE
26	Alabama	0.0	1	Arizona	17.0
27	Alaska	(0.5)	2	Utah	16.2
1	Arizona	17.0	3	Nevada	13.6
18	Arkansas	4.4	4	New Mexico	13.5
48	California	(19.3)	5	Tennessee	12.8
33	Colorado	(3.5)	6	Idaho	12.4
47	Connecticut	(16.5)	7	Oregon	12.1
16	Delaware	5.2	8	Hawaii	9.9
34	Florida	(3.8)	9	Georgia	8.9
9	Georgia	8.9	10	Mississippi	8.3
8	Hawaii	9.9	11	South Carolina	8.2
6	Idaho	12.4	12	Oklahoma	8.0
37	Illinois	(5.8)	13	Louisiana	7.8
29	Indiana	(2.2)	14	Missouri	6.4
39	Iowa	(6.9)	15	Kentucky	5.6
42	Kansas	(9.5)	16	Delaware	5.2
15	Kentucky	5.6	17	Washington	4.7
13	Louisiana	7.8	18	Arkansas	4.4
31	Maine	(3.0)	18	Montana	4.4
23	Maryland	1.5	20	Nebraska	3.5
49	Massachusetts	(23.2)	21	North Carolina	3.2
38	Michigan	(5.9)	22	South Dakota	2.5
24	Minnesota	0.8	23	Maryland	1.5
10	Mississippi	8.3	24	Minnesota	0.8
14	Missouri	6.4	25	Pennsylvania	0.2
18	Montana	4.4	26	Alabama	0.0
20	Nebraska	3.5	27	Alaska	(0.5)
3	Nevada	13.6	28	Ohio	(1.3)
35	New Hampshire	(4.2)	29	Indiana	(2.2)
44	New Jersey	(12.2)	30	Wyoming	(2.9)
4	New Mexico	13.5	31	Maine	(3.0)
50	New York	(27.8)	32	Virginia	(3.2)
21	North Carolina	3.2	33	Colorado	(3.5)
40	North Dakota	(7.2)	34	Florida	(3.8)
28	Ohio	(1.3)	35	New Hampshire	(4.2)
12	Oklahoma	8.0	36	West Virginia	(4.5)
7	Oregon	12.1	37	Illinois	(5.8)
25	Pennsylvania	0.2	38	Michigan	(5.9)
46	Rhode Island	(14.1)	39	Iowa	(6.9)
11	South Carolina	8.2	40	North Dakota	(7.2)
22	South Dakota	2.5	41	Wisconsin	(9.0)
5	Tennessee	12.8	42	Kansas	(9.5)
44	Texas	(12.2)	43	Vermont	(9.8)
2	Utah	16.2	44	New Jersey	(12.2)
43	Vermont	(9.8)	44	Texas	(12.2)
32	Virginia	(3.2)	46	Rhode Island	(14.1)
17	Washington	4.7	47	Connecticut	(16.5)
36	West Virginia	(4.5)	48	California	(19.3)
41	Wisconsin	(9.0)	49	Massachusetts	(23.2)
30	Wyoming	(2.9)	50	New York	(27.8)

| | | | | District of Columbia | 1.4 |

Source: Morgan Quitno Press using data from Federal Bureau of Investigation
    "Crime in the United States" (Uniform Crime Reports, 1992 and 1996 editions)
*Property crimes are offenses of burglary, larceny-theft and motor vehicle theft.

Property Crime Rate in 1992

National Rate = 4,902.7 Property Crimes per 100,000 Population*

ALPHA ORDER				RANK ORDER		
RANK	**STATE**	**RATE**		**RANK**	**STATE**	**RATE**
26	Alabama	4,396.4		1	Florida	7,151.0
17	Alaska	4,909.0		2	Arizona	6,357.8
2	Arizona	6,357.8		3	Texas	6,251.6
33	Arkansas	4,185.2		4	Hawaii	5,853.5
8	California	5,559.8		5	Georgia	5,672.3
11	Colorado	5,379.9		6	Washington	5,638.3
23	Connecticut	4,557.6		7	Louisiana	5,561.9
31	Delaware	4,227.3		8	California	5,559.8
1	Florida	7,151.0		9	Nevada	5,506.9
5	Georgia	5,672.3		10	New Mexico	5,499.2
4	Hawaii	5,853.5		11	Colorado	5,379.9
41	Idaho	3,714.7		12	Utah	5,368.0
21	Illinois	4,788.1		13	Oregon	5,310.7
35	Indiana	4,178.5		14	Maryland	5,224.5
42	Iowa	3,679.2		15	North Carolina	5,121.2
19	Kansas	4,809.1		16	South Carolina	4,948.6
49	Kentucky	2,788.1		17	Alaska	4,909.0
7	Louisiana	5,561.9		18	Michigan	4,840.5
43	Maine	3,392.7		19	Kansas	4,809.1
14	Maryland	5,224.5		20	Oklahoma	4,808.8
32	Massachusetts	4,223.8		21	Illinois	4,788.1
18	Michigan	4,840.5		22	New York	4,736.3
30	Minnesota	4,252.7		23	Connecticut	4,557.6
40	Mississippi	3,870.7		24	New Jersey	4,438.5
28	Missouri	4,356.7		25	Montana	4,426.2
25	Montana	4,426.2		26	Alabama	4,396.4
38	Nebraska	3,975.5		27	Tennessee	4,389.6
9	Nevada	5,506.9		28	Missouri	4,356.7
46	New Hampshire	2,954.8		29	Wyoming	4,255.6
24	New Jersey	4,438.5		30	Minnesota	4,252.7
10	New Mexico	5,499.2		31	Delaware	4,227.3
22	New York	4,736.3		32	Massachusetts	4,223.8
15	North Carolina	5,121.2		33	Arkansas	4,185.2
47	North Dakota	2,820.0		34	Rhode Island	4,183.5
36	Ohio	4,139.6		35	Indiana	4,178.5
20	Oklahoma	4,808.8		36	Ohio	4,139.6
13	Oregon	5,310.7		37	Wisconsin	4,043.3
45	Pennsylvania	2,965.7		38	Nebraska	3,975.5
34	Rhode Island	4,183.5		39	Virginia	3,923.6
16	South Carolina	4,948.6		40	Mississippi	3,870.7
48	South Dakota	2,804.4		41	Idaho	3,714.7
27	Tennessee	4,389.6		42	Iowa	3,679.2
3	Texas	6,251.6		43	Maine	3,392.7
12	Utah	5,368.0		44	Vermont	3,300.5
44	Vermont	3,300.5		45	Pennsylvania	2,965.7
39	Virginia	3,923.6		46	New Hampshire	2,954.8
6	Washington	5,638.3		47	North Dakota	2,820.0
50	West Virginia	2,398.2		48	South Dakota	2,804.4
37	Wisconsin	4,043.3		49	Kentucky	2,788.1
29	Wyoming	4,255.6		50	West Virginia	2,398.2
					District of Columbia	8,574.2

Source: Federal Bureau of Investigation
   "Crime in the United States 1992" (Uniform Crime Reports, October 3, 1993)
*Property crimes are offenses of burglary, larceny-theft and motor vehicle theft.

Percent Change in Property Crime Rate: 1992 to 1996

National Percent Change = 9.3% Decrease*

ALPHA ORDER			RANK ORDER		
RANK	STATE	PERCENT CHANGE	RANK	STATE	PERCENT CHANGE
25	Alabama	(3.2)	1	Hawaii	7.7
28	Alaska	(3.8)	2	Tennessee	6.5
12	Arizona	1.2	3	Louisiana	6.3
17	Arkansas	(0.2)	4	South Carolina	5.4
48	California	(21.8)	5	Utah	5.3
42	Colorado	(12.4)	6	Oklahoma	5.1
46	Connecticut	(16.3)	7	New Mexico	4.8
15	Delaware	0.0	8	Mississippi	4.2
39	Florida	(9.9)	8	Oregon	4.2
15	Georgia	0.0	10	Missouri	3.1
1	Hawaii	7.7	11	Kentucky	2.1
13	Idaho	0.8	12	Arizona	1.2
34	Illinois	(7.5)	13	Idaho	0.8
29	Indiana	(5.2)	14	Nebraska	0.7
36	Iowa	(8.2)	15	Delaware	0.0
40	Kansas	(11.3)	15	Georgia	0.0
11	Kentucky	2.1	17	Arkansas	(0.2)
3	Louisiana	6.3	17	Pennsylvania	(0.2)
26	Maine	(3.6)	19	South Dakota	(0.4)
20	Maryland	(1.8)	20	Maryland	(1.8)
49	Massachusetts	(24.4)	21	Montana	(2.1)
33	Michigan	(7.4)	22	Ohio	(2.7)
24	Minnesota	(3.0)	23	Washington	(2.8)
8	Mississippi	4.2	24	Minnesota	(3.0)
10	Missouri	3.1	25	Alabama	(3.2)
21	Montana	(2.1)	26	Maine	(3.6)
14	Nebraska	0.7	26	North Carolina	(3.6)
31	Nevada	(5.9)	28	Alaska	(3.8)
38	New Hampshire	(8.4)	29	Indiana	(5.2)
45	New Jersey	(14.4)	29	West Virginia	(5.2)
7	New Mexico	4.8	31	Nevada	(5.9)
50	New York	(28.1)	31	Wyoming	(5.9)
26	North Carolina	(3.6)	33	Michigan	(7.4)
37	North Dakota	(8.3)	34	Illinois	(7.5)
22	Ohio	(2.7)	35	Virginia	(7.6)
6	Oklahoma	5.1	36	Iowa	(8.2)
8	Oregon	4.2	37	North Dakota	(8.3)
17	Pennsylvania	(0.2)	38	New Hampshire	(8.4)
44	Rhode Island	(12.8)	39	Florida	(9.9)
4	South Carolina	5.4	40	Kansas	(11.3)
19	South Dakota	(0.4)	41	Wisconsin	(11.7)
2	Tennessee	6.5	42	Colorado	(12.4)
47	Texas	(19.0)	43	Vermont	(12.7)
5	Utah	5.3	44	Rhode Island	(12.8)
43	Vermont	(12.7)	45	New Jersey	(14.4)
35	Virginia	(7.6)	46	Connecticut	(16.3)
23	Washington	(2.8)	47	Texas	(19.0)
29	West Virginia	(5.2)	48	California	(21.8)
41	Wisconsin	(11.7)	49	Massachusetts	(24.4)
31	Wyoming	(5.9)	50	New York	(28.1)
				District of Columbia	9.9

Source: Morgan Quitno Press using data from Federal Bureau of Investigation
"Crime in the United States" (Uniform Crime Reports, 1992 and 1996 editions)
*Property crimes are offenses of burglary, larceny-theft and motor vehicle theft.

Burglaries in 1992

National Total = 2,979,884 Burglaries*

RANK	STATE	BURGLARIES	% of USA
21	Alabama	49,053	1.65%
46	Alaska	5,170	0.17%
18	Arizona	54,095	1.82%
32	Arkansas	26,214	0.88%
1	California	427,491	14.35%
25	Colorado	37,853	1.27%
26	Connecticut	36,372	1.22%
44	Delaware	6,598	0.22%
3	Florida	254,755	8.55%
9	Georgia	97,402	3.27%
37	Hawaii	13,006	0.44%
42	Idaho	7,934	0.27%
5	Illinois	125,306	4.21%
19	Indiana	53,907	1.81%
34	Iowa	21,197	0.71%
30	Kansas	32,639	1.10%
31	Kentucky	27,378	0.92%
14	Louisiana	58,574	1.97%
41	Maine	10,156	0.34%
17	Maryland	55,520	1.86%
12	Massachusetts	64,318	2.16%
8	Michigan	98,257	3.30%
24	Minnesota	39,859	1.34%
28	Mississippi	33,533	1.13%
16	Missouri	57,127	1.92%
45	Montana	5,306	0.18%
38	Nebraska	11,477	0.39%
35	Nevada	17,108	0.57%
43	New Hampshire	6,909	0.23%
11	New Jersey	75,508	2.53%
33	New Mexico	23,896	0.80%
4	New York	193,548	6.50%
6	North Carolina	113,117	3.80%
50	North Dakota	2,487	0.08%
7	Ohio	104,357	3.50%
23	Oklahoma	43,678	1.47%
29	Oregon	32,945	1.11%
10	Pennsylvania	75,834	2.54%
40	Rhode Island	10,529	0.35%
20	South Carolina	49,669	1.67%
48	South Dakota	3,849	0.13%
13	Tennessee	63,665	2.14%
2	Texas	268,928	9.02%
36	Utah	16,045	0.54%
47	Vermont	4,706	0.16%
22	Virginia	45,217	1.52%
15	Washington	57,612	1.93%
39	West Virginia	11,287	0.38%
27	Wisconsin	34,645	1.16%
49	Wyoming	3,127	0.10%

RANK	STATE	BURGLARIES	% of USA
1	California	427,491	14.35%
2	Texas	268,928	9.02%
3	Florida	254,755	8.55%
4	New York	193,548	6.50%
5	Illinois	125,306	4.21%
6	North Carolina	113,117	3.80%
7	Ohio	104,357	3.50%
8	Michigan	98,257	3.30%
9	Georgia	97,402	3.27%
10	Pennsylvania	75,834	2.54%
11	New Jersey	75,508	2.53%
12	Massachusetts	64,318	2.16%
13	Tennessee	63,665	2.14%
14	Louisiana	58,574	1.97%
15	Washington	57,612	1.93%
16	Missouri	57,127	1.92%
17	Maryland	55,520	1.86%
18	Arizona	54,095	1.82%
19	Indiana	53,907	1.81%
20	South Carolina	49,669	1.67%
21	Alabama	49,053	1.65%
22	Virginia	45,217	1.52%
23	Oklahoma	43,678	1.47%
24	Minnesota	39,859	1.34%
25	Colorado	37,853	1.27%
26	Connecticut	36,372	1.22%
27	Wisconsin	34,645	1.16%
28	Mississippi	33,533	1.13%
29	Oregon	32,945	1.11%
30	Kansas	32,639	1.10%
31	Kentucky	27,378	0.92%
32	Arkansas	26,214	0.88%
33	New Mexico	23,896	0.80%
34	Iowa	21,197	0.71%
35	Nevada	17,108	0.57%
36	Utah	16,045	0.54%
37	Hawaii	13,006	0.44%
38	Nebraska	11,477	0.39%
39	West Virginia	11,287	0.38%
40	Rhode Island	10,529	0.35%
41	Maine	10,156	0.34%
42	Idaho	7,934	0.27%
43	New Hampshire	6,909	0.23%
44	Delaware	6,598	0.22%
45	Montana	5,306	0.18%
46	Alaska	5,170	0.17%
47	Vermont	4,706	0.16%
48	South Dakota	3,849	0.13%
49	Wyoming	3,127	0.10%
50	North Dakota	2,487	0.08%
	District of Columbia	10,721	0.36%

Source: Federal Bureau of Investigation
"Crime in the United States 1992" (Uniform Crime Reports, October 3, 1993)
*Burglary is the unlawful entry of a structure to commit a felony or theft. Attempts are included.

Percent Change in Number of Burglaries: 1992 to 1996

National Percent Change = 16.1% Decrease*

ALPHA ORDER			RANK ORDER		
RANK	STATE	PERCENT CHANGE	RANK	STATE	PERCENT CHANGE
32	Alabama	(12.7)	1	Nevada	14.3
8	Alaska	(1.0)	2	Idaho	6.3
5	Arizona	2.8	3	South Dakota	5.9
20	Arkansas	(8.7)	4	Utah	5.7
48	California	(27.0)	5	Arizona	2.8
21	Colorado	(9.0)	6	Wyoming	1.8
46	Connecticut	(24.2)	7	Washington	1.6
27	Delaware	(11.6)	8	Alaska	(1.0)
36	Florida	(14.0)	9	New Mexico	(1.3)
38	Georgia	(15.8)	10	Hawaii	(1.7)
10	Hawaii	(1.7)	11	Kentucky	(2.3)
2	Idaho	6.3	12	Tennessee	(2.8)
35	Illinois	(13.7)	13	Louisiana	(3.7)
37	Indiana	(15.1)	14	Oregon	(3.9)
23	Iowa	(10.6)	15	South Carolina	(4.4)
43	Kansas	(22.7)	16	Oklahoma	(5.1)
11	Kentucky	(2.3)	17	Montana	(7.5)
13	Louisiana	(3.7)	18	Mississippi	(8.3)
19	Maine	(8.4)	19	Maine	(8.4)
22	Maryland	(9.3)	20	Arkansas	(8.7)
50	Massachusetts	(33.3)	21	Colorado	(9.0)
31	Michigan	(12.6)	22	Maryland	(9.3)
25	Minnesota	(10.9)	23	Iowa	(10.6)
18	Mississippi	(8.3)	23	Ohio	(10.6)
40	Missouri	(16.1)	25	Minnesota	(10.9)
17	Montana	(7.5)	26	Nebraska	(11.5)
26	Nebraska	(11.5)	27	Delaware	(11.6)
1	Nevada	14.3	27	West Virginia	(11.6)
47	New Hampshire	(26.7)	29	Pennsylvania	(12.3)
41	New Jersey	(16.2)	30	Wisconsin	(12.4)
9	New Mexico	(1.3)	31	Michigan	(12.6)
49	New York	(32.9)	32	Alabama	(12.7)
33	North Carolina	(12.9)	33	North Carolina	(12.9)
42	North Dakota	(19.9)	34	Virginia	(13.2)
23	Ohio	(10.6)	35	Illinois	(13.7)
16	Oklahoma	(5.1)	36	Florida	(14.0)
14	Oregon	(3.9)	37	Indiana	(15.1)
29	Pennsylvania	(12.3)	38	Georgia	(15.8)
43	Rhode Island	(22.7)	38	Vermont	(15.8)
15	South Carolina	(4.4)	40	Missouri	(16.1)
3	South Dakota	5.9	41	New Jersey	(16.2)
12	Tennessee	(2.8)	42	North Dakota	(19.9)
45	Texas	(24.0)	43	Kansas	(22.7)
4	Utah	5.7	43	Rhode Island	(22.7)
38	Vermont	(15.8)	45	Texas	(24.0)
34	Virginia	(13.2)	46	Connecticut	(24.2)
7	Washington	1.6	47	New Hampshire	(26.7)
27	West Virginia	(11.6)	48	California	(27.0)
30	Wisconsin	(12.4)	49	New York	(32.9)
6	Wyoming	1.8	50	Massachusetts	(33.3)
				District of Columbia	(8.3)

Source: Morgan Quitno Press using data from Federal Bureau of Investigation
  "Crime in the United States" (Uniform Crime Reports, 1992 and 1996 editions)
*Burglary is the unlawful entry of a structure to commit a felony or theft. Attempts are included.

Burglary Rate in 1992

National Rate = 1,168.2 Burglaries per 100,000 Population*

ALPHA ORDER				RANK ORDER		
RANK	STATE	RATE		RANK	STATE	RATE
15	Alabama	1,186.0		1	Florida	1,888.8
35	Alaska	880.7		2	North Carolina	1,653.0
6	Arizona	1,411.7		3	Texas	1,523.2
22	Arkansas	1,092.7		4	New Mexico	1,511.4
7	California	1,384.9		5	Georgia	1,442.8
23	Colorado	1,090.9		6	Arizona	1,411.7
19	Connecticut	1,108.6		7	California	1,384.9
30	Delaware	957.6		8	South Carolina	1,378.5
1	Florida	1,888.8		9	Louisiana	1,366.3
5	Georgia	1,442.8		10	Oklahoma	1,359.8
18	Hawaii	1,121.2		11	Kansas	1,293.7
39	Idaho	743.6		12	Nevada	1,289.2
24	Illinois	1,077.3		13	Mississippi	1,282.8
31	Indiana	952.1		14	Tennessee	1,267.2
38	Iowa	753.8		15	Alabama	1,186.0
11	Kansas	1,293.7		16	Maryland	1,131.2
40	Kentucky	729.1		17	Washington	1,121.7
9	Louisiana	1,366.3		18	Hawaii	1,121.2
37	Maine	822.3		19	Connecticut	1,108.6
16	Maryland	1,131.2		20	Oregon	1,106.7
25	Massachusetts	1,072.3		21	Missouri	1,100.1
28	Michigan	1,041.2		22	Arkansas	1,092.7
33	Minnesota	889.7		23	Colorado	1,090.9
13	Mississippi	1,282.8		24	Illinois	1,077.3
21	Missouri	1,100.1		25	Massachusetts	1,072.3
45	Montana	643.9		26	New York	1,068.2
41	Nebraska	714.6		27	Rhode Island	1,047.7
12	Nevada	1,289.2		28	Michigan	1,041.2
48	New Hampshire	621.9		29	New Jersey	969.4
29	New Jersey	969.4		30	Delaware	957.6
4	New Mexico	1,511.4		31	Indiana	952.1
26	New York	1,068.2		32	Ohio	947.3
2	North Carolina	1,653.0		33	Minnesota	889.7
50	North Dakota	391.0		34	Utah	885.0
32	Ohio	947.3		35	Alaska	880.7
10	Oklahoma	1,359.8		36	Vermont	825.6
20	Oregon	1,106.7		37	Maine	822.3
46	Pennsylvania	631.5		38	Iowa	753.8
27	Rhode Island	1,047.7		39	Idaho	743.6
8	South Carolina	1,378.5		40	Kentucky	729.1
49	South Dakota	541.4		41	Nebraska	714.6
14	Tennessee	1,267.2		42	Virginia	709.1
3	Texas	1,523.2		43	Wisconsin	691.9
34	Utah	885.0		44	Wyoming	671.0
36	Vermont	825.6		45	Montana	643.9
42	Virginia	709.1		46	Pennsylvania	631.5
17	Washington	1,121.7		47	West Virginia	622.9
47	West Virginia	622.9		48	New Hampshire	621.9
43	Wisconsin	691.9		49	South Dakota	541.4
44	Wyoming	671.0		50	North Dakota	391.0
				District of Columbia		1,820.2

Source: Federal Bureau of Investigation
  "Crime in the United States 1992" (Uniform Crime Reports, October 3, 1993)
*Burglary is the unlawful entry of a structure to commit a felony or theft. Attempts are included.

Percent Change in Burglary Rate: 1992 to 1996

National Percent Change = 19.3% Decrease*

ALPHA ORDER			RANK ORDER		
RANK	STATE	PERCENT CHANGE	RANK	STATE	PERCENT CHANGE
31	Alabama	(15.5)	1	South Dakota	2.9
5	Alaska	(4.3)	2	Wyoming	(1.3)
17	Arizona	(11.0)	3	Hawaii	(3.7)
24	Arkansas	(12.8)	4	Utah	(4.1)
46	California	(29.3)	5	Alaska	(4.3)
34	Colorado	(17.4)	6	Idaho	(4.6)
44	Connecticut	(24.0)	7	Louisiana	(5.2)
32	Delaware	(16.0)	8	Nevada	(5.4)
40	Florida	(19.5)	9	Kentucky	(5.6)
43	Georgia	(22.7)	10	Washington	(5.7)
3	Hawaii	(3.7)	11	South Carolina	(6.9)
6	Idaho	(4.6)	12	Oklahoma	(7.7)
30	Illinois	(15.2)	13	Tennessee	(8.2)
35	Indiana	(17.7)	14	New Mexico	(8.9)
19	Iowa	(11.8)	15	Maine	(9.0)
45	Kansas	(24.1)	16	Oregon	(10.7)
9	Kentucky	(5.6)	17	Arizona	(11.0)
7	Louisiana	(5.2)	18	Mississippi	(11.7)
15	Maine	(9.0)	19	Iowa	(11.8)
21	Maryland	(12.3)	19	Ohio	(11.8)
50	Massachusetts	(34.3)	21	Maryland	(12.3)
26	Michigan	(14.0)	21	West Virginia	(12.3)
28	Minnesota	(14.3)	23	Pennsylvania	(12.7)
18	Mississippi	(11.7)	24	Arkansas	(12.8)
39	Missouri	(18.7)	25	Montana	(13.3)
25	Montana	(13.3)	26	Michigan	(14.0)
26	Nebraska	(14.0)	26	Nebraska	(14.0)
8	Nevada	(5.4)	28	Minnesota	(14.3)
47	New Hampshire	(29.9)	29	Wisconsin	(15.0)
36	New Jersey	(18.3)	30	Illinois	(15.2)
14	New Mexico	(8.9)	31	Alabama	(15.5)
49	New York	(33.2)	32	Delaware	(16.0)
38	North Carolina	(18.6)	33	Virginia	(17.1)
41	North Dakota	(20.9)	34	Colorado	(17.4)
19	Ohio	(11.8)	35	Indiana	(17.7)
12	Oklahoma	(7.7)	36	New Jersey	(18.3)
16	Oregon	(10.7)	37	Vermont	(18.5)
23	Pennsylvania	(12.7)	38	North Carolina	(18.6)
42	Rhode Island	(21.6)	39	Missouri	(18.7)
11	South Carolina	(6.9)	40	Florida	(19.5)
1	South Dakota	2.9	41	North Dakota	(20.9)
13	Tennessee	(8.2)	42	Rhode Island	(21.6)
47	Texas	(29.9)	43	Georgia	(22.7)
4	Utah	(4.1)	44	Connecticut	(24.0)
37	Vermont	(18.5)	45	Kansas	(24.1)
33	Virginia	(17.1)	46	California	(29.3)
10	Washington	(5.7)	47	New Hampshire	(29.9)
21	West Virginia	(12.3)	47	Texas	(29.9)
29	Wisconsin	(15.0)	49	New York	(33.2)
2	Wyoming	(1.3)	50	Massachusetts	(34.3)
				District of Columbia	(0.6)

Source: Morgan Quitno Press using data from Federal Bureau of Investigation
    "Crime in the United States" (Uniform Crime Reports, 1992 and 1996 editions)
*Burglary is the unlawful entry of a structure to commit a felony or theft. Attempts are included.

Larcenies and Thefts in 1992

National Total = 7,915,199 Larcenies and Thefts*

RANK	STATE	THEFTS	% of USA
24	Alabama	117,801	1.49%
45	Alaska	20,728	0.26%
15	Arizona	158,053	2.00%
33	Arkansas	66,288	0.84%
1	California	968,534	12.24%
22	Colorado	131,169	1.66%
28	Connecticut	89,463	1.13%
46	Delaware	20,419	0.26%
3	Florida	598,093	7.56%
8	Georgia	246,619	3.12%
36	Hawaii	50,544	0.64%
39	Idaho	30,023	0.38%
5	Illinois	359,618	4.54%
16	Indiana	157,181	1.99%
30	Iowa	77,788	0.98%
29	Kansas	80,526	1.02%
32	Kentucky	69,186	0.87%
17	Louisiana	152,938	1.93%
40	Maine	29,966	0.38%
14	Maryland	165,244	2.09%
20	Massachusetts	141,610	1.79%
7	Michigan	299,486	3.78%
21	Minnesota	134,750	1.70%
34	Mississippi	58,851	0.74%
19	Missouri	143,288	1.81%
41	Montana	29,243	0.37%
37	Nebraska	49,144	0.62%
38	Nevada	46,714	0.59%
44	New Hampshire	23,754	0.30%
12	New Jersey	206,686	2.61%
35	New Mexico	57,072	0.72%
4	New York	495,708	6.26%
10	North Carolina	217,717	2.75%
49	North Dakota	14,498	0.18%
6	Ohio	299,774	3.79%
27	Oklahoma	94,180	1.19%
26	Oregon	109,274	1.38%
9	Pennsylvania	224,150	2.83%
43	Rhode Island	24,052	0.30%
25	South Carolina	116,186	1.47%
48	South Dakota	15,371	0.19%
23	Tennessee	127,934	1.62%
2	Texas	689,780	8.71%
31	Utah	76,964	0.97%
50	Vermont	13,507	0.17%
13	Virginia	185,506	2.34%
11	Washington	207,755	2.62%
42	West Virginia	29,200	0.37%
18	Wisconsin	146,198	1.85%
47	Wyoming	16,003	0.20%

RANK	STATE	THEFTS	% of USA
1	California	968,534	12.24%
2	Texas	689,780	8.71%
3	Florida	598,093	7.56%
4	New York	495,708	6.26%
5	Illinois	359,618	4.54%
6	Ohio	299,774	3.79%
7	Michigan	299,486	3.78%
8	Georgia	246,619	3.12%
9	Pennsylvania	224,150	2.83%
10	North Carolina	217,717	2.75%
11	Washington	207,755	2.62%
12	New Jersey	206,686	2.61%
13	Virginia	185,506	2.34%
14	Maryland	165,244	2.09%
15	Arizona	158,053	2.00%
16	Indiana	157,181	1.99%
17	Louisiana	152,938	1.93%
18	Wisconsin	146,198	1.85%
19	Missouri	143,288	1.81%
20	Massachusetts	141,610	1.79%
21	Minnesota	134,750	1.70%
22	Colorado	131,169	1.66%
23	Tennessee	127,934	1.62%
24	Alabama	117,801	1.49%
25	South Carolina	116,186	1.47%
26	Oregon	109,274	1.38%
27	Oklahoma	94,180	1.19%
28	Connecticut	89,463	1.13%
29	Kansas	80,526	1.02%
30	Iowa	77,788	0.98%
31	Utah	76,964	0.97%
32	Kentucky	69,186	0.87%
33	Arkansas	66,288	0.84%
34	Mississippi	58,851	0.74%
35	New Mexico	57,072	0.72%
36	Hawaii	50,544	0.64%
37	Nebraska	49,144	0.62%
38	Nevada	46,714	0.59%
39	Idaho	30,023	0.38%
40	Maine	29,966	0.38%
41	Montana	29,243	0.37%
42	West Virginia	29,200	0.37%
43	Rhode Island	24,052	0.30%
44	New Hampshire	23,754	0.30%
45	Alaska	20,728	0.26%
46	Delaware	20,419	0.26%
47	Wyoming	16,003	0.20%
48	South Dakota	15,371	0.19%
49	North Dakota	14,498	0.18%
50	Vermont	13,507	0.17%
	District of Columbia	30,663	0.39%

Source: Federal Bureau of Investigation
"Crime in the United States 1992" (Uniform Crime Reports, October 3, 1993)
*Larceny and theft is the unlawful taking of property without use of force, violence or fraud. Attempts are included.
Motor vehicle thefts are excluded.

Percent Change in Number of Larcenies and Thefts: 1992 to 1996

National Percent Change = 0.3% Decrease*

ALPHA ORDER				RANK ORDER		
RANK	STATE	PERCENT CHANGE		RANK	STATE	PERCENT CHANGE
22	Alabama	4.7		1	Arizona	19.1
34	Alaska	(0.8)		1	Tennessee	19.1
1	Arizona	19.1		3	Missouri	17.9
14	Arkansas	10.1		4	Mississippi	17.8
48	California	(14.3)		5	Oregon	17.7
32	Colorado	(0.5)		6	Georgia	17.1
46	Connecticut	(9.1)		7	Oklahoma	16.3
19	Delaware	6.1		8	New Mexico	14.1
29	Florida	1.2		9	Utah	13.7
6	Georgia	17.1		10	Louisiana	13.3
16	Hawaii	8.2		11	Idaho	12.8
11	Idaho	12.8		12	Nevada	11.9
31	Illinois	(0.3)		13	South Carolina	11.6
28	Indiana	2.3		14	Arkansas	10.1
45	Iowa	(7.6)		15	North Carolina	9.6
37	Kansas	(3.0)		16	Hawaii	8.2
18	Kentucky	6.5		17	Pennsylvania	7.4
10	Louisiana	13.3		18	Kentucky	6.5
35	Maine	(1.4)		19	Delaware	6.1
21	Maryland	5.2		20	Montana	5.8
49	Massachusetts	(15.6)		21	Maryland	5.2
44	Michigan	(7.5)		22	Alabama	4.7
26	Minnesota	2.9		23	Ohio	3.8
4	Mississippi	17.8		23	Washington	3.8
3	Missouri	17.9		25	New Hampshire	3.6
20	Montana	5.8		26	Minnesota	2.9
27	Nebraska	2.4		27	Nebraska	2.4
12	Nevada	11.9		28	Indiana	2.3
25	New Hampshire	3.6		29	Florida	1.2
41	New Jersey	(6.2)		30	South Dakota	1.0
8	New Mexico	14.1		31	Illinois	(0.3)
50	New York	(19.4)		32	Colorado	(0.5)
15	North Carolina	9.6		33	Virginia	(0.7)
43	North Dakota	(7.3)		34	Alaska	(0.8)
23	Ohio	3.8		35	Maine	(1.4)
7	Oklahoma	16.3		36	Rhode Island	(2.8)
5	Oregon	17.7		37	Kansas	(3.0)
17	Pennsylvania	7.4		38	West Virginia	(3.1)
36	Rhode Island	(2.8)		39	Wyoming	(3.7)
13	South Carolina	11.6		40	Texas	(4.4)
30	South Dakota	1.0		41	New Jersey	(6.2)
1	Tennessee	19.1		42	Wisconsin	(7.0)
40	Texas	(4.4)		43	North Dakota	(7.3)
9	Utah	13.7		44	Michigan	(7.5)
47	Vermont	(10.2)		45	Iowa	(7.6)
33	Virginia	(0.7)		46	Connecticut	(9.1)
23	Washington	3.8		47	Vermont	(10.2)
38	West Virginia	(3.1)		48	California	(14.3)
42	Wisconsin	(7.0)		49	Massachusetts	(15.6)
39	Wyoming	(3.7)		50	New York	(19.4)
					District of Columbia	2.4

Source: Morgan Quitno Press using data from Federal Bureau of Investigation
  "Crime in the United States" (Uniform Crime Reports, 1992 and 1996 editions)
*Larceny and theft is the unlawful taking of property without use of force, violence or fraud. Attempts are included.
Motor vehicle thefts are excluded.

Larceny and Theft Rate in 1992

National Rate = 3,103.0 Larcenies and Thefts per 100,000 Population*

ALPHA ORDER

RANK	STATE	RATE
29	Alabama	2,848.2
13	Alaska	3,531.2
4	Arizona	4,124.6
33	Arkansas	2,763.2
21	California	3,137.8
7	Colorado	3,780.1
36	Connecticut	2,726.7
25	Delaware	2,963.6
1	Florida	4,434.3
9	Georgia	3,653.1
2	Hawaii	4,357.2
30	Idaho	2,813.8
22	Illinois	3,091.9
31	Indiana	2,776.1
32	Iowa	2,766.3
18	Kansas	3,191.7
49	Kentucky	1,842.5
11	Louisiana	3,567.5
40	Maine	2,426.4
16	Maryland	3,366.8
43	Massachusetts	2,361.0
20	Michigan	3,173.5
24	Minnesota	3,007.8
45	Mississippi	2,251.4
34	Missouri	2,759.3
12	Montana	3,548.9
23	Nebraska	3,060.0
14	Nevada	3,520.3
47	New Hampshire	2,138.1
38	New Jersey	2,653.6
10	New Mexico	3,609.9
35	New York	2,735.8
19	North Carolina	3,181.6
44	North Dakota	2,279.6
37	Ohio	2,721.3
26	Oklahoma	2,932.1
8	Oregon	3,670.6
48	Pennsylvania	1,866.5
41	Rhode Island	2,393.2
17	South Carolina	3,224.7
46	South Dakota	2,161.9
39	Tennessee	2,546.5
6	Texas	3,906.8
3	Utah	4,245.1
42	Vermont	2,369.6
28	Virginia	2,909.0
5	Washington	4,045.1
50	West Virginia	1,611.5
27	Wisconsin	2,919.9
15	Wyoming	3,434.1

RANK ORDER

RANK	STATE	RATE
1	Florida	4,434.3
2	Hawaii	4,357.2
3	Utah	4,245.1
4	Arizona	4,124.6
5	Washington	4,045.1
6	Texas	3,906.8
7	Colorado	3,780.1
8	Oregon	3,670.6
9	Georgia	3,653.1
10	New Mexico	3,609.9
11	Louisiana	3,567.5
12	Montana	3,548.9
13	Alaska	3,531.2
14	Nevada	3,520.3
15	Wyoming	3,434.1
16	Maryland	3,366.8
17	South Carolina	3,224.7
18	Kansas	3,191.7
19	North Carolina	3,181.6
20	Michigan	3,173.5
21	California	3,137.8
22	Illinois	3,091.9
23	Nebraska	3,060.0
24	Minnesota	3,007.8
25	Delaware	2,963.6
26	Oklahoma	2,932.1
27	Wisconsin	2,919.9
28	Virginia	2,909.0
29	Alabama	2,848.2
30	Idaho	2,813.8
31	Indiana	2,776.1
32	Iowa	2,766.3
33	Arkansas	2,763.2
34	Missouri	2,759.3
35	New York	2,735.8
36	Connecticut	2,726.7
37	Ohio	2,721.3
38	New Jersey	2,653.6
39	Tennessee	2,546.5
40	Maine	2,426.4
41	Rhode Island	2,393.2
42	Vermont	2,369.6
43	Massachusetts	2,361.0
44	North Dakota	2,279.6
45	Mississippi	2,251.4
46	South Dakota	2,161.9
47	New Hampshire	2,138.1
48	Pennsylvania	1,866.5
49	Kentucky	1,842.5
50	West Virginia	1,611.5
	District of Columbia	5,205.9

Source: Federal Bureau of Investigation
"Crime in the United States 1992" (Uniform Crime Reports, October 3, 1993)
*Larceny and theft is the unlawful taking of property without use of force, violence or fraud. Attempts are included. Motor vehicle thefts are excluded.

Percent Change in Larceny and Theft Rate: 1992 to 1996

National Percent Change = 4.1% Decrease*

ALPHA ORDER			RANK ORDER		
RANK	STATE	PERCENT CHANGE	RANK	STATE	PERCENT CHANGE
19	Alabama	1.4	1	Missouri	14.2
33	Alaska	(4.1)	2	Mississippi	13.3
13	Arizona	3.1	3	Oklahoma	13.1
11	Arkansas	5.3	4	Tennessee	12.5
49	California	(17.0)	5	Louisiana	11.6
44	Colorado	(9.6)	6	Oregon	9.4
41	Connecticut	(8.9)	7	South Carolina	8.7
21	Delaware	0.8	8	Georgia	7.5
36	Florida	(5.2)	9	Pennsylvania	7.0
8	Georgia	7.5	10	Hawaii	6.0
10	Hawaii	6.0	11	Arkansas	5.3
20	Idaho	1.2	11	New Mexico	5.3
30	Illinois	(2.1)	13	Arizona	3.1
23	Indiana	(0.8)	13	Utah	3.1
41	Iowa	(8.9)	15	Kentucky	2.9
34	Kansas	(4.8)	16	North Carolina	2.4
15	Kentucky	2.9	17	Ohio	2.3
5	Louisiana	11.6	18	Maryland	1.8
29	Maine	(2.0)	19	Alabama	1.4
18	Maryland	1.8	20	Idaho	1.2
48	Massachusetts	(16.9)	21	Delaware	0.8
43	Michigan	(9.0)	22	Nebraska	(0.5)
26	Minnesota	(1.0)	23	Indiana	(0.8)
2	Mississippi	13.3	24	Montana	(0.9)
1	Missouri	14.2	24	New Hampshire	(0.9)
24	Montana	(0.9)	26	Minnesota	(1.0)
22	Nebraska	(0.5)	27	Rhode Island	(1.4)
38	Nevada	(7.3)	28	South Dakota	(1.9)
24	New Hampshire	(0.9)	29	Maine	(2.0)
39	New Jersey	(8.5)	30	Illinois	(2.1)
11	New Mexico	5.3	31	Washington	(3.6)
50	New York	(19.7)	32	West Virginia	(3.8)
16	North Carolina	2.4	33	Alaska	(4.1)
39	North Dakota	(8.5)	34	Kansas	(4.8)
17	Ohio	2.3	35	Virginia	(5.1)
3	Oklahoma	13.1	36	Florida	(5.2)
6	Oregon	9.4	37	Wyoming	(6.7)
9	Pennsylvania	7.0	38	Nevada	(7.3)
27	Rhode Island	(1.4)	39	New Jersey	(8.5)
7	South Carolina	8.7	39	North Dakota	(8.5)
28	South Dakota	(1.9)	41	Connecticut	(8.9)
4	Tennessee	12.5	41	Iowa	(8.9)
46	Texas	(11.8)	43	Michigan	(9.0)
13	Utah	3.1	44	Colorado	(9.6)
47	Vermont	(13.1)	45	Wisconsin	(9.8)
35	Virginia	(5.1)	46	Texas	(11.8)
31	Washington	(3.6)	47	Vermont	(13.1)
32	West Virginia	(3.8)	48	Massachusetts	(16.9)
45	Wisconsin	(9.8)	49	California	(17.0)
37	Wyoming	(6.7)	50	New York	(19.7)
				District of Columbia	11.0

Source: Morgan Quitno Press using data from Federal Bureau of Investigation
    "Crime in the United States" (Uniform Crime Reports, 1992 and 1996 editions)
*Larceny and theft is the unlawful taking of property without use of force, violence or fraud. Attempts are included.
Motor vehicle thefts are excluded.

Motor Vehicle Thefts in 1992

National Total = 1,610,834 Motor Vehicle Thefts*

ALPHA ORDER					RANK ORDER			
RANK	STATE		THEFTS	% of USA	RANK	STATE	THEFTS	% of USA
27	Alabama		14,983	0.93%	1	California	320,112	19.87%
41	Alaska		2,918	0.18%	2	New York	168,922	10.49%
13	Arizona		31,481	1.95%	3	Texas	145,071	9.01%
33	Arkansas		7,900	0.49%	4	Florida	111,685	6.93%
1	California		320,112	19.87%	5	Illinois	71,976	4.47%
23	Colorado		17,662	1.10%	6	New Jersey	63,524	3.94%
19	Connecticut		23,700	1.47%	7	Michigan	59,057	3.67%
43	Delaware		2,109	0.13%	8	Pennsylvania	56,171	3.49%
4	Florida		111,685	6.93%	9	Ohio	51,886	3.22%
11	Georgia		38,913	2.42%	10	Massachusetts	47,416	2.94%
37	Hawaii		4,351	0.27%	11	Georgia	38,913	2.42%
46	Idaho		1,679	0.10%	12	Maryland	35,654	2.21%
5	Illinois		71,976	4.47%	13	Arizona	31,481	1.95%
17	Indiana		25,496	1.58%	14	Tennessee	28,935	1.80%
36	Iowa		4,474	0.28%	15	Louisiana	26,926	1.67%
31	Kansas		8,169	0.51%	16	Missouri	25,831	1.60%
32	Kentucky		8,128	0.50%	17	Indiana	25,496	1.58%
15	Louisiana		26,926	1.67%	18	Washington	24,214	1.50%
45	Maine		1,778	0.11%	19	Connecticut	23,700	1.47%
12	Maryland		35,654	2.21%	20	Wisconsin	21,605	1.34%
10	Massachusetts		47,416	2.94%	21	North Carolina	19,613	1.22%
7	Michigan		59,057	3.67%	22	Virginia	19,488	1.21%
25	Minnesota		15,911	0.99%	23	Colorado	17,662	1.10%
30	Mississippi		8,797	0.55%	24	Oklahoma	16,601	1.03%
16	Missouri		25,831	1.60%	25	Minnesota	15,911	0.99%
44	Montana		1,923	0.12%	26	Oregon	15,881	0.99%
39	Nebraska		3,225	0.20%	27	Alabama	14,983	0.93%
29	Nevada		9,255	0.57%	28	South Carolina	12,443	0.77%
42	New Hampshire		2,165	0.13%	29	Nevada	9,255	0.57%
6	New Jersey		63,524	3.94%	30	Mississippi	8,797	0.55%
35	New Mexico		5,974	0.37%	31	Kansas	8,169	0.51%
2	New York		168,922	10.49%	32	Kentucky	8,128	0.50%
21	North Carolina		19,613	1.22%	33	Arkansas	7,900	0.49%
47	North Dakota		950	0.06%	34	Rhode Island	7,463	0.46%
9	Ohio		51,886	3.22%	35	New Mexico	5,974	0.37%
24	Oklahoma		16,601	1.03%	36	Iowa	4,474	0.28%
26	Oregon		15,881	0.99%	37	Hawaii	4,351	0.27%
8	Pennsylvania		56,171	3.49%	38	Utah	4,313	0.27%
34	Rhode Island		7,463	0.46%	39	Nebraska	3,225	0.20%
28	South Carolina		12,443	0.77%	40	West Virginia	2,968	0.18%
48	South Dakota		719	0.04%	41	Alaska	2,918	0.18%
14	Tennessee		28,935	1.80%	42	New Hampshire	2,165	0.13%
3	Texas		145,071	9.01%	43	Delaware	2,109	0.13%
38	Utah		4,313	0.27%	44	Montana	1,923	0.12%
50	Vermont		600	0.04%	45	Maine	1,778	0.11%
22	Virginia		19,488	1.21%	46	Idaho	1,679	0.10%
18	Washington		24,214	1.50%	47	North Dakota	950	0.06%
40	West Virginia		2,968	0.18%	48	South Dakota	719	0.04%
20	Wisconsin		21,605	1.34%	49	Wyoming	701	0.04%
49	Wyoming		701	0.04%	50	Vermont	600	0.04%
						District of Columbia	9,118	0.57%

Source: Federal Bureau of Investigation
    "Crime in the United States 1992" (Uniform Crime Reports, October 3, 1993)
*Includes the theft or attempted theft of a self-propelled vehicle. Excludes motorboats, construction equipment, airplanes and farming equipment.

Percent Change in Number of Motor Vehicle Thefts: 1992 to 1996

National Percent Change = 13.4% Decrease*

ALPHA ORDER				RANK ORDER		
RANK	STATE	PERCENT CHANGE		RANK	STATE	PERCENT CHANGE
25	Alabama	4.3		1	Utah	98.7
26	Alaska	2.5		2	Nebraska	75.0
8	Arizona	30.3		3	New Mexico	66.9
30	Arkansas	(0.6)		4	Hawaii	64.5
44	California	(24.3)		5	Delaware	49.3
39	Colorado	(13.9)		6	Vermont	47.5
48	Connecticut	(32.4)		7	Idaho	32.8
5	Delaware	49.3		8	Arizona	30.3
35	Florida	(7.1)		9	North Dakota	28.8
17	Georgia	18.8		10	South Carolina	27.4
4	Hawaii	64.5		11	North Carolina	25.3
7	Idaho	32.8		12	Kentucky	24.8
42	Illinois	(19.3)		13	Iowa	21.8
31	Indiana	(2.7)		14	Nevada	21.0
13	Iowa	21.8		15	Washington	19.3
43	Kansas	(21.8)		16	Tennessee	19.0
12	Kentucky	24.8		17	Georgia	18.8
27	Louisiana	2.1		18	Montana	16.9
29	Maine	(0.1)		19	South Dakota	16.0
28	Maryland	1.2		20	Michigan	13.8
47	Massachusetts	(32.1)		21	Minnesota	12.6
20	Michigan	13.8		22	West Virginia	8.9
21	Minnesota	12.6		23	Mississippi	8.3
23	Mississippi	8.3		24	Oregon	7.1
35	Missouri	(7.1)		25	Alabama	4.3
18	Montana	16.9		26	Alaska	2.5
2	Nebraska	75.0		27	Louisiana	2.1
14	Nevada	21.0		28	Maryland	1.2
41	New Hampshire	(18.6)		29	Maine	(0.1)
45	New Jersey	(26.9)		30	Arkansas	(0.6)
3	New Mexico	66.9		31	Indiana	(2.7)
50	New York	(46.8)		32	Oklahoma	(4.0)
11	North Carolina	25.3		33	Virginia	(4.5)
9	North Dakota	28.8		34	Wyoming	(4.6)
38	Ohio	(12.3)		35	Florida	(7.1)
32	Oklahoma	(4.0)		35	Missouri	(7.1)
24	Oregon	7.1		37	Pennsylvania	(11.5)
37	Pennsylvania	(11.5)		38	Ohio	(12.3)
49	Rhode Island	(38.4)		39	Colorado	(13.9)
10	South Carolina	27.4		40	Wisconsin	(17.4)
19	South Dakota	16.0		41	New Hampshire	(18.6)
16	Tennessee	19.0		42	Illinois	(19.3)
46	Texas	(27.7)		43	Kansas	(21.8)
1	Utah	98.7		44	California	(24.3)
6	Vermont	47.5		45	New Jersey	(26.9)
33	Virginia	(4.5)		46	Texas	(27.7)
15	Washington	19.3		47	Massachusetts	(32.1)
22	West Virginia	8.9		48	Connecticut	(32.4)
40	Wisconsin	(17.4)		49	Rhode Island	(38.4)
34	Wyoming	(4.6)		50	New York	(46.8)
					District of Columbia	9.4

Source: Morgan Quitno Press using data from Federal Bureau of Investigation
"Crime in the United States" (Uniform Crime Reports, 1992 and 1996 editions)
Includes the theft or attempted theft of a self-propelled vehicle. Excludes motorboats, construction equipment, airplanes and farming equipment.

Motor Vehicle Theft Rate in 1992

National Rate = 631.5 Motor Vehicle Thefts per 100,000 Population*

ALPHA ORDER				RANK ORDER		
RANK	STATE	RATE		RANK	STATE	RATE
29	Alabama	362.3		1	California	1,037.1
21	Alaska	497.1		2	New York	932.3
5	Arizona	821.5		3	Florida	828.0
33	Arkansas	329.3		4	Texas	821.7
1	California	1,037.1		5	Arizona	821.5
19	Colorado	509.0		6	New Jersey	815.6
10	Connecticut	722.3		7	Massachusetts	790.5
35	Delaware	306.1		8	Rhode Island	742.6
3	Florida	828.0		9	Maryland	726.4
15	Georgia	576.4		10	Connecticut	722.3
28	Hawaii	375.1		11	Nevada	697.4
45	Idaho	157.4		12	Louisiana	628.1
14	Illinois	618.8		13	Michigan	625.8
25	Indiana	450.3		14	Illinois	618.8
44	Iowa	159.1		15	Georgia	576.4
34	Kansas	323.8		16	Tennessee	575.9
40	Kentucky	216.5		17	Oregon	533.5
12	Louisiana	628.1		18	Oklahoma	516.8
48	Maine	144.0		19	Colorado	509.0
9	Maryland	726.4		20	Missouri	497.4
7	Massachusetts	790.5		21	Alaska	497.1
13	Michigan	625.8		22	Washington	471.5
30	Minnesota	355.2		23	Ohio	471.0
32	Mississippi	336.5		24	Pennsylvania	467.7
20	Missouri	497.4		25	Indiana	450.3
39	Montana	233.4		26	Wisconsin	431.5
41	Nebraska	200.8		27	New Mexico	377.9
11	Nevada	697.4		28	Hawaii	375.1
42	New Hampshire	194.9		29	Alabama	362.3
6	New Jersey	815.6		30	Minnesota	355.2
27	New Mexico	377.9		31	South Carolina	345.4
2	New York	932.3		32	Mississippi	336.5
37	North Carolina	286.6		33	Arkansas	329.3
47	North Dakota	149.4		34	Kansas	323.8
23	Ohio	471.0		35	Delaware	306.1
18	Oklahoma	516.8		36	Virginia	305.6
17	Oregon	533.5		37	North Carolina	286.6
24	Pennsylvania	467.7		38	Utah	237.9
8	Rhode Island	742.6		39	Montana	233.4
31	South Carolina	345.4		40	Kentucky	216.5
50	South Dakota	101.1		41	Nebraska	200.8
16	Tennessee	575.9		42	New Hampshire	194.9
4	Texas	821.7		43	West Virginia	163.8
38	Utah	237.9		44	Iowa	159.1
49	Vermont	105.3		45	Idaho	157.4
36	Virginia	305.6		46	Wyoming	150.4
22	Washington	471.5		47	North Dakota	149.4
43	West Virginia	163.8		48	Maine	144.0
26	Wisconsin	431.5		49	Vermont	105.3
46	Wyoming	150.4		50	South Dakota	101.1
					District of Columbia	1,548.0

Source: Federal Bureau of Investigation
   "Crime in the United States 1992" (Uniform Crime Reports, October 3, 1993)
*Includes the theft or attempted theft of a self-propelled vehicle. Excludes motorboats, construction equipment, airplanes and farming equipment.

Percent Change in Motor Vehicle Theft Rate: 1992 to 1996

National Percent Change = 16.7% Decrease*

ALPHA ORDER				RANK ORDER		
RANK	STATE	PERCENT CHANGE		RANK	STATE	PERCENT CHANGE
23	Alabama	1.0		1	Utah	80.2
27	Alaska	(0.8)		2	Nebraska	70.1
13	Arizona	12.8		3	Hawaii	61.2
30	Arkansas	(5.0)		4	New Mexico	54.1
44	California	(26.7)		5	Vermont	42.7
41	Colorado	(21.8)		6	Delaware	41.8
46	Connecticut	(32.2)		7	North Dakota	27.2
6	Delaware	41.8		8	South Carolina	24.1
37	Florida	(13.0)		9	Kentucky	20.6
19	Georgia	9.0		10	Iowa	20.1
3	Hawaii	61.2		11	Idaho	19.1
11	Idaho	19.1		12	North Carolina	17.1
40	Illinois	(20.8)		13	Arizona	12.8
31	Indiana	(5.6)		14	South Dakota	12.7
10	Iowa	20.1		15	Tennessee	12.4
43	Kansas	(23.3)		16	Michigan	11.9
9	Kentucky	20.6		17	Washington	10.8
24	Louisiana	0.6		18	Montana	9.6
27	Maine	(0.8)		19	Georgia	9.0
29	Maryland	(2.1)		20	Minnesota	8.3
47	Massachusetts	(33.2)		21	West Virginia	8.0
16	Michigan	11.9		22	Mississippi	4.2
20	Minnesota	8.3		23	Alabama	1.0
22	Mississippi	4.2		24	Louisiana	0.6
35	Missouri	(10.0)		25	Nevada	0.1
18	Montana	9.6		26	Oregon	(0.5)
2	Nebraska	70.1		27	Alaska	(0.8)
25	Nevada	0.1		27	Maine	(0.8)
42	New Hampshire	(22.2)		29	Maryland	(2.1)
45	New Jersey	(28.7)		30	Arkansas	(5.0)
4	New Mexico	54.1		31	Indiana	(5.6)
50	New York	(47.0)		32	Oklahoma	(6.6)
12	North Carolina	17.1		33	Wyoming	(7.5)
7	North Dakota	27.2		34	Virginia	(8.8)
38	Ohio	(13.5)		35	Missouri	(10.0)
32	Oklahoma	(6.6)		36	Pennsylvania	(11.9)
26	Oregon	(0.5)		37	Florida	(13.0)
36	Pennsylvania	(11.9)		38	Ohio	(13.5)
49	Rhode Island	(37.5)		39	Wisconsin	(19.8)
8	South Carolina	24.1		40	Illinois	(20.8)
14	South Dakota	12.7		41	Colorado	(21.8)
15	Tennessee	12.4		42	New Hampshire	(22.2)
47	Texas	(33.2)		43	Kansas	(23.3)
1	Utah	80.2		44	California	(26.7)
5	Vermont	42.7		45	New Jersey	(28.7)
34	Virginia	(8.8)		46	Connecticut	(32.2)
17	Washington	10.8		47	Massachusetts	(33.2)
21	West Virginia	8.0		47	Texas	(33.2)
39	Wisconsin	(19.8)		49	Rhode Island	(37.5)
33	Wyoming	(7.5)		50	New York	(47.0)
					District of Columbia	18.7

Source: Morgan Quitno Press using data from Federal Bureau of Investigation
"Crime in the United States" (Uniform Crime Reports, 1992 and 1996 editions)
*Includes the theft or attempted theft of a self-propelled vehicle. Excludes motorboats, construction equipment, airplanes and farming equipment.

Hate Crimes in 1996

National Total = 8,759 Reported Hate Crimes*

RANK	STATE	HATE CRIMES	% of USA
49	Alabama	0	0.00%
38	Alaska	9	0.10%
10	Arizona	250	2.85%
47	Arkansas	1	0.01%
1	California	2,052	23.43%
17	Colorado	133	1.52%
18	Connecticut	114	1.30%
23	Delaware	67	0.76%
14	Florida	187	2.13%
35	Georgia	28	0.32%
NA	Hawaii**	NA	NA
22	Idaho	72	0.82%
8	Illinois	348	3.97%
32	Indiana	36	0.41%
28	Iowa	43	0.49%
35	Kansas	28	0.32%
19	Kentucky	109	1.24%
39	Louisiana	6	0.07%
25	Maine	58	0.66%
6	Maryland	387	4.42%
5	Massachusetts	454	5.18%
4	Michigan	486	5.55%
9	Minnesota	268	3.06%
43	Mississippi	3	0.03%
16	Missouri	150	1.71%
37	Montana	10	0.11%
43	Nebraska	3	0.03%
26	Nevada	44	0.50%
47	New Hampshire	1	0.01%
3	New Jersey	839	9.58%
26	New Mexico	44	0.50%
2	New York	903	10.31%
33	North Carolina	34	0.39%
46	North Dakota	2	0.02%
11	Ohio	234	2.67%
21	Oklahoma	83	0.95%
15	Oregon	172	1.96%
12	Pennsylvania	205	2.34%
31	Rhode Island	40	0.46%
30	South Carolina	42	0.48%
43	South Dakota	3	0.03%
34	Tennessee	33	0.38%
7	Texas	350	4.00%
24	Utah	59	0.67%
40	Vermont	4	0.05%
20	Virginia	100	1.14%
13	Washington	198	2.26%
40	West Virginia	4	0.05%
28	Wisconsin	43	0.49%
40	Wyoming	4	0.05%

RANK	STATE	HATE CRIMES	% of USA
1	California	2,052	23.43%
2	New York	903	10.31%
3	New Jersey	839	9.58%
4	Michigan	486	5.55%
5	Massachusetts	454	5.18%
6	Maryland	387	4.42%
7	Texas	350	4.00%
8	Illinois	348	3.97%
9	Minnesota	268	3.06%
10	Arizona	250	2.85%
11	Ohio	234	2.67%
12	Pennsylvania	205	2.34%
13	Washington	198	2.26%
14	Florida	187	2.13%
15	Oregon	172	1.96%
16	Missouri	150	1.71%
17	Colorado	133	1.52%
18	Connecticut	114	1.30%
19	Kentucky	109	1.24%
20	Virginia	100	1.14%
21	Oklahoma	83	0.95%
22	Idaho	72	0.82%
23	Delaware	67	0.76%
24	Utah	59	0.67%
25	Maine	58	0.66%
26	Nevada	44	0.50%
26	New Mexico	44	0.50%
28	Iowa	43	0.49%
28	Wisconsin	43	0.49%
30	South Carolina	42	0.48%
31	Rhode Island	40	0.46%
32	Indiana	36	0.41%
33	North Carolina	34	0.39%
34	Tennessee	33	0.38%
35	Georgia	28	0.32%
35	Kansas	28	0.32%
37	Montana	10	0.11%
38	Alaska	9	0.10%
39	Louisiana	6	0.07%
40	Vermont	4	0.05%
40	West Virginia	4	0.05%
40	Wyoming	4	0.05%
43	Mississippi	3	0.03%
43	Nebraska	3	0.03%
43	South Dakota	3	0.03%
46	North Dakota	2	0.02%
47	Arkansas	1	0.01%
47	New Hampshire	1	0.01%
49	Alabama	0	0.00%
NA	Hawaii**	NA	NA
	District of Columbia	16	0.18%

Source: Federal Bureau of Investigation
   "Hate Crime Statistics 1996" (Uniform Crime Reports)
*Figures are for reporting law enforcement agencies. Participating agencies covered 84 percent of the U.S. population. Sixty-two percent of the incidents were motivated by racial bias; 16 percent by religious bias; 12 percent by sexual-orientation bias; and 11 percent by ethnicity/national origin bias.
**Not available.

Rate of Hate Crimes in 1996

National Reported Rate = 3.9 Hate Crimes per 100,000 Population*

ALPHA ORDER				RANK ORDER		
RANK	STATE	RATE		RANK	STATE	RATE
48	Alabama	0.0		1	Vermont	11.3
21	Alaska	3.5		2	New Jersey	10.5
12	Arizona	5.9		3	Delaware	9.2
48	Arkansas	0.0		4	Kansas	9.0
8	California	6.5		5	Maryland	7.6
21	Colorado	3.5		6	Massachusetts	7.5
17	Connecticut	4.1		7	Georgia	6.8
3	Delaware	9.2		8	California	6.5
35	Florida	1.3		9	Illinois	6.4
7	Georgia	6.8		10	Michigan	6.1
NA	Hawaii**	NA		11	Idaho	6.0
11	Idaho	6.0		12	Arizona	5.9
9	Illinois	6.4		13	Minnesota	5.8
42	Indiana	1.0		14	Oregon	5.5
32	Iowa	1.5		15	New York	5.1
4	Kansas	9.0		16	Maine	4.7
26	Kentucky	2.8		17	Connecticut	4.1
46	Louisiana	0.2		18	Rhode Island	4.0
16	Maine	4.7		19	Nevada	3.8
5	Maryland	7.6		20	Washington	3.6
6	Massachusetts	7.5		21	Alaska	3.5
10	Michigan	6.1		21	Colorado	3.5
13	Minnesota	5.8		21	Missouri	3.5
46	Mississippi	0.2		24	New Mexico	3.4
21	Missouri	3.5		25	Utah	3.0
36	Montana	1.2		26	Kentucky	2.8
34	Nebraska	1.4		27	Ohio	2.6
19	Nevada	3.8		28	Oklahoma	2.5
36	New Hampshire	1.2		29	West Virginia	2.2
2	New Jersey	10.5		30	Texas	1.8
24	New Mexico	3.4		31	Pennsylvania	1.7
15	New York	5.1		32	Iowa	1.5
36	North Carolina	1.2		32	Virginia	1.5
45	North Dakota	0.3		34	Nebraska	1.4
27	Ohio	2.6		35	Florida	1.3
28	Oklahoma	2.5		36	Montana	1.2
14	Oregon	5.5		36	New Hampshire	1.2
31	Pennsylvania	1.7		36	North Carolina	1.2
18	Rhode Island	4.0		36	South Dakota	1.2
40	South Carolina	1.1		40	South Carolina	1.1
36	South Dakota	1.2		40	Tennessee	1.1
40	Tennessee	1.1		42	Indiana	1.0
30	Texas	1.8		43	Wisconsin	0.8
25	Utah	3.0		43	Wyoming	0.8
1	Vermont	11.3		45	North Dakota	0.3
32	Virginia	1.5		46	Louisiana	0.2
20	Washington	3.6		46	Mississippi	0.2
29	West Virginia	2.2		48	Alabama	0.0
43	Wisconsin	0.8		48	Arkansas	0.0
43	Wyoming	0.8		NA	Hawaii**	NA
					District of Columbia	2.9

Source: Morgan Quitno Press using data from Federal Bureau of Investigation
    "Hate Crime Statistics 1996" (Uniform Crime Reports)
*Figures are for reporting law enforcement agencies. Rates calculated using only the population of reporting jurisdictions. Participating agencies covered 84 percent of the U.S. population. Sixty-two percent of the incidents were motivated by racial bias; 16 percent by religious bias; 12 percent by sexual-orientation bias; and 11 percent by ethnicity/national origin bias. **Not available.

VII. APPENDIX

Criminal Victimization in 1996

Each year the Bureau of Justice Statistics conducts the National Criminal Victimization Survey (NCVS). Unlike the FBI's Uniform Crime Reports which collects crime data from law enforcement agencies, the NCVS information is obtained through interviews with victims of crime. In 1996, approximately 45,400 households were represented and 94,000 people age 12 or older were interviewed.

Type of Crime	Number of Victimizations	Victimization Rates*
All crimes	36,796,000	NA
Personal crimes	9,443,000	43.5
Crimes of violence	9,125,000	42.0
Completed violence**	2,700,000	12.4
Attempted/threatened violence	6,425,000	29.6
Rape/Sexual Assault	307,000	1.4
Rape/attempted rape	197,000	.9
Rape	98,000	.4
Attempted rape	99,000	.5
Sexual assault	110,000	.5
Robbery	1,134,000	5.2
Completed/property taken	757,000	3.5
With injury	250,000	1.1
Without injury	508,000	2.3
Attempted to take property	377,000	1.7
With injury	79,000	.4
Without injury	298,000	1.4
Assault	7,683,000	35.4
Aggravated	1,910,000	8.8
With injury	513,000	2.4
Threatened with weapon	1,397,000	6.4
Simple	5,773,000	26.6
With minor injury	1,240,000	5.7
Without injury	4,533,000	20.9
Personal theft**	318,000	1.5
Property crimes	27,353,000	266.3
Household burglary	4,845,000	47.2
Completed	4,056,000	39.5
Forcible entry	1,511,000	14.7
Unlawful entry without force	2,545,000	24.8
Attempted forcible entry	789,000	7.7
Motor vehicle theft	1,387,000	13.5
Completed	938,000	9.1
Attempted	449,000	4.4
Theft	21,120,000	205.7
Completed**	20,303,000	197.7
Less than $50	7,580,000	73.8
$50-$249	7,374,000	71.8
$250 or more	4,216,000	41.1
Attempted	818,000	8.0

Source: U.S. Department of Justice, Bureau of Justice Statistics
   "Criminal Victimization 1996: Changes 1995-96 with Trends 1993-96" (Bulletin, November 1997, NCJ-165812)
*Rates are per 1,000 persons age 12 or older or per 1,000 households. In 1996, there were 217,234,280 persons age 12 or older and 102,697,490 households.
**Completed violent crimes include rape, sexual assault, robbery with or without injury, aggravated assault with injury, and simple assault with minor injury. The NCVS is based on interviews with victims and thus cannot measure murder. Personal theft includes pick pocketing, purse snatching and attempted purse snatching not shown separately. Completed theft includes thefts with unknown losses.

Population in 1997

National Total = 267,636,061*

ALPHA ORDER

RANK	STATE	POPULATION	% of USA
23	Alabama	4,319,154	1.61%
48	Alaska	609,311	0.23%
21	Arizona	4,554,966	1.70%
33	Arkansas	2,522,819	0.94%
1	California	32,268,301	12.06%
25	Colorado	3,892,644	1.45%
28	Connecticut	3,269,858	1.22%
46	Delaware	731,581	0.27%
4	Florida	14,653,945	5.48%
10	Georgia	7,486,242	2.80%
41	Hawaii	1,186,602	0.44%
40	Idaho	1,210,232	0.45%
6	Illinois	11,895,849	4.44%
14	Indiana	5,864,108	2.19%
30	Iowa	2,852,423	1.07%
32	Kansas	2,594,840	0.97%
24	Kentucky	3,908,124	1.46%
22	Louisiana	4,351,769	1.63%
39	Maine	1,242,051	0.46%
19	Maryland	5,094,289	1.90%
13	Massachusetts	6,117,520	2.29%
8	Michigan	9,773,892	3.65%
20	Minnesota	4,685,549	1.75%
31	Mississippi	2,730,501	1.02%
16	Missouri	5,402,058	2.02%
44	Montana	878,810	0.33%
38	Nebraska	1,656,870	0.62%
37	Nevada	1,676,809	0.63%
42	New Hampshire	1,172,709	0.44%
9	New Jersey	8,052,849	3.01%
36	New Mexico	1,729,751	0.65%
3	New York	18,137,226	6.78%
11	North Carolina	7,425,183	2.77%
47	North Dakota	640,883	0.24%
7	Ohio	11,186,331	4.18%
27	Oklahoma	3,317,091	1.24%
29	Oregon	3,243,487	1.21%
5	Pennsylvania	12,019,661	4.49%
43	Rhode Island	987,429	0.37%
26	South Carolina	3,760,181	1.40%
45	South Dakota	737,973	0.28%
17	Tennessee	5,368,198	2.01%
2	Texas	19,439,337	7.26%
34	Utah	2,059,148	0.77%
49	Vermont	588,978	0.22%
12	Virginia	6,733,996	2.52%
15	Washington	5,610,362	2.10%
35	West Virginia	1,815,787	0.68%
18	Wisconsin	5,169,677	1.93%
50	Wyoming	479,743	0.18%

RANK ORDER

RANK	STATE	POPULATION	% of USA
1	California	32,268,301	12.06%
2	Texas	19,439,337	7.26%
3	New York	18,137,226	6.78%
4	Florida	14,653,945	5.48%
5	Pennsylvania	12,019,661	4.49%
6	Illinois	11,895,849	4.44%
7	Ohio	11,186,331	4.18%
8	Michigan	9,773,892	3.65%
9	New Jersey	8,052,849	3.01%
10	Georgia	7,486,242	2.80%
11	North Carolina	7,425,183	2.77%
12	Virginia	6,733,996	2.52%
13	Massachusetts	6,117,520	2.29%
14	Indiana	5,864,108	2.19%
15	Washington	5,610,362	2.10%
16	Missouri	5,402,058	2.02%
17	Tennessee	5,368,198	2.01%
18	Wisconsin	5,169,677	1.93%
19	Maryland	5,094,289	1.90%
20	Minnesota	4,685,549	1.75%
21	Arizona	4,554,966	1.70%
22	Louisiana	4,351,769	1.63%
23	Alabama	4,319,154	1.61%
24	Kentucky	3,908,124	1.46%
25	Colorado	3,892,644	1.45%
26	South Carolina	3,760,181	1.40%
27	Oklahoma	3,317,091	1.24%
28	Connecticut	3,269,858	1.22%
29	Oregon	3,243,487	1.21%
30	Iowa	2,852,423	1.07%
31	Mississippi	2,730,501	1.02%
32	Kansas	2,594,840	0.97%
33	Arkansas	2,522,819	0.94%
34	Utah	2,059,148	0.77%
35	West Virginia	1,815,787	0.68%
36	New Mexico	1,729,751	0.65%
37	Nevada	1,676,809	0.63%
38	Nebraska	1,656,870	0.62%
39	Maine	1,242,051	0.46%
40	Idaho	1,210,232	0.45%
41	Hawaii	1,186,602	0.44%
42	New Hampshire	1,172,709	0.44%
43	Rhode Island	987,429	0.37%
44	Montana	878,810	0.33%
45	South Dakota	737,973	0.28%
46	Delaware	731,581	0.27%
47	North Dakota	640,883	0.24%
48	Alaska	609,311	0.23%
49	Vermont	588,978	0.22%
50	Wyoming	479,743	0.18%
	District of Columbia	528,964	0.20%

Source: U.S. Bureau of the Census
Press Release (CB97-213, December 30, 1997)
*Includes armed forces residing in each state.

Population in 1996

National Total = 265,284,000*

ALPHA ORDER					RANK ORDER			
RANK	STATE	POPULATION	% of USA		RANK	STATE	POPULATION	% of USA
23	Alabama	4,273,000	1.61%		1	California	31,878,000	12.02%
48	Alaska	607,000	0.23%		2	Texas	19,128,000	7.21%
21	Arizona	4,428,000	1.67%		3	New York	18,185,000	6.85%
33	Arkansas	2,510,000	0.95%		4	Florida	14,400,000	5.43%
1	California	31,878,000	12.02%		5	Pennsylvania	12,056,000	4.54%
25	Colorado	3,823,000	1.44%		6	Illinois	11,847,000	4.47%
28	Connecticut	3,274,000	1.23%		7	Ohio	11,173,000	4.21%
46	Delaware	725,000	0.27%		8	Michigan	9,594,000	3.62%
4	Florida	14,400,000	5.43%		9	New Jersey	7,988,000	3.01%
10	Georgia	7,353,000	2.77%		10	Georgia	7,353,000	2.77%
41	Hawaii	1,184,000	0.45%		11	North Carolina	7,323,000	2.76%
40	Idaho	1,189,000	0.45%		12	Virginia	6,675,000	2.52%
6	Illinois	11,847,000	4.47%		13	Massachusetts	6,092,000	2.30%
14	Indiana	5,841,000	2.20%		14	Indiana	5,841,000	2.20%
30	Iowa	2,852,000	1.08%		15	Washington	5,533,000	2.09%
32	Kansas	2,572,000	0.97%		16	Missouri	5,359,000	2.02%
24	Kentucky	3,884,000	1.46%		17	Tennessee	5,320,000	2.01%
22	Louisiana	4,351,000	1.64%		18	Wisconsin	5,160,000	1.95%
39	Maine	1,243,000	0.47%		19	Maryland	5,072,000	1.91%
19	Maryland	5,072,000	1.91%		20	Minnesota	4,658,000	1.76%
13	Massachusetts	6,092,000	2.30%		21	Arizona	4,428,000	1.67%
8	Michigan	9,594,000	3.62%		22	Louisiana	4,351,000	1.64%
20	Minnesota	4,658,000	1.76%		23	Alabama	4,273,000	1.61%
31	Mississippi	2,716,000	1.02%		24	Kentucky	3,884,000	1.46%
16	Missouri	5,359,000	2.02%		25	Colorado	3,823,000	1.44%
44	Montana	879,000	0.33%		26	South Carolina	3,699,000	1.39%
37	Nebraska	1,652,000	0.62%		27	Oklahoma	3,301,000	1.24%
38	Nevada	1,603,000	0.60%		28	Connecticut	3,274,000	1.23%
42	New Hampshire	1,162,000	0.44%		29	Oregon	3,204,000	1.21%
9	New Jersey	7,988,000	3.01%		30	Iowa	2,852,000	1.08%
36	New Mexico	1,713,000	0.65%		31	Mississippi	2,716,000	1.02%
3	New York	18,185,000	6.85%		32	Kansas	2,572,000	0.97%
11	North Carolina	7,323,000	2.76%		33	Arkansas	2,510,000	0.95%
47	North Dakota	644,000	0.24%		34	Utah	2,000,000	0.75%
7	Ohio	11,173,000	4.21%		35	West Virginia	1,826,000	0.69%
27	Oklahoma	3,301,000	1.24%		36	New Mexico	1,713,000	0.65%
29	Oregon	3,204,000	1.21%		37	Nebraska	1,652,000	0.62%
5	Pennsylvania	12,056,000	4.54%		38	Nevada	1,603,000	0.60%
43	Rhode Island	990,000	0.37%		39	Maine	1,243,000	0.47%
26	South Carolina	3,699,000	1.39%		40	Idaho	1,189,000	0.45%
45	South Dakota	732,000	0.28%		41	Hawaii	1,184,000	0.45%
17	Tennessee	5,320,000	2.01%		42	New Hampshire	1,162,000	0.44%
2	Texas	19,128,000	7.21%		43	Rhode Island	990,000	0.37%
34	Utah	2,000,000	0.75%		44	Montana	879,000	0.33%
49	Vermont	589,000	0.22%		45	South Dakota	732,000	0.28%
12	Virginia	6,675,000	2.52%		46	Delaware	725,000	0.27%
15	Washington	5,533,000	2.09%		47	North Dakota	644,000	0.24%
35	West Virginia	1,826,000	0.69%		48	Alaska	607,000	0.23%
18	Wisconsin	5,160,000	1.95%		49	Vermont	589,000	0.22%
50	Wyoming	481,000	0.18%		50	Wyoming	481,000	0.18%
						District of Columbia	543,000	0.20%

Source: U.S. Bureau of the Census
     Press Release (CB96-224, December 30, 1996)
*As of July 1, 1996. Includes armed forces residing in each state.

Population in 1992

National Total = 255,001,827*

	ALPHA ORDER					RANK ORDER		
RANK	STATE	POPULATION	% of USA		RANK	STATE	POPULATION	% of USA
22	Alabama	4,138,254	1.62%		1	California	30,892,326	12.11%
48	Alaska	586,684	0.23%		2	New York	18,080,098	7.09%
23	Arizona	3,868,075	1.52%		3	Texas	17,680,335	6.93%
33	Arkansas	2,394,165	0.94%		4	Florida	13,500,517	5.29%
1	California	30,892,326	12.11%		5	Pennsylvania	11,980,586	4.70%
26	Colorado	3,461,744	1.36%		6	Illinois	11,600,640	4.55%
27	Connecticut	3,276,760	1.28%		7	Ohio	11,000,035	4.31%
46	Delaware	688,975	0.27%		8	Michigan	9,466,017	3.71%
4	Florida	13,500,517	5.29%		9	New Jersey	7,823,660	3.07%
11	Georgia	6,761,159	2.65%		10	North Carolina	6,832,827	2.68%
40	Hawaii	1,149,524	0.45%		11	Georgia	6,761,159	2.65%
42	Idaho	1,066,457	0.42%		12	Virginia	6,383,268	2.50%
6	Illinois	11,600,640	4.55%		13	Massachusetts	5,991,456	2.35%
14	Indiana	5,647,853	2.21%		14	Indiana	5,647,853	2.21%
30	Iowa	2,806,665	1.10%		15	Missouri	5,193,872	2.04%
32	Kansas	2,515,760	0.99%		16	Washington	5,144,193	2.02%
24	Kentucky	3,751,866	1.47%		17	Tennessee	5,012,606	1.97%
21	Louisiana	4,271,460	1.68%		18	Wisconsin	4,991,485	1.96%
39	Maine	1,234,973	0.48%		19	Maryland	4,904,117	1.92%
19	Maryland	4,904,117	1.92%		20	Minnesota	4,472,264	1.75%
13	Massachusetts	5,991,456	2.35%		21	Louisiana	4,271,460	1.68%
8	Michigan	9,466,017	3.71%		22	Alabama	4,138,254	1.62%
20	Minnesota	4,472,264	1.75%		23	Arizona	3,868,075	1.52%
31	Mississippi	2,609,953	1.02%		24	Kentucky	3,751,866	1.47%
15	Missouri	5,193,872	2.04%		25	South Carolina	3,592,567	1.41%
44	Montana	822,555	0.32%		26	Colorado	3,461,744	1.36%
36	Nebraska	1,602,759	0.63%		27	Connecticut	3,276,760	1.28%
38	Nevada	1,332,714	0.52%		28	Oklahoma	3,204,161	1.26%
41	New Hampshire	1,113,375	0.44%		29	Oregon	2,975,198	1.17%
9	New Jersey	7,823,660	3.07%		30	Iowa	2,806,665	1.10%
37	New Mexico	1,581,873	0.62%		31	Mississippi	2,609,953	1.02%
2	New York	18,080,098	7.09%		32	Kansas	2,515,760	0.99%
10	North Carolina	6,832,827	2.68%		33	Arkansas	2,394,165	0.94%
47	North Dakota	635,443	0.25%		34	Utah	1,820,648	0.71%
7	Ohio	11,000,035	4.31%		35	West Virginia	1,805,606	0.71%
28	Oklahoma	3,204,161	1.26%		36	Nebraska	1,602,759	0.63%
29	Oregon	2,975,198	1.17%		37	New Mexico	1,581,873	0.62%
5	Pennsylvania	11,980,586	4.70%		38	Nevada	1,332,714	0.52%
43	Rhode Island	1,000,812	0.39%		39	Maine	1,234,973	0.48%
25	South Carolina	3,592,567	1.41%		40	Hawaii	1,149,524	0.45%
45	South Dakota	715,218	0.28%		41	New Hampshire	1,113,375	0.44%
17	Tennessee	5,012,606	1.97%		42	Idaho	1,066,457	0.42%
3	Texas	17,680,335	6.93%		43	Rhode Island	1,000,812	0.39%
34	Utah	1,820,648	0.71%		44	Montana	822,555	0.32%
49	Vermont	570,023	0.22%		45	South Dakota	715,218	0.28%
12	Virginia	6,383,268	2.50%		46	Delaware	688,975	0.27%
16	Washington	5,144,193	2.02%		47	North Dakota	635,443	0.25%
35	West Virginia	1,805,606	0.71%		48	Alaska	586,684	0.23%
18	Wisconsin	4,991,485	1.96%		49	Vermont	570,023	0.22%
50	Wyoming	463,560	0.18%		50	Wyoming	463,560	0.18%
						District of Columbia	584,686	0.23%

Source: U.S. Bureau of the Census
    Press Release (CB97-213, December 30, 1997)
*Includes armed forces residing in each state. This updates earlier 1992 population estimates.

Urban Population in 1996

National Total = 233,249,003 Urban Population*

ALPHA ORDER

RANK	STATE	POPULATION	% of USA
22	Alabama	3,490,410	1.50%
43	Alaska	415,902	0.18%
18	Arizona	4,086,168	1.75%
29	Arkansas	1,704,359	0.73%
1	California	31,248,738	13.40%
21	Colorado	3,505,420	1.50%
23	Connecticut	3,080,642	1.32%
40	Delaware	631,969	0.27%
NA	Florida**	NA	NA
9	Georgia	5,905,558	2.53%
37	Hawaii	918,519	0.39%
39	Idaho	793,067	0.34%
NA	Illinois**	NA	NA
14	Indiana	4,783,462	2.05%
27	Iowa	1,966,385	0.84%
NA	Kansas**	NA	NA
NA	Kentucky**	NA	NA
20	Louisiana	3,664,992	1.57%
38	Maine	895,261	0.38%
13	Maryland	4,805,157	2.06%
8	Massachusetts	6,080,935	2.61%
6	Michigan	8,538,054	3.66%
19	Minnesota	3,781,711	1.62%
30	Mississippi	1,605,338	0.69%
17	Missouri	4,149,531	1.78%
NA	Montana**	NA	NA
33	Nebraska	1,231,592	0.53%
31	Nevada	1,416,488	0.61%
35	New Hampshire	1,011,659	0.43%
7	New Jersey	7,988,000	3.42%
32	New Mexico	1,410,651	0.60%
3	New York	17,329,534	7.43%
10	North Carolina	5,633,465	2.42%
42	North Dakota	420,916	0.18%
5	Ohio	9,843,446	4.22%
26	Oklahoma	2,665,802	1.14%
25	Oregon	2,689,485	1.15%
4	Pennsylvania	10,997,011	4.71%
36	Rhode Island	990,000	0.42%
24	South Carolina	2,907,476	1.25%
41	South Dakota	439,675	0.19%
15	Tennessee	4,220,891	1.81%
2	Texas	17,497,582	7.50%
28	Utah	1,786,000	0.77%
45	Vermont	348,533	0.15%
11	Virginia	5,613,208	2.41%
12	Washington	5,022,848	2.15%
34	West Virginia	1,042,847	0.45%
16	Wisconsin	4,169,883	1.79%
44	Wyoming	355,091	0.15%

RANK ORDER

RANK	STATE	POPULATION	% of USA
1	California	31,248,738	13.40%
2	Texas	17,497,582	7.50%
3	New York	17,329,534	7.43%
4	Pennsylvania	10,997,011	4.71%
5	Ohio	9,843,446	4.22%
6	Michigan	8,538,054	3.66%
7	New Jersey	7,988,000	3.42%
8	Massachusetts	6,080,935	2.61%
9	Georgia	5,905,558	2.53%
10	North Carolina	5,633,465	2.42%
11	Virginia	5,613,208	2.41%
12	Washington	5,022,848	2.15%
13	Maryland	4,805,157	2.06%
14	Indiana	4,783,462	2.05%
15	Tennessee	4,220,891	1.81%
16	Wisconsin	4,169,883	1.79%
17	Missouri	4,149,531	1.78%
18	Arizona	4,086,168	1.75%
19	Minnesota	3,781,711	1.62%
20	Louisiana	3,664,992	1.57%
21	Colorado	3,505,420	1.50%
22	Alabama	3,490,410	1.50%
23	Connecticut	3,080,642	1.32%
24	South Carolina	2,907,476	1.25%
25	Oregon	2,689,485	1.15%
26	Oklahoma	2,665,802	1.14%
27	Iowa	1,966,385	0.84%
28	Utah	1,786,000	0.77%
29	Arkansas	1,704,359	0.73%
30	Mississippi	1,605,338	0.69%
31	Nevada	1,416,488	0.61%
32	New Mexico	1,410,651	0.60%
33	Nebraska	1,231,592	0.53%
34	West Virginia	1,042,847	0.45%
35	New Hampshire	1,011,659	0.43%
36	Rhode Island	990,000	0.42%
37	Hawaii	918,519	0.39%
38	Maine	895,261	0.38%
39	Idaho	793,067	0.34%
40	Delaware	631,969	0.27%
41	South Dakota	439,675	0.19%
42	North Dakota	420,916	0.18%
43	Alaska	415,902	0.18%
44	Wyoming	355,091	0.15%
45	Vermont	348,533	0.15%
NA	Florida**	NA	NA
NA	Illinois**	NA	NA
NA	Kansas**	NA	NA
NA	Kentucky**	NA	NA
NA	Montana**	NA	NA
	District of Columbia	543,000	0.23%

Source: Morgan Quitno Press using data from Federal Bureau of Investigation
"Crime in the United States 1996" (Uniform Crime Reports, October 4, 1997)
Estimated totals for urban areas, defined by the F.B.I. as Metropolitan Statistical Areas and other cities outside such areas. National total includes states not shown separately.
**Not available.*

Rural Population in 1996

National Total = 32,034,997 Rural Population*

ALPHA ORDER					RANK ORDER			
RANK	STATE	POPULATION	% of USA		RANK	STATE	POPULATION	% of USA
19	Alabama	782,590	2.44%		1	North Carolina	1,689,535	5.27%
38	Alaska	191,098	0.60%		2	Texas	1,630,418	5.09%
28	Arizona	341,832	1.07%		3	Georgia	1,447,442	4.52%
16	Arkansas	805,641	2.51%		4	Ohio	1,329,554	4.15%
22	California	629,262	1.96%		5	Missouri	1,209,469	3.78%
29	Colorado	317,580	0.99%		6	Mississippi	1,110,662	3.47%
37	Connecticut	193,358	0.60%		7	Tennessee	1,099,109	3.43%
42	Delaware	93,031	0.29%		8	Virginia	1,061,792	3.31%
NA	Florida**	NA	NA		9	Pennsylvania	1,058,989	3.31%
3	Georgia	1,447,442	4.52%		10	Indiana	1,057,538	3.30%
33	Hawaii	265,481	0.83%		11	Michigan	1,055,946	3.30%
26	Idaho	395,933	1.24%		12	Wisconsin	990,117	3.09%
NA	Illinois**	NA	NA		13	Iowa	885,615	2.76%
10	Indiana	1,057,538	3.30%		14	Minnesota	876,289	2.74%
13	Iowa	885,615	2.76%		15	New York	855,466	2.67%
NA	Kansas**	NA	NA		16	Arkansas	805,641	2.51%
NA	Kentucky**	NA	NA		17	South Carolina	791,524	2.47%
20	Louisiana	686,008	2.14%		18	West Virginia	783,153	2.44%
27	Maine	347,739	1.09%		19	Alabama	782,590	2.44%
32	Maryland	266,843	0.83%		20	Louisiana	686,008	2.14%
43	Massachusetts	11,065	0.03%		21	Oklahoma	635,198	1.98%
11	Michigan	1,055,946	3.30%		22	California	629,262	1.96%
14	Minnesota	876,289	2.74%		23	Oregon	514,515	1.61%
6	Mississippi	1,110,662	3.47%		24	Washington	510,152	1.59%
5	Missouri	1,209,469	3.78%		25	Nebraska	420,408	1.31%
NA	Montana**	NA	NA		26	Idaho	395,933	1.24%
25	Nebraska	420,408	1.31%		27	Maine	347,739	1.09%
39	Nevada	186,512	0.58%		28	Arizona	341,832	1.07%
40	New Hampshire	150,341	0.47%		29	Colorado	317,580	0.99%
44	New Jersey	0	0.00%		30	New Mexico	302,349	0.94%
30	New Mexico	302,349	0.94%		31	South Dakota	292,325	0.91%
15	New York	855,466	2.67%		32	Maryland	266,843	0.83%
1	North Carolina	1,689,535	5.27%		33	Hawaii	265,481	0.83%
35	North Dakota	223,084	0.70%		34	Vermont	240,467	0.75%
4	Ohio	1,329,554	4.15%		35	North Dakota	223,084	0.70%
21	Oklahoma	635,198	1.98%		36	Utah	214,000	0.67%
23	Oregon	514,515	1.61%		37	Connecticut	193,358	0.60%
9	Pennsylvania	1,058,989	3.31%		38	Alaska	191,098	0.60%
44	Rhode Island	0	0.00%		39	Nevada	186,512	0.58%
17	South Carolina	791,524	2.47%		40	New Hampshire	150,341	0.47%
31	South Dakota	292,325	0.91%		41	Wyoming	125,909	0.39%
7	Tennessee	1,099,109	3.43%		42	Delaware	93,031	0.29%
2	Texas	1,630,418	5.09%		43	Massachusetts	11,065	0.03%
36	Utah	214,000	0.67%		44	New Jersey	0	0.00%
34	Vermont	240,467	0.75%		44	Rhode Island	0	0.00%
8	Virginia	1,061,792	3.31%		NA	Florida**	NA	NA
24	Washington	510,152	1.59%		NA	Illinois**	NA	NA
18	West Virginia	783,153	2.44%		NA	Kansas**	NA	NA
12	Wisconsin	990,117	3.09%		NA	Kentucky**	NA	NA
41	Wyoming	125,909	0.39%		NA	Montana**	NA	NA
						District of Columbia	0	0.00%

Source: Morgan Quitno Press using data from Federal Bureau of Investigation
"Crime in the United States 1996" (Uniform Crime Reports, October 4, 1997)
Estimated totals for rural areas, defined by the F.B.I. as other than Metropolitan Statistical Areas and other cities outside such areas. National total includes states not shown separately.
**Not available.*

Population 10 to 17 Years Old in 1996

National Total = 30,321,174

ALPHA ORDER

RANK	STATE	POPULATION	% of USA
22	Alabama	487,568	1.61%
47	Alaska	81,044	0.27%
23	Arizona	486,311	1.60%
34	Arkansas	305,042	1.01%
1	California	3,553,724	11.72%
24	Colorado	449,931	1.48%
31	Connecticut	339,944	1.12%
48	Delaware	76,159	0.25%
4	Florida	1,479,252	4.88%
9	Georgia	852,571	2.81%
42	Hawaii	128,284	0.42%
39	Idaho	166,700	0.55%
5	Illinois	1,361,721	4.49%
13	Indiana	681,396	2.25%
30	Iowa	345,140	1.14%
32	Kansas	319,063	1.05%
25	Kentucky	449,557	1.48%
20	Louisiana	573,505	1.89%
40	Maine	143,802	0.47%
21	Maryland	549,578	1.81%
17	Massachusetts	610,016	2.01%
8	Michigan	1,145,564	3.78%
19	Minnesota	583,685	1.93%
29	Mississippi	350,529	1.16%
15	Missouri	641,474	2.12%
43	Montana	114,416	0.38%
36	Nebraska	208,323	0.69%
38	Nevada	174,250	0.57%
41	New Hampshire	133,998	0.44%
10	New Jersey	837,413	2.76%
35	New Mexico	227,503	0.75%
3	New York	1,905,397	6.28%
11	North Carolina	797,131	2.63%
46	North Dakota	82,165	0.27%
7	Ohio	1,299,367	4.29%
27	Oklahoma	413,803	1.36%
28	Oregon	373,987	1.23%
6	Pennsylvania	1,312,811	4.33%
44	Rhode Island	103,145	0.34%
26	South Carolina	419,307	1.38%
45	South Dakota	97,662	0.32%
18	Tennessee	592,575	1.95%
2	Texas	2,372,685	7.83%
33	Utah	312,220	1.03%
49	Vermont	69,270	0.23%
12	Virginia	712,106	2.35%
14	Washington	649,435	2.14%
37	West Virginia	205,152	0.68%
16	Wisconsin	636,792	2.10%
50	Wyoming	67,313	0.22%

RANK ORDER

RANK	STATE	POPULATION	% of USA
1	California	3,553,724	11.72%
2	Texas	2,372,685	7.83%
3	New York	1,905,397	6.28%
4	Florida	1,479,252	4.88%
5	Illinois	1,361,721	4.49%
6	Pennsylvania	1,312,811	4.33%
7	Ohio	1,299,367	4.29%
8	Michigan	1,145,564	3.78%
9	Georgia	852,571	2.81%
10	New Jersey	837,413	2.76%
11	North Carolina	797,131	2.63%
12	Virginia	712,106	2.35%
13	Indiana	681,396	2.25%
14	Washington	649,435	2.14%
15	Missouri	641,474	2.12%
16	Wisconsin	636,792	2.10%
17	Massachusetts	610,016	2.01%
18	Tennessee	592,575	1.95%
19	Minnesota	583,685	1.93%
20	Louisiana	573,505	1.89%
21	Maryland	549,578	1.81%
22	Alabama	487,568	1.61%
23	Arizona	486,311	1.60%
24	Colorado	449,931	1.48%
25	Kentucky	449,557	1.48%
26	South Carolina	419,307	1.38%
27	Oklahoma	413,803	1.36%
28	Oregon	373,987	1.23%
29	Mississippi	350,529	1.16%
30	Iowa	345,140	1.14%
31	Connecticut	339,944	1.12%
32	Kansas	319,063	1.05%
33	Utah	312,220	1.03%
34	Arkansas	305,042	1.01%
35	New Mexico	227,503	0.75%
36	Nebraska	208,323	0.69%
37	West Virginia	205,152	0.68%
38	Nevada	174,250	0.57%
39	Idaho	166,700	0.55%
40	Maine	143,802	0.47%
41	New Hampshire	133,998	0.44%
42	Hawaii	128,284	0.42%
43	Montana	114,416	0.38%
44	Rhode Island	103,145	0.34%
45	South Dakota	97,662	0.32%
46	North Dakota	82,165	0.27%
47	Alaska	81,044	0.27%
48	Delaware	76,159	0.25%
49	Vermont	69,270	0.23%
50	Wyoming	67,313	0.22%
	District of Columbia	41,388	0.14%

Source: U.S. Bureau of the Census
"State Population Estimates by Age" (http://www.census.gov/population/www/estimates/st_s95ag.html)

IX. SOURCES

Administrative Office of the U.S. Courts
Statistics Division
One Columbus Circle
Washington, DC   20544
202-273-2290
www.uscourts.gov

American Correctional Association
4380 Forbes Blvd.
Lanham, MD   20706-4322
800-222-5646
www.corrections.com/aca

Bureau of the Census
3 Silver Hill & Suitland Roads
Suitland, MD   20746
301-457-2794
www.census.gov

Bureau of Justice Assistance Clearinghouse
Box 6000
Rockville, MD   20850
800-688-4252
www.ojp.usdoj.gov/BJA/

Bureau of Justice Statistics Clearinghouse
Box 179
Annapolis Junction, MD   20701-0179
800-732-3277
Internet: http://www.ojp.usdoj.gov/bjs/

Drugs and Crime Clearinghouse of the Office of National Drug Control Policy
Box 6000
Rockville, MD   20850
800-666-3332
www.whitehousedrugpolicy.gov

Federal Bureau of Investigation
J. Edgar Hoover FBI Building
935 Pennsylvania Avenue, NW
Washington, DC   20535
202-324-3000
Internet: http://www.fbi.gov

Juvenile Justice Clearinghouse
Box 6000
Rockville, MD   20850
800-638-8736
www.ncjrs.org/ojjhome.htm

National Archive of Crime and Justice Programs
Inter-University Consortium for Political
  and Social Research
P.O. Box 1248
Ann Arbor, MI   48106
800-999-0960
www.icpsr.umich.edu/NACJD/home.html

National Association of State Alcohol and Drug Abuse Directors, Inc.
444 North Capitol Street, NW
Suite 642
Washington, DC   20001
202-783-6868

National Center for State Courts
300 Newport Avenue
Williamsburg, VA   23185
757-253-2000
www.ncsc.dni.us/

National Institute of Justice
810 7th Street, NW.
Washington, DC   20531
(202) 307-2942
www.ojp.usdoj.gov/nij

National Clearinghouse on Child Abuse and Neglect
P.O. Box 1182
Washington, DC   20013-1182
800-394-3366
www.calib/nccanch/

National Criminal Justice Reference Service (NCJRS)
Box 6000
Rockville, MD   20850
800-851-3420
www.ncjrs.org

Substance Abuse and Mental Health Services Administration
U.S. Department of Health and Human Services
5600 Fishers Lane
Rockville, MD   20857
301-468-2600
www.samhsa.gov

Victims of Crime Resource Center
810 7th Street, NW.
Washington, DC   20531
800-627-6872
www.ojp.usdoj.gov/ovc/

X. INDEX

X. INDEX (continued)

X. INDEX (continued)

X. INDEX (continued)

CHAPTER INDEX

Arrests

Corrections

Drugs and Alcohol

Finance

Juveniles

Law Enforcement

Offenses

HOW TO USE THIS INDEX

Place left thumb on the outer edge of this page. To locate the desired entry, fold back the remaining page edges and align the index edge mark with the appropriate page edge mark.